The SMALL PRESS Book Club

Dustbooks also operates the Small Press Book Club which offers some 75 or more small press titles a year. We issue a "Selectionlist" every other month showcasing a dozen titles or so (including the famous "mag bag"). To become a member and receive the bi-monthly mailing you simply buy one item from the current Selectionlist (or from our "Past Selections" list). To stay a member you must buy one book every six months -- that's all the membership rules there are. No titles published or otherwise distributed by Dustbooks are included in the Club lists, nor will purchase of one of these titles fulfill membership requirement.

WRITE FOR THE LATEST SELECTIONLIST TODAY!

See order form

SMALL PRESS INFORMATION

THE BOOKS AND AUTHORS!

Small Press Record of Books in Print

6th Edition - 1977-78

A full in-print-and-available listing of over 5,000 books broadsides and pamphlets from more than 700 small presses

This is a 300+ page paperbound volume of the full in-print listings of over 700 of the world's small presses. It contains data on books, pamphlets, broadsides, posters and poemcards which are available now by mail and through other distribution channels. Each listing carries the following information: title, author(s), editor(s), translator(s), size in inches, number of pages, binding(s) and price(s), date published, ISBN numbers, and a descriptive comment. The Record has four indexes for 100% access: Author Index, Title Index, Publisher Index (with address) and Subject Index.

$8.95/paperback
$27/4 year subscription
ISBN 0-913218-03-0

DUSTBOOKS Paradise, CA 95969

1977-78

Thirteenth Edition

INTERNATIONAL DIRECTORY OF Little Magazines and Small Presses

Editors/Publishers
Len Fulton, Ellen Ferber

Dustbooks also publishes the *SMALL PRESS REVIEW* (monthly), the *Directory of Small Magazine/Press Editors and Publishers*, the *Small Press Record of Books in Print*, and chapbooks of poetry and prose.

CONTENTS

INTRODUCTION
1/LISTINGS
359/SUBJECT INDEX
394/REGIONAL INDEX
424/DISTRIBUTORS, JOBBERS, AGENTS
430/ORGANIZATION ACRONYMS

db

Dustbooks would like to thank Richard Centing for his advice and for helping to make this Directory a more useful and readable publication.

COVER BY GEORGE MATTINGLY

Systems design, typesetting format and computer programming by Neil McIntyre, Data Service Co., P.O. Box 2066, Marysville, CA 95901.

©1977 by Len Fulton, Dustbooks

Published annually by Dustbooks
P.O.Box 1056, Paradise, CA 95969

PAPER	CLOTH
$8.95/copy	$11.95/copy
$27/4 year subsc.	$36/4 year subsc.
ISBN 0-913218-04-9	ISBN 0-913218-05-7

Three-across pressure sensitive mailing labels are available from the *International Directory*. These labels can be sorted alphabetically or by Zip Code. Price is $50.00 per thousand ($50.00 minimum). A zip code tabulation is available with each group of labels for an additional charge of $10.00.

///DBKS//Paradise/CA

frycount 13

Making a list of little magazines, literary magazines and small, independent presses is like counting fry under a waterfall — the fry in this case are what used to be referred to as "ephemeral" or "clandestine" or "underground" or "fugitive" publishing operations. The words "small" and "little" seem to be used now more out of habit, and because they are most familiar, but "independent" is coming more and more to signify what is really meant. "Independent", for one thing, is not loaded with implications for that greatest of all virtues, *size;* and for another *is* loaded with implications for a virtue I do value — *energy,* and its rather tribal source. vehicle, destiny and recyclability.

The first count made for this Directory was in 1965. It turned up 250 fry, and made a Directory of Little Magazines (First Edition) of 40-odd pages — still available (at a collectors' price of about $5), and with what remains as still one of the prettiest covers of any of the first dozen editions (a collage of covers from a flock of small mags of the day). Yet the difference between that First Edition and this Thirteenth is a graphic as well as a literal chronologue of the change and growth of the small press and magazine publisher. The majority of publications listed in the First *looked* like the Directory itself — set on a typewriter, saddle-stitched in format, and, other than its cover collage, minimally "produced". Most publishers here in the Thirteenth, on the other hand, are likely to produce a slicker product — coated-stock covers in two or three colors, squarebacked (and/or case) bindings, professional typesetting and graphic presentation — in short, a highly viable "object" for the marketplace. Inside the small press/magazine movement itself all of this creates a certain nostalgia (almost bordering on woe) even amongst those whose own publications over the years have made the most radical "improvements", and the only way to handle *this* syndrome is to see it as a consistent and healthy self-assessment that has always been integral to independent publishing (see Ellen Ferber's *"QUO VADIS"* in *SMALL PRESS REVIEW* 48-49). The limited-edition fine printers have remained, but their counterparts in the hand-painted covers and mimeo pages have faded into offset, half-tone illustrations and glossy covers. The independent press has simply seized upon certain technological advances in the past eight or ten years — low-cost, short-run concepts in book printing, the narrow-web offset press, typesetting machines like the Compuwriter, etc. The difference in actual size of the First and Thirteenth Directories is the show-and-tell of the growth of the movement.

The difference is also in diversity. A subject index in the 1965 edition would have had one major category: poetry. In the back of this 1977 edition you will find more than 140 categories. Poetry is still big, but it is not big alone. Other subjects claim the technical and creative energies of the independent publishers; these publishers have become a force in publishing itself, as well as in literature. It might be said that the thrust has turned from a rather clenched-fist drive for a revolutionary form of poetry and art in the Sixties outward toward a revolution in the form of publishing itself. More and more of the ground that the Sixties had only begun to illuminate is enclosed: the women's movement, how-to, Native Americans, Blacks, Chicano/as, ecology, prisoners, communal living. Entire magazines and presses are now devoted to material only touched upon earlier.

Another diversity is evident too, a geographic one, as the Regional Index demonstrates in this edition. In 1965 it would have been New York and California; now, though independent publishing tends to nest toward those two locales, they are by no means dominant on the small press map. The Committee of Small Magazine Editors and Publishers (COSMEP), which was founded in 1968 by forty or fifty editors, mostly from California and New York, has in the past year or two found itself breaking into regions — west, south, east and midwest, partly of course as a function of its size (over 1,200 members), and partly as a result of the spiritual and commercial strength which regionalization brings. The list of organizations itself — last year a bare dozen acronyms long — has in this edition multiplied itself severalfold. Whereas in 1965 there was virtually no collective movement in independent publishing, there is in 1977 almost a frenzy of it. Again, this seems to indicate a serious and somewhat more commercial drive.

The subject of *distribution* is not a new one to any kind of publishing, though in the small press movement it has come in for heavier and heavier treatment since the early Seventies. Through help from grants — and the simple growth and commercial visibility of small presses — there are now some twenty small distributors engaged in almost exclusive distribution of small press books and magazines. Those, taken together with the more than one hundred larger agents, jobbers and distributors which Dustbooks regularly deals with, constitute the list in the back of this edition. In 1965 there was no such list.

The information which Dustbooks collects on publishers, as those of you who have followed the *INTERNATIONAL DIRECTORY* for even two or three years have probably noted, has expanded every year in quality and quantity (and quality in this business of fry counting is often a function of quantity), until now a complete data record for any one small press or magazine involves maintenance of more than thirty items, from name, address and type of material used, to subject indexing information and org membership. For years the information was kept on index cards and the Directory was typeset from those and from the forms sent in by publishers. For the past two years this data has been stored on a computer disc just to make it manageable (they don't make index cards that big!) and, with three month's worth of nit-picking updates, the Directory is typeset by computer directly from the disc storage.

The small publishers in this Directory are still fry, and they move with the same speed and grace as always. But they grow big, and they live longer, and the waters show increasing evidence of their presence. And Dustbooks, too, is still a fry. Ninety percent of the work here still gets done on the kitchen table because that table is the most consistently clear surface available. If someone were to suggest that it be reserved for meals only — or even meals primarily — they should have to be thrown out. When the Directory is being compiled everyone eats from their laps.

But most important, the small presses and magazines have retained the spirit of Harriet Monroe, who founded *POETRY* in 1912, and Margaret Anderson, who founded *THE LITTLE REVIEW* in 1913. The thirst for wholeness, relatedness, personalization and experiment, having reawakened in the Sixties, are still here. There is still intoxication with the belief in the freedom of language and in the notion that it belongs to the person using it, that the world is full of good literature, and that the small presses can and will publish it.

—Len Fulton

This introduction includes excerpts from "The Psychologique of Small Press Publishing", an "Occasional Paper" with introduction by Benjamin Weintraub, published by and available from the Graduate School of Library Service, Rutgers University, New Brunswick, NJ ($3.00/copy).

KEY TO DIRECTORY LISTINGS:

Listings are of three basic kinds: those for **magazines** (periodicals), those for **presses** (book publishers), and **cross-references**.

The **cross-references** are simply publisher imprints (usually presses but sometimes magazines) which have no listing data of their own but which are designed to lead you to a listing for that publisher which does have such data.

A complete **magazine** listing would include, in the following order: Name of magazine, name of press, name(s) of editor(s), address, phone number, type of material used (see Index in the back), additional comments by editors including recent contributors, frequency of publication, one-year subscription price, single copy price, sample copy price, founding year, average number of pages, page size, production method (mi-mimeo; lo or of-offset; lp-letterpress), circulation, length of reporting time on manuscripts, payment rates, rights purchased and/or copyright arrangements, ad rates (page/half page), discount schedules, back issue prices, number of issues published in 1976, expected in 1977 and 1978, areas of interest for review materials, and membership in small mag/press organizations (see special list of acronyms).

A complete **press** listing would include, in the following order: Name of press, name of magazine (if any), name(s) of editor(s), address, type of material used, additional comments by editors including recent contributors, average copy price in cloth, paperback and "other", founding year, average number of pages, page size, production method, average press run, length of reporting time on manuscripts, payment or royalty arrangements, rights purchased and/or copyright arrangements, number of titles published in 1976, expected in 1977 and 1978, and membership in small press/mag orgs.

Certain special abbreviations apply to listings from the United Kingdom: px-postage is extra; pf-postage is free; pp-pages; p-pence.

In some cases in this edition we received no report but had a reasonable sense that the magazine or press was still going. In such cases a ‡ is used before the name. Query before sending money or material however.

The following additional indicators are used in this edition to simplify yes or no in the listings: † means that the magazine or press does its own printing; § before a listing of areas of interest for review materials indicates that the magazine wishes to receive materials for review.

For those who wish to list a magazine or press in future editions of this *Directory*, Dustbooks provides a special form. Please write to us for it. Write to us also for a form to list books, pamphlets, broadsides, posters and poem-cards (i.e. *non*-periodicals) in our annual *Small Press Record of Books in Print*. Deadline for this *Directory* is April 1st of each year; for the *Record* it is January 1st.

A, A Press Ltd., William Oandasan, Box 311, Laguna, NM 87026, 505-455-7692. "We are essentially a poetry periodical, 'A,' and have decided interest in native American poetry, but are seeking poetry of contemporary excellence as well, regardless of locale, region, or school or philosophy of poetry. We are, in short, looking for the best poetry being written today. We will also accept letters, articles, reviews, interviews and essays on contemporary life and literature. We like our fiction short and prefer to solicit it—inquire first." irreg.; 1-yr sub price: $2.50 regular; $5.00 for libraries and institutions; add $2.00 to foreign subscriptions for postage and handling.; per copy: $1.50; sample: $1.00 or $2.50. 1976. 32pp; 7 x 10. of. Reporting time: 6 wks. Payment: copies. Copyrighted. Back issues: $1.00 or $2.50. Pub'd 1 issue 1976; expects 2 issues 1977, 2 or 3 issues 1978. Pub's reviews. CCLM, COSMEP, RGWA, SRPS, NCBA, COSMEP-SOUTH, COSMEP-WEST.

A, Alphabox Press, Jeremy Adler, 47 Wetherby Mansions, Earls Court Square, London SW5 9BH, United Kingdom. "A (1970); AB (1973); ABC (1975). Envelope magazine of visual poetry. Pages usually supplied by respective contributors. Contributors include: Bob Cobbing, Peter Finch, Bill Griffiths, D.S.H., Jackson MacLow, Peter Mayer, B. P. Nichol, Nannuci, P. C. Fencott, Paul Outton, Paula Claire etc." irreg.; 1-yr sub price: 50p plus p&p; per copy: 50p plus p&p; sample: 50p plus p&p. 1969. 40pp; A4. mi/of/silkscreen, etc. circ. 150/200. Reporting time: 2 mos. Payment: 3 copies. Copyright with author throughout. no ads accepted. Expects 1 issue 1977. ALP, CULP.

A Harmless Flirtation With Wealth, Helen McKenna, P.O. Box 9779, San Diego, CA 92109, 714-270-3908. avg. price, paper: $3.00. 1975. 80pp; 5½ x 8½. of. avg. press run 3,000. Not accepting ms. right now. Payment: Standard: 10-15 percent. Copyrights for author. Discounts: Distributors: to be arranged; 10 percent libraries; 40 percent bookstores. Pub'd 1 title 1976; expects 1 title 1977, 2 titles 1978. COSMEP.

A Press Ltd. (see also A), William Oandasan, Director, Box 311, Laguna, NM 87026. "A Press is seeking manuscripts of poetry and short stories, as well as works of educational importance and on social-political issues. A Press has published *Earth & Sky,* by William Oandasan, a booklet of haiku and contraries, $1." 1976.

A SHOUT IN THE STREET: a journal of literary and visual art, Queens College Press, Joseph Cuomo, Ed.; Frederick Buell, Marie Ponsot, Poetry; Beverly Gross, Fiction; Richard Schotter, Raymond Gasper, Drama; Herb Goro, Marvin Bileck, Visual Art, English Dept. Queens College, Flushing, NY 11367, 212-520-7238. Poetry, fiction, art, photos, interviews, long-poems, plays, non-fiction. "We are most interested in writing and art that is rooted in particular places and times. We print: long poems, long short stories, portfolios of visual art, & photoessays. Recent contributors: A.R. Ammons, James Dickey, John Gardner, Allen Ginsberg, Aileen M. Smith, W. Eugene Smith, Gary Snyder, Roman Vishniac, Diane Wakoski." 3/yr; 1-yr sub price: $6.00; per copy: $2.50; sample: $2.50 or 10 day trial copy on request to libraries. 1976. 96pp; 6 x 9¼. †of. circ. 1,000. Reporting time: 8 weeks. Payment: in copies. Copyrighted, reverts to author. Ads: $100.00/$50.00/20% discount to small presses. Discounts: To libraries: 10 day trial copies on request. To bookstores: 30 percent discount on consignment; 40 percent discount when bought outright—both discounts off single copy price on orders of 5 or more. Back issues: $2.50. Expects 3 issues 1977, 3 issues 1978. COSMEP.

AB INTRA, Hellric Publications, Dolores Stewart, 39 Eliot St., Jamaica Plain, MA 02130. Poetry. "Latest issue, #3 includes work by Ellen Bass, Nick Dager, Judith Steinbergh, J.J. Clarke, John Kay, Rennie McQuilkin, Clarke Wells, Patricia Cumming, David Leviten, etc. #4, at press, will present Frank Nisetich, Sally McCluskey, Matt Field, Lyn Lifshin, & others. Mss must be accompanied by SASE. International reply coupons are not acceptable. Well-crafted poetry of the imagination & the intellect, any subject any form. Traditional & experimental welcome." irreg.; sub price: $2.50/4 issues; per copy: $.75; sample: $.75. 1972. 28pp; 8½ x 11. †of. circ. 500. Reporting time: 2-3 weeks. Payment: 5 copies plus sub. Discounts: 50% on 20 or more copies of issue. §poetry only.

1

ABBEY, White Urp Press, David Greisman, 5011-2 Green Mountain Circle, Columbia, MD 21044. Poetry, fiction, articles, art, photos, interviews, criticism, reviews, letters, parts-of-novels, plays. "ABBEY is the Molson's Ale of Small Press rags. Recent contributors-Ann Menebroker, Merritt Clifton, Eric Greinke, Steve Sneyd, Susan Fromberg Schaeffer, Charlie McDade." 3-4/yr; 1-yr sub price: $2.00; per copy: $.50; sample: $.50. 1971. 10pp; 8½ x 11. of/other. circ. 200. Reporting time: 2 minutes-2 years. Payment: nothing. Ads: $10/$5. Back issues: 50 ¢. Pub's reviews. §poetry/fiction/fanzines (sci-fi)/rock/beer-drinking.

Aberdeen Peoples Press, Editorial Group, 163 King St, Aberdeen, Scotland, 0224 29669. Fiction, articles, art, photos, cartoons, interviews, criticism, reviews, letters, news items, non-fiction. "Additional interest in material suitable for pamphlets 12pp-100pp. Libertarian socialist politics and scottish political comment." avg. price, other: 20p community papers. 1973. 16pp; 8½ x 12. †of. avg. press run 1,000. Reporting time: 14 days. Payment: negotiable. Copyrights for author. Discounts: discounts given. Pub'd 10 titles 1976; expects 4 titles 1977. APS.

ABERDEEN UNIVERSITY REVIEW, Aberdeen University Press Ltd., E. E. Morrison, Dept Of Mathematics, Edward Wright Building, Dunbar Street, Aberdeen AB9 2TY, United Kingdom. Articles, poetry, reviews. "In general c. 3000-4000 words for articles." 2/yr; 1-yr sub price: $7.00; per copy: $3.50. 1913. 96pp; 15 x 24½ cm. circ. 1400. Reporting time: 1 month. Payment: none. Back issues: At publ. price. Pub'd 2 issues 1976; expects 2 issues 1977, 2 issues 1978.

ABOUT UNIONS, Si Dardick, Jim Best, Brenda Lynn, Janet Desbarets, Alain Brunel, Dick Matthews, Sue Robertson, 3564B Clark Street, Montreal, Quebec, Canada. "Articles concerning healthy trade unionism and community issues. Articles focus on Quebec and Canada but there is also contact with activities outside of Canada. Recent articles have included reports on different union congresses, national vs American unions, boycotts, safety in the workplace. Exchanges with other similar publications welcome." 2-4/yr; sub price: instit: $8/6 issues, newstand: $.35, indiv: voluntary contrib.; per copy: $.35; sample: free. 1973. 20pp; 8.5 x 11. †of. circ. 1,200. Reporting time: 2 weeks. Payment: none. Back issues: cost of copying plus $1.00 otherwise $.75. Pub's reviews. §labour/urban politics/business monopolies/third world.

ABRAXAS, Warren Woessner, 2322 Rugby Row, Madison, WI 53705. Criticism, reviews. "After issue 14 (due summer 1977), *ABRAXAS* will convert to an all-review format. We are interested in reading reviews and criticism of books of small press poetry and fiction. *Abraxas Press* has published Darrell Gray's *Essays And Dissolutions* and is presently not considering unsolicited manuscripts. Reviewers in future issues will include Ron Slate, David Hilton, Douglas Blazek and Jim Stephens." 2/yr; 1-yr sub price: $3.00; per copy: $1.00; sample: $1.00. 1968. 50pp; 5½ x 7. of. circ. 400. Reporting time: 3 wks. Payment: copies. no ads. Discounts: 40 percent trade discount on orders of more than 5 copies. Back issues: Nos. 4-13 available as a set for $30.00. Pub'd 2 issues 1976; expects 2 issues 1977, 2 issues 1978. Pub's reviews: 14 in 1976. §reviews and criticism of small press poetry and fiction. CCLM, COSMEP.

"Absolutely Furious" Productions (see MAGIC SAM)

‡**Aburi Press,** PO Box 130, Corona A, Flushing, NY 11368.

ABYSS, Abyss Publications, Gerard Dombrowski, Michael Standish, P.O. Box C, Somerville, MA 02143. Articles, photos, cartoons, interviews, criticism, reviews, music, letters, collages. "Send no poetry 1976-1977." irreg.; 1-yr sub price: individual: $5.00/yr; institution: $10.00; per copy: varies; sample: $2.00. 1966. pp varies; 8½ x 11. of. Reporting time: 1 month. Payment: Copies. Copyrighted. Ads: none. Discounts: none. Expects 2 issues 1977, 4 issues 1978. Pub's reviews.

Abyss/Augtwofive (see also ABYSS), Gerard Dombrowski, Abyss; Michael Standish, Art Editor; Craig Ellis, Augtwofive, PO Box C, Somerville, MA 02143, 617-666-1804. Poetry, fiction, articles, art, photos, cartoons, interviews, satire, criticism, music, letters, long-poems, collages, plays, concrete art. "Abyss will begin activity again in the Fall of 1977 which will include co-publications with Augtwofive. Do not send ms. with an inquiry which includes mss." 1966/1969. 1-1,000pp;

Varies. of. avg. press run 100-1,000. Reporting time: 6-8 weeks. Payment: Copies. Copyrights for author. Discounts: Standard 40%. Expects 1 title 1977, 2 titles 1978.

ACA REPORTS, Ellen S. Daniels, 570 Seventh Ave., 1546 Broadway #820, New York, NY 10018, 212-354-6655. Articles, art, news items. "Interested in material on arts administration, legislation affecting all the arts, news on all art forms." Approximately 6/yr; 1-yr sub price: Only available with membership.; per copy: $3.00; sample: $3.00. 1968. 40pp; 8½ x 11. circ. 3,000. Payment: none. Not copyrighted. Back issues: $3.00. Pub'd 4 issues 1976; expects 6 issues 1977, 6 issues 1978. Pub's reviews: 100 in 1976. §Arts administration; visual art books; performing arts books; architecture; historic preservation; photography; foundations; grantsmanship; printing; financial management.

ACADEMY AWARDS OSCAR ANNUAL, ESE California, Robert Osborne, 509 N. Harbor Blvd., Lattabra, CA 90631. Articles, art, photos, interviews, reviews. 1/yr; price per copy: $4.95. 1968. 100pp; 8-3/8 x 11. Discounts: 2-5: 20%; 6-10: 25%; 11-29: 30%; 30 & up: 40%.

Academy Press Limited, Anita Miller, Jordan Miller, Jill Sellers, 360 N. Michigan, Chicago, IL 60601, 312-782-9826. Fiction, non-fiction. "Strong anti-sexist bias." avg. price, cloth: $7.95; paper: $3.95. 1975. 150pp; 5½ x 8½. of. avg. press run 5,000. Reporting time: 2 weeks. Payment: Standard paperback/hardcover royalties: c. 7-10 percent. Copyright: own or author's, as decided. Pub'd 2 titles 1976; expects 11 titles 1977.

ACCEPTANCE, Conceptual Non-Press, Loren-Paul Caplin, 230 San Juan, Venice, CA 90291. "Looking for anything & everything of Artistic Expression. Body of work to be shown (displayed) publicly at galleries & reading." 2/yr.

ACID SWITCH, Acid Switch Press, Carl D. Clark, 3007 University Avenue, Austin, TX 78705, 512-472-7415. Poetry, fiction, art, photos, cartoons, satire, reviews, music, letters, parts-of-novels, long-poems, collages, plays, concrete art. "*ACID SWITCH* publishes creative works in all genres, modes, fields, styles, schools, patterns and biases." 4/yr; 1-yr sub price: $10.00; per copy: $2.50. 1977. 90pp; 8½ x 5½. of. Reporting time: 3 mos. Payment: copies. Copyrighted, reverts to author. Ads: none. Discounts: 30 percent trade, 40 percent bulk, agent or jobber; sell at our cost for classroom; libraries should enquire about rates. Expects 4 issues 1977. Pub's reviews: none in 1976. §art, literature, drama, music.

Acid Switch Press (see also ACID SWITCH (ASP is an operation of Nous Ent, which is not a press)), Carl D. Clark, 3077 University, Austin, TX 78705, 512-472-7415. Poetry, fiction, articles, art, photos, cartoons, interviews, satire, criticism, reviews, music, letters, parts-of-novels, long-poems, collages, plays, concrete art. "If we like it or think it's good and can afford to publish it, we will." avg. price, paper: depends. 1977. pp Depends: in addition to books we do postcards, pamphlets, posters, broadsides. etc.; varies. mi/of/silkscreen, typewritten, hand written. avg. press run depends. Reporting time: 1 week to 6 months. Payment: Author gets 10 percent of the copies, 50 percent of the net profit; payed on February 25 of each year. Copyrights for author. Discounts: 40 percent trade, 45 percent bulk, agent or jobber, our cost to classrooms; libraries should write concerning special rates.

Acrobat Books, Tony Cohan, Gordon Beam, 409 N. Las Palmas, Los Angeles, CA 90004, 213-933-7796. Fiction, art, photos. "Short fiction (up to novella size) only — basically open to: 1. strong documentary ideas having to do with Southern California 2. extraordinary original artistic work — fiction, art, photography, & occassionally poetry" avg. price, paper: $4.95. 1975. 96pp; 7¾ x 7¾. lp. avg. press run 3,000. Reporting time: 60 days. Payment: one third of profits. Does not copyright for author. Discounts: 1-5 copies, 20 percent; 6-49, 40 percent. Expects 2 titles 1977. COSMEP, LPSC, SCBP.

Ad Hoc Press (see also BRILLIANT CORNERS: A MAGAZINE OF THE ARTS), Art Lange, 1372 W. Estes No. 2N, Chicago, IL 60626, 312-761-3702. Poetry, fiction, parts-of-novels, non-fiction. avg. price, paper: $1.00-$2.00. 1975. 30pp; 5½ x 7½. of. avg. press run 200-500.

3

Reporting time: 2 weeks. Payment: neg. Copyrights for author. Discounts: 60-40 percent. Expects 2 titles 1977, 2 titles 1978. CCLM.

Adams Publishing (see THE MONTHLY JOURNAL OF GREAT QUOTATIONS)

Addrummer Press (see A DIFFERENT DRUMMER)

The Adobe Press, S.F. Morrow, 264 Cottonpatch, El Cajon, CA 92020. Poetry. "THE ADOBE PRESS publishes books about the American Southwest. Non-fiction, fiction, history, arts and crafts, practical arts, ecology and poetry are subjects that we will consider as long as they relate to the Southwest in theme, application, or experience. David K. Gast's *The Tents Of The King Of Arizona* and other poems is available ($1.25 postpaid) under The Adobe Press paperback imprint. Please send query letter before submitting manuscripts." 1976. 70pp; varies. of. Reporting time: 1-3 weeks.

Adventure Trails Research and Development Laboratories, T. D. Lingo, DIRECTOR, Laughing Coyote Mt., Black Hawk, CO 80422. "Published *Consciousness Science Syllabus* by T.D. Lingto. Fundamental neurology to method of brain self-control, backward self-therapy and forward self-circuiting into the 403/8 bulk of dormant frontal lobes. Since 1957, a new order of advanced problem-solving intelligence, multiple orgasm and species conferencing telepathy to consensus democratic action has been observed to emerge automatically." 1957. 8½ x 11. mi.

THE ADVOCATE, Robert I. McQueen, Editor; David B. Goodstein, Publisher, 1730 S. Amphlett, Suite 225, San Mateo, CA 94402, 415-573-7100. Articles, art, photos, interviews, letters, news items, non-fiction. "Query first, most materials assigned." 26/yr; 1-yr sub price: $12.00; per copy: $.75; sample: $.75. 1967. 88pp; tab. of. circ. 60,951. Reporting time: 6 weeks. Payment: $20.00 per published column, on publication. Copyrighted. Ads: $728.00/$406.00/42 spaces - $2.00. Pub'd 26 issues 1976; expects 26 issues 1977, 26 issues 1978. Pub's reviews. §all. ABC.

AEOLIAN-HARP, Geneva Verkennes, 1395 James St., Burton, MI 48529. "Want rhymed poems, no single sentences, prefer 12 lines." 1/yr; 1-yr sub price: $2.00; per copy: $2.00; sample: $2.00. 1968. 20-40pp; varies. of. circ. 100 up to 500. Reporting time: right away. Payment: none; print for subscribers only. Ads: $.10 word. Back issues: three different issues $5.00. §will review poetry booklets if on nature or religion No Pornography. CCLM.

AFRICA NEWS, Africa News Service, Inc., Charles W. Ebel, P.O. Box 3851, Durham, NC 27702, 919-286-3910. Articles, interviews. 48/yr; price per copy: $0.75; sample: $5.00. 1973. 22pp; 7 x 8½. of. circ. 200. Copyrighted. Discounts: 3 rates, basically: $75.00/yr profit; $48.00/yr non profit; $28.00/yr individuals. Back issues: $0.75/copy. Pub'd 104 issues 1976; expects 48 issues 1977. Pub's reviews: none in 1976. §Africa.

AFRICA TODAY, Africa Today Associates, Edward A. Hawley, Exec. Editor; George W. Shepherd Jr., Ezekiel Mphahlele, Tilden J. LeMelle, Cherrington Hall, Univ of Denver, Denver, CO 80210. Articles, reviews, letters. "Scholarly articles on AFRICA ONLY-2000-6000 words, book reviews (AFRICA titles only)-450-1800 words, occasionally use poetry, but only by African authors or based on first hand experience of Africa." 4/yr; 1-yr sub price: individuals $8.00/institutions $12.00; per copy: $2.50 plus $.50 postage and handling charge; sample: no charge. 1954. 110-112pp; 5½ x 8-3/8. of. circ. 2,000. Reporting time: 3-4 months. Payment: copies in which article appears. Ads: $140/$75/1/4-$40. Discounts: 15% to established sub. agencies only; bulk rates available. Pub's reviews. §contemporary Africa-various aspects:political, economic, geographic, literary.

THE AFRICAN BOOK PUBLISHING RECORD, Hans Zell Publishers, Ltd., Hans M. Zell, P.O. Box 56, Oxford OX13El, United Kingdom. Articles, reviews, news items, interviews, criticism. "Largely a bibliographic tool, providing information on new and forthcoming African published materials; plus 'Notes & News', 'Magazines', 'Company Profiles' sections and interviews; normally one major article on aspects of publishing and book development in Africa per issue. Since 1977 also features short concise book reviews." 4/yr; 1-yr sub price: £18-$40.00; per copy: £4.50-$10.00; sample: free. 1975. 84pp; A4. of. circ. 1,500. Reporting time: 6-8 wks. Payment:

£25/$50 for major feature article. Copyrighted. Ads: £60-$125.00/£35-$75.00. Discounts: 15% to adv. agents/10% to subs. agents. Pub'd 4 issues 1976; expects 4 issues 1977, 4 issues 1978. Pub's reviews.

AFRICAN LITERATURE TODAY, Heinemann (London) Africana Publishing Corporation (New York), Eldred Durusimi Jones, Fourah Bay College, Univ. of Sierra Leone, Freetown, Sierra Leone. Articles, reviews. 1/yr; price per copy: £3.50/cl., £1.80/pa. 1968. 160pp; 5½ x 8½. lp. circ. 3,500. Discounts: 1/3 trade. Pub'd 1 issue 1976; expects 1 issue 1977, 1 issue 1978. Pub's reviews. §Africa.

Africana Publishing Corp. (see AFRICAN LITERATURE TODAY)

AFRO-AMERICANS in NEW YORK LIFE & HISTORY, The Afro-American Historical Association Of The Niagara Frontier, Inc., Monroe Fordham, Ed.; Melvin Watkins, Managing Ed.; Lillian S. Williams, Assoc. Ed., P.O. Box 1663, Buffalo, NY 14216. Articles, art, reviews, music, letters. "13-30 pages dbl. spaced typed, Afro-American Life & History, only non-fiction articles, black authors and social scientists, with material of the highest quality always welcomed, local and regional studies always needed, urban studies, New York black history and culture." 2/yr; 1-yr sub price: $6.00; per copy: $3.50; sample: $4.50. 1975. 110-135pp; 6 x 9. of. circ. 500. Reporting time: 2 - 6 months. Payment: 2 copies. Copyrighted, reverts to author. Ads: $25.00/$15.00. Discounts: 20% over ten copies. Back issues: $5.00. Pub'd 2 issues 1976; expects 2 issues 1977, 2 issues 1978. Pub's reviews: 10 in 1976. §Afro-American Life & History – Urban and Regional Studies.

‡**Afro-Am Publishing Co.,** 1727 S. Indiana Ave., Chicago, IL 60616.

‡**Afropress Ltd.,** Box 3502 Saldanha, Nairobi, Kenya, Africa.

AFTER-IMAGE, Word-Camera Press, Joe Magri, Ray Sibol, PO Box 10144, Towson, MD 21204. Poetry, fiction, articles, satire, parts-of-novels, plays. "Poetry and Prose with emphasis on experimentation and brevity. But quality writing in any style will be considered. Also, short articles/essays on Music, Art, Dance, etc. (For example, our 1st issue will contain a re-print of a short piece (on Ethnic Music) by Steve Reich. But we prefer not to re-print too often.) In general, AFTER-IMAGE is a magazine 'in process'. That is, by keeping costs at a minimum, we hope (in the future) to be able to do many things normally considered outside the scope of a 'magazine'. (e.g. A Sound—cassette tape—Magazine. This would be intended to couple with our printed version, containing 'realizations' of some of the works printed—text sound, etc.)" 1-yr sub price: $0.00; per copy: $0.75; sample: $0.75. 1976. 32-40pp; 8½ x 11. †mi. Reporting time: immediate. Payment: contributor's copy. Copyrighted, reverts to author. §Anything to do with the arts. If good, will review.

AGAINST THE WALL, C. William George, Ed.-Publ., PO Box 444, Westfield, NJ 07091. Poetry, fiction, articles, art, cartoons, interviews, satire, criticism, reviews, music, letters. "Usually publish in 200-500 word range. Philosophically libertarian, anything from laissez faire capitalism to voluntary communalism ok, with preference for anarchism over limited statism subclassification. Recent contributors include Robert Anton Wilson, Robert Brakeman, Tom Palven, Vincent Drosdik, Phyliss Shanken, Pete McAlpine, Barb Mraz." 10/yr; price per copy: $.75; sample: $.75. 1972. 30pp; 8½ x 11. of. circ. 5,200. Reporting time: Varies considerably. Payment: Negotiable, usually copies. We do not believe in "copyright" laws!. Ads: $30.00/$18.00/$0.40, $0.75 for 3x. Discounts: $35/100 copies. Back issues: $1, 3/$2.50. Pub'd 10 issues 1976; expects 10 issues 1977, 10 issues 1978. Pub's reviews: 10 in 1976. §Libertarianism as applied to education, politics, psychology, etc. LPS, COSMEP.

Agape, Bernard Broussard, P.O. Box 192, Franklin, LA 70538. Fiction. "Interested in all matters dealing with struggle for human rights, in response to the Gospel's imperative of love. Recent contributors include Raymond Broussard." 1977. of. Reporting time: 1 month. COSMEP.

AGENDA, Agenda Editions, William Cookson, Peter Dale, 5 Cranbourne Court, Albert Bridge Road, London, England SW11 4PE, United Kingdom. Articles, poetry, art, photos, satire, reviews, interviews, long-poems. "Poetry must be in recongnizable contemporary English. No 'concrete' or sound poetry considered." 1-yr sub price: £3 ($9); per copy: 75p ($2). 1959. 96pp; 7 x 5. lp. circ. 2,000. Reporting time: 1 month. Payment: £3 per page of poetry. Ads: £30/£15. Discounts: 33-1/3%. Pub'd 4 issues 1976; expects 4 issues 1977, 4 issues 1978.

THE AGNI REVIEW, The Agni Press, Sharon Dunn, Askold Melnyczuk, Tia Kimberk, P.O. Box 349, Cambridge, MA 02138. Poetry, fiction, parts-of-novels, long-poems. "Terry Stokes, Russell Edson, Clarence Major, Kenneth Rexroth, David Bosworth, Peter Klappert, David Ignatow, Linda Pastan, and Barbara Eve (feature poet in AGNI 7) are among past contributors." 2/yr; 1-yr sub price: $4.00; per copy: $2.50; sample: $2.50. 1972. 120pp; 5½ x 8½. of. circ. 500. Reporting time: 2-6 weeks. Payment: 3 copies. Ads: $40/$20. Back issues: $2.00. Pub'd 2 issues 1976; expects 2 issues 1977, 2 issues 1978. CCLM.

‡**AGORA,** Caixa Postal 79, Divinopolis, MG, Brazil.

Ahsahta, D. Boyer, O. Burmaster, T. Trusky, Boise State University, Department of English, Boise, ID 83725, 208-385-1246. Poetry. "We publish only work by Western poets-this does not mean paeans to the pommel or songs of the sage, but quality verse which clearly indicates its origin in the west. Our first three volumes include older poets, the next three will be contemporary (and we hope to alternate this way in the future)." avg. price, paper: $2.50. 1975. 60pp; 6 x 8½. †of. avg. press run 500. Reporting time: 1 month. Payment: copies of book. Copyrights for author. Discounts: 30 percent to trade, bulk, jobber, classroom. Pub'd 3 titles 1976; expects 3 titles 1977, 3 titles 1978. COSMEP.

AIEEE, Alphaville Books, Orlan Cannon, Jack Grady, Carolyn Cultural Cannon, PO Box 3424, Charlottesville, VA 22903. "Experimental art & poetics. (Current issue remains free to individuals requesting with SASE or IRC, $0.28/3rd class mail). Art exchange program and archives." 1-12 issues/yr plus supplements (varies)/yr; price per copy: Individuals—free; institutions—$1.00-$1.50; sample: Individuals—free; institutions-$1.00 w-supplements. 1974. 2-100pp; 3 x 5 - 10 x 12. †of. circ. 900 plus. Reporting time: Same day to 3 months. Payment: copies. Ads: $100.00/$55.00/$1.00. Back issues: No. 1, $50.00; No. 2, $20.00; No. 3, $5.00; No. 4, $3.00. Pub'd 1 issue 1976; expects 2 issues 1977, 2 issues 1978. Pub's reviews. §Experimental, surreal, avant, dada, concrete. CCLM, AA of A.

Air Press, Bertrand Lachance, Arthur Richardson, Box 48688 Station Bentall, Vancouver, British Columbia V7X1A6, Canada, 684-9641. Poetry, fiction, art, photos, long-poems, collages, concrete art. "50 page minimum no maximum length—no biases." avg. price, cloth: $10.00; paper: $5.00. 1971. 50-300pp; varies. of. avg. press run 1,000-1,500. Reporting time: 3 weeks. Payment: 10 percent. Copyrights for author. Discounts: 1-19, 33-1/3 percent; over 20, 40 percent. Pub'd 3 titles 1976; expects 4 titles 1977. BCPG, AOCP, LPG.

AIS EIRI, Edmund A. Vitale, 553 W. 51st St., New York, NY 10019, 212-757-3318. Cartoons. "Anything relating to Irish & Irish related things, tho more controversial the better." 2-3/yr; 1-yr sub price: $5.00; per copy: $1.50; sample: Free. 1974. 56pp; 8½ x 11. of. circ. 2,500-3,000. Reporting time: 3 months. Payment: none. Copyrighted, reverts to author. Discounts: 50 percent. Back issues: $2.00/issue. Pub'd 2 issues 1976; expects 3 issues 1977, 3 issues 1978. Pub's reviews: 5 in 1976. §International politics & Irish subjects. CCLM, COSMEP.

AISLING, Paul Shuttleworth, PO Box 998, LaMarque, TX 77568. Poetry, interviews, criticism, reviews. "Recent contributors: James Liddy, James Simmons, Michael Casey, Knute Skinner, Norman H. Russell, William Dickey, Vern Rutsala, Terry Stokes, Dave Kelly, Tom McKeown, Gary Gildner, Barbara Brinson, Adrianne Marcus, Servin Housen, Doug Flaherty, Anick O'meara, James Lee Hubert, Kay Boyle, Jane Bailey, Elaine Dallman, Alan Britt, James White." irreg; sub price: $4.00/4 issues; per copy: $1.00. 1973. 24pp; 8½ x 11. of. circ. 400. Reporting time: 2 weeks.

Payment: copies only (2). Discounts: 50% off for orders of 20 or more. CCLM, COSMEP.

AKROS, Akros Publications, Duncan Glen, 14 Parklands Avenue, Penwortham, Preston, Lancashire PR1 0QL, United Kingdom. Articles, poetry, satire, reviews, interviews, criticism, letters, long-poems. "Mainly Scottish poetry and criticism. Contributors include Alexander Scott, Edwin Morgan, George Bruce, Alastair Mackie, Donald Campbell, Maurice Lindsay, Duncan Glen, John Herdman, D.M. Black." 3/yr; 1-yr sub price: £2.00 for 3; per copy: 60p. 1965. 96pp; 9 x 7. offset litho with occasional letterpress. circ. 1,300. Reporting time: a few days. Payment: £3 per page. Copyrighted, reverts to author. Ads: £40.00/£25.00. Discounts: 25% below & 33 -1/3% over 4. Back issues: nos. 1-9 kraus $22. Pub'd 3 issues 1976; expects 3 issues 1977, 3 issues 1978. Pub's reviews. ALP, ALMS.

AKWESASNE NOTES, Rarihokwats, Editor; Peter Blue Cloud, Poetry Editor, Mohawk Nation, Rooseveltown, NY 13683. Poetry, fiction, articles, art, photos, cartoons, interviews, satire, reviews, letters, long-poems, collages. "Vine Deloria, Jr./Stan Steiner/Jack Forbes" 5/yr plus books and pamphlets; 1-yr sub price: donation basis; per copy: $.50; sample: on request. 1969. 48pp; 17 x 11. of. circ. 75,000. Reporting time: usually promptly. No payment-a participant newspaper. Discounts: 30% on consignment, 50% prepaid. Back issues: 50 cents. Pub's reviews. §ecology, native american, colonialism, etc. APS.

‡**ALA,** Jean Jaures, 453 Pbte, Buenos Aires, Argentina.

ALA/SRRT NEWSLETTER, ALA Social Responsibilities Round Table, Linda Katz, 60 Remsen St, #10E, Brooklyn, NY 11201. "News-no outside material solicited. Bias-small press & movement press for libraries." 5-6/yr; 1-yr sub price: individual $3.00/yr; institution $20.00; sample: 1 free. 1969. 7pp; 11 x 17, fold. of. circ. 1,200. Back issues: $1.00 ea. Pub's reviews. §Movement-general, literary-only gay, women. COSMEP.

‡**ALABAMA REVIEW, Univ. Of Alabama Press,** History Dept., Auburn Univ., Auburn, AL 36830.

ALALUZ, Ana Maria Fagundo, Apartado Postal 5289, Barcelona, Spain, 321-19-51. Poetry, fiction, art. 2/yr; 1-yr sub price: $15.00; per copy: $8.00. 1969. 50pp. lp. circ. 1,000. Payment: none. Copyrighted, does not revert to author. Ads: none. Pub's reviews. §Spanish language materials.

‡**ALASKA REVIEW,** Ala Methodist Univ., Anchorage, AK 99504.

ALBATROSS, Stacey M. Franchild, P.O. Box 2046, Central Station, East Orange, NJ 07019, 201-OR-4-4111. Poetry, fiction, articles, art, photos, cartoons, interviews, satire, criticism, reviews, music, letters, plays. "We try to print all sides of feminist or lesbian issues that our readers express any interest in and keep an open forum going for women to learn to express themselves in print—we prefer short things because we don't have much of an attention span but will also do long ones." 4/yr; sub price: $7.00 (6 issues); per copy: $1.50; sample: $1.50. 1974. 40pp; 8½ x 11. of. circ. about 5,000. Reporting time: 1 week. Payment: We pay in contributors copies, ads & subs. Copyrighted, reverts to author. Ads: $77.00/$47.00/$0.77. Discounts: We try to offer a 25% discount and will go lower if getting money up front—mostly we work on consignment. Back issues: Price varies depending on how scarce the issue is. Pub's reviews §Lesbianism-Women-Women's Movement—& like that. CCLM.

ALBERTA HISTORY, Historical Society of Alberta, Hugh A. Dempsey, 95 Holmwood Ave NW, Calgary Alberta T2K 2G7, Canada, 403-289-8149. Articles, reviews, non-fiction. "3500 to 7000 word articles on Western Canadian History" 4/yr; 1-yr sub price: $6.00; per copy: $2.00; sample: free. 1953. 40pp; 7 x 10. lp. circ. 3,000. Reporting time: 1 month. Payment: nil. None. Ads: none. Discounts: 1/3 off. Back issues: $1.00. Pub'd 4 issues 1976; expects 4 issues 1977, 4 issues 1978. Pub's reviews: 19 in 1976. §In our field-Western Canadian History. AASLH, CHA.

7

THE ALCHEMIST, Marco Fraticelli, Box 123, LaSalle, Quebec, Canada. Poetry, fiction, art, photos, collages, concrete art, non-fiction. "No biases in terms of length of material or number of works submitted. Although we publish good 'traditional' works we are more interested in those which explore the possibilities. We especially need graphics (pen & ink)." 2/yr; 1-yr sub price: $5.00; per copy: $1.50; sample: free. 1974. 40pp; 5½ x 8½. of. circ. 300. Reporting time: 1 mo. Payment: copies only. Copyrighted, reverts to author. Pub'd 1 issue 1976; expects 2 issues 1977, 2 issues 1978. COSMEP.

Alchemist/Light Publishing, Bil Paul, 231 Dorland St, P.O. Box 5530, San Francisco, CA 94101, 415-863-3421. Poetry, art, photos, cartoons, fiction. "Books. Also mini poetry books for city buses." 1972. 100pp; 8½ x 11. of/lp. avg. press run 2,000. Reporting time: 1 week. Discounts: 45 percent. Expects 1 title 1977.

ALCHERINGA:ETHNOPOETICS, Alcheringa, Dennis Tedlock, 745 Commonwealth Ave., Boston, MA 02215, 617-353-4026. Poetry, articles, photos, interviews, reviews. "Innovative translations of oral texts; visions, riddles, dreams; essays on questions of oral and written expression." 2/yr; 1-yr sub price: $9.00-$14.00; per copy: $4.95; sample: $4.95. 1970. 148pp; 8¼ x 9. of. circ. 1,500. Reporting time: 2 months. Payment: $2.00 per page. Copyrighted, does not revert to author. Ads: $85.00/$50.00/none. Discounts:401/3 to (trade) bookstores, 20 percent text, 10 percent agency. Back issues: Old series 3, 4 and 5: $2.50 each; new series $4.95 each. Pub'd 2 issues 1976; expects 2 issues 1977, 2 issues 1978. Pub's reviews: 10 in 1976. §Poetry, anthropology interface. CCLM.

Aldebaran Review, John Oliver Simon, 2209 California, Berkeley, CA 94703. Poetry, art, photos, long-poems. "Aldebaran Review has become a series of chapbooks & small anthologies of poetry. The editor feels especially close to—work by inmates at Folsom Prison, by a group of teenagers in Berkeley, the collected poems of a 6-year-old girl, long-poems & sequences by Alta, Pancho Aguila, Steve Sanfield, etc." 2.7/yr; avg. price, cloth: $6.00-4 issues, $8.00 for institutions; paper: $2.00. 1968. 56pp; 5½ x 8½. †of. avg. press run 1,000. Reporting time: quickly. Payment: copies only. Copyrights for author. Discounts: 20-40% to trade, up to 50% to distributors. Back issues: inquire. Pub'd 4 titles 1976; expects 4 titles 1977, 3 titles 1978. CCLM, COSMEP, COSMEP-WEST.

ALDEBARAN, Staff, Roger Williams College, Bristol, RI 02809. Poetry, fiction, art, photos, interviews. "Recent issues have focused on our own students, which, after all, is how it should be. We don't read during the summer months (May-August), so save your postage. Like everyone else, we're looking for quality material, have no biases, and are doing the best we can." 2/yr; 1-yr sub price: $2.00; per copy: $1.00; sample: $1.00. 1971. 48pp; 8½ x 5½. of. circ. 400. Reporting time: 2 months. no ads. Discounts: 40% bookstores. Back issues: $1.25 for all numbers.

ALEPH, Mel Raff, 7319 Willow Ave, Takoma Park, MD 20012. Poetry, fiction, articles, art, parts-of-novels, long-poems, collages, plays. "Carlo Parcelli, Merrill Leffler, John Pauker, Wm. Claire, Jack Foley, George Zabriskie, Barbara Lefcowitz, Juli Douglass" 2-3/yr; sub price: $5.00/4 issues; per copy: $1.50; sample: $1.50. 1975. 100pp; 8.5 x 7. †xerox 9200 system. circ. 250-500. Reporting time: 6 weeks. Payment: issues. Copyrighted. Ads: $50/$35. Discounts: 40%. Pub'd 2 issues 1976; expects 3 issues 1977, 3-4 issues 1978. COSMEP, CCLM.

Alex Aiken, 48 Merrycrest Avenue, Glasgow G46 6BJ, Scotland. "Publish own writing solely." 1971. 8 x 5½. Discounts: trade 34 percent, libraries 10 percent. Expects 1 title 1977. SGPA.

ALGOL: The Magazine About Science Fiction, Algol Press, Andrew Porter, P.O. Box 4175, New York, NY 10017, 212-643-9011. Fiction, articles, art, photos, cartoons, interviews, criticism, reviews, letters, parts-of-novels, non-fiction. "ALGOL is published for the SF reader interested in the behind-the-scenes aspects of SF. It regularly publishes articles, interviews, criticism by award winning authors. ALGOL has been awarded the Hugo Award by The World SF Convention. Regular columnists: Frederik Pohl (publishing), Richard Lupoff (books), Vincent Difate (art), and Susan Wood (fanzines). Some recent contributors: Ursula K. Le Guin, Samuel R. Delany, Jack Williamson, Robert Silverberg, Arthur C. Clarke, Robert A. Heinlein. Length of material 3-15,000 words.

ALGOL also attempts comprehensive coverage of Canadian SF publishing." 3/yr; 1-yr sub price: $5.40 (academic & libraries); $4.50 (individuals); per copy: $1.95; sample: $1.95. 1963. 68pp; 8¼ x 11. of. circ. 5,000 plus. Reporting time: 2-3 weeks. Payment: 1 cent/word for nonfiction; 3 cents/word for fiction. Ads: $114.00/$60.00/$0.15. Discounts: 40 percent trade discount. Write: F&SF Book Co., Box 415, Staten Island NY 10302. Back issues: Winter, Summer 76 - $1.50 each; Winter, Spring, Summer 1977 - $1.95. Pub'd 2 issues 1976; expects 3 issues 1977, 3 issues 1978. Pub's reviews: 45 in 1976. §S.F., children's fantasy, Canadian SF. COSMEP.

Algol Press, Andrew Porter, Editor & Publisher; Susan Wood, Canadian Literature Editor, P.O. Box 4175, New York, NY 10017, 212-643-9011. Articles, art, photos, interviews, criticism, non-fiction. avg. price, paper: $2.50. 1974. 36pp; 5.5 x 8.5. of. avg. press run 1,000. Reporting time: 3-5 weeks. Payment: Royalties percentage of gross cover price. Copyrights for author. Discounts: 40 percent trade discount. Write: F&SF Book Co., P.O. Box 415, Staten Island NY 10302. Pub'd 2 titles 1976; expects 4 titles 1977, 6 titles 1978. COSMEP.

Alice James Books, Cooperative, 138 Mount Auburn St., Cambridge, MA 02138. Poetry. "We are a small press, publishing books of poetry. We emphasize the publication of women, but have had 2 men as members. As a cooperative we make decisions collectively. When we accept a new manuscript the poet becomes a member of the cooperative and participates in work and policy-making. Members are limited to a geographic area close enough to participate in weekly meetings." 1973. 72pp; 5½ x 8½ (can vary). of. Reporting time: 2 months. Discounts: 20% jobbers, 50% distributors, no discounts for libraries, 40% bookstores. COSMEP.

‡**ALIVE, Alive Press Ltd.,** P.O. Box 1331, Guelph, Ont., Canada.

ALIVE & KICKING!, Selma Sklar, 35-50 85th St., Jackson Heights, NY 11372, 212-HA6-8788. Poetry, art, photos, cartoons. "A magazine for the elderly, but everyone is welcome to submit work. Mostly poetry (including translations) & old family album photos, snapshots (4 x 7 or smaller). Must use editor's name in address. Recent (1st issue) contributors: Dorothy Good; Rocco; Leonard Opalov; Pat Garst; Morty Sklar." 2/yr; 1-yr sub price: $1.30; per copy: $0.65; sample: $0.65. 1976. 24pp; 5½ x 8½. of. circ. 300. Reporting time: 1 week to 2 months. Payment: 2 copies. Copyrighted, reverts to author. Ads: $10.00/$6.00/$0.10. Discounts:40 1/3 to bookstores & bulk to classroom orders. Back issues: not applicable yet.

ALL ABOUT BOATING, Ann Snook, Managing Editor; Marlene Smith, Asst. Editor, 136 Adelaide St. E., Toronto, On M5C1L6, Canada. Fiction, articles, art, photos, interviews, reviews. "—2,000 words, including photos—all must be 'Boating' related—prefer technical articles—eg's:-Spars and Sail Control—The 470-Olympic Boat—Wheel Steering" 4/yr; 1-yr sub price: $2.95. 1974. issue 1: 250pp/issues 2-4: 30pp; 8¼ x 10¾. of. circ. 40,000. Payment: negotiable. Ads: issue 1-$1095 (1x) issue 2-4-$395 (1x)/issue 1-$650 (1x) issue 2-4-$250 (1x). Back issues: n/c. Pub's reviews. §books on boating.

All About Us (see also NOUS JOURNAL), Russ Hazzard, Box 1985, Ottawa, Ontario, Canada, 234-2919. Poetry, fiction, art, photos, plays. "Most books are anthologies by young, unpublished writers." avg. price, cloth: $3.00. 1972. 120pp; 6 x 9. of. avg. press run 3,000. Reporting time: depends on submission. Payment: no royalties. Author retains all rights. Discounts: trade—classroom. Pub'd 1 title 1976; expects 2 titles 1977.

All This & Less Publishers (see also STAR-WEB PAPER), Thomas Michael Fisher, Regents 509 NMSU, Las Cruces, NM 88003. Poetry, fiction, articles, art, photos, cartoons, interviews, satire, criticism, reviews, music, letters, parts-of-novels, long-poems, collages, plays, concrete art, news items, non-fiction. "All This & Less Publishers is planning to publish the best of george montgomery, *the living underground; memoirs,* by hugh fox, and *the machine* by jim mcCurry. a booklet is planned by loren-paul caplin, as well as a series of postcards by ken saville and a postcard by joel deutsch/craig ellis. the press is not soliciting material-we have enough to do for now, anyway. full information on the above books can be obtained by a simple request. our books, we hope, will prove to be valuable documents as american writing continues to evolve." avg. price, cloth:

9

Undetermined.; paper: Undetermined. 1973. 60pp; 8½ x 11. †of/mi. avg. press run 500. Reporting time: 2 weeks. Payment: Copies. Copyrights for author. Expects 2 titles 1977, 1 title 1978. CCLM, COSMEP.

ALL-TIME FAVORITE POETRY, J. Mark Press, Barbara Fischer, Box 2057, N. Babylon, NY 11703. Poetry. "Sincere, sensitive poetry, 1-3 poems, 3-16 lines & return envelope. No smut." quarterly; price per copy: $7.00 paper/$11.00 hardcover; sample: $3.95. 1963. 40pp; 8½ x 5½. †of. circ. 4,000. Reporting time: 2-4 weeks. Payment: $.60 a poem & prizes. Ads: none. Back issues: $3.95 paperback/$9.95 hardcover. §poetry.

Allegany Mountain Press (see also UROBOROS), Ford F. Ruggieri, Helen Ruggieri, 111 N. 10th St., Olean, NY 14760, 716-372-0935. Poetry, fiction, long-poems. "We will be reading manuscripts for publication in our UROBOROS books & the Rebis chapbook series; see UROBOROS magazine for biases." avg. price, paper: $3.50; other: Chapbooks $1.00. 1974. 5½ x 8½. †of. avg. press run 500. Reporting time: 4 to 6 weeks. Payment: Chapbooks pay copies; books by arrangement. Chapbooks secures right for author, books by arrangement. Expects 3 titles 1977, 6 titles 1978. CCLM, COSMEP, NYSSPA.

ALLEGRA, Allegra Press, Nona Fox, Riley Trumbull, 526 Forest, E. Lansing, MI 48823, 517-351-5977. Poetry, fiction, articles, art, photos, interviews, satire, criticism, reviews, letters, parts-of-novels, collages, plays. 4/yr; 1-yr sub price: $3.50; per copy: $1.00; sample: $0.75. 1976. 48pp; 5½ x 8½. †of. Reporting time: 2 weeks. Payment: two copies; cash if we become solvent. Not copyrighted. Ads: $50.00/$25.00. Expects 3 issues 1978. Pub's reviews. §anything in the arts.

Allegra Press (see also ALLEGRA), Nona Fox, Riley Trumbull, 526 Forest, E. Lansing, MI 48823, 517-351-5977. Poetry, fiction, articles, art, photos, interviews, satire, criticism, reviews, letters, parts-of-novels, collages, plays. avg. price, cloth: $7.95; paper: $2.95. 1976. 48-250pp; 5½ x 8½. †of. avg. press run 500. Reporting time: 2 weeks for mag, longer for books. Payment: mag—two copies; books—10 percent quarterly. Copyrights for author. Expects 2 titles 1977.

Alleluia Press, Dr. Jose M. de Vinck, 672 Franklin Tpke Box 103, Allendale, NJ 07401, 201-327-3513. Poetry, criticism. "Very few outside MSS. are accepted since we have our own authors. We produce books and offer our imprint and distribution *only* in the case of scholars whose works are up to our high standards and who can finance first costs of production. No limit to length: we have 1,250 pp. and 850 pp. books. Some recent contributors: Rev. Casimir Kucharek, Rama, Sask., Can.; Liturgical Commission, Rutheian Dioceses of Pittsburgh, Parma & Passaic; Archbishop Joseph Raya, Combermere, Ont., Can., etc. We specialize in very high quality religious books, generally printed in Belgium, but accept other works, for instance a photographic album for account of Mr. Covington Hardee, Chairman of the Board, Lincoln Savings Bank, Brooklyn & NYC. Our distribution, however, is geared mainly to religious customers of the Byzantine Rite, Orthodox and Catholic, and to the general Christian readership." avg. price, cloth: $6.00-$15.00; paper: $2.00-$9.00; other: $30.00-Deluxe Morocco. 1969. from 32 to 1,250 pp depending on type of book; Varies. of/lp. avg. press run from 1,000 to 10,000. Reporting time: 1 week. Payment: Individual contracts. Does not copyright for author. Discounts: Below $20.00, 25 percent; $20.00 or over, 40 percent; except 20 percent on all codes BW and on first printing of WJ. Special discounts on very large orders. Pub'd 3 titles 1976; expects 4 titles 1977. COSMEP.

THE ALLEY CAT READINGS, Bombshelter Press, Michael Andrews, Marcus J. Grapes, 1092 Loma Drive, Hermosa Beach, CA 90254, 725 Sweetzer, Los Angeles, CA 90069. Poetry, art, cartoons. "The Alley Cat Readings is an anthology published in conjunction with a reading by the poets in the book. Sale of the book pays the poets. The book is paid for by local advertising. We are only interested in manuscripts as a way of selecting poets for the readings. We are biased toward oral poetry &, for the moment, local poets as we cannot pay transportation. Ron Koertge, Joseph Hansen, John Thomas, Eloise Healy, Deena Metzger, Doraine Poretz, Michael C. Ford, Kate Braverman, James Krusoe, Dennis Ellman." 4/yr; 1-yr sub price: $8.00; per copy: $2.00; sample: $2.00. 1975. 130pp; 8 x 5½. of. circ. 1,000. Reporting time: varies. Payment: $10-25 a reading. Ads: $35/$25/$15-1/4 pg/$8-1/8 pg. LPSC.

ALLIN, Allin, Nina Carroll, 31 Headlands, Kettering, Northants, United Kingdom. Poetry, art, concrete art. "Ted Hughes, Brian Patten, George McBeth, James Kirkup, each ALLIN is illustrated." irreg.; sub price: £1/4 issues; per copy: 30p; sample: 20p. 1968. 1pp; 15 x 20. of. circ. limited. Payment: commissions. Expects 1 issue 1977, 1 issue 1978. ALP.

Allonge Press, Dana Shilling, 215 Thompson St No. 13, New York, NY 10011, 212-868-3330. Poetry. "1 book so far—120 pp. *Anthology-Bromberg,* Clark, Jacobs, Orchid, Shilling. Will do another book of poetry in late '77 if I can get the money together." avg. price, paper: $2.00. 1976. 120pp; 5½ x 8½. of. avg. press run 500. Reporting time: 3 wks. Payment: 15 percent of profits (probably none). Copyrights for author. Discounts: 60/40 to bookstores & libraries.

The Ally Press, Paul Feroe, 1764 Gilpin St, Denver, CO 80218. Poetry. "Poetry only. Have been doing small (2-12 poem) quality collector's edition and will probably stay with this format for awhile. Past contributors include Robert Bly ('Grass From Two Year/Let's Leave, sold out) Ted Kooser (Shooting a Farmhouse/So This Is Nebraska, $2.50, $5.00 signed,) Martin Booth (Yogh, $1.50, $5.00 signed) and Norbert Krapf (The Playfair Book of Hours, $2.50, $5.00 signed.) 'An Ally is a power capable of carrying a man beyond the boundaries of himself.' From the teachings of Don Juan." 1973. †of/lp. Reporting time: 3 weeks. Payment: in copies. COSMEP.

ALPHA, Either/Or Publications, Lynda C.H. Russell, Box 1269, Wolfville, Nova Scotia B0P1X0, Canada, 542-2201 Ext 421. Poetry, fiction, articles, art, photos, cartoons, interviews, satire, criticism, reviews, music, letters, plays. "Short stories - 1,000 words up. Would very much like to see more humor, satire, etc." 7/yr; 1-yr sub price: $3.00; per copy: $0.50; sample: $0.50. 1976. 32pp; 8½ x 11. of. circ. 300-500. Reporting time: 1 month. Payment: None at present. Copyrighted, reverts to author. Ads: Rates presently under revision. Discounts: Negotiable. Back issues: to Jan. '77 - $0.15; $0.25 Feb. '77 on. Pub's reviews §Fiction, anthologies, nonfiction on the arts.

Alphabox Press (see also A), Jeremy Adler, 47 Wetherby Mansion, Earls Court Square, London SW5 9BH, United Kingdom. Poetry, art, criticism, long-poems, collages, concrete art. " *Fenster Sieben Gedichte* by H. G. Adler, *Acht Gedichte In Faksimile,* by Franz Wurm, *The Amsterdam Quartet* by Jeremy Adler. Forthcoming publications by Peter Mayer and Andrew Lloyd. Other publications in association with Pirate Press and Writers Forum. To publish otherwise unpublishable visual poetry; poetry combining traditional techniques with experimentation; translations; at cost (non profit-making) prices. Contributions not solicited, but considered if accompanied by SAE." 1974. 10pp plus; Quarto. dupl. avg. press run 100-200. Reporting time: 2 months. Payment: copies. Pub'd 1 title 1976. ALP, CULP.

Alphaville Books (see also AIEEE), Jack Grady, Orlan Cannon, Editors (Alphaville Academy of Archetypes), Box 3424, Charlottesville, VA 22903. "Avant-garde press publishing experimental literature & related graphics. Titles include: *'12 Surrealist Fairytales'-Jack* Grady $1.50; *'Toujours La Truite & Quantum Fantasies'-Orlan* Cannon-$1.50; *'Post Taste'* postcard series-first series 8 cards-$2.00; ' *Palace Of Weariness'* (poster) 11 x 17 - C. Cultural Canon-$2.00. Various formats planned for 1977-78. Inquiries and exchanges welcomed." 1975. pp varies; varies. †of/xerox. Reporting time: Every 0.8 seconds. Payment: by arrangement w/authors. Discounts: enquire. Pub'd 1 title 1976; expects 1 title 1977, 1 title 1978.

The Alternate Press (see NATURAL LIFE)

THE ALTERNATIVE PRESS, Ann Mikolowski, Ken Mikolowski, 3090 Copeland Rd, Grindstone City, MI 48467. Poetry, art. "No. 7 includes John Alfaro, Robert Bly, Gloria Dyc, Steve Foust, Donald Hall, Lyn Hejinian, Grace Hartigan, Jim Nawara, Pat Nolan, Bob Sestok, George Tysh, & Anne Waldman. No. 8 includes: Bill Berkson, Donna Brook, D. Clinton, Susan Forthman, Jim Gustafson, Gerard Malanga, Futzie Nutzle, Richard Sweeney, Eric Torgerson, Anne Waldman & Tom Wayman." 3/yr; 1-yr sub price: $10.00; per copy: 3.50; sample: 3.50. 1969. †lp. circ. 500. Reporting time: 1-3 months. Payment: copies. Not copyrighted. Pub'd 2 issues 1976; expects 3 issues 1977, 3 issues 1978. CCLM, COSMEP.

ALTERNATIVE SOURCES of ENERGY MAGAZINE, Alternative Sources of Energy, Inc., Staff, Network Contributors, Rt. 2, Box 90A, Milaca, MN 56353. Poetry, fiction, articles, art, photos, cartoons, interviews, satire, criticism, reviews, letters, news items. "Need alternative energy related material with photos, art, graphics, solar, wind, water, thermo electric topics. Wood/organic fuels, greenhouses architecture, integrated systems, much more." Bimonthly.; sub price: 6 issue price $10.00/Foreign $22.00 for air mail or $12.00 for surface.; per copy: $1.25 to $2.00; sample: $1.75. 1971. 64pp; 7½ x 10½. of. circ. 5,600. Reporting time: 2 weeks. Payment: $20.00/page (30 col. in.) or more. Copyrighted. Ads: $340.00/$170.00/$0.25. Discounts: Bulk: 7 copies plus 40 percent. Back issues: $1.25/$2.00; set of No. 1-10 $5.00, 11-25 $23.00. Pub'd 4 issues 1976; expects 6 issues 1977, 6 issues 1978. Pub's reviews. §Alternative energy topics & appropriate technology. COSMEP.

ALTERNATIVE TO ALIENATION, Alternative Typesetting Ltd, Bill Holloway, Louise Dorfman, Tom Field, David Rubenstein, Ernie Barr, Nancy Christpoulous, Carol Komarowsky, Paul Trapp, Box 46 Stn M, Toronto, On M6S4T2, Canada. Poetry, fiction, articles, art, photos, cartoons, interviews, satire, criticism, reviews, letters. "We'd like concise and to-the-point material, though not necessarily short, which explains and illustrates aspects of humanistic radical philosophy in a concrete manner." 6 times a year; 1-yr sub price: $2.25; per copy: $.35; sample: $.35. 1974. 24pp; 10 x 15. of. circ. 4,000. Reporting time: 2 weeks. Payment: subscription. Ads: $150/$80/$2.00. Discounts: 40% on consignment, 50% for distributors. Back issues: $.50 each. Pub's reviews. §human liberation. COSMEP.

ALTERNATIVES- Perspectives on Society and Environment, Alternatives, Inc, Robert C Paehlke, Trent University, c/o Traill College, Peterborough, On K9J7B8, Canada. Articles. "Environmental-ecological emphasis, topics cover philosophical, social, political, economic and other considerations. Articles submitted should be typewritten, modest footnoting at end of article. Two copies should be submitted." quarterly; 1-yr sub price: $4.00 ($4.25 U.S.); per copy: $1.00; sample: $1.00. 1971. 44pp; 8½ x 11. of. circ. 12-1,500. Payment: none. Ads: $250/$125. Discounts: 40% bookstores and orders of 20 plus. Back issues: $1.00/ea except $3.00/vol. 1,1: 2,1: 2,2; $2.00/vol. 1,2 (Available to Libraries only). Pub's reviews.

Altruistic Enterprises (see also THE SLOUGH), Charles Taylor, Pat Taylor, Nuane Carr, Pat Carr, 184 Q Street 2, English Department, Univ. of Utah, Salt Lake City, UT 84103. Poetry, fiction. avg. price, paper: $1.50. 1974. 64pp; 5 x 4. †of. avg. press run 500. Reporting time: 2 months. Payment: Negotiable. Copyright negotialbe. Discounts: Varies. COSMEP.

‡**Am Hakkert Ltd.,** 554 Spadina Crescent, Toronto, Ont. M5F 2J9, Canada.

Amen-Ra Publishing Co, P.O. Box 481, New York, NY 10462, 212-824-3122. Poetry. "At present publisher has no desire to publish any works other than that of it's present author." avg. price, paper: $4.00. 1975. 104pp; 5½ x 8½. of. avg. press run 1,000. not accepting works from other authors at present. Does not copyright for author. Discounts: standard 40 percent discount to retail store owners & postage & handling. Pub'd 1 title 1976.

American Academy of Arts and Sciences (see DAEDALUS)

AMERICAN ARTS PAMPHLET SERIES, American Arts Documentation Centre, Mick Gidley, Queens Bldg., Univ. of Exeter, Exeter EX4 4QH, United Kingdom. Articles, interviews, criticism. "The American Arts Pamphlet Series is an irregular series publishing specially commissioned items on the arts in America. Titles include A CHRONOLOGICAL CHECKLIST OF THE PERIODICAL PUBLICATION OF SYLVIA PLATH; A SELECTED BIBLIOGRAPHY OF BLACK LITERATURE; THE HARLEM RENAISSANCE; A CATALOGE OF AMERICAN PAINTINGS IN BRITISH PUBLIC COLLECTIONS; CHARLES IVES AND THE AMERICAN BAND TRADITION." 1-2/yr; price per copy: varies. 1970. 33pp; A4. lp. circ. 1,300. Discounts: 33% booksellers.

American-Canadian Publishers, Inc., Arthur Goodson, Ed. Director; Arlene Zekowski, Stanley

Berne, Herman Zaage, Art Director, Drawer 2078, Portales, NM 88130, 505-356-4082. Poetry, fiction, articles, art, photos, interviews, satire, criticism, reviews, music, letters, parts-of-novels, long-poems, collages, plays, concrete art, news items, non-fiction. "We believe through the practice of 25 years and 42 completed works (15 published books with many soon forthcoming) that the language/literature/criticism of the year 2,000 will be a celebration of the multilinear dimensions of verbal consciousness - non-exclusive, genrebreaking and open structured new frontiers of literary possibility. Beyond grammar and the sentence and the visual. A truly perceptual extension in many media. Newest titles: Arlene Zekowski, *Image Breaking Images;* Stanley Berne, *Future Language,* 2nd printing, fall 1977. Also available: 'Literary Best Sellers' *Seasons Of The Mind* (Zekowski); *The Unconscious Victorious* (Berne). Now available on cassettes: interviews readings radio shows on: neo-narrative, poetry-prose open structure & the grammarless language. Send for free kit/catalog on 'The Grammarless Language.' Discounts available for bookstores, distributors & class adoptions." avg. price, cloth: $15.00; paper: $5.00; other: $10.00-$100.00. 1972. 200pp; 6 x 9. of. avg. press run 1,500 per title to 3,000 per title. Payment: negotiable. Copyrights for author. Discounts: 40 percent to dealers; 50 percent bulk-class adoptions: rates negotiable. Pub'd 2 titles 1976; expects 2 titles 1977, 2 titles 1978. Rio Grande Writers Assoc, COSMEP, LPSC, COSMEP-WEST, NESPA.

The American Conference of Therapeutic Selfhelp/Selfhealth/Social Clubs (see CONSTRUCTIVE ACTION FOR GOOD HEALTH)

AMERICAN DANCE GUILD NEWSLETTER, American Dance Guild, Inc. (see also DANCE SCOPE), Nancy Reynolds, 1619 Broadway, Rm. 603, New York, NY 10019. Articles, criticism, reviews, letters, news items. 9-10/yr; sub price: regular membership: $25.00; per copy: not available. 1955. 18pp; 8½ x 11. of. circ. 1,000. Payment: none. Ads: $20. §performing arts, arts management, arts education. CCLM.

AMERICAN FIDDLERS NEWS, American Old Time Fiddlers Assoc., De Lores "Fiddling De" De Ryke, 6141 Morrill Avenue, Lincoln, NB 68507, 402-466-5519. Poetry, articles, cartoons, interviews, reviews, music, letters, criticism, news items, non-fiction. "We can use anything about Music played on the violin-fiddle. Writing must be by someone who knows the subject-(or interviewee must be expert). Must be sympathetic to fiddler-violinist. Must be authentic information-well researched, also review Records and Music books of Music, report contests and conventions." 4/yr; 1-yr sub price: $5.00; per copy: $2.00; sample: $2.00. 1965. 40pp; 8½ x 11. †mi. circ. International Mailing List 5,000. Reporting time: 1 month or less. Payment: copies. We do not copyright for author. Ads: $25/$13 (1/4 page $6.50)/$1 per inch. Discounts: $4.00 per year. Back issues: $5.00 per year's volume. Expects 11 issues 1977, 4 issues 1978. Pub's reviews: 100 in 1976. §Music-folk lore, dancing (folk), violin making-music books, classical violin. All violin-fiddle records/All violin-fiddle music.

AMERICAN LITERATURE, Duke University Press, Arlin Turner, 6667 College Station, Durham, NC 27708. Articles, criticism, reviews. quarterly; 1-yr sub price: $8, individuals/$10, institutions; per copy: $2.50. 1929. 175pp; 6 x 9. lp. circ. 6,000. Reporting time: 2-3 months. Payment: 50 reprints. Pub's reviews. §American literary criticism, scholarship, bibliography.

American Old Time Fiddlers Assoc. (see AMERICAN FIDDLERS NEWS)

‡**AMERICAN POET, Prairie Poet Press,** 902 10th St., Box 35, Charleston, IL 61920.

AMERICAN POETRY REVIEW, Stephen Berg, David Bonanno, Rhoda Schwartz, Arthur Vogelsang, Eleanor Wilner, 1616 Walnut St., Room 405, Philadelphia, PA 19103, 215-732-6770. Poetry, fiction, articles, art, photos, cartoons, interviews, satire, criticism, reviews, music, letters, parts-of-novels, long-poems, collages, plays, concrete art, news items, non-fiction. 6/yr; 1-yr sub price: $5.00; per copy: $1.00; sample: $1.00. 1972. 48pp; 9¾ x 13¾. of. circ. 26,000. Reporting time: 6 weeks. Payment: $0.50 line for poetry; $25.00 tabloid page for prose. Copyrighted, reverts to author. Ads: $500.00/$295.00. Discounts: Through Eastern News for stores and newsstands. Back issues: $5.00 and $2.00. Pub'd 6 issues 1976; expects 6 issues 1977, 6 issues 1978. Pub's reviews: 60 in 1976. §Literary. CCLM.

13

American Revolutionary Political Pamphlets, Melvyn Freilicher, 704 Nob Avenue, Del Mar, CA 92014, 755-1258. Fiction, art. "Mostly I print my own work. When I do print someone else, the ms. is solicited." avg. price, cloth: free. 1974. 45pp; 8½ x 11. of. avg. press run 300. Discounts: These pamphlets are distributed free, so far. Pub'd 1 title 1976. COSMEP.

THE AMERICAN SCHOLAR, Joseph Epstein, 1811 Q St., NW, Washington, DC 20009, 202-C05-3808. Poetry, articles, criticism, reviews, letters. "3,000 to 4,000 words best" Quarterly; 1-yr sub price: $8.00; per copy: $2.00; sample: $2.00. 1932. 144pp; 5½ x 8. of. circ. 40,000. Reporting time: 4 weeks. Payment: $250.00 per article. Copyrighted. Ads: $425.00/$235.00. Discounts: Vary. Back issues: $2.50 and up. Pub'd 4 issues 1976; expects 4 issues 1977, 4 issues 1978. Pub's reviews: 30 in 1976.

AMEX-CANADA MAGAZINE, Editorial Board, Po Box 189 Station P, Toronto, On, Canada. Articles, interviews, reviews. "Our material is related to anti-imperialist struggles, particularly the U.S. role in world affairs: economic and military. We are a publication of U.S. war exiles in Canada and give special attention to the amnesty issue." 6/yr; 1-yr sub price: $5.00; per copy: $.60; sample: free. 1968. 40pp; 8½ x 11. of. circ. 8,000. Payment: none. Pub's reviews. §World & U.s. politics, economics. APS, LNS.

Ana-Doug Publishing, S. J. Scholl, 2830 Chicago St, San Diego, CA 92117, 714-275-2211. Articles, art, photos, cartoons. avg. price, cloth: $12.00; paper: $7.00. 1975. 200pp; 8½ x 11. lp. avg. press run 2,500. Reporting time: 30 days. Payment: 15 percent. Copyrights for author. Discounts: 20 to 50 percent. COSMEP.

‡**ANA EXCETERA,** Vix Montallegro, Genova, Italy.

ANAESTHESIA REVIEW, Trouser Press, Philip E. Mirowski, Cynthia Huntington, 732 S. Forest St no. 5, Ann Arbor, MI 48104. Poetry, fiction, art, interviews, satire, parts-of-novels. "Recent contributors: David Ignatow, Stephen Dunn, Norm Williams, John Glowney (recipient of a pushcart prize). But mainly, we want fiction (especially) and poetry from writers who do not feel compelled to become famous in the next few years." 2/yr; 1-yr sub price: $4.00; per copy: $2.00; sample: $1.00. 1975. 60pp; 9 x 5½. of. circ. 350. Reporting time: 3-4 weeks. Payment: copies. Discounts: none. §For "Fictional Reviews" contemporary non-fiction which lends itself to speculative reaction, like "Zen and the Art of Motorcycle Maintanance" or a book on Indian Medicine. COSMEP.

Ananda Publications, 900 Alleghany Star Rt., Nevada City, CA 95959, 916-265-5877. "Books by Swami Kriyananda: i.e. YOUR SUN SIGN AS A SPIRITUAL GUIDE, 1971; YOGA POSTURES FOR SELF AWARENESS, 1968; TALES FOR THE JOURNEY, 1975; EASTERN THOUGHTS, WESTERN THOUGHTS, 1973." 1968. †mi/of. Pub'd 2 titles 1976. COSMEP.

ANDROGYNE, 1250 Press, Ken Weichel, 930 Shields, San Francisco, CA 94132, 586-2697. Poetry, fiction, art, collages. 1/yr; 1-yr sub price: $1.00; per copy: $1.00; sample: $1.00. 1971. 40pp; 5 x 8. †of. circ. 500. Reporting time: 3 weeks. Payment: 2 copies. Copyrighted, reverts to author. Discounts: 40/60. §Poetry-Collages-Criticism. COSMEP, COSMEP-WEST.

Angel Hair Books, Lewis Warsh, Box 718, Lenox, MA 01240. Poetry. 1966. CCLM.

Angst World Library, Tom Carlisle, Kathie McKie, 2307 22nd Ave. E, Seattle, WA 98112. Fiction, parts-of-novels. "We are a literary press with macabre overtones and interested in science fiction. Recently published: *Bonstonofavitch!* by Thomas Carlisle; *Mystery Of The Pig Killer's Daughter* by Lawrence Russell; *Death Of A Whale* by A.E. Sutton. Please query prior to submitting ms. and *always* enclose SASE." 1974. 5 x 8. of. avg. press run 500. Reporting time: 1-2 mos. Payment: 25% of net profit + 5 copies. Discounts: 40% on purchases over 5 copies. COSMEP.

ANIMA, Conococheague Associates, Inc., John Blair, Karin Blair, Harry Buck, Rebecca Nisley, 1053 Wilson Avenue, Chambersburg, PA 17201. Poetry, articles, art, photos, interviews, criticism, reviews, music, long-poems. "ANIMA, An Experimental Journal celebrates the sources of our separate identity in the common soul of us all. Authors from the Teilhard Research Institute and the Foundation for Mind Research; anthropologists, musicologists, and philosophers explore frontiers of awareness between fields of conventional scholarship. A feminist forum, ANIMA features 'Daughters of the *New* American Revolution,' a clearing house for feminist action, women active in business, teaching, and the arts. Articles on Eastern religion and dance, French folk music, and initiation rites present a cross-cultural perspective centered on the question of creativity in a cultural source. The magazine is itself a physical example of its themes, with experimental design and art work by many new photographers, poets, and artists. Authors creating new traditions from immediate experience are welcome." 2/yr; 1-yr sub price: $7.50; per copy: $4.00; sample: free. 1974. 80pp; 8½ x 8½. of. circ. 400-growing. Reporting time: 8 weeks. Payment: copies and offprints only. Ads: $50/$30. Back issues: $2.50. §psychology, religion, women. COSMEP.

ANN ARBOR REVIEW, Ann Arbor Review Press, Fred Wolven, Editor; Gerald Clark, Assoc Editor; Darlene Hargreaves, Assistant, Washtenaw Community College, Fred Wolven, editor, Ann Arbor, MI 48106, 313-971-6300 ex 407. Poetry, fiction, articles, art, photos, interviews, criticism, reviews, parts-of-novels, plays, concrete art, non-fiction. "New and younger writers, and women writers. Also 1-act plays. New and different directions in poetry and fiction. Especially interested in writer interviews and critical essays, and Canadian, European and South American writing. Duane Locke, Richard Kostel Anetz, Peter Wild, Alvaro Cardona-Hine, Deborah Tall, Linda Wagner, Elisavietta Ritchie, Robert Stilwell. See recent issue." 3/yr (July-June); 1-yr sub price: $4.50 ($5.00 foreign); per copy: $1.50; sample: $1.50. 1967. 96pp; 5 x 7. of. circ. 750-1,000. Reporting time: 1 wk-2 months. Payment: contributor's copies. Ads: $75.00/$40.00. Discounts: 20 - 40 percent (inquire). Back issues: $2.00 per copy. Pub'd 3 issues 1976; expects 3 issues 1977, 3 issues 1978. Pub's reviews: 10 in 1976. §New women writers, anthologies, Canadian writers, articles on writing and teaching of writing. CCLM, COSMEP.

Anonymous Owl Press (see MARGERINE MAYPOLE ORANGOUTANG EXPRESS)

ANTAEUS, The Ecco Press, Daniel Halpern, Susan Dwyer, 1 West 30th St., New York, NY 10001, 212-736-2599. Poetry, fiction, art, interviews, letters, parts-of-novels, long-poems. "Contributors: Michael Rothschild, Louise Gluck, James Merrill, Flann O'Brien, Brian Swann, Sanford Chernoff, Carolyn Forche, William Kotzwinkle, Norman Dubie, Octavio Paz, Robert Hass, Italo Calvino, William Harrison." 4/yr; 1-yr sub price: $12.00; per copy: $3.50; sample: free to reviewers and college professors. 1970. 160pp; 6½ x 9. of. circ. 5,000. Reporting time: 1 month. Payment: $10.00 per page. Copyrighted, will assign copyright upon author's request. Ads: $250.00/$150.00. Discounts: 33-1/3% trade; 40% classroom orders. Back issues: Issues still in print 1-24, $47.00. Pub'd 3 issues 1976; expects 3 issues 1977, 3 issues 1978. CCLM, NYSSPA.

The Antares Foundation (see PARAGRAPH)

Anthelion Press, Inc., Wm. Whitney, Encice King, 101 Townsend St., San Francisco, CA 94107, 415-957-1277. Poetry, fiction, art, photos, non-fiction. avg. price, cloth: $7.95; paper: $2.25. 1971. 160pp; 6 x 9. †of. avg. press run 2,000-5,000. Reporting time: 6-8 wks. Payment: open. Copyrights for author. Discounts: Trade: 10 percent; 40 percent; 41 percent; 42 percent; 43 percent; 44 percent; 45 percent. Pub'd 28 titles 1976; expects 22 titles 1977, 20 titles 1978. COSMEP, COSMEPA.

Anthology: Montreal Poets (see SUNKEN FORUM PRESS)

Anti-Ocean Press (see also SHIRHADASH/NEW SONG), Sol P. Lachman, 148 Pasadena, Highland Park, MI 48203, 313-869-6663. Poetry. "Emerging traditions in Judaism. 1977 title is *Camptown Spaces* by David Shevin (satirical poetry on America)." avg. price, paper: $2.95. 1975. †lp. avg. press run 1,000. Reporting time: 30 days. Payment: by arrangement. Copyrights for author. Discounts: 40 percent to stores. Expects 1 title 1978.

THE ANTIGONISH REVIEW, R. J. MacSween, St Francis Xavier University, Antigonish, Nova Scotia B2G1CO, Canada. Poetry, fiction, articles, art, interviews, criticism, reviews. 4/yr; 1-yr sub

15

price: $5; per copy: $1.50; sample: free. 1969. 110pp. of. circ. 600. Reporting time: 2 months. Payment: copies only. Pub's reviews.

THE ANTIOCH REVIEW, The Antioch Review, Inc., Paul Bixler, Editor; Ira Sadoff, Poetry Ed. Baker, Wm.; Bk. Rev. Ed.; Nolan Miller, Fiction Ed., PO Box 148, Yellow Springs, OH 45387, 513-767-7386. Poetry, fiction, articles, satire, criticism, long-poems, non-fiction. "Recent contributors: James Purdy, Stephen Dixon, Annie Dillard, Tess Gallagher, Heather McHugh, Charles Simic, Constance Scheerer, Thomas J. Cottle, Landrum Bolling, John J. Gilligan, Alvin Greenberg, Arno Karlen." 4/yr; 1-yr sub price: $8.00 ($9.00 for Foreign); per copy: $2.00; sample: $2.00. 1941. 128pp; 9 x 6. of. circ. 3,500. Reporting time: 1-6 weeks. Payment: $8.00 per page (approx. 425 words). Copyrighted. Ads: $120.00/$65.00. Discounts: 2 percent to agent. Back issues: sold at price marked. Pub'd 3 issues 1976; expects 4 issues 1977, 4 issues 1978. Pub's reviews. §General interest social science, fiction, contemporary affairs. CCLM, COSMEP, OAC.

ANTIQUE PHONOGRAPH MONTHLY, APM Press, Allen Koenigsberg, 650 Ocean Ave., Brooklyn, NY 11226, 212-941-6835. Articles, art, photos, cartoons, interviews, criticism, reviews, music, letters, news items, non-fiction. "Ray Wile, George Blacker, Ken Barnes, Jay Gandy, Robert Feinstein, Tim Brooks 500-3,000 words—Articles on the history of recorded sound and development of recording technology, both from a scientific and cultural point of view. Also articles on popular music, vaudeville, opera, politics, etc. Anything recorded 1877-1929. Articles on the development and restoration of antique phonographs." 10/yr; 1-yr sub price: $7.50; per copy: $0.75; sample: free. 1973. 16-20pp; 5½ x 8½. of. circ. 1,200. Reporting time: 2 wks. Payment: $10 to $50. Buys American or reverts to author. Ads: $65/$35/$.10-$.15 per wd/classified. Discounts: free samples for clubs, classroom, etc. Back issues: $7.50 for complete year. Pub'd 10 issues 1976; expects 10 issues 1977, 10 issues 1978. Pub's reviews: 20 in 1976. §Music history, music biography, history of sound recording. ARSC.

THE ANTIQUER, Gary W. Schueler, 318 Highland Ave, Syracuse, NY 13203. Articles, reviews. "1) all material related to collectibles 2) between 700 and 2,000 words (always with photos) 3) interesting angles on old subjects" monthly; 1-yr sub price: $5.00; per copy: $.60; sample: $.60. 1971. 30pp; 16 x 11. of. circ. 10,000. Reporting time: 1 week. Payment: $10 per article. Ads: $175.00/$100.00/$.10. Pub's reviews. §antiques, history, crafts, collectibles.

ANYART JOURNAL, Anyart Contemporary Arts Center, Christiane C. Westlake, Lois Graboys, Michael Kill, Jeanne Sturim, James Humphrey, 259 Water Street, Warren, RI 02885, 245-9005. Poetry, fiction, articles, art, photos, cartoons, interviews, satire, criticism, reviews, music, letters, parts-of-novels, long-poems, collages, plays, concrete art. "Most articles are under 1,600 words. Visual artists are featured regularly with a photo or drawing/print plus a 250 word statement by the artist. Recent contributors: Hugh Townley, James Humphrey, Andrew Glaze, Edward Koren, Lee Hall, James Schevill" 6/yr; 1-yr sub price: $6.00; per copy: $1.50; sample: $1.50. 1975. 44pp; 7 x 8½. of. circ. 1,000. Reporting time: varied. Payment: currently none. Copyrighted, reverts to author. Ads: $40.00/$25.00. Discounts: no discounts except following: one year subscription $6.00, two years $10.00 newstand price $1.50 per unit. Back issues: $7.75.

APALACHEE QUARTERLY, D.D.B. Press, P.V. Leforge, Don Caswell, David Morrill, Len Schweitzer, Po Box 20106, Tallahassee, FL 32304. Poetry, fiction, articles, art, photos, parts-of-novels, long-poems, plays. "We always need manuscripts of poetry and fiction very badly: but we're often flooded by manuscripts from one author. Try not to do this. Send 3-8 poems and prose up to 30 pages. We often write short criticisms on our rejection notices, but unless we specifically ask you to try us again it would be better if you tried your luck elsewhere after the first attempt. We, as well as anyone else, have our prejudices. Submissions without SASE are kept for 2 years, then used for scratchpaper. We have a game where we sit around in a circle and ridicule long vitas and absurd lists of previous publications, so include these accordingly. Don't send manuscripts that are so dog-eared and gravy stained that it's obvious 19 other magazines have amused themselves by making paper airplanes and little hats out of them. We're extremely selective about what goes in to the A.Q. Be selective in submitting. We would prefer to publish quality from an unknown rather than garbage from someone with a name." 3/yr; 1-yr sub price: $3.00; per copy: $1.00; sample: $1.00. 1972.

40pp; 6 x 9. of. circ. 300. Reporting time: 6-8 weeks. Payment: 2 copies. Copyrighted, reverts to author. Ads: $50.00/$30.00. Back issues: $2.50 each. Pub'd 2 issues 1976; expects 4 issues 1977, 4 issues 1978. Pub's reviews. §fiction, poetry. CCLM, COSMEP.

APHRA, Elizabeth Fisher, Edith Konecky, Claire Sawitsky, Box 893 Ansonia Station, New York, NY 10023. Poetry, fiction, articles, art, photos, interviews, criticism, parts-of-novels, plays. "A non-commercial, non-profit literary quarterly edited and written by and for women. As the first feminist literary magazine, APHRA has been coming out regularly for over six years, publishing the work of women like Alta, Margaret Atwood, Rita Mae Brown, Susan Griffin, Marilyn Hacker, Susan Hall, Ann Healy, Eva Hesse, Erica Jong, Audre Lorde, Marisol, Kate Millett, Louise Nevelson, Tillie Olsen, Marge Piercy, Adrienne Rich, Alix Kates Shulman, and Alice Walker, many of them for the first time. We want to go on discovering new women writers and artists." 4/yr; 1-yr sub price: $5.50; per copy: $1.75; sample: $1.75. 1969. 72pp; 6¾ x 8½. of. circ. 4,000. Ads: $200/$125. CCLM, COSMEP.

APM Press (see also ANTIQUE PHONOGRAPH MONTHLY), Allen Koenigsberg, 650 Ocean Avenue, Brooklyn, NY 11226, 212-941-6835. Articles, art, photos, cartoons, interviews, criticism, reviews, music, letters, news items, non-fiction. "Books on the history of recorded sound: 1877-1929. Discographies, manuals, posters, etc., development of the phonograph, lives of the inventors and artists. Also APM Monograph series." avg. price, cloth: $10.00; paper: $5.00. 1968. 100pp; 6 x 9. of. avg. press run 1,000. Reporting time: 2 weeks. Payment: Negotiable. Copyrights for author. Discounts: 40 percent. Pub'd 2 titles 1976; expects 2 titles 1977, 2 titles 1978. ARSC.

Apocalypse (see TAMARISK)

Apocalypse Press (see THE FAMOUS SCIENCE FICTION CHAPBOOK)

Appalachian Press (see WHAT'S A NICE HILLBILLY LIKE YOU . . .?)

Apple-wood Press, Philip W. Zuckerman, Box 2870, Cambridge, MA 02139, 617-868-5408. Poetry, fiction, art, photos, long-poems, non-fiction. "Limited editions of books on: bookmaking, medieval & classical literature. Paper editions of poetry, and novellas, broadsides of poetry—modern and medieval." avg. price, cloth: $20.00; paper: $3.00; other: $7.50 (broadside). 1976. pp impossible to determine. †of/lp/silkscreen. avg. press run Limited: 100-250. Paper: 1,000-2,500. Reporting time: 1 month. Payment: 10 percent. Copyrights for author. Discounts: 40 percent trade. Pub'd 4 titles 1976; expects 15 titles 1977, 15 titles 1978. NESPA, AIGA.

Applegarth Follies (see also APPLEGARTH'S FOLLY, BRICK, and TWELFTH KEY), Jill Jamieson, MacLean Jamieson, Michael Niederman, Box 40, Station B, London, Ontario N6A4V3, Canada, 519-432-6137. Poetry, fiction, articles, art, photos, cartoons, interviews, satire, criticism, reviews, music, letters, parts-of-novels, long-poems, collages, plays, concrete art, non-fiction. "Preferably connected works rather than miscellaneous collections. No chapbooks. Poetry will be looked at with a jaundiced eye. Books are generally illustrated: we make necessary connections between form and content. We don't have many stylistic biases, but have some subject-matter reservations: on, for instance, politics & how-to, which tend to bore us. The merely competent distresses us greatly. The 'another fine product from APPLEGARTH FOLLIES' symbol on all our publications is a quality claim we take seriously." avg. price, cloth: $10.00; paper: $5.00. 1973. 100pp; 6 x 9. †of. avg. press run 300-800 poetry, 500-1,000 other. Reporting time: 30 days on good days. Payment: Generous royalties; no advance. Copyrights for author. Discounts: Trade, agent, jobber: 40 percent discount on 3 or more copies (no discount on less); otherwise: full list except for quantity discount of 20 percent on 15 copies or more. Pub'd 2 titles 1976; expects 18 titles 1977, 24 titles 1978.

APPLEGARTH'S FOLLY, Applegarth Follies, Jill Jamieson, MacLean Jamieson, Michael Niederman, Box 40, Stn. B, London, Ontario N6A 4V3, Canada, 519-432-6137. Poetry, fiction, articles, art, photos, cartoons, interviews, satire, criticism, reviews, music, letters, parts-of-novels, long-poems, collages, plays, concrete art, non-fiction. "Only unpublished material. Each issue is thematic: poetry submitted to Folly that isn't specifically designated as for a particular issue of Folly

17

will be automatically re-routed to Follies' poetry journal, Twelfth Key. Although we are aiming at 2-3 issues per year, each issue takes 2-3 years to put together from start to finish, so don't send us work you want to see in print yesterday; we promise to treat it with reverence, but not necessarily with dispatch: that's not what it's for. Special interest: regionalism (any region)." 1/yr; 1-yr sub price: $0.00; per copy: $4.50; sample: $4.50. 1973. 150-180pp; 7 x 10. †of. circ. 800. Reporting time: 30 days, all going well. Payment: one copy of the issue concerned. Copyrighted, reverts to author. Ads: none. Discounts: see Applegarth Follies. Back issues: $4.50 where available. Expects 3 issues 1977, 1 issue 1978.

Applied Probability Trust (see MATHEMATICAL SPECTRUM)

April Dawn Publishing Company, Po Box 4433, Falls Church, VA 22044. COSMEP.

AQUARIAN AGENT-ASTROLOGY 77 (78), ASI, H. Weingarten, B. Somerfield, 127 Madison Ave, New York, NY 10016, 212-679-5676. Articles, cartoons, interviews, reviews, letters, news items. "Contributions *must* be knowledgeable in astrology. No sun sign garbage." Quarterly.; 1-yr sub price: $8.00; per copy: $2.00; sample: $2.00. 1968. 64pp; 6 x 9. of. circ. 1,500. Reporting time: up to 1 month. Payment: up to $2.00 a page. Copyrighted. Ads: $75/$40/$.25. Discounts: 5-49, 40 percent; 50 plus, 50 percent. Back issues: $10 a volume. Pub'd 4 issues 1976; expects 4 issues 1977, 4 issues 1978. Pub's reviews: 30 in 1976. §astrology.

AQUATIC WORLD, World Publications, Sue Turner, Po Box 366, c/o World Publications, Mtn. View, CA 94040. Articles, art, photos, cartoons, interviews. "The editor reserves the right for complete control over all published material. 'AQUATIC WORLD' contains information on techniques, new training methods, motivation." bi-monthly; 1-yr sub price: $4.50; per copy: $.75; sample: free. 1972. 32pp; 9 x 11. of. Reporting time: varied. Payment: inquire. Back issues: $1.00 each. §sports, recreation and leisure activities.

AQUILA MAGAZINE, Roq Press, Bob Quarteroni, Box 174-B, Petersburg, PA 02725, 814-667-2336. Poetry, fiction, articles, art, photos, interviews, satire, reviews, music, letters, parts-of-novels. "Still looking for the truly different. AGUILA was started with the hope that it could be a repository of the uniquely different. Poems that talk about eating pus-filled crotches are not *different,* they're just silly. I want to see anything that has a fresh perspective, or handling, no matter how twisted. Poems, short fiction, photos, art, reviews." Varies: shoot for 3/yr; 1-yr sub price: $6.00; per copy: $2.00; sample: $2.00. 1975. 32pp; 5¼ x 8½. various methods. circ. 200. Reporting time: 1-4 months. Payment: copies-prizes-some small ($1-3) payments. Ads: $35.00/$17.50. Discounts: no discounts. Back issues: $2.00. Pub'd 1 issue 1976; expects 2 or 3 issues 1977, 2 or 3 issues 1978. COSMEP.

The Aquila Publishing Co. Ltd. (see also PROSPICE), J.C.R. Green, Michael Edwards, P.O. Box 1, Isle of Skye, Portree, Isle of Skye, Scotland IV 51 9BT, United Kingdom. Articles, poetry, fiction, interviews, criticism, long-poems, art, photos, cartoons, satire, reviews, music, letters, parts-of-novels, non-fiction. "Aquila publishes books, (paper & cloth), booklets, pamphlets, broadsheets, etc. Main interest is in poetry, but some literature also used, in other spheres. Recommend that an initial letter is sent detailing work to be offered, ensure IRC or SASE (UK only) is sent otherwise no answer. Aquila publishes several series, including Aquila Pamphlet Poetry; Aquila/The Phaeton Press; Aquila Poetry; Essays on Literature ; Aquila Critical Library. Recent published writers include Martin Booth, Nick Toczek, Stephen Morris, Bryn Griffiths, George MacBeth, Pete Morgan, Peter Finch, E.A. Markham, Paul Matthews, etc. Forthcoming books in the Critical Library from Berryman, Moore, Dickey, Duncan, etc, etc. Aquila also publishes records and cassette tapes." avg. price, cloth: £3.00 ($5.00); paper: £1.50 ($2.50); other: £5.00 ($10.00) signed ltd edition. 1968. 60pp; A5 normally. †lp/mi/silk screen/of. avg. press run 1,250. Reporting time: varies. Payment varies. Discounts: bkshps 25% single copies, 35% other. Pub'd 48 titles 1976; expects 50 titles 1977, 50 titles 1978. COSMEP, SGPA.

ARARAT, Leo Hamalian, 628 Second Ave, New York City, NY 10016. Poetry, fiction, articles, criticism, reviews, parts-of-novels. "We prefer material in some way pertinent to Armenian life and culture." 4/yr; 1-yr sub price: $6.00; per copy: $2.00; sample: $1.00. 1960. 48pp; 9 x 12. lp. circ. 850-1,000. Reporting time: month. Payment: $10.00 a printed page (roughly). Copyrighted; reverts to author. Ads: $100.00. Discounts: 20 percent. Back issues: $1.50. Pub's reviews. §Ethnic, CCLM.

Arbor (see also TREES), Joan Dibble Shambaugh, Old Winter Street, Lincoln, MA 01773. Poetry, fiction, art. "'Submissions are by invitation only.'" avg. price, paper: $1.50. 1975. 20pp; 5½ x 8½. of. avg. press run 250. Copyrights for author.

Arbitrary Closet Press (see SCREEN DOOR REVIEW)

Arc Publications, Tony Ward, 3 & 4 Oldroyd, Todmorden, Lancs, United Kingdom. Poetry, long-poems, concrete art. "Any style considered as long as in high standard. Unfortunately unable to accomodate any mss. for publication during 1977/78." avg. price, paper: 75p. 1969. pp varies; variable. †of. avg. press run 450. Reporting time: 1 month. Payment: Negotiable. Right remains with authors unless otherwise requested. Discounts: 33-1/3 5 or more copies. Pub'd 10 titles 1976; expects 10 titles 1977, 11 titles 1978. ALP, COSMEP, BAAA (Beau & Aloes, Arc Association).

ARCADE-THE COMICS REVUE, The Print Mint, Inc., Bill Griffith, Art Spiegelman, Po Box 40474, San Francisco, CA 94140. Fiction, articles, cartoons, satire, parts-of-novels. "R. Crumb, S. Clay Wilson, Spain Rodriguez, Willy Murphy, Gilbert Shelton, Charles Bukowski, William Burroughs, George di Caprio, Justin Green, Jim Hoberman, M. K. Brown, Michelle Brand." quarterly; 1-yr sub price: $6.00; per copy: $1.50; sample: $1.50. 1975. 48pp; 8¼ x 10½. of. circ. 15,000. Reporting time: three weeks. Discounts: trade-retail less 40%, bulk (over 1500 assorted) retail less 60%.

Arcane Order (see JACKSONVILLE POETRY QUARTERLY)

Archangel Books, Barbara Gravelle, 2922 Otis C, Berkeley, CA 94703, 415-843-0169. Poetry, art, parts-of-novels, long-poems, plays. "Want to eventually publish poetry books, art books, short novels, long poems, and plays. As well as anthologies of work by persons in care facilities and poets working in care facilities for developementary and emotionally disadvantaged persons. Also want to publish a definitive autobiography of contemporary women writers since 1940." 1976. †of/lp. avg. press run 750-1,000 copies. Reporting time: 1 month. Copyrights for author. COSMEP.

THE ARCHER, Camas Press, Elinor Henry Brown, Wilfred Brown, Leone Stitt, Assoc. Editor, P.O. Box 9488, No. Hollywood, CA 91609, P.O. Box 30-383, Taipei 107,ROC, China. Poetry. "Rarely-cover art-very brief prose but that is so rare it probably should not be mentioned. We have enough difficulty handling verse ms.!!" 2/yr in China/4/yr (usually) in US; sub price: 8 issues $4.00; per copy: $.50 (so far); sample: $.50. 1951. 28pp; 5½ x 8½. †of in China/lp. circ. 500. Reporting time: recently indefinite. Payment: only in copies.

THE ARDENT SABOTEUR: a journal of amnemonics, Carl D. Clark, Eric S. Vogel, 3007 University, Austin, TX 78705, 512-472-7415. Poetry, fiction, articles, art, photos, cartoons, interviews, satire, criticism, reviews, music, letters, parts-of-novels, long-poems, collages, plays, concrete art. "*THE ARDENT SABOTEUR* is the artistic journal of the Amnemonic Revolution which is dedicated to overthrowing the constraints of memory and attendant vices such as nostalgia, regionalism, revolutions, politics and other areas of pornography. *THE ARDENT SABOTEUR* lives in a constant state of destruction by incomprehensibility." 3/yr; 1-yr sub price: $3.00; per copy: $1.25. 1977. pp varies erratically; 5½ x 8½. mi/of. Reporting time: 2 mos. Payment: copy; cash when available. Copyrighted, reverts to author. Ads: $50.00/$30.00/$2.00. Discounts: 30 percent to anybody engaged in resale; at cost to classrooms. Expects 3 issues 1977. Pub's reviews. §Literature, graphics, music, philosophy, linguistics, ethics.

Ardis (see RUSSIAN LITERATURE TRIQUARTERLY)

AREITO, PO Box 1124, New York, NY 10009. Poetry, fiction, articles, interviews. "Articles mostly on Cuban topics-either on the revolutionary govt. or about the exile community. Articles will

19

be published in Spanish with an English summary in the English supplement. Length limited to less than 29 double spaced 8½ x 11 pages. Interview with Sen. McGovern, Dancer Alicia Alonso." 4/yr; 1-yr sub price: $4; per copy: $1.00. 1974. 60pp; 8½ x 11. of. circ. 3,000. Pub's reviews. §Cuba, the Cuban exile community in the U.S.

ARETE, Curt F. DeBor, Lou Horvath, Associate, 830 Hyde St. #6, San Francisco, CA 94109. "The title, ARETE refers to the ancient Greek concept of the pursuit of excellence. Contributors should feel free to explore this pursuit in their own style, genre, etc. Explore, explore, explore! *Some ms. are held over for future issues but only after the contributor has been contacted by mail." quarterly; 1-yr sub price: $5.50; per copy: $1.25; sample: $1.50 (ppd). 1975. 40pp plus; 8½ x 5. of. circ. 500. Reporting time: immediate to 1 mo. Payment: copies. Pub's reviews. §literature, art, photography. COSMEP.

Ariel Press, Mary Mackey, Box 9183, Berkeley, CA 94709. "We regret that we can not accept new manuscripts at present. Our poets do their own lay-out, etc, and we help one another on a collective basis! Please do not send single poems since we are *not* a magazine and have no way to print them." avg. price, paper: $2.00. 1973. 64pp. of. Reporting time: 2 mo. Copyright: author. Discounts: 40% to bookstores. COSMEP.

ARION, A Journal of Humanities and the Classics, William Arrowsmith, D.S. Carne-Ross, Boston University, 270 Bay State Rd, Boston, MA 02134. Articles, criticism, reviews. " *ARION* publishes literary essays dealing with the Greek and Latin classical authors, especially the *former.* Style: follow *Chicago Manual,* Webster's Second, Fowler, Follett, Strunk and White." quarterly; 1-yr sub price: $10.00 individuals/$15.00 institutions; per copy: $3.00; sample: $3.00. 1962. 128pp; 4 -7/8 x 8-3/8. of. circ. 1,000. Reporting time: 2-6 mos. Payment: none. Ads: $75/$50. Pub's reviews. §classical literature.

Arion Press, Andrew Hoyem, 566 Commercial St, San Francisco, CA 94111, 415-981-8974. "We specialize in limited editions of 150 to 500 copies; issuing 2 or 3 books a year, at a cost of $100-150 annually. Our editorial policy is to develop our own books from materials which interest us." 1974. †lp. Copyrights for author. Discounts: 20 percent on orders of 1 book; 30 percent on multiple orders. Pub'd 2 titles 1976; expects 1 title 1977, 1 title 1978.

ARION'S DOLPHIN, Dolphin Editions, Stratis Haviaras, Box 313, Cambridge, MA 02138. "A new series is planned, each issue of which will focus on the work of one poet, with writings by and about that poet. Solicited only." irreg.; sub price: $4.00 (4 issues); per copy: $1.00; sample: $1.00. 1971. 32pp; 8.5 x 5.5. lp. circ. 1,000. Reporting time: 1 month. Payment: none. Ads: none. Back issues: Nos. 1-14 still available at $1/ea. Pub's reviews CCLM.

Arizona Jim Co-op (see THE VELVET LIGHT TRAP)

ARIZONA QUARTERLY, Albert F. Gegenheimer, Univ. Of Arizona, Tucson, AZ 85721, 602-884-1029. Poetry, fiction, articles, reviews, non-fiction. 4/yr; 1-yr sub price: $2.00; per copy: $0.50. 1945. 96pp; 6 x 9. of. Reporting time: 3-4 weeks. Payment: Copies. no ads. Back issues: Regular price available. Pub'd 4 issues 1976; expects 4 issues 1977, 4 issues 1978. Pub's reviews: 20 in 1976. §Modern literature.

THE ARK RIVER REVIEW, A.G. Sobin, Jonathan Katz, c/o A.G. Sobin Box 14 WSU, Wichita, KS 67208, 316-832-1075. Poetry, fiction, long-poems, criticism. "We work with a number of readers but with a system that does not require a concensus thus we are open to a very wide range of material. We always prefer to take a chance with something really new than to print what is 'highly competent' but usual—this is especially true of fiction (conventional fiction stands little chance). Recent contributors are: Maura Stanton, Albert Goldbarth, George Chambers, Stephen Dunn, Kenneth Rexroth, Stuart Friebert, James Tate, Michael Ryan, Lyn Lifshin, Harley Elliott, and you will be pleasantly surprised at our good taste!" 2-4/yr; 1-yr sub price: $4.00; per copy: $1.00; sample: $1.00. 1971. 52pp; 5½ x 8½. of. circ. 1,000. Reporting time: 1-3 weeks. Payment: poetry 20 cents line/$5.00 poem minimum/fiction $3.00 page/$20.00 story minimum. Copyrighted, we will grant any request to reprint made by the author. Back issues: Vol. 1 complete $20.00, Vol. 2 complete $18.00. Pub'd 2 issues 1976; expects 4 issues 1977, 4 issues 1978. CCLM, COSMEP.

Armchair Press (see also BROADSIDE, Writers in Residence), Mark Berman, P.O. Box 393, Tiffin, OH 44883, 419-447-4167. Poetry, long-poems. "Publish 4 chapbooks/books each year." avg. price, paper: $1.50; other: Varies. 1975. 16-32pp; Varies. of/lp. avg. press run 750-1,000. Reporting time: 4 months. Payment: 10% of print run. Share copyright with author. Pub'd 2 titles 1976; expects 4 titles 1977, 4 titles 1978. CCLM.

Around Publishing (see also LITTLE AROUND JOURNAL), Janos Szebedinszky, Patricia Walsh, 541 Mentone, Mentone, IN 46539. Poetry, fiction, articles, art, photos, cartoons, interviews, satire, criticism, reviews, music, letters, parts-of-novels, long-poems, plays. "The 1984 Calendar and assorted fantasy directed projects." 1975. of. avg. press run 2-5,000. Reporting time: 3-6 weeks. Payment: 50-50 on profits. Copyrights for author. Discounts: 25-35 percent.

ART AND ARCHAEOLOGY NEWSLETTER, Otto F. Reiss, Publisher, Otto F. Reiss, Editor, 243 East 39th Street, New York, NY 10016. Articles, photos, reviews. "Recent Contributors: Victor W. Von Hagen; David Reese, Harvard Univ; Dale R. Grieb. Length of Material:300 to 3000 words; we often *condense* contributions. Style: not unlike 'Science' department in 'Time' magazine. We return 90%-95% of all submissions as unsuitable, often too naive, and because would-be contributors confuse us with a travel magazine and send reports from an American Express tour of Mexico and similar on-the-beaten-track spots." 4 x yr.; 1-yr sub price: $4.50; per copy: $1.50; sample: 10 13-cent stamps. 1965. 16-20pp; 8½ x 5½. of. circ. 1,800. Ads: $55.00/$30.00. Discounts: subscription agents 20%. Back issues: vary from $.75 to $3.00. Pub's reviews. §ancient history esp. lands around the Mediterranean; archaeology (same area). CCLM, COSMEP.

ART & LITERARY DIGEST, Canada Publishing Company, Roy Cadwell, Tweed, Ont K0K3J0, Canada. "Payment 1 cent a word for material used. We need digests of art, crafts, and general interest articles. Some clippings of general or exceptional interest that would appeal to Canadian readers. Payment for poetry in copies of the magazine." quarterly; 1-yr sub price: $3.00; per copy: $1.00; sample: $1.00. 1969. 4 - 24pp; 8½ x 11 or 5½ x 8. of. circ. 1,000. Reporting time: 30 days. Payment: $.01 a word. Poetry-copies. Ads: $25/$15/$.05. Discounts: 40 percent. Pub's reviews. §art, music, good literature. No off beat books or magazines.

Art Official Inc. (see also FILE), 241 Yonge St, 3rd Floor, Toronto, Ontario M5B1N8, Canada, 416-368-7787. Art, photos, interviews, reviews. "We do not usually publish unsolicited material." avg. price, paper: $5.00. 1971. pp varies; varies. of. avg. press run 3,000. Reporting time: varies. Payment varies. Copyright reverts to authors. Discounts: 40 percent bulk orders. Pub'd 2 titles 1976; expects 7 titles 1977, 3 titles 1978. CPPA.

Art Press (see HARVEST)

ARTE QUINCENAL, Teodoro Perez Peralta, Apartado 19211, Quinta Crespo, Caracas, 101, Venezuela. 18/yr; 1-yr sub price: $20.00; per copy: $0.35; sample: $0.50. of. Copyrighted, reverts to author.

Arterial Books, Martha Henrickson, Thomas Henrickson, 16A Elgin St-Unit 131, Toronto, Ontario L3T4T4, Canada, 416-881-5423. Art, photos. "1st title: *The Organic Zucchini-Thomas* & Martha Henrickson conceptual art book, mainly photographic, also contains cooking section." avg. price, cloth: $6.50. 1976. 80pp; 10 x 8½. of. avg. press run 1,000. presently not soliciting manuscripts. Copyrights for author. Discounts: 40 percent trade/47 percent bulk. Pub'd 1 title 1976; expects 2 titles 1977.

Artistic Endeavors, Inc., PO Box 8916, Boston, MA 02114, 617-227-1967. "Publish material used for children in & out of schools. Our current project is books on major American cities—2 are published & they are being used in schools throughout the country as well as bookstores & museums on the East Coast—oversized paperbacks." avg. price, paper: $3.98. 1975. 48pp; 8½ x 11. avg.

21

press run 1,000-2,500. Discounts: depends on quantity for jobber, trade & classroom.

Artists & Alchemists Publications, Adele Aldridge, 215 Bridgeway, Sausalito, CA 94965, 914-332-0326. Art, concrete art, poetry. avg. price, paper: $5.00. 1975. 8½ x 11. of. avg. press run 2,000. not looking for ms. now. Copyrights for author. Discounts: 45 percent on orders of 5 or more when payment is enclosed and 10 percent on 1-4 books, 40 percent 5 or more without prepayment. No returns - we pay shipping. Pub'd 1 title 1976; expects 1 title 1977, 1 title 1978. COSMEP, NESPA.

‡**ARTS IN SOCIETY,** 610 Langdon St., #728, Madison, WI 53706. CCLM.

AS IS, As Is, L. Pablo Gamson, Paul Parsons, 6302 Owen Pl., Bethesda, MD 20034, 301-229-0142. Poetry, fiction. "Not interested in diatribes, deliberate obscurity, obscenity or superficial pious work. 'The fault of most poetry is not that it is bad but that it is boring.'" irreg; 1-yr sub price: $0.00; per copy: $1.50. 1971. various methods. circ. varied. Reporting time: any time. Payment: copy only. Not copyrighted. Discounts: not yet. Back issues: not yet. §poetry. Glen Echo Writers Center, Glen Echo, MD.

ASCENT, Daniel Curley, Mark Costello, Paul Friedman, Larry Lieberman, Michael VanWalleghen, Jean Thompson, English Dept,, U of Illinois, Urbana, IL 61801. Poetry, fiction. "Fiction up to 5-6 thousand words we have used some very short fiction. We haven't discovered our biases yet or haven't had them pointed out. Recent Contributors: M M Liberman, Manoj Das, Bink Noll, Dave Smith, Ralph Mills, Lloyd Goldman, Anthony Ostroff, Michael VanWalleghen, Mae Briskin, Audrey Borenstein, Jean Thompson, Carolyn Osborn, Alan Hewat, Peter Serchuk, Terry Spohn, William Knight, Jim Lindstrom, Harry Stessel." 3/yr; 1-yr sub price: $3.00; per copy: $1.00; sample: $1.00. 1975. 60pp; 9 x 7. of. circ. 300. Reporting time: 2 months. No payment. Discounts: Book stores 20%.

Ash Lad Press, Bill Romey, P.O. Box 396, Canton, NY 13617, 315-386-8820. Non-fiction. avg. price, paper: $4.95. 1975. 150pp; 6 x 9. of. avg. press run 1,500. Cooperative sharing of costs and income. Copyrights for author. Discounts: trade 40% for orders of over 5, 20% for 1-4, texts 20%, libraries 25%. Pub'd 2 titles 1976; expects 1 title 1977, 2 titles 1978. COSMEP.

‡**Ashland Poetry Press,** Box 171, Ashland College, Ashland, OH 44805.

ASI (see also AQUARIAN AGENT), Henry Weingarten, Barbara Somerfield, 127 Madison Ave., New York, NY 10016, 212-679-5676. Non-fiction. "Astrology, acupuncture, yoga, natural healing." avg. price, cloth: $15.00; paper: $5.95. 1969. 160-320pp; 6 x 9. of. avg. press run 2,000-3,000. Reporting time: 1-2 months. Payment: 7.5 percent plus royalty. Copyrights for author. Discounts: 5 plus books, 40 percent. Pub'd 6 titles 1976; expects 7 titles 1977, 6 titles 1978.

ASI Publishers, Inc. (see also ASTROLOGY '77—The New Aquarian Agent), Henry Weingarten, Barbara Somerfield, 127 Madison Ave, New York, NY 10016, 212-679-5676. "ASI publishes in a variety of subject areas. Our general requirements for new books are (1) the material is accurate (2) the material is unique and adds to the existing literature something not already available, and for which there is a real need (3) the material (explanations and diagrams) are clear and understandable. If you are interested in submitting a manuscript to us, your initial letter should be accompanied by an abstract, table of contenes, detailed description, or outline, including if possible, information relative to approximate page length and number of tables and illustrations. Please do not send a complete manuscript to us until we have made a specific request for it." avg. price, cloth: $15.00; paper: $5.00. 128-256pp; 6 x 9. of. avg. press run 2,000-4,000. Reporting time: 6 months. Payment: Semi-annual payment; standard author contract. All copyrights held by publisher. Discounts: 40 percent retail; higher—dependent on quantity ordered (see ABA redbook). COSMEP.

THE ASIA MAIL, Potomac Asia Communications, Edward Neilan, Editor & Publisher, P O Box 1044, Alexandria, VA 22313. Poetry, articles, art, cartoons, interviews, satire, criticism, reviews, music, letters, parts-of-novels, long-poems. "1,000 word top. We'll send a sample. Write for writer's guidelines, Associate Editor Donna Gays, c/o Asia Mail." 12/yr. 1976. of. circ. 30,000. Reporting time: 3 weeks. Payment: $150.00 Major articles; $50.00 Reviews. Copyrighted. Ads: $1150.00/$875.00/$0.50. Discounts: on request. Back issues: $1.00. Pub's reviews. §Asia interest.

Asian Studies Center (see JOURNAL OF SOUTH ASIAN LITERATURE)

Aslan Enterprises, Steve Saran, P.O. Box 1858, Boulder, CO 80306, 303-449-1515. "Health, natural lifestyle." avg. price, other: $2.25 poster. 1973. 17 x 22. †of. avg. press run 5,000. Reporting time: 1 month. Payment: 2 percent net 10 e.o.m, net 30. Copyrights for author. Discounts: 40 percent. Pub'd 1 title 1976; expects 1 title 1977, 2 titles 1978. COSMEP.

Asociacion Poncena Pro Arte Y Cultura (see CREACION)

ASPECT, Edward J. Hogan, Miriam Sagan, 66 Rogers Ave., Somerville, MA 02144. Poetry, fiction, articles, art, photos, cartoons, interviews, satire, criticism, reviews, letters, parts-of-novels, collages, plays, news items, non-fiction. "We are looking for the finest poetry and fiction, whether by name or unknown writers. We are not looking for any special kind of poetry, or political, critical, or other viewpoint. We try to read work on its own terms. We're still looking for more critical writing focused on small magazines, presses, and their best writers. We'd like to see more experimental work. All mss. must include SASE of sufficient size to return the work. We'd like to read more Canadians, include IRC (avail at your post office). Small presses and magazines should send us their special manuscript needs and news of prize contests, for listing (60-90 day lead time advisable). Ellen Wittlinger, Walter Cummins, Michael Hogan, Frederic Will, Albert Frank Moritz, John Stevens Wade, Christine Zawadiwsky, Jeannine Dobbs." 4/yr; 1-yr sub price: $6.00; per copy: $1.50; sample: $1.50. 1969. 80-100pp; 5½ x 8½. of. circ. 750. Reporting time: 60-120 days. Payment: 2 contributors copies. Buys first serial rights and one-time anthology rights (not exclusive). Ads: $40.00/$20.00/$0.05. Discounts: 40% trade; 20% classroom. Back issues: $1.50. Pub'd 3 issues 1976; expects 4 issues 1977, 4 issues 1978. Pub's reviews: 30 in 1976. §Alternative literary publications of all types; some social/political publications. CCLM, COSMEP, NESPA.

ASPEN ANTHOLOGY, The Aspen Leaves Literary Foundation, Kurt N. Brown, Box 3185, Aspen, CO 81611, 303-925-8750. Poetry, fiction, articles, art, photos, interviews, criticism, reviews, long-poems, plays. "Poems usually no more than 40 lines, stories 1-10,000 words. All forms, themes, subjects considered. Joyce Carol Oates, Kurt Vonnegut, Marge Piercy, Kathleen Fraser, Michael Dennis Browne, James Salter, Karen Swenson." 2/yr; 1-yr sub price: $4.50; per copy: $2.50; sample: $2.50 plus $0.25 postage. 1972. 120pp; 6 x 9. of. circ. 1,000. Reporting time: 2 mo. max. Payment: 2 copies. Copyrighted, reverts to author. Ads: $50.00/$25.00. Discounts: 30% trade & private over 10 copies. Back issues: $2.00/all back issues. Pub'd 2 issues 1976; expects 2 issues 1977, 2 issues 1978. Pub's reviews: 15 in 1976. §all literature, arts, criticism. CCLM.

ASPO NEWSLETTER, Carole Terwilliger Meyers, PO Box 6112, Albany, CA 94706, 415-527-5849. Poetry, articles, art, cartoons, criticism, reviews, letters, news items, non-fiction. "This newsletter is published for pregnant and new parents. ASPO is a national organization which promotes Lamaze prepared childbirth. Articles should be no longer than two pages, double spaced. Include return postage." 4/yr; 1-yr sub price: $2.00; per copy: Free, include return postage.; sample: Free, include return postage. 1966. 16pp; 8½ x 11. of. circ. 5,000. Reporting time: 2 months, include return postage. Payment: none. Not copyrighted. Ads: $140.00/$80.00. Discounts: none. Back issues: Free if available, include SASE. Pub'd 4 issues 1976; expects 4 issues 1977, 4 issues 1978. Pub's reviews. §childbirth, parenting. COSMEP.

Assembling Press, ASSEMBLING, Henry Korn, Richard Kostelanetz, Box 1967, Brooklyn, NY 11202. Poetry, fiction, articles, art, photos, cartoons, interviews, satire, criticism, reviews, music, letters, plays, concrete art. "ASSEMBLING is collaborative. Contributors print 1M copies of up to three 8½ x 11 pages of anything they wish at their own expense. Contribution is by invitation. An invitation will be sent to anyone whose work demonstrates a commitment to 'alternate' style or substance. Those wishing invitations are invited to send manuscripts. Editors of ASSEMBLING are really compilers-they are not interested in authoritarian procedures. Seven ASSEMBLING annuals

23

annuals have collected an unprecedented variety of avant-garde printed art. Individual books extend the bias and principles of the press. Send SASE for check-list." avg. price, paper: $3.95. 1970. 300pp; 8½ x 11. mi/of/lp. avg. press run 1,000. Reporting time: 1 mo. Payment: copies only. Pub'd 3 titles 1976; expects 4 titles 1977. CCLM, COSMEP.

ASSERT NEWSLETTER, Impact Publishers, Inc., Robert E. Alberti, PO Box 1094, San Luis Obispo, CA 93406, 805-543-5911. Articles, interviews, reviews, photos, cartoons, letters, news items, non-fiction. "Special interest: assertive behavior" 6/yr; 1-yr sub price: $3.00; per copy: $0.50; sample: free. 1970. 6pp; 8½ x 11. of. circ. 1,800. Reporting time: 4 weeks. Payment: none. Copyrighted. Ads: $125.00. Discounts: none. Back issues: no discount-$.50 per issue. Pub'd 6 issues 1976; expects 6 issues 1977, 6 issues 1978. Pub's reviews: 2 in 1976. §Assertive Behavior Therapy & Psychology in general.

Astro Black Books, Charles Luden, Julie Yaroch, P O Box 46, Sioux Falls, SD 57101, 605-338-0277. Poetry. "Our first book published is VIRGIN DEATH by Charles Luden (Feb. 1977)" avg. price, cloth: $6.00; paper: $3.00; other: signed, numbered edition $15.00. 1976. 75 to 130pp; 5½ x 8½. of. avg. press run 1,000. Reporting time: 1 month. Payment: negotiable. Copyrights for author. Discounts: 35 percent to trade (stores) 45 percent to jobbers. COSMEP.

ASTROLOGY '77—The New Aquarian Agent, ASI Publishers, Inc., Henry Weingarten, 127 Madison Ave, New York, NY 10016, 212-679-5676. Articles, art, cartoons, satire, criticism, reviews, letters. "Dedicated to the promotion of scientific astrological research practice" 6/yr; 1-yr sub price: $10.00; per copy: $2.00; sample: $1.50. 1969. 64pp; 6 x 9. of. circ. International; 2,000. Reporting time: 1 month. Payment: none. Copyrighted, does not revert to author. Ads: $75.00/$45.00/$0.25. Discounts: 40 percent to retail outlets; 30 percent to retailers with full returns priveleges; 50 percent to jobbers. Back issues: $10.00 Volume; $32.00 for all 4 printed volumes. Pub's reviews. COSMEP.

Asylum Publishing (see also Hh), Tom Konyves, 5355 Walkley No. 40, Montreal, Canada, 481-3580. "Experimental—minimal art." avg. price, paper: $1.50. 1975. 50pp. avg. press run 500. Reporting time: 2 weeks. Payment: tbd. Copyrights for author. Discounts: trade-40 percent; bulk-10 percent. Pub'd 1 title 1976; expects 1 title 1977.

Asylum's Press, Charles Bernstein, 464 Amsterdam Ave, New York, NY 10024, 212-799-4475. Poetry, fiction, articles, criticism, letters, long-poems, concrete art. "'It will be as much like granite as it can be.' Self—contained, with a gravity that weighs it down, thick, embedded, in itself, for itself: reproducing not the look of nature but its conditions. A poetry of borders, of structures, its limits the limits of a—of our—of the—world." avg. price, paper: $2.00. 1975. 200pp; 8½ x 11. of/xerox. avg. press run 100. Reporting time: 6 weeks. Payment: none at this time. Copyrights for author. Discounts: 40% discount to all booksellers.

ATARAXIA, The Madisonian, Madison, Ga. 30650, Philip L. Williams, Linda R. Williams, 204 Highland Ave., Madison, GA 30650, 404-342-0820. Poetry, fiction, articles, art, photos, interviews, criticism, reviews, parts-of-novels, long-poems, collages, concrete art, "Have no restrictions on length. Prefer poems and fiction tending towards craft drawn down lines from Pound, Eliot, W. C. Williams, Stevens, etc." 3/yr; price per copy: $1.00. 1973. 50pp; 8½ x 11. †of. circ. 300. Reporting time: 2 weeks. Payment: two copies of publication. Copyrighted, reverts to author. Discounts: none. Back issues: $0.50. Pub's reviews. §mainly poetry, fiction and criticism. CCLM, COSMEP.

ATHAENA, Paula D. Rubenstein, 2 Sadore Lane, Yonkers, NY 10710. Poetry, art, long-poems. "Innovative or traditional, top-quality material." 3/yr; 1-yr sub price: $5.00; per copy: $2.00; sample: $2.00. 1976. 28pp; 5½ x 8½. †of. circ. 300. Reporting time: 4-6 weeks. No payment. Copyrighted, reverts to author. Back issues: $3.50. §poetry, articles, reviews, criticism, interviews. COSMEP.

Athens Center Of Ekistics (see EKISTICS)

ATLANTIC PROVINCES BOOK REVIEW, John H. Battye, Robie Street, Halifax, Nova Scotia B3H3C3, Canada. Photos, interviews, criticism, reviews. 4/yr; sub price: free; per copy: free; sample: free. 1974. 4pp; 11¼ x 15. of. circ. 5,000. Reporting time: 7 days. Payment: none. Not copyrighted. no ads. Back issues: free. Pub'd 4 issues 1976; expects 4 issues 1977. Pub's reviews: 32 in 1976. §Books about, or by authors living in Atlantic Canada.

Atlantis Editions, Richard O'Connell, P.O. Box 2776, Philadelphia, PA 19120. Poetry. "Poetry of the highest quality. No biases. Contributors include: Elliott Coleman, Calliepe Doxiadis, Alexandra Grilikhes, Jack Lindeman, Howard Meroney, Richard O'Connell, Eric Sellin." lp. Pub'd 4 titles 1976; expects 3 titles 1977, 4 titles 1978. COSMEP.

Atlatl Press (see ROCKY MOUNTAIN REVIEW)

ATTENTION PLEASE, Hearthstone Press, Harold Leland Johnson, 708 Inglewood Drive, Broderick, CA 95605. Poetry. "Average 32 lines-Longer must be good, very, to justify space required. Recent Contributors: Hale Chatfield, Joseph McLaughlin, George Enos, Stella Worley, Arthur Winfield Knight, Ann Menebroker, Michael Scott Cain, Ramona Weeks, James Magorian, Paul Fericano, Guy Beining, Glenn Bacon, Edan Keane, Joyce Odam...." Tri-annual.; 1-yr sub price: $3.00; per copy: $1.00; sample: $1.00. 1975. 36pp plus; 5½ x 8½. †mi/lp. circ. 500. Reporting time: 2-3 weeks. Payment: $10.00 to 2 best of issue, 1 copy to each contrib, 3 issue subs. to 3 or more next best. Copyrighted. Ads: none. Discounts: 40 percent trade only. Back issues: $1.00. Pub'd 2 issues 1976; expects 3 issues 1977, 3 issues 1978. COSMEP, COSMEP-WEST.

AUDIT/POETRY, Audit, Mac Hammond, Editor; Betty Choen, Assoc. Editor; Ansie Baird, Assoc. and Managing Editor, 18 Allenhurst Rd, Buffalo, NY 14214. Poetry. "We publish 2 poets per issue, in some depth. We consider only book-length mss. from submitting poets and we select about 20 poems from each of 2 poets to make up a particlular issue. We are interested in unpublished poets with unusual voices. Recent poets published have been: Alan Feldman, Mike Finn, Gail Fischer, Thomas Frosch, Gary Margolis. In the sixties we had individual issues by Frank O'Hara, Robert Creeley, and Robert Duncan, among others." 1 or 2/yr; sub price: free. 1961. 50pp; 6 x 9. of. circ. 1,000. Reporting time: 1-2 months. Payment: copies. Back issues: $2.00

Augtwofive (see ABYSS/AUGTWOFIVE)

AUNTIE BELLUM, Womens Heritage Association Trust, Merry Bateman, 615 Woodrow St, Columbia, SC 29205, 803-799-4012. Poetry, fiction, articles, art, photos, cartoons, interviews, satire, criticism, reviews, letters. "Material must have some interest to southern women. Emphasis on artistic avenues; photography, poetry and art." 4/yr; 1-yr sub price: $7.00; per copy: $2.00; sample: $2.00. 1976. 32pp; 8½ x 11. of. circ. 1,000. Reporting time: 2 weeks. Payment varies. Copyrighted, reverts to author. Ads: $250.00/$150.00. Discounts: 40 percent usual trade discount. Pub's reviews. §Women oriented.

AURA Literary Arts Review, The University of Alabama In Birmingham, Steven Ford Brown, Box 348 NBSB, University Station, Birmingham, AL 35294, 205-934-3618. Poetry, fiction, art, photos, interviews. "Serious poetry, fiction, prose poetry, experimental prose, interviews, etc. Like good images, interesting use of language. Would like to see more prose poems, good fiction. Interviews with Jesse Hillford, Sonya Dorman. Special issue, Spring 1977 with Robert Bly, Michael McMahon, Sonya Dorman, Howard Nemerov, Victor Contoski. Other contributors in the past include, Greg Kuzma, Pier Giorgio DiCicco, Sandra S. Thompson, John Tagliabue, Konla Hammond, Lyn Lifshin, D C Berry, Alan D. Perlis, and others." 2/yr; 1-yr sub price: $2.50; per copy: $1.00; sample: $1.25. 1974. 60pp; 8½ x 11. of. circ. 2,000. Reporting time: 2 months. Payment: 2 copies. Copyrighted, reverts to author with acknowledgment to the magazine. Ads: $100/$50. Back issues: not available. §poetry mags. COSMEP, COSMEP-SOUTH.

AUSTIN PULPWOOD, Red Bean Revue, Jefferson Woodruff, Cathleen Day, Richard Maurer, 501 Park Blvd, Austin, TX 78751, 512-247-3706. Poetry, fiction, articles, art, photos, cartoons, interviews, satire, criticism, reviews, music, letters, parts-of-novels, collages, plays, concrete art. "Loris Essary, Carl D. Clark, David Gene Fowler (of Austin), Eleanor Crockett, Mark Laeffler, Jefferson Woodruff. No memory verse. Prefer a low rate of syntactical mush to imaginative language." 1-6/yr; 1-yr sub price: $3.00; per copy: $0.25; sample: $1.00. 1972. 28pp; 7½ x 11. mi/of. circ. 250. Reporting time: Indefinite. Payment: 2 copies-10 copies. Copyrighted. Ads: $50.00/$35.00. Back issues: no. 1 $50.00; no. 2 $75.00; no. 3 $35.00; no. 4 $2.00; no. 5 $1.00. Pub's reviews. §Poetry, fiction, new forms, experimental. COSMEP.

AUSTRALASIAN SMALL PRESS REVIEW, Second Back Row Press, Tom Whitton, Wendy Whitton, P.O. Box 197, North Sydney, NSW 2060, Australia. Articles, cartoons, interviews, criticism, reviews, letters. "Any length, style or bias. Recent contributors include Grahame Rowlands, John Ewers, George Turner, Michael Dugan, Ian Stubbin." irregular; sub price: $8 — 5 issues/$11 — 5 (institutions); per copy: $2.00; sample: free. 1975. 44pp; 8 x 5. of. circ. 500. Reporting time: 1 month. Payment: nil. Ads: $15/$8. Discounts: 10 percent to subscription agents; 35 percent bookstores. Pub'd 2 issues 1976; expects 2 issues 1977, 3 issues 1978. Pub's reviews. §small press from Aust. NZ, South Pacific. COSMEP, COSMEPA.

Autumn Press, Inc., Nahum Stiskin, 7 Littell Road, Brookline, MA 02146, 617-738-5680. Poetry. "A.P. Books cover all 'new age' concerns, with a bias toward East-West cultural confluence. Book of Tofu and Book of Miso, by Bill Shurtleff & Akiko Aoyage exemplary: cover natural foods, Zen and meditative practices, alternative lifestyles, self-sufficiency, low-energy technologies. Forthcoming titles to deal with Kundalini-and-science, zen and music, ecology, feminist poetry, Oriental medicine (accuptuncture, etc.). Developing a random list (7 titles now in print) with above focus." avg. price, cloth: $15.00; paper: $5.00. 1972. 216pp. of. avg. press run 3,000-5,000. Payment: standard. Copyrights for author. Discounts: Distributed to the retail and library trade by Independent Publishers Group, Port Washington, N.Y.

AVALANCHE, Center for New Art Activities Inc, Liza Bear, 93 Grand Street, New York, NY 10013. Interviews. "Editorial content consists of: Interviews (done by Liza Bear & Willoughby Sharp), documentation (sections produced by artists in collaboration with Avalanche), and rumbles (news, notes, photographs on recent art projects)." irreg.; sub price: $10/5 issues; per copy: $2.00 + postage; sample: $2.00 plus postage. 1970. 48pp tabloid; 11 x 17. circ. 5,000. Reporting time: 3 months. Payment: nil. Ads: $300/$175/1/4 page $125. Discounts: 40%. Back issues: $5 per issue + 50¢ p&h. §video, performance, film, art.

Ave Victor Hugo Publishing (see also FICTION, GALILEO), Galileo Fiction, 339 Newberry St., Boston, MA 02115. "Published one novel in 1976, *Milk Of Wolves* by Frederick Manfred."

The Avondale Press, Gerda Napier, Ronald Napier, P.O. Box 451, Willowdale, Ontario M2N5T1, Canada. †lp.

AXIOM (Atlantic Canada's Magazine), D.T. Murphy, P.O. Box 1525, Halifax, Nova Scotia B3J 2Y3, Canada. Poetry, fiction, articles, art, photos, cartoons, interviews, satire, criticism, reviews, music. "All material must be oriented toward 4 Atlantic Provinces-N.S., N.B., P.E.I., & NFLD. — BY Lines — Harry Bruce, Dalton Camp, David Coles, Kent Thompson. — Official In-Flight Magazine for Eastern Provincial Airways." 6/yr; 1-yr sub price: $3.00; per copy: $.75; sample: $1.00. 1974. 64pp; 8½ x 11. of. circ. 25,000. Reporting time: 2 months prior to publication. Payment: $25-$300. Ads: $500/6 times, $355/6 times/$15, min. 20 words. Discounts: 20% for ads; 75% for subs. Back Issues: Vol. 1 no. 2 & 3 out of print. 75¢ for all others. Available on microfilm from Micro-Media Ltd. Toronto, Ont. Pub's reviews §must be on Eastern Canada or by Eastern Canadians. CPPA.

Ayanna Press (see BOPP)

AZU-THE INFINITE MAN, Azu Press, Equus Publishers, Zahur Zapata, P.G. Montoya, 146 West 29th St, New York, NY 10001, 212-947-0528. Poetry, fiction, articles, art, photos, interviews, criticism, reviews, parts-of-novels, long-poems, plays, concrete art. "Stefan Baciu, John Horvath,

Jr. Raul Henao, Edgardo Ferreyra, Blanca Luz Sierra, Pablo Gilberto Montoya." 4/yr; 1-yr sub price: $6.00; per copy: $1.50; sample: $1.50. 1966. 40 to 60pp; 8½ x 11. †of. circ. 2,000 copies—The American Continent. Reporting time: 15 to 20 days. Copyrighted, reverts to author. Ads: $75.00/$40.00. Discounts: 30 percent. Back issues: $2.00. Pub's reviews. §American and Latinamerican literature and art.

AZU Press (see also AZU-THE Infinite Man), Zahur Zapata, P.G. Montoya, 146 West 29th St, New York, NY 10001, 212-947-0528. Poetry, fiction, articles, interviews, criticism, plays, concrete art. "Stefan Baciu, J. Luis Panizza, Sahur Zapata, Jose Puben, Hugo Hanriit Perez, Jaime Mejia Duque, Mauricio Reyes." avg. price, paper: $2.50. 1966. 130-200pp; 5 x 8. †of. avg. press run 5,000. Reporting time: 10 to 15 days. Payment: yes, individually. Copyrights for author. Discounts: 30 percent.

B **B & H BOOKS, Fur Line Press,** E.L. Chandler, 330 Paloma Ave, San Rafael, CA 94901, 415-456-0941. Poetry, non-fiction. "We are distributors of 6 small presses: Fur Line, Perivale, VPC Press, Nanroot. Fur Line Press is a subsidiary of B and H Books. The other presses are separate. We are now listing 19 books." 1971. 70pp; varies. of. Discounts: 40% trade, 10% to libraries. Pub'd 4 issues 1976; expects 5 issues 1977. COSMEP.

The B & R Samizdat Express, Barbara Hartley Seltzer, Richard Seltzer, Robert Richard Seltzer, PO Box 161, West Roxbury, MA 02132, 617-469-2269. Fiction. "We publish two titles. 1) The Lizard of Oz, a fable for all ages 2) Now & Then & Other Tales from Ome, a short collection of children's stories." 1974. Lizard-128pp/Now & Then-64pp; 5½ x 8½. of. Copyrights for author. Discounts: trade 40% (orders of 5 or more copies) 20% (orders of less than 5). Pub'd 1 title 1976. COSMEP.

BA SHIRU, Oluropo Sekoni, Richard Lepine, Beverly Mack, University of Wisconsin, 1456 Van Hise, Madison, WI 53706. Poetry, fiction, articles, reviews. "Journal devoted to African Languages, literatures and linguistics. Unique in its emphasis on African Oral traditions. We publish oral narratives in original African language and critical articles as well." bi-annual; 1-yr sub price: indiv. $5.00/yr; instit. $15.00; per copy: $2.50 indiv/$7.50 instit. 1970. 90pp; 6 x 9. of. circ. 150. Reporting time: ASAP. Ads: $50/$25/$15. Back issues: cost. Pub's reviews. §African Studies. CCLM.

The Babbington Press, Eric Kraft, Mark Dorset, Martha Dorset, Margot Dorset, P.O. Box 98, Stow, MA 01775, (617) 568-8024. Poetry, fiction, articles, art, photos, interviews, criticism, music, letters, parts-of-novels, collages, plays, news items, non-fiction. "The Babbington Press and all its publications are pieces of one fiction: The Life Of Peter Leroy, author of *The Unlikely Adventures Of Larry Peters.*" avg. price, paper: $0.90. 1975. 12-16pp; 5½ x 8½. of. avg. press run 500 to 1,000. no unsolicited manuscripts. Payment: authors are fictional characters. Copyright is held by The Babbington Press. Discounts: none. Pub'd 3 titles 1976; expects 6 titles 1977, 6 titles 1978.

BACHY, Papa Bach Paperbacks, John Harris, Poetry; Bob Mehlman, Fiction; Rick Lowitz, Art; Rod Bradley, Poetry; Robert M. Aber, Sports and Religion, 11317 Santa Monica Blvd., Los Angeles, CA 90025. Poetry, fiction, articles, art, photos, cartoons, interviews, satire, criticism, reviews, music, letters, parts-of-novels, long-poems, collages, plays, concrete art. "'BACHY combats the 'Battered Writer Syndrome'—applies to those previously unpublished and neglected writers and artists of merit whose ability currently exceeds their reputations. BACHY has reserved a substantial portion of each issue for new writers who haven't cracked either the underground or the overground establishment. Aims and orientation: editorial approach is eclectic and chooses the best submissions received without regard for current fads, etc; orientation is regional with a predominance of California writers and artists; attempt to maintain the highest standards in layout, design, printing and binding, and to integrate graphic art and photos with the text; contributors include Douglas Blazek, Joseph Hansen, Charles Bukowski, Joseph Bruchac, Sam Eisenstein, John Haines, Jack

Hirschman, James Holmstrand.''' 2/yr; 1-yr sub price: $4.50; per copy: $2.50; sample: $2.50. 1972. 96pp; 8½ x 11. of. circ. 800. Reporting time: about 8 weeks. Payment: author's copies only. Ads: $20/$10. Discounts: 40% off. Back issues: #'s 1,3&4/$2.00; #'s 5&6/$2.50; #2/$4.00. Pub's reviews. CCLM, COSMEP.

BACK DOOR, Dave Smith, Bob DeMott, P.O. Box 481, Athens, OH 45701. Poetry, interviews, criticism, reviews, long-poems. "Because we publish on an irregular schedule and because we have no wish to be involved with the subscription/distribution apparatus, we think of ourselves as a kind of samizdat. Consequently, most of our contributors, though certainly not all, are solicited. As editors we are often poles apart in our inclinations, though committed to quality we hope, and we believe this is reflected in an eclectic body of contributors and a diversity of poetic styles, voices and intentions. Among those contributors in issue 7/8 (Spring, 1975) are Paul Metcalf, Josephine Jacobsen, Richard Hugo, Clayton Eshleman, John Haislip, Herb Scott, Ted Enslin, Michael Heffernan, Carolyn Kizer and Beth Bentley. Issue No. 9/10 (Fall, 1976) includes Stephen Dunn, Grace Butcher, Linda Pastan, Tess Gallagher, Roland Tharp, Robert Kelly, Keith Wilson, and others. We are interested in seeing statements on contemporary poetry, reviews, prose poems, and interviews.'' irregular, 1 double issue/year; price per copy: $2.00; sample: $2.00 when copies available. 1969. 90pp; 8½ x 5½. of. circ. 450. Reporting time: 1 month. Payment varies. Ads: none. Discounts: none. Back issues: No. 9/10 available at $2.00 each. Pub'd 1 issue 1976; expects 1 issue 1977. Pub's reviews: 10 in 1976. §poetry, critical or scholarly books on contemporary poetry; essays on poetics. CCLM.

BACK ROADS, Back Roads Press, Stella Monday Nathan, Box 543, Cotati, CA 94928, 707-937-0618. Poetry, fiction, articles, art, photos, cartoons, interviews, satire, criticism, reviews, parts-of-novels, collages, concrete art, non-fiction. "Each issue has a theme (No. 8 Play & Games, No. 9 Technology & Culture). Write for info on upcoming themes. No more than 5 poems or one story per submission. Welcome original & unique perspectives on the theme. Recent contributors include Robert Bly, Sherrill Jaffe, David Bromige, Alta, Michael Rossman, George Hitchcock, Carol Berge, Opal Nations." Annual.; price per copy: $1.00; sample: $1.00. 1971. 128pp; 5½ x 8½. of. circ. 1,500. Reporting time: 3 months. Payment: Copies, small payments for solicited ms. Copyrighted. Ads: $70.00/$40.00. Discounts: 40 percent to bookstores, 40 percent to prisons & hospitals & small non-profit educational or art organizations. Back issues: $5.00 ea. Pub'd 1 issue 1976; expects 1 issue 1977, 1 issue 1978. Pub's reviews: 1 in 1976. §Related to theme - write for info. CCLM, COSMEP.

Back Roads Press, Steila Monday Nathan, Box 543, Cotati, CA 94928, 707-937-0618. Fiction, poetry. "Ms. considered only on editor's request, write for information." avg. price, paper: $2.50. 1976. 120pp; 5½ x 8½. of. avg. press run 500-1,000. Reporting time: 3 months. Payment: Copies, royalties. Copyrights for author. Discounts: 40 percent bookstores, 40 percent classroom orders of 10 or more, 40 percent to prisons, hospitals, small non-profit or low-budget organizations; inquire for additional discount info. Pub'd 2 titles 1976; expects 2 titles 1977, 2 titles 1978. CCLM, COSMEP.

Back Row Press, M. R. Ritter, PO Box 12845, St. Paul, MN 55112, 612-633-1685. Fiction, plays. "Interested in metaphysical religion, bisexuality—especially lesbianism" avg. price, cloth: $8.95. 1976. 280pp; 5½ x 8½. †mi. avg. press run 350. Not currently accepting submissions. Payment: Authors have collective stock in press. Author owns copyright. Discounts: 40 percent to stores, 25 percent to libraries. Expects 1 title 1977. COSMEP.

BACONIANA, Commander Martin Pares, Noel Fermor, Canonbury Tower, Islington, London, England N1, United Kingdom. Articles, letters. "General maximum: 3,500 words." 1/yr; 1-yr sub price: $5.00; per copy: £1 ($1.75); sample: £1 ($1.75). 1885. 70-100pp; 8½ x 5½. Reporting time: 2-3 wks. No payment. Copyrighted. Ads: Not accepted. Discounts: Depends on size of bulk orders. Back issues: Inquire. Pub'd 1 issue 1976; expects 1 issue 1977, 1 issue 1978. Pub's reviews: 1 in 1976. §Elizabethan & Jacobean literature, philosophy, etc.

Badger Creek Press, Peggy Flynn, James Singer, PO Box 728, Galt, CA 95632, 916-687-7295. Articles. "Essentially two kinds of things: How-to pamphlets, called Badger Creek Notebooks (such as *Badger Creek Farm Food Drier-How to Build It*) of whatever length is necessary and sufficient for which we pay $75.00 and up (query first), and technical books and manuals on health care organization and delivery, of which we have two in the works. Latter are published on 10-12½-15 percent royalty contract. Biased against sloppy, unclear writing; biased toward practical things we need to know to survive.'' avg. price, paper: $2.00. 1976. 12 to 24pp; 8 x 10¾. of. avg. press run 5,000. Reporting time: week. Payment: outright purchase: $75.00 up. Copyright for press. Discounts: 1-9, net; 10-99, 40%; 100 & up, 50%.

Baja Trail Publications, Inc. (see MEXICO WEST!)

‡**Bakke Press,** Rt. 3, Box 119-A, Hillsborough, NC 27278.

Baleen Press (see INSCAPE)

BALL OCCASIONAL, Crosscut Saw Unltd., Bob Adler, C.C. Saw, Michael Wojczuk, Tom Plante, 1806 Bonita, Berkeley, CA 94709. ''Mostly poetry, shorter lengths, very short prose pieces, graphics, photos. We're pretty open editorially, having printed something from almost everyone who has submitted. (That doesn't mean we print everything, or anything.) (Good, tailored, 'Language loaded'.) Recent contributors: Tom Plante, Summer Brenner, Leslie Simon, Andy Clausen, Merritt Clifton, Cynthia Genser, Thom Hover, Susan Efros, & many more.'' irreg.; sub price: $4.00-3 issues; per copy: $1.75; sample: $1.00. 1971. 32pp. of. circ. 400. Reporting time: 3-4 weeks. Payment: 2 copies. Copyrighted, reverts to author. no ads. Back issues: $1.00 each. Pub'd 3 issues 1976; expects 3 issues 1977. CCLM.

BALL STATE UNIVERSITY FORUM, Francis Mayhew Rippy, Merrill Rippy, Ball State Univ., Muncie, IN 47306. Poetry, fiction, articles, interviews, satire, criticism, parts-of-novels, long-poems, plays. ''An eclectic journal, publishing articles of general interest in any field, esp. literature, language, education, history, social sciences; also short stories, poetry, one-act plays.'' 4/yr; 1-yr sub price: $5.00; per copy: $1.50; sample: free. 80pp; 10 x 6½. lp. circ. 1,500. Reporting time: 3 mos. Payment: 10 copies. Ads: $50/$30. CCLM, COSMEP.

BAMCA, Scott Mace, Dave Robison, 1505 Lochinvar Ave., Sunnyvale, CA 94087, 408-248-7220. Articles, photos, cartoons, interviews, reviews, letters. ''BAMCA is the newsletter of the Bay Area 'Matchbox' Collectors Association, a group that collects 'Matchbox' models, made by Lesney Products & Co. of England. We print 1) All material about 'Matchbox' and 2) Local collecting news. Nat'l members welcome.'' 4/yr; 1-yr sub price: $2.00; per copy: $0.75; sample: $0.75. 1971. 10pp; 8½ x 11. †mi/xerox. circ. 75. Reporting time: 2 weeks. Payment: copies. Copyrighted, reverts to author. Ads: $10.00/$5.00/$0.10. Discounts: trade 1 for 1. Back issues: $0.75. Pub'd 3 issues 1976; expects 4 issues 1977. Pub's reviews: 2 in 1976.

Banana Productions (see also BANANA RAG, VILE), Anna Banana, 1183 Church St., San Francisco, CA 94114, 415-648-5174.

BANANA RAG, Banana Productions, Anna Banana, 1183 Church St., San Francisco, CA 94114. ''Any type of material with one important criteria, must be about or contain significant references to Bananas: newstories, information, facts, fantasies, poems, photos, artworks, slang usage, such as 'going bananas', 'top banana', 'banana nose'.'' 1/yr; 1-yr sub price: $2.00; per copy: $2.00; sample: $2.00. 1971. 3pp; 8½ x 14 Often, but varies with material. of. circ. 200. Reporting time: 2 mo. Payment: copies only. Not copyrighted. Back issues: Not available. Pub'd 1 issue 1976; expects 1 issue 1977, 1 issue 1978. CCLM.

Banyan Tree Books, 2300 Le Conte Avenue, Berkeley, CA 94709, 415-548-0737. ''We are not accepting any mss. at present.'' 1975.

BARATARIA REVIEW, The New South Press, David Hershkovits, Louis Gallo, Richard LeMon, Ralph Adamo, 1918½ Dauphine, New Orleans, LA 70116. Poetry, fiction, articles, art, photos, cartoons, interviews, satire, music, long-poems, collages, plays, concrete art. irreg; price per copy: $1.00; sample: $1.00. 1974. tabloid. of. Reporting time: 2 months. Ads: $100/$75. Discounts: 30%.

BARBEQUE PLANET, Project House Foundation, Inc., Bob Millard, Editor; Sue Kaman Millard, Associate Editor, 2513-B Ashwood, Nashville, TN 37212. Poetry, fiction. "We are looking for serious, humorous, imaginative, straightforward, to-the-point poetry and short stories. We are interested in writers with something to share with readers, something of their own vision. No limit as to style or form. The insights into people and their lives yielded through serious reflection or the humor of the ironies of man in society are a few of the many things we appreciate at BBQ P. The human animal is an odd can of worms, we are seeking writers with a can opener." 4/yr; 1-yr sub price: $5.00; per copy: $1.00; sample: $1.00 per copy. 1975. 28-36pp; 8½ x 7. of. circ. 300-500. Reporting time: 2-6 weeks. Payment: copies. Copyrighted, reverts to author. Ads: Rates available on request. Back issues: Issues 1-7 available at single copy rate. Pub'd 4 issues 1976; expects 4 issues 1977, 4 issues 1978. §Contemp. poetry, short stories.

THE BARD, Metloc, The Reverend Francis Edwards S.J., Chairman, Editorial Board, 10 Uphill Grove, Mill Hill, London NW7 4NJ, United Kingdom. Articles, reviews, criticism. "Recent contributors: Peter Milward SJ, Francis Edwards SJ, Eliot Slater. Scholarly articles on all aspects of Shakespearean studies, with special reference to the authorship problem. 3,000-7,000 words." 2/yr; 1-yr sub price: £3.00; per copy: £1.50; sample: £1.50. 1975. 40pp; 9 x 6½. of. circ. 400. Reporting time: 1-2 mos. No payments. Copyrighted. no ads. Discounts: 10 percent to trade. Back issues: Vol. 1, Nos. 1,2,3, supplement to 3. Pub'd 2 issues 1976; expects 2 issues 1977, 2 issues 1978.

BARDIC ECHOES, Bardic Echoes Brochures, Clarence L. Weaver, 1036 Emerald Ave., N.E., Grand Rapids, MI 49503, 616-454-9120. Poetry, art, reviews, news items. "40 lines or less; any style; good taste; poems in the weave form & members of bards given preference. Recent contributors: Jack Ashby, Robert Casper, Charles Cline, Alice Dondiego, Eleanore-Melissa, Jaye Giammarino, Liboria Romano, Lester Rutsky, Louise Kidder Sparrow, Jan Brevet, Guanetta Gordon, Henry Hubert Hutto, Magny Landstad Jensen, James Magorian, Errol Miller, P. C. Niblette, Leonard Opalov, Jess Perlman, Marie J. Post, Alice Mackenzie Swaim, James Hagood, Arnold McLean, Mabelle A. Lyon, Raymond Stark, Robert Ambacher, Nel Modglin, Monica Boyce, Catharine Albright Waldraff, M. K. Kulilowski." 4/yr, occasional extra issue; 1-yr sub price: $2.00; per copy: $.50; sample: $0.50. 1960. 32pp; 5½ x 8½. of. circ. 500. Reporting time: 1-3 mos. Payment: copies only. Not copyrighted. no ads. Discounts: 25% to periodical sub agencies. Back issues: $.50/ea. Pub'd 4 issues 1976; expects 4 issues 1977, 4 issues 1978. Pub's reviews: 141 in 1976. §poetry. CCLM, COSMEP.

BARTHOLOMEW'S COBBLE, Rod Steier, 19 Howland Rd., West Hartford, CT 06107, 203-521-6053. Poetry. "Each poet has full artistic control over his book, this includes length, cover design, material, etc. We normally do not seek unsolicited manuscripts, and have published books by Russell Edson, Rod Steier, Terry Stokes, Charles Simic, Dave Kelly, Pat Bizzaro and Cynthia MacDonald." 3-5 books/yr; price per copy: varies; sample: $1.50. 1974. 24pp; 8½ x 7. of. circ. varies. We only solicit. Ads: None. Discounts: 60-40 usually. COSMEP.

BARTLEBY'S REVIEW, Albert Stainton, Rita Tomasallo Stainton, 3152 Lyon St., San Francisco, CA 94123. Poetry, reviews. 2/yr; 1-yr sub price: $3.00 individuals/$3.00 libraries; per copy: $1.50 individuals/$1.75 libraries; sample: $1.50. 1972. 48pp; 5½ x 8. of. circ. 500. Reporting time: 1-3 months. Payment: copies. Discounts: 40%. Back issues: $5.00 ea. for issues 1 and 2. Pub'd 1 issue 1976; expects 2 issues 1977, 1 issue 1978. Pub's reviews. §poetry. CCLM.

Basement Workshop, Inc., Fay Chiang, 199 Lafayette St., New York, NY 10012. "The Basement Workshop Small Press serves as a vehicle for the publication of literary as well as graphic artists, principally Asian Americans and the disenfranchised culturally in this society. Product:. chapbooks, books, childrens books, social and political analysis. Unlike Bridge Magazine, which is one of our regular publications, the other publications we have produced have been somewhat sporadic. They included: YELLOW PEARL, The Chinatown Children's Coloring Book, THE SOCIAL SERVICE GUIDE OF CHINATOWN and several small brochures. Presently we are in the process of starting off on our small press venture of producing regularly 4 chapbooks a year of new and upcoming poets, short story writers, playwrights, as well as two children's books, and a collection of old photographs of New York Chinatown with the translated oral histories of the community's elderly citizens. This first chapbook will be edited with the help of Lawson Inada and Frank Chin.The writers or rather poets are participants in basement's writers workshop." 1972.

The Basilisk Press, David Lunde, Editor; Suzanne Johnson, Associate Editor, P.O. Box 71, Fredonia, NY 14063. Poetry. "We publish only full length books of poetry. So far have published Bruce Woods, T.C. Burtt, Jr., Phyllis Janik, David Lunde, Dave Kelly, Dave Smith, Greg Kuzma, Tom McKeown, Bruce Guernsey, Tom Disch, Peter Warren. Books forthcoming by Toni Zimmerman, David Rafael Wang, Harley Elliott, Lyn Lifshin. (Have published one set of poem postcards but don't know if this will continue. No unsolicited poems for cards.)" 1970. 50-75pp; 5½ x 8½. of. Reporting time: 1day-1month. Payment: contributor copies only. Discounts: 20% to libraries, 40% to retailers on orders of 5 or more copies. COSMEP.

BASTARD ANGEL, Harold Norse, PO Box 3449, San Francisco, CA 94119. Poetry, fiction, art, photos, cartoons, reviews, collages, concrete art, non-fiction. "Beat, surrealist, raw meat, DADA preferred. No longer accept unsolicited material." Irregular.; price per copy: $3.00 to individuals, $4.00 to libraries (includes postage); sample: $3.00 to individuals, $4.00 to libraries (includes postage). 1971. 52pp; 8½ x 11. of. circ. 1,200. Reporting time: Irregular. Payment: 2 free copies. Copyrighted, reverts to author. Ads: $100.00/$50.00/$1.00. Discounts: None except to bookstores: 40 percent. Back issues: BA No. 1: $50.00. BA No. 2: $10.00. BA No. 3: $25.00. Expects 1 issue 1977, 1 issue 1978. Pub's reviews: none in 1976. §Poetry, fiction. CCLM, COSMEP.

‡**Bay Books,** c/o C. Peterson, 3665 Clay St., San Francisco, CA 94118.

BB Books (see GLOBAL TAPESTRY JOURNAL)

THE BEAD JOURNAL, Robert K. Liu, Carolyn L. E. Benesh, Assist. Editor, P.O. Box 24c47, Los Angeles, CA 90024, 213-838-7539. Articles, art, photos, interviews, reviews. "semi-scholarly" 4/yr; 1-yr sub price: $12.00; per copy: $3.00; sample: $3.00. 1974. 48-56pp; 8½ x 11. of. circ. 2,000. Reporting time: 1-2 months. Payment: none. Copyrighted, reverts to author. Ads: $325.00/$180.00/$15.00-$25.00. Discounts: 40 percent for min order of 10. Back issues: same as current except vol 2, which are $2.50 each. Pub'd 4 issues 1976; expects 4 issues 1977. Pub's reviews: numerous in 1976. §jewelry & personal adornment. COSMEP.

Bear Cult Press (see GREAT CIRCUMPOLAR BEAR CULT)

Bear Hug Books, Chuck Miller, 1636 Ocean View, Kensington, CA 94707, 524-2107. Poetry, fiction, art, photos, cartoons, satire, collages. "This is a small operation focusing on fiction and extensive use of illustration. My aim is to do books that are tailored to content rather than create a constant format. Future plans include silk screen broadsides, post cards, letter press chapbooks (mostly poetry) and continued production of 80 to 100 page fictional works done by offset. Currently at press I have Bobbie Louise Hawkins' *Back to Texas* (120 pages in the $4.00 range) and the soon to begin *The Lost Key* by Sherril Jaffe. Other plans include works by Jack Shoemaker and Michael Palmer. As usual, my output will depend on monies available from past publication ventures. First book available now is *Prose Ocean* by Gus Blaisdell" avg. price, cloth: $3.50. 1975. 60/100pp; 6 x 9. of. avg. press run 600. Reporting time: 2 weeks. Payment: standard 10% with advance. Copyrights for author. Discounts: Standard Serendipity Books Distribution discount.

Bear Tribe (see MANY SMOKES)

BEAU FLEUVE SERIES, Intrepid Press, Allen De Loach, P.O. Box 1423, Buffalo, NY 14214. Poetry, criticism. "Blackburn, De Loach, Mottram, Orlovsky, Bremser, Cirocco, Coleman, Kerman." varies. 16pp; 5 x 8. of. circ. 500-1M. Reporting time: 3 mos. by request. Payment: 10%. COSMEP.

Beau Geste Press/Libro Accion Libre (see also SCHMUCK ANTHOLOGICAL), Felipe Ehrenberg, David Mayor, Apdo, Postal 27, Xico, Veracruz, Mexico, Barhatch Farm, Barhatch Lane, Cranleigh, Surrey, United Kingdom. Articles, poetry, fiction, art, cartoons, news items, interviews, music, criticism, letters, collages, concrete art, photos. "STOP reading this garbage!! Spend your time more profitably by rushing us a request for our latest mail order catalogue." 1971. rubber stamp/of. Reporting time: so quick you hardly notice. Payment: copies. ALP, COSMEP.

Beauregard (see also CANADIAN SLAVONIC PAPERS), 373 Coventry Rd., Ottawa, Canada.

THE BEAUREGARD BUGLE BOY HERALD-TRIBUNE, Carl D. Clark, Paul B. Miner, 3007 University, Austin, TX 78705, 512-472-7415. Poetry, fiction, art, cartoons, satire, criticism, letters, collages, concrete art. 6/yr; 1-yr sub price: $1.50; per copy: $0.30. 1977. 4pp; 8½ x 5½. of. circ. who knows. Reporting time: 1 month. Payment: copy. Not copyrighted. Ads: none. Discounts: none. Pub'd 3 issues 1976.

Beaver Lodge Press (see THE NORTH WIND)

BEDFORDSHIRE MAGAZINE, White Crescent Press, B. Chambers, Crescent Rd., Luton Beds., United Kingdom, Mrs. B. Chambers, 50 Shefford Rd., Meppershall, Shefford Beds. SG17 5LL, United Kingdom. Articles, poetry, art, reviews, news items, letters. "Restricted to material of Bedfordshire interest-history, biography, topography, literature, etc. Articles 800-2000 words, with illustrations." 4/yr; sub price: £4.32 3 years; per copy: 25p. 1947. 64pp; 8½ x 5½. lp. circ. 3M. Payment: Il per 1000 words. Ads: contact publisher. Back issues: 25p plus 11p postage. Pub'd 4 issues 1976; expects 4 issues 1977, 4 issues 1978.

Being Incorporated, Michael Hathaway, Felicity Harley, Box 641, Santa Barbara, CA 93102. Articles, art, interviews, satire. "We're interested in creating and making available what could be called 'cosmic toys' or tools, anything that may effectively foster the marvelous and varied personal, social, planetary evolution now unfolding. Our appointment book & authentic calendar of contemporary Saints for 1977 is a rich brew, blended from lives well-led (Chavez, Margaret Mead, Buffy Ste. Marie, Castaneda, Bronowski, Nader, Indian Saint Sai Baba, ecological and sexual radicals...), with New American holy days (Earth Day, Attica) and places of pilgrimage, all well-spiced with political and cultural commentary. It's also a practical date book. We are concentrating on this one book at the moment, but pamphlets, posters, games, video all interest us. We are compiling a New Age Dictionary, and experimented in a completely different realm by putting on a magical Tibetan Spring Festival. 'We are as gods, & may as well get good at it.'" of. Discounts: 40% for 5 and up. COSMEP.

Bell Springs Publishing Company, Bernard Kamoroff, Bernard Bear, Box 322, Laytonville, CA 95454, 707-984-7117. "We've only published one book, a 192 page paperback called '*Small Time Operator: How To Start Your Own Small Business, Keep Your Books, Pay Your Taxes And Stay Out Of Trouble'*. We are interested in publishing other works, particularly self-help books or similar books with a ready market and good commercial potential. We are not particularly interested in poetry or fiction or short, article-length pieces." avg. price, paper: $6.95. 1976. 192pp; 8½ x 11. of. avg. press run 5-10,000 copies. Reporting time: 2 weeks. Payment: negotiable. Copyright in author's name if author so wishes. Discounts: Discount schedule is flexible; presently have exclusive bookstore distr. contract w/Bookpeople. Pub'd 1 title 1976; expects 1-3 titles 1977, 1-3 titles 1978.

Bellevue Press, Gil Williams, Deborah H. Williams, 60 Schubert St., Binghamton, NY 13905, 607-729-0819. Poetry, art, photos. "Chapbook publication by our invitation only. Poetry post-cards always needed. Recently published artists and authors include: John Yau, Bradford Stark, Matt Phillips, Marcia Falk, Ursula K leguin, Stephen Sandy, Philip Dow, et al." avg. price, paper: $2.50 to $10.00 for books (many autographed editions); other: $4.00 to $5.00 for broadsides. $0.15 for art cards, $0.20 for poetry cards. 1973. 25 to 30 pp for books. of/lp. avg. press run 65 to 125 on broadsides, 500 to 2,500 on post-cards, 220 to 750 on books. Reporting time: Usually within 8 weeks concerning manuscripts, longer for letters and misc. correspondence. Payment: 10 percent of published edition to authors, plus $5.00 for each accepted poetry post-card poem, $10.00 for broadside poems. Payments to illustrators or for introductions varies. Copyright remains with authors. We only print one edition of our books or cards, no reprints. Discounts: 20 percent on orders of $10.00 - $49.00. 40 percent on orders over $50.00, to private collectors. 40 percent off to all bookdealers. No discount to libraries, and no postage added except on large shipments. NESPA.

THE BELLINGHAM REVIEW, Signpost Press, Peter Nicoletta, Editor; Knute Skinner, Editor; Richard Dills, Assistant Editor, 2600 Hampton Place, Bellingham, WA 98225. Poetry, fiction, art, photos, parts-of-novels, plays. "No fiction over 5,000 wds. Open to all types of poetry. Contributors to first two issues: Mark McCloskey, Scott C. Cairns, Lawrence Kearny, Edward Field, Patricia Ver Ellen, Phyllis Janowitz, Samuel Green, Lyn Lifshin, Deborah Larsen, George A. Freek, Laurel Soshnick, Arthur Winfield Knight, Mary Moore, William Stafford, Joan Swift, Virginia Brady Young, A. J. Hovde, L. W. Michaelson, Tom Montag, Robert Huff, Diana Morelli, Robert Matte, Jr., Colleen J. McElroy, Bruce Berlind, Lawrence P. Spingarn, Louis Gallo, Philip Booth, R. A. Gregory, James Simmons, T. R. Jahns, Edeltraud Harzer, Richard Eberhart, Mauga Wahl, Jim Barnes, Wendy Bishop, James Liddy, Dora Polk, John Liddy, Eugene Garber, & Antoni Gronowicz." quarterly; sub price: $8.00-4 issues ($7.00 if payment accompanies order); per copy: $2.00; sample: $2.00. 1975. 50pp; 5½ x 8½. of. circ. 500. Reporting time: 1-2 months. Payment: copies. Copyrighted, reverts to author. Discounts: 25 percent. Back issues: $2.00. Expects 4 issues 1977, 4 issues 1978. Pub's reviews. §Poetry volumes & anth. books of fiction. COSMEP.

Bellrock Press (see JOURNAL OF CANADIAN FICTION)

BELOIT POETRY JOURNAL, Beloit Poetry Journal, Robert Glauber, David M. Stocking, Marion K. Stocking, P.O. Box 2, Beloit, WI 53511. Poetry. "We publish the best of the poems submitted. No biases as to length, form, subject, or school. Occasional chapbooks, such as the recent chapbook of poems in honor of David Ignatow. Some recent contributors: Jerald Bullis, Albert Goldbarth, Philip Dacey, Sanford Weiss, A.G. Sobin, Richard Jackson, T. Alan Broughten." quarterly; 1-yr sub price: $4.00; per copy: $1.00; sample: $.75. 1950. 40pp; 5½ x 8½. of. circ. 1,200. Reporting time: immediately to 4 mos. Payment: 3 copies. Copyrighted, reverts to author. Ads: $100. Discounts: by arrangement. Back issues: $2.00 for chapbooks, most others $1.00. List available. Pub'd 4 issues 1976; expects 4 issues 1977, 4 issues 1978. Pub's reviews: 9 in 1976. §books by and about poets. mags with poetry. CCLM.

BERGEN POETS, Alice Kolb, 218 Gramercy Place, Glen Rock, NJ 07452, 201-652-7016. Poetry, art. "We are a poetry co-op. Annual publication-open to members of Co-op only-30 to 40 poets. *Diversity* our vitality." 1/yr; 1-yr sub price: $0.00; per copy: $2.50; sample: $0.00. 1973. 52 pp perfect bound; 5½ x 8½. of. circ. 250. Payment: copies. Copyrighted, reverts to author. Ads: none. Discounts: none. Back issues: $2.50 each. CCLM.

BERKELEY BARB, Ray Riegert, P.O. Box 1247, Berkeley, CA 94701. Poetry, articles, art, photos, cartoons, interviews, satire, criticism, reviews, parts-of-novels. "Most BARB articles and reviews fall into the 500 to 1,000 word category. Full-page pieces average 1,500 words. Most writing styles are acceptable, providing they are not overly academic or highly experimental as to be inaccessible to a general newspaper readership." weekly; 1-yr sub price: $10.00; per copy: Bay Area-$.25/outside S.F. Bay Area- $.50; sample: Free. 1965. 28pp; 11½ x 17½. of. circ. 15,000. Reporting time: 4 weeks. Payment: 3¢ a word. Ads: $360.00/$190.00/$1.50 per line. Discounts: 15%. Back issues: 25¢, plus postage, if necessary. Pub's reviews. §A broad range of counter-cultural and non-sectarian leftist political issues. APS.

BERKELEY JOURNAL OF SOCIOLOGY, What's Your Line Graphics, Department of Sociology Graduate Students, 410 Barrows Hall, University of California, Berkeley, CA 94720. Articles, criticism. annual; 1-yr sub price: $5.50 institutions/$2.50 individual; per copy: $5.50 institutions/$2.50 individual. 1955. 200pp; 5 x 8. of. circ. 2,000. Reporting time: 2 months. We hold copyright. Ads: Available on request. Discounts: $0.50 ea.; bulk rates available. Back issues: 40-60 percent discount. Pub'd 1 issue 1976; expects 1 issue 1977, 1 issue 1978. Pub's reviews: 1 in 1976. §sociology.

BERKELEY POETRY REVIEW, Christopher Hewitt, Principle Editor, c/o Office of Student Activities, 103 Sproul Hall, Univ of Calif, Berkeley, CA 94720. Poetry, articles, art, photos, reviews. "Manuscripts should be no longer than 5-6 pages, and should include no more than 3 poems; most poems in the magazine are 10-25 lines, although longer and shorter poems can be considered. Prose poems and translations are encouraged; the originals should accompany translations. Reviews and articles should be under 3 pages. Lyrical, moral, erotic, political, comical, magic etc." 2-3/yr; 1-yr sub price: $3.00; per copy: $1.50; sample: $0.00. 1973. 75pp; 6 x 8½. lp. circ. 500-750. Reporting time: 2 weeks. Payment: free copy. Copyrighted, reverts to author. Ads: $50.00. Discounts: none. Back issues: $1.50. Pub's reviews. §new poetry books (not anthologies).

BERKELEY POETS COOPERATIVE, Berkeley Poets Workshop and Press, P.O. Box 459, Berkeley, CA 94701, 415-652-6386. Poetry, fiction, art, photos, parts-of-novels, long-poems, plays. 2/yr; 1-yr sub price: $3.00; per copy: $1.50; sample: $1.25. 1969. 80pp; 5½ x 8½. of. circ. 2,500. Reporting time: 6 mos. Payment: 2 copies plus free subscription. Copyrighted. no ads. Discounts: 40% trade. Back issues: Prices vary, write for information. Pub'd 1 issue 1976; expects 2 issues 1977, 3 issues 1978. CCLM, AAP.

Bern Porter Books, Bern Porter, 22 Salmond Road, Belfast, ME 04915, 207-338-3763. "Owing to death of partner, Margaret Eudine Porter for past twenty years, manuscripts are no longer solicited. Type of material used vanguard, experimental and classic contempory." avg. price, cloth: $8.50; paper: $2.10; other: $12.50. 1911. 167pp. lp. avg. press run 1,750 copies. Reporting time: 3 weeks. Payment: 10 percent royalty on all sales. Copyright in authors name. Discounts: Normal or all current standard. Pub'd 413 titles 1976; expects 467 titles 1977, 482 titles 1978. COSMEP, NESPA, MPW, STWP.

Best Cellar Press (see PEBBLE)

BEST FRIENDS, Best Friends, Carolyn Maisel, Nancy Staley, 329 Montclaire NE, Albuquerque, NM 87108, 268-9105. Poetry, art. 1-2/yr; 1-yr sub price: $0.00; per copy: $2.25; sample: $0.00. 1970. 80-100pp; 7½ x 9. of. circ. 800 plus. Reporting time: 1 week to several months. Payment: 2 copies. Copyrighted, reverts to author. Discounts: Wholesale to book dealers 40 percent; bulk to classes etc. 15 percent. Pub's reviews. §new poetry esp. women. CCLM, COSMEP.

BEST IN POETRY, J. Mark Press, Barbara Fischer, Box 2057, N. Babylon, NY 11703. Poetry. "1-3 poems, 3-16 lines, & return envelope. Sincere, sensitive poetry. No smut." quarterly; price per copy: $7.00 paper/$11.00-hardcover; sample: $3.95. 1963. 40pp; 8½ x 5½. †of. circ. 4,000. Reporting time: 2-4 weeks. Payment: 60¢ a poem & prizes. Ads: none. Back issues: $3.95 paperback/$9.95 hardcover. §poetry.

BEST POETS OF THE 20th CENTURY, Winston-Paramount Books, B.W. Paramount, Drawer J, Babylon, NY 11702. Poetry. "1-3 poems, 3-16 lines, & return envelope. Sincere, sensitive poetry. No smut." quarterly; price per copy: $7.00 paper/$11.00 hardcover; sample: $3.95. 1969. 40pp; 8½ x 5½. †of. circ. 3,000. Reporting time: 2-4 weeks. Payment: 60¢ a poem and prizes. Ads: none. Back issues: $3.95 paperback/$9.95 hardcover. §poetry.

BETELGEUSE CHAPBOOK SERIES/NEWEDI FICTION SERIES, Newedi Press, Kent R. Mahan, Dept. of English, Bowling Green University, Bowling Green, OH 43403. Poetry, fiction, art, parts-of-novels. "Any length manuscripts desired; poetry cannot be 'traditional'; Recent contributors in chapbook series include: David Lloyd Whited, Kent R. Mahan, David Shevin, Judith Dunaway, Frederick Eckman, Mordecai Marcus, D. Clinton." 4/yr; 1-yr sub price: $5.00; per copy: $2.00; sample: $2.00. 1975. 72pp; 5½ x 8½. †of. circ. 750. Reporting time: 1 month. Payment: 10 contributors copies. Copyrighted, reverts to author after 90 days. Ads: $100.00/$50.00. Discounts: 40% to dealers. §poetry, fiction, small press interest.

Bethesda Books, Leo Young, Fay Young, PO Box 34567, Bethesda, MD 20084, 301-320-4675. "Our publication is a book 'Everything You Should Know About Pension Plans' by Fay and Leo Young." 1-yr sub price: $4.95. 1976. 180pp; 5½ x 8½. of/lp. circ. 2,000 copies. We only print our own work at the moment.

Beyond Baroque Foundation Publications, includes Beyond Baroque/newforms, NEW Magazine. Arts & Letters (formerly NeWLetterS), and NewBooks, George Drury Smith, Editor & Publisher; James Krusoe, Associate Editor; Peter Kreiner, Asst. Editor; Alexandra Garrett, Asst. Editor; Kathy McManus, Staff Editor, 1639 W. Washington Blvd., Venice, CA 90291, 213-392-5763. Poetry, fiction, articles, art, photos, cartoons, interviews, satire, criticism, reviews, parts-of-novels, long-poems, collages, plays, news items, non-fiction. "*Beyond Baroque* is devoted to experimental writing. New magazine: *Arts & Letters* is devoted to contemporary fiction, poetry and articles on the creative arts. Newbooks seeks short novels, poetry collections." avg. price, cloth: Institutional subscriptions & memberships $15.00. Also available for smaller donations or free on request. Subscriptions include *all* Beyond Baroque Publications. 1968. 64pp; 8½ x 11. of. avg. press run 15,000. Reporting time: 4-6 weeks. Payment: copies only. Buys first serial rights only. ads: inquire for rates. Discounts: none. Pub'd 6 titles 1976; expects 8 titles 1977, 10 titles 1978. CCLM, COSMEP, LPSC.

BEYOND BAROQUE LIBRARY of SMALL PRESS PUBLICATIONS, Beyond Baroque Foundation, 1639 W. Washington Blvd., Venice, CA 90291, 213-392-5763. "*BEYOND BAROQUE LIBRARY* presently consists of over 12,000 small press publications usually found only in restricted university libraries. The Library serves as an important link between the independent publisher and the public. It strongly urges publishers to contribute books and magazines to the library as a means of better circulation. In exchange *BEYOND BAROQUE* will send its literary magazines and books. The Los Angeles Public Library System has put *BEYOND BAROQUE LIBRARY* on the scan system, one of California's two regional resource centers." 1973.

BEZOAR, Fred Buck, Thorpe Feidt, Paul Kahn, P.O. Box 535, Gloucester, MA 01930. Poetry, fiction, long-poems. 10-20/yr; 1-yr sub price: $5.00; per copy: $1.00; sample: $1.00. 1975. 10pp; 8½ x 11. †mi. circ. 300. Reporting time: instantaneous to never. Payment: 10 copies. Not copyrighted. Ads: none. Discounts: 60/40 trade.

THE BIBLIOTHECK, Douglas S. Mack, University Library, Stirling, Scotland FK9 4LA, United Kingdom. Articles, reviews. 3/yr + supplemental; 1-yr sub price: £4.00; per copy: £1.50; sample: free. 1956. 30pp; 6 x 8. lp. circ. 300. Reporting time: c. 1 month. Payment: 6 offprints. Ads: £10.00/£7.

BIBLIOTHEQUE D'HUMANISME ET RENAISSANCE, Librairie Droz S.A., Geneva, A. Dufour, Librairie Droz S.A., 11r.Massot, 1211 Geneve 12, Switzerland. "history of 16th century" 3/yr; 1-yr sub price: 75 SW.FR ($30.00)-yr; per copy: 25 sw.fr. ($10.00). 1934. 600pp; 16 x 24 cm. typography. circ. 1,000. Pub'd 3 issues 1976; expects 3 issues 1977, 3 issues 1978. Pub's reviews: 60 in 1976.

The Bieler Press, Gerald Lange, 124 North Page Street, Stoughton, WI 53589. Poetry, fiction, long-poems. "Finely printed Chapbooks and Broadsides. Recent and forthcoming: *Roadsalt* by Albert Drake, *The New World* (Broadside) by Gerald Lange. *Demon Letting* by Gayle Feyrer w/serigraphy by Cathie Ruggie, *The World At Large* by Christine Zawadiwsky." avg. price, other: $15.00-$20.00. 1975. 20pp; varies. †lp/hand press. avg. press run 50-200. Reporting time: varies; please inquire w/sample and SASE before submitting manuscript. Payment: 10% of edition. Copyrights for author. Discounts: 10 percent individuals and libraries; 10-40 percent trade. Pub'd 3 titles 1976; expects 3 titles 1977. COSMEP, APHA.

BIG DEAL, Big Deal Press, Barbara Baracks, P.O. Box 830, Peter Stuyvesant Sta., New York, NY 10009. Fiction, articles, art, photos, interviews, satire, cartoons, reviews, music, parts-of-novels, criticism, non-fiction. "Interested in a wide range of styles, unifying criterion a commitment to clear expression. 'Expression' itself a debatable word! A bias towards prose, both fiction and non-fiction, essays, disquisitions, criticism. Reproductble artwork and photos. Recent contributors include: Maureen Owen, Michael Lally, Lee Breuer, Jane Brakhage, Paul Metcalf, Guy Davenport, Bob Ashley, Alvin Lucier, Rudy Burkhardt, Beth Anderson, Mimi Albert. 'Please, don't submit work untii you've bought the magazine.'" Serial.; sub price: 6 issue sub: $18.00 Indiv.; $21.00 Instit.; per copy: $3.00 indiv/$3.50 institutions; sample: $3.00 indiv/$3.50 institutions. 1973. 136pp; 8½ x 11.

†of. circ. 1,500. Reporting time: 2 months. Copyrighted. Discounts: Trade: 40 percent; Jobber: 10 percent. Back issues: Negotiable, inquire for prices. Pub'd 1 issue 1976; expects 2 issues 1977, 2 issues 1978. CCLM.

Big Deal Press (see CHERNOZEM)

BIG MAMA RAG, Tearraleen Woodsharp, 1724 Gaylord, Denver, CO 80206. Poetry, articles, art, photos, cartoons, interviews, satire, cartoons, letters. "Radical Feminist Theory and Women's issues." monthly; 1-yr sub price: $6.00/individual; per copy: $.45 in state/$.55 outside Co. 1972. 16pp; 61 picas x 16 in. of. circ. 9,000. Reporting time: 3 mos. Payment: free sub. Ads: $200/$105/$3-col. in./$.10/wd. Pub's reviews §written by or for women. COSMEP.

BIG MOON, Christine Kyckelhahn-Wilkins, Estelle Milligan, 167 Riverside Dr, Boulder Creek, CA 95006, PO Box 2024, Modesto, CA 95354. Poetry, fiction, articles, art, photos, cartoons, criticism, reviews, letters, parts-of-novels, long-poems, collages, concrete art. "No biases in terms of style, school,etc. The emphasis is on poetry, but i love fiction, & reserve approx. 1/3 of each issue for short stores. I have a regualr section titled New Voices, which features the work of unknown writers. . . usually, this consists of several pgs. of poems by 4 or 5 poets & one short story; some recent contributors include: Richard Hugo, Morton Marcus, Andrei Codrescu, Marge Piercy, Lyn Lifshin, Michael S. Harper, Linda Pastan, Stuart Friebert, Barbara Szerlip, George Barlow, Miriam Levine." 4/yr; 1-yr sub price: $7; per copy: $2. 1974. 130pp; 5½ x 8½. lo. circ. 500. Reporting time: 2-3 wks. Payment: 3 copies. Ads: $28/$15/class-wd: negotiable. Discounts: 60/40. CCLM, COSMEP.

Big River Association (see RIVER STYX)

BIG SCREAM, Nada, David Cope, Susan Cope, 696 48th St SE, Grand Rapids, MI 49508, 616-531-1442. Poetry, fiction, art. "We include at least 5 pages of each writer publ.- some longpoems tend to have imagist bias tho some surrealism; prefer *personal* poems. Contributors: Michael McMahon, Eric Greinke, Dave Montgomery, Jim McCurry, David Cope." 2-3/yr; 1-yr sub price: $5.00; per copy: $1.00; sample: $1.00. 1974. 30pp; 8 x 8½. †mi. circ. 100-150. Reporting time: 1 week - 1 month. Payment: 3 copies. Discounts: 5-10 copies 25 percent, more than 10 40 percent. Back issues: $1.00 per copy.

BIG SKY, Bill Berkson, Box 389, Bolinas, CA 94924. Poetry, fiction, art, photos, cartoons, interviews, criticism, reviews, letters, parts-of-novels, long-poems, collages, plays. "Any length-Experimental-Editor prints what suits him-Unsolicited rarely rings bells—No 'Schools'—Bias of personal interest and sense of 'writing' as standard." 1-2-3/yr; 1-yr sub price: $10.00 (incl. back issues, continuation, plus books); per copy: $2.00-$2.50. 1971. 100-150pp; 7 x 10. of. circ. 1,000. Reporting time: 1 month. Payment: copies (except when special funding allows authors' payments). Discounts: trade/stores:40%. CCLM, COSMEP.

BIKE WORLD, World Publications, John Potter, P.O. Box 366, Mtn. View, CA 94040. "BIKE WORLD contains new approaches to diet and exercise, first person accounts of outstanding tours, training, and racing information, technical reports, and equipment. Evaluations, interviews and personality profiles and features on how to build and maintain your bike-No matter what kind of biking, there's something for you. The editor controls all publishing and printing." 12/yr; 1-yr sub price: $8.50; per copy: $.75; sample: free. 1972. 56pp; 9 x 11. of. circ. 21,000. Ads: inquire. Discounts: bulk rates. Back issues: $1.00 each. Pub's reviews. §sports, recreation and leisure activities.

‡**BILINGUAL REVIEW,** Dept. Of Romance Languages, City College Of New York, New York, NY 10031. CCLM.

Bing America Publications, D.K. Gast, 1555 Murray Avenue, El Cajon, CA 92020. "'How-to media for the Aware. So far we have re-issued Ross H. Gast's 1933 farm-home movement classic, VEGETABLES IN THE CALIFORNIA GARDEN, 59pp; $1.25 and FOOD FOM YOUR SOIL, A

Practical Guide for the Backyard Gardener and Semirural Home Owner, 108pp; $2. Discounts on quantity orders. Please query before submitting manuscripts."

Biography Press, Fremont Johnson, 1240 W. Highland Ave., Rt. 1 Box 745, Aransas Pass., TX 78336, 512-758-3870. avg. price, cloth: varies; paper: Various. 1970. pp varies; varies. †of. avg. press run 500. Reporting time: 2 weeks. Copyrights for author on request, $10.00 including Library of Congress fee. Pub'd 15 titles 1976; expects 20 titles 1977, 25 titles 1978. COSMEP.

Biohydrant Publications, R.F.D. 3, St. Albans, VT 05478. Poetry, art. "Publish primarily the art and writings of sculptor/poet David R. Wheeler." avg. price, cloth: $9.00. 1976. 250pp; 8½ x 11. avg. press run 500. Copyrights for author. Discounts: straight 20 percent. Pub'd 1 title 1976; expects 1 title 1977.

BIRD EFFORT, Bird Effort Press, Robert Long, Josh Dayton, 25 Mudford Avenue, Easthampton, NY 11937, 516-324-4156. Poetry, fiction, articles, art, interviews, satire, criticism, reviews, letters, parts-of-novels, long-poems, collages, plays, concrete art. "Contemporary writing. David Ignatow, Robert Peters, Thomas Berger, John Hall Wheelock, Kathy Acker, George Hitchcock, Stephen Dobyns, Jack Matthews, William Matthews, John Unterecker, H.R. Hays, Joseph Bruchac, Ron Padgett." 2 double issues/yr; 1-yr sub price: $4.00; per copy: $2.00. 1975. 120pp; 8½ x 7. of. circ. 500. Reporting time: 10-20 days. Payment: 2 copies. Copyrighted. Ads: $50.00/$25.00. Discounts: 40% trade. Back issues: Issue 1/2 rare; write for details. Expects 2 issues 1977, 2 issues 1978. Pub's reviews. §Poetry/fiction/criticism/translation. COSMEP.

Bird In The Bush (see TYPEWRITER)

BIRTHSTONE, Dan Brady, Peter Marti, Karen Wegner, Pam Duval, Eve Yorker, PO Box 27394, San Francisco, CA 94127. Poetry, art, photos, long-poems, collages. "Poetry: any subject, graphics: pen and ink any subject. Photos: B/W-no stated biases any subject fine." 2-4/yr; 1-yr sub price: $5.00; per copy: $1.00; sample: $1.00. 1975. 16pp; 8½ x 11. of. circ. 500 plus. Reporting time: 8 weeks plus. Payment: in copies. Not copyrighted. Ads: $70.00/$35.00. Back issues: not available. Pub's reviews. §poetry, graphics, photography. COSMEP-WEST.

Biscuit City Press, Robert M. Gutchen, 146 Biscuit City Road, Kingston, RI 02881, 401-783-8851. "The principal activity of the Biscuit City Press is fine printing on a hand-press (an 1870 Albion hand-press) in limited editions of short pieces, with or without illustrations. Editions have run from a low of 15 copies to a maximum of 250 copies, most running about 60 copies—all numbered. Most pieces deal with printing history, or with English or American History. One publication was a poem by a contemporary US poet, Paul Petrie. Most works consist of fewer than 12 pages. Much emphasis is placed on choice of paper, on typography, inking, and on the quality of the printed impression. Because the Biscuit City Press is an extra-curricular activity, only one or two items—of the proprietor's choice—are issued each year." avg. price, paper: $3.50. 1970. 5 x 8. †op. Discounts: No discounts on single items. 10 percent discount on 5 or more items.

BITS, Bits Press, Robert Wallace, Dennis Dooley, Nicholas Ranson, Frederik N. Smith, c/o Dept of English, Case Western Reserve University, Cleveland, OH 44106, 216-368-2359. Poetry. "Twelve lines or under. The shorter, the better. Recent contributors: Leonard Nathan, David Ray, Stephen Sandy, Albert Goldbarth, Philip Booth, Rosmarie Waldrop, John Ciardi, Daniel Hoffman, Carl Rakosi, Mary Oliver, Peter Wild, Linda Pastan, etc." 2/yr; 1-yr sub price: $2.00; per copy: $1.00; sample: $1.00. 1975. 32pp; 6¼ x 4¾. †lp. circ. 800. Reporting time: two to four weeks. Payment: two contributor's copies. Buys first serial only. no ads. Discounts: class orders, 10 or more, 50 cents each. Back issues: $1.00. Pub'd 2 issues 1976; expects 2 issues 1977, 2 issues 1978. CCLM.

Bits Press (see also BITS). Poetry. avg. price, paper: $2.00. 28pp; 8½ x 5¼. avg. press run 1,200. Payment: by arrangement (usually copies). Copyrights for author. Expects 2 titles 1977, 2 titles 1978. CCLM.

THE BITTER OLEANDER, The Bitter Oleander Press, Paul Roth, 310 Bradford Parkway,

Syracuse, NY 13224. Poetry, art. "This magazine hopes to make up for such a scarcity of devotion, among the small presses, to presenting a format of contemporary international poetry. We are very much interested in translations and have published those from the work of du Bouchet, Bonnefoy, Supervielle, Follain, Trakl, Huchel, Meister, Bobrowski, Goll, Neruda, Andrade, Prospero, Suarez, Locke, Scheibli, Britt, McDonald. We ask only that poems be of a short nature and that submissions be quite large (15 poems minimum)." 3/yr; 1-yr sub price: $5.00; per copy: $2.00; sample: $2.00. 1974. 62pp; 7 x 10. †of. circ. 500. Reporting time: one to two months. Payment: $5/page for poetry & 2 copies. Ads: $35/$15. Discounts: 40% off for bookstores. Back issues: $2.00, few available. CCLM, COSMEP, NESPA.

BITTERROOT, Menke Katz, Blythbourne Station, P.O. Box 51, Brooklyn, NY 11219. Poetry, reviews, concrete art. 4/yr; 1-yr sub price: $5.00; per copy: $1.50; sample: $1.50. 1962. 50pp. Reporting time: immediately. Payment: one copy. Ads: $100/$50. Discounts: 10%. Back issues: complete set of 55 issues/$125.00. Pub's reviews. §poetry. CCLM.

BITTERSWEET, Ellen Massey, Lebanon High School, 777 Brice St., Lebanon, MO 65536, 417-532-9829. Poetry, fiction, articles. "Most material is done by staff, but do accept authentic ozark material." 4/yr; 1-yr sub price: $6.00; per copy: $2.00; sample: free. 1973. 68pp; 8½ x 11. of. circ. 2,700. Reporting time: 1 month. Payment: sample of magazine. Copyrighted, does not revert to author. no advertizing. Back issues: $2.00. Pub'd 4 issues 1976; expects 4 issues 1977, 4 issues 1978.

‡**BkMk Press,** 8700 West 63rd St., Shawnee Mission, KS 66202.

BLACK/AMERICAN LITERATURE FORUM, Indiana State University, Joseph Weixlmann, Indiana State University, Parsons Hall 237, Terre Haute, IN 47809, 812-232-6311, Ext. 2664. Poetry, articles, art, photos, interviews, criticism, reviews. 4/yr; 1-yr sub price: $4.00; per copy: $1.00; sample: $0.25. 1967. 36pp; 8½ x 11. †of. circ. 800. Reporting time: 3 months. Payment: 3 copies. Indiana State Univ. holds copyright. Discounts: 40 percent. Back issues: $1.00. Pub'd 4 issues 1976; expects 4 issues 1977, 4 issues 1978. Pub's reviews: 3 in 1976. §Black/American literature. CCLM, COSMEP.

‡**BLACK AND RED,** Box 9546, Detroit, MI 48202.

BLACK BOOK, J. Garmhausen, Dept. of English, Bowling Green State Univ., Bowling Green, OH 43403. "Each issue contains the work of one writer: poetry, essays, notebooks-whatever fits. The first issue was a collection of poems by Anselm Hollo. Please no unsolicited mss. at present." 3/yr; 1-yr sub price: $4.00; per copy: $1.50. 48pp. of. circ. 1M.

‡**BLACK BOOKS BULLETIN,** 7848-50 South Ellis Ave., Chicago, IL 60619. CCLM.

BLACK BOX MAGAZINE, Watershed Intermedia, Alan Austin, Frances Lang, Ahmos Zu-Bolton, PO Box 4174, Washington, DC 20015. Poetry, reviews, music, long-poems, plays. "We are an audio magazine publishing the whole range of contemporary poetry-including tape-poetry, sound poetry, songs & other collaborations between poets and musicians, binaural translations. Issues are two to three hours long, on a pair of cassettes, in a special box. We're convinced that the age of the page is ending (at least where poetry's concerned), and that a new kind of poetry rooted in the voice and in performance is more and more the norm. Poetry submissions should be made to us on tape only-no manuscripts, please! But for interviews and dramatic material, we'd rather read first, it saves time." 6/yr; 1-yr sub price: individuals, $22.50 institutions, $50; per copy: $7.95-ea while current; $9.95 thereafter.; sample: $5. 1972. circ. 5M. Payment: $2.00 minute. Discounts: Trade, 40 percent on min. order of 10; on instit. subs., there is a 25 percent disc. on the second yr of a 2 yr order, and on the additional copies in a multiple-copy order. Back issues: No. 1 & No. 2 $14.95; others $9.95. Pub'd 5 issues 1976; expects 6 issues 1977, 6 issues 1978. §also records & tapes. CCLM, COSMEP.

THE BLACK CAT, Black Cat Books, Richard Morgan, Phyllis Fischer, PO Box 4926, Albuquerque, NM 87106. Poetry, fiction, articles, art, interviews, criticism, reviews. "We are an international journal, and welcome overseas submissions. We try not to be biased. Material of any style, mode, or matter acceptable. Contributors: Kenneth Patchen, Ted Enslin, Richard Kostelanetz, Lynn Strongin, Brian Swann, Janis Rapoport (Canada), Susan Musgrave (Canada), Vivian Smith (Aus.), Philip Neilen (Aus.), and many others, both noted and new." 2/yr; 1-yr sub price: $4.00 for two issues; per copy: $2.00; sample: $2.00. 1975. varies; 32-64pp; 5½ x 8½. of. circ. 500. Reporting time: 1 month or less. Payment: generally copies; occasional cash by arrangement. Copyrighted. Ads: please inquire. Pub's reviews. §poetry, fiction, art, photography, criticism, counterculture, general non-fiction.

Black Cat Books (see also THE BLACK CAT), Phyllis L Fischer, Richard G Morgan, PO Box 4926, Albuquerque, NM 87106. Poetry, criticism. "We are interested primarily in chapbook-size collections of poetry and short critical monographs in the area of contemporary poetry. Open to general non-fiction as well." avg. price, cloth: varies. 1975. of/or other means, depending on type of material. avg. press run varies. Reporting time: varies. Payment: copies. Copyrights for author. Discounts: 40 percent discount to booksellers. Pub'd 2 titles 1976; expects several titles 1977, 10 titles 1978.

BLACK FORUM, Black Forum Magazine, Horace Mungin, Revish Windham, Julia Coaxum, Fred Richardson, Reggie Ward, PO Box 1090, Bronx, NY 10451. Poetry, fiction, articles, art, photos, interviews, satire, criticism, reviews, letters. "Nikki Grimes, Sylvia Mularchyk, Ron Hill, Carma." 2/yr; 1-yr sub price: $3.00; per copy: $2.00; sample: $1.50. 1975. 48pp; 8½ x 11. circ. 2,000. Reporting time: 2 months. Payment: No payment for poetry. SS $15.00, articles $15.00, profiles & essays $15.00. Copyrighted, reverts to author. Ads: $75.00/$40.00/$0.20. Back issues: $1.25. Pub'd 1 issue 1976; expects 2 issues 1977, 2 issues 1978. Pub's reviews: 3 in 1976. CCLM, COSMEP.

BLACK GRAPHICS INTERNATIONAL, Black Graphics International, Ibn Pori, P.O. Box 732, Detroit, MI 48206. Poetry, fiction, articles, art, photos, cartoons, interviews, satire, criticism, reviews, music, letters, parts-of-novels, long-poems, collages, plays, concrete art. "Art work should be ready to print 'as is,' or a photo." 4/yr; 1-yr sub price: $5.50 in North America/$4.50 outside N.A.; per copy: $1.75; sample: $1.00. 1967. 90pp; 8½ x 11. of. circ. 10,000. Reporting time: 2 months. Payment: $25 max; 5-10 copies. Back issues: $3.00. Pub's reviews. §art, literature, poetry, music, film, dance.

BLACK LITE, John DiPrete, Box 8214, Cranston, RI 02920, 401-944-8867. Poetry, fiction, articles, art, photos, cartoons, interviews, criticism, reviews, letters. "*Black Lite* is bringing something new and exciting to the field of science fiction and fantasy. Our recent contributors have appeared in the pages of *Science Fiction Review, Amazing,* and other professional journals. Every issue we offer a comprehensive package of entertainment, information and enlightenment. With some of the best art work in the genre." 5/yr; 1-yr sub price: $4.75; per copy: $1.00. 1976. 36pp; 8½ x 11. of. circ. 400. Reporting time: a few days, at most. Payment: one quarter cent word for fiction; one half cent word for book reviews; $4.50 full page art. Copyrighted, reverts to author. Ads: $15.00/$8.00/$0.25. Discounts: Do not accept trades. Distributors and book dealers welcome, 40 percent on 10 or more copies. Back issues: $2.50/copy. Pub's reviews. §fantasy, science fiction, fantastic art books.

BLACK MARIA, Collective, 815 W. Wrightwood, Chicago, IL 60614. Poetry, fiction, articles, art, photos, interviews, reviews, plays. "We accept work done by women only. Interested in redefining women's position in society, family & herself. Enclose SASE for return of submissions; prefer original copies. Black & white photos specifications: 2x3 to 8x10 glossy & magazine format 6x9. Poets should submit at least 3 examples of work; 4 to 75 lines." 4/yr; 1-yr sub price: $5.50; Institution $8.00; per copy: $1.50; sample: $1.50. 1971. 64pp; 6 x 9. †of. circ. 1,000. Reporting time: 1-2 months. Payment: Contributors copies and 1 yr. subscription to BLACK MARIA. Ads: $60/$30/$.25 per word. Back issues: $1.50. Pub's reviews. §any material done by or about women. CCLM, COSMEP.

BLACK MOSS, Black Moss Press, Marty Gervais, RR 1, Coatsworth, Ont, Canada. Poetry, fiction, articles, art, photos, interviews, criticism, reviews. 2/yr; 1-yr sub price: $6.00; per copy: $2.95; sample: free. 1968. 98pp; 6 x 9. circ. 1,000. Reporting time: 2 wks. Ads: $100/$50/$.10. Discounts: 40%. Pub's reviews. §poetry/fiction/art/criticism.

‡**BLACK ORPHEUS, Longman's Of Nigeria,** PMB 1036, Ikeja, Nigeria, Africa.

THE BLACK POSITION, Broadside Press, Gwendolyn Brooks, 7428 S. Evans Ave., Chicago, IL 60619. 1/yr. 1971. 5 x 8. Discounts: 10 copies 40%. CCLM.

THE BLACK SCHOLAR: Journal of Black Studies and Research, Robert L. Allen, Editor, P.O. Box 908, Sausalito, CA 94965, 415-332-3130. Poetry, articles, art, photos, interviews, criticism, reviews, music. "Manuscripts for full-length articles may range in length from 2,000 to 5,000 words, include brief biographical statement, typewritten, double spaced. Articles may be historical and documented, they may be analytic and theoretical; they may be speculative. However, an article should not simply be a 'rap'; it should present a solid point of view convincingly and thoroughly argued. Recent Contributors: John Conyers, Jr.: Ronald Walters; William Stricland, Shirley Chisholm, Imamu Amiri Baraka; Robert Staples; Daphne Muse; Vincent Harding; Arthur Ashe, William W. Sales, Jr.; Shirley Graham DuBois." 10/yr; 1-yr sub price: $12.00; per copy: $1.50; sample: free. 1969. 64pp; 5¾ x 8½. of. circ. 12,000. Ads: $400.00/$225.00/$50.00 (1st 50 words) $10.00 (per line, extra). Discounts: Publishers discount of 25% off above rates. Back issues: $2.00. Pub'd 9 issues 1976; expects 10 issues 1977, 10 issues 1978. Pub's reviews. §the black experience or black related books. CCLM.

Black Sparrow Press, PO Box 3993, Santa Barbara, CA 93105. Poetry, fiction. "See our publications." avg. price, cloth: $14.00; paper: $4.00. 1966. 125-150pp; 6 x 9. lp/of. avg. press run 2,500. Reporting time: 60 days. Payment: Royalty on sales. Copyrights for author. Discounts: Trade: 40 percent - 46 percent. Pub'd 20 titles 1976; expects 20 titles 1977, 20 titles 1978. COSMEP.

Black Stone Press (see MONTANA GOTHIC)

THE BLACK WARRIOR REVIEW, Sarah Teal DeMellier, Editor-in-Chief; Ric Dice, Fiction; Richard Weaver, Poetry, P.O. Box 2936, University, AL 35486, 205-348-7839. Poetry, fiction, interviews, reviews, parts-of-novels, long-poems. "Publish high quality contemporary poetry and fiction. Lee Zacharias, Norman Dubie, Thomas Rabbitt, Barry Hannah, Siv Cedering Fox." 2/yr; 1-yr sub price: $4.00; per copy: $2.00; sample: $1.50. 1974. 80pp; 5½ x 8½. of. circ. 750 per issue. Reporting time: 2 weeks to 2 months. Payment: 2 copies of magazine. Copyrighted, transferred on request. Ads: $80.00/$50.00. Discounts: none at present. Back issues: $1.00. Pub'd 2 issues 1976; expects 2 issues 1977. Pub's reviews: 2 in 1976. §Serious poetry and fiction. CCLM, COSMEP, AWP.

BLACKBERRY, Jeanne Shannon, P.O. Box 4757, Albuquerque, NM 87106. Poetry, reviews. "Partial to poems about the natural world or in which the natural world is more than just 'scenery.' Recent contributors include: Karen McKinnon, David Hopes, Nancy Culbertson, Tom Gardner. Please enclose S.A.S.E. with any communication requesting a reply. May suspend publication in 1978." 3/yr; price per copy: $2.00; sample: $2.00. 1974. 30pp; 5½ x 8½. of. circ. 150. Reporting time: 1 week or less. Payment: 1 contributor's copy. Copyrighted. no ads. Discounts: 40%. Back issues: 5 & 6 only. Pub'd 3 issues 1976; expects 2 issues 1977, 1 issue 1978. Pub's reviews: 4 in 1976. §poetry.

BLACKBERRY, Gary Lawless, Box 186, Brunswick, ME 04011. Poetry. "Chapbooks by Enslin, Sanfield, Beltrametti, Gifford, Deemer, Koller, Lawless, Ferraris, Byrd, BlueCloud. One Anthology-Sitting Frog—poetry from Naropa Institute Summer '75, edited by Rachel Peters, Eero Ruittila" 10/yr; price per copy: $1.75; sample: $1.75. 1974. 16-20pp; 8½ x 7. of. circ. 200. Reporting time: 2-4 weeks. Payment: copies + %. Back issues: Sitting Frog-$3.25. §ethnopoetics/back country/Amer. Indian. NESPA.

THE BLACKBIRD CIRCLE, The Blackbird Press, Inc., Dean Deter, Robt. Conley, Ellen Deter, Box 99112, Jeffersontown, KY 40299. Poetry. "No preconceptions about style or form. Our tone is informal, and we like to give young poets a first hearing as well as see what older poets are doing. Please try to read our magazine before submitting. We can't accept xeroxed poems, ones without SASE, or with postage due. Contributors include Elisavietta Ritchie, Laurie Spier, Anthony Piccione, Donald Levering." irreg.; sub price: $6/3 issues. 1970. 32pp; 8½ x 5½. lo. circ. 500. Reporting time: 6 wks. Payment: copies only. Ads: $50/$25. Discounts: 20-40% agent, trade. CCLM, COSMEP.

BLACKSMITH ANTHOLOGY, The Blacksmith Press, Gail Mazur, 5 Walnut Ave, Cambridge, MA 02140, 868-5753. Poetry. "Submissions are for readings; poems by participants are selected—Linda Pastan, Alan Dugan, Rosellen Brown, Donald Hall, Jean Valentine, Robert Pinsky" 1/yr; 1-yr sub price: $0.00; per copy: $2.00; sample: $2.00. 1974. 72pp; 5 x 7. of. circ. 800. Payment: copies. Copyrighted, reverts to author. Discounts: up to 5-10 issues 40% discount; 50% above 10. Back issues: $2.00 for 1st anthology. COSMEP, NESPA.

The Blacksmith Press (see also BLACKSMITH ANTHOLOGY), Gail Mazur, 5 Walnut Ave., Cambridge, MA 02140. Poetry. "At this point, the Press publishes only the anthologies. The contributors are selected from among the poets who give poetry readings at the Blacksmith House." avg. price, paper: $2.00. 1974. 72pp; 5 x 7. of. avg. press run 800. Payment: copies. Copyrights for author. Discounts: 40% disc. on orders from 5-10; 50% above 10. COSMEP, NESPA.

Blackstaff Press (see also IRISH BOOKLORE), Diane Gracey, Carmel McQuaid, 16 Donegall Square South, Belfast BT1 5JE, United Kingdom. Poetry, fiction, art, cartoons, photos, satire, long-poems, plays, concrete art. Reporting time: 1 month.

BLACKWOOD'S MAGAZINE, William Blackwood & Sons Ltd., David Fletcher, 32 Thistle St, Edinburgh EH2 1HA, United Kingdom, 031-225-3411. Articles, poetry, fiction, non-fiction. "BLACKWOOD'S is Britain's oldest monthly, specializing in a wide range of high-quality material. Would-be contributors are advised to study the magazine. Articles and stores are between 3000 and 9000 words in length." 12/yr; 1-yr sub price: £7($17.00); per copy: 60p $1.50; sample: 60p-$1.50. 1817. 96pp; 230 x 150mm. †lp. circ. 10M. Reporting time: immediate. Payment: According to merit. Not copyrighted. Ads: £50.00/£30.00. Discounts: 25% trade orders. Back issues: Prices on application. Pub'd 12 issues 1976; expects 12 issues 1977.

Blafigria Press (see THE GREAT BLAFIGRIA IS/THE GREAT COMPASSION)

BLAKE, AN ILLUSTRATED QUARTERLY, Morris Eaves, Morton D. Paley, Dept. of English, Univ. of New Mexico, Albuquerque, NM 87131, 505-277-3103. Articles, art, photos, criticism, reviews, letters. "Our orientation is scholarly, though we have published some non-scholarly material. Blake was both poet and artist, and we welcome material on either or both aspects of his work: news items on exhibitions, publications, etc.; essays, and notes that run from one to many pages, discussion articles for the exchange of opinion; minute particulars, which are mini-notes; reviews of books about Blake; biographical material. Many of the articles are illustrated." 4/yr; 1-yr sub price: $7.00; per copy: $2. 1967. 40pp; 8½ x 11. lo. circ. 600. Reporting time: 4-6 wks. Payment: copies only. Ads: $80/$55. Discounts: Agency disc. 10 percent; Individual subs. $6.00/yrly. Back issues: whole nos. 17-18/$5; whole no. 20/$3. Pub'd 4 issues 1976; expects 4 issues 1977, 4 issues 1978. Pub's reviews: 20 in 1976. COSMEP.

BLANK TAPE, Permanent Press, Keith Rahmmings, Box 371, Brooklyn, NY 11230. Poetry, fiction, articles, art, photos, cartoons, music, letters, parts-of-novels, long-poems, collages, plays, concrete art. "A couple of changes this time around. Firstly, have dropped One Size Fits All Press for new handle, PERMANENT PRESS. Secondly, have thrown concept of quarterly mag out the window. From now on, BLANK TAPE is a serial anthology, published as often as I can get enough material to constitute an issue. Am on the lookout, as usual, for poetry with a BANG. I'd also like to see more good fiction, any kinda fiction. 'specially the kind you don't generally read in litmags. F'rinstance, speculative fiction. If your stuff's been rejected by AMAZING, ANALOG, &c, try me.

Same goes for comic strips, mysteries, westerns, love stories, dirty stories, fairy stories, photo stories, anti stories, non stories, twenty stories...but here I go again." Irregular; sub price: $6.00/3 issues; per copy: $2.00; sample: $2.00. 1976. 50-60pp; 8½ x 11. †of. circ. 1,000. Reporting time: 2 wks-mo. Payment: Copies and autographed photo of Mister Ed. Buys 1st serial rts. Discounts: 40 percent on 5 copies or more. Back issues: Inquire. Pub'd 1 issue 1976; expects 2 issues 1977, 3 issues 1978. Pub's reviews. §Poetry, fiction, and you name it. COSMEP.

BLEB, Bleb Press, Geoffrey Gardner, Box 322 Times Square Station, New York, NY 10036, 612-339-5162. Poetry, fiction, reviews, long-poems, criticism, letters. "Recent contributors have included Lyn Lifshin, Lucien Stryk, Robert Dana, Faye Kicknosway, Tom McKeown, Stephen Kessler, Hayden Carruth, Paul Mann, Edouard Roditi, Barry MacDonald, Yunus Emre, Leon Felipe, Cid Corman. Excellent work of any style or form. Especially interested in translation. Prospective contributors are advised to look at an issue before submitting their work to us." 2/yr; 1-yr sub price: $1.50; per copy: $0.75; sample: $0.75 while limited supply of back numbers lasts. 1970. 60pp; 6 x 9. †of. circ. 500 plus. Reporting time: At once to 3 months. Payment: Copies only, but generously. Copyrighted, reverts to author. no ads at all. Discounts: 30 percent to bookstores, otherwise none. Back issues: No's. 1-12 $20.00 the set; number's 7-10 $2.00 each. Pub'd 1 issue 1976; expects 2 issues 1977, 2 issues 1978. Pub's reviews. §All poetry, fiction & translation of both as well as magazines printing any or all of these. CCLM.

Blewointmentpress, Bill Bissett, Allan Rosen, Box 48870 Station Bentall, Vancouver, British Columbia, Canada. Poetry. "Cathy Ford, Candas Jane Dorsey, Hart Broudy, Stephen Miller, Lionel Kearns, David S. West, John Cook, Gwen Hauser, Allan Rosen, bill bissett, Gerry Gilbert, Barry McKinnon, Lynne Kokke, Ken West, Joy Zemel Long, David UU, Susan Musgrave, Bertrand Lachance, Earle Birney, john curry, Dorothy Livesay, Michael Lally, P.K. Page, Gerald Lampert, n many othrs." avg. price, paper: $3.00. 1967. 50pp; Varies. †mi/of. avg. press run 500. Reporting time: 1-2 months. Payment: $100.00 advance plus th rest uv th 10 percent in copees. Author holds copyright. Discounts: 40 percent bookstores & wholesalers; 10 percent library. ACP, LPG.

BLOODROOT, Joan Eades, Editor; Linda Ohlsen, Assistant Editor, 316 Harvard St, Grand Forks, ND 58201, 701-777-4300. Poetry, fiction, articles, art, parts-of-novels, long-poems. "Although we have published men, we prefer work by women or about women's concerns. Most of our contributors, though not all of them, are from the Northern Plains." 2/yr; 1-yr sub price: $3.00; per copy: $1.50; sample: $1.00 for back issue. 1976. 64pp; 6 x 9. of. circ. 600. Reporting time: 1 month. Payment: 1 copy. Copyrighted, reverts with credit given. Discounts: standard. Back issues: $1.00. Pub'd 1 issue 1976; expects 2 issues 1977, 2 issues 1978.

Blue Crow Press (see also DECARABIA), D. R. Meiklejohn, Dawn Meiklejohn, D. K. Lamont, Steve Meiklejohn, Jesse Daniels, 48 Salmon Falls Rd. (Box A), Rochester, NH 03867. Poetry, fiction, art, news items. "Most mss accepted on an anthology type basis for the *Blue Crow Equinox* which we plan to publish annually, where a good amount of material will be accepted from recent contributors/subscribers to Blue Crows publications; *Faculty X:* Parapsychology/Occult Newsletter and *DECARABIA.* Feel free to submit anything in the Decarabian line." avg. price, paper: $1.50. 1977. 24-96pp; 5½ x 8½. †mi/of. Reporting time: 1 month. Payment: 10 percent. Copyrights for author. Discounts: 40 percent trade, bulk, etc. Expects 2 titles 1977, 4 titles 1978. CCLM, COSMEP, NESPA.

Blue Horse, Jacqueline T. Bradley, Patrick Kelly, P.O. Box 6061, Augusta, GA 30906. Poetry, fiction, photos, interviews, satire, criticism, parts-of-novels, collages, concrete art. "BLUE HORSE (Redivivus) is a tax exempt, non-profit group anthology, an ancillary publication of BLUE HORSE MOVEMENT and represents the essence of the MOVEMENT. Material length: negotiable. Style: neither simple romantic nor political cant. 'Fade them out with ESOTERICA,' BH says. Biases, Universal—none, yet all. Contributors: primarily educated, proletariat Southerners, but, in Vol ii, Dr. G. Warren Weissmann, Warner Robinson, engraver, J.T. Bradley, U.S. Army advisor on Privacy Act of 1974; Robert Head, editor *NOLA Express/neo-express;* Russian poet, Yevgeny Yevtushenko; Lonnie Barkoot, Lonnie's Chopper Shop, Salinas, Ca., (deceased); Louis Ebert, Kierkegaard Scholar and ward of city of San Francisco; John Quinnett, Poet Laureate Western

Carolina, woodsman crappie authority; Regulars, Patrick Kelly, Media Specialist, U.S.GOVT; Marita Quinnett, retired Small Person and Richard Ross, homilist and counter-propagandist, USIS, Far East." 1966. 76pp; 5½ x 8½. of. Reporting time: irreg. 1 month. Payment: copies or barter. Discounts: Prisoners pay postage only. Expects 3 titles 1978. COSMEP.

BLUE MOON NEWS, Blue Moon Press, Inc., James Hepworth, Criss Cannady, Pat Skinner, c/o English Dept., University of Arizona, Tucson, AZ 85721, 602-884-1387. Poetry, fiction, articles, art, photos, interviews, criticism, reviews, long-poems. "We are mainly interested in poetry and fiction, but are open to all good writing in whatever form it may appear. Some recent contributors include Norman Dubie, Pamela Stewart, Joseph Bruchac, William Stafford, William Pitt Root, and Seamus Heaney." 1 or 2/yr; 1-yr sub price: $3.00; per copy: $2.00; sample: $1.00. 1976. 36pp; 8½ x 11. of. circ. Unknown at this time. Reporting time: 6 weeks to 3 months. Payment: 2 contributor's copies each. Copyrighted, reverts to author. Ads: $75.00/$50.00. Discounts: 30 percent to bookstores, subscription rates are less than direct sales. Back issues: $1.00 if still in print or unless otherwise stated. Pub's reviews §Poetry.

Blue Moon Press, Inc. (see also BLUE MOON NEWS), James Hepworth, Criss Cannady, Pat Skinner, c/o English Dept., University of Arizona, Tucson, AZ 85721, 602-884-1387. Poetry, fiction, articles, art, photos, interviews, criticism, reviews, long-poems. "We are mainly interested in poetry and fiction, but are open to all good writing in whatever form it may appear. Some recent contributors include Norman Dubie, Pamela Stewart, Joseph Bruchac, William Stafford, William Pitt Root, and Seamus Heaney." avg. price, cloth: $7.00 - $10.00; paper: $2.00 - $3.00. 1972. 24pp; 5½ x 8½. avg. press run 250-500. Reporting time: 6 weeks to 3 months. Payment: Authors receive 10 percent of press run. Copyrights for author. Discounts: 30 percent to bookstores, subscription rates are discounted over direct sales.

Blue Mountain Press (see also SKYWRITING), Martin Grossman, 511 Campbell St., Kalamazoo, MI 49007, 349-3924. Poetry. avg. price, paper: $2.00. 1974. 28pp; 9 x 6. of. avg. press run 500. Reporting time: 2-4 mo. Payment: 10 percent of run. Copyrights for author. Discounts: 40 percent/5 copies minimum. Expects 2 titles 1977.

The Blue Oak Press, D. A. Carpenter, Judith Shears, Bill Hotchkiss, Reuben Brewster, 2555 Newcastle Road, Newcastle, CA 95658, 916-663-3474. Poetry, fiction, criticism, long-poems. "Recent contributors: Cornel Lengyel, Edith Snow, William Everson, Robinson Jeffers, Marlan Beilke, Bill Hotchkiss, K'os Naahaabii, Stan Hager. Our bias would be toward the poetry of contemporary Western America; and we have drawn significant focus on the work of Robinson Jeffers as the seminal figure of this developing tradition. Price is extremely variable, from one special edition at $75.00 to paperbacks at $3.95." avg. price, cloth: $10.00; paper: $3.95. 1967. 80-100 pp: but this is also extremely variable, upward.; 6 x 9. †of/lp. avg. press run 500. We do not invite submissions. No specific payment policy. Copyrights for author. Discounts: 40 percent to bookstores and dealers; 10 percent to libraries; 30 percent on consignment; no discounts on special editions.

BLUE PIG, Sand Project Press/US, David Ball, 23 Cedar Street, Northampton, MA 01060. Poetry, art, collages, concrete art. "Tom Raworth, Phillip Lopate, Merrill Gilfillan, Jack Collom. 20-25 pages/issue. Issues rare & irregular. Choice eccentric & unyielding." 1-2/yr; sub price: Free to people; institutions pay through the nose. 1968. 20-25pp; 8½ x 11. of. circ. 250. Reporting time: 1 month to never for unsolicited submissions. Payment: $25.00 - $50.p0 when we have a grant. Copyrighted, reverts to author. Back issues: Prices variable. First issues out of sight. CCLM.

BLUE UNICORN, Ruth G. Lodice, B. Jo Kinnick, Harold Witt, 22 Avon Road, Kensington, CA 94707, 415-526-8439. Poetry, art. "Shorter poems preferred; contributors to first issue include Stafford, Wagoner, Sarton, De Longchamps, Charles Edward Eaton, Diana O'Hehir, Joan Swift, others." 3/yr; 1-yr sub price: $7.00; per copy: $2.50. 1977. 32-60pp; 4¼ x 5½. of. circ. 500 most issues. Reporting time: 1-3 months. Payment: 1 copy. Copyrighted, reverts to author. Expects 1 issue 1977. §Poetry.

Blue Wind Press (Dynamite Books; Overdrive Books), George Mattingly, Lucy Farber, Liza

43

Cohen, 820 Miramar, Berkeley, CA 94707, 415-526-1905. Poetry, fiction, art, photos, satire, collages, non-fiction. "Titles for 1977: *Sojourner Microcosms, Selected Poems* 1959-1976 by Anselm Hollo; *Night Shift* by Maria Gitin; *Erase Words* by Keith Abbott; *She Who Is Alive* by Robert Harris; *Light Years* by Merrill Gilfillan; *Traveling Light* by Steve Toth; (others). Other recent titles: *Bits Of Thirst* by Jack Marshall; *Rotwang* by Tim Hildebrand; *The Book Of Breeething* by William S. Burroughs; *Gush, A Comic Novel About Unemployment* by Keith Abbott. We rarely publish unsolicited manuscripts: Query first. Our emphasis is moving into fiction & non-fiction. No poetry read before summer 1978." avg. price, cloth: $8.95; paper: $2.95. 1970. 100pp. of. avg. press run 1,500. Reporting time: 1-3 months. Payment: royalty-10% paper 15% cloth. Copyrights for author. Discounts: Individual: Prepay plus $0.50 postage required; special discounts available; No Institutional discounts except 15 percent library standing-order. Library jobbers: 1-19, 20 percent; 20 plus, 40 percent. Retail trade: 1-4, 20 percent; 5-19, 40 percent; 20-49, 42 percent; 50-99, 43 percent. Pub'd 4 titles 1976; expects 6 titles 1977, 8 titles 1978. CCLM, COSMEP, AIGA, AIP.

Boa Editions, A Poulin Jr., 92 Park Avenue, Brockport, NY 14420, 716-637-3844. "Generally not accepting unsolicited manuscripts. Major poets invited to select and introduce new poets. Forthcoming contributors include: W. D. Snodgrass, Barton Sutter, M. L. Rosenthal, Barry Wallenstein, Anthony Piccione, Archibald MacLeish, Henry Miller, Bertrand Mathieu, Anne Sexton, Suzanne Berger Rioff, Edward Byrne, John Ashbery." avg. price, cloth: $6.95; paper: $3.95; other: $15.00-$20.00 signed. 1976. 40-60pp; 6 x 9. of. avg. press run 600-1,000 half in paper and half in cloth. Reporting time: 2-4 weeks. Payment: copies and negotiated royalty. Copyrights for author. Discounts: 20 percent to subscribers; Bookstores: 40 percent for 5 or more copies; 20 percent for 1-4 copies of trade and for signed editions. COSMEP, NESPA, NYSSPA.

THE BODY POLITIC- Gay Liberation Journal, Pink Triangle Press, The Body Politic Editorial Collective, Box 7289, Station A, Toronto, Ontario M5W1X9, Canada, 416-863-6320. Poetry, fiction, articles, art, photos, cartoons, interviews, criticism, reviews, letters, news items, nonfiction. "Required: material from people conversant with gay liberation politics and principles-able to translate those ideas into imaginative formats" 10/yr; 1-yr sub price: $5.00 Canada; $8.50 U.S.; per copy: $0.75 Canada; $1.00 U.S.; sample: $0.75 Canada; $1.00 U.S. 1971. 28pp; tabloid. of. circ. 10,000. Reporting time: 1 month. Ads: $225.00/$130.00/$0.10 personal, $0.30 business. Discounts: 33-1/3% trade. Back issues: $0.75 Canada; $1.00 U.S. Pub'd 8 issues 1976; expects 10 issues 1977, 10 issues 1978. Pub's reviews: 120 in 1976. §gay liberation, sexuality, sexual politics, homosexual themes. CPPA.

BOMBAST POETRY REVIEW, Robin Calitri, Carl Zimmermann, P.O. Box 3752, Modesto, CA 95352. Poetry, interviews, criticism, reviews, letters, long-poems, collages, concrete art, news items. "A quarterly devoted to poetry of fine quality. Also invitive surrealism with open arms, collage, critiques & found poetry. Our title serves with an implication that what poets have to say will ring far & wide." 4/yr; 1-yr sub price: $4.00; per copy: $1.00. 1977. 50pp; 6 x 8. of. circ. 300-500. Reporting time: 2 weeks, include a S.A.S.E. Payment: 2 copies. Copyrighted, reverts to author. Ads: $30.00/$15.00. Discounts: subscription trades welcome. Pub's reviews: none in 1976. §poetry. COSMEP.

BOMBAY DUCK, 3035 Fillmore, San Francisco, CA 94123. "BOMBAY DUCK is a new photo mag that's out to publish lively photography. The idea is to provide photographers with a new avenue for getting their work published...A new vehicle to get photography that has spark and character out and into the public. If you're interested, send photos or articles dealing with photography." sub price: $8.00/5 issues; per copy: $2.00. 1976. of.

Bombshelter Press (see THE ALLEY CAT READINGS)

Bonefold Imprint (see also RABIES), Bernard J. Kelly, 68 Parkhill Road, Buckingham Palace, London, England NW3, United Kingdom. "Late late late dada/early early early thoughtism, poems, musings, visuals, natterings, manifestos, on goings, etc. RABIES is wonderful." avg. price, cloth: £2.95; paper: 50p. 1976. 30 to 50pp; A4. of. avg. press run 400. Reporting time: Always. Payment: Fame. None unless stated. Discounts: Friends 50 percent. Pub'd 1 title 1976; expects 1 title 1977.

BONES, White Bones Press, Katherine Greef, Terence Anderson, Box 333, Islip, NY 11751. Poetry, fiction, cartoons, parts-of-novels, long-poems, collages, concrete art. "We welcome new & unpublished writers with at least some experience, i.e. don't send your very first poem. We also include those who have published. We are now especially interested in works by women and in visual poetry." at intervals; sub price: $2.00/2 issues; per copy: $1.00; sample: $1.25. 1967. 80pp; 7 x 8½. of. circ. 1M. Reporting time: up to 2 yrs. Payment: 2 copies. no ads. Discounts: none. CCLM, COSMEP.

BONSAI. A Quarterly of Haiku, Bonsai Press/Jama Press, Jan Streif, Mary Streif, P. O. Box 7211, Phoenix, AZ 85011. Poetry. "'*BONSAI* invites all schools of haiku, but the standard is high. Seeking haiku which 'capture' a moment, not just talk about it. Also very much interested in penetrating essays dealing with the haiku of the 1970's, some reviews, and other contemporary work in the haiku/senryu field. Length: short or long, no limit. Among recent contributors: Jean Battlo, Ross Figgins, Sanford Goldstein, LeRoy Gorman, Elizabeth Searle Lamb, Geraldine Clinton Little, Stanley Morner, Frank K. Robinson, Selma Stefanile, Virginia Brady Young. Also doing book printing, publishing: '*Shedding The River*' by V.B. Young and '*The Best Of Bonsai: HAIKU*, will be out in the near future.'" 4/yr; 1-yr sub price: $5.00 USA & Canada (Other $6.00); per copy: $1.50; sample: $1.00. 1976. 36pp; 8½ x 5½. of. circ. 350. Reporting time: 1-3 weeks. Payment: (10 $2.00 awards per issue). Copyrighted, first rights only. Ads: $25.00/$15.00/$0.05 a word - $1.00 minimum. Discounts: Bookstore 35 percent and up. Back issues: $1.50 (when available). Pub'd 4 issues 1976; expects 4 issues 1977, 4 issues 1978. Pub's reviews: 1 in 1976. §HAIKU. COSMEP, COSMEP-WEST, CCLM.

BOOK ARTS, The Center for Book Arts, Patricia Nedds, Alexandra Soteriou, 15 Bleeker St, New York, NY 10012. Articles, art, photos, interviews. "Articles/Interviews on: books, book sculptures/art, bookbinding, the history of some aspect of books, book restoration, papermaking, printing, calligraphy, wood engraving etc." 4/yr; 1-yr sub price: $7.50; per copy: $2.00; sample: $2.00. 1975. 60pp; 8¼ x 10½. †lp. circ. 10,000. Reporting time: 3 mo. Payment: in copies. Ads: $180/$115/$.35. Discounts: sub agency: 15%; adv. discounts: 20% to rare bookdealers, galleries, art suppliers. §books/mags on books & their arts: bookbinding, calligraphy, fine printing, wood-engraving etc.

BOOK BUYER'S GUIDE/MARKETPLACE, Franklin Book Company, Kevin K. Kopec, PO Box 208, East Millstone, NJ 08873, 201-873-2156. Articles. "Advertisements, buying tips" 3/yr; 1-yr sub price: $5.00; per copy: $1.25; sample: free. 1975. 20pp; 8½ x 11. of. circ. 3,000-5,000. Reporting time: 3 months. Copyrighted. Ads: $90.00/$50.00/$10.00 (50 word) $0.20 per word. Discounts: None, $5.00 annual subscription, $7.00 outside U.S.A. Back issues: $1.00. Expects 4 issues 1977, 4 issues 1978. Pub's reviews. §all areas. COSMEP.

The Book Concern (see THE COPPER COUNTRY ANTHEM)

BOOK EXCHANGE, W. K. Fudge, Sardinia House, Sardinia St., London WC2A 3NW, United Kingdom. 12/yr; 1-yr sub price: £2.50. 1948. 32pp; 8½ x 5½. lp. Ads: £30/page pro rata 1p/word.

Book Publishing Co., Matthew McClure, 156 Drakes Lane, Summertown, TN 38483, 615-964-3571. Articles. 1970. †of.

BOOK REPORT, Book Report, Albert Matzye, P.O. Box 266, Campbell, OH 44405. Reviews, letters. "Book Report is a personal journal devoted to books and writing in general. All reviews, comments, opinions, etc. reflect the biases of the editor (who happens to be the typist, the printer, the researcher, the mail boy, the financial backer, chief clerk, bottle washer, stamp-licker, janitor, etc.). Willing to look at anything in print. Originally founded to serve book collectors, and since anyone is apt to collect anything, no subject, style, form or idiosyncracy is denied consideration." Irregular.; price per copy: $.25; sample: $.25. 1972. 12pp; 8½ x 7. †of. Pub'd 4 issues 1976; expects 4 issues 1977, 4 issues 1978. Pub's reviews: 4 in 1976. §all. COSMEP.

BOOKLEGGER MAGAZINE, Booklegger Press, Celeste West, Sue Critchfield, Valerie Wheat,

Carole Leita, 555 29th St., San Francisco, CA 94131. Articles, art, photos, cartoons, reviews. "We are a feminist collective of information freaks. BKLG reviews the independent, alternative press, mainly to increase librarians' awareness of it. BKLG includes resource guides on social change & creative life styles-such as radical therapy, decriminalizing prostitution, self-publishing, energy, worker self-management, etc. We believe information is action, and should be accessible to all people for control over their own lives." 6/yr; 1-yr sub price: $8; per copy: $1.50; sample: free. 1973. 48pp; 7 x 10. lo. circ. 2M. Reporting time: 1 mo. Payment: $5/resource guide. Pub's reviews. §material advocating social charge, esp. androgyans, socialistic, non racist. CCLM, COSMEP.

BOOKS & BOOKMEN, Cix Amaral, Artillery Mansions, 75 Victoria, London SW1Hohz, United Kingdom, 01-799-4452. Articles, interviews, criticism, letters. "All work is commissioned. No unsolicited MSS please." 12/yr; 1-yr sub price: $26.30; per copy: $0.75; sample: free. 1955. 68pp; 11 x 8½. lp. circ. Not disclosed. Payment: House scale or by arrangement. Copyrighted. Ads: $175.00/$100.00/$0.10. Discounts: 10% publisher/agent. Back issues: Twice current cover price if over 6 months old. Pub'd 12 issues 1976; expects 12 issues 1977, 12 issues 1978. Pub's reviews: 1,500 in 1976. §New books.

BOOKS IN CANADA: A National Review Of Books, Canadian Review of Books Ltd., D Marshall, Pier Giorgio DiCicco, 366 Adelaide St East, Toronto, Ontario, Canada. Poetry, fiction, articles, art, photos, cartoons, interviews, satire, criticism, reviews, music, letters, parts-of-novels. 12/yr; 1-yr sub price: $9.95; sample: free. 1971. 40pp; 7 x 11. of. circ. 40,000. Reporting time: 2 weeks. Payment varies. Ads: $450/$300. Discounts: 15% advertising agency commissions. Back issues: negotiable. Pub's reviews. §literature.

BOOKSELLER, Philothea Thompson, 13 Bedford Square, London WC1B3JE, United Kingdom. 52/yr; 1-yr sub price: £8.50. 1858.

The Bookstore Press, Gene Boyington, Gerry Hausman, Lorry Hausman, Box 191, RFD 1, Freeport, ME 04032, 207-963-7071. "We do not accept unsolicited mss. We have enough contracted books to publish for the next two years. We are exclusively distributed to the trade by The Benjamin & Matthew Book Company, Route 1, Ashville, Maine 04607. Children's books and nonfiction." avg. price, cloth: $5.95; paper: $2.95. 1970. of. avg. press run 3,000. Reporting time: 3 months. Discounts: 40% trade/46% jobbers. Pub'd 2 titles 1976; expects 4 titles 1977, 4 titles 1978. COSMEP.

BOOKSWEST, BooksWest, Inc., George Trinkaus, George Warren, 3757 Wilshire Blvd, Los Angeles, CA 90010, 213-383-8362. Reviews. "*'BOOKSWEST'* is an alternative trade magazine of book publishing: trade news, 50 short-notice reviews, 1 full-length review by major author, per issue. Plus: bestsellers (critiqued), letters (a few)." 12/yr; 1-yr sub price: $15; per copy: $1.25; sample: free. 1976. 48pp; 8½ x 11. of. circ. 10,000. Payment: $100.00 for major review. $5.00 for short notice no unsolicited reviews. Ads: $450.00/$340.00/$1.25 per line. Discounts: 15 percent to agencies. Pub'd 3 issues 1976; expects 8 issues 1977, 12 issues 1978. Pub's reviews: 100's in 1976. §fiction, nonfiction, poetry. COSMEP.

Bookworm Publishing Company, Maisie C. Meier, Editor-In-Chief, P.O. Box 3037, Ontario, CA 91761, 714-984-9419. Non-fiction. "We publish books of interest in the fields of natural and social ecology, broadly defined. Current titles include '*Earthworms For Ecology And Profit*', '*Don't Call It Dirt!*', '*Improving Garden Soil*', by Gordon Baker Lloyd, and '*Begonias For Beginners*' by Elda Haring. Other titles cover the fields of vermology, gardening, and botany. We are looking for well-written how-to-do-it type books on any topic related to gardening & agriculture, including business, and family self-sufficiency." avg. price, cloth: $9.95; paper: $4.95. 1975. 200pp; 5½ x 8½. Reporting time: 6 weeks. Payment: royalty, 5% of revenue. Copyrights for author. Discounts: 1-4, 20 percent, 5-49, 40 percent; 50-149, 44 percent; additional discounts available. Pub'd 3 titles 1976; expects 4 titles 1977, 10 titles 1978. BPASC, BPSC.

BOPP, Ayanna Press, Kambon Obayani, 542 W. 112 No. 5-f, New York, NY 10025, 749-7844. "Michael Harper, Gayl Jones, Ezekial Mphalele, James Baldwin, Ntozake Shange, Jayne Cortez,

Clarence Major, Victor Hernandez Cruz, Mongane Serote etc. Material should be double spaced, typed with a return address. Fiction should not be over fifteen pages, poems not over three pages and essays not over 15 pgs." 2/yr; 1-yr sub price: $7.00; per copy: $3.00. 1971. 120pp; 8½ x 11. Reporting time: 2 weeks. Payment: we pay in copies. Copyrighted, reverts to author. Ads: none. Discounts: 5 percent. Back issues: $2.50. Pub'd 1 issue 1976. Pub's reviews: 1 in 1976. §Literature, music, politics, history, dance, art. CCLM, COSMEP.

Border-Mountain Press, Bill Robinson, P.O. Box 1296, Benson, AZ 85602. Poetry, fiction, articles, art, photos, cartoons, interviews, satire, criticism, reviews, letters, parts-of-novels, long-poems. "Mainly a book publisher, but publishing 1 undated series—book and publishing bulletin. Use magazine type material. No more mss. accepted until 1979." 1975. †of. Reporting time: 2 wks. Payment varies. Copyrights for author. Discounts: 40% to bookstores and agents. Pub'd 7 titles 1976; expects 10 titles 1977, 10 titles 1978. COSMEP-WEST, LPSC.

BOREAL, John Flood, P.O. Box 580, Hearst, Ontario P0L1N0, Canada. Poetry, fiction, articles, art, photos, interviews, criticism, reviews, plays. "Boreal is a trilingual—French, Cree and English—journal of Northern Ontario studies. It is published by Le College Universitaire de Hearst in Hearst and focuses primarily on the northern situation in Canada, particularly in Ontario." 4/yr; 1-yr sub price: $6.00; per copy: $2.00; sample: $2.00. 1974. 80pp; 7¼ x 4¾. of. circ. 500. Reporting time: 1 mo. Payment: $5 per page. Ads: $100/$50. Back issues: $2.00. Pub's reviews. §studies of northern environments, societies, etc.

BOSS, Boss Books, Reginald Gay, Box 370, Madison Square Station, New York, NY 10010. Poetry, fiction, articles, art, photos, interviews, criticism, reviews, parts-of-novels, plays. irregular; price per copy: $2.00; sample: $2.00. 1966. 70pp; 6 x 9. of. circ. 1,000. Reporting time: 4-8 weeks. Payment: copies. Copyrighted, reverts to author. Discounts: trade/bulk/less 40%. Back issues: Prices variable. Expects 1 issue 1977, 1 issue 1978. Pub's reviews. §Poetry, novels, art. CCLM.

Boston Critic, Inc. (see NEW BOSTON REVIEW)

‡**BOSTON PHOENIX,** 1108 Boylston St., Boston, MA 02215.

BOSTON UNIVERSITY JOURNAL, Paul Kurt Ackermann, 775 Commonwealth Ave., Boston, MA 02215. Poetry, fiction, articles, art, interviews, satire, criticism, reviews, letters, parts-of-novels. "Av. length of articles: 10-25 typed, double-spaced pp. Articles should be well-written, lively, devoid of jargon, can be specialized or general, but must be intelligible to educated laymen. Recent Contributors: poetry: Ted Hughes, James Tate, Denise Levertov, lesser-known poets. Short Stories: Joyce Carol Oates, Penelope Mortimer. Articles: Alasdair MacIntyre, Maxwell Geismar, Dore Ashton, lesser-known writers & scholars whose work is of a high quality." 3/yr; 1-yr sub price: $6.00; per copy: $2.00; sample: $2.00. 1966. 72-76pp; 7 x 9¾. of. circ. 3,000. Reporting time: few days to two mos. Payment: $10 printed page/$25 mininum. Ads: $150, inside cover $175/$90. Discounts: agency commission 15%. Back issues: all $2 each. Pub's reviews. §literature, philosophy, history, actually all the arts & sciences. CCLM, COSMEP.

BOTH SIDES NOW, Free People Press, Staff, 1232 Laura St., P. O. Box 13079, Jacksonville, FL 32206. Poetry, fiction, articles, art, photos, cartoons, interviews, satire, criticism, reviews, music, letters, news items, non-fiction. "An alternative paper having magazine-type content with a unique spiritual/political syntheses. Analysis of current events and thinkpieces, plus general coverage of all areas of alternatives and counterculture. Reprinting important articles which deserve wide circulation. Emphasis on transformations related to the new age & aquarian frontier 1976 authors & columnists included Ralph Nader, Sean Devereux, Joe Klein, T. B. Mechling, Robert Sherrill, Dorothy Maas, Eve Pell, Rep. Elizabeth Holtzman, Gar Smith & Elihu Edelson.'' irregular; sub price: 5 issues $1, etc.; per copy: $.25; sample: $.25. 1969. 20pp; tabloid. of. circ. 4,000. Reporting time: erratic. Payment: copies. Authors retain rights. Ads: $100.00/$55.00/$0.50 48 characters-line, $3.00 col. in. Discounts: $10/100 plus postage. Back issues: Most available at reg. prices. Pub'd 2 issues 1976; expects 6 issues 1977, 12 issues 1978. Pub's reviews: 2 in 1976. §counterculture, spiritual, political. APS.

47

BOTTOMFISH MAGAZINE, Bottomfish, Frank Berry, 21250 Stevens Crk., Cupertino, CA 95014, 408-996-4550. Poetry, fiction, art, photos, music, parts-of-novels, long-poems, plays. "Adrianne Marcus, Daniel Langton, Adam David Miller, Thom Gunn, Jessica Hagedorn, Stephen Vincent, Paul Shuttleworth, Frank Cady" 2/yr; 1-yr sub price: $4.50; per copy: $1.75; sample: $1.75. 1976. 50pp; 7 x 8½. †of. circ. 100. Reporting time: 2 months, (not operating during the summer). Payment: two copies of magazine. Copyrighted, reverts to author. Ads: none. Discounts: None, free to prisoners. Pub'd 1 issue 1976; expects 2 issues 1977, 2 issues 1978. CCLM, COSMEP.

BOUNDARY 2, William V. Spanos, Robert Kroetsch, State University of New York, Binghamton, NY 13901. Poetry, fiction, articles, interviews, criticism, reviews. "Frequent special issues, such as Vol. 4, no. 2: 'Martin Heidegger and Literature;' Vol 3, no. 3: 'The Oral Impulse in Contemporary American Poetry.' No length limit, although 50 pages is a good rule of thumb for upper limit. Criticism submitted should deal primarily with postmodern concerns. Recent contributors: Robert Bly, David Ignatow, Jerome Rothenberg, Diane Wakoski, David Antin, Nathaniel Tarn, Jerome Mazzaro, Joseph Riddel, Roy Harvey Pearce, Richard Palmer, Albert Hofstadter, George Economou." 3/yr; 1-yr sub price: Individuals: $7.00/Institutions: $9.00; per copy: $3.00; sample: $3.00. 1971. 300pp plus; 9 x 6. †of. circ. 1,000. Reporting time: 1-3 months. Payment: copies plus offprints. Ads: $65/$40. Discounts: 33-1/3% to bookstores, etc. Pub's reviews §modern and contemporary literature, critical theory, film. CCLM, COSMEP.

Bourne Press (see SELF AND SOCIETY)

Boustrophedon (see LOVE LIGHTS)

BOX 749, Seven Square Press of The Printable Arts Society, Inc., David Ferguson, Editor In Chief; P. Raymond Marunas, Art Editor; Mary Maud Ferguson, Anderson Craig, Elizabeth Culbert, Marc Rangel De Algeciras, Lester Afflick, Steve Crawford, Miesje Jolley, Art Kleiner, Stanley Kurz, Box 749, Old Chelsea Station, New York, NY 10011. Poetry, fiction, art, photos, cartoons, satire, music, parts-of-novels, long-poems, collages, plays. "*BOX 749* is a magazine of the printable arts—open to all kinds of writing, graphic art and music. We have no particular stylistic or ideological bias. We will consider—and have serialized—long fiction; we have published one-act plays and will consider plays that are full length. (We have also printed the first two poems, with art work, of a six-part broadside series.)" 1/yr; sub price: $7.00/4 issues; per copy: $2.00; sample: $2.00. 1972. 64-84pp; 8½ x 11. of. circ. 2,500. Reporting time: 1 to 2 months. Payment: copies. Copyrighted. no ads. Discounts: 4-issue subscription is $6 to libraries. No discounts for single copies. Back issues: $4 each. Pub'd 1 issue 1976; expects 1 issue 1977, 2 issues 1978. CCLM, COSMEP, NESPA.

BOXSPRING, Kathleen Anderson, Scott Haas, Debbie Sklarew, Laurence H. Roberts III, Caaron Belcher, Hampshire College, Amherst, MA 01002. Poetry, fiction, art, photos, interviews, criticism, reviews, letters, parts-of-novels, collages, plays. "BOXSPRING is designed to represent both new and established writers. Recent contributors include: Michael Benedikt, Robert Hershon, Terry Stokes, James Tate, Peter Viereck, William Packard, Linda Pastan, Gerard Malanga" 2/yr; 1-yr sub price: $3.00; per copy: $1.50; sample: $1.50. 1974. 64pp; 6 x 8. of. circ. 1,000. Reporting time: 2 weeks to 1 month. Payment: copies only. Ads: $50/$30. Back issues: $5.00-1st issue. Pub's reviews. §poetry, fiction, first books. COSMEP, NESPA.

The Boxwood Press, Dr Ralph Buchsbaum, 183 Ocean View Blvd, Pacific Grove, CA 93950. "*Books*: science & natural history" 1952. of. Reporting time: 30 days. Payment: 10% royalty. Discounts: 20% on texts;/40% trade.

Boyd & Fraser Publishing Company, Jack Taylor, Joan H. Parsons, 3627 Sacramento St., San Francisco, CA 94118, 415-346-0686. "Publish college level text books only." avg. price, cloth: $15.00; paper: $6.25. 1970. 400pp; 6 x 9. of. avg. press run 3,000 - 5,000. Reporting time: as soon as possible. Payment varies. We own copyright. Discounts: Text short discount.

‡**BRANCHING OUT,** Box 4098, Edmonton, Alberta T6E 4T1, Canada.

‡**Branden Press,** 221 Columbus Ave, Boston, MA 02101.

BRAVADO, Bravado Feature Service/BFS Press, Marc Rangel de Algeciras, Marc Rangel Jr., Diana Eng, Lisa Marzano, 37-40 75th St., Jackson Heights, NY 11372. Poetry, fiction, articles, art, cartoons, satire, criticism, letters. "BRAVADO is a forum for creative work that is free of cant & countercant, those tiresome characteristics of contemporary intellectual faddism. We welcome humorous or serious fiction (750-3m wds) & poems; sardonic poetry or prose; historical whimsy; satire as well as serious social comment; artwork in general, b-&-w or wash, no color; & cartoons, cartoons! The only requirements are that these works be articulate & devoid of apocalyptic dogmatism. In short, we're not interested in paranoiac outpourings, pro forma political rhetoric or conventional expressions of angst. Past contributors include Patricia Eakins, Anderson Craig, Susan Schell & James Mancham, a poet & self-styled philosopher who also happens to be Prime Minister of the Seychelles." 1/yr; 1-yr sub price: $1.50; but recommend 2-yr subsc., at $3; per copy: $1.50; sample: $1.50. 1974. 24-30pp; 8½ x 11. of. circ. 1-2M. Reporting time: approx. 2 mos. Payment: copies only. Ads: $100.00/$60.00. Discounts: 40% on orders of 5 or more. Back issues: $3 per copy. COSMEP, NESPA.

BRIARPATCH REVIEW: A Journal of Right Livelihood and Simple Living, Portola Institute, Annie Styron, Michael Phillips, Kristin Anundsen, 330 Ellis Street, San Francisco, CA 94102. 4/yr; 1-yr sub price: $5.00; per copy: $1.00; sample: $1.00. 1973. 40pp; 8½ x 7. of. circ. 2,000. Ads: we pay our advertisers $25.00 an ad. Discounts: 50%. Pub's reviews. §business, living on less, simple living, sharing resources.

BRICK: A Journal Of Reviews, Applegarth Follies, Stan Dragland, Jean McKay, Box 40, Stn. B, London, Ontario N6A 4V3, Canada, 519-432-6137. Articles, criticism, reviews. "The review finds its own length. Experiment with form, according to what the book requires: consider, for instance, the visual. No book is unreviewable." 3/yr; 1-yr sub price: $9.00; per copy: $3.50; sample: $3.50. 1976. 120pp; 8½ x 11. †of. circ. 500. Reporting time: 21 days. Payment: one copy of the issue concerned. Copyrighted, reverts to author. Ads: $75.00/$40.00. Discounts: see Applegarth Follies. Expects 3 issues 1977, 3 issues 1978. Pub's reviews. §all.

BRIDGE MAGAZINE, Priscilla Chung, C.N. Lee, Merle Motooka, Bill Wong, N.T Yung, 199 Lafayette St. 7th fl., New York, NY 10012. Poetry, fiction, articles, art, photos, cartoons, interviews, criticism, reviews, letters, plays. "Contents: articles on social, political and cultural interest, regular features: news, dance, editorial, film, and book reviews, letters from the readers. Additional information: publish new writers as well as established. Some contributors: David Wand, Noam Chomsky, Diana Chang, Frank Chin, Frank Ching." 24/yr; 1-yr sub price: $5.00; per copy: $1.00; sample: free. 1971. 55pp; 8 x 11. circ. 5,000. Ads: $300/$150. Discounts: none. Back issues: $1.00. Pub's reviews. §Asian Americans Related Issues.

THE BRIGHT MEDUSA, The Bright Medusa Press, Nancy Stockwell, Nila Assiter, Box 9321, Berkeley, CA 94709. Poetry, fiction, articles, art, photos, interviews, satire, criticism, letters, parts-of-novels. 4/yr; 1-yr sub price: $6.50; per copy: $1.50. 1976. 50pp; 6 x 6. of. circ. 500-1,000. Reporting time: 2-3 weeks. Payment: copies. Copyrighted, reverts to author. Ads: $20.00/$10.00/no. Pub's reviews. §women's literature.

"BRILLIANT CORNERS": A Magazine of The Arts, Ad Hoc Press, Art Lange, 1372 W. Estes #2N, Chicago, IL 60626, 312-761-3702. Poetry, fiction, articles, art, photos, cartoons, interviews, satire, criticism, reviews, music, letters, parts-of-novels, long-poems, collages, plays, concrete art, non-fiction. "The magazine prints large selection (10-20 pages) of poetry per poet. Thus submissions of poetry should be 15-20 pages of material. Essays & reviews 600-3,000 words. Recent contributors include: Ted Berrigan, Alice Notley, Richard Kostelanetz, Peter Kostakis, Frank O'Hara, Charles Henri Ford, Ned Rorem, Kenward Emslie, Tony Towle, Philip Whalen, Anthony Braxton." 3-4/yr; 1-yr sub price: $5.00 individuals/$10.00 institutions; per copy: $2.00; sample: $2.00. 1975. 100pp; 8½ x 7. of. circ. 300-500. Reporting time: 2 weeks. Payment: 2 copies. Copyrighted, reverts to author. Discounts: 60-40 percent. Back issues: available only w/$50.00 lifetime sub. Pub'd 3 issues 1976; expects 3 issues 1977, 3-4 issues 1978. Pub's reviews: 5 in 1976. §poetry, fiction, music, painting, etc. CCLM.

Bristol Arts Centre (see also CIRCLE IN THE SQUARE BROADSHEET), Bill Pickard, Bristol Arts Centre, 415 King Square, Bristol, Avon BS28JG, England. Poetry. "Members only" avg. price, paper: 10p plus postage. 1966. 4pp; 12 x 8. professional photo litho. avg. press run 500. Copyright to authors. Pub'd 2 titles 1976; expects 2 titles 1977, 2 titles 1978. ALP.

BRITH, Frank Coupe & Co., Ltd.; Preston Lanes, Rev. Francis Thomas, 87 St Barnabas Rd, Woodfork Creek, Essex, United Kingdom, 01-504-3737. Articles. "Articles on Bible Prophecy and Christian Ethics." 12/yr; 1-yr sub price: free; per copy: Nil. 1945. 32pp. lp. circ. 3,000 plus. Reporting time: Soon as possible. The magazine articles are copyrighted to the Covenant Peoples Fellowship. Pub'd 12 issues 1976; expects 12 issues 1977, 12 issues 1978.

BRITISH BOOK NEWS, British Council, Gillian Dickinson, 65 Davies St., London W1Y 2AA, United Kingdom. Articles, reviews. 12/yr; 1-yr sub price: £7.20, $18.00-yr; per copy: 60p, $1.50. 1940. 100pp; 24½ x 18½. of. circ. 9,000. Ads: £105.00/£55.00/£30.00. Discounts: 5 percent on 3, 10 percent on 6, 12 percent on 9, 15 percent of 12 ads with 12 months, 10 percent on 6-12 ads with 12 months.

BRITISH COLUMBIA HISTORICAL NEWS, British Columbia HISTORICAL ASSOCIATION, Philip A. Yandle, 3450 West 20th Ave., Vancouver, B.C. V6S1E4, Canada. Art, reviews. "Strictly relating to history of British Columbia." 4/yr; 1-yr sub price: $5.00; per copy: $1.00; sample: $1.00. 1968. 28pp; 8½ x 11. ..mi. circ. 1,200. Payment: none. Pub's reviews. §British Columbia history only.

BRITISH JOURNAL OF AESTHETICS, Oxford University Press, Harold Osborne, 90A St Johns Wood, High St, London NW8, United Kingdom. Articles, reviews, letters. 4/yr; 1-yr sub price: £22.00; per copy: £6.00; sample: free. 1960. 96pp; 228 x 115mm. of. circ. 2M. Ads: £50.00/£30.00. Discounts: 10% series. Back issues: available from Thames & Hudson. Pub'd 4 issues 1976; expects 4 issues 1977, 4 issues 1978.

BRITISH NATURALISTS' ASSOCIATION (PUBLISHERS), Country-Side, Anthony Wootton, 40 Roundhill, Stone, Aylesbury, Bucks, England HP17 8RD, United Kingdom. Articles. "Occasional publications in paperback form—prices 10p-40p—on all aspects of wild life. List on request." irregular. 1905. 16pp; 14 x 22. lp. Payment: none. Copyrighted, reverts to author.

British Science Fiction Assoc. Ltd. (see also VECTOR), Christopher John Fowler, 72 Kenilworth Avenue, Southcote, Reading, Berkshire RG3 3DN, United Kingdom, 0734-594890. Poetry, fiction, articles, art, photos, cartoons, interviews, satire, criticism, reviews, letters, news items. "Official journal of British SF Association. Serious critical journal. Contributions by many leading science fiction writers." avg. price, paper: 60p. 1958. 32pp; A4. of. avg. press run 800. Reporting time: 3-6 weeks. No payment. Copyrights for author. Discounts: 33-1/3 to dealers. Pub'd 8 titles 1976; expects 6 titles 1977, 6 titles 1978.

BRITISH THEATRE INSTITUTE NEWSLETTER & REPORT, BTI, c/o 125 Markyate Road, Dagenham, Essex RM8 2LB, United Kingdom. Articles, reviews, interviews, criticism, news items. "To establish a theatre institute in the United Kingdom." 6/yr; 1-yr sub price: £12-50; per copy: £1. 1974. 10pp; A4. Payment: copies. Ads: £30. Discounts: 33-1/3%. Back issues: 33-1/3.

BROADSHEET, Broadsheet Collective, P.O. Box 47561, Auckland, New Zealand, 378954. Poetry, fiction, articles, art, photos, cartoons, interviews, satire, criticism, reviews, letters, news items, non-fiction. "New Zealand's only feminist magazine covering the women's movement. Comment on current events mainly in New Zealand, theoretical articles on feminism, fiction and poetry. Trying to get a mass of women as well as feminists so present attractively with good graphics and photos." 10/yr; 1-yr sub price: $8.00 NZ Overseas/$6.00 NZ Inland; per copy: $.60 N.Z.; sample: $.60 N.Z. 1972. 40pp; 20½cm x 26½cm. of. circ. 3,500. Ads: $75/$41.25/$1.65 per col cm. Discounts: 33-1/3%. Back issues: complete set $11.00 N.Z. plus postage. Pub'd 10 issues 1976; expects 10 issues 1977, 10 issues 1978. Pub's reviews: 26 in 1976. §women, feminism, abortion, women's art-culture, novels by women, poetry, children's books.

BROADSIDE, Armchair Press, Mark Berman, P.O. Box 393, Tiffin, OH 44883, 419-447-4167. Poetry. "Experimental one page/one poem magazine." 12/yr; 1-yr sub price: $6.00; per copy: $0.50; sample: $.25. 1974. 1pp; Varies. 1p/of. circ. 200. Reporting time: 1 month. Payment: copies. Copyrighted. Back issues: $.25 per issue. Pub'd 8 issues 1976; expects 5 issues 1977, 12 issues 1978. CCLM, COSMEP.

Broadside Press (see THE BLACK POSITION)

Brombacher Books, John Tullis, 691 South 31st Street, Richmond, CA 94804, 415-232-5380. Photos, non-fiction. "Strong on gardening and how-to, consumer help books." avg. price, paper: $2.95. 1974. 160pp; 8¼ x 5¼. †of. avg. press run 3,000 to 5,000. Reporting time: 30 days. Payment: Usually straight sale of rights. Does not copyright for author. Discounts: Discounts to trade: 1-4 copies, 20 percent; 5-24, 40 percent; 25-49, 43 percent; 50-99, 44 percent; 100-249, 45 percent; 250 plus, 46 percent. No library discounts except bulk purchase. Pub'd 6 titles 1976; expects 5 titles 1977, 6 titles 1978. ABA.

BRONTE SOCIETY TRANSACTIONS, Charles H. Lemon, c/o Bronte Parsonage Museum, Haworth, Keighley, West Yorkshire, United Kingdom. Articles, reviews, letters. "500/800 words. Recent contributors: Miss Rachel Trickett M.A., Miss Margaret Drabble, Lord David Cecil, Miss Margaret Lane etc. etc." 1/yr; sub price: Not on sale, but issues to members annual sub £6.00. 1893. 70pp; 5¼ x 8½. circ. 2,200. Reporting time: up to 1 year. Payment: none. Ads: none. Back issues: Available. Pub'd 1 issue 1976; expects 1 issue 1977, 1 issue 1978.

BROWNING SOCIETY NOTES, Browning Society of London, A.N. Kincaid, 29 Southmoor Road, Oxford OX2 6RF, United Kingdom, 0865-53189. Articles, reviews, criticism. "Articles should be about 10-15 double-spaced typed pages in length, though slightly longer acceptable if merit warrants, and shorter is often necessary if subject requires (we don't want extra padding to make articles longer than they need be.) Notes published. Reports of work in progress desired. Original bias was biographical, but at present we are running two concurrent critical series, one on the poems of Elizabeth Barrett Browning and one Robert Browning's Asolando Volume. This does not exclude continued interest in biographical, bibliographical and social material connected with these two poets. Persons wishing to act as reviewers should contact review editor, Dr. Ian Small, Univ. of Birmingham. Recent contributors: Philip Drew, W. David Shaw, James T. Loucks, Barbara Melchiori, Park Honan." 3/yr; 1-yr sub price: £1.75/sub; £2/sub instit; per copy: 70p. 1970. 35pp; 8 x 10. †lo. circ. 200. Reporting time: 1-3 wks. Payment: 1 copy of journal; offprints if available. Ads: £30/£16. Discounts: 10 percent for advertising in series of 3 issues. 20 percent if camera-ready copy supplied. Back issues: £1.75 vol, 70p single copy. Pub'd 3 issues 1976; expects 3 issues 1977, 3 issues 1978. Pub's reviews: 6 in 1976. §Robert and Elizabeth Barrett Browning: life, works, contemporaries.

Brownstone Publishers, Inc., Andrew O. Shapiro, John M. Striker, 360 Lexington Avenue, New York, NY 10017. "We are interested in book-length material—or proposals for book-length material—on nonfiction subjects. Our particular interest lies in the area of hard-information, how-to, self-help type books."

BTI (see BRITISH THEATRE INSTITUTE NEWSLETTER & REPORT)

BUCKLE, Bernhard Frank, State Univ/1300 Elmwood Av, English Dept., Buffalo, NY 14222, 716-886-7033. Poetry, art, photos, long-poems. "First issue anticipated in July. Excellence only criteria for poetry. Minority poetry (Black, Indian Gay, Women's) welcome, but not propaganda." 2/yr; 1-yr sub price: $1.50; per copy: $1.00; sample: $1.00. 1977. 60pp; 5½ x 8½. of. circ. 1,500. Reporting time: 4/6 wks. Payment: contributor copies. Copyrighted, reverts to author. Expects 2 issues 1977, 2 issues 1978. COSMEP.

‡**BUCKNELL REVIEW,** Bucknell University, Lewisburg, PA 17837.

51

Buddhist Text Translation Society (see also VAJRA BODHI SEA), Sino American Buddhist Assn., 1731 15th Street, San Francisco, CA 94103, 415-861-9672. Poetry, fiction, articles, art, photos, non-fiction. "The Buddhist Text Translation Society began publishing in 1972 with the goal of making the principles of Buddhist wisdom available to the American reader in a form that can be put directly into practice. BTTS translators are not only scholars but are practicing Buddhists who encounter every day the living meaning of the works they translate. Each translation is accompanied by a contemporary commentary. On the publishing list are standard Buddhist classics such as the *Shurangama Sutra*, the *Lotus Sutra*, and the *Vajra Sutra;* esoteric works such as the *Earth Store Bodhisattva Sutra* and the *Great Compassion Dharani Sutra;* books of informal instruction in meditation; and books, including fiction, that have grown out of the American Buddhist experience." avg. price, paper: $5.95. 1968. 200pp; 5½ x 8½. of. avg. press run 4,000. Payment: none-non profit org. Copyrights for author. Discounts: on orders of one book, no discount; 2-4 books, 20 percent; 5-9 books, 30 percent; 40 percent thereafter. Pub'd 6 titles 1976; expects 5 titles 1977, 5 titles 1978.

Buffalo Books, Fred Thaballa, 15 Gladstone Dr., San Francisco, CA 94112, 415-586-2247. Poetry. "5 books published to date: 1) *The Convict Poems* by Jim Schreier 2) *Saying Yes* by Rosella Felsenfeld 3) 15 *Poems* by Fred Thaballa 4) *United States, An Anthology Of Political Poetry*, Thaballa, ed. 5) *American Dusk* by David C. Childers." 1975. lp/of. Pub'd 3 titles 1976; expects 2 titles 1977, 2 titles 1978.

BUFFALO GNATS, Buffalo Gnats Press, Alice Kolb, Dorothy Lee, PO Box 163, Glen Rock, NJ 07452, 201-652-7016. Poetry, interviews, criticism, reviews. "Our space—finances—limited. We aim to get good poems into print beginning with poets/writers in our own region (NJ-NY). Recent contributors: Issue No. 1: William J. Higginson, Morty Sklar, Joe Johnson." 4/yr; 1-yr sub price: $4.00; per copy: $1.00; sample: $1.00. 1976. 24pp; 5½ x 8½. of. circ. 100-150. no submissions wanted-we request material. Payment: copies (3) only. Copyrighted, reverts to author. Discounts: none. Pub'd 1 issue 1976; expects 4 issues 1977, 4 issues 1978. Pub's reviews. §poetry, short fiction. COSMEP.

BUGLE-AMERICAN, Collective, P.O. Box 12318, Milwaukee, WI 53212. Poetry, articles, art, photos, cartoons, interviews, satire, criticism, reviews, music, letters. 52/yr; 1-yr sub price: $7.50; per copy: $.25; sample: $.35. 1970. 54pp; 8½ x 11. of. circ. 12,000. Ads: $150/$85/$.10. Pub's reviews. §politics/ecology/counter culture/women/music/film. APS.

Bull Publishing Co., David C. Bull, P O Box 208, Palo Alto, CA 94302, 415-322-2855. "Texts in health sciences." avg. price, cloth: $7.00; paper: $5.00. 1974. 200pp. avg. press run 7,000. Reporting time: 1 week. Copyrights for author. Discounts: Trade: 1-3 30 percent, 4-9 40 percent, 10-49 42 percent, 50 plus 44 percent, jobber: 1-3 30 percent, 4 plus 50 percent, text 20 percent, bulk 10-49 10 percent 50 plus 20 percent. COSMEP.

THE BULLETIN BOARD, Lee Miller, 190 East 21st St. 6D, Brooklyn, NY 11226. Poetry, fiction, articles, letters, news items, non-fiction. "Short poetry, no longer than 12 lines—all styles welcome. Seeking more humorous material. Short articles no longer than 250 words—various subjects—how-to, crafts, health, humor, educational—no smut or porno." 6/yr; 1-yr sub price: $5.00; per copy: $1.00; sample: $0.60. 1974. 12-15pp; 8½ x 11. †mi. circ. 500. Reporting time: within 1 month. Payment: copies. Not copyrighted. Ads: $0.25. Pub'd 6 issues 1976; expects 6 issues 1977, 6 issues 1978. §how-to, crafts, writing, poetry, fiction.

BULLETIN OF CONCERNED ASIAN SCHOLARS, Steve Andors, Christine White, 604 Mission #1001, San Francisco, CA 94105. Poetry, fiction, articles, art, photos, cartoons, criticism, reviews, letters, parts-of-novels, plays. " *BCAS* is an academic journal dealing with Asia. We have also, however, experimented with special issues on single themes: 1.'Asian America'(1972) 2.'South Asia in Crisis'(1972) 3.'Women in Asia' 2 issues(1975) 4.'Imperialism & Development in Asia'(1975) 5.'The Development of Revolutionary Literature in China'(1976)-forthcoming." 4/yr; 1-yr sub price: $7.00/students $5.00/libraries $12.00; per copy: $2.00. 1969. 72pp; 8½ x 11. of. circ. 2,000. Reporting time: 2-5 months. Payment: none. Ads: $75/$40. Discounts: bulks-up to 40% on orders of 10 copies. Back issues: pre-1975: $1.00 each. §Asia. COSMEP.

THE BULWER LYTTON CHRONICLE, High Orchard Press, Howard Cooper-Brown, Eric F. J. Ford, High Orchard, 125 Markyate Rd, Dagenham, Essex RM8 2LB, United Kingdom. "Dissemination of works, life, times, contemporaries, influences on and from, upon and about Bulwer Lytton and his family. Bulwer Lytton British Author (1803-1973) Statesman, Dramatist and Poet." 1/yr; 1-yr sub price: £2; per copy: £1. 1973. 40pp; A5. of,dupl. circ. 100. Reporting time: 6 mos. Payment: copies. Ads: £15/pro rata. Discounts: 20%. Back issues: bulk issues 20% list. COSMEP.

‡**Burning Deck Press,** 71 Elmgrove Ave., Providence, RI 02906.

BUSH LEAGUE, Bush League, Richard Bangs, 7777 W. 91st #E-1144, Playa del Rey, CA 90291. Poetry, fiction, articles, art, photos, cartoons, interviews, satire, criticism, reviews. "Designed to represent the actual voices of youg people involved in wilderness-adventure. Its scope encompasses whitewater sports, spelunking, mountaineering, skiing, trekking, and on and on. Our parameters are wide, though. We're looking for different material; anything unusual, and that includes the bizarre, radical, environmentally militant, satirical, droll, lewd, avant garde, lampoonish and on and on. We want the actual perspectives of people who go out and do things in the wilderness that 'ordinary folk' find crazy." 4/yr; 1-yr sub price: $4.00; per copy: $1.00; sample: $.50. 1976. 32pp; 8½ x 11. of. circ. 5,000. Reporting time: 2 weeks. Payment: $5 per 250 wds upon publication. Ads: $200/$125/$.30. Pub's reviews. §wilderness, adventure, ecology, environment. COSMEP.

BUTT: A Quarterly, Butt Press, Len Andersen, Robert Sherman, Contributing Editor, 156 Pleasant St., Arlington, MA 02174. Poetry, fiction, art, interviews, criticism, reviews, parts-of-novels, long-poems. "Particularly interested in long sections of work(s)-in-progress. Prefer submissions to be 9-15 pages so that we can see more of the poet, as well as the writing. Would like to receive more works of literary analysis, E.G. of magazines, of poets, of writing (it's direction, it's relevancy to life, (culture) what is the basis of 'good', of 'bad' and the relationship created by this bi-polarization. Recent contributors have been Stratis Haviaris, William Corbett, Katli Aguero, Ifeanyi Menkiti, Gerard Malanga." 4/yr (irregular basis); 1-yr sub price: $5.00; per copy: $1.25; sample: $1.25. 1975 80pp; 5½ x 7½. †of. circ. 600-800. Reporting time: 1-2 months. Payment: copies. Ads: $20/$10. Discounts: 60/40. Back issues: No 1-out of print/No. 2-$1.00/No. 3-4 out of print. Pub'd 3 issues 1976; expects 4 issues 1977, 4 issues 1978. Pub's reviews: 6 in 1976. §anything of and about little mags, presses; any book, small publisher or big, of literary value. NESPA, COSMEP.

Butterfly Press, Naomi Watson, PO Box 19571, Houston, TX 77024, 713-464-7570. "I publish only my own books." avg. price, cloth: Varies; paper: Varies; other: Varies. 1974. pp varies; Varies. of. avg. press run Varies. Reporting time: 2 weeks. Payment varies. Does not copyright for author. Discounts: 40 percent to bookstores. Pub'd 1 title 1976; expects 2 titles 1977. COSMEP.

C

C.E.N.S.I.T. (see SHINAKI)

C.I.S.S., Canadian Information Sharing Service, 51 Bond Street, Toronto, Ontario, Canada, 363-8944. "We are an abstract service linking groups working for social justice-we are interested in documents for limited distribution that include reflection, analysis, report on action —always with a *Canadian* Focus." 6/yr; 1-yr sub price: $10.00; per copy: $2.00. 1976. 30pp; 8½ x 11. †mi. circ. 600. Reporting time: 3 months maximum. Payment: none. Not copyrighted. Ads: none. Discounts: 10 subscriptions, $70 (Can.); 100 subscriptions, $500 (Can.). Back issues: $2.00. Pub'd 6 issues 1976. §Social justice struggles/analysis.

C.S.P. WORLD NEWS, Guy F. Claude Hamel, P.O. Box 2608, Station D. Ottawa K1P5W7, Canada. Poetry, satire, reviews. "Recent Contributors: Alexander L. Amprimoz, 'C.S.P. World News Poet of the Year' for 1975" 12/yr; 1-yr sub price: $6.00; sample: $1.00. 1965. 12pp; 8 x 14. †of. circ. 2,000. Reporting time: 2 weeks. Payment: $1 per typewritten page. Ads: $25/$15/$.02. Discounts: 10%. Back issues: $1 per copy. Pub's reviews. §all types books and LP's and tapes.

CAFE SOLO, Solo Press, Glenna Luschei, 1209 Drake Circle, San Luis Obispo, CA 93401. Poetry, fiction, articles, art, photos, interviews, criticism, letters. "We have just bought a small letter press and are teaching a course in fine printing called belle lettres. CAFE SOLO is now part of our Community Arts Center, SOLO FLIGHT. Both are incorporated under India, Inc., as part of our poetry in the schools." irreg.; price per copy: $2.00. 1969. 44pp; 8 x 11. of. circ. 1,000. Reporting time: punctual. Discounts: 40% orders over 5. Pub's reviews. CCLM, COSMEP.

CAFETERIA, Cafeteria Press, Gordon Preston, Rick Robbins, P.O. Box 16191, San Diego, CA 92116. Poetry, interviews, criticism, reviews. "Recent Contributors: Ai, Peter Wild, Robert Bly, Tom Wayman, Stuart Friebert, Edward Harkness, Franz Douskey, Dennis Saleh, Rick DeMarinis, Mark Jarmon." enough; 1-yr sub price: fair; per copy: fairer; sample: fairest. 1970. 60-80pp; 6 x 9. of. circ. selective. Reporting time: soon. Back issues: collector's rates. Pub's reviews. §books of poetry & little magazines. COSMEP.

CAIM, Dolphin-Moon, Bernard Taylor, Muriel Ashley, James Taylor, 1829 Colonial Road, Baltimore, MD 21207. Poetry, art, photos. "Format: Folder of broadsides. Length: Majority are one page, although two and three page poems have been published. Contributors: Ann Darr, John Unterecker, Daniel Berrigan." 2/yr; 1-yr sub price: $3.00; per copy: $1.75; sample: $1.50. 1973. 32pp; 8½ x 11. of. circ. 750. Reporting time: 3 to 4 weeks. Payment: 3 copies plus some broadsides. Discounts: 40%-bookstores or more than 4 copies. Back issues: #2-$1.50/#3-$1.50. CCLM, COSMEP.

Cal-Syl Press (see LOOSE LIPS SINK SHIPS)

Calculators/Computers (see DYMAX)

CALIFORNIA PELICAN MAGAZINE, John Stodder, Eshelman Hall, University of California, Berkeley, CA 94720. Poetry, fiction, articles, art, photos, cartoons, interviews, satire, criticism, reviews, parts-of-novels, long-poems. "For prose writers, mostly non-fiction, avoid stylistic and materialistic conventions of 'straight' journalism, in favor of writing that is potent, personal, speculative and sensitive. Poetry must be good. Slight Bay-area bias, easily overcome." 3/yr; 1-yr sub price: $1.50; per copy: $.50-$.75; sample: $.75. 1903. 48pp; 8½ x 11. †of. circ. 3,000-7,000. Reporting time: 3 months. Payment: copies only. Ads: $135/$81. Pub's reviews. §anything crucial to masses of people, which is as yet going unread.

The California/Pendleton Press, David Spencer, Peter Gilman, P.O. Box 731, Carmel Valley, CA 93924, 408-659-2886. 1975.

THE CALIFORNIA QUARTERLY, Elliot Gilbert, Sandra Gilbert, Diane Johnson, 100 Sproul Hall, Univ of Calif, Davis, CA 95616. Poetry, fiction, articles, art, photos, reviews, criticism, interviews, parts-of-novels, long-poems. "Stories should not exceed 5,000 words, though we make exceptions. We like 'California material' however you care to define that, but don't insist on it. We publish whatever we think is good and recommend that authors glance at past issues. Recent contributors include Charles Simic, Robert Kelly, Karl Shapiro, James Bertolino, Marjorie Grene, Jerry Bumpus, Sandra Gilbert, Rosellen Brown, Ann Stanford." 4/yr; 1-yr sub price: $5.00; per copy: $1.50. 1971. 83pp; 8½ x 5½. of. circ. 400. Reporting time: 4-6 weeks. Payment: $3/page poetry & graphics; $2/page prose. Ads: $40 page/$25 1/2. CCLM, COSMEP.

CALIFORNIA STATE POETRY QUARTERLY, Ruth G. Iodice, Ed. in Chief; Harold Witt, B. Jo Kinnick, Assoc. Editors, 22 Avon Road, Kensington, CA 94707, 526-8453. Poetry, art, photos, collages. "Shorter poems more usable for our space, accept all kinds and forms of poetry, main criterion is excellence; use mainly Californians' MSS, but a few others." 4/yr; 1-yr sub price: $6.00; per copy: $2.00. 1972. of. circ. 500 most issues. Reporting time: 3—6 months. Payment: one contributor's copy of CQ. Copyrighted, does not revert to author. Back issues: no back issues available prior to IV, copy 1.

CALIFORNIA STATE POETRY QUARTERLY, Thomas Piekarski, 3218 Impala Dr. 9, San Jose, CA 95117, 408-379-0303. Poetry, art, interviews, reviews, long-poems, concrete art. "No inspirational or light verse. Send SASE. Recent contributors: Harold Witt, Josephine Miles, Richard Eberhart, Lawrence Ferlinghetti." 4/yr; 1-yr sub price: $8.00; per copy: $2.00; sample: $2.00. 1968. 50pp; 5½ x 8½. of. circ. 500. Reporting time: 1-6 weeks. Payment: 1 copy. Copyrighted, reverts to author. Pub's reviews. §Poetry.

California Syllabus Press (see LOOSE LIPS SINK SHIPS)

California Tomorrow (see CRY CALIFORNIA)

Caligula Books, Steve Wheatley, 45 Canterbury Grove, London SE23, England. Poetry, art, collages, concrete art. "The press is mainly devoted to pamphlets and books which explore the visual and sequential possibilities of what a book could be, such that the physical form of the book seeks to illuminate the contents. Thus, while I use written material (poems etc) and visual material, the criteria on which I select is that of an overall concept for each book. The press is based on my own work but I do accept three to four books each year from artists/writers working on similar lines. The bias in the work is mainly towards dada, concrete, imagism and surrealism." avg. price, paper: £0.40-£1.00. 1974. up to 30pp; varies. of. avg. press run 200 copies. Payment: this is a non-profit making enterprise. Copyrights for author. Discounts: 30 percent. Pub'd 12 titles 1976; expects 6 titles 1977.

THE CALL/EL CLARIN, Call Publications, Dan Burstein, Box 5597, Chicago, IL 60680. News items. "Published weekly with a section in Spanish." 50/yr; 1-yr sub price: $12.00; per copy: $.25; sample: free. 1972. 20pp; 11 x 15½. lp/of. circ. 20,000. Discounts: bulk discount-40% off. Pub'd 38 issues 1976; expects 50 issues 1977, 50 issues 1978. Pub's reviews: 5 in 1976. §politics/international news/mass movements.

Calliopea Press, Carol Lea Denison, 701 Longstaff, Missoula, MT 59801, 406-549-6945. Poetry, fiction, art, parts-of-novels, long-poems, plays. "1976. David Ernst. Poetry, *Windy Road, Narrow Bridges* 4 vo. 40 pgs. Handmade paper. Illustrated by Deborah Padrick. $10.00 hardbound. (out of print) 1977. Lynn Watson. Fiction, *Rehearse & The Grandmother Story.* 4 vo. 14 pgs. Hardbound $3.50; softbound $2.00. 300 copies" avg. price, cloth: varies. 1976. pp varies depending on book; varies. †lp. avg. press run 300-500. Payment: individual arrangements with each author. Copyrights for author. Discounts: 30 percent to bookstores. Pub'd 3 titles 1976; expects 5 titles 1977.

CALYX, Calyx, A Northwest Feminist Review, Barbara Baldwin, Poetry; Elizabeth McLagan, Poetry; Margarita Donnelly, Prose; Meredith Jenkins, Art, Route 2, Box 118, Corvallis, OR 97330, 503-753-8891. Poetry, fiction, articles, art, photos, criticism, reviews, parts-of-novels. "Prose no more than 5,000 words. Poetry. Art work suitable for reproduction in black and white. Submit 35 mm slides or 8 x 10 black and white glossy photo. We publish only work by women. Not limited to women living in NW. Recent contributors published: Olga Broumas, Ingrid Wendt, Gwen Head, Marge Piercy." 3/yr; 1-yr sub price: $5.00; per copy: $2.00; sample: $2.00. 1975. 60pp; 8 x 7. of. circ. 100 subscribers-40 bookstores. Reporting time: 8-10 weeks. Payment: free copy to each contributor accepted. Copyrighted, reverts to author. Ads: none. Discounts: Trade 30 percent, we do our own distribution. Back issues: $2.00 ea or 3 for $5.00. Pub'd 1 issue 1976; expects 3 issues 1977, 3 issues 1978. Pub's reviews.

Camas Press (see THE ARCHER)

Cambric Press (see also FIRELANDS ARTS REVIEW), Joel Rudinger, Publisher, 912 Strowbridge Dr., Huron, OH 44839, 419-433-4221. "No restrictions, looking for humor (literary humor)

55

in *FIRELANDS ARTS REVIEW*. No restrictions for co-op publication. We are a co-op press. High quality poetry, fiction, non-fiction, Pix Paperbacks. Query first." avg. price, paper: $2.95. 1975. 80pp; 5½ x 8½. of. avg. press run 1,000. Reporting time: 2-8 weeks. Payment: varies: co-op runs 100 percent to author; FIRELANDS ARTS REVIEW copies only. Copyrights for author. Discounts: 30 percent on bulk orders over 10; 30 percent for classroom orders. Pub'd 3 titles 1976; expects 2 titles 1977, 3 titles 1978. CCLM.

CAMELS COMING NEWSLETTER, Richard Morris, PO Box 703, San Francisco, CA 94101. "CAMELS COMING NEWSLETTER is the second series of this publication. The first series was a poetry magazine published 1965-68. Although we will print any type of material if we like it well enough, about 90% of each issue will be devoted to criticism. It is a waste of time to submit poetry. We have printed two poems in the last three years, and only one of those was unsolicited." irreg; sub price: $7.00/12 issues; sample: free. 1965. 8pp; 8½ x 11. of. Reporting time: immediate. Payment: copies only. COSMEP, NESPA.

Campaign For Homosexual Equality (see OUT)

Campaign for Nuclear Disarmament, Brian Deer, Eastbourne House, Bullards Place, London, England E20PT, United Kingdom, 01-980-0937. Poetry, articles, photos, cartoons, interviews, satire, criticism, reviews, letters, news items, non-fiction. "Paper concentrates on peace, foreign & defence policy, disarmament." avg. price, paper: 10p. 1961. 16pp; 12½ x 9½. of. avg. press run 7,000. Copyrights for author. CND.

Canada Publishing Co. (see ART & LITERARY DIGEST)

CANADA WEST, Stagecoach Publishing Co Ltd., I. W. Paterson, P.O. Box 3399, Langley, British Columbia V3A4R7, Canada. Articles, photos. "Preferred length 2,000-3,000 words. Photos must be included." 4/yr; 1-yr sub price: $4.00, Canada; $6.00, U.S.; per copy: $1.50; sample: free. 1969. 40pp; 8½ x 11. of. circ. 5,000. Reporting time: 6 weeks. Payment: 1½ cent per word-$5.00 per photo. Copyrighted, reverts to author. Ads: $0.10. Discounts: 20 percent. Back issues: $1.00-$7.00. Pub'd 4 issues 1976; expects 4 issues 1977. Pub's reviews. §history or outdoor topics. CPPA.

CANADIAN AUTHOR & BOOKMAN, Canadian Authors Association, Duncan S. Pollock, P.O. Box 120, Niagara On The Lake L0S1J0, Canada, 416-468-7391. Poetry, articles, criticism, reviews. "Want Canadian literary doings-writing craft articles from any writer." 4/yr; 1-yr sub price: $4.00; per copy: $1.00; sample: $0.25. 1921. 48pp; 8½ x 11. of. circ. 3,000. Reporting time: 1 week. Payment: 1 cent a word. Copyrighted. Ads: $180.00/$110.00/$0.25 word. Discounts: 15 percent. Back issues: on microfilm. Pub'd 4 issues 1976; expects 4 issues 1977, 4 issues 1978. Pub's reviews: 40 in 1976. §all areas.

CANADIAN CHILDREN'S LITERATURE, Canadian Children's Press, John R. Sorfleet, P.O. Box 335, Guelph, Ontario N1H 6K5, Canada. Articles, interviews, criticism, reviews. "CCL publishes critical articles and in-depth reviews of books written for Canadian children and adolescents." 4/yr; 1-yr sub price: $9.00 (plus $2.00 postage outside Canada); per copy: $2.95; sample: $2.95 (plus 50 cents postage outside Canada). 1975. 100pp; 6 x 9. of. circ. 1,000. Reporting time: 2 mos. Payment: nil. Ads: $75/$45. Discounts: 10% to agencies. Back Issues: $2.95 ea plus 50¢ postage outside Canada, 25¢ postage in Canada. Pub's reviews. §books written for Canadian children and adolescents. CPPA.

CANADIAN CHILDREN'S MAGAZINE, Evelyn Samuel, 4150 Bracken Avenue, Victoria B.C. V8X3N8, Canada, 604-479-6906. Poetry, articles, photos, cartoons, interviews, reviews, letters. "We are interested in strictly Canadian-oriented material: History, inventions, biographies, museums, animals, etc. geared to children 6-12. Illustrations commissioned for specific articles." 4/yr; 1-yr sub price: $5.00; per copy: $1.25; sample: $1.25. 1976. 48pp; 8¼ x 10¾. web. circ. 25,000. Reporting time: 2 months. Do not pay. Copyrighted, reverts to author. Discounts: 10 percent to agents for individual subscriptions. Orders to one address: 50 or more equals $1.00 each; 100 or more equals $0.75 each. Back issues: $1.50 per issue, $6.00 for a full year. Pub's reviews §Children's materials, Canadian oriented.

CANADIAN DIMENSION, Canadian Dimension Publishers, John Gallagher, Box 1413, Winnipeg, Manitoba, Canada. Articles, art, photos, cartoons, criticism, reviews, music. 10/yr; 1-yr sub price: $7.00/inst-$10.00/pensioners & students $5.00; per copy: $.75; sample: $.75. 1965. 48pp; 8½ x 11. †of. circ. 8,000. Ads: $195/$105. Discounts: 25% discount to bookstores 1/3 discount to distributors. Back issues: 50 ¢ per issue. Pub's reviews. §politics/economics/contemp. topics.

CANADIAN FICTION MAGAZINE, Canadian Fiction Magazine, Geoffrey Hancock, P.O. Box 46422, Station G, Vancouver, B.C. V6R4G7, Canada. Fiction, interviews, criticism, reviews, parts-of-novels. "We publish only the work of writers and artists resident in Canada and Canadians living abroad. No restriction on length, subject matter or style though we tend to prefer fiction that astonishes both through technique & meaning. We offer an annual $250.00 contributors prize. Recent contributors include Derk Wynand, Michel Tremblay, Jacques Ferron, Felix Leclerc, George Woodcock, Matt Cohen, Rikki, Joyce Marshall, Leon Rooke, Hugh Hood, Robert Harlow, Jane Rule, John Metcalf, Yves Theriault, Robert Kruetsh." 4/yr; sub price: Canada $9.00-yr; U.S.A. $10.00-yr; per copy: $2.50; sample: $2.50 in Canadian funds. 1971. 128pp; 6 x 9. of. circ. 1,800. Reporting time: 4-6 weeks. Payment: $5 per printed page on publication. Buys first North American serial rights. Ads: $100/$65. Discounts: 5% agent, 40% consignment to stores. Back issues: price on request. Pub'd 4 issues 1976; expects 4 issues 1977, 4 issues 1978. Pub's reviews: 35 in 1976. §Surrealism & magic realism in short fiction; also short stories & novellas, French-Canadian writers in translation; interviews. CPPA.

THE CANADIAN FORUM, Denis Smith, Editor; Jane Somerville, Mang. Editor, 3 Church St. #401, Toronto, Ontario M5E1M2, Canada, 416-364-2431. Poetry, fiction, articles, art, photos, cartoons, interviews, satire, criticism, reviews, music, letters. 10/yr; 1-yr sub price: $9.00; per copy: $1.00; sample: $2.00. 1920. 44pp; 8½ x 11. of. circ. 23,000. Reporting time: 2 mo. Payment: $50-article $10-review. Ads: $600/$400/$.20. Pub'd 10 issues 1976; expects 10 issues 1977, 10 issues 1978. Pub's reviews: 120 in 1976. CPPA.

CANADIAN FRONTIER, Nunaga Publishing Co. Ltd., Brian Antonson, P.O. Box 157, New Westminister, B.C. V3L4Y4, Canada. Photos, reviews. 4/yr; 1-yr sub price. $3.50; per copy: $1.00; sample: $1.00. 1971. 40pp; 8½ x 11. of. circ. 2,000 plus. Reporting time: 1 month. Payment: approx $30.00. Ads: $120/$65. Back issues: $1.00. Pub's reviews.

CANADIAN LITERATURE, George Woodcock, University of British Columbia, Vancouver, B.C. V6T 1W5, Canada. Criticism, reviews. "Only criticism and reviews relating to Canadian writers are used." 4/yr; 1-yr sub price: $7.50 Canada/$8.00 abroad; per copy: $2.50; sample: $2.50. 1959. 120pp. lp. circ. 2,500. Reporting time: 1 month. Payment: $6.00 a page. Ads: $80. Back issues: $2.50   Pub's reviews. §Canadian writers and writing.

Canadian Photopress Publishing Ltd. (see KRZYK)

CANADIAN PUBLIC POLICY- Analyse de Politiques, University of Toronto Press, J. Vanderkamp, Arts Building, University of Guelph, Guelph, Ontario N1G2W1, Canada. Articles, reviews. "A journal for the discussion of social and economic policy. Recent contributors include: C.E. Beigie, C.M. Drury, S. Gordon, F. Hawkins, H.G. Johnson, E. Kierans, R. Lacroix, M. Pelletier, I.A. Stewart" 4/yr; 1-yr sub price: $10.00 individual/$8.00 members of sponsoring associations/$5.00 students/$12.00 institutions; per copy: $4.00; sample: $4.00. 1975. 150pp; 6½ x 9¾. of. circ. 2,000. Reporting time: 35 days. Ads: $150/$95. Discounts: can be arranged. Pub's reviews. §public policy.

Canadian Review of Books Ltd. (see BOOKS IN CANADA)

CANADIAN SLAVONIC PAPERS, Beauregard, R.C. Elwood, 256 Paterson Hall, Carleton

University, Ottawa K1S5B6, Canada. Articles, reviews. "We publish scholarly articles in all disciplines of Russian, Soviet & East European studies. Manuscripts-no longer than 30 typewritten double spaced pages. Directory" 4/yr; 1-yr sub price: $15.00; per copy: $4.00. 1956. 150pp; 6 x 9. circ. 1,000. Reporting time: 3 mos. Payment: none. Copyrighted, rights remain with journal. Ads: $75/$40/outside back cover $100. Discounts: none. Back issues: $4.00. Pub'd 4 issues 1976; expects 4 issues 1977, 4 issues 1978. Pub's reviews: 146 in 1976. §in Russian & East European studies.

CANADIAN STEAM MAGAZINE, Richard L. Coulton, Richard L. Coulton, Bentley, Alberta T0C0J0, Canada. Poetry, articles, reviews. "Articles should be kept short (a few hundred words); in general, references should be included (usually a bibliography alone is sufficient). All material should be factual, concise, and must deal with Canadian steam power; it's uses, past history, future possibilities, etc. (Subjects may include steam locomotives, steam traction engines, steam boats and steamships, etc.)" 4/yr; 1-yr sub price: $1.00; per copy: $.25; sample: $.25. 1972. 7pp; 8½ x 11. †mi. Reporting time: a few months. Payment: 1 cent/word upon publication. Ads: 1 cent/word. Pub's reviews. §Canadian steam power-it's history, uses, etc.

CANADIAN THEATRE REVIEW, CTR Publications, Don Rubin, York University, Downsview, Ontario M3T1P3, Canada, 416-667-3768. Articles, plays. "Documents & analysis of professional theatre with emphasis on Canadian Theatre. A full-length playscript is published in each issue. An international journal." 4/yr; 1-yr sub price: $10.00; per copy: $3.00; sample: $3.00. 1973. 144pp; 6 x 9. of. Reporting time: 3 weeks. Payment varies. Not copyrighted. Ads: $300.00/$175.00/$0.50. Back issues: $3.00 each. Pub'd 4 issues 1976; expects 4 issues 1977, 4 issues 1978. Pub's reviews. §drama. CPPA.

Canadian Women's Educational Press, 280 Bloor St. W. Suite 305, Toronto, Ontario, Canada. Discounts: 40% trade, 20% educational.

CANNIBAL, Carl D. Clark, Eric S. Vogel, 3007 University, Austin, TX 78705, 512-472-7415. Poetry, fiction, articles, art, photos, cartoons, interviews, satire, criticism, reviews, music, letters, parts-of-novels, long-poems, collages, plays, concrete art. "*CANNIBAL* is the propaganda arm of the Rita Hayworth Liberation Army. Each issue will be devoted to radical (non-politically so) treatments of subjects; *CANNIBAL* originates from but goes beyond Dada/Absurdism. Future issues include *If Joyce Kilmer Were Alive Today He'd Sniff Exhaust Pipes, A Different Love* (poems of consummated affairs outside normal straight or gay relationships." 6/yr; 1-yr sub price: $3.00; per copy: varies; sample: $1.00. 1977. 4pp; 8½ x 11. of. circ. 5-20,000. Reporting time: 1 day-1 year. Payment: copies. Not copyrighted. Ads: forget it. Discounts: none. Expects 3 issues 1977.

Canongate Publishing Ltd., Stephanie Wolfe Murray, Charles Wild, James Maxtone-Graham, Canongate Publishing, 17 Jeffrey St., Edinburgh, Scotland EH1 1DR, United Kingdom, 031-556-0023. Poetry, fiction, long-poems, non-fiction. "Some books for 1977: *Springtide and Neaptide* (anthology of poems in English and Gaelic by Sorley MacLean); *Men On Ice* (metaphysical poem by Andrew Greig); *The Greatest Breakthrough since Lunchtime* (racy medical novel by Colin Douglas); *Island on the Edge of the World* (by Charles MacLean—about the lonely islanders of St. Kilda; *A Sense of Freedom* (biography of a convicted murderer); *Festival* (topical novel about the Edinburgh Festival)" avg. price, cloth: £4; paper: £2. 1973. pp varies; varies. of/lp. avg. press run 2,000-5,000. Reporting time: 6 weeks. Payment varies. Copyrights for author. Discounts: 35-60 percent depending on quantity. Pub'd 6 titles 1976; expects 15 titles 1977, 20 titles 1978. SGPA, NBL.

CANTO LIBRE-A Bilingual Quarterly of Latin American Peoples Art, Center for Cuban Studies, Susan Ortega, Sandra Levinson, 220 East 23rd St, New York, NY 10010. Poetry, articles, art, photos, interviews, criticism, reviews, music. 4/yr; 1-yr sub price: $5.00; per copy: $1.25. 1974. 48pp; 8½ x 11. of. Discounts: bulk discount available. §arts/Latin America/political science.

THE CAPE ROCK, Southeast Missouri State Univ., Bob Burns, English Dept, Southeast Missouri State, Cape Girardeau, MO 63701, 314-334-8211 ext. 278. Poetry, photos. "We consider poems of any style on almost any subject. Although our first criterion for selection is the quality of the poetry (and our standards are high), we must avoid any obscene or profane diction. We like to feature the work of a single photographer in each issue; submit 30 thematically organized 8 x 10 B & W glossies, or send five pix with query. We favor poems under 70 lines. SASE required for return of submissions. Submissions should bear authors' names and complete addresses in the upper right-hand corner of each page." 2/yr; 1-yr sub price: $1.50; per copy: $1.00; sample: $1.00. 1964. 56-64pp; 5½ x 8¾. †of. circ. 500. Reporting time: 1-4 mos. Payment: copies only. Magazine is copyrighted. Rights to contents released to authors and artists upon request, subject only to their giving credit to *The Caperock* whenever and wherever else the work is placed. no ads. Discounts: 25 percent off on orders of 25 or more (our cost plus postage). Back issues: $1.00 per copy. Pub'd 2 issues 1976; expects 2 issues 1977, 2 issues 1978. CCLM, COSMEP, NESPA.

THE CAPILANO REVIEW, The Capilano Review, Bill Schermbrucker, 2055 Purcell Way, North Vancouver, B.C. V7J3H5, Canada, 604-986-1911. Poetry, fiction, art, photos, interviews, criticism, reviews, music, parts-of-novels, long-poems, collages, plays, concrete art. "Contributors: Stan Persky, John Bentley Mays, Margaret Atwood, Michael Ondaatje, George Bowering, Audrey Thomas, Robin Blaser, BP Nichol, Victor Coleman, Jack Spicer, Robert Duncan, Beverley Simons" 2/yr; 1-yr sub price: $5.00 individual/$6.00 libraries/add $1.00 postage for U.S. & overseas.; per copy: $3.00. 1972. 200pp; 8 x 5½ (approx). of. circ. 1,000-1,500. Reporting time: one month. Payment: $10.00-$40.00. Copyrighted, reverts to author. Ads: exchange ads only. Discounts: 30 percent to bookstores. Back issues: $5.00 per copy. Pub'd 2 issues 1976; expects 3 issues 1977, 1 issue 1978. §poetry/fine art/fiction.

Capra Press, Noel Young, 631 State St., Santa Barbara, CA 93101, 805-966-4590. Fiction, interviews, satire, criticism, parts-of-novels, non-fiction. "Eclectic booklist, a western press in the broadest sense of the word." avg. price, cloth: $10.00; paper: $4.00. 1970. 84-160pp; varies. †of/lp. avg. press run 5,000. Reporting time: 1-6 weeks. Payment: royalties negotiated. Copyright in author's name. Discounts: 1-4, 20 percent; 5-49, 40 percent; 50-99, 42 percent; distributors, 50 percent. Pub'd 12 titles 1976; expects 12 titles 1977, 12 titles 1978. COSMEP.

Caprice Out of Sight (see OUT OF SIGHT)

CARACOL, Caracol, Cecilio Garcia-Camarillo, PO Box 7577, San Antonio, TX 78207, 512-228-9838. Poetry, fiction, articles, art, photos, cartoons, interviews, satire, criticism, reviews, music, letters, parts-of-novels, plays, concrete art. "There's something like 10 million Chicanos in the country and only about 4 or 5 magazines; so Caracol is aimed primarily to our people—we do 2 types of reductions on the material here at Caracol: 80 and 69 percent reductions. Can fit approx. 950 words (80 percent red) per page and 1,260 words (69 percent red) per page. We encourage 1,000, 1,500 or 2,000 word things. If over we swtich to 69 percent red. We can fit in anything over 2,000 words and up to 3,500. We just did a 6,000 word thing, but don't encourage such lengths." 12/yr; 1-yr sub price: $3.50 persons-$5.00 institutions; per copy: $0.35; sample: free. 1974. 24pp; 8½ x 11. of. circ. 1,500. Reporting time: 20 days. Payment: payment only with copies of Caracol—5 through 10 copies, depending on what was submitted. Copyrighted, reverts to author. Ads: $100.00. Discounts: Caracol is $3.50 per person & $5.00 for institutions. No exceptions (except for Chicano prisoners), no reductions or special prices. Back issues: 35 cents. Pub's reviews. §Educational, political, literary—but they have to be Chicano, not watered down Mexican American.

‡CARLETON MISCELLANY, Jones Press, Carleton College, Northfield, MN 55057. CCLM.

Carma Press, Florence Nelson, Box 12633, St Paul, MN 55112, 612-633-6845. Articles, art. "We are looking for material in one area only: HELP FOR THE NON-PROFESSIONAL TEACHER OF ADULTS. We deal with techniques, problem situations, how to construct and use teaching materials, etc. We would like to see various subject areas (i.e., How to teach Real Estate, Astrology, Writing, Crafts...anything!). Our recent publication, YES YOU CAN TEACH! deals with teaching in general. Now we'd like to get more specific. Length: from 20 to 60 pages." avg. price, paper: $5.00. 1976. 50pp; 8½ x 11. of. avg. press run Varies. Reporting time: Query first-immed. reply, ms-2 weeks. Payment: Outright payment or standard royalty. Copyrights for author. Discounts: Standard.

CARN (a link between the Celtic nations), Padraig O Snodaigh, Celtic League, 9 Br Cnoc Sion, Ath Cliath 9, Republic of Ireland, Dublin 373957. Articles, reviews, criticism, news items. "500-1M words per article, 2000 for one or two in each issue.401/3 to401/4 of the material in Celtic languages, rest in English, CARN is the organ of the Celtic League which fosters co-operation & solidarity between the Celtic nations." 4/yr; 1-yr sub price: £2.00 (Ireland, Gt. Britain), $5.50 USA and other non-European countries.; per copy: 30p; sample: 17p. 1973. 24pp; 8½ x 10½. of. circ. 2M. No payment. Copyrighted, remains with CARN. Ads: £4.00 column inch. Discounts: 20-25 percent bookshops. Back issues: 25p per copy. Pub'd 4 issues 1976; expects 4 issues 1977, 4 issues 1978. Pub's reviews: 6 in 1976.

CAROLINA QUARTERLY, Robert Gingher, PO Box 1117, Chapel Hill, NC 27514, 919-933-0244. Poetry, fiction, art, photos, reviews, parts-of-novels, long-poems. "'Looking for the well-crafted poem or story, with an emphasis on original language use'. Recent contributors: John Tagliabue, Anthony Burgess, Judith Moffett, D.W. Baker, Greg Kuzma, Lee Smith, William Harmon, Howard McCord, John Hollander, Arthur Vogelsang, Douglas Blazek, Paul Smyth, Graham Petrie, Fred Chappell, Joyce Carol Oates, Doris Betts, Marianne Gingher, Jessie Schell, Albert Goldbarth." 3/yr; 1-yr sub price: $4.50; per copy: $1.50; sample: $1.50. 1948. 120pp; 6 x 9. of. circ. 1,500. Reporting time: 4-6 weeks. Payment: $3/page; $5/poem. Ads: $80/$50. Discounts: 20% local stores; 40% out of state; agent, 10%. Back issues: $2.00. Pub'd 3 issues 1976; expects 3 issues 1977, 3 issues 1978. Pub's reviews: 3 in 1976. §Short stories, poems, novels. CCLM, COSMEP.

The Carolina Wren Press, Judy Hogan, P O Box 209, Carrboro, NC 27510, 919-967-8666. Poetry, fiction, plays. "I am primarily publishing new North Carolina writers; am going to publish my first novel this summer and hope to do one a year. Bias toward writing capable of bringing about cultural change but I evaluate it as writing (poetry or whatever). Among early titles; *Chrome Grass* (Liner); *Milky Way Poems* (Rigsby); *American Peasant* (Herron); *dead on Arrival* (Jaki Shelton)." avg. price, paper: $3.00. 1976. 50pp; 5½ x 8½. of. avg. press run 500 for poetry; 1,000 for novels. Reporting time: 6 months to 1 year. Payment: 50 percent off on copies plus 20 free copies. Copyrights for author. Discounts: 40 percent to bookstores. COSMEP, COSMEP-SOUTH.

Carolyn Bean Associates, Publishing, Lawrence M. Barnett, John C.W. Carroll, 48 Second Street, San Francisco, CA 94105, 415-398-6011. Art, photos, cartoons. "We publish books. Our direction in publishing seems to be to publish books that deal, usually in a visual way, with problems in the Human Condition. Our first book, *Smile in a Mad Dog's i,* by Richard Stine, and our second book (coming out in May 1977), *PUPPETS,* by Ardeshir Mohassess, are books of drawings depicting cliches and stereotypes of our contemporary life. We seek works of 'Heart'." avg. price, cloth: Varies. 1976. pp varies; Varies. of. avg. press run Varies. Payment varies. Copyright: sometimes. Discounts: trade, 40 percent: agents, 55 percent: jobbers, 50-65 percent. COSMEP.

Carousel Press, Carole Terwilliger Meyers, P.O. Box 6061, Albany, CA 94706, 415-527-5849. Art, photos, cartoons, non-fiction. "We are interested in books on parenting, including family travel guides. 75-100 pages." avg. price, cloth: $8.95; paper: $3.95. 1976. 96pp; 5½ x 8½. of. avg. press run 2,500. Reporting time: 6 weeks, include return postage. Payment: Royalties and flat payments. Copyrights for author. Discounts: trade, bulk, jobber; 40 percent for five or more books, libraries 10 percent. Pub'd 2 titles 1976; expects 1 title 1977, 1 title 1978. COSMEP.

CAROUSEL QUARTERLY OF POETRY, Carousel Publishers, Jay B. Isaacs, Box 111, Mt Laurel, NJ 08054, 609-871-0612. Poetry, reviews. "no biases, any length,—Geraldine Clinton Little, Elizabeth Bartlett, Mordecai Marcus" 4/yr; 1-yr sub price: $10.00; per copy: $3.00; sample: $3.00. 1976. 3pp; 5½ x 8½. of. Reporting time: 3 weeks. Payment: $0.10 per line. Copyrighted, reverts to author. Ads: $25.00/$15.00/$1.00. Discounts: none. Back issues: $1.40. Pub's reviews. §poetry. COSMEP.

Carpenter Press, Bob Fox, Susan Fox, Route 4, Pomeroy, OH 45769, 614-992-7520. Poetry, fiction, art, photos. "Plan to publish primarily fiction with maybe one or two poetry chapbooks a year. Watch for ads. Already backlogged. Won't read new mss. for a year. Xeroxed queries waste your money here." avg. price, paper: $5.00; other: $1.50 - Chapbooks. 1973. 6 x 9. of/lp. avg. press run 500-1,500. Reporting time: immediate. Payment: Royalty contracts. Copyrights for author. Discounts: Trade. Expects 3 titles 1977, 3 titles 1978. COSMEP.

CARTA ABIERTA, Juan Rodriguez, 3408 Dwinelle Hall-UC-, Berkeley, CA 94720, 415-642-0240. Reviews, letters. "News about the Chicano literary world." 4/yr; 1-yr sub price: $5.00 institutions-$3.00; per copy: $0.75; sample: $0.75. 1975. 10pp; 8 x 11½. †of. circ. 350. Reporting time: immediate. Pub's reviews. §Chicano literature.

‡**CASA DE LAS AMERICAS,** G Y Tercers, Vedado Habana, Cuba.

Casa del Sensitive (see LOST AND FOUND TIMES)

Casa Editorial, Leland Mellott, Maria Tello, 3128 24th Street, San Francisco, CA 94110. "CASA EDITORIAL is interest primarily in publishing Raza and/or Spanish-speaking writers, with emphasis on a bi-lingual format. We will consider manuscripts in poetry, short story and drama. CASA EDITORIAL is also a non-profit mail order bookstore which sells small press poetry and magazines through catalogues."

Casa Fun Dada (see LE JARDIN DU MONDE)

Cascade Farm Enterprises, L. W. Fortner, Ethel N. Fortner, Route 1, Box 259, Estacada, OR 97023, 503-630-4690. Poetry. "We do poetry books only—will publish on invitation only—our present thinking is in terms of Oregon poets whose work we admire and who have never had but deserve publication. Possibly in 1977 or 1978 we will be able to do 1 or 2 books per year." avg. price, cloth: $4.00; paper: $2.00 - $5.00. 1973. 32-80pp; 5½ x 8. of. avg. press run 500 copies. not open to submissions. Payment: on individual basis. Copyrights for author. Discounts: 35 percent.

Cassandra Publications (see also NOE VALLEY POETS WORKSHOP), Stephanie Mines, 160 Caselli Avenue, San Francisco, CA 94114, 626-6047. Poetry. avg. price, paper: $3.00. 1972. 50-150pp; 6 x 9. of/lp. avg. press run 500. Payment: very loose. Copyrights for author. Discounts: 60/40. COSMEP.

Cat Anna Press, V. MacLeod, E. Firth, P.O. Box 301, Dexter, MI 48130. Poetry, fiction, art, long-poems. "We also use selections from women's journals, dreams, meditations, visions. The first catalogue contained erotic feminist fiction. The next will be devoted to fiction from area women. Each catalogue will specialize in a different type of women's writing. Themes planned are fairy tales, poetry (each book a separate author), goddess myths & prophecies, & illustrated children's books." avg. price, paper: $2.00. 1977. 25-100 pp. All our editions are small & handbound; 4½ x 6. †of. avg. press run 500 copies. So far we have printed only local women, altho' this may change soon. Payment: no arrangements yet-to be worked out. The authors hold all copyrights. Discounts: we have not worked these out yet. Expects 10 titles 1977.

Catalyst, Ian Young, 315 Blantyre Ave., Scarborough, Ontario M1N2S6, Canada. Poetry, fiction, long-poems, plays. "We are a non-profit co-operative with emphasis on gay writing and Canadian writing. We have recently published books by: Ian Young, Graham Jackson, Gavin Dillard, Oswell Blakeston, Wayne McNeill, Tom Meyer, E.A. Lacey." 1967. of. Reporting time: within one week. Payment: 10% royalty. Discounts: 40% (less than 10 items, 30%). IPA.

CATALYST 1987, Catalyst 1987 Cooperative, Etienne Boisjoli, Brantford, Ontario, Canada, 519-752-1557 (Editorial), 416-783-8830 (Advertising). Poetry, fiction, articles, art, photos, cartoons, interviews, satire, criticism, reviews, music, letters, parts-of-novels, long-poems, collages, plays, concrete art. "Recent contributors include novelists Norma West Linder & Hugh Garner. Upcoming international editions will feature works by young (some unpublished) authors & poets from more than 150 countries-in their own languages with side-by-side English & French adaptations. The publication sponsors autonomous catalyst clubs in penal centers & educational institutions for the joint promotion of 'catalytic literature' and the development of more effective '21st-century communicative arts'. Specification sheets free for the asking. We publish excerpts of unpublished novels, circulate these to prospective publishers; in several instances, we have been successful in getting beginners published. Only publication with predetermined lifespan due to 'special project' nature; last edition to be published December, 1986. Some delays in 1977 caused by Canadian postal slowdowns, other factors now corrected. Editorial dept: Catalyst 87 Park, Box 1987, Brantford, Ont. N3T5W5; Ad dept: Catalyst 1987, The Hallmark Bldg., 1912A Avenue Rd., Toronto, Ont., M5M4A1." 12/yr; 1-yr sub price: $5.00; per copy: Can & U.S. $.60; U.K. 30p; sample: $.60. 1975. 16pp; 11½ x 17. of. circ. 17,500. Reporting time: 10-60 days (depending on speed of regional editors). Payment: poetry $5-$200; fiction $200 up. Ads: $175/$90/$.50 ($8 minimum). Discounts: 50%; free to prison addresses. Pub'd 8 issues 1976; expects 12 issues 1977, 12 issues 1978. Pub's reviews: 116 in 1976. §catalytic literature (poetry, fiction)/otherwise, no restrictions. COSMEP.

Catex Press, Jack Clifton, 1150 Spruce St, Berkeley, CA 94707. "Children's literature, fiction, non-fiction, poetry. Things of interest to children of all ages" 1975. of. Reporting time: 1 week. COSMEP.

THE CATHARTIC, Patrick M. Ellingham, 76 Hinman, Buffalo, NY 14216. "No biases except won't use rascist or sexist material and this is not a very arbitrary selection, it's pretty obvious what is rascist/sexist. Any length of poem, any style, favor work that deals with human feelings, awareness that can be meaningful for readers whether they are poets or not. There are no taboos as to words used or feelings expressed. Recent contributors are: Jess Perlman, Margaret Kaminski, Joy Walsh, Polly Joan, Lyle Glazier, Tom Weigel, Errol Miller, Marilyn McComas, Martha Bower, Ilka Scobie. There are people both known and unknown. I'm interested in new and young writers but there is a place for everyone." 3/yr; 1-yr sub price: $1.25; per copy: $.50; sample: $.50. 1974. 16pp; 5½ x 8½. of. circ. 100. Reporting time: less than 1 week. Payment: copies. Discounts: 30%. Back issues: no special price. Pub's reviews. §poetry/original views on art. CCLM.

Cat's Pajamas Press (see also MOJO NAVIGATOR(E)), John Jacob, 527 Lyman, Oak Park, IL 60304. Poetry, fiction, criticism, parts-of-novels, long-poems. "Recently we have published poetry by Thomas Michael Fisher, John Oliver Simon, and Stephen Leggett. We have published prose fiction by Ken Smith and Eric Felderman, and non-fiction prose by John Jacob and Tom Montag. We prefer short manuscripts, and will look closely at material working through texts—usually of anthropological or historical source. In 1976-77 we are committed to an anthology drawn from an already-closed selection of manuscripts, a fiction book by Ken Smith, and one or two undecided projects. Regardless of how broke we become, we have made a commitment to publish at least one book and one broadside each year. Beginning in 1976 we will provide an author's state arts council with at least 5% of an author's print run in a small press education effort." 1968. 8-32pp; 5 x 8; 8 x 11. mi/of/lp/other. avg. press run 100-1,000. Reporting time: 4-6 weeks. Payment: min. 20% print run. Discounts: 40% on multiples. Pub'd 1 title 1976; expects 1 title 1977.

Caveman Publications Ltd., Trevor Reeves, P.O. Box 1458, Dunedin, New Zealand. 1971. 52pp; 8½ x 5¼. of/lp. Payment: 10% on retail, royalties. Discounts: library—retail; bookshops—33-40% retail terms. COSMEP, COSMEPA.

Caxton Press (see NEW ZEALAND MONTHLY REVIEW)

Cedar Creek Press, John G. Henry, P.O. Box 1051, Stillwater, OK 74074. Poetry. avg. price, cloth: $5.00; paper: $2.00. 1966. 32-48pp; 6 x 9. †lp. avg. press run 500. Reporting time: 3-4 weeks max. Payment: 10 percent of press run. Copyrights for author. Discounts: 20 percent on orders for more than 5 copies. Pub'd 2 titles 1976; expects 5 titles 1977, 6 titles 1978.

Cedar House Enterprises, Janet Wherry, PO Box 70, El Granada, CA 94018, 415-726-4096. Fiction. "I prefer things that do well at trade fairs like cookbooks, coloring books, books with local interest appeal." avg. price, paper: $4.95. 1976. 20 to 250pp; 8½ x 11. †mi. avg. press run 300. Reporting time: 2 weeks. Payment: author receives percent of profit by check in mail bimonthly. Copyrights for author. Discounts: classroom. COSMEP.

CEDAR ROCK, Cedar Rock, Inc., David C. Yates, Bob Watson, Asst. Ed., 1121 Madeline, New Braunfels, TX 78130, 512-625-6002. Poetry, articles, art, photos, reviews, long-poems. "Emphasis on readable poetry-although any form-conventional or free verse-considered. Recent contributors include: Judson Jerome, Naomi Shihab, Marge Piercy, Paul Zimmer, R.S. Gwynn." 4/yr; 1-yr sub price: $3.50; per copy: $1.00; sample: $1.00. 1975. 24pp; tabloid. of. circ. 800. Reporting time: 2 wks. Payment: 2 contributors copies, plus occasional prizes as finances allow. Copyrighted, reverts to author. Ads: $120.00/$60.00. Discounts: $2.25 per student. Back issues: $1 per issue. Pub'd 4 issues 1976; expects 4 issues 1977, 4 issues 1978. Pub's reviews: 12 in 1976. §poetry. COSMEP, CCLM.

CELEBES, Sicilian Antigruppo, Costantino Petralia, Nat Scammacca, Largo dei Giacinti, 38, Trappani, Sicily. Articles, interviews, satire, criticism, reviews, letters, collages, concrete art. "3 to 5 typewritten pages, cultural in every field. Recent contributors: Antonio Noto, Enrico Crespolti, Guiseppe Zagarrio, Nicolo DAlessandro, Nat Scammacca, Francesco Carbone, Giacomo Baragli, Franco DiMarco, *only* Italian." 3/yr; 1-yr sub price: $5.00; per copy: $2.00; sample: $1.50. 1975. 64pp; 5 x 8. of. circ. 500-750. Reporting time: 1 month. Payment: none. Copyrighted, reverts to author. Ads: $100.00/$50.00/0. Discounts: 33 percent. Back issues: $2.00. Pub's reviews. §all areas.

CELEBRATION, Wm. J. Sullivan, 2707 Lawina Road, Baltimore, MD 21216. "All styles, we hope to be as unbiased as contributors will permit. Recent contributors: Karen Donnelly, Lora Dunetz, Don Harrold, Michael R. Pashall." occasionally; price per copy: $1.00; sample: $1.25. 1975. 30pp; 5½ x 8½. of. circ. 300. Reporting time: 8 weeks. Payment: copies. Back issues: $1.25. COSMEP.

Celestial Arts, Hal Kramer, President, 231 Adrian Rd., Millbrae, CA 94030. "Publishes quality paperback originals. Query first with outline and sample chapters. Include descriptions and examples of artwork and photos. SASE. Awareness/sensitivity poetry and philosophy-subjects of unique interest or unique approach to subject of general interest." Reporting time: 6 weeks. Payment: standard royalty contract.

THE CENTENNIAL REVIEW, David Mead, 110 Morrill Hall, Mich. State Univ., E. Lansing, MI 48824, 517-355-1905. Poetry, articles. "Topics cover English literature, soc. sci, sciences, humanities, 3,000 words, double-spaced. Contributors:Joseph Needham, Susan Fromberg Schaeffer" 4/yr; 1-yr sub price: $3.00; per copy: $1.00; sample: $1.00. 1955. 100pp; 6 x 9. of. circ. 1,000. Reporting time: 3-6 months. Payment: year's free subscription. Copyrighted, reverts to author. Back issues: $1 copy.

CENTER, Carol Berge, 2617 Benvenue, Berkeley, CA 94704, 415-845-2860. Fiction, articles, satire, criticism, reviews, letters, parts-of-novels, non-fiction. "Experimental & innovative prose only. No poetry ever. As of 1977 format changes from short sections to longer prose 'chapbooks'. New writers must query w/sample of work—before submitting. Enclose SASE." 2/yr; price per copy: $2.00 to individuals, $2.50 to libraries.; sample: $2.00. 1971. 80pp; 8½ x 11. of. circ. 1,000. Reporting time: 2 wks. Payment: $3.00-$4.50 pg. Copyrighted, revert to authors 6 mos. after pubn. Discounts: None. Back issues: First 3 issues, $50.00 to libraries; negotiable to writers. Other back issues: $3.00 each, when available. Pub'd 2 issues 1976; expects 2 issues 1977, 2 issues 1978. Pub's reviews. §Innovative prose & fiction only. CCLM.

The Center For Book Arts (see BOOK ARTS)

Center For Contemporary Poetry, John Judson, Murphy Library, Univ of Wisconsin, La Crosse, WI 54601, 608-784-6050, Ext 237. Poetry, articles, interviews. "We publish an annual volume under the title *Voyages To The Inland Sea;* emphasis is on midwestern poetry. Each volume includes two or three poets, with representative poems and an essay by each. Prices for Vols 3-6, $6.00 reg & $10.00 signed. For 1977 & after are $8.00 reg ed & $15.00 signed. Vol VII features poets Hale Chatfield & Wm. Kloefkorn. Vol I and II are O.O.P. MSS. are not solicited." avg. price, cloth: $8.00; other: $15.00 signed. 1971. 65pp; 8½ x 5½. of. avg. press run 500 vols. Discounts: 20% to dealers, jobbers. Pub'd 1 title 1976; expects 1 title 1977, 1 title 1978.

Center For Cuban Studies (see also CANTO LIBRE, CENTER NEWSLETTER), 220 East 23rd St, New York, NY 10010. "Areas of interest, arts, Cuba, Latin America"

Center for Educational Reform, Inc. (see EDCENTRIC MAGAZINE)

Center for New Art Activities Inc. (see AVALANCHE)

Center for Women's Studies & Services (see FEMINIST BULLETIN)

CENTERGRAM, Centergram Press, Terry Gross, 401 N Plank Rd, Newburgh, NY 12550. Poetry. "To 25 lines - only the toughest stuff around, nothing sappy." 4/yr; 1-yr sub price: $4.00; per copy: $1.00; sample: $1.00. 1977. 24-36pp; 5 x 8. †lp. circ. 100. Reporting time: Immediate. Payment: copies. Not copyrighted. Ads: none. §Poetry.

Centergram Press (see also CENTERGRAM), Terry Gross, 401 N Plank Rd, Newburgh, NY 12550. Poetry. "Collections, mostly short work, but any length is o.k." avg. price, paper: $3.00. 1977. pp varies; 5 x 8. †lp. avg. press run Varies. Reporting time: 1 month. Payment: copies. Does not copyright for author.

CENTER NEWSLETTER, Center for Cuban Studies, 220 East 23rd St., New York, NY 10010. "Documents in translation from Cuba."

CENTERING: A Magazine of Poetry, Years Press, F. Richard Thomas, ATL EBH, Michigan State University, E. Lansing, MI 48824. Poetry. "Unlike many little magazines, CENTERING contains at least 10 pages of each poet's work. Because of limitations of time and money, I rarely accept unsolicited material." 1/yr; 1-yr sub price: $1.00; per copy: $1.00; sample: $1.00. 1973. 48pp; 7 x 8½. of. circ. 300. mss. solicited. Payment: 5 copies. Copyrighted, reverts to author. Pub'd 1 issue 1976; expects 1 issue 1977, 1 issue 1978. COSMEP.

Challenge Press (see also CONFRONTATION/CHANGE REVIEW), Frederick M. Finney, C/O Economic Research Center, Inc., 32 College St., Dayton, OH 45407, 513-275-8637. Poetry, fiction, articles, art, photos, interviews, satire, criticism, reviews, music, letters, parts-of-novels, plays, non-fiction. "Urban sociology, urban planning, urban problems—interested in subjects that have economic-social implications on the history and life of Blacks in the United States and The Third-World Community. Good fiction and poetry with Black and/or Third World experience." avg. price, cloth: $4.95-$15.95; paper: $3.95-$6.95. 1973. poetry, 60pp., nonfiction 320, fiction 240pp; 5½ x 8. of. avg. press run 500 poetry, 1,000 other. Reporting time: 4-6 weeks. Payment: Negotitated. Royalty rates, will enter into cooperative subsidy arrang. on occissions. Copyrights for author. Discounts: trade, 40 percent; libraries 45 percent. Expects 4 titles 1977, 10 titles 1978. COSMEP.

Chandler & Sharp Publishers, Inc., Jonathan Sharp, Howard Chandler, 5643 Paradise Drive Suite 10, Corte Madera, CA 94925, 415-924-7822. "We are strictly book publishers-Adult non fiction trade books and college textbooks in the social sciences and humanities." 1972. of. avg. press run 4,000. Payment: royalties. Discounts: Trade books: 40 percent; textbooks: 20 percent; wholesalers: 50 percent. Pub'd 7 titles 1976; expects 8 titles 1977, 10 titles 1978. COSMEP, AAA.

THE CHANEY CHRONICAL, London Northwest, David H Schlottmann, 929 South Bay Rd, Olympia, WA 98506. "Devoted to study of William H. Chaney (1821-1903) who is generally believed to be father of author Jack London. A companion paper to WHAT'S NEW ABOUT LONDON, JACK? Future items will include articles written by Chaney on spiritualism, astrology, etc, a horoscope cast for a Salem, Oregon resident, and bibliographies." irreg; price per copy: $.50. 1972. 10pp; 8½ x 11. mi. circ. 30. Payment: none. Ads: 1 cent/wd classified. Back issues: xerox available.

CHANGE, Art Coulter, 1825 North Lake Shore Dr, Chapel Hill, NC 27514, 919-942-2994. Articles, criticism, reviews, letters. "Synergetics is the art and science of evoking synergy in the human mind, in small groups, and in other complex systems." 6/yr; 1-yr sub price: $5.00; per copy: $1.00; sample: $1.00. 1954. 25pp; 8½ x 11. †mi. circ. 200. Reporting time: 30 days. Payment: copies only. Pub'd 6 issues 1976; expects 6 issues 1977, 6 issues 1978.

Chaosium (see WYRD)

THE CHARIOTEER, Parnassos, Greek Cultural Society Of New York, Andonis Decavalles, Bebe Spanos Ikaris, PO Box 2928, Grand Central Station, New York, NY 10017. Criticism, reviews. "We are a review of modern Greek culture and 75 percent to 80 percent of each issue consists of translations from modern Greek authors." 1/yr; 1-yr sub price: $4.00; per copy: $4.00; sample: $4.00. 1960. 100pp; 5½ x 8½. lp. circ. 1,500. Reporting time: 3 months. Payment: none. Copyrighted, reverts by arrangement. Ads: $150.00/$100/none. Discounts: 10 percent for recognized agencies provided check accompanies order. Back issues: $3.00 regular issues; $6.00 double-issues. Discounts on multiple issues. Pub'd 1 issue 1976; expects 1 issue 1977, 1 issue 1978. Pub's reviews. §Greek culture, especially modern. CCLM.

CHARITON REVIEW, Andrew Grossbardt, Jim Barnes, Language & Literature, Northeast Missouri St. Univ., Kirksville, MO 63501, 816-665-5121. Poetry, fiction, art, photos, reviews. "We try to keep open minds, but admit a bias to work that relies more on strong imagery than talkiness. We are very interested in translation, particularly translations of modern poets and especially those from languages other than French or Spanish though we have used numerous translations from those two languages. Recent contributors include Richard Hugo, John Haines, Phil Levine, Maura Stanton, David Ray, Madeline Defrees, James Tate, Tess Gallagher, Raymond Carver, Quinton Duval, James Welch, Paul Zimmer, Dennis Schmitz, Russel Edson; translations of Supervielle, Lorca, Rozewicz. No xerox or carbons!" 2/yr; sub price: $4.00/yr ($7.00 2/yr); per copy: $2.00; sample: $2.00. 1975. 96pp; 6 x 9. lp. circ. 650. Reporting time: 1 month. Payment: $5.00 page up to $50.00 and 2 copies. Copyrighted, returned to author on request. Ads: $40/$20. Discounts: on request. Back issues: Vol. 1 No. 1 $5.00; Vol. 1 No. 2 $2.00; etc. Pub'd 2 issues 1976; expects 2 issues 1977, 2 issues 1978. Pub's reviews. §Modern poetry, fiction, translation. CCLM.

CHAUCER REVIEW, The Pennsylvania State University Press, Robert W. Frank Jr., 215 Wagner Bldg., University Park, PA 16802.

CHELSEA, Sonia Raiziss, Editor; Helene Dworzan, Alfredo de Palchi, Brian Swann, Associate Editors, Box 5880, Grand Central Station, New York, NY 10017. Poetry, fiction, articles, art, interviews, criticism, reviews, parts-of-novels, long-poems, plays, concrete art. "Stress on quality, originality, style, variety...(superior translations). No special biases, no requirements on length (according to suitability). Catholic attitudes, eclectic material. Recent contributor: Laura (Riding) Jackson." 1/2/yr; sub price: $4.50/2 consecutive issues as published; per copy: $2.50; sample: $3.00 or more. 1958. 185pp; 5½ x 8½. of. circ. 1,000. Reporting time: 2 mos. Payment: copies, or token fee. Discounts: agency discount: 40%; bookstores : 30%. Back issues: prices range from $3.00 to $15.00 if rare. Pub'd 2 issues 1976; expects 2 issues 1977, 2 issues 1978. Pub's reviews. §poetry, prose, art, architecture. CCLM.

THE CHELSEA JOURNAL, Marian Press, Battleford, Sask., A. de Valk, 1437 College Drive, Saskatoon, Saskatchewan S7N0W6, Canada. 306-343-4561. Poetry, fiction, articles, interviews, reviews, letters, plays, news items, non-fiction. 6/yr; 1-yr sub price: $8.00 Canada/$10.00 U.S. & Foreign; per copy: $1.50. 1975. 52pp; 8 x 11. circ. 1,300. Reporting time: 2 to 6 weeks. Copyrighted. Ads: $100/$60. Discounts: consignment sales-30%. Back issues: $1.50 each. Pub'd 6 issues 1976; expects 6 issues 1977, 6 issues 1978. Pub's reviews: 30 in 1976. §politics, good fiction, possibly religious. CPPA.

CHERNOZEM, Big Deal Press, Steven L. Deal, Susan L. Deal, Gen. Delivery, No. Platte, NB 69101. "Not accepting manuscripts until further notice. Temporarily suspending publication. Moving." irreg.; price per copy: $1.00; sample: 2 13-cent stamps. 1973. 15pp; 9½ x 11. †mi. circ. $1.00 each. 100. Reporting time: 30 days. Payment: copies. Back issues: one thru nine

Cherry Tree Press, Box 121, White Rock, B.C. V4B1N4, Canada. of. Reporting time: 6 mos. Payment: 10%. COSMEP.

Cherry Valley Editions (see also NORTHEAST RISING SUN), Box 303, Cherry Valley, NY 13320, 607-264-3204. Poetry, fiction, long-poems, collages. "1975 saw the publication of chapbooks (one a translation from French), another a chapbook by one of the few women writing in cut-up. Three poetry chapbooks by men and 4 by women. We definitely lean towards experimental writing in our books. We are looking for something new and exciting-for 1978. We plan books by Paul Grillo (with collages), Brown Miller, Margot de Silva." avg. price, paper: $3.00; other: Signed $15.00. 1974. 56pp; 5½ x 8½. of. avg. press run 1,000. Reporting time: A.S.A.P. Payment: 10 percent royalty. Copyrights for author. Discounts: 1-4: 20 percent; 5-19: 40 percent; 20 plus: 50 percent. Pub'd 6 titles 1976; expects 8 titles 1977. NESPA, COSMEP, COSMEP-EAST, NYSSPA.

Cheshire Books, Michael Riordan, Schorr Berman, Linda Goodman, P.O. Box 7616, Menlo Park, CA 94025, 415-854-0393. "We are not presently accepting submitted material from the writing public at large. We are publishing our own material or that solicited specifically for our books. Area of concentration is environmental & energy books. Most recent (& only) book is *The Solar Home Book* by Bruce Anderson. Two others in the works but it's too early to give notice." avg. price, cloth: $7.50. 1976. 304pp; 11 x 8½. of. avg. press run 20,000. Payment: split profits 50-50. Does not copyright for author. Discounts: trade distribution exclusively through RPM distributors (40 percent retail; 50 percent wholesale). Pub'd 1 title 1976; expects 1 title 1977.

CHIAROSCURO, Chiaroscuro Press, John Latta, Chris Henkel, 2624 Roseland Dr., Ann Arbor, MI 48103, 313-761-5530. Poetry, interviews, reviews, long-poems. "'We seek poems—the bright red communist, the blindly moribund, the static other, the persistently aberrant...our 'editorial policy' rides protectively, indian style, between a horse of irrepressible scoffing and one of final amazement and awe'. Recent contributors include Charles Wright, Robert Morgan, William Matthews, Danny Rendleman." 2/yr; 1-yr sub price: $2.00; per copy: $1.25; sample: free. 1975. 40pp; 6 x 9. †lp. circ. 125. Reporting time: 2-4 weeks. Payment: 2 copies. Copyrighted, reverts to author. Discounts: 20 percent off on orders of 10 copies or more. Pub'd 1 issue 1976; expects 1 issue 1977. Pub's reviews. §poetry, translations, small mags.

Chicago New Art Association (see also NEW ART EXAMINER), Jane Allen, Editor; Derek Guthrie, Associate Editor, 230 E. Ohio, RM. 207, Chicago, IL 60611, 312-642-6236. avg. price, paper: $700.00. 1973. 11½ x 17. of. avg. press run 4,500. Payment: $8.00, 350 word reviews, $25.00 article. Discounts: 3x, 5x plus 10x rates.

CHICAGO REVIEW, Richard Vine, Alina Romanowski, Julis Siegal, University of Chicago, Faculty Exchange Box C, Chicago, IL 60637. Poetry, fiction, articles, art, photos, interviews, criticism, reviews, parts-of-novels, concrete art. "We have an international readership interested in contemporary literature and graphic arts. We look for material with sophistication and integrity. Recent contributors include; Euganio Montale, John Mella, Jean Ricardou, Alain Robbe-Grillet, Susan Fromberg Schaeffer" 4/yr; 1-yr sub price: $8.95; per copy: $2.45; sample: $2.45. 1946. 160-240pp; 5¾ x 9. of. circ. 3,000. Reporting time: 3 months. Payment: mostly in contributors copies. Copyrighted, does not revert to author. Ads: $120.00/$70.00. Discounts: agency-10 percent subscription. Pub's reviews. §literature & the arts. CCLM, COSMEP.

‡**CHICANO COMMUNICATIONS,** PO Box 6086, Albuquerque, NM 87107.

Children's Art Foundation, Inc. (see STONE SOUP)

Children's Book Press/Emprenta de Libros Enfantiles, Harriet Rohmer, Roger I. Reyes, Robin Cherin, 1461 9th Ave., San Francisco, CA 94122, 415-664-8500. "We publish myths, legends, and folklore of the different peoples who live in America today. Most of our books are bilingual in Spanish, Chinese, or Tagalog (Filipino)." avg. price, paper: $2.95. 1975. 24pp; 8 x 9. of. avg. press run 4,400. We do not solicit manuscripts. Payment: yes. Copyrights for author. Discounts: 40 percent trade discount, other rates on request.

CHIMERA-A Complete Theater Piece, HS Press, Harry William Saffren, 340 East Mechanic St., Philadelphia, PA 19144. Fiction, plays. "CHIMERA is a complete theater piece, including: the theater, sets, characters, and script; to cutout, put together and perform. Issue No. 1 (April 1976) contains Kenneth Marcus Lipman's *This Is Money-A Story Told To An Audience Of Two.* Issue No. 2 (Dec. 1976) contains Edgar Allan Poe's *The Cask Of Amontillado.* Issue No. 3 (due Sept. 1977) will be *The Jeniper Tree* from Grimms' Tales." 2/yr; 1-yr sub price: £7.00; per copy: $3.95. 1976. 8½ x 11. of. circ. 1,000. Discounts: 20% on 2-4 issues, 40% 5 or more. Back issues: $3.95. Pub'd 2 issues 1976; expects 1 issue 1977, 2 issues 1978.

CHOMO-URI, Collective, 506 Goodell Hall, University of Mass, Amherst, MA 01003, 413-545-0883. Poetry, fiction, articles, art, photos, interviews, satire, criticism, reviews, plays. "'Please' limit number of submissions to five. Interested in perspectives on a changing society. We publish only women. Some recent contributors include: Polly Joan, Karen Glenn, Cheryl H. Kindernecht, Margaret R. Sackman, Marjorie Abel, Jane Flanders, Margaret Kaminski, Jane Kogan, Chocolate Waters, Jean Emmons, Barbara Johnson. Annual thematic issue-Fall/Winter issue." 3/yr; 1-yr sub price: $4.00; per copy: $1.50; sample: $1.00 (back issue). 1974. 44pp; 5½ x 8½. of. circ. 1,500. Reporting time: up to 4 months. Payment: copies. Copyrighted, reverts to author. Ads: None. Discounts: $1.20 for bookstores & subscription agency. Back issues: $1.00 except special issues always $1.50. Pub'd 3 issues 1976; expects 3 issues 1977, 3 issues 1978. Pub's reviews: 3 in 1976. §Women's work published by women's presses and by small presses as in accordance with the philosophy of CHOMO-URI. CCLM, COSMEP, NESPA, WIP.

CHOOMIA - COLLECTIONS OF CONTEMPORARY POETRY, Yarrow Press, Ann Guido, Jay Barwell, P.O. Box 107, Framingham, MA 01701. Poetry, art, interviews, reviews. "We are open-minded. Recent contributors: Philip Booth, Ruth Whitman, Michael McMahon, Ruth Stone, James Schevill, Brendan Galvin, Peter Viereck, John Engels, May Sarton, Marie Harris, Alan Feldman..." 2/yr; sub price: 2 yr, 4 issues for $5.00; per copy: $1.50; sample: $1.50. 1975. 60-80 pp perfect bound; 5 x 8. †of. circ. 500. Reporting time: 1 to 2 months. Payment: usually copies per poem or page. Copyrighted, reverts to author. Ads: none. Discounts: 40 percent to bookstores in bulk orders over 10 copies; 40 percent to classes over 10 copies. Back issues: $1.00 for Nos. 2 & 3; $2.00 special New England issue 100 pp. Pub'd 3 issues 1976; expects 3 issues 1977, 2 issues 1978. Pub's reviews: none in 1976. §poetry. CCLM.

CHOUTEAU REVIEW, W. Conger Beasley Jr., David Perkins, 10016, Kansas City, MO 64111, 816-444-0060. Poetry, fiction, articles, art, photos, cartoons, interviews, satire, criticism, reviews, music, parts-of-novels, long-poems, concrete art. "Prefer poems 1 or 2 pages, no more than 5; stories from 5-20 pages (our pages). Catholic taste; we want clarity, excitement, intelligence, novel forms. Contributors include: Bly, Anderson, Codrescu, A.S. Hamilton, Barry Lopez, R. Kostelanetz, S. Dunn, A. Salkey, T. Veitch, C. Coolidge, J. Tate, A. Feldman." 2/yr; 1-yr sub price: $10.00 two years; per copy: $2.50; sample: $2.00. 1975. 116pp; 5½ x 8½. of. circ. 1,000. Reporting time: 1 week—1 month. Payment varies. Copyrighted, does not revert to author. Ads: $100.00/$60.00. Discounts: none estbl. Pub's reviews §Poetry, film, novels, interviews, musical scores, graphics, photography.

THE CHOWDER REVIEW, Ron Slate, 2858 Kingston Dr, Madison, WI 53713. Poetry, articles, interviews, criticism, reviews. "We publish poems that give as much as they demand, that try to accomplish more than present a series of observations connected by mood. But there are even good poems in that category. Length: any. Leonard Nathan, Theodore Weiss, Ann Darr, Dave Etter, Harley Elliott." 2/yr; sub price: $4.00/3 issues; per copy: $1.50; sample: $1.50. 1973. 80pp; 8½ x 5½. of. circ. 600. Reporting time: 2 weeks. Payment: copies or subscription. Ads: $35/$20. Discounts: 40% stores. Back issues: Special issue: best poems of Nos. 1-3 $1.00 all others (4,5) $1.50. Pub's reviews. §poetry/poetics/review maps. CCLM.

Christopher Davies Publishers Ltd. (see POETRY WALES)

Chronicle Books, Phelps Dewey, Dick Schuettge, 870 Market Street Suite 915, San Francisco, CA 94102, 415-777-7240. "Chronicle Books has published, and will continue to publish many regional travel titles, outdoors and nature titles, as well as an expanding list of general non fiction. With the recent addition of Dick Schuetgge to our staff, we look forward to publishing more visual books on current themes, with full color, beginning in the Spring of 1978." avg. price, cloth: $7.95; paper: $4.95. 1968. of. avg. press run 5,000. Reporting time: one month. Payment: 10 percent paid yearly. Copyrights for author.

Chthon Press, Paul J.J. Payack, 39 Hawthorne Village, Concord, MA 01742. Poetry, fiction. "By invitation only. Meta fiction." 1973. of. Pub'd 2 titles 1976. COSMEP.

Cibola Studio (see COQUI QUARTERLY)

Cider Press, Wm Stage, Naomi Cargill, Griswold Otter, 1821 Burton St. S.E., Grand Rapids, MI 49506, 616-243-6840. Poetry, fiction, satire, reviews, letters. "Cider Press, presently in nascent form, is a collective operation devoted to the publication of traditional & innovative poetry and prose. This publication encompasses all subjects and all submissions are taken into consideration. Always happy to see philosophic meanderings on biologic oneness. The god concept, caprice and the existential universe. Animal stories, too." avg. price, paper: $1.00. 1976. 60pp; 5½ x 8½. †mi/of. avg. press run 250. Reporting time: 3 weeks. Payment: yes. Does not copyright for author. Discounts: open to negotiation.

CIE, Museroom, Michael D. Hazard, 8 Longford St, Philadelphia, PA 19136, 612-222-2096/227-2240. "No unsolicited material accepted or returned poetry, prose & other forms of intelligent writing every 'issue' of our 'magazine' comes in a different form, from postcards to 'regular' mags to video tapes." 12/yr; 1-yr sub price: varies; per copy: varies; sample: varies. 1974. variespp; varies. †Some silkscreen, offset jobbed, mimeo, letterpress in house. circ. 2,500-5,000. Payment: varies with project. Rights stay with author. no ads. Back issues: sold out. Pub'd 12 issues 1976; expects 12 issues 1977, 12 issues 1978. Pub's reviews. §international/media/literature. COSMEP.

CIMARRON REVIEW, Okla. State University Press, Clinton Keeler, Ed-in-Chief; Jeanne Adams Wray, Managing Editor, Oklahoma State University, Stillwater, OK 74074. Poetry, fiction, articles, art, interviews. 4/yr; 1-yr sub price: $10; per copy: $4; sample: free. 1967. 64-72pp; 6 x 9. †of. circ. 500. Reporting time: 4-6 months. Payment: payment in copies. Discounts: 50% off to international booksellers. Back issues: half-price.

Cincinnati Chess Federation (see J'ADOUBE)

Cincinnati Women's Press (see SYZYGY)

CINEASTE MAGAZINE, Gary Crowdus, Dan Georgakas, Ruth McCormick, Lenny Rubenstein, 333 Sixth Ave, New York, NY 10014. Articles, photos, interviews, satire, criticism, reviews, letters. "Offers a social & political perspective on the cinema—everything from the latest hollywood flicks & the American independent scene to political thrillers from Europe and revolutionary cinema from the Third World." 4/yr; 1-yr sub price: $4.00; sample: $.50. 1967. 56pp; 8½ x 11. of. circ. 5M. Reporting time: 2-3 wks. Payment: copies only. Ads: $150/$75 1/2. Discounts: 25%. Back issues: $.75/ea to subscribers; $1 to others. COSMEP.

CINEMA/QUEBEC, Editions Cinema/Quebec, Jean-Pierre Tadros, c.p. 309, Station Outremont, Montreal, Quebec H2V 4N1, Canada. 12/yr; 1-yr sub price: $9.00; per copy: $1.00; sample: free. 1971. 54pp; 7 x 10. †of. Ads: $275/$150.

CIRCLE, Circle Forum, J.M. Gates, P.O. Box 176, Portland, OR 97207. Poetry, long-poems. "*CIRCLE* IS NOW AN *ANNUAL* PUBLICATION SUPPLEMENTED BY AN OCCASIONAL NEWSLETTER *CIRCLETS*. The 1975-1976 circle will be released May 1976 and the 1976-1977 issue in September 1976. CIRCLE is exclusively dedicated to poetry readable, line by line, both forwards and backwards. Minimum length eight lines. First-time publication of reversible poetry on heritage themes, environmental themes, general themes, protest themes in standard English. Long poems, which are reversible, are particularly welcome. A bibliography of reversible poetry is in progress. 'Circlets' Newsletter is provided gratis to Circle subscribers; for others, a self addressed stamped envelope is required." 1/yr; sub price: 4 issues for $4.50; per copy: $1.50; sample: $1.50. 1973. 40pp annual; 5½ x 8½. of. circ. 200. Reporting time: 4 months. Payment: 2 contributor's copies. no advertising. Discounts: Normal discounts to educational institutions on bulk orders. Back issues: $2 each when available. Pub's reviews. §Reversible poetry, narrative poetry and long poems. COSMEP.

CIRCLE IN THE SQUARE BROADSHEET (see Bristol Arts Centre)

Circle Press, Andrew Towe, Ken McCullough, 419 So. Grand, Bozeman, MT 59715. Poetry, fiction, art, long-poems. "Interested in ms. reflecting life in Northwest area, past or present; poetry, fiction, nonfiction, art, etc. Poetry limited to chapbooks-No anthologies at present. Patrick Todd, Julie Reid, Bob Love, Beth Chadwick will have chapbooks of poetry published by Circle Press in 1976." 1976. †lp. Reporting time: 2 mos. Payment: copies + royalties. Discounts: trade-library.

Circle Press (see also ROUND NOTES), Frank Hamsher, PO Box N, Boulder Creek, CA 95006, 408-338-2141. "We have been printing our own material which comes out of the communal experience that the Press is a adjunct to. We are primarily involved in the raising of the Conscious level of man, using principles for evolvement which have their roots in pre-history, but are still functional today. We are dedicated to using ourselves as individuals to bring about these changes within our own consciousness, and in the group consciousness. We have printed books for other individuals involved in the same kinds of activities, at reasonable rates. We do not at this time plan on subsidizing to any greater extent book or pamplet length material. Suitable submissions of shorter length might be submitted to our magazine." avg. price, cloth: $8.50; paper: $5.00; other: (pamphlets) $1.00, (pamp) $0.50. 1975. 152pp; 5-3/8 x 8¼. †of. avg. press run 1,000-2,000 copies. Reporting time: 30-60 days. Copyrights for author. Discounts: standard discount schedule; multiple copies up to 10: 20 percent discount, 11 or more copies: 40 percent. COSMEP.

Circle Publications, Carl Fredricks, PO Box 34, Lyndhurst, NJ 07071, 201-438-1326. 1976.

CIRCULAR LETTER, Carl D. Clark, 3007 University, Austin, TX 78705, 512-472-7415. Poetry, fiction, articles, art, photos, cartoons, interviews, satire, criticism, reviews, music, letters, parts-of-novels, long-poems, collages, plays, concrete art. *"CIRCULAR LETTER* is an operation that exists to (1) circulate work of writers, artists, musicians, etc. and (2) get responses from readers commenting upon that work. We send around poems, fiction, plays, tapes, drawings, paintings, essays etc. Readers are responsible for forwarding material to next subscriber. Special section on 1960's." 10/yr; 1-yr sub price: $1.00. 1977. napp. circulates in manuscript. Reporting time: 1 day-6 months. Payment: none. Copyrighted, reverts to author. Ads: none. Expects 10 issues 1977. Pub's reviews: none in 1976. §art, music, literature, philosophy, current history.

CIRCUS MAXIMUS, Garretson Graphics, Pete Garretson, P O Box 3251, York, PA 17402. Poetry. "We prefer imaginative language poems which use concrete imagery to create a 'scene' with a beginning, a middle and an end which suddenly comes alive for the reader. We don't want diary poems that come from nowhere and lead to nowhere. No sermons, end-rhymes that say nothing or furry friend nonsense." 4/yr; 1-yr sub price: $6.00; per copy: $2.00; sample: $2.00. 1975. 44pp; 5½ x 8½. of. circ. 500. Reporting time: 2-3 weeks. Payment: (Starting with 12/77 issue) $2.00/poem. Copyrighted, reverts to author. Ads: none. Discounts: Inquire. (We've never been approached about quantity orders.). Pub's reviews. §Poetry only. COSMEP.

CITY 4, Faculty Press, Neal Abramson, Nora Roberts Wainer, 152 Finley Hall, CCNY 138 St & Convent Ave, New York, NY 10031. Poetry, fiction, articles, art, photos, interviews, criticism, reviews, parts-of-novels, long-poems, plays. "Hugh Seidman, Joel Oppenheimer, Francine Gray." 2/yr; 1-yr sub price: $3.00; per copy: $1.50; sample: $.90. 96pp. Pub's reviews. §poetry, fiction. CCLM, COSMEP.

City Lights Books, Lawrence Ferlinghetti, Nancy J. Peters, 261 Columbus Ave., San Francisco, CA 94133. Poetry, fiction, articles, non-fiction. 1955. of. Pub'd 3 titles 1976; expects 5 titles 1977, 5 titles 1978. COSMEP.

CITY MINER, City Miner, Michael Helm, P.O. Box 176, Berkeley, CA 94701, 415-524-1162. Poetry, fiction, articles, photos, cartoons, interviews, satire, letters. "Bay area focus (strong prejudice toward writers in this area) with focus on Berkeley and East Bay. Ideal length for articles 2-3,000 words. Bias towards decentralism, experimentation, community, humanism. Alta Ferlinghetti, Bruce Boston, Malcolm Margolin, Frank Polite, Herb Kohl, Jenifer Stone, Michael Helm, Bruce Hawkins." 4/yr; 1-yr sub price: $2.75; per copy: $0.75; sample: $0.50. 1976. 48pp; 7-1/8 x 10¼. of. circ. 5,000. Reporting time: 2—3 weeks. Payment: 1 cent word for articles and prose, 10 cents line poetry. Ads: $150.00/$85.00,401/4 page $45.00,401/8 page $30.00/25% dis—2 issues. Discounts: 40% trade, 40% bulk, 40% classroom. Back issues: $2.00 each (for Vol 1-3). Pub'd 3 issues 1976; expects 4 issues 1977, 4 issues 1978. §Community, psychology, poetry.

THE CITY MOON, The City Moon, David Ohle, James Grauerholz, Roger Martin, PO Box 842, Canal St. Station, New York, NY 10013, 212-674-0288. Articles, art, photos, satire, letters, parts-of-novels, collages. "The City Moon is a tabloid from 8 to 24 pages long. It purports to be a newspaper but is rather dadaesque, mixing 'fact' and 'fiction' with a fine disregard for distinctions as artificial as these in our time." 8/yr; 1-yr sub price: $5.00; per copy: $0.50; sample: free. 1972. 12pp; 17 x 22. of/xerox. circ. 450. Reporting time: 3-4 weeks. Payment: payment in copies. Copyrighted, sometimes reverts. Ads: $50.00/$1.00. Discounts: 40 percent on consignment, 50 percent for net sales, 50 percent on bulk (30 copies or more). Back issues: all back issues very rare, priced from $1.00 to $10.00. Pub's reviews. §serious prose, nonfiction, pornography. CCLM.

The City Moon (see also THE CITY MOON), James Grauerholz, PO Box 842, Canal St. Station, New York, NY 10013, 212-674-0288. Fiction. "The City Moon so far has published five City Moon Broadcasts, all of them pamphlets from 8 to 40 pages long. Eventually larger books are anticipated. So far we have published Richard Elovich, Steven Low, Claude Pelieu-Washburn, John Wellman, and William S. Burroughs. Manuscripts are in hand from Brion Gysin, John Hopkins, David Ohle, Ed Sanders and others. The emphasis is very strongly on writing that avoids pointless experimentality and that has a crisp moral tone so to speak. Book design is considered extremely important." avg. price, paper: $2.00. 1975. 35pp; 5½ x 8½. of/xerox. avg. press run 1,500 copies. Reporting time: 1 month. Payment: no advance, 10 percent of net (advance for some authors). Copyrights for author. Discounts: 40 percent standard trade discount, 50 percent to a jobber. CCLM.

City Slicker Press, Leonard Palmer, 2325 52 St, Kenosha, WI 53140, 414-657-7883. Poetry, fiction. "City Slicker is a series of three for 1976, authored and published by Leonard Palmer. The next (no. 2), will be titled 'Bare Knuckles'—stories of bar brawling and boozing." avg. price, paper: $1.00. 1976. 50pp; 5½ x 8. of. avg. press run 500 copies. Reporting time: 1 week. Discounts: 25% library/40% bookstore/50% jobber. COSMEP.

CLAIMANTS NEWSPAPER (Claimants Unite), National Federation of Claimants Unions Publications, Co-operative, NFCU Publications (International), 134 Villa Rd, Birmingham, England B191NN, United Kingdom. Articles, news items, letters, plays, photos, satire, reviews. "No subscriptions. Current list on request (stamped addressed envelope). (IPRC)" 4/yr; price per copy: 15p plus 15p postage; sample: 15p plus 15p postage. 1970. 8pp; A4. of. circ. 1,000. Payment: None. Ads: rates on application. Discounts: usual. Back issues: Same as above. Issues 1-12 published to date 4/5/77. Pub'd 4 issues 1976; expects 4 issues 1977, 4 issues 1978. Pub's reviews: 2 in 1976. §Social security, welfare rights.

CLARITY, J.M. Sprague, 3 Greenway, Berkhamsted, Herts HP4 3JD, United Kingdom. Articles, poetry, criticism, letters. "Length of material approx. 750-2500 words. Aimed at intelligent non-specialist who is interested in Christianity; interdenominational, covering a broad spectrum of views & attitudes. CLARITY is the house magazine of the MENSA Christian Group, for MENSA members who are interested in Christianity. Contributors are mainly group members, but outside contributors & subscribers are welcome." 6/yr; 1-yr sub price: £1.00. 1968. 20-24pp;401/2 flscp.

dupl. circ. 100 plus. Copyrighted. Pub'd 6 issues 1976; expects 6 issues 1977, 6 issues 1978. Pub's reviews: 2 in 1976. §religious, social science, psychology. MCG.

CLASSIC FILM COLLECTOR, Samuel K. Rubin, 734 Philadelphia St, Indiana, PA 15701. Articles, art, photos, cartoons, interviews, criticism, reviews, letters. "No standard." 4/yr; 1-yr sub price: $6.00; per copy: $1.75; sample: $1.00. 1962. 72pp; 11 x 15. of. circ. 2,000. Ads: $90/$45/$.10. Back issues: $2.00 each. Pub's reviews. §film. COSMEP.

Clatworthy Colorvues, Mike Mandel, Larry Sultan, 111½ Riverview St, Santa Cruz, CA 95062, 408-426-6401. "We do not solicit contributors. We are artists and publish our own work. We have at present five titles published. Much of the work has been supported by grants from the National Endowment for the Arts. We also have disigned four billboard (non-commercial) exhibitions in San Francisco since 1973." avg. price, cloth: $12.95; paper: $3.00. 1973. 5½ x 8½. of. avg. press run 1,000 copies. Copyrights for author. Discounts: 40 percent to retailer. Pub'd 1 title 1976; expects 1 title 1977.

CLAUDEL STUDIES, Moses M. Nagy, University of Dallas Station, Irving, TX 75061. Criticism. "Our journal dedicates itself to the promotion of the writings of Paul Claudel (playwright and prose writer), and we accept articles, papers in English or in French. Some of our contributors in 1975: Edwin Marie Landau (Switzerland). Jacques Cassar (France), Ann Bugliani (Chicago), Elsie M. Wiedner (Rutgers), Moses M. Nagy (Dallas), Georgia K. Shurr (Idaho)." 2/yr; 1-yr sub price: $5.00; per copy: $3.00; sample: free. 1972. 80-100pp; 4.5 by 7 inches. of. circ. 500. Reporting time: 2 months. Payment: none. Back issues: $3.00. Pub's reviews. §Books concerning Paul Claudel's works or books on theater.

Clean Energy Press, Howard C. Wiig, 3593-a Alani Dr, Honolulu, HI 96822, 808-988-4155. Articles, non-fiction. "Editor is now seeking material on alternative energy sources, and on energy-saving original material. Emphasis is on clean-energy vehicles." avg. price, paper: $1.65. 1975. 176pp; 7 x 4¼. of. avg. press run 2,000. Reporting time: 2 weeks. Payment: 5 cents per word. Copyrights for author. Discounts: $1.00 per copy to dealers. COSMEPA, COSMEP-WEST.

Clearwater Publishing Company, Inc., Norman A. Ross, 75 Rockefeller Plaza, New York, NY 10019. "We publish books, microfiche and audio tape cassettes on American Indians and Peace Studies" avg. price, cloth: $18.00; paper: $7.00. 1973. 6 x 9. of. avg. press run 1,000. Discounts: 20 percent. Pub'd 7 titles 1976; expects 13 titles 1977. COSMEP.

Cleveland State Univ. Poetry Center, Alberta Turner, Leonard Trawick, Dept English, Cleveland State Univ, Cleveland, OH 44115, 216-687-3986. Poetry, concrete art. "1 local poetry series—14 published since 1969—32 pp-50. 1 national series; 1 vol. per year; have already published Stuart Friebert, Thomas Lux, Stratis Haviaris; David Young and Jan Haageusen in press. Query before submitting. About 50-100 pp." avg. price, cloth: $2.95. 1962. 32-100pp; varies. †of. avg. press run 500 local series; 1,500 national series. Reporting time: 4-8 weeks. Payment: 10 percent national series; 100 copies local series. Copyrights for author. Discounts: 20 percent for bulk orders. National series distributed by National Association of College Stores, Oberlin, Ohio 44074. Pub'd 3 titles 1976; expects 4 titles 1977.

Cloud Marauder Press, David Bullen, Don Cushman, 5153 Shafter Ave., Oakland, CA 94618, 415-654-7116. Poetry, fiction. avg. price, paper: $2.50. 1968. 48-88pp; 6 x 9. †of. avg. press run 750. Reporting time: 3 months. Payment: Copies or royalties - cash payment when possible. Does not copyright for author. Pub'd 7 titles 1976; expects 6 titles 1977.

THE CLOVER PATCH, The Clover Patch, Inc., Jan Quackenbush, Virginia Quackenbush, 75 Church St., Montrose, PA 18801, 717-278-3950. Poetry, fiction, art, interviews. "We are mainly a regional magazine focused on writers of the Northern Tier Region five counties of NE Pennsylvania, although we do include work from other sources. We have received grants from the state arts council and CCLM. Members of CCLM and COSMEP. We distribute magazines free of charge." 2/yr; 1-yr sub price: free; per copy: free. 1974. 25pp; 5½ x 8-1/i. of. circ. 600. Reporting time: 1 month. Payment: none. Copyrighted, reverts to author. Ads: $10.00. Back issues: none available. §poetry & prose. CCLM, COSMEP.

Clover Press (see also GREEN'S MAGAZINE), David Green, Box 313, Detroit, MI 48231. "Capable of limited-run production; type by compositor; no reduction capability; noncoated stock. Will not undertake distribution except in conjunction with GREEN'S MAGAZINE. Mail, art extra." avg. price, paper: $2.00 per 100 page 5¼ x 8½ - staple binding. 1975. up to 11 x 14 (full sheet). †of. avg. press run 1,000. Reporting time: 6 weeks. Copyrights for author. Pub'd 1 title 1976.

CLOWN WAR, Clown War Press, Bob Heman, P.O. Box 1093, Brooklyn, NY 11202. Poetry, art, long-poems, concrete art. "CLOWN WAR has doubled its press run & is now distributed free in bookstores & galleries. We are especially interested in experimental poetry & prose, in prosepoems, & in works that touch the 'sense of wonder.' Also very interested in pen & ink drawings that do the same. We like to have sections of three or four writers per issue, but special issues are always a possibility. Recent contributors include Lyn Hejinian, Ray Dipalma, David Gitin, John Jacob, A.F. Caldiero." 4-8/yr. 1971. 24-28pp; 5 x 7. †of. circ. 500-1,000. Reporting time: 1 week - 3 months. Payment: copies. Back issues: No back issues available. Pub'd 1 issue 1976; expects 6 issues 1977, 8 issues 1978. §Poetry, experimental prose, narrative graphics. CCLM.

Club Leabhar Highland Book Club, Frang Macthomais, 31 Braeside Park, Balloch, Inverness IV1 2HJ, United Kingdom. Poetry, fiction. "Publishers of Gaelic and English fiction, non-fiction and Gaelic-based products. Exists to encourage writers in the Gaelic language. English-language publications sales subsidise Gaelic titles."

CM Publications (see SPORTSWOMAN MAGAZINE)

Coach House Press (see LAOMEDON REVIEW)

Coach House Press (see RUNE)

COASTLINE MAGAZINE, New Horizons Communications Group Press, R. M. Benn, S. L. Berger, Charles Price, P.O. Box 914, Culver City, CA 90230. Poetry, fiction, articles, art, cartoons, interviews, satire, criticism, reviews.

Cobblesmith, Gene H. Boyington, General; Gerald Hausman, Juvenile Poetry, Route One, Ashville, ME 04607, 207-963-7071. "We are a general non-fiction publisher. The thread that runs through all our publications is personal growth & a greater responsibility of each individual for him/herself & for others in the human community. If each of us is personally fulfilled and nearly self-sufficient, each will be able to contribute more of himself to the betterment of the community as a whole." avg. price, cloth: $8.95; paper: $3.95. 1974. 8½ x 11. of/lp (later). avg. press run 4,500. Reporting time: 1 week to 6 months. Copyrights for author. Discounts: on request. Pub'd 4 titles 1976; expects 3 titles 1977, 5 titles 1978. COSMEP.

Cobra Press, G.W. Sherman, 15381 Chelsea Dr, San Jose, CA 95124. "The Cobra Press has printed 4 titles, the most recent is: *Ballad of Twelfth Night.*"

CODA: Poets & Writers Newsletter, Poets & Writers, Inc., Poets & Writers, Inc., 201 West 54th St., New York, NY 10019. Articles, photos, news items. "*CODA* publishes factual articles of interest to writers, editors, publishers, and all others interested in contemporary American literature. Most articles are researched and written by the staff of Poets & Writers Inc., few outside articles are solicited. However, *CODA* welcomes all news our readers might think of interest to the writing community and encourages our readers to send us information. Recent articles have included writers' colonies, taxes and the writer, publishing coops, and copyright information. Regular columns include grants and awards, publishing opportunities, and writers in need of work." 5/yr; 1-yr sub price:

$6.00; per copy: $1.25; sample: $1.50. 1973. 32-36pp; 8½ x 11. of. circ. 6,500. Ads: $320/$175/$100 1/4. Discounts: 2-49 subscriptions, 40 percent: 50 or over, 46 percent: $4.50/yr to authors listed with Poets & Writers. Back issues: $1.50. Pub'd 5 issues 1976; expects 5 issues 1977, 5 issues 1978. §especially technical or practical books. COSMEP.

CODA: Canada's Jazz Magazine, Coda Publications, John Norris, Box 87 Stn. J., Toronto, Ont. M4J4X8, Canada. Photos, interviews, criticism, reviews, music. "Our emphasis is on the art rather than the commerce of the music (i.e. we concentrate on non-commercialism) and we cover jazz of all styles and areas." 10/yr; 1-yr sub price: $10.00 Canada/$11.00 other countries; per copy: $1.50; sample: free. 1958. 40pp; 8¼ x 11¼. of. circ. 3,500. Reporting time: 1 month to 2 years. Payment: none. Ads: $90/$40/$.05 (min.$3). Discounts: agency discount (subscriptions only) 25%. Back issues: $1.50. Pub's reviews. §jazz, blues. CPPA.

COE REVIEW, Fiction & Poetry Workshops at Coe College, 1220 First Ave NE, Cedar Rapids, IA 52402, 319-398-1563. Poetry, fiction, articles, long-poems, satire, reviews, parts-of-novels. "The COE REVIEW is interested in publishing good experimental writings. We believe that brevity is the soul of wit to facilitate the inclusion of more writers' works, though all materials accompanied by an SASE will be considered. Fiction should be held to 10,000 wds.; poems - 40 lines; long poems - 4 pp.; articles - 10 pp.; and sections of plays or reviews - 15 pp or less." 3/yr; sub price: $5.00-4 issues; per copy: $1.50; sample: $.75. 1965. 166pp; 6 x 9. of. circ. 1,500. Reporting time: 2 months. Payment: copies. Temporary-reprinting is allowed; but no simultaneous submissions. Back issues: $0.75 per copy (except Winter '75 issue $1.00). Pub'd 2 issues 1976; expects 2 issues 1977, 3 issues 1978. Pub's reviews: 1 in 1976. §Works of quality.

COEVOLUTION QUARTERLY, Stewart Brand, Box 428, Sausalito, CA 94965, 415-332-1716. Poetry, fiction, articles, art, photos, cartoons, interviews, reviews, parts-of-novels, plays, non-fiction. 4/yr; 1-yr sub price: $8.00; per copy: $2.50. 1974. 144pp; 6 x 9. of. circ. 35,000. Reporting time: 1 month. Ads: We do not accept advertising. Discounts: 50-60 percent to distributors. Back issues: Available at same price. (Issues 5, 6, 7, 9 are out of print.). Pub'd 4 issues 1976; expects 4 issues 1977, 4 issues 1978. Pub's reviews: 100 in 1976. §Soft tech., craft, architecture, sports & travel, educational mat'ls. COSMEP, ABA.

THE COFFEEHOUSE, The Wire Press, Dino Siotis, 392 San Jose Ave, San Francisco, CA 94110. Poetry, fiction, articles, art, photos, music, collages, plays. "Contemporary Greek Arts & Letters" 2/yr; 1-yr sub price: $5.00; per copy: $2.00; sample: $1.20. 1975. 70pp; 7 x 8½. †of. circ. 1,000. Payment: no. Not copyrighted. Ads: $30.00/$18.00. Discounts: 40 percent for bookstores. Back issues: no, two only at $2.00 each. Pub'd 2 issues 1976; expects 2 issues 1977, 2 issues 1978. CCLM.

Cold Mountain Press, Ryan Petty, Editor; Michael Hogan, Associate, 4705 Sinclair Ave, Austin, TX 78756. Poetry, fiction. "We have published poetry post cards (29), broadsheets (7), and pamphlets (by James Tipton, Joseph Bruchac, Michael Delp, Wendell Berry and Michael Hogan). Last Winter Cold Mountain Press published a 90 minute tape cassette of Michael Hogan reading his poetry while incarcerated in the Arizona State Prison at Florence. Soon we will publish our first novel: *The Dreams Of Jesse Bowman* by Joseph Bruchac. Twice a year we issue a catalogue of rare literary items and poetry publications currently available from other small presses. We are open to submissions for collections of poems, essays, letters, interviews, very fine short fiction etc. Small press editors should send for our open letter describing *Cold Mountain* as a distribution outlet. We are currently interested in working out the details involved in the legal relationship between small presses and authors, with a view toward promoting fair play and harmony in the small press community. Late in 1977 we will publish a *Model Contract* proposal which we hope will be both widely used and useful. In the meantime we are interested in hearing from small presses and authors who have experiences or observations in this subject area." 1973. lp. Reporting time: 60 days. Payment: negotiated with the author.

COLLABORATION, Matagiri, Eric Hughes, Matagiri, Mt. Tremper, NY 12457. Poetry, articles, letters. "*COLLABORATION* is devoted to the philosophy of Sri Aurobindo, with extracts from his

73

works and relevant material by others. Also includes news of the city of Auroville and Sri Aurobindo centers around the world." 4/yr; 1-yr sub price: free; per copy: free; sample: free. 1974. 16pp; 8¾ x 11¼. of. circ. 4,800. Back issues: Some available. Pub'd 4 issues 1976; expects 4 issues 1977, 4 issues 1978. COSMEP.

A. COLLECTOR'S ITEM, Padre Productions, A. Robert Connolly, Ms. Shan Wallace, PO Box 1275, San Luis Obispo, CA 93406, 805-543-5404. "Both newsletters are scheduled to begin Jan-Feb, 1977. A. is national and international coverage of collectibles and antiques as an industry, investment, phenomena—an insider's report with much forecasting. B. is regional, covering 13 Western states and all media, but especially books, presses large and small." 12/yr; 1-yr sub price: $18.00; sample: charter issue only, on request. 1977. 8pp; 8½ x 11. circ. 1,500. Reporting time: 10 days—2 weeks. Payment: by arrangement. Copyrighted, reverts on req. Ads: none available. Discounts: Subscription rate for 12 monthly issues, $18.00 each title. Back issues: per year rate. Pub's reviews. COSMEP.

COLLECTORS' NETWORK NEWS, James P. Danky, Acq Sec/State Histrcl Soc, 816 State Street, Madison, WI 53706, 608-262-9584. 6/yr; 1-yr sub price: $6.00; per copy: $1.00; sample: $1.00. 1977. 16pp; 8½ x 11. of. circ. about 50. Payment: none. Not copyrighted. Ads: $50.00. Discounts: none. Pub's reviews. §Underground or alternative papers, right wing materials and anything in between.

COLLEGE ENGLISH, National Council of Teachers of English, Richard Ohmann, Editor; Susan McAllester, Poetry Editor, Wesleyan University, Middletown, CT 06457, 203-347-9411, EX 491. Poetry, articles, cartoons, satire, criticism, reviews. 8/yr; 1-yr sub price: $20.00; per copy: $2.50. 1939. 128pp; 7½ x 9½. of. circ. 12,000. Reporting time: up to 3 mos. Payment: copies only. Copyrighted. Ads: $340/$225. Back issues: $2.50. Pub'd 8 issues 1976; expects 8 issues 1977, 8 issues 1978. Pub's reviews.

College V, UCSC (see QUARRY WEST)

THE COLORADO QUARTERLY, University of Colorado, Walter G. Simon, Editor; Claudine Seever, Managing Editor; Alex Warner, Associate Editor, Hellems 134, University of Colorado, Boulder, CO 80309. Fiction, articles. "Articles and stories 6,000-20,000 words generally; however, we will have a prize issue once a year beginning in 1977 for which longer pieces (40,000 words)—in-depth articles, novellas, etc.—will be considered. We are looking for articles written by professional writers for the intelligent general reader. We prefer stories with plots and well-defined characters." 4/yr; 1-yr sub price: $6.50; per copy: $2.00; sample: free. 1952. 135pp; 6 x 9. of. circ. 700. Reporting time: 4-6 weeks. Payment: $50 minimum for a story or article. Copyrighted. Discounts: 25% for agencies. Back issues: $1.50 per copy prior to spring 1977 & later issues $2.75 per copy. Pub'd 4 issues 1976; expects 4 issues 1977, 4 issues 1978. CCLM.

COLORADO-NORTH REVIEW, David F. Leonard, Editor; George Almon, Advisory Editor, University Center, Greeley, CO 80639, 303-353-4647. Poetry, fiction, articles, art, photos, cartoons, satire, reviews, long-poems, collages, plays. "On written request of author copyright is reassigned." 3/yr; 1-yr sub price: $3.00; per copy: $1.00; sample: $1.00. 1964. 80pp; 5½ x 8½. of. circ. 6,000. Reporting time: two months. Payment: $5.00 per page. Copyrighted, does not revert to author. Ads: $100.00/$50.00/not done. Discounts: none. Back issues: $1.00. Pub's reviews. §literature, poetry, drama, art. COSMEP.

DE COLORES, Pajarito Publications, Jose Armas, 2633 Granite NW, Albuquerque, NM 87104. Poetry, fiction, articles, art, photos, criticism, interviews, satire, criticism, reviews, music, letters, long-poems, collages, plays, concrete art. "We are currently one of two independent quarterlies in the country publishing limited editions of the best in Chicano expression and thought. We publish both known and new Raza talent and have strived to fill a large void publishing art as well as scholarly work which contribute to Chicano-self-awareness and affirmation. Recent contributors: Octavio Paz, Jose Armas, Sylvia Gonzales, Juan Bruce-Novoa, Guadalupe Anguiano." 4/yr; 1-yr sub price: individuals $8.00; institutions $16.00; per copy: $2.25. 1973. 75pp; 9 x 6. of. circ. 500.

Discounts: 30% discount on multiple orders (10 or more). Back issues: $2.25 per issue. Pub's reviews. §Socio/Political, Mexican American Education, Chicano Lit & Poetry. CCLM, COSMEP.

COMBINATIONS, A JOURNAL OF PHOTOGRAPHY, Combinations Press, Mary Ann Lynch, Middle Grove Road, Greenfield Center, NY 12833, 518-584-4612. Poetry, fiction, articles, photos, interviews, criticism, reviews, letters. "Issue I: Jacqueline Livingston, Roger Williams, Ted Orland, Sue Robinson, Merry Moor Winnett, Margaretta Mitchell, Dave Read, Ron Rosenstock (photographs) poetry by Joseph Bruchac, Margaretta Mitchell, (Duane Niatum—issue 2) interview with Clarence John Laughlin by John Messina (issue 2) we accept work during specific times only. $3.00 consideration fee & SASE reqd. Next accepting period, Sept. 15-Oct. 15, 1977." 4/yr; 1-yr sub price: $11.00 overseas-$15.00 (includes postage); per copy: $3.00 overseas-$4.00 (includes postage); sample: $3.00 overseas-$4.00 (includes postage). 1976. 44-48pp; 8 x 10. of. circ. 1,000. Reporting time: 2-4 weeks. Payment: copies. Copyrighted, reverts to author. Ads: $100.00/$50.00. Discounts: discounts to contributors, galleries, bookstores (rates being set). Expects 3 issues 1977, 4 issues 1978. Pub's reviews. §photographic photography/small press publishing in photography. COSMEP.

‡**COME-UNITY, Unity Press,** 13 East 17 St., New York, NY 10003.

Commander Martin Pares (see BACONIANA)

The Commentators Press (see also IMPACT, LITERARY CONTESTS AND AWARDS NEWSLETTER), Gary Lagier, Editor; Judson Jerome, Consulting Editor; Gordon Curzon, Consulting Editor, P.O. Box 61297, Sunnyvale, CA 94088. "The Commentators' Press is the publishing arm of the commentators, a poet group of greater San Francisco Bay area residents (who meet at Stanford University) trying through the poetic mode to provide a chrysalis from which ideas may flutter new-born and possibly strengthen their wings by contact with diverse opinions. We invite poetry, essays, criticism, reviews and line-drawings. We publish the quarterly, IMPACT; the annual anthology, FEEDBACK; and chapbooks. Also do commentapes (taped poetry for radio stations). If you send us a tape or section of one please include a sequential manuscript with it. Prefer open reel to reel tapes, but can handle others if necessary. We sponsor 4 contests per year with prizes ranging from $50.00 for 1st to $10.00 for 5th plus 20 honorable mentions. Founded 1975, pay in copies, report in less than six weeks. All correspondence of any kind without SASE cannot be answered." avg. price, paper: $3.50. 1975. 48-60pp; 5½ x 8½. of. avg. press run 500 plus. Reporting time: Less than 6 weeks. Payment: 10 percent of run. Copyrights for author. Pub'd 1 title 1976; expects 3 titles 1977, 4 titles 1978. CCLM, COSMEP, COSMEP-WEST.

COMMON SENSE, Northern California Alliance, 2811 Mission St., San Francisco, CA 94110. Articles, art, photos, cartoons, interviews, reviews, music, letters. "Newsmonthly-Socialist perspective; non-sectarian, non-rhetorical, news, reviews & analysis-aimed at mass audience, primarily S.F." 12/yr; 1-yr sub price: $5.00; per copy: $.25; sample: donation. 1973. 20pp; 11 x 17½. of. circ. 12,000. Payment: none. Ads: $4.50-col inch. Back issues: donations. Pub's reviews. §history/progressive movements(eg. women, Chicano, Black, Native American, Asian).

Commoners' Publishing (see AUGURIES)

Communication Creativity, Ann Markham, P O Box 17120, San Diego, CA 92117, 714-276-7171. "Communication Creativity Books are designed to be both entertaining and informational. They deal primarily with subjects in the fields of leisure and business." avg. price, cloth: $8.95; paper: $4.95. 1977. 72-144pp; 5½ x 8½. of. avg. press run 5,000. Not soliciting submissions. Payment: Negotiable. Copyrights for author. Discounts: From 20 percent to 52 percent. COSMEP.

The Communications Co. (see ROCK-N-ROLL NEWS)

The Communication Press, Randall Harrison, P O Box 22541, San Francisco, CA 94122, 415-566-3921. Cartoons. "Our focus is on humorous how-to, such as our *How To Cut Your Water Use - and Still Stay Sane and Sanitary*. Primarily we collaborate with content area specialists, e.g.,

Ph.D.s in specific technical areas. Our general concern is with ecologically sound topics. We're probably a poor market for free lancers as we already have as many projects as we can handle for the next few years; and we hope to stay small and quality oriented." avg. price, cloth: $3.95; paper: $1.95. 1977. 64 to 128pp; 4 x 7. of. avg. press run 5,000. Reporting time: 6 to 8 weeks. Payment variable. Copyrights for author. Discounts: 40 percent trade. COSMEP.

Communities (see SERIATIM)

COMMUNITIES, Community Publications Cooperative, Cooperating Editorial Board, Box 426, Louisa, VA 23093, 703-894-5126. Poetry, fiction, articles, art, photos, cartoons, interviews, reviews, letters. "Bias: limited to contributions relating to aspects of cooperative living" 6/yr; 1-yr sub price: $6.00; per copy: $1.25; sample: yes. 1972. 60pp; 8½ x 11. of. circ. 5,000. Reporting time: 2 months. No payment. Copyrighted, reverts to author. Ads: $100.00/$50.00/free. Discounts: trade 30%–50% bulk 55%. Back issues: $1.00, recent issue $1.25. Pub's reviews. §cooperative living; farming; building. COSMEP.

COMMUNITY ACTION, Collective, P.O. Box 665, London SW1X 8DZ, United Kingdom. Articles, news items. 6/yr; 1-yr sub price: £1.50, £2.50 for libraries, etc.; per copy: 25p plus 9p post; sample: 25p plus 9p post. 1972. 40pp; A4. of. circ. 4,750. Ads: No charge for ads but we have strict policy on which ones we do put in. Back issues: reduced rates for various packages. Pub'd 6 issues 1976; expects 6 issues 1977, 6 issues 1978. Pub's reviews.

COMMUNITY SERVICE NEWSLETTER- in serial with: COMMUNITY COMMENTS, Community Service, Inc., Griscom Morgan, Staff, Box 243, Yellow Springs, OH 45387. "The single series includes bi-monthly newsletters, which are replaced in series by occasional Community Comments, which differ in that they each treat of a single subject and are longer than the newsletters, 10-30 pp." 24/yr; 1-yr sub price: $5.00; per copy: $.50/$1.50 for COMMUNITY COMMENTS; sample: free. 1940. 6pp; 8½ x 11. mi/of. circ. 1,200. Back Issues: list for Community Comments indiv. newsletters free on request. Pub's reviews. §community, alternatives in community, society, economy, education, governance, technology, land and land reform.

COMPASS, Sam Bradley, RD 1 Box 584, Honey Brook, PA 19344. "Articles up to 5,000 words; low as 500 words. Style desired is that of the essay, without elaborate footnoting. Subjects must be on current countries being presented-at present, forthcoming issues are on Mexico and Japan." 2/yr; 1-yr sub price: $2.00; per copy: $1.00 current/$2.00 back copies; sample: $1.00. 1971. 56pp; 6 x 9. †lp. circ. 300. Reporting time: 3 months. Payment: none. Ads: not presently taking advertising. Discounts: on application. Back issues: $2.00 each. Pub's reviews. §area studies. COSMEPA.

COMPUTER MUSIC JOURNAL, People's Computer Co., John Snell, 1263 El Camino, P. O. Box E, Menlo Park, CA 94025, 415-323-3111. Articles, reviews, music. "Devoted to development of computer systems capable of high fidelity music." 6/yr; 1-yr sub price: $14.00; per copy: $2.75. 1977. 64pp; 8½ x 11. of. circ. 1,000 per issue. We are just starting-only the first issue is out. Payment: none. Copyrighted, reverts to author. Discounts: discounts to resellers and subscription agencies. Back issues: none yet. Expects 6 issues 1977, 6 issues 1978. Pub's reviews. §computer music, acoustics of musical instruments, music theory, psychoacoustics, computer design, electronics.

Conceptual Non-Press (see ACCEPTANCE)

CONCERNING POETRY, L.L. Lee, Editor; Robert Huff, Poetry Editor, English Department, Western Wash. State College, Bellingham, WA 98225. Poetry, articles, criticism, reviews. "Articles not over about 10-12 type-written, double-spaced pages. Poems rarely longer than two type-written pages." 2/yr; 1-yr sub price: $3.00; per copy: $1.50; sample: $1.50. 1968. 85pp; 9 x 6. of. circ. 400. Reporting time: 2-3 months. Payment: copies only. Copyrighted, reverts to author. Ads: $40/$20. Discounts: none; agents may add 20 percent to our base prices. Back issues: $2.00 per copy. Pub'd 2 issues 1976; expects 2 issues 1977. Pub's reviews: 7 in 1976. §poetry books; books about poetry (criticism). COSMEP.

Conch Magazine Ltd. (Publishers) (see also CONCH and THE CONCH REVIEW OF BOOKS), Dr. S. O. Anozie, General Editor, 102 Normal Avenue, (Symphony Circle), Buffalo, NY 14213, 716-885-3686. Articles, interviews, criticism, non-fiction. "Law, medicine, semiotics, linguistics, sociology, history, children's literature, politics, anthropology, structuralism. Conch Magazine, Ltd. is an indigenous African publisher of scholarly monographs and periodicals. Our editorial interest, reflected in our program of independent series of studies, is to present authentic African viewpoint through an original analysis and interpretation of current and significant issues in Africa." avg. price, cloth: $8.00; paper: $5.00. 1972. 150pp; 6 x 9. of. avg. press run 2M. Reporting time: 30-60 days. Payment: Terms negotiable. Copyrights for author. Discounts: Quantity discounts available upon request. Pub'd 3 titles 1976; expects 5 titles 1977, 6 titles 1978. COSMEP.

CONCH MAGAZINE, Conch Magazine, Ltd., Dr. S.O. Anozie, 102 Normal Avenue, Buffalo, NY 14213, 716-885-3686. Articles, criticism. "Unsolicited articles are not acceptable for publication in the CONCH journal." 2/yr; 1-yr sub price: Ind $9.00, library $12.00, foreign add $2.00. 1969. 100pp; 5½ x 8½. of. circ. 2½M. Payment: copies only. Copyrighted. Ads: General adv. $300.00/$200.00/$0.50; Pub rate $200.00/$150.00. Discounts: details available upon request. Back issues: 50¢ for catalogue. Pub'd 4 issues 1976; expects 2 issues 1977, 2 issues 1978. COSMEP.

CONCH REVIEW OF BOOKS, Conch Magazine, Ltd., Dr. S.O. Anozie, 102 Normal Ave., Buffalo, NY 14213, 716-885-3686. Reviews. "Writers may submit book reviews, film reviews, music reviews for possible publication in CONCH REVIEW OF BOOKS: A Literary Supplement on Africa. We request that authors comply with the MLA style sheet, and that a review do not exceed 1000 words. It is desirable that prospective contributors contact the editor before making a submission." 4/yr; 1-yr sub price: $10.00 (Indiv); $15.00 (Lib); Foreign add $2.00. 1973. 50pp; 6½ x 9½. of. circ. 2M. Reporting time: 30 days. Payment: copies only. Copyrighted. Ads: General adv. $300.00/$200.00/$0.50; Publishers $200.00/$150.00. Discounts: Details available upon request. Back issues: 50¢ for catalogue. Expects 7 issues 1977, 4 issues 1978. Pub's reviews: 100 in 1976. §African studies, incl all areas of books (children's lit, history, literature, etc.). COSMEP.

Concilio Mujeres (see LA RAZON MESTIZA/LA MUJER ES LA TIERRA)

CONDITIONS, Conditions, Elly Bulkin, Jan Clausen, Irena Klepfisz, Rima Shore, PO Box 56, Van Brunt Sta., Brooklyn, NY 11215, 212-857-5351/768-2453. Poetry, fiction, articles, interviews, criticism, reviews, parts-of-novels, long-poems, plays, letters, non-fiction. "*Conditions* is a magazine of women's writing with an emphasis on writing by lesbians." 3/yr; 1-yr sub price: $6.50; per copy: $2.50; sample: $2.50. 1976. 125pp; 5½ x 8½. of. circ. 1,500. Reporting time: up to 2 months. Payment: copies. Copyrighted, reverts to author. Discounts: 40 percent discount on bookstore orders of 5 or more. Expects 3 issues 1977, 3 issues 1978. Pub's reviews. §special bias in favor of women's & lesbian press.

Confluence Press, Inc. (see THE SLACKWATER REVIEW)

LA CONFLUENCIA, Patricia D'Andrea, Susan Dewitt, P.O. Box 409, Albuquerque, NM 87103. Poetry, fiction, articles, art, photos, interviews, reviews, letters, non-fiction. "Query before sending ms. of more than 5,000 words. Prints English, Spanish, S.W. Indian languages. Interviews, teacher's observations, and community case studies." 4/yr; sub price: 4 issues $8.00; per copy: $2.50. 1976. 40pp; 8½ x 11. of. circ. 1,000. Reporting time: 1 month. Copyrighted, reverts to author. Discounts: classroom (teachers, students) $6.00 per volume (4 issues). Pub'd 1 issue 1976; expects 2 issues 1977, 2 issues 1978. Pub's reviews. §southwest...anthropology, history, folklore, teaching. COSMEP.

CONFRONTATION, Martin Tucker, English Dept., Long Island University, Brooklyn, NY 11201. Poetry, fiction, articles, interviews, parts-of-novels, long-poems, plays. 2/yr; 1-yr sub price: $3.50; per copy: $2.00; sample: $1.50. 1968. 160pp; 5 x 9. lp. circ. 2,000. Reporting time: 6 weeks. Payment: $50 stories, $10-25 poetry. Back issues: $2.00. §fiction, poetry. COSMEP.

CONFRONTATION/CHANGE REVIEW, Challenge Press, Frederick M. Finney, 32 College

St., Dayton, OH 45407, 513-275-8637. Poetry, fiction, articles, photos, cartoons, criticism, reviews, parts-of-novels, plays, news items, non-fiction. "Articles preferred on social and applied economics with Black and Third World prespective; Black fiction and poetry in high demand (looking for new Black writers — The New Baraka's); book reviews on economics, Black history and economics; fiction — 500 to 10,000 words. Recent contributors Baruti Nkrumah, Mary Browning Johnson, Archibald Henderson, Neil Setoule, George Yeargon, and R. M. Vera." 4/yr; 1-yr sub price: $10.00; per copy: $3.00; sample: $2.00 1976. 80-126pp; 8½ x 11. of. circ. 1,000. Reporting time: 2-4 weeks. Payment: contributors copies, one year subscription (first contributor), cash payments on occassion ($10-$200.00). Copyrighted. Ads: $250.00/$100.00. Discounts: trade 40 percent; classrooms and libraries 50 percent. Back issues: $2.00. Pub'd 2 issues 1976; expects 4 issues 1977, 4 issues 1978. Pub's reviews: 9 in 1976. §social & applied economics, Black history, literature, fiction & poetry. COSMEP.

CONNECTICUT FIRESIDE, Fireside Press, Albert Callan, P.O. Box 5293, Hamden, CT 06518. Poetry, fiction, articles, art, photos, cartoons, satire, criticism, reviews, letters, parts-of-novels. "Fireside is becoming more literary and less general. We will have more fiction and fewer articles. Prefer articles on literary subjects, as piece on HP Lovecraft and Raymond Chandler piece in Fireside #6." 4/yr; sub price: 4 issues-$4.00/6 issues-$6.00; per copy: $1.00; sample: $1.00. 1972. 80pp; 7 x 9½. †of. circ. 500. Reporting time: 2 weeks. Payment: copies. Ads: none. Discounts: none. Back issues: cover price when available. Pub's reviews. §literary, politics, esoteric. CCLM, COSMEP.

Conococheague Associates, Inc. (see ANIMA)

CONQUEST, Robert Hertz, 318 Summit Ave., St. Paul, MN 55102. "This is a radically reactionary newsletter. We are pro-slavery, pro-vengeance, pro-cannibalism. Sample articles: Cruelty and Evolution, Manson and the future of Satanism. Articles should be no more than 1,000 words on these themes. Inquiries are welcome." 8/yr; 1-yr sub price: $1.75; per copy: $.25; sample: free. 1975. 4pp; 8 x 11. of. circ. 100. Reporting time: 2 wks. Payment: copies only. Ads: none. Discounts: none. Back issues: 25¢ each.

CONRADIANA, Texas Tech Press, David Leon Higdon, Dept. of English, Box 4530, Texas Tech University, Lubbock, TX 79409. Articles, photos, interviews, criticism, reviews. 3/yr; 1-yr sub price: $7.50; per copy: $2.50; sample: $2.00. 1968. 95pp; 6 x 9. †lp. circ. 800. Reporting time: 50 days. Payment: 15 offprints. Copyrighted. Ads: $100.00/$50.00. Discounts: None. Back issues: Available. Pub'd 3 issues 1976; expects 3 issues 1977, 3 issues 1978. Pub's reviews: 6 in 1976. §books related to Joseph Conrad. CCLM, COSMEP.

CONSTRUCTIVE ACTION FOR GOOD HEALTH, The American Conference of Therapeutic Selfhelp/Selfhealth/Social Clubs (ACT), Sr. Shirley Burghard, R.N., A.A.S., B.A., O.S.L., O.O.H., B 1104 Ross Towers, 710 Lodi St., Syracuse, NY 13203, 315-471-4644. "We prefer material that shows people how they can help themselves to new and better lives via the use of selfhelp poetry therapy, selfhelp art therapy, selfhelp creative writing therapy, selfhelp pet therapy, selfhelp horticulture therapy, selfhealth natural food recipe therapy, selfhealth supplemental vitamin and mineral therapy etc. We are primarily constructive in nature, but we are against the therapeutic state, the new gods known as psychiatrists, the great mental illness-mental health rip off of the psychoquackiatrists, the psychofrauds and the mental health racketeers. We are against state mental institutions because of the abuse, assaults, atrocities committed in them by the staff against the patient. We believe not only in the right to treatment but the right to refuse treatment when it consists of brain cell destroying electric convulsive shock treatment and over tranquilization to a zombie state and brain surgery." 6/yr; 1-yr sub price: $5.00; per copy: $.50; sample: $0.50 plus $0.25 postage. 1960. 26pp; 8½ x 11. †mi. circ. 500. Reporting time: about 3 weeks. Payment: copy. Not copyrighted. Ads: $1.00 and up for classified ads: $5.00 and up for businesses and industries. Discounts: none. Back issues: $0.50 each plus $0.25 postage. Pub'd 12 issues 1976; expects 6 issues 1977, 6 issues 1978. Pub's reviews: 2 in 1976. §Selfhelp/Selfhealth or the fucking over of little people by the big psychiatric profession. COSMEP, North American Conference on Human Rights and Psychiatric Oppressions.

CONTACT/11: A Bimonthly Poetry Review Magazine, Contact/11 Publications, Maurice Kenny, J. G. Fosciak, 11 Broadway, New York, NY 10004, 212-425-5979. Poetry, articles, art, photos, cartoons, interviews, satire, criticism, reviews, letters, news items, non-fiction. "*CONTACT/11: A Bimonthly Poetry Review* gives voice in magazine format to poetry and poets regardless of region, school, or subject matter. We try to be as open-minded and fair as humanly possible with all comers. We try to limit material (other than poems) to a 2-page spread. Poems are poems and we do not edit. We are always interested in reviews, criticism, articles on poetry. Recent contributors include: Barbara A. Holland, Rochelle Rattner, Patricia Wilcox, Phyllis Holliday, Lyn Lifshin, Siv Cedering Fox, Richard Longchamps, John Brandi, Kirby Congdon, James Purdy, Duane Niatum, Wendy Rose, Theodore Enslin, Keith Wilson, Joseph Bruchac, Joe Johnson, William Packard, Robert Peters, Norman Russell, Tom Montag, George Hitchcock, Mei-Mei Berssenbrugge, Morgan Gibson, John Yau, Miguel Algarin, Carol Lee Sanchez." 6/yr; 1-yr sub price: $5.00; per copy: $0.75; sample: $0.75. 1976. 32pp; 8½ x 11. †of. circ. 750-1,000. Reporting time: 6 weeks. Payment: in copies. Ads: $100.00/$50.00/$0.25. Back issues: $1.50 each where available. Pub'd 1 issue 1976; expects 6 issues 1977, 6 issues 1978. Pub's reviews: 6 in 1976. §poets/poetry/works by or about poets.

CONTEMPA, PO Box 115, Armadale, Victoria 3143, Australia.

‡**CONTEMPORA,** PO Box 673, Atlanta, GA 30301.

CONTEMPORARY ART/SOUTHEAST, Contemporary Art/Southeast, Inc., Julia Ann Fenton, Editor, PO Box 7873, Station C, Atlanta, GA 30357. Articles, art, photos, interviews, criticism, reviews, letters. "First issue was published in April/May 1977. The magazine is concerned with the visual arts, from the traditional media through more experimental art forms. It's to have a regional focus & will deal with issues & problems in the total visual art system, using the Southeastern U.S. as a model for examining those problems. We will encourage the development of substantive critical writing on the visual arts and provide a medium for the exchange of information in the arts." 6/yr; 1-yr sub price: Individual $9.00-yr; Institutional $12.00-yr; per copy: $2.00. 1976. 64pp; 8½ x 11. of. circ. 10,000. Reporting time: 2 months. Payment: none yet. Ads: $300.00/$165.00. Expects 6 issues 1977, 6 issues 1978. Pub's reviews: none in 1976. §visual arts (including video & experimental film, performance art), art & culture.

CONTEMPORARY KEYBOARD MAGAZINE, Keyboard Players International, Tom Darter, Box 907 (12333 Saratoga-Sunnyvale Rd.), Saratoga, CA 95070. Articles, photos, interviews. "Length: 6-12 pages, doublespaced typescript. *CK* publishes articles on a wide variety of topics pertaining to keyboard players and their instruments (acoustic and electric piano, harpsichord, organ, synthesizer, accordion, etc.) In addition to interviews with keyboard artists in all styles of music, we are interested in historical and analytical pieces, how-to articles dealing either with music or with equipment, profiles of well-known instrument makers and their products—in general, anything that amateur and professional keyboardists would find interesting and/or useful. *CK* is a music magazine, not a pop culture magazine. Interviews with artists include as much information as possible about the equipment they use, their instrumental technique, and the influences that have shaped their musical style. Please include a self-addressed, stamped envelope with all unsolicited manuscripts." 24/yr; sub price: $6.00 for 6 issues/$11.00 for 12 issues; per copy: $1.00; sample: free. 1975. 52pp; 8-3/8 x 10¾. of. circ. 50,000. Reporting time: one week. Payment: $50-$100. Ads: $800/$570. Back issues: 1st issue-$2.00; 2nd issue-$1.50; all others-$1.25. Pub's reviews. §music—keyboard related.

THE CONTEMPORARY LITERARY SCENE, Salem Press, Inc., Frank Magill, Walton Beacham, Dept. of English, Va. Commonwealth Univ., Richmond, VA 23284. 1/yr; price per copy: $8.95. 1973. 300pp. Reporting time: 1 month. Payment: $1.00 per article.

CONTEMPORARY LITERATURE, University of Wisconsin Press, L.S. Dembo, 7141 Helen C. White Hall, University of Wisconsin, Madison, WI 53706. "Scholarly literary criticism" 4/yr; 1-yr sub price: individuals $10.00/yr; institutions $20.00; per copy: varies. 1960. 136pp; 6 x 9. of. circ. 2,000 plus. Payment: none. Ads: $150/$80. Discounts: 5% subscription agency. Back issues: write for details. Pub's reviews.

CONTEMPORARY LITERATURE IN TRANSLATION, Andreas P. Schroeder, PO Box 3127, Mission City, BC V2V4J3, Canada. Poetry, fiction, photos, parts-of-novels, long-poems, plays. "Accept for consideration contemporary literature from any language translated into English, New translations of classics sometimes considered as well. All submissions must contain short biographical notes on both original author and translator." 3/yr; 1-yr sub price: $6.50; per copy: $2.50. 1967. 45pp; 8½ x 11. lp. circ. 5M. Reporting time: 2 mos. Payment: copies only. Ads: $75 page/$40 1/2. Discounts: 35% for orders over 20. COSMEP.

CONTEMPORARY POETS, Gloria Bromberg, 100 Sullivan St., New York, NY 10012. Poetry. "Poetry submissions only. We are devoted to publishing quality work only by new upcoming poets, known and unknown. No biases on style, or length. 1st issue Nov. 1975 will feature Joan Babbage, Beverly Lesch, Peter Wortsman." 1-yr sub price: $5.00; per copy: $1.00; sample: $1.00. 1975. 25pp; 5½ x 8½. of. circ. 250. Reporting time: 1 month. Payment: copies only. no ads.

CONTEMPORARY POETS, JOURNAL OF, Eileen Reed, Box 444, Brentwood, NY 11717. Poetry. "1-3 poems, 3-16 lines, & return envelope, Sincere, Sensitive poetry. No smut." 40yr; avg. price, cloth: $11.00; paper: $7.00; other: $3.95. 1973. 40pp; 8½ x 5½. †of. avg. press run 3,000. Reporting time: 2-4 weeks. Payment: 60¢ a poem. Ads: none. Back issues: $3.95 paperback-$9.95 hardcover. §poetry.

CONTRABAND MAGAZINE, Contraband Press, Kilgore, Holsapple, Empfield, P.O. Box 4073, Sta. A, Portland, ME 04101. Poetry, fiction, articles, art, photos, cartoons, interviews, satire, criticism, reviews, music, letters, parts-of-novels, long-poems, collages, plays, concrete art, news items, non-fiction. "Experimental" 2/yr/yr; 1-yr sub price: $2.00; per copy: $.50; sample: free. 1971. 60pp; 7 x 8½. of. circ. 500. Reporting time: 3 weeks. Payment: 2 copies. Copyrighted, reverts to author on publication. Ads: none. Discounts: 40%. Pub'd 2 issues 1976; expects 1 issue 1977, 2 issues 1978. Pub's reviews: 2 in 1976. §Any area. CCLM, MWPA.

Contraband Press (see also CONTRABAND MAGAZINE), Kilgore, Holsapple, Empfield, P.O. Box 4073, Sta A, Portland, ME 04101. Poetry, fiction, long-poems, plays, non-fiction. avg. price, paper: $1.50. 1971. 80pp; 5½ x 8. †lp. avg. press run 500. Reporting time: 2 months. Payment: 100 copies. Copyright not library of congress. Discounts: 40 percent. Pub'd 5 titles 1976; expects 2 titles 1977, 2 titles 1978.

CONTRACULTURA, David Grinberg, C C Central 1332, Buenos Aires 1000, Argentina. Articles. 2/yr; price per copy: $1.00. 1970. 16pp; 13 cm x 18 cm. lp. circ. 2,000. no ads. Back issues: Free. Expects 2 issues 1977, 2 issues 1978. Pub's reviews. §Counterculture. APS.

CONTRIBUTORS BULLETIN (also FREELANCE WRITING), Freelance Press Services, Arthur Waite, FREELANCE WRITING; S.E. Williams, CONTRIBUTORS BULLETIN, Forestry Chambers, 67 Bridge Street, Manchester M3 3BQ, United Kingdom. Articles. 4/yr (FLW) 12/yr (CB); 1-yr sub price: £1.50 FLW - £5.85 CB; per copy: 50p. 1962. 12 pp CB, 28 pp FLW; 13 x 8. †of. circ. CB 800, FLW 2,500. Reporting time: 1 week. Payment: £4.00 per 1,000. Ads: 5p word.

‡**Cookie Press,** 4225 University, Des Moines, IA 50311.

Copley Books, 7776 Ivanhoe Avenue, P O Box 957, La Jolla, CA 92038, 714-454-1842. "We want submissions *only* in our publishing area. We publish no poetry, childrens stories, or non-fiction. Specialty authentic (non-fictional) history of California, the Southwest, and Mexico." avg. price, cloth: $12.50; paper: $6.50. 200-300pp; 8½ x 11. avg. press run 3,000. Payment: As arranged. Copyright per arrangement with author. Discounts: Booksellers 40 percent; libraries 25 percent.

Copper Beech Press, Edwin Honig, Box 1852 Brown Univ., Providence, RI 02912, 401-863-2393. Poetry, fiction, long-poems. avg. price, paper: $2.50 - $7.50. 1973. Poetry 40-75, fiction 150-275.pp; Varies. of. avg. press run Varies between 350 and 1,000. Reporting time: ASAP, usually within 3 months. Payment: copies. Does not copyright for author. Discounts: 1-5 20 percent, 6 33 percent.

Copper Canyon Press/Copperhead, Sam Hamill, Tree Swenson, P.O. Box 271, Port Townsend, WA 98368. Poetry, long-poems. "We publish full-length books of poems and chapbooks. We are interested especially in 'first' books by younger poets. We do not want mss from writers who have not studied the *Ta Hsio.* No SASE, no reply. Suggest poets query with a few extracted poems from the mss. Recent poets include: W.M. Ransom, Robert Hedin, James Masao Mitsue, McCord, Bertolino, Richard Hugo, Primus St. John, Gladys Cardiff, Nancy Steele, Cheryl Van Dyke." 1973. 64pp; varies (6x10). †of/lp. Reporting time: 1 month. Payment: 10% of edition. Discounts: standard 40 percent, returnable; 50 percent on standing orders and more than 10 copies combined. Also distributed by Bookpeople.

THE COPPER COUNTRY ANTHEM, The Book Concern, Don Kilpela, Publisher; Brenda Rubens, Editor, Box 330, Hancock, MI 49930, 906-482-1250. Poetry, fiction, articles, art, photos, cartoons, interviews, letters. "We solicit articles, poetry, fiction, and art work relating to Michigan's Upper Peninsula and the Copper Country. We are also interested in other areas of the country similar to our own in arts, crafts, sports, and other interests. We are interested in winter sports, especially hockey; outdoor activities such as sailing, camping, and hiking; and human interest stories." 12/yr; 1-yr sub price: $12.00; per copy: $1.00; sample: $1.00. 1976. 50pp; 8½ x 11. †of. circ. not determined yet. Reporting time: 2-4 weeks. Payment: up to $50.00 depending on material. Copyrighted. Ads: $200.00/$100.00. Back issues: $1.00. Pub's reviews. §vacation areas, hiking, camping, fishing, winter sports, winter camping, ice fishing, copper mining lore, ecology, artisans, crafts and craftsmen.

COPY CORNUCOPIA, The Direct Marketing Writers Guild, Andi Emerson, Herb Ahrend, 516 Fifth Avenue, New York, NY 10016. Poetry, fiction, articles, cartoons, interviews, criticism, reviews, letters. "The Guild is the only nonprofit group devoted to the interests of direct response copywriters (freelance and employed by others). Mostly staff written because we can't find enough good material on effective writing (the major thrust of the newsletter)." monthly; 1-yr sub price: $18.00. 1964. 8pp; 8½ x 11. of. circ. 600 paid. Reporting time: 2 weeks. Payment: none. Ads: $20.00. Discounts: none. Pub's reviews. §Techniques of effective writing, especially as to direct response copywriting.

COQUI QUARTERLY, Cibola Studio, E. W. Northnagel, P O Box E, Carolina, PR 00630, 809-726-8382. Poetry, articles, art, photos, interviews, satire, criticism, reviews, letters, collages. "An individual review concerned with man's culture and environment. Thus, heavy interest in anthropology, geography, belle letres, arts and crafts, ethnology, ecology, natural history, travel. Prefer imagistic poetry. Artwork should be black & white; calligraphy liked. Will consider any material but *COQUI* will not be *singing* about terrorism, racism, gay lib, drug addiction, fire & brimstone; still, any well-written material will be seriously considered. Garden verses, having affairs 'afar' with a 'star,' are *not* wanted. Defeatism is *not* wanted. Please send SASE with all submissions. Biographical (rather, autobiographical) notes sought. NOTE: Puerto Rico is a Commonwealth of the U.S. and has the same postage, currency, and citizenship." 4/yr; 1-yr sub price: $4.50; per copy: $1.25; sample: $1.25. 1977. 40pp; 6 x 9. of. circ. (starting) 500. Reporting time: 1 week (unless traveling). Payment: Contributors copies plus $1.00 or (hopefully) more per page, acceptance. Copyrighted, reverts to author. Ads: $0.10. Discounts: Libraries, schools, booksellers—40 percent. Pub's reviews. §Poetry, art & photography, ethnology, natural history, anthropology, travel.

‡**Corinth Books Inc.,** 228 Everit St., New Haven, CT 06511.

‡**CORMORAN Y DELFIN,** 1805 1-5 Olivos, Buenos Aires, Argentina.

Cornerstone Press (see also IMAGE MAGAZINE), Anthony J. Summers, James A. Fredericks, Peter Carlos, P.O. Box 28048, St. Louis, MO 63119, 314-225-3892. Poetry, fiction, art, cartoons, plays. "We have published 4 books to date. One by George Buggs, one by Michael Castro, Al Montesi and Peter Carlos. We are looking for works of art no matter how they are produced. Submit only things that will stand on their own. For '77 we have 3-5 books planned or already in the works." avg. price, cloth: $4-5.00; paper: $1.00 - $3.00. 1974. 48-72pp; 5 x 11. of. avg. press run 500-600. Reporting time: 2 weeks to 6 months. Payment: money and copies to be arranged. Copyrights for author. Discounts: one free copy to any prison requesting.

Corporate Press (see PARACHUTIST)

COSMEP NEWSLETTER, Richard Morris, PO Box 703, San Francisco, CA 94101. "Published for COSMEP members. Membership is $20 per year. Library subscription rates on request."

Cosmic Brain Trust (see COSMIC CIRCUS)

COSMIC CIRCUS, Cosmic Brain Trust, Rey King, 521 33rd St., Oakland, CA 94609, 415-658-0203. Poetry, fiction, articles, art, photos, criticism, interviews, satire, reviews, collages, plays. "We publish as follows: 50 percent underground comix, 25 percent short stories, 10 percent poetry, 10 percent photos. This publication presents material which may be considered strange or 'beyond human comprehension.' (Example-all copies of issue No. 1 are signed on the back with the editor's blood). Subscription includes membership. Submissions by members are given primary consideration but others are welcomed to try. Also available are hour long tapes for the blind or those who may wish to indulge audio mind food." 2-3/yr; 1-yr sub price: $5.00; per copy: $2.00; sample: $2.00. 1972. 40pp; 8½ x 10. †of. circ. 1M. Reporting time: 1 month to 6 weeks. Payment: in books. Ads: $25/$15/$.15. Back issues: $2.50 issue 1-20$2.00 issue 3-4. Pub'd 1 issue 1976; expects 2 issues 1977, 4 issues 1978. Pub's reviews. §Occult, comics, science fiction, film, poetry, bisexuality. CCLM.

COSMOPOLITAN CONTACT, Pantheon Press, Romulus Rexner, P. O. Box 1566, Fontana, CA 92335. Articles, cartoons, interviews, criticism, reviews, letters. "COSMOPOLITAN CONTACT-A polygot magazine promotes intercultural understanding & intellectual growth as means toward the reduction of intergroup and international tension and conflict. Worldwide, friendly exchange of letters, hobbies, gifts, ideas, hospitality, information and other mutual travel or trade assistance among members. As a result of listings in this directory, in Writers' Markets, etc. more and better literary material is being contributed and more space will be allocated to literary material relevant to the philosophy and objectives of planetary legion for peace (P.L.P.) and planetary universalism." 2-3/yr; 1-yr sub price: $2.00; per copy: $1.00. 1962. 32pp; 6 x 9. of. circ. 1,500. Reporting time: 2 wks. Payment: copies only. Ads: $3.00 per inch/$0.10. Back issues: $1.00. Pub'd 2 issues 1976; expects 2-3 issues 1977, 2-3 issues 1978. §Public affairs.

Coteau Books, Bob Currie, Gary Hyland, Geoff Ursell, Barbra Ursell, 1188 Duffield Cr., Moose Jaw, Saskatchewan S6H5M4, Canada, 692-8540. Poetry, fiction, long-poems, plays. "We publish material by Saskatchewan writers only, although distribution is Canada wide." avg. price, paper: $3.00. 1975. 55pp; 6 x 9. avg. press run 1,000. Reporting time: 3-4 weeks. Payment: 10 free copies and 10 percent of all sales. Copyrights for author. Discounts: 15 percent for all. Pub'd 2 titles 1976; expects 3 titles 1977. Literary Press Group (Canada).

COTTONWOOD REVIEW, Cottonwood Review, Mike Smetzer, Box J, Kansas Union, Univ. of Kansas, Lawrence, KS 66045. Poetry, fiction, art, photos, interviews. "We publish a wide variety of styles but tend not to accept academic writing, workshop produce, or rhymed couplets. We generally prefer work that comes from experience. We are particularly interested in work from or about the 'Kansas midwest'. Poetry submissions should be limited to the five best, as a rule, we are interested in translations of contemporary writers not available in the commercial press. Past issues have included interviews with Ginsberg, Creeley, William Gass, William Stafford and Robert Kelly. We've had recent work by Danny Rendleman, Victor Contoski, Jonathan Katz, and Mark Rudman. We also publish a tabloid, *Open House,* intended in part as a proving ground for local work, in part as an outlet for less dignified forms of creativity, in part as a source of local news, and generally for fun." 2/yr; 1-yr sub price: $4.25; per copy: $1.90; sample: $1.00. 1965. 80pp; 8½ x 11. of. circ. 800. Reporting time: 2 mos. Payment: copies. Copyrighted. no ads. Discounts: 40% trade disc., bulk negotiable. Back issues: $2.00. Pub'd 1 issue 1976; expects 2 issues 1977, 2 issues 1978. Pub's reviews: 8 in 1976. §Kansas Midwest. CCLM, COSMEP.

COUNCIL ON INTERRACIAL BOOKS FOR CHILDREN BULLETIN, Bradford Chambers,

1841 Broadway, New York, NY 10023, 212-757-5339. Articles, art, photos, cartoons, reviews. 8/yr; 1-yr sub price: Indiv. $10.00, Instit. $15.00; per copy: $1.35. 1967. 24pp; 8½ x 11. of. circ. 10,000. Copyrighted, does not revert to author. Back issues: $0.75. Pub's reviews. §Children's books 1-10 yrs. Educational-Racism/Sexism. Third World Children's Books. COSMEP, LPS.

COUNTERSPY, Fifth Estate Publishing Company, Julie Brooks, Winslow Peck, Ellen Ray, 647 Ben Franklin Station, Washington, DC 20044, 202-466-3424. Articles, art, photos, cartoons, interviews, satire, criticism, reviews, letters. "Material ususally 10-15 pp. typed, double space. Anti-CIA humanitarian, socialist, anti-fascist. Recent contributers: Philip Agee, Robert Friedman, Philip Wheaton, Tony Rasso, William Turner, Sid Lens" 6/yr; 1-yr sub price: $10.00; per copy: $1.75; sample: $2.00. 1973. 65pp; 7 x 9½. of. Reporting time: 3 weeks to 3 months. Copyrighted. Ads: $250.00/$150.00/$0.35. Discounts: for advertising there's a 15 percent cash disc., distributers discounts vary, bookstores on consignment. Back issues: $2.00/copy. Pub's reviews. §Repression, US Foreign Policy, CIA, FBI, Right Wing. COSMEP.

COUNTRY-SIDE, British Naturalists' Assoc. (Publishers), Anthony Wootton, 40 Roundhill, Stone, Nr. Aylesbury, Bucks HP17 8RD, United Kingdom. Articles, reviews, news items, letters, photos. "Length varies. Factual, original material, preferably based on first-hand observation. Contributors: Academics, professionals & amateur nature lovers. No material on blood sports, except as condemnation of same. Natural history generally (mainly British) ecology, conservation. B.N.A. has 20+ branches in different parts of England." 3/yr; 1-yr sub price: £1.50; per copy: 60p; sample: 25p. 1905. 52pp; 14 x 22cm. lp. circ. 2,500. Reporting time: varies. No payment. Copyright for author/British Naturalists Association. Ads: £12/£6.50/£3.50 1/4/2p wd prepaid advertisements (unclassified). Discounts: 10% publishers, 15% adv. agencies. Back issues: 25p. Pub'd 3 issues 1976; expects 3 issues 1977, 3 issues 1978. Pub's reviews: 150 plus in 1976. §natural history (animals, plants, ecology, conservation, geology etc. etc.).

COUNTRY WOMEN, Country Women Press, Operated Collectively, P.O. Box 208, Albion, CA 95410. Poetry, articles, art, photos, interviews, reviews. "Material should be from 1,000-6,000 words. We are interested in practical how-to articles about country skills and personal experience articles by feminist women. Each issue is half practical articles (gardening, animal care, tools, etc.) and half theme (e.g. relationships, sexuality, women working)." 5/yr; sub price: $4.00 - 5 issues; per copy: $1.25; sample: $1.00. 1972. 64pp; 8½ x 11. of. circ. 10,000. Reporting time: 2 months. Payment: copies. Copyrighted, reverts to author. Ads: none. Discounts: trade 20-50% depending on order size: books-40%. Back issues: prior to Oct. 1975-75¢. Pub'd 4 issues 1976; expects 5 issues 1977, 1 issue 1978. Pub's reviews: 13 in 1976. §material by, for, or about women. COSMEP.

THE COUNTRYMAN, Crispin Gill, Sheep Street, Burford, Oxford OX8 4LH, United Kingdom, Burford 2258. Articles, poetry, art, cartoons, photos, reviews. "1,500 words max. Concern with country life of all kinds, but no Townie sentimentalising." 4/yr; 1-yr sub price: £7.50; per copy: 50p. 1927. 224pp; 125 x 182. of. circ. 70,000. Reporting time: 1-2 wks. Payment: £12 a 1,000 words. Full copyright kept by magazine. Ads: £126-£155/£65/17p. Pub'd 4 issues 1976; expects 4 issues 1977, 4 issues 1978. Pub's reviews. §Country life.

‡**Countryman Press,** Taftsville, VT 05073.

COUNTRYSIDE, Countryside Publications Ltd., Jerome D. Belanger, Route One, Waterloo, WI 53594. Articles, art, photos, cartoons, interviews. "Freelance articles should be typed, double-spaced, approx. 2400 words; especially interested in articles on organic farming methods and success stories; have a livestock/small farm focus (homesteading); interested in craft articles and methods of home food production, preservation and storage and alternative sources of energy; have a workshop section for carpentry and equipment features. Articles should reflect factual reasons for methods prescribed and authors expertise—conversational style preferred." 12/yr; 1-yr sub price: $9.00 ($10 Canada); per copy: $1.00; sample: $1.00. 1917. 64pp; 8¼ x 10-7/8. of. circ. 30,000. Reporting time: 6-8 wks. Payment: $25 articles/$2.50-$10 artwork/$35 color covers. Back issues: all back issues are $1. Pub's reviews. §agriculture, conservation, alternative energy, ecology. COSMEP.

Court Street Chap-Book Series, C.S. Giscombe, S. Sommer, 114 West Court Street, Ithaca, NY 14850, 607-273-0509. Poetry, fiction, long-poems. "Prefer manuscripts under 30pp., though exceptions will be made for extraordinary material. Biased against work that is self-consciously cerebral, verbose, or precious." avg. price, cloth: varies. 1976. 20—30pp; varies. of/lp. avg. press run 500. Reporting time: 1 month. Payment: copies; royalties after break-even. Copyrights for author. Discounts: varies. COSMEP.

CP Graham Press, C.P. Graham, Box 5, Keswick, VA 22947. Poetry, photos, reviews, music, letters, long-poems, collages, concrete art. 1974. 100pp. of.

CQ, CONTEMPORARY QUARTERLY: POETRY AND ART, L/A House, Kenneth John Atchity, Box 41110, Los Angeles, CA 90041, 213-254-4455. Poetry, art, photos, cartoons, long-poems, collages, concrete art. "Long & short poems, single criterion is excellence. Submit only to one of the contributing editors listed in CQ. Recent contributors include Amiri Baraka, Gerald Locklin, Mark McCloskey, Marcus J. Grapes, Sam Eisenstein, Joyce Odam, Howard Stern (ed.), Ben Pleasants (ed.), Howard Lachtman (ed.)." 4/yr; 1-yr sub price: $7.00US-$9.00; per copy: $2.00; sample: $2.00. 1976. 72pp; 5½ x 8½. of. circ. 1,000. Reporting time: 3 months. Payment: 1 contributor's copy per poem or artwork. Copyrighted, reverts to author. Discounts: 40 percent discount to bookstores on consignment, 50 percent for outright sale. Back issues: cover price-$2.00. Pub'd 4 issues 1976; expects 4 issues 1977, 4 issues 1978. CCLM, COSMEP-WEST.

CRAWL OUT YOUR WINDOW, Crawl Out Your Window Press, Paul Dresman, Melvyn Freilicher, Rex Pickett, 704 Nob Ave, Del Mar, CA 92014, 714-755-1258. Fiction, art, photos, music, parts-of-novels, long-poems, collages. "Try to give 10 pages to all contributors." l/yr; price per copy: $2.00. 1975. 105pp; 8½ x 11. of. circ. 350-500. Payment: Several issues of magazine. Copyrighted, reverts to author. §New fiction, visual art. COSMEP.

Crawl Out Your Window Press (see also CRAWL OUT YOUR WINDOW), Melvyn Freilicher, Paul Dresman, 704 Nob Ave, Del Mar, CA 92014, 714-755-1258. Fiction, art, photos, parts-of-novels, long-poems, collages. "Mostly interested in California avant-garde art. Intermedia and collaborative works especially." 1975. Varies widely. of. avg. press run 350-500.

CRCS Publications, Stephen Arroyo, 111 G Street, Suite 29, Davis, CA 95616, 916-756-5074. Art. "We are specializing in the production of high-quality, aesthetically-pleasing astrological books, with a psychological and spiritual slant. Art should be book length mss." avg. price, paper: $4.95 - $6.95. 1975. 200 pluspp; Varies. of. avg. press run 5,000. Reporting time: 4 weeks. Payment: Royalties plus large discounts on books. Copyrights for author. Discounts: 40 percent off on orders of 5 or more books to dealers; 40 percent off on all pre-paid orders from dealers, in any quantity; 10 percent disc. to libraries if requested. Pub'd 1 title 1976; expects 2 titles 1977, 3 titles 1978. COSMEP.

CREACION, Asociacion Poncena Pro Arte Y Cultura (APPAC), Cirilo Toro-Vargas, Hector J. Martell-Morales, Box 111, Estacion 6-UCPR, Ponce, PR 00731. Poetry, fiction, articles, art, photos, cartoons, interviews, criticism, reviews, letters. "Objectives: (1) to establish a link of communication; mutual understanding and acceptance between creators and the people. (2) to work towards the individual and collective improvement of the creators by means of the *APPAC*. (3) to help cultural workers (both graphic and literary) be known, especially those who remain anonymous because no help is given to them. Printed in Spanish, but works in other languages may be submitted." 4/yr; 1-yr sub price: $4.00 (P.R. and U.S.; $7.00 other countries); per copy: $0.60 (plus $0.35 mail charges in P.R. and U.S.; other countries add up the proper mail charges). 1975. 32pp; 4 x 7. of. circ. 1,000. Reporting time: One to three months, depending on our time available since we manage to work on the magazine on our leisure time. Payment: in copies. Copyrighted, copyright reverts to author upon publication. Ads: $100.00/$50.00. Discounts: 20 percent for trade. Back issues: same as single copy price. Pub'd 2 issues 1976; expects 4 issues 1977, 4 issues 1978. Pub's reviews. §art and literature (especially from and about Latin America). CCLM.

Creative Arts Book Company, Don Ellis, Barry Gifford, 833 Bancroft Way, Berkeley, CA 94710,

415-848-4777. Fiction, articles, art, photos, interviews, criticism, letters, non-fiction. "We publish mainly non-fiction material, but remain open to anything. Recent and forthcoming works include: *Heart Beat, My Life With Jack* [Kerovac] & *Neal* [Cassady] by Carolyn Cassady; *Selected Writings Of Edward S. Curtis/The Portable Curtis,* edited by Barry Gifford; *The Collected Correspondence Of Allen Ginsberg & Neal Cassady; The Autobiography Of An American Communist* by Peggy Dennis; and *The Creation Of The Sun & The Moon* by B. Traven." avg. price, cloth: $12.95; paper: $4.00. 1976. pp varies; 5½ x 8½. †of. avg. press run varies: 1,500 to 10,000. Reporting time: 1 week to 3 months. Payment varies. Copyrights for author. Discounts: Single copies no discount. 2-4, 10 percent; 5-9, 30 percent; 10 or more 40 percent. Distrib. to the trade by bookpeople; RPM, The Distributors, The Whirlwind Book Company and McBride & Broadley (UK & Europe). Pub'd 6 titles 1976; expects 6 titles 1977, 6 titles 1978.

Creative Book Company, Sol H. Marshal, PO Box 21-4998, Sacramento, CA 95821, 916-489-4390. Articles. "Our general fields are those of community organization and education. Leasership for individuals in those fields. Agency and school development and promotion. Public relations for those fields. Personal and professional development for people in those fields. Education, especially adult education and gerontology. It is quite difficult to reduce all of this to two numbers as you request for line 26." avg. price, paper: $1.95 - $5.95. 1965. 32 to 48pp; 8 x 10½. avg. press run First run 300 copies. After that 1,000 or 2,000. Reporting time: 2 weeks. Payment: flat fee. Copyright for Creative Book Company. Discounts: 20 percent on 1 to 9 copies, mixed titles okay. 40 percent on 10 or more copies; mixed titles okay. Additional 10 percent for annotated listings in catalogs.

Creative Books, John Hicks, Regina Hicks, P.O. Box 5162, Carmel, CA 93921. "CONCEPTOGRAPHY, CANNERY ROW, A Pictorial History, MONTEREY, A Pictorial History." 1973. of. COSMEP.

Creative Communications (see TIME/OUT)

CREATIVE COMPUTING, Creative Computing Press, David H. Ahl, Publisher; Steven B. Gray, Editor in Chief; Burchenal Green, Managing Editor, P.O. Box 789-M, Morristown, NJ 07960, 201-540-0445. Poetry, fiction, articles, art, photos, cartoons, interviews, satire, reviews, letters. "Magazine is for students, educators, hobbyists, and anyone curious about computers. Articles and stories about the effect of the computer on society, privacy, art, science, etc. Human interest side of computers. Lots of games, classroom activities, things to do, with complete program listings and microcomputer profiles. Fiction: stories about runaway computers, robots, computers gaining human intelligence, etc. Book reviews, cartoon, humor, sf, fantasy, some poetry." 6/yr; 1-yr sub price: $8.00; per copy: $1.50; sample: $1.50. 1974. 128pp; 8½ x 11. of. circ. 30,000. Reporting time: 4-6 weeks. Payment: Fiction: 3 ¢/word—Cartoons: $15. Copyrighted, reverts, but we hold rights to anthologize. Ads: $900.00/$525.00/$40.00 inch. Discounts: agent:10%, bulk: up to 50% bookstores: 40%. Back issues: Available for March 1975 on, at $1.50. Pub'd 5 issues 1976; expects 6 issues 1977, 6 issues 1978. Pub's reviews: 25 in 1976. §Computers, technology, sf, microcomputer kits and equipment. COSMEP.

Creative Computing Press (see also CREATIVE COMPUTING), David H. Ahl, Publisher; Steven B. Gray, Editor-in-Chief; Burchenal Green, Managing Editor, 51 Dumont Place, Morristown, NJ 07960, 201-540-0445. Poetry, fiction, articles, art, photos, cartoons, interviews, satire, reviews, letters. "Publish books about how to understand and use a micro computer, innovative, fun, programs for a micro computer, computer fiction and cartoons, with emphasis on computers in the home and the effect that will cause in society." avg. price, cloth: $10.00; paper: $8.95. 1974. 336pp; 8½ x 11. of. avg. press run 10,000. Reporting time: 4-6 weeks. Copyrights for author. Discounts: Bulk & bookstores-from 40 to 50 percent. Pub'd 7 titles 1976. COSMEP.

CREATIVE GUITAR INTERNATIONAL, Mockingbird Press, Jerry Mock, Ruth Mock, Box 7, Alpine, TX 79830. Articles, art, photos, interviews, criticism, reviews, music, letters. "A classic guitar magazine covering the international scene. Past articles have featured Alirio Diaz, the Omega

Quartet, Julian Carrillo, Leo Brouwer, Mangore, Siegfried Behrend. Unique articles on the physics of sound production with nylon strings, teaching guitar to young children, sources for music, reading 20th century music, developing sight reading, bibliography of music for four guitars. *CGI* attracts such noteworthy contributors as Peter Danner, Colin Cooper, John Tanno, Gilbert Biberian, Richard Stover, Graham Wade, Michael Wright, Reed Maxson, Frank Wagner, and Konrad Wolk." 3/yr; 1-yr sub price: $8.50; per copy: $3.00; sample: $3.00. 1973. 40pp; 8½ x 5½. †of. Reporting time: 2 weeks. Copyrighted. Ads: $50.00/$30.00/$0.90 word for 3 consecutive issues, minimum $13.50. Discounts: none. Back issues: $3.00. Pub'd 3 issues 1976; expects 3 issues 1977, 3 issues 1978. Pub's reviews: 14 in 1976. §We are looking for new music, records, books to review on classic guitar.

CREATIVE MOMENT, Poetry Eastwest, Syed Amanuddin, Editor; M. Diesendorf, Assoc. Editor; H. B. Kulkarni, Assoc. Editor, Box 391, Sumter, SC 29150. Poetry, interviews, criticism, reviews. "We have received too many poetry manuscripts, but we would like to concentrate on criticism, reviews and interviews of world poets in English." 2/yr; 1-yr sub price: $3.00; per copy: $1.50. 1972. 40pp; 5½ x 8½. of. circ. 300-500. Reporting time: 6-8 months. Payment: 1 copy. Copyrighted, reverts to author. Back issues: $3.00. Pub's reviews. §Poetry, poetry criticism. CCLM, COSMEP.

Creative Ventures, R. Brian Regehr, Publisher, 1000 East Kaweah, Visalia, CA 93277, Route 8, Box 8835, Bainbridge Island, WA 98110, 209-734-3503. "First-time publishing venture, 1976 *Winds Of Imagination,* and 1977 forthcoming titles: *Sea Shadows & Solitude; Mountain Meandering's* by Petie W. Baldwin. Illustrations by R. Brian Regehr. Poetry, graphics, posters, awareness, nature, whatever." avg. price, cloth: $6.95; paper: $3.50. 1976. 48pp; 6 x 9. avg. press run 1,000. Pub'd 1 title 1976; expects 2 titles 1977. COSMEP, COSMEP-WEST.

CRIME AND SOCIAL JUSTICE, ISSUES IN CRIMINOLOGY., Greg Shank, Paul Takagi, Suzie Dod, Tony Platt, Michael Hannigan, P.O. Box 4373, Berkeley, CA 94704. Poetry, articles, art, photos, cartoons, interviews, criticism, reviews. "30pp. Manuscript maximum-bias-marxist and radical perspectives." 2/yr; 1-yr sub price: ind-$6.00/instit $10.00; per copy: $3.00; sample: $3.00. 1974. 72pp; 8¼ x 10½. lp. circ. 1,200. Reporting time: 1 month. Copyrighted, does not revert to author. Discounts: 20% off to bookstores. Back issues: Indiv. $2.50, Instit. $5.00 (Issue No. 1); all others $3.00, $5.00. Pub'd 2 issues 1976; expects 2 issues 1977, 2 issues 1978. Pub's reviews: 5 in 1976. §Criminology, Occupational Health and Safety.

THE CRISIS, Crisis Publishing Company, Inc., Warren Marr ii, Editor; Maybelle Ward, Assistant Editor, 1790 Broadway, New York, NY 10019. "About 2,500 words. Well-researched, literary approach." 10/yr; 1-yr sub price: $6.00; per copy: $.75; sample: $.75. 1910. 36pp; 8½ x 11. of. circ. 112,539. Reporting time: 4 weeks. Payment: Author's copies only. Ads: $1100/$605/$55-col. in. Discounts: 15% to agencies; 2% 10 days. Pub's reviews. §Books by or about black people.

CRISS-CROSS ART COMMUNICATIONS, Criss-Cross, Richard Kallweit, Clark Richert, Fred Worden, Charles DiJulio, PO Box 2022, Boulder, CO 80302, 442-5832 (303). Art, criticism, reviews. "Criss-Cross seeks out and supports new work and encourages cross-communication among artists—in the remote areas as well as the population centers. We emphasize the straight forward presentation of art rather than critical analysis. Interviews, articles, essays and original work. Recent work by Barbara Dilley, Ed Lowe, Joe Clower, A.R.C., Donald Lipski." 4/yr; 1-yr sub price: $10.00; per copy: $2.50; sample: free. 1975. 60pp; 8¾ x 8. of. circ. 3,000. Payment: not yet. Not copyrighted. Ads: $120.00/$70.00. Discounts: $1.50 ea. $2.50 retail. Back issues: $5.00. §contemporary art.

THE CRITICAL LIST, Jerry Green, Publisher, 32 Sullivan St., Toronto, Onatrio M5T1B9, Canada. Articles, photos, cartoons, interviews, satire, criticism, reviews, letters. "Magazine analyses & criticizes the health care system as it relates to the everyday experiences of patients." 12/yr; sub price: $8.00 12 issues Canada/$14.00 12 issues outside Canada; per copy: $.75; sample: $1.00. 1975. 40pp; 10¾ x 8¼. of. circ. 12,000. Reporting time: 2 mos. Payment: 3¢ word. Ads:

$300/$175/$.15 (min $2.70). Discounts: agency 15, cash 2%. Back issues: $.75. Pub's reviews. §health/illness/politics/if such. COSMEP, APS, CPPA.

THE CRITICAL REVIEW, The Critical Review, S. L. Goldberg, Editor; T. B. Tomlinson, Managing Editor, Australian National University, P.O. Box 4, Canberra, A.C.T. 2600, Australia. Criticism. "c. 7,000-8,000 words or less. No footnotes or notes at end. Critical articles on English literature and related topics; also review articles, commentaries, etc." 1/yr; 1-yr sub price: $3.00 U.S. 1958. 130pp; A5. lp. circ. 1,600. Reporting time: 2 months. Payment: 6 off prints of article. Discounts: 10%. §English literature.

CRITIQUE: Studies in Modern Fiction, James Dean Young, Dept. of English, Georgia Tech, Atlanta, GA 30332. Criticism. "Particular consideration will be given to critical essays on the fiction of writers from any country who are alive and without great reputations." 3/yr; 1-yr sub price: $7.50; per copy: $3.00. 1956. 112pp; 9 x 6. of. circ. 1,500. Reporting time: 4 to 6 mos. Payment: 25 offprints; 5 copies of issue. Copyrighted by editor. Discounts: 10 percent. Back issues: $2.50 per issue (from Vol. 13 only). Pub'd 3 issues 1976; expects 3 issues 1977, 3 issues 1978.

Critiques Livres, Rosalind Boehlinger, Jean Claude Salomon, 173 avenue de la Dhuys, Bagnolet 93170, France, 858 56 86. "So far, all research and editorial work has been done by the above founders/editors. Basically, we work from publishers' catalogues since our bibliographies include only available works in all fields, except scientific/medical/technical, in English, French, German, and Italian. (We welcome cooperation from publishers, adding us to their mailing lists.) We have attempted to use a Marxist approach to the organisation and presentation of books ideologically in a bibliography." avg. price, paper: $4.00. 1976. 88pp; 8½ x 11. of. avg. press run 3,000. Discounts: 1-3 copies, 25 percent; 3-10 copies, 33 percent; 10 plus copies, 40 percent; 50 copies or more, 50 percent. Expects 1 title 1977.

Croissant & Company, Duane Schneider, Route 1, Box 51, Athens, OH 45701, 614-593-8339. Poetry, news items. "Usually not able to handle unsolicited material, at least not in the near future, because of commitments through 1978." avg. price, paper: $2.50. 1968. 10pp; 5½ x 8. of. avg. press run 300 copies. Reporting time: variable. Payment: negotiable. Does not copyright for author. Discounts: trade disc 40 percent. Pub'd 1 title 1976; expects 2 titles 1977.

Cross Country Press, Ltd. (see also CROSSCOUNTRY), Robert Galvin, Jim Mele, Ken Norris, PO Box 21081, Woodhaven, NY 11421, 212-896-7648. Poetry. "We publish Canadian & U.S. poetry chapbooks. This year we will be reprinting two long out of print chapbooks by Terry Stokes & David McFadden. Our small budget & production schedule means that we cannot really consider new manuscripts at this time. Our first chaps are *An Oracle Of Love* by Jim Mele & *Under The Skin* by Ken Norris. Please note that we have two addresses-U.S. & Canadian: 2365 Hampton Ave., No. 7; Montreal, Quebec, H4A2K5, Canada." avg. price, cloth: $1.00 to $3.00. 1975. 24 to 40pp; 5½ x 8½. of. avg. press run 500. Reporting time: 6 months. Payment: by arrangement with individual author. Copyrights for author. Discounts: 50 percent bulk & 40 percent trade. Pub'd 2 titles 1976; expects 4 titles 1977, 4 titles 1978. CCLM.

CROSSCOUNTRY, Cross Country Press, Ltd., Robert Galvin, Jim Mele, Ken Norris, PO Box 21081, Woodhaven, NY 11421, 212-896-7648. Poetry, art, photos, criticism, reviews, letters. "CC is a magazine of Canadian-U.S. poetry. We only are able to use a few unsolicited manuscripts each year. Recent contributors have included Terry Stokes, David McFadden, David Ignatow, William Bronk, Louis Dudek, David Bromige & Opal Nations. Please note that we have two addresses-U.S. & Canadian 2365 Hampton Ave., No. 7; Montreal, Quebec, H4A2K5, Canada" 3/yr; 1-yr sub price: $6.00; per copy: $2.00; sample: $1.00. 1975. 72pp; 5½ x 8¼. of. circ. 500. Reporting time: 6 to 12 weeks. Payment: 2 copies. Copyrighted, reverts to author. Discounts: 50 percent bulk, 40 percent trade, 25 percent subscription agency. Back issues: No. 1-$10.00, No. 2-$1.00, No. 3/4-$2.00. Pub'd 3 issues 1976; expects 3 issues 1977, 3 issues 1978. Pub's reviews. §poetry, both Canadian & U.S. CCLM.

CROSSCURRENTS, Greenwich-Meridian Press, Bob Fink, 516 Ave K South, Saskatoon,

Saskatchewan, Canada. Criticism. "Crosscurrents themes are interdisciplinary.They deal with concrete events, but also with lasting or universal aspects surrounding any event. Issues include one on inflation, on modern Art Galleries, Population, you name it. I see no reason why a serious sheet can't be made about science, anthropology, art, music, ecology—a kind of 'leaflet-college' aimed at everyone, and always aimed at a theme of freedom. I don't pretend to be an expert on anything, but I do intend to speak out anyway. Crosscurrents even prints free musical scores (like Greensleeves)—put a little music in your life. Greenwich-Meridian press has published two books (by myself). One is *Continuum-The Evolution of Matter into Humankind*. A left-wing, cross-discipline approach to art, science, ecology and current social issues, It should be read by the old and new left. It's 400 pages, 7 x 10, 2-colors, limited numbered edition, illustrated, hand insets on cover, and a special fold-out section of precise hand-illustrations on architecture. H.C., Black and Gold, index, $25. Another section is on the modern 'cultural revolution' now going on in the West. The other book is *The University of Music* (on the origin of music) $5 & $10. Write for brochures and review comments. Do small books and printing at very low cost." occassional; sub price: $5.00 for 10 issues; per copy: $.25 plus postage (25¢). 1975. 1pp; 8½ x 11. †mi/of. circ. 500 to 5,000. Reporting time: sometimes forever. Payment: copies. Back issues: $5 for 9 from 1975.

Crosscut Saw Unltd. (see BALL OCCASIONAL)

The Crossing Press, John Gill, Elaine Gill, R.D. 3, Trumansburg, NY 14886, 607-387-6217. Poetry, fiction. 1966. of. avg. press run 1,000-5,000. Reporting time: 4-6 wks. Payment: percent of run or royalties. Copyrights all material. Discounts: 1-4 books, 25 percent: 5 or more titles 40 percent: wholesale-jobbers negociable. Pub'd 6 titles 1976; expects 8-10 titles 1977, 8-10 titles 1978. CCLM, COSMEP, NESPA.

CROSSROADS QUARTERLY, Suncat Enterprises, Thor Denton, Geneva Steinberg, Accomplice, 1471 Second Avenue Apt. 19, New York, NY 10021. Articles, art, photos, cartoons, interviews, satire, criticism, reviews, letters. 4/yr; 1-yr sub price: $3.00; per copy: $.75; sample: $1.00. 1976. 28-32pp; 8½ x 11. of. Reporting time: within a month. Payment: subscription. Ads: $20/$11/$.05. Pub's reviews. §SF, Occult, (especially paganism), UFO'S weird stuff.

‡**Croupier Press,** Box 270 Rt. 4, Golden, CO 80401.

The Crow's Mark Press, Hayden Carruth, Johnson, VT 05656. "Very irregular publication of limited edition books and booklets for free distribution." 1967.

CROW'S NEST, Scarecrow Books, Paul F. Fericano, Editor; Thelma Scarce, Fiction Editor; Dan Poppers, Fiction Editor; Roger W. Langton, Poetry Editor; Paula Jackson, Poetry Editor; Florine Mill, Poetry Editor, 1050 Magnolia 2, Millbrae, CA 94030. Poetry, fiction, articles, art, cartoons, satire, criticism, reviews, plays. "We consider manuscripts between Oct. 1 and April 30 of each year only. CROW'S NEST is interested in publishing quality material, regardless of whether or not you have a 'name.' The magazine is a stepchild of a writer's workshop (a very informal one), so chances are when you submit material, it will be read by several people. If you believe in yourself and your work, then try us. We might connect. We try to be very open. Recent contributors: Sidney Tyler, Emilie Glen, A.D. Winans, Josephine Meadows, Miriam Metters, Barbara Maeder, William Bly, Paul Foreman, Lyn Lifshin, Barry Chamish, Robert Murphy, Ben Hiatt, Teresinka Pereira, John Elsberg, Don Eulert, Stella Worley, Ann Menebroker, Joyce Odam, Dorrel Diricco, Leon Spiro, Anna Moresi, Patrick O'Neil, D.G.H. Schramm, Hester Schartz, Gene Fehler, and more." 1/yr Annual/Summer; 1-yr sub price: $2.00; per copy: $2.50; sample: free to impoverished writers. 1974. 80-100pp; 6 x 9. †of. circ. 500. Reporting time: 1-2 weeks. Payment: copies. Copyrighted, reverts to author. Ads: (negotiable). Discounts: usual. Back issues: Nos. 1, 2 sold out; No. 3 available. Pub'd 1 issue 1976; expects 1 issue 1977, 1 issue 1978. Pub's reviews. COSMEP.

CRY CALIFORNIA, California Tomorrow (nonprofit, educational foundation), Richard A. Grant, Associate Editor, 681 Market Street, Room 1059, San Francisco, CA 94105. Photos, cartoons. 4/yr; sub price: $12.00/yr membership; $9.00/students; $9.00 library subscription; per copy: $1.00 to members/$2.00 to non-members; sample: $2.00. 1965. 40pp; 7 x 10. of. circ. 3,500.

CS JOURNAL, R.S.H. Publications Worldwide, Rita Sublett Hawkins, Suite 302, 818 Roeder Road, Silver Spring, MD 20910, 301-588-7896. Poetry, fiction, articles, art, photos, cartoons, interviews, criticism, reviews, music, letters. "Audience is christian and potential christian people of all ages. Material must drill into the bone of human problems and tell how to solve them from a christian standpoint. Length: open. Is a market for christian and potential christian unpublished writers. Publication is designed to promote the anointed writers of GOD who, for circumstances and lack of recognition, cannot do what they know GOD has called them to do. Simultaneous submissions are taboo. Recent contributors are Rev. Oral Roberts, Rev. R.W. Schambach, John Tissot, O.J. Robertson, Gertrude Katz, a syndicated columnist for the Tribune Newspaper, and many more well-known writers and ministers, but we are primarily looking for unknown writers who need an outlet for their creative ideas. *CS JOURNAL* has a sister companion, *CS GLOBE REPORTER NEWSPAPER*. Query first." 12/yr; 1-yr sub price: $10.00; per copy: $3.00; sample: $2.50. 1975. 56pp; 8½ x 11. †of/lp. Reporting time: 4 to 6 weeks. Payment varies with author. Ads: $675.20 1x/vertical 1/2: $378.67 1x/horizontal 1/2: $361.45 1x. Back issues: $1.00 and $0.50 to help defray postage rates. Pub's reviews §Christianity, especially mags. COSMEP.

CTHULHU, Spectre Press, Jon M Harvey, 18 Cefn Road, Mynachdy, Cardiff CF4 3HS, United Kingdom. Poetry, fiction, art, long-poems, satire. "Fantasy-orientated material in the Cthulhu mythos genre (re. the stories of H.P. Lovecraft). However, I am not looking for or printing the usually dull rehash of the old mythos stories, but am interested in new, off-beat ideas. Recent contributors: Glen Singer, Andrew Darlington, Brian Mooney, Brian Lumley and David A. Sutton." infrequent; sub price: £2/4 issues; per copy: 50p; sample: 50p. 1976. 30pp; 5½ x 8¼. of. circ. 750. Reporting time: 1-2 mos. Payment: copies only. Buys first U.K. rights only. no ads. Discounts: agent, 50 percent; bulk, 40 percent for 10-49 copies; 50 percent, for 50 or more copies. Pub'd 1 issue 1976.

CTR Publications (see also CANADIAN THEATRE REVIEW), Don Rubin, York University, Downsview, Ontario M3T1P3, Canada. Articles, plays, reviews. avg. price, paper: $3.00. 1973. 144pp; 6 x 9. †of. avg. press run 3,000. Reporting time: 3 weeks. Payment varies. Discounts: 40 percent to bookstores. Pub'd 4 titles 1976; expects 4 titles 1977, 4 titles 1978. CPPA.

Cumbria Poetry Centre (see also POETRY CUMBRIA), Selected from committee for each issue, Charlotte Mason College, Rydal Road, Ambleside, Cumbria, United Kingdom. Poetry, reviews. "None" avg. price, paper: £0.35 to £0.60. 1975. 48pp; A5. of. avg. press run 500. Reporting time: Maximum of six months. Payment: free copies to contributors. Copyrights for author. Discounts: 33-1/3 percent. Pub'd 3 titles 1976; expects 3-4 titles 1977, 3-4 titles 1978.

Cupola Productions (see ROCKINGCHAIR)

Curbstone Press, Alexander Taylor, 321 Jackson Street, Willimantic, CT 06226, 456-2432. "For the most part we publish short books (32—48pp) of poetry and translations of poetry. We have a bias toward poetry of the left that rises above political invective. We also have a Danish series. American poets we have published include James Scully, Richard Schaaf, Margaret Gibson and Marion Metivier. Danish: Ole Sarvig & Klaus Rifbjerg. We have done some broadsides & will do more this year, as well as poetry postcards. Writers scheduled for cards and broadsides are: Victor Contoski, James Scully, Roberta Metz, Phil Paradis, and George Butterick." avg. price, cloth: $5.00-$10.00; paper: $2.50-$6.50; other: Signed, limited $10.00-$15.00. 1973. 32-84—usually we expect about 48pp; 6 x 9. †of. avg. press run 850. We do not ask for unsolicited ms. If they come in, it may take 2—3 months to respond. Payment: We lose money on the books & do not pay a royalty, except in copies. The author retains all rights. Copyrights for author. Discounts: 40% off to bookstores; 50% off to distributors; no library discount. Pub'd 3 titles 1976; expects 5 titles 1977, 5 titles 1978.

The Curlew Press (see also POETRY QUARTERLY), Jocelyne Precious, Harecott, Kettlesing, Harrogate, Yorkshire, United Kingdom. Poetry, fiction, articles, art, photos, cartoons, interviews, satire, criticism, reviews, letters, parts-of-novels, long-poems, collages, plays, concrete art, news items, non-fiction. "One poet collections, broadsheets, pamphlets. So many produced free by the press, so many published on poet/press basis. All work accepted on merit only. Further details on request. Poets published by the press include: Nigel Gray, Colin Simms, Barry Edgar Pilcher, Steve Sneyd, Max Noiprox, Paul St. Vincent, E.A. Markham." avg. price, paper: £1.75. 1975. Variable. up to 100pp; varies. of. avg. press run Variable. up to 500. Reporting time: By return of post when possible. Payment: None. Copyrights for author. Pub'd 8 titles 1976; expects 8 titles 1977.

CURRENT (a reprint magazine), Grant S. McClellan, Editor, Plainfield, VT 05667. "Reprints articles and book excerpts on social-political affairs." 12/yr (combined May-June-July-Aug); 1-yr sub price: $11.00/$15.00 institutions; per copy: $1.50; sample: free. 1960. 60pp; 7 x 10. circ. 7,900. §political-eco-social affairs.

CURTAINS, Pressed Curtains, Paul Buck, 12 Foster Clough, Hebden Bridge, West Yorkshire HX7 5QZ, United Kingdom, 042-283-3900. Poetry, fiction, articles, art, interviews, criticism, music, parts-of-novels, long-poems, non-fiction. "Presents mainly French writings in translation. Blanchot, Bataille, Noel, Laporte, Faye. Though English & American poetry also strongly featured." 1/yr; price per copy: $5.00. 1971. 215pp; A4. of/colored inks. circ. 350. Reporting time: days. Payment: copies. Copyrighted. Ads: none. Pub'd 1 issue 1976; expects 1 issue 1977, 1 issue 1978. Pub's reviews: 1 in 1976. §same as content material.

‡**Curveship Press**, St. Andrew's Presbyterian College, Laurinburg, NC 28352.

CUTBANK, SmokeRoot, Lex Runciman, Rick Robbins, English Dept., U. of Montana, Missoula, MT 59801. Poetry, fiction, articles, art, photos, interviews, criticism, reviews, parts-of-novels, long-poems. "Charles M. Fair, Jim Heynen, Tess Gallagher, William Stafford, Richard Hugo, Raymond Carver, Roberta Hill, Thomas Johnson, John Haines, Madeline Defrees, Ira Sadoff." 2/yr; 1-yr sub price: $3.50; per copy: $2.00; sample: $2.00. 1973. 100pp; 5½ x 8½. of. circ. 600. Reporting time: 3-5 weeks. Payment: copies. Copyrighted. Ads: $50.00/$30.00. Back issues: No. 1, $1.50: Nos. 3-7, $9.00. Pub'd 2 issues 1976; expects 2 issues 1977, 2 issues 1978. Pub's reviews: 8 in 1976. §poetry/fiction/criticism. CCLM.

‡**Cycle Press**, 18 Warren Place, Brooklyn, NY 11201.

CYCLO * FLAME, Cyclotron Press, Vernon Payne, 212 W. First St., San Angelo, TX 76901. Poetry. "Submissions/acceptances first 6 months of odd-number years." 1/ea. 2 yrs; price per copy: $5.00 paper/$10.00 cloth. 1940. 200pp; 8¼ x 10½. of. circ. 500 plus. Reporting time: one month. Payment: $1 on acceptance. no ads. Discounts: 40% on clothbound. Pub's reviews.

Cyclotron Press (see CYCLO * FLAME)

D

D.D.B. Press (see APALACHEE QUARTERLY)

THE D.H. LAWRENCE REVIEW, James C. Cowan, Box 2474, University of Arkansas, Fayetteville, AR 72701. Articles, art, photos, interviews, criticism, reviews. "THE D.H. LAWRENCE REVIEW publishes scholarly and critical articles, review essays, bibliography, and news relating to D.H. Lawrence and his circle. We are not a journal of imaginative writing, but we have on three occasions in nine years published poetry relating to Lawrence. The average length of an accepted article is about 15 pages in manuscript, double-spaced, but we are flexible enough on special occasions to accept larger and sometimes smaller articles. Material submitted should follow *The MLA Style Sheet* and be accompanied by return self-addressed envelope and postage. We are eclectic in approach from various critical perspectives and in subjects treated within our area of interest." 3/yr; 1-yr sub price: $7.00; per copy: $2.50; sample: $2.50. 1968. 130pp; 6 x 9. circ. 550. Reporting time: 3 months. Payment: 2 copies of issue plus about 25 offprints of article. Discounts: 20% discount to dealers and subsciptions agencies. Back issues: $2.50 single copy and $7.00 annual volume. Pub'd 3 issues 1976; expects 3 issues 1977, 3 issues 1978. §D.H. Lawrence and his circle, modern literature.

DACOTAH TERRITORY, Territorial Press, Mark Vinz, Ed.; Grayce Ray, Assoc. Ed., P.O. Box 775, Moorhead, MN 56560. Poetry, art, photos, interviews, reviews. "Not interested in unsolicited reviews or graphics; interested in all types of poetry, though space is highly limited. Have published very few translations, long poems or concrete poems." 2/yr; 1-yr sub price: $2.50; per copy: $1.50; sample: $1.50. 1971. 96pp; 7 x 8½. of. circ. 1M. Reporting time: 1 week-2months. Payment: 2 copies. Copyrighted, reverts to author. no ads. Discounts: 20-40%. Back issues: issue 1-12 available at $1.00 ea, issue 13 available at $1.50 each. Pub'd 2 issues 1976; expects 2 issues 1977, 2 issues 1978. Pub's reviews: 15 in 1976. §Midwestern poets. CCLM, COSMEP.

DADAZINE, Dadaland Press, William J. Gaglione, 1183 Church St., San Francisco, CA 94114. Art, photos, interviews, letters, collages, plays, concrete art. "DADAZINE is an international magazine on the avant-garde activities. 1) Opal L. Nations (Canada) 2) Richard Morris (U.S.A.) 3) Anna Banana (U.S.A.) 4) Tip Top (U.S.A.) 5) Dick Higgins (U.S.A.) 6) COUM (England) 7) General Idea (Canada) 8) Richard Kostelanetz (U.S.A.) 9) Edgardo-Antonio-Vigo (Argentine) 10) Herta (Hungary)" 2/yr; 1-yr sub price: $4.00; per copy: $2.00; sample: $1.00. 1975. 20-50pp; 8½ x 11 or 5 x 7. of. circ. 500. Payment: free subs. Discounts: 40 percent for over 5 copies. Back issues: $3.00. Pub'd 1 issue 1976; expects 2 issues 1977, 4 issues 1978. §avant garde literature/news. AAP.

DAEDALUS, Journal of the American Academy of Arts and Sciences, American Academy of Arts and Sciences, Stephen R. Graubard, Editor; Geno A Ballotti, Managing Editor, 7 Linden Street, Cambridge, MA 02138. 4/yr; 1-yr sub price: $10.00; per copy: $2.95; sample: $2.50. 1958. 225pp; 6¾ x 9¾. lp. circ. 35,000.

DAIMON, House of Keys, Kay Leigh Hagan, Norman Finkelstein, Kathryn E. Meyer, Terrill S. Soules, P O Box 7952, Atlanta, GA 30357, 404-876-0529. Poetry. "Typed submissions of at least 3 poems. Four poets per issue. Our unique broadside format provides four large panels, giving each poet a singular focus. Submissions are reviewed by all four editors; each submission receives a personal reply with editorial comment. A sample copy will best represent our preferences. Recent contributors: Gita Maritzer Smith, Nat Anderson, Anthony Harrington, Scott Wilson, Beryl Arroyo, Gary Corseri, Pearl Cleage Lomax." 4/yr; sub price: To receive *Daimon,* simply ask to be on our mailing list. 13 cent stamp. 1976. 4pp; 7½ x 17. of. circ. 2,000. Reporting time: 1 week to 1 month. Payment: $10.00 per panel. Copyrighted, reverts to author. Discounts: Distributed for free. Back issues: Issues 2, 3, & 4 available for postage. CCLM, COSMEP-SOUTH.

Dakota Press (see also SOUTH DAKOTA REVIEW), John R. Milton, Swes, University of South Dakota, Vermillion, SD 57069, 605-677-5281. avg. price, cloth: $9.00; paper: $3.00. 1968. Has run from 50 to 400.pp; varies. lp/of. avg. press run 1,000. (Not considering material at present time). Discounts: 40 percent to bookstores. Pub'd 1 title 1976; expects 2 titles 1977.

THE DALHOUSIE REVIEW, Dalhousie University Press Ltd., Dr. A.R. Bevan, Prof R.L. Raymond, The Dalhousie Review, Killam Library, 4413 Halifax, Nova Scotia B3H4H8, Canada. "5,000 words, W.K. Thomas, John W. Bilsland, Clarence Karr, Beverly Rasporich, Hans-Peter Breuer, David Alexander, Harold R.W. Morrison, Ronald S. Librach, S.V. Pradhan and James Gray" 4/yr; 1-yr sub price: $6.00; per copy: $2.00 plus handling; sample: free. 1921. 200pp; 9 x 6½. lp. circ. 1,100. Reporting time: varies. Payment: $1 per page (honorarium only) $3 for each poem used. Ads: $50 (45 ea. for 4)/$30 (25 ea. for 4). Discounts: agent 25% subs. only 15% advt. Pub's reviews §all areas would be examined.

DAMASCUS ROAD, Damascus Road Press, Charles Shahoud Hanna, 6271 Hill Drive, Wescosville, PA 18106. Poetry, fiction, articles, art, photos, criticism, letters. "DAMASCUS ROAD was born in the late 50's an offspring of Ginsberg/Kerouac, New York/San Francisco, Peace/& the Bomb, Pollack/Kline, Beat/vs. Mad Ave., Gotham/8th Street/City Lights, began as a representative world voice that included many translations as part of contemporary scene. Continues to be a voice for 'today's' writing while trying to be reflective of the many diverse sounds of modern words. Last issue dedicated to Paul Blackburn & featured: William Bronk, Gregory Corso, Diane DiPrima, Theodore Enslin, Allen Ginsberg, Marguerite Harris, Michael Heller, Barbara Holland, Robert Kelly, Galway Kinnell, Jackson MacLow, Thomas McGrath, Toby Olson, Rochelle Owens, Allen Planz, Rochelle

Ratner, Adrienne Rich, Jerome Rothenberg, Mark Strand, Diane Wakoski, & 45 other poets and writers." 1/yr; price per copy: $2.25; sample: $1.25. 1959. 143pp; 5½ x 8½. of. circ. 750. Reporting time: 3 months. Payment: $2 page. Ads: none. Discounts: 40% stores/50% cash. Back Issues: #1-$3.50 #2 & 3-$1.95 #4-$3.50 #5-$3.25 full set #1-#5 $12.75. CCLM, COSMEP.

DANCE DIMENSIONS, Wisconsin Dance Council, Diane Milhan Pruett, M.D. Hart, 3236 N. Bartlett Ave., Milwaukee, WI 53211. Poetry, articles, art, photos, reviews. "DANCE DIMENSIONS strives to be a forum for dancers and dance writers in Wisconsin. Recent Contributors: Ellen Moore, Curtis Carter, Sharon Haas." 4/yr; 1-yr sub price: $3.50; per copy: $1.00; sample: free. 1972. 32pp; 7 x 11. of. circ. 250. Reporting time: immediate. Ads: $35/$25 1/4 $15/$.50. §arts/dance/music/women.

DANCE HERALD, Dance Herald Press, William Moore, 243 West 63st, New York, NY 10023. Articles, art, photos, cartoons, interviews, criticism, reviews, letters. "Due to length of publication everything must be very *short*." 4/yr; 1-yr sub price: $3.00; per copy: $.75; sample: $.75. 1975. 6pp; 8½ x 12. of. circ. 300. Reporting time: 4 months. Payment: none. Pub's reviews. §black dance/black music/art.

DANCE IN CANADA, Susan Cohen, 314 Jarvis St. #103, Toronto, Ontario M5B2C5, Canada. Articles, photos, interviews, criticism, reviews, music, letters. "Canada's only national bilingual dance magazine. Exclusive coverage of ideas, events, personalities and criticism from coast to coast." 4/yr; 1-yr sub price: $6.50; per copy: $2.00; sample: $2.00. 1973. 32pp; 8½ x 11. circ. 1,000. Reporting time: 6 weeks. Payment: $25-$50. Ads: $315/$200. Discounts: 40% on consignment. Pub's reviews. §dance/performing arts.

DANCE SCOPE, American Dance Guild, Inc., Richard Lorber, 1619 Broadway, Rm. 603, New York, NY 10019. Poetry, fiction, articles, art, photos, cartoons, interviews, satire, criticism, reviews, letters. 2/yr; 1-yr sub price: $3.50; per copy: $2.00; sample: $2.00. 1965. 80pp; 6 x 9. of. circ. 6,000. Reporting time: 3 mos. Payment: $25.00 plus 5 issues. Ads: $100.00/$58.00. Discounts: 30-40%. Back issues: $2.00. Pub'd 2 issues 1976; expects 2 issues 1977. Pub's reviews. §dance, theatre, music, film, video, etc. CCLM.

THE DANDELION, Michael E Coughlin, 1985 Selby Ave, St Paul, MN 55104, 612-646-8917. Articles, cartoons, satire, criticism, reviews, letters. "This is a libertarian/anarchist magazine. Well-written pro-freedom, anti-state articles desired. Length not necessarily a handicap, though short, punchy articles are preferred." 4/yr; 1-yr sub price: $3.50; per copy: $1.00; sample: free. 1977. 28pp; 5½ x 8½. of. circ. about 400. Reporting time: one month. Payment: payment in copies of the magazine. Not copyrighted. Ads: $15.00/$10.00. Discounts: 25 percent off listed price for bulk orders. Back issues: same as single copy price. Pub's reviews. §Anarchist/libertarian history, biographies, philosophy.

Daniel Stokes, Publisher (see EAST RIVER REVIEW)

Daran Inc. (see HUERFANO)

DARK FANTASY, Shadow Press, Howard Gene Day, Con. Editor; C. R. Saunders, Gale Jack, Box 207, Gananoque, Ontario K7G2T7, Canada, 613-382-2794. Poetry, fiction, art. "Generally tales of fast moving adventure, S-R & S&S or horror. No heavy sex—very light in that aspect. 3,000 words preferred but always willing to compromise. R. C.-R. E. Howard. Neal Adams." 4-6/yr; sub price: $5.00 for 5 issues; per copy: $1.00; sample: $1.00. 1973. 40-52pp; 5½ x 8½. of. circ. 500-600. Reporting time: 4-6 weeks. Payment:40 1/2 cent per word, $1.00 per poem, $5.00 for art use. Copyrighted, reverts to author. Ads: $8.00/$5.00/none. Discounts: 40 percent flat discount on orders over 10. Back issues: usually $1.25. Pub'd 4 issues 1976; expects 5-6 issues 1977.

DARK HORSE, Jane Barnes, Ricky Funkhouser, Bob Knox, Anne Sheffield, Joyce Thompson, c/o Barnes, 47a Dana St., Cambridge, MA 02138. Poetry, fiction, articles, art, photos, cartoons, interviews, satire, criticism, reviews, letters, parts-of-novels, long-poems, collages, plays, concrete art. "Recent Contributors: Dora Stein, Ron Schreiber. Seldom use poems over 60 lines, but will if exceptional. We are biased in favor of contributors from *New England;* seek to maintain 'regional' tone and use only a minimum of work from outside the region. We are particularly interested in articles on all aspects of small press publishing, reviews of sm.pr. publications, articles on publication process, personal experiences with sm.press publishing. Also very interested in receiving news of info. about literary activity of all sorts; readings, prizes, new publications, etc for our regular news column. Also interested in letters, responses, will print source." 4/yr; 1-yr sub price: $3.00; per copy: $.50 on newsstand/$.75 thru mail; sample: $.75. 1974. 16pp; 11½ x 17 (tabloid). of. circ. 2,000. Reporting time: 1-12 wks. Payment: 10 copies. Ads: exchange. Discounts: 40%-bookstores, 40%-classroom orders of 20 or more. Pub's reviews. §poetry/literature. CCLM, COSMEP, NESPA.

DARK TOWER, Linda Unger, University Center Rm. 7, Cleveland State University, Cleveland, OH 44115. Poetry, fiction, photos, interviews, long-poems, plays. "We're looking for fresh treatment of subject matter. Lynn Lifshin, David Citino, Daniel Kaminsky, James Kilgore, Richard Frost, Judson Crews." 2/yr; 1-yr sub price: $1.75; per copy: $1.00; sample: $1.00. 1972. 48pp; 6 x 9. of. circ. 1,500 copies-primarily local. Reporting time: 4-6 wks. Payment: in copies or up to $5.00. Back issues: no back issues available for sale.

Daughters Publishing Co., Inc., Parke Bowman, June Arnold, 22 Charles St., New York, NY 10014, 212-243-8252. Fiction. "Full-length finished (completed) novel manuscripts with passionate feminist content. Letter of query first." avg. price, paper: $4.25. 1972. 300pp; 5¼ x 8½. webb. avg. press run 5,000. Reporting time: 6 weeks. Payment: 10% on cover price with advances. Copyrights for author. Discounts: 50% distributors; 40% to bookstores (10 copy mixed); 25% libraries, feminist studies teachers. Pub'd 4 titles 1976; expects 5 titles 1977, 5 titles 1978. COSMEP, AAP.

Davinci Magazine (see VEHICULE PRESS)

DAWN, 331 Ormeau Road, Belfast 7, Northern Ireland BT7, United Kingdom. Articles, art, photos, cartoons, interviews, reviews, letters, news items, non-fiction. "Dawn exists to explore relevance of nonviolence to struggle for peace & justice in Ireland, and to promote concrete nonviolent actions." 12/yr; 1-yr sub price: £2.00; per copy: 10p; sample: free. 1974. 12pp; a4. of. circ. 1,000. Payment: none. Pub'd 12 issues 1976; expects 12 issues 1977, 12 issues 1978. Pub's reviews: 6 in 1976. §nonviolence, pacifism, community action, ecology, sexual politics, anarchism, mutual aid, third world. APS.

Dawn Horse Press, Saniel Bonder, Billy Taikanois, P.O. Box 99637, San Francisco, CA 94109, 621-1158. avg. price, cloth: $9.00; paper: $4.00. 1970. 250pp; 5¼ x 8½. †of. avg. press run 5,000. Reporting time: 2-3 weeks. Payment: royalties 10 percent. Copyrights for author. Discounts: 1-2 copies 20%/3-9 copies 40%/10-24 copies 41%/25-49 copies 42%/50-99 copies 43%/100 up copies 44%. Pub'd 2 titles 1976; expects 5 titles 1977.

Dawn Valley Press, Nancy E. James, Box 58, New Wilmington, PA 16142. Poetry, fiction. "Dawn Valley's fourth and fifth titles, to be published in 1977, will be an anthology by fourteen women poets including Jeannine Dobbs, Barbara Friend, Judy Neeld, and Joan Shapiro; and a collection of short stories by James Ashbrook Perkins. At present manuscripts are read by invitation only." avg. price, paper: $3.00-$4.00. 1976. of. Discounts: Retail: 1 copy, 20 percent; 2-5, 25 percent; 6-25, 40 percent; 26 or more, 50 percent. Wholesale: 1 copy, 25 percent; 2-5, 40 percent; 6 or more, 50 percent. Pub'd 2 titles 1976; expects 2 titles 1977. COSMEP.

DAY BY DAY, Loverseed Press, Ronald Mallone, Woolacombe House, 141 Woolacombe Rd., Blackheath, London SE3, United Kingdom, 01-856-6249. Articles, poetry, fiction, art, satire, reviews, interviews, criticism, letters. "Poems or stories must be short. Intending authors are advised to study a copy or copies first. Use mainly factual material which must be carefully authenticated." 13-14/yr; 1-yr sub price: $6.00; per copy: 23p; sample: 23p. 1962. 18pp; 13 x 8. mi. circ. 11,500. Reporting time: 7-20 days. Payment: by arrangement. Ads: 5p. Pub'd 12 issues 1976; expects 14 issues 1977, 15 issues 1978.

Daylight Press, U. Carrion, c/o Other Books and So, Herengracht 227, Amsterdam, The Netherlands. Poetry, art, concrete art. "I publish *only* experimental language-art." 1975. of/lp.

de la Ree Publications, Gerry de la Ree, Helen de la Ree, 7 Cedarwood Lane, Saddle River, NJ 07458. "We publish books and art folios in the fantasy-weird-and science fiction fields. Mainly nonfiction articles dealing with various authors, artists, or other facets of these fields." avg. price, cloth: $15.00; paper: $7.50. 1972. Varies. of. Reporting time: Immediate. Copyrights for author. Discounts: 40 percent on 10 or more copies. Pub'd 3 titles 1976; expects 3-4 titles 1977.

DECARABIA, Blue Crow Press, D. R. Meiklejohn, 48 Salmon Falls Rd (Box-A), Rochester, NH 03867. Poetry, fiction, art, reviews, news items. "We will look at all mss. Especially like to see clear cut 'needles & glass' poetry that builds on the senses and brings them alive (what fingernails on a chalkboard do for your ears). We have a soft heart for surrealism in short fiction/in simple art that accents the multidimensional nature of all things." 4/yr; sub price: $4.00, 4 issues; per copy: $1.25; sample: $1.25. 1977. 48pp; 5½ x 8½. †mi/of. circ. 200. Reporting time: 2-4 weeks. Payment: copies/some gifts/awards. Copyrighted, reverts to author. Ads: $25.00/$15.00. Discounts: 40 percent trade, bulk, etc. Expects 2 issues 1977, 4 issues 1978. Pub's reviews: none in 1976. §poetry, short fiction, talismanic art, occult. NESPA.

DECEMBER MAGAZINE, December Press, Curt Johnson, Robert Wilson, 4 E. Huron, Chicago, IL 60611. Poetry, fiction, articles, art, photos, interviews, satire. irregular; sub price: 4-issues $10.00; per copy: $3.00; sample: $2.00. 1958. 228pp; 5½ x 8½. of. circ. 1,500. Reporting time: 6-8 weeks. Payment: free copies. Ads: $100/$60. Discounts: 20% 10 or more-agency 20%. Back issues: twice over cover price. Pub'd 4 issues 1976; expects 3 issues 1977. Pub's reviews. §fiction. CCLM, COSMEP.

Deciduous (see also EVERYMAN), Christopher Franke, 4208½ Whitman Avenue, Cleveland, OH 44113, 216-631-1454. Poetry, art, photos, cartoons, collages, concrete art. "*Up Against The Wall,* 15 poems by Christopher Franke on a 20' x 26' broadside, is available for $1.00. Various poem-collage leaflets are available for a S.A.S. envelope. *Deciduous* is dormant in the winter and estivates in the summer. As for spring and fall, ?. Some future issues of *EVERYMAN* will be guest edited. Cyril A. Dostal will do the first guest edited issue in 1978." 1970. 1pp plus; varies. Reporting time: varies. Payment: copies. Expects 2 titles 1977. CCLM.

THE DEKALB LITERARY ARTS JOURNAL, William S. Newman, 555 N. Indian Creek Dr, Clarkston, GA 30021. Poetry, fiction, articles, art, photos, criticism, reviews, music, plays. 4/yr; 1-yr sub price: $6.00; per copy: $1.50; sample: $1.40. 1966. 100pp; 6 x 9. of. circ. 1M. Reporting time: 6-8 wks. Payment: copies only. Copyrighted, reverts to author. no ads. Back issues: upon request. Pub'd 4 issues 1976; expects 4 issues 1977, 4 issues 1978. Pub's reviews: 4 in 1976. §The arts. CCLM, COSMEP.

DELAP'S F & SF REVIEW, Richard Delap, Frederick Patten, 11863 West Jefferson Blvd., Culver City, CA 90230, 213-432-1192. Reviews. "A monthly illustrated book-review journal designed for libraries & schools, specializing in coverage of science-fiction & fantasy. Includes novels, collections, hardcover & paperback, adult & juvenile, S-F literary studies, S-F cinema, S-F poetry, spoken records & S-F movie sound track recordings, etc. Reviewers include Richard Delap, Tom Reamy, Harlan Ellison, Susan Wood, Marion Zimmer Bradley, Beverly Friend, Frederick Patten, Bill Warren, Fritz Leiber, George Barr & others. Also a monthly S-F calendar of all announced titles from all publishers. No unsolicited material." 12/yr; 1-yr sub price: $13.50 individuals-$18.00 institutions-yr; per copy: $1.50; sample: $1.50. 1976. 40pp; 8½ x 11. of. circ. 1,650. Payment: free subscription to magazine/free books sent to our reviewers. Copyrighted, reviews copyrighted in name of reviewer if requested. Ads: $100.00 (7' x 10' image area)/$60.00 (7' x 5' image area). Discounts: 10% to subscription agents, 40% to dealers, others ordering 6 copies or more per issue. Back issues: $1.50 each. Pub'd 12 issues 1976; expects 12 issues 1977, 12 issues 1978. Pub's reviews: 485 in 1976. §science-fiction & fantasy/incl. studies of, works on s-f cinema/poetry/juvenile fantasy/s-f spoken records or s-f movie soundtracks/etc.

DELIRIUM, Libra Press, Jim Mc Curry, 1827 Elm St., Denver, CO 80220. "No biases in a restrictive sense. Recent contributors include Douglas Blazek, Sandra Case, Jack Collom, David Cope, Melissa Cummings, Thomas Michael Fisher, Hugh Fox, Marilyn Krysl, Lyn Lifshin, Lewis MacAdams, Phoebe MacAdams, Christopher Middleton, David Plante, Charles Plymell, Stephen Ruffus, Arlene Zekowski & Stanley Berne. 3rd issue ready for printing. Filled thru no. 6." try for 4/yr; 1-yr sub price: $4.00; per copy: $1.50; sample: 2 free while they last. 1975. 54pp; 8½ x 11. of. circ. 300 (so far). Reporting time: immediately; one week maximum. Payment: 3 copies plus lifetime subscription. Copyrighted, reverts to author. Ads: exchange ads. Back issues: no. 2 free while they last. Pub's reviews. §poetry, prosepoems, fiction. CCLM, COSMEP.

THE DELPHYS FORUM, S. M. Schneble, Editor-Publisher, P.O. Box 677, Pacific Palisades, CA 90272, 213-454-8659. "Articles, interviews, reviews, (black and white photos), occasionally poetry (cetacean related). Our subject matter is scholarly and scientific—anything having to do with whales, dolphins and propoises for an international audience comprised of academics, scientists, marine biologists, environmentalists, and government institutions, etc. Query best bet. Include S.A.S.E. for prompt return." 12/yr; 1-yr sub price: $35.00; per copy: $3.00. circ. 5m to 10m. Reporting time: 2 weeks. Payment: copies only; will reset rates after one year. Ads: $95.00 for 401/6th of page only. Discounts: sub agent, $25.00/yr; bkstr., $2.00/copy. $25/year for colleges and universities.

DENTAL FLOSS MAGAZINE, Toothpaste Press, Allan Kornblum, P.O. Box 546, 626 E. Main, Westbranch, IA 52358, 319-643-2604. Poetry. "Submissions mostly by invitation. Unsolicited will be considered, but not encouraged. There are just so many Iowa city poets. We like to keep that geographical focus for the mag. more open with the press. Recent contributors: David Hilton, John Sjoberg, Sheila Heldenbrand, Morty Sklar, Cinda Kornblum, Jim Mulac. Coming soon: Josephine Clare, Bob Perelman & Brad Harvey." 2/yr; sub price: $5.00 Vol.; per copy: $1.50; sample: $1.50. 1975. 16pp; 6¼ x 9. †lp. circ. 375. Reporting time: 6-8 weeks. Payment: 2 copies. Discounts: 1-4 copies-25%/2 & over 40%. Pub'd 1 issue 1976; expects 1 issue 1977, 2 issues 1978. COSMEP.

THE DENVER QUARTERLY, Gerald Chapman, Editor; Robert D. Richardson Jr, Burton Feldman, Robert Pawlowski, Burton Raffel, Associate Editors, University of Denver, Denver, CO 80210. Poetry, fiction, articles, criticism, reviews, parts-of-novels, long-poems. "Poems: John Ashbery, Allen Mandelbaum,. Essays: Rene Wellek, Laura Riding, Owen Barfield, David Kalstone. Fiction: Tom O'Brien, John Humma, Baine Kerr. Reviews: symposium on Eric Voegelin, Berel Lang, Gabriel Gersh." 4/yr; 1-yr sub price: $8.00; per copy: $2.00; sample: $2.00. 1966. 125-160pp; 6 x 9. circ. 1,000. Reporting time: 6 wks. Payment: fiction and essays $5.00 page poetry $10.00 page. Back issues: $3.00 copy over one year old. Pub's reviews. §literary & philosophic culture of last 100 years. CCLM.

Derwyddon Press (see also LODGISTIKS). avg. price, paper: $3.00. 60pp; Varies. Pub'd 2 titles 1976; expects 2 titles 1977, 2 titles 1978.

DESCANT, Texas Christian University Press, Betsy Feagan Colquitt, English Department, TCU, Fort Worth, TX 76129. Poetry, fiction, articles. 4/yr; 1-yr sub price: $3.00; per copy: $1.00; sample: $1.00. 1955. 48pp; 6 x 9. of. circ. 650. Reporting time: about six weeks. Payment: in copies. Copyrighted. COSMEP.

DESCANT, Karen Mulhallen, P.O. Box 314 Station P, Toronto, Ontario M5S1S8, Canada. Poetry, fiction, articles, art, photos, cartoons, interviews, satire, criticism, reviews, music, parts-of-novels, long-poems, collages, plays, concrete art. 3/yr; 1-yr sub price: $5.00-$10.00; per copy: $2.00; sample: $1.00. 1970. 96pp; 6 x 8. of. circ. 700. Reporting time: 4-6 months. Payment varies. Copyrighted. Ads: None. Pub'd 3 issues 1976; expects 3 issues 1977, 4 issues 1978. Pub's reviews: none in 1976. §Poetry, fiction, graphics. COSMEP, CPPA.

Desert First Works, Inc., Ann M. Huck, Sylvia R. Lafferty, Sonja J. Young, 3870 N. Vine Ave., Tucson, AZ 85719, 602-793-2859. Poetry. "List of books: *Becoming,* by Ann Marie Huck, *We Shall Curse The Dead,* by Thomas Cobb, *We Do What We Can,* by Rita Garitano, *All That Is Left,* by Susan North, *Taking Chances,* by Jefferson Carter, *Flying At Night,* by Paul Stein. 1977-78 books by: Stephanie Hallgren, Jeannette Spavieri Subhas, Gregory Nelson Forker, Sonja Reisen. Autographed copies of all books published during the year sent to friends ($25/yr) and sponsors ($50/yr). Donations are tax deductible." avg. price, paper: $2.50 plus $0.45 postage/handling. 1975. 40pp; 5½ x 8½. of. avg. press run 500-1,000. Reporting time: 1 month. Payment: 10 percent of run in copies. Copyright in author's name. Discounts: 40% to retailers (25% on consignment). Pub'd 3 titles 1976; expects 4 titles 1977, 4-6 titles 1978. COSMEP.

Desserco Publishing, Roquita French, P.O. Box 2433, Culver City, CA 90730, (213) 320-9101. Articles, criticism, reviews, collages. "Recently published book: 'God Rejected.'" avg. price, cloth: $4.95; paper: $2.95. 1975. 128pp; 5½ x 8½. of. avg. press run 2,000. Payment: none—author published. Copyrights for author. Discounts: various up to 55%.

Deuce of Clubs Press, Marseille Spetz, P.O. Box 4682, Sacramento, CA 95825. Poetry, fiction, satire.

Dharma Publishing (see also GESAR), 5856 Doyle St., Emeryville, CA 94608. "20 titles currently in print; over 50 Tibetan reproductions in full color. Sepcializes in books on Buddhism. We have our own photo-typesetting and offset printing facilities. We published 12 new titles in 1975 and will do 12 more in 1976."

DHARMA SARA, Dharma Sara Publications, Ravi Dass, Anand Dass, Narendra Dass, P.O. Box 247, Sumas, WA 98295. Articles, art, photos, interviews, letters, non-fiction. "We're interested in material relevant to the spiritual unfoldment current in North America-not so much sociological but subject areas that deal with new age. We're concerned with presentation of traditional ideas in a context acceptable in modern western society. Our usual frame of reference is Yoga and eastern mysticism but we're also interested in being 'spiritual' in the world." irreg; 1-yr sub price: $5.50; sample: $1.25. 1974. 48-200pp; 6 x 9 and 8½ x 11. of. circ. 3,500. Reporting time: 1 month. Payment: 7½% sales. no ads. Discounts: 50% distributors, 40% bookstores. Back issues: Vol 1-$1.25. §new age spiritual.

‡**DIAGONAL CERO,** Calle 7, #546, 2E La Pl., Buenos Aires, Argentina.

DIAL-A-POEM POETS LP'S, Giorno Poetry Systems Records, John Giorno, 222 Bowery, New York, NY 10012, 212-925-6372. Poetry. "LP records of over 75 poets reading their work." 4 LPs/yr; price per copy: $4.98 single album/$7.98 double album. 1969. circ. 2,000. CCLM, COSMEP.

Diana Press, Inc, Coletta Reid, Casey Czarnik, 12 West 25th St., Baltimore, MD 21218. Non-fiction. "We publish feminist books by women, for women." 1972. †of. Reporting time: 6 mos. Payment: 10% retail price or 50% net profit. Discounts: trade 40%.

DIANA'S BIMONTHLY, Tom Ahern, 71 Elmgrove Ave., Providence, RI 02906. Poetry, fiction, art, photos. "For 1976, will print mostly folios, single poems and single authors. *All* material solicited. In 1975 published pamphlets by Keith and Rosemarie Waldrop, Charles Hine, David Ball, Walter Hall, and Hannah Weiner. In 1976: Terry Stokes, Bill Zavatsky, Jaimy Gordon, Bruce Andrews & others." 6/yr; 1-yr sub price: $4.50; per copy: $.75; sample: $1.25. 1972. 12pp. †of/lp/silkscreen. circ. 500. Reporting time: 1 week. Payment: 15% of press run or $25. Discounts: 40% to dealers on orders of 5 or more. Back issues: $20 for complete Vol 1/$20 for Vol 2/$25 for Vol 3. CCLM, CRISP.

The Dickens Fellowship (see THE DICKENSIAN)

THE DICKENSIAN, The Dickens Fellowship, Andrew Sanders, 48 Doughty St., London WC1N 2LF, United Kingdom, Birkbeck College, Malet St., London WC1, United Kingdom. Articles, criticism. "Specialist journal referring to Dickens, his life & works, with Victorian background information and book reviews, reports on Fellowship (International) activities and strong critical and academic articles." 3/yr; 1-yr sub price: £3(UK)/£3.50 (overseas). 1905. 68pp. lp. circ. 2,000 plus.

Payment: nil. Ads: £40.00/£45.00(overseas) pro rata. Pub'd 3 issues 1976; expects 3 issues 1977, 3 issues 1978.

THE DICKINSON REVIEW, William Fleming, L. Ray Wheeler, Div. of English, Dickinson State College, Dickinson, ND 58601. Poetry, articles, criticism. "James Tate & Miller Williams." 1/yr; 1-yr sub price: $1.50; per copy: $2.00; sample: $2.00. 1967. 70pp; 6½ x 9. of. Reporting time: 2 mo. Payment: 5 copies. Discounts: 40% discount to agents. §philosophy/film/fiction.

A DIFFERENT DRUMMER—THE POET'S JOURNAL, Addrummer Press Ltd., Samuel Evins Brown, 18 Union St Rt, Toms Rvr., NJ 08753, 201-341-0835. Poetry. "Preferably short poems/25 lines maximum. Personal, existential themes only. Unpublished poets who have never been in print & are continually receiving rejection slips are welcome to submit to our poetry journal. Query first. [SASE] No more than 3 poems submitted! Three publishing plans. Contests. Subscribers wanted. Prefers positive subjective themes. [Dedicated to Thoreau & individualistic thinking & creativity.]" 12/yr; 1-yr sub price: $20.08; per copy: $1.99; sample: $1.99. 1975. 24pp; 6 x 9. †of. circ. 5,000 & growing fast!. Reporting time: 1 month. Payment: Contributor copies. Copyrighted, reverts to author.

DIGNITY, Wayne Ward, 755 Boylston St. Room 413, Boston, MA 02116. Poetry, articles, interviews, satire, criticism, reviews, letters. "Recent contributors: Gregory Baum, Bob Nugent, Bill Roberts, John McNeill, Norman Pittenger, Jeannine Gramick, Thomas Oddo, Paul Diederich, Bob Fournier, Peg Barry." monthly; 1-yr sub price: $15.00; sample: free. 1969. 12pp; 8½ x 11. of. circ. 5,000 plus per issue. Copyrighted. Back issues: negotiable. Expects 12 issues 1977, 12 issues 1978. Pub's reviews. §gay Catholic experience.

‡**DIMENSION,** Box 7939, Austin, TX 78712. CCLM.

The Direct Marketing Writer's Guild (see COPY CORNUCOPIA)

DIVINE TOAD SWEAT, The Neo-American Church, Inc., Art Kleps, 423 Northgate, North Ave, Burlington, VT 05401. 1-yr sub price: $10.00; per copy: $1.00; sample: $.25. 6pp; 8½ x 11. of. circ. 79. §psychedelic drugs/religion/philosophy.

DR. DOBB'S JOURNAL OF COMPUTER CALISTHENICS & ORTHODONTIA, People's Computer Co., Jim Warren, 1263 El Camino, P. O. Box E, Menlo Park, CA 94025, 415-323-3111. Articles, interviews, criticism, reviews, letters. "Considered the source of software for personal and home computing." 10/yr; 1-yr sub price: $12.00; per copy: $1.50. 1976. 48 to 64pp; 8½ x 11. of. circ. 11,000 copies sold per issue. Payment: none. Copyrighted. Ads: none accepted. Discounts: discounts to resellers and subscription agencies. Back issues: $13.00 for all of 1976. Pub'd 10 issues 1976; expects 10 issues 1977, 10 issues 1978. Pub's reviews. §computers & computer software.

Dodo Press, P.O. Box 167 Wentworth Bldg., Sydney Univ. NSW 2006, Australia.

DOGS IN CANADA, Elizabeth M. Dunn, 59 Front St. E., Toronto, Ontario M5E1B3, Canada, 363-2018. Articles, cartoons, reviews, letters. 13/yr; 1-yr sub price: $9.00; per copy: $0.75. 1889. 28pp; 10¼ x 16. of. circ. 17,000. Payment: $.20 per printed line. Copyrighted. Ads: $896.00/$448.00/$0.25 per word with $4.00 min. Pub's reviews §dogs-breeding, training, anything re purebred dogs. CPPA.

DOGSOLDIER, Dogsoldier Press, William Hudson, E. 2933 Queen, Spokane, WA 99207. Poetry, fiction, articles, interviews, reviews, parts-of-novels, long-poems. "Contributors should be forewarned that we have a wealth of material on hand: will take strong MSS to break in, and new acceptances can expect a year's wait before seeing print. (Publication very irregular now as time & energies devoted toward establishing small press center—library? store? —locally. Suggestions and support welcomed.) Recent Contributors: Judson Crews, Joan Colby, Susan Fromberg Schaefer, Al Drake, Brian Swann, Barbara Holland, many others." 2-3/yr; sub price: $5.50/4 issues; per copy: $1.75; sample: $1.00. 1974. 100pp; 5½ x 8½. of. circ. 500. Reporting time: 4-6 weeks. Payment:

copies only. Ads: exchange/exchange/none. Discounts: 40% (5 or more copies)/20% to subscription agents. Pub's reviews. §fiction/any northwest-based mags. CCLM, COSMEP.

Dollar of Soul Press, Owen Davis, Jeremy Hilton, 4 Alexandra Terrace, Swanage, Dorset, United Kingdom. Poetry. avg. price, paper: 45p. 1975. 30pp; a5. photo-litho. avg. press run 200. no unsolicited mss. Payment: nil. Author. Discounts: 33-1/3 percent trade. Expects 4 titles 1977.

Dolphin Editions (see also ARION'S DOLPHIN), Stratis Haviaris, William Corbett, Paul Hannigan, John Bakti Box 313, Cambridge, MA 02138. "A cooperative non-profit outfit for poetry monographs. The first 4 books will be out within two weeks, and are the following: Allan Dugan, *SEQUENCE.* Cover designed & silkscreened by Judy Shahn, Paul Hannigan, *BRINGING BACK SLAVERY.* Cover by Steven Trefonides, John Batki, *FALLING UPWARDS.* Poems & drawings; Jay Boggis, *TURGOR.* Cover by Philip Guston." 1976.

Dolphin-Moon (see also CAIM), 1829 Colonial Rd, Baltimore, MD 21207. "Books and chapbooks by poets, fiction writers and dramatists. In addition, anthologies as well as childrens' books are in the planning stages. A book of poems by Peter Wild is in the planning stages-due to appear in late '76 or early '77."

Dorset Poets Society (see also UNDER DORSET SKIES), Malc Payne, 14 Bryanston St, Blandford, Forum, Dorset DT117AZ, United Kingdom, Blandford 25082 3409. Poetry. "Poems solicited from Dorset folk only (worldwide) average 30-35 lines." avg. price, paper: £1. 1975. 64pp. litho. avg. press run 250. No payments. Copyright retained by authors. Discounts: 33-1/3 percent only on bulk. Pub'd 250 titles 1976; expects 250 titles 1977, 250 titles 1978. Dorset Poets (1972) Society.

Dovetail Press, D. Cushman, Publisher, 627 West 113th Street, New York, NY 10025. Poetry, fiction. "Poetry almost exclusively will be published; fiction contemplated. *REST IN LOVE* by D. H. Melhem (paperback, 103 pg, $2.95) a sequence of poems. 1975 is the first publication. Submissions not solicited." 1975. of.

DOWN RIVER, World Publication's, Bob Anderson, World Publications, P.O. Box 366, Mtn. View, CA 94040. Fiction, articles, art, photos, cartoons, interviews. "The editor has complete control over all published material. 'DOWN RIVER' covers canoeing, kayaking, rafting and other forms of transportation on Americas waterways. There's also information on river safety, and every issue tells of someone's adventure on a river." 12/yr; 1-yr sub price: $8.00; per copy: $.75; sample: free upon request. 1974. 32pp; 9 x 11. of. circ. 5,000. Reporting time: variable. Discounts: bulk rate available. Back issues: $1.00 ea. Pub's reviews.

Down There Press, Joani Blank, PO Box 2086, Burlingame, CA 94010, 415-342-9867. "So far I have published three books which I wrote myself. They are *The Playbook For Women About Sex, The Playbook For Men About Sex,* and *Good Vibrations; The Complete Women's Guide To Vibrators.* In 1977 I will be publishing *A Sexuality Play/Work Book For Children, Ages 8-12.*" avg. price, paper: $3.00. 1975. 48pp; 8½ x 11. of. avg. press run 2,000. COSMEP.

DPG Publishing Co./Dumont Press Graphics, 97 Victoria St. N, Kitchener, Ontario, Canada. avg. price, cloth: $10.00 - $12.00; paper: $5.00 - $7.00. 1971. 200pp; 5 x 8. †of. avg. press run 3,000. Copyrights for author. Expects 4 titles 1977, 4 titles 1978. COSMEP, IPA.

DRAGONFLY:A Quarterly Of Haiku, J & C Transcripts, Lorraine Ellis Harr, Assoc; Carl F. Harr, Kametaro Yagi, (Japan); Kazuo Sato, (Japan); Gustave Keyser, 4102 N.E. 130th Pl., Portland, OR 97230. Poetry. "Classical/traditional Haiku only. 300 word articles on pertinent subjects. Forum page: 300 word (or less) Articles on points of Haiku writing. Must be concise and to the point. Paul O. Williams, Carl F. Harr, Kazuo Sato, Prof. K. Yagi, Oliver Statler, Alan Watts, Richard Hansen, Robert Draper." 4/yr; 1-yr sub price: $6.00; per copy: $1.50; sample: $1.50. 1967. 68pp; 5½ x 8½. lp. circ. over 500. Reporting time: usually by return mail within 30 days. Payment: Many cash & book prizes, awards. n.p. Discounts: 10 percent off yearly sub. Back issues: $1.25 until Jan. 1977, then $1.50. Pub's reviews. §Oriental poetry, anything relating to Haiku-Senryu-Haibun, Zen/Am. Indian, etc. WWHS.

‡**DRAGONFLY, Dragonfly Press,** 3415 Bell Ave., Eugene, OR 97402. CCLM.

Dragon's Teeth Press, Cornel Lengyel, Adams Acres, El Dorado Nat. Forest, Georgetown, CA 95634. Poetry, music. 1970. 64-128pp; 5½ x 8½ or 8½ x 11. of. Reporting time: 6 wks. Payment: 10% royalty.

THE DRAMA REVIEW, Michael Kirby, Editor; Kate Davy, Managing Editor, 51 West 4th St. Room 300, New York, NY 10012, 212-598-2597. Articles, photos, plays. "TDR documents new trends in contemporary avant-garde performance. (plays are published only as partial documentation of historically significant productions). TDR is interested in performance analysis, not dramatic evaluation, interpretation or criticism." 4/yr; 1-yr sub price: $12.50; per copy: $3.50; sample: $3.50. 1955. 144pp; 7 x 10. of. circ. 10,000. Reporting time: 2 weeks. Payment: 2 cents a word; $10.00/photo. Copyrighted, does not revert to author. Ads: $287.00/$172.00. Discounts: 40 percent bookstores; 10 percent subscription agencies. Back issues: $3.50-$6.00, depending on no. of copies still in print & available. Pub's reviews. §Theatre, drama, art performance, avant-garde performance indigenous drama. CCLM, COSMEP, ASME, CELJ.

DRAMATIKA, Dramatika Produce, John Pyros, Janice Pyros, 390 Riverside Dr., New York, NY 10025. Plays. "Performable pieces only (plays, songs, etc.)" 2/yr; 1-yr sub price: $5.00; per copy: $2.50. 1968. 50pp; 8 x 11. Reporting time: 2 mos. Payment: copies only. CCLM, COSMEP.

Dramatika Produce (see also DRAMATIKA), John Pyros, Janice Pyros, 390 Riverside Dr., New York, NY 10025. "Solicit biographies of performing arts, avant-garde figures, especially from previously unpublished M.A. or PH.D. theses-also off-beat novella length pieces."

DREAMS AND INNER SPACES, Gerald Joseph, Patricia Pirmantgen, Edendale PO 26556, Los Angeles, CA 90026. "Contents based primarily on personal experiences of author-editors. We call the periodical a newsletter but personal journal would probably be more accurate. Submissions not accepted." 10/yr; 1-yr sub price: $6.00; per copy: free/sase; sample: free/SASE. 1973. 4pp printed, 8pp mimeo; 8½ x 11. †mi. Back issues: $5/volume. COSMEP.

DREMPLES, Jaap Boerdam, Stewart Florsheim, Scott Rollins, Paul Wilcox, Joh. Verhulststr. 102, Amsterdam, The Netherlands. Poetry, fiction, articles, art, photos, interviews, letters, parts-of-novels, long-poems. "Recent contributors include: Michael Hamburger, Ray Rudnik, Anthony Rudolf. Publishes poetry in original and english translation; We will 'supply' english translation if you cannot. Have published work in Dutch, German, Spanish. The rest of the mag is published in English." 4/yr; 1-yr sub price: $9.00; per copy: $2.50; sample: free. 1975. 48pp; 14½ x 21 cm. of. circ. 500. Reporting time: 2-4 wks. Payment: 2 issues.

A DRIFTGLIDE IN TIME, Waystar Books, Rick Lawler, 3138 W. Dakota, 229, Fresno, CA 93711. Poetry, fiction, articles, art, reviews. "Length: Open/Enclose SASE" 1/yr; 1-yr sub price: $1.00; per copy: $1.00; sample: $1.00. 1975. 28pp; 5½ x 8¼. of/le. circ. 500. Reporting time: month. Payment: copy/$if possible. Discounts: 35% discount on orders of 10 or more. §Science Fiction, Poetry, Film.

DRIFTWOOD-EAST, Marjorie L. Drake, 95 Carter Avenue, P.O. Box 2262, Pawtucket, RI 02861, 401-723-5184. Poetry, reviews. "Poems, any style; not over 20 lines. Dr. Max Barker, Henry P. Beechhold, Michaelena Buonocore, Liboria Romano, Roberta Goldstein, Gertrude M. Lutz, Dr. Raymond Stark, A. De Pietro, Dr. Louis J. Cantoni, Angelo De Luca, Florence Ungarst, Jaye Giamarino, Frederick Raborg, J. T. Stigner, M. J. Richardson, Edna Jones Kayser, M. C. Rosner, Mary T. Brizzi, Madeline Mason - (of Mason Sonnet)." 4/yr; 1-yr sub price: $6.00; per copy: $1.50; sample: $1.00 (2 back issues). 1973. 76pp; 6 x 9. of. circ. 1000. Reporting time: 2weeks. Payment: Services, book awards, contests. 3 subscriptions each issue, 5 poets chosen & paid. Page poets receive 3 extra months, center fold poets receive 6 months addition to subscription.

Copyrighted. no ads. Discounts: $1.00 off to colleges if purchased through *me, not* thru Ebsco!. Back issues: 2 for $1.00. Pub'd 4 issues 1976; expects 4 issues 1977, 4 issues 1978. Pub's reviews: 24 in 1976. §Poetry.

DRINKWATCHERS' NEWSLETTER, Gullistan Press, Ariel Winters, PO Box 179, Haverstraw, NY 10927, 914-429-4844. Cartoons, reviews. "Interested in outstanding alcoholic spirit recipes, hints on controlled drinking, news about alcohol treatment programs, etc. Short material only." 12/yr; 1-yr sub price: $12.00; per copy: $1.00; sample: free. 1975. 4pp; 9 x 11. circ. about 1,000. Payment: $5.00-$10.00, or higher, varies, Most contribute free. Copyrighted. Discounts: 30-40 percent according to no. Back issues: $1.00 ea. §Books related to alcohol and related problems.

Druid Books, Jon Reilly, Ephraim, WI 54211. Poetry, fiction, photos. 1969. 50pp; 5½ x 8½ usually. of. Payment: Author's royalties 10% of retail price, plus copies. Discounts: 40% book retail, 50% book distributors.

Druid Heights Books, 685 Camino Del Canyon, Muir Woods, Mill Valley, CA 94941.

Drunken-Juggler Press (see also SMALL MOON MAGAZINE), Ed Cates, Ron Vachon, 12 Cooney St, Somerville, MA 02143. Poetry, art, photos, interviews, criticism, reviews, concrete art. *"The Insect In The Rose Of The Heart,* selected poems of Jean Follain." 1977. of. Reporting time: Closed to submission right now.

‡**Dryad Press,** c/o Lehrman, 2943 Broderick St., San Francisco, CA 94123. CCLM.

Duck Down Press (see also SCREE), Kirk Robertson, Nila Northsun, Box 761, Fallon, NV 89406. Poetry, fiction, art, collages, concrete art. "Titles in print: *Chase* - Gerald Locklin; *Red Work Black Widow* - Steve Richmond; *Men Under Fire* - Ronald Koertge; *The Kid Comes Home* - Leo Mailman; *The Man In The Black Chevrolet* - Todd Moore; *Diet Pepsi & Nacho Cheese* - Nila Northsun; *Whiplash On The Couch* - John Bennett; *Asylum Picnic* - Robert Matte, Jr." avg. price, paper: $2.00 $3.00; other: Signed lettered editions - $25.00 (no discount). 1973. 24-72pp; varies. †of. avg. press run 500-750. Reporting time: Fast. Payment: Copies plus share of £ above expenses. Copyrights for author. Discounts: 5 or more, 40 percent. Pub'd 5 titles 1976; expects 3 titles 1977, 3-4 titles 1978. CCLM, COSMEP-WEST, LPSC.

Duende Press (see also FERVENT VALLEY), Box 571, Placitas, NM 87043. "Avant garde song. Submissions will be burned."

Duke University Press (see AMERICAN LITERATURE)

THE DURHAM UNIVERSITY JOURNAL, J.M.I. Rogister, 43 North Bailey, Durham DH1 3EX, United Kingdom. Criticism. "Mss. and books for review should be sent to the editor, 43 N. Bailey, Durham, England. All correspondence on other matters relating to the journal should be sent to the chief clerk, Univ. Office, Old Shire Hall, Durham. Subscriptions should be made payable to University of Durham." 2/yr; 1-yr sub price: £2.50 plus 35p (postage); per copy: £1.25 plus 15p (postage). 1876. 250-300pp; 7¼ x 4. lp. circ. 800. Reporting time: 3 mos. No payment. Copyrighted. Ads: £50.00/ £30.00/£4.00401/4 page. Pub'd 2 issues 1976; expects 2 issues 1977, 2 issues 1978. Pub's reviews. §Literature, history, philosophy, classical studies, theology, poetry.

Dustbooks (see also SMALL PRESS REVIEW), Len Fulton, Ellen Ferber, Box 1056, Paradise, CA 95969, 916-877-6110. "We have a small general trade list and will continue to do poetry (2 titles a year), novels, anthologies, non-fiction prose, how-to, etc. But it should be remembered that our real expertise & commitment is small press-mag info. On January 1st of every year we face a full year of publishing without looking at one new manuscript. We do three annuals:this Directory you're holding which takes 5 months from start to finish and $25,000; its companion volume, the DIRECTORY OF SMALL MAGAZINE-PRESS EDITORS and PUBLISHERS, and the SMALL PRESS RECORD OF BOOKS In Print (latest edition-240 pp). We do one monthly, the SMALL

PRESS REVIEW which we also print ourselves in the back yard. We've done a nice string of general trade books (see ads) and will do many more, but our space is severely modified by our mainstay titles above. Best to query & send sample pages of anything along." avg. price, cloth: $7.95; paper: $2.95. 1963. 64-200pp; 5½ x 8½. of. avg. press run 1-2 M. Reporting time: 3-6 months. Payment: royalty (15%). Copyrights for author. Discounts: 2-10, 25 percent; 11-25, 40 percent; 26 plus, 50 percent (bookstores), distributors by arrangement, jobbers 25 percent. Pub'd 8 titles 1976; expects 8 titles 1977, 10 titles 1978. ALP, CCLM, COSMEP, LPS.

Dymax (see also CALCULATORS/COMPUTERS), Don Inman, PO Box 310, Menlo Park, CA 94025, 415-323-6111. Art, photos, cartoons, reviews, non-fiction. "Books written for all ages; games & tricks for calculators, as well as books for computer programming." avg. price, paper: $2.00. 1969. 75pp. Composer. avg. press run 10,000. Payment: 15 percent. Our books are copyrighted. Ads: $200.00/$120.00. Discounts: resalers (bookstores) 1-4 copies-25 percent; 5-99-40 percent; 100-499-42 percent; 500-999-45 percent; 1,000 plus-50 percent. Back issues: $2.00. Expects 2 titles 1977. COSMEP.

Dynamite Books (see BLUE WIND PRESS)

E & E Enterprises, P.O. Box 405, Howell, NJ 07731. "Recent book: DYNAMICS OF THE FAMILY UNIT, by Edmond Knowles."

E & R Marlin, Publishers, 1 Regent St, Ottawa, 1 K1S2R4, Canada. "The Ottawa Newspaper Review has not been published since January 1973. However, it may be revived at any time, and we have just published a booklet, *The Home Daycare Manual*." †mi.

E.M. Press (see SPANNER)

Eads Street Press, Mort Castle, 402 Stanton Lane, Crete, IL 60417. Poetry, fiction. "In 1976, EADS STREET PRESS will publish only chapbooks. Hate slop lock lyrics claiming to be poetry, Hallmark soft-focus sentiment, all manner of unk-jay. Especial interest in the work of young poets, and, while submissions are not sought at this time, queries are welcome. Upcoming books, *Specimen Hunting*, by Lisa Smith, *The Morning House*, by Chris Amati, *Is Cold Oatmeal Like Life?* by Mark Harmon, first publication for all three poets who are seventeen years old. Submissions not sought at this time." 1975. pp varies; 8½ x 5½. Payment: generous batch of copies. Discounts: 40 percent bookstores agents. COSMEP.

THE EAR IN A WHEATFIELD, Kris Hemensley, "Clifton", 24 Urquhart St., Westgarth, Victoria 3070, Australia. "Anglo-American, Australasian, work in translation (French, German, Japanese, Italian), poetry and prose. (UK): J. Riley, Longville, Hall; (USA): Koller, Coolidge, Palmer, Bromige, Davidson; (Austr-NZ): Tranter, Billeter, Maiden; (Transl): Jabes, Ponge, Celan, Elgner, Dawson. I ought to emphasize that most work in 'THE EAR' is solicited. Air or S.A.L. for contributors; sea-mail for others." irreg.; price per copy: A$.50-A$1.50. 1973. 60-100pp; A-4. †mi. circ. 150. Reporting time: prompt. Payment: 0 to $2/page. Copyrighted. Ads: None. Discounts: Nil. Back issues: Back issues are available. Pub'd 3 issues 1976; expects 3 issues 1977. Pub's reviews: 6 in 1976.

EAR MAGAZINE, Ear, Beth Anderson, Richard Hayman, 32 East Second St., apt 22, New York, NY 10003. Poetry, fiction, articles, art, photos, cartoons, interviews, satire, criticism, reviews, music, letters, parts-of-novels, collages, concrete art. "Short is best. Avant-garde bias. Contributors: Nam June Paik, Anna Lockwood, Alison Knowles, Dick Higgins." 10/yr; 1-yr sub price: $10.00; per copy: $1.00; sample: $.50. 1973. 8pp; 16 x 11½. of. circ. 1,000. Reporting time: 4 mos. Payment: none available. Ads: $100/$50/$1. Discounts: 50 cents each. Back issues: Price varies (approx $2 each).

101

EARTH'S DAUGHTERS, Judith Kerman, Lillian Robinson, Elaine Rollwagen, 944 Kensington Ave, Buffalo, NY 14215. Poetry, fiction, art, photos, parts-of-novels, long-poems, plays. "We are a feminist arts periodical." 2/yr; 1-yr sub price: varies; per copy: $1.50; sample: $1.50. 1971. pp varies; Varies. of. circ. 1,000. Reporting time: 3-6 months. Payment: 6 copies of issue. Copyrighted, reverts to author. Discounts: trade 30-35%; bulk 35%; jobber-straight rates. Back issues: no special price. Pub'd 1 issue 1976; expects 2 issues 1977, 2 issues 1978. §Work by women or in feminist themes. CCLM, COSMEP.

East African Publishing House, Lennard Okola, Richard C. Ntiru, Sald Mzee, Nyoike Waiyaki, PO Box 30571, Nairobi, Kenya, Africa, 557417 & 555694. avg. price, cloth: Ksh. 60.00; paper: Ksh. 30.00. 1965. lp/of. avg. press run 7,500. Discounts: 20 percent, 25 percent, 30 percent, 35 percent. Pub'd 35 titles 1976; expects 25 titles 1977, 35 titles 1978.

East Carolina University Poetry Forum Press (see TAR RIVER POETS)

East 128 (see PIANETA FRESCO)

EAST RIVER REVIEW, Daniel Stokes, Publisher, Daniel M. J. Stokes, 1807-60th St, Brooklyn, NY 11204. Poetry, fiction, plays. "No Biases. Recent contributors: Barbara A. Holland, Duane Locke, Alan Britt, Eugene Mcnamara, Patricia Eakins, Bob Arnold, etc., etc." irreg.; price per copy: $.50-$1.00; sample: $.75. 1974. 18-48pp; 5½ x 8½. of. circ. 300. Reporting time: 1 month. Payment: 2 copies. Discounts: 10 plus 40%.

East River Anthology, Jan Barry, W. D. Ehrhart, 114 N 6th St., Perkasie, PA 18944. Poetry, fiction, art, photos. "Currently distributing *Demilitarized ZONES: Veterans After Vietnam*, East River Anthology, 1976; 100 contributors, 177pp, $2.95; and *WINNING HEARTS AND MINDS: War Poems by Vietnam Vetrans*, 1st Casualty Press (now defunct), 1972; 33 contributors, 108pp, $2.00. Not now seeking new material; would like to branch out from Indochina themes, but have no definite plans yet; our orientation: anti-war; peace and freedom through non-violent social action. Recent contributors: Philip Appleman, John Balaban, Jan Barry, D.C. Berry, Steven Ford Brown, Michael Casey, Merritt Clifton, Horace Coleman, W.D. Ehrhart, George Knowlton, Gerald McCarthy, Stephen Sossaman, Bruce Weigl and 120 others." 1975. 5¼ x 8. of. avg. press run 5,000. Reporting time: varies, as soon as possible. Payment: contributors copies. Copyright to East River Anthology, but place no restrictions on future use by individual authors. Discounts: bulk orders of 10 or more: 50 percent plus shipping; bookstores: 50 percent plus shipping, pay in advance; no other discounts (all orders are pay in advance except libraries). COSMEP.

Eberhard Ebner (see S.H.Y.)

Ecart Publications, John M. Armleder, 6, Rue Plantamour, Geneva CH -1201, Switzerland, 022-32.67.94/022-45.73.95. Poetry, art, photos, interviews, music, letters, collages, concrete art. "Fluxus, post fluxus, intermedia, mail-art, rubber-stamp. Recent publications by: Endre Tot, Herve Fischer, Paul-Armand Gette, Dan Graham, Genesis P. Orridge/Coum, Robert Filliou, Tamas Sentjoy, Al Souza, James W. Felter. Planning 2 magsin 1976-77." avg. price, cloth: $5.00-$10.00; paper: $5.00-$10.00; other: $5.00-$10.00. (1969) 1973. 30/100pp; din a5-a4. †of/other. avg. press run 500. Payment: no standards. Copyright to the author, usually. Discounts: trade: 33 -1/3%. Pub'd 10 titles 1976; expects 10 titles 1977, 10 titles 1978.

The Ecco Press (see also ANTAEUS). Poetry, fiction. avg. price, cloth: $6.95; paper: $2.95. pp varies; Varies. avg. press run 4,000. Payment: advance and royalties. Copyrights for author. Discounts: Distributed by Viking - their discount schedule. Pub'd 7 titles 1976; expects 7 titles 1977, 8 titles 1978.

ECHO, Echo Books, Hank Johnsen, P.O. Box 728, Station A, Vancouver, B. C. V6C2N7, Canada. Poetry. "Generally under 100 lines. No concrete or nursery rhymes. Contributors, so far, include George Bowering, Bill Bissett, Rosalind Macphee, John Ditsky." every 8 mos.; sub price: 3 issues $3.00 (or donation); per copy: $1.00; sample: $1.00. 1975. 100pp; 4¼ x 5½. of. circ. 1,000.

Reporting time: 3-10 wks. Payment: (Contest; $.50 entry fee per poem). Ads: $40/$25. Discounts: none, yet. Back issues: none, yet. Pub's reviews. §Primarily poetry mags & books.

ECO CONTEMPORANEO, Eco Contemporaneo Press, Miguel Grinberg, C C Central 1933, 1000 Buenos Aires, Argentina. Poetry. Quarterly; price per copy: $1.00; sample: Free. 1961. 50pp; 20 cm x 15 cm. †mi. circ. 1,000. Reporting time: Immediate. Payment: None. Copyrighted. no ads. Discounts: None. Expects 4 issues 1977, 4 issues 1978. APS.

Eco Contemporaneo Press, Miguel Grinberg, C C Central 1933, 1000 Buenos Aires, Argentina. Poetry. avg. price, paper: $1.00. 1961. 50pp; size varies. †mi. avg. press run 1,000. Reporting time: Immediate. Pub'd 3 titles 1976.

THE ECOLOGIST, Edward Goldsmith, Ruth Lumley-Smith, Managing Editor, 73 Molesworth St., Wadebridge, Cornwall PL27 7DS, United Kingdom. Articles, cartoons, reviews, interviews, criticism, letters. "Articles of a serious and well researched type up to 6,000 words. Shorter reports. Journal should be studied for style and content." 10/yr; 1-yr sub price: £6.00 (Sterling) ($14.50); per copy: 50p ($1.40 post free); sample: free. 1970. 36pp; A4. of. circ. 10,000 plus. Reporting time: 2-6 wks. Payment: £10.00 per thousand (Sterling) or by arrangement. Ads: apply advertising agent. Discounts: agents 20%. Back issues: 60p (post free $1.40).

EDCENTRIC MAGAZINE, Center for Educational Reform, Inc., Wendy Young, Ken Miller, Linda Duggan, PO Box 1802, Eugene, OR 97401. Poetry, articles, art, photos, interviews, criticism, reviews, letters. "Edcentric is a journal of educational change. We attempt to draw links between movements for educational change and movements for social change, and between educational institutions and social structure, from a progressive perspective. We attempt to serve as a forum for people working for change in education and through education. Especially interested in original investigation and analysis, reports of current projects, resources and experiences of people working for change. Length ranges from very short to about 5000 words. Recent contributors include Diane Divoky & Peter Schrag, Jonathan Kozol, Miriam Wasserman, Harry Braverman, Charles Isaacs and many people who had never previously published." 4-6/yr; sub price: $6 (6 issues); per copy: $1; sample: $1 (free to librarians). 1969. 32pp; 8½ x 11. of. circ. 4,000. Reporting time: 2-3 mos. Payment: copies of magazine. Ads: $300/$165/$.25. Discounts: 40% off bulk orders. Back issues: $.60 for older issues. Pub's reviews. §Education, children, relationships to political movements & society. COSMEP, APS.

EDDY, Eddy Dance Foundation, Inc., Tom Borek, 124 Chambers St, New York, NY 10007, 212-962-1327. Poetry, fiction, articles, art, photos, cartoons, interviews, satire, criticism, reviews, music, letters, collages, plays, concrete art. "Mainly, about dance." irregular, but at least 3/yr; sub price: $9/six issues; per copy: $2; sample: $2. 1973. 80pp; 8 x 10½. of. circ. 600. Reporting time: open. Payment: 7 copies. Copyrighted. no ads. Back issues: $2/copy. Pub'd 2 issues 1976; expects 3 issues 1977, 3 issues 1978. Pub's reviews: 3 in 1976. §especially dance. COSMEP.

Eden Valley Press, Inc. (see THE EMISSARY)

EDGE, The Edge Press, D. S. Long, 161 Taylor's Mistake Road, Christchurch 8, N Zlnd, Sumner 5084. Poetry, fiction, articles, art, photos, interviews, criticism, reviews, parts-of-novels, long-poems, collages, plays, concrete art. "Charles Simic, Gary Snyder, William Stafford, W. S. Merwin, Jorge Luis Borges, Rene Char, George Hitchcock, Gary Langford, Ian Wedde" irregular; 1-yr sub price: $0.00; per copy: $2.00; sample: $2.00. 1971. 64pp; 6 x 8½. †lp. circ. 1,000 to 2,000 (varies). Reporting time: mss. back to post same week received. Payment: about $8.00 a page plus 2 copies. Copyrighted, reverts to author. Ads: advertising now excluded. Discounts: NZ stores 33-1/3%/overseas stores 40%. Back issues: $2.00 a copy. Pub's reviews. §poetry the most. COSMEP, COSMEPA, NZ book council and assoc. of handcraft printers.

The Edge Press (see also EDGE), D. S. Long, 161 Taylor's Mistake Road, Christchurch 8, N Zlnd, Sumner 5084. Poetry. "William L. Fox, D. S. Long, Trevor Reeves, Bert Meyers, John Haines (all broadsheets)" avg. price, paper: $1.00. 1971. pp varies. †lp. avg. press run 100 printed and set by

103

hand broadsheets. Reporting time: mss. back to post same month received. Payment: many copies. Copyright if desired. Discounts: NZ stores 33 -1/3%/overseas stores 40%. COSMEP, COSMEPA, Nz book council and assoc of handcraft printers.

Edgepress (see also EVALUATION NEWS), Michael Scriven, Box 64, Point Reyes, CA 94956, 415-663-1511. Non-fiction. "Usually only consider book length manuscripts in the philosophy of science, practical logic, contemporary moral issues. Check before sending. Will evaluate, also publish in all fields at author's expense." avg. price, cloth: $12.50; paper: $8.50. 1975. 300pp; 5½ x 8½. of. avg. press run 2,000. Reporting time: preliminary within a few days. Payment: either straight 15 percent or 25 percent of profits. Copyrights for author. Discounts: trade 25 percent/bulk 20 percent/classroom 25 percent/agent 35 percent/jobber 35 percent. Pub'd 1 title 1976; expects 2 titles 1977, 2 titles 1978. COSMEP.

Editions Cinema/Quebec (see CINEMA/QUEBEC)

‡Editions De Femmes, 2 Rue De La Roquette, Paris 75011, France.

Editorial Pocho Che (see TINTAN)

EDWARDIAN DRAMA & LITERATURE, Edwardian D&L Assn, Eric Ford, High Orchard, 125 Markyate Road, Dagenham, Essex RM8 2LB, United Kingdom. "Promote interest in Edwardian drama & literature." 1/yr; price per copy: £3 p.a. 1976. A5. lo/dupl. Payment: copies. Ads: £15/pro rata (new journal check rates, please). Discounts: 20%.

EEL, Eel Press, P. Inman, 3314 Mt. Pleasant NW No. 2, Washington, DC 20010. Poetry, fiction, photos, parts-of-novels, long-poems. "Bias toward non-referential and/or procedural works. Contributors: Hanah Weiner, Allen Fisher, Susan Howe, Lynne Dreyer, Michael Lally, Tina Darragh, Lennart Bruce, Doug Lang, Kathy Acker, Michael Sappol, Terence Winch, Opal Nations." 2/yr; price per copy: $1.00; sample: $1.00. 1974. 40pp; 8½ x 11. of. circ. 250. Reporting time: month. Payment: none. Not copyrighted. Ads: no. Discounts: 40 percent trade. Back issues: $1.00 for No. 3, all others op. Pub'd 1 issue 1976; expects 2 issues 1977. CCLM.

‡EEN HAND, Morsestraat 24, Den Haag, Holland.

EFRYDIAU ATHRONYDDOL, University of Wales Press, T.A. Roberts, 6 Gwennyth St., Cathays, Cardiff, Wales, United Kingdom. 1/yr; 1-yr sub price: 37p. Discounts: trade 25%.

EH?, Clayton S. Fisk, 3007 University, Austin, TX 78705, 512-472-7415. Poetry, fiction, articles, art, photos, cartoons, interviews, satire, criticism, reviews, music, letters, parts-of-novels, long-poems, collages, plays, concrete art. "*EH?* is a magazine devoted to contemporary dada/surrealism and applications of such schools of thought to 'real-world' situations. We approach d/s from a sceptical point of view even though we encourage its development. NB: we do not consider gratuitous scatology, pornography or obscenity to be anything other than scatology...etc." 4/yr; 1-yr sub price: $6.00; per copy: $2.00. 1977. pp: who knowspp; 8½ x 11. mi/of. Reporting time: 3 mos. Payment: copies, money will be worked out as it becomes available (haha). Not copyrighted. Ads: none. Discounts: none. Pub'd 2 issues 1976. Pub's reviews: none in 1976. §any and all.

Eight Miles High Press (see LUDD'S MILL)

Either/Or Publications (see ALPHA)

EKISTICS, Athens Center of Ekistics, Gwen Bell, Editor; Rebecca Packard, Assistant Editor; J. Tyrwhitt, Consultant Editor, Page Farm Road, Lincoln, MA 01773, 617-259-9144. Articles, art, photos, cartoons. "Each issue of EKISTICS covers a single aspect of human settlements. The articles describe new methodological approaches, the findings of original empirical research, and prescriptions for the future. It is recommended that all textual material be supplemented with illustrations." 12/yr; 1-yr sub price: $24.00; per copy: $3.00. 1955. 62pp; 8 x 11. †of. Reporting time: 1 day to 1 year. Payment: none. Not copyrighted. Discounts: 20 percent agent; 40 percent trade. Back issues: $4.00 after one year. §public affairs/community.

ELAN POETIQUE LITTERAIRE ET PACIFISTE, Louis Lippens, 31 Rue Foch, Linselles 59126, France, (20)78.30.68. "Poesie et temoignages au service du pacifisme integral, de la non-violence active et de l'objection de conscience permanente." trimestriel; 1-yr sub price: abonnement annuel: 20 francs (soit 4 dollars environ); sample: specimen gratuit. 1955. 12pp. of. circ. 2,000 exemplaires. Not copyrighted. §Pacifisme. APS.

ELAN VITAL: Journal of Creative Adventures, Elan Vital Publications, Mark S. Winn, P O Box 209, Hermosa Beach, CA 90254, 372-0190. Poetry, fiction, articles, art, photos, cartoons, interviews, satire, criticism, reviews, music, letters, parts-of-novels, long-poems, collages, plays, concrete art. "Approx. 5,000 word max. Only positive growth oriented material. Recent contributors: R. Buckminster Fuller, Ray White, John Douglas." 6/yr; 1-yr sub price: $15.00; per copy: $3.00; sample: Flexible. 1977. 75-100pp; 8 x 10. circ. Growing. Reporting time: 2 months. Payment: Percentage of profits. Copyrighted, reverts to author. Ads: $200.00/$100.00/0. Discounts: Not established exactly. Estimate 1-5 issues 25 percent, 5 and up 40 percent. Back issues: No back issues yet. Pub's reviews §Art, Science, Philosophy, Fantasy, Fiction.

ELBOW DRUMS, Ms. Pat Burnett, 140 2 Ave S.W., Calgary, Alberta T2P0B9, Canada, 403-264-1155. Poetry, fiction, articles, art, cartoons, letters, photos, interviews, long-poems, news items, non-fiction. 12/yr; 1-yr sub price: $3.50; per copy: $.35. 1971. 12pp; 8½ x 11. †of. circ. 600 copies. Reporting time: 2 weeks ahead. Pub'd 12 issues 1976; expects 12 issues 1977, 12 issues 1978. §indian culture.

Electronic Music Enterprises (see XENHARMONIC BULLETIN)

THE ELEMENTS, The Elements, James Ridgeway, Ed; Bettina Connor, Managing Ed; Catherine Lerza, Agriculture Ed., 1901 Q St N.W., Washington, DC 20009. "2,000 words max." Monthly, except in August; 1-yr sub price: $5 ind, $10 inst; sample: free. 1974. 12-16pp. †of. circ. 2,100. Reporting time: One month. Payment: $.10 a word. §Energy, agriculture, natural resources.

The Elizabeth Press, James L Weil, Editor & Publisher; Carroll Arnett, Associate Editor; Simon Perchik, Associate Editor, 103 Van Etten Blvd, New Rochelle, NY 10804. Poetry, non-fiction. "Mss. by solicitation only." 1961. lp. Copyright for author. Pub'd 13 titles 1976; expects 8 titles 1977, 6 titles 1978.

Ellen's Old Alchemical Press (see HARD PRESSED)

ELLIPSE, Larry Shouldice, Richard Giguere, Univ. de Sherbrooke, Box 10 Faculte des Arts, Sherbrooke, Quebec J1K2R1, Canada, 819-565-4576. 3/yr. 1969. of. Pub'd 19 issues 1976; expects 22 issues 1977, 25 issues 1978.

Elm Tree Press, Jay Rick, P O Box 1364-185, La Crosse, WI 54665. "Elm Tree Press formed to publish a book I wrote on Daycare and Head Start. Have only done one edition so far, handbound, using used paper-printed on the clean side (reviewed in North Country Anvil). Getting ready to go into 2nd edition. Will do conventional paperback and cloth if I can come up with the loot." avg. price, cloth: $5.50. 1976. 280pp; 7 x 10. of. avg. press run 500 - 1,000. Payment: none-will be doing own books and community education pamphlets. Discounts: sell direct 15 percent—30 percent to jobbers & bookstores.

Elpenor Books, Donna Mills, P O Box 3152, Chicago, IL 60654, 312-929-0906. Poetry. avg. price, cloth: $7.00; paper: $3.50. 1974. 64pp; 6 x 9. of. avg. press run 500 copies. Reporting time: 6 weeks. Payment: 12 percent. Copyrights for author.

Ember Press (see LITTACK)

Emerald City Press (see YELLOW BRICK ROAD)

EMERGENCY LIBRARIAN, Emergency Librarian, Sherrill Cheda, Phyllis Yaffe, 46 Gormley Ave, Toronto, Ontario M4V1Z1, Canada, 486-0866. Articles, art, criticism, reviews, letters. "About 1,200 words with feminist approach." 6/yr; 1-yr sub price: $9.00; per copy: $1.50; sample: $2.00. 1973. 28pp; 8½ x 11. of. circ. 1,300. Reporting time: 1 month. Payment: $25.00/article. Not copyrighted. Discounts: none. Back issues: $1.50 each. Pub'd 6 issues 1976. Pub's reviews: 100 in 1976. §feminism, library-oriented materials with Canadian emphasis. CPPA.

EMILY DICKINSON BULLETIN, Higginson Press, Frederick L. Morey, 4508 38th St., Brentwood, MD 20722. Articles, criticism, reviews. "4000 word maximum; MLA style sheet; contributors: Jay Leda, Lawrence Perrine, William White, George Monteiro (all professors). Also academics from Finland, Japan, and India." 2/yr; 1-yr sub price: $5.00 individuals $10.00 libraries; per copy: $3.00; sample: $3.00. 1968. 50pp; 5 x 8. of. circ. 250. Reporting time: 1 mo. Payment: 1 copy only. Ads: $90/$50. Discounts: 10%. Back issues: $10/yr $60 for 25 currently in print. COSMEP.

THE EMISSARY, Eden Valley Press, Inc., Robert Moore, Theodore Black, Jerry Kvasnicka, P.O. Box 328, Loveland, CO 80537, 303-667-0599. Poetry, fiction, articles, art, photos, cartoons, interviews, reviews, letters, non-fiction. "We would encourage prospective contributors to write us for a complimentary copy of the magazine (and writers' guide sheet), so that they may become familiar with the special nature of this journal. THE EMISSARY is a journal dedicated to the practical art of living. Recent contributions have included an interview with the founder-director of a boys' adventure school in the Canadian wilderness; a description of a successful communal group; articles by a doctor, a nurse and a counselor on the subject of death; articles of personal experience." 12/yr; 1-yr sub price: $7.50 (non-U.S. $8.50); per copy: $.75; sample: free. 1975. 48pp; 5¾ x 9. †of. circ. 2,500. Reporting time: month. Payment: copies. Copyrighted by Eden Valley Press, first rights only. Ads: No advertising, since we are non-profit. Discounts: 50% distributor on large orders. 40% bookstores and other retailers. Back issues: 50¢ an issue. Pub'd 12 issues 1976; expects 12 issues 1977, 12 issues 1978. Pub's reviews: 9 in 1976. §Victorious experience of living; special creativeness in fiction or in non-fiction (professional). COSMEP-WEST.

‡**EN HAA,** #19211 Quinta Crespo, Caracas 101, Venezuela.

EN PASSANT POETRY QUARTERLY, James A. Costello, 1906 Brant Rd, Wilmington, DE 19810. Poetry, art. "Insight and clear imagery should characterize the poetry. The poetry should not be self-conscious. Also takes poetry in translation. Several detailed, imaginative line drawings are used with the vertical dimension being the longest. All submissions are carefully and promptly considered and comments are offered where they might be of help. *EN PASSANT* believes that poetry is the highest form of communication, the most elemental. It is the purest distillation of speech; it is song. It is a transfusion of emotion from poet to reader. Poetry touches the mind, which imposes order on emotion, by reaching deeper than the mind." 4/yr; 1-yr sub price: $6.00; per copy: $1.75; sample: $1.50. 1975. 40pp; 5½ x 8½. of. circ. 500. Reporting time: 1 to 3 weeks. Payment: 2 copies. Takes first rights, shares remaining rights with author. Ads: none. Discounts: $1.00-per copy for orders of 6 copies or more accompanied by payment. Back issues: $1.50. Pub'd 2 issues 1976; expects 4 issues 1977, 4 issues 1978. COSMEP.

‡**ENCRES VIVES,** Castillon 09800, France.

Encuentro Ediciones (see also ENCUENTRO), Alberto Luis Ponzo, Italia 830, Castelar 1712, Buenos Aires, Argentina. Poetry, articles, interviews, criticism, letters. avg. price, cloth: $5.00. 1966. 16pp; 5½ x 8½. of. avg. press run 3,000 issues. Discounts: 30 percent discount.

ENDYMION, Linda Stern, David M. Katz, 562 W. End Ave Apt 6A, New York, NY 10024. Poetry, long-poems. "Recent contributors: Helen Adam, William Bronk, Theodore Enslin, Joan Larkin, David Levine, Joel Oppenheimer, Michael Perkins, Konstantinos Lardas, Jonathan Sterling." 1/yr; 1-yr sub price: $1.00; per copy: $1.00. 1972. 20pp; 5½ x 8½. of. circ. 500. Reporting time: 3 to 6 months. Payment: copies. Copyrighted. Discounts: 40% to trade. Pub'd 1 issue 1976; expects 1 issue 1977, 1 issue 1978. CCLM, NYSSPA.

Energy BlackSouth Press (see also HOO-DOO BLACK SERIES/SYNERGY MAGAZINE/IN ORBIT), A. Zu-Bolton, E. E. Miller, J. Ward. 1973. of.

Engendra Press Ltd., Ronald Rosenthall, 4277 Esplanade, Montreal, Quebec H2W1T1, Canada, 514-845-7502. Poetry, fiction, satire, criticism, parts-of-novels, plays. "It should be noted that we are a small press (proceeding one volume at a time) that does 'big press' books. Our area of specialization is the translation into English of important modern European writing. Ideas for books tend to originate in house; we will not consider unsolicited manuscripts. Given the costs of purchasing English-language rights from foreign publishers, translators/editors are rarely remunerated unless special funds are made available for the purpose by some outside body. Indeed, the point has been reached where publication of a book has become financially impracticable unless the translator/editor (invariably an academic) can obtain a grant from his or her university, or again, if sufficient funds are made available by some other establishment or agency. Also enclosed is a recent write-up of the press in a Canadian trade journal." 1975. of. avg. press run 1,500 - 2,000 copies. Copyrights for author. Discounts: Trade and wholesalers' discounts on request; institutional discount, 10 percent; discount to individuals, nil.

Engine Press (see SHELLY'S)

ENGLISH DANCE AND SONG, English Folk Dance And Song Society, Tony Wales, Cecil Sharp House, 2 Regents Park Rd, London NW1 7AY, United Kingdom. Articles, cartoons, photos, criticism, music, letters, reviews, non-fiction. 3/yr; sample price: 40p. 1936. 40pp; 9¾ x 7¼. lp. circ. 12,000. Ads: £60.00/£35.00/5p. Discounts: agency 10%. Pub's reviews. §English folk music, dance, or customs.

English Language Literature Association (see LINQ)

ENGLISH STUDIES IN AFRICA-A Journal of the Humanities, Witwatersrand University Press, Professor B.D. Cheadle, Witwatersrand University Press, 1 Jan Smuts Ave., Johannesburg 2001, South Africa. Criticism, reviews. 2/yr; 1-yr sub price: R. 5.00; per copy: R. 2.50; sample: free. 1958. 56pp; 19.5 x 13 cm. le. circ. 500. Reporting time: 3 months. Ads: R. 25/R. 15. Discounts: 25% discount for agents. Pub's reviews. §African & South African literature only.

ENSAYO CULTURAL, Chacabuco 1291, 2B, Buenos Aires, Argentina.

ENTROPY NEGATIVE, Les Recherches Daniel Say Cie., Daniel Say, Box 65583, Vancouver 12, B.C. V5N5K5, Canada. Articles, art, interviews, criticism. "Articles related to SF or fantasy, 1000 to 10,000 words usually of a serious mean. We cannot use U.S. stamps. Use i reply coupons for return postage" 4/yr; 1-yr sub price: $2.00; per copy: $.75; sample: $.75. 1970. 40pp; 28 cm x 21. †mi/of. circ. 500. Reporting time: month. Payment: copies. Pub's reviews.

EPOCH, 251 Goldwin Smith Hall, Cornell Univ., Ithaca, NY 14850. CCLM, COSMEP.

EPOS, Michael Blanchard, Department of English, Troy State University, Troy, AL 36081. Poetry, fiction, photos. price per copy: $1.00. 1970. 58pp; 10 x 6. of. circ. 500. Reporting time: 4-6 weeks.

Equal Time Press, Hugh Seidman, Frances Whyatt, 463 West St. Apt D 1016, New York, NY 10014. 1972. NESPA.

Equus Publishers (see also AZU, The Infinite Man), Zahur Zapata, 146 West 29th St., New York, NY 10001. Poetry, fiction, articles, criticism. "Print poetry, fiction, etc.—Latin American and America. Recent contributors: Hugo Hamriot, Jose Puben, Jaime Mejia Duque." avg. price, paper: $2.00. 1966. 150 to 500pp; varies. †of. avg. press run 5,000 to 25,000. Reporting time: 1 month.

Payment varies. Copyrights for author. Discounts: 30 percent bulk, trade, libraries, etc. CCLM, COSMEP.

Erebus Press, Anne Witten, 4 Merestone Terrace, Bronxville, NY 10708, 914-793-4663. Poetry, photos. avg. price, other: $6.95. 1969. 9 pages plus recording; circular 7 inches diameter. of/silkscreen. avg. press run 500. do not accept submissions. Payment: 10 percent royalty. Does not copyright for author. Discounts: 40 percent to libraries, bookstores.

Erin Hills Publishers, Dean Trembly, 1390 Fairway Dr, San Luis Obispo, CA 93401. of/le.

Erewon Press, Peter Hjersman, PO Box 4253, Berkeley, CA 94704. Poetry, concrete art, non-fiction. avg. price, cloth: $5.00-$10.00; paper: $1.00 - $7.50. 1975. 8-300pp; 8-1/2 x 11. †of/lp. avg. press run 1,000-5,000. nothing sought at this time. Payment: as appropriate. Copyrights for author. Discounts: no retail through publisher; distributors 50 percent. Expects 2 titles 1977. COSMEP.

ESE California (see ACADEMY AWARDS OSCAR ANNUAL)

ESPONTANEO, Hellric Publications, Ottone M. Riccio, 39 Eliot St, Jamaica Plain, MA 02130. Fiction, parts-of-novels. "Actively seeking good fiction #3, latest issue, includes work by Clark Norton, Hugh Fox, Mary Graham Lund, Jenny Scott, David W. Rea, H. Sedgwick, David Kerr, Thomas Pearson, Leo Korovan, Laura Marlin. No Taboos. Not over 3000 words. MSS not accompanied by SASE are destroyed. Int'l reply coupons are no longer acceptable." irreg; sub price: $2.50/4 issues; per copy: $.75. 1972. 26pp; 8½ x 11. †of. circ. 500. Reporting time: week or less. Payment: 5 copies plus complimentary subscription. Discounts: 50% on 20 or more copies.

ESSAYS ON CANADIAN WRITING, Jack David, s 765 Ross, York University, Downsview M3J1P3, Canada. Articles, interviews, criticism, reviews. "We print intelligent yet readable criticism of Canadian writing of any genre or period. Prefer articles on untouched subjects. Willing to consider experimental criticism. Recent contributors: b p Nichol, George Bowering, Robert Lecker, Keath Fraser." 3/yr; 1-yr sub price: $6.00; per copy: $1.50. 1974. 80pp; 8½ x 5½. of. circ. 550. Reporting time: 2 weeks. Payment: in copies. Ads: $40/$25. Discounts: 40% trade. Pub's reviews. §Canadian topics or by Canadian authors or publishers only. CPPA.

ETC: A Review of General Semantics, International Society for General Semantics (ISGS), Thomas M. Weiss, Ed-in-Chief; Elizabeth Bartlett, Poetry Editor, Univ of Wyoming, Laramie, WY 82070, Aptdo. 19, Comala, Colima, Mexico. Poetry, articles, art, photos, cartoons, reviews, letters. "Poetry should be submitted with International Coupon & self-addressed envelope. Short poems preferred—not doggerel, haiku, concrete. Name & address to be typed in upper left corner of each sheet. 1975 included Mark Byers, Barbara Holland, Steven Kellman, Richard O'Connell, Joan Colby." 4/yr; 1-yr sub price: $6.00; per copy: $1.50. 1943. 110pp; 6 x 9. le. circ. 4,000. Reporting time: promptly. Payment: 2 contributor-copies. Pub's reviews. §education, language, communication, semantics. COSMEP.

ETC Publications, Richard W. Hostrop, P.O. Drawer 1627-A, Palm Springs, CA 92262, 714-325-5352. Non-fiction. "Considers timely topics in all non-fiction areas." avg. price, cloth: $10.00; paper: $7.00. 1972. 256pp; 6 x 9. of. avg. press run 3,500. Reporting time: 4 weeks. Payment: standard book royalties. Copyrights for author. Discounts: usual trade. Pub'd 9 titles 1976; expects 12 titles 1977, 15 titles 1978. COSMEP.

The Eternal Network (see IS)

EUREKA REVIEW, Orion Press, Roger Ladd Memmott, P.O. Box 366, Willows, CA 95988. Poetry, fiction, articles, art, photos, reviews, parts-of-novels. "*Eureka Review* is published by Orion Press, an independent organization devoted to furthering the literary arts. The magazine publishes fiction primarily, some poetry, artwork, photographs, articles, and reviews. It is receptive to both established as well as previously unpublished and relatively unknown writers of worth. Editorial policy is eclectic. Although word count alone will never be responsible for a manuscript's rejection, stories beyond 7,500 words may run into problems of space. Material must be well-written, honest, and 'literarily sound,' whether conventional or avant-garde. The best literature achieves a balance of content and form. *No* sentimentality, academicism, or work with a cheap metaphysical slant. Recent contributors: Raymond Carver, Raymond Federman, Richard Kostelanetz, Leonard Michaels, Lyn Lifshin, James Bertolino, Greg Kuzma, Ron Silliman." 2-3/yr; sub price: $7.00/4 issues; per copy: $2.00; sample: $1.50. 1975. 110pp; 5½ x 8½. of/le. circ. 1,000. Reporting time: 1-6 weeks. Payment: 2-3 copies. Ads: $40/$20. Discounts: 25-50%. Back issues: $2.00. Pub's reviews. §fiction & poetry. CCLM, COSMEP.

EUROPEAN JUDAISM, Marcel Marcus, Kent House, Rutland Gardens, London SW71BX, United Kingdom, UAHC, European Judaism, 838 5th Ave, New York, NY 10021. Articles, poetry, fiction, interviews, criticism, letters, reviews. "Recent contributors include George Oppen, Edmond Jabes, Elaine Feinstein, Jakov Lind, A. Alvarez, M. Hamburger, F. T. Prince, Jean Starobinski. The name of the magazine describes its orientation." 2/yr; 1-yr sub price: £1.70 ($5.00 U.S.)-yr, £3.00 ($9.00 U.S.)-2; per copy: 95p ($2.50). 1966. 52pp; 9½ x 7. lp. Reporting time: 6 wks. Payment: by agreement. Ads: £30/page £18/1/2. Back issues: On application. Pub'd 2 issues 1976; expects 2 issues 1977, 2 issues 1978. Pub's reviews: 13 in 1976. §Judaism spec. plus religion, philosophy plus history in general. Literary expression by Jews (poems, short stories, novels). Middle East politics.

Evaluation News (see EDGEPRESS)

EVENT, John Levin, Douglas College, P.O. Box 2503, New Westminster, B.C. V3L5B2, Canada. Poetry, fiction, articles, art, photos, reviews, parts-of-novels, long-poems, plays, interviews. "George Woodcock, Bill T. O'Brien, Charles Bukowski, Alden Nowlan, George McWhirter, Pat Lowther, Gordon Pinsent, Harvey Shapiro, Cynthia Ozick, Jacob Zilber, Kevin Roberts, Ken Stange" Bi-annual Spring, Winter; 1-yr sub price: $5.00; per copy: $2.50; sample: $2.50. 1970. 135pp; 6 x 9. of. circ. 500. Reporting time: 4 months. Payment: $5.00-$10.00. Ads: $100/$50. Discounts: 20%. Back issues: $2.50. Pub'd 3 issues 1976; expects 2 issues 1977, 2 issues 1978. Pub's reviews §Poetry, fiction, photography, drama. COSMEP, CPPA.

The Evergreen Publishing Company (see GLASS)

Everyman (see DECIDUOUS)

Ex Libris (see MOUNTAIN SUMMER)

Excello & Bollard (see also SANDWICHES), Paul Lamprill, Graeme Carter, 10, Minden Close, Danesholme, Corby, Northants NN189EW, United Kingdom. Poetry, art, long-poems, concrete art, fiction. "All cheques payable to '*Excello & Bollard*'. *Excello & Bollard* is a required trade mark and business name. £1 or $2 for copy of all current booklets. *Excello & Bollard* produced largest number of non-vanity poetry titles in U.K. in 1976 [ref Poet's Yearbook '77]." avg. price, paper: 10p. 1973. 20pp; a4 or less. †duplicator. avg. press run 100. Reporting time: 1 month. Payment: nil. Pub'd 22 titles 1976; expects 20 titles 1977.

EXIT, Rochester Routes/Creative Arts Projects, Frank Judge, Ben Gray, Don Schimizzi, 50 Inglewood Drive, Rochester, NY 14619, 271-8552. Poetry, fiction, art, photos, interviews. "*EXIT* publishes poetry, fiction, translations, interviews, and art work. We are interested primarily in *quality* and prefer shorter pieces. Past numbers have included Feldman, Rimanelli, Fitzgerald, Cimatti, Bonazzi, and Rastafolk. Back issues 1-3 can be purchased for $2/ea." 2/yr. 1976. 60pp; 5½ x 8½. litho. circ. 600. Reporting time: 1 month. Payment: 3 copies. Copyrighted, reverts to author. Ads: $30.00. Back issues: $2.00. Pub'd 2 issues 1976.

EXPLORATION, Exploration Press, Steve Kagle, James Scrimgeour, Dept. of English, Illinois State University, Normal, IL 61761. "EXPLORATION magazine has in the past consisted of scholarly articles on science fiction literature (which are still welcome) but is expanding to include creative material, especially poetry, dealing with spiritual and/or physical exploration of past present and future. The press also puts out books of poetry (Anthologies and single authors). All styles welcome." 1974. COSMEP, NESPA.

ExPress, Ed Buryn, Box 31123, San Francisco, CA 94131, 824-8938. Non-fiction, photos. "Presently a one-book (*Vagabonding in America),* one-man (Ed Buryn) business. The future is unknowable, but welcome." avg. price, paper: $4.50. 1976. 256pp; 6 x 8. of. avg. press run 5,000. Reporting time: varies—presently not considering any submissions. Payment: 10%; no advance; semi-annual. Copyrights for author. Discounts: 40% thru distributor (book people). Pub'd 1 title 1976; expects 1 title 1978.

EXPRESSION, Ontario Library Association, Peggy White, 2397A Bloor St West, Toronto, Ontario M6S1P6, Canada, 416-762-7322. Articles, photos, interviews. 2/yr; 1-yr sub price: $5.00; per copy: $3.00; sample: free. 1976. 8½ x 11. of. circ. 2,500. Payment: none. Copyrighted, reverts to author. Discounts: agent, jobber 10 percent. Back issues: as above. Pub'd 1 issue 1976; expects 2 issues 1977.

EXPRESSIVE ARTS REVIEW, Robert Alexander, Box 444, Brentwood, NY 11717. "1-3 poems, 3-16 lines & return envelope, Sincere, sensitive poetry. No smut." 4/yr; price per copy: $7 paper $11 cl.; sample: $3.95. 1973. 40pp; 8½ x 5½. †of. circ. 3,000. Reporting time: 2-4 wks. Payment: 60¢ a poem. Ads: none. Back issues: $3.95 paper/$9.95 cl. §poetry.

F

Faculty Press (see CITY 4)

FAG RAG, Fag Rag Varieties, Inc., Fag Rag Collective, Box 331, Kenmore Station, Boston, MA 02115, 617-426-4369. Poetry, fiction, articles, art, photos, cartoons, interviews, satire, criticism, reviews, music, letters, parts-of-novels, long-poems, collages, plays, concrete art. "prefer short contributions; need new b & w art always" 4/yr; sub price: $7.00 10 issues; per copy: $1.00; sample: $1.00. 1970. 32 tabloidpp; 11 x 17. of. circ. 5,000. Reporting time: max. 3 months. Payment: copies. Copyrighted, reverts to author. no ads. Discounts: $1.00 retail; 40 percent disc. to retailers, 50 percent to distributors. Back issues: $2.00. Pub'd 4 issues 1976. §politics, gay lit., poetry, culture mongering. CCLM, COSMEP, NESPA.

THE FALCON, W. A. Blais, Poetry; T. E. Porter, Fiction, Belknap Hall, Mansfield State College, Mansfield, PA 16933. Poetry, fiction, photos, interviews, parts-of-novels, long-poems. "Some recent contributors: Carol Berge, Albert Goldbarth, Anselm Hollo, Margaret Randall." spring and winter; 1-yr sub price: $2.00; per copy: $1.00; sample: free. 1970. 125pp; 6 x 9. of. circ. 1,500. Reporting time: 1 month. Payment: copies only. Copyright reverts to author upon publication. Ads: exchange ads only. Discounts: 40% to agents. Pub'd 2 issues 1976; expects 2 issues 1977, 2 issues 1978. §poetry and fiction. CCLM.

Falconiforme Press Ltd., Box 4047, Saskatoon, Saskatchewan S7K3T1, Canada. "Books on Natural History, Falconry and Birds of Prey." 1974. Discounts: trade 40%, library 15-25%, agent 50%.

Fallen Angel Press, Leonard Kniffel, 1913 West McNichols C-6, Highland Park, MI 48203, 313-864-0982. Poetry. "No restrictions, just want to put good poetry in print. Authors: Margaret Kaminski, Michael Scott-Burke, Roberta Greifer, A. D. Winans, Lynn Strongin, Helen Duberstein. Would like to publish two or three titles a year." avg. price, paper: $2.00. 1975. 25pp; 5½ x 8½. †mi/hand press/of. avg. press run 500. Reporting time: 1 month. Payment: payment in copies. Copyrights for author. Pub'd 1 title 1976; expects 3 titles 1977, 3 titles 1978.

THE FAMOUS SCIENCE FICTION CHAPBOOK (series), Apocalypse Press, Alan R. Bechtold, P.O. Box 1821, Topeka, KS 66601. "We publish approx. bimonthly chapbooks by the greatest names in science fiction in limited, editions of 500 copies signed personally, 500 copies unsigned.

We have so far published material by The Firesign Theatre, Isaac Asimov and Harlan Ellison, with more of the very best lined up for the near future. We are no longer accepting manuscripts for our earlier projected magazines, LOTION, SPACE EGGS, and MOTHRAYS, as they are no longer planned for publication—discontinued! We would like to see all kinds of artwork and photography that could be published in signed limited editions for our upcoming OCULAR BAZAAR, a signed and numbered art print distribution program. We will produce the prints of worthwhile material and sell ALL existing copies of said print for 50% commission after expenses...no MSS please.'' 4-6/yr; price per copy: $2/signed-$5.00. 1976. 40pp; 5½ x 8½. of/silk-screen. circ. 1,000. no advertising. §science fiction littles, presses.

Fantome Press, C. M. James, 720 North Park Avenue, Warren, OH 44483. Poetry, art. "We prefer short material as this is almost a necessity for letterpress production. At present we are primarily publishing poetry of a weird or macabre nature but will soon expand this into areas of surreal poetry and that of a mainstream nature. We have published Lovecraft, Brennan and Moone. We have also published the work of three local poets and plan on doing some printed conceptual art pieces in the near future.'' avg. price, other: $3.00 (handmade folios). 1976. 6 to 10pp; 4½ x 6. †lp. avg. press run 150 copies or less. Reporting time: 2 weeks. Payment: Depends upon professional status of author. Copyright if requested. Discounts: After June 1, 1977, 25 percent discount will be available to book dealers. COSMEP.

FAS Publishing/Fleetwood Art Studio, Inc., Kenn Flee, 6613 Seybold Rd, Madison, WI 53719. Poetry, fiction, articles, art, photos, cartoons. 1968. 24-48pp; 4¼ x 7 & 5½ x 8½. †of. COSMEP.

THE FAULT, The Fault Press, Rustie Cook, 33513 6th St., Union City, CA 94587. Poetry, fiction, art, photos, parts-of-novels, long-poems, collages, plays, concrete art. "Each issue is a balanced format of fiction, poetry, drama & art.'' Irregular.; 1-yr sub price: $1.50; per copy: $1.50. 1971. 150pp; 8½ x 5½. †of/le. circ. 500. Reporting time: 2-4 weeks. Payment: 3 copies. Discounts: 20% 5 copies or more. CCLM, COSMEP.

Fels and Firn Press, John M. Montgomery, 1036 Colorado Ave., Palo Alto, CA 94303, 415-321-0696. "I published (1977) my own essay about Kerouac whom I knew. This is a more than doubling of a 1970 pamphlet of mine published elsewhere. 2,500 - 2,600 copies.'' 1961. 5½ x 9½. of. Reporting time: Haven't had any yet. Payment: Conventional. Copyrights for author. Discounts: Trade 30-40 percent, bulk 50 percent, jobber various.

FEMALE ARTISTS PAST & PRESENT, Women's History Research Center, Inc., Vicki Lynn Hill, '74 ed; Louisa Moe, '75 ed, 2325 Oak St, Berkeley, CA 94708, 415-548-1770. price per copy: 1974 ed $6, 1975 ed $3. 1971. 1974 150pp, 1975 75pp; 8½ x 11. of. circ. 1,000. Discounts: 30-40 percent discount to book dealers buying at least 5 copies. COSMEP.

THE FEMINIST ART JOURNAL, The Feminist Art Journal, Inc., Cindy Nemser, Chuck Nemser, 41 Montgomery Place, Brooklyn, NY 11215. Poetry, articles, art, photos, interviews, satire, criticism, reviews. *"The Feminist Art Journal* features in-dept articles (1500-2500 words) and interviews on prominent women artists of the past and present, written from a feminist perspective. We also run articles on women in music, filmmaking & dance along the above lines'' 4/yr; 1-yr sub price: $7.00; per copy: $2.00; sample: $2.00. 1972. 44pp; 8½ x 11. of. circ. 5,000. Reporting time: 2 weeks. Payment: $25 for articles; $10-15 for reviews. Back issues: $2.50. Pub's reviews. §women artists, womens' sensibility in art, poetry, anthologies.

FEMINIST BULLETIN, Center for Women's Studies & Services, Lisa Cobbs, 908 F St., San Diego, CA 92101. Articles, art, photos, interviews, criticism, reviews. "This is the newsletter/newspaper of a radical feminist organization: the Center for Women's Studies & Services. Material submitted should ave at least a women's liberation oriented viewpoint and should be no longer than 2000 words.'' 12/yr; 1-yr sub price: $3.00; per copy: free; sample: free. 1971. 25pp; 7 x 8½. of. circ. 1,000. Reporting time: 2 months. Pub's reviews. §women's issues, health, liberation, history, etc. COSMEP.

111

The Feminist Poetry & Graphics Center (see also THE GREATER GOLDEN HILL POETRY EXPRESS), 2561 B Street, San Diego, CA 92102, 714-239-3664. 1976.

The Feminist Press (see also WOMEN'S STUDIES NEWSLETTER), Liz Phillips, Box 334, Old Westbury, NY 11568. "The Feminist Press is a non-profit, tax-exempt publishing house, engaged in educational change. We publish reprints of neglected women's writing, biographies, & materials for nonsexist curriculum at every educational level." avg. price, paper: $1.95-$6.50. 1970. avg. press run 5,000. Payment: small royalty. Discounts: see catalogue. Pub'd 4 titles 1976; expects 3 titles 1977, 4 titles 1978.

Femmes, Les (see LES FEMMES PUBLISHING)

FICTION, Fiction, Inc., Mark Mirsky, Box 112 Stuyvesant Station, New York, NY 10009. Fiction, art, photos, parts-of-novels, collages, concrete art. "We tend slightly towards the so-called 'experimental', though do not limit ourselves to that. Recent contributors have included: Donald Barthelme, Manuel Puig, Ann Beattie, Grace Paley, Ishmael Reed, Julio Cortazar, as well as their emerging (less known) counterparts." 3/yr; 1-yr sub price: $6.00; per copy: $1.00; sample: free. 1972. 32pp; 10 x 14. of. circ. 5,000. Reporting time: 3 months, longer if submitted during summer. Payment: neither our editors nor our contributors receive payment; translators we pay 2 cents per word. Copyrighted, reverts if requested. Discounts: 40 percent discount to bookstores; 50 percent to distributors, 10 percent to teachers (bulk). Back issues: $1.00 apiece except for Vol. 3, 2-3 which is $2.00. §fiction. CCLM.

‡**Fiction Collective,** English Dept., Brooklyn College, Brooklyn, NY 11210.

FICTION INTERNATIONAL, Joe David Bellamy, Dept. of English, St. Lawrence Univ., Canton, NY 13617. Fiction, interviews, criticism, reviews, parts-of-novels. "Because of our editorial commitment to publishing fiction, we are no longer able to read unsolicited poetry submissions. No hard-and-fast length limitaions on fiction, though we rarely use short-shorts or mss. over 30pp. No taboos. Especially receptive to innovative forms and idiosyncratic styles. Contributors: Joyce Carol Oates, Jerry Bumpus, Russel Banks, Ronald Sukenick, George Chambers, Siv Cedering Fox, Michael Benedikt, G.E. Murray, Robley Wilson, Gordon Weaver." 2/yr; 1-yr sub price: $5.00; per copy: $8.00 instit. 1973. 150pp; 5½ x 8½. lp. circ. 5M. Reporting time: 1-2 mos. Payment: $5-$150. Ads: $80/$345. Discounts: 25%. CCLM.

FICTION MAGAZINE, Ave Victor Hugo Publ., Vincent McCaffrey, 339 Newbury St., Boston, MA 02115, 617-266-7746. Poetry, fiction, articles, interviews, criticism, reviews, letters, parts-of-novels, long-poems, plays. "Fiction-storytelling only-articles related to fiction only." Was quarterly—temporarily twice yearly.; 1-yr sub price: $4.00; per copy: $1.50; sample: $1.50. 1972. 96pp; 8½ x 11. of. circ. 4,000. Reporting time: 1-2 months. Payment: $0.01 per word. Copyrighted, reverts to author. Ads: $75.00/$50.00/$0.10. Discounts: 40 percent to bookstore, 50 percent to distributor (over 100 copies), 20 percent to agent. Back issues: Nos. 1-3, $3.00; Nos. 5-9, $1.50; No. 10, $3.00. Pub'd 2 issues 1976; expects 2 issues 1977, 4 issues 1978.

FICTION WEST, Fiction West, R.F. Bruns, 3012 Vichy Ave., Napa, CA 94558. Fiction, articles, interviews, criticism, reviews, letters, parts-of-novels. "We do not presume to define what literature is. Rather, we want good solid prose pieces with an emphasis on balance amongst craft, plot, entertainment and other prose elements. Will consider all kinds of prose, will make hard effort to say why we can't use a given piece. Acceptances will speak for themselves. Genre pieces also considered. Excerpts from novel should be episodic enough to stand on their own. Book reviews average 1,000 words; articles on established prose writers to 3,000 words. Maximum on anything normally 6,000, unless incredibly good. Suggest first class mail in case FW moves again. Mss. will generally be forwarded." 2/yr; sub price: $5.00 - 4 issues; Patron subscribers $10.00 - 4 issues.; per copy: $1.50; Patron subscribers $25.00; sample: $1.50 plus $0.50 postage. 1976. 100-120pp; 8½ x 11. †mi. circ. 750. Reporting time: 1-3 months. Payment: 2 copies. Returns all rights except option on anthology rights for possible best FICTION WEST around 1978. Ads: $75/$345. Discounts: bookstores 40% purchase cash/25% consignment. Back issues: All out of print except No. 1, special green edition, $5.00, yellow or blue $15.00 (five each). Pub'd 2 issues 1976; expects 2 issues 1977, 2-3 issues 1978. Pub's reviews: 17 in 1976. §Prose.

THE FIDDLEHEAD, Roger Ploude, Managing Editor; William Bauer, Poetry Editor; Kent Thompson, Fiction Editor, Dept. of English, Univ. New Brunswick, Fredericton, NB, Canada. Poetry, fiction, art, reviews, parts-of-novels, long-poems, plays. 4/yr; 1-yr sub price: $6.00 Canada $7.00 U.S.; per copy: $1.50. 1945. 120-140pp; 5¼ x 8½. circ. 850. Reporting time: 4-6 wks. Payment: $5 printed page. Ads: $50/$26. Back issues: $2. COSMEP.

FIELD, David Young, Stuart Friebert, Rice Hall, Oberlin College, Oberlin, OH 44074. Poetry, long-poems. "Also essays on poetry and translations of poetry." 1-yr sub price: $4.00; per copy: $2.00. 1969. 100pp; 5¼ x 8½. circ. 1,200. Reporting time: 1-2 wks. Payment: $10 a page. Discounts: bookstores: 40%, agencies: 30%. CCLM, COSMEP.

Fifth Estate Publishing Company (see COUNTERSPY)

FIGHT BACK, Fight Back People's House, Ingrimstr 28, 69 Heidelberg, West Germany. Articles, cartoons, interviews, criticism, reviews. "Journal for, about and by soldiers stationed in the FRG. Stresses struggles for GI rights, plus info on role of U.S. armed forces and the foreign policy of the U.S.A. very critical of U.S. politics as well as treatment of GI'S" 12/yr; 1-yr sub price: $7.00 (to U.S.A.); per copy: $1.00. 1972. 24pp; 4 x 8. †of. circ. 3,000. Discounts: 10 or more $5.00 per sub. Pub's reviews APS, LNS.

FIGHTING WOMAN NEWS, Valerie Eads, 9 East 48th St, New York, NY 10017, 212-868-3330. Articles, art, photos, cartoons, interviews, reviews, letters, news items, non-fiction. "We need articles to 2,000 words, with photos, on martial arts, self defense & combative sports. Our readership is knowledgeable & critical. Also feminist. No 'girls' unless they are under 12. No bikini photos, or 'love your rapist' articles. We have published men including artists Rick Bryant & Sergio Aragones." 12/yr; 1-yr sub price: $6.00 individuals; $10.00 institutional; per copy: $.50; sample: $2.00 set of 3 (incl. post). 1975. 16pp; 8½ x 11. of. circ. 650. Reporting time: asap. Payment: From contributors' copies to honorarium (rarely), cover photo $10.00. Copyrighted. Ads: $100/$50/$.20. Discounts: 10 or more prepaid 50 percent off, 40 percent to bookstores on consignment. Back issues: $0.75 (incl. post). Pub'd 10 issues 1976; expects 10 issues 1977, 12 issues 1978. Pub's reviews: many in 1976. §martial arts, self defense, combative sports, women's history in these areas.

FIGMENT, Jacob L. Bloom, 34 Andrew St, Newton, MA 02161, 617-628-4571. Poetry, fiction, art, letters. "Poetry from 2 to 100 lines, Porse up to 2,200 words. Leaning towards surrealism and science fiction. Recent issues have included works by John Calabro, Andrew Darlington, Errol Miller and Kathryn Ramsay." 1/yr; 1-yr sub price: $0.75; per copy: $0.75; sample: free. 1970. 40pp; 5½ x 8½. †mi. circ. 300. Reporting time: 3 months. Payment: copy of issue. Copyrighted, reverts to author. Ads: none. Discounts: 40 percent bookstore, 20 percent jobber. Back issues: $0.75 each. Pub'd 1 issue 1976; expects 1 issue 1977, 1 issue 1978. COSMEP.

The Figures, Laura Chester, Geoffrey Young, 2016 Cedar, Berkeley, CA 94709, 415-843-3120. Poetry, fiction. "Stan Rice, poems SOME LAMB; David Benedetti, prose-poems NICTITATING MEMBRANE; Summer Brenner, poems, FROM THE HEART TO THE CENTER; Julia Vose, poems & fictions, MOVED OUT ON THE INSIDE; Tom Clark, baseball writings, BASEBALL; Paul Auster, poems WALL WRITING; Artie Gold & Geoffrey Young, combination poems MIXED DOUBLES." avg. price, cloth: $10.00; paper: $3.50. 1975. 75pp; 5½ x 8½. of. avg. press run 750. Reporting time: 1 month. Payment: 10 percent edition, 40 percent off on extra sales. Copyrights for author.

FILE MAG, Art Official Inc., 241 Yonge St., 3rd Floor, Toronto, Ont. M5B 1N8, Canada, 416-368-7787. Art, photos, interviews, reviews. "We do not usually publish unsolicited material." 2/yr; 1-yr sub price: $5.00; per copy: $3.00; sample: $3.00. 1972. 64pp; 10¾ x 14. of. circ. 3,000. Reporting time: varies. Payment varies. Copyrighted, reverts to author. Ads: $400.00/$200.00. Discounts: bulk orders-40 percent. Back issues: on request. Pub'd 1 issue 1976; expects 2 issues

1977, 2 issues 1978. Pub's reviews: 10 in 1976. §art, books by artists. CPPA.

FILM, Peter Cargin, 81 Dean St., London W1A6AA, United Kingdom, 01 437 4355. Articles, photos, interviews, criticism, news items. "Film news, criticisms, etc. advertising managers: address, 81 Dean St. London W1A6AA" 12/yr; 1-yr sub price: $12.00-yr £5.00; per copy: 30p; sample: free. 1954. 24pp; A4. of. circ. 3,000. Reporting time: 2 wks. Payment: by arrangement. Ads: £50/£28. Pub'd 12 issues 1976; expects 12 issues 1977, 12 issues 1978.

FILM CULTURE, Film Culture Non-Profit Inc., Jonas Mekas, P. Adams Sitney, G. P. O. Box 1499, New York, NY 10001. Poetry, articles, photos, letters. "We are a magazine devoted to avantgarde cinema and classical cinema. Recent contributors have been James Broughton, John G. Hanhardt, Richard Foreman, P. Adams Sitney, Regina Cornwall, etc. The next three issues will be devoted to the LEGEND OF MAYA DEREN, a documentary biography in three volumes, edited by VeVe Clark, Millicent Hodson and Catrina Neiman." 4/yr; 1-yr sub price: $8.00; per copy: $2.00-$6.00; sample: free. 1955. 90-200pp; 5½ x 8. of. circ. 4,500. Payment: At present articles are submitted without payment. Copyrighted, reverts to author. Ads: $300.00/$150.00/none. Discounts: We give 25 percent to 40 percent discount to bookstores. Back issues: inquire. Pub's reviews. §Cinema, poetry. CCLM.

Film Culture Non-Profit, Inc. (see also FILM CULTURE), Jonas Mekas, P. Adams Sitney, G. P. O. Box 1499, New York, NY 10001. Poetry, fiction, articles, photos, letters. "Film Culture publishes anything that it deams important to avantgarde cinema—journals, poetry, fiction, prose, articles on film, etc." avg. price, cloth: Varies. 1955. pp varies; Varies. of. avg. press run 5,000. Reporting time: Varies. Payment: Negotiated individually after production costs are paid. Copyrights for author. Discounts: 25-40 percent discount to bookstores. other discounts must be negotiated individually.

FILM HERITAGE, University of Dayton, F. Anthony Macklin, Box 652, University of Dayton, Dayton, OH 45469. Articles, photos, interviews, criticism, reviews. "FILM HERITAGE is a quarterly journal devoted to analyses of films and rediscoveries of underrated films. Length of material: approx. ten pages double spaced, typed. style: Univ. of Chicago: A Manual of Style. Recent contributors: Interviews with John Wayne, Charlton Heston, Marty Scorsese, Alfred Hitchcock, Molly Haskell." 4/yr; 1-yr sub price: $3.00/$3.50 Foreign & Canada; per copy: $.75; sample: free. 1965. 40pp; 5½ x 8½. of. circ. 2,000. Reporting time: 6-8 weeks. Payment: copies only. Ads: $100/$60. Back issues: v.1-$4 ea; v.2&3-$3 ea; v.4-8-$2 ea; all others-$1 ea. Pub's reviews §film. COSMEP.

FILM INDEX, John Howard Reid, 2 E Mosman St, Mosman Bay, NSW 2088, Australia. Articles, photos, interviews, criticism, reviews, letters. 12/yr; 1-yr sub price: $12.00; per copy: $1.25; sample: free. 1967. 16pp; 6½ x 9½. le. circ. 2,000. Reporting time: immediate. Payment: copies. Ads: $100/$60. Discounts: 20%. Back issues: $2.00 each. Pub's reviews. §film.

FILM LIBRARY QUARTERLY, William Sloan, Emma Cohn, Box 348, Radio City Station, New York, NY 10019. "Articles and reviews on noncommercial cinema-documentary, avant-garde, childrens, and on video." 4/yr; 1-yr sub price: $10.00; per copy: $2.50; sample: free. 1967. 56pp; 6 x 9 inches. of. circ. 1,900. Reporting time: 10 days. Ads: $150/$90/none. Back issues: $2.00 per issue. Pub's reviews. §cinema, video.

FILM QUARTERLY, Univ. of California Press, Ernest Callenback, University of California Press, Berkeley, CA 94320. 4/yr; 1-yr sub price: $5.00; per copy: $1.25. 1945. 62pp; 5½ x 7. lp. circ. 8M. Reporting time: 2-3 weeks. Payment: 1½¢ per word. Ads: $170/$115.

Films By And/Or About Women (see WOMEN'S HISTORY RESEARCH CENTER)

FINE PRINT; A Review for the Arts of the Book, Sandra Kirshenbaum, D. Steven Corey, Assoc. Ed.; Linnea Gentry, Assoc. Ed.; George F. Ritchie, Assoc. Ed.; Elaine Ginger, Assoc. Ed., 2107 Van Ness Ave. 303, San Francisco, CA 94120. Articles, interviews, criticism, reviews. "The first

114

review medium devoted to the finely printed limited editions of private and specialized presses, giving full bibliographic description and comments. Plus newsnotes, trade reviews and feature articles on typography, papermaking, calligraphy, hand-bookbinding, book-illustration and the history of the book. Send all mail to: P.O. Box 7741, San Francisco, California 94120." 4/yr; 1-yr sub price: $10.00 to individuals; $14.00 to institutions; per copy: $2.50; sample: $2.50. 1975. 28pp; 8 x 11. le. Reporting time: 3-4 weeks. Payment: author's copies. Ads: $150.00/$75.00/$0.30. Discounts: 50% on bulk orders to bookstores, $1.00 off institutional orders from agents. Back issues: All except vol. 1, no. 1 & 2 avail. $3.00 each. Pub'd 4 issues 1976; expects 4 issues 1977, 4 issues 1978. Pub's reviews: 12-16 in 1976. §book arts; history, craft.

FIRELANDS ARTS REVIEW, Cambric Press, Joel Rudinger, Firelands Campus, Huron, OH 44839, 419-433-4221. Poetry, fiction, photos. annual; 1-yr sub price: $3.00; per copy: $3.00; sample: $2.00. 1972. 80pp; 8½ x 5½p. of. circ. 1M. Reporting time: 4-8 wks. Payment: copies. Copyrighted. Ads: $500.00/$250.00. Discounts: 30 percent over 10 copies. Back issues: 1972 $1.25; 1973 $1.25; 1974 $1.50; 1975 $2.00; 1976 $2.00. Pub'd 1 issue 1976; expects 1 issue 1977, 1 issue 1978. CCLM.

Fireside Press (see CONNECTICUT FIRESIDE)

FIREWEED, Fireweed Press, Galen Green, Box 9888, Columbus, OH 43206, 614-262-3395. Poetry, fiction, articles, art, cartoons, interviews, satire, letters, parts-of-novels. 4/yr; 1-yr sub price: $3.00; per copy: $1.00; sample: $1.00. 1975. 40pp; 5½ x 8½. of. circ. 500-400. Reporting time: 2-4 wks. Payment: 2 copies. Not copyrighted. Ads: $50.00/$25.00. Discounts: 30 percent discount to all wholesalers (bookstores etc.). Back issues: $1.50. §all.

Fireweed Press (see also FIREWEED), Galen Green, Box 9888, Columbus, OH 43206, 614-262-3395. Poetry, fiction, articles, art, cartoons, interviews, satire, letters, parts-of-novels. "Books: You're Never The Same Person Twice by Galen Green; Naked Charm by Lyn Lifshin (eleven postcard poems; 1976); An Amnesiac On The Verse Of Heaven by George Myers, Jr. (32 pp., 1976); Meat Watch by John M. Bennett (?4pp.; 1977); World-Weary Polka by Galen Green (32pp.; 1977)." avg. price, paper: $1.00. 1975. 40 pp for mag..but varies widely for books; 5¼ x 8½. of. avg. press run 500-400. Reporting time: 2-4 wks. Payment varies (negotiable). Does not copyright for author. Discounts: 30 percent discount to all wholesalers (bookstores etc).

FIREWEED, Fireweed Ltd., David Craig, Nigel Gray, 99 Dale St., Lancaster, United Kingdom, Lancaster 60229/66893. Poetry, fiction, art, cartoons, photos, satire, music, parts-of-novels, long-poems, plays. "Socialist and working class arts. Edward Bond, Ian Campbell, Leon Rosselson, Berthold Brecht, Pablo Neruda, Archie Hill, Gunther Wallraff, George Hallett, Renato Guttuso, Arthur Miller, Trevor Griffiths, Adrian Mitchell as well as unknown writers and artists." 4/yr; 1-yr sub price: £3.50-$10.00; per copy: 75p-$2.00 [add 15p or 50 cents for p&p]; sample: 75p [add 15p or 50 cents for p&p]. 1975. 112pp; A5. photo print. circ. 2,000. Reporting time: 2 months. Payment varies-min £5. Copyrights remains with author. Ads: £40/£20. Back issues: 75p [plus 15p p&p]. Pub'd 4 issues 1976; expects 4 issues 1977, 4 issues 1978.

FIRST ENCOUNTER, Allan Cooper, C/O Eng. Dept., Mt. Allison University, Sackville, New Brunswick, Canada. Poetry, art, photos. "The magazines basic emphasis is student work. However, in the past we have received contributions from most major Canadian poets, but none from American poets. It would be good to hear from American poets, known or unknown...Interested in anything new, moving, non-concrete, non-confessional...Looking for work (poetry) basically trans-world, eastern, translations, prose-poems, small poems...like Bly, Ignatow, Knott, Haines, Simpson, Snyder, Wright, Li Po, Rilke, etc. etc." 1/yr; 1-yr sub price: $1.50; per copy: $1.50; sample: free. 1968. 50-100pp; 6 x 9. le. Reporting time: quick (1 month). Payment: 1 copy. no advertising. §poetry journals, poetry books.

First Feather Press (see THE MACROBIOTIC)

The First Ozark Press (see TOTAL LIFESTYLE, REBUTTAL:)

First Person, M. D. Elevitch, Washington Springs Rd, Palisades, NY 10964. Fiction, art, photos, cartoons, satire, parts-of-novels. "Travel, memoirs, humor—'The Literature of Personality'—A commemorative anthology on person/place is anticipated. current: *Americans At Home* by M. D. Elevitch—a novel. Early contributors: Barthelme, Dahlberg, Gorey, Lorca. No unsolicited manuscripts please." 1960. book-128pp; book-6 x 8. of. Reporting time: query. Discounts: 40%. COSMEP.

Fish (see ROXBURY POETRY ENTERPRISES)

FISH & GAME SPORTSMAN, J. B. (Red) Wilkinson, P.O. Box 737, Regina, Sask. S4P3A8, Canada. "The Fish and Game Sportsman is a regional outdoor magazine covering two distinct areas-Alberta and Saskatchewan. We are basically interested in material relating to these two western Canadian provinces, however, we do purchase how-to and other informational articles if they are of sufficient interest to our western audience. As the title of the magazine suggests, most of the editorial content is devoted to fishing and hunting articles, although we do publish many articles on camping, snowmobiling, canoeing, fly tying, dogs, and other outdoor-related subjects. We prefer to receive articles up to 2,500 words, accompanied by up to 10 black and white 8 x 10 glossy photos." 4/yr; 1-yr sub price: $3.25 U.S. $3.75; per copy: $1.00. 1968. 96pp; 7 x 10. of. circ. 13,650 ABC. Reporting time: 3 to 4 weeks. Payment: $40 to $175. Ads: $450.00/$275.00. Pub'd 4 issues 1976; expects 4 issues 1977, 4 issues 1978. Pub's reviews. OWC, OWAA, ABC, CPPA.

FIT, The Fit Press, Brent Spencer, Cathrine Spencer, John Bonner, 4 Riverside Drive, Wilkes-Barre, PA 18702, 717-822-3024. Poetry, articles, interviews, criticism, reviews. "Besides printing the best poetry we receive, we also serve Pennsylvania, New York, and New Jersey by listing upcoming readings in the tri-state area and reviewing many of them. We solicit information and reviews of such readings in addition to the needs listed above." 4/yr; 1-yr sub price: 4 SASE; per copy: SASE; sample: SASE. 1977. 4pp; 17 x 11. of. circ. 300. Reporting time: 3 weeks. Payment: 2 copies. Copyrighted, reverts to author. Ads: Exchange. Discounts: none. Back issues: SASE. Pub's reviews. §Poetry and poetics, small press publication.

Five Trees Press, Cheryl Miller, Jaime Robles, Kathy Walkup, 660 York St, San Francisco, CA 94110. Poetry, fiction, parts-of-novels, long-poems, collages. †le. Reporting time: 4-6 weeks. Payment: 10% royalty on net.

FLEA MARKET QUARTERLY ALMANAC, Maverick Publications, Ken Asher, Box 243, Bend, OR 97701. Articles, photos, cartoons. "Nonfiction and Photos: 'Short items of wit; money-making, money-saving tips; recycling ideas; practical ecological news; collecting trends; alternate lifestyle ideas; consumer affairs and health briefs. Use inspirational, optimistic approach, but be frank. There is no other nationwide flea market publication. We particularly like articles giving money-making ideas that require little capital to get started.' Informational, how-to, personal experience, interview, profile, inspirational, humor, nostalgia, photo, travel, book reviews, successful business operations, new product, and merchandising techniques. Recent articles include 'Hitler's Historical Droppings' (gave details, prices, information and market sources for a different and unusual collecting field)." 4/yr; 1-yr sub price: $6.00; per copy: $2.00; sample: $1.00. 1973. 48pp; 8½ x 11. †of. circ. 10,000. Reporting time: 6 weeks. Payment: $20 published page. Ads: $99/$56/$.10. Pub's reviews. §money-making, money-saving, alternate lifestyles. COSMEP.

FLOATING ISLAND, Floating Island Publications, Michael Sykes, P.O. Box 516, Point Reyes Station, CA 94956. Poetry, fiction, articles, art, photos, cartoons, parts-of-novels, long-poems, collages. "Floating Island is pub. 1x per yr. Fall-8-1/2 x 11, 160pp, perfectbound cover in color, text B&W, 24pp of photographs (full-page) on coated stock, approx. 50 percent of text is poetry, 25 percent fiction & prose, 25 percent graphics-poetry fiction & prose is frequently illustrated, engravings, woodblocks, pen & pencil etc.-some artwork halftoned to retain fidelity, most is line-shot-contributors include well-known poets & writers as well as previous unpublished artists-subscribers $5/yr also receive advance notice of other pubs. from Floating Island Pub. & receive a 20 percent discount on all orders including issues of Floating Island." 1/yr; 1-yr sub price: $5.00; per copy: $6.95; sample: $3.50. 1976. 160pp; 8½ x 11. of. circ. 500. Reporting time: 2-4 weeks.

Payment: Copies. Copyrighted, all rights revert to authors upon request. no ads. Discounts: 50% to dist.; 40% to retail outlets. Pub'd 1 issue 1976; expects 1 issue 1977, 1 issue 1978. COSMEP, COSMEP-WEST.

Florida Sun-Gator Publishing Co., Mrs. Sheril K. Charba, Emil Klosinski, P.O. Box 365, Oviedo, FL 32765, 671-6543, 671-3633. Non-fiction. "No requirements as to length of material. October 1976 release: 'Notre Dame, Chicago Bears and Hunk' football memoirs in highlight by Heartley 'Hunk' Anderson in collaboration with Emil Klosinski. Also Microbiology text by Dr. Julius F. Charba is in the process of completion—no publication date set." avg. price, cloth: $7.95; paper: $5.95; other: science text books not established as yet. 1976. 180-210pp; 5½ x 8½. of. avg. press run anticipate 2,000-10,000. Will accept submissions in 1977 (reporting time within 10 days on outlines) invited manuscripts—4 to 6 weeks. Payment: 10%. Copyrights for author. Discounts: agent—open, others 40%, generous orders additional 5-10%.

FOCUS ON FILM, The Tantivy Press, Allen Eyles, 136-148 Tooley Street, London SE12TT, United Kingdom, 407 7566. Articles, reviews, interviews, criticism, letters. "A magazine that documents the history of the cinema in close detail and specialises in subjects and areas generally neglected elsewhere. Contributors need to be exceptionally well informed on their subjects. Magazine includes reviews of new films, film books, soundtracks, sponsored films, interviews, career articles." 4/yr; 1-yr sub price: $7.00; per copy: $1.75. 1970. 60pp; 9½ x 6½. 1p. Reporting time: 2 weeks. Payment variable. Ads: on application. Back issues: current issue price (5 or more 50p each). Pub'd 3 issues 1976; expects 4 issues 1977, 4 issues 1978.

FOCUS/ MIDWEST, Focus/ Midwest Publishing Co., Inc., St. Louis Journalism Review, Charles Klotzer, Dan Jaffe, 928a N. McKnight, St. Louis, MO 63132, 314-991-1698. Poetry, articles, interviews, satire, criticism, letters. bi-monthly; 1-yr sub price: $5.00; per copy: $.85; sample: $.85 plus postage. 1962. 32-48pp; 8½ x 11. †of. circ. 5,500. Reporting time: 4-8 weeks. Payment: upon publication. Copyrighted. Ads: $350.00/$185.00/$.16. Discounts: sub./agencies: 20%. Back issues: $1.50 plus postage. Pub's reviews. §politics, social, literary, urban, etc.

FOLIO, Russell Leong, Editor; Janet Chann, Art Director, 2207 Shattuck Ave., Berkeley, CA 94704. Poetry, fiction, articles, art, photos, letters. "Material used relates to programming, as this is basically a program guide. However, we have had feature articles on Chile, Portugal, the Chinese 'Long March' as well as contemporary prose and poetry by Third World writers." 12/yr; 1-yr sub price: $30.00; sample: free. 1949. 20pp; 15 x 11¾. of. circ. 19,000. Ads: $250/$125/$1.50—line. §politics, social criticism, 3rd world authors.

FOLK MASS AND MODERN LITURGY, Resource Publications, William Burns, Jake Empereur, Liturgy; Paul F. Page, Music, 7291 Coronado Dr. #3, San Jose, CA 95129. Poetry, fiction, articles, art, photos, cartoons, criticism, reviews, music, letters, plays, concrete art. "Inquire before submitting articles. Other content may be submitted unsolicited. Include SASE. All content relates to creative ideas for religious ritual (worship). Fiction 'with a point' or for children, and any content useful for religious education will be considered." 8/yr; 1-yr sub price: $16.00; per copy: $2.25; sample: $2.25. 1973. 36pp; 8½ x 11. of. circ. 10,000. Reporting time: 6 wks. Payment: 2 copies to $100. Ads: $393.00/$275.00/$1.00. Discounts: 1-9/$2.50, 10-24/$2.00, 25-49/$1.50, 50-99/$1.10, 100 or more/$1.00. Back issues: $2.50 prepaid. Pub'd 8 issues 1976; expects 8 issues 1977, 8 issues 1978. Pub's reviews: 6 in 1976. §religious arts. COSMEP, CPA.

FOLLIES, Terry Cannon, P O Box 5231, Pasadena, CA 91107, 213-358-6255. Poetry, articles, art, photos, cartoons, interviews, criticism, reviews, letters, collages. "A community journal of arts and opinion. Heavy on criticism and reviews of films, art, rock and jazz record reviews. Small amount of poetry and cartoons." 12/yr; 1-yr sub price: $5.00; per copy: free; sample: free. 1975. 16pp; 10 x 16. of. circ. 10,000 - 12,000. No payment at this time. Copyrighted, reverts to author. Ads: $135.00/$75.00/free. Back issues: Will mail special back issues for postage. Pub's reviews §Any small press publications.

Food For Thought Publications, Dick McLeester, PO Box 331, Amherst, MA 0x002,

117

413-584-7984. Non-fiction. avg. price, paper: $3.00. 1976. 124 pppp; 7 x 8½. Discounts: trade 3-4 copies—30 percent; 5 or more copies—40 percent. 30 day billing. COSMEP.

THE FOOLKILLER, The Foolkiller, Verle Muhrer, Editor; Elijah P Lovejoy, Managing Editor; H L Dellinger, Associate Editor, 2 W 39th, Kansas City, MO 64111, 816-531-9226. Poetry, fiction, articles, art, photos, cartoons, interviews, satire, criticism, reviews, music, letters, parts-of-novels, long-poems, plays. "Popular culture, special emphasis on Midwest—history of radical writing and folk culture, literary contributions of current writers, political analysis. Midwest-based but will consider material from anywhere. SASE required with submissions." 4/yr; 1-yr sub price: $2.00; per copy: $0.50; sample: $0.25. Reestablished 1976. 12 pp (16 soon); 11½ x 16. of. circ. 3,000. Reporting time: 2 wks. Payment: copies. Copyrighted, reverts to author. Ads: $80.00/$45.00/$1.00 for½ inch. Discounts: 40 percent to bookstores and individuals who wish to act as agents. Back issues: yes-see ad each issue. Pub's reviews §Popular culture, poetry, literature, politics, history. Joining COSMEP.

FOR THE TIME BEING, R. D. Swets, editor; David denBoer, poetry editor, P.O. Box 7144, Grand Rapids, MI 49507. Poetry, fiction, art, photos, interviews, criticism, reviews, music, parts-of-novels, long-poems, collages, plays, concrete art. "Published by the Fine Arts Fellowship, a non-profit association of artists and writers. Enclose SASE. Occasional color. Only quality work will be considered for publication." 4/yr; 1-yr sub price: $10.00; per copy: $2.50. 1969. 48pp; 7 x 8½. of. circ. 1,000. Reporting time: 2 wks-2 months. Payment: copies only. Ads: $100/$60/none. Discounts: group (10 or more to 1 address): $6/yr. Back issues: $1.50. Pub's reviews. §poetry, fiction, music. CCLM, COSMEP.

FORESIGHT MAGAZINE, John W.B. Barklam, J. Barklam, 29 Beaufort Av., Hodge Hill, Birmingham, England B346AD, United Kingdom, 021-783-0587. Articles, reviews, letters, news items. "Articles of approx 1000 words welcomed. A bias towards philsophy as related to life. Dealing also in mysticism, occultism, U.F.O.S and allied subjects. Aims are to help create peace and encourage spiritual awareness and evolution in the world." 6/yr; 1-yr sub price: £1.29/$2.50; per copy: 22p/50 cents; sample: 22p/50 cents. 1970. 20pp; 5¾ x 8¼. †dupl. circ. 1500. Reporting time: immediately. Ads: £9.00-$13.50/£5.00-$7.50/2p-3 cents. Discounts: none. Back issues: 15p (incl. postage)-40 cents. Pub'd 6 issues 1976; expects 6 issues 1977, 6 issues 1978. Pub's reviews: 10 in 1976.

Forum Literati (see also SAGEBLOOM), Guida Jackson, P.O. Box 79464, Houston, TX 77079, 467-2398. Poetry, fiction, articles, art, cartoons, satire, criticism, letters. "Prose 1,500 words, poetry 22 lines by writers age 70 and older. No preaching. Nostalgia o.k. if it is relevant to the present. Our premise is that you've only just learned enough at 70 to begin to live, and at 90 you're just beginning to mellow. Please don't submit if you are younger than 70." avg. price, paper: $1.50. 1974. 28pp; 8½ x 11. of. avg. press run 1,000. Reporting time: 1 month. Payment: copies only. Copyrights for author. Discounts: 45 percent for 20 or more. Expects 4 titles 1977.

Foundations for the Redefinition of Sanity, Claire Burch, Mark Weiman, 463 West St. Apt 318C, New York City, NY 10014, 212-929-3833. Poetry, art, satire, music, parts-of-novels, long-poems, collages, plays. "We have 3 works in print at the moment. Two anthologies of work by people involved with the organization and one play." avg. price, cloth: $5.00; paper: $3.00. 1973. 150pp; 6 x 8. of. avg. press run 500. We are not accepting submissions at the moment. Payment: through the Foundation. Does not copyright for author. Discounts: 40% discount for all orders over 10 copies.

The Four Humours Press, Susan Turner, Myron Turner, St. Paul's College, University of Manitoba, Winnipeg. man., Canada. Poetry, fiction, long-poems. "Publishing poetry in illustrated, finely designed, limited editions; all binding, press-work and type-setting by hand." †le. Discounts: trade: 40 percent.

FOUR QUARTERS, John J. Keenan, LaSalle College, Philadelphia, PA 19141. Poetry, fiction articles. 4/yr; 1-yr sub price: $3.00; per copy: $.75; sample: $.75. 1951. 48pp; 6 x 9. lp. circ. 700. Reporting time: 6 wks. Payment: $5 poem; story, article up to $25 + 3 copies. Back issues: $1. CCLM.

‡**Four Seasons Foundation,** PO Box 159, Bolinas, CA 94924.

THE FOUR ZOAS JOURNAL OF POETRY & LETTERS, The Four Zoas Press, M. Gordon, P. Daniels, H. Ehrenfeld, RFD, Ware, MA 01082. Poetry, letters, long-poems. "We are a limited edition press, printing our books by hand, often using rag papers. The *Journal* is a *Contemporary* magazine and has published Jon Silkin, Gary Gach, Ken Smith, Alicia Ostriker, John Stevens Wade, Jack Hirschman, Diane Stevenson, among the many. And we believe what Oscar Wilde said, that 'a beautiful thing helps us by being what it is.'" 1-yr sub price: $7.50; per copy: $3.00; sample: $2.00. 1971. 50pp; 9 x 6. †le. circ. 1,000. Reporting time: 3-6 weeks. Payment: 2 copies. Ads: $50 or exchange/$25. Discounts: 10 or more-50% disc cash basis. Back issues: issue 1 & 2 (amnesty) $10. Pub's reviews. §contemporary poetry magazines, books of poems, letterpress pub. CCLM, COSMEP, NESPA.

‡**FOXFIRE,** Rabun Gap, GA 30568.

FPS: A MAGAZINE OF YOUNG PEOPLE'S LIBERATION, Youth Liberation Press, Inc., Keith Hefner, 2007 Washtenaw, Ann Arbor, MI 48104. Articles, art, photos, cartoons, interviews, satire, criticism, reviews, letters. 4-6/yr; sub price: $10.00-6 issues (1 year or more); per copy: $0.95; sample: $0.60. 1970. 48pp; 7 x 10. †of. circ. 1,750. Reporting time: 2 months. Payment: none. Copyrighted. Ads: $50.00/$30.00/$3.00 col. inch (about 25 words). Discounts: 20 percent off to subscription agencies. Back issues: $1.00 each. Pub'd 5 issues 1976; expects 5 issues 1977, 5 issues 1978. Pub's reviews: 10 in 1976. §Youth, education, social change. COSMEP, APS.

Fragment Press (see PLOUGHMAN)

Franklin Book Company (see also BOOK BUYER'S GUIDE/MARKETPLACE DIRECTORY), Kevin K. Kopec, PO Box 208, East Millstone, NJ 08873, 201-873-2156. Articles. "Consumer orientation material. Source directories." avg. price, paper: $3.95. 1975. 50-100pp; 8½ x 11. of. avg. press run 3,000-5,000. Reporting time: 3 months. Payment: 25 percent. Copyrights for author. Discounts: 50 percent. COSMEP.

Free Books Inc (see also WINDOWS IN THE STONE), Ronnie Lane, Pres. Treas.; Eric Greinke, V.P. Sec., 7437 Eastern SE, Grand Rapids, MI 49508. Poetry, fiction, art, photos, cartoons. 1976. †of. Payment: copies.

FREE LANCE, A Magazine of Poetry & Prose, Casper L. Jordan, Russell Atkins, 6005 Grand Ave., Cleveland, OH 44104. "Vol. 17, 1975: Alan Britt, Barbara Holland, J. Hollander, Glee Knight, Kenneth Rosen, Emilie Glen, etc." 2/yr; 1-yr sub price: $2.00; per copy: $1.00. 1950. 80-100pp; half 8½ x 11. of. circ. 500. Reporting time: irreg. Payment: copies only. no ads. CCLM, COSMEP.

Free Life Editions, Chuck Hamilton, Robert Rossi, Valerie Sayers, 41 Union Square West, New York, NY 10003, 212-989-3750. Art, non-fiction. "We publish books which examine political and social authoritarianism in practice and theory as well as texts which teach and suggest ways to subvert hierarchical relations. We have published a book on libertarian education, several books on the European political scene and one book which concerns domestic fascism. We have also printed two posters on anti-authoritarian themes. Forthcoming books of great interest will be three volumes of Paul Goodman's essays and poetry and a book of maxims by Raoul Vaneigem. We will also be publishing a book on aging by Bonnie Bluh in 1978." avg. price, cloth: $11.50; paper: $4.15. 1973. 303pp. of. avg. press run 2,500. Reporting time: 1-4 months. Payment: advance varies, standard royalties. Copyrighted by author. Discounts: 20 percent 1-4, 40 percent 5 or more. Expects 7 titles 1977, 2 titles 1978. COSMEP.

Free People Press (see BOTH SIDES NOW)

FREEDOM, Freedom Press, Collective, In Angel Alley, 84B Whitechapel High St, London E1, United Kingdom, 01 247 9249. Articles, cartoons, reviews, news items, criticism, letters. fortnightly; 1-yr sub price: £5.00 [$10.00 per yr seasonal] air mail rates on request.; per copy: 15p; sample: SAE. 1886. 16pp; 12 x 8½. †of. circ. 1,500. Reporting time: normally by return. Payment: none. Discounts: 25% to indiv/bulk order, 33% to shops. Back issues: available at price of current issue (or of sub. for year sets). Pub'd 26 issues 1976; expects 26 issues 1977, 26 issues 1978. Pub's reviews: 60 in 1976. §anarchism.

FREEDOMWAYS, Freedomways Associates, Inc., Esther Jackson, Managing Editor; John Henrik Clarke, Associate Editor; J. H. O'Dell, Associate Editor, Ernest Kaiser, Associate Editor, 799 Broadway, Suite 542, New York, NY 10003. Poetry, articles, cartoons, reviews. 4/yr; 1-yr sub price: $4.50 (US)/$6.00 (outside US); per copy: $1.25; sample: free. 1961. 96pp; 4½ x 7¼. le. circ. 7,000. Reporting time: several months. No payment. Ads: $150.00/$75.00. Discounts: 30% discount-bulk, agent only. Back issues: $2.00 except for special back issues $2.50 each. Pub'd 4 issues 1976; expects 4 issues 1977, 4 issues 1978. Pub's reviews. §Black culture, economics.

Freelance Press Services (see CONTRIBUTORS BULLETIN)

Frick and Friends (see TUGBOAT)

Friends of Malatesta, Inc., Robert S. Dickens, Anne B. Dickens, Ron LaFrance, P.O. Box 937, Ellsworth, ME 04605. "We also publish: Little People Publications." 1973. of. Reporting time: 1 mo. No payment. Discounts: 25% on orders over $7. COSMEP.

Friends of the Earth (see NOT MAN APART)

Friends Of The Washington Review Of The Arts (see THE WASHINGTON REVIEW)

FROM HERE, From Here Press, William J. Higginson, Box 2702, Paterson, NJ 07509. Poetry, fiction, criticism, reviews, parts-of-novels, long-poems, plays. "First issue summer '76, another to follow shortly. Among early contributors: Alicia Ostriker, Weatherly, Celestine Frost, etc. Looking for clarity, intensity, otherwise no particular biases here. No submissions before Nov. 1976, please, so we get the first two issues out before becoming swamped. FH Press also publishes a series of miniature chapbooks called wee!editions, selling for 10¢ to 50¢, as well as XTRAS and HAIKU MAGAZINE (which see). Catalogue requests invited. VIEWS FROM HERE, opinion sheet/newsletter, free for s.a.s.e." irreg.; sub price: $6.00 4 issues/$10.00 institutions 4 issues; per copy: $2.00; sample: $2.00. 1976. 40pp; 5.5 x 8.5. †of. circ. 500. Reporting time: immed. Payment: 1 copy. Pub's reviews. §poems, avant-garde, prose, translations, esp fm Asian lang. COSMEP.

From Here Press (see FROM HERE, HAIKU MAGAZINE, XTRAS)

FROM THE FIELD: A Magazine of Art and Verse, Staff Press, Dr. Suhail Hanna, Box 295, Sterling, KS 67579. Poetry, art, photos, concrete art. "We're looking for excellence in traditional and experimental art and verse. We're small, but we value the best, the enduring, the spirtually uplifting. If it has no spirituality, it belongs to another domain, certainly not to our harvest from the fields." 2/yr; 1-yr sub price: $3.00; per copy: $1.50. 1976. 48pp; 5½ x 8½. †le. circ. 500. Reporting time: one month. Payment: copies. Pub's reviews. §little magazines.

THE FRONT, The Front Press, Jim Smith, P.O. Box 1355, Kingston, Ontario K7L5C6, Canada. Poetry, fiction, articles, art, photos, cartoons, interviews, satire, criticism, reviews, letters, parts-of-novels, long-poems, collages, plays, concrete art. "Bias towards post-modernist & experimental, exploratory work (slight). Length no matter (as long as contributors understand that longer pieces might be broken into 2 or more numbers). Open to any style. Recent contributors: Stuart MacKinnon, Jim Smith, David McFadden, Wayne Clifford, b p Nichol." Irreg. (at least 2 per year); 1-yr sub price: $5.00; per copy: $1.00; sample: $1.00. 1974. 30-50pp; 8½ x 11. †mi/of. circ. 250-500. Reporting time: 3 wks. Payment: Copies (5). Buys first serial publication only. Ads: Free/exchange. Discounts: 40 percent. Back issues: $5.00 ea. Expects 3 issues 1977, 3 issues 1978. Pub's reviews: 5 in 1976. §poetry/fiction/avant-garde & experimental arts. Joining COSMEP.

FRONT STREET TROLLEY, Molly McIntosh, 2125 Acklen Ave., Nashville, TN 37212, 615-297-8025. Poetry, fiction, articles, art, cartoons, interviews, satire, criticism, reviews. "Short fiction (maximum 2,500), short articles, etc., poetry (any length)-works of a satirical nature especially welcome, preferance given to Southern writers." Quarterly.; 1-yr sub price: $3.00; per copy: $0.50; sample: $0.50 or free. 1974. 32pp; 8½ x 11. of. circ. 300-500. Reporting time: one to two months. Payment: copies. Copyrighted. no ads, except of the announcement nature. Back issues: $0.50. Pub'd 4 issues 1976; expects 4 issues 1977, 4 issues 1978. Pub's reviews: 4 in 1976. §Poetry, films. COSMEP, CCLM.

Frontier Press, Harvey Brown, Elizabeth Warner, 1419-12th Ave., San Francisco, CA 94122, 415-665-6071. Poetry. avg. price, cloth: $8.00; paper: $2.00. 1964. 100pp; 6 x 8. lp/of. avg. press run 2,000. Copyrights for author. Discounts: 40 percent. Expects 3 titles 1977, 2 titles 1978. COSMEP.

FROZEN WAFFLES, Pitjon Press/Backback Media, Bro. Dimitrios, David Wade, 321 N. Indiana, Bloomington, IN 47401, 813-336-9117. Poetry, fiction, articles, art, interviews, reviews, collages, concrete art. "Want poems using the magic of the banal, subreal, 'everyday' (cf Prevert, Zen poetry, Brautigan at his best, D. Wade & Richard Gombar's poems in *Stoney Lonesomes* No. 4 & 5, Spike Jones writing about Stravinsky's shoes squeaking, etc.) or the magic of the 'meta-real' (cf Breton, Neruda, Bly when he's not bull shitting, the school of Duane Locke at it's best, etc.) Frags from diaries (names changed to protect the guilty), anectotes, weird observations, fresh interviews, art work (India ink only!) will also be appreciated. Ditto: book & mag reviews (short!). Due to various delays, we'll be coming out (Nos. 1-3) in late '77 and/or early '78. Would like black India ink sketches of poets accepted by us. Preferably self-portraits: or by fellow-artists of poets." 2-3/yr; 1-yr sub price: Not set. But figure about $3.50 per copy. Plan to print special issues of a single poet, also.; per copy: About $3.50 per copy. 1976. 36-50pp. mi/of. circ. 200-400. Reporting time: 2 weeks-2 months. Payment: 1 copy. Copyrighted. no ads: not yet, anyway. Discounts: 10% off five or more. Back issues: $5.00 each (after 2 years: $10.00 each). Expects 2-3 issues 1977, 2-3 issues 1978. Pub's reviews. §poetry, poetics, bios of poets.

EL FUEGO DE AZTLAN, Oscar Trevino, 3408 Dwinelle Hall, Univ of Calif, Berkeley, CA 94720. Poetry, fiction, articles, art, photos, cartoons, interviews, satire, criticism, reviews, parts-of-novels, long-poems, plays. "Short stories over 10 doublespaced typewritten pages have little chance of being considered. Looking for unusual, original Chicano material. Free to prisoners (as long as we can afford it)." 4/yr; 1-yr sub price: $8.00 institution-$3.50; per copy: $1.50. 1976. 32pp. of. Reporting time: 6 weeks. Payment: contributor's copies. Copyrighted, reverts to author. Discounts: 10 or more, 25 percent off. Pub'd 2 issues 1976; expects 4 issues 1977, 4 issues 1978. Pub's reviews. §Chicano/Mexican American. CCLM.

FULCRUM, Socialist Party of Canada, Committee (Editorial), Box 4280 Station A, Victoria, B.C. V8X3X8, Canada. 4/yr; 1-yr sub price: $2.00 libraries $4.00 (2 year); per copy: $.25; sample: Free. 1968. 12-16pp; 8½ x 14. †of. circ. 700. no ads.

Full Court Press (see also GOODFELLOW REVIEW OF CRAFTS), Christopher Weills, Jon Stewart, Bill Netzer, Box 4520, Berkeley, CA 94704, 415-845-7645. Art. 1973. of. avg. press run 10,000 (tabloid). Reporting time: 3 weeks. Discounts: 50 percent. COSMEP.

Funch Press, Seth Wade, 1101 Tori Lane, Edinburg, TX 78539. "I have pubd THE HORBLY GNOME & THE PAN AMERICAN REVIEW & a few other things including a couple of bks. But divorce, heart attack, & bourgeois insanity in general have taken their toll. Still, I expect to get out a bk this year & eventually mail things to those who shd get them. That is, the concrete-fluxus-etc experimentalist mostly. The business distribution end of this enterprise can go to hell. Funch Press, THE HORBLY GNOME, & THE PAN AMERICAN REVIEW are still recovering. Will be heard from. Still interested in international avant-garde activities."

Fur Line Press (see B&H BOOKS)

THE FURTHER RANGE, Adele Kenny Kookogey, 27 Oval Road, Milburn, NJ 07041. Poetry. "*Further Range* is a new magazine associated with the Robert Frost Society. We make it clear that our tastes in content and style are not necessarily those of Robert Frost. We want good contemporary work that reflects strong poetic vision and sophistication. Up to 35 lines. Send S.A.S.E. Recent contributors: Madeline Bass, Penny Bihler, William Higginson, Alicia Ostriker." 1-2/yr; price per copy: $1.50 plus postage; sample: $1.50 plus postage. 1976-77. 30pp; 5½ x 8½. of. circ. 400. Reporting time: 1-3 months. Pays in a contributor's copy. Copyrighted, reverts to author. Back issues: none available this year. §poetry.

The Future Press, Richard Kostelanetz, P.O. Box 73, Canal St., New York, NY 10013. "Committed exclusively to radically alternative materials for books and radically alternative forms of books. Have so far done a ladderbook, a cut-out book, a collection of cards containing numerals, a one-man collection of visual poetry. What we can do depends, alas, largely on grants; and since U.S. funding agencies have been notoriously ungenerous toward experimental work and its practitioners, *The Future Press* is scarcely sanguine. The artists are there; the audience is there; the trouble lies in the middle." avg. price, paper: $2.00. 1976. 1-48pp; varies. of. avg. press run 600-1,000. We can't encourage submissions. Payment: generous percentage of edition. Copyrights for author. Discounts: usual. Pub'd 2 titles 1976.

FUTURES INFORMATION INTERCHANGE, The Future Studies Program, 166 Hills South, University of Massachusetts, Amherst, MA 01003, 413-545-0981. Fiction, articles, criticism, reviews. "Our magazine is unique in that it is the only (that we know of) university periodical to deal specifically with educational futures studies. Articles are usually 4-7 pages in length, written mostly by members of the future studies program with subscriber participation encouraged. Recent contributors include Harvey Scribner and Dwight Allen, who were the former Chancellor of The New York City Schools and the former Dean of The Mass School of Education, respectively." 2/yr; 1-yr sub price: $2.00; per copy: $1.00; sample: $0.50 (individual article reprints). 1970. 25-30pp; 8½ x 11. of. circ. 300. Payment: none so far. Copyrighted. Discounts: bulk rate. Back issues: $1.00 per back issue. Pub's reviews. §All areas relating to future studies: bio-ethics, technology, forecasting, design science, aesthetics, education, etc.

Futurum Forlag (see GATEAVISA)

G

G P Enterprises—JOB HUNTER'S FORUM, I. Norman Johanson, 132 Pinecrest Drive, Annapolis, MD 21403, 301-261-2320. "We are a career counseling consulting firm and a small press publisher. We specialize in providing people with information and tools to help them find satisfying jobs and careers (with employers or in their own businesses). We have published two how-to books on job hunting and career planning ('WRITE YOUR TICKET TO SUCCESS—A DO-IT-YOURSELF GUIDE TO EFFECTIVE RESUME WRITING & JOB HUNTING'—$7.95 and 'TIPS ON LANDING A FEDERAL GOVERNMENT JOB'—$2.95). We are interested in being contacted by distributors, jobbers, libraries, and bookstores." avg. price, paper: $2.95-$7.95. 1974. 8½ x 11. of. avg. press run varies with book orders. Copyrights for author. Discounts: up to 40% to bookstores, distributors up to 50%, bulk orders up to 20% (retail sales). Pub'd 2 titles 1976; expects 1 title 1977. COSMEP.

GAIRM, Gairm Publications, Derick S. Thomson, 29 Waterloo St., Glasgow, Scotland G2, United Kingdom. Articles, poetry, fiction, cartoons, photos, reviews, interviews, criticism. "All matter printed is in Gaelic" 4/yr; 1-yr sub price: $4.00; per copy: $1.00. 1952. 100pp; c. 8vo. lp. circ. 2,000. Payment: nominal. Ads: £35/£20. Back issues: available in most cases. Pub'd 4 issues 1976; expects 4 issues 1977, 4 issues 1978. Pub's reviews: 11 in 1976.

GALAXIA 71, Grupo Escritores De Venezuela, Modesto Vargas Lopez, P.O. Box 4023, Carmelitas 101, Caracas, Venezuela. Poetry, articles, art, photos, interviews, criticism, reviews, parts-of-novels. "Dionisio Aymara; A. Garibaldi; German Pardo Garcia; Aleixo Leite Filho" 2/yr; 1-yr sub price: $6.00 U.S.; per copy: $4.00. 1970. 25pp; 11.4 x 8.2½. †of. Reporting time: two weeks. Ads: $100/$65/$.15. Discounts: 10-15 %. Pub's reviews. §poetry, art, novels and photos.

GALILEO, Ave Victor Hugo Publ., 339 Newberry St, Boston, MA 02115. "Science fiction and fantasy magazine." 4/yr.

GALLERY SERIES/POETS, Harper Square Press, Phyllis Ford-Choyke, Arthur Choyke, 401 W. Ontario St., c/o Artcrest Products, Chicago, IL 60610. *"Gallery Series Five/Poets-To An Aging Nation (with occult overtones)* is last of present series. No unsolicited material.' 1-yr sub price: $2.25 each; per copy: $2.25. 1967. 104pp; 4¼ x 11. of. circ. 1,000 plus. Payment: 6 copies. Back issues: GS I, $1.25; GS II, $1.50; GS III, $1.75; GS IV, $2.00. CCLM, COSMEP.

GALLIMAUFRY, Gallimaufry, Mary MacArthur, Fiction; Mary Mackey, Plays, 3208 N. 19th Rd., Arlington, VA 22201. Fiction, art, photos, criticism, reviews, parts-of-novels, collages, plays, concrete art. "Primarily fiction." 2/yr; 1-yr sub price: $4.00; per copy: $2.25; sample: $2.25. 1973. Approx. 100pp; 6 x 9. of. circ. 1,500. Reporting time: 3 mos. max. Payment: Copies and/or nominal cash payment. Copyrighted. Ads: $50.00/$25.00. Discounts: 40 percent trade (minimum 5 copies); to prisoners & workshops for postage only. Back issues: Available on request. Pub'd 3 issues 1976; expects 2 issues 1977, 2 issues 1978. CCLM, COSMEP.

Galloping Dog Press, Peter Hodgkiss, 25 St Albans Road, Swansea, West Glamorgan, United Kingdom. Poetry, fiction, long-poems, non-fiction, criticism. "GDP is an *unsubsidised* press operated completely separately from poetry information. Publications. Jim Burns-PLAYING IT COOL; David Tipton-A GRAPH OF LOVE" avg. price, cloth: Vary; paper: varies; other: varies. 1976. 30-40pp; A5/A4 (mimeo). †of/mi. avg. press run 300-500. Payment: Copies. Copyrights for author. Discounts: 25 percent. Expects 2 titles 1977, 2 titles 1978. ALP.

Ganglia Press (see GRONK)

GARGOYLE, Gargoyle, Jeffrey Kelly, Claudia Buckholts, 160 Boylston St. no. 3, Jamaica Plain, MA 02130. Poetry, art. "Poetry from the New England area. We prefer poems with craft and vision. We are receptive to new writers." 2/yr; 1-yr sub price: $3.00; per copy: $1.00; sample: $1.00. 1975. 44pp; 5½ x 8½. of. circ. 300. Reporting time: deadlines March 1 and Sept. 1—report up to 3 mo. Payment: copies. Copyrighted, reverts to author but if material republished prefer note that it first appeared in Gargoyle. Discounts: 40% to trade. Back issues: no. 1 and no. 2 sold out. no. 3 $1.00. NESPA.

GARLIC TIMES, Lovers Of The Stinking Rose/Midpress Books, L. J. Harris, 1043 Cragmont Av., Berkeley, CA 94708, 527-1958. Articles, art, photos, cartoons, interviews, satire, reviews, letters, collages. "We celebrate the cuisine, folklore, herbalism cultivation and humor of garlic & onions. We use recipes, remedies, interviews with herbalism, chefs, medical doctors, etc. Members keep us informed of various media attention payed to garlic. Jeanne Rose, the popular herbalist, writes a column in each issue, our approach is light-hearted, but our information is quite serious." 1-2/yr; sub price: $9.00 (lifetime); per copy: $0.50. 1976. 25pp; 7 x 10. of. circ. 3,000. Reporting time: 6 weeks. Payment varies. Copyrighted. Ads: $40.00/$25.00. Discounts: trade, 40 percent; bulk, 50-55 percent; wholesale, 50-60 percent. Pub'd 1 issue 1976. Pub's reviews: 3 in 1976. §cookbooks, herbal books, natural history: garlic & onion related.

Garrett Park Press, Willis L. Johnson, Garrett Park, MD 20766. avg. price, cloth: $9.00; paper: $7.50. 1968. 400pp; 8½ x 11. of. avg. press run 4,000. Payment: 10 percent 1,000-15 percent above that. Copyrights for author. Discounts: 30 percent.

Garretson Graphics (see CIRCUS MAXIMUS)

GATEAVISA, Futurum Forlag, The Collective, Hjelmsgt 3, Oslo 3, Norway. Articles, photos, cartoons, interviews, criticism, reviews, music, letters, collages, news items. "Biases: libertarians socialist/cultural." 10/yr; 1-yr sub price: $6.00 (KR 30)-yr; per copy: $0.80 (KR 4); sample: $1.00 (KR 5). 1970. 24pp; 42.27 cm. of. circ. 10,000. Payment: none. Ads: $300.00/$150.00. Back issues: 13 issues $6.00. Pub'd 4 issues 1976; expects 10 issues 1977, 10 issues 1978. Pub's reviews: plenty in 1976. §political/counter-culture/arts. APS.

A GAY BIBLIOGRAPHY, Task Force on Gay Liberation, Barbara Gittings, P.O. Box 2383, Philadelphia, PA 19103. revised approx. every 18 months; price per copy: $.25 5 for $1.00. 8pp; 8½ x 11. of. circ. 15,000. Discounts: 6-30 copies 15¢ each, 31 or more 12¢ each. §gay/lesbian material.

GAY COMMUNITY NEWS, GCN Inc., Neil Miller, 22 Bromfield St., Boston, MA 02108, 617-426-4469. Articles, art, photos, interviews, reviews, music, letters, cartoons, news items, non-fiction. "Also includes weekly news of and about gay people including news commentaries." 52/yr; 1-yr sub price: $15.00; per copy: $.35; sample: $0.35. 1973. 20pp; 10¼ x 15½. of. circ. 5,500. Reporting time: 1 week. Copyrighted. Ads: $200/$140/$3/4 lines. Pub'd 52 issues 1976; expects 52 issues 1977, 52 issues 1978. Pub's reviews. §gay, sexual, feminist. COSMEP, NEPA.

GAY LEFT, Collective, 36a Craven Rd, London W2, United Kingdom. "Articles on gay liberation and socialism. Theoretical articles on sexuality. Reviews. News of gay socialist activity internationally." Irregular.; price per copy: 40p. 1975. 32pp; A4. of. circ. 2,600 plus. Payment: None. Copyrighted. Ads: Exchange ads only. Pub'd 2 issues 1976; expects 2 issues 1977. Pub's reviews: 10 in 1976. APS.

GAY LITERATURE, Daniel Curzon, English Dept./CSUF, Fresno, CA 93740. Poetry, fiction, articles, art, photos, interviews, satire, criticism, reviews, parts-of-novels, plays. "We want quality writing, chiefly fiction and essays, on gay life. We don't want pulp or slick work." 4/yr; 1-yr sub price: $8.00 (library $10.00); per copy: $2.00. 1974. 56pp; 8½ x 9½. of. circ. 500-1,000. Reporting time: 2 months. Payment: in copies. Back issues: $2.00, #1-5. Pub's reviews. §gay material. COSMEP.

GAY NEWS, Denis Lemon, 1A Normand Gardens, Greyhound Road, London W14 9SB, United Kingdom, 01-381-2161. Articles, poetry, fiction, art, cartoons, photos, satire, reviews, news items, interviews, criticism, letters. "Maximum length of contributions-3,000 to 3,500 words" fortnightly; sub price: £4.00/13 issues £7.50/26 issues; per copy: 20p; sample: 40p. 1972. 40pp; 26cm x 39.4 cm. of. circ. 22,500. Reporting time: 2-6 weeks. Payment: by negotiation. Ads: £150/£80. Back issues: 35p.

GAY SUNSHINE: A Journal of Gay Liberation, Gay Sunshine Press, Winston Leyland, P.O. Box 40397, San Francisco, CA 94140. Poetry, fiction, articles, art, photos, cartoons, interviews, satire, criticism, reviews, letters. "'Gay Sunshine' is a cultural gay liberation journal. We concentrate on poetry, interviews, political literary articles, graphics, photos. We need good material. Manuscripts should be double spaced, typed & less than 15 pages. Recent contributors include Jonathan Williams, Allen Ginsberg, Gore Vidal, Taylor Mead, John Wieners. We also sponsor a Gay Liberation Book Service. Free list in return for SASE." 4/yr; sub price: $10.00/12 issues; per copy: $1.00. 1970. 32pp; 17½ x 11¼. circ. 8,000. Reporting time: 1 month. Payment: copies/free subs. Ads: $200/$100/$1.00 line. Discounts: 35% off cover, postpaid, for 10 or more copies. Back issues: $10 for packet #1 (10 issues). Pub's reviews. §poetry, some fiction, literary essays, biog. CCLM, COSMEP.

Gay Sunshine Press, Inc. (see also **GAY SUNSHINE: A Journal Of Gay Liberation**), Winston Leyland, P.O. Box 40397, San Francisco, CA 94140. Poetry, fiction, interviews, non-fiction. "*Gay Sunshine Press* was founded in 1970 to publish cultural, literary, political material by Gay people. During the first five years of its existence it published only the tabloid cultural journal, *Gay Sunshine*. Since 1975 it has been publishing chapbooks and books. It was incorporated as non-profit in 1976." avg. price, cloth: $15.00; paper: $5.95; other: $2.50. 1970. 200pp; 6 x 9. avg. press run 2,000. Reporting time: 1 month. Payment: royalties. Copyrights for author. Discounts: distributors to the Book Trade (book stores): (at 40 percent discount) No discounts to individuals or libraries. Discounts to book jobbers & specialty shops: Orders of 1: 20 percent; 2-4: 25 percent; 5 up: 30 percent.

GAY TIDE, Gay Alliance Toward Equality, P.O. Box 14638 Station A, Vancouver, British Columbia V5L1X5, Canada. Poetry, fiction, articles, photos, interviews, satire, reviews, letters. "Gay Tide is a gay liberation newspaper. Although fiction etc. are included, central focus is on the independent political action taken by gays in British Columbia, Canada and USA to achieve liberation of homosexuals." irreg.; sub price: 6-issue $2.00/supporting 6-issue sub: **$5.00**; per copy: $.25; sample: $.50. 1973. 12pp; 15½ x 10¼. of. circ. 2,000. Reporting time: 1 month. no advertising. Discounts: institutional price $5.00/6 issues agents retain 1/3 of copies sold. Back issues: $.50. Pub's reviews. §gay liberation, homosexuality, related areas.

GAYELLOW PAGES, Renaissance House, Frances Green, box 292 Village Station, New York City, NY 10014. "Directory of organizations, businesses, publications, bars, baths, churches etc. of interest to gay women and men in USA & Canada." 1-yr sub price: $10.00 ($18 outside USA/CANADA); per copy: $5.00 ($7 outside USA/CANADA). 1973. 80pp; 8½ x 11. of. circ. 1,500. Ads: $100/$60. Discounts: minimum 3 copies, 50% prepaid and nonreturnable, 40% prepaid returnable, 40% regular consignment. Pub's reviews. §gay-related topics; gay-supportive feminist.

GAZEBO, Marsha Mills, Editor-in-Chief; Barbara Bihlmaier, Editor; Robert Bush, Editor, Wichita State Univ Post Office, Wichita State University, Wichita, KS 67208, 316-689-3130. Poetry. "Contributions restricted to members of Wichita State University community (students, faculty, staff members, administrators) only genre form accepted is poetry." 2/yr; 1-yr sub price: free. 1974. 16pp; 9 x 6. of. circ. 800. Reporting time: 1 month. Payment: 3 copies. no advertising. Back issues: will be mailed on request; all issues available. Pub'd 2 issues 1976; expects 2 issues 1977, 2 issues 1978. COSMEP.

GCN Inc. (see GAY COMMUNITY NEWS)

GEGENSCHEIN, 6 Hillcrest Ave., Falconbridge, New South Wales 2776, Australia. Reviews, criticism, letters. "Editor written. No outside contributors except art, cartoons." sample price: $1.00. 1971. 40pp; 8 x 10. †mi. circ. 250. Copyrighted. no ads. Back issues: Expected to be out of stock soon. Pub'd 3 issues 1976; expects 3 issues 1977, 2 issues 1978. Pub's reviews: 100 plus in 1976. §Science fiction.

GEGENSCHEIN QUARTERLY, NeoNeo Do-Do, Phil Smith, Phil Demise, 291-293 7th Ave, 10th Floor, New York, NY 10001. Poetry, fiction, art, music, long-poems, poetry, collages, plays, concrete art. "The Gegenschein Quarterly & NeoNeo Do-Do are now only part of a large performing space known as the GEGENSCHEIN Vaudeville Placenter. Gegenschein Quarterly will continue to publish the written word while NeoNeo Do-Do will publish performing material that will be performed at the Placenter. We are not really open to any unsolicited material at this point but if you are interested in knowing more about our concept, please write and we will respond." 2-4/yr. 1971. 100pp; 8½ x 11. of. circ. 300-600. Reporting time: 2 wks-1 month. Payment: copies. Discounts: 40% consign, 50% cash. Back issues: GQ #'s 1-14-$100. §any areas. CCLM, COSMEP.

Gen Guides Book Co., Alfred Mayerski, 5409 Lenvale, Whittier, CA 90601, 213-692-5492. avg. price, paper: $2.95. 1964. 100pp; 5½ x 8½. Does not copyright for author. Discounts: trade-40 percent wholesale only.

Gemini (see MADRONA)

The Generalist Assn., Inc. (see THE SMITH)

THE GENEVA POND BUBBLES, Leathern Wing Scribble Press, John M. Armleder, 6 Rue Plantamoor, Geneve CH-7207, Switzerland, 022-32-6784. Poetry, art, photos, music, collages, concrete art. 1977. †mi/of/lp. Discounts: 33-1/3.

GENRE, University of Oklahoma, Ronald Schleifer, General Editor; Paul G. Ruggiers, Robert Murray Davis, Assoc. Eds., Dept. of English 760 Van Vleet Oval, Norman, OK 73069. "Articles in the journal will focus on questions dealing with genre in relation to specific major literary texts, historical development of specific genres, and theoretical discussions on the concept of genre itself. The last issue of each year will be a special publication in order to treat specific topics for which prominent scholars will be invited to be guest editors. Recent contributors to the journal have been: Charles Muscatine, A.K. Nardo, George T. Amis, Kenny Marota and Avrom Fleishman. Paul G.

Ruggiers will be the guest editor for the upcoming special issue ('76) which will treat the subject of comedy before Shakespeare. Please direct correspondence to Donald Rose, Business Manager, Dept. of English, University of Oklahoma." 4/yr; 1-yr sub price: indiv $6.00/yr, libraries $7.00; per copy: $1.50 for each issue/$3.00 for special issue. 120pp. of. circ. 550. Reporting time: 2-3 weeks. Back issues: special issue which comes out yearly will cost $3.00.

George Sroda, Publisher, George Sroda, Amherst Jct., WI 54407. "Has published one book, *Facts About Nightcrawlers."*

THE GEORGIA REVIEW, Univ. of Georgia, Athens, GA 30602, 404-542-3481. Poetry, fiction, articles, art, photos, interviews, criticism, reviews. "Robert Penn Warren, Harold Bloom, Stanley Cavell, John Ashbery, Guy Davenport, Geoffrey Hartman, Richard Howard." 4/yr; 1-yr sub price: $3.00; per copy: $1.50. 1947. 270pp; 7 x 10. lp. circ. 2,032. Reporting time: 1-2 mos. Payment: $4 page prose; $.50 line poetry. Copyrighted by University of Georgia, who holds copyright. Ads: $60/$35/no. Discounts: agency sub. 25% ads 15%. Back issues: $1.50. Pub'd 4 issues 1976; expects 4 issues 1977, 4 issues 1978. Pub's reviews: 19 in 1976.

GESAR- The Magazine of Buddhism in the West, Dharma Publishing, Judy Robertson, 5856 Doyle St., Emeryville, CA 94608. Articles, photos. "News from Buddhist organizations accepted." 4/yr; 1-yr sub price: $5.00; per copy: $1.50. 1973. 42pp; 7 x 9¼. †of. circ. 2,000. Reporting time: 2 months. Discounts: 40%. Back issues: $1.00/copy. Pub's reviews. §Buddhist. LPS.

Ghost Dance: **THE INTERNATIONAL QUARTERLY OF EXPERIMENTAL POETRY, Ghost Dance Press,** Hugh Fox, Paul Ferlazzo, N.W. Werner, 526 Forest, E. Lansing, MI 48823, 351-5977. Poetry. "Recent contributors: Richard Morris, Helen Duberstein, Bill Costley. Looking for new foms, new ideas, *really* new. *Not* looking for warmed-over Concretism, Dadaism, Futurism, etc." 4/yr; 1-yr sub price: $3.00; per copy: $1.00; sample: $1.00. 1968. 32pp; 5½ x 8½. †of. circ. 300. Reporting time: 1 hour. Payment: copies. Not copyrighted. Ads: none. Discounts: none. Back issues: $1.00. CCLM, COSMEP.

Ghost Dance Press (see also GHOST DANCE MAG), Hugh Fox, N.W. Werner, Paul Ferlazzo, 526 Forest, E. Lansing, MI 48823. Poetry. "Anything breaking new formal ground. We want to stay the forever-about-to-break newest wave you can ride into *Nirvana."* avg. price, paper: $1.00; other: $1.00. 1968. 32-36pp; 5½ x 8½. †of. avg. press run 200-500. Reporting time: 1 day. Payment: copies. Common law copyright. Discounts: 50 percent to trade. CCLM, COSMEP.

Giorno Poetry Systems Records (see DIAL-A-POEM POETS LPs)

GLASS, The Evergreen Publishing Corporation, Fred Abrams, 7830 S.W. 40th Avenue, Portland, OR 97219, 503-245-4444. Articles, art, interviews, criticism, reviews, letters. 12/yr; 1-yr sub price: $20.00; per copy: $2.00; sample: free. 1973. 56pp; 8½ x 11. circ. 3,200. Reporting time: 1 month. Payment: 4 cents/word, $125.00 max. on publication. Copyrighted, reverts if so arranged. Ads: $350.00/$225.00/n/a. Discounts: 5 or more copies, 40 percent; 50 or more, 50 percent; 250 or more, 60 percent. 2 percent 10 net 30. Returns accepted for full credit for up to one year from invoice date, complete copies only. Pub's reviews §Art-oriented ones. COSMEP.

Glass Bell Press, Margaret Kaminski, 5053 Commonwealth, Detroit, MI 48208, 414-898-7972. Poetry. "Glass Bell hand sets & hand prints original work by women poets. It is named after a book by Anais Nin, who printed her work in the 40's. For 1975, International Women's Year, Glass Bell was awarded a grant from Mich. council for the arts to print poems by Mich. women poets; this project is now out of print. *Sisters And Other Selves,* by Judith McCombs, was the press's 1976 project, an offset production with cover art by Catherine Claytor-Becker. 1974 poets included Ellen Bass, Audre Lorde, Susan Fromberg Schaeffer, Toni Ortner Zimmerman, Lili Bita, Gloria Dyc, Gail Steslick, and Judith McCombs. These hand-set broadsides are still in print for $0.10 each plus $0.50 postage. (1 pp., 8½ x 11). 1977 Project: *Journal Of A Woman Almost* 30, by Gloria Dyc - $2.00, pap." 1974. 8½ x 11 or 5-3/8 x 8¼. †of/lp. Reporting time: 1 to 2 weeks. Payment: copies only for broadsides;15% for books. Discounts: Bookstores & distributors, classroom: 50%. Pub'd 1 title

1976; expects 1 title 1977, 1 title 1978.

GLASSWORKS, Glassworks Press, Betty Bressi, Estelle Visconti, Managing Editor, PO Box 163, Rosebank sta, Staten Island, NY 10305. Poetry, art, concrete art, long-poems, collages, fiction, photos. "Established and new writers/artists. Recent contributors: Colette Inez, Robert Hass, Richard Shelton, Lyn Lifshin, Brian Swann, Helen Saslow, Alfred Starr Hamilton, Richard Kostelanetz, Natale S. Polly." 3 issues yr; 1-yr sub price: $4.00; per copy: $1.50; sample: $1.50. 1975. 64pp; 5½ x 8½. of. circ. 500. Reporting time: 4 weeks. Payment: 2 copies. Copyrighted, reverts to author. Ads: $30/$15. Discounts: bulk 30% libraries, subscription $6.00, single copy $2.00. Pub'd 3 issues 1976; expects 3 issues 1977, 3 issues 1978. CCLM, COSMEP, NESPA.

Glebe Press (see OLD FRIENDS)

Gleniffer Press, Ian Macdonald, 11 Low Road, Castlehead, Paisley PA2 6AQ, United Kingdom, 041-889-9579. Poetry, art, photos, letters, long-poems, plays. "Willing to look at anything new in art, poetry, stories (short), essays, specialist in miniature books, bookplate designs, limited editions. Mailing list of private buyers now established. Recently published ' *Smallest Book In The World*'. Elected 'printer of the year 1976 by British Printing Society." avg. price, cloth: Varies; paper: Varies; other: Varies. 1968. 20pp; up to quarto. †lp/of. avg. press run 250-1,000. Reporting time: 2 wks. Payment: Single fees. Copyrights for author. Discounts: 33-1/3%. Pub'd 3 titles 1976; expects 2 titles 1977, 1 title 1978. BPS, COSMEP, SGPA, PLA.

Glide Publications, Ruth Gottstein, Noah Levin, 330 Ellis St, San Francisco, CA 94117. "Glide Publications for 1976: Battered Wives, The Kids Ko It Book, Alternatives in Print 4th Ed." Discounts: standard. COSMEP.

GLOBAL TAPESTRY JOURNAL, BB Books, Dave Cunliffe, 1 Spring Bank, Salesbury, Blackburn, Lancs, England BB1 9EU, United Kingdom. "Mainly concerned with creative poetry & prose. Also those energy communications networks which liberate human animal beast mind. Be it psychedelics, mutant vampires or dead history memory recall." irreg.; sub price: £6/4 issues; per copy: £1.50 plus post; sample: £1.00. 1971. 64pp; A4. of. circ. 1,000. Reporting time: soon. Payment: one copy. Ads: none. Discounts: one third trade.

Glouchester Press, William R. Tudor, PO Box 1044, Fairmont, WV 26554, 304-366-1441. Poetry, music. "So far we publish only College Music text books and serious music." avg. price, cloth: $17.50 (notebook style). 1971. 200pp; 8½ x 11. of. avg. press run 1,000. Reporting time: 1 month. Payment: 10 percent annual. Copyrights for author. Discounts: 40 percent (trade, agent & jobber) 20 percent (classroom). ASCAP.

GNOSTICA, Llewellyn Publications, C. L. Weschcke, Box 3383, St. Paul, MN 55165. Articles, art, photos, reviews. "*GNOSTICA* is geared to the intelligent beginner as well as the advanced student. Articles should be well-researched and well-thought out. Recent issues of GNOSTICA have centered around various occult themes such aas magic, astrology, paganism and para-psychology. All articles must have an occult theme and usually run 5/10,000 words in length, poetry and fiction are used as filler only. Recent contributors include: Colin Wilson, Israel Regardie, Robert Anton Wilson, Brad Steiger, Gareth Knight, Stuart Holroyd and Fritz Leiber. Most articles are solicited." bi-monthly; 1-yr sub price: $10.00; per copy: $2.00; sample: free. 1971. 120pp; 8½ x 11. of. circ. 7,000. Reporting time: 8 wks. Payment: $.02 per word. Copyrighted. Ads: $160/$90/$.25 wd. Discounts: Agency, frequency, CWO, will trade. Back issues: $2.00 per copy. Pub'd 5 issues 1976; expects 6 issues 1977, 6 issues 1978. Pub's reviews: 25-30 in 1976. §All occult fields, e.g. astrology, parapsychology, magic, witchcraft, graphology, palmistry, tarot, etc.

Goat Hair Press (see QUEEN STREET MAGAZINE)

GOETHE'S NOTES, Goethe's Notes Press, Jesse Glass Jr., 254 N. Gorsuch Rd, Westminister, MD 21157, 848-3690. Poetry, fiction, art, plays. "*GOETHE'S NOTES* appears when the money does. It has no price therefore no owners & no deadlines. I'm looking for poetry with explosive images. No S.A.S.E. no return. Recent contributors: Roland Flint, Beth Joselow, Robert Lawler, Jeff Whittaker, Joe Gainer. Query first w/sample." 1/yr. 1974. mi. circ. 500. Reporting time: varies-immediate to years. Payment: 3 copies of the mag. Copyrighted, reverts to author. Discounts: none. §poetry, fiction, plays.

Goethe's Notes Press (see also GOETHE'S NOTES), Jesse Glass Jr., 254 N Gorsuch Rd., Westminister, MD 21157, 848-3690. Poetry, long-poems, plays. "Do mostly things by myself & my friends like Artavd—a broadside playlet by Jesse Glass, Jr. G's NS is a poor man's press—doing small books in cheapo editions distributed without charge to friends of the press. If it has no price it has no owner—so friends lay it on friends until the book falls apart. I'm looking for the calculated explosion that shatters the prisms from the face of God. Query first, w/sample. No S.A.S.E. no return." avg. price, paper: free/donation to press. 1974. pp varies; varies. mi. avg. press run 100. Reporting time: varies. Payment: copies. Does not copyright for author. Discounts: none.

GOLD TURKEY, Carl D. Clark, 3007 University, Austin, TX 78705, 512-472-7415. Articles, photos, interviews, criticism, reviews, music, collages, plays. "*GOLD TURKEY* is a journal of news and works in the field of music and other non-literary, non-graphic arts. Each issue will consist of a brief printed section containing news, biblio-/disc-/ographies in the fields of jazz, rock, avantegarde, classical, etc. music, oral/sound poetry etc. In addition, each issue will have scores and a tape of original works." 4/yr; sub price: $3.00 plus a tape/issue; per copy: $0.75 plus a tape; sample: none. 1977. 4pp; 5½ x 8½. mi/of/tape. Reporting time: 2 weeks. Payment: copies. Not copyrighted. Ads: none. Discounts: none: libraries should write concerning institutional rates and arrangements. Pub'd 1 issue 1976. §any records and tapes.

Golden Atom Publications, Larry Farsace, Duverne Farsace, P.O. Box 1101, Rochester, NY 14603. Poetry, fiction, articles, art, photos, reviews, letters. "We publish many oneshots, and have several magazines, including: 7 STAR POEMS, POETRY DAY MAGS, DARK SHADOWS mags, etc. (some 8 times a year). Enquiries for information (with SASE) welcome." 1939. 12-100pp. mi. Reporting time: 2 wks. Payment: $4-$12 fiction $.25 line poetry.

Golden Mountain Press, Harold Graves, PO Box 2387, San Francisco, CA 94126.

Golden West Books, Donald Duke, PO Box 8136, San Marino, CA 91108, 213-283-3446. Non-fiction. avg. price, cloth: $10.00; paper: $3.95. 1963. 265pp; 8½ x 11. of. avg. press run 5,000. Reporting time: 3 weeks. Payment: Royalties. Copyrights for author. Discounts: 40 percent. Pub'd 8 titles 1976; expects 8 titles 1977, 8 titles 1978.

Golden West Publishers, Hal Mitchell, 4113 N. Longview, Phoenix, AZ 85014. "ARIZONA COOK BOOK, Al Fischer and Mildred Fischer; MEXICO'S WEST COAST BEACHES, Al Fischer and Mildred Fischer."

Goldermood Rainbow Press (see also NITTY GRITTY), Bill Wilkins, Editor, 331 W. Bonneville, Pasco, WA 99301, 509-547-5525. Poetry, fiction, articles, art, photos, cartoons, interviews, satire, criticism, reviews, letters, concrete art, non-fiction. "Articles, commentary, fiction, maximum 10,000. Poetry-mostly short. Reviews-short-maximum 500 words. Cartoons-humor-photos." avg. price, paper: $4.00; other: $3.00. 1974. 100pp; 8½ x 11. †of. avg. press run 2,000. Reporting time: 60-90 days. Payment: fiction $15.00, poetry & photos $2.00, cartoons & art work $5.00, commentary-personal experience-reviews-articles $10.00. Copyrights do not revert. Discounts: trade 40 percent. Pub'd 2 titles 1976; expects 5 titles 1977, 4 titles 1978. COSMEP.

THE GOLIARDS, Goliards Press, Jerry Burns, 3515 18th St, Bellingham, WA 98225. Poetry, art, photos. "Energies previously expended in pursuit of the business of printing, politics, ladies, motorcycles, bars, etc., have been refocused to photography, poetry, printing, sailing & gardening. GOLIARDS has enjoyed several miscarriages and or stillbirths, but is now reasonably functional. But i am mot overjoyed at the prospect of wading through piles of illiterate emotional orgasisms. I am receptive to creative expression: poetry and photography. Current issue indicates strong interest in graphics & quality reproduction. Future issues will be smaller & more frequent." irreg.; price per copy: $3.00; sample: $3.00. 1964. 112pp; 7 x 10. †of. circ. 1,200. Payment: copies. Discounts: 40% 10 days, trade. Pub's reviews. COSMEP.

Good Gay Poets Press, Good Gay Poets Collective, Box 277, Astor Station, Boston, MA 02123. Poetry. avg. price, cloth: $15.00; paper: $3.00-$5.00; other: $3.00-$5.00. 1973. 72pp; 5½ x 8½. of. avg. press run 500 copies of each book. Reporting time: 3 months to 2 years. Payment: 10 percent of run to author; payment only after costs have been returned. Copyrights for author. Discounts: 40 percent disc to retailers; 50 percent to distributors. Pub'd 10 titles 1976.

THE GOODFELLOW REVIEW OF CRAFTS, Full Court Press, Christopher Weills, Jon Stewart, Bill Netzer, PO Box 4520, Berkeley, CA 94704, 415-845-7645. Art. "Articles covering traditional & contemporary crafts." 12 issues a year (as of July); 1-yr sub price: $8.00; per copy: $0.75; sample: Free. 1973. 28pp; 10 x 14. of. circ. 10,000 (printed). Reporting time: 3 weeks. Payment: $20.00. Copyrighted, reverts to author. Ads: $250.00/$150.00/$0.10 a word. Discounts: 50 percent. Back issues: $1.00. Pub'd 7 issues 1976; expects 8 issues 1977, 12 issues 1978. Pub's reviews: 14 in 1976. §Arts & crafts. COSMEP.

GPU NEWS, Liberation Publications, Inc., Eldon E. Murray, PO Box 92203, Milwaukee, WI 53202, 414-276-0612. Poetry, fiction, articles, art, photos, cartoons, interviews, satire, criticism, reviews, music letters, plays, news items, non-fiction. monthly; 1-yr sub price: $7.00 ($8.00 Foreign); per copy: $0.75; sample: $1.00. 1971. 52pp; 8½ x 11. of. circ. 3,000. Reporting time: 1 month. Copyrighted, does not revert to author. Ads: $48/$30/$.10. Discounts: $0.30 copy - 10 or more copies. Back issues: $.50 each in lots of five or more. Pub'd 12 issues 1976; expects 12 issues 1977, 12 issues 1978. Pub's reviews. §Must be of interest to gay readers.

THE GRACKLE: Improvised Music In Transition, The Grackle, Ron Welburn, Edit. Director; Roger Riggins, Jim Stewart, Victor Rosa, Joseph Banks, Box 244 Vanderveer Station, Brookly, NY 11210. Articles, interviews, criticism, music, photos. "Interviews w/ Marion Brown, Steve Lacy, David Murray. We lean more toward 'free improvisational jazz' but of course are interested in all. Interested in discography, bibliography, international jazz. Moving toward black music/jazz scholarship." appx 3/yr; 1-yr sub price: $4.00 ($7.50 Foreign); per copy: $1.35 ($2.25 Foreign); sample: $1.35 ($2.25 Foreign). 1976. 50pp; 8½ x 11. of. circ. 1,000. no unsolicited ms. Payment: copies. Copyrighted. Back issues: Only No. 3 available. Pub'd 3 issues 1976; expects 2 issues 1977, 2 issues 1978. Pub's reviews: 35 in 1976. §Music-jazz, R&B, 20th C. internat'l.

GRAFIKTRAKTS, Ted Smith/Graphics, Eugene Warren, 300 W. 3rd, Rolla, MO 65401. "We are doing 16 to 24 page chapbooks, folders, etc, of poetry, prose, graphics-from a Christian perspective. No bias as to form, but it should be tight, with sharp images. Especially interested in fiction. #1, RUMORS OF LIGHT, Eugene Warren, $.75; #2 WEIGHT OF RESURRECTION, Lionel Basney, $1. Forthcoming: John Leax, Jennifer Thomas." 3/yr; sub price: $3.50/6 titles; sample: $.75. 1974. 20pp. of. circ. 500. Reporting time: 4 mos. Payment: copies only. Discounts: 40% trade. Expects 1 issue 1977.

GRAHAM HOUSE REVIEW, Graham House Press, Peter Balakian, Bruce Smith, Box 489, Englewood, NJ 07631, 201-871-4498. Poetry. "Our aim is to publish good poetry wherever we find it, poetry from the unknown and the well-established. We believe the best poetry struggles with language for music, image, and voice; is well made and attached with integrity to experience. Some recent contributors include: Hugo, Goldbarth, Soto, Wheatcroft, Stern, Blessing, Pierson, Broughton, E. Knight and others." 2/yr; 1-yr sub price: $2.50; per copy: $1.25; sample: $1.25. 1976. 40-50pp; 5½ x 8½. of. circ. 500. Reporting time: 2-4 wks. Payment: copies only. Copyrighted, does not revert to author. Discounts: trade discount 20-40 percent, negotiable. Pub'd 2 issues 1976; expects 2 issues 1977, 2 issues 1978. CCLM, COSMEP.

The Grail (see IN TOUCH)

GRAND RIVER REVIEW/CAPITOL CITY MOON, Grand River Review, Gary R. Andrews,

129

PO Box 15052, Lansing, MI 48901. "Preferred length less than 2500 words, most any topic considered, mostly into historical or relevant local area material that presents views other than those generally found in either the straight or underground media. Sometimes we just put a bunch of stuff in an envelope and send it to the folks on our list." irreg.; price per copy: $1.00. 1972. 24pp plus; little to tabloid. †of. circ. 500 to 5,000. Reporting time: 3 months. Back issues: $1.00 each for Nos. 1, 2, 3, 4. Pub's reviews

GRANITE, Granite Publications, Anselm Parlatore, Box 1367, Southampton, NY 11968. Poetry, fiction, interviews, criticism, reviews, letters, parts-of-novels, long-poems. "Ammons, Morgan, Bertolino, Matthews, Merwin." 2/yr; 1-yr sub price: $6.00; per copy: $3.00. 1971. 120pp; 9 x 6. †of. circ. 1,000. Reporting time: 2 wks. Payment: copies. Back issues: $100.00 full set. Pub's reviews. §poety. CCLM, COSMEP.

Granny Soot Publications, Colin Browne, Box 171, Sannichton, BC V0S1M0, Canada. Poetry, long-poems. of. Reporting time: 2 wks. Discounts: over 5 copies 40%.

GRANTS AND AWARDS AVAILABLE TO AMERICAN WRITERS, P.E.N. American Center, Mel Mendelssohn, Exec. Secretary, 156 Fifth Ave, New York, NY 10010. "The GRANTS AND AWARDS . . . booklet is a directory of financial assistance for the writer. The 1977 edition is considerably updated, and is appearing in a new, more compact format." 1/yr; price per copy: $2.00 per copy. 64pp; 6 x 9. COSMEP.

GRASS ROOTS, Grass Roots General Store, David Miller, Meg Miller, Box 900, Shepparton, Victoria 3630, Australia. Reviews, non-fiction. "Aim is to be completely Australian." 4 issues/yr; 1-yr sub price: $a8 yr for overseas subs. $6.60 local sub; per copy: $2.00; sample: $2.00. 1973. 60pp; quarto. of. circ. 10,000. Reporting time: 3 months. Payment: nil. Copyrighted, reverts to author. Ads: $a 125.00/$a 65.00/$2 per classified ad. no word rate. Back issues: $a 2.00. Pub'd 2 issues 1976; expects 4 issues 1977, 4 issues 1978. Pub's reviews: 30 in 1976. §alternatives. COSMEP, COSMEPA, APS.

Grasshopper Press, Gregory J. Tetrault, Maxine W. Davis, P.O. Box 331, DeWitt, NY 13214. "One book: THE ORGANIC TRAVELER: A Guide to Organic, Vegetarian, & Health Food Restaurants in the U.S. and Canada" 1975. 178pp; 5 x 8. of.

GRAVIDA, Gravida, Ltd., Lynne Savitt, Romaine Murphy, Ina Wilde, Abby Luttinger, Natale Polly, Box 118, Bayville, NY 11709. Poetry, reviews. "Our bias is excellence of craft, fresh imagery. Diane Wakoski, Andre Codrescu, Colette Inez, Michael McMahon, A.D. Winans, etc. etc. Bukowski, Ignatow, Sam Hamill, Malanga, Stainton etc. etc." 4/yr; 1-yr sub price: $4.00; per copy: $1.25; sample: $1.00. 1973. 60pp; 5½ x 8½. of. circ. 500-1,000. Reporting time: 6 weeks. Payment: copies only. Pub's reviews: 2 in 1976. §poety. CCLM, COSMEP.

GRAYDAY MAGAZINE, Point Blanc Press, Roger Charles, Garland Burnette, 2830 Napier Ave., Macon, GA 31204. "Poems & stories that illuminate. Prose to 3,500 words." 2/yr; 1-yr sub price: $2.00; per copy: $1.00. 1975. 44pp; 5½ x 8½. †of. circ. 350. Reporting time: 5 wks. Payment: copies only. Discounts: 50%. CCLM.

Gray Flannel Press, Adrian C. Louis, P.O. Box 9181, Providence, RI 02740. Poetry, fiction. "Looking for eclectic, heavy, emotional, excellent poetry. Query first." 1974. of. Reporting time: 4 wks. CRISP.

The Graywolf Press, Scott Walker, P.O. Box 142, 2210 S. Peabody, Port Townsend, WA 98368, 206-385-1160. Poetry, fiction. avg. price, cloth: $12.00; paper: $4.00. 1974. Varies, 12-86pp; Varies. †lp. avg. press run 200-2,000. Reporting time: 1 wk to 4 wks. Payment: Negotiable. Usually 10 percent of edition in copies. Copyrights for author. Discounts: 1 copy, 10 percent; 2 copies, 20 percent; 3-5 copies, 30 percent; 6 or more 40 percent. 20-25 percent on cloth. 10 percent on handbound in boards. Pub'd 7 titles 1976; expects 7-9 titles 1977, 8 titles 1978.

Great Basin Press, Eric N. Moody, Lee Mortensen, Phillip I. Earl, Box 11162, Reno, NV 89510, 702-329-0709. "Interested, primarily, in history and literary criticism pertaining to Great Basin region." avg. price, paper: $4.00. 1976. 150pp; 5½ x 8½. of. avg. press run 300 copies. Reporting time: 1-2 months. Payment: percentage of sales. Copyrights for author. Discounts: 40 percent to retailers, regardless of volume. Pub'd 2 titles 1976; expects 3 titles 1977.

THE GREAT BLAFIGRIA IS/THE GREAT COMPASSION, Blafigria Press, John R. Boland, PO Box 1054, Santa Fe, NM 87501. Poetry, fiction, articles, art, photos, cartoons, interviews, satire, criticism, reviews, music, letters, parts-of-novels, long-poems, collages, plays, concrete art, news items, non-fiction. "THE GREAT BLAFIGRIA IS, is as you are, this spirit motion of culture continuing and coming, is to being a common edition of seeings, of those with all sensitivities in the arts, in music, in science, in philosophy, in the living, seeings given through journals, essay, diary, poetry, story, letter and especially combinations, and through picture, drawing and photo. THE GREAT BLAFIGRIA IS is a network of selves, dancers, naturalists, writers, parents, actors, children . . . who are readers/editors, hesheis to becoming an example of energy and human spirit. Send inquiry first." 2/yr; sub price: $9.00 (3 issues); per copy: $3.50; sample: $1.00. 1975. 140pp; 8½ x 14 & 7¼ x 10¾. of. circ. 2,000. Reporting time: 2-3 wks. no ads. Discounts: 40% 5 or more. Back issues: $2.25/Free. Pub'd 2 issues 1976; expects 1 issue 1977, 2 issues 1978. Pub's reviews.

GREAT CIRCUMPOLAR BEAR CULT, Bear Cult Press, Rick Penn, David Kubach, Box 468, Ashland, WI 54806. Poetry, fiction, articles, art, interviews, criticism, reviews, long-poems. 2/yr; 1-yr sub price: $3.00; per copy: $2.00. 1976. 64pp; 7 x 8½. of. circ. 500. Payment: 2 issues. Copyrighted. Pub'd 1 issue 1976; expects 2 issues 1977, 2 issues 1978. Pub's reviews. §poety. COSMEP.

Great Granny Press, M. Truman Cooper, 829 West Anapamu, Santa Barbara, CA 93101, 805-966-9532. "All Great Granny publications are FREE on request. The Great Granny no. 1, a poetry post card by Ted Kooser is out of print. Great Granny no. 2 is by Marjorie Hawksworth, available as a poetry post card. Have plans for a broadside, a modest 2-poem booklet in addition to more cards. I am completely open on submissions & try to give each one careful personal attention." avg. price, paper: free. 1976. 1pp; 6 x 9. 1p. avg. press run 1,000 copies. Payment: copies. Will copyright a booklet. NESPA.

Great Raven Press, Paul Martin, P.O. Box 1112, Lewiston, ME 04240, 784-0523. Poetry, long-poems. "Books from Theodore Enslin, Keith Wilson, Michael Hogan, Paul Martin, Martin Rosenblum, Monica Wood, Kendall Merriam, Gary Lawless, Leo Connellan, John Brandi, and Winslow Durgin. Translations, poems, and prose-poems preferred. Query before any submissions. Publish what appeals to my particular tastes...'regional' poetries." avg. price, paper: $3.00; other: $6.00 signed. 1976. 24-36 pp-photo of poet along with bio information; 6 x 9. of. avg. press run Limited editions 300 to 500 copies-4 books published per set. Reporting time: 1 month. Payment in copies. Copyrights for author. Discounts: 40 percent to trade. Expects 8 titles 1977, 8-12 titles 1978. MWPA, NESPA.

Great Society Press, Angelo De Luca, 451 Heckman St. Apt. 308, Phillipsburg, NJ 08865, 201-859-6134. 1960. 17pp; 5 x 7. lp/of.

Great Star Press, N. J. Brown, 1117 High Court, Berkeley, CA 94708. "One title thus far: *Rag Theater*." 1975. of/lp.

GREAT WORKS, Great Works Editions, Peter Philpott, 25 Portland Road, Bishops, Stortford, Hertfordshire, United Kingdom. Poetry, fiction, articles, art, criticism, reviews, letters, long-poems. "No. 6 includes: Kevin Porman, Andrew Crozier, John Freeman, Martin Harrison, Yann Lovelock, Paul Matthews, David Miller, Opal L Nations, Elaine Randell, John Welch: No. 7 will include: David Chaloner, Michael Haslam, Rod Mengham, David Miller, Peter Riley, Nigel Wheale, John Wilkinson." 2-3/yr; 1-yr sub price: £1.80; per copy: 60p; sample: 30p. 1973. 80pp; A4. †duplicated. circ. 175. Reporting time: 1 month. Payment: none. Copyright to author. Ads: negotiable. Discounts:

1/3 for trade. Back issues: 1-5 60p. Pub'd 1 issue 1976; expects 2 issues 1977, 3 issues 1978. Pub's reviews: 3 in 1976. §contemporary writing.

Great Works Editions (see also GREAT WORKS), Peter Philpott, 25 Portland Rd., Bishops, Stortford, Herts, United Kingdom. Poetry, fiction, parts-of-novels, long-poems. "Could publish anything but prefers to publish contemporary English writing. Current publisher Andrew Crozier: *Pleats,* Neil Oram: *The Golden Forgotten,* Lorand Caspar: *Ground Absolute* (trans. Peter Riley). Forthcoming works include Allen Fisher: *Docking,* John Hall: *Couch Grass,* Louis Patler: *Eloisa.*" avg. price, paper: 75p. 1973. 30pp; a4 usually. †mi/of. avg. press run 200 or more. Reporting time: 1 month. Payment: 50 percent any profits. Copyright to author. Discounts: 1/3 trade sale or return accepted. Pub'd 3 titles 1976; expects 8 titles 1977.

THE GREATER GOLDEN HILL POETRY EXPRESS, The Feminist Poetry & Graphics Center, Carolyn Hull, Joyce Nower, Shelley Savren, 2829 Broadway, San Diego, CA 92102, 714-239-3664. Poetry. "Recent contributors: Pat Traxler, Bobbie Bishop, Barbara Mor, Kathleen Fraser, Joyce Nower, Shelley Savren, Deena Metzger, Margaret Kaminski. Manuscripts being solicited." 3-4 x's per yr; price per copy: $1.50 out of town. 1975. 45pp; 7 x 8½. of. circ. 400. Reporting time: up to 1 mo. Copyrighted, reverts to author. Ads: none. Back issues: Summer 1976-National issue.

‡**GREEN EGG,** PO Box 2943, St. Louis, MO 63130.

THE GREEN FUSE, Hearthstone Press, Stella Worley, 708 Inglewood Dr, Broderick, CA 95605. Poetry, satire, reviews. "No fixed line limits; depends on the poems. Do not accept haiku, light verse, sentimental poetry, or seasonal verse. Poems with imagery, and meaning to others besides the writer are welcome. Also like surrealism, and satire. Contributors are George Enos, Harold L. Johnson, Guy Beining, Arthur Knight, William Bly, Paul Fericano, Ann Menebroker, Joyce Odam and others." 2/yr; price per copy: $1.00; sample: $1.00. 1976. 36pp plus; 5½ x 8½. †mi/lp. circ. 300 plus. Reporting time: 1 wk to 1 mo. Payment: copy. Copyrighted. Ads: none. Back issues: $1.00. Pub'd 2 issues 1976; expects 2 issues 1977, 2 issues 1978. Pub's reviews: 2 in 1976. §Poetry only. COSMEP.

THE GREEN HORSE FOR POETRY, The Green Horse Press, Richard Behm, Kerry Thomas, c/oCreative Writing Program, Bowling Green Univ., Bowling Green, OH 43403. Poetry. "THE GREEN HORSE FOR POETRY was discovered with the intent of publishing young poets and providing a representative forum of craft and idea as they are made new in creative writing programs throughout the country. Ideally, we like to publish five to seven poems of each of the poets included in the magazine, though we do publish longer poems. Aside from time and money, our biggest problem is that most poets send only five or six poems. We would prefer more substantial mss of what you think is your best work, or that represents a series of poems which you are excited about, rather than the four poems the New York Quarterly rejected. We try to over-power or finesse our own biases, realizing ultimately that it is impossible to do so. We have published large chunks of poems by Howard McCord, Bruce F. Kawin, Clark Baker, Robert Vander Molen, James Grabill, Phil Smith, Michael McMahon, and D. Clinton and shorter works by many others." 1/yr; 1-yr sub price: $3.00; per copy: $3.00; sample: $3.00. 1973. 100pp; 8½ x 9. of. circ. 200. Reporting time: 1-3 mos. Payment: 1 copy. no ads. Discounts: 20% to creative writing classes on orders of 10 or more. Back issues: not available. CCLM, COSMEP.

Green Horse Press, Wm. Greenwood, Tom Maderos, Lynn Mally, Paul Mann, PO Box 1691, Santa Cruz, CA 95061. Poetry. "The Press is devoted to the discovery and translation of outstanding collections of poems not yet available in English. Each issue is a finely printed, Bilingual Book. We are interested in chapbook-size manuscripts of translations only. Send query letter. Sase. Our titles include: G.H. 1 The Dog of Hearts-Rene Char, G.H. 2 Peace Has Yet To Be Won-Arguelos Morales, G.H. 3 (at press) Destruction or Love-Vincente Aleixandre." 1972. 60pp. 1p. Reporting time: 3-6 weeks. No payment for translators.

Green Horse Press (see PLATFORM)

Green Horse Publications, Andrew Cozens, 28 The Crescent, Andover, Hampshire, England, United Kingdom. Poetry. "All mss. are considered though usually solicited mss. receive preference. Recent and planned booklets include: Welch, Tipton, Tweedale, Ward (UK), Eigner (US), Kondos (Greece), and traditional Bengali poetry. Inexpensively but neatly produced. The only bias, we hope, is for talent as opposed to mediocrity." 1971. 20pp; 7 x 5. †lp. avg. press run 150-300 plus. Reporting time: 1 month. Payment: By arrangement. Discounts: By arrangement. Pub'd 5 titles 1976; expects 5 titles 1977, 5 titles 1978. ALP.

The Green Hut Press, Janet Wullner Faiss, Publisher & Editor; Rosalie Heacock, Associate Editor, 24051 Rotunda Rd, Valencia Hills, CA 91355, Book Orders: P.O. Box 55144, Valencia Hills, CA 91355, 805-259-5290. "The work (writing & art) of Fritz Faiss. Limited editions. Thus far we work by mail order only, except for a few selected bookstores. Enquiries welcome. We have prices ranging between $4.00 and, for a hand-colored-by-artist edition, $125.00." 1972. 75pp; Varies. †mi/of. avg. press run 200 copies. We do not accept manuscripts. Copyrights for author. Pub'd 1 title 1976; expects 2 titles 1977, 2 titles 1978.

Green Knight Press, Ritchie Darling, P.O. Box 512, Amherst, MA 01002. Poetry, fiction, satire, criticism. "Francis Golffing" 1965. 8½ x 5½ or 9 x 6. of. Reporting time: 6 months. Payment: $10 per poem. COSMEP, NESPA.

GREEN MOUNTAIN QUARTERLY, Green Mountain Editions, Lee Baxandall, et. al., 460 N. Main Street, Oshkosh, WI 54901. Articles, art, photos, cartoons, interviews, criticism, reviews, letters. "GREEN MOUNTAIN QUARTERLY takes a socialist and anarchist perpective and seeks to present outstanding analyses on issues of social urgency. Fiction or nonfiction may be the medium. The clarity, practicality, and imaginativeness of thought, expression or documentation is of the essence. Keep a carbon of what is submitted and do not expect return if you don't supply a stamped self-addressed envelope" 4/yr; 1-yr sub price: $6.00 foreign/$5.00 U.S. & Canada; per copy: $1.50; sample: $1.50. 1975. 64pp; 8½ x 10¾. lp. circ. 500. Reporting time: 15-60 days. Payment: none, except. commissioned pieces. Ads: $100/$55. Discounts: 40% on 10 or more copies. §socialist/anarchist/labor. COSMEP.

THE GREEN REVOLUTION, The School of Living, F. Paul Salstrom, Larry Lack, c/o School of Living, Freeland, MD 21053. Articles, art, photos, cartoons, interviews, satire, criticism, reviews. "We are into *Social Decentralism* and act as a journal with that orientation for N. Amer. interested in back-to-the-land whys & hows" 12/yr; 1-yr sub price: $6.00; per copy: $.50; sample: $.50 free by special request. 1962. 28pp; 8½ x 11. of. circ. 1,500. Payment: usually none. Ads: $40/$25/$.50 line. Discounts: Bulk 40% Agents 20%. Pub's reviews.

GREEN RIVER REVIEW, Green River Press, Raymond Tyner, SVSC Box 56, University Center, MI 48710. Poetry, reviews. 3/yr; 1-yr sub price: $6.00; per copy: $2.00; sample: $2.00. 1968. 96pp; 6 x 9. of. circ. 450. Reporting time: 2-3 months. Payment: in copies. Copyrighted, reverts to author. Ads: $50.00/$25.00. Discounts: 20 percent agent and jobber. Back issues: $5.00 per copy. Pub's reviews. §Contemporary poetry. CCLM.

Green River Press (see also GREEN RIVER REVIEW, INTERNATIONAL POETRY REVIEW), Raymond Tyner, Evalyn P. Gill, SVSC Box 56, University Center, MI 48710. "We publish poetry." avg. price, cloth: $10.00; paper: $5.00. 1968. 56 to 130pp; 6 x 9. of. Reporting time: 2-3 months. Payment: yes. Copyrights for author. Discounts: trade, 40; bulk, 40; classroom, 40; agent, 20; jobber, 20. CCLM.

GREEN'S MAGAZINE, Clover Press, David Green, Box 313, Detroit, MI 48231. Poetry, fiction. "Stories to approx 3,500 poems to 40 lines. Want deep characterization in complex conflicts. Prefer to avoid profanity, explicit sexuality. Recents: Marjorie Holmes, Stanley Field, Leonard Guardino, Timothy Wade Black, Marjorie Deiter Keyishian, Warren C. Miller, Wayne Barton, Lyn Lifshin, A. E. Darmsky, Gary Fincke, Terry Kennedy. No carbons or photostats please." 4/yr; 1-yr sub price: $5.00; per copy: $1.50; sample: $1.50. 1972. 100pp; 5¼ x 8½. †of. circ. 1,000. Reporting time: 6 wks. Payment: up to $25.00. Copyrighted, will reassign rights. Ads: $100/$60. Discounts: $4.50

libraries; $4.00 schools etc./orders of 10 or more. Pub'd 4 issues 1976; expects 4 issues 1977, 4 issues 1978. §general. CCLM, COSMEP.

THE GREENFIELD REVIEW, The Greenfield Review Press, Joseph Bruchac, Michelle Sullivan, Carol Bruchac, Ossie Enekwe, P.O. Box 80, Greenfield Center, NY 12833, 518-584-1728. Poetry, reviews. "Open to both new and established poets. Some of our special features in past and forthcoming issues include prison writing from Auburn, Modern African poetry, Asian-American poets, new Caribbean poets. Contributors lately include Michael Hogan, Joan Colby, Gayl Jones, Alvin Aubert, Christine Zawadisky, Colette Inez, Ross Talarico, Freya Manfred, Ary Feeney, Geraldine Kudaka, Michael McMahon, Thomas Johnson, Tony Moreno, Victor Hernandez Cruz, Alan Chong Lau, Leslie Silko, Walt Shepperd." 2 double issues/yr; 1-yr sub price: $4; per copy: $2.00. 1968. 136pp; 5½ x 8½. of. circ. 750. Reporting time: 1 wk-6 wks. Payment: Copies. Copyrighted, reverts to author after first printing. Ads: $50.00/$25.00/None. Discounts: standard discounts. Back issues: Issue #1-$20. Pub'd 2 issues 1976; expects 2 issues 1977, 2 issues 1978. Pub's reviews. §poetry. CCLM, COSMEP, NESPA.

GREENHOUSE REVIEW, Greenhouse Review Press, Gary Young, 126 Escalona Dr., Santa Cruz, CA 95060, 408-426-4355. Poetry, fiction, long-poems. "Recent work by Charles Wright, Diane Wakoski, James McMichael, Russell Edson, D.J. Waldie and others." 2/yr; 1-yr sub price: $2.00; per copy: $1.00; sample: $1.00. 1975. 40pp; 5-1/2 x 8½. †of. circ. 500. Reporting time: 4 weeks. Payment: copies. Copyrighted. Pub'd 2 issues 1976; expects 2 issues 1977, 2 issues 1978. Pub's reviews. §poetry.

Greenhouse Review Press (see also GREENHOUSE REVIEW), Gary Young, 126 Escalona Dr., Santa Cruz, CA 95060, 408-426-4355. Poetry. "Greenhouse Review Press publishes a chapbook and broadside series. We are interested in manuscripts of up to 20 pages." avg. price, paper: $1.50. 1975. 16-32pp; 5½ x 8½. †lp. avg. press run 300. Reporting time: 4 weeks. Payment: copies. Copyrights for author. Pub'd 1 title 1976; expects 3 titles 1977, 4 titles 1978.

GREENPEACE, c/o 6 Endsleigh St., London WC1, United Kingdom. "Environmental/pacifist" Bimonthly; 1-yr sub price: £1.00 minimum; per copy: Stamped addressed envelope; sample: Stamped addressed envelope. A4. †mi. circ. 500. Pub'd 6 issues 1976; expects 6 issues 1977, 6 issues 1978. APS.

Greenwich-Meridian (see CROSSCURRENTS)

Grist Press (see also GRIST), Lucy Bate, Carole Oles, Elizabeth McKim, Alice Ryerson, Miriam Goodman, Judith Steinbergh, Estelle Leontief, 195 Lakeview Ave., Cambridge, MA 02138. Poetry, art, photos. "Grist is a cooperatively published press; does not usually consider submissions. At present we publish only women writers; mainly poetry, but not exclusively." 3/yr; avg. price, cloth: $1.00; paper: $0.35; other: $0.35. 1975. 8pp; 11 x 17. of. avg. press run 1,000. Grist does not normally accept submissions. Payment: copies; contributors usually help pay expenses of the issue in which their work is being published. Copyrights for author. Discounts: 60% plus postage on orders of 10 or more. Back issues: Vol I, Nos. 1 & 2, 25 cents each; Vol II, Nos. 1, 2 & 8, 35 cents each. CCLM.

GRIST, Grist Press, Estelle Leontief, Carole Oles, Elizabeth McKim, Lucy Bate, Miriam Goodman, Judith Steinbergh, Alice Ryerson, 195 Lakeview Ave., Cambridge, MA 02138. Poetry. 3/yr; 1-yr sub price: $1.05; per copy: $0.35; sample: $0.35. 1975. 8pp; 11 x 17. of. circ. 1,000. We do not ordinarily consider submissions. Payment: copies. Copyrighted, reverts to author. Back issues: 3 for $1.00. CCLM.

GRITO DEL SOL: A Chicano Quarterly, Tonatiuh International Inc., Octavio I. Romano, 2150 Shattuck Ave, Berkeley, CA 94704. Poetry, fiction, articles, parts-of-novels, plays. 4/yr; 1-yr sub price: individuals $7.00/yr; institutions $8.00; per copy: $2.00; sample: free. 1976. 125pp; 6 x 9. of. circ. 1,600. Reporting time: 2 mos. max. Payment: pro-rate per page. no advertising. Discounts: Bookstores-35%/Agencies-15%. Back issues: $2.00 per issue. Pub'd 4 issues 1976; expects 4 issues

1977, 4 issues 1978. §Publications relating to chicanos.

GRONK, Ganglia Press, bp Nichol, 239 Queen St West, Toronto, Ont, Canada. Poetry, fiction, cartoons, parts-of-novels, long-poems, collages, plays, concrete art. "I tend to publish single author issues. Border-blur material preferred" 1/2yr; sub price: 8 issues/$12.00 institutional/$10.00 individual. 1967. of/other. circ. 100. Payment: authors copies.

Grossmont Press, Inc., 7071 Convoy Court, San Diego, CA 92111. 1970. of/lp. Reporting time: 4wks. Payment: Standard royalty on books; 40% royalty on subsidized books.

GROUND SKIMMER, Rich Grigsby, Box 66304, 11312½ Venice Blvd, L. A., CA 90066. Poetry, fiction, articles, art, photos, cartoons, interviews, satire, criticism, reviews, letters. 12/yr; 1-yr sub price: $10.00; per copy: $1.00. 1972. 50pp; 8½ x 11. of. circ. 9,000. Ads: $150.00/$80.00/$.15 wd. Back issues: Mimeo 1-10-50 cents each, 19-36-$.75 each, 37-$1.00. Pub's reviews.

THE GROVE, Naturist Foundation, Editorial Committee, Naturist Headquarters, Sheepcote, Orpington, Kent BR5 4ET, United Kingdom, Orpington 71200. Articles, cartoons, photos, news items, letters, non-fiction. "House journal of Naturist Foundation & Sun Societies, circulating internationally to naturists. Contributions on subjects of interest to naturists welcome-with or without illustrations. But no payment offered!" 3/yr; 1-yr sub price: £3.00 ($6.00); per copy: £1.00 ($2.00); sample: £1.00 ($2.00). 1950. 16pp; 9½ x 7½. lp. circ. 800. Payment: none. Ads: £20.00 ($40.00)/£12.00 ($24.00). Discounts: 10% for 3 inserters. Back issues: $1.00. Pub'd 3 issues 1976; expects 3 issues 1977, 3 issues 1978.

Growing Room Collective (see ROOM OF ONE'S OWN)

GRUB STREET, Grub Street, Alan Ball, Patricia Russell, P.O. Box 91, Bellmore, NY 11710, 212-733-3922. Poetry, fiction, articles, art, photos, cartoons, interviews, satire, criticism, reviews, music, letters, parts-of-novels, long-poems, collages, plays, concrete art. "Main interest is poetry, fiction, graphics." 2/yr; 1-yr sub price: $2.50; per copy: $1.50; sample: $0.50. 1969. 44-56pp; 5½ x 8½. of. circ. 1,000. Reporting time: 3 weeks-3 months. Payment: 3 copies; we will pay cash if we are successful in getting a grant for that purpose. One featured poet in each issue receives $10.00 and 10 copies. Copyrighted, reverts to author. Ads: inquire. exchange ads possible. Discounts: 40 percent on 5 or more copies to same address. 40 percent to bookstores in any quantity. Will accept consignment orders from bookstores. Distributor discounts by arrangement. Back issues: No. 1-4 50 cents ea. No. 5 $1.50. No. 6 $2.00. Pub'd 1 issue 1976; expects 2 issues 1977, 2 issues 1978. Pub's reviews: none in 1976. COSMEP, CCLM.

Grupo Escritores de Venezuela (see GALAXIA 71)

GUARD THE NORTH, Les Recherches Daniel Say Cie, Daniel Say, Box 65583, Vancouver 12, B. C. V5N 5K5, Canada. Articles, art, interviews, criticism, reviews, letters. "500 to 3000 word light writing of science, writing, SF, fantasy etc. etc." 8/yr; 1-yr sub price: $4.00; per copy: $.50; sample: $.25. 1971. 20pp; 21 x 28 cm. †mi. circ. 300. Reporting time: 1 month. Payment: copies. Pub's reviews. §Science or Science Fiction.

GUARDIAN, Weekly Guardian Associates, Irwin Silber, Jack Smith, 33 W 17th St, New York, NY 10011, 212-691-0404. Articles, photos, cartoons, interviews, criticism, reviews, letters, news items. 50/yr; 1-yr sub price: $17.00; per copy: $0.50; sample: free. 1948. 24pp; 10¼ x 15. of. circ. 20,000. Ads: $350.00/$210.00/$0.85. Discounts: none. Back issues: $0.65. Pub'd 50 issues 1976; expects 50 issues 1977, 50 issues 1978. Pub's reviews: 40 in 1976. §Politics, history, current events.

Guildford Poets Press (see also WEYFARERS), 10 Ashcroft, Shalford, Guildford, Surrey, United Kingdom. Poetry. avg. price, paper: 50p. 1972. 32pp; 8 x 6. of. Pub'd 3 titles 1976; expects 2 titles 1977.

Gullistan Press (see also DRINKWATCHERS' NEWSLETTER), Laurette Brown, Ariel Winters, P.O. Box 179, Haverstraw, NY 10927, 914-429-4844. "Published books: *Seashell Craft* (1977 booklet $4.00). *Drinkwatchers* by Ariel Winters ($6.95, 245 pp. paperback), illustrated with introduction by Dr. M. A. Hartman, Psychiatrist." avg. price, paper: $6.95. 1976. 250pp; 5 x 9. of. avg. press run 1,000-2,000 or more. Reporting time: 1 month. Payment: by special arrangement. Discounts: 40 percent or by arrangement. Pub'd 2 titles 1976; expects 6 titles 1977, 12 titles 1978.

GYMNASTICS WORLD, World Publications, Pam Goforth, c/o World Publications, P.O. Box 366, Mtn. View, CA 94040. "Please write directly to the editor for information on publishing articles. 'Gymnastics World' is a magazine about gymnastics, by the athletes themselves, their coaches, trainers and others directly involved in the sport." 24/yr; 1-yr sub price: $4.50; per copy: $.75; sample: free upon request. 1975. 28pp; 9 x 11. of. circ. 25,000. Back issues: $1.00 each magazine. §Sports, recreation and leisure activities.

THE GYPSY SCHOLAR: A Graduate Forum for Literary Criticism, Peter C. Mott, Managing Editor, Dept. of English, Michigan State U., East Lansing, MI 48824. "Manuscripts should not exceed 30 typed pages and conform to the *MLA Style Sheet*. 'The editors invite any graduate students to submit manuscripts which employ venturesome, speculative, inquiring, or controversial approaches to the study of literature. Brief forum articles dealing with the problems and professional concerns of English graduate students are also encouraged.' We also publish an *Annual Bibliography of Doctoral Dissertations in British and American Literature*." 3/yr; 1-yr sub price: Stud: $3.00/Fac: $5.00/Lib: $7.00; per copy: $3.50; sample: free. 1973. 55-60pp; 9 by 6. of. circ. 750. Reporting time: 3-4 weeks. Payment: none. no advertising. Discounts: Agents: 20%. Back issues: $3.50. §Texts on the teaching of writing; reading methodology; anthologies for use in the classroom.

Gyst Publications (see RUFUS)

H

HAIKU MAGAZINE, From Here Press, William J. Higginson, Box 2702, Paterson, NJ 07509. Poetry, fiction, criticism, reviews, letters. "Dormant in 1975; one issue plus supplement out already in 1976, two more to follow. HM is the leading journal of the new haiku, begun in Toronto by Eric W. Amann, led away from gushy 5-7-5s toward crystal-cutting haiku and other poems in English, traditional and contemporary work from Japanese, Spanish, French, German in translations by Cid Corman, the editors, others. Edited by WJH since 1971, pushing further into senryu/sequences/haibun/renga (collaboratives)/poems in organic form. Criticism & reviews. Special issue, HAIKU CHECKLIST, will give annotated list of over 160 books and other items of/on haiku—-free with subscription in 1976. Recent contributors incl. Anita Virgil, V.B. Young, Michael McClintock, Cor van den Heuvel, Rod Tulloss." irreg.; sub price: $6.00 4 issues/$10.00 institution 4/issues; per copy: $2.00; sample: $2.00. 1967. 48pp; 5.5 x 8.5. †of. circ. 500. Reporting time: 1 month. Payment: 1 copy. Back issues: rare, expensive. Pub's reviews. §haiku and related/translations from Asian languages. COSMEP.

Haiku Society of America, Inc. (see MINUTES AND PROCEEDINGS)

Halty Ferguson Publishing Co., William Ferguson, Raquel Ferguson, 376 Harvard Street, Cambridge, MA 02138, 617-868-6190. Poetry, fiction. "We do not encourage unsolicited material at the moment. To date we have published Jorge Guillen (in Spanish), James Tate (two titles), Tim Reynolds, William Ferguson, Peter Davison, Mark Strand, and John Updike." avg. price, cloth: $25.00; paper: $4.00. 1970. 60-100pp; 6 x 9. †lp. avg. press run 500-1,000. Reporting time: asap. Payment: 10 percent of list. Copyrights for author. Discounts: 40 percent on trade books, 30 percent on luxury signed editions.

THE HAMPDEN-SYDNEY POETRY REVIEW, Tom O'Grady, P.O. Box 126, Hampden-Sydney, VA 23943, 804-223-4381. Poetry. "W. D. Snodgrass, David Ignatow, Peter Viereck, Louis Simpson, Howard Moss, William Stafford, Josephine Jacobsen, Kenneth Rexroth, Denise Levertov." 2/yr; 1-yr sub price: $3.00; per copy: $2.00; sample: free. 1975. 40pp; 9 x 5. †of/lp. circ.

500. Reporting time: 6 weeks. Payment: copies. Copyrighted. Ads: none. Discounts: none. §poetry. CCLM.

HAND BOOK, Susan Mernit, Rochelle Ratner, C/O Mernit, 72 Spring St., Delaware, OH 43015, 72 Spring St, Delaware, OH 43015. Poetry, fiction, articles, art, photos, interviews, music, letters, parts-of-novels, long-poems. "A gathering of the spirit. A magazine of the internal. A piece of the network. An attempt to collect the energy of the spirit that works behind our poetry, our art, our science. A capturing of the Holy we find in the artist and the work. A magazine of reinforcement—a garden of those words and interest in the sacred that powers the world. Our wish is to add energy to energy, shaping the page into incant and force. Issue No. 1: *Prayer;* Issue No. 2: *Silence;* Issue No. 3: *The Spritual Sword* (Darkside, ruach) winter 78. Hand book as a gathering place & for shared concern. Some contributors: David Meltzer, Rose Drachler, William Stafford, Diane Diprima, Faye Kicknosway, Marc Kaminsky." 1-2/yr; sub price: $6.00 (an issue); per copy: $4.00; sample: $3.00. 1976. 220pp; 6 x 9. of. circ. 1,200. Reporting time: 2 weeks-2 months. Payment: contrib. copies. Copyright; reverts to authors on publication. Ads: Query for ad rates. Discounts: 40 percent trade. Back issues: No. 1 Spring 1977 Prayer. Expects 2 issues 1977, 2 issues 1978. Pub's reviews: none in 1976. §poetry, social sci.

HANGING LOOSE, Hanging Loose Press, Robert Hershon, Emmett Jarrett, Dick Lourie, Ron Schreiber, Denise Levertov, Contrib. Ed., 231 Wyckoff St, Brooklyn, NY 11217. Poetry, fiction. "Emphasis remains on the work of new writers-and when we find people we like, we stay with them. Among recent contributors: Harley Elliott, John Gill, Jacqueline Lapidus, Helen Adam, Kathy Akin, Jim Gustafson, Faye Kicknosway, Sam Kashner, Stephen Vincent, Lyn Lifshin, Michael Lally. We welcome submissions to the magazine, but artwork & book mss. are by invitation only." 4/yr; sub price: $5.50-4 issues (to individuals); per copy: $1.50. 1966. 80pp; 7 x 8½. of. circ. 1,200. Reporting time: 2-3 Months. Payment: 3 copies. Copyrighted. no ads. Discounts: Standard. Available on request. Back issues: Prices on request, including complete sets. Pub's reviews. CCLM, COSMEP.

HAPPINESS HOLDING TANK, Stone Press, Albert Drake, Barbara Drake, 1790 Grand River, Okemos, MI 48864. Poetry, articles, criticism, reviews, letters. "We've emphasized poetry, information, printing processes, & people. Any information of a literary nature will be passed along. The current issue (No. 18) lists dozens of new mags, dead mags, contests, etc. (in addition to poetry, commentary, essays, etc.) only $1.25. Still doing posters, post cards, pamphlets, books. A poetry pack brings a lot ($4.00). Philip Whalen, Earle Birney, Wm. Matthews, Wm. Stafford, Anselm Hollo, and more than 300 known/unknown poets. No mss during summer." 3/yr; 1-yr sub price: $3.50; per copy: $1.00-$1.25; sample: $1.00. 1970. 50pp; 8½ x 11. †mi/of. circ. 300-500. Reporting time: 1-3 weeks. Payment: copies. Ads: $15/$8. Discounts: 40%. Pub'd 1 issue 1976; expects 2 issues 1977. Pub's reviews. §poetry & fiction. CCLM.

HARBINGER, Robert Israel, Miles Parker, John Fedorowicz, P.O. Box 235, Annex Sta, Providence, RI 02901. Poetry, fiction, articles, art, photos, interviews, satire, criticism, reviews, long-poems, plays. "We have a slight bias towards realism, but the editors are open to any work of quality. Unknown writers are welcome to submitt. Harbinger is presently funded by a matching grant from the CCLM" 2/yr; 1-yr sub price: $2.50; per copy: $1.50. 1969. 36pp; 6 x 9. of. circ. 500 copies. Reporting time: 3-4 months. Payment: 1 yr subscription. Discounts: 40%-all. Back issues: 1/2 unit price. Pub's reviews. §Poetry, fiction, biography, & criticism. CCLM, COSMEP.

Harbour Publishing (see RAINCOAST CHRONICLES)

HARD PRESSED, Ellen's Old Alchemical Press, Ellen Rosser, C.B. Davis, Jane Conant-Bissell, Ray Hadley, 2850 3rd Ave, Sacramento, CA 95818. Poetry, art. "Portfolio format. Each poem (40 lines or fewer) on a separate page suitable for display. Recent contributors: Rosellen Brown, Marge Piercy, Gary Snyder, Jack Hirschman, Robert Bly, Mary Mackey." 2/yr; 1-yr sub price: indivual: $2.50/institutional:$5.00; per copy: $1.00 ea plus $0.25 postage; sample: $1.00 ea plus $0.25 postage. 1975. 24pp; 8½ x 11. †lp. circ. 500. Reporting time: 4 weeks. Payment: 2 copies. Copyrighted.

137

Discounts: 40%. Back issues: Ind. $5.00; inst. $10.00. Pub'd 2 issues 1976; expects 2 issues 1977, 2 issues 1978. COSMEP.

The Harian Press, Harry Barba, 47 Hyde Blvd, Ballston SPA, CT 12020, 518-885-7397. Poetry, fiction, articles, parts-of-novels. "1) 3,000-20,000 fiction & monograph essays 2) 20-50 poems by one author 3) socially functional fiction, poetry & monographs on education, literature, art and culture 4) Harry Barba, Harold Bond, Leo Hamalian & others." avg. price, cloth: $7.95; paper: $2.95; other: $0.95-$1.25 (offprints). 1967. 200pp; 8½ x 5½. of/lp. avg. press run 2,000-3,000. Reporting time: 2-3 months. Payment: by arrangement. Copyright, if individual book. Discounts: trade 40 percent cash, 30 percent consignment; bulk 50 percent; classroom 20 percent; jobber 50 percent. Pub'd 3 titles 1976. COSMEP, ALP, COSMEPA, NESPA, PWI, AWP, PEN, MLA, CEA.

Harlo Press, Jimmie Osborne, PO Box B-65577, E-207, Soledad, CA 93960. Poetry. "'The River of Many Minds' is just the first of many anthologies and books that Publisher Jimmie Osborne, himself a convict, plans to publish to showcase the outstanding talent of prisoners across the nation; a book that will be the forerunner of a whole new genre of exciting, informative essays, poems and short stories written by the men who *really* know and understand the total prison experience. 'The River of Many Minds' has authors within its cover that you have never heard or read about, but the publication of this important book will change all of that. We promise that you will be moved — deep within — by the writings of these young authors who have looked within themselves and have had the guts to write what they feel. An initial run of 2,000 copies of this 72-page ll be a book you will read and share with your friends. Or, better yet, encourage them to order a copy for themselves." avg. price, paper: $4.00. 1976. 72pp; 6 x 9. avg. press run 2,000. Payment: by arrangement. Copyrights for author. Discounts: 10 percent in 30 days on orders of 30 or more copies. COSMEP.

HARMONY, University of New Hampshire Student Press, John Grady, Jon Ring, Jeff Katz, Associate Editors, M.U.B. Rm. 153, University of N.H., Durham, NH 03824. Poetry, fiction, articles, art, photos, cartoons, interviews, satire, criticism, reviews, music, letters, parts-of-novels, long-poems, collages, plays, concrete art. "We welcome all material on the theme of: Religion, Spirituality, Higher Consciousness, Universal Brotherhood, from all races, creeds, countries beliefs or dispositions. Our goal is to harmonize the widely varying viewpoints on this theme. We want to open channels of communication through this magazine with other interested people around the world. We also sponsor events on campus i.e. sufi dancing, meditations, talks etc. and welcome ideas for events. Concerts, talks, whatever." 2/yr; 1-yr sub price: free. 1976. 32pp; 8 x 10. of. circ. 500. Reporting time: 40 days. Payment: $20 for article. Pub's reviews. §Religious, spiritual, higher consciousness, human potential, brotherhood.

Harper Square Press (see GALLERY SERIES/POETS)

THE HARVARD ADVOCATE, Marc Granetz, Prose; April Bernard, Poetry; Emily Kane, Art, 21 South St., Cambridge, MA 02138, 617-495-7820. Poetry, fiction, articles, art, photos, interviews, criticism, reviews, parts-of-novels, long-poems, plays. "THE HARVARD ADVOCATE publishes work from Harvard affiliates and alumni. We regret we cannot read manuscripts from other sources." 5/yr; sub price: $5.00 Indiv.; $7.50 for Institutions (for 6 issues); per copy: $1.00; sample: $1.00. 1866. 32pp; 8½ x 11. of. circ. 4,000. Reporting time: 2-3 weeks. Payment varies. Copyrighted, does not revert to author. Ads: $200.00/$120.00. Discounts: none. Back issues: Price varies. Pub'd 5 issues 1976; expects 5 issues 1977, 5 issues 1978. Pub's reviews. §literature.

HARVEST, Art Press, New Britain, Conn., Robert T. Casey, 238 Meriden Ave, Southington, CT 06489. Poetry, fiction, articles. "Deadline for submitted material is May 7, 1976. Submitters must be members of Connecticut writers league. Membership open to all. Dues $10.00/year." 1/yr; 1-yr sub price: $2.95; per copy: $2.95. 1974. 8½ x 11. lp. circ. 500-600. Payment: none. Ads: none. Discounts: 20% to stores 50% to members of CWL. Back issues: $1.50.

Harvest Press, Patty Dunks, Thom Dunks, P.O. Box 1265, Santa Cruz, CA 95061, 415-335-5015. "One title at this time-*Gardening With Children*." avg. price, paper: $4.95. 1976. 176pp; 8½ x 5½. avg. press run 5,000. Copyrights for author. Discounts: 40 percent trade, 45-50 percent bulk. Pub'd 1 title 1976.

Harvest Publishers (see also HARVEST QUARTERLY), Ann Baxandall Krooth, Editorial Collective; Richard Krooth, Editorial Collective; Jackie Greenberg, Editorial Collective; Bill Brady, Art Director, 907 Santa Barbara Street, Santa Barbara, CA 93101. Poetry, articles, art, photos, cartoons, interviews, criticism, reviews, letters, long-poems, concrete art, plays, non-fiction. "3 classic titles are available: *Poets & Players,* including an interview *'Simone de Beauvoir Questions Jean-Paul Sartre'; A Classic Poem About Alaska's Historical Conquest* by Richard Dauenhauer; and *Afro-American Poetry* by Nandi Jordan. *Empire: A Bicentennial Appraisal,* by Richard Krooth, covering the historical roots of the U.S. empire. *Japan: Five Stages Of Development,* a short & concise history of Japan & its place in the world today." avg. price, paper: $2.50; other: $1.50. 1975. 60pp. of. avg. press run 3,500-4,000. Reporting time: 10-14 days. Payment: To be negotiated. Copyrights for author. Discounts: Jobber discounts on trade, terms for books in bulk. Pub'd 2 titles 1976; expects 2 titles 1977, 4 titles 1978. COSMEP.

HARVEST QUARTERLY, Harvest Publishers, Ann Baxandall Krooth, Editorial Collective; Richard Krooth, Editorial Collective; Jackie Greenberg, Editorial Collective; Bill Brady, Art Director, 907 Santa Barbara Street, Santa Barbara, CA 93101. Poetry, articles, art, photos, cartoons, interviews, criticism, reviews, letters, long-poems, concrete art, plays, non-fiction. "HARVEST QUARTERLY: Classic studies of society and social movements. On our first birthday, we invite you to receive any earlier issue of the QUARTERLY free with your order for a one year subscription. Outstanding features in Quarterly No. 1, *Essays On Movement Projects;* Quarterly No. 2, *Classics On The Division Of Labor;* Quarterly Nos. 3-4, *Oral History & Women In Struggle;* Quarterly No. 5, *Questions About The Social Order;* Quarterly No. 6, *Alternative Institutions & Classic Radical Essays;* Quarterly No. 7, (Fall 1977) Features Flora Tristan: *Socialist Feminist Of 1840 On The Emancipation Of Women;* Quarterly No. 8, (Winter 1977) Features *The Great Homestead Strike Of 1892: An Analysis Of The Most Important Strike In The 19th Century.*" 4/yr; 1-yr sub price: $5.00 U.S. & $6.00 Canada, $7.00 elsewhere; per copy: $1.50; sample: $1.50. 1976. 52pp; 8½ x 11. of. circ. 1,000-1,500. Reporting time: 10-14 days. Payment: 3 copies of edition where author's work appears. Copyright right to reprint by permission of HARVEST Quarterly. Ads: $120.00/$60.00/$2.00 for ten words. Discounts: 30% 10 or more for resale, organizations, study-groups or classrooms. Back issues: Same as original price, see special offer on HARVEST birthday. Pub'd 3 issues 1976; expects 4 issues 1977, 4 issues 1978. Pub's reviews. §Political economy, literary radicalism, philosophical notes, Marx to Mao, Sartre to Beauvoir, socialist feminist history to labor struggles. COSMEP.

HAWK PRESS Hawk Press, Alan Loney, 10 Repo Street, Paraparaumu, N Zld. Poetry. "All work—design, handsetting type, printing on a treadle platen, & binding—is done by the sole owner of the press. General aim—to produce poetry in limited editions, & have the labour of the book appropriate to the poetry. I can take mss up to 50 pages or so, & I have no desire to print only New Zealand work. Poets printed so far, are: Ian Wedde, Stephen Oliver, Alan Loney, Alan Brunton, Graham Lindsay, and Robert Creeley, Rhys Pasley." avg. price, paper: $5.00. 1975. 36 to 40pp; 6½ x 9¼. †lp. avg. press run 300 copies limited editions. Reporting time: 1 month. Payment: Some have waived payment, but else, 10 percent monthly. Copyrights for author. Discounts: Trade 33 -1/3%, Libraries 10%, Trade Standing Orders 40%, Libraries Standing Orders 20%.

Headland Publications (see also NEW HOPE, PROMONTORY), Gerald England, Gladys Mary Coles, 38 York Ave, West Kirby, Wirral, Merseyside L483JF, United Kingdom, (editorial) 103 Clarksfield Rd., Oldham, Lancs OL4 1LJ, United Kingdom, 051-625-9128. Poetry, art, criticism, long-poems, concrete art, non-fiction. "Original poetry by writers who are usually just about to become well-known. Authors include Colin Simms, Penelope Shuttle, David Grubb, Anna Adams, James Kirkup, David Jaffin, Wes Magee, B.C. Leale." avg. price, paper: 50p. 1970. 16pp; A5. lp/of. avg. press run 500. Reporting time: up to 3 mos. Payment: 10% royalties. Discounts: usual trade. Pub'd 2 titles 1976; expects 5 titles 1977, 3 titles 1978. ALP.

HEALTH/PAC BULLETIN, Ronda Kotelchuck, 17 Murray Street, New York, NY 10007. Articles, art, cartoons, criticism, reviews, letters. 6/yr; 1-yr sub price: $7.00; per copy: $.75; sample: free.

Hearsay Press (see also RAT ATTACK; MOVEABLE NICHE (occasionals)), John Love, 115 West Broadway, New York City, NY 10013, (212) 349-4234. Poetry, art. "HEARSAY PRESS silkscreens single poems on to 22 x 26 sheets of either charcoal paper or 100-lb. cover stock. Typefaces are chosen by each author, who also consults with the press as to layout and ink color. Point sizes of the type are large: from 36-point to as large as 120-point. Editions of 500 are printed, with 100 copies signed by the author. *The author retains 100% of net profit of signed copies.* Broadsides already in print include poems by David Ignatow, Russell Edson, Robert Bly, Susan Sherman, James Tate, John Love, Bill Knott, Terry Stokes, Mei-Mei Berssenbrugge, W. S. Merwin, Galway Kinnell, Thomas Lux, and Andrei Codrescu. The current series is an attempt to find out what the American love poem is....." avg. price, other: broadsides: $1.00 unsigned/$10.00 signed. 1974. one lonely page; 22 x 26. †silkscreen. avg. press run 500 copies. Reporting time: Gestation period of the Quark. Payment: All the unsigned copies he/she can use; plus 100% of net profit of signed sheets; that's $6 on a $10 sheet, with $4 for the dealer. Copyrights for author. Discounts: 40% discount to dealers and booksellers; 400% mark-up to Patrons & Heirs. CCLM.

Hearthstone Press (see also THE GREEN FUSE, ATTENTION PLEASE), Stella Worley, Harold Leland Johnson, 708 Inglewood Drive, Broderick, CA 95605, 916-372-0250. Poetry. "Book production limited 2-3 annually." avg. price, paper: $2.00 - $3.00. 1975. 48pp; 5½ x 8½. †mi/lp. avg. press run 200-500. Reporting time: 2-3 weeks. Payment: By agreement. Copyrights for author. Discounts: 40 percent trade. Pub'd 2 titles 1976; expects 2 titles 1977, 2 titles 1978. COSMEP, COSMEP-WEST.

HECTOR AND HECTOR, Lois Hamilton, Francesca Moghari, K & K Stilwell, Liz Nygard, Fred Gulden, 1112 ISU Station, Ames, IA 50010. Poetry, fiction, articles, art, photos, cartoons, interviews, satire, criticism, reviews, music, letters, parts-of-novels, long-poems, plays. "Design by Francesca Moghari... Center set by Liz Nygard. Articles on holography, numerology, forteanna. Citizens for responsible energy on nuclear energy. Poets: Gayle Emmel, Ibraby, Michael Kehoe, Kathleen Stilwell, W. Mark Burrow, James Hiduke. Quarterly chess column: Fred Gulden. Fiction by: George Rutledge, Joel T. Conner, Gregg Suddeth. Photographs by: Lynn Purcell, Keith Stilwell, Jill Jensen." 4/yr; 1-yr sub price: $3.00; per copy: $.75; sample: $1.00. 1974. 50pp; 11 x 8½. of. circ. 400. Reporting time: Quarterly. Payment: in copies. Ads: $8. Discounts: 40% trade, 25% consignment. Back issues: $1.00 each. Pub's reviews. §Anything interesting. COSMEP.

Heidelberg Graphics (see also PHANTASM), Larry S. Jackson, P.O. Box 3404, Chico, CA 95927, 916-342-6582. "Heidelberg Graphics is not accepting unsolicited material at this time except for publication in *PHANTASM*. The Native American calendar is my main publication along with a few limited editions of books by myself or friends. Write for prices, wholesale and retail." 1972. †of/lp. Payment: Negotiable. Copyrights for author. Pub'd 2 titles 1976; expects 3 titles 1977. COSMEP, CCLM, SCCIPHC.

Heinemann (see AFRICAN LITERATURE TODAY)

HEIRS, Heirs Press, Alfred Durand Garcia, Jil Immerman, Ernst J. Oswald, 657 Mission St., San Francisco, CA 94105. Poetry, fiction, articles, art, photos, interviews, criticism, reviews, music, parts-of-novels, long-poems, collages, plays, concrete art. "Quality and variety is the major focus—translations encouraged—essays dealing with art and humanism encouraged. Major articles on artists, etc. appear in English, Spanish, and Chinese. Contributors include: John Morita, Bruce Hutchinson, Dan Georgakas, Kenneth Lee, Luciano Mezzetta, Dadaland, Lorraine Tong, Andrei Codrescu, Sandra Case, Daniel Clay II, Jessica Hagedorn, et. al.." 2/yr; sub price: $6.00/2 issues; per copy: $3.00; sample: $2.50. 1968. 80pp; 8½ x 11. of. circ. 2,000. Reporting time: 6-8 wks. Payment: copies & token $ if available. Ads: $115/$75/$30 1/4. Back issues: #9-$5, #8-$3, #6,7-$3, #5-$2, #4-$2, #1-$5, #2,3-$7. §visual art/plays/fiction. CCLM, COSMEP.

Helikon Press, Robin Prising, William Leo Coakley, 120 West 71st Street, New York City, NY 10023. Poetry, art, long-poems. "We try to publish the most vital contemporary poetry in the tradition of English verse—using the work of the finest artists, designers, and printers and the best materials possible. We cannot now encourage submissions—we read a wide variety of magazines and ask poets to build a collection around particular poems we have selected. We hope to continue without government subsidy. Poets: Helen Adam, George Barker, John Heath-Stubbs, and Michael Miller." avg. price, cloth: $7.00-$12.00; other: limited eds. $5.00 or $10.00. 1972. 16 pages limited editions, 60 pages trade edition; No standard size: each book is designed to suit the particular poems & poet. of/lp. avg. press run 100 for limited editions; 500 for 1st printing of trade ed. Reporting time: 2 weeks. Payment: yes. Copyrights for author. Discounts: discount to the book trade: 30% for limited editions and 1-4 of trade edition; 40% for 5 or more of trade edition. Pub'd 1 title 1976; expects 1 title 1977.

Helix House, Ken Kuhlken, Terrill Luitjens, 1520 Helix St, Spring Valley, CA 92077, 714-461-1185. Poetry, fiction, parts-of-novels, long-poems, plays. "Looking for collections of verse, novellas, short novels, story collections, traditional or experimental. We'd like to see some long poems, 30 pages or up." avg. price, cloth: $5.95; paper: $2.95. 1974. 50 pp for poetry. 125 pp for fiction.; 8 x 5. †of. avg. press run 1,000 first printing. Reporting time: 1 mo. Payment: By arrangement. Discounts: 50% on purchase. 40% consign. Pub'd 1 title 1976; expects 3 titles 1977, 5 titles 1978. COSMEP.

HELLCOAL ANNUAL, Hellcoal Press, John Silbersack, Box 4 SAO, Brown University, Providence, RI 02912. Poetry, fiction, parts-of-novels, long-poems, plays. 1/yr; 1-yr sub price: $4.00; per copy: $4.00. 1970. 200pp; 8½ x 9½. of. circ. 1,500. Reporting time: 1 month. Payment: 2 copies. Discounts: 40% trade 5 or more.

Hellcoal Press, John Silbersack, Box SAO, Brown Univ., Providence, RI 02912. Poetry, fiction, parts-of-novels, long-poems, plays. "Our focus is on creative experimental work by young authors. Our purpose is to give those authors space to expand and develop their work comfortably, unencumbered by the restrictions of anthology form so that they would best benefit from publication as a single piece." 1965. of/lp. Reporting time: 1 month. Payment: copies. Discounts: 40% on 5 or more.

Hellric Publications (see also PYRAMID, AB INTRA, and ESPONTANEO), 39 Eliot St, Jamaica Plain, MA 02130. "We are not currently reading mss."

HENNEPIN COUNTY LIBRARY CATALOGING BULLETIN, Sanford Berman, 7001 York Ave. S., Secretary, Technical Services Division,Hennepin Co. Library, Edina, MN 55435, 612-830-4980. Articles, news items. "Purpose of publication: variously to report what we're doing at HCL (e.g., new or altered cross-references, format-rules, DDC-NUMBERS, and subject descriptors, citing authorities, precedents, & applications), to relate cataloging to total library service & the 'real world,' to involve both readers & our own staff in the cataloging process, & to provide a genuinely open vehicle for cataloging-related ideas, news, innovations, criticism, and even muckraking. To the extent that the bulletin succeeds in achieving these things, it may also transform the 'image' of cataloging itself from that of a stodgy, tradition-mired, static routine to that of a lively, responsive, access-expanding art, something at once creative, vital, and personally satisfying. Two-year rates: $10.00 Individuals, $20.00 Institutions. Indexes: No. 1-10 ($3.00), No. 11-20 ($5.00)." 6/yr; 1-yr sub price: Individuals $6.00; Institutions $12.00; per copy: $1.50 (Including all back-issues); sample: free. 1973. 40pp; 8½ x 11. †of. circ. 500. Reporting time: 1 week. Payment: 2 copies. Discounts: none. Back Issues: all back issues available each $1.00 indexes: #1-10 $3, #14-16 $1.50, #11-20 (due July 1976 each $5). Pub'd 6 issues 1976; expects 6 issues 1977, 6 issues 1978. Pub's reviews: 9 in 1976. §Cataloging & classification of library and information-center materials. Also: social impact/consequences of language, terminology (e.g., sexist/ageist/racist nomenclature), and catalog access to alternative and small press materials. COSMEP.

Henry Philips Publishing Company, Vicki E. Walton, 19316-3rd Avenue N.W., Seattle, WA 98177, 206-542-8483. Photos, non-fiction. "Fields of health concerns (particularly related to women), consumerism in health-related fields. Non-fiction book-length or pamphlet-length material" avg. price, paper: $5.95. 1976. 150-300pp; 6 x 9. of. avg. press run 5,000. Reporting time: 1 month. Payment: Deal with each individually. Copyrights for author. Discounts: 40% to bookstores, 50-55% to distributors. Pub'd 1 title 1976; expects 5 titles 1977. COSMEP.

HERA, INC., Collectively Edited, 328 South 17th St, Philadelphia, PA 19103, 215-732-2420. Poetry, fiction, articles, art, photos, cartoons, interviews, satire, criticism, reviews, music, letters. "1200 wd max; prefer article, etc. by women, original material preferred. We are dedicated to reporting revolutionary struggles which contribute to the personal & political growth of women." 4/yr; 1-yr sub price: $3.00; per copy: $0.50; sample: $0.75. 1975. 24pp; 12 x 18. of. circ. 4,000. Reporting time: 2-3 months. Payment: 5 issues to contributors. Copyrighted. Ads: $275.00/$150.00/$2.00. Discounts: min bulk order of 5-40 percent discount; consignment allowed. Back issues: $0.75 each. Pub's reviews. §books from small presses dealing with revolutionary struggles on all fronts, especially women 's struggles all over the world.

HERESIES: A FEMINIST PUBLICATION ON ART AND POLITICS, Heresies Collective, PO Box 766 Canal St. Station, New York, NY 10013. Poetry, fiction, articles, art, photos, interviews, satire, criticism, letters, parts-of-novels, long-poems, collages, plays, concrete art. "First issue: Adrienne Rich, Eva Cockcroft, Ruth Iskin, Carol Duhammond, Arlene Ladden, May Stevens, Nancy Spero, Joan Braderman, Carol Muske, Assata Shakur etc." 4/yr; 1-yr sub price: $10.00; per copy: $2.50. 1976. 128pp; 8½ x 11. of. Reporting time: depends on process for individual issues. Payment: $25-50 so far; would like to raise them. Copyrighted, reverts to author. §Feminsm, art, politics, the arts in general.

Hero Press (see THE WICA NEWSLETTER, WITCHCRAFT DIGEST)

The Heron Press, B. Chandler, 36 Bromfield St., Boston, MA 02108. Poetry, art, satire, long-poems, plays. "Most recent books: Jon Silkin, *The Peaceable Kingdom,* 1975 and Armand Schwerner, *The Tablets XVI-XVII,* 1976." avg. price, cloth: $65.00; paper: $5.00. 1968. 24-32pp; varies. †lp. avg. press run 300-500. Reporting time: 1 mo-4 mos. Payment: copies. Author must copyright. Discounts: 20-30 percent. Pub'd 1 title 1976; expects 3 titles 1977, 2 titles 1978. NESPA, APHA (Amer Printing Hist Assoc), New York.

Heyday Books, Malcolm Margolin, Box 9145, Berkeley, CA 94709. "I'm not a magazine, but a small publisher. So far I've published only my own stuff. The East Bay Out (a local guidebook for hikers & campers) in 1974: updated 1975. This year i plan to publish another of my books. Dancing on The Brink of the World (the story of the Indians of San Francisco Bay)" 1974. of.

The Heyeck Press, Robin Heyeck, 25 Patrol Ct., Woodside, CA 94062. Poetry. "Plan to publish collection of women's poetry this summer." 1976. †lp. Reporting time: as soon as possible. Payment: copies.

Hh, Asylum Publishing, Tom Konyves, 5355 Walkley No. 40, Mtl., Canada, 514-481-3580. Poetry, articles, art, photos, interviews, satire, criticism, reviews, parts-of-novels, long-poems, collages, concrete art. "quality experiments" 2/yr; 1-yr sub price: $3.00; per copy: $1.50. 1976. 16pp; 8½ x 11. of. circ. 500. Reporting time: 2 weeks. Payment: copies. Copyrighted, reverts to author. Ads: $50.00/$35.00/$0.25. Discounts: trade, 40 percent; bulk, 40 percent; classroom, 10 percent; agent, 10 percent; jobber, 40 percent. Back issues: $5.00. Pub'd 5 issues 1976. Pub's reviews: none in 1976. §poetry, art.

Hibiscus Press (see also IN A NUTSHELL), Margaret Wensrich, Fiction; Joyce Odam, Poetry, P.O. Box 22248, Sacramento, CA 95822. Poetry, fiction, cartoons, art. "Write before sending a manuscript" avg. price, paper: $3.00. 1972. 36pp; 5½ x 8½. of. avg. press run 2m. Reporting time: 2-4 weeks. Payment:401/2 cent fiction/$2 min poetry/$5 min cartoons. Discounts: Write for discount. Pub'd 1 title 1976; expects 1 title 1977, 2 titles 1978. CCLM, COSMEP.

Hiddigeigei Books, R. A. Wolf, P.O. Box 5031, San Francisco, CA 94103. "Hiddigeigei does not solicit any materials (Ms. or other) at this time" avg. price, paper: $2.50. 1976. 56pp; 8 x 10. Discounts: 40% retail/50% wholesale. COSMEP.

Hierophant Press, Thomas Kerrigan, 15141 Sutton St., Sherman Oaks, CA 91403. Poetry. "HIEROPHANT Magazine folded in 1972 after 7 issues. In the future, Hierophant Press will publish one book of poetry a year. It will accept no unsolicited manuscripts of poetry." 1970. 50pp; 5 x 9. lp. Reporting time: 3 wks. Payment: 2 copies. Discounts: none.

HIGGINSON JOURNAL OF POETRY, Higginson Press, Frederick L. Morey, 4508 38th St., Brentwood, MD 20722. Poetry, articles, art, criticism, reviews. "4,000 words, popular middle style (chiefly Emily Dickinson overflow from EDB), contemporary poets considered if crafted, recently George Monteiro, Inder Kher, Howard Meyer, Gladys Wenk, Glenn Swetman, Doris Wight, Penny Bihler, Florence Elon, Kelly Cherry, Cynthia Roberts, Martha Vertreace, Ralph Setian, Jean Rodenbough, Terrance Lisbeth, Margaret Hillert." 2/yr; 1-yr sub price: $10.00 libraries (invoiced)/$5.00 individuals; per copy: $3.00. 1971. 50pp; 8½ x 11. of. circ. 200. Reporting time: 1 month. Payment: 1 copy. Ads: none. Discounts: 10% to any agent. Back issues: $30.00 for all in print: nos. 4 thru 12. Pub's reviews. §E. Dickinson and poetry in general.

Higginson Press (see EMILY DICKINSON BULLETIN, HIGGINSON JOURNAL OF POETRY)

HIGH COUNTRY NEWS, Joan Nice, Managing Editor; Marjane Ambler, Associate Editor, Box K, 331 Main St., Lander, WY 82520, 332-4877 (307). Articles, art, photos, cartoons, interviews, criticism, reviews, letters. "We're after hard-hitting, environmental journalism with a regional slant. We cover Montana, Wyoming, Colorado, Utah, Idaho and, occasionally, the Dakotas and Arizona and New Mexico." 25/yr; 1-yr sub price: $12.00; per copy: $0.40; sample: free. 1969. 16pp; 10 x 14. of. circ. 3,500. Reporting time: 2 weeks. Payment: 1½ cents to 4 cents per word. $1.00-$4.00 per published B&W photo. Not copyrighted. Ads: $218.40/$112.00/$0.10, $1.00 min. Discounts: sell in bulk to schools, libraries, organizations. Back issues: $0.50 each if over one month old otherwise $0.40. Pub's reviews. §Conservation, wildlife, energy, land use, and other natural resources issues. COSMEP.

The High Foundation (see THE INTERNATIONAL NEW AGE NEWSLETTER)

High Orchard Press (see THE BULWER LYTTON CHRONICLE, SHAVIAN, WELLSIANA)

HIGH/COO: A Quarterly of Short Poetry, High/Coo Press, Randy Brooks, Shirley Brooks, 26-11 Hilltop Dr., W. Lafayette, IN 47906, 463-6969. Poetry, reviews, concrete art. "We are interested in short poetry—13 lines or less. Especially interested in experimental forms—experimental high/coo, senryu, tanka, epigrams with a rockbed of images. Recent contributors include Sanford Goldstein, Lee Perron, Raymond Roseliep, John Judson, James Weil, R. Clarence Matsuo-Allard." 4/yr; 1-yr sub price: $4.00; per copy: $0.75; sample: $0.50. 1976. 40pp; 4¼ x 5½. of. circ. 250. Reporting time: 1 month. Payment: 2 copies. Copyrighted, reverts to author. Ads: $20.00/$10.00. Discounts: 40 percent discount to bookstores and schools. Back issues: all sold out. Pub'd 4 issues 1976; expects 4 issues 1977. Pub's reviews: 2 in 1976. §haiku, tanka, short lyric books.

High/Coo Press (see also HIGH/COO), Randy Brooks, Shirley Brooks, 26-11 Hilltop Dr., W. Lafayette, IN 47906, 463-6969. Poetry, reviews, concrete art. "We publish chapbooks every six months—Raymond Roseliep's *Sun In His Belly* and Bill Pauly's *Wind The Clock By Bittersweet* are two we have done so far. We favor American high/coo and tanka, but are also interested in short poetry of all kinds. We also produce a poemcard with each issue of *HIGH/COO*. Recent contributors include John Judson, Michael Tarachow, James Weil, Carrow DeVries, R. Clarence Matsuo-Allard, Jeffrey Winke, Gary Hotham, and Gary Hines." avg. price, paper: $1.50. 1976. 40-48pp; 4¼ x 5½. of/lp. avg. press run 350. Reporting time: 1 month. Payment: copies and 15 percent after costs are met. Copyrights for author. Discounts: 40 percent bookstores. Pub'd 2 titles 1976; expects 2 titles 1977.

Highlands Press (see NEW RIVER REVIEW)

Highway Book Shop (see also LIFELINE), Patricia Moffat, Cobalt, Ontario P0J1C0, Canada. "Primarily publishing Northern Ontario authors." Reporting time: 1 month. Payment: 10% royalty.

Hilltop Press, Steve Sneyd, 4 Nowell Place, Almondbury, Huddersfield, West Yorks, England HD5 8PB, United Kingdom. Poetry, fiction, art, long-poems, plays. "'76 quiet, one booklet only, *Hunter* by Keith Dearn. '77 *Definitely Booklets* by Wilson Stapleton, David Banks (poems re Kurdistan), also one theme anthology, *Subject & Object).* Other hopes in pipe line. Unsolicited mss. W. Sae irc will be read, but little chance of new work being accepted in near future. Forsythia have flowers before they have leaves: This was *Hilltop's* past mistake." avg. price, paper: future publications 25p(UK), 50 cents (US). 1966. a5 or a4. of. avg. press run 200. Reporting time: varies; asap. Copyrights remain with author. Discounts: 1/3 bookshop or bulk. Pub'd 1 title 1976; expects 4 titles 1977.

HINDSIGHT, And/Or (alternative gallery space, not a press), Katherine Grosshans, 1525 10th Ave., Seattle, WA 98122, 324-5880. Poetry, fiction, articles, art, photos, interviews, music, letters, collages, concrete art. "This is a documentary publication of the events which occur at *and/or*. Its contents are compiled from comments by the artists who perform/show/speak at *and/or*, photographs xeroxes, interviews etc. Its purpose is to attempt to provide through as broad a net of impressions as possible the activities which center around our space." 1/yr. 1976. 90-100pp; 11 x 8½. of/xerox. circ. we will print 200 at the end of the year. Copyrighted, reverts to author. Ads: none. Discounts: and/or members can obtain the magazine for $5.00, non-members $7.50. Back issues: there are no back issues as of yet.

Hipparchia Press, Eileen Callahan, Netzahaulcoyotl Historical Society, 2845 Buena Vista Way, Berkeley, CA 94708. Poetry, fiction. avg. price, cloth: $10.00; paper: $4.00. 1976. 32pp. †lp. avg. press run 350. Reporting time: 2 weeks. Payment: 10 percent. Copyrights for author. Discounts: 40 percent to the trade. Pub'd 1 title 1976; expects 4 titles 1977.

Hippopotamus Press, Roland John, B.A. Martin, Business Manager, 26 Cedar Road, Sutton, Surrey SM25DG, United Kingdom, 01-643-1970. Poetry, long-poems. "Size, number of pages, cost will vary with the material. Against: concrete, typewriter, neo-surrealism and experimental work. For: competent poetry in recognisable English, a knowledge of syntax and construction, finished work and not glimpses into the workshop, also translations. Recent pamphlets include G.S. Sharat Chandra (U.S.A.), David Summers (Canada), Stan Trevor (S. Africa) Shaun McCarthy, Neil McNeil, Peter Dale, William Bedford, Humphrey Clucas, William Cookson." avg. price, cloth: $6.00 (£1.50); paper: $2.00 (£0.60). 1974. 26pp; Variable. lp. avg. press run 1,000. Reporting time: 1 month. Payment: by arrangement/royalty. Standard UK copyright. Remaining with author. Discounts: 33-1/3 off singles, 40 percent off bulk orders. Pub'd 2 titles 1976; expects 2 titles 1977. ALP.

HIRAM POETRY REVIEW, David Fratus, Box 162, Hiram, OH 44234, 216-569-3211. Poetry, fiction, articles, reviews. "Reviews, essays, art, photos, etc. Only by invitation. Poetry is 95 percent of what we accept." 2/yr; 1-yr sub price: $2.00; per copy: $1.00; sample: free. 1967. 40pp. circ. 500. Reporting time: 6-8 wks. Payment: 2 copies plus yr's. subscription. Copyrighted, reverts by request. Discounts: 50-50 to subscription agencies; 60-40 to retail bookstores. Back issues: No. 1 unavail.; others vary; send for info. Pub's reviews CCLM, COSMEP.

Historical Society of Alberta (see ALBERTA HISTORY)

Hit & Run Press, Larry Rafferty, P. O. Box 1041, Ft. Bragg, CA 95437, 707-964-0843. Poetry. avg. price, cloth: $10.00; paper: $3.00. 1974. 20pp; 6 x 9. †lp. avg. press run 200. Reporting time: 1 month. Copyright secured by/for author. Pub'd 1 title 1976; expects 5 titles 1977.

Hoddypoll Press, James Mitchell, 226 Rose St., San Francisco, CA 94102. Poetry. "Poetry chapbooks." avg. price, other: $2.00. 1968. 25pp; 5½ x 8½. of. avg. press run 350. Reporting time: 1 mo. Copyrights for author. Pub'd 2 titles 1976; expects 3 titles 1977, 4 titles 1978.

THE HOLLINS CRITIC, John Rees Moore, P.O. Box 9538, Hollins College, VA 24020. Poetry. "Essay on particular work of one author; several poems. Essay approximately 5000 words, no footnotes. No unsolicited essay mss. Short poems are published in almost every issue. Other features are a front picture of the author under discussion, a checklist of his writing and a brief sketch of career." 5/yr; 1-yr sub price: $3.00; sample: $.65. 15pp. lp. circ. 850. Reporting time: 1 month. Payment: $20 for poems. Back issues: $.65 ea (U.S.A.). CCLM, COSMEP.

HOLLOW SPRING REVIEW OF POETRY, Hollow Spring Press, Alex Harvey, PO Box 76, Berkshire, MA 01224, 413-499-2709. "Open to new writers of poetry as well as established poets. Open to all subjects and poetic forms. Recent contributors: Sternlieb, Ackerson, Atkinson, Eakins, Finley, Niatum, Erhart." 2/yr; 1-yr sub price: $5.00; per copy: $3.00; sample: $2.50. 1975. 64pp; 8½ x 5½. circ. 900. Reporting time: 2-6 weeks. Payment: copies. Ads: $100.00/$60.00. Discounts: 40% bookstores. Back issues: Vol. 1 No. 1 $3.25. §Poetry, criticism. COSMEP, CCLM, NESPA.

Holmgangers Press, Gary Elder, Editor; Jeane Elder, Editor; Mary Maurer Morgan, Mg Editor, 11 El Centro, Diablo, CA 94528. Poetry, fiction, art, photos, long-poems, collages, plays, concrete art. "Bus. address as given above. Editorial address: Rodney Nelson, Assoc. Ed., 3101 Skillman Lane, Petaluma, CA 94952. Phone: 707-763-1395." 1974. of. avg. press run 500. Reporting time: 1-4 weeks. Payment: 10 percent net-after recovery. Copyrights for author. Discounts: 20% off 4 or less; 40% off 5 or more. Pub'd 3 titles 1976; expects 9 titles 1977.

HOLY BEGGARS' GAZETTE, Judaic Book Service, Steven E. Maimes, Elana Rappaport, 3726 Virden Ave., Oakland, CA 94619. Poetry, articles, art. "We are a journal of Chassidic Judaism. Our issues have contained teachings from Rabbi Shlomo Carlebach & Rabbi Zalman Schachter, stories from Chassidic Rebbes, Jewish mysticism and poetry." 1/yr; price per copy: $2.50 appx.; sample: $2.00. 1971. 7 x 10. of. circ. 1,000. Reporting time: 2 weeks. Payment: copies only. Discounts: trade—40%. Back issues: $1.25 each. Pub'd 1 issue 1976; expects 1 issue 1977, 1 issue 1978. CCLM, COSMEP.

HOO-DOO BlackSeries, Energy BlackSouth Press, Ahmos Zu-Bolton, E.E. Miller, Jerry Ward, 2805 Southmore, Houston, TX 77004, Box 4174, Washington, DC 20015. Poetry, fiction, articles, art, photos, cartoons, interviews, satire, criticism, reviews, music, letters, parts-of-novels, long-poems, poetry, plays, concrete art. "Black works aimed at Southern lore." 1/yr; sub price: $10.00 for No. 6 - No. 13 (13 is exit & emerging No. in *HOO-DOO* rituals - completes the series).; per copy: $2.50. 1973. 80pp. of. circ. 2,000. Reporting time: 2 weeks to 2 months. Payment: copies. Copyrights for contributors. Discounts: 40% to bookstores. Back issues: vol. one valued at $10.00. Pub'd 1 issue 1976; expects 2 issues 1977, 2 issues 1978. Pub's reviews. §Black, third-world, spiritual, open workings. CCLM.

The Hosanna Press, Cathie Ruggie, 405 South Ann St, Columbia, MO 65201, 314-442-6755. Poetry, fiction, art, concrete art. "New titles in 1976: 'This Living Alone' by Andrea Musher. Broadside. *Harry's Second Debut* by Cathie Ruggie. Booklet. 'Presenting Harry's Second Debut...' Poster. Still in process: *Flown* (a chapbook of Gerald Lange's poetry with an original serigraph by Cathie Ruggie)." 1974. †1p. avg. press run 25-100. Expects 1 title 1977.

HOT WATER REVIEW, Hotwater, Joel Colten, Peter Bushyeager, 42 W. Washington Lane, Philadelphia, PA 19144. Poetry, articles, photos, plays. 1/yr.; price per copy: $2.00; sample: $2.00. 1976. 88pp; 8½ x 5½. of. circ. 1,000. Reporting time: 1-2 months. Payment: copies. Ads: $90/$50. Discounts: 60/40.

House of Anansi Press Limited/Publishing Co., Ann Wall, Managing Editor; James Polk, Editorial Director, 35 Britain St., Toronto M5A1R7, Canada, 416-363-5444. Poetry, fiction, criticism. "*Anansi* is a small, Canadian, literary publisher. We will consider non-fiction manuscripts that have contemporary, social criticism themes. We publish only Canadian authors." avg. price, cloth: $9.00; paper: $4.00. 1967. 60-200pp; 5¼ x 8½. of. avg. press run 1,000-20,000. Reporting time: 4-6 weeks. Payment varies; advance plus royalties. Copyrights for author. Discounts: Set by our distributor; usual industry discounts. Pub'd 4 titles 1976; expects 6 titles 1977, 6 titles 1978. COSMEP, ACP, LPG.

House of Keys: The Atlanta Poetry Collective, Inc. (see also DAIMON), Kay Leigh Hagan, Norman Finkelstein, Kathryn E. Meyer, Terrill S. Soules, P O Box 7952, Atlanta, GA 30357, 404-876-0529. Poetry. "We are starting a series of chapbooks this year with the assistance of a city grant. We will publish two chapbooks this year, and if our distribution and sales are successful, we will publish four chapbooks in 1978. A sample of our magazine, DAIMON, will outline editorial preferences. Chapbooks are up to 34 pages in length, perfect-bound, 5½ x 8, with illustrations if desired by poet. We want to involve the poet in the production of the book as much as possible." avg. price, paper: $2.00. 1977. 34pp; 5½ x 8. of. avg. press run 500 copies. Reporting time: 1 week to 1 month. Payment: 50 copies to author. All sales return to press. We are a non-profit, tax-exempt organization. One poet's success allows another poet to be printed. Copyrights for author. Discounts: Unresolved at present. CCLM, COSMEP-SOUTH.

House Of Paz (see PAZ PRINT/PERIPHERY)

House Of Words (see also THIRD COAST ARCHIVES), C. Rossiter, Jeffrey Winke, 207 E. Buffalo St. No. 518, Milwaukee, WI 53202. Poetry, art, long-poems, concrete art. "We do *Third Coast Archives* quarterly, also 'Littlebooks' series, which are small format, paper cover, 8-24 short poems, as well as 'foldsheets', 5-10 short poems, and poetic postcards." avg. price, paper: $0.50 - $1.00. 1976. 20-35pp; 4¼ x 5-1/2. of. avg. press run 150. Reporting time: 2 weeks to 2 months. Payment: copies. Copyrights for author. Discounts: 40% plus postage on 5 or more. Pub'd 1 title 1976.

Houston Writers Workshop (see also TOUCHSTONE), Guida Jackson, Managing Editor, Drawer 42331, Houston, TX 77042. Poetry, fiction, articles, art, photos, cartoons, interviews, satire, criticism, reviews, music, letters, non-fiction. avg. price, paper: $1.50. 1976. 32pp; 8½ x 11. of. avg. press run 1,000. Reporting time: 6 weeks. Payment: copies only. Copyright assigned to author on request. Discounts: 45 percent-20 or more copies. Pub'd 3 titles 1976; expects 4 titles 1977, 4 titles 1978.

HS Press (see CHIMERA-A Complete Theater Piece)

Hub Publications Ltd. (see also ORBIS, IPSE), Robin Gregory, Cal Clothier, Youlgrave, Bakewell, Derbyshire, England, United Kingdom. Poetry, articles, reviews. lp/of. avg. press run 1,000.

THE HUDSON REVIEW, The Hudson Review, Inc., Paula Deitz, Frederick Morgan, 65 East 55th St., New York City, NY 10022, 212-755-9040. Poetry, fiction, articles, criticism, reviews, parts-of-novels, long-poems. "Although we have developed a recognizable group of contributors who are identified with the magazine, we are always open to new writers and publish them in every issue. We have no university affiliation and are not committed to any narrow academic aim; nor to any particular political perspective." 1-yr sub price: $9.00; per copy: $2.50. 1948. 160pp; 4½ x 7½. of. circ. 3,500. Reporting time: 8-10 weeks maximum. Payment: 2½ cents per word for prose; 50 cents per line for poetry. Copyrighted, reverts only upon the author's request. Ads: $175.00/$20.00 depending on rarity of issue. Discounts: bulk rates and discount schedules on request. Pub's reviews. §Literature, fine and performing arts, sociology and cultural anthropology. CCLM, COSMEP.

Hudson River Press (see 3RD THING MAGAZINE OF POETRY AND GRAPHICS)

HUERFANO, Daran, Inc., Randell Shutt, Editor; Vicki Thompson, Poetry Editor, Box 49155, Tucson, AZ 85717. Poetry. "Annual Daran Award of $50.00" 2/yr; 1-yr sub price: $2.00. 1974. 30-40pp; 5½ x 8½. of. circ. 200. Reporting time: 2-3 weeks. Payment: copies only. Copyrighted, reverts to author. Ads: $10.00/$5.00. CCLM.

The Huffman Press, Katherine Gekker Huffman, 110 S. Columbus St., Alexandria, VA 22314, 703-836-7160. Poetry, fiction, art, photos, music, parts-of-novels, long-poems. "Send inquiries first." avg. price, cloth: $15.00. 1974. 12pp; 7½ x 6. †lp. avg. press run 100 copies. Reporting time: 2-4 weeks. Payment: open. Copyrights for author. Discounts: standard. Expects 2 titles 1977, 2 titles

1978. COSMEP.

THE HUMANIST, Paul Kurtz, 923 Kensington Ave., Buffalo, NY 14215, 716-837-0306. Poetry, articles, art, photos, cartoons, interviews, criticism, reviews, long-poems. 6/yr; 1-yr sub price: $12.00; per copy: $2.00. 1940. 64pp; 8½ x 11. of. circ. 28,500. Ads: $395.00/$215.00/$0.40. Discounts: 40% bulk discount. Back issues: $2.50. Pub'd 6 issues 1976; expects 6 issues 1977, 6 issues 1978. Pub's reviews: 20 in 1976. §Philosophy, Psychology, Social Science, & Religion.

HUMANIST IN CANADA, Pacific Northwest Humanist Publications, J. Lloyd Brereton, Rod Symington, P.O. Box 157, Victoria, B.C. V8W2M6, Canada, 604-388-5323. Poetry, articles, photos, criticism, reviews, letters. "The magazine explains and advocates the humanist philosophy." 4/yr; 1-yr sub price: $3.00; per copy: $.75; sample: $.85. 1967. 48pp; 8 x 11. of. circ. 1,800. Discounts: 33%. Back issues: $1. Pub'd 4 issues 1976; expects 4 issues 1977, 4 issues 1978. Pub's reviews. CPPA.

Humble Hills Press (see THE NEW MOON)

Hummingbird Press (see HYACINTHS AND BISCUITS)

HUMPTY DUMPTY, Collective, 32 Parkholme Rd, Dalston, London E83AG, United Kingdom. Articles, cartoons, reviews, interviews, letters. "Length: max 2,000 words. Style: non-academic, fairly punchy, libertarian socialist, but other biases considered. Content: critical of psychology theory & practice." occasional; sub price: £1 for 3 issues (post included); per copy: 30p (plus postage); sample: free. 1972. 32pp; A4. of. circ. 2,000. Reporting time: 1 mo. Discounts: 1/3 bookshops or for orders over 10. Back issues: sub. can include back issues. Expects 2 issues 1977, 1 issue 1978.

HUNDELOCH, Carl D. Clark, 30C7 University, Austin, TX 78705, 512-472-7415. Poetry, fiction, articles, art, photos, cartoons, interviews, satire, criticism, reviews, music, letters, parts-of-novels, long-poems, collages, plays, concrete art. "*HUNDELOCH* (black hole?) prints non-sciencefiction accounts of possible phenomena; we are interested in what's in your head, not what's around you or what you do. Confessional poets need not apply." 3/yr; 1-yr sub price: $3.00; per copy: $1.00; sample: none. 1977. 8-12pp; 8½ x 11. mi/of. Reporting time: 2 mos. Payment: copy. Not copyrighted. Ads: none. Discounts: none. Pub'd 1 issue 1976.

Hunter Publishing, Co., Diane Thomas, P.O. Box 9533, Phoenix, AZ 85068, 602-944-1022. Non-fiction. "We publish creative Ojo books—4 separate titles now. Interested in undertaking publishing venture for good craft oriented ideas-resale to craft & hobby shops, book stores, museum gift stores, etc. Also 2 books pub. on Japanese silk flower making." avg. price, paper: $1.50-$2.95. 1975. 24-52pp; 8½ x 11. avg. press run 10m-20m plus. Reporting time: 1-2 weeks. Copyrights for author. Discounts: 40-50 percent retail. Higher disc. to distributors. Pub'd 2 titles 1976; expects 2 titles 1977.

Huntsville Literary Association (see POEM)

HURON REVIEW, Walden Press, Frank Hamilton, 423 South Franklin Ave., Flint, MI 48503. Poetry, fiction. "I receive much good work to read for HURON REVIEW- more, of course, *than I can use*. Much more poetry comes than fiction. Walden Press is still alive and healthy; most of sales still come for work on Thoreau from libraries." 2/yr; 1-yr sub price: $3.00; sample: free. 1974. 32pp; 13½ x 21½. †of. circ. 350. Reporting time: 1 wk. Payment: copies only. Copyrighted, reprint rights remains with authors. no ads. Discounts: 50 percent libraries and jobbers. Back issues: free for postage. Pub'd 2 issues 1976; expects 2 issues 1977, 2 issues 1978. COSMEP.

Hurtig Publishers, Eva Carlson, 10560-105st, Edmonton, Alberta T5H2W7, Canada. "Canadian interest only." Reporting time: 6 weeks.

HYACINTHS AND BISCUITS, Hummingbird Press, Jane R. Card, box 392, Brea, CA 92621. Poetry, articles, art, photos, cartoons, satire, reviews. "Poems from 1 to 100 words; quality wanted, but no particular school. It is a mixture of traditional and modern forms, sonnets and free verse. Includes haiku, light verse, and limericks. Short, short stories, an unusual incident or locale are accepted to 300 words. Poet biographies to 300 words, about modern poets (1930 to present) original and well-written. Contributors to #20:(some) Geraldine C. Little, Ramona E. Vernon, Catherine Wardlaw, Paul Rider, Doris Wight, Daniel O'Connell, Jessie Hraska, Karla M. Hammond, Jerry Lipman, Katherine B. March, Carl Woods, M.L. Hester Jr., Kosrof Chantikian, Jesse Reichman, Val Richardson, P.C. Niblette, Leonard B. Gray, Barbara Holland, Maria Berl Lee, Toni Ortner Zimmerman, Leonard Opalov, Frank Foster." 6/yr; sub price: $5.00/6 issues; per copy: $1.00; sample: $1.00. 1969. 56pp; 8 x 10½. †of. circ. 1,000. Reporting time: 1 week to 1 month. Payment: $2 more than 5 lines $1 five or less lines. Ads: $45/$25. Discounts: 50% to agent, classrooms, etc. Pub's reviews §poetry, black, women, chicano, other minorities, oral poetry, tapes. CCLM, COSMEP.

HYPERION A Poetry Journal, Thorp Springs Press, Paul Foreman, Judy Hogan, Foster Robertson, 2311-C Woolsey, Berkeley, CA 94705, Subs: 2-D Chase Park, Chapel Hill, NC 27514. Poetry, criticism, reviews, long-poems. "Would like to see essays on poetics, esp concerned with American tradition." 2-3/yr; 1-yr sub price: $4.00; per copy: $1.00 ea usual issue, $2.00 or $4.00 combined issues; sample: $1.00. 1969. 100pp; 8½ x 5½. †of. circ. 2,000. Reporting time: 2-6 mos. Payment: copies only. Copyrighted. Discounts: bookstore 40%, jobbers 10% 1-10 copies, 20% 11-50 copies. Back issues: One & two $25.00 each, 3-10 $5.00 each, 11 & 12 & 13 $10.00 each. Pub'd 1 issue 1976; expects 2 issues 1977. Pub's reviews. §Poetry, literature, languages, Asian literature, Greek literature, modern poetry. CCLM, COSMEP.

I **ICARUS, Icarus Press,** Margaret Diorio, 1015 Kenilworth Drive, Towson, MD 21204, P.O. Box 8, Riderwood, MD 21139. Poetry, reviews. "John Tagliabue, Lyn Lifshin, Susan Fromberg Schaeffer, Don Gordon, Barbara A. Holland, Laurence Moffi, Mark Rudman, Aaron Kramer, Lora Dunetz, Carl Bode, Arlene Stone, Daisy Alden, Elizabeth Bartlett, Dave Etter, Larry Rubin, Willis Barnstone, Alan Britt, Michael McMahon, Christine Zawadiwsky, Charles Edward Eaton." 3/yr; 1-yr sub price: $3.00; per copy: $1.00. 1973. 28pp; 5½ x 8 -1/2. †of. circ. 600. Reporting time: 1-2 months. Payment: 4 copies. Back issues: $1.00. Expects 3 issues 1977, 3 issues 1978. Pub's reviews: 3 in 1976. §poetry. CCLM, COSMEP.

ICARUS, Michael S. McIntosh, Missouri Western State College, St. Joseph, MO 64507. Poetry, fiction, articles, plays. "We are not able to accept manuscripts. The college pays our printing costs and insists that we publish only people associated with the college." 1/yr; 1-yr sub price: $1.00; sample: free with exchange. 1972. 60pp; 6 x 9. of. circ. 500. no ads.

ICONOCLAST, Douglas D. Baker Jr., P.O. Box 7013, Dallas, TX 75209. Articles, art, photos, cartoons, interviews, satire, criticism, reviews, music, letters. 52/yr; 1-yr sub price: $10.00; per copy: $.25. 1967. 32pp; 14½ x 10½. of. circ. 8,000. Reporting time: 30 days. Payment: $10.00 up. Ads: $218.40/$118.30/$.10. Back issues: 35¢. Pub's reviews. §art/political science/ecology/books, etc. APS.

ICONOMATRIX, Iconomatrix, J.A. Brebner, J.C Mahanti, P.O. Box 2, Postal Station A, Fredericton, N.B. E3B4Y2, Canada. Poetry, articles, interviews, satire, criticism, reviews, letters. "10-20 page articles accepted; short poems used as fillers; zesty non-academic style preferred, no footnotes or end notes please; recent contributors—Robert Lowell, George Woodcock, Irving Layton, D.S. Savage, Bela Egyedi." 4/yr; 1-yr sub price: $9.00; per copy: $3.00; sample: $1.50. 1975. 100pp; 8½ x 5½. circ. 560. Reporting time: 1-2 weeks. Ads: $250/$150/$.50. Discounts: $2.00 per issue/$6.00 for subscription. Back issues: $1.50. Pub's reviews. §fiction, poetry, criticism, general literature.

IDAHO HERITAGE, Idaho Heritage, Inc., Alan Minskoff, P O Box 9365, Boise, ID 83707, 208-345-0060. Poetry, fiction, articles, art, photos, cartoons, interviews, reviews, letters, parts-of-novels. "Publish a calendar, books are still in planning stage. Subject matter is not limited to Idaho but should relate to the magazine's general concerns. See past copies. Our policy is to publish widely divergent opinions on all aspects of life in Idaho, except politics, which we try to ignore. Fiction should not exceed 3,000 words and shorter stories are preferred. Non-fiction, 500 to 2,000 words, but we are open-minded about such things. Recent contributors: Ted Trueblood, L. J. Davis, Diane Wakoski, William Stafford, Richard Shelton, Frank Church, Cecil Andrus." 6/yr; 1-yr sub price: $7.50; per copy: $1.50; sample: Free to qualified contributor. 1975. 64pp; 8½ x 11. of. circ. 12,500. Reporting time: 5 weeks. Payment: $1.00 per column inch for fiction & non-fiction, $10.00 per poem, $10.00 per drawing, $7.50 per photo. Copyrighted, reverts on request. Ads: $525.00/$262.50. Discounts: $1.00 per for agents, $0.75 jobbers. Back issues: $1.30 each, issue 2 is unavailable. Pub's reviews §Photography, poetry, preservation, architecture, fiction, history, conservation. COSMEP.

IF LIFE, THEN ONE AMONG AT LEAST FOUR, Horace G. Oliver Jr., P.O. Box 282, Palisades Park, NJ 07650. "Monthly magazine of Epistemology." 12/yr; 1-yr sub price: $5.00; per copy: $1.00. 1975. 16pp; 4½ x 7¼. †of. circ. 100. Reporting time: 1 month. Back issues: $1.00 each.

Igloo Press, Box 4555, Vancouver, BC V6B4A1, Canada.

Ilkon Press, Ilse Bing, 210 Riverside Drive No. 6G, New York, NY 10025, 212-663-2579. Poetry, art, concrete art. avg. price, cloth: $10.00; paper: $7.00. 1975. 180pp; 12 x 9. of. avg. press run 1,000 books. Copyrights for author. Discounts: Libraries 20 percent; bookstores 40 percent; jobbers 50 percent when ordering 5 books minimum - otherwise 40 percent. Pub'd 1 title 1976. NESPA.

ILLINOIS LIBERTARIAN, Libertarian Party of Illinois, Robert Osterlund, (press address) Box 1776, Chicago, IL 60690, (editor) 5301 S. Kimbark Ave., Chicago, IL 60615. "2,000 words max; Libertarian Party of Illinois news, Midwest Libertarian activities, news analysis, opinion, informative articles, etc. Bias: Libertarian, local, and original material. Contributors: Joe Cobb, Richard Suter, et al." 12/yr; 1-yr sub price: $6.00; per copy: gratis; sample: gratis. 1975. 8pp; 8½ x 11. of. circ. 250. Reporting time: 2 wks. No payment.

ILLUMINATIONS, Illuminations Press, N. Moser, 1900 9th Street 8, Berkeley, CA 94710, 415-849-2102. Poetry, fiction, articles, art, photos, reviews, letters, long-poems, collages, plays. "Fiction not usually over approx. 10 pp., plays not over 20 pp., reviews and short articles not over 7-8 pp. No biases, entirely eclectic. Contributors: Walsoski, J. Hays, F. Alexander, W. Witherup, Bukowski, Blazek P. Wild, Ginsberg, etc. Plan 1-2 issues more if NEA grant comes thru." 1/yr; 1-yr sub price: Indiv. $20.00 - Instit. $30.00; per copy: $1.50; sample: $1.50. 1965. 30-60pp; 8 x 11. of. circ. Varies, 500-2,000. Reporting time: 3-6 months. Payment: copies. Copyrighted, reverts to author. Ads: $75.00/$40.00/$15.00/$8.00. Discounts:40⅓ discount to retail outlets. No other discounts. Back issues: $100.00 complete set minus No. 1; $75.00 No. 3. Pub's reviews. CCLM, COSMEP.

Illuminations Press (see also ILLUMINATIONS), N. Moser, 1900 9th Street 8, Berkeley, CA 94710, 415-849-2102. Poetry, fiction, long-poems, plays. "The magazine and book releases are in suspension awaiting outcome of beginning NEA grant schedule soon. The mss. are here; funds are not. Both books and magazines are planned if funds come thru; if don't, have no idea what I'll do or whether I'll continue. Big on planning boards is an *ILLUMINATIONS* Reader anthology. ($5.00 paperback; $10.00 cloth)." avg. price, paper: $1.50. 1965. 30-40pp; 3 x 5. of. avg. press run 1,000 - 2,000. Reporting time: 3-6 months. Payment: Agreed percentage. Copyrights for author. Discounts:40⅓ discount to retail outlets. No other discounts. CCLM, COSMEP.

THE ILLUSTRATED ORB, The Trauma Works, Jerry Provan, Dewey McCulloch, P.O. Box 111, Royal Oak, MI 48068. Articles, art, cartoons, interviews, satire, criticism, reviews, music. "50% or more illustrated cartooning, art, comics, pictorial satire— *NO* PHOTOS. Any photos sent here will be *shot*." 12/yr; 1-yr sub price: $4.00; per copy: $.50; sample: for stamp. 1976. 16pp; 10½ x 14½. †of. circ. 10,000. Reporting time: 1 month. Payment: up to 2¢ word/$5 & up art work. Ads:

149

$140/$75/$.10. Discounts: 50% off to the small press. Pub's reviews. §All areas, especially illustrated materials.

ILLYRIAN REVUE, Kneechee Press, Joseph J. DeCanto, Andrew Norman Luria, Dean Nappi, Arthur Hoffman, P.O. Box 450, Saddle Brook, NJ 07662. Poetry, articles. "We print poetry; essays and articles relevant to philosophy, film, and aesthetics. Although shorter essays and poems are preferred, ultimately quality is our only standard." 4/yr; 1-yr sub price: $5.00; per copy: $1.50; sample: $1.50. 1977. 50pp; 5½ x 8½. †lp. circ. undetermined. Reporting time: 3-4 weeks. Payment: copies. Copyrighted, does not revert to author. no ads. Discounts: 10 percent on orders of five or more; 20 percent on orders of 10 or more; classroom rates upon request. Back issues: Price undetermined. Pub'd 2 issues 1976. Pub's reviews: none in 1976. §poetry, philosophy, film, fiction & anything else relevant to aesthetics.

IMAGE MAGAZINE, Cornerstone Press, Anthony J. Summers, James A. Fredericks, Peter Carlos, P.O. Box 28048, St. Louis, MO 63119, 314-225-3892. Poetry, fiction, articles, art, photos, cartoons, interviews, satire, reviews, letters, parts-of-novels, long-poems, plays, concrete art. "We want stuff that will make us scream or otherwise perform unnatural acts. It must be good, and daring, no sloppy attempts. Some recent contributors: check back issues." 3/yr; 1-yr sub price: $4.50; per copy: $1.50; sample: $1.50. 1972. 40-60pp; 5 x 11. of. circ. 300-400. Reporting time: 2 weeks to infinity. Payment: 2 copies to contr. plus $10.00 for best poem/s. story per issue. Copyrighted, does not revert to author. Discounts: 1 free copy to any prison that requests it. Back issues: $5.00 per copy if I can find them. They are collectors items. Pub's reviews §anything.

IMAGES, Gary Pacernick, Bruce Pilgrim, English Dept, Wright State Univ., Dayton, OH 45435. "Millen Brand, Robert Peters, Peter Cooley, Daniel Langton, Arlene Stone, Josephine Jacobsen, Lyn Lifshin, Milton Kessler, Opal Nations." 3/yr; 1-yr sub price: $1.50; per copy: $.50; sample: $0.50. 1974. 12pp; 16 (L) x 11½ (W). of. circ. 500. Reporting time: 1 month. Payment: copies. Back issues: $0.50. Pub'd 3 issues 1976; expects 3 issues 1977. CCLM, COSMEP.

IMAGES AND INFORMATION (Sort of an Art Magazine), Don Mabie, 4236 Worcester Dr SW, Calgary, Alberta T2P2B3, Canada, 262-6241. Art, criticism, collages. "The magazine is supported by myself and occasional contributions from interested parties. I am not interested in receiving unsolisited contributions—Images published as time, energy, and money allow." When time, energy, and money come together.; sub price: 6 issues for $5.00; per copy: $2.00; sample: $2.00. 1975. 18-20pp; 14 x 8½. of. circ. 500 copies. Payment: none at present. Not copyrighted. no advertising. Discounts: none. Back issues: $2.00. Pub's reviews. §art. COSMEP.

Images Press, Robert Leverant, David Bratman, P.O. Box 9444, Berkeley, CA 94709, 415-843-8834. Art, photos, non-fiction. avg. price, paper: $3.50. 1968. 64pp; varies. of. avg. press run 2,000. Reporting time: 2 weeks. Copyrights for author. Discounts: 40 percent 5 books or more. Pub'd 1 title 1976; expects 2 titles 1977, 3 titles 1978. COSMEP, COSMEP-WEST.

IMK (see MAYBE)

IMPACT, AN INTERNATIONAL QUARTERLY OF CONTEMPORARY POETRY, The Commentators' Press, Gary Lagier, Editor; Jess Irwin, Associate Editor; Judson Jerome, Consulting Editor; Gordon Curzon, Consulting Editor; and 21 Foreign Editors, Vange Peterson, Art Editor; Kenneth Atchity, Review Editor, P.O. Box 61297, Sunnyvale, CA 94088. Poetry, articles, art, cartoons, interviews, satire, criticism, reviews. "Our only criteria is: excellence. We are contemporary in content, not necessarily form. Do not like poetry with unrelieved howling. Manuscripts should have something to say, and get at it with a minimum of fuss. L. Ferlinghetti, Harold Witt, Paul Fericano, Harold Johnson, Stella Worley, Jim Martin, Crary Elwood, Authur Winfield Knight, Ed Falkowski, A.D. Winans, Gertrude May Lutz, Joan George, Tom Piekarski, Gary Lagier. Manuscripts & correspondence not accompanied by SASE are not read! 4 contests held each year, with $50.00 1st prize plus other awards. Write for details. Each issue we feature, in the center section, an as yet 'undiscovered' poet. Candidates for featured poet should submit a minimum of 12 poems, showing full range & interests of talent." 4/yr; 1-yr sub price: $6.00; $9.00 Foreign.; per copy:

$2.00; sample: $2.00. 1975. 60pp; 5½ x 8½. of. circ. 1,000 plus. Reporting time: Under 6 weeks. Payment: Copies (featured poet: copies & $ as available). Copyrighted. Ads: None. Discounts: None. Back issues: Over 3 months old: $3.00 plus $0.25 postage. Pub'd 4 issues 1976; expects 4 issues 1977, 4 issues 1978. Pub's reviews. §well-written material on any subject. CCLM, COSMEP, COSMEP-WEST.

Impact Publishers, Inc. (see also ASSERT NEWSLETTER), Robert E. Alberti, President, PO Box 1094, San Luis Obispo, CA 93406, 805-543-5911. Photos, cartoons, non-fiction. "Personal development/social change/health." avg. price; cloth: $7.95; paper: $3.95. 1970. 200-300pp; 5¼ x 8. of. avg. press run 5,000-10,000. Reporting time: 4-6 weeks. Payment: standard royalty contract. Copyrights for author. Discounts: Bookstores & wholesale distributors: up to 4 copies, 20 percent; 5-99 copies 40 percent; 100 plus copies, contact Impact re terms. Libraries paper 10 percent; cloth 15 percent. Pub'd 4 titles 1976; expects 3 titles 1977, 3 titles 1978.

IMPEGNO '70, Sicilian Antigruppo, Rolando Certa, Nat Scammacca, Gianni Diecidue, Corso Umberto, 22, Casella Postale N. 30, Mazara Del Vallo, Trappani, Sicily, 9-45492. Poetry, fiction, articles, art, photos, interviews, satire, criticism, reviews, letters, long-poems, collages, plays. "Materials within 10 pages. Contributors: Nat Scammacca, Sam Guibilato, Ignazio Navarra, Rolando Certa, Gianni Diecidue, Robert Bly, Lawrence Ferlinghetti, Sacca, Roberto Roversi, Rafaeli Alberti. A Populist Magazine of the Sicilian Antigruppo, a literary movement." 3/yr; 1-yr sub price: $5.00; per copy: $2.00; sample: $1.50. 1968. 150 pluspp; 5 x 8½. of/lp. circ. 1,500. Reporting time: 1 month. No payment, copies of review offered. Copyrighted, author. Ads: $100.00/$50.00. Back issues: $2.00. Pub's reviews. §Poetry, literary reviews, essays.

Impress Inc. (see PRIMIPARA)

IMPRESSIONS, Impressions Photographic Society, Isaac Applebaum, Shin Sugino, Box 5, Station B, Toronto, Ontario M5T2T2, Canada. Poetry, articles, photos. 4/yr; 1-yr sub price: $11.00. 1970. 52pp; 9 x 11. duotone printing. circ. 3,000 per issue. Reporting time: 3 months. Ads: $300/$175. Discounts: 10% agents/15% classroom.

IMPULSE, Eldon Garnet, Box 901, Station Q, Toronto, Ontario, Canada. Poetry. "Bias for the innovator—Les Levine, Mark Prent, Joe Hall, Michael Snow" 4/yr; 1-yr sub price: $10.00; per copy: varies. 1971. 65pp; varies. circ. 1,000. Reporting time: 1 month. Payment: negotiable. Ads: $100.00/$50.00. Discounts: 40 percent. Back issues: normal prices except for those which are limited. Pub'd 4 issues 1976. §experimental. CPPA.

IN A NUTSHELL, Hibiscus Press, Margaret Wensrich, Fiction; Joyce Odam, Poetry, P.O. Box 22248, Sacramento, CA 95822. Poetry, fiction, art, cartoons. "Poetry by: B.J. Kinnick, Harold Witt, Stella Worley, Ann Menebroker, Paul F. Fericano, Susan A. Coons. Stories 1,500-2,000 words: Jesse F. Knight, Robert D. Easton, John Rasmussen. Poetry by: Errol Miller, Susan A. Coons, Sandra Case, Ann Petrick. Annual short story and poetry contest Send S.A.S.E. after Aug. 15th for rules and entry form. Cash prizes. Closes Oct. 31st. Send S.A.S.E. with all submissions." 4/yr; 1-yr sub price: $4.00; per copy: $1.25; sample: $1.25. 1975. 36pp; 5½ x 8½. of. circ. 5m. Reporting time: 3-4 wks. Payment:401/2 cent fiction/$2 minimum poetry/$5 minimum cartoons. Copyrighted, right reverts to author upon publication. Ads: no ads. Discounts: Write for discount. Order must be for 5 or more copies of the same issue. Back issues: $1.25. Pub'd 4 issues 1976; expects 4 issues 1977, 4 issues 1978. CCLM, COSMEP.

In Between Books, Karla Margaret, Star Route, Box 271, Sausalito, CA 94965, 388-8048. Poetry, non-fiction. avg. price, cloth: depends. 1974. 100pp; 5 x 8. of. avg. press run depends. Reporting time: query first. Copyrights for author. Discounts: 20 percent to libraries; 40 percent to bookstores; 50-55 percent to distributors. Expects 1 title 1977. CCLM, COSMEP.

IN ORBIT: A Journal of Earth Literature, Energy BlackSouth Press, Rava X. Nelson, 2805 Southmore, Houston, TX 77004. "Science fiction plus." 1/yr. 1977. circ. 2,000. Reporting time: 2 weeks to 2 months. Copyrighted, reverts to author. Pub's reviews. §Science future fiction poetry. COSMEP.

IN TOUCH, The Grail, Jackie Rolo, The Grail, 125 Waxwell Lane, Pinner, Middx HA5 3ER, United Kingdom. Articles, poetry, photos, reviews, news items, interviews. "700-750 words. Personal & immediate-human interest, educational, spiritual-housewives, business men, professional men/women, young people, volunteers, clergy, religious." 4/yr; 1-yr sub price: 75p; per copy: 20. 1969. 12pp; 10 x 7½. of. circ. 1,200. Payment: nominal. Back issues: 10p each.

Incunabula Collection Press (see also ROOTS OF CREATION), Paul Meinhardt, Lela Meinhardt, 277 Hillside Ave, Nutley, NJ 07110. Articles. "Title planned for Dec. '77, *Cinderella And The Housework Dialectics* by Lela Meinhardt & Paul Meinhardt. Erik Meinhardt (illustrations & caligraphy). A radical analysis of housework, household and family." avg. price, cloth: $12.00; paper: $5.00. 1977. 300pp; 5½ x 8½. †of. avg. press run 3,000. Discounts: library and classroom-teaching less 25 percent; trade (bookstores) less 45 percent. COSMEP.

INCUS (see also Incus Press), Thomas Masiello, Gretchen Masiello, 457 Avenue Y, Brooklyn, NY 11223, 214-375-5801. Poetry, fiction, articles, art, photos, interviews, satire, criticism, reviews, music, letters, parts-of-novels, long-poems, collages, plays, concrete art, non-fiction. "We are a new magazine to appear for the first time in the Summer of 1977. We have absolutely no biases, but will of course only accept what we judge to be the best of the material submitted. We are open to all forms from the most concrete to the most abstract and will consider all submissions as carefully as possible, no matter how alien the form or subject. We hope to be able to do chapbooks in the future." semiannual for 1977, quarterly thereafter; avg. price, cloth: $1.75; paper: $6.00 4 issues. 1977. 50-100pp; 8½ x 5½. of. avg. press run 300. Reporting time: immediately. Payment: copies. Copyrights for author. Ads: $25.00/$15.00. Discounts: arranged for libraries, schools, etc. Expects 2 titles 1977, 2 titles 1978.

THE INDEPENDENT JOURNAL OF PHILOSOPHY, The Independent Philosophy Press, George Elliott Tucker, Cobenzlgasse 13/4, A-1190 Vienna, Austria. Articles, criticism, reviews, letters, news items. "We are attempting to forge and further a 'third force' in philosophy, beyond analyticism and existentialism/Marxism. Articles in German or English of 20 to 30 double-spaced typewritten pages, as well as short notices and replies, are welcomed. Prospective book-reviewers should consult the editor first. Would especially like information on books that are 'philosophical' in the broad but strict sense; and which cut across the usual, narrow 'disciplines', without however becoming merely eclectic. Issues planned for 1977: *'What Is Philosophy'*, *'Leo Strauss—Essays On The Issues And Themes Of His Life-Work'*, and Wittgenstein. Only high quality material will be considered. First issue to appear in June, 1977." 4/yr; 1-yr sub price: $18.50 Individuals/$21.00 Institutions; per copy: $5.25; sample: $5.25. 1976. 100-140pp; 11-5/8 x 8¼. of. circ. 1,000. Reporting time: 2 months. Payment: 50 offprints. Copyrighted, does not revert to author. Ads: $60.00/$40.00. Discounts: By arrangement. Back issues: Same as singles. Expects 3 issues 1977, 4 issues 1978. Pub's reviews. §Philosophy, political science, classical studies, economics, education, science, etc.

INDEX ON CENSORSHIP, Writers & Scholars International, Michael Scammell, George Theiner, 21 Russell St., Covent Garden, London WC2B 5HP, United Kingdom, 01-836-0024. Articles, poetry, fiction, cartoons, satire, news items, interviews, criticism, letters, parts-of-novels, plays, reviews, non-fiction. "US sub price includes air-surface postage. Magazine is an outlet for manuscripts by authors who cannot be published in their own countries; and publishes reports on threats to freedom of expression-such as the censorship or persecution or torture of writers, scholars, journalists, artists, film-makers etc. Also publishes interviews, discussions and questionnaires. Scope is international-West and East. Contributors 1975-6 include: Viktor Nekrasov, A. Tverdokhlebov, Ludvik Vaculik, Vaclav Havel, V. Fainberg, Kim Chi-ha, George Mangakis, Reza Baraheni, Amnesty International, Arthur Miller, Robert Birley, James Michener, Nadine Gordimer." 6/yr; 1-yr sub price: £6.00 ($14.00); per copy: £1.25 ($2.45); sample: free. 1972. 80pp; 24 x 17cms. lp. circ. 4,500. Reporting time: variable. Payment: £20 per thou to authors. Authors' copyrights by arrangement. Ads: £75.00 ($150.00)/£40.00 ($80.00). Discounts: [Publishers 20 percent, non profit 40 percent. These discounts apply only to advertisements placed in INDEX.] Agent 10 percent. Bookshops variable (supplied via Random House). Back issues: $3.00 or £1.50. Pub'd 4 issues 1976; expects 6 issues 1977, 6 issues 1978. Pub's reviews: 17 in 1976. §Censorship, human rights.

The Independent Philosophy Press (see also THE INDEPENDENT JOURNAL OF PHILOSOPHY), George Elliott Tucker, Cobenzlgasse 13/4, A-1190 Vienna, Austria. Articles, criticism. "We are attempting to forge and further a 'third force' in philosophy, beyond analyticism and existentialism/marxism. We are interested in translations, scholarly reprints (basic texts and monographs) as well as first rate contemporary work. Authors should send a detailed outline before submitting manuscripts." 1977. of. Reporting time: 2 months. Payment: by arrangement. Copyrights for author. Discounts: by arrangement. Expects 1-2 titles 1977, 2-6 titles 1978.

Indian Academy of Letters (see INDIAN LITERATURE)

INDIAN HOUSE, Indian House, Tony Isaacs, Ida Isaacs, Box 472, Taos, NM 87571. Photos, music. "We specialize in recordings of traditional American Indian music, published in LP Phonodisc, Cassette, and 8-track formats." 6/yr; price per copy: $6.98 list. 1966. of. Discounts: wholesale to record stores, 37½%.

INDIAN Literature, Indian Academy of Letters, Keshav Malik, Rabindra Bhavan, 35 Feroze Shah Road, New Delhi 110001, India. Poetry, fiction, articles, criticism, reviews, parts-of-novels, long-poems. "Articles about 5,000 words maximum." 4/yr; 1-yr sub price: Rs.8, $4.00; per copy: Rs.2. 1958. 150pp; 21cm x 13½cm. lp. circ. 1,100. Pub's reviews. §literary/poetry.

INDIAN TRUTH, Indian Rights Association, Theodore B. Hetzel, Elaine P. Lariviere, 1505 Race St., Philadelphia, PA 19102, 215-563-8349. Articles, photos, reviews. 4/yr; 1-yr sub price: $15.00; per copy: free; sample: Free. 1924. 6pp; 8½ x 11. lp. circ. 3,000. no ads. Pub'd 2 issues 1976; expects 4 issues 1977, 4 issues 1978. Pub's reviews. §Native American/American Indians.

THE INDIAN VOICE, The Indian Voice, Donna Doss, 201-423 West Broadway, Vancouver, British Columbia V5Y1R4, Canada. Poetry, articles, art, photos, interviews, reviews, letters, collages. "THE INDIAN VOICE newspaper was founded to serve as a communications vehicle for native Indians of the North American continent. Because we are funded by the Secretary of State we ask our contributing writers to do the work gratis. We have, at other times, given a nominal fee which varies according to the money in the bank." 12/yr; 1-yr sub price: Canadian $4.00/overseas and U.S. $4.50; per copy: $.35. 1969. 12-16pp; 15 inch tabloid. of. circ. 1,500. Ads: $220/$110. Discounts: (Can) $3.80 (Foreign) $4.30. Back issues: 35¢. §all areas affecting the native Indian.

Indiana State University (see BLACK AMERICAN LITERATURE FORUM)

INDIVIDUAL LIBERTY, David Walter, Donald Ernsberger, P.O. Box 1147, Warminster, PA 18974, 215-675-6830. Poetry, fiction, articles, art, photos, cartoons, interviews, satire, criticism, reviews, letters. "Libertarian movement." avg. price, cloth: $0.25; paper: $0.25. 1969. 6pp; 8½ x 11. of. avg. press run 2,000. Reporting time: 1 wk. Payment: Neg. Does not copyright for author. Ads: $35.00/$20.00/$0.10. Discounts: agents 10%. Back issues: $0.25. Pub'd 12 titles 1976; expects 12 titles 1977, 12 titles 1978. LPA.

INDOCHINA CHRONICLE, Indochina Resource Center, Staff of Indochina Resource Center, P.O. Box 4000-D, Berkeley, CA 94704, 415-548-2546. Articles, art, photos, cartoons, interviews. "Main article usually approx. 10,000 words. Interprets current situation in/related to Indochina and throughout Southeast Asia. Sympathetic to revolutionary regimes in Indochina/supports friendly relations between U.S. and Vietnam, Laos, Cambodia. Recent authors: Banning Garrett, Linda and Murray Hiebert, Lou and Eryl Kubicka, Gary Porter and George Hildebrand, David Marr, E. Thadeus Flood, Khieu Samphan." 8/yr; 1-yr sub price: $8.00 Domestic; $10.00 Foreign; $15.00 Foreign Airmail.; per copy: $.75. 1971. 20pp; 8½ x 11. of. circ. 600. Reporting time: 2-3 weeks. Discounts: 10 plus copies 50 cents/100 plus copies 40 cents. Pub'd 8 issues 1976; expects 8 issues 1977, 8 issues 1978. Pub's reviews: 1 in 1976.§Indochina, Southeast Asia.

INDOCHINA RESOURCE CENTER, Indochina Chronicle, P.O. Box 4000 D, Berkeley, CA 94704, 415-548-2546. "TRADITION AND REVOLUTION IN VIETNAM. Nguyen Khac Vien.

The first serious political analysis by a Vietnamese writer available to a general English-language audience. CHILDREN OF VIET-NAM Tran Khanh Tuyet, editor. Stories and poems, with line drawings. Ages 4-9. BANH CHUNG BAHN DAY (The New Year's Rice Cakes). Vietnamese children's folktale, with line drawings. Ages 6-10." 1971. Discounts: 40 percent to booksellers.

INDUSTRIAL WORKER, Patrick Murfin, 752 W. Webster, Chicago, IL 60614, 312-549-5045. Articles, art, photos, cartoons, interviews, reviews, letters. 12/yr; 1-yr sub price: $5.00 institutional-$2.50 individual; per copy: $0.25; sample: free. 1912. 8pp; 8½ x 17. circ. 2,500. Not copyrighted. Discounts: discount 60 percent of cover price for 5 or more copies. Back issues: 50 cents 1 copy. Pub's reviews. §labor, labor history, economics. APS.

INLET, Joseph Harkey, Virginia Wesleyan College, Norfolk, VA 23502. Poetry, fiction. "Poems: 2 lines-200 lines; very short & very long poems must be especially good. Open on style, subject, form. Short fiction: 1,000-3,000 words. We seek as much diversity as possible in the writing we publish. Peter Meinke, Robert Stock, P.B. Newman, Peter Cooley, Bernell MacDonald." 12/yr; 1-yr sub price: Free, enclose 25 cent stamp for postage. 1971. 30pp; 8½ x 8½. of. circ. 500. Reporting time: 2wks-2mos. Payment: copies. Copyrighted. Back issues: Free, enclose 25 cent stamp for postage. Pub'd 1 issue 1976; expects 1 issue 1977, 1 issue 1978.

INQUEST, Quest Publishing, Jon Tuschen, Sherry Morse, Suni Caylor, 853 Williamson St., Madison, WI 53703. Poetry, art, reviews, plays. "Few biases but that rhyming, pipe smoking stuff is out. Very interested in graphics and short plays. Also reviews. New material from such writers as Marilyn Hacker, George Barker, Henri Michaux (translated by Michael Fineberg), Roy Watkins, and Ruth Stone." 4/yr; 1-yr sub price: $3.00; per copy: $1.00. 1970. 40pp; 8½ x 11. of. circ. 500. Reporting time: 1 mo. Payment: copies only. Ads: $20/$10/no class. Discounts: none. COSMEP.

THE INQUIRER, The Inquirer Publishing Co Ltd., Fred M. Ryde, 1-6 Essex Street, London WC2R 3HY, United Kingdom. Articles, poetry, cartoons. 26/yr; 1-yr sub price: £3.25; per copy: 10p. 1842. 4pp. of. Payment: £5 per author above 1,000 wds. Ads: 60p cm.

Inquiry Press, P.O. Box 1766, E. Lansing, MI 48823. 1975. mi/lp. Discounts: 40% trade/20% textbook.

‡**INSCAPE, Baleeen Press,** Box 13448, Phoenix, AZ 85002.

Institute for Local Self-Reliance (see SELF-RELIANCE)

Institute for Southern Studies (see SOUTHERN EXPOSURE)

THE INSURGENT SOCIOLOGIST, Cora Fisher, Paul Fitzgerald, Sara Goodman, Harry Humphries, Marty Landsberg, Kitty Leonard-Humphries, Jerry Lembcke, Ray Nelson, Carla Orcutt, Al Szymanski, c/o Department of Sociology, Univ. of Oregon, Eugene, OR 97403. Poetry, articles, art, criticism, reviews, letters. 4/yr; 1-yr sub price: indiv. $6.00 low income $10.00 sustaining; per copy: $2.00; sample: free. 1969. 100pp; 7½ x 10-3/8. of. circ. 1,800. Reporting time: 90 days. No payment. Ads: $150/$80. Discounts: 30% booksellers. Back issues: $3.00 except Vol V, No 3 $4.00. Pub's reviews. §politics/history/sociology.

INTEGRITY: Gay Episcopal Forum, Integrity, Inc., William A. Doubleday, 99 Brattle St., Cambridge, MA 02138. Articles, reviews, poetry, art, news items. "'Official publication of INTEGRITY, Inc., national org. of Gay Episcopalians and our friends. Articles from 100-1000 words. All material affirms God's love of all Gay people. Highly literate audience, largely with Anglican theological background; many of us are street queers, prisoners, and other people whom God loves. We are not seeking acceptance; we already have it, purchased at Calvary. We do not worship respectability, and we seek to bring the Church to our knees, as the meek at last inheriting the earth. We are often sassy, enjoy camp, and believe that the Holy Spirit chooses to make Her presence known to all persons. S.A.S.E.'" 10/yr; 1-yr sub price: $10.00; per copy: $1.25; sample: $1.00. 1974. 11pp; 8½ x 11. of. circ. 1,000. Reporting time: 2-4 weeks. Payment: copies. Ads:

$75/$50/none. Back issues: $2. Pub'd 10 issues 1976; expects 10 issues 1977, 12 issues 1978. Pub's reviews. §gay, religious, episcopalian, sexuality in general. COSMEP.

INTERCONTINENTAL PRESS, Joseph Hansen, P.O. Box 116, Varick Street Station, New York, NY 10014. News items. "Contributors: Ernest Mandel, George Novack, Livio Maitan, Pierre Frank." 49/yr; 1-yr sub price: $24.00; per copy: $.75. 1963. 32pp; 8½ x 11. of. Reporting time: 2 weeks. Copyrighted. Back issues: $0.75. Pub'd 49 issues 1976; expects 49 issues 1977, 49 issues 1978. Pub's reviews: 20 in 1976. §politics/ecology.

INTERFACE JOURNAL: Alternatives in Higher Education, Interface, Carl Ginsburg, P.O. Box 970, Utica, NY 13503. Articles, interviews, reviews. "We accept articles from people engaged in projects for change in post-secondary education. Special issue 3-4 was devoted to alternative concepts of the learning process. Some authors published include, Carol Berge, Lewis Hyde, Bill Romey and David Zeller. SASE for return of unused material." 2/yr; sub price: $8.00/4 issues, $10.00 institutions; per copy: $2.00/$4.00 double issue. 1975. 56pp; 8½ x 11. of. circ. 300. Reporting time: 2 mo. Payment: copies. Ads: $65/$40. Discounts: 25%. Pub'd 2 issues 1976; expects 1 issue 1977, 2 issues 1978. Pub's reviews: 2 in 1976. §education/innovative education.

Interface Unlimited, Dennis Oblander, P.O. Box 8583, Toledo, OH 43623. "Not soliciting manuscripts, probability of future books contingent on success of first." 1975. photocopy. COSMEP.

Interim Books, Kirby Congdon, Box 35, Village Station, New York, NY 10014. Poetry. "Doing broadsides until money is forthcoming for next issue." 1962. Payment: Copies.

Interim Press, Peter Dent, 4 Northcroft Villas, Northcroft Rd., Englefield Green, Egham, Surrey TW20 0DZ, United Kingdom, EGHAM 5538. Poetry. "Gerald Duff, Robin Fulton-most recent contributors. Translations of Andre Frenaud and Eleni Vakalo due shortly." avg. price, paper: £0.40. 1975. 16-32pp; varies. lo. avg. press run 250 copies. Reporting time: 2 wks. Payment: copies only. All material copyrighted for author (translators also). Discounts: 33 percent to trade. Pub'd 2 titles 1976; expects 3 titles 1977.

INTERMEDIA, Intermedia, Harley W. Lond, 243 Grand View Ave, San Francisco, CA 94114. Poetry, fiction, articles, art, photos, satire, criticism, reviews, music, collages, plays, concrete art. "Will be publishing special experimental literary issues and visual art chapbooks." irregular; 1-yr sub price: $5.00; per copy: $1.50-$3.00; sample: issue 5/6/7-$3.00. 1974. 60pp; 8½ x 11. of. circ. 3,000. Reporting time: max-1½ mo. Payment: contrib. copies. Copyrighted, reverts to author. Discounts: 40% trade, bulk institutions: $8.00. Back issues: all sold out. Pub'd 2 issues 1976; expects 3 issues 1977, 2 issues 1978. Pub's reviews: 50 in 1976. §experimental literature/art. COSMEP, LPSC.

Intermedia Press (see THE POEM COMPANY)

International Books International Writing Program, Univ of Iowa, Iowa City, IA 52240, 319-353-5920. Poetry. "International Books is a very small publishing and distributing organization operated by the International Writing Program. It is a non-profit operation designed to make available work that would not usually be published in the U.S. International Books publishes individual poets in translation, usually in conjunction with small publishers in England, sometimes in the U.S. The primary publisher (e.g. Anvil Carcanet) takes care of the entire production of the book, which we subsidize. Then we distribute copies in the U. S." avg. price, paper: $2.50. 1973. 50pp; 5½ x 9. avg. press run 300-500. By primary publisher.

International Center for Environmental Research-ICER Press, Ingeborg U. VanDeVenter, T. Robert Kendall, 141 Emerald Bay, Laguna Beach, CA 92651. Articles, art, photos, non-fiction. avg. price, cloth: $24.50. 1970. 104pp; 8½ x 11. of. avg. press run 2,000. Copyrights for author. Discounts: 2-4 copies 20 percent; 5-99 copies 40 percent, more than 100-30 percent. Pub'd 1 title 1976; expects 1 title 1977, 1 title 1978.

THE INTERNATIONAL FICTION REVIEW, International Fiction Association, Dr. Saad Elkhadem, Dept. of German & Russian, UNB, Fredericton, nb, Canada. "The *IFR* is a biannual periodical devoted to international fiction. Mss. are accepted in English and should be prepared in conformity with the second edition of the *MLA Style Sheet* and submitted to the Editor." 2/yr; 1-yr sub price: $6.00; per copy: $3.00; sample: $3.00. 1973. 90pp; 6 x 9. circ. 500. Reporting time: 6 weeks. Copyrighted. Ads: $60/$40. Discounts: none. Back issues: the same rate. Pub'd 2 issues 1976; expects 2 issues 1977, 2 issues 1978. Pub's reviews. §fiction. IFA.

International Marine Publishing Co. (see also NATIONAL FISHERMAN), Peter Spectre, Kathleen Brandes, 21 Elm Street, Camden, ME 04843, 207-236-4326. "We publish non-fiction marine books, especially practical boating books." avg. price, cloth: $12.50; paper: $5.95. 1969. 225pp; 7 x 10. of. avg. press run 5,000. Reporting time: 6 weeks. Payment: 10 percent of list price. Copyrights for author. Discounts: trade 40 percent; wholesale 46 percent. Pub'd 15 titles 1976.

THE INTERNATIONAL NEW AGE NEWSLETTER, The High Foundation, Dr. Carey Carpenter, P.O. Box 1137, Harrison, AR 72601. Poetry, articles, interviews, letters. "Monthly lessons by a Master Teacher telling how to combine progress on the spiritual path with a well-motivated and fulfilling life among fellow humans—comment on human problems here and abroad—non-denominational spiritual directions for all seekers in the Light—meditation, spiritual healing, natural living—The-Way of Light and Love." 12/yr; 1-yr sub price: $10.00; per copy: $1.00. 1966. 8pp; 8½ x 11. †of. circ. 5,000 plus. Reporting time: 30-60 days. No payment. Pub's reviews. §The govtter Life, Spiritual Awareness, Meditation, Success Motivation, Eastern Religions, Christianity & Judiasm & Lesser Groups, ESP, Healings, Medical & Science, books and magazines on what lies beyond this life and universe.

International New Thought Alliance (see NEW THOUGHT)

INTERNATIONAL POETRY REVIEW, Green River Press, Evalyn P. Gill, Raymond Tyner, SVSC Box 56, Univ. Center, MI 48710. Poetry. "Primary interest in translations from modern foreign language poetry. Section of poetry in English, Bilingual publication." 2/yr; 1-yr sub price: $4.50; per copy: $2.25; sample: $2.25. 1974. 115pp; 6 x 9. of. circ. 350. Reporting time: 2-3 months. Payment: in copies. Copyrighted, reverts to author. Ads: $50.00/$25.00. Discounts: 20 percent to agents and jobbers. Back issues: $5.00 per copy. §contemporary poetry. CCLM.

International Poetry Society: Hub Publications (see ORBIS, IPSE)

International Publishers Co., Inc., Louis Diskin, 381 Park Ave. South, New York, NY 10016. of/lp.

INTERNATIONAL SOCIALIST REVIEW, Caroline Lund, 14 Charles Lane, New York, NY 10014. Articles, interviews, reviews, letters. 12/yr. 1934. 12pp; 11½ x 17½. of-webb. circ. 20,000. Pub's reviews. §labor movement/black struggle/women's movement/Marxism.

International Society for General Semantics (see ETC)

‡**Intersection Inc.,** 756 Union St., San Francisco, CA 94133.

INTERSTATE, Noumenon Press, Loris Essary, Mark Loeffler, P.O. Box 7068, U.T. Sta., Austin, TX 78712. Poetry, fiction, art, reviews, music, parts-of-novels, long-poems, collages, plays, concrete art. "Experimental. We are primarily interested in new writing which explores forms and themes not usually found in publications in this country. Recent contributors: Stanley Berne, John Cage, Neal Cassady, Robert Deweese, Larry Eigner, J. Christopher Jones, Gottfried Honegger, Henry Korn, Richard Kostelanetz, Charles Levendosky, Gerard Malanga, Paul Miner, Frank Parman, Tom Raworth, Ken Saville, Edwin Schlossberg, Ian Tarnman, Nick Toczek, John Interecker, Valton Tyler, Jeff Woodruff, J. Michael Yates, Arlene Zekowski." 4/yr; 1-yr sub price: $5.00 individual/$6.00 institutional; sample: $2.00. 1974. 80pp; 8.5 x 5.5. of. circ. 500. Reporting time: 1-2 weeks or sooner. Payment: copies. Copyrighted. Ads: none. Discounts: 40% to bookstores. Back issues: By arrangement. Pub's reviews §all genres of the arts. CCLM, COSMEP.

INTREPID, Intrepid Press, Allen De Loach, P.O. Box 1423, Buffalo, NY 14214. Poetry, fiction, articles, art, photos, cartoons, interviews, satire, criticism, letters, parts-of-novels, long-poems, collages, plays, concrete art. "Contributors indexed in #23/24 include Ginsberg, Blackburn, Mottram, Wantling, Bremser, DeLoach, Shaetter, di Prima, Rothenberg." irreg.; sub price: $6.00/4 issues; per copy: $2.00. 1964. 8½ x 11. of. circ. 1M. Reporting time: 3 mos. Payment: copies only. Back issues: Available. CCLM.

Intrepid Trips Information Service (see SPIT IN THE OCEAN)

Intrepid Press (see BEAU FLEUVE SERIES, INTREPID, 23 CLUB SERIES)

INVICTUS, J & A Publications, Anna Trotta, c/o Iacono, 4521 West Greenway Rd., Glendale, AZ 85306. Poetry, fiction, interviews, satire, reviews, letters. "Articles, fiction, humor etc maximum of 300 words. Poetry-20 lines maximum. We have our own Book Reviewer-Dorothy L. Bostwick, 6512 N. Lake Rd., Brooklyn, Mich 49230" 4/yr; 1-yr sub price: $4.00; per copy: $1.20. 1974. 32pp; 5½ x 8½. of. circ. 300 plus. Reporting time: 2 weeks. Payment: contributor copies. Ads: $.10 per word. Discounts: $3.00/yr libraries. Back issues: $1.00. Pub's reviews. §all except Erotica. COSMEP.

INVISIBLE CITY, Red Hill Press, John McBride, Paul Vangelisti, 6 San Gabriel Drive, Fairfax, CA 94930. Poetry, articles, photos, criticism, reviews, letters. "Nos. 21-22 (August '77) features translations of Mohammed Dib, Antonio Porta, Adriano Spatola, Vicente Huidobro, several Polish & Latin-American poets; a post-World War II essay by Tristan Tzara and an interview with Kenneth Rexroth. Collages, graphics ('*Forbidden Words*' by Paul Eluard), notes, controversies & samples of forthcoming Red Hill Press books. No. 23 will resume publishing of U.S. poets and much more." 3-4/yr; sub price: 3/$3.00; per copy: $1.00; sample: $1.00 ppd. 1971. 16pp; 11 x 17. of. circ. 1,500. Reporting time: 2-3 months at worst. Payment: copies for sure. Authors, translators retain rights. Back issues: Sampler: $3.00/3 ppd. Bound sets available shortly (with index). Pub'd 1 issue 1976; expects 1 or 2 issues 1977, 2 plus issues 1978. Pub's reviews. §translation & criticism. CCLM, COSMEP.

‡**Inwood Press,** 128 Post Ave., New York, NY 10034.

IO, North Atlantic Books, Richard Grossinger, RFD 2 Box 135, Plainfield, VT 05667, 802-454-7845. "Above categories don't fit that well because we do issues by subject matter. In the near future we plan to be re-doing the baseball and alchemy issues as sourcebooks, but only want work from people who have read and digested previous editions." variable; sub price: $12.00 for 4 consecutive issues; per copy: $4.00. 1964. 250pp; varies. of. circ. 1500. Reporting time: Immediate—but do not want unsolicited submissions. Payment: copies only except where stated otherwise. Copyrighted, reverts to author. Ads: $50.00/$30.00. Discounts: none, only to bookstores. Back issues: All back issues still available at original prices (current issue is 23) full set is $89.50 (thru 23). Pub'd 2 issues 1976; expects 1 issue 1977, 2 issues 1978. CCLM.

IOWA REVIEW, U of Iowa Printing Service, William Matthews, Poetry; Robert Coover, Fiction; T.R. Whitaker, Criticism, 321 EPB, Univ. Of Iowa, Iowa City, IA 52242. Fiction, poetry, criticism. Quarterly.; 1-yr sub price: $7.50 ($8.50 outside USA); per copy: $2.00; sample: $2.00. 1970. 120pp; 6 x 9. circ. 750. Reporting time: 2 wks 3 months. Payment: Fiction & criticism $5.00/pg; poetry $0.50/line on publication. Copyrighted. Ads: $100.00/$60.00. Back issues: All available still. Pub'd 4 issues 1976; expects 4 issues 1977, 4 issues 1978. CCLM.

Iowa State University Press (see POET & CRITIC)

IPSE, International Poetry Society: Hub Publications Ltd., Robin Gregory, Youlgrave, Bakewell, Derbyshire, England, United Kingdom. Articles, poetry, reviews, criticism, long-poems. 4/yr; 1-yr sub price: $7.00; per copy: $2.00; sample: $2.00. 1975. 48pp; A5. of. circ. 500. Payment: Small. Copyrighted. Ads: £15.00 or ($25.00). Pub'd 4 issues 1976; expects 4 issues 1977.

Iris Press, Patricia Wilcox, 27 Chestnut St., Binghamton, NY 13905, 607-722-6739. Poetry, fiction. "*Iris Press* intends to publish poetry and the shorter forms of prose fiction on a roughly equal basis. Because we bring out only one or two titles per year, we cannot look at new manuscripts until 1978. Our goal is to bring out significant and readable literature in handsome editions. In 1977 we published, both in cloth & soft cover, *George Scarbrough: New and Selected Poems,* a 324-page work with illustrations and a photographic essay by Faith Decker. In 1975 we published fine soft-cover editions of a first collection of poems by Don Revell and a novella by E. V. Austin. In 1976 we published John Vernon's first collection of poems, *Ann,* also in fine soft-cover format. Authors should write ahead of sending a manuscript, including SASE." avg. price, cloth: $7.00; paper: $4.00. 1975. 85pp; 6 x 9. of. Reporting time: 1 month. Payment: negotiated individually. Copyrights for author. Discounts: 40 percent on 5-50 copies. Book services will be given 20 percent on any order. Pub'd 1 title 1976; expects 1 title 1977. COSMEP, COSMEP-SOUTH, NYSSPA.

IRISH BOOKLORE, Blackstaff Press, Wesley Mc Cann, Department of Library Studies, Queen's University, Belfast BT1 5JF, United Kingdom, 0232-45133 EXN 3622. Articles, reviews, news items, photos, letters. "Articles on Irish bibliography up to 25,000 words. Reporting, informative style. Librarian of National Library of Ireland, Archbishop of Armagh, Librarian of Ulster, Folk Museum-contributors." 2/yr; 1-yr sub price: £3.50; per copy: £2.50. 1970. 130pp; 9¾ x 6¼. of. circ. 750. Reporting time: 1 month. Payment: none. Ads: £40 per page. Pub'd 2 issues 1976; expects 1 issue 1977, 2 issues 1978. Pub's reviews: 12 in 1976. §Bibliography, printing, publishing (both Irish and general).

IRON, Iron Press, Peter Mortimer, Editor; Pete Swan, Art Editor, 5 Marden Terrace, Cullercoats, Northumberland, United Kingdom, 0632-531901. Poetry, fiction, art, letters, long-poems. "In its first four years *IRON* has published 280 authors from more than 20 countries. While actively encouraging poetry, it also recognises the short story as a neglected form, and considers these up to 6,000 words. It is also interested in featuring the work of photographers and artists, and lays great stress on the visual side of the magazine. All work submitted is commented upon." 4/yr; 1-yr sub price: $3.00-£1.20; per copy: $0.75-30p; sample: free. 1973. 48pp; A4. of. circ. 700. Reporting time: 2 weeks. Payments rare. Rights remain with author. Ads: $25.00/$15.00. Discounts: trade discount 33 percent. bulk discount negotiable. Back issues: 30p (70 cents) post free. Pub'd 4 issues 1976; expects 4 issues 1977, 4 issues 1978. Pub's reviews: 23 in 1976. §poetry, all small press publ.

Iron Mountain Press, Robert Denham, Box 28, Emory, VA 24327, 703-944-5363. "I am interested in publishing chapbooks of excellent poetry. All printing is done from handset type using high quality paper. The Iron Mountain Press Poetry Chapbooks average 28 pages in length, and include the poetry of Ann Deagon, Kate Jennings, Mike Martin, Robert Cluett, and Elizabeth Fisher. I also publish poetry post cards, illustrated with linocuts. All printing is done by hand on a C & P letterpress. Bindings are handsewn." avg. price, paper: $3.00. 1975. 28pp; 5½ x 8½. †op. avg. press run 400 copies. Reporting time: 1 week. Payment: Author receives 50 percent of the copies. I keep 50 percent. Does not copyright for author. Pub'd 3 titles 1976; expects 3 titles 1977, 3 titles 1978. COSMEP, South Books Arts Society.

‡**Ironwood Press,** PO Box 49023, Tucson, AZ 85717. CCLM.

IS (pronounced 'eyes'), The Eternal Network, Vic d'Or, 101 Kendal Ave, Toronto, Ontario M5R1L8, Canada. Poetry, fiction, art, photos, satire, letters, long-poems, collages, concrete art. "No unsolicited manuscripts please." 3/yr; 1-yr sub price: $10.00; per copy: $2.50-$4.00; sample: $3.00. 1966. 84pp. of. circ. 500.

Isat Pragbhara Press, Loring Johnson, Rt. 1, Box 143-C, Houma, LA 70360, 504-872-9701. Poetry, fiction, long-poems. "I am basically interested in poetry, book-length mss, tho fiction and/or essays will be considered. I also publish a postcard & a broadside series. My bias is toward the conquest of meaning over mere sound & rhythm, & toward poetry that expresses hope over poetical disillustionment." 1976. †lp/of. avg. press run 300. Reporting time: 4-8 weeks. Payment: Copies. Copyrights for author. Discounts: 40% to distributors. Pub'd 2 titles 1976; expects 2 titles 1977, 3 titles 1978. COSMEP.

Ishtar Press, Inc. (see also PAINTBRUSH), B. M. Bennani, Comparative Literature, State Univ of

New York, Binghamton, NY 13901, 607-798-2319. Poetry. "Richard Eberhart, Denise Levertov, David Ignatow, George Keithley, Joseph Bruchac, Douglas Blazek, Charles Levendosky, Sam Hamill, G. Wilson Knight, and others." 1974. 65pp; 5½ x 8½. of/lp. avg. press run 500. Reporting time: 1-2 weeks. Payment: 10 percent of sales. Copyright is author's. Discounts: 20-40 percent. CCLM, COSMEP, Associated Writing Programs.

ISLANDS, A New Zealand Quarterly of Arts & Letters, Islands, Robin Dudding, 4 Sealy Road, Torbay, Auckland 10, New Zealand. Poetry, fiction, articles, art, photos, cartoons, interviews, satire, criticism, reviews, music, letters, parts-of-novels, long-poems, collages, plays, concrete art. "Basically New Zealand-related material." 4/yr; 1-yr sub price: $8.00 (NZ)-$10.00 (NZ) overseas; per copy: $2.10 (NZ)- $2.60 (NZ) overseas. 1972. 112pp; 8½ x 6. of/lp. circ. 2,000. Reporting time: A.S.A.P. Payment: No set rate. Ads: $40(NZ)/$18(NZ). Discounts: 33-1/3% trade 2 or more copies 25% single copies. Back issues: First 5 vols available. Pub'd 4 issues 1976; expects 4 issues 1977, 4 issues 1978. Pub's reviews.

ISTHMUS, Isthmus Poetry Foundation, Pablo Satora, J.R. Willems, PO Box 6877, San Francisco, CA 94101, 415-668-5605. "Third world literature also black improvisational music, Marxist culture." 1/yr; sub price: $10.00 Instit; $6.00 private (3 copies); per copy: $2.50; sample: $2.50. 1971. 150pp; Stnd book size. of. circ. 500. Reporting time: 3-4 months. Payment: None. Copyrighted. Ads: None. Discounts: To bookstores 40 percent. Back issues: Not for 1 or 5, all others $2.50. Pub'd 1 issue 1976; expects 2 issues 1977, 1 issue 1978. Pub's reviews: several in 1976. §Politics, Third world culture. CCLM, COSMEP, TDS.

IT COMES IN THE MAIL, Purple Mouth Press, Cuyler Warnell "Ned" Brooks Jr., 713 Paul Street, Newport News, VA 23605. Art, cartoons. "I write the contents myself, only outside material is the cover art." 2/yr. 1972. 18pp; 8½ x 11. circ. 200-250. Reporting time: a week. Payment: free copy. Back issues: trade. Pub's reviews. §science fiction/fantasy/fantasy art/science fiction reference.

Ithaca House, Baxter Hathaway, Lynn Shoemaker, Joseph Freedman, 108 N. Plain St, Ithaca, NY 14850, 607-272-1233. Poetry, fiction. "High-quality work, no trend or style or philosophy excluded." avg. price, paper: $3.50. 1970. 64pp; 6 x 9. †of/lp. avg. press run 500. Reporting time: 3 months. Payment: 10 copies. Discounts: 1, 10 percent; 2-4, 20 percent; 5 or more, 40 percent. Pub'd 9 titles 1976; expects 9 titles 1977, 9 titles 1978. COSMEP.

Ithaca Press, Charles E. Jarvis, Paul Jarvis, P.O. Box 853, Lowell, MA 01853. *"Visions of Kerouac; The Life of Jack Kerouac,* by Charles E. Jarvis. *Zeus Has Two Urns,* by Charles E. Jarvis." of. Pub'd 1 title 1976; expects 1 title 1977. COSMEP, NESPA.

J

J&A Publications (see INVICTUS)

J&C Transcripts (see also DRAGONFLY), Box 15, Kanona, NY 14856.

J and J House, Carl Hackerman, P.O. Box 15019, Baltimore, MD 21209. Poetry. 1975. of.

J and J Printing (see WOMEN STUDIES ABSTRACTS)

J. Buchs Publications, June Buchs, 5301 Richmond, 24B, Houston, TX 77056. 1975. of.

J. Mark Press (see ALL-TIME FAVORITE POETRY, BEST IN POETRY, NATIONAL BOOK REVIEW, POETIPS, SUNSHINE)

J STONE PRESS WEEKLY, The Stone Press, G.P. Skratz, 5399½ Bryant, Oakland, CA 94618. "This here's a weekly postcard series featuring Jerome Rothenberg, Bobbie Louise Hawkins, Allen

Ginsberg, Robert Creeley, Diane Kruchkow, Ed Dorn, Liz Zima, John Giorno, Andrei Codrescu & lots of other fine people. Unfortunately, tho, I'm so full up with poems to print that I can't take any more unsolicited manuscripts for a while. But dig: ask for a free sample. I'll bet you'll dig it. Maybe even subscribe." 52/yr; 1-yr sub price: $10.00; sample: free. 1974. 1pp; 4 x 6. †of/lp. Payment: lots of copies. Discounts: 40%. §poetry. COSMEP.

JABBERWOCKY, Mary S. Johnston, 530 Lakeshore Rd, Sarnia, Ontario M4Y1R6, Canada, 336-2143. Poetry, fiction. "Children's literature only-length 1,500 words max." 4/yr; 1-yr sub price: $6.00; per copy: $1.50; sample: $1.50. 1974. 28pp; 8 x 11. of. circ. 500. Reporting time: 6 months max. Payment: $5.00 plus contributor copy. Not copyrighted. no advertising. Discounts: none. Back issues: not generally available. Pub'd 4 issues 1976.

The Jacek Publishing Company, Mike F. Holodnak, Author, 38 Morris Lane, Milford, CT 06460, 203-874-4544. Articles. "Has pub'd a selection of some of Holodnak's best *Brass Tacks* columns published in modern times from 1971 to 1976." avg. price, cloth: $1.50; paper: $1.50. 1976. 47pp; 6 x 9. of. avg. press run 1,000. Copyrights for author. Discounts: 40 percent bulk, jobber, classroom. Pub'd 1 title 1976; expects 1 title 1977. COSMEP, ASW (am. society of writers).

The Jackpine Press, A.R. Ammons, Gen. Ed.; Emily Wilson, Isabel Zuber, Betty Leighton, Ed. Board, 3381 Timberlake Lane, Winston-Salem, NC 21706. Poetry. "1st book: *Balancing On Stones,* poems by Emily Wilson. 2nd book: *Out In The Country, Back Home,* poems by Jeff Daniel Marion. *Orion,* poem by Jerald Bullis. *Sidetracks,* poems by Clint McCown." avg. price, cloth: $6.95; paper: $3.95. 1975. 50pp; 7 x 9. of. avg. press run 1,000-1,500. Reporting time: 2-3 months. Copyright by author. Pub'd 2 titles 1976. COSMEP.

JACKSONVILLE POETRY QUARTERLY: Proclamations of the Arcane Order, Arcane Order, John Sulik, General Editor; William H. Cohen, Poetry Editor, 5340 Weller Ave., Jacksonville, FL 32211, 904-724-4185. Poetry, articles, art, satire. "We publish only material by members: Steve Lotz, Thomas Charles Chimes, Elihu Edelson, Elizabeth Hunter." 2-4/yr. 1950. 2-10pp; 8½ x 11. †mi/of. circ. Over 1,010 members. We publish only material by members. No payment. Not copyrighted. no advertising. Discounts: Distributed gratis to members. Back issues: Available to members at $1.00 to $2.00. §Poetry, art, satire.

J'ADOUBE!, Cincinnati Chess Federation, David Moeser, P O Box 30072, Cincinnati, OH 45230, 513-232-3204. Articles, art, photos, cartoons, interviews, satire, criticism, reviews, letters. 9/yr; 1-yr sub price: $4.00; per copy: $0.50; sample: $0.50. 1972. 30pp; 8½ x 11. †mi. circ. 350. Reporting time: Variable. Payment: none-generally. Copyrighted, reverts to author. Ads: $12.00/$7.00/$0.03. Discounts: none. Back issues: not available. Pub's reviews. §Chess. COSMEP.

Jalmar Press, Inc., John Dickinson Adams, Editor-in-Chief, 391 Munroe Street, P. O. Box 255038, Sacramento, CA 95825, 916-481-1134. "Primarily interested in works dealing with Transactional Analysis. Have two series: *Transactional Analysis For Everybody, Warm Fuzzy Series* vol. 1. Recent contributions: Claude Steiner, *A Warm Fuzzy Tale;* Dennis Look, *Joy Of Backpacking: People's Guide To The Wilderness;* Margaret DeHaan Freed, *A Time To Teach, A Time To Dance.* Vol. 1 Warm Fuzzy Series for children - average length, 60 pages with illustrations." avg. price, paper: $5.00. 1973. 200pp; 8 x 11. of. avg. press run 25,000. Reporting time: 2½ weeks. Payment: 4 percent - 12 percent. Copyrights for author. Discounts: yes. COSMEP, WPA.

JAM TO-DAY, Don Stanford, Judith Stanford, Floyd Stuart, P.O. Box 249, Northfield, VT 05663. Poetry, art. "Interested in any style of poetry from traditional to avant garde." 1-2/yr; sub price: $2.75/2 issues; per copy: $1.50; sample: $1.50. 1973. 48pp; 5½ x 8½. of. circ. 300. Reporting time: 3-6 weeks. Payment: $5.00/poem plus 2 copies of mag. Copyrighted. Ads: $30.00/$20.00. Discounts: 40% to bookstores. Back issues: $1.50. Pub'd 1 issue 1976; expects 1 issue 1977, 2 issues 1978. Pub's reviews: 1 in 1976. §poetry. CCLM, NESPA.

JAMES JOYCE QUARTERLY, Thomas F. Staley, University of Tulsa, 600 S. College, Tulsa, OK 74104. Articles, criticism, reviews. "Academic criticism of Joyce's works and of his critics:

book reviews, notes, bibliographies; material relating to Joyce and Irish Renaissance and Joyce's relationship to other writers of his time. Articles should not normally exceed 20 pp. Notes should not excceed 6 pp. Please consult MLA *Style Sheet* and 'Special Note to Contributors' which appears on p.2 of each issue of the *JJQ* regarding style & preparation of manuscript." 4/yr; 1-yr sub price: $7.00; per copy: $2.25-U.S., $2.50-Foreign; sample: $2.25. 1963. 120pp; 6 x 9. of. circ. 1,200. Reporting time: 6-12 weeks. Payment: contributors' copies & offprints. Ads: $100.00 ($135 includes copy of *JJQ* subscription list on set of self-adhesive address labels)/$60.00. Back issues: $2.25. Pub's reviews. §Joyce studies.

‡**Janus Press,** Claire Van Vliet, Rt #2, West Burke, VT 05871.

LE JARDIN DU MONDE: The Journal of International Casafundada, Casafundada, P.O. Box 5385, Seattle, WA 98105. Poetry, fiction, articles, art, photos, interviews, criticism, reviews, music, letters, parts-of-novels, long-poems, collages, plays, concrete art. "Casafundada is pan-historic and post-historic: the final step to plateau: the discovery of ourselves. It believes that all myth is an impediment to this discovery, and that beauty—the projection of the human towards the non-human—is the measure of all things. Its journal is concerned with the selfless aspiration to beauty in all areas of existence. There are no other restrictions on materials received." 2/yr; 1-yr sub price: $4.00; per copy: $2.25; sample: $2.00. 1976. Varies. †of. Reporting time: 4 weeks max. Payment: copies. Ads: $50.00/$35.00. Discounts: 10%, five copies and above. Expects 2 issues 1977, 2 issues 1978. Pub's reviews. §all verbal, pictorial, plastic arts, music, drama, dance, film, criticism, and the history of criticism and the arts.

JAWBONE, Jawbone Press, Samuel Green, Editor; Sara Birtch, Assistant Editor, 17023 5th Avenue NE, Seattle, WA 98155. Poetry, articles, interviews, criticism, reviews, letters, long-poems. "No restrictions: All varieties of poetry will be considered. Recent contributors include: John Hurd, Frank Maloney, Duane Niatum, Joseph Bruchac, Beth Bentley, Dan Masterson, Peter Nicoletta, Lyn Lifshin, and others." Uncertain.; price per copy: $1.50; sample: $0.50. 1975. 35pp; 5½ x 8½. of. circ. 300. Reporting time: immediately. Payment: copies. Pub'd 1 issue 1976. Pub's reviews. §poetry only. COSMEP.

JEFFERSONIAN REVIEW, Frank Conneen III, PO Box 3864, Charlottesville, VA 22903. "Have been suffering from financial doldrums and do not expect to publish anything in the near to distant future. Currently returning all mss." CCLM.

JEOPARDY, Western Washington State University, Fay Jewell, Humanities 362 W.W.S.C., Bellingham, WA 98225. Poetry, fiction, art, photos, long-poems. "1) prefer poetry of no more than 3 single spaced, legal-paper pages in length. 2) prefer stories of no more than 10 single spaced, legal-paper pages in length. 3) open to nearly any style, with the possible bias against Haiku. 4) recent well known contributors: William Stafford, James Bertolino, Ron Bayes, Daniel Halpern, Joyce Odam, Madeline DeFrees, and Richard Hugo." 1/yr; 1-yr sub price: $1.00; per copy: $1.00; sample: free. 1966. 120pp; varies. of. circ. 2,500. Reporting time: as long as 4 months. Payment: none. Back issues: $1.00. CCLM, COSMEP.

JOHN BERRYMAN STUDIES, Rook Press, Inc., Ernest Stefanik, Cis Stefanik, Richard J. Kelly, Gary Q. Arpin, Contributing Editors, 805 West First Avenue, Derry, PA 15627. Poetry, articles. "JOHN BERRYMAN STUDIES is a quarterly journal devoted to critical works on John Berryman and other middle-generation American poets (Roethke, Jarrell, Schwartz, etc.). We feature annual symposia on individual poems and regular primary and secondary bibliographical updates. Recent contributors include Jack Barbera, Jo Brans, John Haffenden, Ann Hayes, J.M. Linebarger, Charles Molesworth, Sergio Perosa, Peter Stitt, Larry Vonalt, Linda Wagner, Ann Warner. We publish a few poems, usually by invitation. Recent contributors include Michael Dennis Browne, Margaret Carney, Mark Halperin, Samuel Hazo, William Heyen, Delora Shaw, William Stafford. We also publish occasional supplements of prose or poetry." 4/yr; 1-yr sub price: $5.00; per copy: $1.50; sample: $1.50. 1975. 40-64pp; 8½ x 7. of. circ. 300. Reporting time: 3-6 weeks. Payment: 2 copies additional copies 50¢ prior to pub. Ads: $40/$20/n/a. Discounts: 10% agencies/40% bookstores. Back issues: $1.50. Pub's reviews.

John Muir Publications, Ken Luboff, Barbara Luboff, P.O. Box 613, Santa Fe, NM 87501, 505-982-1387. Non-fiction. avg. price, paper: $6.00. 1969. of. avg. press run 5,000-10,000. Reporting time: 4-6 weeks. Payment: by individual contract. Copyrights for author. Discounts: 50 percent. Pub'd 1 title 1976; expects 1 title 1977. COSMEP.

John Parke Custis Press, David L. Chapman, 875 Fifth Avenue, Los Angeles, CA 90005. "The JPC Press is interested in publishing short, richly bound, limited editions of unusual or rare works especially dealing with late nineteenth century English literature." 1974. of.

"JOINT" CONFERENCE, King Publications, Kathryn E. King, P.O. Box 19332, Washington, DC 20036. Poetry, fiction, articles, art, cartoons. "This is an inmate-written literary magazine and I accept material *ONLY* from inmates. I'd like to receive more work by women. There will be a short story contest in 1977. Recent contributors: David L. Rice, Carl L. Harp, Michael Hogan, Daniel L. Klauck, and John P. Minarik." 4/yr; 1-yr sub price: $4.00 $2.00 for inmates; per copy: $1.50; sample: $1.00. 1974. 60-64pp; 6 x 9. of. circ. 250. Reporting time: 4-6 weeks. Payment: $3.00-$30.00 plus copy. Copyrighted, reverts to author upon request. Discounts: 40% to libraries and bookstores. Back issues: $1.50. Pub'd 3 issues 1976; expects 4 issues 1977, 4 issues 1978. CCLM, COSMEP, COSMEP-SOUTH.

Jones Press (see CARLETON MISCELLANY)

JOURNAL OF CALIFORNIA ANTHROPOLOGY, Malki Museum Press, Philip Wilke, Editor; Harry W. Lawton, Managing Editor; Michael Kearney, Assistant Editor, Business Offices Malki Museum, Inc., 11-795 Fields Road Morongo Indian, Banning, CA 92220, 714-787-3885 or 787-3346. Articles. "Papers on ethnology, ethnohistory, archaeology, and linquistics of the Native Americans of California and Baja California. Editorial offices for manuscripts is in care of the Department of Anthropology, University of California, Riverside, California 92521. If you can only use one address use this one. The business address above is for the publisher, Malki Museum, Inc., a non-profit educational institution on the Morongo Indian Reservation. The journal is published by Malki Museum Press in cooperation with the Department of Anthropology at the University of California, Riverside. Renewals or new subscriptions by individuals after March 1 of any year are billed at 2 rate of $10.00." 2/yr; 1-yr sub price: $7.50 Individual - $12.00 Institutions up to March 1.; per copy: $5.00; sample: $5.00. 1974. 144pp; 8½ x 11. of. circ. 800. Reporting time: 2 months. Payment: none. Copyrighted, rights revert to author where authorized by the Editorial Board. Ads: $150/$75. Discounts: None. Back issues: $5.00 plus postage. Pub'd 2 issues 1976; expects 2 issues 1977, 2 issues 1978. Pub's reviews: 26 in 1976. §only books on California Indians (or mags).

JOURNAL OF CANADIAN FICTION, Bellrock Press, John R. Sorfleet, Managing Ed.; D. Arnason, J. Moss, Box 338, Guelph, Ontario N1H 6K6, Canada. Fiction, criticism, reviews. "*Primary* focus is *Canadian* fiction & criticism & reviews thereof." 4/yr; 1-yr sub price: $11.00 plus $2.00 postage outside Canada; per copy: $2.95 plus $0.50 postage outside Canada; sample: $2.95 plus $0.50 postage outside Canada. 1972. 200pp; 5 x 8. of. circ. 1,500. Reporting time: 3-6 months. Payment: $100.00/stories, $10.00/reviews. Ads: $75/$50. Discounts: 10% to agencies. Pub'd 4 issues 1976; expects 4 issues 1977, 4 issues 1978. Pub's reviews: 28 in 1976. §Fiction, criticism of fiction writers. CPPA.

JOURNAL of CANADIAN STUDIES, Trent University, Ralph R. Heintzman, Trent Univ., Peterborough, Ont., Canada. Articles, criticism, reviews. 4/yr; 1-yr sub price: $6.00, individuals/yr; $10.00, institution; per copy: $2.50. 1966. 64pp; 7½ x 10¼. of. circ. 1,600. Ads: $100/$60. Discounts: 30%. Back issues: $2.50 issue.

JOURNAL OF THE HELLENIC DIASPORA, The Wire Press, Nikos Petropoulos, Dino Siotis, P.O. Box 22334, Indianapolis, IN 46222. Poetry, fiction, articles, art, photos, cartoons, interviews, satire, criticism, reviews, music, letters, parts-of-novels, long-poems, news items, non-fiction. "Alternative content." 4/yr; 1-yr sub price: Institutional $15.00; Regular $10.00; Low income students $5.00; Foreign add $3.00 to above.; per copy: $1.50; sample: $1.00. 1973. 80pp; 5½ x 8½. †of. circ. 1,000. Reporting time: 2-3 months. Payment: None. Ads: Varies, negotiable. Discounts:

none. Back issues: At cost for individuals, negotiable for institutions. Pub'd 4 issues 1976; expects 4 issues 1977, 4 issues 1978. Pub's reviews: 7-8 in 1976.

JOURNAL OF MODERN LITERATURE, Maurice Beebe, Temple Univ., Philadelphia, PA 19122. Articles, interviews, criticism, reviews. 4/yr; 1-yr sub price: $8.00. 1970. 160pp; 7 x 10. of. circ. 2,200. Reporting time: 6 wks. Payment: $100 articles. no ads. COSMEP.

JOURNAL OF NARRATIVE TECHNIQUE, George Perkins, English Dept, Eastern Michigan University, Ypsilanti, MI 48197. Criticism. "JNT is a scholarly magazine with a small international circulation. Essays run generally from 15 to 30 typed pages. Contributors should follow MLA style." 3/yr; 1-yr sub price: $6.00; per copy: $2.00; sample: free. 1970. 65pp; 6 x 9. of. Reporting time: 1-4 mos. Payment: copies only. Back issues: $1.00.

JOURNAL OF NEW JERSEY POETS, W. Cummins, A. Decavalles, V. Halpert, M. Keyishian, W Zander, Fairleigh Dickinson Univ., English Dept., Madison, NJ 07940, 01-377-4700. Poetry. "Open to submission of poetry from present and past residents of New Jersey; no biases concerning style or subject." 3/yr; 1-yr sub price: $3.00; per copy: $1.00; sample: $1.00. 1976. 40pp; 8½ x 11. †of. circ. 500. Reporting time: 1-4 months. Payment: 2 copies. Copyrighted, reverts to author. Discounts: 40 percent. Pub'd 2 issues 1976; expects 4 issues 1977, 3 issues 1978.

THE JOURNAL of PSYCHOHISTORY, Psychohistory Press, Lloyd DeMause, Editor, 2315 Broadway, NY, NY 10024. Articles, reviews. "Psychohistory of individuals and groups, history of childhood and family." 4/yr; 1-yr sub price: $16.00/individual $22.00 organization; per copy: $4.00; sample: $4.00. 1973. 150pp; 7 x 9. of. circ. 3000. Reporting time: 2 weeks. Payment: none. Ads: $150/$90. Discounts: 10% agency. Pub's reviews. §psychology & history.

JOURNAL OF SOUTH ASIAN LITERATURE, Asian Studies Center, Carlo Coppola, Surjit Dulai, C. M. Haim, Mich State Univ, Asian Studies Ctr., E. Lansing, MI 48823. Poetry, fiction, articles, interviews, satire, criticism, reviews, parts-of-novels, long-poems, plays. 4/yr; 1-yr sub price: $10.00; per copy: $2.50-$5.00. 1964. 200-400pp, 8½ x 11. †of. circ. 300. Reporting time: 2 wks. Back issues: $2.50 $5.00. Pub's reviews. §South Asian. CCLM.

JOURNAL OF WORLD EDUCATION, Leah R. Karpen, 3 Harbor Hill Dr, Huntington, NY 11743, 516-427-0723. Poetry, articles, art, photos, cartoons, reviews, letters. "Articles must be related to cross cultural education, world view in education, or world problems. Recent contributors: Harold Taylor, Eric Hecksher, Marc Schreiber, Rene V. L. Wadlow, students." 4/yr; 1-yr sub price: $15 membership; $10 libraries; $7 students; sample: $1.00 plus postage. 1970. 16pp; 8½ x 11. of. circ. 4,000-5,000. Reporting time: 3-4 weeks. No payment. U.S. copyright-each issue. Ads: $200.00/$100.00/$5.00-3 lines. Back issues: $1.00. Expects 4 issues 1977, 4 issues 1978. Pub's reviews: 23 in 1976. §Cross-cultural education, cross-cultural experiences, educational innovations, world problems; especially interested in material by non-Americans. COSMEP, EDPRESS, ICIE.

Journalism Laboratory Press (see SHENANDOAH)

Joyful World Press, Gina Allen, 468 Belvedere Street, San Francisco, CA 94117, 415-566-2787. Fiction, art, photos. "We do not solicit manuscripts." avg. price, paper: $2.95. 1971. 24 pp plus cover; 8½ x 11. of. avg. press run 3,000. We write our own material.

Judaic Book Service (see HOLY BEGGARS' GAZETTE, TZADDIKIM)

JUICE, Juice Press, Stephen Morse, Judy Brekke, 5402 Ygnacio, Oakland, CA 94601, 415-532-5621. Poetry, fiction, art, photos, cartoons, interviews, satire, criticism, reviews, music, parts-of-novels, long-poems, plays. "No length limits. Recent issues have been primarily poetry & fiction, but we're open. Tend to like poetry as written and influenced by R. Creeley, R. Bly, James Tate, W. S. Merwin, T. Roethke, C. Simic, etc., mostly contemporary and suspicious of verse. Recent contributors: Gary Ligi, Glee Knight, Ron Koertge, Emilie Glen, Patrick White, Susan Fromberg Schaeffer, Hugh Fox, Nellie Hill, Blazek. Looking for poetry with energy, not overly fond of doom/gloom political poems, though quality anything has a good chance at Juice. New people welcome—We don't even look at the name 'til we've read the submission." 2/yr; 1-yr sub price: $4.00; per copy: $2.35; sample: $1.00. 1970. 48pp; Varies. of. circ. 900. Reporting time: 4 weeks. Payment: 2 copies. Copyrighted. Discounts: 40% classrooms or orders of 10 or more. Back issues: $1.50 except Juice 1, 1975 which is $5.00. Pub'd 2 issues 1976; expects 2 issues 1977, 2 issues 1978. Pub's reviews. §Poetry, fiction, art. CCLM, COSMEP, COSMEP-WEST.

Jules Verne Circle (see also JULES VERNE VOYAGER), F. James, Editor, 125 Markyate Road, Dagenham, Essex RM82LB, England. Poetry, fiction, articles, art, photos, cartoons, interviews, satire, criticism, reviews, music, letters, parts-of-novels, long-poems, collages, plays, concrete art, news items, non-fiction. avg. price, paper: $5.00. 1977/78. 10pp; A5. †of. avg. press run 100. Reporting time: 6 months. Pays in copies. Copyrights for author. Discounts: Agents 20 percent.

JULES VERNE VOYAGER, Jules Verne Circle, F. James, Editor, 125 Markyate Road, Dagenham, Essex RM82LB, England. Poetry, fiction, articles, art, photos, cartoons, interviews, satire, criticism, reviews, music, letters, parts-of-novels, long-poems, collages, plays, concrete art, news items, non-fiction. "Research and scholarship on and about Verne and his life works, times, contemporaries, influences, inc SF." 2/3 pa/yr; 1-yr sub price: $5.00 pa. 1977/78. 10pp; A5 upright. †of. circ. 100. Reporting time: 6 months. Pays in copies. Copyrighted. Ads: $15.00 pro rata. Discounts: Agents 20 percent. Pub's reviews

JUMP CUT, A Review of Contemporary Cinema, John Hess, Chuck Kleinhans, P.O. Box 865, Berkeley, CA 94701. Articles, art, photos, cartoons, interviews, criticism, reviews, letters. "Interested in commercial and independent film since 1970. Length as needed to make points, but shorter preferred; we strive for clarity in style. Biased to radical criticism, esp. Marxist and feminist. No cute and superficial reviews. Strongly suggest reading an issue before submission. Send sase for 'Notice to Writers'." irreg.; 1-yr sub price: $4.00-Canada & abroad $5.00; per copy: $0.75; Canada & abroad $1.00; sample: $0.75; Canada & abroad $1.00. 1974. 28-36pp; 16½ x 10¼. of. circ. 4,000. Reporting time: 3 wks-3 mos. Payment: copies. Contributor may retain c-right. Ads: $100.00/$50.00. Discounts: Institutional rate is $7.00; Canada & abroad $8.00; Agency discount is 10 percent. Back issues: Nos. 1 & 2 sold out. $1.00 ($0.75 with a sub); Canada & abroad $1.25 ($1.00 with sub). Also they are available from [Xerox International Microfilm]. Pub'd 4 issues 1976; expects 4 issues 1977, 4 issues 1978. Pub's reviews: 43 in 1976. §On the subjects of film and marxist culture and criticism. COSMEP.

Jungle Garden Press, Marie C. Dern, 47 Oak Rd, Fairfax, CA 94930. Poetry, art. "Susan Efros, *TWO-WAY STREETS/* Jana Harris, *THIS HOUSE THAT ROCKS WITH EVERY TRUCK ON THE ROAD"* 1973. 30-40pp. †lp. avg. press run 500. Expects 1 title 1977. COSMEP.

Juniper Press (see NORTHEAST/JUNIPER BOOKS)

K

K-State Press (see also EDUCATIONAL CONSIDERATIONS), Charles Litz, Mary Kahl Sparks, College of Education, K.S.U., Manhattan, KS 66506, 913-532-5533. Articles. "Current issues in educational theory, practice and administration. Also moral issues in education. Walter Mathews, *'Homosexuality: Out Of The Educational Closet'*. Jonathan Levine, *'Politics and Education'."* avg. price, cloth: $4.00; paper: $1.50; other: Free. 1973. 26-30pp; 21½ cm x 28 cm. †of. avg. press run 1,200. Reporting time: 4-8 weeks. No payment. Does not copyright for author. Discounts: Fifty cents off $4.00 p.a. subscription for institutions if requested. Pub'd 3 titles 1976; expects 3 titles 1977, 3 titles 1978. EPAA.

KALDRON, Rainbow Resin Press, Karl Kempton, 441 North 6th St., Grover City, CA 93433, 805-481-2360. Poetry, art, reviews, long-poems, collages. "To borrow from kandinsky—there iz a floo from the poet/artist to the reeder/vuuer: emotion-sensation-work-sensation-emotion. hence, the work must kontain, az fokal point, one hell of a charj to tranzfer that emotion-sensation thru to reeder/vuuer. otherwize, the work will have a tendencee to kreate negativ space, pollution. each issue featurez at leest one poet with a 2 page spred; featured poets/vizual poets thus far: Will Inman, D. R. Wagner, James Minor, Michael Hannon, Charles Doria, Loris Essary, Morgan Nyberg. other poets/vizual poets given much space: Howard McCord, Charles Potts, Michael Bell, Kirk Robertson, Robert Head, Len Roberts. being a free tabloid, *KALDRON* iz an xampl of free enterprize. enkourij xchanj." sample price: kost of a 3rd klass stamp. 1976. 12pp; 11 x 17. of. circ. 1,000. Reporting time: 1-14 days. Payment: 10-20 kopeez. Copyrights belong to kontributor. Pub'd 1 issue 1976; expects 4 issues 1977, 3 issues 1978. People against nuclear power.

The Kanchenjunga Press (San Francisco & Vancouver), Miki Sheffield, Managing Editor, 22 Rio Vista Lane, Red Bluff, CA 96080. Poetry, fiction, criticism, long-poems. "Bi-National Press (U.S. & Canada); also U.S. distributor for the Sono Nis Press of Victoria B.C. publications include books, chapbooks and broadsides, usually in limited editions. Please do not send unsolicited manuscripts." avg. price, cloth: $10.00-$15.00; paper: $4.00-$5.00. 1972. of/lp. avg. press run 500-2,000. Payment: standard royalties. Discounts: trade discount: single-copy 25%; multiple orders 40%.

KANSAS QUARTERLY, Harold W. Schneider, Ben Nyberg, Denison Hall, Kansas St. Univ., Manhattan, KS 66506, 913-532-6716. Poetry, fiction, art, criticism. "We prefer excellent fiction and poetry, aimed at an adult audience. We have no preference between what might be termed classic or experimental, but we have no interest in either for its own sake. We do special numbers in literary criticism, art, and history, but contributors should note special announced topics before submitting. Recent contributors: Joyce Carol Oates, Jim Heynen, Greg Kuzma, James Hashim, Stephen Dixon, Jerry Bumpus, Jesse Stuart, Jay Meek, Dan Curzon, Rodney Nelson, etal." 4/yr; 1-yr sub price: $7.50; per copy: $2.50; sample: $2.50. 1968. 128pp; 5 x 8. of. circ. 1,000. Reporting time: 2 to 6 months. Payment: 2 subscription copies-and yearly awards to short fiction & poetry (two each). $300.00/$150.00; $200.00/$100.00. Copyright held by K.Q. Ads: $100/$55. Discounts: 10 percent to subscription agencies, 40 percent to bookstores with regular accounts (on consignment). Back issues: $2.50 each. Pub'd 4 issues 1976; expects 4 issues 1977, 4 issues 1978. CCLM, KAC.

Kanthaka Press, Alex Jack, Ann Fawcett, P.O. Box 696, Brookline Village, MA 02147, 617-734-8146. "Publishers of *The Adamantine Sherlock Holmes: The Adventures in Tibet & India* by Hapi, *Shanti, the Game of Lasting Peace,* and *The New Age Dictionary*." 1973. of. Discounts: 40 percent. Pub'd 1 title 1976; expects 1 title 1977, 1 title 1978. COSMEP.

KARAKI, Ken Fernstrom, Ed.; David Clarke, Design; Wendy Burton, Contributing Editor, Box 1900, Victoria, BC V8W2Y3, Canada, 604-931-5417. Poetry, fiction, articles, art, cartoons, satire, reviews, letters, parts-of-novels, plays, interviews, concrete art. "We are slow. If you have submitted the same material to other mags than don't bother to submit it to us as we don't want to get into silly copyright problems. We don't care about length but we do mind having 35 or 100 poems sent to us. And no xeroxs. Would like to see plays (preferably produced), short stories and translations. As far as biases i guess we go for surrealism and wit coupled with intelligence. If you're impotent, had a bad love affair or a bad trip of any sort we don't particularly want to hear about it. Read editorial in #5. Recent contributors: Bryan Wade, Colin Partridge, Marco Fraticelli, Eugene McNamara, Leslie Fernstrom, Christopher Heide, etc." irreg.; price per copy: $2.95; sample: $1.50 min. 1971. 52pp; 8½ x 5½. of. circ. 250. Reporting time: Long. Payment: 2 copies. Copyrighted. Ads: Exchange. Expects 2 issues 1977, 2 issues 1978. Pub's reviews. §The usual arty regions, but most especially collections of short stories or plays.

KARAMU, Allen Neff, Editor; Carol Elder, Poetry Editor; Ray Schmudde, Fiction Editor, English Dept, Eastern Illinois Univ., Charleston, IL 61920, 217-581-5013. Poetry, fiction, articles. "Prefer articles on very contemporary literature (after 1960) will look at experimental stories (2,000-8,000 words) but prefer stories with beginning, middle and end. Enjoy traditional poems but prefer poems that are a fresh act of language, that wake up the eye." 1/yr; 1-yr sub price: $1.50; per copy: $1.50; sample: $1.50. 1967. 76pp; 9 x 6. of. circ. 300. Reporting time: 3 mos. Payment: 2 copies. Copyrighted, reverts to author. Back issues: $1.00. Pub'd 1 issue 1976; expects 1-2 issues 1977, 1 issue 1978.

KAYAK, Kayak Press, George Hitchcock, 325 Ocean View, Santa Cruz, CA 95062. Poetry, criticism. 3-4/yr; 1-yr sub price: $4.00; per copy: $1.00; sample: $1.00. 1964. 70pp; 5½ x 8½. †of. circ. 1,400. Reporting time: 2 wks. Ads: $40/$20. Back issues: $2.00 ea. Pub's reviews CCLM.

KEEPSAKE POEMS, Keepsake Press, R. Lewis, S. Toulson, 26 Sydney Road, Richmond, Surrey TW9 UEB, United Kingdom, 01 940 9364. Poetry, art, cartoons, satire, long-poems, plays. "We publish books rather than a magazine. KEEPSAKE POEMS are a series of single poems but are only one of our interests. But we dislike unpoetry by non-communicators." irreg.; 1-yr sub price: varies; per copy: $1.00; sample: $1.00. 1957. 4-50pp; varies. †various methods. circ. 200-300. Reporting time: 3 weeks. Payment: by agreement if any. Buys first serial rights. Discounts: 33% to bookseller. Back issues: when available. Pub'd 6 issues 1976; expects 6 issues 1977. ALP.

Kelsey St. Press, Patricia Dienstfrey, Kit Duane, Karen Brodine, Rena Rosenwasser, Marina LaPalma, 2824 Kelsey St., Berkeley, CA 94705, 841-2044. Poetry, art. "We don't like submissions through the mail. Don't have time to read so much. We are particularly interested in work by women and are doing a letter press series of translations of women writers. In Summer of 1976 published *Hair-Raising,* a book of poems and graphics about hair. In the Fall of 1976 we published *Making The Park,* a letterpress edition of poetry with an introduction by Susan Griffin, as well as a children's book, *A Girl Named Hero,* by Kit Duane, who uses rubber stamps in the illustrations. Nellie Wong's book, *Dreams In Harrison Railroad Park,* and Karen Brodine's *Workweek* are available now, both offset." avg. price, paper: $3.00. 1975. 48pp; 5 x 7, 9. †of/lp. avg. press run 350, letterpress, 750 offset. Reporting time: 1 month. Payment: In copies. Copyright retained by author unless otherwise agreed. Pub'd 3 titles 1976; expects 3 titles 1977, 2 titles 1978.

Kent Publications, Kent School, Richard Cloke, Lori C. Smith, 18301 Halsted St, Northridge, CA 91324, 213-349-5088. Fiction. "Richard Cloke-Mister Pistol-John; Vegtor-Lee." avg. price, cloth: $1.95-$3.50; paper: $1.75. 1976. 200pp; 5½ x 8½; 6 x 9. Instant Press. avg. press run 1,000. Reporting time: Faculty or students only—immediate. Payment: 50 percent to author as received. Copyrights for author. Discounts: jobber-50 percent; trade-40 percent; lib., colleges-25 percent. Pub'd 1 title 1976; expects 1 title 1977, 1 title 1978. COSMEP.

KENTUCKY FOLKLORE RECORD, Kentucky Folklore Society, Charles S. Guthrie, Box u-169, Western Ky. University, Bowling Green, KY 42101, 502-745-3043. "No fiction or original poetry used. Articles should be about the folklore (in the widest sense of the word) of Kentucky and surrounding areas. Some pictures. Articles up to 12 double-spaced pages. Use MLA Style Sheet and a sample copy of KFR to get proper format ready for typesetting." 4/yr; 1-yr sub price: $4.00, foreign add 1.50 postage; per copy: $1.50; sample: $0.30 (stamps) for postage. 1955. 28pp; 5-7/8 x 8¾. of. circ. 400. Reporting time: 4 wks. Payment: 3 copies. All rights reserved. Discounts: 25% to agents. Back issues: $4.00 per volume plus postage. Single copies, $1.50 postpaid. Pub'd 3 issues 1976; expects 4 issues 1977, 4 issues 1978. Pub's reviews. §All areas of folklore and folklife.

KENTUCKY FOLKLORE SERIES, Kentucky Folklore Society, Charles S. Guthrie, Box U-169, Western Ky. Univ., Bowling Green, KY 42101, 502-745-3043. "Folklore material of 50 typed pages up to 100 pages." irreg. 1964. 6 x 9. of. circ. 150-200. Reporting time: 4-8 wks. Payment: copies only. All rights reserved.

Keyboard Players International (see CONTEMPORARY KEYBOARD MAGAZINE)

Killaly Press (see STUFFED CROCODILE)

King Publications (see "JOINT" CONFERENCE)

Kitchen Harvest, Sue Anderson Gross, Sidney A. Gross, 3N 681 Bittersweet Drive, St. Charles, IL 60174, 312-584-4084. "Cookbooklets: Sourdough Rye and Other Good Breads; The Honey Book; Holiday Baking; Bagels, Bagels, Bagels; The Early Spring Garden Book; Fruit Flavored Yogurt & More; The Roll Basket; Old World Breads." avg. price, paper: $2.50. 1973. 16-40pp; 5-1/8 x 8½. †mi/of. avg. press run 1,000. All material copyrighted. Discounts: 1-4 copies, 20 percent; 5 or more copies, 40 percent. Pub'd 1 title 1976; expects 1 title 1977, 2 titles 1978.

Kitchen Sink Enterprises (see SNARF)

‡**Kite Books,** John Domini, 423 Franklin St., Cambridge, MA 02139.

Kneechee Press (see ILLYRIAN REVUE)

Knollwood Publishing Company, Box 735, Willmar, MN 56201, 612-235-4950. "Currently a one-book, one-record publishing house—*'Silver Spurs', Santa's Smallest Brightest Elf*. Record, sheet music, 4 full color posters (scenes from book), t-shirt stencil (5 x 8-full color)." avg. price, cloth: $4.95 (record $1.00). 1973. 39pp; 8½ x 11. Discounts: libraries, schools, bookstores-40 percent; fund raisers & distributors-60 percent. ASCAP, Society of Children's Book Writers.

Know, Inc., Anne Pride, Poetry; Jo-Ann Evans Gardner, Articles, P.O. Box 86031, Pittsburgh, PA 15221. Poetry, articles, reviews. "Know, Inc. is a small but growing feminist publishing company. We were founded in 1969 and currently publish both hard and soft cover books, pamphlets, a newsletter for members (6/yr) and a poetry series. Our list is very broad, covering subjects in all areas of the women's movement." 1969. of. Discounts: try to make 50% for distrib. 40% for other bulk sales. COSMEP.

The Kober Press, P.O. Box 4155, Berkeley, CA 94704, 415-845-1790. "One book a year." 1975. avg. press run 2,500. Discounts: 40 percent for 2 bks or more; 20 percent or less to bkstr; 20 percent library; 50 percent wholesalers. Expects 1 title 1977, 1 title 1978. COSMEP.

Kol Hai, Inc. (see 613 MAGAZINE)

KONGLOMERATI, Konglomerati Press, Richard Mathews, Barbara Russ, 5719 29th Avenue South, Gulfport, FL 33707, 813-343-3633. Poetry, art, cartoons, collages, concrete art. "Recent contributors include F.A. Nettelbeck, Jim Hall, Peter Meinke, David Shevin, Jerred Metz. We look for clear, original, innovative voices." Irregular.; 1-yr sub price: $8.00; per copy: $2.50/$5.00; sample: No special rate for sample copies. 1972. 45pp; 6¼ x 9¾. †of/lp/other. circ. 150-300. Reporting time: 1 month-6 weeks. Payment: copy. Copyrighted, reprint rights by permission. Ads: $40.00/$20.00. Discounts: 1-4 copies, 20 percent; 5 or more copies, 40 percent to bookstores. Back issues: No. 1 *Faces* $2.50/No. 2 *Concrete* 1-$25.00 (only five copies remain). Expects 1 issue 1977, 1 issue 1978. Pub's reviews. §Literary, poetry, avant garde, fine printing. COSMEP, COSMEP-SOUTH, WMS, PHS.

Konglomerati Press (see also KONGLOMERATI), Richard Mathews, Barbara Russ, 5719 29th Avenue South, Gulfport, FL 33707, 813-343-3633. Poetry, art, cartoons, collages, concrete art. "Exploring visual poetry, letterpress typography and the hand made book. A series of Poetry Pamphlets (up to 300 copy edition) with work from recognized as well as new voices. Bird Chit Books (500 copy editions) chapbooks with illustrations, handsewn binding, soft cover, letterpress-printed, some hand-made papers. Two-Bit Bird Sheets (single poems) and post cards." avg. price, cloth: $15.00; paper: $5.00. 1971. 60pp; 6 x 7. †lp/of/other. avg. press run 300-500. Reporting time: 1 month - 6 weeks. Payment: up to 10% of the edition plus 40% disc on add. copies. Discounts: 1-4 copies, 20 percent; 5 or more 40 percent to bookstores. Pub'd 2 titles 1976; expects 4 titles 1977, 4 titles 1978. COSMEP, COSMEP-SOUTH, WMS, PHS.

Konocti Books (see also SIPAPU), Noel Peattie, Route 1, Box 216, Winters, CA 95694. avg. price, paper: $2.00. 1973. lp. avg. press run 500. Reporting time: 3 weeks. Discounts: 40 percent booksellers. Pub'd 1 title 1976.

KONTAKTE, Phenomenon Press, Richard Truhlar, John Riddell, 76 Admiral Road, Toronto, Ontario M5R2L5, Canada, 922-8206. Poetry, fiction, long-poems, collages, concrete art. 4-5/yr; 1-yr sub price: $10.00; per copy: $4.00. 1976. 50pp; 8½ x 11. †of. Reporting time: 1-3 months. Payment: none. Copyrighted, reverts to author. Ads: none. Pub'd 3 issues 1976.

167

Kontexts Publications, Michael Gibbs, Eerste Van Der Helststraat 55, Amsterdam, Nthlnd, (020) 768556. Poetry, articles, art, interviews, criticism, reviews, letters, concrete art, photos, collages. "Concerned with visual/experimental poetry and language arts. The magazine has now folded. Last number 9/10 Winter 76/77, but Kontexts Publications will be continuing with the production of books and book-objects by individual writers/artists. Recent books: *6 Plays* by Ulises Carrion; *Pages* by Michael Gibbs." avg. price, other: average book price: $3.00. 1969. †mi/of/lp. avg. press run 100. Copyright for books. Discounts: 33-1/3% on 6 or more. Back issues: 9/10 - $4.00. Pub'd 2 titles 1976; expects 2 titles 1977.

KOSMOS, Milky Way-Kosmos, Kosrof Chantikian, 130 Eureka, San Francisco, CA 94114, 415-863-4861. Poetry, fiction, art, parts-of-novels, long-poems, plays. "KOSMOS is reborn twice yearly and aspires to publish the best poetry and fiction now being imagined and written. Bring or send your work in the original with SASE to the address above. Poetry is the invitation to go to the ching the well to the very foundations of life. Recent contributors: Joan Murray, Rochelle Owens, Ruth Lisa Schecter, Jana Harris, Douglas Blazek, John Tagliabue, Robert Enright, Colette Inez, Lyn Lifshin, Rochelle Ratner, Alfred Starr Hamilton, Brian Vanderlip." 2/yr; 1-yr sub price: $3.50-Libraries $5.00; per copy: $1.75; sample: $1.75 plus $0.25 postage. 1975. 64pp; 5½ x 8½. of. circ. 300. Reporting time: 7-9 weeks. Payment: 2-3 copies, except when grant money becomes available. no ads. Discounts: 40% trade. Back issues: $2.00. Expects 3 issues 1977, 2 issues 1978. §Poetry, fiction, children. COSMEP, NESPA.

KRAX, Andy Robson, 63 Dixon Lane, Leeds, Yorkshire LS12 4RR, United Kingdom. Articles, poetry, fiction, art, interviews. "Favour younger writers and fantasy art" 2/yr; price per copy: 40p incl. post.; sample: 15p incl. post. 1971. 40pp; A5. litho. Reporting time: 1 week. Payment: cover design only £1. Ads: £6. Pub'd 1 issue 1976; expects 3 issues 1977, 2 issues 1978.

Kropotkin's Lighthouse Publications, Jas Huggon, c/o Housmans Bookshop, 5 Caledonian Rd., London N19DX, United Kingdom. Poetry, fiction, art, non-fiction. "We do not require unsolicited mss. Recent publication incl. postcards (4), calendars (2), poetry, anthologies, bibliography, fiction, pamphlets, posters." 1969. †lp/mi. Reporting time: by return. Payment: none. Discounts: 33-1/3% plus postage. Pub'd 2 titles 1976; expects 2 titles 1977, 2 titles 1978. ALP.

KRZYK (OUTCRY), Canadian Photopress Publishing Limited, Janurz J. Uiberall, P.O. Box 113, Stn "M", Toronto, Ontario M6S4T2, Canada. Poetry, articles, art, photos, cartoons, interviews, criticism, reviews, music, letters, parts-of-novels. 12/yr; 1-yr sub price: $6.00; per copy: $.50; sample: $.50. 1974. 20pp; 10¼ x 15¼. of. circ. 3,500. Ads: $320/$170. Discounts: 30%. Back issues: 25¢. Pub's reviews. §art/entertainment/etc.

KUKSU: Journal of Backcountry Writing, Kuksu Press, Dale Pendell, Box 980 Alleghany Star Rt., Nevada City, CA 95959. Poetry, fiction, articles, art, photos, interviews, criticism, reviews, parts-of-novels. "Please see an issue before submitting material." 1-2/yr; sub price: $5.00/2 issues; per copy: $2.50; sample: $2.50. 1972. 140pp; 5 x 8. of. circ. 1,500. Reporting time: 1-3 mos. Payment: copies. Discounts: 40%-trade, bulk. Pub's reviews. §poetry/anthropology/western American/counter culture. CCLM, COSMEP.

Kulchur Foundation, Lita Hornick, 888 Park Ave., New York, NY 10021, 988-5193. Poetry. avg. price, cloth: $7.00; paper: $3.50. 1970. 128pp; 7½ x 10. of. avg. press run 1,000. Reporting time: varies. Payment: $500.00 a book. Copyright in author's name. Discounts: 40 percent to bookstores, 20 percent to libraries. Pub'd 2 titles 1976; expects 2 titles 1977.

Kurios Press, Barbie Engstrom, Publisher, 743 Woodleave Rd./Box 946, Bryn Mawr, PA 19010, 215-527-4635. "All our books so far have been ones that I've written. My hope is to do one a year and have done two so far. So I do not solicate other manuscripts unless I know the person or they are really outstanding. My first book 'Faith To See' is going into its third printing, so I have my hands full with just my own business." avg. price, paper: $3.00 - $4.00. 1974. 64-96pp; varies. of. avg. press run 5,000 to 10,000 but it has been as low as 500 to begin with. Payment: none. Copyrights for author. Discounts: all books, even one copy are given a 46 percent discount.

Kylix Press, Emery E. George, Editor; Mary W. George, President, 1485 Maywood, Ann Arbor, MI 48103, (313) 761-5399. Poetry, art, photos, criticism. "Please see statement on rear panel of enclosed brochure." avg. price, cloth: $4.95; paper: $2.45. 1974. pp varies; have been doing books 64, 72 pp. More to follow.; 6 x 9. of. avg. press run 1,000. Reporting time: 3—6 months. Payment: yes: 10—15%. Copyrights for author. Discounts: Jobbers, 40%; libraries and other institutions, on direct orders: 20%. COSMEP.

L

‡**L MAGAZINE,** 34 Franciscan Way, Kensington, CA 94707.

L-A House (see CQ)

LA-BAS: A Newsletter of Experimental Poetry & Poetics, La-bas, Douglas Messerli, Box 509 Hollywood Sta., College Park, MD 20740, 301-864-6921. Poetry, reviews, letters, long-poems, collages. "*La-bas* is interested in any poem that excites & holds the reader's interest. The newsletter is sent free to poets who have continued to achieve these qualities in their poetry, and the magazine is *sold* only to libraries by subscription. McClure, Codrescu, Loewinsohn, Norse, Roditi, Eigner, Andrews, Davidson, Greenwald & Ratner are among its contributors." 6/yr; 1-yr sub price: $8.00 (libraries only); per copy: $0.00; sample: $0.00. 1976. 50pp; 8½ x 11. †mi. circ. 350. Reporting time: 1-3 weeks. No payment—all contributors are sent all issues of the newsletter. Copyrighted, reverts to author. Pub's reviews. §All aspects of contemporary or experimental poetry. CCLM.

La-bas (see also LA-BAS: A Newsletter of Experimental Poetry & Poetics), Douglas Messerli, Box 509 Hollywood Sta., College Park, MD 20740, 301-864-6921. Poetry, long-poems, collages. "*La-bas* publishes chapbooks of long poems or series of related poems only. We do not publish *selected* poems. Experimental poetry (poetry that experiments with form, subject or language) is considered only. Recent books published are: Guy Beining's CITY SHINGLES & Lou Horvath's inter-related, surrealist poems, VU." avg. price, paper: $3.00. 1976. 30pp; 8½ x 11. †mi. avg. press run 500. Reporting time: 1 month. Payment: Royalty: 25-30 percent. Copyrights for author. Discounts: 20 - 40 percent. CCLM.

Labor Arts Books, Emanuel Fried, 1064 Amherst St., Buffalo, NY 14216, 716-873-4131. "For the moment not seeking submissions. Still working on distribution of present publication: 'The Dodo Bird'." avg. price, paper: $1.50. 1975. 72pp; 4¼ x 7. Print Press. avg. press run 5,000. Payment: individual arrangement. Discounts: 40 percent to bookstores—to others: 0-19 copies-$1.50 ea. 20-99 $1.25 ea.; over 100-$1.00 ea. COSMEP.

LAD (see SOURCE)

THE LAKE SUPERIOR REVIEW, Faye Korpi, Cynthia Willoughby, Lee Merrill, Box 724, Ironwood, MI 49938. Poetry, fiction, art, satire. "Prefer manuscripts kept under 3,000 words. No limit on length of poetry. All styles considered. We publish writings that we feel are intellectually and emotionally stimulating and revealing. Cover letters not wanted. Send no more than 6-8 poems or 2 short stories per submission. Do not send mss. during June, July, August. Send original copies of mss. No simultaneous or photocopied submissions." 3/yr; 1-yr sub price: $4.00; per copy: $1.50. 1970. 48pp; 8½ x 5½. circ. 400. Reporting time: 2 weeks - 4 months. Payment: copies only. Copyrighted, returned to writer upon request with acknowledgement. Discounts: 10 percent on orders of 20 or more; 20 percent agent, jobber. Back issues: All available at $4.00/mag. Pub'd 3 issues 1976; expects 3 issues 1977, 3 issues 1978. CCLM, COSMEP.

LAKES & PRAIRIES; A Journal of Writings, Pioneer Press, Edward Haggard, Constance Leininger, P.O. Box A 3454, Chicago, IL 60690. Poetry, fiction, long-poems. " *Lakes & Prairies* places no limitation on length, only quality work is accepted. *Lakes & Prairies* devotes its space to the work of 3-5 writers/issue. Occasionally, anthologized or theme issues are printed. Writers published to date include Denise Levertov, Diane Wakoski, Lucy Swope, Martin J. Rosenblum, Karl

Young, Angela Pecken Paugh, Michael Tarachow and Mary Shumway." varies; sub price: $1.85/3 issues; per copy: $.75; sample: $.75. 1974. 48pp; 8 x 11. of. circ. 500. Reporting time: 4-6 weeks. Payment: 2 copies. Ads: $15/$9. Discounts: 40% (5,10 or 25 copies). Back issues: 60¢ ea. Pub'd 1 issue 1976; expects 1 issue 1977.

Lame Johnny Press, Associates (see also SUNDAY CLOTHES), L. M. Hasselstrom, Box 66, Hermosa, SD 57744, 605-255-4228. "No limits; lean toward Great Plains writers, fiction, poetry." avg. price, cloth: $4.95; $5.50 postpaid; paper: $2.95; $3.50 postpaid; other: $1.95 (chapbooks). 1971. 32-120pp; 8 x 8. of. avg. press run 1,500. Reporting time: 3-10 weeks. Payment: LJP is a cooperative subsidy press; brochure on request with SASE; payment varies, is percentage of sale price. Copyright rests with author. Discounts: Bookstores and distributors only: 1-24, no discount, 25-49, 30 percent; 50-99, 40 percent; 100 plus, 46 percent. Expects 2 titles 1977, 2 titles 1978. COSMEP.

THE LAMPETER MUSE, Lampeter Editions, Lori Chips, William Wilson, Bard College, Annandale-On-Hudson, NY 12504. Poetry, fiction, articles, art, photos, interviews, criticism, music, letters, parts-of-novels, long-poems. "It would be best to look at a sample copy of the MUSE. We're not in the habit of working with unsolicited material, but we do consider it. The furthest from what we want is the brief, clever one-shot poem. We look for poetry that comes out of a poet's long, deep & broad interaction with & commitment to his work. This precludes a stylistic bias. Tear out a clump of grass & take the dirt and the roots that come up with it." 1/yr; 1-yr sub price: $3.00; per copy: $2.50; sample: $2.50. 1966. 80-120pp; 6 x 9. lp. circ. 2,000. Payment: copies. Back issues: $2.50. §poetry.

Lamplighters Roadway Press, J.B. Grant, Freestone Box #1, 500 Bohemian Hwy., Freestone, CA 95472. Poetry, fiction, articles, art, photos, interviews, criticism, reviews. avg. price, paper: $3.00. 1972. 100pp; varies. of. avg. press run 2,500. ms. not solicited. Copyrights for author. Discounts: trade. Expects 1 title 1978. COSMEP.

Landmark Publishing (see also 1977 TRAVELER'S TOLL-FREE DIRECTORY), Jerome T. Smith, Robert R. Harding, Box 3287, Burlington, VT 05401, 802-863-5333. Articles. avg. price, paper: $2.25. 1976. 128pp; 4 x 9. of. avg. press run 5,000. Reporting time: first time. Payment: none as of yet. Copyrights for author.

LANELLE'S LETTER BOX, Lanelle M. Greer, 142 West Brookdale Place, Fullerton, CA 92632. Poetry, letters, long-poems. "Want poetry about all aspects of life, all ages and stages, fresh - (and, appealing to the emotions). Strong reader indentification. No explicitly sexual poems or 'angry' atheistic poems desired, as over half of my subscribers are Catholic. Catholic themes invited." 5/yr; 1-yr sub price: $5.00; per copy: $1.00; sample: $1.00. 1976. 24-36pp; 5½ x 8½. of. circ. 500. Reporting time: 2 weeks. Payment: small cash awards & prizes. no ads. Discounts: none.

LAOMEDON REVIEW, Coach House Press, L.J. Kuschnir, Erindale College, 3359 Mississauga Road, Mississauga, Ontario L5L1C6, Canada. Poetry, fiction, articles, art, photos, cartoons, satire, criticism, long-poems, plays, interviews, reviews, parts-of-novels. 1-2/yr; 1-yr sub price: $5.00; per copy: $3.00. 1974. 112pp; 6 x 9. of. circ. 2,500. Reporting time: 3 months. Payment: none. Copyrighted, reverts to author. Ads: $150/$80. Back issues: $5.00. Pub'd 1 issue 1976; expects 1 issue 1977, 1 issue 1978. Pub's reviews: none in 1976. §literary/cultural/educational.

‡**Larkspur Press**, Rt. 3 Severn Creek, Monterey, Owenton, KY 40359.

LAST POST, Drummond Burgess, Managing Editor; Editorial Board, 454 King St. W Suite 302, Toronto, Ontario M5V1L6, Canada. Cartoons, satire, reviews. "LAST POST is a news magazine, dealing with topical questions relating to Canada, with some coverage of international affairs. We do book, film, and occasionally theatre reviews." 8/yr; 1-yr sub price: $5.00 personal/$7.00 institutional; per copy: $.75. 1969. 48pp; 7 x 10. of. circ. 20,000. No payment. Ads: $400/$300. Discounts: 30% on 10 plus/50% on 25 plus. Back issues: $20.00/set. Pub's reviews. §political.

Latitudes Press, Robert Bonazzi, Rochelle Bonazzi, 3514 Lafayette Ave, Austin, TX 78722. Poetry, art. "Our primary interest is in fiction that cuts against the conventional grain. We're trying to give experimental fiction a good name. We've brought out three anthologies of such fiction (Banks, Greenberg, Berge, Dixon, Roth, Cohen, Buzzati, Elizondo among fifty contributors) in our 'New Departures in Fiction' series, but we want to abandon the anthology format and go on to individual titles, under the 'Further Departures in Fiction' series, which will include short novels (120-140 pages) by Brian Swann, Russell Hardin and Nick Ranieri in 1977. Presently we are not looking for any manuscripts. We can't consider anything until 10-77, and only then ms. of experimental fiction preceded by a query letter. There are just too many projects in the works and not enough time and money to consider more." 1972. 6 x 9. of. avg. press run 1,000. Reporting time: 3 months. Payment: copies. Pub'd 2 titles 1976; expects 3 titles 1977.

LAUGHING BEAR, Laughing Bear Press, Tom Person, Editor, Box 14, Woodinville, WA 98072, 206-524-2314. Poetry, fiction, articles, interviews, reviews, letters, long-poems, plays, concrete art, criticism, news items, non-fiction. "Some of the contributors are: Toby Lurie, Richard Kostelanetz, Peter Finch, Ian Tarnman, and R. Clarence Matsuo-Allard. Long poems, stories, etc., are welcome but query first about anything over six pages. *Laughing Bear* is an eclectic magazine. If something shows up that doesn't seem to fit in with where the magazine is usually at, and I like it, I'll fit it in somehow. I'm interested primarily in experimental materials and in all phases of literary history. I also publish *Laughing Bear Newsletter* which needs short, nonfiction articles." 4/yr; 1-yr sub price: $5.00; per copy: $1.50; sample: Send S.A.S.E. (25 cents postage) 6 x 9 envelope for free sample. 1976. 64pp; 6 x 9. of. circ. 1,000. Reporting time: 1 day to 6 weeks. Payment: copies. Buys all rights, but will negotiate. Ads: $35.00/$20.00/$2.00/10 words, $0.25 each word thereafter. Discounts: 40% trade; 20% libraries. Back issues: $1.00. Pub'd 1 issue 1976; expects 5 issues 1977, 4 issues 1978. Pub's reviews: 13 in 1976. §Experimental literature, nonfiction on about anything; traditional poetry, fiction, drama; reference material. COSMEP.

THE LAUREL REVIEW, Mark De Foe, West Virginia Wesleyan College, Buckhannon, WV 26201, 303-473-8006. Poetry, fiction, articles, interviews, parts-of-novels, plays, reviews. "Although we seek to encourage writers in Appalachia, THE LAUREL REVIEW does not want to become a 'spit and whittle' magazine. We will publlish anything by anyone if it strikes our fancy, from the avant garde to the traditional. We are interested in intelligent, lucid, provocative writing. We would like to see some articles or essays on Appalachian subjects. In any case, whether, poetry, drama, fiction or article, craftmanship and meaning do count!" 1-2/yr; 1-yr sub price: $3.00; per copy: $1.50; sample: $1.50. 1960. 60pp; 5½ x 8. of. circ. 500. Reporting time: 1 week to 3 months. Payment: 3 copies. Copyrighted. Ads: $80/$40/$.10. Expects 1 issue 1977, 2 issues 1978. Pub's reviews.

Lava Mt, John Taylor Gatto III, Janet MacAdam, 235 W 76th St, New York City, NY 10023, 874-3631. Art, interviews, music. "Currently we're attempting to reduce the horror tales of H.P. Love Craft to dramatic form and issue LP records of same; also, we're following up our Richard Nixon LP with others in a series called *'The Nixon Years '*—next scheduled is *Spiro Agnew*. We also offer a free descriptive catalogue of *'Golden-age'* radio shows on cassette for a self-addressed stamped envelope." avg. price, cloth: $7.00. 1974. of/lp. avg. press run 2,000. Reporting time: 6 weeks. Payment: 10%. Copyrights for author. Discounts: Trade 50%, Schools & Libraries 25%. Pub'd 2 titles 1976; expects 3 titles 1977, 4 titles 1978. ASCAP.

Lawhead Press (see THE NEW LAUREL REVIEW)

Lawrence Hill & Company, Publishers, Inc., Lawrence Hill, Mercer Field, 24 Burr Farms Road, Westport, CT 06880, 203-226-9392. Poetry, fiction, art, photos, cartoons, interviews, satire, criticism, music, letters, non-fiction. "Have strong Black Studies list but are equally interested in other materials." avg. price, cloth: $6.95; paper: $3.95. 1972. 192pp; 5½ x 8½. of. avg. press run 5,000. Reporting time: 2-3 weeks. Payment: standard royalty arrangements. Copyrights for author. Discounts: See ABA handbook; 10 percent discount with prepayment on single-copy orders; also SCOP 40 percent. Pub'd 8 titles 1976; expects 14 titles 1977, 10 titles 1978. AAP, CBPA.

Lawton Press, Susan Lawton, 230 Pelham Road 5P, New Rochelle, NY 10805, 914-576-1435. Poetry, art, photos. "Lawton Press is still in the embryonic stages. In 1976, I published *Conceptus,* my own book of poetry. Since then I have become associated with *Stone Country,* a magazine published out of Madison, New Jersey by Judy Neeld. I will be printing *Stone Country* beginning with the fall issue, and have an advertisment for Lawton Press in the Spring issue. Future prospects include three individual poets whose books I will be designing, publishing, and printing. I see Lawton Press as the kind of press that individual poets can use to publish their own works at a reasonable cost, and where the quality of that publication will meet the highest standards. Lawton Press is not limited to poets. I will be publishing a booklet on Journal writing next month, and am presently in negotiations for a childrens book." avg. price, cloth: Varies according to copy preparation necessary and stock used. 1976. 20 pages plus the cover.; 5½ x 8½. †of. avg. press run 200-1,000 copies. Reporting time: 1 week. Payment: No royalties. 50 percent before printing, 50 percent upon delivery. Copyrights for author. Discounts: None at this time. COSMEP.

League Books (see POETS' LEAGUE OF GREATER CLEVELAND NEWSLETTER)

Leathern Wing Scribble Press (see also THE GENEVA POND BUBBLES), John M. Armleder, 6 Rue Plantamoor, Geneve CH-7207, Switzerland, 022-32-6794. Poetry, art, photos, music, collages, concrete art. 1977. †mi/of/lp. Discounts: 33-1/3.

Leaves of Grass Press, Inc., Stephen Gorstman, P.O. Box 129, Bolinas, CA 94924. of.

LEAVES OF TWIN OAKS, Twin Oaks Community, David Oaks, Mikki Oaks, Rt. 4 Box 17, Louisa, VA 23093, 703-894-5126. Poetry, articles, art, photos, cartoons, letters. "Material published in the *LEAVES* is entirely about our experiences in trying to create a mini-society based upon egalitarian principles." 4/yr; 1-yr sub price: $3.00; per copy: $0.75; sample: free. 1967. 22pp; 7 x 8½. †of. circ. 600. Back issues: $0.75. Pub'd 6 issues 1976; expects 4 issues 1977, 4 issues 1978. §communal living. COSMEP.

LEFT CURVE, Left Curve Publications, Richard Olsen, Csaba Polony, 1230 Grant St. Box 302, San Francisco, CA 94133. Poetry, fiction, articles, art, photos, cartoons, interviews, criticism, reviews, music, letters, long-poems, collages, concrete art. "*LEFT CURVE* focuses on theoretical & practical issues concerning art & revolution. Average length of main articles, 8 pages. All styles from avant-garde to traditional. Recent contributors: E. San Juan, Jr., Willis H. Truitt, Ian Burn, Margaret Randall, Eva Cockcroft. Including editors, Richard Olsen, Csaba Polony." 3/yr; 1-yr sub price: $5.00 indiv/$7.00 institutions; per copy: $2.00; sample: $2.00. 1974. 85pp; 8½ x 11. of. circ. 1,000. Reporting time: max. 3 months. Payment: 5 copies. Ads: $100/$50. Discounts: 1/3 trade. Back issues: $1.50 each. Pub's reviews. §contemporary art.

LEMMING, Rex Burwell, 1125 H St. Apt. 22, Davis, CA 94616. Poetry. "Edson, Ignatow, Levertov, Stafford." 4/yr; 1-yr sub price: $5.00; per copy: $1.50; sample: $.75. 1970. 26pp; 8½ x 7½. of. circ. 200. Reporting time: 1 wk. Payment: copies only. no ads.

Lenape Publishing Ltd., Sandra S. Michel, 608 Whitby Dr., Wilmington, DE 19803, 302-652-1248. Poetry, fiction. "We are concentrating on childrens books" avg. price, paper: $2.00. 1973. 32pp; varies. of. avg. press run 1,000. Reporting time: 4 weeks. Payment: 10 percent royalty normal-can vary-but will be determined before publishing. Copyrights for author. Discounts: trade 30 percent 2-10 copies; 40 percent 11-49; 50 percent 50 plus copies; schools & library-special rates vary with each book; jobber & bulk-can be negotiated. Pub'd 5 titles 1976; expects 2 titles 1977, 3 titles 1978. COSMEP.

L'Epervier Press, Bob McNamara, 1219 East Laurel, Fort Collins, CO 80521. Poetry. "Full length books only. In 1977, we will publish books by: Paul Nelson, Lynn Strongin, Pamela Stewart, Jack Myers, Bob Herz, Michael Burkard, Christopher Howell, Carolyn Maisel, and Robert Morgan. Books available as series. Subscription: $19.00 for whole year." 1977. 64pp; 6 x 9. of. avg. press run 500. Reporting time: Varies. We try for 2-3 months. Payment: 12 percent sales. Copyrights for author. Discounts: none.

Les Femmes Publishing, Ruth Kramer, Publ., 231 Adrian Road, Millbrae, CA 94030, 415-692-4500. "Our major editorial needs are for manuscripts that complement or relate to our existing booklist and for photography and art work which supplement them. We have no immediate plans to publish fiction but are willing to look at ms. Our standard book format is 5½ x 8½, about 160 pages in length. Some variation is possible when warranted. Short works should be submitted in full; outline or synopsis and sample chapters may be submitted for longer works. All manuscripts should be typewritten and double spaced, if possible. Include a description or samples of artwork or photography available. Be sure to label all materials submitted." 1974. 160pp; 5401/2 x 8401/2. Payment: Standard Royalty. Discounts: 1-4, 20 percent prepaid only; 5-24, 40 percent; 25-49, 41 percent; 50-99, 42 percent. Pub'd 24 titles 1976; expects 9 titles 1977.

LESBIAN CONNECTION, Ambitious Amazons, P.O. Box 811, E. Lansing, MI 48823. Articles, art, photos, criticism, reviews, letters. "We only print material relevant to lesbians, by lesbians. We don't print fiction or poetry. The length of the article should not exceed 2 typed pages-single spaced." 8/yr; 1-yr sub price: free; per copy: free. 1974. 28pp; 8½ x 11. †mi/of. circ. 6,000. Reporting time: 6 wks before publication of issue. Payment: none. Ads: donations. Discounts: libraries & institutions $13.00. Pub's reviews. §all areas if relevant to lesbians. COSMEP.

THE LESBIAN TIDE, Tide Publications, Jeanne Cordova, Shirl Buss, Sharon McDonald, 8855 Cattaragus Ave., Los Angeles, CA 90034. Poetry, fiction, articles, art, photos, cartoons, interviews, satire, criticism, reviews, letters, parts-of-novels, long-poems, plays. "Oldest and largest lesbian publication in the U.S., we present material by and for the international lesbian, feminist, and gay communities. Submissions sought from 1 to 5 pages (double-spaced), with exceptions for special materials. Radical feminist perspectives especially encouraged, but all women's view points welcomed. No male contributors." 6 issues/yr; 1-yr sub price: $6.00; per copy: $1.00; sample: $1.25. 1971. 40pp; 8½ x 11. of. circ. 7,000. Reporting time: Bimonthly. Payment: $5.00-$25.00. Ads: $80.00/$40.00/$3.00 col. inch. Discounts: bulk (10 copies min.) 30% off; institutions/overseas $10.00/yr. Back issues: $1.00. Pub'd 6 issues 1976; expects 6 issues 1977, 6 issues 1978. Pub's reviews. §lesbians/feminists/women/gay movement.

LESBIAN VOICES, Ms. Atlas Press, Rosalie Nichols, Editor; Johnie Staggs, Associate Editor, 120 E. San Carlos Street, San Jose, CA 95112, 408-289-1088. Poetry, fiction, articles, photos, interviews, reviews, parts-of-novels, long-poems, plays, non-fiction. "All views expressed in this publication are the ideas and opinions of the individual contributor. Favorable treatment of any idea, ideology, product, etc. in *LESBIAN VOICES* does not constitute an endorsement by this magazine, its editors or publisher. We welcome differing points of view on controversial issues, but request that ideas be expressed clearly and rationally and in a tone and style compatible with *LESBIAN VOICES*. We attempt to present a dignified format and a positive, constructive sense of life, in keeping with our belief that lesbianism (and indeed life itself) can be and should be good, wholesome, fulfilling and joyful. We reject the view of lesbianism as material for psychiatric study, religious censure, or pornography..all of which treat lesbianism as sick, sinful or salicious. We reject this view of lesbianism whether it is promulgated by straight society, voyeristic men, or by lesbians themselves." 4/yr; 1-yr sub price: $5.00; per copy: $1.50; sample: $1.50. 1973. 60pp; 7 x 8½. †of. circ. 5,000. Reporting time: 2 weeks. Payment: copies. Copyrighted, reverts to author. Ads: $20.00/$12.50/$0.10. Discounts: 40 percent on orders of five or more. Send for list of back issues. Pub'd 4 issues 1976; expects 4 issues 1977, 4 issues 1978. Pub's reviews: 6 in 1976. §women's history/lesbian novels. COSMEP.

LETTERS, Mainspring Press, G. F. Bush, Publisher; Helma Nash, Editor, Box 82, Stonington, ME 04681, Box 175, Princeton, NJ 08540, 207-367-2484. Poetry, fiction. "For readers of general literary interests. Quality, no unethical submissions invited with SASE for submissions and sample copy." quarterly; 1-yr sub price: $4.00; per copy: $1.00; sample: Free. 1964. 4 pp minimum; 8½ x 11. †of. circ. 4,500. Reporting time: one month. Payment: moderate; some payment always made. Copyrighted, buys first rights only (write for details). Ads: $300/$165/none. Discounts: none. Back issues: available on request. Pub's reviews. §any, including technical.

Levenson Press, P.O.B. 19606, Los Angeles, CA 90019. "Staff written only, doesn't accept

173

outside ms. Press publishes books only." avg. price, paper: $12.50. 1972. pp varies.; 8½ x 11. of. Copyrights for author. Discounts: 23 percent wholesalers, institutions. Pub'd 1 title 1976; expects 1 title 1977.

LIBERAL NEWS, David Deeley, 1 Whitehall Place, London SW1A2HE, United Kingdom, 01 839 3658. Articles, photos, news items. "Newspaper" 52/yr; 1-yr sub price: $20.00; per copy: 10p. 1946. 8pp; 17 x 11. of. circ. 8,500. Payment: nil. Ads: £1.00/£.50/5p. Discounts: 6 for price of 5 on advertisements; 15 percent agency commission on advertisements. Back issues: not available. Pub'd 51 issues 1976; expects 51 issues 1977, 51 issues 1978. Pub's reviews: 10 in 1976. §political.

LIBERATION MAGAZINE, Jan Edwards, Michael Nill, 186 Hampshire St., Cambridge, MA 02139, 617-354-0492. Poetry, fiction, articles, art, photos, cartoons, interviews, satire, criticism, reviews, music, letters. "We are an independent radical magazine which publishes informational, critical, and impressionistic articles on a broad range of subjects. Our emphasis is on understanding the assumptions underlying our personal/social/political realities and on developing visions and practical alternatives by which we might create a non-authoritarian society." 10/yr; 1-yr sub price: $10.00; per copy: $1.25; sample: $1.00. 1956. 36pp; 8½ x 11. of. circ. 9,500. Reporting time: 6 weeks. Payment: 10 copies plus sub. Ads: No paid ads-exchanges only. Discounts: 40% off on 10 or more; 50% for agents. Back issues: $2.00. Pub'd 5 issues 1976; expects 7 issues 1977, 9 issues 1978. Pub's reviews.

Liberation Publications, Inc. (see GPU NEWS)

Liberator Press, Douglas Rae, P.O. Box 7128, Chicago, IL 60680. News items, non-fiction. "We produce books and pamphlets on the working-class movement in the U.S. and around the world. Liberator Press was founded in order to aid and strengthen the worldwide struggle against imperialism." avg. price, paper: $2.00. 1975. 200pp; 5½ x 8½. †of. avg. press run 5,000. Reporting time: 3 months. Copyrights for author. Discounts: 40 percent bookstores, 25 percent individuals ordering 10 or more, special distributor discounts available. Pub'd 3 titles 1976; expects 3 titles 1977, 5 titles 1978.

Libertarian Party of Illinois (see ILLINOIS LIBERTARIAN)

LIBERTE, Box 2932, LaFayette, LA 70502. Photos, cartoons, reviews, letters. 8/yr; 1-yr sub price: $5.00; sample: free in Louisiana. 1972. 4-6pp; 7½ x 10. of. circ. 300 plus. Reporting time: 2 weeks. Payment: none. Ads: $20/$10. Pub's reviews. §libertarian. LPS.

Libra Press (see also DELIRIUM), Jim McCurry, 1827 Elm St., Denver, CO 80220, 309-399-1644. Poetry, fiction, art, photos, cartoons, letters, parts-of-novels, long-poems, collages. "No length restrictions, although I like to edit prose: no biases. Recent contributors: Hugh Fox, Stanley Berne, Linda Bohe, Jack Collom, David Cope, Thomas Michael Fisher, John Giorno, Christy Kyckelhahn, Lyn Lifshin, Christopher Middleton, Toby Olson, Sandra Case, Melissa Cummings, Stephen Ruffus, David Plante, Ron Silliman, Dan Raphael, Bruce Andrews, Paul Vangelisti, Charles Plymell, Marc Weber, Arlene Zekowski & others. Issue 3 will be out this month (December, 1976). Issues 4 & 5 are filled. Issue 6 is half-filled. I will be issuing the first in a series of chapbooks in 1977: DIFFICULT TO SLEEP IN THE QUIET WORLD, by Melissa Cummings." avg. price, paper: $1.50. 1975. 60pp; 8 x 10. of. avg. press run 500. Reporting time: immediately to 2 weeks. Payment: 3 copies plus lifetime subscription. Power of copyright reverts to author. CCLM, COSMEP.

LIBRARIANS FOR SOCIAL CHANGE, John L. Noyce, Publisher, John L. Noyce, Ed. Coordinator, PO Box 450, Brighton, Sussex BN1 8GR, United Kingdom. Articles, poetry, fiction, art, cartoons, satire, news items, interviews, photos. "Anything on librarianship and social change; sexism, racism, workers' control in librarianship and related areas such as info work, publishing, etc." 3/yr; 1-yr sub price: libraries £3.50; individuals £1.50; per copy: £1.00 libraries (50p individuals); sample: £1.00 libraries (50p individuals). 1972. 32pp; A4. †dup/lo. circ. 400. Reporting time: we try. Payment: free copy. Ads: on application. Discounts: 20 percent to trade.

Back issues: £1.00 libraries (50p individuals). Pub'd 3 issues 1976; expects 3 issues 1977, 3 issues 1978. Pub's reviews: 40 in 1976. §libraries, social change, alternative society/work/ideas.

Librairie Droz S.A. (see BIBLIOTHEQUE D'HUMANISME ET RENAISSANCE)

Library Research Associates, Matilda A. Gocek, Dunderberg Road, Monroe, NY 10950, 914-783-1144. Non-fiction. "I attempt to give authors of non-fiction local history (N.Y.) a chance to be published." avg. price, cloth: $9.00; paper: $3.00. 1968. 150pp; 5½ x 8½. of. avg. press run 1,000. Reporting time: 1 month. Payment: 10 percent royalties. Copyrights for author. Discounts: 40% to book sellers. Pub'd 3 titles 1976; expects 4 titles 1977, 4 titles 1978.

LIBRARY REVIEW, J. D. Hendry, G. Jones, 30 Clydeholm Road, Glasgow G14 OBJ, United Kingdom. Articles. 4/yr; 1-yr sub price: £3.00; per copy: 1927. 48pp. lp. Reporting time: 1 month. Payment: by arrangement usually £5/1500 words. Ads: £35/£18. Discounts: 16-2/3% to agents.

LIBRE PRESS, Scranton Theatre Libre, John J. White, 512-514 Brooks Bldg, Scranton, PA 18510, 717-342-3608. Poetry, fiction, articles, art, photos, cartoons, interviews, satire, criticism, reviews, letters, plays. 3/yr; price per copy: $1.00. 1976. 13pp; 8 x 11½. of. circ. 500. Reporting time: 6 months. Payment: none. Copyrighted, reverts to author. Ads: $50.00. Pub's reviews. §Theatre, Satire, Political Reviews. CCLM.

LIFELINE, Highway Book Shop, Douglas C. Pollard, Cobalt, Ontario P0J1C0, Canada. Articles. "Always interested in short articles (500 words or less) on any aspect of writing and/or publishing." 24/yr; 1-yr sub price: $15.00; per copy: $1.00; sample: $1.00. 1974. 16pp; 8½ x 11. †of. circ. 700. Reporting time: 1 week. Payment: 1 year sub. Ads: $.10. Pub's reviews. §Writing and/or publishing. COSMEP.

LIGHT, Roberta C. Gould, P.O. Box 1105 Stuyvesant, New York City, NY 10009. Poetry, photos, collages, concrete art. "An ecclectic selection in regard to both content & form. Not biased against political statements but the poem must make it as a poem. Looking for line drawings and translations. Plan reviews-would like more submissions by women. Contributors: Ree Dragonette, Daisy Aldan, Robert Stock, Barbara Holland, Vinnie Marie D'Ambrosio. No. 3-special translation issue. No zerox or large envelope submissions." 1/yr; sub price: $4.50 - 4 issues; per copy: $1.25; sample: $1.00. 1973. 64pp; 8½ x 5½. of. circ. 500. Reporting time: 3 days-3 mos. Payment: copies. Copyrighted, reverts to author. Discounts: $5/4 issues to libraries; 40% off to bkstrs. Back issues: $1.25 except No. 1 - $5.00. Pub'd 1 issue 1976; expects 1 issue 1977, 1 issue 1978. Pub's reviews. §Poetry. CCLM, COSMEP.

LIGHT TIMES, St. John's Bread Church, Art Wand, Karl Harpon Confusion, 3028 Stanford, Venice, CA 90291, 823-6233. Poetry, fiction, art, satire, letters, collages, concrete art. "Anyone who contributes material laid out on stencils is considered an editor. Material usually under 2,000 words. Recent contributors: Robert Anton Wilson (Mordecai the Foul), Ron Cobb (Elder the Junger). All material appears anonymously or under pseudonyms reflecting writer's mythic identity." 2/yr; 1-yr sub price: free. 1969. 24pp; 8½ x 11. †mi/of. circ. 500. Reporting time: 1 week to 8 months. Payment: none. Not copyrighted. Ads: none. Discounts: *LIGHT TIMES* is free. Back issues: none available.

LIMIT! (The National Newsletter Of The Libertarian Republican Alliance), Joseph L. Gentili, Publisher; Elliott Capon, Editor, 1811 East 34th St, Brooklyn, NY 11234. Articles, interviews, criticism, reviews, letters, news items, non-fiction. "750-1,500 words preferable, non-pedantic style. Topic should be politically oriented. Slant should appeal to Libertarians Conservatives, Republicans (or any combination thereof). Recent contributors: Scott Royce, Donald M. McLean, Vincent A. Drosdik III, Fred Stein, Hon, Ronald E. Paul M.D., George Chapman, John McClaughry, Daniel Williams, Jack R. Patterson, Mark Frazier, Nelson A. Pryor, Karl E. Peterjohn, Rep. Larry McDonald, Herald G. Beale." 12/yr; 1-yr sub price: $5.00; per copy: $0.50; sample: free. 1974. 6-8pp; 8½ x 11. of. circ. 500 plus. Reporting time: 1-2 weeks. Payment: pay in copies. Ads: $25.00/$14.00/$8.50-¼ page. Pub'd 12 issues 1976; expects 12 issues 1977, 12 issues 1978. Pub's reviews: 6 in 1976. §Politics with a libertarian, Conservative, Republican slant, individualistic sci. fi. LPS.

Lincoln Publishing Company, D. L. David, Box 5249, Santa Monica, CA 90405. Non-fiction. "We are interested in non-fiction titles, especially of a how-to-nature: including self-improvement, money-making, better health, self-help, popular psychology, and sex and marriage. Payment rates vary. Please send us a letter first: do not send manuscript." avg. price, cloth: $15.95; paper: $7.95. 1973. pp varies; varies. of. avg. press run 23,000 copies. Reporting time: 4 wks. Payment varies. Copyrights for author. Discounts: 40%. Pub'd 6 titles 1976; expects 9 titles 1977, 15 titles 1978. COSMEP, APS.

LINES REVUE, M. McDonald, Robin Fulton, M. McDonald, Edgefield Rd, Loanhead, Midlothian EH20 9SY, United Kingdom. Articles, poetry, reviews, long-poems. 4/yr; 1-yr sub price: £1.50; per copy: 30p. 1952. 48pp; 8½ x 5½. lp. circ. 850. Reporting time: by return. Payment: approx £2.00 per page. Ads: £16/£10/£6 1/4 page.

LINQ, English Language Literature Assoc., Cheryl Frost, Coordinating Editor, English Dept., James Cook University of North Queensland, Townsville 4811, Australia. Poetry, fiction, articles, interviews, criticism, reviews, parts-of-novels, long-poems, plays. "Critical articles about 3000 words. Reviews 1000 words." 4/yr; 1-yr sub price: $a4-20; per copy: $a1-00; sample: $a1-00. 1971. 60pp; 5½ x 8½. of. circ. 70. Reporting time: 2 mo. Back issues: $a0-50. Pub's reviews. §any area of contemporary interest, political, sociological, literary.

LITERARY CONTESTS & AWARDS NEWSLETTER, The Commentators' Press, Gary Lagier, Joan George, P.O. Box 61297, Sunnyvale, CA 94088. "Bi-monthly newsletter, each containing hundreds of contests, grants, foundations, work-shops, scholarships, and awards for the poet and writer. A real, no-nonsense, writers' and poets' working tool! The original contest/resource calendar! We are dedicated to the wide dissemination of writers' information and offer FREE LISTINGS to the sponsor who sends us a rule sheet and/or application forms at least 3 months in advance of closing date. Out-of-date 'teaser' issue sent free to anyone requesting information. No current copies given free." 6/yr; 1-yr sub price: $12.00; sample: $2.00.

THE LITERARY MONTHLY (formerly Pacific Sun Literary Quarterly), Linda Ferguson, PO Box 1445, Ross, CA 94957, 415-383-4500. Poetry, fiction, articles, criticism, reviews. "The Literary Monthly is the successor to the Pacific Sun Literary Quarterly. Although it is primarily a book review publication, 25% of each issue is devoted to fiction and poetry. Contributors: Ferlinghetti, Boyle, Connell, Aram Saroyan, Herbert Gold, Richard Morris" 10/yr; 1-yr sub price: $6.00; per copy: $0.75; sample: $0.75. 1974. 24pp; 11 x 17. of. circ. 20,000. Reporting time: 1 month. Payment: 50 cents/column inch. Copyrighted, reverts to author. Ads: $504.00/$252.00/$6.00 column inch. Discounts: inquire. Back issues: prices on request. Pub's reviews. §all areas. COSMEP.

The Literary Review, Martin Green, Harry Keyishian, Fairleigh Dickinson University, 285 Madison Avenue, Madison, NJ 07940. "We consider fiction and poetry submissions of any type and of any length (within reason) from new and established writers. We welcome critical articles on any aspect of American and international literature and are anxious to have submissions of essays that are written for a general literary audience and not aimed at the academic quarterly market. We are preparing some special issues on the following themes and particularly welcome essays on these topics: *The Great Depression* and *Its Literary Impact;* the modern practice of tragedy in fiction, drama, and film; medieval literature as international culture and its continuities; popular genres in the U.S. and abroad. *TLR* has always had a special emphasis on contemporary writing abroad (in translation) and we welcome submissions from overseas." avg. price, cloth: $9.00 U.S., $10.00 foreign; paper: $3.50 U.S., $4.00 foreign. avg. press run 1,000-1,200. Reporting time: 2-3 months. Payment: copies.

LITERARY SKETCHES, Mary Lewis Chapman, Box 711, Williamsburg, VA 23185, 804-229-2901. Articles, interviews, reviews, letters. "1,000 word maximum" 11/yr; 1-yr sub price:

$2.50; per copy: $.25; sample: $.25. 1961. 16pp; 7 x 4. †of. circ. 500. Reporting time: month. Payment: 1/2 cent per word. Ads: $10/$6/$.05. Back issues: $0.25. Pub's reviews. §Literary Biographies only. COSMEP, NESPA.

‡LITERATURE & IDEOLOGY, Progressive Books & Periodicals, Box 727, Adelaide Stn., Toronto, Ont., Canada.

Litmus, Inc., Charles Potts, Editor, 574 3rd Ave, Salt Lake City, UT 84103. Poetry, photos, long-poems, plays. "Charles Bukowski, Mike Finley, Edward Smith, Karen Waring. Inquire before submitting." avg. price, paper: $3.00. 1966. 64pp; 5½ x 8½. †of/lp. Reporting time: 6 months. Payment: 10%. Copyrights for author. Discounts: 40 percent on 5 or more, mixed titles OK.

LITTACK SUPPLEMENT, Ember Press (Brixham), William Oxley, 6 The Mount, Furzeham, Brixham, South Devon, United Kingdom. Poetry, reviews. "No bias on length; quality only criterion. But tired of the lie that splits the modern from the traditional. Contributors: Robert Graves, Kathleen Raine, Ian Hamilton Finlay, Hugh MacDiarmid, Lawrence Durrell, Rigby Graham, Anthony L. Johnson, Ronald Duncan, Anthony Rudolf, Hugo Manning, Duncan Glen, Tom Scott, David Jaffin, Cal Clothier, Kathleen Abbott. objective: to establish a climate of new poetry of UK." 2/yr; 1-yr sub price: 50p ($1.00); per copy: 25p. 1972. 16pp; 11-7/10 x 8 -5/10. lo. circ. 400. Reporting time: US 4wks; UK 1wk. Payment: by negotiation. no advtg. Discounts: 33-1/3 trade. Back issues: first editions, available at cost.

THE LITTLE AROUND JOURNAL, Around Publishing, Janos Szebedinszky, Patricia Walsh, PO Box 541, Mentone, IN 46539. Poetry, fiction, articles, art, photos, cartoons, interviews, satire, criticism, reviews, music, letters, parts-of-novels, long-poems, collages, plays, concrete art, news items. "Length of material determines size of publication. Biases are toward less 'down' information, more toward entertainment, and access to things." 12/yr; 1-yr sub price: $5.00; per copy: $0.50; sample: free. 1975. 16-28pp; 6 x 9. †of. circ. 2,000 to 5,000. Reporting time: 2-5 weeks. Payment: Promissory notes, and an occasional check. Copyrighted, reverts to author. Ads: $200.00/$100.00/$0.15. Discounts: general 25-35 percent discount. Back issues: $1.00 each. Pub's reviews. §Ecology, philosophy, anthropology, sci-fi, poetry, science, homemaking, humor, and all other good things.

LITTLE CAESAR, Dennis Cooper, Jim Glaeser, 231 W. Olive, Monrovia, CA 91016, 213-358-1556. Poetry, fiction, art, photos, cartoons, interviews. "We like work that's on fire. Originality catches our eyes. We want to reach everyone from poetry fans to rock'n'rollers to the Dodgers, so keep that in mind. We hope our biases are against dullness and didacticism, and pro-energy. Recent contributors: Tom Clark, Ron Koertge, Ian Young, Greg Kuzma, Jean Genet, Ron Padgett, Robert Peters." 3/yr; 1-yr sub price: $4.00; per copy: $1.50; sample: $1.50. 1976. 45pp; 5½ x 8½. of. circ. 300 and growing. Reporting time: 1 to 6 weeks. Payment: 3 copies. Copyrighted, reverts to author. Ads: $1.00. Discounts: 40 percent discount for trade, libraries, schools, etc. Back issues: $1.50 per issue. Pub's reviews §Literature publications chiefly.

LITTLE FREE PRESS, Larry F. Johnson, 715 E. 14th St., Minneapolis, MN 55404. "Anything logical utopian. Information for dropping out of Rat Race." 12/yr; 1-yr sub price: $10.00; per copy: $.05; sample: $.13 stamp. 1969. 8pp; 3½ x 8½. of. circ. 2M. no ads. Discounts: 3 cents each in quantities. Back issues: 3¢ plus postage.

THE LITTLE MAGAZINE, Barbara Damrosch, David G. Hartwell, Box 207 Cathedral Station, New York, NY 10025. Poetry, fiction, articles, interviews, criticism, reviews, parts-of-novels, long-poems. "No bias-just the best. Recent special issues: Women's Issue, Peter Wild, Maralyn Hacker, Tom Wayman, Albert Goldbarth." 4/yr; 1-yr sub price: $6.00; per copy: $1.50; sample: $1.50. 1964. 66pp; 5½ x 8½. of. circ. 1,000. Reporting time: 1 month. Payment: 2 copies. CCLM.

THE LITTLE REVIEW, Little Review Press, John McKernan, Marshall University, English Department, Huntington, WV 25701. "Modern poetry & translations." 2/yr; 1-yr sub price: $2.50; per copy: $1.25; sample: $1.25. 1968. 24-32pp; 8½ x 11. of. circ. 1,200. Reporting time: 2 mos.

Payment: copies. Pub's reviews. §poetry. CCLM.

Little Wing Publishing, Gloria J. Leitner, 865-E Emb. del Mar, Isla Vista, CA 93017. Poetry, art. "At present, publishing only the editor's own work. One book, 1975, *Poems Of Song & Passion* (paperback), hand-colored cover, 112 pp., illustrated. Love, nature, and spiritual poetry - $2.50. 1977 poemcards." 1975. 112pp; 4½ x 6. of. Discounts: 30%.

LIVE FREE QUARTERLY, Uphill Underground Press, James C. Jones, James Koller, Live Free Inc., PO Box 743, Harvey, IL 60426. Poetry, articles, cartoons, reviews, letters. "*Psychosurvival*-technical/*Position Paper #1*- philosophy/*Wind Power For Independence*- science/*The Endless Beginning*- philosophy/*The Three Little Pigs Revisited*- philosophy/*Chinese Wall*- poetry" 4/yr; 1-yr sub price: $3.00; per copy: $1.00; sample: $1.00. 1974. 20pp; 8½ x 11. †of. circ. 400. Reporting time: 3 to 4 months. Ads: $18.00/$10.00/$.05. Discounts: Group: 10 copies/$15.00 per year. Back issues: 4 issues $3.00. Pub's reviews. §Survival, Alt Life Style, Camping, Philosophy, Energy, Ecology. COSMEP.

LIVING BLUES, Jim O'Neal, Amy O'Neal, 2615 N. Wilton, Chicago, IL 60611. Articles, photos, interviews, criticism, reviews, letters. 6/yr; 1-yr sub price: $4.00; per copy: $.75; sample: $1.00. 1970. 52pp; 8¼ x 10-5/8. of. circ. 5,500. Ads: $120/$70/$.15. Back issues: $1.00 each. Pub's reviews. §blues & black music, black culture.

Living History Classrooms Pub. Co. (see MASTHEAD)

LIVING IN THE OZARKS NEWSLETTER, Living In The Ozarks, Joel Davidson, Sherri Davidson, Pettigrew, AR 72752. Articles, art, cartoons, interviews, satire, criticism, reviews, letters. "50 to 1000 word articles on back to the land homesteading in ozark region, any regional material, decentralist." 12/yr; 1-yr sub price: $8.00; per copy: $.75; sample: $.75. 1974. 18pp; 8½ x 11. †mi. circ. 3,000. Payment: copies. Ads: NC paid ads. Back issues: $.75. Pub's reviews. §How-To, Gardening, Energy,; Bulling; Farming. COSMEP.

Living Poets Press, Samuel Mandelbaum, Laura Mandle, S.J. Mandle, 838 Carroll St., Brooklyn, NY 11215. Poetry, fiction, photos, plays. "Leo Connellan-*Another Poet In New York*- poetry. Allen Planz-*Wild Craft*- poetry. William Packard-*Four Plays*- plays. *A Harvest Of Ideas*- ed. Leo Connellan-anthology." 1975. Discounts: 40%.

Llewellyn Publications (see GNOSTICA)

LOCAL TENDERNESS, Old Marble Press, Terry Henry, P.O. Box 1701, E. Lansing, MI 48823. Poetry, art, photos, cartoons, collages. "David Highsmith, Al Drake, David Ignatow, Franze Douskey, Rochelle Owens, Lyn Lifshin, A.D. Winans, Ted Enslin...others. Like Creative force Craziness/Poems that have movement...Am tending towards doing the thing quarterly and am going toward Black Book and sparrow and several others. That is one poet per issue/it makes it a lot easier for me." 4/yr; 1-yr sub price: $3.00; per copy: $1.00; sample: postage. 1973. 44pp; half 8½ x 11. circ. 250. Payment: 2 copies. Ads: $30/$20/$.10 wd classified. Discounts: regular. COSMEP.

LOCUS: The Newspaper of the Science Fiction Field, Locus Publications, Charles N. Brown, Dena C. Brown, Box 3938, San Francisco, CA 94119, 415-339-9196. Articles, photos, interviews, reviews, letters, news items. "News stories, reports on SF events." 12/yr; 1-yr sub price: $6.00, individual/yr; $10.00, institution; per copy: $0.75; sample: $0.75. 1968. 16pp; 8½ x 11. of. circ. 3,500. Ads: $100.00/$60.00/$1.00 per line. Discounts: 40% plus postage on 10 or more. Back issues: from 50¢. Pub'd 15 issues 1976; expects 12 issues 1977, 12 issues 1978. Pub's reviews: 190 in 1976. §only S.F.

Lodestar Press, John Gierach, John Moulder, P.O. Box 4657, Boulder, CO 80306. Poetry. "*Broadsides* by: Creeley, Coolidge, Aram Saroyan, Tom Clark, Jack Collom, Eigner, Charley George, Charles Potts, Maria Gitin, Marilyn Thompson, Theodore Enslin. *Books* by: Jack Collom, John Moulder, Marc Campbell, John Gierach. No specific biases. Book mss: 48 pages or less. Single exceptional poems will be considered for Broadside series." 1974. 30pp; 6 x 8½. †lp. Reporting time: 2-4 wks. Payment: copies. Copyrights for author. Discounts: 40 percent on orders over $20. Pub'd 2 titles 1976; expects 1 title 1977.

Lodestar Publishing, 3075 West Seventh Street, Los Angeles, CA 90005, 213-387-9781. "First book 4-28-77 a family story craft book with pre-assigned library of Congress catalogue card number. 1978 begins the first of a bilingual series on Southwest. Interested in hearing from deeply involved economic botanists and/or aspiring young naturalists." avg. price, cloth: $8.95; paper: $6.95. 1974. 85-100pp; 8½ x 7. of/silk screening. avg. press run 500 copies. Discounts: Postage prepaid 40 percent-no limit on number for trade. Special considerations to professional library story-tellers on family story craft books.

LODGISTIKS, Derwyddon Press, David Uu, Lodge North, Box 764, Kingston, Ontario K76 4X6, Canada. Poetry, fiction, articles, art, photos, parts-of-novels, long-poems, collages, plays, non-fiction. "No restrictions on length. Inclined towards language experimentation (visual poetry, etc.) surrealism and fantastic art. Particularly interested in philosophy and occult philosophy (alchemy, etc.) expressed through the arts. Past contributors include: Bill Bissett, Jack Wise, Alan Neil, Paul de Vree, Gerry Gilbert, Ivo Vroom, Gary Lee-Nova, Edwin Varney, etc." irreg.; sub price: $10.00/4 issues; per copy: Varies. 1972. 40pp; 8½ x 11. †of/mi. circ. 100-500. Reporting time: 6 weeks. Payment: 2 copies. Copyrighted, reverts to author. Discounts: 1-5 20%/6-10 27%/over 10 33-1/3%. Back issues: Prices available on request. Pub'd 1 issue 1976. DOL.

THE LONDON COLLECTOR, Wolf House BOOKS, Richard Weiderman, Frank Girard, James E. Sisson, P.O. Box 209, Cedar Springs, MI 49319. Poetry, articles, art, photos, cartoons, interviews, criticism, reviews, letters. "THE LONDON COLLECTOR publishes articles of interest to fans and students of Jack London. One topic is discussed each issue. Wolf House Books reprints rare ephemera & other scarce London material. Future plans call for further reprinting of desirable material as well as a series of monographs by contemporary London scholars." irreg.; 1-yr sub price: $1.00; per copy: $.50; sample: none. 1970. 20pp; 5½ x 8½. of. circ. 130. Reporting time: immediate. Payment: 12 copies. Discounts: 40% five or more.

London Northwest (see THE CHANEY CHRONICAL, WHAT'S NEW ABOUT LONDON, JACK?)

Lonely Planet Publications, Tony Wheeler, P.O. Box 88, South Yarra, Victoria 3141, Australia, 03 42 5928. Non-fiction. "Travel guides for the low budget traveler-& to exotic, unusual countries." avg. price, paper: $3.00. 1972. 192pp; 5 x 7¼. of. avg. press run 10,000. Copyrights for author. Ads: $350.00-$500.00 full page, 4 color. Discounts: generally 55 percent to my overseas accounts. Pub'd 2 titles 1976; expects 5 titles 1977, 8 titles 1978. IPA.

Long Island Poetry Collective, Inc. (see NEWSLETTER)

LONG ISLAND REVIEW, Box 900, Chicago, IL 60690. Poetry, fiction, articles, interviews, criticism, reviews, parts-of-novels, long-poems, plays. "Still looking for purposeful, well-crafted material, form and content worthy of each other. Criticism and reviews of contemporary writers, not literary history. Still object to the purely didactic, the sentimental, the artificially structured. Where are the writers of experimental fiction? No more stories about English professors, please. Anyone out there know Anne Hussey's whereabouts? Giles Gordon?" 2/yr; 1-yr sub price: $2.00; per copy: $1.00; sample: $1.00. 1973. 48-64pp; 5½ x 8½. of. circ. 300. Reporting time: 5-6 wks. Payment: 2 copies. Ads: $10/$6. Discounts: 40%. Back issues: $1. §poetry/fiction/criticism of contemporary literature. COSMEP.

LONG POND REVIEW, Vince Clemente, Joe Hilyard, Ed Joyce, Russell Steinke, Dan Murray, Pat Powers, Steve Lewis, Ivan Sanders, John Gabosch, English Dept, Suffolk Community College, Selden Long Island, NY 11784. "LONG POND REVIEW prints what's best in contemporary poetry, fiction, and criticism. Some recent contributors: May Swenson, David Ignatow, John Hall Wheelock, William Heyen, Aaron Kramer, Allen Planz, Robert DeMaria, Greg Kuzma, Tom

Snapp." 2/yr; 1-yr sub price: $3.00; per copy: $1.50; sample: $1.00. 1974. 86pp; 6 x 9. lp. circ. 1M. Reporting time: 1 mo. Payment: copies only. no ads. Discounts: none. Back issues: $1.

Longman's Of Nigeria (see BLACK ORPHEUS)

LOOK QUICK, Quick Books, Robbie Rubinstein, Joel Scherzer, P.O. Box 4434, Boulder, CO 80306. Poetry, fiction, music. "We seek material with a feel for the bizarre and the erotic. Original use of language is a top priority. Much of what we publish has urban themes, often with an eye to the cinema. We can relate to writing with strange and even unwholesome undercurrents. Among other things, we're devotees of the hard-boiled school of American fiction and its modern derivatives. Blues lyrics are always welcome, as are imaginative line drawings. Recent contributors include: Roger Aplon, Guy R. Beining, Judson Crews, Stuart Dybek, Barbara Holland, Thomas Johnson, Arthur Winfield Knight, Allen Kovler, Lyn Lifshin, Errol Miller, Okie Tony and Philip Whalen." 2 or 3/yr; sub price: $2.50 - 4 issues.; per copy: $.75; sample: $0.75. 1975. 24pp; 5½ x 8½. †of. circ. 500. Reporting time: As soon as possible up to one month. Payment: copies. no ads. Back issues: $.75. Expects 2 issues 1977, 3 issues 1978. COSMEP, COSMEP-WEST.

LOON, D.L. Emblen, Richard Speakes, Richard Welin, P.O. Box 11633, Santa Rosa, CA 95406. Poetry. "No limit on length, style, or subject matter: we simply want the best poems we can find. We also want good translations of foreign poets. Some recent contributors: Douglas Blazek, Robert Gibb, Patricia Goedicke, Peter Wild, William Talcott, Thomas Johnson, Tomas Transtromer, John Vernon, David Waggoner, Werner Aspenstrom, Jeanne Kammer, Lucien Stryk." 2/yr; 1-yr sub price: $3.00; per copy: $1.50; sample: $1.50. 1973. 60pp; 5½ x 8½. of. circ. 500. Reporting time: 2-8 weeks. Payment: 2 copies. All rights reserved; copyright reassigned to authors on request. Pub'd 2 issues 1976; expects 2 issues 1977, 2 issues 1978. Pub's reviews: 2 in 1976. §poetry. CCLM, COSMEP.

LOOSE LIPS SINK SHIPS, California Syllabus (Cal-Syl Press), Madonna Datzman, Mark Ross, Tobey Kaplan, P.O. Box 2764, Oakland, CA 94602. Poetry, fiction, articles, art, cartoons, satire, music, letters, parts-of-novels, long-poems, collages, plays. "We refer to LLSS as 'literary vaudeville'; all possibilities are considered. Esp. experimental materials. No unsolicited material will henceforth be accepted." 2/yr; sub price: $1.50/2 issues.; per copy: $0.50 plus $0.25 postage. 1975. 64pp; 5½ x 8½. †of. circ. 700. Reporting time: Indefinite. Payment: None. Copyrighted, reverts to author. Ads: None. Discounts: None. Back issues: $0.50 plus $0.25 P & H. Pub'd 1 issue 1976; expects 1 issue 1977, 2 issues 1978.

LORE AND LANGUAGE, J.D.A. Widdowson, The Centre of English Cultural Tradition and Language, The University, Sheffield S10 2TN, United Kingdom, Sheffield 79555 ext 211. Articles, reviews. "Articles and items for those interested in language, folklore, cultural tradition and oral history." 2/yr; 1-yr sub price: £1; per copy: 50p. 1969. 54pp; 15 x 21cm. lo. circ. 1,000. Reporting time: 3 wks. Payment: none. Ads: none. Discounts: none. Back issues: Vol. 1 25p each, Vol 2 50p each. Pub'd 2 issues 1976; expects 2 issues 1977, 2 issues 1978. Pub's reviews: 62 in 1976. §Language, folklore, cultural tradition, oral history. CECTAL.

LOST AND FOUND TIMES, Luna Bisonte Prods, Casa Del Sensitive, John M. Bennett, Douglas C. Landies, 137 Leland Ave, Columbus, OH 43214, 118 E. Longview, Columbus, OH 43202. Poetry, fiction, articles, art, photos, cartoons, satire, reviews, letters, parts-of-novels, long-poems, collages, concrete art. "Opal Nations, Klaus Groh, Charles Johnson, Reality Reality, Whitson, J. Hyder, Frank Ferguson, Music Master, Smokie Topaz, Mango Dave, Jim Jordan, Gregg Puchalski. New expanded format makes room for anything: make it meaty, outrageous." irreg; sub price: $5.00 for 5 issues; sample: $1.00 for sample packet. 1975. 15-20pp; 8½ x 5½. of. circ. 300. Reporting time: 2 wks. Payment: copies. Discounts: 40% for resale. Pub's reviews. §Literature, Art, Reviews. COSMEP.

LOVE LIGHTS, Boustrophedon Deserted X (Mag), David Moe, #354 1230 Grant Ave, San Francisco, CA 94133. "Send poems typed on a dark ribbon (if possible) with your name on each page. Recent contributors: Janice Blue, Harold Norse, Jack Hirschman, Irving Stettner, Kristen

Wetterhahn, Summer Brenner, Luke Breit, Dan Propper, Julius Caesar, Neelie Cherkovski, Tom Plante, Stephen Kessler, Kaye McDonough, Lawrence Ferlinghetti, Tommy Trantino, Mike Koch, Suzanne Freedman, Tom Dawson." irreg; 1-yr sub price: $5.00; per copy: $.25-$.50; sample: $1.00. 1968. 12-16pp; 10¼ x 16½. of. circ. 40,000. Reporting time: long time. Payment: copies. Ads: $375/$200. Back issues: $5000.00 for complete set. §Plays, fables, music compositions, poetry, photo-collages.

The Love Project (see THE SEEKER NEWSLETTER)

Love Street Books, Jim Wortham, P.O. Box 58163, Louisville, KY 40258. Poetry, plays. "Send inquiry before sending manuscript." avg. price, paper: $2.50. 1974. 64pp; 5½ x 8½. of. avg. press run 1,000 copies. Reporting time: 1 month. Payment: 10% royalty. Copyright in author's name. Discounts: 40% to trade. Pub'd 6 titles 1976; expects 6 titles 1977, 6 titles 1978. COSMEP.

Lovers Of The Stinking Rose/Midpress Books (see GARLIC TIMES)

Loverseed Press (see also DAY BY DAY), Woolacombe House, 141 Woolacombe Rd., Blackheath, London SE3, United Kingdom, 01-856-6249. "Publishes pamphlets on politics, religion, economics, poetry & magazines." 1959.

LOWLANDS REVIEW, Tom Whalen, Nancy Harris, 8204 Maple No. 1, New Orleans, LA 70118. Poetry, fiction, art, interviews, reviews, parts-of-novels, long-poems. "We like the experimental/surreal, but are not adverse to good work in any vein. Recent contributors include Ralph Adamo, Peter Cooley, Stuart Dybek, Leon Stokesbury, Brian Swann, Julia Randall, Christopher Middleton, Robert Walser, etc." 2/yr; 1-yr sub price: $3.00; per copy: $1.50; sample: $1.50. 1974. 48pp; 6 x 9. of. circ. 400. Reporting time: 2 wks to 2 mos. Payment: 3 copies. Copyrighted, reverts to author. Pub'd 2 issues 1976; expects 2 issues 1977, 2 issues 1978. Pub's reviews: none in 1976. §fiction, poetry (contemporary).

LSM Information Center (see also LSM NEWS), LSM Information Center, P.O. Box 2077, Oakland, CA 94604, 635-4863. Articles, art, photos, interviews, criticism, reviews. "We publish our own material on the national Liberation Struggles in Southern Africa. Recent publications are *The People In Power* and *Road To Liberation* documenting, from first-hand experience, the recent conflict in Angola." avg. price, paper: $1.50. 1970. 50-125pp; 5¼ x 8¼. †of. avg. press run 3,000. Payment: none. Copyright sometimes. Discounts: bookstores only-40 percent discount on prepaid orders; 25 percent invoiced postage & handling. Pub'd 3 titles 1976; expects 4 titles 1977.

LSM NEWS, LSM Press, Carol Barnett, LSM Information Center, P.O. Box 2077, Oakland, CA 94604. Articles, art, photos, interviews, criticism, reviews, music, letters. "Political organ of pro-socialist, anti-imperialist, marxist-leninist organization, i.e., we mostly write our own material. Most of what we print is on national liberation movements and our own work." 4/yr; 1-yr sub price: $2.00; per copy: $.50; sample: $0.75. 1974. 40pp; 8½ x 5½. †of. circ. 2,500. Copyrighted. Discounts: 1-5 copies 25%, 6 or more 50%-trade only. Back issues: $1.00 each except for 1st 2 issues-$.50 to individuals. Pub'd 4 issues 1976; expects 4 issues 1977, 4 issues 1978. Pub's reviews. §Left political.

LUCILLE, Lucille Press, Stephen Harrigan, Alice Gordon, Sue Ellen Line, No. 5 Kern Ramble, Austin, TX 78722. Poetry, reviews. "We're interested in seeing strong, serious poems of any reasonable length. We don't belong to any 'school' that we're aware of. Recent contributors: John Ramington, Thomas Whitbread, Glenn Hardin, Vassar Miller, James Whitaker." 2/yr; sub price: $2.00/2 yr; per copy: $.50; sample: $0.50. 1973. 80pp; 5½ x 8½. of. circ. 1,000. Reporting time: 2 mos. Payment: 2 copies. Copyrighted; reverts to author after publication. Ads: $40/$20. Back issues: $1.00. Pub'd 2 issues 1976; expects 2 issues 1977, 2 issues 1978. Pub's reviews: 2 in 1976. §poetry. CCLM.

LUCKY HEART BOOKS, Salt Lick Press, James Haining, Box 1064, Quincy, IL 62301. "Letters to Obscure Men. Verse by Gerald Burns. Catch My Breath. Verse, prose, and fiction by

Michael Lally. George Washington Trammell. Verse by Robert Trammell. Two Kids & The Three Bears. Prose narrative by John Dennis Brown." irreg.; 1-yr sub price: $5.00; sample: $1.00. 1939. †of/other. circ. 1,500. Reporting time: 10 days. Payment: copies and $ if available. Discounts: 65%-35%. CCLM, COSMEP.

LUDD'S MILL, Eight Miles High Press, Andrew Darlington, 44 Spa Croft Road, Teall Street, Ossett, West Yorkshire WF50HE, United Kingdom, Ossett 275814. Articles, poetry, fiction, art, cartoons, reviews, music, non-fiction. "Emphasis on general counter-culture, dada, beat, bebop, working class, rock, anarchist, psychedelia, creative literature, S.F., Bohemian et al. Short biog. with submissions. Not returned without S.A.S.E." erratic; sub price: £1.00/4 issues; per copy: 25p plus post future; sample: 10p plus post. 1971. 20pp past (plan 32pp future); A5 future (A4 past). of. circ. 600. Reporting time: varies, asap. No payment. Ads: £4 pro rata smaller. Discounts: 1/3 indiv orders 6 copies or more, bookshops. Back issues: sold out. Pub'd 1 issue 1976; expects 3 issues 1977, 3 issues 1978. Pub's reviews: numerous in 1976. §Anything within the areas specified in comments. (emphasis on poetry, alternative arts, rock/jazz, science fiction).

LUNA, Luna Publications, Ann F. Dietz, 655 Orchard St., Oradell, NJ 07649. Articles, cartoons, interviews, reviews. "Title and frequency changed from LUNA Monthly in mid-1976, so current information is completely new. Have dropped some features and added some new ones, but the emphasis is still science fiction and fantasy news, reviews, bibliography, etc." 4/yr; 1-yr sub price: $3.00; per copy: $.75; sample: $.75. 1969. 48pp; 5½ x 8½. of. circ. 600. Reporting time: 1 month. Payment: copies. Ads: $10.00/$5.00/$.05. Back issues: $.50, $.75, $1.00. Pub's reviews. §science fiction, fantasy, space and related subjects.

Luna Bisonte Prods (see also LOST AND FOUND TIMES), John M. Bennett, 137 Leland Ave, Columbus, OH 43214. Poetry, art, cartoons, satire, letters, collages, concrete art. "Mostly dedicated to work of JMB and Nick L. Nips, but enjoy reading anything. Interested in exchanges. We print broadsides and labels, chapbooks, poetry products. Have published work of Richard Kostelanetz, Lyle Lee, Kirk Robertson, Thomas Michael Fisher and others." 1974. of/rubber stamps. Reporting time: 2 wks. Payment: copies. Discounts: 40% for resale. COSMEP.

LUNCH, Geoffrey Nulle, 220 Montross Ave, Rutherford, NJ 07070. Poetry, fiction, articles, art, cartoons, interviews, satire, criticism, letters, parts-of-novels, long-poems, plays, concrete art. "Long works are subject to editing because of space. No biases. Must have style of the seventies." 6/yr; 1-yr sub price: $3.00; per copy: $.50; sample: free. 1975. 25-30pp; 8 x 11. †mi. circ. 500. Reporting time: 3 wks. Payment: copies. Ads: $25/$12.50. Discounts: 50% schools 100 copies. Back issues: $.25. §poetry, fiction.

Lynx House Press, Robert Abel, Christopher Howell, PO Box 800, Amherst, MA 01002, 413-367-2865. Poetry, fiction. "We publish poetry and fiction of excellent quality; these are primarily first books by 'young' writers with substantial magazine/journal publication whose first book is long overdue. We have published Floyce Alexander, Ray Amorosi, Tomai O'Leary, Wayne Ude, Hal Stowell, Valerie Martin, Robert Hahn, Don Hendrie, Jr., and David Unson; and hope to publish Joyce Thompson, Robbie Gordon, and Margaret Robison as soon as funds are available. We also have a chapbook series, with titles by Robert Bohm, Robert Collen, Murry Crow, Cynthia Tveinblay, and Molly Ice." avg. price, paper: $2.50. 1971. 64pp; varies. of. avg. press run 500. Reporting time: 1 month-6 weeks. Payment: 10 percent of press run. We copyright for author. Discounts: 30-40 percent. Pub'd 5 titles 1976; expects 5 titles 1977, 5 titles 1978. NESPA.

M **M.O. Publishing Company (see also MODUS OPERANDI),** Sheila R. Jensen, P.O. Box 136, Brookeville, MD 20729. "We do not want to receive book manuscripts. Queries are welcome if accompanied by No. 10 SASE." avg. price, paper: $1.00 to $3.00. 1970. 100pp; 8½ x 5½. avg. press run 300.

THE MACROBIOTIC, First Feather Press, Herman Aihara, 1544 Oak St, Oroville, CA 95965. Poetry, fiction, articles, art, photos, cartoons, interviews, satire, criticism, reviews, music, letters, parts-of-novels, long-poems, collages, plays. "Material should be oriented around macrobiotic experiences and/or theorizing of philosophical dialectical, or traditional life, thought, which stresses or brings out the yin/yang aspects of phenomena or daily experience in Biology, Chemistry, Physics, Geology, Anatomy, Medicine or other fields of study. Any level of social or emotional experience coming from those who are trying the macrobiotic experience are welcomed and encouraged." 12/yr; 1-yr sub price: $10.00; per copy: $1.00; sample: $.50. 1970. 32pp; 8½ x 11. †of. circ. 1,200. Reporting time: no report made. No payment. Ads: $25.00/$15.00/$.01. Discounts: 40% on order over 10. Back issues: $.50 each. Pub's reviews. §Biology, Physiology, Diet, Philosophy, Dialectics, Medicine, etc.

The Madisonian (see ATARAXIA)

MADRONA, Gemini, Charles Webb, Editor; Gretchen Wigton, J. K. Osborne, Vasselis Zambaras, John Levy, Associate Editors, 4730 Latona N.E., Seattle, WA 98105. Poetry, fiction, art, photos, interviews, satire, letters, long-poems. "Editorial pearls: We want work that grabs the reader's interest and holds on. All-out war on dullness! 'Serious' literature should not be boring literature. Sterile academic and sloppy 'street' stuff gets the same cold shoulder. Good writing doesn't mirror experience, it creates it. Entertain us! We're sick of writers sounding alike. Good writers are influenced; bad writers parrot. A good thing may be fashionable, but fashionable things are rarely good. We're looking for people who've found their own voice and mastered its use. Good writing is so well crafted that it seems spontaneous. If we see the writer laboring, his labor is wasted. We want to meet powerful minds swarming with new ideas. Getting excited is a good way to forget we're dying. Contributors: Hugo, Levertov, Zimmer, Finkel, Bly, Edson, Stafford, Bukowski, Benedikt, Locklin, Koertge, Kessler, Matte, Robertson, Northsun, Grossbardt." irregular-when we get enough material for a good issue.; sub price: $5.00/volume; per copy: $2.50; sample: $2.00. 1971. 75pp; 7 x 8. †of. circ. 500. Reporting time: 1 wk-3 months-longer when we're out of town. Payment: copies. Ads: $40.00/$20.00/none. Discounts: 40% dealers, 40% classrooms. Back issues: query. Pub'd 2 issues 1976; expects 2 issues 1977. Pub's reviews. §poetry, fiction. CCLM.

Magic Circle Press, Valerie Harms, 10 Hyde Ridge Rd, Weston, CT 06880. Fiction, art, photos, criticism, concrete art. "Not accepting mss. at this time. Recent contributors are children's authors Ann McGovern and Ruth Krauss; Diarist and novelist Anais Nin, Erika Duncan, Susan Thompson, Sas Colby. Also have done special projects such as poetry of women from prison." 1972. of. Reporting time: 2 mos. Payment: depends. Discounts: 40% trade, 15% library. Pub'd 3 titles 1976; expects 3 titles 1977. COSMEP, NESPA.

MAGIC SAM, Asbolutely Furious Productions, Ken Bolton, Box 164 Wentworth Building, Darlington, N.S.W. 2037, Australia. Poetry, fiction, art, interviews, reviews, parts-of-novels, long-poems. "'Modern', - in the sense of being stylistically self conscious, even to the point of exhibiting this awareness." 2-3/yr; price per copy: $2.00 (Australian); sample: $2.00 (Australian). 1975. 180pp; quarto. †of. circ. 300-400. Reporting time: 6-8 weeks, or less. Payment: none. Back issues: $2.00 a. Pub's reviews.

Magna Publishing Co. (see NATIONAL ON-CAMPUS REPORT)

MAIL ORDER USA, Dorothy O'Callaghan, PO Box 19083, Washington, DC 20036. 1/yr; 1-yr sub price: $4.00; per copy: $4.00; sample: $2.00. 1972. 144pp; 5 x 8. of. circ. 5,000. §mail order/consumerism.

MAINE EDITION, Stephen Cook, 22 Bridge St, Topsham, ME 04086. Poetry, articles, interviews, criticism, reviews, letters, long-poems. 4/yr; sub price: $1.00/3 issues; per copy: $.50; sample: $.50. 1972. 20pp; 7½ x 10. circ. 1,000. Reporting time: 2 month. Payment: copies. §poetry.

Mainespring Press (see also LETTERS), G. F. Bush, Publisher; Helma Nash, Editor, Box 82, Stonington, ME 04681, 207-367-2484. "George Garret, Carlos Baker, G.F. Bush, Helen Nash,

Janet McCroskey, typical authors." avg. price, cloth: $6.95. 1965. 50 pp minimum; varies. †of. avg. press run 4,500 min. Reporting time: one month. Payment: usual. We retain first rights only; details available. Discounts: none. ALP, COSMEPA.

THE MAINSTREETER, The Scopcraeft Press, Antony Oldknow, Dept of English, Univ of Wisc, Stevens Pt, WI 54481. Poetry, art. "Wish to print regular-meter poems as often as possible; welcome translations (but must see original text); recent contributors: Mark Vinz. Richard Lyons, William Virgil Davis, Robin Hemley, Carla Hoffman, Gerald Gallant, Sherree Houston, Joan Eades, Dan Eades, Rise Smeall, Karen Locke, Ann Dunn, John Gidmark etc." irreg.; price per copy: $1.00; sample: $1.00. 1971. 44pp; 8 x 5. †of. circ. 400. Reporting time: 2 months. Payment: 2 copies. Ads: $50/$25. Discounts: bulk, classroom-both 15% off face value. Back issues: Combined volume reprint: MAINSTREETERS 1-5 $5.00 each. §modern poetry, fiction, criticism, books on movies.

MAJORITY REPORT, Nancy Borman, Joanne Steele, 74 Grove St, New York, NY 10014, 212-691-4950. Articles, interviews, criticism, reviews. "Newspaper, tabloid, in two colors. National international and local coverage of feminist events and women's issues. Habits of rapists. Calendar of feminist events. Subversive medical information. Feminist reviews of books, poetry, drama, film, media. Galleries listing. Women's business listing." 26/yr; 1-yr sub price: $5.00 indiv./$10.00 institutions; per copy: $.25; sample: $.50. 1971. 20pp; 11 x 17. of. circ. 25,000. Reporting time: immed/4 wks. Payment: none. Buys one-time rights. Ads: $745.00/$380.00/$0.50 ($7.50 min). Discounts: bulk, 40%; agent subscriptions, 20%. Back Issues: Jan-Dec 72 (as available) $15.00/Jan-Dec 73, $15.00/Jan-Dec 74 $12.50/Jan-Dec 75 $10.00. Pub'd 26 issues 1976; expects 26 issues 1977, 26 issues 1978. Pub's reviews. §feminist/women's/lesbian etc. COSMEP.

MAKARA, Makara Publishing & Design Cooperative, 1011 Commercial Dr, Vancouver B. C. V5L 3X1, Canada. Poetry, fiction, articles, art, photos, cartoons, interviews, satire, criticism, reviews, music, letters, parts-of-novels, long-poems, collages, plays, non-fiction. "A Makara is any composite beast-this MAKARA combines the relevance and innovation of alternative publications with the high quality of big budget magazines. Social issues, education, children, whatever the subjects, MAKARA handles them with a positive outlook, reflecting our belief that with real dialogue and a willingness to explore alternatives we can make the changes survival demands of us. MAKARA also reflects our belief that change comes from both inside and outside, and that it comes as a result of all kinds of pressures-humour as well as documented attack." 6/yr; 1-yr sub price: $6.00; per copy: $1.25; sample: $1.25. 1975. 48pp; 8½ x 11. of. circ. about 6,500. Reporting time: up to 2 months. Payment varies. Mag is copyrighted; rights revert to artist/author on publication. Ads: $300.00/$180.00. Discounts: Agents are granted a 10 percent discount. Bookstores buying outright from us-$0.75/copy. Bookstores buying on consignment-$0.88/copy. Back issues: *MAKARA'S* first year (6 issues)-$6.00. Pub'd 6 issues 1976; expects 6 issues 1977, 6 issues 1978. Pub's reviews. §all(emphasis on Canadian works). CPPA.

MAL DE MER, Press of Arden Park, Budd Westreich, 861 Los Molinos Way, Sacramento, CA 95825. Cartoons, satire. "This is a miniature magazine devoted to *humor,* not over 750 words." 12/yr; 1-yr sub price: $6.00; per copy: $.75. 1974. 12pp; 3¼ x 5½. †of/lp. circ. 200. Reporting time: 2 weeks. Payment: $1 to $5. Discounts: none. §if they're funny. COSMEP.

THE MALAHAT REVIEW, University of Victoria, B.C., Robin Skelton, Editor; William David Thomas, Charles Lillard, Asst. Editors, P.O. Box 1700, Victoria, British Columbia, Canada. Poetry, fiction, art, photos, interviews, criticism, letters, long-poems, plays, concrete art. "Short works preferred." 4/yr; 1-yr sub price: $8.00; per copy: $2.00; sample: $2.00. 1967. 150pp; 9 x 6. of. circ. 900. Reporting time: 8 to 10 weeks. Payment: $10.00 per poem page, $25.00 per thousand words-prose. Ads: $50. Discounts: 33-1/3%, agents and bookstores only. Pub's reviews.

Malki Museum Press (see also JOURNAL OF CALIFORNIA ANTHROPOLOGY), Katherine Siva Saubel, President of Malki Museum, Inc.; William Bright, Acting Director; Harry W. Lawton, Chairman of Editorial Board, Malki Museum Press, 11-795 Fields Road, Morongo Indian Reservation, Banning, CA 92220, 714-849-7291. "Books and phamphets of a scholarly or popular nature on the Native American peoples of California. Malki Museum Press has published 17 books, including

Carobeth Laird's best-selling *Encounter With An Angry God*, and numerous booklets." avg. price, cloth: $8.95; paper: $6.50; other: $1.50. 1965. pp varies.; Varies. of. avg. press run 1,500-2,000. Reporting time: 3 months. Payment: 10 percent royalties to authors. Copyrights for author. Discounts: Dealer discounts of 40 percent. Pub'd 3 titles 1976; expects 2 titles 1977, 3 titles 1978.

Malpelo, Lee Mallory, 1916 Court Avenue, Newport Beach, CA 92663. Poetry. "Latest offering is a broadside series featuring known and unknown writers. A majority of broadsides in each edition are numbered and signed by the poet. Recent contributors include: Thomas Kerrigan, Mike Finley, Lyn Lifshin, and Gordon Preston. All copies of this initial series are free. No unsolicited manuscripts." 1969. of. COSMEP.

The Mandeville Press, Peter Scupham, John Mole, The Mandeville Press, 2 Taylor's Hill, Hitchin, Hertfordshire SG49AD, United Kingdom. Poetry. "The Mandeville Press publishes pamphlet collections of poets both new and established, in runs of approximately 200. The pamphlets are printed in letterpress, by hand, and sewn into card-covers. Recent collections by Neil Powell, C. H. Sisson, Donald Ward, William Bedford, & Joan Downar." avg. price, paper: 50p. 1974. 16pp; 8 -5/8 x 5½. †lp. avg. press run 200-250. Reporting time: 2-3 wks. Payment: copies. Pub'd 2 titles 1976; expects 5 titles 1977.

MANGO, Lorna Dee Cervantes, 329 So. Willard A, San Jose, CA 95126, 297-2077 (408). Poetry, fiction, art, cartoons, interviews, satire, criticism, reviews. "Chicano litmag—no editorial biases, political or otherwise—publishes graphics bilingual—reads all material, answers all in the form of personal correspondence—(Ano I, Num. I) features the work of Ricardo Sanchez, Jose Antonio Burciaga, Ray Gonzalez, Lorna Dee Cervantes, Paul Fericano, Orlando Ramirez, Juan Bruce-Novoa, Wendy Rose, Jose Saldivar & Teresinka Pereira." 4/yr; 1-yr sub price: $3.00; per copy: $1.00; sample: $1.00. 1976. 40pp; 5½ x 8½. †of. circ. 500. Reporting time: 2 weeks. Payment: copies. Copyrighted, reverts to author. Ads: $15.00/$7.50/none. Pub's reviews. §Chicano literature.

MANITOBA NATURE (formerly ZOOLOG), Robert E. Wrigley, Manitoba Museum, 190 Rupert Ave., Winnipeg, Manitoba R3B0N2, Canada. Poetry, articles, art, photos, cartoons, satire, letters. "Mostly local content so do not seek submissions." 4/yr; 1 yr sub price: $2.50; per copy: $1.00 1966. 48pp; 6 x 9. circ. 3,500. Payment: none. Ads: $100/$65. Discounts: $.65/copy.

MANROOT, ManRoot Books, Paul Mariah, Richard Tagett, Box 982, South San Francisco, CA 94080. "Overstocked. We will be converting MANROOT into an annual because we do not like the topicality tag involved with magazine as we feel like we are more of an anthology or an annual than a magazine. Each will be thematic. Some back copies are available, please query. No ads used. An anthology of contemporary poetry will be available in 1977 in LARGE PRINT for the visually handicapped. Send self addressed stamped envelope for complete catalog listing and free poems that are available. We've published Robert Peters' THE POET AS ICESKATER, Helen Luster's YEAR OF THE HARE POEMS, Paul Mariah's Selected Poems 1960-1975,Jack Micheline's Selected Poems 1958-1975." 1-2/yr; 1-yr sub price: $5.00; per copy: $2.50; sample: $2.50. 1969. 120pp; 8½ x 5½. of. circ. 1,000. Reporting time: 3 months. Payment varies. Ads: None. Discounts: 40% bookstores & bulk available for classroom. Pub's reviews. §poetry/gay/prison/theatre. CCLM, COSMEP.

MANY SMOKES, Bear Tribe, Wabun, SunBear, P.O. Box 9169, Spokane, WA 99209. Poetry, articles, art, interviews, reviews. "Short stuff-Native American religions emphasis. Some earth . Must be constructive in attitude. Not scholarly, but accurate." 4/yr; 1-yr sub price: $2.00; per copy: $.50; sample: $.50. 1966. 20pp; 8½ x 11. †of. circ. 5,000. Reporting time: depends on kind. Payment: none. Copyrighted. Ads: $300/$150/$.15. Discounts: 30 percent agent, 50 percent jobber. Back issues: $0.75-$1.50. Pub'd 4 issues 1976; expects 4 issues 1977, 4 issues 1978. Pub's reviews. CCLM.

THE MARGARINE MAYPOLE ORANGOUTANG EXPRESS, Anonymous Owl Press, Carl Mayfield, Editor; Morrow Baker, Editorial Consultant, 3213 Wellesley, NE 2, Albuquerque, NM 87107. Poetry. "Dedicated to the short poem. Very short. Recent contributors: David Kherdian,

185

Theodore Enslin, Gene Frumkin, Larry Goodell, John Brandi." 6/yr; 1-yr sub price: $1.00; per copy: $0.25; sample: $0.25. 1973. 1pp; 5½ x 8½. of. circ. 50-100. Reporting time: 3 days to 1 week. Payment: 3 free copies. Not copyrighted. Discounts: none. Back issues: First issue: $10.00 most back issues: $1.00. CCLM.

MARGINS, P.O. Box A, Fair Water, WI 53931.

MARILYN: A Magazine of New Poetry, Jeffrey Wells-Powers, P. Schneidre, 150 West Ninth Street, Claremont, CA 91711. Poetry, long-poems. "James Merrill, W.D. Snodgrass, James Tate, Ira Sadoff, Peter Everwine, Bert Meyers, Lawrence Raab, Charles Martin, Greg Kuzma, Mark Strand, Charles Wright, Fanny Howe, Charles Simic, Richard Shelton, Michael Benedikt, Leonard Nathan, Charles Webb, Herbert Morris, Charles Bukowski, Stuart Friebert, Howard Moss, Lyn Lifshin, Philip Levine, Gary Soto, Norman Dubie, Robert Mezey, Ann Stanford, Gerard Malanga, F.D. Reeve, Tom Lux, Barry Spacks, Peter Wild, Jack Anderson, Peter Payack, Mike Finley." 2/yr; 1-yr sub price: $3.50; per copy: $1.95. 1975. 64pp; 8¼ x 5¼. of. circ. 500. Reporting time: 3 weeks. Payment: Contributor's copies. Copyrighted. Ads: $40/$25. Discounts: 40% trade discount/consignment 30%. Pub'd 2 issues 1976; expects 2 issues 1977. CCLM, COSMEP.

MARK TWAIN JOURNAL, Cyril Clemens, Mark Twain Journal, Kirkwood, MO 63122. 1-yr sub price: $3.00; per copy: $1.00; sample: $1.00. 1936. 21pp; 10 x 8. Reporting time: 10 days. Ads: $100. Back issues: all $1 a copy. §literary/biography/criticism.

MARKET FOR LIBERTY, Richard R. Gray, 1903 E. 38th, Albany, OR 97321. "MARKET FOR LIBERTY has primarily three focuses. One is to include articles on political philosophy relevant to the libertarian movement. A second is to cover the news of events both within the state and elsewhere which would be of interest or Oregon libertarians. The third is to cover editorials relevant to the Oregon Libertarian Party, its policies, prodeedures, etc." 12/yr; 1-yr sub price: $4.00; per copy: $.40; sample: free on request. 1975. 6pp; 8½ x 11 inches. of. circ. 57. Reporting time: 2 weeks. LPS.

THE MARKHAM REVIEW, Joseph W. Slade, Horrmann Library, Wagner College, Staten Island, NY 10301. "Need articles on history of technology; minor writers; popular culture. Maximum length—6000 words. MLA Style Sheet. Contributors generally academics." 4/yr; 1-yr sub price: $3.00; per copy: $1.00; sample: free. 1968. 20pp; 8½ x 11. of. circ. 1,000. Reporting time: 4 weeks. Payment: 18 copies. Copyrighted, subsequent copyright negotiable with author. Back issues: $1.00 per issue. Pub'd 4 issues 1976; expects 4 issues 1977, 4 issues 1978. Pub's reviews: 2 in 1976. COSMEP.

Maro Verlag, Benno Kaesmayr, Christiane Kaesmayr, Bismarckstr, 7½, D-8900 Augsburg, West Germany, 0827-577131. Poetry, fiction. "We are one of the 'German Alternative-Presses'. We are editing young German poets (Fauser, Derschau) and important American writers (in translation by Carl Weissner: Charles Bukowski, Harold Norse). Each year we arrange a complete catalogue of German Small Presses and Little Magazines ('books you cannot find everywhere'). *Turpentine On The Rocks* is called a new anthology edited by Charles Bukowski and Carl Weissner (1977)." avg. price, paper: dm 10.00. 1969. 150pp; 20.5/13.5 cm. †of. avg. press run 1,000-25,000. Reporting time: 6 months. Payment: 10-15 percent of retail prize. Copyrights for author. Discounts: 35-50 percent. Pub'd 3 titles 1976; expects 4 titles 1977, 4 titles 1978. AGAV.

Maryland Historical Press, Vera R. Rollo, 9205 Tuckerman St, Lanham, MD 20801, 301-577-2436. "We publish material for schools in Maryland on free-lance basis. History, Govt., Geog., Biography, and Black History. Our books are mostly set in type, printed via off-set process, illustrated, and about 50 percent are casebound, 50 percent paperback" avg. price, cloth: $6.00-$8.00; paper: $3.00 - $5.00. 1965. 100-400pp; 8½ x 11. of. avg. press run 2,000 copies on paperbacks, 5,000 on casebound. We buy almost nothing, sorry. Payment: None. Author is partner. Copyright in name of Vera Rollo or in one case Md H'l Press. Discounts: 33 percent to jobbers/dealers.

THE SUPPLEMENT TO THE BULLETIN OF THE MARYLAND WRITERS COUNCIL, Maryland Writers Council, Denis Boyles, 16 West Franklin St, Baltimore, MD 21201. Criticism, reviews, letters, concrete art, poetry, fiction. "Mostly news and commentary on collaborative literary activity and alternative publishing. Capsule reviews of all titles received. Circulates to libraries, mags and individuals in the mid-Atlantic area. Reprints from selected periodicals. Recent contributors: Douglas Messerli, Michael Scott Cain, Richard Kostelanetz, Diane Wakoski (from Gravida), Stephen Wiest, Bob Friedman, others." monthly except August; sub price: $10.00/yr; free to MWC members and exchanging periodicals. Membership: $7.50; per copy: $1.00; sample: gratis. 1974. 24pp (varies according to format); varies. †of/mi/silkscreen. circ. 500. Reporting time: 6 wks. Payment: copies. Ads: $10.00 any size (varies according to format) or exchange. Discounts: none. Back issues: No back issue available. Pub's reviews. §all areas.

THE MASSACHUSETTS REVIEW, John Hicks, Lee Edwards, Robert Tucker, Memorial Hall, Univ. of Mass, Amherst, MA 01003, 413-545-2689. Poetry, fiction, articles, art, photos, interviews, satire, criticism, reviews, letters, long-poems, plays, non-fiction. 4/yr; 1-yr sub price: $9.00; per copy: $2.50; sample: $2.50 plus $0.30 postage. 1959. 200pp; 6 x 9. lp. circ. 2M plus. Reporting time: 4-6 wks. Payment: $50 stories $10 min poetry. Ads: $125/$75/$50 1/4. Discounts: 15 percent discount on ads for univ. presses, adv. agencies, small presses; 40 percent bookstores. Back issues: $4 & $5. Pub'd 4 issues 1976; expects 4 issues 1977, 4 issues 1978. CCLM, COSMEP.

Master Calendar For Australian Growth Groups (see S.A. GROWTH PRESS)

MASTHEAD: A Journal For Teaching History With Old Newspapers, Living History Classrooms Pub. Co., Walter A. Day Sr., Walter A. Day Jr., P O Box 1009, Marblehead, MA 01845, 617-581-0198. Articles, reviews. "Can be any where between 500-5,000 words. Must be history of printing, history of journalism, paper americana hobbies; history teaching." 9/yr; 1-yr sub price: $9.00; per copy: $0.75; sample: $1.00. 1977. 20 - 24pp; 10 x 16. of. circ. 6,500 - 7,900. Reporting time: Within 3 weeks. Payment: Free subscriptions, ad space, complimentary copies other merchandise. No cash as of yet. Not copyrighted. Ads: $45.00/$24.00/$0.05. Discounts: Classroom: 50 copies or more can be purchased for $0.25 each. Back issues: $0.75 by mail; $1.25 by air mail in envelope. Pub's reviews §History or techniques in teaching history.

Matagiri (see COLLABORATION)

THE MATCH, P.O. Box 3488, Tuscon, AZ 85722.

MATHEMATICAL SPECTRUM, Applied Probablity Trust, H. Burkill, Dept of Pure Mathematics, The University, Sheffield S3 7RH, United Kingdom. Articles, reviews, letters. 3/yr; 1-yr sub price: £4.00. 1968. 100pp. circ. 2,500. Back issues: on request. Pub'd 3 issues 1976; expects 4 issues 1977, 4 issues 1978. Pub's reviews: 3 in 1976. §books on mathematics suitable for senior student's in schools and beginning undergraduates in colleges and universities.

MATI, Ommation Press, Effie Mihopoulos, 5548 N. Sawyer, Chicago, IL 60625. Poetry, articles, art, photos, interviews, reviews, letters, long-poems. "Very open to experimental poetry and especially poems by women. The magazine was established to provide another source where new poets can see their work in print. The work doesn't have to be perfect, but show potential. MATI wants to encourage young poets to see as much of their work in print as possible. Open to exchange (magazines and ads) with other magazines. Recent contributors: Anne Waldman, Alice Notley, Ron Padgett, Lawrence Ferlinghetti, Ted Berrigan, Opal L. Nations, John Tagliabue, Faye Kicknosway, Richard Kostelanetz, Ed Dorn, Lyn Lifshin." 4/yr; 1-yr sub price: $6.00; per copy: $1.50; sample: $1.50. 1975. 80-100pp; 8½ x 11. of. circ. 500. Reporting time: Immediately - 2 weeks. Payment: 1 copy. Ads: $30/$15. Discounts: 40%. Pub'd 1 issue 1976; expects 4 issues 1977, 4 issues 1978. Pub's reviews. §poetry, fiction, art. CCLM, COSMEP.

Matrix (see PRIMAVERA)

Mattole Press, Ray Porter, PO Box 22324, San Francisco, CA 94122. Articles, art, photos, cartoons, interviews. "Mattole Press is interested in book production developing out of intimate relationships between author, publisher, designer, editor. Plan to create a few fine books that grow out of personal experiences. At this time I am working on several projects and do not expect to start any new ones for at least two years." avg. price, cloth: $13.00. 1976. 250 pp varies; 8 x 8. of. avg. press run 2,000-5,000. Payment varies. Copyright varies. Discounts: trade.

Maverick Publications (see FLEA MARKET QUARTERLY ALMANAC)

MAYBE, Worlds of Fandom, IMK, Irvin M. Koch, c/o 835 Chatt. Bk. Bg., Chattanooga, TN 37402, 615-267-2000. Articles, art, cartoons, interviews, reviews, letters, parts-of-novels. "600-2000 words, of interest or info to the SF & F related fan." 4/yr. 1969. 20pp; 4¼ x 5½. of. circ. 200. Reporting time: Sase-immediately, otherwise—someday if & when. Payment: copies. Not copyrighted. Ads: $10.00/$5.00. Pub'd 6 issues 1976; expects 1 issue 1978. Pub's reviews: 20 in 1976. §science fiction, fantasy & related.

Mayer Press (see PIVOT)

M. McDonald (see LINES REVIEW)

MCLEAN COUNTY POETRY REVIEW, The Worn-Out Press, Terence M. Fitzgerald, Ruth A. Wantling, 101 East Sycamore, Normal, IL 61761. Poetry, art, photos, long-poems. "Judson Crews, James Scrimgeour, Steve Richmond, Erroll Miller" 2/yr; 1-yr sub price: $2.00; per copy: $1.00; sample: $1.00. 1975. 50pp; 8½ x 11. †mi. circ. 250-300 copies. Reporting time: 1-2 months. Payment: free copies. §poetry, photography.

Meanings Press, Stephen Alan Saft, 36 Megunticook St., Camden, ME 04843. 1975. of. Reporting time: one month plus.

MEANJIN QUARTERLY, Meanjin Company in association with the University of Melbourne, J.H. Davidson, Kris Hemensley, Poetry, University of Melbourne, Parkville, Victoria 3052, Australia. 4/yr; 1-yr sub price: $10.00; per copy: $2.50; sample: $2.50. 1940. 112pp; 9½ x 6½. lp. circ. 3,000. Reporting time: 2 months. Payment: for articles from $75. Ads: $220/$120. Pub's reviews. §cultural politics.

MEASURE, The Tribal Press, Howard McCord, P.O. Box 161, Bowling Green, OH 43402. Poetry, fiction, parts-of-novels, long-poems. "Each issue of MEASURE is devoted to the work of one writer. Recent issues include: Gus Blaisdell, *Dented Fenders;* Laura Chester, *Nightlatch;* Marie Harris, *Herbal,* Howard McCord, *The Arctic Desert.*" 2/yr; 1-yr sub price: $6.00; per copy: $3.00. 1971 (magazine) 1965 (press). 60pp; varies 5½ x 8 usually. of. circ. 400. Mss. by invitation only. Payment: copies (10% of run). Discounts: 40% to bookstores and dealers. CCLM.

MEDIA REPORT TO WOMEN, Donna Allen, Editor; Martha Leslie Allen, Associate Editor, 3306 Ross Pl. N.W., Washington, DC 20008, 202-363-0812. News items. "We publish annually an annotated, cumulative index of all past volumes of MEDIA REPORT TO WOMEN and a directory of women's media [periodicals, presses, publishers, news service, media columns, radio/tv groups and regular programs, video and cable groups, film, multi-media, art/graphic/theater groups, music (groups, recording companies, etc)] including women's albums, speakers bureaus, media courses, media organizations/media change/guidelines, distributors, bookstores and mail order, special library collections, selected directories and catalogs. Also includes directory of media women who ask to be included. Descriptions of women or groups in their words, with address, phone, contact people and other vital information. Brochure available." 12/yr; 1-yr sub price: $15.00; per copy: $1.00; sample: $1.00-ea. 1972. 16pp; 8½ x 11. of. circ. 1,500. Ads: $0.75. Discounts: bulk-40% on 5 or more. Back issues: $1.25. Pub'd 12 issues 1976; expects 12 issues 1977, 12 issues 1978. Pub's reviews: 20 in 1976. §media/women.

The Mediaworks, P.O. Box 4494, Boudler, CO 80303, 303-494-1439. Fiction. avg. price, paper: $4.00. 1975. 45pp; size varies. of. avg. press run 3,000 books. Payment varies. Does not copyright for author. Pub'd 3 titles 1976. COSMEP.

MEDICAL HISTORY, Edwin Clarke, Wellcome Institute for the History of Medicine, 183 Euston Rd., London NW1 2BP, United Kingdom. Articles, reviews, news items. 4/yr; 1-yr sub price: £10.00 yr ($25.00); per copy: £2.50. 1957. 116pp; 5 x 8. lp. circ. 1,300. Reporting time: 2 wks. No payment. Copyrighted. Ads: £30/ £16. Discounts: 10% for four consecutive issues. Back issues: £3.00 if available. Pub'd 4 issues 1976; expects 4 issues 1977, 4 issues 1978. Pub's reviews: 240 in 1976. §All aspects of history of medicine and allied sciences.

‡MELE, Univ. Of Hawaii, European Languages, Honolulu, HI 96822. CCLM.

Membrane Press (see also STATIONS), Karl Young, Publisher, P.O. Box 11601-Shorewood, Milwaukee, WI 53211. "Not looking for unsolicited material at this time. Books currently available by: Toby Olson, Martin J. Rosenblum, Kathleen Wiegner, Hilary Ayer, John Shannon, Tenney Nathanson, Barbara Einzig, Jerome Rothenberg, Nathaniel Tarn, Harris Lenowitz, Jackson Mac-Low, Karl Young, Charles Doria. Also: Monaural cassettes ($6) and Membrane Press post cards (sample pack of at least 8 cards-50 cents)." avg. price, paper: $2.50. 80pp; varies. †of. avg. press run 700. Payment varies. Discounts: 40 percent trade. Pub'd 6 titles 1976; expects 6 titles 1977.

MEN'S, M.E.N. International, Richard Doyle, P.O. Box 189, Forest Lake, MN 55025. 12/yr; 1-yr sub price: $15.00 (to non-members); per copy: $1.00; sample: Free to distributors. 1975. 14pp; 7 x 8½. of. circ. 2,000. Reporting time: 30 days. Ads: $10.00-column inch. Discounts: 10 percent to agents. Back issues: $0.50 each. Pub's reviews. §Law men's, women's lib, divorce.

The Menard Press, Anthony Rudolf, Brenda Rudolf, 23 Fitzwarren Gardens, London N19, United Kingdom. Poetry. "1) poetry, poetics, translated poetry. 2) 15 books were published in 1976. 3) the press's books are distributed in the USA by Serendipity Books, Berkeley, California." avg. price, paper: $3.00. 1971. 48pp. of/lp. avg. press run 600. no new manuscripts can be considered for time being. ALP.

Mercer House Press, P.O. Box 681, Kennebunkport, ME 04046. Discounts: 40% to wholesalers.

MERIP REPORTS, P.O. Box 3122, Columbia Heights Station, Washington, DC 20010. Articles, art, photos, cartoons, interviews, reviews. 10/yr; 1-yr sub price: $10.00; per copy: $1.00; sample: free. 1971. 28pp; 8½ x 11. of. circ. 1,500. Payment: none. Copyrighted. Discounts: 40%. Back issues: $1.00 (for all back issues). Pub'd 10 issues 1976; expects 10 issues 1977, 10 issues 1978. Pub's reviews: 10 in 1976. §middle east politics, economics, international economics, oil. APS, COSMEP.

MERLIN PAPERS, Merlin Press, Milton Loventhal, Jennifer McDowell, PO Box 5602, San Jose, CA 95150. Poetry, fiction, art, photos, reviews, music, parts-of-novels, plays. "Prose pieces should not exceed 10 pages. Two to 6 poems per submission is preferred. Enclose SASE. Recent contributors. Julia Vinograd, George Kauffman, Nancy Gaugier." Irregular; 1-yr sub price: 5 issues $2.00-institutions; 5 issues $5.00; per copy: $0.50; sample: $0.25. 1969. 8pp; 19 x 11. of. circ. 1,000. Reporting time: 6 months. Payment: Copies. Copyrighted, reverts to author. Ads: $50.00/$25.00/$10.00 for 2 x 2. Discounts: One-third off. Back issues: Issues 1-6 $3.00, each others $1.00 each. Expects 1 issue 1977, 1 issue 1978. Pub's reviews: 1 in 1976. CCLM.

Merlin Press (see also MERLIN PAPERS), Milton Loventhal, Jennifer McDowell, P. O. Box 5602, San Jose, CA 95150. Poetry, music, non-fiction. avg. price, paper: $7.95. 1977. of. avg. press run 1,000. Reporting time: 6 months. Copyrights for author. Discounts: 1-10 copies, 10 percent; 11-20 copies, 20 percent; above 20, 30 percent. Expects 1 title 1977. CCLM.

METAMORPHOSIS, Metamorphosis Books, T. Fallon, Rumford, ME 04276. Poetry, fiction, satire, parts-of-novels, long-poems, plays, concrete art. "Will study *any* literary work. Writers should *stand* on work/*contradict* editor's criticism if they feel they're right. Will read legible xerox, carbon and handwritten works. Editor does *not* stand on ceremony with honest writers. Recent contributors: McMahon, Burns, Ferlinghetti, McLean, Knight, O'Niell." 2/yr; 1-yr sub price: $2.00; per copy: $1.00; sample: $1.00. 1973. 50pp plus; 5¼ x 7. 1p. Reporting time: 1-3 mos. Payment: copies. Ads: $25/$18/none. §fiction/poetry. COSMEPA.

METANOIA, An Independent Journal of Radical Lutheranism, Douglas C. Stange, 1018 9th Street No. 47, University Village, Albany, CA 94710. Articles, art, photos, interviews, reviews, letters. "Material-articles that run about 5-6 double space typewritten pages. Style-interpretative rather than descriptive, forceful rather than milk-toast. Biases-leftist, in the old Christian Socialist tradition. Non-violent unless...Contributors include Joseph Fletcher, Harvey Cox, Martin Niemoeller, John C. Cooper, Connie Parvey, et. al." 4/yr; 1-yr sub price: $3.00; per copy: $1.00; sample: $1.00. 1969. 12-16pp; 8½ x 11. of. circ. under 1M. Reporting time: 2-3 wks. Payment: copies only. Ads: no paid ads, sometimes carry free ads for selected "causes". Discounts: bulk rates available. Back issues: Most still available at $1.00 each plus postage. Pub'd 4 issues 1976; expects 4 issues 1977, 4 issues 1978. Pub's reviews: 3 in 1976. §Religion and politics/Social problems.

Metloc (see THE BARD)

MEXICO WEST, Baja Trail Publications, Inc., Tom Miller, Elmar Baxter, P.O. Box 6088, Huntington Beach, CA 92646, 714-836-9203. Articles, news items. "500-750 words. Current travel and recreational information on Baja and west coast of Mexico-story style." 6/yr; 1-yr sub price: $5.00; per copy: $1.00; sample: $.25. 1975. 12pp; 8 x 10½. of. circ. 1,000. Reporting time: 2 weeks before 1st of Feb., Apr., June, Aug., Oct., Dec. Payment: $20. Ads: none. Discounts: none. Back issues: $1.00 each. Pub'd 6 issues 1976; expects 6 issues 1977, 6 issues 1978. Pub's reviews: 4-6 in 1976. §Mexico/travel/Baja. COSMEP.

Micah Publications, Robert Kalechofsky, Roberta Kalechofsky, 255 Humphrey St, Marblehead, MA 01945. Fiction, articles, criticism. "Micah Publications publishes prose: scholarly, fictional, lyrical; a prose that addresses itself to issues without offending esthetic sensibilities, a prose that is aware of the esthetics of language without succumbing to esthetic solipsism. Two books a year. No unsolicited mss." avg. price, paper: $4.50. 1975. 200pp; 5½ x 8½. of. avg. press run 600 books. Reporting time: 3 months. Payment: none. Discounts: 1-5 books 30%/6-50 books 40%/51 books and up 50%. Pub'd 2 titles 1976; expects 1 title 1977, 1 title 1978. COSMEP, NESPA.

MICHIGAN GERMANIC STUDIES, Michigan Germanic Studies, Inc., Emery E. George, Editor; Thomas L. Markey, Managing Editor, Department of German, University of Michigan, Ann Arbor, MI 48109, (313) 764-5357. Articles, art, photos, criticism, reviews. "MICHIGAN GERMANIC STUDIES is a journal of academic scholarship in the field of Germanic Languages and Literatures, published twice a year. Recent contributors: Rudolf Arnheim, Einar Haugen, Oskar Seidlin & others." 2/yr; 1-yr sub price: $15.00; per copy: $5.00; sample: free, is sent out on assumption that subscription will follow. 1975. 140 pp per issue.; 6 x 9. of. circ. 500; may increase. Reporting time: 2 months. Payment: None. Contributors receive one free copy of issue. Copyrighted, does not revert to author. Ads: $50.00-$75.00/$35.00. Discounts: none. We sell copies to individuals and libraries (mostly university) by subscription only. Complimentary copies available on request. Back issues: All back issues $5.00 apiece. Pub's reviews §German Literature; Germanic Linguistics; studies on interrelation between lit. and art with a German orientation.

THE MICKLE STREET REVIEW, Geoffrey M. Sill, Frank McQuilken, 330 Mickle St., Camden, NJ 08103. Poetry, fiction, articles, art, photos, interviews. "A journal dedicated to preserving and furthering the influence of Walt Whitman on American poetry, published from Whitman's last residence." 1976. COSMEP.

MICROMEGAS, Frederic Will, Associate Editor; Fritz Konig, Associate Editor, 84 High Point Dr., Amherst, MA 01002, 413-256-8637. Poetry, criticism, long-poems. "Want language which pushes English to its limits; and so is revolutionary." 2/yr; 1-yr sub price: $3.50; per copy: $1.25. 1966. 50pp; 8½ x 5½. of. circ. 500. Reporting time: 2 months. No payment, copies. Back issues: Any two back issues; $2.00. Pub'd 1 issue 1976; expects 1 issue 1977, 3 issues 1978. CCLM, COSMEP.

THE MIDATLANTIC REVIEW, Stephen Baily, Walter Blanco, Billy Collins, P O Box 398, Baldwin Place, NY 10505. Poetry, fiction. "In poetry we favor clean-edged images and language that's up to something; in fiction, particularity grounded in dramatic narrative. Recent contributors: Charles Bukowski, Robert Peters, Ramon Sender, Ruth Jespersen." 4/yr; 1-yr sub price: $4.00; per copy: $1.00; sample: $1.00. 1975. 80pp; 5½ x 8½. †of. circ. 1,000. Reporting time: 3-5 weeks. Payment: Two copies on publication. Copyrighted, reverts to author. Ads: $50.00/$25.00/none. Discounts: 40 percent. Back issues: Prices vary. §Poetry and fiction. CCLM.

The Middle Atlantic Press, Karen Waldauer, Box 263, Wallingford, PA 19086, 215-565-2445. Non-fiction. "We are a trade book publisher. Our material is oriented to the Middle Atlantic region, but all of our books are sold nation-wide." avg. price, cloth: varies with title. 1968. pp varies with title; varies with title. of. avg. press run varies with title. Reporting time: 2 months. Payment: 10 percent royalty to author. Copyrights for author. Discounts: 40% to retailers for 3 plus copies.

Middle Earth Books Inc., Samuel Amico, 1134 Pine St, Phila, PA 19107. Poetry, fiction, art, photos, interviews, criticism. "Infrequent 'guerrilla' publishing of pamphlets, chapbooks, broadsides, and limited editions of poetry and fiction, concepts and design growing out of working interelationship with authors and publisher-no submissions please." 1972. pp varies. no submissions. Discounts: 40% trade/20% libraries & institutions.

MIDNIGHT, Moon publications, Chris Lovette, PO Box 7574, Van Nuys, CA 91409. Poetry, art, photos. "Open to all styles & forms, but most easily impressed by *modern,* perhaps experimental work that reflects a certain sense of Poetic Astonishment, a keen originality in perception. . ." 4/yr; 1-yr sub price: $4.00; per copy: $1.25; sample: $1.25. 1974. 40pp; varies. †mi/of. circ. 200-300. Reporting time: 2 months. No payment. Ads: $10/$5.

Midpress Books, L. J. Harris, 1043 Cragmont Ave., Berkeley, CA 94708, 527-1958. Art, photos, cartoons, collages. "*MIDPRESS BOOKS* co-publishes general non-fiction with *Panjandrum Press.* From 100 pages to 300 plus pages. How-to, cooking, health, biography, musical instrument construction, psychology, etc. Our next book is by Jeanne Rose, the herbalist." avg. price, cloth: $10.00; paper: $4.95. 1976 250pp; 6 x 9. of. avg. press run 4,000. Reporting time: 1 month. Payment: 7½ percent, 10 percent, 12½ percent, twice annually. Copyrights for author. Discounts: our discounts are typical—available on request. Pub'd 2 titles 1976; expects 2 titles 1977.

MIDWEST CHAPARRAL, Marguerite Kingman, 5508 Osage, Kansas City, KS 66106. Poetry. "Haiku (3 lines) to 20 lines free, blank or rhymed. 4-8 line light verse-no juvenile verse." 3/yr; 1-yr sub price: $3.00; per copy: $1.00; sample: $.75. 1942. 32-36pp; 6 x 9. circ. 250. Reporting time: wk-10 days. Back issues: $.50. Pub's reviews. §poetry (traditional) & (contemporary).

THE MIDWEST QUARTERLY, Pittsburg State University, V.J. Emmett Jr., Editor; Michael Heffernan, Poetry, Pittsburg State University, Pittsburg, KS 66762. Poetry, articles, criticism, reviews. "Scholarly articles on history, literature, the social sciences (especially political), art, music, the natural sciences (in non-technical language). Most articles run 4,000 to 5,000 words. Can use a brief note of 1,000 to 2,000 words once in a while. Chief bias is an aversion to jargon and pedantry. Instead of footnotes we use a minimum of parenthetical documentation and a short bibliography. Reviews are assigned. Poems in both formal and free verse. Few poems longer than one page. Contributors: Goldbarth, Kuzma, Dave Smith, Katz, Etter, O'leary, Ruark, Turco, Kennedy" 4/yr; 1-yr sub price: $4.00; per copy: $1.50; sample: free. 1959. 110pp; 6 x 9. lp. circ. 1,000. Reporting time: 3-5 mo. articles, longer for poems. Payment: copies only. Copyrighted, rights sometimes released to author after publication on request. no ads. Discounts: 10% to agencies. Back issues: $1.50. Pub'd 4 issues 1976; expects 4 issues 1977, 4 issues 1978. Pub's reviews: 3 in 1976. §poetry, non-fiction, fiction by authors we have published.

MIKROKOSMOS, Mikropress, Theodora Todd, Marsh Galloway, Terry Sellers, Box 14 Dept of English, Wichita State University, Wichita, KS 67208. Poetry, fiction, art, photos, interviews, satire. "Loose 5,000 wd. limit on fiction, no limit on length of verse. Experimental prose & poetry prefered. Recent contributors: Donald Finkel, Lyn Lyfshin, Albert Goldbarth, Stuart Friebert." 2/yr; 1-yr sub price: $2.00; per copy: $1.00; sample: $.75. 1958. 50pp; varies. lp. Reporting time: 3-4 weeks. Payment: contributors' copies. Ads: $75.00/$45.00/$.50. Discounts: 10 issues $9.00, 25 $20.00. Back issues: vol 20, 1975 (retrospective), .75; vol 19, 1974, .50. Pub'd 1 issue 1976; expects 1 issue 1977, 2 issues 1978. Pub's reviews: none in 1976. §poetry chapbooks, new little mags. CCLM.

THE MILITANT, Mary-Alice Waters, 14 Charles Lane, New York, NY 10014, 212-929-3486. 52/yr; 1-yr sub price: $9.00; per copy: $0.35; sample: free. 1928. 32pp; 11½ x 18. of. circ. 30,000. Discounts: Bulk $0.25 copy; Agent $0.175. Back issues: $.50. Pub'd 50 issues 1976; expects 48 issues 1977, 48 issues 1978. Pub's reviews: 20 in 1976. §politics, economics, black studies, women's studies.

MILK QUARTERLY, The Yellow Press, Richard Friedman, Peter Kostakis, Darlene Pearlstein, 2394 Blue Island Ave, Chicago, IL 60608. Poetry, fiction, art, photos, cartoons, music, long-poems, collages, plays. "The magazine has evolved more toward the concept of 'theme project' issues: e.g. 'Chicago, Poets' and 'Special Hat Issue'. Contributors include Claes Oldenburg, Erica Jong, Robert Creeley, Bill Knott, Alice Notley, Jayzey Lynch, composer Marion Brown, John Wieners, David Henderson, Gwendolyn Brooks, Paul Metcalf and Thomas McGuane." irreg.; sample price: $1.00. 1972. 95pp; 8½ x 11, to 5½ x 8½. lp. circ. 1,500. no new submissions please. Discounts: bulk only. CCLM.

Milky Way-Kosmos (see also KOSMOS), Kosrof Chantikian, 130 Eureka, San Francisco, CA 94114, 415-863-4861. Poetry, fiction. "Milky Way-Kosmos was founded in July 1974 by Kosrof Chantikian. The first book printed was done by hand on letter press by the poet in a limited signed & numbered edition: *Imaginations & Self-Discoveries:* poems 1971-73. Milky Way is in the process of establishing a modern poets chapbook series. This will be a series of books by talented known & unknown poets. Milky Way-Kosmos is also seeking poems by children (twelve years & younger) for its children's poetry anthology to be published in early 1978 poems should be sent in the original (along with drawings) with SASE." 1974. 64pp; 5 x 8½. of. avg. press run 1,000. Reporting time: 7 weeks. Payment: Negotiable. Copyright reverts to author upon written permission of Milky Way-Kosmos. Discounts: 40 percent. Expects 2 titles 1977.

THE MILL, The White Ewe Press, Donna Jenkins, Art Editor; Kevin Urick, Box 996, Adelphi, MD 20783. Poetry, fiction, art, cartoons, satire, parts-of-novels, long-poems. "Prefer short fiction (3,000 words or less). Will consider anything author has enough faith in to send us. Would like to see more satire. Recent contributors: Poets E. Ethelbert Miller, Walter Kerr, Arlene Stone, Pat O'Neill; fiction by Jean Jaszi, John Winston, Albert Drake." 1-2/yr; 1-yr sub price: $5.00; per copy: $1.25; sample: $1.00. 1976. 40-60pp; 6 x 9. of. circ. minute. Reporting time: 2 days to 1 month. Payment: copies only. Copyrighted, reverts to author. Ads: negotiable. Discounts: 40 percent to retailers, and 10 percent any order of five or more copies. Back issues: 2. Pub'd 1 issue 1976; expects 2 issues 1977, 2 issues 1978. COSMEP, Washington Writers Center.

‡**Mill Mountain Press,** R. Irv Broughton, 1425 9th West, Seattle, WA 98119.

Miller Pond Books, Timothy Matson, RFD, Thetford Center, VT 05075. "Our focus is on Northern New England" 1975. of. Reporting time: month or less. Payment: 1/2 signing 1/2 delivery-negotiable. Discounts: standard 40% off to bookstores.

MIME JOURNAL, Thomas Leabhart, Route 3, Spring Green, WI 53588, 608-588-2514. Articles, art, photos, interviews, criticism, reviews. "MIME JOURNAL publishes articles relating to mime and movement for theatre in the broadest sense. Articles of 1,500 words and up, illustrated with photographs and drawings." 2/yr; 1-yr sub price: Libraries & Inst. $14.00, Indv. $7.00; per copy: varies. 1974. 36 - 80pp; 7 x 8½. of. circ. 250. Reporting time: Immediate. Payment: none. Copyrighted. Ads: $125.00/$75.00/none. Discounts: 30 percent to Booksellers and Subscription services. Back issues: No. 2 "Masked Theatre", Inst. $7.00-Indv. $3.50: No. 3-4 "Mime in Czech" Inst. $12.00-Indv. $6.00. Pub's reviews §Mime and movement for the theatre.

MINI-TAUR SERIES, Taurean Horn Press, Bill Vartnaw, 601 Leavenworth 45, San Francisco,

CA 94109. Poetry, art, cartoons. "Will include: Carol Lee Sanchez, Tim Jacobs, Bill Vartnaw, Gary A. Blackman, Poetry For The People (SFCC group), Robert Matte Jr." 10/yr; price per copy: $0.25; sample: $0.25. 1977. 12-24pp; 8½ x 7. †mi. circ. 100. Reporting time: No unsolicited ms. Expects 10 issues 1977.

Minicomputer Press, Charles Moore, Box 1, Richboro, PA 18954, 215-355-6084. "Hobby computing." avg. price, cloth: $10.00. 1977. 200pp; 5½ x 8½. avg. press run 500 copies. Reporting time: 2 weeks. Payment: depends. Copyrights for author. Discounts: Universal.

THE MINNESOTA REVIEW, Roger Mitchell, Editor; Lyman Andrews, Paul Buhle, Victor Contoski, Fredric Jameson, David Peck, M.L. Raina, Scott Sanders, Assoc. Eds., Box 211, Bloomington, IN 47401. Poetry, fiction, articles, art, photos, cartoons, interviews, satire, criticism, reviews, letters, parts-of-novels, long-poems, plays. "Interested in committed writing. Recent contributors include: LIVING NEWSPAPER, Jon Silkin, Walter Benjamin, Heiner Muller, Graham Good, James Hazard, James Scully, John Williams, Stanley Arondwitz, Roy Fuller, Marge Piercy, Tom Wayman, Lola Haskins, Albert Goldbarth, Antler, Darko Suvin, Fredric Jameson, David Peck, Victor Contoski, Dave Wagner, Donald Wesling, Carol Papenhausen, Barry Pritchard, Margaret Randall, David Craig, Kathleen Wiegner, Bart Friedman, Yannos Ritsos, Scott Sanders, Terry Eagleton, David Bathrick, Shiela Delaney, many more." 2/yr; 1-yr sub price: $3.50; per copy: $2.00; sample: $2.00. 1960. 150pp; 8½ x 5½. of. circ. 1,200. Reporting time: 1-3 mos. Payment: copies. Copyrighted. Ads: $40/$20. Discounts: 40%. Back issues: Available; price $1.00 more than single copy price. Pub'd 2 issues 1976; expects 2 issues 1977, 2 issues 1978. Pub's reviews: 8 in 1976. §poetry, fiction, drama, very interested in marxist literary & cultural criticism. CCLM.

MINORITY RIGHTS GROUPS REPORTS, MRG Press, B. Whitaker, MRG, 36 Craven St., London WC2N5NG, United Kingdom, 01-586-0439. "Specially commissioned reports only. Reports already published include those on the Basques, The Africans predicament in Rhodesia, What future for the Amerinidians of South America, The Two Irelands, Namibians of S.W. Africa, Arab Women etc. for complete list please contact M.R.G." 5/yr; 1-yr sub price: $7.00 (£3.50); per copy: 75p. 1970. 30pp. Circ. 1,000.

MINOTAUR, Minotaur Press, Jim Gove, Editor; Charles Mitchell, Associate Editor, 2923B Rose, Anchorage, AK 99504. Poetry, fiction, articles, art, long-poems, plays. "Please be alive and real." 4/yr; 1-yr sub price: $8.00; per copy: $2.00; sample: $2.00. 1975. 40pp; 5½ x 8½. of. circ. 300 plus. Reporting time: erratic (2 week target). Payment: poetry-copies, articles $20 pay on pub., cover $5.00 on pub., fiction $10.00. Discounts: 20%. Pub's reviews. §poetry only. COSMEP.

MINUTES & PROCEEDINGS, Haiku Society of America, Inc., William J. Higginson, Pres; Tadashi Kondo, Sec'y, 333 East 47th St., New York, NY 10017. "The HSA is a group of poets and others interested in promoting and studying haiku, and related literatures, both in Japanese and in the modern proliferation of the genre, throughout Western poetry. Membership is open to *anyone* interested in haiku, upon payment of annual dues (presently $6). Members receive the MINUTES & PROCEEDINGS, and whether they can make the eight meetings yearly (held in NYC) or not, they can contribute to the discussions of the Society through correspondence and other activities. The Society also gives several Biennial Awards for excellence in published work in the genre, and conducts an annual open contest—the Harold G. Henderson Memorial. No submissions from non-members, please." 8/yr; sub price: incl in membership. 1968. 12pp; 7 x 8½. of. circ. 200. Payment: none. Back Issues: new members receive M&P back to January of the year joining.

Miocene Press, Roland Neave, 634 Tunstall Cres., Kamloops, BC V2C 3J1, Canada, 604-372-7280. "We publish only books, non-fiction dealing with regions and in travelogue style. Minimum book length is 40,000 words." 1974. avg. press run 5,000 but depends on book content. Reporting time: acknowledge immed. report 1 month. Payment: 9% royalty on retail price. Discounts: 35% retailer, 55% distributor, 20% library.

MIORITA, New Quarterly Cave, Outrigger Publ., Norman Simms, Charles Carlton, University Of Waikato, Hamilton, New Zealand. Criticism, reviews, non-fiction. "Scholarly." price per copy:

193

$2.00. 1973. 60-100pp; a4. mi. circ. 250. Reporting time: 2 months. Payment: copies. Copyrighted. Discounts:40l/3 to retail; 10 percent sub agents. Pub'd 2 issues 1976; expects 2 issues 1977, 2 issues 1978.

THE MISSISSIPPI MUD, Mud Press, Joel Weinstein, 3125 S.E. Van Water, Portland, OR 97202. Poetry, fiction, art, photos, cartoons, interviews, satire, criticism, reviews, parts-of-novels, long-poems, collages, plays. *"THE MISSISSIPPI MUD* is a quarterly magazine featuring the work of northwest writers & artists. The magazine welcomes contributions of all kinds by the fifth of the month prior to publication. Prose & poetry should not exceed 2,500 words.'' 4/yr; 1-yr sub price: $5.00; per copy: $1.00; sample: $0.25. 1973. 32pp; 8½ x 11. of. circ. 500. Reporting time: 1-2 mos. Copyrighted. Back issues: $.50 per copy vol 2 #6 & 7, vol 3 #1 & #2. Pub's reviews. §arts & politics.

MISSISSIPPI REVIEW, Mississippi Review, Jean Todd Freeman, Fiction; D.C. Berry, Poetry, Box 37, Southern Station, Hattisburg, MS 39401. Poetry, fiction, reviews. "We use both mainstream and experimental fiction and both traditional and free verse. We may be concentrating more heavily on metrical poetry and fixed forms-we will announce this in a future issue.'' 3/yr; 1-yr sub price: $3.00; per copy: $1.50; sample: $1.75. 1971. 150-175pp; 6 x 8½. †of. circ. 350. Reporting time: 8 to 10 weeks. Payment: $5 per poem/$3 per printed page of poetry. Ads: $60/$30. Discounts: none. Back issues: $1.50. Pub's reviews. CCLM, COSMEP.

MISSISSIPPI VALLEY REVIEW, Forrest Robinson, Editor; Loren Logsdon, Fiction; John Mann, Poetry, Dept. of English, Western Ill. University, Macomb, IL 61455. Poetry, fiction. "Little, if any, ms. reading during summer. No long poems and no novella-length stories. MVR has published work by Jack Matthews, Lucien Stryk, Laurence Lieberman, Daniel Curley, Ralph Mills, Jr., James Ballowe, John Judson, Lester Goldberg, Paul Bartlett, Winston Weathers, & John Craig Stewart. We prefer that poets submit no more than five poems at one time; fiction writers: one story at a time. We usually solicit our reviews.'' 2/yr; 1-yr sub price: $3.00; per copy: $1.50; sample: $1.50. 1971. 64pp; 6 x 9. lp. circ. 400. Reporting time: 3 months. Payment: 2 copies of issue in which work appears plus 1 copy of succeeding 2 issues. Pub's reviews. CCLM, COSMEP.

MR. COGITO, Robert A. Davies, John Gogol, Box 627, Pacific Univ., Forest Grove, OR 97116, John Gogol, 8744 SE Rural, Portland, OR 97226. Poetry, art, long-poems. "We will publish the best poetry from the most varied schools of poetry. We are particularly interested in good translations of foreign poetry, both modern and ancient. Among recent poets in our pages were Norman Russell, Peter Wild, Walt Curtis, Ursula LeGuin, Patrick Gray, Kenneth O. Hanson & Zbigniew Herbert.'' 3/yr; 1-yr sub price: $3.00; per copy: $1.00. 1973. 24pp; 4½ x 11. of. circ. 500. Reporting time: 2 wks to 3 mos. Payment: copies only. no ads. Discounts: 40%. CCLM.

Mockingbird Press (see CREATIVE GUITAR INTERNATIONAL)

THE MODERN LANGUAGE JOURNAL, Charles L. King, McKenna 30A, University of Colorado, Boulder, CO 80309, 303-492-7036. Articles, reviews, news items. 6/yr; 1-yr sub price: $9.00; per copy: $3.00. 1916. 80pp; 7½ x 10. circ. 8,000. Pub'd 6 issues 1976; expects 6 issues 1977, 6 issues 1978.

MODERN LANGUAGE QUARTERLY, William H. Matchett, 4045 Brooklyn Ave. N.E., Seattle, WA 98195. Criticism, reviews. "No unsolicited reviews. Literary criticism by and for scholars.'' 4/yr; 1-yr sub price: $8.00; per copy: $2.25. 1940. 112pp; 6-5/8 x 9 -5/8. of. circ. 1,975. Reporting time: 1 to 3 mos. Payment: none. Ads: $100/$75. Discounts: 10%. Pub's reviews. §only literary criticism.

MODERN LITURGY, Resource Publications, William Burns, Editor; Jake SJ Empereur, Liturgy Editor; Paul F. Page, Music Editor; Brian Casey, Poetry Editor, Box 444, Saratoga, CA 95070. Poetry, articles, art, photos, cartoons, reviews, music, letters, plays, concrete art. 8/yr; 1-yr sub price: $16.00; per copy: $2.25; sample: $2.25. 1973. 36pp; 8½ x 11. of. circ. 10,000. Reporting time: 6 weeks. Payment: $1.00 to $100.00. Copyrighted, does not revert to author. Ads:

$393.00/$275.00/$1.00. Discounts: 40 percent trade & bulk, $0.50 per subscr. Back issues: $2.50. Pub'd 8 issues 1976; expects 8 issues 1977, 8 issues 1978. Pub's reviews. §Religious arts, music, religious education. COSMEP, CPA.

MODERNIST STUDIES: Literature & Culture 1920-1940, Shirley Rose, University of Alberta; Ernest G. Griffin, York University, Department of English, University of Alberta, Edmonton, Alberta T6G2E1, Canada. Articles, photos, interviews, criticism, reviews, letters. *"MODERNIST STUDIES* serves as a continuing forum on the Twenties and Thirties, the vital centre of the modern period, by emphasizing the two decades as a phenomenon of Western Humanism. Discussions are encouraged that cross conventional discipline lines, probe traditional units, and further a comparative approach to literature, not only in and by itself, but also in relation to the other arts and to cultural developments in Great Britain, the European continent, the United States, Canada, and the Commonwealth. Mss. should be double-spaced throughout, including quotations and footnotes, and comply with the *MLA Style Sheet*. Self-addressed, stamped envelopes (Canadian postage or International Reply Coupons) must accompany mss. Recent articles by Geoffrey Bullough, Barbara Hardy, George Woodcock, Edward Engelberg, John Vickery, Desmond Maxwell. ame period, including the two World Wars." 1-yr sub price: $6.00, individual/yr; $10.00, institutions/yr (Canada-USA); $11.00, foreign institutions. 1974. 72pp; 7 x 10. of. circ. 300. Reporting time: 2-6 months. Payment: none. Pub's reviews. §all humanities areas relevant to the 1920s and 1930, literary criticism and theory, philosophy, history, art, music; social sciences relevant to the same period, including the two World Wars.

THE MODULARIST REVIEW, Wooden Needle Press, R.C. Morse, 65-45 Yellowstone Blvd., Forest Hills, NY 11375, 212-896-4103. Poetry, fiction, articles, art, photos, interviews, criticism, reviews, letters, parts-of-novels, long-poems. "*TMR* is the only magazine to publish the work of the Modularists, a transnational movement of poets, writers, painters, architects, filmmakers, sculptors and other artists." 1/yr; 1-yr sub price: $3.00; per copy: $3.00; sample: $2.00. 1972. 96pp; 5 x 8. of. circ. 1,000 plus. Reporting time: 1-2 months. Payment: copies, subscription. Copyrighted. Ads: $100/$50. Discounts: trade-40%. Back issues: None (out of print). Pub'd 1 issue 1976; expects 1 issue 1977, 1 issue 1978. Pub's reviews: 1 in 1976. §poetry, prose, art, architecture, sculpture, etc. CCLM, NESPA.

MODUS OPERANDI, M.O. Publishing Company, Sheila R. Jensen, P.O. Box 136, Brookeville, MD 20729, 301-774-2900. Fiction, articles, satire, criticism, letters, cartoons, non-fiction. "Prose 500 to 1,000 words, no profanity. Guideline for writers will be sent to anyone sending us a No. 10 SASE. Manuscripts not accompanied by SASE are destroyed." 12/yr; 1-yr sub price: $6.00 U.S./$8.00 foreign; sample: $1.00. 1970. 34 pp (December issue includes author index and is at least 40 pp).; 8½ x 11. †mi/Electronic Stencils/Silk Screening Process. circ. 1,000. Reporting time: Fast!. Payment: Some features pay cash. Three favorite writers in each issue are paid cash & prizes. Copyrighted. Ads: $0.10. Discounts: Bookstores: 40 percent; dealers: negotiable. 3 year subscriptions: $17.00 U.S., $23.00 Foreign. Back issues: Volume (12 issues) $20.00. Pub'd 12 issues 1976; expects 12 issues 1977, 12 issues 1978. CCLM, COSMEP, LPSC, NESPA, WIFP.

Mojave Books, Judith R. Bazol, Sr. Editor; Ruth B. Franklin, 7040 Darby Ave., Reseda, CA 91335, 213-342-3403. Poetry, fiction, plays, non-fiction. "We are book publishers-general subjects, poetry, political science, etc." 1969. 5½ x 8½. of. Reporting time: 3 weeks. Copyrights for author. Discounts: 10-25 percent paperback; 25-40 percent hard back, based on quantities purchased. Pub'd 45 titles 1976; expects 60 titles 1977. COSMEP.

MOJO NAVIGATOR(E), Cat's Pajamas Press, John Jacob, Martha Jacob, Fiction, 527 Lyman, Oak Park, IL 60304. Poetry, fiction, articles, art, photos, criticism, reviews, parts-of-novels, long-poems. "Issue #5, to be published no later than summer 1976, will be the final issue of MOJO. We will continue to fill orders for #4 and #5, and we will continue our presswork, but the magazine bites the dust. We have done 5 issues in 7 years, but they have all been really fine, we think, Continuing to expend the energy necessary to maintain the quality of publication offered in the past will be impossible. Our response to manuscripts recently has been terribly slow, a condition we will not allow to continue. And the politics of publishing from the sorts of material usually seeing print to the facts of 'distribution' necessitate a long hard look at the scene. We finally decided it was ludicrous to publish a magazine that is read by maybe 50 people outside of contributors. If you don't make choices you get driven out. Be well. We will be on the streets too." irreg.; price per copy: $1.00; sample: $1.00. 1969. 40pp; 5½ x 8½. of. circ. 500. Payment: copies plus-has varied. Discounts: usual 40% on multiple orders. Back issues: issue #1: $5.00. §ethnohistory, anthropology, poetry relative to above. CCLM.

MOLE EXPRESS, 178 Oxford Rd., Manchester 13, United Kingdom. Articles, fiction, cartoons, photos, satire, news items, interviews, criticism, music, letters. "Nothing longer than say 2500 words unless really sensational. Could say we were politically biased left-wing." 12/yr; 1-yr sub price: £.80; per copy: 6p; sample: free. 1970. 20pp; 13 x 8. litho. circ. 2,000. Reporting time: vary. Ads: £20 pro rata. Discounts: 10%.

Mole Press, F. Whitney Jones, C/O English Program, St. Andrews College, Laurinburg, NC 28352. Poetry, art. "Recent publications: Paul Metcalf, *Land, Skin & Blindness;* Jonathan Williams & Fielding Dawson, *Hot What?;* Basil Bunting, program for reading at St. Andrews; books; broadsides; postcards." avg. price, paper: $3.00; other: signed, limited $10.00. 1975. of. avg. press run 500. manuscripts by invitation only. Discounts: 40 percent to the trade. Pub'd 3 titles 1976.

MOMENTUM, Momentum Press, William Mohr, 10508 W. Pico Blvd., Los Angeles, CA 90064. Poetry, fiction, criticism, letters, long-poems, plays. "I want poetry which is as distinct in its voice & vision as the work of Charles Olson, Lew Welch, and Diane di Prima. If your writing would blend in with the poetry in Daniel Halpern's *The American Poetry Anthology* (an updated version of the 1950's Hall-Pack-Simpson anthologies), of Los Angeles poets and writers, including Leland Hickman, Kate Ellen Braverman, Holly Prado, James Krusoe, John Thomas (whose excellent book is still available from Red Hill Press), Dennis Ellman, Harry Northup, Peter Levitt, Sandra Tanhauser, and Wanda Coleman. Poets from other parts of the country include James Grabill, Lynn Shoemaker, Mary Haynes, and Jack W. Thomas. I should emphasize that work from other areas of the country must be of outstanding quality in order to catch my attention. The work must make you want to sing." 2/yr; 1-yr sub price: $4.00; per copy: $2.00; sample: $2.00. 1974. 70pp; 8½ x 5½. of. Reporting time: 2 wks-2 months. Payment: copies. Copyrighted, reverts to author. Ads: $25/$15. Discounts: 40% off to classrooms, bulk, institutions, bookstores. Back issues: issues #1,2,3 $2.00 each. Pub'd 1 issue 1976; expects 2 issues 1977, 2 issues 1978. Pub's reviews. §poetry/especially by younger poets. CCLM, COSMEP.

Momentum Press (see also MOMENTUM), William Mohr, Editor, 10508 W. Pico Blvd., Los Angeles, CA 90064. "MOMENTUM PRESS has published nine books of poetry and prose (Summer, 1977) and will publish five more books during the coming year, including the definitive underground anthology of Los Angeles poets. I am not interested in any manuscripts until the Fall of 1978." 1975. 60pp; Varies. of. avg. press run 500. Payment: Copies. Copyrights for author. Discounts: 40 percent.

Momo's Press (see SHOCKS)

Monad Press, George Novack, 410 West Street, New York, NY 10014. "Publishes 5 books a year." 1970.

‡**Montana Books, Publishers, Inc.,** 1716 North 45th, Box 30017, Seattle, WA 98103.

MONTANA GOTHIC, Black Stone Press, Peter Koch, P.O. Box 756, Missoula, MT 59801. Poetry, fiction, articles, art, criticism, reviews, letters. "Becoming more occasional, more selective-move towards quality printing letterpress-eventually will appear only once a year/all letterpressed; pre-eminently interested in the imagination and its mythological power and sympathetic conjuration with nature, MONTANA AND ALCHEMY- the same goes for other places. Recent contributors include Michael Poage, David Thomas, Jane Bailey, Robert Bly, Albert Goldbarth, Siv Cedering Fox, Tess Gallagher, Blazek, Milo Miles and Charles Plymell." 1-2/yr; 1-yr sub price: $5.00; per copy: $1.50; sample: $1.50. 1974. 100pp; 6½ x 9. †of/lp. circ. 500. Reporting time: 1-2 mos. Payment: contrib. copies. Ads: none. Discounts: none. Back issues: 1-3 $25 a set. Pub's reviews. §surrealism, imaginative, mythological, MONTANA, letterpress. CCLM.

MONTEMORA, The Montemora Foundation, Eliot Weinberger, Box 336, Cooper Station, New York, NY 10003, 212-255-2733. Poetry, art, criticism, reviews, letters, long-poems, interviews. "In our first three issues we've published interviews with Charles Reznikoff and Basil Bunting, and a wide variety of work by poets known and unknown, including George Oppen, Octavio Paz, Amiri Baraka, William Bronk, Lorine Niedecker, Basil Bunting, Cid Corman, Jerome Rothenberg, Hugh MacDiarmid, Vicente Huidobro, Kenji Miyazawa, Charles Reznikoff, Homero Aridjis, Jonathan Griffin, Carl Rakosi, as well as translations from the Chinese and Japanese by Burton Watson, A. C. Graham, and Hiroaki Sato. Translations are often published bilingually, and longer poems or selections are stressed. There are normally four or five reviews in each issue, and a list of recommended new books. Unsolicited manuscripts, accompanied by the usual SASE, are certainly welcome. However, if your only knowledge of Montemora is this notice, please don't waste your time and postage. The courtesy of a 'cover' letter is frankly essential. We particularly like to hear from barely, rather than widely, published poets." 3/yr; 1-yr sub price: $9.00; per copy: $3.50; sample: $3.50. 1975. 180pp; 9 x 6. of. circ. 1,000. Reporting time: immediate. Payment: When possible. Copyrighted. Ads: $100.00/$50.00. Discounts: 40% trade. Back issues: $3.50. Pub'd 1 issue 1976; expects 2 issues 1977, 2 issues 1978. Pub's reviews. §poetry/literary/criticism.

THE MONTHLY JOURNAL OF GREAT QUOTATIONS, Adams Publishing, Frank Adams, Box 512, Manchester, VT 05255, 803-362-9890. "A monthly newsletter of quotations of upbeat, unfamiliar wisdom and wit of the ages." 12/yr; 1-yr sub price: $4.00; per copy: $0.50; sample: free. 1975. 4pp; 8½ x 11. of. circ. exactly 28 subscribers. Payment: none. Not copyrighted. Discounts: 33% off to anyone.

‡**MONTHLY REVIEW,** Box 345, Christchurch, New Zealand.

NEWSLETTER - MONTREAL POETS' INFORMATION EXCHANGE, Mattie Falworth, Vanier College, 821 Ste. Croix Blvd., Montreal, Quebec H4L 3X9, Canada, 514-333-3980. Articles, interviews, reviews. "Major emphasis is on present day Montreal poetry. News items and publication information should be as brief as possible—25 words or less. Articles between 250 and 500 words. Contributors, Ari Snyder and Fran Davis." 10-12/yr; 1-yr sub price: $5.00; per copy: $0.50; sample: $0.25. 1975. 8pp; 5½ x 11. of. circ. 500. Reporting time: 1 month or less. Payment: 2 cents per word. Not copyrighted. Ads: $25.00/$15.00/$0.10. Discounts: 30 percent. Back issues: generally, not available. Pub'd 11 issues 1976; expects 12 issues 1977, 7 issues 1978. Pub's reviews: 7 in 1976. §Magazines publishing poetry only.

MONUMENT IN CANTOS AND ESSAYS, Monument Press, Victor Myers, 508 Mexico Gravel Road, Columbia, MO 65201. Poetry, fiction, articles, photos, parts-of-novels. "5 poems each submission, 1 fiction piece (max. 12 typed pages), require SASE. Prefer poetry with vivid imagery, carefully chosen language, concise, strong particularity. Only interested in fiction of similar character with impact." irreg; 1-yr sub price: $1.00 individual/$2.00 institutional; per copy: $1.00; sample: $1.00. 1968. 50pp; 5½ x 8½. of. circ. 300. Reporting time: 3 months. Payment: 2 copies. Back issues: $2.00. §poetry as described above, esp dealing with nature, Zen perceptions, American Indian, monistic philosophical inclinations.

Moon Books, Anne Kent Rush, Anica Vesel Mander, PO Box 9223, Berkeley, CA 94709, 444-0465. Poetry, fiction, articles, art, photos, cartoons, interviews, satire, criticism, reviews, letters, long-poems, plays. "We specialize in Feminist material . Anne Kent Rush, Eva Forest, Dorothy Bryant, Anica Vesel Mander" avg. price, cloth: $6.00. 1975. 350pp. of. avg. press run 10,000. Reporting time: 6 weeks. Payment: standard. Copyrights for author.

Moon Publications (see MIDNIGHT)

Moon Publications, Bill Dalton, P.O. Box 88, South Yarra, Victoria 3141, Australia, 03 42 5928. avg. price, paper: $3.50. 1973. 200pp; 5 x 7¼. of. avg. press run 5,000. Discounts: agent, 52½ percent. Pub'd 1 title 1976.

Moonbeam Publications (see MOONDANCE)

MOONDANCE, Moonbeam Publications, Thom Daniel, 1321 Swallow Lane, Memphis, TN 38116. Poetry, fiction, articles, art, photos, interviews, criticism, parts-of-novels, plays. "More serious poetry than light, up to 50 lines. Short stories up to 10-15 type written pages. Lean toward more traditional styles. Recent contributors: Michael Hogan, Greg Kuzma, Ernest J. Oswalt, Thomas Johnson, Raphael Rudnik, B.A. Holland, Rod Taylor, R. Daniel Evans, John Jacob, David Lee, Kenneth J. Cook, Duane Ackerson." 2/yr; 1-yr sub price: $5.00; per copy: $2.75; sample: $2.75. 1975. 48pp; 8½ x 5. of circ. 200. Reporting time: 2-3 months. Payment: in copies only-1 copy. Ads: $50/$25. Discounts: 1-5: 25%; over 5: 50%. Back issues: $2.50. Pub's reviews. §poetry, fiction, literary crit., books. COSMEP.

MOONS AND LION TAILES, Permanent Press, H. Schjotz-Christensen, Linda Beth Cantor, Assistant Editor, Box 8434, Lake Street Station, Minneapolis, MN 55408, 612-377-4384. Poetry, art, photos, criticism, reviews, letters. "Robert Bly, David Ignatow, Thomas McGrath, James Wright, James Moore, Patricia Hampl, Freya Manfred, Candyce Clayton, Gregory Orr, Douglas Blazek, Maridel Lesueur, Russell Edson, Denise Levertow, Philip Levine. No biases in poetry. Each issue publishes an essay on a significant contemporary poet, comments on contemporary poetry, and several reviews and translations." 4/yr; 1-yr sub price: $5.00 ind./$6.00 institution; per copy: $1.95; sample: $1.95. 1974. 100pp; 5½ x 8½. of. circ. 2,000. Reporting time: 2 months. Payment: $10.00 a page nonfiction prose; copies for poetry. Ads: $50.00/$25.00. Back issues: $1.95. Pub'd 3 issues 1976; expects 4 issues 1977, 4 issues 1978. Pub's reviews: 18 in 1976. §Contemporary poetry and criticism. CCLM.

THE MOOSEHEAD REVIEW, Robert Allen, Jan Draper, Stephen Luxton, Box 287, Waterville, Quebec, Canada, 819-837-2222. Poetry, fiction, articles, art, photos, cartoons, satire, criticism, reviews, parts-of-novels, long-poems, plays. "This is a new magazine, first issue due out June 1977. We will consider anything, regardless of length, but are especially interested in long poems, parts of novels, political articles (especially Marxist Literary Theory)." 2/yr; 1-yr sub price: $3.50; per copy: $2.00. 1977. 80pp; 5 x 8. Payment: copies. Copyrighted, reverts to author. Pub's reviews. §poetry, fiction, political.

More Waters (see WATERS)

Morning Star Press (see also THE PHOENIX), James Cooney, Poplar Hill Road, RFD, Haydenville, MA 01039, 413-665-4754. Poetry, letters, parts-of-novels, long-poems, plays, non-fiction. "Best to write for full details on our American Poets Co-Operative Publications & American Novelists Co-Operative Publications." 1970. †lp. avg. press run 500-5,000. Reporting time: 2-4 weeks.

Mosaic Press/Valley Editions, S. Mayne, H. Aster, M. Walsh, P. Potichnyj, PO Box 1032, Oakville, Ontario L6J 5E9, Canada. Poetry, fiction, criticism. Discounts: 40% to bookstores.

Mota Press (see MUSEUM OF TEMPORARY ART MAGAZINE)

THE MOTHER EARTH NEWS, John Shuttleworth, Kas Thomas, PO Box 70, Hendersonville, NC 28739. Articles, interviews. 6/yr; 1-yr sub price: $12.00; per copy: $2.50. 1969. 180pp; 11 x 8. of. circ. 440,000. Ads: $4,800.00/$2,840.00. Back issues: $2.00 per copy. Pub'd 6 issues 1976; expects 6 issues 1977, 6 issues 1978. §ecology, self-help, gardening, alternate energy.

MOUNTAIN REVIEW, Betty Edwards, Box 660, Whitesburg, KY 41856. Poetry, fiction, articles, art, photos, cartoons, interviews, criticism, reviews, music, non-fiction. "Fiction, non-fiction: 1000-3000 wds. Poetry: printable on one page or less. Material must be related to life in Southern Appalachians." 4/yr; 1-yr sub price: $5.00; per copy: $1.50; sample: $1.50. 1974. 48pp; 8½ x 11. of. circ. 2,000. Reporting time: 2 wks. Copyrighted, reverts on request. Ads: $85.00/$50.00, quarter $25.00,401/8 $15.00. Discounts: wholesale price: $1.00 per copy. Back issues: $1.75. Pub's reviews. §Southern Appalachians. CCLM, COSMEP.

MOUNTAIN SUMMER, Ex Libris at the University Press, Don Keck Du Pree, Michael William Jones, 'Glen Antrim', Sewanee, TN 37375. Poetry, criticism. "MOUNTAIN SUMMER is concerned with presenting material which represents a reinterpretation of traditional form in English verse. Although experimentation can be a re-interpretion of traditional form, the editors seek material in the tradition which captures lyric grace and dramatic power." 1/yr; 1-yr sub price: $1.75; per copy: $1.75; sample: $1.75. 1973. 40-60pp; 8½ x 5. lp. circ. 600. Reporting time: 2 weeks. Payment: copies. Is copyrighted/rights revert to author on request. no ads. Pub'd 1 issue 1976; expects 1 issue 1977, 1 issue 1978. §Magazines of verse and collections which could be mentioned in a state of letters essay. COSMEP.

MOUTH OF THE DRAGON, Andrew Bifrost, Box 107, New York, NY 10003. Poetry, art, cartoons. *"The New Voice In Poetry."* 4/yr; 1-yr sub price: $6.00; per copy: $1.50; sample: $1.50. 1974. 80pp; 6 x 9. of/lp. circ. 1,000. Reporting time: 2 months. Payment: 2 copies. Ads: none. Discounts: 40%. Back issues: 2 through 10 inclusive, $1.50 ea.; 11/12 (double issue), $3.00. Pub'd 4 issues 1976; expects 4 issues 1977, 4 issues 1978. CCLM.

MOVEMENT, Nationalist, Mary Condren, Tim O'Neill, SCM Publications, 168 Rathgar Road, Dublin 6, Ireland, Dublin 970975. Articles, cartoons, reviews, news items, letters, interviews, satire, criticism. "Av. length 2,500 words, each issue carries 30,000 word 'in depth' study; theology & gay liberation; theology & sexual politics; feminist theology; christianity & mental health care; the christian church & its revoltionary role (in Cuba, Ireland, S. Korea, Namibia, USA especially). Liberation theology, the rise of fascism, materialist, reading of Bible, christian marxism. Biases-radical christian ideas & actions. Contributors include: Daniel Berrigan, Thomas Szasz, Rosemary Ruether, Mary Daly, Bruce Kent, Rictor Norton, Walter Hollenweger, Des Wilson, Gustavo Gutierrez, Helder Camara, etc." 6/yr; 1-yr sub price: Britain & Ireland £3/overseas £3.25 (airmail £6.50); per copy: 35p; sample: 35p. 1971. 48pp; A4. of. circ. 10,000. Reporting time: 4 weeks. Payments very rare. We usually hold copyright unless author requests reversion. Ads: £54/£30/3p a word. Discounts: on request/negotiation. Back issues: upon enquiry. Pub'd 6 issues 1976; expects 6 issues 1977, 6 issues 1978. Pub's reviews: 20 in 1976. §radical christianity/marxism/fascism/alternative society/peace movements/gays. APS, LNS, WSCF, SPC, USI, NUS, EPS, IFOR, CNOE.

MOVING ON, New American Movement, Roberta Lynch, Richard Healey, Nick Rabkin, 4327 N Milwaukee, Chicago, IL 60647, 312-252-7151. Poetry, articles, photos, interviews, criticism, reviews, letters. "This magazine a continuation of New American Movement newspaper reflects a democratic socialist viewpoint." 10/yr; 1-yr sub price: $4.00; per copy: $0.40. 1977. 24pp; 8 x 11. of. circ. 4,000. Payment: none. Not copyrighted. Ads: exchange ads only. Discounts: copies to individual distributors and bookstores - $0.25 each. Pub's reviews. §major political and cultural trends.

MOVING OUT: Feminist Literary & Arts Journal, Gloria Dyc, Margaret Kaminski, 4866 Third & Warren, Wayne State University, Detroit, MI 48202. Poetry, fiction, articles, art, photos, interviews, criticism, reviews, parts-of-novels, long-poems, plays. "We publish quality work by women. LIBRARY JOURNAL recently described our journal as one with a 'well-defined aesthetic sense which considers all facets of women's lives and literature...first choice for librarians who must make such a choice.' Please do not double submit or send work which has been published elsewhere. Enclose SASE. Plans for 1978 unstable. Please query before submitting." 2/yr; 1-yr sub price: $3.50; per copy: $1.75; sample: $1.25. 1970. 60pp; 8½ x 11. circ. 2500. Reporting time: 3 to 6 months. Payment: none. Pub'd 2 issues 1976; expects 2 issues 1977. Pub's reviews. §women's writings. COSMEP.

MRG Press (see MINORITY RIGHTS GROUPS REPORTS)

Ms. Atlas Press (see also LESBIAN VOICES), 120 E. San Carlos, San Jose, CA 95112, 408-289-1088. Poetry, fiction, long-poems, non-fiction. 1975. †of. avg. press run depends on the copy. Reporting time: 2 weeks. Discounts: 40 percent on orders of 5 or more. Pub'd 1 title 1976; expects 2 titles 1977.

Mu Publications, G. Dunbar Moomaw, Publisher, Box 612, Dahlgren, VA 22448. "*Mu Publications* presently operates for advancing the works of Poet—G. Dunbar Moomaw. Thru books, posters, and bookmarks. Released thus far: (Books) *A Collection Of Poems,* Cloth $2.95, Paper $1.25; *Communion Poetics,* Cloth $2.95, Paper $1.00. (Posters) *Declaration Of Love,* 8½ x 11 Multicolor, $2.00; *Declaration Of* life, 5½ x 8½ Multicolor, $1.50. Scheduled for summer release are two books of poetry. For Fall release, one. Several posters in the works; release dates uncertain at this time." avg. price, cloth: $2.95; paper: $1.25. 1976. 22pp; 4¼ x 7. mi/of. avg. press run 200. Discounts: 40 percent for: bookstores, libraries. Pub'd 1 title 1976; expects 3 titles 1977.

Mud Press (see THE MISSISSIPPI MUD)

Mudborn Press (see also ROCKBOTTOM), Sasha Newborn, Judyl Mudfoot, 209 W. De la Guerra, Santa Barbara, CA 93101, 805-962-9996. Poetry, fiction, articles, parts-of-novels, long-poems. "Medium-length poetry (50 pp., letterpress) and prose (150 pp., offset) books in the first person. No style limitations; our bias is toward intimate, serious writing. Projected: a chapbook series of translations (Aztec, Sanskrit, Greek, Sumerian) and short essays on language/culture." avg. price, cloth: $7.50; paper: $3.00. 1975. 50 pp, poetry, 150 pp, prose.; Quarto & 6 x 9. †of/lp/silkscreen. avg. press run 700. Reporting time: 1 month. Payment: 5 percent cash or 10 percent press run, books only. Copyrights for author. Discounts: 40 percent bulk or trade. Pub'd 2 titles 1976; expects 6 titles 1977, 8 titles 1978. LPSC, COSMEP.

Multinational Media, Gordon McShean, Sensu, Dirk Gordon, 228 Burlwood Dr., Scotts Valley, CA 95066, 408-438-0253. Fiction, non-fiction. "Emphasis will be books on showbusiness, the occult, sexual behavior, and children's books." 1976. of. Reporting time: 30 days. Copyrights for author. Discounts: 10% libraries. Pub'd 2 titles 1976; expects 1 title 1977.

MUNDUS ARTIUM: A Journal of International Literature & Art, Mundus Artium Press, Rainer Schulte, Box 688, Richardson, TX 75080. Poetry, fiction, art, photos, criticism, parts-of-novels, long-poems, plays. "Foreign poetry in bi-lingual format. Interdisciplinary focus on contemporary arts. Interested in translation of younger international writers. Conceptual rather than representational. Recent contribs: Benny Anderson, Jean Breton, Angel Gonzalez, Ilse Aichinger." 2/yr; 1-yr sub price: $6.00; per copy: $3.50; sample: $3.00. 1967. 180pp; 6 x 9. lp. circ. 1,000-1,200. Reporting time: 1-2 months. Payment varies. Ads: $100/$60. Back Issues: vol 1&2 rare $20 ea, single issues $3.50, volumes $6.00 each. Pub's reviews. §International art scene, translations. CCLM, COSMEP.

Museroom (see CIE)

Museum of New Mexico Press (see EL PALACIO)

MUSEUM OF TEMPORARY ART (MOTA) MAGAZINE, Mota Press, Janet Schmuckal, Eric Baizer, 1206 G Street NW, Washington, DC 20005, 202-296-6689. Poetry, fiction, articles, art, photos, cartoons, interviews, satire, criticism, reviews, music, letters, collages, concrete art. "1 - 2 page material preferred on 5½ x 8½ format; we like visual, multimedia, offbeat and satirical material." 4-6/yr; 1-yr sub price: $3.00; per copy: $0.50; sample: $0.50. 1975. 20-40pp; 5½ x 8½. of. circ. 200-500. Copyrighted, reverts to author. Ads: $40.00/$25.00. Back issues: Anti-Communism issue $1.00. Pub's reviews. §Multimedia, avant'-garde' magazines.

MUSIC AND LETTERS, Oxford Univ. Press, Denis Arnold, Edward Olleson, 32 Holywell, Oxford, United Kingdom. Articles, reviews, music, letters. "Not specialized in scope, being open to the discussion of anything from primitive music to the latest experiments in the laboratory. But preference is given to contributors who can write, who have a respect for the English language and are willing to take the trouble to use it effectively." 4/yr; 1-yr sub price: £5.70 ($14.00); per copy: £1.75 ($4.00); sample: free. 1920. 120pp; 6 x 9¾. of. circ. 2,000. Payment: £1.00 per printed page. Ads: £40.00 & pro rata/£23.00. Pub'd 4 issues 1976; expects 4 issues 1977, 4 issues 1978. Pub's reviews: 100 in 1976. §Music, musical criticism, musical history, etc.

Mustang Press, Karl Edd, Marjorie Appell, P.O. Box 9007, Denver, CO 80209.

THE MYSTERIOUS BARRICADES, Rainbow Press, Henry Weinfield, 1332 Riverside Drive, New York, NY 10033, 212-928-8108. Poetry, fiction, articles, criticism, reviews, music, parts-of-novels, long-poems. "Serious contributors will have read the magazine, and will feel a kinship with its aims. Our judgments are based solely on our perception of value." irreg.; 1-yr sub price: $4.00; per copy: $2.00; sample: $2.00. 1972. 100pp; 5½ x 8½. of. circ. 500. Reporting time: 2 weeks. Payment in copies. Copyrighted, reverts to author. Ads: $100.00/$50.00/none. Discounts: 40 percent bookstore; otherwise varies. Back issues: issue no. 4 - $2.00. others o.p. Pub's reviews §Poetry, music, politics, (general). CCLM.

N **Nada (see also BIG SCREAM),** David Cope, Susan Cope, 696 48th St SE, Grand Rapids, MI 49508, 616-531-1442. Poetry, fiction, art. avg. price, paper: $1.00. 1974. 30pp; 8 x 8½. †mi. avg. press run 100. Reporting time: 1 week - 1 month. Payment: 3 copies. Discounts: 5-10 copies 25 percent; more than 10 40 percent.

The Naiad Press, Inc., Barbara Grier, P.O. Box 5025, Washington Stn., Reno, NV 89513, 816-633-4136. "Small press publishing material by and for women. Publishes only Lesbian/Feminist novels and poetry. Nine titles to date. We are expanding, and will be publishing 3 other titles in the next 9 months. Writers of Lesbian/Feminist novels are invited to inquire." avg. price, paper: $4.50. 1973. of. avg. press run 3,000 copies. Reporting time: 4 weeks. Payment: 50 percent. Copyrights for author. Discounts: 40 percent dealers - 5 or more copies. Pub'd 4 titles 1976; expects 2 titles 1977, 2-4 titles 1978. COSMEP.

Nairn Publishing House, Stan Dragland, Don McKay, Box 40, Stn. B, London Ont. N6A 4V3, Canada. Poetry, fiction. "This is just a hobby. Nairn isn't honestly looking for unsolicited mss." avg. price, cloth: $7.95; paper: $2.50. 1972. 80pp; 8½ x 5½. of/lp. avg. press run 500. Payment: nil. Discounts: 40% trade, no other discount except 20% on 15 or more copies. Expects 2 titles 1977, 1 title 1978.

NANTUCKET REVIEW, Richard Cumbie, Richard Burns, P.O. Box 1444, Nantucket, MA 02554. Poetry, fiction, articles, art, satire, criticism, parts-of-novels, long-poems. 3/yr; 1-yr sub price: $5.00; per copy: $1.75; sample: $1.00. 1973. 60-70pp; 6 x 9. of. circ. 500. Reporting time: 2 mos. Payment: copies. Ads: $50/$25. Discounts: 40%. Back issues: $100. COSMEP.

NATIONAL BOOK REVIEW, J. Mark Press, Barbara Fischer, Box 2057, N. Babylon, NY 11703. Reviews. "NBR is sent free to all major book reviewers, librarians, book clubs, teachers, & authors, as well as those seeking to discover lesser-known authors. It is a showcase." 2/yr; 1-yr sub price: $2.00; per copy: $1.00; sample: 2 First Class postage stamps. 1976. 20pp; 8½ x 5½. †of. Payment: copies. Ads: $350.00/$175.00/$.50.

National Council of Teachers of English (see COLLEGE ENGLISH)

National Federation Of Claimants Unions Publications (see CLAIMANTS NEWSPAPER)

NATIONAL FISHERMAN, International Marine Pub Co, David R. Getchell, 21 Elm St., Camden, ME 04843, 207-236-4344. Articles, art, photos. "journal of the American fishing industry (commercial) and custom boat building." 13/yr; 1-yr sub price: $8.00; per copy: $0.75; sample: n/c. 1903. 104pp; 10 x 14¼. †of. circ. 60,000. Payment: 2 cents per word. Copyrighted, does not revert to author. Ads: $1,175.00/$910.00/$0.25. Discounts: none. Back issues: $1.00. Pub'd 13 issues 1976. Pub's reviews: 30 in 1976. §marine non-fiction.

NATIONAL ON-CAMPUS REPORT, Magna Publishing Co., William Haight, 621 N. Sherman Ave, Madison, WI 53704. Articles. "News clips." 12/yr; 1-yr sub price: $18.00; per copy: $1.50;

sample: $1.50. 1972. 8pp; 8½ x 11. of. Reporting time: 30 days. Payment: $.05 & up/word. Back issues: $2.00.

Nationalist (see MOVEMENT)

NATURAL LIFE, The Alternate Press, Wendy Priesnitz, Box 640, Jarvis, Ontario N0A1J0, Canada, 519-587-4821. Articles, art, photos, cartoons, interviews, letters. "Down-to-earth, how-to-do-it, self-sufficiency oriented articles. Access to alternatives in Canada." 12/yr; 1-yr sub price: $6.00; per copy: $0.75; sample: $1.00. 1976. 56pp; 7 x 10. of. circ. 25,000. Reporting time: 2 wks. Payment: 2 to 5 cents/wd. approx-varies per article. Copyrighted, reverts to author. Ads: $300.00/$160.00/$0.20. Back issues: full cover price. Expects 12 issues 1977. Pub's reviews. §self-sufficiency, alternate energy. CPPA.

Naturegraph Publishers, Inc., Sevrin Housen, P. O. Box 1075, Happy Camp, CA 96039, 916-496-5353. "We publish mainly paperback books on natural history and indian lore." avg. price, cloth: Varies.; paper: Varies. 1946. Varies. †of. Reporting time: 1-8 weeks. Payment: Royalties. Discounts: Write for our free catalog.

Naturist Foundation (see THE GROVE)

NAUSEA, Russ Haas Press (Nausea Publications), Leo Mailman, P.O. Box 4261, Long Beach, CA 90804. Poetry, fiction, art, photos, cartoons, reviews, long-poems, plays. "I tend toward poetry with a minimum of poetic diction, and that is socially relevant and/or humorous: the epitome of this style would be the poetry of Edward Field. Recent contributors: Gerald Locklin, Ronald Koertge, Edward Field, Charles Bukowski, Steve Richmond, Linda King, Charles Webb, Fritz Hamilton & Opal L. Nations." 2-3/yr; sub price: $3.50 (4 iss)/$5.50 (institutions, 4 iss); per copy: $1.50; sample: $1.00. 1972. 48pp; 5½ x 8½. †of. circ. 400. Reporting time: 4-8 wks. Payment: 2 copies. Discounts: 40% to bookstores. Back issues: 1st (9) issues available for $10.00. Expects 2 issues 1977, 2 issues 1978. Pub's reviews. §po/fi/small press efforts. CCLM.

NEBULA, Nebula Press, Ken Stange, Ed; Ursula Stange, Associate Editor; Ian McCulloch, Associate Editor, 970 Copeland, North Bay, Ontario P1B3E4, Canada. Poetry, fiction, articles, art, photos, cartoons, interviews, satire, criticism, reviews, music, letters, parts-of-novels, long-poems, collages, plays, concrete art. "We are interested in formal innovation: the carefully crafted but originally structured work is always of interest to us. We do thematic issues, so a would-be contributor is advised to send a buck for a sample of latest issue, wherein he/she will find a statement of our immediate thematic interests. (And those dollars will help keep us alive) Next issue deals with theme of 'eros', considering future issue devoted to the long-poem. Our contributors range from the very established to the totally unknown. Some names, Robert Kroetsch, Michael McMahon, Martin Booth, Charles Plymell, Garcia Lorca, Glen Sorestad, Alfie McConnkell, John Kellnhauser, Allan Brown, Len Gasparini, Opal Nations, Brian Shein, David McFadden, George Amabile, Andy Suknaski." 2/yr; sub price: $5.00-2 yrs, institutions $10.00-2; per copy: $1.25; sample: $1.00. 1974. 88pp; 5½ x 8½. of. circ. 750. Reporting time: one month. Payment: contributor copies. Copyrighted. Ads: $50.00/$25.00. Discounts: 40%. Back issues: Nos. 1, 4 sold out; Nos. 2, 3 $2.00. Pub'd 2 issues 1976; expects 2 issues 1977, 2 issues 1978. §extremely eclectic. COSMEP, CPPA.

The Neo-American Church, Inc. (see DIVINE TOAD SWEAT)

Neon Sun, P.O. Box 2191, Station A, Berkeley, CA 94702.

Nevada Publications, Stanley W. Paher, Box 15444, Las Vegas, NV 89114. Poetry, articles, art, photos, cartoons. "We publish books on Nevada, California and Arizona, mostly guides to scenic areas and ghost towns. All are lavishly illustrated and are solidly based in orginal research and are well edited."

New American Movement (see MOVING ON)

‡**NEW ARGOT,** PO Box 6368, Wellington, New Zealand.

NEW ART EXAMINER, Chicago New Art Association, Jane Addams Allen, Derek Guthrie, Associate Editor, 230 E. Ohio, Chicago, IL 60611, 312-642-6236. Art, articles, interviews, criticism, reviews, letters, news items. "Commentary on and analysis of the exhibtion and making of art, film, photographs, including humor, occasional cartoons, Jack Burnham, Joshua Kind." 10/yr; 1-yr sub price: $6.00; per copy: $0.70; sample: free. 1973. 24pp; tabloid 11. of. circ. 5,000. Reporting time: three months. Payment: $8 350 word reviews/$25 article. Ads: $450.00/$225.00/$0.10. Discounts: 3x, 5x plus 10x rates. Back issues: Volume I $1.25 each, Volume II $1.00 each, Volume III $0.85 each, Vol. IV $0.70 each. §visual art/film photography/architecture.

NEW BOSTON REVIEW, Boston Critic, Inc., J.M. Alonso, Gail Pool, 77 Sacramento St., Somerville, MA 02143. Poetry, fiction, articles, interviews, criticism, reviews, parts-of-novels. "Essays—2,000-4,000 words covering art, literature, music, film, photography, theater. Contributors range from Geoffrey Barraclough, Glenn Gould, Octavio Paz to free-lance writers." 4/yr; 1-yr sub price: $3.00; per copy: $1.00; sample: $1.00. 1975. 36pp; 11¼ x 15¼. of. circ. 11,000. Reporting time: 3 months. Payment: none. Ads: $300.00/$175.00. Discounts: bookstores 50%. Back issues: $1.00. Pub'd 4 issues 1976; expects 4 issues 1977. Pub's reviews. §poetry/fiction/criticism. COSMEP, NESPA, CCLM.

NEW COLLAGE MAGAZINE, New Collage Press, A. McA. Miller, 5700 North Trail, Sarasota, FL 33580, 919-355-7671, Ex 203. Poetry. "We want poetry with clear focus and strong imagery. Would like to see fresh free verse and contemporary slants on traditional prosodies. Issues are often thematic; so query before sending poems." 3/yr; 1-yr sub price: $3.00; per copy: $1.00; sample: $1.00. 1970. 32pp; 5½ x 8½. of. circ. 1,000. Reporting time: 3 weeks. Payment: copies or token payment cash. Copyrighted, reverts to author. Ads: none. Back issues: All available, 8 volumes at $1/issue or $3.00 per volume. Pub'd 3 issues 1976; expects 3 issues 1977, 3 issues 1978. Pub's reviews: 5 in 1976. §Poetry, some interviews. CCLM, COSMEP, COSMEP-SOUTH, NESPA, FSWC.

NEW DIRECTIONS FOR WOMEN, New Directions For Women, Inc., Vera Goodman, Trustee, 223 Old Hook Road, Westwood, NJ 07675, 201-666-4677. Articles, art, photos, cartoons, interviews, satire, criticism, reviews, letters. "Maximum length 1,000 words. Must be from a feminist perspective or to help women." 4/yr; 1-yr sub price: $3.00; per copy: $0.00; sample: free. 1971. 16pp; 10 x 16. of. circ. 30,000. Reporting time: 3 months. Payment: none-free copies. Not copyrighted. Ads: $500.00/$280.00/$0.40. Back issues: $1.00 each. Pub'd 4 issues 1976; expects 4 issues 1977, 4 issues 1978. Pub's reviews. §By, for and about women & feminism.

New Earth Books, Michael Largo, 58 St. Marks Pl., New York City, NY 10003, 212-673-1682. Poetry, fiction, plays. "A collective for writers" 1976. lp. Reporting time: varies.

THE NEW EARTH REVIEW, New Earth Books, Michael Largo, Thomas Kitts, Carl Larsen, 58 St. Marks Pl, New York, NY 10003. Poetry, fiction, articles, art, photos, cartoons, interviews, satire, criticism, reviews, music, letters, parts-of-novels, long-poems, collages, plays, concrete art. "A magazine which is a whale going slowly through blue water. It has no biases either." 2/yr; 1-yr sub price: $5.00; per copy: $2.50. 1974. of. circ. 1,000. Reporting time: 1 month. Payment: copies. Copyrighted, reverts to author. Ads: $25.00/$12.00. Back issues: none left. Pub's reviews. §all (but very interested in books concerning the lost tribe of New Zealand. New Earth Collective.

NEW EARTH TRIBE NEWSPACK, R.V.K. Publishing Co., S.P. Stavrakis, P.O. Box 264, Menomonee Falls, WI 53051. Poetry, fiction, articles, art, photos, cartoons, satire, parts-of-novels, concrete art. "Looking for poetry, short-short stories, all types. Photos, graphics. Emphasis is on fantasy, erotic, erratic, experimental. Send 2 stamps with submissions, no envelopes." 10/yr; 1-yr sub price: $10.00; per copy: $1.25. 1972. 20pp; 8½ x 11. of. circ. 500. Reporting time: 2 wks-2 mos. Ads: $50/$25/free if we like it. COSMEP.

NEW EDINBURGH REVIEW, Edinburgh University Student publications Board (EUSP), 1 Buccleuch Place, Edinburgh, Scotland EH8 9LW, United Kingdom. Articles, poetry, art, photos, reviews, interviews, criticism, long-poems. "Member of Scottish Assocn of Magazine Publishers. Contributors, recent & future include: J. P. Mackintosh M. P., I. MacCormick M. P., Prof. L. A. Gunn; Murray Grigor; Sorley MacLean." 4/yr; 1-yr sub price: UK £1.50 o/s eas £2.00; per copy: 35p. 1969. 40pp; A4. litho. circ. 2,500. Reporting time: 1 month. Payment: by negotiation. Ads: £40 per page. Discounts: 33-1/3% to trade. Back issues: list available on application.

NEW GERMAN STUDIES, Department Of German, Unv. Hull, Rex Last, Alan Best, Dept Of German, Univ. Hull, Hull HU6 7RX, United Kingdom, 0482 46311 (extn 7652). Articles. "Up to 4,000 words on German language, literature, culture." 3/yr; 1-yr sub price: £2.50 (indiv) £3.50 (institution); per copy: £1.20; sample: £1.20. 1973. 60pp; A5. of. circ. 200. Reporting time: 1-2 months. Payment: nil. Copyrights with editors. Discounts: 15 percent. Back issues: £2.00 (indiv) £2.50 (institution) vols 1-4. Pub'd 3 issues 1976; expects 3 issues 1977, 3 issues 1978. Pub's reviews. §German language, literature, culture.

THE NEW HARBINGER: A JOURNAL OF THE COOPERATIVE MOVEMENT, North American Student Cooperative Organization (NASCO), Margaret Lamb, Editor; Jonathan Klein, Associate Editor, Box 1301, Ann Arbor, MI 48106, 313-663-0889. Articles, interviews, satire, reviews, letters, news items, non-fiction. "1,000-4,000 words. Articles should be related to consumer cooperatives or similar efforts at social change." 4/yr; 1-yr sub price: $8.00; per copy: $2.00; sample: $1.00. 1971. 64pp; 6 x 9. of. circ. 1,500. Reporting time: two weeks. Payment: none currently/policy may change. Copyrighted, does not revert to author. no advertising currently/policy may change. Discounts: 40 percent. Pub'd 4 issues 1976; expects 4 issues 1977, 4 issues 1978. Pub's reviews. §co-ops; social change; economic democracy. COSMEP.

NEW HOPE, Headland Publications, Gerald England, 103 Clarksfield Road, Oldham, Lancs OL41LJ, United Kingdom, 061-624-3439 & 051-625-9125. Articles, poetry, reviews, news items, interviews, criticism, letters, fiction, art, non-fiction. "NEW HOPE will print poetry of a high standard, informative articles on all aspects of poetry/literature/christianity, (cover designs welcome) & reviews of books and magazines." 3/yr; 1-yr sub price: £1.25 ($3.00); per copy: 40P plus postage. 1972. 24pp; A4. mi. circ. 1,500. Reporting time: Up to 3 months. Ads: 2P/word (min 50P) box nos 25P. Discounts: 33 percent to shops (cash with order). Expects 1 issue 1977, 3 issues 1978. Pub's reviews: 80 in 1976. §Poetry, literature, christianity, general. ALP, APS.

New Horizens Communications Group Press (see COASTLINE MAGAZINE)

THE NEW INFINITY REVIEW, James R. Pack, Ron Houchin, Manuscript Editor, P.O. Box 554, South Point, OH 45680, 614-377-4182. Poetry, fiction, articles, art, photos, interviews, satire, criticism, reviews, letters, parts-of-novels, long-poems, concrete art. "*Fiction:* 2,000 to 4,000 words-we seek stories that are mentally exciting and germinal with ideas. Science fiction, fantasy and mystery find an eager eye. *Poetry:* no length limit—we try to feature at least one poet every issue. *The New Infinity Review* is dedicated to the new and unknown writer." 4/yr; 1-yr sub price: $3.50; per copy: $0.95; sample: free to any writer upon request. 1974. 52pp; 5½ x 8½. of. circ. 500. Reporting time: 2-4 weeks. Payment: two copies, art $5.00 up. Copyrighted, reverts to author. Discounts: subscription agency discount: subscription-$3.00 per year. Back issues: $1.25. Expects 4 issues 1977, 4 issues 1978. §poetry, short stories, fantasy of any length. CCLM.

NEW JERSEY POETRY MONTHLY, New Jersey Poetry Press, George W. Cooke, Katharine Glynn, Geoffrey Sill, Rosalyn J. Wolff, James A. Harrington, Art, P.O. Box 824, Saddle Brook, NJ 07662, 201-445-9436. Poetry. "We prefer 4 to 5 short poems of high quality submitted at one time. ISSN 0146-1087" 12/yr; 1-yr sub price: $12.00; per copy: $1.50; sample: $1.50. 1977. 16-32pp; 5½ x 8½. of. circ. 500. Reporting time: 4 weeks. Payment in copies. Copyrighted, does not revert to author. Discounts: 40 percent to trade. Back issues: $1.50. Expects 12 issues 1977, 12 issues 1978. COSMEP.

THE NEW KENT QUARTERLY, Quarterly Press, Rob Tomsho, 239 Student Center, Kent State University, Kent, OH 44240, 216-672-7951. Poetry, fiction, articles, art, photos, cartoons, interviews, satire, criticism, reviews, music, parts-of-novels, collages, plays, concrete art. "Primarily interested in students and area artists, but we welcome outside submissions (as many as we can handle). No biases as long as we get a SASE. Don't send us 30 pages of poetry or 50 page novellas. Make sure your stuff is typed. Do not send in anything during summer. Contributors: Ralph La Charity, Thomas Kinsella." 2/yr; price per copy: $1.00; sample: $1.00. 1955. 50pp; 8 x 11. of. circ. 400. Reporting time: 2 months. Payment: copies. Copyrighted, reverts to author. no advertising. Back issues: $0.50 to $0.20. Pub's reviews. §Poetry and fiction.

THE NEW LAUREL REVIEW, Lawhead Press, Alice Moser Claudel, Editor; Dr. Calvin A. Claudel, Assistant Editor, PO Box 1083, Chalmette, LA 70044, 504-271-4209. "Biased only toward work which seems to us to be *alive*. We have the usual antipathies, I think: against vague abstractions, too much personal confession, smart-alec scholarship (as opposed to sound research and ideas); nature for decoration's sake; etc. Tom O'Grady, James P. White, Lyn Lifshin, Bernice Larson Webb, Jesse Stuart, Joshua Norton, Michael Anderson, Laurence Perrine, Herb Francis, Guy Owen." 2/yr; 1-yr sub price: $3.50-$4.00 for libraries & institutions; per copy: $2.00; sample: $1.50. 1971. 60pp; 6 x 9. of. circ. 500. Reporting time: Varies-longer time for interesting work. Somewhat crowded with poetry (about 3 weeks). Payment: two copies of the magazine in which their work appears. Copyrighted. Back issues: $4.00 for back numbers; $2.00 for more recent numbers; that is, 1974,75,& 76. Pub's reviews. §poetry and books about poets and related matter. CCLM.

NEW LETTERS, University of Missouri, David Ray, 5346 Charlotte, Kansas City, MO 64110, 816-276-1168. Poetry, fiction, articles, parts-of-novels, long-poems, art, photos, satire. "The best in contemporary fiction, poetry, personal essay, art, and photography. Contributors include Bly, Ignatow, Stafford, Gildner, Mayo, Colter, Levertov, Kumin. Special issue on Paul Goodman." 4/yr; 1-yr sub price: $8.00; per copy: $2.50; sample: $2.50. 1971 (Predecessor, *University Review*, 1934). 128pp; 6 x 9. of. Reporting time: 2 wks to 2 mos. Payment: small, upon pub. Ads: $100/$60/$.25. Discounts: 14% agencies, 2% 10 days, 25% disc. on contract of 4 ads. Back issues: $5. Pub'd 4 issues 1976; expects 4 issues 1977, 4 issues 1978. Pub's reviews: 39 in 1976. §Lit, art. CCLM, COSMEP.

NEW LITERATURE & IDEOLOGY, People's Canada Publishing House, Norman Bethune Institute, Publ., PO Box 727, Adelaide Station, Toronto, Ontario, Canada. Poetry, fiction, articles, art, photos, cartoons, interviews, satire, criticism, reviews, music, letters, parts-of-novels, long-poems, plays. 4/yr; price per copy: $2.25; sample: free. 1968. 130pp; 5 x 8. Back issues: $1.25. Pub's reviews. §Culture, politics, labour.

New London Pride, Elaine Fisher, Allen Fisher, 18 Hayes Court, London SLY2 EX, United Kingdom, 01 674 4364. Poetry, long-poems. "Recent work from: Pierre Joris, Eric Mottram, Clayton Eshleman, Bill Sherman, Barry MacSweeney, Antony Lopez. Fully booked into August 1978. No unsolicited mss. Distributed by Truck Distribution in USA." avg. price, paper: $1.30 incl postage; other: 60p. 1975. 35pp; 7½ x 10½. †mi/of. avg. press run 250. Reporting time: 3 months. Payment: by mutual agreement. Copyrights for author. Discounts: trade 33-1/3 percent; bulk 33 -1/3 percent. Pub'd 3 titles 1976. ALP, BAAA.

NEW MAGAZINE: Arts & Letters (see also Beyond Baroque Foundation Publications).

New Mexico News Cooperative (see SEERS)

‡**NEW MEXICO QUARTERLY,** Univ. Of New Mexico, Albuquerque, NM 87106.

THE NEW MOON, Humble Hills Press, Michael Lefabre, David Whitehall, David M. Marovich, Assoc. Ed., 2147 Oakland Dr, Kalamazoo, MI 49008. Poetry. "We like poems that ride around the essential mystery on the backs of vivid natural images." 1-2/yr; sub price: $3.50/2 issues; per copy: $2.00; sample: $1.25. 1975. 40pp; 5½ x 8½. of. circ. 400. Reporting time: 1 month. Payment: 2 copies/poem. Ads: $25/$15. Discounts: bulk + trade 40% classroom and institutional 30% agent 50%. Back issues: $1.25.

New Oregon Publishers, Inc. (see OREGON TIMES MAGAZINE)

NEW ORLEANS REVIEW, Marcus Smith, Shael Herman, Poetry Ed.; Dawson Gaillard, Fiction Ed., Loyola University, New Orleans, LA 70118, 504-865-2294. Poetry, fiction, articles, art, photos, interviews, criticism, reviews, plays. "Walker Percy, Susan Fromberg Schaeffer, Peter Wild, Christopher Isherwood, David Madden, Annie Dillard, Rosemary Daniell, Natalie Petesch, Doris Betts, Larry Rubin, Greg Kuzma, Harry Taylor, John William Corrington. We like to see high quality material in all aspects of human endeavor and culture." 3/yr; 1-yr sub price: 4 issues, $6.00: 8 issues, $10.00: 12 issues, $14.00.; per copy: $1.50; sample: $1.50. 1968. 96pp; 8½ x 11. of. circ. 1,000. Reporting time: 2 wks-2 mos. Payment: $50.00 fiction/articles; $10.00 poetry/art work. Copyright release available on request. Discounts: Sub agencies: $5.00/4 issues $8.00/8 issues $11.00/12 issue. Back issues: Vol 2-Vol 3, No. 1-$1.25 each issue, Vol 3-Vol 4 $1.50 each issue. Pub's reviews. §all areas. CCLM, COSMEP.

NEW PERIODICALS INDEX, The Mediaworks Ltd., Michael Haldeman, Bobi Haldeman, Mary Peckham, P.O. Box 4494, Boulder, CO 80305, 303-494-1439. "Semi-annual subject-author index to all articles in some 70 alternative and new age periodicals." 2/yr; 1-yr sub price: $25.00. 1977. 260pp; 6½ x 10. of. Copyrighted. Expects 1 issue 1977. §ecology, spiritual, alternative technology, community. COSMEP, SOI.

New Plays for Children, Pat Hale Whitton, Publisher, Box 273, Rowayton, CT 06853. "Children's plays and creative dramatic books."

NEW POETRY, Workshop Press Ltd., Norman Hidden, 2 Culham Court, Granville Rd, London N4 4JB, United Kingdom, 01-348-4054. Articles, poetry. "Heavily overstocked. Do not submit without first studying the magazine carefully to ascertain its style and standards. Recent contributors have included: Brownjohn, Hamburger, Gunn, Hughes, Heaney etc." 4/yr; 1-yr sub price: $6.00; per copy: $1.50; sample: $1.50. 1967. 48pp; 8 x 5. lp. circ. 2M. Reporting time: up to 1 mo. Payment: pays by arrangement. Copyright with author. Ads: $50.00/$25.00. Discounts: 33-1/3 percent on bulk orders. Back issues: 2-10 at $2.00 (few only); onwards $2.00. Pub'd 4 issues 1976; expects 4 issues 1977, 4 issues 1978. ALP, ALMS.

NEW POETRY, The Poetry Society of Australia, Prism Books, Cheryl Adamson, Box N110 Grosvenor St Post Office, Sydney, N.S.W. 2000, Australia. Poetry, fiction, articles, art, photos, interviews, criticism, reviews, long-poems. "NEW POETRY is at the centre of Australian poetry. We are primarily interested in contemporary poetry with a bias to the Black Mountain/post-Black Mountain influences, but we do publish a fairly extensive range of poetry and would like to extend our publication of criticism and reviews. NEW POETRY has published the most important new poets working in Australia alongside the established poets. Recent contributors include Robert Duncan, Michael McClure, Donald Davie, Charles Tomlinson, Robert Adamson, Jennifer Maiden, Charles Bukowski, Sylvia Kantarizis, Max Williams and Michael Wilding et al. Although the magazine has been around for a while now, it is continually changing and growing, self-consciously perhaps with the rest of Australian art. It is internationally significant. Essentially. Look, the length of material generally doesn't worry us—articles up to 17 pages (25 quarto typed) etc etc. More graphics? Interviews? We're pretty open ended inside our biases. Have a look for $2.00 (sample). Essential before submitting material to look at an issue." 4/yr; 1-yr sub price: $20.00(Australian) includes post.; per copy: $4.50 (incl. post); sample: $2.00 (Aust.). 1954. 80pp; 22 cm x 14½ cm. of/lp. circ. 2,000. Reporting time: 6 weeks. Payment: min. $10.00 up to $200.00. Ads: $50/$25. Discounts: trade 40%; bulk 25%. Back issues: Pre 1972 are rare & about $5-$10 post 1972-$3.00/copy. Pub's reviews. §Black Mountain & Post Black Mountain-Olson, Duncan, Pound, Creeley—et al.

The New Poets Series, Clarinda Harriss Lott, 541 Piccadilly Rd., Baltimore, MD 21204, 301-828-8783. Poetry. "NPS chapbooks contain enough poems (or poems plus graphics) to make about 42 pp. of type. Editorial bias in favor of excellent material in an original voice. Most recent issue: THE HOUR BETWEEN DOG AND WOLF, poems by Laura Wallace. All NPS poets have exhibited a high degree of professionalism, not only by writing top quality material but by publishing in magazines, giving readings working hard at their poetry and in related fields (several have been Poets-in-the-Schools)." avg. price, paper: $1.95. 1970. 50pp; 5½ x 8½. of. avg. press run 750-1,000. Reporting time: 6 mos. Payment: none: all revenue from sales goes to publish the next issue. Author holds own copyright. Discounts: $1.50 cost to bookstores; $1.95 retail; $1.75 to mail subscribers. CCLM, COSMEP, Maryland Writers Council.

NEW POLITICS, Julius Jacobson, 507 Fifth Ave, New York, NY 10017. 4/yr; 1-yr sub price: $5.00; per copy: $1.25; sample: $1.25. 1961. 100pp; 6 x 9. lp. circ. 5,000. Ads: $200/$125. Discounts: 20% for 5 or more. Pub's reviews. §political, social, economic.

THE NEW QUARTERLY, World University Service, Dr. K.B. Rao, World University Service, 20 West 40th St, New York, NY 10018. Poetry, fiction, parts-of-novels, long-poems, plays. "Devoted exclusively to creative writing about Asia. A stamped self-addressed is required for the return of manuscripts." 4/yr; 1-yr sub price: $10.00; per copy: $3.00; sample: $3.00. 1976. 100-125pp; 8½ x 11. †of. Reporting time: 4 weeks. Payment: Negotiable. Ads: Inquiries invited. Pub's reviews §creative writing exclusively. COSMEP.

NEW QUARTERLY CAVE, Outrigger Publishers Ltd., Norman Simms, Tim Pickford, Sefulu Ioane, 1 Von Tempsky St., Hamilton, New Zealand. Poetry, fiction, articles, criticism, reviews, music, long-poems. "Oral and literary traditions, translations, synthetic and creative reviews." 4/yr; 1-yr sub price: $8.00 indiv; $12.00 institution in NZ funds-yr; per copy: $2.00; sample: $2.00. 1973. 80-100pp; A5. of. circ. 400. Reporting time: 3 mos. Payment: copies. Copyrighted. Ads: $50.00/$30.00. Discounts: trade retail 33-1/3 percent; subscription services 10 percent. Back issues: Cave 6-8:$6.00/outrigger 3-9 $3.50 (NZ funds). Pub'd 4 issues 1976; expects 4 issues 1977, 4 issues 1978. Pub's reviews: 30 in 1976. §Literature, ethenic, tribal, oral traditions, music, art, crafts.

THE NEW RENAISSANCE, A Magazine of Ideas & Opinions, Emphasizing Literature & The Arts, Louise T. Reynolds, Harry Jackel, Olivera Sajkovic, (thru 9); Louise E. Reynolds, Stanwood Bolton, Poetry (10 & 12); Lloyd (11) Van Brunt, 9 Heath Road, Arlington, MA 02174. Poetry, fiction, articles, art, photos, interviews, satire, criticism, reviews, music, letters, parts-of-novels, collages, plays, non-fiction. "(Currently overstocked & oversubmitted in fiction. (Mss destroyed w/o SASE) Our only prejudice is toward writing which has something to say, says it w/some style and grace and speaks in a personal voice. We're not biased toward any age group (17 or 70, it makes no difference); sex; ethnic background; colour, or political stance, etc. We're prejudiced vs sloppy, careless writing, can't phrases or attitudes, & propaganda of any political or sociological set international interests. Recent contributors include: E.J. Neely, Barbara Holland, Tambuzi, G.P. Vimal, Saul Gilson, Barry M. Lally, Brad Darby, Alyce Ingram, James Hearst, Robert Henson, Ruskin Bond, Harriet Gay, Thomas Frosch, Richard Davidson, Wm. Aiken & Jean Pedrick." 2/yr; sub price: $6.00 - 3 issues (U.S. & Canada) -$7.00 Foreign; per copy: $2.65 - U.S. & Canada - $3.00 other; sample: $1.80 (back issues). 1968. 80-96pp; 6 x 8¾. of. circ. 1,300. Reporting time: 26-40 weeks or more (when oversubmitted). Payment: $5.00-$10.00 poems/$15.00-$30.00 fiction/$15.00-$50.00 non-fiction/$12.50-$25.00 essays & reviews. Ads: $150/$85. Discounts: Agents, etc.: 25%, 20 copies-20%, 50 or more, 30%. Back issues: TNR No. 1—$4.25; Nos. 2-7, $1.80; No. 8-$2.30. Pub'd 2 issues 1976; expects 2 issues 1977, 2 issues 1978. Pub's reviews: 2 in 1976. CCLM.

THE NEW REVIEW (formerly THE REVIEW), Ian Hamilton, 11 Greek St, London W1LV5LE, United Kingdom, 01-437-4494. Articles, poetry, fiction, interviews, criticism, reviews, letters, long-poems, plays. "The first new literary monthly to be founded in Britain for more than a decade. There is an extensive and topical reviews section, regular literary bulletins from abroad, lively and informed coverage of news and controversy and regular articles on painting, music, theatre and cinema. Contributors include A. Alvarez, Roy Fuller, Douglas Dunn, Robert Lowell, Brian Aldiss, Peter Porter, Melvyn Bragg, Harold Pinter, Simon Gray." 12/yr; 1-yr sub price: £12($30); per copy: 75p ($2.00). 1962 (as The Review); 1974 (as the new Review). 64pp; 257 mm x 175 mm. †of. Reporting time: 6 weeks. Ads: £75.00/£52.00. Discounts: Subscription agents 10 percent.

New Review Books (see also NEW REVIEW OF EAST-EUROPEAN HISTORY), Alexandra Pidhainy, Publisher, P.O. Box 31, Sta. E, Toronto, Ontario M6H, Canada, 416-536-5083. Articles, reviews, non-fiction. 1,000/yr; avg. price, cloth: $35.00; paper: $10.00. 1962. 400pp; 7 x 10. lp.

Reporting time: 3 months. Payment: by contract. Copyrights for author. Discounts: 15 percent to jobbers. Expects 4 titles 1977 8 titles 1978.

NEW REVIEW OF EAST-EUROPEAN HISTORY, New Reviews Books, Oleh Pidhainy, M. Mladenovic, Box 31, Station E, Toronto, Ontario M6H4E1, Canada, 416-536-5083. Articles, reviews, non-fiction. "Articles with fresh new interpretations are especially welcome. Average length: 12 printed pages." 4/yr; 1-yr sub price: $10.00; per copy: $2.50; sample: free. 1961. 64pp; 6 x 9. lp. circ. 1,000 Reporting time: 1 month. No payment. 10 copies of the issue free to the author. Copyrighted. Ads: $300.00/$180.00. Discounts: 10 percent to magazine jobbers only. Back issues: same as the price of that issue. Pub's reviews. §East-European and Russian History.

NEW RIVER REVIEW, Highlands Press, Charles L. Hayes, Fiction; Philip Pierson, Poetry, Radford College Stat., Radford, VA 24142. Poetry, fiction, art, photos, parts-of-novels, longpoems, plays, concrete art. "No. 1 had: Butrick, Chappell, Dodd, Rugin, Reiss, & others. No. 2 had: Bartlett, Cooley, Zawadiwsky, Clinton, Inez, Newman & many others. No. 3, Dranow; interview with Chappell on poetry, Frost, Colby, Hearst." 2/yr; 1-yr sub price: $4.00; per copy: $2.00; sample: $2.00. 1975. 64pp plus; 5½ x 8½. of. circ. 500 plus. Reporting time: 1-6 wks. Payment: copies (2). Ads: $50/$25. Discounts: none. Back issues: $3.00. Pub'd 1 issue 1976; expects 2 issues 1977, 2 issues 1978. §Poetry, & fiction (short stories) books, plays.

New Rivers Press, Inc., C. W. Truesdale, PO Box 578, Cathedral Sta., New York, NY 10025. "We publish new writing of merit and distinction, mostly poetry, some combinations of prose & poetry, & a fair number of translations. We like to use graphics in as many books as possible. We inaugurated a new children's series in 1976, 3-4 per year." avg. price, cloth: $10.00; paper: $2.50; other: $1.25. 1968. 48-96pp. of. Reporting time: 1-6 months. Payment: 100 copies of book to author commissions (variable for art work). Discounts: 40% trade discount; 25% discount to subscribers to all our publications. Pub'd 12 titles 1976; expects 12 titles 1977, 12 titles 1978. COSMEP, CCLM, PC.

THE NEW SCHOLAR: Studies, Essays, Reviews, The New Scholar, Vernon H. Kjonegaard, Editor; Michael T. Arguello, Reviews Editor, Center for Iberian and Latin American Studies, University of California, San Diego, CA 92093. Articles, interviews, criticism, reviews. "We publish articles, essays, and reviews in an *americanist* context" 2/yr; 1-yr sub price: $10 institution $7 individual; per copy: $4.00; sample: $4.00. 1969. 200pp; 6 x 9. of. circ. 1,000. Reporting time: 6 wks. Payment: 10 offprints. Ads: $75/$40. Back issues: $4.00. Pub's reviews. §Latin American studies, Native American and New World immigrant. CCLM, COSMEP.

NEW SCHOOLS EXCHANGE NEWSLETTER, Bill Harwood, Grace Dailey, Pettigrew, AR 72752. Articles, art, photos, cartoons, interviews, reviews, letters. 10/yr; 1-yr sub price: individuals-$12; institutions-$15; per copy: $1.00; sample: $1.00. 1969. 30pp; 8½ x 11. of. circ. 2,500. Payment: none. Discounts: bookstores 20%. Back issues: $1.00. Pub's reviews. §education, society, human development, alt. energy, community, etc.

New Seed Press, We are a feminist collective & make decisions together, P.O. Box 3016, Stanford, CA 94305. Fiction, art. "We are a small feminist collective commited to publishing non-sexist, non-racist stories for children which actively confront issues of sexism, racism, classism. We are currently soliciting manuscripts by and about Third World women and children or stories by and about children of lesbians (or lesbian living situations). Manuscripts should be typed and sent with return stamped envelope. We will consider any length ms. though our budget usually forces us to limit the size of those we accept." avg. price, paper: $1.25. 1972. pp varies; varies. †of. avg. press run 2,000. Reporting time: 2 months. Payment: varies. Our material is copyrighted only to prevent misuse; feminist, left, and movement groups/people working with children will be given permission to reprint. Discounts: 40 percent to bookstores and distributors. Pay in advance including 10 percent postage. Pub'd 1 title 1976.

The New South Company, Nancy Stone, P.O. Box 3891, Dilworth Station, Charlotte, NC 28203, 704-334-3440. "Our first book is *White Trash,* an anthology of contemporary Southern poets. Our second is *Bear Crossed;* this is an anthology of poems also-the serious, archetypal type. Submissions closed June 1." avg. price, cloth: $5.50. 1976. lp. avg. press run 1,500. Reporting time: Varies. Payment: None, unless the books make money. Copyrights for author. Discounts: We sell direct for the same price we sell to bookstores, etc. They are advised to take their usual mark-up. Pub'd 1 title 1976; expects 2 titles 1977.

The New South Press (see BARATARIA REVIEW)

NEW STORIES, Geoff Tomlinson, College of Education, Co. Durham, Middleton St. George, England. Fiction, parts-of-novels. "Short stories & self-contained extracts from novels 500-10,000 wds." 4/yr; 1-yr sub price: $1.75; per copy: 40p. 1977. 40pp; 8 x 10. of/lp. circ. 400. Reporting time: 2 weeks. Payment: nominal payment only (£2-5 per story). Ads: £20.00/£10.00. Discounts: trade, bulk, classroom, 20 percent. Expects 4 issues 1977. Pub's reviews. §fiction & fiction-writers, literary crit.

NEW THOUGHT, International New Thought Alliance, Dr. Blaine C. Mays, 4533 Scottsdale Rd. 208, Scottsdale, AZ 85351, 602-945-0744. Articles, interviews, non-fiction. "NEW THOUGHT is a self-help, metaphysical publication with articles designed to increase the creative fulfilling, and healing energies in each one of us. Material written from a philosophical and religious point of view is used in the magazine. Emphasis is always upon the positive, constructive, and inspirational." 4/yr; 1-yr sub price: $5.00; per copy: $1.50; sample: $1.50. 1913. 64pp; 8½ x 11. of. circ. 7M. Reporting time: 3-4 wks. Payment: Contributors' copies only. Copyrighted. Ads: $349.69/$175.06. Back issues: Not offered. Pub'd 4 issues 1976; expects 4 issues 1977, 4 issues 1978. Pub's reviews: 12 in 1976.

New Vegetarian Press, Paul Feroe, 1764 Gilpin St, Denver, CO 80218. "Art, short essays, quotes and recipes. Concentrating exclusively on material favorable to vegetarianism. Have printed two postcard sets (8/$1.00) featuring quotes from famous people and on the food crises. Plan five more sets in 1977, recipe postcards, illustrated greeting cards and stationary." 1975. Reporting time: 3 weeks. Payment in copies (for now).

NEW VOICES, Don Fried, P. O. Box 308, Clintondale, NY 12515. Poetry, fiction, satire, parts-of-novels, long-poems, plays. "NV is dedicated to airing the work of unpublished or little known writers. Although some photographs and graphics are used, only those which can be clearly reproduced by offset should be submitted." 1/yr; 1-yr sub price: $3.50; per copy: $3.50; sample: $3.50. 1972. 300pp; 5½ x 8½. of. circ. 500 plus. Reporting time: 1 month. Payment: copy. Copyrighted, reverts to author. Back issues: $2.00. Pub'd 1 issue 1976; expects 1 issue 1977, 1 issue 1978. CCLM, COSMEP.

New Woman Press, Jean Mountaingrove, Ruth Mountaingrove, Box 56, Wolf Creek, OR 97497. "Book Published: *Turned-On Woman Songbook,* 34 pages, 27 original songs, feminist bent, photos and drawings. 1975, $3.00 tapes available: 12 songs-custom-$6.50; 18 songs-pre-chosed $5.00." 1975. of. Payment: royalties/15% on songbook. Expects 2 titles 1977.

NEW WORLD JOURNAL, Turtle Island Foundation, Bob Callahan, 2845 Buena Vista Way, Berkeley, CA 94708. Poetry, fiction, articles, art. "New world history and literature: Anderson, Barlow, Callahan, Cardenal, Dorn, Dawson, DeAngulo, DiPrima, HD, Irey, Metcalf, Olson, Sauer, Tarn." 2/yr; price per copy: $3.00; sample: $3.00. 1975. 64-96pp; 5½ x 8½. †lp. circ. 1,000. Discounts: 40% trade. §New World Letters. CCLM, COSMEP.

‡**NEW WRITING FROM ZAMBIA, New Writers Group,** PO Box 1889, Lusaka, Zambia, Africa.

NEW YORK ARTS JOURNAL, Richard Burgin, 560 Riverside Drive, New York, NY 10024. Poetry, fiction, articles, art, photos, cartoons, interviews, satire, criticism, reviews, music, letters, parts-of-novels, long-poems, collages, plays, concrete art. "NEW YORK ARTS JOURNAL tries to achieve a balance between worthwhile creative achievement and critical reflection in dealing with the major art forms. As such it is open to different styles of work. Contributors in our first issue included: John Cage, Alain Robbe-Grillet, Duane Michals, David Shapiro, Robert Bly, John Updike, Jonathan Baumbach and George Stude." 6/yr; 1-yr sub price: $4.00; per copy: $.75; sample: price of postage. 1976. 44pp; 11½ x 15½. of. circ. 13,500. Reporting time: maximum 1 month. Payment: poetry $1.00-line/prose $3.00-page. Ads: $150/$75. Discounts: classroom-institutions 15%/ad agencies 15%. Back issues: $.75 plus postage. Pub's reviews. §criticism, fiction, poetry, music, art.

THE NEW YORK CULTURE REVIEW, The New York Culture Review Press, Daniel M. J. Stokes, 1807 60th St, Brooklyn, NY 11204. Articles, interviews, criticism, reviews, letters. "Recent contributors: Robert Peters, Clifton Snider, Norman Lederer, Janice L. Ross, Colin Ross, Arthur Knight, Yves Barbero, Joseph McLaughlin. Book reviews should be a min. of 200 words and a maximum of 1,000 words." irreg.; sub price: $9/12 issues libraries; $7 others; $4 unemployed; per copy: $.35-$1.00; sample: $1.00. 1974. 14pp; 8½ x 11. of. circ. 1,000 plus. Reporting time: 1 month. Payment: copies. Discounts: 10 plus copies—40%. Back Issues: Newsletter issues available for $.50 in stamps. Others $1.00. Pub's reviews. §all areas. CCLM.

‡**NEW YORK QUARTERLY,** PO Box 2415 G Central Stn., New York, NY 10017. CCLM.

NEW ZEALAND MONTHLY REVIEW, Caxton Press, Box 345, Christchurch, New Zealand. 11/yr; 1-yr sub price: $5.00; per copy: $0.50. 1959. 24pp; crown. print. circ. 2,100. Payment: nil. Copyright: ours. Ads: $50.00/$25.00. Back issues: difficult.

NewBooks (see also Beyond Baroque Foundation Publications).

Newedi Press (see also BETELGEUSE CHAPBOOK SERIES/NEWEDI FICTION SERIES), Kent R. Mahan, Dept. of English, Bowling Green University, Bowling Green, OH 43403. Poetry, fiction, art, letters, long-poems. avg. price, paper: $2.00. 1975. 72pp; 5½ x 8½. †of. avg. press run 500-1,000. Reporting time: 1 month. Payment: 10 contributor's copies. Copyright reverts to author after 90 days. Discounts: 40 percent to dealers. Pub'd 8 titles 1976; expects 6 titles 1977, 8 titles 1978.

NEWEST REVIEW, Newest Press, George Melnyk, 13024-109 Ave, Edmonton, Alberta T5M3N3, Canada. Poetry, fiction, articles, art, photos, cartoons, interviews, satire, criticism, reviews, letters, parts-of-novels, long-poems, plays. "The Newest Review has as its main focus Western Canada. Through book reviews, film reviews, essays, poetry, political commentary, art etc. it has provided since Sept. 75 a monthly overview of politics, society, culture in the West. It restricts its contributors to Western Canadians, except for a special 'A Letter From. . .' section which is open to everyone. The Newest Review is a commercial publication which operates without government grants and supports itself by advertising and subscription/sales." 10/yr; 1-yr sub price: $4.00-Canada, $6.00-US, $8.00-foreign (airmail), $6.00-institutional, $8.00-institutional (US), $10.00-foreign institutional-yr; per copy: $0.50. 1975. 12pp; demi-tab. of. circ. 700. Reporting time: 1 month. Payment: $15.00 per page printed. Ads: $200/$100. Discounts: none. Pub's reviews: 30 in 1976.

NEWORLD, Fred Beauford, 1308 S. New Hampshire Ave, Los Angeles, CA 90029. Poetry, fiction, articles, art, photos, interviews, criticism, reviews, letters, parts-of-novels. 4/yr; 1-yr sub price: $15.00; per copy: $1.25; sample: $1.25. 1974. 56pp; 8½ x 11. of. circ. 10,000. Reporting time: 1 month. Payment: $50.00 article. Ads: $500/$350. Back issues: $3.00 each. Pub's reviews. §The arts.

NEWSLETTER, Long Island Poetry Collective, Inc, George William Fisher, 2441 Riverside Drive, Wantagh, NY 11793, 516-826-8724. Criticism, reviews, news items. "Features include: calendar of regional literary events (Long Island-NY City), 2-4 reviews per issue, an extensive small press markets column, and other informational materials of useto readers/writers of poetry." 10/yr; 1-yr sub price: $3.00; per copy: $0.25; sample: $0.25. 1974. 16pp; 5½ x 8½. of. circ. 450. Reporting time: 2-4 weeks. Payment: none. Not copyrighted. Ads: none. Back issues: vol 3 only (1976-1977) $5.00/ 10 issues. Pub'd 10 issues 1976; expects 10 issues 1977, 10 issues 1978. Pub's reviews. §poetry (or poetry in combination with short fiction, graphics, etc.).

Newsnovel Publishers, Darlene Wheeler, 3969 University Ave, Riverside, CA 92501. Poetry, fiction, articles, art, satire, criticism, parts-of-novels. "We publish news novel in newsprint-1st novels, novelettes, fiction, fact-whichever we choose" 1970. 12pp; 17 x 21. of. Reporting time: 1 mo.

NEXUS, Wright State University, Dayton, OH 45431, 513-873-2782. Poetry, fiction, articles, art, photos, cartoons, interviews, satire, criticism, reviews, long-poems, plays. "The emphasis in our articles is local—Wright State University and the surrounding community in the Miami Valley region of Ohio—but we consider poetry and fiction from anywhere. Query after July 1 for possible theme issues in 1976-77. With the switch to a new tabloid format, NEXUS has been liberated. It is now given away free in exchange for just about anything, and also to anyone who sends a self-addressed, stamped manilla envelope. Art (must be high contrast block and white) and reviews are also considered for publication." 3/yr; 1-yr sub price: free; per copy: free. 1965. 32pp; 11½ x 16 (tabloid). of. circ. 4,000. Reporting time: 3 months. Payment: copies. Ads: none. Pub'd 3 issues 1976; expects 3 issues 1977, 3 issues 1978. Pub's reviews: 3 in 1976. §Poetry books, fiction (novels). COSMEP.

THE NIAGARA MAGAZINE, Neil Baldwin, 369 Pennsylvania Street, Buffalo, NY 14201. Poetry. "We are looking for poetry which reflects a deep commitment to temporal and/or spiritual landscapes. We continue to seek a dynamic poetry which uses space, enjambments, tensions in unusual ways; I have a personal aversion to 'flat,' sentence like, genteel poems. We are very interested in Canadian poetry, and are trying to bridge the cultural gaps between the borders. I encourage young Canadian poets to get in touch. We publish the very well-known and also the very new—as long as it's exciting, projective, positive poetry. Although we have shifted locales from Buffalo to NYC, I consider the force and vitality of 'NIAGARA' to be a state of mind. I suggest you send for a sample copy before submitting work." 2/yr; sub price: $7.00/4 issues; per copy: $2.00; sample: $1.50. 1974. 52pp; 8½ x 6¾. of. circ. 500 plus. Reporting time: 8 weeks at most. Payment: copies. Copyrighted, we will transfer copyright in writing, upon request. no ads. Discounts: 40% trade discount. Back issues: No. 3. (Irish issue,) $1.50. No. 7, (Winter 1977), $2.00. Pub'd 3 issues 1976, expects 2 issues 1977, 2 issues 1978. §Interested in translations—and new Canadian poetry. COSMEP, CCLM.

NICOTINE SOUP, Sea of Storms, Laura Brown, P.O. Box 22613, San Francisco, CA 94122, 567-9091. Poetry, fiction, art, photos, cartoons, satire, long-poems, collages, concrete art. "We generally don't print more than 10 pages of material from an artist. We prefer printing more than 1 or 2 poems by a poet. We tend to gravitate towards under published artists." 4/yr; 1-yr sub price: $4.00; per copy: $1.00; sample: $1.00. 1974. 36pp; 7 x 8½. of. circ. 500. Reporting time: 1 month. Payment: none. Copyrighted, reverts to author. Ads: none. Discounts: 40 percent discount to bookstores & distributors for orders of 1-50. Over 50, 50 percent. Back issues: $1.00 a copy. Pub'd 2 issues 1976; expects 4 issues 1977, 4 issues 1978. COSMEP.

NIMROD, University of Tulsa, Francine Ringold, Nimrod University of Tulsa, 600 S. College, Tulsa, OK 74104. Poetry, fiction, articles, art, photos, interviews, parts-of-novels, long-poems, plays. "Recent contributors: David Ray, Winston Weathers, Stephen Kennedy, Paulette Millchap, Carol Haralson, H.L. Van Brunt, E.M. Broner, Lance Henson, Paul Scott, Stanley Sulkin, Ellen Bass, Isaac Bashevis Singer, Victoria Ocampo, Judith Johnson Sherwin, Cynthia MacDonald, Peter Viereck, Jorge Luis Borges." 2/yr; 1-yr sub price: $4.00; per copy: $2.25; sample: $2.25. 1956. 125pp; 6 x 9. of. circ. 1,000 (counting subscriptions & direct sales). Reporting time: 12-16 weeks. Payment: up to $5 a page. Copyrighted, reverts to author. Ads: $85/$50. Back issues: $1.50 each up through Vol. 19, No. 2. Pub'd 2 issues 1976; expects 2 issues 1977, 2 issues 1978. §Poetry. CCLM, COSMEP.

1977 Traveler's Toll-Free Directory (see LANDMARK PUBLISHING)

"NITTY GRITTY", Goldermood Rainbow Press, Bill Wilkins, Editor, 331 W. Bonneville, Pasco, WA 99301, 509-547-5525. Poetry, fiction, articles, art, photos, cartoons, interviews, satire, criticism, reviews, letters, concrete art, non-fiction. "Articles, commentary, fiction: maximum

10,000. Poetry-mostly short. Reviews-short: maximum 500 words. Cartoons-humor-photos." 3/yr; 1-yr sub price: $10.00; per copy: $4.00. 1974. 120pp; 8½ x 11. †of. circ. 4,000. Reporting time: 60-90 days. Payment: fiction $15, poetry & photos $2, cartoons & art work $5, commentary-personal experiences-reviews-articles $10. Copyrighted, rights do not revert. Ads: $50/$30/$20 1/4/none. Discounts: trade 40%. Pub'd 2 issues 1976; expects 4 issues 1977, 3 issues 1978. Pub's reviews: 20 in 1976. §all small press. COSMEP.

No Dead Lines, John Daniel, Venetia T. Gleason, 241 Bonita, Portola Valley, CA 94025. Poetry, fiction, art. "We experiment with alternative forms of fine book publishing. Emphasis on poetry and graphics. We've had particular success with co-operative anthologies. Each of our books is unique. Write for free catalog." avg. price, paper: $3.00. 1975. of. avg. press run 300. Discounts: 40% to bookstores & contributors. Pub'd 4 titles 1976; expects 6 titles 1977.

Nobodaddy Press (see also POETRY IN MOTION), David Lehman, Stefanie Green, 20 College Hill Rd., Clinton, NY 13323, 315-853-6946. Poetry, long-poems. *"The Reading of an Ever-Changing Tale,* a chapbook of poems by John Yau. *The Conquest of Appetite,* a pamphlet of poems by David Lehman. Special limited editions of avant-garde poetry, 'High Quality Publishing.' The first 50 copies of an edition are signed by author and by artist (cover design)." avg. price, paper: $3.50. 1976. 24-32pp; 5½ x 8½. †of/lp. avg. press run 500 copies. Reporting time: It varies. Payment: Author receives 100 copies. Copyrights for author. Discounts: The usual trade discount of 40 percent. CCLM.

NOE VALLEY POETS WORKSHOP, Cassandra Publications, 160 Caselli Ave, San Francisco, CA 94114. "We publish only books by workshops members."

NOMAD, Other Scenes, John Wilcock, BCM-Oscenes, London WC1V 6XX, United Kingdom. "Occasional travel newsletter issued. $1.00 brings sample issue plus NOMAD press card 'good for what you can get away with'. Useful travel info. Box 4137 Grand Central P. O., New York, NY 10017." 1968. of.

NOMEN, Sunyata Press, Jak English, Susan Clark, Box 278, Brentwood Bay, British Columbia VO51AO, Canada. Poetry, articles, art, photos, interviews, reviews, letters. Irreg.; 1-yr sub price: Inquire; per copy: Inquire; sample: Inquire. 1975. 30-60pp; 8½ x 5½. circ. 3-500. Reporting time: 3-4 weeks. Payment: 2 copies. Discounts: Trade etc. 30 percent. §Esp. oriental relig. & poetry. Nuclear resistance, oriental lang. anthro & mysticism.

NORDIC WORLD, World Publications, Dave Prokop, PO Box 366, Mtn. View, CA 94040. Fiction, articles, art, photos, cartoons, interviews. "The editor controls all published material. 'Nordic World' is the only magazine in the country devoted exclusively to the sport. It provides thorough coverage of Nordic skiing, snow camping, ski mountaineering, safety, equipment, and racing." 9/yr; 1-yr sub price: $6.50; per copy: $.75; sample: free upon request. 1973. 48pp; 9 x 11. of. circ. 10,000. Reporting time: variable. Payment: write for info. Back issues: $1.00 each issue. §sports, recreation 2nd leisure activities.

NORTH AMERICAN MENTOR MAGAZINE, Westburg Associates, Publishers, John Westburg, Mildred Westburg, General Editors; Martial Westburg, Art Editor, Post Office Drawer 69, Fennimore, WI 53809. Poetry, fiction, articles, art, photos, satire, criticism, reviews, parts-of-novels, long-poems, plays. "We offer an annual poetry contest, with cash awards and certificates of merit. Contestants must be paid subscribers. Write for contest rules." 4/yr; 1-yr sub price: $9.00; per copy: $3.00; sample: $1.25. 1964. 60-90pp; 8½ x 11. †of. circ. Between 350 and 500 for 1977-1978. Reporting time: 2 to 3 months. Payment: 1 copy. Copyrighted. Ads: none. Discounts: None. Back Issues: Volume 1-2, $150.00; Volume 3-4, $50; all others, $3.00 per number. Pub'd 4 issues 1976; expects 4 issues 1977, 4 issues 1978. Pub's reviews: 4 in 1976. §Art, anthropology, poetry, fiction, history, literary criticism, and political science. CCLM, COSMEP.

THE NORTH AMERICAN REVIEW, Robley Jr. Wilson, Univ. Of Northern Iowa, Cedar Falls, IA 50613, 319-266-8487/273-2681. Poetry, fiction, articles, reviews, long-poems. "Environmental focus." 4/yr; 1-yr sub price: $6.00; per copy: $1.50; sample: $1.00. 1815. 80pp; 8½ x 11. of. circ. 3,000. Reporting time: 8 weeks. Payment: $10.00 per published page; 50 cents a line for poetry. Copyrighted, assigned on request of author. Ads: $300.00/$175.00. Discounts: Agent 20 percent; bulk (10 or more) 33-1/3 percent. Back issues: face price. Pub'd 4 issues 1976; expects 4 issues 1977, 4 issues 1978. Pub's reviews. §poetry & fiction. CCLM, COSMEP.

North American Student Cooperative Organization (see THE NEW HARBINGER)

North Atlantic Books (see also IO), Richard Grossinger, RFD 2, Box 135, Plainfield, VT 05667, 802-454-7845. Poetry, fiction, non-fiction. "Authors: Richard Grossinger, Diane Di Prima, Edward Sanders, Lindy Hough, Irene McKinney, Bernadette Mayer, Don Byrd, Gerrit Lansing, Wayne Turiansky, Theodore Enslin, Paul Kahn, Josephine Clare, Bobby Byrd, Alex Gildzen." avg. price, paper: $4.00. 1973. 250pp; 6 x 9. of. avg. press run 1500. no unsolicited manuscripts. Payment: 10%. Copyrights for author. Discounts: none, bookstores only. Pub'd 4 titles 1976; expects 3 titles 1977, 3 titles 1978.

THE NORTH CAROLINA REVIEW, The N. C. Review Press, Carol Lynn Wilkinson, 3329 Granville Dr., Raleigh, NC 27609. Poetry, fiction, reviews. "Recent contributors: Guy Owen, Fred Chappell, Robert Watson, Leon Rooke, Gordon Weaver, Albert Goldbarth" 2/yr; sub price: $7.00/4 issues; per copy: $2.00; sample: $2.00. 1975. 85pp; 6 x 9. †of. circ. 900. Reporting time: 2 wks on rejections longer on acceptances and near misses. Payment: $.50 a line for poetry, $5.00 a page for fiction. Pub's reviews. §fiction, poetry. COSMEP.

NORTH COAST POETRY, North Coast Press, Rotating Editorship, PO Box 56, East Machias, ME 04630. Poetry. "Some recent contributors: Michael McMahon, Kris Larson, Thomas Johnson, Mark Mendel, Timothy Wright, Myrna Bouchey, Albert Stanton, Rita Stanton." 2/yr; 1-yr sub price: $2.00; per copy: $1.00; sample: $1.00. 1972. 30pp; 8½ x 11. mi. circ. 100. Reporting time: Up to 2 months usually. Payment: copies only. Discounts: 40% bulk, trade, etc. Back issues: Nos. 2 & 8 available. Pub'd 2 issues 1976. §poetry. CCLM.

NORTH COUNTRY, Richard Foss, Dept English, U. of N.D., Grand Forks, ND 58201. Poetry, fiction, photos, parts-of-novels. "Contributors include: Anthony Oldknow, Wendell Berry, Wm. Gass." 2/yr. 1966. 72pp; 6 x 9. of. circ. 400. Reporting time: 1-6 weeks. Payment: 1 copy. Back issues: $.50 each.

‡NORTH COUNTRY ANVIL, North Country Alternatives, Box 37, Millville, MN 55957.

North Country Press, P.O. Box 12223, Seattle, WA 98112. "We are only a book publisher, not a magazine. Our only book is The World Of A Giant Corporation, an unauthorized report on General Electric, by John Woodmansee with Ralph Nader, Derek Sheaver, and others, paperback $2.95." 1975. Discounts: 40 percent trade thru us or our distributor, bookpeople; please write for info on higher discounts to wholesalers, indicating quantity & payment schedule to be used.

NORTH COUNTRY STAR, North Country Star, Eleanor Lewallen, John Lewallen, PO Box 24081, Oakland, CA 94611, 415-655-1335. Articles, photos. "Northern California back-to-the-land environmentally sound lifestyle is our beat." 8/yr; sub price: 12-issue subs. price $3.50; per copy: $0.25; sample: $0.50. 1976. 8pp; 10 x 16. of. circ. 2,500. Reporting time: 1 week. Payment: nothing. Copyrighted, reverts to author. Ads: $340.00/$180.00/$0.10. Discounts: 15 cents each to any seller (cover price: 25 cents). Back issues: 50 cents each. Pub'd 6 issues 1976; expects 8 issues 1977, 8 issues 1978. Pub's reviews: 25 in 1976. §back-to-the-land movement, ecology.

‡NORTH DAKOTA QUARTERLY, Dept. Of History, Univ. Of North Dakota, Grand Forks, ND 58201.

‡NORTH STONE REVIEW, Tendon Press, University Stn. 14098, Minneapolis, MN 55414. CCLM.

THE NORTH WIND, Beaver Lodge Press, Susan Walsh, Box 65583, Vancouver 12, B. C. V5N 5K5, Canada. Articles, art, reviews. "We would like articles on medieval and renaissance crafts, skills, manners etc. of about 500 to 1,000 words, from *any* culture. This is a newsletter/research organ of the Canadian Society for Creative Anachronism. People associated with SCA (and there are about 4,000 of them) will know what we want. Rigour demanded, i.e. proper footnotes and references are required." 10/yr; 1-yr sub price: $7.00. 1974. 24pp; 21 x 28 cm. †mi. circ. 150. Reporting time: 2 weeks. Payment: copies. Pub's reviews. §If they relate to medieval skills or history.

NORTHEAST/JUNIPER BOOKS, Juniper Press, John Judson, 1310 Shorewood Dr., LaCrosse, WI 54601. Poetry, fiction, articles, art, interviews, criticism, reviews, parts-of-novels, long-poems. "We solicit any work of quality that has a human being behind it whose words help shape his and our awareness of being human. This has always come before fashion, reputation or ambition in our eyes. Juniper books are chapbooks. A subscription includes two NE's and 4 Juniper books per year, plus gifts." 2/yr; sub price: $10.50-$18.00 for complete sub including 2 fine printed poetry bks per-yr plus NE and all Juniper Books.; per copy: $1.75; sample: $1.75. 1962. 40-60pp; varies. †of/lp. circ. 4-500. Reporting time: 4-6 wks. Payment: 2 copies. no ads. Back issues: write for information/most are available but in very small quantities. Pub'd 10 issues 1976; expects 10 issues 1977, 10 issues 1978. Pub's reviews. §poetry, crit., experimental fiction. CCLM.

NORTHEAST RISING SUN, Charles Plymell, Pamela Beach Plymell, Joshua Norton, Michael Scott Cain, Box 303, Cherry Valley, NY 13320, 607-264-3204. Articles, criticism, reviews, interviews, letters. 8/yr; 1-yr sub price: $8.00; per copy: $1.50; sample: $1.50. 1976. 32pp; 8½ x 11. of. circ. 2,000. Reporting time: a. s. a. p. Payment: eventually plan to pay at going rate for reviews. Ads: $35/$20. Discounts: 40 percent - 50 percent. Pub'd 5 issues 1976; expects 8 issues 1977, 8 issues 1978. Pub's reviews. §all literary, particularly in Northeast. COSMEP, CCLM, NESPA, NYSSPA.

NORTHERN JOURNEY, Northern Journey Press, Craig Campbell, David McDonald, Valerie Kent, Fraser Sutherland, PO Box 4073, Station "E", Ottawa, Ontario K1S 5B1, Canada. Poetry, fiction, articles, art, photos, interviews, criticism, reviews, parts-of-novels, concrete art. 2/yr; 1-yr sub price: $3.50; per copy: $1.95. 1971. 120pp; 6 x 8¾. of. circ. 1,500. Reporting time: 2 months. Pub's reviews. §literary.

NORTHERN LIGHT, University of Manitoba Press, George Amabile, Editor; Pamela McLeod, Managing Editor., 605 Fletcher Argue Bldg., Univ. of Manitoba, Winnipeg, Manitoba R3T2N2, Canada, 204-474-8145. Poetry, reviews. "Any length poem is possible, though we've found that few longpoems are really sustained. We want poetry which uses the subtle rhythms of speech, strong images, fresh metaphor, intense patterns of verbal music, which are original and subtle, and a central coherent theme or context. We don't like chatty poems, 'street' poetry which is often illiterate and boring, literary puzzles, word games, typographical doodling, abstract prose laid out in lines to look like poetry, or meaningless 'free association'. Manuscripts without SASE will be destroyed. Recent contributors include Pat Lane, Elizabeth Brewster, Alan Safarik, Kenneth McRobbie, Thomas McGrath, Susan Musgrave, Peter Wild, Robert Bagg, Richard Emil Braun, etc. We prefer to publish young Canadian Poets, and also do reviews of recent books of Canadian poetry." 2/yr; 1-yr sub price: $3.25; per copy: $1.85; sample: $1.50. 1968. 64pp; 8-5/8 x 5-5/8. of. circ. 1,200. Reporting time: 1 mo. Payment: 5 copies. Copyright: NL & U. of M. Press. Ads: $100.00/$65.00. Discounts: 10% agencies 40% student rate (bulk) for classroom use. Back issues: Full set (far point 1-8) $75.00. Pub'd 1 issue 1976; expects 2 issues 1977, 2 issues 1978. Pub's reviews: 3 in 1976. §Recent books of Canadian poetry. COSMEP, CPPA.

NORTHERN NEIGHBORS, Northern Neighbors, Dyson Carter, PO Box 1210, Gravenhurst, Ont. P0C 1G0, Canada. "Staff produced-we do not accept submissions." 12/yr; 1-yr sub price: $3.00; per copy: $.50; sample: $.25. 1949. 28pp; 9 x 11. of. circ. 12,000. Payment: none. Back issues: $1.00 per copy.

NORTHERN NEW ENGLAND REVIEW, J. W. Morgan, PO Box 825, Franklin Pierce College,

Rindge, NH 03461. Poetry, fiction, articles, art, photos, satire, criticism, reviews, parts-of-novels. 2/yr; 1-yr sub price: $4.00; per copy: $2.00; sample: $2.00. 1973. 80pp; 8½ x 11. of. circ. 400. Reporting time: 4 months. Payment: copies. Back issues: No. 2 $1.00. Pub's reviews. §any publication in New England. COSMEP, NESPA.

Northland Library (see WRITE ON)

NORTHWEST CHESS, Kennedy Poyser, P O Box 2951, Olympia, WA 98507, 206-753-3841. Fiction, articles, art, photos, cartoons, interviews, reviews, letters. "We are interested in chess-related material of all kinds. There's no need for a 'regional slant'; chess is much the same in the Northwest as it is elsewhere. Longer material would probably be held for the larger issues (March, June, September & December). Fritz Leiber is one noteworthy recent contributor." 12/yr; 1-yr sub price: $5.00; per copy: $0.50; sample: $0.50. 1947. 32pp; 7 x 11. of. circ. 1,000 mostly in the Northwest. Reporting time: 2 weeks. Payment varies from contributors' copies to about $15.00 for articles. Not copyrighted. Ads: $20.00/$10.00/$0.05. Discounts: Free subs. to prisons/Free exchange with other chess mags/30 percent disc. to agents/$2.50 per year to prisoners. Back issues: from $0.25 to $1.00 each, depending on year. Pub's reviews. §chess and other board games. COSMEP, AUSCJ.

Northwest Matrix, Charlotte Mills, Bobbie Moore, Nancy Clark, 1628 E. 19th, Eugene, OR 97403, 503-687-8660. Fiction, articles, criticism, reviews. "NW Matrix is a feminist publishing house. We only publish woman authors now. See   *Publishing Philosophy* for the time being. 1. We're interested in women's history, anthropology, politics and literature; 2. Essays or short papers on same topics for essay series 'Current feminist topics'. 3. Fiction, biography, history (non-sexist) for young adults." avg. price, paper: $4.00. 1975. 150pp; 5¼ x 8¼. of. avg. press run 1,000. Reporting time: 1-3 mos. Payment varies. Copyrights for author. Discounts: 40 percent for all orders over 5 for each title. COSMEP, WIP.

NORTHWEST PASSAGE, Collective, Box 105, South Bell Station, Bellingham, WA 98225. Poetry, fiction, articles, art, photos, cartoons, interviews, satire, criticism, reviews, music, letters, collages, plays, concrete art. "We are a non-hierarchical collective of people concerned with giving voice/support to the struggle for human, freedom, economic self-control, & environmental sanity. We will not publish any sexist, racist, ageist, or oppressive submissions which run contrary to this theme." Every 2 wks.; 1-yr sub price: $8.00; per copy: $.35; sample: $.35. 1968. 32pp; 16 x 13. circ. 12,000. Reporting time: one wk. prior to issue publ. Payment: none. Ads: $115/$63.50/$.12 institutions/$.05 personal word. Back issues: $.50 within one year. Pub's reviews. §Radical thought, alternative economics, internation 3rd world, radical environmentalism.

NORTHWEST REVIEW, University of Oregon Press, Michael Strelow, Editor; Christine McQuitty, Fiction Ed.; John Ackerson, Poetry Ed., 369 P.L.C., University of Oregon, Eugene, OR 97405, 503-686-3957. Poetry, fiction, art, photos, reviews, parts-of-novels, long-poems, plays. "Recent contributors: Wm. Stafford, John Woods, Greg Kuzma, Douglas Blazek, in poetry; Albert Drake, Jerry Bumpus, Joyce Carol Oates in fiction. Bias: Quality in whatever form. No other predisposition." 3/yr; 1-yr sub price: $5.00; per copy: $2.00; sample: $1.50. 1957. 132pp; 6 x 9. of. circ. 2,000. Reporting time: 6 weeks. Payment: around $6/poem and $1.50 page fiction. Copyrighted. Ads: $50.00/$30.00. Discounts: bookstore/agencies:20% consignment & 40% wholesale. Back issues: $2.00 all. Pub'd 3 issues 1976; expects 3 issues 1977, 3 issues 1978. Pub's reviews: 20 in 1976. §literature/poetry fiction:special Northwest interest materials. CCLM, COSMEP.

NORTHWOODS JOURNAL, Northwoods Press, Inc., Robert W. Olmsted, Editor; Paul Hodges, Reviews Editor, RR 1, Meadows of Dan., VA 24120, 703-952-2388. Poetry, fiction, articles, art, cartoons, interviews, satire, criticism, reviews, letters, long-poems. "We want stuff that will teach the writer that New York slicks are not reality. That the small press world is their only chance. Stuff of interest to writers who haven't discovered us (small press) yet. Also, just fine writing." 8/yr; 1-yr sub price: $4.00; per copy: $1.00; sample: $0.25. 1972. 32pp; 5½ x 8½. †of. circ. 1,000-1,500. Reporting time: 15th of each month. Payment: $1.00 per page minimum. Buys all rights, but releases on specific request. Ads: $40.00/$25.00/$0.10. Discounts: None. Back issues: $1.00 ea, as available. Pub'd 8 issues 1976; expects 8 issues 1977, 8 issues 1978. Pub's reviews: 35 in 1976. §all small press or self published works.

Northwoods Press, Inc. (see also NORTHWOODS JOURNAL), Robert W. Olmsted, RR 1, Meadows of Dan, VA 24120, 703-952-2588. Poetry, fiction, news items, non-fiction. avg. price, cloth: $8.95; paper: $2.95. 1972. 80pp; 5½ x 8½. of. avg. press run 500. Reporting time: 30 days or less. Payment: Royalties. Copyrights for author.

Nosferatu (see STONEY LONESOME)

NOSTOC, Marshall Brooks, Editor; Bill Costley, Editor-At-Large; Stephen Halpert, Contrib. Editor; Brenda Halpert, Contrib. Editor, 101 Nehoiden Rd, Waban, MA 02168. Poetry, fiction, articles, criticism, reviews, parts-of-novels, non-fiction. "We have no biases; no special requirements. We publish both known and unknown writers. Interested in small press history. Recent contributors are Herschel Silverman and Menke Katz·.." Minimum of 2 issues/yr.; sub price: $1.00-4 issues; libraries $2.50; per copy: $.25; sample: SASE. 1973. 25pp; 5½ x 8½. †lp. circ. 500. Reporting time: immediately. Payment: copies. Ads: rates on request. Discounts: usual trade discount. Back issues: rates on request. Pub'd 2 issues 1976; expects 2 issues 1977. Pub's reviews: 8 in 1976. §small press history.

Not-For-Sale-Press, Lew Thomas, 243 Grand View Ave, San Francisco, CA 94114, 415-647-4290. Photos. "*8 x 10,* 1975, compiled by Lew Thomas, 48 pgs. 21 photos. *PERFORMANCES AND INSTALLATIONS,* Kesa. 1976, 62 pages, 50 photos." avg. price, paper: $4.00. 1975. 48 to 62pp. of. avg. press run 500. Discounts: 40% trade, 55% wholesale.

NOT MAN APART, Friends of the Earth, Tom Turner, Ed; David Gancher, Mary Lou Seaver, Assoc. Eds., 529 Commercial St, San Francisco, CA 94111. Articles, art, photos, cartoons, reviews, letters. "No poetry, confound it. Suggest reading a sample issue before submitting. We concentrate on national and global environmental issues, with a political perspective." 24/yr; 1-yr sub price: $10.00; per copy: $.50; sample: free. 1970. 16pp; 11½ x 15 (tabloid). of. circ. approx. 25,000. Reporting time: varies 2-8 wks. Payment: copies. Ads: $300 1x/$180 1x. Back issues: $.25 copy. Pub's reviews. §environment, food, eco-fiction (whatever you take that to mean). COSMEP.

NOTABLE AMERICAN POETS, Winston-Paramount Books, Linda Nash, Box j, Babylon, NY 11702. Poetry. "1-3 poems, 3-16 lines & return envelope. Sincere, sensitive poetry. No smut." 4/yr; price per copy: $7.00 paper $11.00 hardcover; sample: $3.95. 1970. 40pp; 8½ x 5½. †of. circ. 3,000. Reporting time: 2-4 weeks. Payment: $.60 per poem. Back issues: $3.95 paperback $9.95 hardcover.

THE NOTEBOOK & OTHER REVIEWS, Notebook Press, Michael O'Neill, P O Box 180, Birmingham, MI 48012. Poetry, fiction, articles, art, cartoons, satire, criticism, reviews, letters. "Best to examine issues." when material is available; sub price: $10.00/10 issues; per copy: $2.00; sample: $1.00. 1975. 32pp; 8½ x 11. of. circ. 300 plus. Reporting time: 2 wks. Payment: negotiable. Copyrighted, does not revert to author. Ads: $40.00/$25.00/$0.10. Discounts: none. Back issues: query (expensive). Pub's reviews. §all esp. poetry & fiction. COSMEP.

Notebook Press (see also NOTEBOOK & OTHER REVIEWS), Michael O'Neill, P O Box 180, Birmingham, MI 48012. Poetry, fiction, criticism, reviews. avg. price, cloth: $7.95; paper: $3.95. 1976. 56pp; 5½ x 8½. of. avg. press run 1,000. Reporting time: 1 month. Payment variable usually 10 percent. Copyrights for author. Discounts: standard bookstore. COSMEP.

Noumenon Press (see also INTERSTATE), Loris Essary, Mark Loeffler, PO Box 7068, University Station, Austin, TX 78712. Poetry, fiction, art, photos, music, long-poems, collages, plays, concrete art. "Available titles are Carl D. Clark, *Desire, Chasing A Cow;* Susan Bright Buchanan, *Container;* Tamara O'Brien, *Affairs;* Jeff Woodruff, *Farm To Market;* Paul B. Miner, *Your Mother Wears Combat Boots;* Loris Essary, *Ending.* Manuscripts are currently by invitation only and writers should submit their work to INTERSTATE magazine. A sample copy of a book is available for $1.25."

1974. of. Reporting time: Immediately. Payment: copies. Copyrights for author. Pub'd 3 titles 1976; expects 6 titles 1977. COSMEP.

NOUS: a journal of arts and ideas, Carl D. Clark, 3007 University, Austin, TX 78705, 512-472-7415. Poetry, fiction, articles, art, photos, cartoons, interviews, satire, criticism, reviews, music, letters, parts-of-novels, long-poems, collages, plays, concrete art. 3/yr. 1977. 5½ x 8½. mi/of. Reporting time: 1 week-6 months. Payment: copies. Copyrighted, reverts to author. Ads: none. Discounts: no discount schedule at present. Pub'd 1 issue 1976. Pub's reviews: none in 1976. §arts, philosophy (especially avante-garde/radical).

NOUS JOURNAL, All About Us/Nous Autres Inc., Russ Hazzard, P.O. Box 1985, Ottawa, Ontario KIP5R5, Canada, 613-234-2919. Poetry, fiction, articles, art, photos, cartoons, interviews, reviews, letters, long-poems, concrete art. "Most material (poems, stories) written by young writers (6-18 years)" 4/yr; 1-yr sub price: $1.50; per copy: $0.50; sample: $0.50. 1974. 16pp; 11½ x 15½. of. circ. 5,000. Reporting time: 2 months. Payment: none-except expenses where applicable. Copyrighted, reverts to author. Discounts: single subscription $1.50—group subsc. (10 issues postpaid ($12.00)—group subsc. 20 issues postpaid $20.00). Back issues: $0.50. Pub'd 4 issues 1976. §art, education.

John L Noyce, Publisher (formerly Smoothie Pub) (see also LIBRARIANS FOR SOCIAL CHANGE, STUDIES IN LABOUR HISTORY), John L. Noyce, P.O. Box 450, Brighton, Sussex BN1 8GR, United Kingdom. "Bibliographies, directories, etc. of use to the Alternative Community, etc; recent pubns. inc. Alternative Bookshops, Alternative Publishers, a series of indexes to various Alternative Periodicals, eg. Inside Story, Peace News and a series on Alternative Technology (10 titles in this series so far). Also Librarianship." avg. price, paper: £1.50. 1970. 10-200pp; a4. †mi/of. avg. press run varies. Reporting time: we try. Payment: 10 percent royalty plus free copy. Copyrights for author. Discounts: 25 percent. Pub'd 20 titles 1976; expects 20 titles 1977, 30 titles 1978.

NRG, Dan Raphael, David Whited, 30½ Dewey No. 4, Ashland, OR 97520. Poetry, fiction, art, music, letters, parts-of-novels, long-poems, collages, concrete art. "Solid bias—spatial (in Communicative Cybernetics)—to be reacted w/—the work as 4 dimensional resultant of words/meaning/energy rampant in the associational/re-membering matrix-organism of mind; gut-sense disorientation/travel. Dipalma, Kempton, Shevin, Grabill, McCurry, Andrews, Wiater." 3/yr; 1-yr sub price: $2.00; per copy: $.75; sample: stamps. 1975. 8pp; 11 x 17. of. circ. 400. Reporting time: less than 1 month. Payment: copies. Copyright reverts to author. Back issues: $.50. Expects 3 issues 1977, 4 issues 1978. CCLM.

Nunaga Publishing Co. Ltd. (see CANADIAN FRONTIER)

O O Press, Michael Lally, 138 Sullivan St, New York, NY 10012. Poetry. "I do only books-no unsolicited ones-all 'poetry'-titles include: *Vowels* by Bruce Andrews and *Facade* by David Drum-Forth coming: Books by Tim Dlugos, Doug Lang, etc." avg. price, paper: Varies, but nothing over $2.50. 1974. 32pp; Varies. of. avg. press run 300. Pub'd 3 titles 1976; expects 2 titles 1977, 2 titles 1978.

O Press/Heavy Evidence (see also SOFT TIMES), E. T. Caldwell, Jim Spenker, Basil Tozer, Carol Line, 1338 N. Astor, Milwaukee, WI 53202. Poetry, fiction, articles, art, photos, cartoons, interviews, satire, criticism, reviews, music, letters, collages, concrete art. "Particularly interested in submissions from victims of Scrivener's Palsy. Masculist, sexist, and affiliated with I.L.I.E. (international league of idlers & eccentrics). Recent contributors; E. T. Caldwell, Jim Spencer, Charles O. Dynzof, Kathleen Wiegner, Roger Skrentny, Rich Manglesdorff, El Gilbert, Bob Watt, Roger Steffen, & John Pflaum" avg. price, paper: $0.50. 1975. 60pp; varies. †of. avg. press run 5,000. Reporting time: 2 weeks-2 months. Payment: 2 copies or cash, if available. Copyrights for author. Discounts: to be negotiated.

O. O. L. P. (Out of London Press), Luigi Ballerini, Richard Milazzo, Brunetta Carena, 12 West 17th St, New York, NY 10011. Poetry, art, criticism. "OOLP (Out of London Press) is a critical exercise in publishing. It operates within English & Italian cultural markets. Texts are selected independently of the existing forms of acculturation & proposed as instances of rhetorical dialectical research. Its activity encompasses analogical criticism, aesthetics, philosophy of language & poetry. Kostelanetz, Richard, ed. *Essaying Essays* (anthology of experimental essays) Diacono, Mario, *Vito Acconci* (art critcism).'' 1975. 7¾ x 6-1/16. of. Payment: percentage of list price. Discounts: 40% to bookstores on 2-3 month consignment basis. COSMEP.

OASIS, Oasis Books, Ian Robinson, Antony Lopez, 12 Stevenage Road, London SW6 6ES, United Kingdom. Articles, poetry, fiction, art, photos, reviews, interviews, criticism, music, letters, long-poems, plays, collages, concrete art. "Any length & style, high quality essential. International in content; we publish a good proportion of material in translation. We do not favour 'big name' contributors, but beginners face stiff competition. Submissions must be accompanied by usual return postage—sorry, no time to comment on rejections. Some contributors: UK: Martin Booth, Lee Harwood, David Grubb. N. America: Frederick Matteson, Len Fulton, Walter Cummins. Greece: George Seferis, Yannis Ritsos, Takis Sinopoulos. Germany: Horst Bienek, Hans-Jurgen Heise, Herbert Eisenreich. East Europe: Anna Akhmatova, Attila Jozsef, Natalia Gorbanevskaya. Also Max Jacob, Fernando Pessoa, Manuel Bandeira, etc.'' 6/yr; 1-yr sub price: £1.20; per copy: 25p; sample: 25p plus p & p. 1969. 40pp; A5. litho. Reporting time: as soon as possible. Payment: copies. Ads: £8/£4/£2 1/4 page. Discounts: books-trade 25 percent single copies, 5 or more 40 percent. Back issues: 50p. ALMS, ALP.

Oasis Books (see also OASIS), Ian Robinson, Antony Lopez, 12 Stevenage Rd., London, England SW6 6ES, United Kingdom. Poetry, long-poems. "Oasis Books publish high-quality poetry from the UK, North America and from other languages in translation, by both established and less well known poets in the form of booklets or full-length volumes. Mostly solicited mss only. Some recent titles: SIX MODERN GREEK POETS (tr. John Stathatos); SNATH, Martin Booth; THE TWELVE WORDS of the GYPSY, Kostes Palamas; ACCIDENTS, Ian Robinson; LOG BOOK, John Stathatos.'' 1969. lo/lp. Reporting time: 1 wk to 1 mo. Payment: by arrangement. Discounts: 40% over 5 copies, 25% otherwise (trade only).

OBSIDIAN: BLACK LITERATURE IN REVIEW, Alvin Aubert, 10 Georges Place, Fredonia, NY 14063, 716-672-2082. Poetry, fiction, articles, interviews, criticism, reviews, parts-of-novels, long-poems, plays. 3/yr; 1-yr sub price: $5.50; per copy: $2.00; sample: yes. 1975. 100pp; 5½ x 8½. of. Reporting time: 2 - 4 weeks. Payment in copies. Copyrighted, reverts to author. Ads: $50.00/$30.00/$0.30. Discounts: 10 percent discount to subscription agencies. Back issues: $2.00. Pub's reviews. §Black literature in English worldwide. CCLM, COSMEP.

OCCULT AMERICANA, Barb Mraz, Box 667, Painesville, OH 44077. "Subject for articles must be historical or contemporary marginal American religious movements or personalities, with supportive data. Poems on a spiritual theme.'' 6/yr; 1-yr sub price: $3.00; per copy: $.50; sample: postage $.13. 1973. 20pp; 8½ x 7. of. circ. 350. Reporting time: 2 wks to 1 month. Payment: $5.00 article/copies for poems, reviews, graphics. Ads: $.10. Pub's reviews. §Very much, but only about American religions.

OCCURRENCE, John Wilson, 928 Pine, Apt 12-B, Philadelphia, PA 19107. Poetry, criticism, reviews. "Theodore Enslin, John Taggart, Michael Heller, Toby Olson, Jane Augustine, Russell Edson, Frank Samperi, Carol Frost, Lyn Hejinian, Cid Corman, Ray DiPalma.'' Pub's reviews CCLM.

Tom Ockerse Editions, Thomas Ockerse, 37 Woodbury Street, Providence, RI 02906, 401-331-0783. Poetry, fiction, articles, art, photos, collages, concrete art. "The intended purpose of T.O.E. is to publish monographs of works by artists whose work is structured by a primary commitment to concrete language, i.e., self-describing/self-referal.'' avg. price, cloth: $20.00; paper: $4.00. 1967. pp varies/no limit; varies. †of/lp/silkscreen, xerox. avg. press run 300-1,000. Payment varies. Copyrights for author. Pub'd 2 titles 1976.

‡OCOTILLO, Brad Harvey, PO Box 304, Iowa City, IA 52240.

OFF OUR BACKS, Off Our Backs, Margie Crow, Carol Anne Douglas, Janis Kelly, Fran Moira, Wendy Stevens, Jan Braumaller, Alice Henry, Terri Poppe, 1724 20th st. N.W., Washington, DC 20009, 202-234-8072. Articles, photos, cartoons, interviews, criticism, reviews, fiction, letters, news items. "Consider ourselves a radical feminist *news* journal, with prison, struggle, culture, & heath & reviews section. Free to prisoners." 12/yr; 1-yr sub price: $6.00 Indiv.; $20.00 Institutions (Inc. libraries); per copy: $0.60; sample: $0.60. 1970. 32pp; 8½ x 11 (tabloid). of. circ. 8,000. Reporting time: 2 months. Ads: $192.28/$100.32/$0.10-word. Back issues: $.50. Pub's reviews. §women. COSMEPA, NESPA.

THE OHIO REVIEW, Wayne Dodd, Stanley W. Lindberg, Ellis Hall, Ohio University, Athens, OH 45701, 614-594-5889. Poetry, fiction, articles, interviews, reviews, non-fiction. 3/yr; 1-yr sub price: $7.00; per copy: $2.50; sample: $2.00. 1959. 130pp; 6 x 9. lp. circ. 900. Reporting time: 90 days. Payment: Rates vary: copies plus min. $5.00 per page prose; $10.00 per poem. Copyrighted. Ads: $75.00/$50.00. Back issues: $2.50 per or $1.00 each with subscription. Pub'd 2 issues 1976; expects 3 issues 1977, 3 issues 1978. Pub's reviews: 33 in 1976. §Poetry, fiction, books, including all chapbooks. CCLM.

The Ohio State University Libraries Publications Committee (see UNDER THE SIGN OF PICES)

OHIOANA QUARTERLY, James P. Barry, 1105 Ohio Dept Bldg., 65 S. Front St, Columbus, OH 43215, 614-466-3831. Reviews. "Reviews by staff and guest reviewers. Length of review varies from 40 to 400 words. Ohio authors only." 4/yr; 1-yr sub price: $8.50 (membership); per copy: $2.50; sample: $2.50. 1929. 48pp; 6 x 9. of. circ. 1,200. Ads: none. Discounts: $6.00 to libraries. Back issues: $2.50. Pub'd 4 issues 1976; expects 4 issues 1977, 4 issues 1978. Pub's reviews. §Books about Ohio or Ohioans.

OINK!, Oink! Press, Paul Hoover, Maxine Chernoff, 7021 N. Sheridan Rd, Chicago, IL 60626. Poetry, fiction, art, long-poems, collages. "Unsolicited contributors *must* examine a copy of OINK! before submitting. We are open to any kind of modernist poetry but favor 'soft-core' surrealism. We have published Russell Edson, Michael Benedikt, Kenneth Rexroth, Charles Simic, Ted Berrigan, Alice Notley, Bill Knott, Douglas Blazek, Anne Waldman, and Peter Schjeldahl, among others. The editors are very interested in seeing translations. See #12 for translations of Tymoteusz Karpowicz, Pierre Jean Jouve, Max Jacob, and Nicolas Guillen." 2/yr; 1-yr sub price: $4.00; per copy: $2.00; sample: $2.00. 1971. 75pp; 8½ x 7. of. circ. 400. Reporting time: 1 wk-1 month. Payment: copies only. Ads: $50/$10. Discounts: 60/40 to bookstores. Back issues: #1-$20, #2-$20, #3-$15, #4-$5, #5-11-$2.00. §poetry, prose poems, especially, translations. CCLM.

Oklahoma State University Press (see CIMARRON REVIEW)

Old Adobe Press, G. Haslam, B. Young, J. Molinaro, J. Hasley, P.O. Box 115, Penngrove, CA 94951, [Haslam]707-763-7362. "We plan to publish one book in 76, *Masks*, a novel by Gerald Haslam. In 77 we will publish *Heartland: Writing from California's Great Central Valley*. Those two projects will absorb all our money, so no submissions now, please. We try to work carefully, one project at a time, and give each all our attention and the best distribution we can manage. Our last publication, a scholarly book, *The Language of the Oilfields*, sold steadily for four years and gave us the money for our next project." avg. price, paper: $1.95-$4.95. 1971. 150pp; 5 x 8. of/lp. avg. press run 500-1,000 1st printing; 2,500 2nd printing. Payment: standard. All titles copyrighted in authors name. Discounts: 1 copy 20%, 2-3 30% 4 or more 40%. Pub'd 1 title 1976; expects 1 title 1977, 1 title 1978. COSMEP, COSMEP-WEST.

OLD FRIENDS, Glebe Press, David Allen, Henry Christner, Patty Hardee, c/o Culpeper News, 146 N. Main St, Culpeper, VA 22701. Poetry, fiction, art, photos, satire, letters, parts-of-novels, long-poems, plays, concrete art. "'Our approach is to explore beyond formality in art. We want to reveal the person creating. Writers and artists should send 7-10 samples of their work. A substantial selection is necessary to present the wholeness and diversity of the artist's expression. Some recent contributors have been-David Axlerod, Debbie Berson, Anne Becker, Jim Landry, Jackie Potter.'" irreg.; 1-yr sub price: $5.00; per copy: $1.25; sample: free. 1973. 48pp; 5½ x 8½. of. circ. 250-up. Reporting time: 2 mos. Payment: copies. Discounts: 40% bulk. Back issues: $1.00. §poetry/short fiction/just about anything.

Old Marble Press (see LOCAL TENDERNESS)

Old Time Bottle Publishing Company, S. T. Conatser, Sheldon S. Brown, 611 Lancaster Dr. N.E., Salem, OR 97301. 1963. Discounts: Trade. COSMEP.

Olivant Press (see also WEID), D.V. Smith, P.O. Box 1409, Homestead, FL 33030. "Mss. read by invitation only-no unsol. mss. NOTE: Olivant publishes WEID, but it publishes books by indiv. authors also-over 25 titles in print, over 70 titles published." avg. price, cloth: $8.00; paper: $2.00. 1952. 60pp; varies. †of. avg. press run 250-1,000. Reporting time: 1 month. Payment: Royalty - 15 percent of net. Copyrights for author. Discounts: 30 percent. Expects 6 titles 1977, 6 titles 1978. CCLM, COSMEP.

Olympus Publishing Company, Donald G. Gale, 1670 East 13th South, Salt Lake City, UT 84105. "Non-fiction, book length" 1972. of. Discounts: From 20% to 45%.

Omango d' Press, PO Box 255, Wethersfield, CT 06109, 203-242-4294. "Books on Fruitarianism & Live Food related to Spirituality and Healing. We publish books on healing, vegetarianism, spiritual. Recently published books: V. Kulvinskas, M.S., N.D. *Survival Into 21st Century,* introduction by Dick Gregory, art: Peter Max. $8.00—*Nutritional Evaluation Of Sprouts,* $2.00—Abramowski, M.D., *Fruitarian Diet For Regeneration* $1.00. *Love Your Body-Poorman's Vegetarianism* $2.50." avg. price, paper: $8.00; other: $2.00. 1974. 320 pp max, 100 pp min; 8 x 11. of. avg. press run 10,000. Reporting time: 3 months. Payment: yes. Copyrights for author. Discounts: jobbers 60 percent, trade 40 percent, agent 10 percent, classroom 25 percent.

OMENS POETRY MAGAZINE, Sam Brown, John Martin, 9 Roundhay Road, Leicester LE32BY, United Kingdom. Poetry. "No prejudice as to length or style. Criteria are simply best of all poetry submitted in quarter. Recent contributors inc. Nicki Jackowska G.S. Fraser, Penelope Shuttle, Glen Cavaliero." 4/yr; 1-yr sub price: £1.50 ($3.00); per copy: £.50 ($1.00); sample: £.20 ($.50). 1971. 36pp; A5. of. circ. 6-700. Reporting time: 1 week of announced deadline. Payment: Rate not fixed-commencing payment September 1977. Rights remain with author. Ads: £20.00/£12.00. Discounts: trade discount 33 percent. Back issues: six £1 or 2 dollars. Pub'd 5 issues 1976; expects 4 issues 1977, 4 issues 1978.

Ommation Press (see also MATI). Pub'd 10 titles 1976; expects 10 titles 1977.

Omphalos Press (J-Jay Publications Ltd.), Martin Booth,401/2, Dorset Bldgs., Dorset Rise, Salisbury Sq, London EC48ES, United Kingdom. Poetry, long-poems. avg. price, cloth: varies; paper: varies; other: varies. 1972. 60pp; a5. †of/lp. avg. press run 500. Reporting time: 2 mos. Payment varies. Copyright according to contract. Discounts: 33% trade. Expects 4 titles 1977, 4 titles 1978.

ONCE, The Country Press, Stephen Baily, P O Box 398, Baldwin Place, NY 10505. Fiction. "We're looking for fiction with a heavy emphasis on dramatic narrative. Experimental work is welcome, but only if it isn't boring. We particularly dislike sloppy, unfocused writing and formula hackwork. Preferred length is under 4,000 words." 4/yr; 1-yr sub price: $4.00; per copy: $1.00; sample: $1.00. 1977. 64pp; 8½ x 11. †of. circ. 1,000. Reporting time: 1-4 weeks. Payment: Five dollars on acceptance, plus two copies on publication. Copyrighted, reverts to author. Ads: $100.00/$50.00/none. Discounts: 40 percent. Pub's reviews. §fiction.

ONE, One Publications, David Chaloner, 16 Rosemary Avenue, London N3 2QN, United Kingdom. Poetry, fiction, articles, criticism, reviews. "Andrew Crozier, Tony Towle, James

Schuyler, Douglas Oliver, Michael Palmer, Peter Riley, Lee Harwood, John James, Anne Waldman, Gerard Malanga, Ian Patterson, John Welch, John Hall, Martin Wright, Anthony Barnett, Peter Schjeldahl, Tim Longville, Jim Burns, Peter Ackroyd, Andre Du Bouchet, Martin Thom, Peter Philpott, Paul Green.'' irreg. 1971. 50pp; A4. mi. Reporting time: varies. Rights remain with authors/credit appreciated. Discounts: 33-1/3% trade. Pub'd 1 issue 1976; expects 2 issues 1977.

ONE: The Writer's Magazine of Fiction and Poetry, One Books, Paul Freeman, PO Box W, Scottsdale, AZ 85252. Poetry, fiction, cartoons, letters. ''ONE is interested in alltypes of fiction and poetry. We have no taboos regarding length, style, or subject matter. We've published mysteries, science fiction, and humor as well as 'straight' literary stories. Each manuscript is carefully read and, when possible, commented upon. We prefer to print stories that are less than five thousand words in length because it allows us to publish more writers, but word count alone will never be responsible for a manuscript's rejection. As a general rule, we look for stories that are well written, honest, and emotionally stimulating. We dislike overly abstract and intellectually pompous material that tends to put down everyone but the author. Recent contributors: Mort Castle, Merritt Clifton, Carla Hoffman, Barbara Holland, Karen Loeb.'' 2/yr; 1-yr sub price: $3.50; per copy: $1.75; sample: $1.75. 1973. 80pp; 5½ x 8½. of. circ. 300. Reporting time: 6 weeks. Payment: 1 copy. Ads: $20/$10/$.05. Back issues: Set of issues 1-7:$10.00;5,9: $1.50 ea.; 10-up $2.50.

ONE DOLLAR, One Dollar Publishing, Mark Christensen, 919 SW Taylor #706, Portland, OR 97205. Poetry, fiction, articles, art, photos, interviews, satire, criticism, reviews, music, letters. 12/yr; 1-yr sub price: $5.35; per copy: $.50. 1973. 40pp; 8 x 10. of. circ. 6,200. Payment: $25-50. Ads: $309.06/$222.81. Discounts: none. Pub's reviews. §Northwest Publications.

ONE SHOT DEAL, Pulpart Forms Unltd., Walt Shepperd, 1530 East Genesee St., Syracuse, NY 13210. ''OSD solicits only inquires for essays on the politics of being a person, reports of non-events, and fullpage comic strips, with return postage. Also, a rating of underground bestsellers each issue, depending largely on what's been sent that season.'' 4/yr; 1-yr sub price: free w/purchase of any pulpartform. 1974. 12pp; 11 x 16 (tabloid). of. circ. 5,000. Payment: 10 copies. Ads: $144/$72/free NB: if space. COSMEP.

Ontario Library Association (see EXPRESSION)

ONTARIO REVIEW, Raymond J. Smith, 6000 Riverside Dr. East, Windsor, Ont. N8S 1B6, Canada. Poetry, fiction, articles, art, photos, interviews, criticism, reviews. 2/yr; 1-yr sub price: $5.00; per copy: $2.50; sample: $2.50. 1974. 112pp; 6 x 9. lp. circ. 750. Reporting time: 3 weeks. Payment: copies. Copyrighted, reverts to author. Ads: $100.00/$60.00. Discounts: 10 percent to agents. Back issues: $2.50. Pub'd 2 issues 1976; expects 2 issues 1977, 2 issues 1978. Pub's reviews: 29 in 1976. §Poetry, fiction. CPPA, COSMEP.

Oolichan Books, Ron Smith, John Marshall, P.O. Box 10, Lantzville, British Columbia V0R2H0, Canada, 604-390-4839. Poetry, fiction, plays. ''*Oolichan Books* generally publishes *full-length* manuscripts of poetry, fiction and drama...although we do plan to publish two chapbooks in the coming year, but only because we believe each is of exceptional quality. Although we prefer letters of inquiry with sample writing we will consider unsolicited mss. Apart from our main interest in poetry and fiction we are also interested in statements on poetics or collections of letters which reveal something of the stance of the writer & language. We attempt to maintain a balance between established and newer authors. Generally we are not interested in the mass market book (unless it has something to say and, to be blunt and pragmatic, will provide us with the means to publish more serious fiction & poetry) but rather in books which indicate how the writer sees through language. Recent contributors include: Robert Kroetsch, John Newlove, Lorna Uher, Robin Skelton, Ken Cathers, Robert Stallman, David Philips & George Woodcock.'' avg. price, cloth: $8.95; paper: $4.50. 1975. 76-160pp; 6 x 9. †of/lp. avg. press run 750-2,000 depending on author. Reporting time: 2 weeks to 1 month. Payment: 10 percent. Copyrights for author. Discounts: (40 percent over 3 copies; 30 percent 1-3 copies trade agent or jobber) 20 percent libraries. Pub'd 6 titles 1976. ACP, LPG, BCPA.

OPEN PLACES, Eleanor M. Bender, Thomas Dillingham, Bk. Review Ed., Box 2085, Stephens College, Columbia, MO 65201, 314-442-2211. Poetry, reviews. "We publish as few as six poets per issue with as many as 12 poems by each poet. We are interested in a variety of styles and techniques. No prejudices that we are aware of. Recent contributors are: Sonya Dorman, Marge Piercy, Laura Jensen, William Stafford, Leslie Ullman, Larry Levis, Marcia Southwick." 2/yr; 1-yr sub price: $4.00; per copy: $2.00. 1966. 64pp; 8½ x 5½. of. circ. 700. Reporting time: 2-6 wks. Payment: $8/page + copies. Copyrighted. no ads. Discounts: 40% trade. Back issues: Nos. 1-23 $24.00 p.p. Pub'd 2 issues 1976; expects 2 issues 1977, 2 issues 1978. Pub's reviews: 10 in 1976. §poetry. CCLM, COSMEP.

Open University Press (see SESAME)

Open Window Books, P.O. Box 949, Chickasha, OK 73018, 405-224-3217. Poetry, photos, letters, parts-of-novels. avg. price, paper: $8.95. 1976. 144pp; 8½ x 11. of. avg. press run 3,000.

Open Window Society Inc. (see THE VOYEUR)

Openings Press, Dom Silvester Houedard, John Furnival, Rooksmoor House, Woodchester, Glos, United Kingdom. Concrete art. "No unsolicited mss." 1964. varied. of/silk-screen. Payment: copies. Discounts: 33-1/3%. ALP.

OPINION, Opinion Publications, James E. Kurtz, Editor, PO Box 1885, Rockford, IL 61110. Articles, satire, criticism, reviews. "We want strong articles on theology, philosophy and sociology-but not long articles. We don't care who you are as long as you know how to write and can back your stuff up with accurate research, facts." 12/yr; 1-yr sub price: $5.00; per copy: $.50; sample: $.30. 1951. 16pp; 8½ x 11. of. circ. 3,000. Reporting time: 3 weeks. Payment: copies only. Not copyrighted. Ads: $25.00/$12.50/$.10. Discounts: none. Back issues: $.50 each. Pub'd 12 issues 1976; expects 12 issues 1977, 12 issues 1978. Pub's reviews. §All areas.

Opportunities Unlimited Publications, Jack Payne, P.O. Box AA, Magalia, CA 95954. Non-fiction. "Will be interested in anything telling Readers *how to do something* in a popular, broad spectrum field, in clear, concise, digested 'how-to' language. How to benefit, *in a monetary way,* is of prime consideration." avg. price, paper: $2.00. 1963. 16pp; 5½ x 8½. of. avg. press run 2,000 on most titles. Reporting time: 30 days. Payment: Flat 10% against all sales—retail or wholesale. All copyrights in name of Opportunities Unlimited Pubs. Discounts: 10% on invoice orders; 20% on cash orders—applies to all bulk orders for resale.

ORBIS, International Poetry Society; Hub Publications, Robin Gregory, Cal Clothier, Youlgrave, Bakewell, Derbyshire, England, United Kingdom. Articles, poetry, reviews, criticism, long-poems. 4/yr; 1-yr sub price: $7.00; per copy: $2.00; sample: $2.00. 1969. 48pp; A5. lp. circ. 1M. Reporting time: varies. Payment: small. Copyrighted. Ads: £20.00 or ($35.00). Pub'd 4 issues 1976; expects 4 issues 1977, 4 issues 1978.

THE ORCHARD, Orchard Press, David Mayers, 2855 Old Gravenstein Hwy South, Sebastopol, CA 95472. Poetry, fiction, articles, art, photos, criticism, reviews, parts-of-novels. "Strong first issue and we will work to make next issues strong. We like gutsy writing and writing which helps us see clearly. Fielding Dawson, Al Masarik, Phil Weidman, Ann Menebroke, R. Hamilton." 2/yr; 1-yr sub price: $3.00; per copy: $1.50; sample: $1.50. 1976. 40pp; 5½ x 8½. of. circ. 250. Reporting time: varies. Payment: free copy of mag. Copyrighted, reverts to author. Back issues: $1.50. Pub'd 1 issue 1976; expects 2 issues 1977, 2 issues 1978. Pub's reviews: 21 in 1976. §Bitter-sweet truths of life, American tribal indians, music, poetry, prose, geography topics, translations.

Orchard Press (see also THE ORCHARD), David Mayers, 2855 Old Gravenstein Hwy. South, Sebastopol, CA 95472. Poetry, fiction, articles, art, photos, criticism, reviews, parts-of-novels. "We are poor and yet have a hunger to publish great writing which deserves a wider audience." avg. price, cloth: $3.00; paper: $1.95. 1976. 40-90pp; 5½ x 8½. of. avg. press run 250-500. Reporting time: varies. Payment: exchange for free copies. Copyrights for author. Pub'd 2 titles 1976; expects

2-3 titles 1977, 2-3 titles 1978.

Oregon Historical Society, Miss Priscilla Knuth, 1230 S.W. Park Avenue, Portland, OR 97205, 503-222-1741. Articles. "Thomas Vaughan, Terence O'Donnell" avg. price, cloth: $8.00; paper: $3.00. 1873. 200pp; varies w/book. of. avg. press run 2,000. Reporting time: 1 year. Payment: 10 percent. Copyrights for author. Discounts: 30 percent paper 40 percent hardbound.

OREGON TIMES MAGAZINE, New Oregon Publishers, Inc., Tom Bates, Editor; Dave Kelly, Man. Editor, 1000 SW 3rd, Portland, OR 97204. Poetry, fiction, articles, photos, interviews, criticism, reviews, plays. "We can use up-to-date news on Oregon and the Pacific Northwest as it applies to the environment and left-leaning politics." 12/yr; 1-yr sub price: $8.00; per copy: $.75; sample: free. 1971. 64pp; 8½ x 11. of. circ. 6,000. Reporting time: 2 weeks. Ads: $234/$117/none. Discounts: Students, senior citizens $6.00 yr. Back issues. $.35 apiece. Pub's reviews. §Oregon and Northwest.

ORGAN DIGEST, Tino Publications, Tino Ciammitti, 4001 East Fanfol, Phoenix, AZ 85028, 602-996-9335. Articles, art, photos, cartoons, criticism, reviews, music, letters. "Most of material printed in magazine is tests and reports on organs and electronic keyboard products as well as entertaining articles of interest to organ hobbyists" 6/yr; 1-yr sub price: $10.00; per copy: $2.00; sample: $2.00. 1976. 40pp; 5¾ x 8¾. of. circ. 5,000. Reporting time: 2 months. Payment: $50.00 to $100.00. Copyrighted, does not revert to author. Ads: $260.00/$150.00/$0.25. Discounts: 40 percent. Back issues: $2.00. §organ products.

ORIEL, Peter Finch, Meic Stephens, ORIEL, The Welsh Arts Council Bookshop, 53 Charles St., Cardiff, Wales CF14ED, United Kingdom, 0222-395548. Poetry, art. "Publications are confined to Welsh and Anglo-Welsh authors together with material about Wales. Unsolicited mss. are not requested. In existence are a number of fine edition poster poems and illustrated book about Dylan Thomas. Projected publications for 1976-77 include futher posters and a new series of spoken work records." 1974. of/lp. circ. 2,000. Payment: By arrangement. Not copyrighted. Ads: None. Discounts: 33-1/3-50%. Pub'd 20 issues 1976; expects 20 issues 1977, 20 issues 1978.

‡**Origin Press,** Cid Corman, 87 Dartmouth St., Boston, MA 02116.

ORIGINS, Ms. L. Wilson, Mr. H. Barrett, Box 5072, Station E, Hamilton, Ontario L8S4K9, Canada, 416-528-0552. Poetry, art. 4/yr; 1-yr sub price: $2.00; per copy: $0.60; sample: $0.60. 1967. 32pp; 6 x 9. of. circ. 500. Reporting time: 4 weeks. Payment: Complimentary copy of issue published in. Copyrighted, reverts to author. Ads: $25.00/$15.00. Discounts: Bulk, classroom. Back issues: $0.60 when available. Pub'd 4 issues 1976.

THE ORIGINAL ART REPORT (TOAR), Frank Salantrie, P.O. Box 1641, Chicago, IL 60690. Criticism, reviews, letters, articles, interviews, news items, non-fiction. "Exclusive interest in fine art (visual) in Midwest and elsewhere in the world as it affects people, society, and art. Material must take advocacy position, one side or another. No puffy previews, reviews, profiles. Prefer controversial subject matter." 12/yr; sub price: $10.00-12 issues; per copy: $1.00; sample: $1.00. 1967. 6pp; 8½ x 11. of. circ. 100-1,000. Reporting time: 1-2 weeks. Payment: 1 cent/word; max 500 words. Discounts: 25 to same address-$7.00 each/special artist discount-25 percent off-pay $7.50 for individual subscription. Back issues: $2.00 each if available. Expects 12 issues 1977, 12 issues 1978. Pub's reviews. §Fine art (visual)/related.

Orion Press (see EUREKA REVIEW)

OSIRIS, Andrea Moorhead, Box 297, Deerfield, MA 01342. Poetry, fiction, interviews, reviews, music, long-poems. "*OSIRIS* is apolitical. Prints texts in English, French, Italian, without translation. Recent contributors: Pierre Morency, (Quebec) Michel Cosem, Raymond Federman, Paola Ceratto (Italy)." 2/yr; 1-yr sub price: $3.50; per copy: $1.75; sample: $0.75. 1972. 40-44pp; 6 x 9. of. circ. 500. Reporting time: 4 weeks. Payment: 2 copies. Copyrighted, reprint with credit line to *OSIRIS*. Ads: none. Back issues: $1.00 *Osiris* 1,2,3. Pub's reviews: 2 in 1976.

OTHER PRESS POETRY REVIEW, Other Press, Paul Gotro, Terry Galvin, 2503 Douglas College, New Westminister, British Columbia, Canada, 522-6038. Poetry, fiction, articles, art, photos, parts-of-novels, long-poems, plays, concrete art. "J. Michael Yates, Eugene McNamara, Harold Enrico, Leona Gom, Eric Ivan Berg, Micheal Bullock, Derk Wynand." 4/yr; 1-yr sub price: $6.00; per copy: $1.50; sample: free. 1976. 32pp. of. circ. 400. Reporting time: 1 month. Payment: in copies. §poetry, short fiction.

Other Scenes (see also NOMAD), John Wilcock, BCM-OSCENES, London WC 1V, United Kingdom. Articles, art, news items, interviews, letters, collages, concrete art, photos. "Literature, alternative, occult, sociology, travel." 1967. pp varies; varies. lo. Reporting time: 48 hours. Payment: low. COSMEP.

Otherworlds Media (see UNEXPECTED)

Otto F. Reiss, Publ. (see ART AND ARCHAEOLOGY NEWSLETTER)

OUR GENERATION, 3934 St. Urbain St., Montreal, Canada. 4/yr; 1-yr sub price: $7.00; per copy: $1.75. 1961. 80pp; 7 x 9¼. of. circ. 5,000. Reporting time: 3 mos. Payment: none. Ads: $100/$50. Back issues: $250.00 a set. Pub's reviews. §public affairs-women-anarchist.

OUT, Campaign For Homosexual Equality, P.O. Box 427, Manchester, England M602EL, United Kingdom. Articles, art, photos, cartoons, interviews, criticism, reviews, letters, news items, non-fiction. "Pro gay only. Journal discusses aims and actions of OUT and the view of its executive committee & annual conference. Material liable to editing." 6/yr; 1-yr sub price: £4.00 ($10.00) air mail; per copy: 30P ($2.00) air mail; sample: 30P ($2.00) air mail. 1969. 12-16pp; A4. of. circ. 6,000 plus. Reporting time: 1 month. Copyrighted. Ads: On application. Discounts: 25 percent on 10 or more. Back issues: Standard prices. Pub's reviews: 4 in 1976. §Gay liberation, some women's rights.

Out & Out Books, Joan Larkin, 476 Second St, Brooklyn, NY 11215, 212-499-9827. Poetry, articles. "Book-length manuscripts of special interest to women. 7 vols. of lesbian poetry and 2 prose non-fiction published. Currently not soliciting manuscripts." avg. price, cloth: $2.00-$3.75. 1975. 72pp; 5½ x 8½. of. avg. press run 2,000. Reporting time: 3 months. Payment: flexible. Copyrights for author. Discounts: 40% trade discount. Pub'd 1 title 1976; expects 3 titles 1977, 3 titles 1978. COSMEP, WDG.

OUT OF SIGHT, Caprice Out Of Sight, James Mechem, Box 32, Wichita, KS 67201. Poetry. "Out Of Sight does not seek out new writers, does not attempt to publish those never published before. Out Of Sight is not intended as a proving ground for poets. Out Of Sight likes the glamour of big names over and above good poetry." 6/yr; sub price: $100.00/series of 100; per copy: free; sample: free. 1971. 12pp; 5½ x 8½. †mi. circ. 300. Reporting time: 6 mos. Payment: $5.00. CCLM, COSMEP.

Out of the Ashes Press, Walt Curtis, Norman Solomon, Catherine J Waechter, P.O. Box 42384, Portland, OR 97242. Poetry, fiction, photos, parts-of-novels, long-poems, collages. "We are interested in radical literature. We do not have interest in printing macho male fantasies, whether of John Wayne, beatnik or hippie varieties. We very much have interest in collections of poetry and fiction which is from an insurgent perspective— non-rhetorical, pro-feminist, anti-imperialist, innovative, non-commercialized, searching, sensitive, explosive, what we can make possible. We cannot consider submissions that are only a few pages long; we cannot really consider extremely long (over about 200 pages) manuscripts either. All stuff sent should have a S.A.S.E. enclosed. Recent books: 'THE SUNFLOWER,' collection of poems and drawings by Walt Curtis; 'COCKROACH,' a novel by Norman Solomon. Upcoming: Feminist anthology. Poetry. Prose." 1971. 64pp; 8 x 10. of. Reporting time: variable. Payment: contributors' copies (for anthologies) authors' copies.

OUT THERE MAGAZINE, Pedestrian Press, Stephen M.H. Braitman, 552 25th Ave, San Francisco, CA 94121. "Formerly science-fiction oriented, OUT THERE is going into the field of music criticism. Surprising, isn't it? The Pedestrian Press imprint will grace (hopefully) any number of publications dedicated to whatever the editor and friends are interested in." irreg.; sub price: $5.00/yr (charity rate); per copy: $.50; sample: $.75. 1967. 25pp; 8½ x 11. of. circ. 500-1M. Reporting time: 1 wk to 1 mo. Payment: copies. Ads: $100/$50. Back issues: $.75-$5.00.

OUT THERE MAGAZINE, Out There Press, Rose Lesniak, 6944 W George St, Chicago, IL 60634, 312-745-8988. Poetry, art, long-poems, interviews, letters, collages, concrete art, reviews. "Especially interested in quality. Experimental, non-sexist." 3/yr; 1-yr sub price: $5.00; per copy: $1.50; sample: $1.00. 1972. 100pp; 8½ x 11. of. circ. 800-1,000. Reporting time: 1-2 months. Payment: copy. Copyrighted. Ads: $200.00/$100.00. Discounts: 40% to bookstores. Back issues: (1-8) $10.00 (No. 8-11 $2.00). Pub'd 3 issues 1976; expects 3 issues 1977, 3 issues 1978. Pub's reviews: 3 in 1976. §Woman's movement/all quality work. CCLM.

Outland Press, Hilary Russell Jr., Jane P. Russell, Lewisville, PA 19351. Poetry. "Though we still favor poetry written from a rural experience, poetry that comes from the land and the lives of a given place, we will consider any work of high quality." 1974. 5½ x 8½. of. Reporting time: 1 month. Discounts: 40% for bookstores.

OUTPOSTS, Outposts Publications, Howard Sergeant, 72 Burwood Road, Walton-On-Thames, Surrey KT12 4AL, United Kingdom. Poetry, reviews, criticism. "OUTPOSTS is the oldest independent poetry magazine in the UK. It was founded to provide a satisfactory medium for those poets, recognised or unrecognised, who are concerned wtih the potentialities of the human spirit, and who are able to visualize the dangers and opportunites which confront the individual and the whole of humanity. Although recent contributors have included famous poets like Ted Hughes, Peter Porter, George MacBeth, Vernon Scannell, Kingsley Amis, Thomas Blackburn & etc the magazine makes a special point of introducing the work of new and unestablished poets to the public." 4/yr; 1-yr sub price: $6.00; per copy: $1.50. 1944. 40pp; demi 800. lp. circ. 1,500. Reporting time: 2 weeks. Payment: $2.00. Ads: $50.00/$25.00. Discounts: 10% publishers 10% series. Back issues: Price varies. Pub'd 60 issues 1976; expects 50 issues 1977, 50 issues 1978. Pub's reviews: 50 in 1976. ALP.

OUTRIGGER, Outrigger Publishers Ltd., New Quarterly Cave, Moirita, Tim Pickford, 4 Miami St, East Mangere, Auckland, New Zealand. Poetry. price per copy: $1.50. 1974. 30-40pp; a5. †mi. circ. 200. Reporting time: 2 months. Payment: copies. Copyrighted. Pub'd 6 issues 1976; expects 6 issues 1977, 6 issues 1978.

Overdrive Books (see Blue Wind Press)

OVERLAND, Overland, Stephen Murray-Smith, GPO Box 98a, Melbourne, Victoria 3001, Australia. Poetry, fiction, articles, art, cartoons, interviews, satire, criticism, reviews, parts-of-novels. "Interest leftish & basically Australian. Not looking for floods of material from overseas." 4/yr; 1-yr sub price: $6.00 aust.; per copy: $1.50 aust; sample: $1.50 aust. 1954. 64pp; quarto. lp. circ. 2,000. Reporting time: 3 months. Payment: by arrangement all contributors paid. First publication only required. Ads: $140 Aust/$70 Aust. Back issues: $1.50 Aust per copy. Pub'd 3 issues 1976; expects 4 issues 1977, 4 issues 1978. Pub's reviews. §interest mainly Australian.

OVO MAGAZINE, Jorge Guerra, P.O. Box 1431, Station A, Montreal, Quebec H3C2Z9, Canada, 514-861-8094. "OVO MAGAZINE is a Quebec based photographic publication which is published quarterly. OVO is dedicated to the promotion of photography as a means of social improvement and communication. Publishes 2 separate versions, French and English. Issues are now thematic (prisons, immigration, etc)." 4/yr; sub price: $6.00 4 issues-U.S. $8.00-for. $10.00-yr; per copy: $2.00. 1970. 48pp; 8½ x 11¾. of. circ. 6,000. Ads: $300.00/$150.00. Back issues: $1.00. Pub'd 4 issues 1976; expects 4 issues 1977, 4 issues 1978. Pub's reviews: 9 in 1976. §photography. CPPA.

Ox Head Press, Don Olsen, 414 N 6th St, Marshall, MN 56258. Poetry. "3 to 6 poems per pamphlet. Robert Bly, *The Loon*. $3.00 ($5.00 signed)." 1966. 20pp; 4¼ x 6¼. †lp. Reporting time: week to a month. Payment: $25 & up plus 25 copies. Discounts: Varies - 33 percent to 50 percent.

225

OXYMORON: Journal Of Convulsive Beauty, Alphaville Books/Sleep & Dream Lab., Jack Grady, P.O. Box 3424, Charlottesville, VA 22903, 804-977-5685. Poetry, fiction, parts-of-novels, collages. "Bulletin of the *Alphaville Sleep & Dream Lab.* International Neosurrealism. Oxysubscribers receive Alphaville supplements free of charge. Airmail delivery outside North America $1.00 additional per number. Magazine exchanges and dream materials with SASE/IRC enclosed are invited. Semiannual." 2/yr; 1-yr sub price: $4.50 individuals; $9.00 institutions (multiple reader); per copy: $3.00 individuals; $5.00 institutions, postpaid; sample: $3.00 individuals; $5.00 institutions, postpaid. 1976. 64pp; 5½ x 8½. †of/lp. circ. 999. reports: in spurts. Payment: pays copies. Copyrighted, reverts to author. Ads: inquire. Discounts: usual. Expects 2 issues 1978. Pub's reviews. §juxtaposed space, disembodied poetics. Global Psychoactivity.

Oxford University Press (see BRITISH JOURNAL OF AESTHETICS)

Oxus Press, John Stathatos, Gail Robinson, 16 Haslemere Rd., London N.8., United Kingdom. Poetry, long-poems. "Recent titles: *Last Days Of The Eagle* by David Grubb; *Maps And Tracings* by John Stathatos; and *The First Volume Of Folio:* work in process an occasional anthology of poetry. Folio is co-published with the Sceptre Press, and includes work by Allan Fisher, D.M. Thomas, Brian Patten, Harry Guest and others. The Oxus Press was founded to publish the best of the new British and European poetry (in translation), and will also be issuing titles from North America. Forthcoming: Roy Fisher, Takis Sindpoulos." 1976. of. avg. press run 500-1,000 plus. Reporting time: Regret no unsolicited mss considered. Payment: 10 percent on full length books. Copyrights for author. Discounts: 33-1/3 off. ALP.

OYEZ, Robert Hawley, PO Box 5134, Berkeley, CA 94705.

OYEZ REVIEW, Al Walavich, 430 S Michigan, Chicago, IL 60605, 312-341-2017. Poetry, fiction, art, photos, criticism, parts-of-novels, long-poems, collages. "OYEZ REVIEW is a magazine of the arts which attempts to offer a showcase for the poet or fiction writer who uses a more innovative approach in his or her work. We are open to material of any length which would be appropriate to a publication of our size, but we do not usually use the extremely short poem. Recent contributors include Jonathan Baumbach, Michael Anania, Eugene Wildman, Elliott Anderson, Skip Rozin, Jerome Klinkowitz, Sharon Spencer, Rhoda Lerman and Lynn Sukenick." 2/yr; 1-yr sub price: $3.00; per copy: $2.00; sample: $2.00. 1966. 120pp; 5½ x 8. of. circ. 750. Reporting time: 4-6 weeks. Payment: in copies. Copyrighted, reverts to author. Discounts: none. Back issues: $2.00 back through Vol 8, No. 1, previous issue prices on request. Pub'd 1 issue 1976; expects 2 issues 1977, 2 issues 1978. Pub's reviews. §Criticism, fiction, poetry and related fine arts, small press - inquire. CCLM, COSMEP.

Oz Publications, Inc. (see 10 POINT 5)

P.E.N. American Center (see GRANTS AND AWARDS AVAILABLE TO AMERICAN WRITERS)

Pacific Northwest Humanist Publications (see HUMANIST IN CANADA)

Pacific Perceptions, Inc. (see STONECLOUD)

PACIFIC POETRY AND FICTION REVIEW, Richard Johnson, Patricia MacInnes, English Office, San Diego State University, San Diego, CA 92182, 714-466-0675. Poetry, fiction, articles, art, photos, interviews, satire, criticism, reviews, parts-of-novels, long-poems, plays. "Contributors: Peter Wild, Jerry Bumpus, David McElroy, Carolyn Forche, Glover Davis. We are seeking poetry, short fiction, graphic art, reviews, plays." 1/yr; 1-yr sub price: $1.50; per copy: $1.50; sample: $1.50 or free with exchange. 1973. 80pp; 6 x 9. of. circ. 500. Reporting time: 4-6 weeks. Payment: copies. Not copyrighted. Discounts: none. Back issues: $1.00. Pub's reviews. §fiction, poetry.

PACIFIC RESEARCH, Pacific Studies Center, Leonard M. Siegel, 867 W. Dam, Mountain View, CA 94041, 415-969-1545. Articles, reviews. 6/yr; sub price: $6.00-U.S.; $7.20-Foreign/2 yr; per copy: $0.60; sample: free. 1969. 16pp; 8½ x 11. of. circ. 800. Pub's reviews. §US economy & foreign policy; Asia; Latin America.

Packard Publications, Gar Packard, 11521 Snow Heights N.E., Albuquerque, NM 87112, 505-293-5493. avg. price, paper: $5.00. 1970. 64pp; 8½ x 11. of. avg. press run 5,000. Discounts: 20 percent library 1-4 copies, 40 percent trade 5 or more copies.

PADAN ARAM, Peter Baker, Harris Collingwood, Peter Freeman, David Godolphin, 52 Dunster Street, Harvard U, Cambridge, MA 02138, 495-2807. Poetry, fiction, art, photos, reviews, long-poems, concrete art. "We try for a sparse, clean layout, and prefer publishing several poems by the same author rather than single pieces. Award winning graphics. Recent contributors include Robert Bly, Peter Mattair, James Richardson, and Cedric Whitman." 4/yr; 1-yr sub price: $4.00; per copy: $.50; sample: $0.14 postage. 1975. 16pp; 11 x 13. lp. circ. 14,000. Reporting time: 3 weeks. Payment: none. Copyrighted. Ads: $134.40/$71.40. Back issues: Price on request for available issues. Pub'd 4 issues 1976; expects 4 issues 1977, 4 issues 1978. §poetry and short fiction.

Padma Press, Carol Stetser, PO Box 56, Oatman, AZ 86433. Photos. *"Padma Press* publishes high-quality black and white photography books. Interested in books by women photographers and books exploring Buddhist philosophy photographically. Forthcoming title; *Chopping Wood, Carrying Water-1978.* In print-*Black And White-1977.* " avg. price, paper: $5.95. 1976. 56pp; 8½ x 11. of. avg. press run 3,000 copies. not accepting unsolicited manuscripts at the present time. Payment: negotiable. Does not copyright for author. Discounts: 40 percent trade. Expects 1 title 1977, 1 title 1978. COSMEP.

Padre Productions (see also COLLECTOR'S ITEM and WESTERN PUBLISHING SCENE), Lachlan P. MacDonald, PO Box 1275, San Luis Obispo, CA 93406, 805-543-5404. Art, photos. "Padre Productions concentrates on Western travel, especially unconventional books illustrated with line drawings, and on antiques and collectibles (illustrated by photos and drawings); however, art, children's, self-help and general titles are of interest. So far no adult fiction or poetry, though one novel is planned for future production." avg. price, cloth: $7.50; paper: $4.95. 1973. 140pp; 5½ x 8. of. avg. press run 3,500, usually 3,000 paperback and 500 hardcover. Reporting time: 10 days-2 weeks. Payment varies according to involvement, usually 10 percent. Copyrights for author. Discounts: 1-4 copies 20 percent; 5-100 40 percent. Payment with order. Fully returnable 90 days to 2 years if resalable condition. Trade. COSMEP.

PAID MY DUES: Journal of Women and Music, Woman's Soul Publishing, Inc., Lucille Allison, Music; Dorothy Dean, Copy, P.O. Box 11646, Milwaukee, WI 53211, 414-263-7792. Articles, art, photos, cartoons, interviews, satire, criticism, reviews, music, letters, news items, non-fiction. "Material must have feminist orientation, or at least, non-sexist. Only print material by women. Must be music-related." irregular; sub price: $8.00-4 issues/$12.00 where invoice necessary; per copy: $2.00; sample: $2.25. 1974. 48pp; 8½ x 11. of. circ. 1,000. Reporting time: 6-8 weeks. Payment: $5.00-$10.00 plus copies. Copyrighted, reverts to author. Ads: none/write details. Discounts: 40 percent discount on bulk orders 5 plus copies. Back issues: $2.50. Pub'd 1 issue 1976; expects 2 issues 1977, 4 issues 1978. Pub's reviews: 5 in 1976. §Recordings, songbooks, music history, musician biography, women & music. COSMEP, WIP.

PAINTBRUSH: A Journal of Poetry, Translations & Letters, Ishtar Press, Inc., B.M. Bennani, Comparative Literature, State Univ of New York, Binghamton, NY 13901. Poetry, articles, interviews, criticism, reviews. "Richard Eberhart, Denise Levertov, David Ignatow, George Keithley, Joseph Bruchac, Douglas Blazek, Charles Levendosky, Sam Hamill, G. Wilson Knight, and others." 2/yr; 1-yr sub price: $5.00 in U.S./$6.00 Foreign; per copy: $3.00; sample: $3.00. 1974. 65pp; 5½ x 8½. of/lp. circ. 500. Reporting time: 1-2 weeks. Payment: copies also monies when available. Ads: $150/$100. Discounts: 20-40%. Back issues: 2,3,4, $2.00/5,6 $3.00. Pub'd 2 issues 1976; expects 2 issues 1977, 2 issues 1978. Pub's reviews: 4-5 in 1976. §poetry & translations. CCLM, COSMEP, Associated Writing Programs.

PAINTED BRIDE QUARTERLY, Painted Bride Press, R. Daniel Evans, Louise Simons, 527 South St, Philadelphia, PA 19147. Poetry, art, photos, reviews, music. "Sorry, we found we cannot do fiction. Would like to have some good art work sent our way. We publish only high quality material, and have priinted many well-known poets, will not list any names so as not to offend any contributors. Please do not send book length manuscripts." 4/yr; 1-yr sub price: $5.00; per copy: $1.50; sample: $2.00. 1973. 6 x 9. of. circ. 1,000. Reporting time: 1 week to 6 mo. Payment: 2 copies. Ads: $50/$25. Pub's reviews. §poetry. CCLM, COSMEP.

Pajarito Publications (see DE COLORES)

EL PALACIO, Museum of New Mexico Press, Carl E. Rosnek, Ed; Phyllis Hughes, Managing Ed., P.O. Box 2087, Santa Fe, NM 87503. "Issues planned yr in advance; alost all articles by commission. Enquiries required in advance on free-lance. College-level popular style; 6,000-8,000 words, less for shorts; art supplied by author. Museum related topics, Southwest or Western slant (usually). Recent contributors: Dr. Charles diPeso, Dr. Stuart Northrop, Dr. Bertha P. Dutton, David Neumann, David Snow, Dr. Michael Pijoan, Dr. Alfred Sunseri, Betty T. Toulouse, others." 4/yr; 1-yr sub price: $6.00; per copy: $1.50. 1913. 48pp; 8½ x 11. of. circ. 2,000 plus. Reporting time: 2 wks-2 mos. No payment. no ads. Discounts: 40% trade-15% inst. Back issues: $1.00 for copies from 1918-1967/face valve there after. Pub's reviews. §anthro, archeology, history, fine arts folk art-western or southwest topic.

PALERMO ANTIGRUPPO, Sicilian Antigruppo, Nat Scammacca, Crescenzio Cane, Villa Scanimac via Argenteria Km 4, Trappani, Sicily, 0923-38681. Poetry, articles, satire, criticism, reviews, letters, long-poems, collages, concrete art. "3-5 pages in English and Italian. A poetry review of the Sicilian Antigruppo, a populist movement of pluralistic commitment, leftist. Contributors: Crescenzio Cane, Nat Scammacca, Lollini, Jack Hirschman, Guiseppe Zagarrio, Mariella Bettarini, Pietro Terminelli, Ignazio Apollonio, Carmelo Pirrera, Santo Cali, V. Bonanno." 3/yr. 1968. 44pp; 6 x 8. of/lp. circ. 1,000. Reporting time: 1 month. Payment: none. Copyrighted, reverts to author. Pub's reviews. §Poetry, poetics, criticism.

PANACHE, Panache Books, David Lenson, Candice Ward, Robert Steiner, PO Box 77, Sunderland, MA 01375, 413-367-2762. Poetry, fiction, art, letters, parts-of-novels, long-poems, concrete art. "Kenneth Rexroth, Robert Coover, Gayl Jones, Maura Stanton, Lyn Lifshin, David Shapiro, George Chambers, Raymond Federman, Richard Kostelanetz, Christopher Howell, Christine Zawadiwsky." 2/yr; 1-yr sub price: $2.50; per copy: $1.50; sample: $1.50. 1965. 64pp; 5½ x 8½. of/lp. circ. 750. Reporting time: one month. Payment: $3.00 page. Copyrighted, reverts to author. Ads: $25.00/$15.00. Discounts: 40%. Pub'd 2 issues 1976; expects 2 issues 1977, 2 issues 1978. §poetry & fiction. CCLM, COSMEP, NESPA.

Pancake Press, Patrick Smith, 54 Aqua Vista Way, San Francisco, CA 94131, 415-648-3573. Poetry, long-poems. "Our principle interest is in first poetry books by writers who have fairly long experience. We want to do small first editions of poetry books which are the product of several years writing, and which have value as an autobiographical account of a significant social role — workers in all fields, sufferers of various passions, role-changers, all the democratic atoms of our national life." avg. price, paper: $5.00. 1973. 35-50pp; 5½ & 7 x 8½. of. avg. press run 150. Reporting time: 1 month. Payment: arranged by mutual consent. Copyrights for author. Discounts: 25% for less than 25; 40% for 26-99; 48% 100 and over. Pub'd 7 titles 1976; expects 12 titles 1977, 15 titles 1978. COSMEP, WCPC.

PANJANDRUM POETRY JOURNAL, Panjandrum Press, Inc., Dennis Koran, Ed-in-Chief; David Guss, Assoc. Ed.; Sean Cotter, Assoc. Ed.; Barbara Luck, Assoc. Ed., 99 Sanchez St, San Francisco, CA 94114. Poetry, fiction, art, photos, cartoons, reviews, collages. "eclectic; Rothenberg, Einzig, de Angulo, Bly, Ferlinghetti, Norse, McClure, Doria, Beausoleil, Vose, Weiss, Fraser, Vinograd, etc." 1/yr; sub price: $14.00/3 issues; sample: $3.00 plus shipping. 1971. 80-120pp; usually 5½ x 8½. of. circ. 2,000. Reporting time: 1 month. Payment: As grants are avail.; $10.00/submission plus 2 copies of issue. no ads. Discounts: Trade: 1, 20 percent; 2-3, 30 percent; 4-25, 40 percent; 25-up, 50 percent. No library disc. Jobbers: 1-3, 20 percent; 4-25, 40 percent;

26-up, 45 percent. Back issues: PAN 1: $5.00; 2-3, o.p.; 4, $3.00. Pub'd 4 issues 1976; expects 5 issues 1977, 6 issues 1978. §all areas. CCLM, COSMEP.

Panland Books, Glenn Knudsen, Box 83, Monte Rio, CA 95462. "Distributes books by Hunce Voelcker"

Pantagraph (see SOU'WESTER)

Pantheon Press (see COSMPOLITAN CONTACT)

Papa Bach Paperbacks (see BACHY)

Paper Tiger Press (see SQUEEZEBOX)

Parable Press (formerly June McLaughlin Press), Bethany Strong, 136 Gray Street, Amherst, MA 01002, 413-253-5634. "Drama, fiction, graphics (category 37 please)." 1976. avg. press run 1,000. Expects 3 titles 1977. COSMEP, NESPA.

Parachuting Publications, Dan Poynter, P.O. Box 4232-Q, Santa Barbara, CA 93103, 805-968-7277. Photos, cartoons. "I write, produce and market my own books." avg. price, cloth: $9.95; paper: $5.95. 1969. 6 x 9. of. avg. press run 5,000. Copyrights for author. Discounts: start at 40 percent. Pub'd 2 titles 1976; expects 8 titles 1977. AWSA.

PARACHUTIST, Corporate Press, Michael F. Truffer, 806 15th St. NW. Suite 444, Washington, DC 20005. Articles, photos, reviews. 12/yr; 1-yr sub price: $7.00 U.S. $8.00 other; per copy: $1.00. 1958. 32pp; 8½ x 11. of. circ. 15,000. Reporting time: two weeks. Ads: $300/$175/$.25, $.30-all caps $3.50 min. Pub's reviews §aviation sports.

Paradoxical Press (see also VELVET WINGS), Sarah Kennedy, 1228 Oxford St, Berkeley, CA 94709, 415-843-4630. Poetry, fiction, art, letters, long-poems. avg. price, paper: $1.50. 1976. 50-70pp; varies. †of. avg. press run 500-750. Reporting time: 2 weeks-3 months. Payment: may do it for press labor or author receives 1/2 books. Discounts: 40 percent of trade, bulk. Pub'd 1 title 1976. COSMEP.

PARAGRAPH: A QUARTERLY OF GAY FICTION, The Antares Foundation, N. A. Diaman, Box 14051, San Francisco, CA 94114. Fiction, art, satire, parts-of-novels. "The emphasis will be on literary excellence; a balance between lesbian and gay male work will be maintained in each issue; innovative, experimental and erotic material will be considered; foreign works in English translation." 4/yr. of. Reporting time: up to 8 weeks. Payment: contributors copies. Copyrighted, reverts to author. COSMEP.

Parallax Press, Richard Uhlich, 1160 South Main St., Middletown, CT 06457. "poetry, fiction" NESPA.

‡PARIS REVIEW, 541 East 72 St., New York, NY 10021. CCLM.

Parnassos (see THE CHARIOTEER)

PARNASSUS: POETRY IN REVIEW, Herbert Leibowitz, 205 West 89th Street, New York, NY 10024, (212) 787-3569. "Length varies from four pages to forty. Editorial policy is intentionally eclectic. Recent and forthcoming contributors: Adrienne Rich, Jonathan Williams, Guy Davenport, Elizabeth Sewell, Ross Feld, Paul Metcalf, Rosellen Brown, R.W. Flint, Michael Harper, Octavio Paz, Hayden Carruth, Alice Walker" 2/yr; 1-yr sub price: $8.00; per copy: $4.00; sample: $4.00. 1972. 250pp; 6 x 9¼. of. circ. 1,500. Reporting time: 1 week to 1 month. Payment: $25.00 average, occasionally more. Copyrighted, reverts on request. Ads: $175.00/$100.00/none. Discounts: 10% to magazine subscription agencies, 30-40% to bookstores. Back issues: $3.75 each, $7.25 for special issues. Pub's reviews. §Poetry. CCLM, COSMEP.

PARTISAN REVIEW, William Phillips, 1 Richardson St., Rutgers University, New Brunswick, NJ 08903. Poetry, fiction, articles, interviews, criticism, reviews, parts-of-novels, long-poems. 4/yr; 1-yr sub price: $7.50; per copy: $2.00; sample: $2.00. 1935. 160pp; 4¼ x 7-3/8. of. circ. 8,500. Reporting time: 3 to 4 months. Payment: 1½¢ word, prose; 40¢ line poetry. Ads: $100/$50/none. Pub's reviews. §books literature, politics, art, general culture. CCLM.

PASS-AGE: A Futures Journal, Robert Kahn, Timothy Wessels, 3617 Powelton Ave, Philadelphia, PA 19104, 215-387-6294. Poetry, articles, art, photos, cartoons, interviews, reviews. "Stewart Brand, Susan Harris" 1/yr; price per copy: $3.50; sample: $0.00. 1975. 100pp; 8¼ x 10¾. †mi. circ. 1,000. Reporting time: several weeks. Payment: no cash, exchange finished copies of journal for contributors. Copyrighted, reverts to author. Discounts: none. Back issues: all back issues out of print. Pub's reviews. §Future studies, appropriate technology, alternative futures. COSMEP.

PASSAGES, Passages Press, John L. Fluent, Box 14, Evanston, IL 60204, 312-492-1288. Poetry, articles, cartoons, interviews, reviews, letters. "We publish articles of interest to free-lance writers, poets and cartoonists. Max. length 800 wds. for features. 300 wds. for fillers. At present we can offer *no* payment for poetry." 12/yr; 1-yr sub price: $15.00; per copy: $1.00; sample: free. 1976. 16pp; 8½ x 11. of. circ. 800. Reporting time: 4 weeks. Payment varies. Minimum of $10.00 for features. No payment for fillers or poetry. Copyrighted, reverts to author. Ads: $80.00/$40.00/$0.30. Discounts: Prisoners - $9.00 year. Back issues: 50 cents per copy. Pub'd 3 issues 1976; expects 12 issues 1977, 12 issues 1978. Pub's reviews. §Writing, publishing, poetry, cartooning, photojournalism. COSMEP.

Pathfinder Press, Inc, Peggy Brundy, Managing Editor, 410 West Street, New York, NY 10014. "Publishers of books and pamphlets in Afro-American studies, women studies, labor history, Marxist philosophy, radical political science and sociology, and Soviet studies. Complete list totals more than 100 books and more than 75 pamphlets. Complete catalog available free upon request. Recent major books: THE HIDDEN HISTORY OF WASHINGTON'S WAR by Harsch & Thomas; *Woman's Evolution* by Evelyn Reed, *Cointelpro: The FBI'S Secret War on Political Freedom* ed by Perkus with intro. by Noam Chomsky." 1970. Reporting time: 2 months. Payment: standard royalties.

PAUNCH, Arthur Efron, 123 Woodward Ave, Buffalo, NY 14214, 716-836-7332. Poetry, articles, photos, criticism, reviews, letters, long-poems. "The one surviving and growing theme in *PAUNCH*, in its many changes since its beginning, is the human body in literature. Issue 42-43 (Dec. 1975) explores the 'heart' and 'water' in Plath's poem, *'Tulips.'* No. 44-45 (1976) was on sensuality in work/love within Marxism, a booklength discussion of Bill J. Harrell's *'Marx And Critical Thought.'* No. 46-47 (April 1977) is on Wayne Burns, the first American critic to connect the reading of novels with the energies and insights of the body. Recent contributors include Gene Frumkin, Marjorie Perloff, Kingsley Widmer, Audre Lorde, Lyle Glazier, Mac Hammond, Alvin Greenberg, Burton Weiss, Raya Dunayevskaya. Our other major interest, which always seems close to the first, is the authority and criminality of the state. Planned 1977 issues include photographs, *'Bodyscapes'* by Oliver Grosz; also complete reprint of rare 1959 book on *Reich And D. H. Lawrence* by David Boadella." 2/yr; 1-yr sub price: $4.00 indiv., $7.00 libraries; per copy: $2.00 single, $4.00 double issue.; sample: No charge. 1963. Double: 172pp Single: 96pp; 5½ x 8½. of. circ. 400. Reporting time: 30 days. Payment: copies. Copyrighted, rights are handed over upon request to authors. no ads. Discounts: agents, $0.75 a year: classrooms, 20 percent: trade, 40 percent. Back issues: Yes. All through No. 21, Oct. 1964; which was the first to be distributed publicly. Pub'd 1 issue 1976; expects 3 issues 1977, 2 issues 1978. Pub's reviews: none in 1976. CCLM, COSMEP.

THE PAWN REVIEW, Michael Anderson, Editor; Rotating panel of fiction judges., 2806 Reagan Apt. 204, Dallas, TX 75219. Poetry, fiction, articles, art, photos, cartoons, interviews, satire, criticism, reviews, music, letters, parts-of-novels, long-poems, collages, plays, concrete art. "THE PAWN REVIEW is published beyond the confines of a university. Dylan gave us our name, and our poems tend toward symbolist; our fiction, toward black humor & fantasy. We demand specific imagery, and all manuscripts, particularly those from Texas writers, are welcomed. No form rejections, and we try to publish one long-25 pp., typescript, dblsp. - work per issue. We have featured Marshall Terry, Ramona Weeks, James P. White, Walt McDonald, Alice Moser Claudel, Edwin Honig, Rainer Schulte & James Schevill. Each Fall issue focuses on specific genres: 1976 on drama and poetry translations; 1977 on songs and fiction translations." 2/yr; 1-yr sub price: $4.00; per copy: $2.00; sample: $2.00. 1975. 84pp; 5½ x 8½ trimmed. †of. circ. 500 paid. Reporting time: 1 month poetry & art, 3 months other mss. Payment: 1 copy; additional40 1/2 price/payment expected by Fall, 1978. Copyrighted, reverts to author. Ads: $50/$25. Discounts: Bookstores-25 percent consignment, 40 percent on purchase of 5 or more copies, small press agents-50 percent. Pub'd 2 issues 1976; expects 2 issues 1977, 2 issues 1978. Pub's reviews: 7 in 1976. COSMEP, CCLM.

PAZ PRINT/PERIPHERY, House of Paz, Jim Goldfeder, Cheryl Goldfeder, P.O. Box 8267, Univ. of Tenn. Station, Knoxville, TN 37916. "We will not begin publication until the end of 1976 or the beginning of 1977. PAZ'S first publication THE GIRL WHO WOULDN'T TALK was sold to the National Association of the Deaf and published by them in 1975. They will also publish the Goldfeder's second book ROBIN SEES A SONG in 1976. Both these publications were originally scheduled to be published by House of Paz but were sold instead to the National Association of the Deaf. Our magazines PAZ PRINTS and PERIPHERY will not begin until next year. We are looking for good poetry and original children's material. Goldfeders review small press materials for the U.T. Beacon. (30,000 circulation). Send review copies to Jim Goldfeder, 1611 Laurel Ave., #807, Knoxville, Tn. 37916" first issue 1977; price per copy: $2.00. 1975. §poetry/children's materials/novels/almost anything!. COSMEP.

PEACE & PIECES REVIEW, Peace And Pieces Foundation, Todd S.J. Lawson, Maurice Custodio, Carol Carter, Ernesto Ferrera, PO Box 99394, San Francisco, CA 94109. Poetry, fiction, articles, cartoons, interviews, satire, criticism, reviews, letters. "We do multi-lingual poetry but require camera-ready copy. No bi-lingual fiction or reviews right now. We are a non-profit corporation (literary-educational) and any donations to us are tax-deductible, both Federal & State. We publish and distribute to prisoners, elderly, multi-cultural communities. Mix knowns with unknowns. Recent contributors include: Robert Bly, a 15 year-old fiction writer, prison inmate and author Ross Laursen, Tina Villanueava, D. Hunter, Allen Ginsberg, Grace Harwood, Opal L. Nations. We are open to all styles and literary forms. Publish mostly in English but several other languages with English translations done also. Short work preferred." 4/yr; 1-yr sub price: $3.50; per copy: $1.50; sample: $1.00. 1971. 66pp; 8 x 10. circ. 500 plus. Reporting time: 2 wks. Ads: $35/$15/$.15/wd/class. Discounts: libraries-20-40%/schools-40%. Back issues: $1/issue. CCLM, COSMEP, COSMEP-WEST, CNS, NCPA.

Peace & Pieces Foundation (see also PEACE & PIECES REVIEW), Maurice M. Custodio, Pres.; Todd S.J. Lawson, Vice-Pres.; William Samolis, Sec.; Efren Ramirez, Carol Carter, Ernesto Ferrera, Contributing Editors, Box 99394, San Francisco, CA 94109. "We publish our magazine irregularly; books and pamphlets free to prisons, elderly institutions, poor people, and operate from tax-deductible donations and grants. 2 new books in 1975-76 include: *Astrolabes* by Elizabeth Keeler, David Hoag & Nellie Hill; *Sweet Tomorrow* by Ross Laursen. We do bi-lingual chapbooks, poetry, short novels and non-fiction books and booklets (depending on grant monies). Your tax-deductible contributions are always welcomed. Our editors are also volunteers. We have volunteer Chinese, Japanese, Filipino (Tagalog), Spanish, etc. Translators for much of our work. Hope to sponsor cassette poetry and literature tapes to hospitals and institutions soon. New 1977 book, *The 69 Days Of Easter* (fiction) by Todd S.J. Lawson - doing films of poets and artists during 1977-78. New book (photography) gay, *In Pursuit Of Images* by Efren Ramirez. Also new book, *Contemporary Fictions: Today's Outstanding Writers* (Dec. 76)."

PEACE NEWS "For Non-Violent Revolution", Editorial Collective, 8 Elm Avenue, Nottingham, United Kingdom, 0602-53587. Poetry, articles, cartoons, photos, news items, letters. 26/yr; 1-yr sub price: £14.00, £22.00 airmail; per copy: 15p; sample: 10p. 1936. 20pp; A4. of. circ. 5,000. Ads: £25. Back issues: 20p inc p&p. Pub'd 25 issues 1976; expects 26 issues 1977, 26 issues 1978. Pub's reviews: 10 in 1976. §Health, conservation. UAPS(E).

Peace Press, Harold Moskovitz, 3828 Willat Ave., Culver City, CA 90230, 213-838-7387. Poetry, fiction, art, photos, parts-of-novels. "Peace Press is an alternative printing & publishing collective.

We do political & commercial work that includes books. Our biases are towards books on ecology, politics, peace and non-sexist material." avg. price, cloth: $10.00; paper: $5.00. 1969. 200pp; Varies. †of. avg. press run 3,000. Reporting time: 3 months. Payment: Quarterly. Copyrights for author. Discounts: Trade: 1-4, 20 percent; 4-50, 40 percent; 50 plus, 45 percent. Text: 20 percent. Wholesalers inquire. Pub'd 3 titles 1976; expects 5 titles 1977, 8 titles 1978. COSMEP, LPSC, COSMEP, WEST.

Peaceweed Press, Thistle Naddour, Charles Henley, Patricia Henley, Tolstoy Farm, Rt. 3 Box 70, Davenport, WA 99122. Poetry, fiction. "PEACEWEED publishes chapbooks of poetry and fiction. At the present time we are not soliciting manuscripts, but that may change by early '77." 1970. †of. Reporting time: 1 month. Payment: 10% of the printing. Discounts: 40% when purchasing five or more copies. COSMEP.

‡**PEBBLE, Best Cellar Press,** 118 South Boswell, Crete, NB 68333.

Pedestrian Press (see OUT THERE MAGAZINE)

PEDESTRIAN RESEARCH, L. Wilensky, 170 Broadway, Rm 201, New York, NY 10038. "Biased giving the *pedestrian* viewpoint." 4/yr; 1-yr sub price: $3.00; per copy: $1.00; sample: $.25. 1973. 4pp; 8 x 11. of. circ. 1,000. Payment: optional. Discounts: 20% discounts. Back issues: $1-each if available. §pedestrian/pedestrian environment/criticism of auto culture. COSMEP.

Pegana Press, Lois Newman, P.O. Box 2148, Boulder, CO 80302. Fiction. "The Pegana Press is a small press publishing fiction, children's and other books which we like. We do first printings of 5,000 and try to have a superior looking product. We are attempting to get as wide a distribution as possible." 1975. Reporting time: 1 mo. Payment: 15% royalty. Discounts: 40-47% trade.

PEMBROKE MAGAZINE, Norman MacLeod, P.O. Box 756, Pembroke, NC 28372. Poetry, fiction, articles, art, photos, criticism, reviews. "Archibald MacLeish, N. Scott Momaday, Simon J. Oritz, John Pauker, Joseph Bruchac, Blyden Jackson, Hugh MacDiarmid, Charles Olson, W.S. Graham, Diana Chang, Kay Boyle, Harald Littlebird, Jonathan Daniels, Guy Owen." 1/yr-occasional supplementary issue; sub price: $3.00/yr-another $3.00 for supplementary issue, if published.; per copy: $3.00 (overseas $3.50); sample: $3.00. 1969. 200pp; 6 x 9. of. circ. 1,500. Reporting time: 1-4 months. Payment: whatever we can. Copyright reverts to author except for right of editor to reprint the magazine and to issue a PM anthology. Ads: $40/$25. Discounts: 40% bookstores. Pub'd 1 issue 1976; expects 2 issues 1977, 1 issue 1978. Pub's reviews. CCLM, COSMEP.

Penmaen Press, Michael McCurdy, Joan Norris, Michael Peich, Old Sudbury Road, Lincoln, MA 01773, 617-259-0842. Poetry, fiction. "First edition wk preferable" avg. price, cloth: $15.00-$20.00; paper: $4.00. 1968. 40pp; 6¼ x 9¾. †lp. avg. press run 1,000. Reporting time: 1-2 weeks. Payment: 10% hardcover/7½% soft. Copyrights for author. Discounts: 1-4 copies 20 percent; 5-24 copies 40 percent; 25-49 copies 42 percent; 50-99 copies 44 percent; 100 or more 46 percent. Pub'd 2 titles 1976; expects 3 titles 1977, 3 titles 1978. NESPA.

Pennsylvania State University Press (see CHAUCER REVIEW)

Pennyworth Press, David Foy, Beverley Foy, 114 7th Ave, N.W., Calgary, Alberta T2M0A2, Canada. Poetry, long-poems, non-fiction. "No requirements as to style, form, theme, or content. High literary quality is essential. It is unlikely that poets previously unpublished in literary magazines will meet our standards, but we welcome all submissions and read all carefully particularly receptive to Canadians. Canadian return postage or Int'l reply coupons an absolute necessity." 1974. †of/lp. Reporting time: up to 2 weeks. Payment: small advance, large royalty after costs. Discounts: Standard. Expects 4 titles 1977. HHFLC.

Pentagram Press, Michael Tarachow, P.O. Box 11609, Milwaukee, WI 53211. Poetry, fiction, interviews, criticism, reviews, long-poems. "Following an interest in the politics of smallpress publishing, *Concern/s*, by Tom Montag, *'The End' Appendix*, by Richard Kostelanetz, and *Toward A Further Definition*, edited by Michael Tarachow, will all appear in 1977 or by early '78. TAFD collects essays by over 40 smallpress people, telling more of what we do without, without nailing the scene down for dissection. Poetry's still a main concern, though: new titles include Enslin, Clewell, Kloefkorn, Kooser, Tarachow, Montag, & Judson. After seeing 25 books into print in the last 2½ years I'm slowing to 3-7 smaller books a year, with luck handset letterpress. Now interested in a very specific poetry: please query with SASE before sending mss. See you on the dark side of the moon.'' avg. price, cloth: $10.00 - $15.00; paper: $3.00. 1974. 16-256pp; 5.25 x 8.25. †of/lp. Please query with SASE. Payment varies. Copyrights for author. Discounts: Standard. Pub'd 7 titles 1976; expects 10 titles 1977, 3-7 titles 1978.

Pentangle Press, Robert Springer, 132 Lasky Dr., Beverly Hills, CA 90212. ''Holography'' avg. price, cloth: $10.00; paper: $8.00. 1974. 100pp; 6 x 9. of. avg. press run 2,000. Reporting time: 30 days. Discounts: retailers: 2-4 20%, 5-29 40%. Expects 2 titles 1977, 2 titles 1978.

The Penumbra Press, Bonnie P. O'Connell, Box 12, Lisbon, IA 52253. Poetry, fiction, art, photos, collages. ''Editions usually number 200-250 copies. All releases are hand printed from hand-set type. Most editions are casebound, some come out in paperback. Recent: *Stepping Outside* by Tess Gallagher, *Sleeping On Doors* by Steven Orlen, *The Prayers Of The North American Martyrs* by Norman Dubie, *Anxiety And Ashes* by Laura Jensen, *Dear Anyone* by William Keens. We also publish *'The Manila Series'*, pamphlets in which each release is housed in a manila envelope.'' avg. price, cloth: $15.00; paper: $7.50. 1971. 35pp. †lp. Payment: 10% of the edition. Discounts: 25% to dealers who purchase 5 or more copies. Pub'd 2 titles 1976; expects 2 titles 1977.

PEOPLE & ENERGY, Ken Bossong, Alan Okagaki, 1757 S Street NW, Washington, DC 20009, 202-332-4252. Articles, art, photos, cartoons, reviews. 12/yr; 1-yr sub price: $10.00; per copy: $1.00; sample: SASE. 1975. 12pp; 8½ x 11. of. circ. 2,000. Not copyrighted. Ads: none. Discounts: Negotiated on an individual basis. Back issues: $0.75 copy. Pub's reviews. §Energy. COSMEP.

PEOPLE'S BOOKSELLER, Bob Broedel, P.O. Box 20049, Tallahassee, FL 32304. ''A newsletter for progressive booksellers.'' 2/yr; 1-yr sub price: $1.00; per copy: $.50; sample: free. 1974. 8pp; 8½ x 11. of. circ. 1,000. Reporting time: slow. Payment: none. Back issues: no back issues available. Pub's reviews. §must have some progressive political content.

People's Canada Publishing House (see NEW LITERATURE & IDEOLOGY)

People's Computer Co. (see also PEOPLE'S COMPUTER CO./DR. DOBB'S JOURNAL OF COMPUTER CALISTHENICS & ORTHODONTIA/COMPUTER MUSIC JOURNAL), 1010 Doyle No. 9, Menlo Park, CA 94025, 415-323-3111. Articles, photos, cartoons, interviews, criticism, reviews, letters. ''A non profit, educational company dedicated to demystifying personal and home computers.'' avg. price, paper: $1.00 - $2.75. 1971. 48-64pp; 8½ x 11. of. avg. press run 5,000-10,000. Payment: none-we are non-profit. Copyrights for author. Discounts: 40 percent off retail to resalers; other discounts occasionally upon arragement.

PEOPLE'S COMPUTERS, People's Computer Co., Phyllis Cole, 1263 El Camino, P. O. Box E, Menlo Park, CA 94025, 415-323-3111. Articles, photos, cartoons, interviews, criticism, reviews, letters. ''A periodical for novices & intermediate uses of personal and home computers. Published by a non-profit, educational company dedicated to demystifying personal and home computers. Publications: *What To Do After You Hit Return* and others.'' 6/yr; 1-yr sub price: $8.00; per copy: $1.50. 1971. 48-64pp. of. circ. 5,000-10,000. Payment: none. Copyrighted. Ads: none accepted. Discounts: discounts to resellers, bulk subscriptions, and subscription agencies. Back issues: $12.00 for all back issues. Pub'd 6 issues 1976; expects 6 issues 1977, 6 issues 1978. Pub's reviews. §computers & computers in education.

PEOPLE'S NEWS SERVICE, PNS, PNS Collective, 182 Upper St., London, N 1, United Kingdom, 01-359-3785. Articles, cartoons, news items. ''We are a fortnightly bulletin of rare & interacial news. We hope to become more of a co-ordinator in the future for the left & alternative

233

press in UK with our radical circulation." 25/yr; 1-yr sub price: $4.37. 1973. 16pp; A4. circ. 400. Reporting time: Variable. Payment: Voluntary. Not copyrighted. Discounts: no. Back issues: Some available. Pub's reviews. §Politics, women, prisons etc. APS.

Peoples Press, Peoples Press Collective, 2680 21st St, San Francisco, CA 94110. Poetry, photos, cartoons, interviews. 1969. of. Usually no payment. COSMEP.

PEOPLE'S YELLOW PAGES of the SAN FRANCISCO BAY AREA, Diane Sampson, Jan Zobel, P.O. Box 31291, San Francisco, CA 94131. Art. "No free lance other than art. No payment for art. Write for information-only local ads accepted." once every 1½ yrs; price per copy: $3.50. 1971. 196pp; 8½ x 11. of. circ. 20,000. Payment: none. Discounts: 40% for 10 or more copies. Back issues: $1 to $1.95 depending on which issue. Expects 1 issue 1978. §alternatives/women/gay/other liberation.

PEQUOD, David Paradis, Fiction; Mark Rudman, Poetry, Fiction, P.O. Box 491, Forest Knolls, CA 94933, Poetry, 282 W. 4th St., New York, NY 10014. Poetry, fiction, articles, criticism, parts-of-novels, long-poems, plays. "A journal of contemporary literature and literary criticism. Contributors: Paul Blackburn, Richard Hugo, Jane De Lynn, Tom McHale, Stephen Dobyns. We are not interested in receiving unsolicited submissions from people who are not familiar with PEQUOD." 2/yr; sub price: 1 yr $4.50; 2 yrs $8.00; per copy: $2.50; sample: $2.50. 1974. 90pp; 5½ x 8½. of. Reporting time: 2-3 months. Payment: $3-pages/$5-min/$30-max/12 copies. Copyrighted, reverts to author. Discounts: 40% trade. Back issues: $2.00 each. Pub'd 2 issues 1976; expects 2 issues 1977, 2 issues 1978. CCLM, COSMEP.

Peradam Publishing House (see also SMALL PRESS WRITER'S REVIEW c/o Peradam Publishing House), Arnold Wolman, Ted Wolter, P.O. Box 85, Urbana, IL 61801, 815-367-7070. Poetry, articles, art. "Keith Hitchcock, Bill Alvarez, Gary Legare, Ted Wolter, Arnold Wolman, K.T. Moore, Joffree Stewart, Bruce Sanders, Bernie Pyron, Elvan, Jimmy Kleinhans." avg. price, paper: $1.00 - $5.00; other: Handmade books $10.00 - $500.00. 1971. pp varies.; Varies. †of/handmade. avg. press run 100 - 10,000. Payment: 5-15% of retail price. Copyright both via publisher and author. Discounts: 40-50%. Pub'd 2 titles 1976; expects 6 titles 1977, 6-10 titles 1978. COSMEP.

Peregrine Smith, Inc., Richard A. Firmage, C. W. Smith, PO Box 667, Layton, UT 84041. "Books on Architecture, Arts, Crafts, History, Native Americans. Reprints." 1970. of.

PERFORMING ARTS JOURNAL, Bonnie Marranca, Gautam DasGupta, P.O. Box 858, Peterstuyvesant Station, New York, NY 10009, 212-260-7586. Articles, art, photos, interviews, criticism, reviews, music, plays. "Maximum length of article: 15 double-spaced typed pages. Biases: criticalorientation towards twentieth-century performing arts. Joseph Chaiken, Richard Schechner, Michael McClure, Edward Bond." 3/yr; 1-yr sub price: $6.00 individuals; $12.00 libraries & institutions; per copy: $2.25; sample: $2.25. 1976. 140pp; 5½ x 8¼. of. circ. 2,500. Reporting time: 1 month. Copyrighted. Ads: $140.00/$85.00. Discounts: trade discount 40 percent. Pub'd 2 issues 1976; expects 3 issues 1977. Pub's reviews: 15 in 1976. §theatre, dance, music, film, video, performance. CCLM, COSMEP.

Performing Arts Society, Inc. (see also UTOPIAN EYES). "Publish *'Far Out West'* comics & ' *The Storefront Classroom'* newspaper as well as *'UTOPIAN EYES'*."

‡**PERIODICAL LITERARIO,** Apartado 410, Merida, Venezuela.

Periphery (see PAZ PRINT/PERIPHERY)

‡**Perishable Press Limited,** Wisconsin Arts Board, PO Box 7, Mt. Horeb, WI 53572.

Perivale Press, Lawrence P. Spingarn, 13830 Erwin Street, Van Nuys, CA 91401, 213-785-4671. Poetry, fiction. "We specialize in translations from foreign poetry by individuals or regional-national groups and in anthologies. Small editions (750-1,000 copies) from 40 pp to 230 pp. Recently published: *Poets West,* edited by L.P. Spingarn. *Yiddish Sayings Mama Never Taught You* by Weltman & Zuckerman. Forthcoming: *The Epigrams Of Martial, Tr.* by Richard O'Connell. *Contemporary French Women Poets, Tr.* by C. Hermey. *The Blue Door & Other Stories* by L.P. Spingarn." avg. price, paper: $3.95. 1968. 100pp; 5½ x 8½. of. avg. press run 1,000. Reporting time: 3 months. Payment: 10%-15% royalty, sliding. Will copyright for author if author pays fee. Discounts: trade: 40%; institution: 10%; student: 10%. Pub'd 3 titles 1976; expects 3 titles 1977, 3 titles 1978. COSMEP.

PERMAFROST, Neil Williams, Box 80625, Fairbanks, AK 99708. Poetry, fiction, articles, art, photos. "The first issue includes Kay Boyce, Lael Morgan, Yvonne Mozee, John Morgan. We wish to publish quality work by known & unknown artists. No editorial biases. One note: Please do not put your name on submissions; we wish to evaluate the work only, not the name." 3/yr; 1-yr sub price: $5.00; per copy: $2.00; sample: $2.00. 1977. 56pp; 5½ x 8. of. circ. 1,000. Reporting time: 3 months. Payment: copy. Copyrighted, reverts to author. no ads. Discounts: None. Back issues: Vol. 1 No. 1. Expects 3 issues 1977, 3 issues 1978.

Permanent Press, Robert Vas Dias, 52 Cascade Avenue, London, N10 England, United Kingdom, 1040 Park Avenue, New York, NY 10028. Poetry, long-poems. "Length: from 10 to 30 pages per booklet. Recent authors: Jackson Mac Low, Edward Dorn, Jennifer Dunbar, Elaine Randell, Pierre Joris, Nathaniel Tarn, Armand Schwerner, Janet Rodney." avg. price, paper: $1.65; other: $4.00 (signed & numbered editions). 1972. 20pp; 6 x 8. of. avg. press run 350. Reporting time: 1 month. Payment: modest, plus copies. Copyrights for author. Discounts: 40% to trade, no returns. Pub'd 2 titles 1976; expects 4 titles 1977, 4 titles 1978. ALP.

Permanent Press (see BLANK TAPE)

Permanent Press (see MOONS AND LION TAILES)

Phillip M. Perry, Phillip M. Perry, P O Box 2319, Springfield, MA 01101, 413-737-1685. "Publishes paperback books in fields of finance and show business. Catalog available." 1977. of. avg. press run Varies. Not currently accepting outside work. Discounts: Booksellers, 40 percent: Libraries, 15 percent: Others, request details.

Petronium Press, Frank Stewart, 1255 Nuuanu Ave, #1813, Honolulu, HI 96817. Poetry, fiction, long-poems. "Biased toward fine printing and/or fine writing (the two together whenever possible). Biased toward the poem rather than the poet. Submissions are not encouraged. Publications to date include signed, limited-edition broadsides and portfolios of Gardner, Stafford, Logan, Merwin; books by Schmitz, Hoge, Edel. Now reading for an anthology of local women poets." 1975. †of/lp. Reporting time: 1 to 6 weeks. Payment: copies. Discounts: 40% to the trade. Pub'd 2 titles 1976; expects 2 titles 1977, 2 titles 1978. COSMEP.

PHANTASM, Heidelberg Graphics, Larry S. Jackson, PO Box 3404, Chico, CA 95927, 916-342-6582. Poetry, fiction, articles, art, photos, interviews, criticism, reviews, concrete art, news items, non-fiction. "As a bi-monthly publication we print more current literary events, features, interviews, guest columns, reviews and editorials. We publish short stories from well know authors like Antoni Gronowicz, Irene Tractenberg and Jamake Highwater as well as promising new writers. Special editions such as our surprise double issue with a 40-page supplement feature of American Indian contributors, add dimension along with our award-winning graphics and illustrated articles. *PHANTASM* welcomes and prints material from many schools of thought including translations. Poets who have published range from Jascha Kessler, John Oliver Simon, Philip Hacket, Al Gowan, Chuck Oliveros, Adrienne Wolfert, Jim Barnes, Wendy Rose, Ralph Salisbury and Helen Ruggier; to those who published for the first time. All issues are preserved in subscribing libraries from coast to coast (ISSN: 0145-5203)." 6/yr; 1-yr sub price: $5.00; per copy: $1.25; sample: $1.25. 1976. 40 pluspp; 8½ x 11. †of. circ. 1,000. Reporting time: 4 to 8 weeks. Payment is by copies. Copyrighted, reverts to author. no ads. Back issues: Varies from $1.25 to $4.00. Pub'd 6 issues 1976; expects 6 issues 1977, 6 issues 1978. Pub's reviews: 3 in 1976. §Poetry, graphics, writing, events. COSMEP, CCLM, SCCIPHC.

Phenomenon Press (see also KONTAKTE), Richard Truhlar, John Riddell, 76 Admiral Road, Toronto, Ontario M5R2L5, Canada, 922-8206. Poetry, fiction, long-poems, collages, concrete art. '' *KONTAKTE* is a periodical devoted to experimental literature: non linear poetry & prose; concrete poetry; sound poetry, etc. We are international; corresponding with Europe & the States. Some issues are devoted entirely to an author's work; while others are anthologies; and others still are thematic issues (we produced an issue devoted to the dadaist sound-poet blugo ball). Recent contributors include-b p Nichol, Dick Higgins, Steve McCaffery, Steven Smith, Paul Sutton, Owen Sound.'' avg. price, paper: $4.00. 1976. 50pp; 8½ x 11. †of. avg. press run 70-100. Reporting time: 1-3 months. Payment: none. Copyrights for author. Pub'd 3 titles 1976.

Philatelic Directory Publishing Co (see also THE PHILATELIC JOURNALIST), Gustav Detjen Jr., Box 150, Clinton Corners, NY 12514. ''The directory is published as a handbook for philatelic writers and advance stamp collectors and students of Philately. In trying to expand its contents will consider the addition of any subject which is helpful to the philatelic writer and journalist.'' avg. price, cloth: $12.00. 1976. 48pp; 6 x 9. lp. avg. press run 1,200. Reporting time: 60 days. Payment: to be negotiated. Does not copyright for author. Discounts: 33-1/3 percent to the trade, larger quantities subject to negotiation.

THE PHILATELIC JOURNALIST, The Philatelic Directory, Gustav Detjen Jr., Box 150, Clinton Corners, NY 12514, 914-266-3150. Articles, letters. ''Articles which are concerned with the problems of philatelic writers, which offer helpful suggestions, and which promote Philately.'' 6/yr; 1-yr sub price: $6.00; per copy: $1.00; sample: $1.00. 1971. 16pp; 5½ x 8½. lp. circ. 1,000 plus. Reporting time: 30 days. Payment: subject to negotiation. We do receive many free contributions in return for additional copies & ads. Not copyrighted. Ads: $40.00/$25.00/$1.00 per line. Discounts: agents, 33-1/3 percent; libraries special rate of $10 for three years. Back issues: $1.00. Pub'd 6 issues 1976. Pub's reviews. COSMEP.

Phillip The Grasshopper, Dorothy L. Tullis, Box 54119, Los Angeles, CA 90074, (213) 662-0188. ''Delightful soft-bound 8½ x 11 inch 17-page children's fairytale with cute illustrations on each page, printed in green color, selling for $1.50 each plus 35 cents tax and postage and handling.'' avg. price, paper: $1.50. 1975. 17pp; 8½ x 11. of. avg. press run only one run, thus far, of 2,000. Reporting time: 1 week. Discounts: 40% wholesale discount to stores; 50% discount to mail order houses.

Philmer Enterprises, Phyliss Shanken, 617 Wayfield Rd, Wynnewood, PA 19096, 215-896-6630. Poetry, fiction, articles, art, long-poems. ''At the moment, we can publish very few publications. Interest in gift books that can be illustrated by top quality artists. Interest in universal appeal for wide market, rather than traditional, elusive poetry.'' avg. price, paper: $2.95. 1976. 56pp; 5½ x 8½. avg. press run 3,000. Reporting time: 1 month. Payment: by arrangement with author. Copyrights for author. Discounts: trade. COSMEP.

PHILOLOGOS, A. Henry Eliassen, PO Box 2586, Tallahassee, FL 32304. Poetry, fiction, articles, satire, criticism, reviews, letters. ''PHILOLOGOS is basically a personal journal of its editor-publisher. Outside contributors (short) accepted as 'Letters to the Editor' so long as they are not in questionable taste (i.e., bland, toothless, non-controversial).'' 12/yr; 1-yr sub price: $5.00; per copy: $0.35; sample: $0.35. 1975. 8pp; 8½ x 11. †mi. circ. 50 per month. Reporting time: 1-2 months. Payment: none. Copyrighted, does not revert to author. Ads: none-do not accept paid advertising. Discounts: none. Back issues: $.35. Pub's reviews. §satire on the state of society & culture.

PHOEBE, Samuel J. O'Neal Jr., G.M.U. 4400 University Dr., Fairfax, VA 22030. 4/yr; 1-yr sub price: $8.00; per copy: $2.00; sample: $2.00. 1971. 70pp; 8 x 10. of. circ. 4,000. Reporting time: 60 days. Payment: copies only. Pub's reviews. COSMEP.

THE PHOENIX, Morning Star Press, James Cooney, American Editor, Morning Star Farm, RFD, Haydenville, MA 01039, 413-665-4754. Poetry, letters, parts-of-novels, long-poems, plays. ''We don't publish 'fiction'. We publish evocations of the human struggle told in stories, poems, diaries, novels, letters, woodcuts, line drawings & photos. We have no restrictions relative to the length of mss. or to the far ranging aspects of the struggle, past and present. We are most receptive to writings which intrinsically encourage uncompromising non-violent resistance to all assaults against the indivisibility of humanity and against the inherent human rights of individual conscience, freedom of speech and dissent. We are equally receptive to writings which nurture international reconciliations and healings of human society and help us find our way past the malign schisms of tribes, nations, races, absolutist religious & ideological dogmas, and the rival anti-human governments of this world." Irregular quarterly.; sub price: $10.00 (4 nos); per copy: $3.00; sample: $2.50. 1938. 264-360pp; 5-3/8 x 7-5/8. †lp. circ. 2,500-2,800. Reporting time: usually 2-3 wks. Payment: copies plus a years subscription. Ads: No paid ads. exchange notices & free notices only. Back issues: Very scant supply of recent issues. All copies of Vol. 1 & Vol. 2 (Spring 1938 through Autumn 1940) are long out of print but available in hardcover 2-volume facsimile reprint edition. Expects 4 issues 1977, 4 issues 1978. Pub's reviews. §radical humanist literature.

PhoeniXongs (see also a songsmith's JOURNAL), James Durst, P.O. Box 622 (orders), 1652 Longvalley Drive (correspondence), Northbrook, IL 60062, 312-498-3981. Poetry, art, photos, cartoons, music, interviews, letters, articles. "We are primarily publishers of the work of songsmith James Durst." avg. price, cloth: $4.95; paper: $1.95. 1973. Varies. of. avg. press run 2,500. Discounts: Standard 40 percent trade. Expects 2 titles 1978. COSMEP.

PHONE-A-POEM, Peter Payack, Box 193, Cambridge, MA 02141, 617-492-1144. Poetry, satire, reviews. "*PHONE-A-POEM* is the Cambridge/Boston 24-hour, free, recorded poetry hotline where you hear 3 minutes of poetry & poetry news. Poems are recorded by the poets themselves. I try to 'play' a broad selection of what's happening in poetry today. If somebody is doing it, you'll eventually hear it on *PHONE-A-POEM!* I change the tape once a week, on Tuesdays." 52/yr. 1976. circ. 1,500-2,000. Pub'd 52 issues 1976. Pub's reviews. §poetry, short short fiction, satire.

PIANETA FRESCO, East 128, Fernanda Pivano, Ettore Sottsass, Allen Ginsberg, 14 Via Manzoni, Milano 20121, Italy. price per copy: lire 2.300. 1967. 100pp. of. circ. 350.

PICK, Pick Publications, Brian Dann, Jerry Orpwood, Michael Rose, Corresponding Editor; Carol Rumens, and associate editor for each issue., 43 Edgar Rd., South Croydon, Surrey CR2 0NJ, United Kingdom, 01-660-6856. Poetry. "PICK publishes a wide range of poetry, and is not restricted to any particular style or type. Both new names and established poets are welcome to contribute." 4/yr; sub price: £2.40 for four issues ($8.00); per copy: 60p each ($2.00); sample: 60p each ($2.00). 1974. 48pp; A5. of. circ. 250. Reporting time: 8-10 weeks at present. Payment: complimentary copy. Copyrighted, reverts to author. Ads: £10.00/£7.00. Discounts: 33 percent to bookshops. Back issues: 50p plus postage ($2.00). Pub'd 2 issues 1976; expects 4 issues 1977, 4 issues 1978. Pub's reviews: 67 in 1976. §Poetry.

Pierian Press (see REFERENCE SERVICES REVIEW)

PIGIRON, Pigiron Press, Jim Villani, Editor; Terry Murcko, Poetry Editor; Rose Sayre, Entourage Editor; Jon Missik, Systems Editor, P.O. Box 237, Youngstown, OH 44501, 216-744-2258. Poetry, fiction, photos, cartoons, letters, long-poems, concrete art, art, collages, plays. "Not a magazine. A concept. That which is life...the crowd, the process, the distillation, the perpetuity. The media as a way of life...not an instrument, not a manipulation, not a job, but..a fullfillment. An exploratory approach to publishing. The editors of PIGIRON believe that the process of creation is as important as the finished product. Length: open. Style/bias: high-energy. Recent contributors: Michael D. Smith, Hale Chatfield, Nancy Harris, Carl Larsen, James Jurado, Terry Wright. Publish chapbooks none in 1976, one in 1977 (expected 1,000 copies. Copyright for author, 10 percent to author. Size varies, paper only)." Irregular, at least once and not more than three times a year.; sub price: $5.00/3 issues; $9.00/6 issues.; per copy: $3.00; sample: $2.00. 1974. 100pp; 8½ x 11. of. circ. 1,000. Reporting time: 3 weeks to 12 weeks. Payment: 2 copies. Copyrighted, reverts to author. no ads. Discounts: booksellers/3 or more copies 40%. Back issues: $3.00. Pub'd 1 issue 1976; expects 2 issues 1977, 3 issues 1978. COSMEP.

Pikeville College Press (see also TWIGS), Leonard Roberts, Pikeville, KY 41501, 432-3161. avg.

price, cloth: $4.50-$10.00; paper: $3.00-$6.00; other: $3.00-$6.00. 1971. 100 to 600pp; 5 x 8. of/lp. avg. press run 500, 1,000. Reporting time: 1 to 2 months. Payment: from 00/10%/12½%. Discounts: 20 edu insti, 40 booksellers; above 200 order 50%. Pub'd 2 titles 1976; expects 2-4 titles 1977, 2-4 titles 1978. CCLM, COSMEP.

PILGRIMS OF THE ARTS, Pilgrim South Press, Stephen Higginson, 80 Holly Road, Christchurch, New Zealand. Poetry, fiction, articles, art, photos, interviews, reviews, letters. "Published work will include short stories, reviews, interviews, correspondence, photographs, art work/articles, essays. Each issue will contain a guest (paid). All mss. for return, include S.A.E and postage." 3/yr; 1-yr sub price: $3.00. Payment: copy.

Pilot Press Books, Eric Greinke, PO Box 2662, Grand Rapids, MI 49501. Poetry, fiction, art, photos, letters, long-poems. "Pilot Press publishes books of poetry & fiction from 48 to 300 pages in length in both paperback and hardcover formats. We are interested in work that is so itself that it's automatically great. Our favorite poets right now are Ben Tibbs, Ronni M. Lane, Dave & Sue Cope, Pam & Eric Greinke, & other poets living & writing in & around Grand Rapids, Michigan, affectionately known as 'Paris On The Grand'. Write for a free list of current titles. Query first before sending any manuscripts. Projects too numerous to mention!" 1972. 48-300pp. of. Reporting time: 1 day-1 wk. Discounts: Bookstores & libraries: 40%, no minimum; classroom: 50% on orders of 20 copies or more. COSMEP.

The Pilot School Co-operative (see also THE PLANET QUARTERLY), Jamie Askins, Mark Camirand, Justin Doebele, Sarah Hart, Alexander Ingle, Gabriel Jackson, Jan Koso, Carla Michelini, Heather A. Ryan, C/O Heather A. Ryan, 2 Bancroft Street, Cambridge, MA 02139, 617-864-9341. Poetry, fiction, art, cartoons, long-poems. "High school aged students (13-19 yrs. old) can send submissions of poetry, fiction, ink drawings." 1976. of. avg. press run 200. Reporting time: 3 mos. Discounts: 10 copies for $4.00 to classes.

Pink Triangle Press (see also THE BODY POLITIC), The Body Politic Editorial Collective & Pink Triangle Press Collective, Box 639, Station A, Toronto, Ontario M5WAG2, Canada, 416-863-6320. Poetry, fiction, articles, art, photos, cartoons, interviews, criticism, reviews, letters, news items, non-fiction. "Will be seeking manuscripts and art works informed by a gay consciousness, the publication of which will in some way advance the cause of gay liberation." 1975. various methods. Reporting time: 1 month for Body Politic. Discounts: to be decided. Expects 1 title 1977.

Pioneer Press (see LAKES & PRAIRIES)

Pirate Press, Bill Griffiths, 107 Valley Drive, Kingsbury, London NW9 9NT, United Kingdom. Poetry. "Publications include a dual-text version of Beowulf in old and modern English; other translations; contemporary poetry. Free catalogue available by post." 1971. of/duplicating. ALP.

Pitcairn Press Inc., John Marten, 388 Franklin St, Cambridge, MA 02139. "Have published one book 1975 'A FLIGHT OF ARROWS' by Jjohn H. Beavais."

Pitjon Press/BackBack Media (see FROZEN WAFFLES)

PIVOT, Mayer Press, Joseph L. Grucci, 221 S. Barnard, State College, PA 16801, 814-238-8887. Poetry. "Length of material usually not more than 40-50 lines. Recent contributors: Eugene J. McCarthy, Paul Nest, John Balaban (Lamont Poetry Prizewinner)." 1/yr; price per copy: $1.25; sample: $1.00. 1951. 48pp; 6 x 9. lp. circ. 1,500 - 2,000. Reporting time: 1-3 months. Copyrighted, reverts to author. Ads: $85.00/$45.00/$25.00. Discounts: Bookstores 33-1/3 percent; Agents 40 percent. Back issues: $2.00; $45.00 for complete file. CCLM.

Place of Herons (see also WOOD IBIS), James Cody, 2404 Riverside Farms Rd., Austin, TX 78741. "The press is interested primarily in Texas and Southern writers within the framework outlined for WOOD IBIS MAGAZINE. This does not mean that we would not like to see mss. from other areas." 1974. 5½ x 8½. of. Payment varies. Copyrights for author. Discounts: 40 percent for bookstores; varies with others. Pub'd 2 titles 1976; expects 6 titles 1977, 3-4 titles 1978.

THE PLANET QUARTERLY, The Pilot School Co-operative, Heather A. Ryan, Justin Doebele, Alexander Ingle, Jamie Askins, Mark Camirand, Sarah Hart, Oabe Jackson, Jan Koso, Carla Michelini, c/o Heather A. Ryan, 2 Bancroft Street, Cambridge, MA 02139, 617-864-9341. Poetry, fiction, art, cartoons, long-poems. "High school age editors, contributors, publishers only. Teachers, and other adults can send work of their students, friends (13-19). Magazine comes from a poetry workshop at the pilot school, an alternative high school in Cambridge. Recent contributors for no. 1 are members of the co-op; no. 2 accept outside submissions. Want to exchange info and copies with other high school magazines." 4/yr; 1-yr sub price: $2.00; per copy: $.25 (to students) $.50 other; sample: $.50. 1976. 44pp; 1/2 a legal page. of. circ. 150. Reporting time: 3 mos. max. Payment: 2 copies. Ads: $20.00/$10.00/$.20. Discounts: 10 copies for $4.00 to classes. Back issues: $.50 each. Pub'd 3 issues 1976; expects 4 issues 1977, 4 issues 1978. §Work by very young (13-19) writers, or about workshops in high schools, publishing efforts of younger people.

PLANTAGENET PRODUCTION, Recording Library of the Spoken Word, Plantagenet Productions, Dorothy Rose Gribble, Westridge, Highclere, Nr. Newbury, Royal Berkshire RG159PJ, United Kingdom. "Recordings of poetry, philosophy, narrative and light work on cassette, tape, lp. Special orders undertaken. New tape/cassette issues; by special permission. Twentieth century writings: Elizabeth Jennings, Douglas Fraser." erratic; price per copy: lp-£2.25, £2, £1 cassette tape £2.25, £1.75 postage extra. 1964. Pub'd 1 issue 1976; expects 1 issue 1977, 3 issues 1978.

PLATFORM, Green Horse Press, Andrew Cozens, Jim Cozens, Duncan Tweedale, c/o 28 The Crescent, Andover, Hampshire, United Kingdom. Poetry, fiction, articles, art, reviews, letters, long-poems. "PLATFORM is a magazine of reviews and poetry edited with a concern for current taste and critical standards. Recent contributors are from world-wide sources. All genuine letters and enquiries receive personal attention." 2-3/yr; sub price: 75p/4 issues; per copy: 20p; sample: postage. 1971. 50pp; 8 x 5. lo. circ. 500. Reporting time: varies but immediate acokowledgement. Payment: none as yet. Ads: All by arrangement. Discounts: by arrangement. Back issues: free for postage.

Platform Poets Geoff Tomlinson, College Of Education, Middleton St. George, Co. Durham, England, Dinsdale 2760. Poetry. avg. price, paper: 35p. 1974. 40pp; 8 x 10. of/lp. avg. press run 400. Reporting time: 2 weeks. Payment: by arrangement-small fee. Copyrights for author. Discounts: trade & educational 20 percent. Pub'd 4 titles 1976; expects 4 titles 1977.

Playwrights Co-op, Shirley Gibson, 8 York Street, 6th Floor, Toronto, Ontario M5J1R2, Cnada, 416-363-1581. Plays. "Are bound by our constitution to only publish the work of Canadian citizens or landed immigrants." avg. price, cloth: $3.00. 1972. 50pp; 8½ x 11. †mi/of. avg. press run 300. Reporting time: 2 months. Payment: $0.25 per copy. Copyrights for author. Discounts: 10-40 percent. Pub'd 12 titles 1976; expects 12 titles 1977. Association of Canadian Publishers & Literary Presses Group.

Pleasant Hill Press, Eugene H. Boudreau, 2600 Pleasant Hill Rd, Sebastopol, CA 95472. "My books are about the Sierra Madre in Mexico." of.

Pleasure Dome Press (Long Island Poetry Collective Inc.) (see also XANADU), George William Fisher, Charles Fishman, Coco Gordon, Beverly Lawn, 2441 Riverside Drive, Wantagh, NY 11793, 516-826-8724. Poetry. "We are primarily interested in Long Island poets who are willing to assist in design and production. Publications include poetry postcards, letterpress chapbook on handmade papers, full-length poetry collection in hard and soft-bound editions. We are not open to unsolicited mss. at this time, but welcome queries from regional poets, and suggestions for collaborative efforts. Recent Title: *Mortal Companions,* by Charles Fishman (96pp hard/soft eds, 1977)" avg. price, cloth: varies; paper: varies; other: varies. 1976. pp varies; 5½ x 8½. †lp/of. avg. press run varies according to project. not currently considering unsolicited material. Payment varies. Buy all rights. Discounts: 10 percent on orders of $20.00 or more (includes XANADU and Newsletter subs.). Pub'd 1 title 1976; expects 3 titles 1977. CCLM.

PLEXUS, Bay Area Women's Newspaper, A. Mac Mahon, C. Orr, K. D. F. Reynolds, J. Starita, N. Stockwell, B. Taber, A. Weinstock, M. Willcox, 2600 Dwight Way 209, Berkeley, CA 94704. Poetry, articles, art, photos, cartoons, interviews, satire, criticism, reviews, letters, collages. "New articles and reviews should be no longer than 500 words. Features can run from 1200 to 2500 words. Material of the feminist persuasion is sought, however, anything relevant to the lives of women struggling against sexism will be considered. Recent contributors have included Alta, June Arnold, Susan Griffin. Articles of specific interest to women are sought." 12/yr; 1-yr sub price: $5.00; per copy: $.35; sample: $.35. 1974. 16pp; 16 x 10. of. circ. 3,500. Reporting time: varies. Payment: none. Ads: $300.00/$175.00/$.50 a line. Back issues: $.50. Pub's reviews. §books by, for, and about women.

‡**PLOUGHMAN, Fragment Press,** PO Box R217, Royal Exchange, Sydney 2000, Australia.

PLOUGHSHARES, DeWitt Henry, Peter O'Malley, Box 529, Cambridge, MA 02139. Poetry, fiction, interviews, criticism, reviews, parts-of-novels, long-poems. "Maximum length for over 6,000 words. We're biased towards new writers, towards writers in the Boston and New England areas, towards 'rediscovery' of neglected writers of interest to same. Because of our revolving editorship, status of issues in progress & contrast of emphasis from issue to issue, we suggest inquiry prior to submission. Recent contributors: Elizabeth Bishop, George Starbuck, Lloyd Schwartz, Jane Shote, John McGahern, Hilma Wolitzer, Linda Pastan, James Richardson, R.D. Skillings, Russell Banks, Andrew Salkey, Fanny Howe, George Bojin, Norman Dubre, Pamela Stewart, Richard Hugo, Maura Stanton, Judith Leet, Michael Ryan, Cora Brooks, Jean Thompson." 3-4/yr; sub price: $8.00/4 issues; per copy: $3.50. 1971. 170pp; 8½ x 5½. of. circ. 3,000. Reporting time: 3 mos. Payment: $5/p prose ($50 max); $10/poem. Ads: $100.00 (non-profit); $175.00 (trade)/$60.00 (non-profit); $95.00 (trade). Discounts: 40% trade (5 copies or more); 10% agent. Back issues: Back issues: 1/1 o.p.; 1/2 $3; 1/3 $3.50; 1/4 $3.50; full set Vol 2 $10.00 or $2.50 each, except 2/4-$2.95; full set Vol 3 $8.00 or 3/1-$2.95, 3/2-$2.50, 3/3 & 4-$3.95. Pub'd 2 issues 1976; expects 4 issues 1977, 4 issues 1978. Pub's reviews: 6 in 1976. §quality poetry, fiction, criticism. CCLM, NESPA.

PMS/King Publishing, Dennis A. King, Norma L. King, 12625 Lido Way, Saratoga, CA 95070. Photos. avg. price, paper: $5.95. 1976. 200pp; 7 x 9. of. avg. press run 5,000. Copyrights for author. Discounts: SCOP: 20 percent, trade: 4-13 $4.00, 14-49 $3.60, 50-99 $3.20, 100-999 $3.00, 1,000-up $2.70, agent: 10 percent of wholesale price.

PNS (see PEOPLE'S NEWS SERVICE)

POCKET PAL, The Pocket Pal Press, Bruce Weigl, Editor; John Mahnke, Editor, 131 E. College Street, Oberlin, OH 44074, 216-774-5548. Poetry, fiction, articles, criticism, reviews, long-poems. "Any length poetry; short (3,500 wds) fiction; essays (*Poetics*). Bias toward *new* work. Also print translations (poetry & short fiction). Recent contributors include: Michael Ryan, Tom Lux, David Young, James Tate, Stuart Friebert, Charles Simic, Rilke, Eich, Russel Edson, James Wright & many young writers..." 3/yr; 1-yr sub price: $3.00; per copy: $1.25; sample: postage. 1975. 16pp; 15½ x 11. of. circ. 200 copies—National. Reporting time: 1 week—ten days. Payment: three copies. Copyrighted, reverts to author. Ads: $10. (or trade)/$5./none. Discounts: 40% to anyone who orders five or more copies. Pub'd 3 issues 1976; expects 3 issues 1977, 3 issues 1978. Pub's reviews. §poetry/short fiction. CCLM.

The Pocket Pal Press (see also POCKET PAL), Bruce Weigl, Editor; John Mahnke, Editor, 131 E. College Street, Oberlin, OH 44074, 216-774-5548. Poetry, long-poems. "Publish short (25 page maximum) chapbooks of poetry & poetry in translation. This year: Stuart Friebert, *Stories My Father Can Tell;* David Young, translator: *Magic Strings:* poems by Li Ho; Erica Pedretti, translated by Franz Wright: *Jarmila. Flies:* 10 prose poems by Erica Pedretti. *From Orphic Songs* by Dino Campana. Versions by Thomas Lux & *Turn,* poems by Jean Valentine. Bias toward new writers with a publishing record..." avg. price, paper: $1.50. 1975. 25pp; varies. of. avg. press run 200. Reporting time: 1 week—ten days. Payment: 20% of press run. Copyrights for author. Discounts: 40% to any order of five or more copies. Pub'd 1 title 1976; expects 2 titles 1977, 5 titles 1978. CCLM.

POCKET POETRY, Pocket Poetry Press, Richard Marsh, PO Box 70, Key West, FL 33040. Poetry, articles, reviews. "Reprint from Small Press Books & Little Mags. No original poems. Reviews, brief articles, commentary welcome. Pocket Poetry will cease publication with issue No. 12, tentatively scheduled for publication late 1977." 4/yr; sub price: $10.00 - 12 issues (No. 1-12) only.; per copy: $1.00; sample: $1.00. 1974. 56pp; 4¼ x 7. of. circ. 600. Reporting time: 1 wk or more. Payment: 2 copies. Ads: $25/$15/$.10. Discounts: 40 percent all retail outlets; 50 percent distributors. Back issues: $1.00. Pub'd 2 issues 1976; expects 3-4 issues 1977, 1 issue 1978. Pub's reviews: 13 in 1976. §poetry only. CCLM, NESPA.

POEM, Huntsville Literary Association, Robert L. Welker, PO Box 1247, West Station, Huntsville, AL 35807. Poetry. "Any length, any style, no biases except against pornography for the sake of pornography, propaganda for right, left, or center and biased for quality poetry. Recent contributors: T. Alan Broughton, Hannah Kahn, Larry Rubin, Charles Edward Eaton." 3/yr; 1-yr sub price: $5.00; per copy: $3.00; sample: $1.50. 70pp; 4½ x 7-1/3. lp. circ. 500. Reporting time: 30 days. Payment: copies. no advertisement. Back issues: $3.00. CCLM.

THE POEM COMPANY, Intermedia Press, Edwin Varney, Henry Rappaport, Box 3294, Vancouver, B. C. V6J 3X9, Canada. Poetry, art, long-poems, collages, concrete art. "The best traditional, avant garde, visual, concrete, dada and classical poetry. Poem. The whole spectrum. Haiku. No bias, no style requirement, any length. Must be good bordering on or actually great." 6/yr; 1-yr sub price: $10.00; per copy: $.50; sample: $.50. 1970. 16pp; 7 x 5¾. †of. circ. 500. Reporting time: 2 month. Payment: copies. Discounts: 20%. Expects 1 issue 1977. §poetry. COSMEP.

POEMCARDS, Realities, Richard A. Jr. Soos, P.O. Box 33512, San Diego, CA 92103, 714-280-8359. Poetry, art, satire. "Short poems only, or portion of long poem. 7 line maximum. Published Rexroth, Kinnell, Ferlinghetti, Bukowski" 52/yr; 1-yr sub price: $5.20; per copy: $0.15; sample: $0.25. 1977. 1pp, 1½ x 3. thermograph. circ. 400. Reporting time: 1-2 weeks. Payment: 20 copies & royalties. Buys all rights. Ads: $15.00. Discounts: 40 percent 10 or more copies. Back issues: $0.25. Expects 25 issues 1977, 52 issues 1978. CCLM.

‡**POESIA ARGENTINA,** 958-3 Cordoba, Argentina.

‡**POESIA DE VENEZUELA,** Apartado 1114, Caracas, Venezuela.

POESIE - U.S.A., Pierre Chanover, P O Box 811, Melville, NY 11746, 516-549-3438. Poetry, art, photos. "POESIE-U.S.A. is a quarterly magazine that encourages unpublished as well as published poets who have written poems in the French language." 4/yr; 1-yr sub price: $8.00; per copy: $2.00; sample: $1.00. 1976. 48pp; 5½ x 8½. of. circ. 500 (circa). Reporting time: four weeks. Payment: in copies. Copyrighted, does not revert to author. Ads: $75.00/$40.00/none. Back issues: $2.00 each. §French Poetry. CCLM, COSMEP.

‡**POESIE VIVANTE,** BP 1211, Geneve 16, Switzerland.

POET, Poet Press India, Dr. Krishna Srinivas, Dr. Mabelle A. Lyon, Edward L. Meyerson, Edwin A. Falkowski, 208 W. Latimer Ave., Campbell, CA 95008, 408-379-8555. Poetry, reviews. "40 line limit (poems only); free form, free verse (couplets thru ballads) in good taste; sase for fact sheet *before* submitting. Translations into English from 30 countries. N. Russell, O. Lysohorsky, R. Menon, M. Dei-Anang, H. McKinley, L. Pasternak-Slater, J. Negalha, L. Pennington, B. Cameron, A. Kastan." 12/yr; 1-yr sub price: $15.00; per copy: $1.25; sample: $1.25. 1960. 80pp; 5½ x 8½. lp. circ. 500. Reporting time: 30 days. Payment: none. Copyrighted, reverts to author. Ads: none. Discounts: none. Back issues: $1.25. Pub'd 13 issues 1976; expects 12 issues 1977, 13 issues 1978. Pub's reviews. World Congress of Poets.

POET & CRITIC, Iowa State University Press, Richard Gustafson, English Dept., ISU, 203 Ross Hall, Ames, IA 50010. Poetry, articles, art, cartoons, satire, criticism, reviews. "Contributors comment on each other's work." 3/yr; price per copy: $1.00; sample: free sample. 1964. 48pp; 6 x 9 lp. circ. 500-1M. Reporting time: up to 8 wks. Payment: copies only. CCLM, COSMEP.

Poet Gallery Press, Mike Pavlos, 224 West 29th St, New York, NY 10001. "A small press, founded originally to publish works of American writers living outside continental USA. Number of books published varies according to year-ECO conditions, etc. Have published a minimum of 2 titles per year since 1970 while have published (novels) fiction, drama, and poetry we have also published some experimental work." 1970. †mi/of/lp. Reporting time: 1 mo. Payment: depends. COSMEP.

‡**POET LORE,** Box 688, Westport, CT 06880.

Poet Papers, P.O. Box 528, Topanga, CA 90290. Poetry, art, photos, long-poems, collages. "Please: If sending materials for consideration enclose stamped self-addressed envelope! No SSAE-NO reply." 1970. 150pp; 7 x 10. of/lp/other. Reporting time: 6 mos-1 year. Payment: copies of book. Discounts: library-trade 20%.

Poet Press India (see also POET), Dr. Krishna Srinivas, Dr. Edwin A. Falkowski, 208 W. Latimer Ave., Campbell, CA 95008, 408-379-8555. Poetry, reviews, long-poems. "Pancontinental Premier Poets (Biennial Anthology of Poetry); Fifth, scheduled for the Fall-1978, 100 pgs. Ondra Lysohorsky, 'Karel Klimsa and Other Poems', foreword by Christopher Fry. Krishna Srinivas, 'Dance of Dust'. 'Poems of Lydia Pasternak Slater and William E. Morris'. 'Great American World Poets, an Assessment', by Dr. Krishna Srinivas, 124 pgs., $6.00. In preparation, a series of a 'Trilogies of Poets'; two issues released featuring, Wallace H. Fuller, Mabelle A. Lyon and Hugh McKinley, and Jeno Platthy, Edward L. Meyerson and Alfarata Hansel. 60 pgs. $1.25. 'Indian Verse in English', an anthology of 39 Hindu poets, Edited by Syed Ar,an ddin." avg. price, paper: $1.25, up to $6.00 (over 100 pp.). 1960. 96pp; 5½ x 8½. lp. avg. press run 500. Reporting time: 30 to 90 days. Payment: open. Copyright open (first rights). Discounts: under 100 pages-$1.25, 3-$3.25, 5-$5.00. over 100 pages-$6.00, 2-$10.00, 5-$20.00. Pub'd 3 titles 1976; expects 2 titles 1977, 3 titles 1978. World Congress of Poets.

THE POETIC HARDWARE PRESS, James C. Jurado, 1815 Riverside Drive 4k, New York, NY 10034, 212-942-4692. Poetry. "Poetry (period.) Prefer ingenious pyrotechnical use of metaphor, emphasizing imagery as 'speech acts' in human situations. Conversation in poetry should sculpt the emotions in the synapse of quotation. Distraction, illiteracy, amnesia, failure—all these should underly words." 1-2/yr; price per copy: $1.50. 1975. 32pp; 5½ x 8½. of. circ. 100-150 (Limited editions). Reporting time: 1-3 months. Payment: copies only (2). Copyrighted, reverts to author. Discounts: none. Back issues: Price upon request.

POETIPS, J. Mark Press, Barbara Fischer, Box 2057, N. Babylon, NY 11703. Articles. "Advice or inspiration for poets. Short, tight writing is a must. 100 to 500 word limit. Our poets are concerned with distributing their books, giving readings, and writing well. POETIPS is sent free of charge with all our manuscript replies, and to all poets who send reply envelopes requesting our guidelines." 4/yr; price per copy: $.25; sample: SASE. 1974. 8pp; 8½ x 5½. †of. circ. 15,000. Reporting time: 2-4 weeks. Payment: copy. Ads: $.20. Pub's reviews. §poetry.

POETRY, Daryl Hine, 1228 N. Dearborn Parkway, Chicago, IL 60610. Poetry, reviews. 12/yr; 1-yr sub price: $18.00; per copy: $1.75 plus post. 1912. 64pp; 5 x 9. of. circ. 10,000. Reporting time: 6 weeks. Payment: $10-page prose/$1-line verse. Back issues: $2 plus 25¢ post. CCLM.

POETRY &, Joann Castagna, P O Box A3298, Chicago, IL 60690. Poetry, fiction, articles, art, photos, cartoons, interviews, satire, criticism, reviews, letters, news items, non-fiction. "Contributors to the first volume included: Mary Lane, John Yau, Mercy Bona, Jessie Ellison, Dan Campion, Elizabeth Eddy, Ruth Moon Kempher, etc. Special thanks to DC, JBM and Michael Brown. Artwork by Sara Counts and Tim Sarro. We also publish postcards. We will continue to be the least expensive." Bimonthly 6/yr & broadsides & postcards. 12; 1-yr sub price: $5.00; per copy: $0.50; sample: $0.50. 1976. 8pp; 11½ x 17. of. circ. 300 - 500. Reporting time: 1 month. Payment: copies. Copyrighted. Ads: $15.00/$0.05. Discounts: 60/40 bookstores. Back issues: $10.00 for Volume I. Pub'd 11 issues 1976; expects 6 issues 1977, 6 issues 1978. Pub's reviews: 24 in 1976. §Only from Illinois writers/presses. COSMEP.

POETRY AUSTRALIA, South Head Press, Grace Perry, 350 Lyons Rd., Five Dock, N.S.W. 2046, Australia. Poetry. 4/yr; 1-yr sub price: $10.00 (Aust)-$12.00 O/S; per copy: $2.50; sample: $1.00. 1964. 80pp. circ. 1,600. Payment: $8-per page. Pub's reviews. §poetry & prose.

POETRY CUMBRIA, Cumbria Poetry Centre, Selected for each issue, Charlotte Mason College, Rydal Rd., Ambleside, Cumbria, United Kingdom. Poetry, reviews. "None" 3/yr; 1-yr sub price: £1; per copy: £0.35 to £0.60. 1975. 48pp; A5. of. circ. 500. Reporting time: Maximun of six months. Payment: None. Copyrighted. Ads: Not used. Discounts: 33-1/3 percent. Back issues: Subject to negotiation. Pub'd 3 issues 1976; expects 3-4 issues 1977, 3-4 issues 1978. Pub's reviews. §Poetry, short stories, prose poems.

Poetry Eastwest (see also CREATIVE MOMENT), S. Amanuddin, Box 391, Sumter, SC 29150. Poetry, interviews, criticism. avg. price, cloth: $5.00; paper: $3.00. 1967. 60 - 80pp of. avg. press run 500 - 1,000. We are not soliciting mss now. Payment: copies only. Copyrights for author. CCLM, COSMEP.

POETRY FLASH, John Ford, Editor-in-Chief; Alan Soldofsky, Contributing Editor; Jana Harris, Contributing Editor; Joseph Flower, Publisher; Harold Lutsky, Publisher; Tim Jacobs, Calendar Editor, 144 Hugo, San Francisco, CA 94122, 415-731-9084. Art, interviews, criticism, reviews, satire, news items. "POETRY FLASH is the monthly review of Bay Area poetry events. We use calendar items, information interesting or useful to poets (places to publish, prizes, workshops, etc.) and reviews of books and readings." 12/yr; 1-yr sub price: $4.00; sample: $1.00. 1972. 6pp; 8½ x 11. of. circ. 3,000. Reporting time: one month. Payment: none. Copyrighted, reverts to author. Ads: $70.00/$35.00/$5.00 Column inch. Back issues: $1 plus postage. Pub'd 12 issues 1976; expects 12 issues 1977, 12 issues 1978. Pub's reviews: 78 in 1976. §poetry/exploratory fiction/incisive thought. CCLM, COSMEP, BAPC.

POETRY IN MOTION, Nobodaddy Press, David Lehman, Stefanie Green, 20 College Hill Rd., Clinton, NY 13323, 315-853-6946. Poetry, long-poems. "We may decide to expand operations and consider works of criticism and fine arts. We are committed to the development of new and unusual forms of publication, i.e. Broadsheets, poem post-cards, poem greeting cards, etc." 1976. †of/lp. circ. 500. Reporting time: It varies. Copyrighted, reverts to author. Discounts: The usual 40 percent off for bookstores, etc. §Poetry and the arts. CCLM.

POETRY INFORMATION, Peter Hodgkiss, c/o 18 Clairview Road, London SW16, United Kingdom. Articles, reviews, interviews, criticism, news items. "Articles on current developments in poetry/poetics in UK & USA. Extensive listings & short reviews of small press material-international. Increasing amount of articles/information on experimental writing." 2/yr; sub price: $8.00-4 issues/£3.00-4 issues; per copy: 75p ea/$2.00; sample: postage. 1970. 100-120pp; A4. of. circ. 1,200. Copyrighted. Discounts: 33-1/3 percent all bookshop orders. Back issues: 50p/$2.00 Nos. 4,6; 50p Nos. 12/3 (remainder o/p) 60p-Nos. 14,15,16. Pub'd 2 issues 1976; expects 2 issues 1977, 2 issues 1978. Pub's reviews: 60 in 1976. §Poetry/exp. writing, etc. COSMEP.

THE POETRY MAILING LIST, The Poetry Mailing List, Stephen Paul Miller, Kenneth Deifik, 77 Franklin St., New York, NY 10013, 212-442-8432. Poetry, fiction, articles, art, cartoons, interviews, satire, criticism, reviews, music, long-poems, collages, plays, concrete art. "William Burroughs, John Cage, Kenward Elmslie, David Shapiro, Jackson Mac Low, Ann Lauterbach, David Lehman, Joseph Ceravalo, Dick Higgins, Joel Oppenheimer,. *The PML* mails a poem or a small bunch of related poetry weekly." 500/yr; 1-yr sub price: $20.00; per copy: $5.00; sample: free. 1975. 8 x 11. †of/ektagraph. circ. 350. Reporting time: 1 month. Payment: pending on grants. Copyrighted, reverts to author. Discounts: 35 percent for any number of subscriptions to same address. Pub's reviews. §poetry. CCLM.

THE POETRY MISCELLANY, Kurt Heinzelman, Richard Jackson, Michael Panori, P.O. Box 175, Williamstown, MA 01267, 413-458-3214. Poetry, criticism, reviews, long-poems. "David Wagoner, Denise Levertov, Maxine Kumin, William Meredith, Laurence Raab, Cynthia Mac-Donald, Robert Pack, James Martin, John Peck, Anthony Hecht, Diane Wakoski, Herbert Morris,

Barbara Howes, Donald Finkel, Dabney Stuart." 1/yr; 1-yr sub price: $2.00; per copy: $2.00. 1971. 80-90pp; 6 x 9. of. circ. 500. Reporting time: 3-4 weeks. Payment: copies. Copyrighted, copyright reverts to author upon request, as for re-publication. Ads: $50. Back issues: Same price as current issues. Pub'd 1 issue 1976; expects 1 issue 1977, 1 issue 1978. Pub's reviews: 7 in 1976. §poetry. CCLM.

POETRY NATION REVIEW, Donald Davie, C.H. Sisson, Michael Schmidt, Department of English, University of Manchester, Manchester M13 9PL, United Kingdom. Articles, poetry, fiction, art, reviews, interviews, criticism, letters, long-poems. 4/yr; 1-yr sub price: £4.90 ($12.00); per copy: £1.25; sample: £1.25. 1973. 65pp; A4. of. circ. 1,800. Back issues: I-VI £12.00 (Casebound 750pp). Pub'd 4 issues 1976; expects 4 issues 1977, 4 issues 1978. Pub's reviews: 30 in 1976. §Poetry and related.

POETRY NEWSLETTER, Richard O'connell, Dept. of English, Temple University, Philadelphia, PA 19122. Poetry, interviews, long-poems, plays. "Poetry newsletter is now a quarterly. Recent contributors: Charles Angoff, Geoffrey Cook, Josephine Jacobsen, Anthony L. Johnson, D. S. Long, William Oxley, Edward Pitcairn, Kenneth Rexroth. The poetry is the news." 4/yr; 1-yr sub price: $3.00; per copy: $1.00; sample: $1.00. 1971. 30-40pp; 8½ x 10. of. circ. 500-1M. Reporting time: 3-4 months. Payment: copies. no ads. Back issues: #1-#36 back issues available at $.50 ea. CCLM.

POETRY NIPPON, The Poetry Nippon Press, Atsuo Nakagawa, 11-2, 5-chome, Nagaike-cho, Showa-ku, Nagoya 466, Japan. Poetry, articles, interviews, criticism, reviews, letters, news items, photos. "Poetry book reviews, poetics, translations of Japanese poems, poems on topical themes or Japan, Tanka, Haiku, one-line poems are solicited from non-members. Guest poems are also printed. Recent contributors: James Kirkup, C. L. Riley, Stephen Tosker, Cyril Patterson." 4/yr; 1-yr sub price: $7.00 (plus $3.00 abroad); per copy: $2.50 (plus $3.00 abroad); sample: 3 ircs. 1967. 40pp; A5. of. circ. 500. Reporting time: 1 year. Payment: Depends on ms. Mss. in all our publications are reserved. Ads: $40/$20. Discounts: 10% for libraries/40% for bulk order. Back issues: $2.00 for single number, $4.00 for double number. Pub's reviews: 4 in 1976. §poetry books and magazines.

‡**POETRY NORTHWEST,** Parrington Hall, Univ. Of Washington, Seattle, WA 98195. CCLM.

POETRY NOW, E.V. Griffith, 3118 K Street, Eureka, CA 95501. Poetry. "POETRY NOW appears in tabloid newspaper format and seeks to publish the best work available to us in all moulds. One 'poet profile' per issue, based on interview with a major contemporary poet. Photos of poets included throughout issue. Book 'reviews' are via sample—a few poems from the book being 'reviewed:-quoted in full without critical comment, just publisher's name, address and price of book. Special features include a 3-page spread in each issue of reprints from other little magazines. Contributors include William Stafford, John Haines, David Ignatow, Michael McClure, Russell Edson, Peter Viereck, Edward Field, Richard Eberhart, Ann Stanford, Mona Van Duyn, Karl Shapiro, Vassar Miller, Maxine Kumin, Edwin Honig, Gary Soto." 6/yr; 1-yr sub price: $5.00; per copy: $1.25; sample: free for $.39 postage. 1973. 48pp; 11½ x 15. of. circ. 2,500 plus. Reporting time: 2 days to 2 wks. Payment: copies only, with three annual cash awards ($250-$100-$50). Copyrighted, reverts to author. Ads: $150/$85/none. Discounts: classroom adoption: 85 cents per copy, with minimum order of 10 copies sent to single address. Back issues: Issues 1 through 14 available at $1.25 each while stock lasts. Pub's reviews: 60 in 1976. §poetry only. CCLM, COSMEP.

POETRY/PEOPLE, R. V. K. Publishing Co., S. P. Stavrakis, PO Box 264 du, Menomonee Falls, WI 53051. Poetry, fiction, art, photos, cartoons, satire, parts-of-novels, concrete art. "Wide spectrum of poetry published. Prefer fantasy, erotic, s.f., experimental types. A response to the current trend on the part of small publishers to stick with elitist, cliqueish attitudes and narrow editorial margins in their publications. Poetry is a people's art, and no one should be excluded because his style doesn't match the editor's or his name isn't well known. Submit with two stamps, no envelope. Short poems-2-30 lines. Looking particularly for photos suitable for offset and short-shorts in addition to all poetry." 2/yr; 1-yr sub price: $18/yr (all publications); per copy: $6.50; sample: $5.00. 1972. 100pp; 5½ x 8½. of. circ. 1M-2M. Reporting time: 2 mos. Ads: $50/$25/free if we like it. Back issues: $5 postpaid. COSMEP.

POETRY QUARTERLY (previously CURLEW), The Curlew Press, Jocelyne Precious, Harecott, Kettlesing, Harrogate, Yorkshire, United Kingdom. Articles, poetry, fiction, art, cartoons, photos, satire, reviews, news items, interviews, criticism, letters, long-poems, plays, concrete art, collages. 4/yr; 1-yr sub price: £5.00 sub includes additional publications; per copy: 50P when available; sample: Free when available. 1975. Varies. up to 100pp; 5 x 8 and 8 x 14. of. circ. Variable. Reporting time: By return of post when possible. Payment: none. Copyrighted, reverts to author. Ads: £10.00/£5.00/10 words £1.00; 20 words £2.00, etc. Back issues: Some available on request. Pub'd 4 issues 1976; expects 4 issues 1977, 4 issues 1978. Pub's reviews: 11 in 1976. §Poetry, literature.

POETRY REVIEW, The Poetry Society, Edwin Brock, Harry Chambers, Douglas Dunn, Roger Garfitt, 21 Earls Court Square, London SW5, United Kingdom, 01-373-7861. Poetry, long-poems, reviews, concrete art. 4/yr; 1-yr sub price: $6.00 w-membership; per copy: $1.50. 1912. 60pp; A5. of. circ. 2,900. Reporting time: 2 mos. Payment: £15 per poet. Ads: £25.00/£13.00/¼ page £7.00. Discounts:401/3 to trade. Back issues: Same as cover price. Expects 4 issues 1977, 4 issues 1978. Pub's reviews: none in 1976. §Poetry, criticism, etc.

The Poetry Society of Australia (see NEW POETRY)

POETRY SURVEY, Poets Yearbook Ltd., S. T. Gardiner, 1 Herbert Rd., London N112QN, United Kingdom. Poetry, articles, reviews, non-fiction. " *POETRY SURVEY* is primarily an updating supplement to the Poets Yearbook but all overseas publications received are listed or reviewed." price per copy: 4 issues $7.00 (£3.65). 1977. 40pp; a4 (8 x 11¾). litho. circ. 1,000. Reporting time: 1 month. Payment: by arrangement. Copyright reserved for authors. Discounts: none. Expects 4 issues 1977, 4 issues 1978.

POETRY TEXAS, Poetry Texas Press, Paul Shuttleworth, Division of Humanities, College of the Mainland, Texas City, TX 77590. Poetry. "We will publish the best poetry available. We will especially encourage poets from Texas or poets living in Texas. Our chapbook series will be, at the start, limited to writers from Texas or living in Texas." 2/yr; 1-yr sub price: $2.00; per copy: $1.00; sample: $1.00. 1976. 60pp; 8 x 7. †of. circ. 600. Reporting time: a month. Payment: 2 copies. no ads. Discounts: 40% on 10 or more. §we will run a list of books & magazines we admire.

POETRY TORONTO NEWSLETTER, Darina Smerek McFadyen, Vaughn Thurman, George Miller, 224 St. George St. Apt 709, Toronto, Ontario M5R2N9, Canada. Poetry, articles, reviews. "Interested in reviews and especially previews of any live poetry events." 12/yr; 1-yr sub price: $3.00; $4.00 institutions; per copy: $.25; sample: free. 1975. 12pp; 8½ x 5½. circ. 500. Reporting time: 2 weeks. Payment: copies only. Pub'd 12 issues 1976; expects 12 issues 1977, 12 issues 1978. COSMEP.

POETRY VENTURE, Valkyrie Press, Inc., Marjorie Schuck, 2135 1st Ave. South, St. Petersburg, FL 33712. Poetry, interviews, criticism, reviews, letters, long-poems. "POETRY VENTURE solicits poetry with intelligible content; form, either organic or traditional; diction that is fresh without depending upon slang or the remnants of Anglo-Saxon for verve. An American or foreign poet's work is usually featured in each issue in both the original and the English translation. Longpoems considered but length of poetry preferred-not over 112 lines. Contributors: Gigi Lord, Lyn Lifshin, Caryl Poeter, Joan White, Emilie Glen, Joan Colby, Fred Wolven, Lee Pennignton, Mary Balazs, Guy Beining, etc." 2/yr; 1-yr sub price: $3; per copy: $1.50; sample: $1.25. 1968. 64-72pp; 6 x 8¾. †of. circ. 1,500. Reporting time: 2-8 mos. Payment: copies + 1 yr sub. Copyright in publisher's name, reprint permission granted on written request. no ads. Discounts: 40%. Back issues: $1.25/copy Free to libraries. Expects 2 issues 1977, 3 issues 1978. CCLM, COSMEP, COSMEP-SOUTH.

POETRY VIEW, Post-Crescent, Dorothy Dalton, 1125 Valley Rd., Menasha, WI 54952. Poetry. "Serious poetry to 24 lines-light verse 4-8 lines. Free verse preferred, fresh use of language-no religious, no overly sentimental. Enclose SASE with submissions, and queries. A tearsheet is sent to out-of-town contributors." 52/yr. 1970.401/2p tabloid. circ. 50M. Reporting time: 2-3 mos.

Payment: $3 poem, month following publication. Not copyrighted. Pub'd 52 issues 1976; expects 52 issues 1977, 52 issues 1978.

POETRY WALES, Christopher Davies Publishers Limited, J.P. Ward, 4/5 Thomas Row, Swansea SA1 1NJ, United Kingdom. Articles, poetry, reviews, criticism, letters, long-poems. "Articles of not less than 2,000 words. All types of poetry considered. Originally biased towards Welsh, Anglo-Welsh poetry, or poetry by persons living in Wales. Now wider approach encompassing all British writers and translations of foreign poets and critiques of same." 4/yr; 1-yr sub price: £3.00; per copy: 75p. 1965. 130pp; 5½ x 8½. of. circ. 1,000. Reporting time: 3-4 wks. Payment: by arrangement. Ads: £25/£15/£8 1/4. Discounts: trade. Back issues: 40.

POETRY-WINDSOR-POESIE, Alexandre L. Amprimoz, William A. Schiller, Box 6 Sandwich P.O., Windsor, Ontario N9C3Z1, Canada. Poetry, fiction, interviews, long-poems. "Tom Marshall, Fred Cogsworth, Rina Lasnier, Cecile Cloutier, etc—-English and French poetry. Occasionally short fiction pieces." 3/yr; 1-yr sub price: $2.50; per copy: $1.00; sample: $1.00. 1974. 30pp; 4½ x 11. of. circ. 300. Reporting time: 2 weeks. Payment: 2 copies. Ads: $40/$20/$.05. Discounts: 20% on 10 copies. Back issues: $6 for volume I. COSMEP.

Poets & Writers, Inc. (see also **CODA: POETS & WRITERS NEWSLETTER**), 201 West 54th Street, New York, NY 10019, 212-757-1766. 1972.

Poets & Writers of New Jersey, 2514 Tack Circle, Scotch Plains, NJ 07076. "P&WNJ is a service organization for writers interested in NJ, and for organizations interested in the services of writers. Established in 1974, P&WNJ publishes a Directory of Members (50¢), giving full professional biographies and interests, and an occasional newsletter for members (sample free for s.a.s.e.). An anthology of members' writing is scheduled for publications within the year. Writers with an interest in NJ, and persons interested in programs of/about NJ writing or workshops are invited to make inquiry at the address above."

POETS' LEAGUE of GREATER CLEVELAND NEWSLETTER, League Books, PO Box 6055, Cleveland, OH 44101. "The newsletter runs reviews of local readings and poetry books, articles on poetry in general, articles on the Cleveland poetry scene, a calendar of poetry events, a poem or two per issue, and whatever else seems germane. Query. League Books is a distributor currently of four poetry titles: *Emergency Exit,* Cyril A. Dostal; title, Christopher Franke; *Big Mama,* Linda Monacelli*Editor, Barbara Angell, Mary Ann Cronin, Meredith Holmes, Sally Pirtle, Marguerite Beck Rex; & *Alone, But Not Lonely,* Elaine Ede Hornsby." 1975. COSMEP.

POETS ON:, Ruth Daigon, Virginia Brady Young, Box 255, Chaplin, CT 06235, 203-455-9671. Poetry. "*Poets On:* explores basic human concerns through crafted poetry our first issue dealt with *Turning Points.* Each subsequent issue will have a basic theme-*Roots, Loving* etc. some of our contributors are William Stafford, Marge Piercy, John Tagliabue, Richard Eberhart, Philip Booth etc." 2/yr; 1-yr sub price: $5.00; per copy: $2.50. 1976. 48pp; 5½ x 8½. lp. circ. 400. Reporting time: up to a month. Payment: 2 copies. Copyrighted, reverts to author. Back issues: $2.00. Pub'd 1 issue 1976; expects 2 issues 1977, 2 issues 1978. COSMEP.

POETS YEARBOOK, Poets Yearbook Ltd., Poetry Survey, S.T. Gardiner, 1 Herbert Rd., London N11 2QN, United Kingdom. News items, non-fiction. 1/yr; price per copy: $5.00 (£2.45) post free. 1975. 204pp; a5 (5¾ x 8¼). litho. circ. 3,100. Ads: $80.00 (£45)/$45.00 (£23). Discounts:401/3 but no discounts on single copies. Back issues: $5.00 (£2.45) post free. Pub'd 1 issue 1976; expects 1 issue 1977, 1 issue 1978.

Pogo Press, George Backler, A. S. Sebastian, PO Box 283 Stn. E., Montreal, Quebec H2T 3A8, Canada.

Point Blanc Press (see also GRAYDAY MAGAZINE). Pub'd 3 titles 1976; expects 2 titles 1977.

POINT OF CONTACT/PUNTO DE CONTACTO, Pedro Cuperman, 110 Bleecker St. 16B, New

York City, NY 10012, 212-260-6346. Poetry, art, photos, interviews, criticism, reviews. "Recent contributors: S.W. Snodgrass, Jean Franco, Eldridge Cleaver, Pedro Cuperman, Michel Beaujour, David Wevill, Christopher Middleton, Carlos Blanco Aguinaga, Raymond Panikkar, Noe Jitrik, Saul Yurkievich." Quarterly; 1-yr sub price: Institutional $14.00; Individual $12.00; per copy: $3.50; sample: $3.50. 1975. 100pp; 8 x 10. of. circ. 1,500. Payment: None. Copyrighted, does not revert to author. Ads: $200.00/$110.00. Back issues: $3.50. Expects 4 issues 1977. Pub's reviews. §Literature, criticism, political theory.

‡**Point Riders Press,** Michael Dirham, PO Box 2731, Norman, OK 73069.

POINTS OF AWARENESS, Christopher Derrett, Lincoln College, Oxford, United Kingdom. "By invitation, Steve Sneyd, Andy Darlington, & Merritt Clifton. Otherwise, 'I'm still waiting for material really worth printing or circulating; people like to throw off any old thing of theirs to get it into print and get known, when what i want to see is material that has been slaved over or polished internally. Poetry in particular.'" occasional. 1975. Payment: copies only.

Poltroon Press, Alastair Johnston, Frances Butler, 2315 Carleton Street, Berkeley, CA 94704. Poetry, fiction, art, photos, interviews, satire, criticism, letters, parts-of-novels, long-poems, collages, concrete art. "Tom Clark, Thomas Love Peacock, Tom Raworth. No bias towards first names of Tom or Tomassina but trend is developing." avg. price, cloth: $15.00; paper: $4.00. 1975. 32pp; 8 x 10. †of/lp. avg. press run 150. Reporting time: Immediately return all unsolicited mss. Payment varies (often 25 percent of net sales). Copyrights for author. Discounts: 40 percent on 5 or more, etc.

The Pomegranate Press, Jeffrey Katz, PO Box 181, N. Cambridge, MA 02140. Poetry, fiction. "Poetry & experimental fiction-Joyce Carol Oates, Adrienne Rich, James Merrill. New translation of Rimbaud w/illustrations by Jime Dine & Sigmund Abeles." Discounts: trade. COSMEP.

‡**POOR FARM, Starvation Studios,** 103 Myrtle St., Methuen, MA 01844.

PORCH, Porch Publications, James V. Cervantes, 1019 E. Pike, Seattle, WA 98122, 206-325-5614. Poetry, art, interviews, reviews, letters, long-poems. "*PORCH'S* form and content will vary according to 1) what we receive 2) what guest editors wish to do with their particular issue 3) who the editor, or guest editor, wishes to invite to submit. Thus, we will appear as invitational issue, selection from unsolicited manuscripts, or chapbook, at least 4 times a year as these assemble. Project announced in each issue." 4/yr; 1-yr sub price: $7.00; per copy: $2.00; sample: $1.50. 1977. 50-60pp; 5½ x 8½. of. circ. 300 copies 1st issue. Reporting time: 1-3 weeks. Payment: 2 copies at present; hope to pay cash (however little) in the future. Copyrighted, reverts to author. Ads: $50.00/$25.00. Discounts: libraries, 20 percent; all others per usual contract. Pub's reviews. §poetry.

Porphyrion Press, Coral Crosman, 4053 Middle Grove Road, Middle Grove, NY 12850, 518-587-9809. Poetry, fiction, art, photos. avg. price, paper: $3.50. 1974. 58pp; 5½ x 8½. of. avg. press run LTD. 100-300, so far. not currently considering material. Copyrights for author. Discounts: standard 40 percent etc. COSMEP.

PORT TOWNSEND JOURNAL, Woolman Press, Deborah Robson, 933 Tyler St, Port Townsend, WA 98368. Poetry, fiction, articles, satire, music, parts-of-novels, long-poems. "Mostly fiction. Some poetry. We like essays (not the kind you wrote in school, unless it was a terrific school). Willing to devote whole issues to something special: not necessarily fiction. No xerox unless very clean and not submitted elsewhere (include a note)." 1/yr; sub price: $6.00/2-3 issues sub.; sample: $1.00 or 9 x 12 SASE. 1973. 75-125pp; 8½ x 11. †mi/of/lp/silkscreen. circ. 200. Reporting time: 1 week- 3 mos. Payment: copies. no ads.

‡**Porter Sargent Publisher,** 11 Beacon St., Boston, MA 02108.

PORTLAND REVIEW, Art Homer, P.O. Box 751, Portland, OR 97207. Poetry, fiction, articles, art, interviews, satire, criticism, reviews, long-poems. "We're looking for new writers with a fresh approach and control over style & technique. Students are encouraged to submit. Recent contributors include Walt Curtis, Ann Darr, Kenneth Hanson, Gwen Head, Christopher Howell, Ken Kesey, Glenna Luschei, Morton Marcus, Anthony Ostroff, W.M. Ransom, and many fine writers nobody's ever heard of." 1/yr; 1-yr sub price: $3.00; per copy: $3.00; sample: $1.50. 1953. 160pp; 6 x 9. of. circ. 1M. Reporting time: 3-6 mos. Payment: copies only. Discounts: 60% to distributors. Back issues: $1.50. CCLM.

Portola Institute (see BRIARPATCH REVIEW)

Post-Crescent (see POETRY VIEW)

POSTCARD ART/POSTCARD FICTION, Martha Rosler, Martha Rosler, RFD 168 Z, Del Mar, CA 92014. Fiction, art, photos. "I do all the writing myself. I chose mail as a means of dissemination because of its directness and because i wanted to raise questions about 'personal' and 'first-personal' communications, fiction, and autobiography. All my work is meant to relate the private, often female sphere to the public, often male, sphere. Current work focuses on food production and consumption." 2/yr; price per copy: $1.50; sample: $1.50. 1974. 12pp; postcard. †mi/of. circ. 350. §arts, film/video, photography.

Potomac Asia Communications (see ASIA MAIL)

‡**Powder House Press,** Richard W. Edelman, 86 Powder House Blvd., Somerville, MA 02144.

Prairie Books, Otto Wood, 501 Park Blvd, Austin, TX 78751, 512-454-6133. Articles, art, photos, plays. "Recent contributors: Nasa, Leon Box, Henri Rousseau." avg. price, paper: $4.00. 1974. 32-128pp; varies. of. avg. press run 750. Reporting time: 6 months. Payment: percent press run plus fame & immortality. Copyrights for author. Discounts: 40 percent on all orders 5 copies or more. Terms: 6 weeks. Pub'd 1 title 1976.

Prairie Poet Press (see AMERICAN POET)

Prairie Publishing Company, Ralph E. Watkins, 65 Carberry Crescent, Winnipeg R2Y 0K3, Canada, 204-832-2818. "We are in the market for book length material dealing with the growth, discovery, and development of Western Canada. Historical material dealing with Manitoba." avg. price, paper: $5.00. 1969. 165pp. avg. press run 2,000 copies. Reporting time: 6 to 8 weeks. Payment: 10 percent. Copyrights for author. Discounts: 40 percent bookstores, 20 percent libraries & schools. Pub'd 1 title 1976; expects 2 titles 1977.

PRAIRIE SCHOONER, Bernice Slote, 201 Andrews Hall, Univ. of Nebr., Lincoln, NB 68588. Poetry, fiction, articles, criticism. 4/yr; 1-yr sub price: $6.00; per copy: $1.75; sample: $.50. 1927. 96pp; 6½ x 10. circ. 1,500. Reporting time: 1-2 months. Payment: copies of magazine, tearsheets, and prizes. Ads: $50/$35. Pub's reviews. §literature/general culture. CCLM, COSMEP.

PRAXIS: A Journal of Radical Perspectives on the Arts, Praxis, Ronald Reimers, Nico Mayo, Gregg Gorton, P.O. Box 207, Goleta, CA 93017. Poetry, articles, art, photos, cartoons, interviews, criticism, reviews. "Publish essays on aesthetics, art and literary criticism, and wide-ranging articles on social radicalism in the arts. Recent articles have included 'The Images Of Power In American Policital Cartoons,' 'Lunacharsky: The Paradoxes Of Art And Revolution,' 'The Role Of Filmmakers In Revolutionary Social Change,' 'Lucien Goldmann And The Sociology Of Culture,' 'Preliminary Notes On The Prison Writings Of Gramsci: The Place Of Literature In Marxian Theory,' 'Brecht And The Dynamics Of Production,' 'Salvation And Wisdom Of The Common Man: The Theology Of The Reader's Digest' and 'Painting And Ideology: Picasso And Guernica'." 2/yr; 1-yr sub price: $7.00; per copy: $3.50; sample: $3.50. 1975. 200pp; 9¼ x 5½. of. circ. 1,750. Reporting time: 6 weeks. Payment: copies. Ads: $50.00. Discounts: 33-1/3%. Back issues: $3.75. Pub'd 1 issue 1976; expects 2 issues 1977, 2 issues 1978. Pub's reviews. COSMEP.

The Pray Curser Press, Erwin R. Bergdoll, c/oErwin R. Bergdoll, Elm Bank, Dutton, VA 23050,

804-693-2823. "An irregular private press involved in graphic arts and lucid letters to produce prints, illustrated broadsides, brochures, portfolios and booklets, mostly in limited, numbered, signed editions. Emphasis is cheerfully on quality (de spiritus et materia), in a world which is, to use J. R. Oppenheimer's quaintly ironic comment, obviously going to hell. Cognoscenti are invited to express interest, make exchanges, contribute ideas & materials." 1976. †lp. avg. press run 107. Pub'd 1 title 1976. BPHS, APHA, EBUWCK.

THE PRE-RAPHAELITE REVIEW, Rat & Mole Press, Francis Golffing, Nathan Cerro, Barbara Golffing, P.O. Box 111, Amherst, MA 01002. Articles, art, photos, interviews, satire, criticism, reviews, letters. "A critical biographical journal. First issue Jan. 1977." 2/yr. 1976. 128pp; 8½ x 5½. of. circ. 300. Reporting time: 2-3 months. Payment: copies. Pub's reviews. §anything to do with Pre-raphaelite. COSMEP, NESPA.

Prescott Street Press, Vi Gale, Editor, Publisher, 407 Postal Building, Portland, OR 97204. "Prescott Street Press will have a dormant period until '77/'78 when we will print again. Meanwhile, we are filling orders from work already in print. If we should come into funding, we will go to press again much sooner." COSMEP.

Press Gang Publishers, Press Gang Collective, 821 East Hastings St., Vancouver, B.C. V6A1R8, Canada. Poetry, fiction, articles, plays. "We are new publishers. Our first book is *Women Look at Psychiatry*, an anthology of articles by Vancouver professionals, paraprofessionals, ex-mental patients. The next book we are working on is Beth Jankola's poetry. Our third book is a play called *Betty Windsor's Blue Plate Special* by Carolyn Bell." †of. Payment varies. Discounts: 40% to bookstores (if over 5 copies), 20% to libraries and schools.

Press of Arden Park (see MAL DE MER)

Press Pacifica, Jane Pultz, Editor; Richard Pultz, Managing Editor, PO Box 47, Kailua, HI 96734, 808-261-6594. Poetry, fiction, non-fiction. "We are a book publisher and will consider all inquires. We will hold all mss sent without return postage until it is sent. Especially interested in women's history and feminist books but open to other fields. This coming year we have a novel about a deliquent boy, a parents guide to sex education and a children's illustrated poetry anthology. This year we published *'Loom And Spindle'* by Harriet H. Robinson, a reprint of an autobiography of a woman who worked in the cotton mills in 1835-47. Also a booklet on Hawaiian postage stamps. Basically we are a general publisher with wide interests." avg. price, cloth: $7.95; paper: $4.50; other: $1.95. 1975. varies from 144 to 250pp. of. avg. press run 1,000-2,500 (past); 2,500-5,500 (1977). Reporting time: 6-10 weeks. Payment: 10 percent first book. Copyrights for author. Discounts: Trade 25-44 percent discount, libraries 15-25 percent, no consignments. Pub'd 1 title 1976; expects 3 titles 1977, 4 titles 1978. COSMEP, WBPA.

Press Porcepic Limited, W.D. Godfrey, Ellen Godfrey, 70 Main Street, Erin, Ontario N0B1T0, Canada. "Publish fiction, poetry, literary criticisms, other books of social and political relevance by Canadian authors. James Reaney, Dorothy Livesay, Eli Mandel, Joe Rosenblatt." 1971. Reporting time: 6 weeks. Payment: 5% of retail price. COSMEP, IPA, APC.

Pressdram Ltd. (see PRIVATE EYE)

Pressed Curtains (see also CURTAINS), Paul Buck, 12 Foster Clough, Hebden Bridge, W Yorkshire HX75Q2, United Kingdom, 042-283-3900. Poetry, fiction, art. "Publish contributors central to magazine" avg. price, paper: $2.40; other: $5.00. 1971. 60pp; A4. †mi. avg. press run 400. Reporting time: days. Payment: copies. Copyrights for author. Pub'd 8 titles 1976; expects 4 titles 1977, 6 titles 1978.

PRIMAVERA, Matrix, Janet Ruth Heller, Ida Noyes Hall, Univ. of Chicago, Chicago, IL 60637. Poetry, fiction, art, photos, satire. "We are committed to encouraging new writers & artists. All work received will be read & *commented on* in a personal letter to you. Only women may submit. Please don't forget to type all literature & include S.A.S.E." 1/yr; 1-yr sub price: $3.70; per copy:

249

$3.70; sample: $3.70. 1974. 90pp; 8½ x 11. of. circ. 1,000. Reporting time: 2 months. Payment: 2 copies. Copyrighted, reverts to author. Ads: $200/$100. Back issues: 1st issue $3.20; 2nd issue $3.70; 3rd issue $3.90. Pub'd 1 issue 1976; expects 2 issues 1977, 2 issues 1978. COSMEP, CCLM.

PRIMER, Primer Press, Ron Wray, 502 E. 38 St, #14F, Indianapolis, IN 46205. Poetry, fiction, articles, art, photos, cartoons, interviews, satire, criticism, reviews, music, letters, parts-of-novels, long-poems, collages, plays, concrete art. "Open to visuals able to be reproduced offset; no maximum length tho currently 10 pages (single space) or less more likely accepted. Contributors for PRIMER #2 are to include Lindy Hough, Theodore Enslin, Paul Metcalf, Douglas Woolf. PRIMER #1 included Clayton Eshleman & Etheridge Knight. This gives some idea of direction of magazine's material. However overall range is fairly wide, provides for inclusion of diverse styles & interests." 2-3/yr; 1-yr sub price: $4.00; per copy: $2.00; sample: $2.00. 1975. 70pp; 8½ x 11. †of. circ. 300. Reporting time: 1-3 weeks. Payment: 2 copies. Ads: $20.00/$10.00/no class. Discounts: 40% to each/libraries regular rate. Pub's reviews. §general interest, tho principally in arts.

PRIMIPARA, Impress Inc, Diane Nichols, PO Box 171, Oconto, WI 54153. "Contributors *restricted* to Wisconsin residents only (anti-feminist work not accepted) — we're trying to establish a viable informal outlet for our state's women rather than leaning on N.Y. or CALIF. area markets." 2/yr; 1-yr sub price: $3.00; per copy: $1.75; sample: $1.00. 1974. 48pp; 8½ x 5½. of. circ. 400. Reporting time: 3 months. Payment: 1 copy. Back issues: $1.00 each. Pub's reviews. §preference given to Wisc authors or Wisc based publications and women oriented.

The Print Mint, Inc. (see ARCADE)

Prism Books (see also NEW POETRY), Cheryl Adamson, Robert Adamson, Box N110 Grosvenor St. P.O., Sydney, N.S.W. 2000, Australia. Poetry, photos, criticism, long-poems. "Published by NEW POETRY for The Poetry Society of Australia. These are well-produced limited editions of poetry from Australia's important new poets. In 1975 we published nine volumes, five of which were first books. To date: Kantarizis, Williams, Murray, Macrae, Maiden, Hewett, Porter, Thorne and Duncan." 1971. 96pp. of/lp. Reporting time: 4 weeks. Payment: 2% (royalties). Discounts: 40% trade.

PRIVATE EYE, Pressdram Ltd., Richard Ingrams, 34 Greek St., London W1, United Kingdom. Cartoons, photos, satire, news items, letters. 26/yr; 1-yr sub price: £8.50; per copy: £7.00; sample: £4.00. 1961. 24pp; A4. of. circ. 100,000. Ads: £450/15p.

ProActive Press, James Craig, Marguerite Craig, P.O. Box 296, Berkeley, CA 94701, 415-549-0839. Non-fiction. "We established the ProActive Press to assist in the co-creation of a caring society through humanistic politics. We are eager to share what skills we have with anyone who has a good, readable manuscript that offers a promising pro-life, pro-active program for humanizing social change. (We're not interested in more re-actions to the horrors we see and sense all about us.) Our *Synergic Power: Beyond Domination and Permissiveness* shows the kind of manuscript we're looking for." avg. price, cloth: $6.95; paper: $2.95. 1973. 144pp; 5½ x 8-1/2. of. avg. press run 2,500. Reporting time: Varies-query. Discounts: 40% trade, 20% text — both for orders of 5 or more books. Pub'd 1 title 1976; expects 3 titles 1977, 3 titles 1978. COSMEP.

Programmed Studies Inc, Dick Whitson, P.O. Box 113, Stow, MA 01775, 617-897-2130. Articles. "Recently published programmed instruction course in seduction and lovemaking techniques: how to meet and bed girls — would like similar material for women" avg. price, other: $29.95. 1975. 200pp; 8½ x 11. of/le. Reporting time: 4 weeks. Payment: $25 to $200. Copyrights for author. Discounts: up to 66%. Pub'd 1 title 1976; expects 3 titles 1977, 3 titles 1978. COSMEP.

Project House Foundation, Inc. (see BARBEQUE PLANET)

Project Press, 710 Wilshire #106, Santa Monica, CA 90401.

PROLETARIAT, Workers' Press, Jonathan Aurthur, PO Box 3774, Merchandise Mart, Chicago,

IL 60654. Articles. "PROLETARIAT is a theoretical journal published by the Communist Labor Party of the United States of North America. We print articles relating to the application of Marxism-Leninism to current world and national conditions, historical studies of the revolutionary movement, etc. We welcome contributions from non-Party members." 2-4/yr; sub price: $3.50/4 issues; per copy: $1.00; sample: free. 1971. 40-60pp; 5½ x 8½. †of. circ. 3,000. Reporting time: 1 month. No payment. Discounts: 40% trade, bulk etc. Back issues: free. §political science, world communist movement.

PROLOG, Theater Sources, Inc., Mike Firth, 104 N. St. Mary, Dallas, TX 75214. Articles, reviews, letters, news items, non-fiction. 4/yr; 1-yr sub price: $4.00 Indiv.-$6.00 Instit.; per copy: $1.00; sample: $1.00. 1973. 08pp; 8½ x 11. of. circ. 200. Reporting time: month. Payment:40 1/2 cents word. Ads: $10.00. Discounts: none set. Back issues: $1.00. Pub'd 4 issues 1976; expects 4 issues 1977, 4 issues 1978. Pub's reviews: 4 in 1976. §writing for theater, the process of writing.

Prologue Publications, Carol Rudoff, P.O. Box 640, Menlo Park, CA 94025, 322-5034. Poetry, fiction. " we are entirely subjective. When we're rich, we publish; when we're poor we fake it." avg. price, paper: $3.95. 1976. 72pp; 5½ x 8½. of. avg. press run 500 on up to several thousand. Reporting time: 6 weeks. Payment: 10 percent on sale. Copyrights for author. Discounts: trade 40 percent, bulk 50 percent, agent 12 percent. Pub'd 1 title 1976; expects 9 titles 1977. COSMEP.

PROMONTORY, Headland Publications, Gerald England, 103 Clarksfield Rd., Oldham OL4 1LJ, United Kingdom, 061-624-3439. Poetry. "Only high-quality poetry required. Unsolicited mss arriving without return postage are destroyed! Contributors include Harriet Rose, Eugenio Montale, Philip Ward, Nicki Jackowska, B.C. Leale, Roger Howson, etc. Merges with NEW HOPE after 1977." 1/yr; sub price: £1.00/4 issues; per copy: 35p. 1974. 12-16pp; A5. of. circ. 250. Reporting time: 3 mos. Discounts: None. Pub'd 1 issue 1976; expects 1 issue 1977. ALP.

The Proof Press, Polly Zane, John Zane, PO Box 1256, Berkeley, CA 94720. "Native American educational materials· 12 portrait drawings of North American Indians, one chart (survey of N.Am. Ind. cultural areas), 36 student booklets representing 12 cultural areas. $20." of.

PROSPICE, The Aquila Publishing Co. Ltd., J.C.R. Green, Michael Edwards, P.O. Box 1, Portree, Isle of Skye, Scotland IV51 9BT, United Kingdom. Poetry, fiction, articles, art, photos, interviews, satire, criticism, reviews, music, parts-of-novels, long-poems. "PROSPICE is a magazine of poetry and poetics. International in scope, its main concern is to foster creative work and also basic reflection about poetry to provide a clear focus for exploration. In particular it seeks to confront English language poetics with Non-English, partly by printing unpublished foreign poems, partly by special numbers devoted to non-English poetry, and by the publishing of essays, articles and reviews. Length varies, contributors in recent issues include, Cid Corman, Robert Bly, George Oppen, Adrian Henri, Peter Redgrove, Douglas Dunn, Carl Rakosi, Charles Tomlinson, Octavio Paz, Nick Toczek, Yves Bonnefoy, Keith Bosley etc etc." 3/yr; 1-yr sub price: £2.50 paper (US $5.00); per copy: Varies; sample: £1.00 or $2.50. 1973. 96pp; A5. of. circ. 1,250. Reporting time: varies. Payment: payment only on commissioned pieces. Ads: No ad carried. Inserts by arrangement. Discounts: trade on application. Pub'd 3 issues 1976; expects 3 issues 1977, 3 issues 1978. Pub's reviews: 19 in 1976. §Poetry, literature, fiction, etc. COSMEP, SGPA.

PROTEUS, Proteus Press, Cathy Gatling, Frank Gatling, 1004 N. Jefferson St., Arlington, VA 22205. Poetry, fiction, articles, reviews, parts-of-novels, plays, art, interviews, criticism, long-poems. "Due to limited funds, concentration on chapbooks, and various problems, we are unable to continue accepting unsolicited manuscripts. Issue No. 6/7 includes Bill Garrison, Richard Cooper, Robert Lax, Richard Kostelanetz, E. Ethelbert Miller, Arnost Lustig, Jim Morrissette, Carlo Parcelli, Stephen McKinney, and others." irreg.; sub price: $5.00/4 issues; per copy: $1.50; sample: $1.50. 1972. 64pp; 7 x 8½. of. circ. 500. Reporting time: 3 months. Payment: 2 copies. Copyrighted, permission for copyright must be requested in writing. Ads: $30.00/$15.00. Discounts: none. Back issues: $2.00 (magazine) $2.50 (chapbooks). Pub'd 2 issues 1976; expects 5 issues 1977, 4 issues 1978. Pub's reviews. §fiction, poetry, criticism. CCLM, COSMEP, WPA, WCI.

PROVINCETOWN POETS, To the Lighthouse Press, Charles Boyle, Louis Postel, Candy Jernigan, Art Editor, 216 Bradford St., Provincetown, MA 02657. Poetry, fiction, articles, art, photos, cartoons, interviews, satire, music, collages, plays, concrete art. "PROVINCETOWN POETS is a mosaic of work produced mainly in town but not always. No style biases but the shorter the better. Recent contributors include Robert Bly, Joshua Norton Gerard Malanga, Mary Oliver, Marge Piercy, Helen Duberstein, The Women's Media Committee, Alan Dugan, Mark Weiss, B. H. Friedman, Walker Evans, Opal Nations. SASE, please (perfectbound, 23 full pages of art, over 45 illustrations)" 3/yr; 1-yr sub price: $6.00; per copy: $1.95 (plus 50¢ postage handling). 1975. 64pp; 6 x 9. of. circ. 2M. Reporting time: 3-4 mos. Payment: copies, maybe money. Ads: $100/$55/$30 1/4. Discounts: 40% discount over 5 copies, 55% to agents. §experimental, multimedia. CCLM, COSMEP, NESPA.

Pruett Publishing Company, Gerald Keenan, Managing Ed.; F.A. Pruett, President, 3235 Prairie Avenue, Boulder, CO 80301, 303-449-4919. Articles, art, photos, criticism, music. "We publish books of interest to the trans-Mississippi west: histories, railroadiana. Also special education titles and textbooks for el-hi and college levels. We are planning an extensive pictorial history of the California Zephyr, an Alaskan railroad book, a history of the American Indian in Colorado and a new social study series for the mentally handicapped child." 1-yr sub price: varies. 1959. pp will vary; 8½ x 11. of. circ. will vary according to each book. Reporting time: Within a few days, if we reject ms. Within 30 days, if ms. is under consideration. Payment: by negotiation. Copyrighted. ABA.

Psychohistory Press (see THE JOURNAL OF PSYCHOHISTORY)

Puckerbrush Press, Constance Hunting, 76 Main St., Orono, ME 04473, 207-866-4868. Poetry, fiction, criticism. "Recent: *A Day's Work,* poems by Michael McMahon; *A Paper Raincoat,* poems by Sonya Dorman; No strictly 'women's' stuff please." avg. price, paper: $3.50. 1971. 50-100pp; 6 x 9. of. avg. press run 150-300. Reporting time: 2-4 wks. Payment: 10% of each retail copy. Copyright to author. Discounts: 40%. Pub'd 1 title 1976; expects 2 titles 1977. NESPA, MWPA.

PUDDINGSTONE, Puddingstone Press, John Coward, Box 8800, University Station, Knoxville, TN 37916. Poetry. "Looking for quality contemporary poetry that is carefully crafted and original. We prefer a literal style of poetry—poetry that makes sense, moves well, and has some impact. Biased toward Southern writers. Any length will be considered, but shorter work generally preferred. Recent poets include Malcolm Glass, Peter Meinke, Jeff Daniel Marion, Floyd Skloot, Mary Balazs, Dave Smith, & Thomas Johnson." 2/yr; sub price: $3.50/4 issues; per copy: $1.20 each; sample: $1.20 each. 1974. 28pp; 8½ x 5½. of. circ. 250. Reporting time: 6-8 weeks. Payment: copies. Back issues: $1.20 each for back issues.

PUERTO DEL SOL, Puerto Del Sol Press, David Apodaca, et. al., Box 3E, Las Cruces, NM 88003, 505-646-3932. Poetry, fiction, art, photos, interviews, reviews, parts-of-novels, long-poems, plays. "Emphasis on Chicano, Nat. Am. & Anglo writers. Some Latin American with trans." 2/yr; 1-yr sub price: $6.50; per copy: $2.00; sample: $2.00. 1961. 100pp; 6 x 9. of. circ. 1,000. Reporting time: 6 weeks. Payment varies. Copyrighted. Discounts: 40 percent general/50 percent jobber. Back issues: complete set $40.00 (vol 1 no. 1-vol 14 no. 2). Pub's reviews. §Chicano, Nat. Am., poetry, fiction. CCLM.

Puerto Del Sol Press (see also PUERTO DEL SOL), David Apodaca, Box 3E, Las Cruces, NM 88003. Poetry, fiction. "Joy Harjo: *The Last Song* $1.50. Leroy Quintana: *Hijo Del Pueblo,* New Mexico poems $2.00. Part of *Del Conejo* series for New Mexico writers." avg. price, paper: $2.00. 1975. 30pp; 6 x 9. of. avg. press run 500. Reporting time: 6 weeks (solicited only). Payment varies. Copyrights for author. Discounts: 40 percent/50 percent jobber.

PULP, Howard Sage, 720 Greenwich St. Apt 4H, New York City, NY 10014, 46-48 Robinson St., Flushing, NY 11355. Poetry, fiction, articles, art, photos, cartoons, interviews, satire, parts-of-novels, long-poems, plays. "Michael Heller, Archibald Henderson, Marge Piercy, Diana Chang, Lyn Lifshin, Philip Appleman, Richard O'Connell, Donald A. Sears. Consider all styles, no biases." 4/yr; 1-yr sub price: $2.00/$5.00 outside U.S.; per copy: $.25; sample: $.25. 1974. 12pp; tabloid 9¾ x 15. of. circ. 2,000. Reporting time: 1 week-1 mo. Payment: copies. Copyrighted, reverts to author upon publication. Ads: $150/$75/$1-for 28 wds. Back issues: $0.50 plus postage. Pub'd 3 issues 1976; expects 4 issues 1977, 4 issues 1978. Pub's reviews: 2 in 1976. §poetry, fiction. CCLM.

‡**PULP CONTENT, Pulp Press,** Box 8806 Stn H, Vancouver 5, Canada.

Pulp Press (see also THREE CENT PULP), Ed. Board, Box 48806 Stn. Bental, Vancouver, Canada, 604-687-4233. Poetry, fiction, art, satire, parts-of-novels, long-poems, plays, non-fiction. avg. price, cloth: $8.95; paper: $3.50; other: $1.00-$2.00. 1971. 108pp; 5¼ x 8. †of. avg. press run 1,200-2,000. Reporting time: 1 month. Payment: royalties negotiated after 1,000 copies sold. Copyrights for author. Discounts: trade 40 percent: libraries 10 percent: wholesale (bulk) 50 percent. Pub'd 5 titles 1976; expects 10 titles 1977, 15 titles 1978.

PulpartForms Unltd. (see ONE SHOT DEAL)

Purple Mouth Press (see IT COMES IN THE MAIL)

Pushcart Press, Bill Henderson, P.O. Box 845, Yonkers, NY 10701. "Pushcart publishes THE PUBLISH-IT-YOURSELF HANDBOOK: Literary Tradition and How-To, edited by Bill Henderson, a complete guide on publishing without assistance of vanity or commercial publishers, including essays by Anais Nin, Stewart Brand, Alan Swallow, Leonard Woolf, Richard Kostelanetz, Len Fulton, Gordon Lish (plus 20 others). Complete bibliography and how-to section. Each year we will publish THE PUSHCART PRIZE: Best of the Small Presses, with the help of our distinguished contributing editors." 300pp; 5½ x 8½. of. COSMEP.

PYRAMID, Hellric Publications, Ottone M. Riccio, 39 Eliot St., Jamaica Plain, MA 02130. Poetry, fiction, articles, art, cartoons, interviews, satire, criticism, reviews, long-poems, collages, plays, collages. "Pyramid is still overstocked and accepting very little. 14, latest issue, includes work by Albert Goldbarth, Ben Tibbs, Sam Grolmes, Robert Joe Stout, M. N. O'Neill, etc. No limits or taboos. MSS not accompanied by SASE are destroyed. International reply coupons are no longer acceptable." irregular; sub price: $5.00/4 issues; per copy: $1.50; sample: $1.50. 1968. 76pp; 8½ x 5½. †of. circ. 500. Reporting time: week or less. Payment: $3 up per printed page plus 5 copies & complimentary subscription. Discounts: 50% on 20 or more copies of title or issue. Back issues: 6-$3.00. §poetry, fiction, literary commentary.

Q

‡**QUADERNI DI POESIA,** Via Corrado Segre 7, Rome, Italy.

Quark Press, Peter Payack, Jane Barnes, Box 193, Cambridge, MA 02141. "All books are 'Minimal' Chapbooks. Editions of 300 printed for all books. Manuscripts solicited only. No submissions." 1976. 20pp; 2½ x 3-7/8. of. Payment: several books. Pub'd 1 title 1976; expects 6 titles 1977, 6 titles 1978.

QUARRY WEST, College V, David Swanger, Bessie Eiermann, Larry Fisher, Kristin Richardson, College v, University of Calif, Santa Cruz, CA 95064. Poetry, fiction, articles, art, parts-of-novels, long-poems. "Joyce Carol Oates, Raymond Carver, J. B. Hall, Gary Ligi, Steven Dixon, Gary Soto, Susan Fromberg Schaeffer, Ronald Wallace, Greg Kuzma, Vern Rutsala, George Hitchcock." 2/yr; 1-yr sub price: $4.00; per copy: $2.00. 1971. 60pp; 7 x 8. circ. 400. Reporting time: 4 weeks. Payment: 3 issues. CCLM.

Quarterly Committee of Queen's University (see QUEEN'S QUARTERLY)

Quarterly Press (see THE NEW KENT QUARTERLY)

QUARTERLY REVIEW OF LITERATURE, Quarterly Review of Literature, Theodore Weiss,

Renee Weiss, 26 Haslet Ave, Princeton, NJ 08540, 921-6976. "Current issue: Vol XX, No. 1/2 30th anniversary special issues retrospective containing poetry, fiction translations and articles by and about Kafka, Moore, Pound, Valery, Holderlin, Leopardi and Montale. Third of a series of 4 retrospectives, the first two being Volume 19, No. 1/2-poetry and No. 3/4-prose, culled from the best of *QRL'S* work published over the past 30 years. Vol XX, No. 3/4 Criticism Retrospective." irregular; 1-yr sub price: $20.00 institutional & hardback $10.00 paper; per copy: $13.00 (hardback) $6.50 (paper); sample: $1.50. 1943. 550pp; 5½ x 8½. of. circ. 3,000. Reporting time: 6 weeks-2 months. New material being accepted after the retrospectives are finished. Check criticism issue for information. Payment to authors. Copyrighted, does not revert to author. Ads: $175.00/$100.00/$0.00. Discounts: Bookstores: 10 percent on 1 copy, 40 percent on 3 or more. Agency subscription discounts: 10 percent. Back issues: Scarce; available through us on request. Not all available; cost-roughly $20.00 per volume. CCLM, COSMEP.

QUARTERLY WEST, Quarterly West, James Thomas, Andrew Grossbarot, 312 Olpin Union, U. of Utah, Salt Lake City, UT 84112, 801-581-3938. Poetry, fiction, art, interviews, reviews, parts-of-novels, long-poems, collages. "To be filled out in February. 'On-the-wall fiction, poetry and reviews. Special interest in the 'creative essay.' Contributors include: (fiction) Jack Matthews, David Kranes, Gordon Weaver, Dan Curley, M. Pabst Battin; (poetry) Peter Wild, Tess Gallagher, Mark McClosky, John Haines, David Ignatow, Howard McCord, Patricia Goedicke, Carolyn Forche, Robert Mezey, David Ray, Joe David Bellamy, Ralph J. Mills, Jr.'" 3/yr; 1-yr sub price: $5.00; per copy: $1.50. 1976. 144pp; 9 x 12. of. circ. 1,000. Reporting time: 10 weeks. Payment: $5.00 to $10.00 a page. Copyrighted, does not revert to author. Ads: $90.00. Back issues: $2.00. Pub'd 3 issues 1976; expects 3 issues 1977, 3 issues 1978. Pub's reviews: 18 in 1976. §fiction and poetry.

QUARTET, Richard Hauer Costa, Editor-Publisher, 1119 Neal Pickett Dr., College Station, TX 77840. Poetry, fiction, articles, art, photos, satire, criticism, reviews. "*Quartet* now publishes only one general issue a year. One other is a *double,* and always has a theme. The fourth is usually for avant-garde material. *Self-contained fiction* (no fragments of novels or sketches or prose poems). Poetry should be along lines of what is now considered contemporary." 4/yr; 1-yr sub price: $4.00; per copy: $1.00; sample: $1.00. 1962. 40pp; 6 x 9. of. circ. 1,000. Reporting time: one to four months. Payment only when and if a grant provides funds. Ads: $50/$30. Discounts: to bookstores, follow their policies—average discount—25%. Back issues: $2.00 per issue. Pub's reviews. §poetry, fiction, belles-lettres. CCLM.

The Quarto Press, Brian Louis Pearce, 69 Swan Rd., Feltham, Middx TW13 6PE, United Kingdom. Poetry. "New poets preferred, but veterans considered for the series of booklets THE QUARTO POETS, which has been highly acclaimed for the quality of production." avg. price, paper: 50p. 1963. 20pp; A5. †lp. avg. press run 300. Reporting time: approx. month. Payment: negotiable. Copyright reverts to author. Discounts: 25% trade & bulk. Pub'd 3 titles 1976; expects 4 titles 1977. ALP.

QUEEN STREET MAGAZINE, Goathair Press, Angelo Sgabellone, Beth Learn, Box 251, Station B., Toronto M5T2W1, Canada. Articles, art, photos, interviews, criticism, reviews, music, parts-of-novels, concrete art. "To encourage the development of experimental/creative expression, and at the same time help cultivate a greater awareness of and receptivity towards the experimental, progressive arts. Generally to do anything which is necessary or incidental to the promotion and encouragement of excellence in Canadian and other cultural forms of activity. Material should be less than 1,000 words or contact the editors and must fall into the innovative levels of the visual or literary arts. Although we accept 'straight' work, poetry/prose it must be stressed it will only be considered as a secondary aspect of our publishing interests. We will *NOT* return nor can be held responsible for unsolicited material therefore please write with an enclosed brief on what you intend to do or the nature of your work. Although we apologize, we neither expected, have the time or financial resources to handle the incredible back log of mail and contributions received over the last three years. This time could be better spent on direct magazine production and as much as we enjoy hearing from you the 'magazine' is non funded by any public agency and therefore takes precedence." 3-4/yr; 1-yr sub price: $5.00; per copy: $2.00; sample: free. 1973. 80pp; 8½ x 11. circ. 5,000. Reporting time: 2-3 wks. Payment: $20 1,000 words or more $10 for less. Ads: $80/$60. Discounts: 60%. Back issues: $2.00 each. Pub's reviews. §only of experimental work/language and visual arts. COSMEP.

Queens College Press (see also A SHOUT IN THE STREET), Joseph Cuomo, General Editor, Writers & Artists Series, English Dept, Queens College, Flushing, NY 11367, 212-520-7238. Poetry, fiction, art, photos, interviews, long-poems, plays, non-fiction. "Send submissions only to A SHOUT IN THE STREET. We do not have staff to read submissions to book series. Our books are hand-set, hand-bound letterpress editions. Books: *Admit Impediment*, poems by Marie Ponsot; *Objective Mysteries*, poems by Fred Buell." avg. price, paper: Books-$4.50; mag-$2.50. 1977. Books-60; mag-96pp; books-5½ x 8½; mag-6 x 9¼. †books-lp/mag-of. avg. press run 1,000. Reporting time: magazine only-8 weeks. Payment: Books-percentage of sales; mag-copies. Copyrights for author. Discounts: Books-40 percent to bookstores; 50 percent to distributors. Mag-30 percent on consignment; 40 percent outright. Pub'd 2 titles 1976; expects 3 titles 1977, 4 titles 1978. COSMEP.

QUEEN'S QUARTERLY: A Canadian Review, The Quarterly Committee of Queen's University, Kerry McSweeney, Queen's University, Kingston, Ontario K7L3N6, Canada. Poetry, fiction, articles, interviews, satire, criticism, parts-of-novels, plays. "Articles: 20-25 double-spaced pp. Recent contributors: Gwendolyn MacEwen, Dorothy Livesay, D. O. Hebb, George Woodcock, Joyce Carol Oates, Edgar Z. Friedenberg, Al Purdy" 4/yr; 1-yr sub price: $8.00($8.25 foreign); per copy: $2.00; sample: $2.00. 1893. 160pp; 5-1/8 x 7-5/8. of. circ. 1,900. Reporting time: max, 1 month. Payment: $3 per printed page (short stories), $10 per poem 50 free offprints (articles), copies. Ads: $150/$85. Pub's reviews. §books only; history, science, politics, philosophy, social science, literary studies, music, art, etc. COSMEP, CPPA.

QUEST: A Feminist Quarterly, Quest: A Feminist Quarterly, Inc., Beverly Fisher, Managing; Charlotte Bunch, Coordinating; Alexa Freeman, Production and Design; Karen Kollias, Promotion; Jane Dolkart, Nancy Hartsock, Mary-Helen Mautner, Sidney Oliver, Gerri Traina, PO Box 8843, Washington, DC 20003. Poetry, articles, art, photos, cartoons, interviews, satire, criticism, reviews. "Only original, unpublished material is acceptable. Major articles should be no longer than 20 double-spaced typewritten pages (8½ x 11). QUEST is a national journal committed to the exposure of feminist political analysis and ideological development. Each issue covers a specific theme in-depth. Authors should write and request list of ideas and questions for particular themes of issues. QUEST is neither a news magazine, literary, or academic journal. We seek to be a forum for political exchange in the feminist movement. Recent contributors: Nancy Hartsock, Charlotte Bunch, Jean Elshtain, Bertha Harris, Linda Phelps, Joan Rothschild." 4/yr; 1-yr sub price: $9.00/individuals; $15.00/institutions; $11.00/overseas, surface mail; $14.50/overseas, air mail.; sample: $2.75 plus $.35 postage. 1974. 80pp; 6 x 8¼. of. circ. 4,000. Reporting time: 4 months. Payment: $50.00 to $150.00. Ads: $120.00/$70.00/none. Discounts: trade 40% through Women in Distribution, 10% bulk, orders under 25, 20% orders 25 or over, agents, 20%. Back Issues: vol. i no. 2-vol. ii no. 3, $2.00 plus 35¢ postage vol. ii no. 4 on-$2.75 plus 35¢ postage. Pub's reviews. §women; feminism; social, political and economic change. COSMEP.

Quest Publishing (see INQUEST)

Quick Books (see LOOK QUICK)

Quickoats (see QUIXOTE, QUIXOTL)

QUILL & QUIRE, Fiona Mee, 59 Front Street East, Toronto, Ontario M5E1B3, Canada. Photos, interviews, reviews. "Q & Q is a trade journal, subscribed to by publishers, librarians, teachers, booksellers, and writers. Articles cover all aspects of publishing, bookselling and librarianship in Canada. Canadian books only are reviewed (approx. 50 a month). There are four special education issues published annually." 12/yr; 1-yr sub price: $12.00; per copy: $1.00; sample: free. 1935. 32pp; 10¼ x 15½. of. circ. 12,000. Reporting time: 2 weeks. Payment: $65-$150. Ads: $910/$560/$3.00 a line. Pub's reviews.

Quintessence Publications, Marlan Beilke, 356 Bunker Hill Mine Road, Amador City, CA 95601, 209-267-5470. Poetry, articles, art, photos, criticism, non-fiction. "Initial publication to be the 356 page *Shining Clarity: God And Man In The Works Of Robinson Jeffers,* [1st September, 1977]. This book (hard-cover) is an indepth consideration of Jeffers' views of the human and the divine; hence, it is literary commentary more so than literary criticism. 50 complete Jeffers poems (one hitherto unpublished) included therein. Contributors: poets: Gary Elder and Bill Hotchkiss. Photographers: Horace Lyon and Karl Bissinger. Artists: Lumir Sindelar and Kenneth Jack. Critic: Dr. James D. Hart, Director, The Bancroft Library. The book will be issued in two states: 900 copies of trade edition; 100 copies in a slip-cased, signed edition featuring; bronze medal [weighing 2¾ths lb.] of Robinson Jeffers, unpublished color & B&W photographs, ms facsimile, etc." avg. price, cloth: $20.00; other: $75.00 (separate edition). 1976. 350pp; 8 x 6¼. of. avg. press run 1,000. Payment: by arrangement. Copyrights for author. Discounts: Trade, 5 or more copies-40 percent: others, by arrangement. Expects 1 title 1977.

QUINTESSENCE, Quintessence Press, Estelle Trust, 166 Albany Ave., Shreveport, LA 71105. "poetry, 20 line limit" 3/yr; 1-yr sub price: $3.00; per copy: $1.00; sample: $.60. 1963. 10pp; 8½ x 11. circ. 200. Reporting time: 2 weeks. Payment: none. no ads. Pub's reviews.

QUIXOTE, QUIXOTL, Quickoats, The anti-capitalist renegade marxist wordslingers collective., 151 E Gilman, Madison, WI 53703. "Continue our anti-fox, anti-Judy Hogan, anti-COSMEP newsletter bias. Recent contributors: D.A. Levy, Pablo Neruda, Leah Tallina, West End & Liberation magazines, Austin lesbians, human beings. Pro Bennett. Against the sin of pride. Making headway against the genteel tradition of Warren Woessner. Interested in keeping Texas writers and thinkers in exile permanently in exile. Like postage stamps, photos, personal letters, beer, and grafitti. Cleveland and Madison work given special attention as is anything relating to Poland, any dirt on the Petit-Bourgeoisie." 3 Angstroms/month-12 issues/yr; 1-yr sub price: $10.00; per copy: $1.00; sample: 50 zlty. 1868. 50pp; varies. †of. circ. 1,000. Reporting time: 4 months to 40 years. Payment: copies, kewpies, cowpies. Copyrighted, to authors to stop that damn Reilly from ripping off. Ads: $3000.00/$150.00/$0.07. Discounts: .001 percent to Bowker agents. Back issues: no, we have some side issues. Pub'd 10 issues 1976; expects 12 issues 1977, 25 issues 1978. Pub's reviews: 5 in 1976. §satire, humor, fiction, marxist leninist maoist thought, anarchism, workers stuff. CCLM, APS, LPS, CIO-AFL, NFL, BBC, PTA, TACL.

QUOZ?, Trinity Press, Carlo Giovanni Cicatelli, Box 1320, San Francisco, CA 94101. Poetry, art, photos, satire, collages, concrete art. 4/yr; 1-yr sub price: $5.00; per copy: $2.00; sample: $2.00. 1973. 40pp; 5¼ x 4-1/8. †of. circ. 500. Reporting time: 1-2 months. Payment: copy or copies. Back issues: $2 complete set (1-12) $100. CCLM, COSMEP.

R **R & D Services,** Ron Playle, PO Box 644, Des Moines, IA 50303, 515-262-5397. Non-fiction. "Publishes *'How-To-Win'* booklets in many fields; money making opportunities, contests, etc." avg. price, paper: $3.95. 1971. 32pp; 8½ x 11. of. avg. press run 15,000. Reporting time: 1 month. Payment: outright purchase (no royalty). Copyrights for author. Discounts: trade: 50 percent & up, libraries: 25 percent. Pub'd 3 titles 1976; expects 12 titles 1977, 12 titles 1978.

R.O. Beatty & Associates, David Beatty, Melissa Dodworth, P.O. Box 763/611 North Fifth, Boise, ID 83701, 208-343-4949. Fiction, photos, letters, non-fiction. "Material must be suitable for general market. Query first to save us all a lot of time and trouble (and postage)." 1974. avg. press run 5,000. Reporting time: 6 weeks. Payment: negotiable. Copyright for author if desired. Discounts: trade 40 percent (1-49), 42 percent (50-99), 43 percent (100 plus); wholesale 50 percent (5 plus); libraries/schools 20 percent. Pub'd 2 titles 1976; expects 2 titles 1977, 3 titles 1978.

R.S.H. Publications (see CS JOURNAL)

R.V.K. Publishing Co. (see POETRY/PEOPLE, NEW EARTH TRIBE NEWSPACK)

RA: A Journal of Popular Culture and the Arts, Ra Press, D. Neale King, A. J. Wright, PO Box 1043, Auburn, AL 36830. Poetry, fiction, articles, interviews, satire, criticism, reviews, long-poems, plays. "Due to financial hassles we have yet to get out our first issue. But the sky is clearing, and we should have one out by the end of 1977." irreg.; sub price: $5.00/5 issues; sample: $1.00. 1975. 50pp; 7 x 8½. of. Reporting time: 3 days-3 mos. Payment: 3-5 copies. Ads: exchange only. Discounts: none. Expects 1 issue 1977, 1-2 issues 1978. Pub's reviews. §literature, music, politics, popular culture.

RABIES, Bonefold Imprint, B. J. Kelly, 68 Parkhill Rd, London NW3, United Kingdom. Poetry, satire, news items, letters, plays. 4/yr; 1-yr sub price: £1.30; per copy: 50p. 1972. 30pp; A4. circ. 200-400. Reporting time: Immediate. ALP.

Racz Publishing Co., Jack A. Cashman, PO Box 287, Oxnard, CA 93032, 805-483-8843. 1973. of. Payment: annually. Copyrights for author.

RADAR, Santa Cruz Poetry Center, Flora Durham, 108 Locust St, Santa Cruz, CA 95060. Poetry, art. "*Radar* is a local publication for local writers & distributed for free in the community. Mail out some when we can afford postage, to anyone interested. Bias is for local folk. Stephen Kessler, Ellen Bass, Fruud, Greg Keith, Tael Thomas." 8-10/yr. 1976. folds out into poster; 8½ x 11. of. circ. 1,200 plus. Reporting time: 1-3 wks. Payment: just copies up to 10 copies. Copyrighted, reverts to author. Discounts: none. Back issues: no back issues, all are given away. CCLM, COSMEP.

RADICAL AMERICA, Collective, Box B, N. Cambridge, MA 02140. 6/yr; 1-yr sub price: $8.00; per copy: $1.50; sample: $1.50. 1967. 90pp; 8 x 10. of. circ. 3,000. Reporting time: month. Payment: none. Ads: $100. Discounts: 40%. Pub's reviews. §politics/history.

THE RAG, The Rag Collective, 2330 Guadalupe, Austin, TX 78705. "Articles should not exceed six double spaced typewritten pages. Style should be good English prose, with readability an important factor. What we most need is sophisticated Marxist analyses of capitalism and imperialism in all its aspects, domestic or foreign, without excessive use of jargon. Sectarian polemics not wanted. The work of Paul Sweezy, Noam Chomsky, Richard E. Ward, Wilfred Burchett, Andre Gunder Frank, Felix Greene, Franz Schurmann, etc. should give an idea of the kind of material we need. Articles on cultural matters are also desired, but they should provide a radical analysis rather than be merely descriptions or reviews." 52/yr; 1-yr sub price: $8.00; $12.00 for institutions; per copy: $.25; sample: free, but contributions appreciated. 1966. 16pp; 10 x 14¾ in. circ. 5,000. Submissions not acknowledged unless used. Payment: none. Ads: $240/$120. Back issues: $.25 per copy. Pub's reviews. §Radical politics, contemporary culture. APS.

THE RAG, Roaring Aardvark Press, R. D. Swets, 850 Reynard St SE, Grand Rapids, MI 49507. Poetry, fiction, art, photos, interviews, music, parts-of-novels, long-poems, collages, plays, concrete art. "We are just beginning. As i am a typesetter by trade, i expect to do a great deal of graphic experimentation. I am not expecting to do a great deal of prose. Concrete poems must be interesting on subsequent readings. I expect the magazine to look good. I want to run the best things i can find." 4/yr; 1-yr sub price: $3.50; per copy: $1.00; sample: free, when available. 1976. 24pp; 5½ x 8. of. circ. 500. Reporting time: 2 weeks. Payment: 2 copies. Ads: $25/$15. Back issues: free, when available.

Ragnarok Press, Rochelle Holt, D. H. Stefanson, 1719 13th Ave So, Birmingham, AL 35205, 205-933-6366. Poetry, fiction, art, photos. "*Valbella, Modern Drama Anthology* (Megan Terry, W. Metzger, etc.) *Mysteries Poems* by Rochelle Ratner; *Song Of A Robin Children's Story* by R. Holt; *Yellow Peers, Smooth As Silk,* 45 rpm record by R. Holt. *Night Raised Her* by Isel Revero; *Wind Songs* by R. Zaller; *Sacrifice Exile Night* by Leli Beta; *Froms One Bird,* poems by Rochelle Holt and *Art-letter Collage* by C.P. Graham." avg. price, cloth: $5.00; paper: $4.00; other: $2.00. 1970. 20 or morepp; 6 x 9. †lp/of. Reporting time: immediately. Payment: copies. Discounts: 40% bookstores. CCLM, COSMEP.

RAIN: JOURNAL OF APPROPRIATE TECHNOLOGY, The Rain Umbrella, Lane de Moll,

Tom Bender, Lee Johnson, 2270 NW Irving Street, Portland, OR 97210, 503-227-5110. Articles, art, photos, cartoons, interviews, reviews, letters, news items, non-fiction. "Entries, blurbs, catalog-style, how-to, living lightly, community communications, short, networks, new ideas, right idea at the right time & place, models, patterns, solar, wind, energy conservation, recycling, small-scale neighborhood businesses, land use, utility rate reform, urban gardening, agriculture, video, alternative lifestyles, appropriate technologies, institutional size, scale & style." 10/yr; 1-yr sub price: $10; per copy: $1.00; sample: Free. 1974. 24-32pp; 8½ x 11. of. circ. 5,000. Reporting time: 2 months. Payment: None. Copyrighted, reverts to author. Ads: None. Discounts: 10 or more, 40 percent (60 percent of retail); 100 or more, 60 percent (40 percent of retail). Back issues: $1.00 each if still available. Pub'd 10 issues 1976; expects 10 issues 1977, 10 issues 1978. Pub's reviews: 500 in 1976. §Appropriate technologies in all areas of U.S. life.

Rainbow Press (see also THE MYSTERIOUS BARRICADES), Henry Weinfeld, 1332 Riverside Drive, New York, NY 10033, 212-928-8108. Poetry, long-poems. "Only one book has thus far been published: *An Unlikely But Noble Kingdom* by Bradford Stark, 1974 (Poetry). At this point we cannot publish more volumes." avg. price, paper: $3.00. 1974. 60pp; 6 x 9. lp. avg. press run 750. Reporting time: 1 month. Payment: 10 percent gross. Copyrights for author. Discounts: 40 percent bookstore regular jobber rates.

Rainbow Resin (see also KALDRON), Karl Kempton, 441 North 6th Street, Grover City, CA 93433, 805-481-2360. Long-poems. "unlike most presses, rr began bii publishing books and later changed to publishing a mag, KALDRON, free poetry & vizual poetry: free enterprize. upkuming projekts books & broadsides dependz upon availabl fundz." 1972. of. avg. press run 1,000. Reporting time: 1 to 14 days. Copyrights belong to kontributor. PANP.

RAINCOAST CHRONICLES, Harbor Publishing, Howard White, Peter Trower, Box 119, Madeira Park, BC V0N2H0, Canada. Poetry, fiction, articles, art, reviews, parts-of-novels. "The magazines prime concern is the history and culture of the British Columbia coast. We publish mainly articles on coast history, with the occasional poem or short story. Literary merit is at least as important as historical accuracy. Recent contributors have been Peter Trower, Pat Lane, John Kelly, Scott Lawrence, and many writers never published before." 4/yr; 1-yr sub price: $5.00; per copy: $1.75; sample: $1.75. 1972. 56pp; 7½ x 10½. of. circ. 8M. Reporting time: 4 wks. Discounts: schools & libraries 20%, bookstores 40%, distributors 50%.

Raincrow Press, Alan Basting, Joe Darwish, Christopher Smith, 501 Vivian, Ft Collins, CO 80521. Poetry. "We are trying to do small finely drawn volumes that will reflect careful thought and quality publishing. We have no biases. Our first book: FALLING TOWARD THANKSGIVING, by David Weissman." 1975. 25-35pp; 8½ x 5½. of. Reporting time: 1-3 mos. Payment: in copies.

Raindust Press, David Briscoe, Frank Higgins, PO Box 1823, Independence, MO 64055. "Have published 3 chapbooks by Dave Etter, Harry Stessel and George Gurley. One dollar a piece. will move to full length books this year." 1975. 5½ x 8½. of. Reporting time: 5 weeks. Payment: standard royalties. Discounts: 50% for classroom adoptions.

Raintree, Fredric Brewer, 4043 Morningside Dr, Bloomington, IN 47401, 812-332-6561. Poetry, letters, long-poems. "Have no interest in obscure, muddled writing. Recent writers: Roger Pfingston, J. V. Ricapito, Ona Siporin, Richard Pflum, Judith Roman, Fredric Brewer, Norman Corwin, Carolyn Ricapito, David Wade, Robert Hill Long, Willis Barnstone. Contributors often assist in production and distribution. *Raintree,* however, assumes all costs. *Raintree Annual* planned for 1978. SASE must accompany all mss." avg. price, paper: varies; from $3 to $15. 1975. pp varies; varies. †lp. avg. press run 150. Reporting time: 6 months. Payment: royalties and/or copies. Copyrighted in name of *Raintree.* Rights are negotiated. Discounts: trade 1-4 copies 30%, 5-49 40%, 50-99 42%, 100-more 43%. Pub'd 4 titles 1976; expects 6 titles 1977, 5 titles 1978.

Ramaclo Brothers (see ZONA)

Ransehc Publishing, Inc. (see also TEXAS COUNTRY MAGAZINE), Lynne Chesnar, Publisher; Guida Jackson, Ed-in-Chief, Box 966, Alief, TX 77411, 713-467-5664. Articles, art, photos, cartoons, interviews, reviews, music, letters, news items, non-fiction. "Country music and country arts. We edit prose." avg. price, paper: $1.00. 1976. 32pp; 8½ x 11. of. avg. press run 15,000. Reporting time: 6 wks. Payment: copies. Buys all rights but will reassign poetry & fiction on request. Discounts: 45 percent-20 copies or more. Pub'd 6 titles 1976; expects 6 titles 1977, 6 titles 1978.

RAPPORT, The Slow Loris Press, Anthony Petrosky, Patricia Petrosky, 6359 Morrowfield Avenue, Pittsburgh, PA 15217. Poetry, art, interviews, long-poems. "*RAPPORT* 10 will feature work by Nils Nelson and translations by Jonas Zdanys and Willard Gingericks, as well as poems by Joseph Bruchac, David Ignatow, Simon Perchik." 2/yr; sub price: $3.50/2 issues; per copy: $2.00; sample: $2.00. 1971. 112-124pp; 6 x 9. of. circ. 750. Reporting time: 1-2 months. Payment: contributor copies of magazine. Copyrighted. Discounts: 40% to trade/30% to institutions/30% to classroom. Pub'd 1 issue 1976; expects 2 issues 1977, 2 issues 1978. §poetry/translations. CCLM.

RASPBERRY PRESS (magazine), Raspberry Press, Susan Hauser, W.H. McDowell, Rte. 6 Box 459, Bemidji, MN 56601, 218-751-8497. Poetry, articles, art, satire, letters, criticism. "No unsolicited submissions-return of unsolicited mss. immediately. Focus of each issue determined by whim of editor. R.P. 3 is of a single poet's work. Work by: Carol Heckman, Rich Behm, Beth Copeland, Tina Matthews, Judith Dunaway. R.P. 4/5 - a double issue, *The Aaron Edition*. Submissions closed." Annual.; 1-yr sub price: $2.00; per copy: $2.00; sample: $2.00. 1974. 50pp; Varies. †mi. circ. 300. Reporting time: 1 week. Payment: copy. Copyrighted. no ads. Discounts: None. Back issues: R.P. 2, $1.00; R.P. 3, $2.00. Pub'd 1 issue 1976; expects 1 issue 1977, 1 issue 1978. CCLM.

Rat & Mole Press (see also PRE-RAPHAELITE REVIEW, STONY HILLS), Ritchie Darling, P.O. Box 111, Amherst, MA 01002. Poetry, fiction, satire, criticism. 1971. of. Reporting time: 6 months. Payment: $10 per poem. COSMEP, NESPA.

Rat Attack (see HEARSAY PRESS)

The Rather Press, Clifton Rather, Lois Rather, 3200 Guido Street, Oakland, CA 94602. "We are a strictly self-contained private press, print only mss. we write ourselves, in editions of 150 usually." †lp. Discounts: 25% for purchase of 2 or more copies.

Raven Publications (see also URBANE GORILLA), Ed Tork, 29 Parkers Road, Sheffield S10 1BN, United Kingdom, Sheff. 664-862. Poetry, fiction, parts-of-novels, long-poems. avg. price, paper: 50p/$4.00. 1970. 68pp; A4. of. avg. press run 1,000. Reporting time: 2-3 months. Payment: None. Copyrights for author. Discounts: Rate on enquiry. Pub'd 2 titles 1976; expects 3 titles 1977, 1 title 1978.

LA RAZON MESTIZA/LA MUJER es la TIERRA, Concilio Mujeres, Dorinda Moreno, P.O. Box 27524, San Francisco, CA 94127. 1/yr; 1-yr sub price: $5.00; per copy: $2.00; sample: none. 1970. 64pp. of. circ. 2,000. §only from or about Chicano/Latin women/La Raza/native American movement. COSMEP.

RE:PRINT (AN OCCASIONAL MAGAZINE), Seven Square Press of the Printable Arts Society, Inc., David Ferguson, c/o BOX 749, Box 749 Old Chelsea Station, New York, NY 10011. Poetry, fiction, satire, long-poems. "*RE:PRINT,* an occasional magazine, has been established to print and sell separately works of general interest that have been published in BOX 749 (another publication of Seven Square Press) and other magazines. We run 5000 of each issue and sell the copies until the print run is sold out. So far two stories have been published in the *RE:PRINT* series; we welcome the calling of our attention to other exceptional already-published work. Submissions only on request." 1/yr; price per copy: $.50. 1973. 8-16pp; 4¼ x 11. †of. circ. 5,000. Payment: copies. COSMEP, NESPA.

Real Free Press Foundation, R. Olaf Stoop, Martin Beumer, Oude Nieuwstr-10, Amsterdam, The Netherlands. "6-8 publications per year. Unasked submissions are unwanted." 1965. of. APS.

Realities (see SEVEN STARS POETRY, SEVEN STARS FICTION QUARTERLY, POEM-CARDS)

Rebis Press, Betsy Davids, Jim Petrillo, 5806 Lawton Ave., Oakland, CA 94618, 415-655-5695. Poetry, fiction, art, parts-of-novels, long-poems, concrete art. "We're overloaded and are not encouraging unsolicited mss. at this time. Publish 1-2 books a year." avg. price, other: $25.00. 1972. 32pp; Varies. †of/lp. avg. press run 150-300. Reporting time: 6 mos. or longer. Payment: royalties. Copyright for author. Discounts: Trade 40 percent. Pub'd 1 title 1976; expects 1 title 1977, 1 title 1978. COSMEP.

REBUTTAL! The Bicentennial Newsletter of Truth, The First Ozark Press, Mary Bell, P.O. Box 1126, Branson, MO 65616. Criticism, reviews. "Vivid comment on national and international people, places, and events...with some emphasis on finding the truth in matters of political, educational, and medical nature. A look behind the mass media into what is really happening from the people's viewpoint. Staff-written." 24/yr; 1-yr sub price: $24.00; per copy: $2.00; sample: $2.00. 1976. 4pp; 8½ x 11. Pub's reviews.

Les Recherches Daniel Say CIE. (see GUARD THE NORTH, ENTROPY NEGATIVE)

RECON, Recon Publications, Chris Robinson, Editor; Lewis Bellis, Business Manager, P.O. Box 14602, Philadelphia, PA 19134. Articles, cartoons, interviews, reviews. " a monthly publication dealing with revolutionary military affairs: expose Pentagon planning, revolutionary strategy & tactics, GI movement, Third World struggles, women in the military." 12/yr; 1-yr sub price: $10.00; sample: $.35. 1973. 12pp; 8½ x 11. of. circ. 2,000. Reporting time: within a week. Payment: copies only. Ads: $40/$20/$.05-word. Back issues: $20/year. Pub's reviews. §politics/the military/history/geography. COSMEP.

THE RECORD SUN, Laimons Juris G, 982 University Avenue, Berkeley, CA 94710. Poetry, articles, art, photos, cartoons, satire, criticism, reviews, music, letters, collages. "All work submitted MUST have Stamped Self-Addressed envelopes - or we do not reply. Most of our contributors are subscribers (whom *The Record Sun* is printed most for!)" 4/yr; 1-yr sub price: $4.00; per copy: $0.00; sample: $1.00. 1969. 3-6pp; 8½ x 14. of. circ. We print 7,000. Reporting time: 2 years (Editorship rotates-and our Editors travel frequently). Payment: copies. Not copyrighted. Ads: $50.00/$1.00. Discounts: Deal with retailers directly. Back issues: First Issue Anniversary Issue $2.00. Pub's reviews. §Poetry, photography, graphics, cartoons, joy, fun, satire, statistics, information.

Red Alder Books, David Steinberg, Box 545, Ben Lomond, CA 95005. "We have published two books to date- YELLOW BRICK ROAD, a collection of writings by people who are developing alternative life styles, and *Welcome,Brothers,* collection of poems on changing men's consciousness other books of the growing men's movement will follow." 1974. of. Reporting time: 2 weeks. Payment varies. Discounts: 40% (5 or more); 20% (2-4). COSMEP.

Red Bean Revue (see also AUSTIN PULPWOOD), Jefferson Woodruff, Cathleen Day, Richard Maurer, 501 Park Blvd, Austin, TX 78751, 247-3503. Poetry, fiction, articles, art, photos, cartoons, interviews, satire, criticism, reviews, music, letters, parts-of-novels, collages, plays, concrete art. "We seek the deranged & derived from the critical praxis of universal evolution. As yet we have not stooped to the perversion of rhyme & meter, however, this policy could change..." avg. price, paper: $0.25. 1972. 28pp; 7½ x 11. mi/of. avg. press run 250 issues. Reporting time: Indefinite. Payment: copies. Copyright left open. COSMEP.

THE RED BOOK, White Bear Books, Gerrye Payne, Box 402, Occidental, CA 95465. Poetry, art. "Strong & exciting images in drawing & poetry. Please include return postage." 1/yr; 1-yr sub price: $2.50; per copy: $2.50; sample: $2.50. 1977. 60pp; 5½ x 8½. of. circ. 500. Reporting time: 2-4 weeks. Payment: none. Copyright White Bear Books, reverts to author/artist on request. Expects 1 issue 1978.

RED CEDAR REVIEW, Randy Roorda, Editor; Rose Arenas, Marilyn Basel, Lynn Domina, Janet Flegg, Ron Mieczkowski, Sam Mills, 325 Morrill Hall, Dept. of English, Mich. State Univ., E. Lansing, MI 48824, 517-355-9286. Poetry, fiction, art, photos, interviews, criticism, reviews, parts-of-novels, long-poems. "We have no particular editorial bias-clarity is appreciated, sentimentality isn't. Some recent contributors: William Stafford, Diane Wakoski, Hugh Fox, Judith McCombs, Barbara Drake, Charles Edward Eaton, Dan Gerber, Herbert Scott. We're also open to new writers; we generally try to comment on promising work that we don't accept. In some cases, we ask for resubmissions-no guarantees, of course. In addition to poetry and fiction, we'd like to receive reviews, interviews, and graphic art for consideration. Our two annual issues come out around Dec./Jan. and May/June, but submissions are considered year-round." 2/yr; 1-yr sub price: $3.50; per copy: $2.00; sample: $2.00 for current issue, $1.00 for previous issues. 1965. 64pp; 7 x 10. of. Reporting time: 2 wks to 1 mo. Payment: 3 copies. Copyrighted, reverts to author. no ads. Back issues: $1.00. Pub'd 2 issues 1976; expects 2 issues 1977, 2 issues 1978. Pub's reviews. §Poetry, fiction, translations, books, chapbooks, magazines, anthologies. CCLM.

Red Clay Books, Charleen Swansea, Barbara Campbell, 6366 Sharon Hills Rd, Charlotte, NC 28210, 704-366-9624. Poetry, fiction, art. avg. price, paper: $3.00. 1964. 72pp; 6 x 9. of/lp. avg. press run 2,000. Reporting time: 3 months. Payment: negotiable. Copyrights for author. Discounts: 40 percent-trade; 20 percent-universities.

Red Dust, Joanna Gunderson, 218 E. 81st St, New York, NY 10028. Poetry, fiction. "We publish as we have money." avg. price, cloth: $10.00; paper: $4.50. 1963. pp varies; varies. of. avg. press run 1,000-1,500. Reporting time: 2 mo. Payment: $300 advance against royalty. We copyright for author in most cases. Discounts: libraries 20 percent; wholesalers & booksellers 1 copy-30 percent, 2 or more-40 percent, paperback 1-4 copies-20 percent, 5 or more-40 percent. Pub'd 1 title 1976; expects 4 titles 1977, 3 titles 1978. COSMEP.

Red Earth Press, Karl Kopp, Jane Kopp, P.O. Box 26641, Albuquerque, NM 87125. Poetry, fiction, articles, art, photos, interviews, criticism, reviews, long-poems, concrete art. "1st book-an anthology of contemporary southwest writing. Our basic interest is in the southwest, though this can change." avg. price, paper: $6.95. 1977. 250pp; 6 x 9. ot. avg. press run 1,000. Reporting time: 2 weeks-but prefer to solicit. Payment: to be decided. Copyrights for author. Discounts: 40 percent bookstores. Expects 2 titles 1978. COSMEP.

RED FOX REVIEW, James Coleman, Mohegan Community College, Norwich, CT 06360. Poetry, fiction, art, photos. "A Regional Publication-Connecticut Writers. We sponsor a poetry contest yearly, $100.00 prize. 157 entries/1975, 246 entries/1977." 1/yr; 1-yr sub price: $2.00; per copy: $2.00. 1974. 90pp; 8½ x 5½. lp. circ. 1,500. Payment: copies only. Copyrighted. Discounts: 40%. Back issues: $1. Pub'd 1 issue 1976; expects 1 issue 1977. COSMEP, NESPA.

Red Hill Press, Los Angeles & Fairfax (see also INVISIBLE CITY), John McBride, Paul Vangelisti, 6 San Gabriel Dr, Fairfax, CA 94930. "Having released 25 chapbooks in 1976-77, Red Hill will concentrate in '77-78 on translations: Mohammed Dib, Sarah Kirsch, Adriano Spatola, Antonio Porta and a large anthology of contemporary Italian poets, those most versed in 'the internal tension of language'. Also further chapbooks and illustrated books (*Hawthorne* by Robert Peters & Carol Yeh; *Instead Of An Animal* by Frances Butler & Leslie Scalapino; *2x2* by Paul Vangelisti) to follow. Distributed by Serendipity Books." avg. price, paper: $2.50. 1969. 48-80pp; varies. of. avg. press run 750. Reporting time: Extended. Payment: Copies. Author's/translator's retain c-right. Pub'd 15 titles 1976; expects 10 titles 1977, 10 titles 1978. COSMEP, CCLM.

Red Ochre Press, Ed Baker, 8215 Flower Ave, Takoma Park, MD 20012. Poetry. "What we like; any style; as we can. We like a run of poems up to 64 pgs. Sound. Movement. Light. Space. The page, the paper, the piece uncluttered." 1970. of. Reporting time: 1 month. Payment: 25% of combination of net sales & number of copies produced. Discounts: 10 copies or more-40% 1-9 copies-30%.

Red Studio Press, Susan Winter, Laurence Winter, Route 1 Box 155, Loretto, MN 55357. Poetry, fiction, art, photos, cartoons, satire. "We are trying to combine the best of the large and small publisher by distributing and promoting our books internationally while including each author in the artistic design of his book. We use the highest quality paper, binding, and printing methods, give our authors generous royalties, print runs of several thousand and keep our books in print. Publ. 4 book a year." 1975. 60pp. of. Payment: 10% royalties plus advance to author.

RED WEATHER, Red Weather Press, Bruce Edward Taylor, Patricia V. Alea, PO Box 1104, Eau Claire, WI 54701, 715-834-9870. Poetry, fiction, articles, interviews, criticism, reviews, parts-of-novels, long-poems. "Marge Piercy, Albert Goldbarth, Charles Wright, Carol Muske, Walter Lowenfels, Maura Stanton, Maxine Kumin." 3/yr; 1-yr sub price: $3.75; per copy: $1.25; sample: $1.25. 1976. 24pp; 11 x 17. of. circ. 1,000 per issue. Reporting time: 60 days. Payment: none. Copyrighted, reverts to author. Ads: $30.00/$15.00. Discounts: 40 percent to bookstores, classrooms, agents, jobbers 6 or more copies. Back issues: $1.25. Expects 3 issues 1978. Pub's reviews. §poetry, short stories. COSMEP.

Red Weather Press (see also RED WEATHER), Bruce Edward Taylor, PO Box 1104, Eau Claire, WI 54701, 715-834-9870. Poetry. "First Chapbook in series, *Everywhere The Beauty Gives Itself Away* by Bruce Edward Taylor" avg. price, paper: $1.25. 1976. 22pp; 5 x 4. of. avg. press run 400. Payment: none on first print, 50 percent on 2nd and subsequent printings. Copyrights for author. Discounts: 40 percent on 6 or more copies. COSMEP.

Reed, Cannon, & Johnson, Ishmael Reed, Steve Cannon, Joe Johnson, 2140 Shattuck #311, Berkeley, CA 94704. avg. price, paper: $2.95-$4.95. avg. press run 2,000. Pub'd 3 titles 1976; expects 2 titles 1977.

Reference Service Press, Gail Schlachter, 9023 Alcott Street, Los Angeles, CA 90035, 213-271-1955. "Only reference books are published. Two books published since inception: *Minorities and Women: A Guide to Reference Literature in the Social Sciences;* and *Directory of Financial Aids for Women.*" avg. price, cloth: $17.50; paper: $5.00. 1976. 275pp; 6 x 9. of. avg. press run 3,000. Reporting time: Varies; on the average: one month. Payment varies; 10-25 percent. Author may copyright, if preferred.

REFERENCE SERVICES REVIEW, Pierian Press, T. Schultheiss, P.O. Box 1808, Ann Arbor, MI 48106, 313-434-5530. "Library/reference." Quarterly.; 1-yr sub price: $25.00; per copy: $7.50; sample: Free. 1972. 100pp; 7¼ x 9¾. of. circ. 3,000. Reporting time: 1 week. Payment: None. Pierian Press holds copyright. Ads: $300.00/$160.00. Discounts: None. Back issues: Available. Pub'd 4 issues 1976; expects 4 issues 1977, 4 issues 1978. Pub's reviews: 200 in 1976. §All subjects in reference format.

Regent Graphic Services, R. Martin Helick, P.O. Box 8372, Swissvale, PA 15218, 412-371-7128. "So far, all self-published but may consider carefully written architectural & environmental critiques, scholarly & highly specialized manuscripts and graphics. Please do not send anything without first submitting detailed inquiry. SASE or we scrap. Titles in print: *Merchant Built Houses In Western Pennsylvania, System Of Townhouse Variations, Varieties Of Human Habitation, Elements Of Preschool Playyards, The Complex Vision Of Philo St. John, Fugue For An October Age.*" avg. price, cloth: $12.00; paper: $5.00. 1966. 300pp; size varies. of. avg. press run 1,000. Reporting time: Varies. Payment: Will negotiate. Will negotiate copyrights. Discounts: 20 percent 1-4; 40 percent 5 plus; some room for negotiation. Expects 1 title 1977, 1 title 1978. COSMEP.

Release Press (see also SOME), Larry Zirlin, Harry Greenberg, Alan Ziegler, Michael Andre, 309 W. 104 St. Apt. 9D, New York, NY 10025. Poetry, fiction, art, photos, collages. "Books in print are *City Joys* by Jack Anderson, *Sleeping Obsessions* by Mercy Bona, *Rome In Rome* by Bill Knott, & *Lucky Darryl*, a collaborative novel by Bill Knott & James Tate. Next project *The Touch Code*, poems by John Love. Hope to have it Sept. 1977. Serendipity Books our distributor. We have all the material we can handle, but if you think it would make a great post card, or an innovative printable, send it along." avg. price, paper: $2.50. 1973. 64pp; 5½ x 8½. †of/lp. avg. press run 1,000. Reporting time: varies. Payment: 50/50 after we break even. Copyrights for author. Discounts: 60/40 for over 5 copies. Pub'd 2 titles 1976; expects 2 titles 1977, 3 titles 1978. CCLM.

RELIX, Jerry Moore, Steve Kraye, PO Box 94, Brooklyn, NY 11229, 212-998-1100. Poetry, fiction, articles, art, photos, cartoons, interviews, satire, criticism, reviews, letters, music, news items. "RELIX covers the 'underground' rock music from the late 1960's to present. With accent on San Francisco groups and off-shoots: i.e. - Grateful Dead, Hot Tuna, Airplane/Starship." 6/yr; 1-yr sub price: $7.00; per copy: $1.50; sample: $1.50. 1972. 32pp; 8½ x 11. of. circ. 6,000. Reporting time: 6 weeks before publication. Payment: Photos $2.00; articles, according to content. Copyrighted, does not revert to author. Ads: $125.00/$75.00/$0.30. Discounts: Open. Back issues: $3.00 and up. Pub'd 6 issues 1976; expects 6 issues 1977, 6 issues 1978. Pub's reviews: numerous in 1976. §rock music.

THE REMINGTON REVIEW, Joseph A. Barbato, Fiction; Dean Maskevich, Poetry, 505 Westfield Ave., Elizabeth, NJ 07208. "THE REMINGTON REVIEW is a magazine of new writing and graphics-short stories, poems, parts-of-novels, and art. We will look at quality fiction and poetry of any school, by new as well established writers. However, we tend to shy away from work that indicates the contributor has just learned how toes freeze when it gets too cold outside. But if you and your work are alive, by all means let us see something. We want to do what we can to bring new talent and an appreciative audience together. Please, no Xerox copies or carbons-they will be returned unread. Thus far, our contributors have included Henry H. Roth, Joyce Carol Oates, Stephen Dixon, Douglas Blazek, Alvin Greenberg, Paul West, John Tagliabue, Patricia Goedicke, Karen Swenson, and Joseph Papaleo. Fiction should be 1500 to 10,000 words in length, poetry not more than 100 lines. Drawings and photographs should be suitable for black-and-white offset reproduction. Submissions must be addressed to appropriate editor and be accompanied by an sase." 2/yr; 1-yr sub price: $2.00; per copy: $1.00; sample: free to librarians $5/3yrs. 1972. 80pp; 5 x 7. of. circ. 500. Reporting time: 2 weeks-2 months. Payment: 2 copies. All rights revert to author upon publication. Ads: $50.00/$25.00. Discounts: 10 percent to agencies. Back issues: $1.00 per copy, with the exception of no. 1 vol 1. Pub'd 2 issues 1976; expects 2 issues 1977, 2 issues 1978. CCLM, COSMEP.

Renaissance House (see GAYELLOW PAGES)

Renaissance Press (see UNDINE)

REPARTEE, Milbish Pute, P.O. Box 3232-A, Birmingham, AL 35205. "We produce our own material." irreg. 1970. 6pp; 8½ x 14. †mi. circ. 250. Reporting time: soon. Payment: none. Pub's reviews. §humor/politics.

Resource Publications (see also FOLK MASS AND MODERN LITURGY, MODERN LITURGY), 7291 Coronado Dr, San Jose, CA 95070. Poetry, fiction, articles, art, photos, cartoons, criticism, reviews, music, letters, plays, concrete art. "Interested primarily in creative ideas or examples of use in planning or leading worship" avg. price, paper: $3.00-$21.95. 1973. 32-200pp; 8½ x 11. of. Reporting time: 6 weeks. Payment: editorial fee or royalty on sales. Copyrights for author. Discounts: standard trade. Pub'd 4 titles 1976; expects 4 titles 1977, 2 titles 1978. COSMEP, CPA.

RESOURCES, Richard Gardner, Box 134, Harvard Square, Cambridge, MA 02138. Satire. "RESOURCES is useful information about new products, services, publications, interesting orgainzations, new ideas and events. What's happening on the cutting edge of our changing society. Also, some amusing items from the trailing edge and a few so-so's from the vast middle of America (and the rest of the World)." sub price: $5.00/12 issues & index; per copy: $.50; sample: $.50. 1973. 8pp; 8½ x 11. of. circ. 10,000. Pub's reviews. §how-to/consumer information/technology. COSMEP, APS.

REVISTA CHICANO-RIQUENA, Nicolas Kanellos, Luis Davila, Indiana University Northwest, 3400 Broadway, Gary, IN 46408, 219-980-6692. Poetry, fiction, articles, art, photos, interviews, satire, criticism, reviews, long-poems, plays. "Revista Chicano-Riquena is a journal of Chicano and

Puerto Rican literature and art that also publishes articles of literary criticism, folklore, and popular culture. We publish the most renown Chicano and Puerto Rican writers as well as beginning writers." 4/yr; 1-yr sub price: $7.00 individuals; $10.00 institutions.; per copy: $2.00; sample: $2.00. 1972. 64-170pp; 6 x 9. of. circ. 1,000. Reporting time: immediate acknowledgement; delayed acceptance or rejection. Payment: only on basis of CCLM grant; no fixed rate. Copyrighted, reverts to author. Ads: $60.00/$30.00/0. Back issues: $2.00. Pub's reviews. §Chicano and Puerto Rican literature, art, culture, etc. CCLM.

REYNARD QUAKER FELLOWSHIP OF THE ARTS, Charles Kohler, Yew Tree Road, Dorking, Surrey, United Kingdom. Articles, poetry, art, cartoons, photos, reviews, criticism. "Reynard is the magazine of the Quaker Fellowship of the Arts (QFA). It is largely a vehicle for members' own work, but would not say 'no' to contributions of quality. Quakers can be very catholic. Recent contributors include Clive Sansom, Laurence Lerner, David Blamires. Subscription includes membership of QFA." 1/yr; 1-yr sub price: £1.25; per copy: 25p; sample: 10p. 1954. 32pp; 8½ x 5½. litho. circ. 500. Reporting time: 1 week. No payment. Ads: by negotiation. Discounts: none. Back issues: 25p.

RFD, The Northwest Collective, 4525 Lower Wolf Creek Rd, Wolf Creek, OR 97497. Poetry, fiction, articles, art, photos, cartoons, interviews, satire, criticism, reviews, music, letters, parts-of-novels, long-poems, collages, plays, concrete art. "RFD is a magazine for country faggots. Any material relevant to building our community is considered." 4/yr; 1-yr sub price: $4.00; per copy: $1.25. 1974. 56pp; 7 x 10. of. circ. 3,000. Reporting time: 2 months. Payment: copies. Copyrighted. Ads: $100.00/$50.00/$0.15. Discounts: Bulk 80 percent, bookstore 32 percent, dist. 48 percent. Back issues: Nos. 3-12. Pub'd 4 issues 1976; expects 4 issues 1977, 4 issues 1978. Pub's reviews: 6 in 1976. §Country concerns, spiritual realities, feminism, faggotry, poetry alternatives. CCLM, COSMEP.

RHINO, Suzanne Brabant, Helen Cohen, Liz Peterson, Sandra Rendleman, 1420 North Av., Bannockburn, IL 60015, 312-945-0382. Poetry. "We're looking for good-excellent work by little-known writers, both short prose and poetry—neither to exceed 3 pgs., dble-spaced. (We would, however, like to see five poems or two prose works per writer.) One poem by an established writer will be solicited for each issue. Reports: 1 mo.; Please supply SASE; Pays: 1 contributor's copy. Expects: 2 issues per year, 40 or more pages, Fall and Spring. $1.50/ea. We print on high-quality paper." sub price: $1.50 (paperback). 1976. 40pp; 5½ x 8½. of. circ. 300. Reporting time: 1 month. Payment: 1 contributor's copy.

Rialto Books, Megan Capelthwaite, Box 343, Geneva, NY 14456. Poetry, fiction, articles, photos, interviews, criticism. "Subject areas include nagualism, masonry, fairy-faith, mystical toponomy: tessellation and geodetics, conspiracy theory and criticism. We are interested in authentic radical scholarship and will support and publish those so engaged. We have thus far printed Michael Hoffman's *Singing Roses* and are continuing with his trilogy." avg. price, paper: $2.45. 1976. 40-120pp; 5 x 8½. of. avg. press run 500 copies. Reporting time: four weeks. Payment: copies and rarely, cash. Copyrights for author. Discounts: bulk rate available on request.

RICH'S SUCCESS NEWS, Richard Fairfield, P.O. Box 587, Santa Cruz, CA 95061, 408-427-3959. Art, interviews, reviews, letters. 5/yr; 1-yr sub price: $5.00; per copy: $2.00. 1976. 24pp; 8 x 10. of. circ. 8,000. Reporting time: 30 days. Payment: Free adv. space. Ads: $60.00/$35.00/$0.15. Discounts: 60 percent. Back issues: $2.00. Pub'd 4 issues 1976; expects 5 issues 1977, 5 issues 1978. Pub's reviews. §self-improvement, financial, psychology, sociology.

Richard L. Coulton (see CANADIAN STEAM MAGAZINE)

Richboro Press, Charles Moore, Box 1, Richboro, PA 18954, 215-355-6084. Articles. avg. price, cloth: $8.00. 1975. 200pp; 5½ x 8½. †of. avg. press run 500. Reporting time: 2 wks. Payment: depends. Copyrights for author. Discounts: 20 percent trade universal-other. Pub'd 3 titles 1976. COSMEP, COSMEPA.

RIKKA, Rikka Publishing House, Ted T. Aoki, Gordon Hirabayashi, Thurlow Setsuko, George Yamada, Managing Editor, 1518 Bayview Ave, Toronto, Ontario M4G3B4, Canada, 416-482-0300. Poetry, letters. 4/yr; sub price: 4 issues-$5.00-yr; per copy: $1.00; sample: $1.00. 1974. 48pp; 6 x 9. †of. circ. 1,000. Reporting time: 5 weeks. Ads: $160/$80. Discounts: 20% on bulk orders over 100 copies of one issue. Back issues: $1.00. Expects 4 issues 1978. Pub's reviews: 5 in 1976. §Asia theatre/Human Rights/Cross-cultural inter-ethnic.

RIPPLES, Shining Waters Press, Karen Schaefer, Editor; Jim Schaefer, Publisher, P.O. Box 52, Ann Arbor, MI 48107. Poetry, long-poems, fiction. "Unique publishing venture for developing poet and short fiction writer, as the first 3 issues are printed as newsletters of material being worked on, then final issue printed in formal format. Eclectic poetry not desired, but are interested in natural, organic images of daily life around the perceiver. We will consider material appropriate to the bicentennial if it is not trite or too obvious." 4/yr; 1-yr sub price: $3.00; per copy: $.50 newsletter/$1.50 magazine. 1973. 40pp; 14 x 7. of. circ. 1,000. Reporting time: 1 day. Payment: copy. §poetry/short fiction. CCLM, COSMEP.

RIVER BOTTOM MAGAZINE (Baseball, Floating and Nickle Times), River Bottom Press, R. Chris Halla, Gary Busha, Janet Halla, Box 252, Iola, WI 54595. Poetry, fiction, art, criticism, reviews, parts-of-novels, long-poems. "We have as our goal, publication of the best poetry, fiction, criticism and comment being written today. So far we have published a lot of good poetry and a few short stories, but there seems to be a real shortage of good prose (of any kind). Editorial policy is based solely on literary merit. Some contributors have been Doug Flaherty, Dorothy Dalton, Greg Kuzma, Dave Etter, Peter Wild, Tom McKeown, Lyn Lifshin, William Kloefkorn, Gary Busha, Peter Fallon, Lewis Turco, Mary Zane Allen, Karl Elder, Thomas Johnson, Elaine Dallman, Franz Dousky and G. E. Murrey. 1977 will be *RIVER BOTTOM'S* last year as a magazine and press. Our plans for the future are to publish a pamphlet/chapbook series under another imprint, beginning in late 1977 after publication of the last *RIVER BOTTOM*. The new series will include poetry, fiction, criticism and anything else that impresses us." 2/yr + 3 broadsides and other misc. publications; price per copy: $1.50. 1973. 50pp; 8½ x 5½ (broadsides 8½ x 11). of. circ. 300 approx. Reporting time: 1 mo. or less. Payment: contributor's copies and prizes. Copyrighted. Discounts: 1-5 20%; 6-10 40%; 11 50 41%; 50 & up 45%. Pub'd 9 issues 1976; expects 10 issues 1977. Pub's reviews: 10 in 1976. §poetry, fiction, literary criticism. CCLM.

RIVER STYX, Big River Association, Michael Castro, Jan Castro, 7420 Cornell Ave., St. Louis, MO 63130, 314-725-0602. Poetry, fiction, art, photos, cartoons. Bi-annual; 1-yr sub price: $5.00; per copy: $3.00; sample: $2.00. 1975. 110pp. †of. Reporting time: 3 weeks. Payment: 2 issues. Copyrighted, reverts to author. Ads: None. Discounts: 40 percent discount to stores, 50 percent discount with orders of 10 or more. Back issues: $2.00. Pub'd 1 issue 1976; expects 2 issues 1977. §Myth & poetics. CCLM.

RIVERSEDGE, Riversedge Press, Brian Robertson, Jan Seale, Dorey Schmidt, Ted Daniels, PO Box 1547, Edinburg, TX 78539. Poetry, fiction, art, photos, interviews, reviews. "All four editors are writers, and our individual biases give riverSedge a very broad scope. We are trying to give immediate and personal response to submissions. We pay careful attention to the magazine's appearance as well as content. Most of our contributions are discovered in the mail from people we don't know. We've published Paul Shuttleworth, Charles Taylor, Lisa Trow, Marie Danti, and others. We publish a poem, graphic, or story if it shows an understanding of the CRAFT, not because of someone's name. Poetry: up to 40 lines; anything over 40 had better be a true vision. Send for our riverSedge no. 1 if you have $1.50 to spare and want to get a feeling for our quality." 4/yr; 1-yr sub price: $5.00; per copy: $1.50; sample: $1.50. 1977. 40pp; 5½ x 8. of. circ. 500. Reporting time: immediately, to two weeks. Payment: copies. Copyrighted, reverts automatically, should cite RIVERSEDGE. Discounts: 40 percent discount to bookstores, bulk discount available. Back issues: all $1.50. Pub's reviews. §open to chapbooks or other collections of poetry.

Riversedge Press (see also RIVERSEDGE), Brian Robertson, Jan Seale, Dorey Schmidt, Ted Daniels, PO Box 1547, Edinburg, TX 78539. Poetry, fiction, articles, art, photos, interviews, reviews. "We publish the magazine riverSedge and plan a series of chapbooks and Broadsides series, as well as numerous publications regarding the craft of poetry, At this point, we aren't taking unsolicited material for the chapbooks or broadside series. Read riverSedge and submit it as soon as you can. We are open to writers and artists and photographens who know their crafts." avg. price, paper: $1.50. 1977. 40pp; 5½ x 8. of. avg. press run 500-1,000. Reporting time: immediately to 2 weeks. Payment: arranges. Copyrights for author. Discounts: 40 percent discount to bookstores, bulk discount available.

RIVERSIDE QUARTERLY, Leland Sapiro, Redd Boggs, Fiction; Sheryl Smith, Poetry, Sapiro Box 14451, University Station, Gainesville, FL 32604, Boggs Box 1111, Berkeley, CA 94701, Smith 1346 W. Howard, Chicago, IL 60626. "RQ prints reviews, essays on all aspects of science-fiction and fantasy, but emphasis is on current scenes rather than, e.g., gothic horror or fantasy in the gilded age. Some recent titles: ' *Science Fiction As Will And Idea: The World Of Alfred Bester,*' *'Ursula Leguin's Archetypal Winter Journey,'* *'Mythology In Samuel Delany's Einstein Intersection.'* No maximum word length for essays or reviews, but fiction is restricted to 3,500 words. But contributors are urged to read several copies of the RQ (available at any major public or university library) before sending an ms — -and are warned that our standards are tough: RQ's rejects appear in professional magazines like amazing stories." irreg.; sub price: $2.00, 4 copies; per copy: $.60. 1964. 84pp; 8½ x 5½. of. circ. 1,200. Reporting time: 10 days. Payment: copies. Back issues: $.60. Pub's reviews. §science-fiction. CCLM.

ROAD/HOUSE, Road/House, Todd Moore, 900 West 9th St., Belvidere, IL 61008, 543-9581. Poetry. "Some recent contributors to Road/House have been Harley Elliott, Kirk Robertson, Nila NorthSun, Tom Montag, Albert Goldbarth, Ron Koertge, Thomas McGrath, etc." 2/yr; 1-yr sub price: $1.50; per copy: $0.75; sample: to people mostly free. 1975. 36-44pp; 5½ x 8½. of. circ. about 200 (this varies). Reporting time: usually 2 weeks. Payment: 2 or 3 copies to contribs depends on quantity available. Copyrighted, reverts when I assign them. Discounts: Road/House has no discount rates because it is given away, except in cases where libraries wish to subscribe. Then it is sold at the listed rate. Back issues: free until gone (libraries pay). Expects 2 issues 1978. Pub's reviews. §poetry only.

ROAD APPLE REVIEW, Anick O'Meara, 3263 Shorewood Dr., Oshkosh, WI 54901. Poetry, art, interviews, reviews. "We want straight-forward, honest, image poetry about man, animals, physical nature. Back we go again to the primitive, the ritual, the mythic. 'The sparrow is a bullet in the heart of the living dead.' We have published Bly, Snyder, Stafford, Merwin, Everson, Brigham, Matthews, McKeown, etc." 4/yr; 1-yr sub price: $4.00; per copy: $1.00. 1969. 40pp; 8½ x 7. of. circ. 500. Reporting time: 1-2 wks. Payment: copies only. Discounts: none. Pub'd 4 issues 1976; expects 4 issues 1977, 4 issues 1978. CCLM.

Roaring Aardvark Press (see THE RAG)

Roberton Publications, Kenneth Roberton, The Windmill, Wendover, Aylesbury, Bucks HP22 6JJ, United Kingdom, 0296-623107. Music. "All types of standard and educational music, no pop or jazz, bias towards choral works of all kinds." avg. price, cloth: £1.00; paper: 15p. 1971. 8 pages octavo leaflets, impossible to average other publications.; varies. of. avg. press run 3,000. Reporting time: 2 months. Payment: 10 percent royalty on retail sp. Equal division of performing on recording fees. Copyrights for author. Pub'd 103 titles 1976; expects 60 titles 1977, 60 titles 1978. ASCAP, MCPS, MPA, PRS.

ROCHDALE'S ALTERNATIVE PAPER, Rochdale's Alternative Press, David Bartlett, John Walker, 230 Spotland Rd, Rochdale, Lancs, United Kingdom, 44981. Articles, cartoons, photos, satire, news items, letters. 12/yr; 1-yr sub price: £1; per copy: 7p. 1971. 16pp; 15 x 9. †of. circ. 6,000. Ads: £40.00/£20.00. Back issues: From editors.

Rochester Routes/Creative Arts Projects (see EXIT)

ROCK-N-ROLL NEWS, Communications Company, The, Mike Farrace, Chuck Woodbury, 2815 J St, Sacramento, CA 95816, 916-446-6455. Articles, photos, cartoons, interviews, reviews, music, letters. 26/yr; 1-yr sub price: $5.75; per copy: $.50; sample: $.50. 1975. 24pp; 10 x 15. of. circ. 15,000. Reporting time: 2 weeks. Payment: $3.00-$25.00 average, sometimes more. Copyrighted, reverts to author. Ads: $450.00/$281.00/$.50. Discounts: inquire. Back issues: prices vary, please inquire for price list. Pub's reviews. §Rock music, jazz.

ROCKBOTTOM, Mudborn Press, Judyl Mudfoot, Sasha Newborn, 209 W. De La Guerra, Santa Barbara, CA 93101, 805-962-9996. Poetry, fiction, art, parts-of-novels, long-poems. "We require emotional honesty in our writers, and craft in their writing. Kerry Tomlinson, Jonathon London, Judy Brown, Millie Mae Wicklund, Al Masarik." 4/yr; 1-yr sub price: $5.00; per copy: $1.50; sample: $1.00. 1976. 72pp; 6 x 9. †of/lp. circ. 400. Reporting time: 1 month. Payment: copies only. Copyrighted, reverts to author. Discounts: 40 percent bulk or trade. Pub'd 2 issues 1976; expects 4 issues 1977, 4 issues 1978. LPSC, COSMEP.

ROCKINGCHAIR, Cupola Productions, John Politis, P.O. Box 27, Philadelphia, PA 19105. Reviews. "*ROCKINGCHAIR* is a review newsletter for popular music fans and librarians who buy records. Its main purpose is to help professional librarians in providing a better collection of recordings to meet the needs of their patrons. Popular recordings are reviewed for their artistic quality and their circulation potential. Please check sample copy before submitting any mss." 12/yr; 1-yr sub price: $6.95 (librarians) $11.95 (non-librn); per copy: $0.60 (librarians) $1.00 (non-librn); sample: $1.00. 1977. 12pp; 7 x 8½. of. circ. not stablized yet. Reporting time: 4-6 weeks or less. Payment: copies for mini-articles, album & copies for record review. Copyrighted, reverts to author. libraries that subscribe are permitted reproduction of reviews for in-house use. no advertising. Discounts: none at this time. Back issues: $1.00 for back issues. Expects 9 issues 1977. Pub's reviews. §popular music, artists, and recordings. COSMEP.

ROCKY MOUNTAIN REVIEW, Atlatl Press, Marianna, Leonard Bird, PO Box 1848, Durango, CO 81301, 303-247-2857. Poetry, fiction, art, long-poems, parts-of-novels. "Any length, as long as it's hard-crafted, polished. About 50 percent of the mag emphasizes Rocky Mountain/Southwest writers, themes, or settings. We're more interested in the work than the reputation." 3/yr; 1-yr sub price: $4.00; per copy: $1.50; sample: $1.50. 1974. 52pp; 8½ x 5½. †of. circ. 700. Reporting time: 2 week-2 months. Payment: $5 page + 1 copy of mag. Copyrighted, reverts to author. Ads: None. Discounts: 33-1/3-40%. Back issues: Nos. 1 & 2, $25.00 each; No. 3, $10.00; Nos. 4 & 5, $5.00. Pub'd 3 issues 1976; expects 3 issues 1977, 3 issues 1978. CCLM, COSMEP, COSMEP-WEST.

‡**ROMANIAN REVIEW,** Strada Ion Ghica 5, Bucharest, Romania.

ROOF, Tom Savage, James Sherry, 300 Bowery, c/o Sherry, New York, NY 10012, 212-677-7911. Poetry, fiction, music, letters, long-poems. "We print mostly poetry—though all of the above have appeared" 4/yr; 1-yr sub price: $7.50; per copy: $2.00; sample: $2.00. 1976. 80pp; 8½ x 11. of. circ. 650. Reporting time: 1-3 mos. Copyrighted, reverts to author. Discounts: 40 percent bookstores. Expects 4 issues 1977, 4 issues 1978. COSMEP, NYSSPA.

Rook Press, Inc. (see also JOHN BERRYMAN STUDIES), Ernest Stefanik, Cis Stefanik, 805 West First Avenue, Derry, PA 15327. Poetry, criticism. "Rook Press publishes broadsides, folios, pamphlets, and books. The first broadside series includes poems by Samuel Hazo, William Heyen, Charles Simic, Richard Wilbur, John Updike, and Karen Swenson. The first folio series includes poems by William Heyen, Czeslaw Milosz, Paul Zimmer, Jon Anderson, Gerald Costanzo, Ed Ochester, Mark Halperin, Daniel Halpern, James Tate, Sandra McPherson, Frederick Morgan, and William Stafford. Works in the monograph series include Gary Arpin on *The Dream Songs,* Susan Berndt on the epigraphs to *The Dream Songs,* John Mann on the Dickinson-Higginson correspondence, and J. M. Linebarger on Arthur Sampley. The first in the chapbook series is Margaret's Carney's *Magaret of Cortona.* We regret that we can no longer accept unsolicited manuscripts." Discounts: 40% to bookstores (less on some items).

ROOM, Gail Newman, Kathy Barr, P.O. Box 40610, San Francisco, CA 94110. Poetry, fiction, articles, art, photos, cartoons, interviews, satire, reviews, parts-of-novels, long-poems, collages. "We would like material with a wide range of styles and subject matter. We are also interested in journals, dream writing, articles on women writers, presses, and so on." 2/yr; 1-yr sub price: $3.00; per copy: $1.75. 1976. 64pp; 5½ x 8½. of. circ. 750. Reporting time: 3 mo. Payment: copies of mag. Copyrighted, reverts to author. Discounts: $1.75 ordered from us. Back issues: $1.75. Pub's reviews. COSMEP.

ROOM OF ONE'S OWN, Growing Room Collective, Laura Lippert, Gayla Reid, Gail VanVarseuelo, 1918 Waterloo St, Vancouver, British Columbia V6R3G6, Canada, 604-733-6276. Poetry, fiction, articles, art, interviews, criticism, reviews, parts-of-novels, long-poems, plays. "Material that promotes positive images of women written with respect of literature in mind. We do publish men as well." 4/yr; 1-yr sub price: $7.00-USA $6.00-CA; per copy: $2.00; sample: free. 1974. 80pp; 5½ x 8½. of. circ. 1,500. Reporting time: 6 weeks. Payment: $3.00. Copyrighted, does not revert to author. Ads: no. Discounts: trade 40 percent, bulk-negotiable, agent-15 percent off institutional orders only. Pub's reviews. §literature, women.

ROOTS OF CREATION, Incunabula Collection Press, Lela Meinhardt, Paul Meinhardt, 277 Hillside Av., Nutley, NJ 07110. "A radical analysis of housework, household and family primarily criticism, articles and interviews but open to all contributions fitting the description above." 4/yr; 1-yr sub price: $4.00; per copy: $1.50; sample: free. 1977. 60pp; 5½ x 8½. †of. Reporting time: 3 mos. Payment: 10 free copies per page accepted. Copyrighted, reverts to author. Ads: $150.00/$80.00/$0.20. Discounts: library and classroom-teaching less 25 percent; trade (bookstores) less 45 percent. Back issues: $1.00. §housework/household/family/radical economics. COSMEP.

ROQ Press (see AQUILA MAGAZINE)

The Rose Bower Press, Tom O'grady, Rt 3, Box 252, Farmville, VA 23901, 804-223-8209. Poetry. "This is a poetry pamphlet series-just one pamphlet of 7-10 related poems by a single author is published each year." avg. price, other: $2.00 pamphlet, limited/signed. 1973. single sheet-7 to 10 folds; varies. †of. avg. press run 200 limited, signed edition. only accept requested submissions. Payment: all money beyond pring cost. Copyrights for author. Discounts: none. Pub'd 1 title 1976; expects 1 title 1977.

The Rosetta Press, Daniel Towner, P O Box 771, Athens, OH 45701, 614-592-4822. Poetry, long-poems. "Our first project will be a chapbook by Hollis Summers. Unsolicited mss. welcome." avg. price, paper: $2.00. 1977. 8-12pp; 5½ x 8½. †lp. avg. press run 100-300. Reporting time: 2 weeks. Payment: arranged. Copyrights for author. Discounts: 40 percent trade.

Rosler, Martha (see POSTCARD ART/POSTCARD FICTION)

Ross-Erikson Publishers, Inc., Robert Walton Brown, 1825 Grand Ave, Santa Barbara, CA 93101, 966-2691. Fiction, criticism. "Book length. See enclosed statement of purpose. Contributors-Agehauda Bhaiati, Kenneth Rexroth, Robert Duncan, Jerry Kamstra" avg. price, cloth: $11.95; paper: $4.95. 1973. 250pp; 5½ x 8½. of/lp. avg. press run 3,000. Reporting time: 1 month. Payment: standard. Copyrights for author. Discounts: jobber 50 percent, salesman 10 percent of net. LPS.

ROT, Edition Rot, Max Bense, Elisabeth Walther, Vorsteigstr 24B, Stuttgart D-7000, Germany, 0744/295435. Irregular; price per copy: DM 5; sample: Free. 1960. 24pp; size varies. of. Copyrighted. Discounts: 33½ percent. Pub'd 1 issue 1976.

Rough Life Press, Collective, 734 Venice Way, Inglewood, CA 90302. Poetry, art. "First book, out now-*no place fast,* by F. A. Nettelbeck is poetry & costs $2.00. All forth coming titles will be solicited. Hopefully to publish in the future: Peter Fenton, C. Marks, Thomas Michael Fisher & Stephen Kessler-although they haven't been told yet. So, just getting started. Dig the nettelbeck book." avg. price, paper: $3.00. 1976. 100pp; 5 x 7, 5½ x 8½. of. avg. press run 1,000. Reporting time: 1 month. Payment: 10%. Discounts: 40%. Pub'd 1 title 1976; expects 2 titles 1977, 2 titles 1978.

ROUND NOTES, Circle Press, Frank Hamsher, PO Box N, Boulder Creek, CA 95006, 408-338-2141. Poetry, articles, art, cartoons. "Our magazine is a non-literary publication which is an adjunct to the communaul living experience which runs CIRCLE PRESS and other activies in the S.F. Bay area. It and we are dedicated to raising the Conscious level of mankind out of the destructive patterns that it has devolved to. Submissions on that basis are welcomed, however we cannot pay for them." 12/yr. 1975. 24pp; 5-3/8 x 8½. †of. circ. 1,200 copies per month. Reporting time: 30 to 60 days. No payment. Copyrighted. Discounts: distributed free to a mailing list, interested groups, libraries and bookstores. Back issues: as available, sent for donation. Pub's reviews. §communal living experience. COSMEP.

ROUNDTABLE, Michael Loveland, Bruce Mensinger, Jose J. Ruiz, Arnold Weiss, 170 So. Hobart, Los Angeles, CA 90004. Poetry, fiction, art, cartoons, letters. "'The editors do not profess powers of comprehension beyond human understanding. When we read something that makes the hackles rise and the breath come quick, that is our quest.' We are looking for good, well integrated writing dealing with the human experience. All submissions must be accompanied by SASE. Unpublished fiction, art, cartoons, (no half tones). Stories-complete stories (no fragments) up to 2000 words, prefer fiction, speculative fiction-humor. Poetry up to 24 lines. Art-line drawings & cartoons Published 1 issue 1974. format-non-experimental." irreg.; 1-yr sub price: $4.50; per copy: $1.50; sample: $1.00. 1974. 50pp; 8½ x 11. of. circ. 300. Reporting time: 2 mo or less. Payment: copies. Ads: $50/$30. §fiction-poetry. COSMEP.

Roxbury Poetry Enterprises (see also FISH?), Peter Ganick, 301 Marked Tree Road, Needham, MA 02192. "RPE publishes chapbooks of poetry, especially on the topic of music. Books available by Larry Eigner, Peter Ganick, Clayton Eshelman, Will Bennett. RPE will accept manuscripts of approximately 30-50 pp for consideration. Poetry should be abstract in nature, whatever that may mean to you. FISH? is an avant-'garde' journal." avg. price, paper: $1.50. 1973. 30pp; 8½ x 5½. of. avg. press run 50-200. Reporting time: 1 week. Payment: 3 copies. COSMEP.

RT: A Journal of Radical Therapy (formerly ROUGH TIMES), Collective, Box 89, W. Somerville, MA 02144. Poetry, articles, interviews, satire, criticism, reviews, letters, long-poems, plays. "We are a radical publication, generally styled along the lines of much of the alternative press. We have a very definite bias-focusing on anti-psychiatry and alternatives to traditional (mental) health practices. We also include a lot on gay & prisoners rights, and are strongly feminist." 6/yr; sub price: $6.00/6 issues; per copy: $1.00. 1970. 24pp; 11 x 16. of. circ. 5,000. Reporting time: about 2 months. Payment: none. Ads: $200/$110/$.10 individual-$.20 commercial. Discounts: 35%-50% (over 50). Pub's reviews. §psychology (radical, or from radical humanistic view point). COSMEP.

RUFUS, Gyst Publications, Patricia Ann Bunin, Editor; Robin Shectman, Managing Editor; Wyn Brookhouse, Art Editor; Francis de Buda, Reinhold Kaebitzsch, Edward Reilly, Howard Stroll, Contributing Editors; Ted Bookey, Book Review Editor, PO Box 16, Pasadena, CA 91102. Poetry, articles, art, photos, interviews, criticism, letters. "Some recent contributors: Emilie Glen, Marcus Grapes, Karl Kopp, Bernice Lever, Lyn Lifshin, Alicia Ostriker, Judith McCombs. We return comments and criticism on all material, accepted or rejected." 3/yr; 1-yr sub price: $5.00; per copy: $2.00; sample: $2.00. 1973. 48pp; 5½ x 8½. of. circ. 300 to 500. Reporting time: 4 to 6 weeks. Payment: copies; cash prizes for 3 best poems of the year. Copyrighted, reverts to author. Discounts: 40 percent to bookstores. Back issues: $1.00. Pub's reviews. §poetry. CCLM, COSMEP.

Rumba Train Press, David Barker, 4497 Barrett Street S., Salem, OR 97302, 399-1640. Poetry, long-poems, collages. "RUMBA publishes two types of material: 1)Poetry chapbooks, 8-48 pages, 5½ x 8½. 2) Magazine half-tone photo-collages with a heavy technological bent, averaging 8 pages, 5½ x 4¼, with or without captions/text. Distributed free in L.A. area via LeCal Document System. Ephemeral. Biases: the non-rational, the personal, the erotic, the humorous, the mysterious, the non-commercial, the amaturish. Whismical tastes, dada leanings. Out for a good time. Recent Contributors: Elliot Fried, David Barker, Joseph Laguar. Characteristic Titles: *Studebaker UFO Confidential, Vegas, Single Life, Laguar's Last Dream, Hot Rods Of Spring, Italy My Love, My Silly Banana.*" avg. price, paper: $1.50. 1972. 16pp; 5½ x 8½. of/xerox. avg. press run 200-300 copies. Reporting time: 3 weeks. Payment in copies only. Copyrights for author. Discounts: negotiable; usually just 50 cents off retail price. Expects 1 title 1977.

RUNE, Coach House Press, E. J. Carson, Brian Henderson, 81 St. Marys St., Box 299, St. Michael's College, Toronto, Ontario M5S1J4, Canada. Poetry, fiction, articles, art, satire, criticism, reviews, concrete art. "Recent contributors-A. R. Ammons, bill bisset, Eli Mandel, Barry Goldensohn, J. M. Cameron, Norman Dubie, bp Nichol, Marshal McLuhan, Guenter Eich (trans), Ernst Jandl (trans), Jon Silkin, Daryl Hine, Louis Dudek" 1/yr; 1-yr sub price: $2.50; per copy: $2.50. 1974. 80pp; 5½ x 8½. lp. circ. 500. Reporting time: 1-2 months (we're in no big hurry). Payment: no. Not copyrighted. Ads: $25.00/$12.50. Discounts: 30-40 percent consignment only. Back issues: $4.00 for No. 3, No. 1 & No. 2 are $6.00. Pub's reviews: 2 in 1976. §poetry. CPPA.

The Runeskald Press, Harry R. Skallerup, P.O. Box 612, Annapolis, MD 21404. "Books only." 1974. lp/of. Discounts: trade 10% off list price. COSMEP.

RUNNERS WORLD, World Publications, Joe Henderson, World Publications, P.O. Box 366, Mtn. View, CA 94040. "RUNNERS WORLD presents solid advice on effective diets and exercises information on technique and equipment, and methods for staying motivated. It gives complete coverage of the best and most interesting races, personality profiles and much, much more." 12/yr; 1-yr sub price: $.50; per copy: $.75; sample: free. 1966. 56pp; 9 x 11. of. circ. 50,000. Back issues: $1.00 regular $2.00 special. §sports/recreation/leisure activities.

Running Press, Lawrence Teacher, 38 South 19th Street, Philadelphia, PA 19103, 215-567-5080. "We publish large format quality trade paperbacks. Many of our books show people how to make or do things (*The Loft Book, The Dome Builder's Handbook, Herb Grower's Guide, Shop Tactics*). *Energybook* 1 was the beginning of an on-going project which was continued with *Energybook* 2, published in the fall of 1976. Running Press has an horticultural authority, Richard Nicholls, who has written *The Plant Doctor, The Plant Doctor In His Vegetable Garden, The Handmade Greenhouse,* and *The Plant Buyer's Handbook*. We have also begun a line of reference works including a set of 12 glossaries on specific languages (i.e. banking, real estate, baseball), the *Running Press Dictionary Of Law, The Complete Encyclopedia Of Needlework, The Barefoot Doctor's Manual,* and *The Illustrated Running Press Edition Of The American Classic Gray's Anatomy*. Running Press is always interested in considering energy-, paramedical-, or medical-related manuscripts, and our interest in how-to is still strong. These manuscripts will be returned if accompanied by a self-addressed, stamped envelope." 1973. of. avg. press run 10,000. Reporting time: 1 month. Payment: negotiable. Discounts: 20% 1-4 to 43% 250 plus 50% wholesale. Pub'd 14 titles 1976; expects 22 titles 1977. AAP, PBC.

Russ Haas Press (see NAUSEA)

RUSSIAN LITERATURE TRIQUARTERLY, Ardis, Carl R. Proffer, Ellendea Proffer, 2901 Heatherway, Ann Arbor, MI 48104, 313-971-2367. 3/yr; sub price: institutions-$35.00 cloth $25.00 pa; individual, $15.95; students $12.95; per copy: $5.00 current year. 1971. 500pp; 6 x 9. of. circ. 1,000. Reporting time: 2 months. Ads: $60.00/$40.00. Back issues: $15.00 cloth/$10.00 pa. Pub'd 2 issues 1976; expects 3 issues 1977, 3 issues 1978. Pub's reviews. §Russian literature/history/politics. CCLM, COSMEP.

S **S.A. Growth Press (see also MASTER CALENDER FOR AUSTRALIAN GROWTH GROUPS),** Herb Seal, Managing Assistant, 20 Seventh Ave., Cheltenham 5014, South Australia. Articles, photos, reviews. "We don't publish any magazine just a newsletter & hopefully a journal this year. We do one book a year." avg. price, paper: $1.00. 1975. 4pp; 6½ x 9. of. avg. press run 1,500 of MASTER CALENDER, 10,000 on book titles. Reporting time: 3 months maximum. We try for 2 weeks. Copyrights for author. Discounts: On books 33-1/3 percent less than 10; 40 percent 10 plus; 1 carton 34 copies 50 percent if paid with order. Pub'd 1 title 1976; expects 1 title 1977. IPA.

S Press Books, Michael Koehler, Uwe Moentmann, D-8 Munchen, Zieblandstrasse 10, West

Germany. Poetry, fiction, art, photos, interviews, criticism, music. "S. Press Books publishes a series of texts (primary as well as secondary) which are thought by the editors to represent or add to the understanding of a post-modern stance in their respective fields, i.e. literature, film, the plastic and performing arts. The texts will be published in a scholarly fashion, with annotations if necessary, as mimeographed fascicles at first. Authors will include Robert Creeley, Charles Olson, John Cage, Jonas Mekas, Stan Brackhage, et.al." 1976. 60pp; 75 x 10cm. †mi/of. Reporting time: 3 wks. Discounts: 25% to the trade. Expects 4 titles 1977, 4 titles 1978.

S-B Gazette (see STAR*WEST)

S.H.Y., Eberhard Ebner, Ann Rivers, Jeffrey Willer, %Poste Restante, Hydra, Greece, Jeffrey Miller, 556 Larkin St., San Francisco, CA 94102. Poetry, fiction, articles, art, photos, interviews, satire, criticism, letters, parts-of-novels, long-poems, plays, non-fiction. "The only periodical soliciting criticism by and from its contributors. Also Greece's only English language literary journal, circulated internationally. Recent contributors: Hugh McKinley, Peter Russell, Richard Burns, Richard O'Connell, Brian Keeble." 4/yr; 1-yr sub price: $5.00; per copy: $1.50; sample: free. 1974. 30pp; 8 x 12. inside pp.-xerox/cover-photo offset. circ. 300. Reporting time: 1-2 months. Payment: none. Copyrighted, reverts to author. Ads: none. Discounts: none. Pub'd 4 issues 1976; expects 4 issues 1977, 4 issues 1978. CCLM, COSMEP.

Sable Publishing Corporation, Judith H. McDowell, Robert E. McDowell, P.O. Box 788, Arlington, TX 76010, 817-265-5001. Music. avg. price, cloth: $20.00; paper: $10.00. 1973. 250pp; 5½ x 8½. of. avg. press run 500. Reporting time: 2 mos. Payment: 10 percent royalties. Copyrights for author. Discounts: 20 percent off to libraries, schools. Pub'd 1 title 1976; expects 1 title 1977, 1 title 1978.

Sagarin Press, Roy H. Sagarin, 26 High St, Chatham, NY 12037, 518-392-3094. "Basically oriented to new ideas, creative non-fiction/poetry Ron Morris-circus writer/Lyn Lifshin/Gary Livingston. Please note: so far I have published only books first under the Omphalos Press imprint and now as Sagarin Press." avg. price, cloth: $8.95 / $9.95; paper: $3.00 / $4.95. 1975. Varies. of. avg. press run 1,000. Reporting time. 6 months or more. Payment: copies/royalties/contracts. Copyrights for author. Discounts: 1 copy-25 percent, 2-4 copies 33-1/3 percent, 5-49 copies 40 percent, etc. Cash with single copy orders-40 percent. Pub'd 3 titles 1976; expects 5 titles 1977, 5 titles 1978. COSMEP, NESPA.

SAGEBLOOM, Forum Literati, Guida Jackson, P.O. Box 79464, Houston, TX 77079, 467-2398. Poetry, fiction, articles, art, cartoons, satire, criticism, letters. "This magazine publishes the wisdom and wit of writers age 70 and older. No preaching. Reminiscences are o.k. if they are well written and have a point. We're out to show the world that *older is better*. (prose length: 1,500 words, poetry: 22 lines)" 4/yr; 1-yr sub price: $6.00; per copy: $1.50; sample: $1.50. 1977 (mag), 1974 (press). 28pp; 8½ x 11. of. circ. 1,000. Reporting time: 1 month. Payment: copies only. Copyrighted, reverts to author. Discounts: 45 percent for 20 or more.

SAILING THE ROAD CLEAR, Jane Creighton, Box 238, Old Mystic, CT 06372. Poetry. "Recent contributors-Carol Berge, Jayne Anne Phillips, Jackson Mac Low, Larry Eigner, Joan Larkin, Jonis Agee, Bobby Byrd, Daphne Marlatt, Rochelle Owens, Tom Raworth, Hilda Morley, William Bronk." irreg.; sub price: $5.00/3 issues; per copy: $2.00; sample: $2.00. 1973. 60pp; 5¼ x 8¼. †of. circ. 500. Reporting time: 4 weeks. Payment: copies. Ads: none. Back issues: $2.00 each. Pub'd 1 issue 1976; expects 1 issue 1977. CCLM.

SAINT ANDREWS REVIEW, F. Whitney Jones, St. Andrews College, Laurinburg, NC 28352, 919-276-3652. Poetry, fiction, articles, art, photos, interviews, criticism, reviews, parts-of-novels, long-poems, collages, plays, non-fiction. "Recent contributors: Bunting, Oppenheimer, Dawson, Rumalar, Jonathan Williams, Metcalf, Mishima plus new, unpublished writers. Bulk of material solicited from authors." 2/yr; 1-yr sub price: $4.00; per copy: $3.00; sample: $3.00. 1970. 186pp. of. circ. 1,000. Reporting time: 2-3 months. Payment: none (pay in copies). Buys first serial rights; copyright reverts to author upon publication. Ads: $60.00/$30.00. Discounts: 40 percent to the trade.

Back issues: all but Vol 1, No. 1 available. Pub'd 2 issues 1976; expects 2 issues 1977, 2 issues 1978. Pub's reviews. §poetry, fiction. CCLM.

ST. CROIX REVIEW, Angus MacDonald, Ed & Publ.; Michael S. Swisher, Book Review Ed., Box 244, Stillwater, MN 55082. Articles, cartoons, criticism, reviews, letters. "19th century liberalism" 6/yr; 1-yr sub price: $10.00; per copy: $2.00. 1968. 48pp; 6 x 9. of. circ. 2,000. Reporting time: 14 days. Payment: none. Ads: $100. Discounts: 50% for bulk orders, of 10. Back issues: $2.00. Pub's reviews.

Saint Heironymous Press, Inc., David Lance Goines, PO Box 9431, Berkeley, CA 94709, 415-549-1405. Poetry, art, concrete art. avg. price, paper: $9.50. 1971. 56pp; (large format). †of/lp. avg. press run 5,000. Copyrights for author. Discounts: trade 40 percent (over $500 - 50 percent), Educational Institutions 20 percent. Pub'd 1 title 1976; expects 1 title 1977, 2 titles 1978.

St. John's Bread Church (see LIGHT TIMES)

ST. LOUIS JOURNALISM REVIEW, FOCUS/ Midwest Publishing Co., Inc., Group Edited, 928A N. McKnight, St. Louis, MO 63132, 314-991-1698. Articles, interviews, satire, criticism, reviews, letters. 6/yr; 1-yr sub price: $5.00; per copy: $.50; sample: $.50 plus postage. 1970. 12-16pp; 11 x 16½. of. circ. 5,000. Reporting time: 2-4 weeks. Payment: $25.00. Ads: $350.00/$185.00/$.16. Discounts: 20% to subagencies. Back issues: $1.00 plus postage. Pub's reviews. §journalism, particularly St Louis area.

St. Luke's Press, Anna Farris, St. Luke's; Gary Martin, Marilou Bonham Thompson, 1474 Harbert, Memphis, TN 38104, 901-276-8028. Poetry, fiction, art, photos, parts-of-novels, long-poems, collages, plays, concrete art. "St. Luke's Press—we are publishers of book-length works in general literature and of books for children. While we are interested in quality work from other sections, our primary function is to provide mid-south writers with a national audience and national distribution." avg. price, cloth: $5.95; paper: $3.95. 1974. pp Varies; size varies. of. avg. press run 2,000. Reporting time: 1-2 months. Payment: 25 percent of profit. Copyrights for author. Discounts: 40 percent trade; bulk, negotiable; institutions, 20 percent; wholesalers, 50 percent. Pub'd 4 titles 1976; expects 1 title 1977, 3 titles 1978. COSMEP, COSMEP-SOUTH.

St. Mawr Jazz Poetry Project (see VEINS)

The Salamander Imprint, Farida Majid, General Editor, 3 Cadogan Square, London SWIXOHT, United Kingdom. Poetry. "We are dedicated to publishing beautifully produced books of high quality poetry by poets who deserve to be published by big publishers but don't. We do not publish collections of less than 25 poems. At this stage of the game we are discouraging unsolicited mss, but next year may be different. Our current catalogue: *Take Me Home, Rickshaw*, poems by contemporary poets of Bangladesh, selected and translated by Farida Majid. *The Horses Of Falaise*, poems on the experiences of a fighting soldier in World War 2 by Victor West. *The Goldfish Speaks From Beyond The Grave*, by Jim Burns, a poetry book society recommendation, summer 1976. *Woods and Mirrors*, by Jack Carey; and *Thursday Evening Anthology*, ed. Farida Majid, illus. Feliks Topolski." avg. price, cloth: £3.50; paper: £2.50; other: specially bound limited editions, numbered and signed by author/s and artist: £9.00. 1973. 48-80pp; 8½ x 5¾ or 6 x 9. lp. avg. press run 1,500. Reporting time: 2 to 3 weeks. Payment: standard royalty to the author or its equivalent in copies of the book at its retail price. Discounts: 33-1/3% in the UK, 40% in the US. Pub'd 1 title 1976; expects 2 titles 1977. ALP.

Salem Press, Inc. (see THE CONTEMPORARY LITERARY SCENE)

Salient Books, Carl D. Clark, Eric S. Vogel, 3007 University, Austin, TX 78705, 512-472-7415. Poetry, fiction, articles, art, photos, cartoons, interviews, satire, criticism, reviews, music, letters, parts-of-novels, long-poems, collages, plays, concrete art. " *Salient Books* will print out of the ordinary (avantegarde?experimental?radical? unbelievable?) chapbooks and eventually books of writing, graphics and music. We will attempt to print mostly what is laughingly called non-fiction/concrete/graphics/music works. We are devoted to information flow first, quality of the manufactured article second and merchandising third. Crayolas and butcher's paper anyone?" 1977. pp varies. mi/of. avg. press run 1-500. Reporting time: varies. Payment varies. Copyrights for author. Discounts: varies.

Saline Productions, Carl D. Clark, 3007 University, Austin, TX 78705, 512-472-7415. Poetry, fiction, interviews, music, parts-of-novels, long-poems, plays. *"Saline Productions* distributes/produces/trades/acts as a clearinghouse for/tapes (and—dream on —hopefully someday records) of 'non-commercial' music, sound poetry, drama, etc." avg. price, other: $1.00 plus reel/cassette. 1970. †tape. avg. press run varies. Reporting time: depends. Payment: depends upon number of composers/performers on tape: they split 75 cents per tape sent out. Does not copyright for author. Discounts: write us.

SALMAGUNDI, Salmagundi, Robert Boyers, Editor; Peggy Boyers, Managing Editor, Skidmore College, Saratoga Springs, NY 12866, 518-584-5000 (ext 302). Poetry, fiction, articles, art, photos, interviews, criticism, reviews, long-poems, plays. "Recent contributors: Robert Lowell, Helen Vendler, Robert Pinsky, John Peek, Bob Hass, Philip Booth, Mary Kinzie, Sanford Pinskea, Christopher Lasch, Tony Tanner, Henry Pachter, Jack Jone, Charles Molesworth." 4/yr; 1-yr sub price: $6.00; per copy: $2.00-$4.00; sample: $2.00-$4.00. 1965. 160pp; 5½ x 8½. of. circ. 3,000. Reporting time: 4-5 months maximum. Copyrighted, does not revert unless specifically requested. Ads: $70.00/$40.00. Discounts: none. Back issues: $3.00-$10.00. Pub'd 4 issues 1976. Pub's reviews: 10 in 1976. §poetry, social sciences, & art history, cultural history & film criticism. CCLM.

SALOME: A LITERARY DANCE MAGAZINE, Effie Mihopoulos, 5548 N. Sawyer, Chicago, IL 60625. Poetry, fiction, articles, art, photos, cartoons, interviews, criticism, reviews, music, plays, concrete art, satire, letters, long-poems, collages. "SALOME is a dance magazine that contains poems, short stories, plays, etc. about the dance; i.e., modern dance or ballet. Please, do not send any material unrelated to the dance. Recent contributors: Bobbie Louise Hawkins, Ted Berrigan, Alice Notley, John Tagliabue, Richard Kostelanetz." 4/yr; 1-yr sub price: $7.50; per copy: $2.00; sample. $2.00. 1975. 100pp; 8½ x 11. of. circ. 500. Reporting time: Immediately - 2 weeks. Payment: contributor's copy. Ads: $30.00/$15.00/$1.00. Discounts: 40%. Back issues: $5.00 each. Pub'd 2 issues 1976; expects 4 issues 1977, 4 issues 1978. Pub's reviews: 13 in 1976. §dance, performing arts. CCLM, COSMEP.

SALT, Tegwar Press, Robert Currie, 1119-13th Ave N.W., Moose Jaw, Sask S6H 4N5, Canada. Poetry, fiction, reviews. "We tend to be eclectic, believing that poetry is the exciting game without any rules. Hence, we print whatever we like, but what we like tends to be concrete and vivid, poetry that communicates thought and emotion. Recent contributors include Szumigalski, Suknaski and Mitchell. We are now printing the occassional short story as well. Guest editors for next 2 issues Geoffrey Ursell & Barbara Sapergia. Editorial address: 2226 McTavish, Regina, Sask., Canada, S4T3X2." 2/yr; 1-yr sub price: $1.50; per copy: $0.75; sample: $0.75. 1969. 26pp; 8½ x 11. mi. circ. 350. Reporting time: 1-2 mos. Payment: copies only. Back issues: $1.00 each. Pub'd 2 issues 1976; expects 2 issues 1977, 2 issues 1978. Pub's reviews. §poetry.

THE SALT CEDAR, Tamarix House, Don Snow, Editor; Lyn Chaffee, Assistant Editor, Route 3, Box 652, Fort Collins, CO 80521, 303-568-7472. Poetry, fiction, articles, art, reviews, parts-of-novels, long-poems. "Preference toward letters with a strong sense of place, environmental statement. Hope to print more non-fiction prose & short stories in upcoming issues. Mostly interested in writing about the West, its landform, biota, community. Contribs: Peter Wild, Reg Saner, Lynn Strongin, Pamela Stewart, Lyn Hejinian, Phil Foss..." 2/yr; 1-yr sub price: $3.50; per copy: $2.00; sample: $2.00. 1976. 30-40pp; 8½ x 11. of. Reporting time: 3-4 weeks. Payment: copies. Copyrighted, does not revert to author. Discounts: 40 percent for all. Expects 2 issues 1977. Pub's reviews. §poetry, non-fiction prose, natural history.

Salt Lick Press (see LUCKY HEART BOOKS)

Salt-Works Press (see also SOMA-HAOMA), Tom Bridwell, Edward Harper, Box 649, Dennis,

MA 02638, 617-385-3948. Poetry, fiction, articles, art, photos, criticism, long-poems, non-fiction. "Fine hand-set letterpress publications, hand-sewn, graphics, often use hand made paper (our own) for covers." avg. price, cloth: $15.00; paper: $3.00-$5.00. 1973. pp varies; 6 x 9. †lp. avg. press run 300-400. Reporting time: 6 weeks. Payment: Copies, plus. Copyrights for author. Discounts: Standard. Pub'd 8 titles 1976; expects 10 titles 1977, 10 titles 1978.

SALTHOUSE, D. Clinton, 1562 Jones Dr., Ann Arbor, MI 48105. Poetry, long-poems. "SALTHOUSE is a magazine of field notes/histories & geographies. Interested in narratives/imagined journeys/popular histories/conceptual development of the American horse/air voyages to the Arctic/historical re-expressions/alongside solstice & blessings of the land & oceanographies & land records & beautiful declarations of love." 2/yr; 1-yr sub price: $2.50; per copy: $1.25; sample: $1.25. 1975. 36pp; 5½ x 8½. of. circ. 300. Reporting time: 2 months. Payment: 2 issues & gift. Copyrighted, reverts to author. Ads: $20/$15/$.20 per word. Discounts: Not enough volume to discount. Back issues: Regular prices. Pub'd 1 issue 1976; expects 1 issue 1977, 2 issues 1978. §Historical & geo/poetics.

SAM HOUSTON LITERARY REVIEW, Sam Houston State University Press, Paul Ruffin, English Department, Sam Houston State University, Huntsville, TX 77340. Poetry, fiction, interviews, reviews. "Because of the size of our magazine, we do not encourage the submission of long poems or exceptionally long short stories. We'll probably expand soon to incorporate photography, critical essays on literature and culture, etc." 2/yr; 1-yr sub price: $3.00; per copy: $1.50. 1976. 64pp; 6 x 9. lp. circ. 500 to 750. Reporting time: 6 weeks. Payment: copies only. Copyrighted. no advertising. Back issues: $1.50. Pub'd 2 issues 1976; expects 2 issues 1977, 2 issues 1978. Pub's reviews: 6 in 1976. §Poetry, fiction, drama. COSMEP.

SAMISDAT, Samisdat Associates, Merritt Clifton, Editor-in-Chief; June Kemp, Assistant Editor; Robin Michelle Clifton, Reviews Editor; Mark Phillips, Contributing Editor; Bill Robinson, Contributing Editor, Box 231, Richford, VT 05476. Poetry, fiction, art, satire, criticism, parts-of-novels, long-poems, plays. "We resemble no other publication, past or present—except our imitators. We are a typewriter/offset, kitchen-printed literary journal, in a loose class with some 2,000 others indexed here. But at this similarity ends. We don't belong to COSMEP, or ACADEMIA. We don't live off grants or donations. We don't print psuedo-authors counting credits like Guinness Book of Records candidates count bounces of the yo-yo. We regard effective communication, not ego-blast, as the first and foremost purpose of writing and publishing. If talented and devoted, the unknown, the disenfranchised, and the alienated may find themselves among friends here—but the hobbyist, the dingaling, and the piss-ant 'name' who thinks we owe him something had better duck. We handle all submissions as personal correspondence, though we receive several hundred a week, and spare neither oaths nor criticism. If we can help, we do so; if something's shit, we say so. We see as our essential duty the preservation of meaning in a world where the medium itself all too often becomes the message—as in television, yes, but also in sonnet, haiku, and conversely much experimental writing, where form or lack thereof takes precedence over content. At the same time, we remain exceptionally sensitive to style. Clumsy writing may sell to the slicks, may be simultaneously an unfortunate small press hallmark, but to us weak style indicates weak commitment; we have room only for the sincerely dedicated. Our measure is greatness—and against the dial, the little review, and others we admire but differ from, we still measure ourselves whiskers ahead. We do seek new contributors—actively and enthusiastically. We will also consider reprints from foreign magazines and magazines defunct for at least three years (to avoid repeating readerships; we do fully acknowledge.) However, the would-be submitting without first having read us stands only one chance in 100, we find from current statistics. There are writers, and then there are *SAMISDAT* writers, among the semi-regulars Lorna Dee Cervantes (San Jose), Barry Chamish (Jerusalem), Miriam Sagan (Cambridge), W. E. Ehrhart (Philadelphia), Mort Castle (Crete, Illinois), Walter Cummins (Morristown, NJ), H. R. Coursen (Brunswick, Maine), Kurt Nimmo (Florida). No clique; just folks doing what we like & often. We publish from love—demanding, consuming, but sustaining as well." 6/yr; sub price: $5.00-500 pages; subscribe in any amount at 1 cent/printed page. $50-all future issues & books.-yr; per copy: $1.00; sample: $1.50. 1973. 80pp; 8½ x 5½. †of. circ. 500. Reporting time: Two seconds to two weeks. Payment: copies. Ads: $15. Discounts: 40% on orders over ten. Classrooms can dicker. Back issues: From $.50 to $2.00. Pub'd 16 issues 1976;

expects 12-15 issues 1977, 12-15 issues 1978. Pub's reviews: 270 in 1976. §We review & rate everything that comes in, if semi-relevant to writing & literature; exchange with anyone. We only review quality at any length, however, and are death on crudzines, vanity, & sheer self-indulgence. CCLM.

Samisdat Associates (see also SAMISDAT), Box 231, Richford, VT 05476. Poetry, fiction, criticism. *"SAMISDAT* chapbooks and novels are published under a cooperative arrangement whereby authors pay for the paper and any necessary outside printing, while we supply the skilled labor. Press runs are proportionately divided. We ask would-be authors to confer with a few of those we've previously published before submitting, as we're proud of our success in bringing new writers before the public, and will fight the clown confusing us with a vanity operation. Our judges and standards are the same as for *SAMISDAT* regular issues. Previous books have included collections of fiction, poetry, and criticism, longpoems, novels, and field guide. Among our authors are H.R. Coursen, Merritt Clifton, June Kemp, Deborah Knaff, James Magorian, Gordon Clark, Fred Merkel, Walter Cummins, Miriam Sagan, Paul Payack, Peter Payack, Gail White, Mort Castle, W. D. Ehrhart, Robert Joe Stout, Robin Michelle Clifton, Kurt Nimmo, and M.K. Kulikowski. We prefer publishing those previously in *SAMISDAT* regular issues, but will consider others. Of our book releases, Maine Times recently stated that though 'the format and typography are hardly as opulent as the products of The New York Publishers', we are 'producing more quality more frequently than any other publisher in the country.' We wouldn't settle for less." 1973. 8½ x 5½. †of. avg. press run 400. Reporting time: 2 minutes to 2 weeks. Copyrights for author. Pub'd 13 titles 1976; expects 12-15 titles 1977, 12-15 titles 1978.

SAMPHIRE, Michael Butler, Kemble Williams, Heronshaw, Holbrook, Ipswich, United Kingdom. Poetry. "Reviews used. Mag should be studied first." 3/yr; 1-yr sub price: £6.00; per copy: £1.50. 1968. 44pp; 8 x 6½. lo. circ. 700 plus. Reporting time: 6-8 wks. Payment: £2.00 per poem/page. Copyrighted. Ads: By arrangement. Discounts: 33-1/3 percent. Back issues: by arrangement. Pub'd 3 issues 1976; expects 3 issues 1977, 3 issues 1978.

SAN FRANCISCO REVIEW OF BOOKS, Ron Nowicki, 2140 Vallejo St., San Francisco, CA 94123. Articles, photos, cartoons, interviews, criticism, reviews, letters. "Book reviews of titles from both large and small presses; current titles, but not best sellers. Not interested in reviews on books dealing with Nixon, Watergate, Patty Hearst. Minimum no. words: 600; Max. 2,000, with editor's ok. Recent contributors: Andrei Codrescu, Leonard Michaels, William Kotzwinkle, Harold Norse, Stanley Weintraub, Gloria Frym, Valerie Miner." 11/yr; 1-yr sub price: $7.50; per copy: $0.75; sample: $0.75. 1975. 40pp; 7 x 10. of. circ. 10,000. Reporting time: 3-4 wks. Payment: 1 yrs. subscription plus copies. Ads: $275.00/$150.00. Discounts: Usually 30 percent on consignments, 40 percent on outright purchases of 5 or more. Back issues: 75¢. Pub'd 11 issues 1976; expects 11 issues 1977, 11 issues 1978. Pub's reviews: 132 plus in 1976. CCLM, COSMEP.

SAN JOSE STUDIES, San Jose State University, A.N. Okerlund, San Jose State Univ., San Jose, CA 95192, 408-277-3460. Poetry, fiction, articles, art, photos, cartoons, interviews, satire, criticism, reviews, letters, long-poems, non-fiction. "*San Jose Studies* is published in February, May, and November. Manuscripts, books for reviewing, photo essays, and editorial communications should be sent to the editor at the above address, subscriptions and business communications should be sent to the managing editor at the above address. *San Jose Studies* publishes articles, literature, photographs, and art appealing to the educated public. Critical, creative, and informative writing in the broad areas of the arts, humanities, sciences, and social sciences will be considered. Please limit contributions to a maximum of 5,000 words and avoid footnotes when possible. All mss. must be typewritten and double-spaced on standard 8-1/2 x 11 white bond. The editorial board will need an original and one copy of the ms. SASE for return. Only previously unpublished work will be considered." 3/yr; 1-yr sub price: $8.00; per copy: $3.50; sample: $3.50. 1975. 120pp; 6 x 9. of. circ. 2M. Reporting time: 2-3 mos. Payment: 2 copies. Copyrighted. Ads: $100/$60/none. Discounts: none. Back issues: $2.00. Pub'd 3 issues 1976; expects 3 issues 1977, 3 issues 1978. Pub's reviews: 3 in 1976. §literature, history. Council of Editors of Learned Journals.

‡**San Marcos Press**, PO Box 53, Cerrillos, NM 87010.

SAN MARCOS REVIEW, San Marcos Press, Gene Frumkin, David Johnson, P.O. Box 4368, Albuquerque, NM 87106. Poetry, articles, art, interviews, reviews, long-poems. "Primarily concerned with poetry of location, poetry of reverie, poetry of anger. As a general policy we are interested in *poets*. We would prefer to publish several poems from a few rather than single poems from many. These 'biases' are not rigid, but more the indication of a course we want to follow." 2/yr; sub price: $4.00/3 issues in U.S.-$5.00/3 issues other countries; per copy: $1.50; sample: free to libraries & educ. institutions. 1976. 80-100pp. †of. circ. 500 initially. Reporting time: 4-6 wks. Payment: 2 copies. Discounts: 40% trade/20% bulk, classroom, etc. Pub's reviews §poetry/fiction.

Sand Dollar, Jack Shoemaker, Vicki Shoemaker, 1205 Solano Avenue, Albany, CA 94706. Poetry, articles, photos. "We are presently unable to consider unsolicited manuscripts. Recent books by Michael Davidson, Bill Berkson, Leslie Scalapino, Theodore Enslin, Wendell Berry, Ronald Johnson." avg. price, cloth: $15.00; paper: $4.00. 1970. †of/lp. avg. press run 1,000. Reporting time: 1 month. Payment: 10% royalty. Pub'd 4 titles 1976; expects 5 titles 1977.

Sand Project Press/US (see BLUE PIG)

SANDWICHES, Excello and Bollard, Paul Lamprill, Mark Williams, 10 Minden Close, Danesholme, Corby, Northamptonshire NN189EW, United Kingdom. Poetry, fiction, articles, art, satire, reviews, news items, criticism, music, letters, long-poems, concrete art, non-fiction. "No limit on length of material or content. Many short poems used, also the tongue-in-cheek throwaway satiricial. Opposed to more academic, styles." 4/yr; 1-yr sub price: £1 ($2.00); per copy: 25p; sample: 10p. 1973. 30pp; A4. †dup. circ. 150. Reporting time: often by return never more than few days. Payment: none. Ads: no advertising. Discounts: free poetry books to £1 subscribers. Back issues: £1 or $2 for collection of all available back issues. Pub'd 5 issues 1976; expects 4 issues 1977, 4 issues 1978. Pub's reviews: 100 in 1976. §all areas-especially art.

Santa Cruz Poetry Center (see RADAR)

SAPPHO, Sappho Publications Ltd., Jacqueline Forster, BCM/PETREL, London WC1V6XX, United Kingdom. Articles, poetry, fiction, art, cartoons, photos, satire, reviews, news items, interviews, criticism, letters. "Contents contributed by readers/subscribers about women's/gays rights. Contributors: Jill Tweedie, Anna Raeburn, & Maureen Duffy." 12/yr; sub price: U.K. subs. £2.50 6 months; overseas subs £6.40 12 months; per copy: 40p plus 10p postage. 1972. 36pp; sixmo. lo. circ. 3,000. Reporting time: 1 month. Payment: none. Ads: £20/£12/£8 1/4. Discounts: 10% minumum on ads. Back issues: £1.00 for 3.

The Saturday Centre (see also SATURDAY CLUB BOOK OF POETRY), Patricia Laird, Kenneth Laird, Box 140 P.O., Cammeray, NSW 2062, Australia. "po/short stories,stories & verse for kids, stories & verse by kids/essays (if we can get them). Publishers of THE SATURDAY CENTRE BOOKS FOR KIDS, THE SATURDAY CENTRE POETS' SERIES & THE SATURDAY CLUB BOOK OF POETRY." 1972. 12-60pp; A4 folded to A5. †of/lp. Reporting time: less than 3 months. Payment: $50 to writer if 500 copies done/$100 to writer if 1,000 copies done. Also 50 copies of book to writer. Discounts: 40% to bookshops & agents.

SATURDAY CLUB BOOK OF POETRY (sub-title: SCOP), The Saturday Centre, Patricia Laird, Joanne Burns, Rae Desmond Jones, Philip Hammial, Box 140 P.O., Cammeray NSW 2062, Australia. Poetry, fiction, art, photos, cartoons, satire, letters, long-poems, collages, concrete art. "Wide age-range of contributors accepted; no restrictions on style; cross-section of known & unknown poets; some recent contributors: Judith Wright, Judith Rodriguez, Philip Hammial, Philip Neilsen, Peter Kocan, Rae Desmond Jones, John Jenkins, Joanne Burns, Peggy Clarke, Colleen Burke, Philip Edmonds, Trevor Reeves, Cathy Warry, etc. No limit on length of poems. 2,000 word limit on prose fiction." 4/yr; 1-yr sub price: $6.00 (Aust); per copy: $1.80 (Aust); sample: $1.80 (Aust). 1972. 48pp; A4 folded to A5. †of. circ. 500. Reporting time: 3 months. Payment: minimum $2 for poems up to 10 lines-10/ each additional line. short stories & prose varies by arrangement. $5p or b & w photo/graphics/cover designs. Discounts: bookshops & agents 40%.

Scarecrow Books (see also THE WEST CONSCIOUS REVIEW, CROW'S NEST), 1050 Magnolia No. 2, Millbrae, CA 94030. "Write for catalog. Titles in 1977 include: *Passport* by Leon Spiro; *ORG* -1 by A. D. Winans; *If I Don't Find Pleasure I Will Die* by Roger W. Langton; *The 'Poets-Card' Series; Cancer Quiz* by Paul F. Fericano; and the huge 120 page *Stoogism* Anthology w/27 photos. Not accepting any new manuscripts at this time." COSMEP.

Scarecrow Press, Eric Moon, President; Robert Franklin, Executive Editor, P O Box 656, Metuchen, NJ 08840, 201-548-8600. Criticism. "Very varied list. Emphasis on reference books, scholarly monographs, some professional textbooks. Dominant subject areas include: Cinema, women, minorities, music, literature, library science, social work, parapsychology." 1950. 150pp; 5½ x 8½. of. avg. press run 1,000. Reporting time: 1 week. Payment: 10 percent first 1,000 copies; 15 percent thereafter. Copyrights for author. AAP, ALA.

The Sceptre Press, Martin Booth, The Sceptre Press, Knotting, Beds MK44 1AF, United Kingdom. Poetry, fiction, long-poems, plays. "Length immaterial: catholic range of style and biases but no 'pop' or concrete work; recent contributors include Robert Creeley, Harry Guest, George MacBeth, Gavin Ewart, Ken Smith, Susan Musgrave, Denis Goacher, Peter Redgrove, Penelope Shuttle. Unknown poets welcome to submit, but always sending sae. The aim is to publish good verse in booklet form. Do please see what we publish before submitting." 1968. 20pp; A5. 1/press. avg. press run 150-250. Reporting time: 6 wks. Payment varies. Copyright retained by author. Discounts: trade only. Pub'd 18 titles 1976; expects 18 titles 1977, 18 titles 1978.

SCHISM: A Journal of Divergent American Opinion, Schism Publishing Company, Jeffrey A. Norris, 3 West Highland Court, Mount Vernon, OH 43050, 614-392-8586. Poetry, articles, art, photos, cartoons, letters. "No longer than 4 printed pages (72 column inches) 2 copies to be submitted, w/*vita*/bio of author. Subject to editorial change of style, grammar, etc., only. No excison of material by editor." 4/yr; 1-yr sub price: $8.50; per copy: $2.25; sample: $2.00. 1969. 64pp; 8½ x 11. of. circ. 1,150. Reporting time: variable 2 mos. Payment: none. Discounts: 10% to magazine subscription agencies. Back issues: $2.50. Pub'd 3 issues 1976; expects 4 issues 1977, 4 issues 1978. §political science/social change/political economy/anything dealing with human & civil rights. COSMEP.

SCHMUCK ANTHOLOGICAL, Beau Geste Press/Libro Accion Libre, Filipe Ehrenberg, David Mayor, Apdo, Postal 27, Xico, Veracruz, Mexico, Barhatch Farm, Barhatch Lane, Cranleigh, Surrey, United Kingdom. Articles, poetry, fiction, art, news items, interviews, music, criticism, letters, collages, concrete art, photos. "Stop reading this garbage!! Spend your time more profitably by rushing us a request for our latest mail order catalogue. . ." irreg.; sub price: £4 for copies to that value plus 10 percent discount; per copy: varies; sample: review only. 1972. 90pp plus; 195 x 280mm. lo/rubber stamp. circ. 550. Reporting time: So slow you'd never notice. Payment: copies. Ads: £3.50 to £20.50 (rates on application). Discounts: usual trade and to collectors; 10% to subscribers. COSMEP, ALP.

SCHOLIA SATYRICA, R.D. Wyly, English Department, University of South Florida, Tampa, FL 33620, 974-2421. Poetry, articles, satire, criticism. 4/yr; 1-yr sub price: $3.50; per copy: $1.00; sample: $1.00. 1974. 40pp; 5-3/8 x 8½. of. circ. 225. Reporting time: 1-2 months. Payment: copies. Copyrighted, copyright reverts to author after pub. Ads: $50/$30. Discounts: 20 percent to subscription agencies, Faxon, Ebsco etc. Back issues: $1.25. Pub'd 3 issues 1976; expects 4 issues 1977, 4 issues 1978.

The School of Living (see THE GREEN REVOLUTION)

SCIENCE FICTION BAZAAR, Robert James Sourk, P.O. Box 11272, San Diego, CA 92111. Fiction, art, interviews, reviews. "This is an S-F advertising trade journal and is distributed to the S-F fans to act as a marketplace to sell and publicize their conventions, books, and magazines related to the S-F field." 24/yr; 1-yr sub price: $1.00; per copy: $.15; sample: free. 1976. 12pp; 8½ x 11. of. circ. 500. Reporting time: 2 weeks. Payment: copies only. Ads: $20/$10/$.05. Discounts: none. Back issues: first come 15¢. Pub's reviews. §science fiction/fantasy/horror/space exploration. COSMEP.

SCIENCE FOR THE PEOPLE, Science for the People, 9 Walden St., Jamaica Plain, MA 02130. Poetry, articles, art, photos, cartoons, criticism, reviews, letters. "SCIENCE FOR THE PEOPLE is the publication of Scientists and Engineers for Social and Political Action, a group which seeks to organize scientists , to seminate and disseminate scientific information, and to present a critique of the scientific estate from a radical, socially conscious viewpoint." 6/yr; 1-yr sub price: $12.00; per copy: $.75; sample: free. 1969. 42pp; 8½ x 11. of. circ. 4M. No payment. Ads: exchange only/no class/wd. Discounts: 40% to bkstrs, free to prisoners.

SCILLONIAN MAGAZINE, Clive Mumford, c/o Newsagent, St. Mary's, Isles of Scilly, Cornwall, United Kingdom. Articles, poetry, fiction, reviews, news items, interviews, letters, photos. "A voluntary local magazine run entirely for the islands." 2/yr; 1-yr sub price: £1.40; per copy: 70p. 1925. 100pp; 8½ x 5½. circ. 2M. Ads: £10.00/£6.00. Back issues: 55p.

The Scopcraeft Press (see THE MAINSTREETER)

Scottish Arts Council, Trevor Royle, Literature Director, 19 Charlotte Square, Edinburgh, Scotland EH2 4DF, United Kingdom.

Scotty Macgreger Publications, Scotty Macgreger, 10 Pineacre Dr., Smithtown, NY 11787. "Publishing poetry-educational books and records for children. Sell to libraries, schools, stores and smart people who want to buy for resale in their area." 1970.

Scranton Theatre Libre (see LIBRE PRESS)

SCREE, Duck Down Press, Kirk Robertson, Nila Northsun, Box 761, Fallon, NV 89406. Poetry, fiction, articles, art, photos, cartoons, interviews, satire, reviews, letters, parts-of-novels, long-poems, collages, concrete art. "We read & consider everything that comes in the mail—open to all schools & types, etc.-poetry & fiction to collages & concrete. Strong poems that can be followed with humor and/or energy probably stand a better chance-but anything that's said well will get in. We want to know what's going on out there. Also receptive to native American material-would like to see. More visual material as well as more strong poetry-stuff that pulls us to the edge & says 'LOOK!' So send & see. Recent contributors include: Bukowski, Micheline, Al Masarik, John Bennett, Todd Moore, Robert Matte, Peter Wild, Judson Crews, Kell Robertson, Peter Blue Cloud, John Calvin Rezmerski, Fritz Hamilton, Charles Potts, Robert Scotellaro, Gerald Haslam, Charles Plymell, & lots of folks we'd never heard of till they arrived in the mailbox." 3-4/yr; 1-yr sub price: $6.00 Individuals - $8.00 Institutions/ 4 issues.; per copy: $2.00; sample: $2.00 or exchange. 1973. 48-72pp; 5½ x 8½. †of. circ. 500. Reporting time: fast. Payment: copies 3-6. Copyrighted, reverts to author. Ads: Inquire. Discounts: 5 or more copies, 40 percent. Back issues: 1-8 $2.00 each. Pub'd 3 issues 1976; expects 3-4 issues 1977, 3-4 issues 1978. Pub's reviews: 40-50 in 1976. §Poetry/contemporary fiction/collage/little mags. CCLM, COSMEP-WEST, LPSC.

SCREEN, Society for Education in Film and Television, Geoffrey Newell-Smith, 29 Old Compton St., London W1V 5PL, United Kingdom. 4/yr; 1-yr sub price: £5 or $18; per copy: £1.20/$4.50. 1969. 128pp; 5½ x 8½ ins. monotype. circ. 3,000. Reporting time: 6 weeks. Payment: £18. Ads: 1/1p £35 1/2p £18.50. Pub's reviews.

SCREEN DOOR REVIEW, Arbitrary Closet Press, Richard Neva, Box 54, Onondaga, MI 49264. Poetry, art, photos. "Art is anything I can get away with. Highly arbitrary biases. Includes the erotic: males, females, children, others. Take a chance. Known, unknown, anonoymous welcome." 1-yr sub price: $1.00; per copy: $1.00; sample: $1.00. 1972. 5 x 8. †lp/of/mi. circ. 200. Reporting time: Immediate. Payment: copies only. Back issues: yes. §poetry (short to medium length).

Scrimshaw Press, Frederick C. Mitchell, 6040 Claremont Ave, Oakland, CA 94618, 415-658-2323. Art, photos. avg. price, cloth: $15.00; paper: $7.00 - $10.00. 1969. pp varies; varies. avg. press run 10,000. Reporting time: 1—2 months. Payment varies. Copyrights for author. Discounts: Trade: 1-4 30%; 5-49 40%; 50-99 42%; 100 or more 43%. Pub'd 3 titles 1976; expects 7 titles 1977.

Sea Of Storms (see NICOTINE SOUP)

Sea Pen Press, Suzanne Ferris, 2216 NE 46th, Seattle, WA 98105, LA2-8113. Poetry, art, long-poems. "Recent contributors: Joan Stone, Beth Bentley. The only biases I have are toward the art of fine printing, with handset type, hand-made papers—and the art of book illustration." avg. price, cloth: $25.00. 1976. 12pp; varies. †lp. avg. press run 100. Reporting time: variable. Payment: 20-25 percent of edition. Copyrights for author. Discounts: none. Pub'd 1 title 1976.

Seagull Books, NOPCO, Ltd., Ernest S. Kelly, Ellen R. Kelly, 150 Lakeshore Road West, Suite 1110, Mississauga, Ontario L5H3R2, Canada, Pending. Art, photos. "Book-length material only. We publish self-help, how-to, hobby, outdoors and inspirational books. Will publish fiction if of high quality." avg. price, cloth: $7.95; paper: $4.95; other: $2.95-$4.95. 1976. pp depends upon length of ms., usually 120-220 pages.; varies. of/lp. avg. press run 5,000-10,000. Reporting time: 6 weeks. Payment: standard royalty contract with 10 percent of retail price. Copyrights for author. Discounts: trade 40 percent, library 15 percent, educational 30 percent, bulk upon agreement, agent & jobber—depending upon contractual arrangements. Pub'd 3 titles 1976. CBPC.

Seagull Publications, Carolyn Bennett, Senior Editor; Margaret Bruno, Associate Editor, 1736 East 53 Street, Brooklyn, NY 11234, 212-338-6622. Poetry, fiction. "We are open to all types of material (but prefer that a person query first if the idea is non-fictional in nature). We generally want manuscripts in fiction to be between 200-250 pages (but how can one put a word count on art?). We will look at any manuscript as long as it is not sexist in nature. We urge women who are writing to send us their manuscripts (although we are not a feminist press) and we urge all men to send their manuscripts along, as long as they are not Henry Miller or Norman Mailer." avg. price, cloth: $6.95; paper: $3.95. 1976. poetry 64-72 pages, fiction 90-200 pages.; 5½ x 8¼. of. avg. press run 1,000 paper and 200 cloth for a first run. Reporting time: 6 weeks. Payment varies. Copyrights for author. Discounts: 40 percent trade and jobbers. Expects 5 titles 1977, 5 titles 1978. COSMEP.

‡**Seamark Press,** Iowa State Arts Council, State Capitol Bldg., Des Moines, IA 50300.

Second Aeon Publications, Peter Finch, 3 Heol Y Waun, Whitchurch, Cardiff, Wales CF41LB, United Kingdom, 0222-68697. Poetry, art, long-poems, collages, concrete art. avg. price, paper: 50p. 1967. 20pp; A5. mi/of. avg. press run 300-1,000. Reporting time: 2 weeks. Payment: by arrangement. Does not copyright for author. Discounts: By arrangement. Pub'd 2 titles 1976; expects 1 title 1977. ALP.

Second Back Row Press (see also AUSTRALASIAN SMALL PRESS REVIEW), Tom Whitton, Wendy Whitton, P.O. Box 197, North Sydney NSW 2060, Australia. "We have published 7 books on bookshops and we would be interested in further practical, how-to material for publication and/or distribution. We distribute over 25 presses from US, UK and Canada in Aust. and are always interested in more in alternative lifestyles area." 1973. Reporting time: 1 month. Payment: 10%. Copyrights for author. Discounts: 35%-40%. Pub'd 1 title 1976; expects 5 titles 1977. COSMEP, COSMEPA.

SECOND COMING, Second Coming Press, A.D. Winans, P.O. Box 31249, San Francisco, CA 94131. Poetry, fiction, art, photos, interviews, letters, long-poems. "Open to all schools of poetry but 'meat' of the poem ranks 60-40 over technique. Past contributors have included the late Wm. Wantling, Gene Fowler, Doug Blazek, Gerald Locklin, Lyn Lifshin, Anne Menebroker, Lynn Savitt, Terry Stokes, Gene Ruggles, Pancho Aguila, Charles Bukowski, Jack Micheline etc." 2-3/yr; 1-yr sub price: $3.75 individual-$5.75 library-yr; per copy: $2.00; sample: $1.50-including postage and handling. 1971. 80pp; 6 x 9. of. circ. 1,000. Reporting time: 1 day-30 days. Payment: copies only. Copyrighted, rights revert back to author upon written request. Discounts: 30 percent, 1-4 copies; 40 percent, 5 or more bookstores; 50 percent, 30 or more copies. Back issues: $5.00 each except Vol 1, No. 1, $30.00 (only 7 left), complete back list available $60.00. Pub'd 1 issue 1976; expects 3 issues 1977, 3 issues 1978. CCLM, COSMEP.

Second Coming Press (see also SECOND COMING), PO Box 31249, San Francisco, CA 94131.

Poetry. "1 title in 1972: *3 Drums For The Lady:* Ann Menebroker. 5 titles in 1975: *Felon's Journal* by Gene Fowler, *7 On Style* by the late Wm. Wantling; *Love Letters* by George Tsongas; *No Capital Crime* by the late Ed. Lipman and *Tales Of Crazy John* by A. D. Winans. 3 titles published 1976. *Last House In America* by Jack Micheline; *To Keep The Blood From Drowning* by Doug Flaherty; *California Poets Anthology* featuring the work of over 70 leading California poets, 224 pages, with photos. 6 titles planned for 1977. Write for 1977-78 catalog." avg. price, cloth: $10.00; paper: $3.00. 1972. 56-80pp; 5½ x 8½. of. avg. press run 1,000. Reporting time: 30 days. Payment: 10 percent of press run, 50 percent of any profit after expenses are met. Copyrights for author. Discounts: Same as magazine: 20 percent library only if this listed source is quoted. Pub'd 3 titles 1976; expects 6 titles 1977, 2-3 titles 1978. COSMEP, CCLM.

SECOND GROWTH, Frederick O. Waage, Karen Racz, Art Editor; Betsy Adams, Science Editor; Richard Lillard, Book Review Editor, 121 Somerset St, New Brunswick, NJ 08903. Poetry, fiction, articles, art, photos, interviews, criticism, reviews. "Environmental literary magazine; all forms of writing which present humanistic approaches to ecology/nature, humans relation to the natural world. Particularly non-scientific writing by scientists. No 'cute' nature writing sought, but rather first-quality fiction (to 3,000/words) poetry, creative essays which evoke conditions that have no easy, pat solutions. Interested in interdisciplinary approaches to ecology, and a mythology of nature in contemporary poetry. Personal correspondence with all interested writers desired; free copy with inquiry and S.A.S.E. Recent contributors: Richard Lillard, Betsy Adams, Dan Gerber, Louis Ginsberg, David Ignatow, Greg Kuzma, Allen Planz." 3/yr; 1-yr sub price: $4.00; per copy: $1.50; sample: free. 1975. 16pp; tabloid. of. Reporting time: 6 weeks. Ads: $50/$25. Pub's reviews. §American poetry, nature, ecology, rural "life-styles". COSMEP.

Second Porcupine, Jack Parsons, PO Box 548, Santa Fe, NM 87501, 505-988-2995. Poetry, non-fiction. "We will be publishing primarily poetry and Southwestern oral history." avg. price, cloth: $15.00; paper: $5.00. 1976. 150pp; Varies. of. avg. press run 1,000 - 5,000. By invitation. Payment: 10 to 15 percent of gross sales. Does not copyright for author. Discounts: 40 percent bookstores, 30 percent libraries. Pub'd 1 title 1976; expects 2 titles 1977, 4 titles 1978. COSMEP.

Seed Center, Deray, Sura, Jeff, PO Box 591, Palo Alto, CA 94302, 493-6121. Poetry, fiction, non-fiction. "Generally oriented but not limited to self-awareness, self-discovery & metaphysical topics." avg. price, cloth: $7.00; paper: $3.00. 1972. 100-150pp; Varies. of. avg. press run 5,000. Reporting time: varies-1 to 4 months. Payment: 8 to 15 percent paid quarterly. Copyrights for author. Discounts: Trade, jobber, bulk individual. Pub'd 3 titles 1976; expects 2 titles 1977. WBPA.

THE SEEKER NEWSLETTER, The Love Project, Arleen Lorrance, Diane K. Pike, PO Box 7601, San Diego, CA 92107. Poetry, articles, photos, cartoons, interviews, letters. 4/yr; 1-yr sub price: $5.00 or more; sample: free. 1972. 28pp; 8½ x 11. of. circ. 500. Payment: none. Discounts: none. COSMEP.

SEEMS, Steven Kosek, Karl Elder, Poetry Editor; Jerome Klinkowitz, Fiction Editor, Dept. of English, Northern Illinois Univ., DeKalb, IL 60115. Poetry, fiction, articles, reviews, parts-of-novels, long-poems. "Send fiction ms. to Klinkowitz, Dept. of English, Univ of Northern Iowa, Cedar Falls, Ia, 50613. Poetry ms. to Elder. Dept. of English, Wichita State Univ. Wichita, ks 67208. #5 includes Abish, Curry, Elliott, Foss, Gustafson, Hershon, Hilton, Pacernick,and Ratner. #6, a special fiction issue includes Baumbach, Federman, Glynn, Hershman, Katz, Krampf, Major, Sorrentino and Wakefield." 4/yr; 1-yr sub price: $4.00; per copy: $1.00. 1971. 60pp; 8½ x 7. of. circ. 500 plus. Reporting time: 1-4 wks. Payment: $1/printed page & copies. Ads: $30/$17.50/no classified. Discounts: 25%. Back issues: #2.3 & 4 are free with a one-year sub. CCLM.

SEER OX: American Senryu Magazine, Seer Ox, Michael McClintock, et. al., PO Box 42893, Los Angeles, CA 90050. Poetry, articles, art, photos, interviews, satire, criticism, reviews. "Recent contributors include Cid Corman, Tadashi Kondo, L. A. Dona, William J. Higginson, Martin Shea, William De Voti. Also publishes booklets, i. e. the American Haiku Poets Series and Pieces Editions. Definitely not interested in the flaccid, flatulent or overwritten, SEER OX is at the heart of the so-called Neo-Imagist movement toward poetry that is self/thing contained experience, without

280

references: pure image: what is. We prefer poetry of absolute essentials and elimination of all extraneous matter, objectivity and subjectivity mutually restraining, *in balance.* We do not wish to hear from 'the haiku ladies'." 5-6/yr; sub price: $2.50/4 issues; per copy: $.65; sample: free when available. 1974. 36pp; from 4¼ x 5½ to 7 x 8½. of. circ. 1,000 plus. Reporting time: 1 month. Payment: copies. Ads: All advertising is negotiable. Discounts: none. Pub's reviews. §Zen, Philosophy, Metacriticism or broad, far-ranging material on the nature of poetry, language, image, being, collections of importance, given our biases. COSMEP.

SEERS RIO GRANDE WEEKLY, New Mexico News Collective, Seers Collective, P.O. Box 4940, Albuquerque, NM 87106, 505-247-1518. Articles, photos. "We rarely accept material submitted from outside. Our objective is to be a reliable news service for the people of our area. Our collective generates all the material we can use." 48/yr; 1-yr sub price: $10.00; per copy: $.25; sample: free. 1971. 16pp; 11½ x 17. of. circ. 7,000. Reporting time: indefinite. Payment: none. Ads: $192.00/$112.00/$3.60 column inch. Pub'd 26 issues 1976; expects 48 issues 1977, 48 issues 1978. §Chicanos, poverty, gays, unions, Indians, ecology, education, women.

SELECT PRESS REVIEW, Select Press Book Service, Inc., Anne M. Conway, 14 South Street, Manchester, NH 03055, 613-673-8255. Reviews. "Reviews of current *(this year)* publications of small presses and lesser known commercial presses. Is geared to acquisitions librarians at public and academic institutions." 2/yr. 1975. 12pp; 8½ x 11. of. circ. 1,000. Reporting time: Immediate acknowledgement of reviews received. Payment: No payment; reviewers keep materials reviewed. Not copyrighted. Ads: No advertising being accepted at this time. Is a possibility for the future. Discounts: Distributed free of charge to about 1,000 libraries/librarians and presses whose works are reviewed. Back issues: Sorry, back issues not available. Pub's reviews §Materials with library potential. Any subject matter is acceptable. COSMEP.

A SELECTED FEW/THE PEOPLE'S GALLERY, Joseph Capobianco, Lawrence VanHeusen, 206 Elm St, Albany, NY 12210. Poetry, fiction, articles, art, photos, reviews. "Unfortunately (for us, i.e.) it appears that we will bring out only one more issue (Christmas 1976). Subject to change of course." 2/yr; 1-yr sub price: free. 1970. 24pp; 7 x 8½. of. circ. 250. Reporting time: 3 weeks. Payment: copies. Copyrighted, reverts to author. Ads: none. Back issues: free. CCLM.

SELF AND SOCIETY, Bourne Press, Vivian Milroy, 62 Southwark Bridge Rd, London SE1 0AU, United Kingdom. Articles, poetry, cartoons, photos, reviews, news items, interviews, criticism, letters. "Material within field of humanistic psychology; length from 500 to 5000 words: popular science approach, not too much jargon. Recent articles on R. D. Laing, Aaron Esterson, Wilhelm Reich, Carl Rogers, Abraham Maslow, Sidney Jourard." 12/yr; 1-yr sub price: £4.00; per copy: 35p. 1973. 32pp; A5. litho. circ. 3,500. Reporting time: 1 month. Payment: nil. Ads: £30 per page. Discounts: 20%. Back issues: 35p (Vol I 50p). Pub'd 12 issues 1976; expects 12 issues 1977, 12 issues 1978. Pub's reviews: 21 in 1976. §psychology (humanistic, growth movement). AHP.

SELF DEFENSE, World Publications, Pam Goforth, P.O. Box 366, Mtn. View, CA 94040. Fiction, articles, art, photos, cartoons, interviews. "Editor assumes complete control over all published material. SELF DEFENSE follows a traditional approach, publishing articles on training methods, strategy, philosophy, history and movement." 6/yr; 1-yr sub price: $4.50; per copy: $.75; sample: free. 1975. 25pp; 9 x 11. of. circ. 15,000. Discounts: bulk rates. Back issues: $1.00 each. §sports/recreation/leisure activities.

SELF-RELIANCE, Institute for Local Self-Reliance, Richard Kazis, 1717 18th St. NW, Washington, DC 20009. "The magazine is, right now, primarily an in-house production. Most articles are written by members of the institute on issues related to urban decentralism and community self-reliance." Bi-monthly.; 1-yr sub price: $6.00 Indiv; $12.00 Instit.; per copy: $1.00. 1976. 16pp; 8½ x 11. of. circ. 6,000. Payment: none. no ads. Back issues: yes, $1.00. Pub'd 4 issues 1976; expects 6 issues 1977, 6 issues 1978. Pub's reviews. §urban decentralism. COSMEP.

SENECA REVIEW, James Crenner, Robert Herz, Hobart & William Smith Colleges, Geneva, NY 14456 poetry/fiction, reviews. 2/yr; 1-yr sub price: $3.50; per copy: $1.75; sample: $1.75. 1970. 84pp; 8½ x 5½. lp. circ. 1,000. Reporting time: 4-6 wks. Payment: $5.00 per pg. poetry/$25.00 per story. Ads: Exchange. Back issues: $1.25. Pub'd 2 issues 1976; expects 2 issues 1977, 2 issues 1978. Pub's reviews. §poetry. CCLM.

SEQUOIA, Michael J. Smith, Prose; Dana Gioia, Poetry, Storke Publications Bldg., Stanford, CA 94305. Poetry, fiction, interviews, criticism, long-poems. "We publish poetry and fiction of the highest quality. We want mature work in any style. When we find a writer with real talent, we do our best to support him or her by calling attention to his work to other editors and publishers. Recent contributors: Alexander Theroux, Robert B. Shaw, Donald Davie, Thom Gunn, N. Scott Momaday, Marcia Falk, Al Young. Next fall we are publishing a special issue on translation." 4/yr; 1-yr sub price: $3.00; per copy: $1.00; sample: $1.00. 1897. 60-100pp; 9 x 6. of. circ. 1,000. Reporting time: 2 months. Payment: multiple copies.

SERIATIM: A Journal of Ecotopia, Communities, Collective, PO Box 117, McMinnville, OR 97128. Poetry, fiction, articles, art, photos, cartoons, interviews, satire, criticism, reviews, music, letters, parts-of-novels, long-poems, collages, plays, concrete art. "There is a country called Ecotopia that lies along the Northwestern edge of the American continent, stretching North from San Francisco to Vancouver and West from the Sierras to the Pacific. Though formerly thought to exist only in the imagination or in the future, Ecotopia exists here and now as an infant society; a succession forest growing toward climax from a thousand clearings. SERIATIM is an Ecotopian journal of research and innovation. It publishes research reports, proposals, accounts of individual practices, and formulations of strategy relevant to the evolution of this stable-state society. Topics may range from the results of an aquaculture or natural energy experiment to a discussion of group decision-making or bodily healing processes, to a comparison of alternative economic ventures to inventories of the region's resources. SERIATIM will pay for solicited material. Inquiries from researchers, practitioners and journalists are welcome. We wish to receive articles during the next 3 months for publication in late spring." 6/yr; 1-yr sub price: $10 regular $12 institutional; per copy: $2.00; sample: $2.00. 1976. 36pp; 10 x 15. of. circ. 1,000. Reporting time: 2 months. Payment: individually set. Ads: $50. Discounts: 5-9 copies 30%, 10-24 35%, 25 & up 40%. Pub's reviews. §All forms of ecology & related areas of health.

Seripress, Barbara Caruso, 686 Richmond Street West, Toronto, Ontario M6J1C3, Canada. Poetry, concrete art. "Titles by: b p Nichol, Mike Doyle, Nelson Ball, Steve McCaffery, Stephen Scobie, David Aylward. Graphics by: P.K. Irwin, Barbara Caruso. We use no unsolicited mss." 1973. †mi/lp/other.

SESAME, Open University Press, Les Holloway, Sesame, The Open University, Walton Hall, Milton Keynes MK76AA, United Kingdom. Articles, cartoons, photos, satire, reviews, news items, interviews, criticism, letters. "Sesame is published to link the students and staff of Open University throughout the U.K. Its contents are almost wholly devoted to university matters and related higher education topics." 9/yr; 1-yr sub price: £1; per copy: free; sample: free. 1972. 16pp; A3. of. circ. 70,000. Reporting time: 1 month. Payment: by arrangement. Ads: £285.00/£150.00/PSCC 4P. Discounts: 10% agency comm. Back issues: On request. Pub'd 8 issues 1976; expects 8 issues 1977, 8 issues 1978.

Sesame Press, Eugene McNamara, Peter Stevens, c/o English Dept Univ of Windosr, Windsor, Ontario N9B3P4, Canada. Poetry. "We publish only poetry by Canadian poets. We started out trying to offer an alternative to the sluggish attitude of the big presses (also their smugness, timidity etc.) and the in-group snobbery and elitism of too many small presses. We wanted to be more open (hence: *sesame*. Also our logo is a winged seed—well, like a sesame seed, or any kind of germ which might be catching—) and definitely not incestuous. We have published nothing from the home front—first four books were from poets in B.C., Moose Jaw, London, Ont. and Switzerland (an emigre Canadian) then we did one from Calgary, one from Hamilton, then Toronto and now finally *Landing* by Claude Liman in Thunder Bay Ont and *The Only Country in the World Called Canada* by Doug Beardsley in Victoria, B.C. We will not publish ourselves or our families." avg. price, paper: $3.00.

1974. 50pp; 6 x 9. lp. avg. press run 500. Reporting time: 6 weeks. Payment: 50 copies on publication as full payment. Copyrights for author. Discounts: 40 percent. COSMEP.

Seven Square Press (see BOX 749, RE: PRINT)

SEVEN STARS FICTION QUARTERLY, Realities, Hans Jr Ebner, 3635 Nottingham, Detroit, MI 48224. Fiction, satire, parts-of-novels. "Only fiction of any type. No Poetry." 4/yr; 1-yr sub price: $8.00; per copy: $2.50; sample: $2.50. 1977. 48pp; 8½ x 5½. †of. circ. 400. Reporting time: 2-3 weeks. Payment: copies. Copyrighted. Ads: $75.00/$50.00. Discounts: 40 percent 5 or more copies. Expects 2-3 issues 1977, 4 issues 1978. CCLM, COSMEP.

SEVEN STARS POETRY, Realities, Richard A. Soos Jr., P.O. Box 33512, San Diego, CA 92103, 714-280-8359. Poetry, fiction, art, interviews, reviews, long-poems, plays. "No minimum or maximum length. No style requirements, although we feel rhyming games are a distinct artform separate from poetry and we accept only poetry. Hans Ebner Jr., L. Ferlinghetti, James Marvelle, Kathleen Keller, K. Rexroth." 12/yr; 1-yr sub price: $12.00; per copy: $1.50; sample: $1.50. 1974. 40pp; 8½ x 5½. †of. circ. 1,000-1,100. Reporting time: 1-2 weeks. Payment: $0.50-$1.00 per poem short stories-$1.00 per printed page. Copyrighted. Ads: $75.00/$50.00/$0.20. Discounts: 5 or more copies, 40 percent. Back issues: $5.00. Pub'd 12 issues 1976; expects 12 issues 1977, 12 issues 1978. Pub's reviews: 60 in 1976. §poetry/fiction. CCLM.

Seven Woods Press, George Koppelman, P.O. Box 32, Village Station, New York, NY 10014. Poetry. "In so far as we have been able to establish an identity as a small press, it would be as a publisher favorable to long book-length poems or collections of poems containing long sequences. In 1977, we will be extending our interest in long poems to a new, abbreviated format with our SansFolio series of poetry pamphlets, each devoted to a single poem of 8 to 12 pages. In addition, we will be doing a series of chapbooks by woman poets." 1972. 72pp. of. avg. press run 1,000. Reporting time: varies. Payment: royalty 10%. Copyrights for author. Discounts: 40% trade wholesale. Pub'd 2 titles 1976; expects 2 titles 1977, 2 titles 1978.

‡**SEVENTIES, Seventies Press,** Odin House, Madison, MN 56256.

75 Press (see THE SPICY MEATBALL)

‡**SEWANEE REVIEW,** Univ. Of The South, Sewanee, TN 37375. CCLM.

SEX NEWS, P.K. Houdek, 7140 Oak, Kansas City, MO 64114. "SEX NEWS is a hobby of mine. It is a non-profit operation. It is a one-man operation. Circulation is almost entirely to professionals in the fields of sex education, marriage and family counseling and writers in the fields. No advertising is accepted. Circulars of books reviewed are often used as inserts at no charge." 12/yr; 1-yr sub price: $4.00; per copy: $.25; sample: free. 1969. 4pp; 8½ x 11. of. circ. 600. Reporting time: 6 weeks. Payment: none. Ads: not accepted. Back issues: any 12 issues $1.00 payment with order. Pub's reviews. §sex education, marriage, family, research in sex, marriage, and the family.

SF COMMENTARY, Bruce Gillespie, GPO Box 5195AA, Melbourne, Victoria 3001, Australia, Australia (03) 419-4797. Articles, interviews, criticism, reviews, letters, news items. "*Style:* Serious, but not standard academic style. 'Straight talk about science fiction', with a bias towards literary rather than scientific side." 5/yr; 1-yr sub price: $6.00; per copy: $1.25. 1969. 24pp; US Quarto. of. circ. 1,200. Reporting time: 3 weeks. Payment: none + copies of books for review/copies of issue where material appears. Ads: $100.00/$60.00. Pub'd 8 issues 1976; expects 5 issues 1977, 5 issues 1978. Pub's reviews: 50 in 1976. §science fiction/criticism of SF/FANTASY cinema/general literature.

SHADES OF LIGHT, Shades of Light Press, Mary Beth Houston, Crete-Monee High School, Crete, IL 60417. Poetry, fiction, art, photos, cartoons, parts-of-novels. 2/yr; 1-yr sub price: $2.00;

per copy: $1.00; sample: $1.00. 1972. 72pp. of. circ. 500. Reporting time: 2-3 months. Payment: copies. Back issues: 75¢ per issue. §small lit. mags.

Shadow Press (see also DARK FANTASY), Howard Gene Day, Box 207, Gananoque, Ontario K7G2T7, Canada, 613-382-2794. Poetry, fiction, art. "Recent contributors include-Tevis Clyde Smith, Charles Saunders, Lew Capos, Thomas Egan, Glenn Rahmen, Robert E. Howard. 3,000 words preferred-but not necessary" avg. price, other: $1.00. 1973. 40-52pp; 5½ x 8½. of. avg. press run 500-600. Reporting time: 4-6 weeks. Payment: no royalty-flat401/2 cent per word. Does not copyright for author. Discounts: 40 percent flat discount. Pub'd 4 titles 1976; expects 5-6 titles 1977.

SHAKESPEARE NEWSLETTER, Louis Marder, Univ. of Illinois, Chicago Circle, Chicago, IL 60680, 312-996-3289. Poetry, articles, criticism, letters. "Short pithy poems-dozen lines or so. For articles-send your conclusions & I will let you know if I want the article." 6/yr; 1-yr sub price: $2.50; per copy: $1.00; sample: $1.00. 1951. 10pp; 9¼ x 12. of. circ. 2,800. Reporting time: less than a month. Payment: 3 copies. Not copyrighted. Ads: $254/$137.50. Discounts: none. Back issues: $1 each $5 per yr for 6. Pub'd 6 issues 1976; expects 6 issues 1977, 6 issues 1978. Pub's reviews: 50 in 1976. SNL.

SHAMAN, Shaman, Inc., Dora Sherwood, 47 Fletcher St, Kennebunk, ME 04043. Poetry, photos. "We publish serious poetry of high quality, all styles. Short and medium length (to 4 or 5 pages) but not epic-length. Recent contributors are Raymond Roselip, Norma Farber, Herbert Morris, Greg Kuzma, Patricia Goedicke, Mordecai Marcus, Colette Inez, Marcia Hastie, Ira Sadoff. Please note that I (the editor) am taking a year off from work on SHAMAN to do my own work...I expect to resume editorial work on SHAMAN in the Spring/Summer of 1977." 1/yr; price per copy: $2.00; sample: $2.00. 1973. 70pp; 6 x 9. of. circ. 500. Reporting time: 6 wks-4 mos. Payment: about $5 per page. Discounts: library, classroom etc 20% disc,agent-dist. 50%. Back issues: #1-2 $1.25 issue. §poetry. COSMEP, NESPA.

‡**SHAMAN DRUM,** Frederic Brunke, 1796 Shattuck, Berkeley, CA 94709.

SHAMELESS HUSSY REVIEW, Shameless Hussy, Angel, Alta, P.O. Box 424, San Lorenzo, CA 94580. Poetry, fiction, art, photos, cartoons, satire, criticism, parts-of-novels, long-poems. "Not accepting ms. until 1979 or 1980." 1/yr; 1-yr sub price: $.95; per copy: $.95; sample: $.95. 1969. 50pp; 8½ x 5½. of. circ. 3,000. Discounts: 40% to bookstores & bulk orders. Back issues: #4 $15.00. COSMEP.

SHANTIH, Box 125, Bay Ridge St., Brooklyn, NY 11220. CCLM.

SHAVIAN—JOURNAL OF BERNARD SHAW, High Orchard Press, Robert Clare, Eric F.J. Ford, 125 Markyate Rd, Dagenham, Essex RM8 2LB, United Kingdom. "Research & scholarship on & about Bernard Shaw." 2-3/yr; 1-yr sub price: $5.00; per copy: $3.00; sample: $3.00. 1941. 10pp; A5. lo. circ. 600. Reporting time: 6 months. Payment: copies. Ads: £15/page & pro rata. Discounts: agents 20%. Back issues: $3.00. Pub'd 1 issue 1976; expects 2 issues 1977, 2 issues 1978. Pub's reviews: 6 in 1976. §Edwardian period.

SHAW NEWSLETTER, Shaw Society, E. Ford, High Orchard, 125 Markyate Road, Dagenham, Essex RM 82 LB, England. Poetry, fiction, articles, art, photos, cartoons, interviews, satire, criticism, reviews, music, letters, parts-of-novels, long-poems, collages, plays, concrete art, news items, non-fiction. "Brief items on and about G. Bernard Shaw, British dramatist. His life works, times, contemporaries, influences, causes which he espoused, e.g. vegetarianism." 3/4 pa/yr; 1-yr sub price: $5.00. 1976. 4 pp per issue; A5 upright. †of. circ. 600. Reporting time: 6 months. Payment: Pays in copies. Copyrighted. Ads: $15.00 pro rata. Discounts: Agents 20 percent. Pub's reviews §Books magazines for review welcomed. See comments for suitable fields.

THE SHAW REVIEW, University Press (Penn State University), Stanley Weintraub, S-234 Burrowes Building, University Park, PA 16802. Articles, interviews, criticism, reviews, letters. 3/yr; 1-yr sub price: $6.75; per copy: $2.25; sample: $2.25. 1951. 50pp; 6 x 9. of. circ. 700.

Reporting time: immed. Payment: none. Ads: none. Discounts: 75 cents to agents. Back issues. Vol I-XI $1 Vol XII-XVII $1.75. Pub's reviews. §connected to Shaw, his contemporaries or environment.

Shaw Society (see also SHAW NEWSLETTER), E. Ford, High Orchard, 125 Markyate Road, Dagenham, Essex RM82LB, England. Poetry, fiction, articles, art, photos, cartoons, interviews, satire, criticism, reviews, music, letters, parts-of-novels, long-poems, collages, plays, concrete art, news items, non-fiction. avg. price, paper: $5.00. 1941. 4 pp per issue; A5 upright. †of. avg. press run 600. Reporting time: 6 months. Payment: Pays in copies. Copyrights for author. Discounts: Agents 20 percent.

SHELL, Jack Kimball, 362 Waban Ave, Waban, MA 02168, 617-244-3258. Poetry, criticism, reviews, long-poems. "Recent contributors to SHELL: John Wieners, Frank Lima, Ann Kim, Larry Eigner, R. Buckminster Fuller, Kenward Elmslie, S. Fox, Donald Quatrale, Gerard Malanga, George Quasha, Susan Ruel, Robert Bly, Charles Stein, Clayton Eshleman, Charles Plymell, Theodore Enslin, Rando, Rochelle Owens, Andrei Codrescu, Robert Kelly, Charles Bernstein, William Burroughs, William Corbett, John Yau, Ira Cohen, Brian George, Jerome Rothenberg, Al Moritz, Jack Kimball." 4/yr; 1-yr sub price: $12.00; per copy: $3.00. 1976. 100pp; 8 x 11. of. circ. 600. Reporting time: varies. Payment: copies. Copyrighted. Expects 4 issues 1978. §poetry. COSMEP, CCLM.

SHELLY'S, Engine Press, Bill Polak, Ralph W. Mills, 501 Franklin St, Kent, OH 44240. Poetry, fiction, art, photos, interviews, satire, parts-of-novels, collages, plays, concrete art. "We are looking for material to form a section of the magazine devoted to outside contributors. Because of space limitations we shy away from long poems, overgrown stories etc. Avoid sentimentality, carefully formulated drivel and mistology. Do *not* send more than 5 poems or 2 stories. We are *looking* for people. What to do? Why do be do be do. DO be do be DO." irreg; price per copy: $2.00; sample: $2.00. 1974. 70pp; 8½ x 11. of. circ. 300-400. Reporting time: 2-3 mos. Payment: copies. Copyrighted, reverts to author. no ads. Back issues: $2.00. Pub'd 2 issues 1976. §poetry and fiction.

SHELTERFORCE, Kathy Aria, John Atlas, Ronald Atlas, Martin Bierbaum, Tom Connell, Pat Morrisy, Phyllis Salowe-Fay, Mary Tasker, Stan Varon, Robert Widriw, 31 Chestnut Street, East Orange, NJ 07018. "SHELTERFORCE is a national housing publication that analyzes housing and urban problems and serves as a forum to exchange ideas concerning short- and long-term tactics and strategies for the housing movement. It is published by a group of housing activists, lawyers and planners in New Jersey, together with the New Jersey Chapter of the National Lawyers Guild." 4-6/yr; 1-yr sub price: $3.00; per copy: $1.00; sample: $1.00. 1975. 16pp; 8½ x 11. lp. circ. 8,500. Discounts: subs. of 25 for $25.00. Back issues: $1. Pub's reviews. §housing, urban problems, politics, cities, environment. APS.

SHENANDOAH, Journalism Laboratory Press, Washington and Lee University, James Boatwright, P.O. Box 722, Lexington, VA 24450. "Literary review featuring fiction, poetry, essays and reviews." 4/yr; 1-yr sub price: $5.00; per copy: $1.50. 1950. 100pp; 6 x 9. †of. circ. 1,200. Payment: by arrangement. Ads: $60/$35. Discounts: 20% discount through agencies/50% bulk rate to bookstores. Back issues: $2.50. Pub's reviews. CCLM.

SHINAKI, C.E.N.S.I.T., Toronto Network of Christian Communities, 63 Beaty Ave, Toronto, Ontario M4M2H5, Canada, 536-6087. Poetry, articles, art, interviews, letters. "We try to reflect on our own experience in Toronto & report experiences of other communities else where." 4/yr; 1-yr sub price: $10.00 community; $3.00 individual; per copy: $0.50. 1974. 30pp; 8½ x 11. †mi. circ. 400. Payment: none. Not copyrighted. Ads: free. Pub'd 4 issues 1976.

Shining Waters Press (see RIPPLES)

Shinn Music Aids, Duane Shinn, PO Box 192, Medford, OR 97501, 664-2317. Music. "Most publications are house-produced. Very little free lance material accepted." avg. price, paper: $3.95. 1966. 40pp; 8½ x 11. of. avg. press run 5m min.-25m max. Reporting time: 4 weeks. Payment: flat rate. Copyrights for author. Discounts: 50 percent basic; single copy 25 percent-over gross 67 percent.

SHIRHADASH/NEW SONG, Anti-Ocean Press, Sol P. Lachman, 148 Pasadena, Highland Park, MI 48203, 313-869-6663. Poetry, fiction, articles, art, photos, interviews, music, letters, long-poems. "Very short fiction. Prayers. Contemporary Jewish poetry and new liturgy, translations from Hebrew and Yiddish, retranslation and commentary." 3/yr; 1-yr sub price: $6.00; per copy: $2.50. 1977. 48pp; 8½ x 11. of. Reporting time: 60 days. Payment: copies. Copyrighted, reverts to author. Expects 1 issue 1977.

SHOCKS, Momo's Press, Stephen Vincent, Box 14061, San Francisco, CA 94114. Poetry, criticism, letters. "We usually do one large issue a year (100-150 pages). The issue has a particular focus. Most recently (1976) we did *The Androgyny Issue,* subtitled 'Men looking at the women in themselves, women looking at the men in themselves'. Just coming up is THE POETRY READING (issue). An exploration of how language can occur in our culture(s), it will contain articles on poetry w/video, dance, tape, pure voice, and a special w/SF Bay Area poetry typographers. Writers have included: Susan Griffin, Jack Anderson, Andrei Codresca, 1/yr; sample: $3.00. 1973. 132pp; 6 x 9. circ. 1,500. Reporting time: 2 months. Payment: copies. Copyrighted, reverts to author. Back issues: Shocks $6.00, The Androgyny Issue: $3.00 (post incl), Shocks $5.00, The Day Book, $2.25 (postage inclu), all other issues OP. CCLM, COSMEP.

THE SHORE REVIEW, Shore Press, Kenn Kwint, Al Moritz, 2931 So. 57 St., Milwaukee, WI 53219. irreg.; 1-yr sub price: $5.50; per copy: $1.50; sample: $1.50. 1968. 120pp; 4 x 6. of. circ. 2,500. Reporting time: 1 month. Payment: copies. Ads: $80/$30. Back issues: $1.50 per copy. Pub's reviews. §poetry, translations, commentary, etc. COSMEP.

Sibyl-Child Press (see also SIBYL CHILD: A WOMEN'S ARTS & CULTURE JOURNAL), Pat Dowell, Peg Downey Kaplin, Candyce Homnick Stapen, 6906 West Park Dr., Hyattsville, MD 20783, 301-422-7493/9140. Poetry, fiction, articles, art, photos, cartoons, interviews, satire, criticism, reviews, letters, parts-of-novels, long-poems, plays, concrete art. "Art submissions should include commentary" 1976. of. New project, now accepting submissions. Discounts: no policy established at present—to be worked out on individual basis. CCLM, COSMEP.

SIBYL-CHILD: A Women's Arts & Culture Journal, Sibyl-Child Press, Pat Dowell, Peg Downey Kaplin, Candyce Homnick Stapen, 6906 West Park Dr., Hyattsville, MD 20783, 301-422-7493/9140. Poetry, fiction, articles, art, photos, cartoons, interviews, satire, criticism, reviews, music, letters, parts-of-novels, long-poems, collages, plays, concrete art. "Women's art and culture—Grace Cavalieri, Margery Goldberg, Barbara Holland, Wendy Stevens, Lois Van Houten, Joyce Tenneson Cohen, Polly Joan, Clarinda Harriss Lott, Candyce Homnick Stapen, Peg Kaplin" 3/yr; 1-yr sub price: $8.00; per copy: $3.00; sample: [same to individuals; free to institutions]. 1974. 64pp; 5½ x 8½. of. circ. 500. Reporting time: within a month. Payment: complimentary copies (2) plus tear sheets. Copyrighted, reverts upon written request provided that Sibyl-Child is credited as 1st published. Discounts: 20% to distributors (trade, jobbers, etc.); 10% to individuals in quantities of 5 or more. Back issues: VI Issue 1,$1.25; Issue 2 and 3 (double issue) $4.00; Issue 4 $2.00. Pub's reviews. §Women's studies, art, culture. CCLM, COSMEP.

Sicilian Antigruppo (see also IMPEGNO '70, PALERMO ANTIGRUPPO, CELEBES), Nat Scammacca, Rolando Certa, Costantino Petralia, Villa Scanimac, via Argenteria Km 4, Trappani, Sicily, 0923-38681. Poetry, fiction, articles, art, photos, interviews, satire, criticism, letters, parts-of-novels, collages, concrete art. "For our newspaper, a weekly, articles are usually up to 3½ typewritten pages. For our reviews any length. For books, essays, criticism on any subject no limit. Books of poetry, 64 pages. Languages: Italian, English and Sicilian. We are doing a series of 20 books of poetry of American poets completely in Italian and English, the languages face to face. Some writers and poets are: Crescenzio Cane, Ignazio Apolloni, Pietro Terminelli, Gianni Diecidue, Rolando Certa, Nat Scammacca, Franco DiMarco, Santo Cali, Carmelo Pirrera, L. Ferlinghetti, R. Bly, Rafaeli Alberti, Guiseppe Zaggario, Beppi DiBella, Ignazio Navarra, Cesare Zavattini." avg. price, paper: $4.00 - $5.00. 1968. 150pp. mi/of/lp/posters etc. avg. press run 2 to 6 months.

Reporting time: 1 month. Payment: Regular contract 10 percent etc. Copyrights for author. Discounts: 33 percent.

SIGNAL, Approaches To Children's Books, The Thimble Press, Nancy Chambers, Lockwood, Station Road, South Woodchester, Glos. GL5 5EQ, United Kingdom. Articles, interviews, criticism, letters. "We do not impose word limits. Prefer evaluative rather than descriptive approaches to articles. Subject matter: as wide as the range of interests in children's literature. January 1976 issue included articles by Ursula Le Guin and Peter Opie plus a reprint of Harry Furniss's 'Recollections of Lewis Carroll'." 3/yr; 1-yr sub price: £2.10 or $5.00 US & Canada; per copy: 70p or $2.00. 1970. 52pp; 8½ x 5½. lo. circ. 1,000 plus. Reporting time: 1-2 weeks. Payment: contributor's copies only. Ads: Ads not taken. Back issues: Listing on request. Pub'd 3 issues 1976; expects 3 issues 1977, 3 issues 1978.

Signpost Press (see THE BELLINGHAM REVIEW)

SIGNPOST, Signpost Publications, Louise Marshall, Barbara Diltz-Siler, 16812 36th Ave W, Lynnwood, WA 98036, 206-743-3947. Poetry, fiction, articles, art, photos, cartoons. "Editorial comment is heavily weighted for Pacific Northwest backpackers, ski tourers, snow shoers, etc. We rarely purchase outside material, but can 'pay' with extra copies." 16/yr; 1-yr sub price: $10.00; per copy: $1.00. 1966. 16pp; 10 x 15. of. circ. 4,000. Reporting time: 3 weeks. Payment: very low. Copyrighted, reverts to author. Ads: $350.00/$180.00/$0.10-wd.$2.00 min. Discounts: 40 percent discount to retailers. Back issues: $1.00 magazine issues; 50 cents newsletter. Pub'd 16 issues 1976; expects 16 issues 1977, 16 issues 1978. Pub's reviews. §outdoor non-motorized activities.

Signpost Publications (see also SIGNPOST), Louise Marshall, Barbara Diltz-Siler, 16812 36th Ave W, Lynnwood, WA 98036, 206-743-3947. Articles. "We publish books on outdoor subjects for non-motorized persons, with emphasis on backpacking, camping, ski touring, snow-shoeing, canoeing, etc. If subject has only regional appeal, it must be for the Pacific Northwest." avg. price, paper. $3.95 - $4.95. 1966. 128-144pp; 5½ x 8½. of. avg. press run 5,000. Reporting time: 4 weeks. Payment: 8-10 percent of retail price. Copyrights for author. Discounts: 10-24 books, 40 percent; 25 or more, 50 percent. Pub'd 4 titles 1976; expects 9 titles 1977, 12 titles 1978.

Simon & Pierre Publishing Co. Ltd., Marian M. Wilson, Rolf Kalman, Box 280, Adelaide St. P.O., Toronto, Ontario M5C2J4, Canada, 416-463-5944 order desk 416-463-5945. Fiction, art, photos, plays, non-fiction. "Publish two illustrated drama series including one act and full length plays, and children's plays in cloth and paper binding, plus new fiction-all Canadian authors, photographic books and non fiction." avg. price, cloth: $12.75; paper: $4.50. 1972. 180-350 pp casebound, 80-120 pp plays in paper; varies. of. avg. press run 2,500. Reporting time: 2 weeks if rejected; 3 months if being considered for publication. Payment: 10 percent royalty. Copyrights for author. Discounts: Trade: 1-5, 20 percent; wholesalers 20 percent, 6 or more 40 percent; some short discount books (20 percent); classroom & bulk discounts. Pub'd 8 titles 1976; expects 8 titles 1977, 8 titles 1978. COSMEP, ACP.

SING OUT! The Folk Song Magazine, Robert Norman, Alan Senauke, Rhonda Mattern, 270 Lafayette Street, New York, NY 10001. Poetry, articles, art, photos, cartoons, interviews, reviews, music, letters. 6/yr; 1-yr sub price: $6.00; per copy: $1.25; sample: $1.25. 1950. 56pp; 5-7/8 x 8-7/8. lp. circ. 10,000. Reporting time: variable. Payment: copies. Ads: $400/$235/$.50 word. Back issues: $1.00 ea. Pub's reviews §music, folklore, politics, printing, arts, minority, ethnic materials, etc. COSMEP.

Singing Wind Publications, Eric Staley, Karlene Gentile, P.O. Box 1426, Columbia, MO 65201, 314-442-6543. Poetry, fiction, articles, art, photos, interviews, parts-of-novels. "*SWP* is a regional press established to promote the writing and the arts in Missouri and is therefore at this time accepting only material on or about Missouri or the manuscripts of Missouri residents. Recent contributors include Speer Morgan and William Peden in fiction; Larry Levis and Tom McAfee in poetry." avg. price, cloth: $11.70; paper: $5.00. 1975. 150pp; 8½ x 11. of/lp. avg. press run 1,000. Reporting time: 2 months. Payment: direct ms. payment or 10 percent; depending upon material & project.

Does not copyright for author. Discounts: single discount rate is 20 percent. Pub'd 2 titles 1976; expects 2 titles 1977.

SINISTER WISDOM, Catherine Nicholson, Harriet Desmoines, 3116 Country Club Dr, Charlotte, NC 28205, 704-377-0333. Poetry, fiction, articles, art, photos, interviews, satire, criticism, reviews, letters, parts-of-novels, long-poems, collages, plays. "Lesbian literary journal; no length limit; recent contributors: Adrienne Rich, Audre Lorde, Julia Stanley, Jacqueline Lapidus, Joan Larkin, Bertha Harris, Barbara Grier, Susan Griffin, Deena Metzger, etc." 3/yr; 1-yr sub price: $4.50; per copy: $2.00; sample: $2.00. 1976. 100pp; 6 x 9. of. circ. 750. Reporting time: 30 days. Payment: 3 copies. Copyrighted, reverts to author. Ads: rates not yet set. Discounts: 40 percent off for 5 or more copies; 30 percent off for 2-4 copies. Back issues: No. 2, *"Lesbian Writing & Publishing"* $2.50; others $2.00. Pub's reviews. §Lesbian & radical feminist. COSMEP.

SIPAPU, Konocti Books, Noel Peattie, Route 1, Box 216, Winters, CA 95694, 916-662-3364; 916-752-1032. Articles, interviews, reviews. "A newsletter for librarians interested in third world studies, the counter-culture & alternative and independent presses. Konocti Books publishing work on similar themes. Make all checks out to Noel Peattie, Editor and Publisher, *SIPAPU.* No stamps accepted." 2/yr; 1-yr sub price: $2.00; per copy: $1.00; sample: $1.00. 1970. 24pp; 8½ x 11. of. circ. 600. Reporting time: 3 weeks. Payment: $0.04 per word. Copyrighted, released to author on request. Discounts: books 40%. Back issues: No special prices, but many back issues out of print. Complete file now being microfilmed at University of Southern California. Pub'd 2 issues 1976; expects 2 issues 1977, 2 issues 1978. Pub's reviews: 30 in 1976. §3d world/regional/special items. COSMEP, APS.

SISTER COURAGE, Collective, Box 296, Allston, MA 02134, 617-661-2689. Articles, photos, cartoons, interviews, reviews, letters. "Socialist—feminist" 11/yr; 1-yr sub price: $4.00; per copy: $0.35; sample: $0.35. 1975. 20pp. of. circ. 3,000. Payment: none. Copyrighted, does not revert to author. Ads: $275.00/$160.00/$3.00 for 4 lines for non-profit, $4.00 for 4 lines for profit, $0.50 each additional line. Back issues: $0.50 per copy. Pub'd 11 issues 1976; expects 11 issues 1977, 11 issues 1978. Pub's reviews. §feminism, women. COSMEP.

651, Carl D. Clark, 3007 University, Austin, TX 78705, 472-7415. Poetry, fiction, articles, art, photos, cartoons, interviews, satire, criticism, reviews, music, letters, parts-of-novels, long-poems, collages, plays, concrete art. "A continuation of the line that runs from Francis Picabia up to Brian Eno; Marcel Duchamp to Terr Riley: every one must use their own ruler." 3/yr; 1-yr sub price: $1.00; per copy: $0.50; sample: free. 1977. 4pp; 8½ x 5½. mi/of. circ. enough. Reporting time: 1 month. Payment: copies. Not copyrighted. Ads: none. Discounts: none; libraries should query. Back issues: write. Pub'd 1 issue 1976.

613 MAGAZINE, Kol Hai, Inc., Meir Abehsera, Yerachmiel Tilles, P.O. Box 168, Brooklyn, NY 11223. Poetry, fiction, articles, art, photos. "Everything from a Jewish perspective." 6/yr; 1-yr sub price: $10.00; per copy: $1.00; sample: $1.00. 1975. 60pp; 8½ x 11. of. circ. 5,000. Ads: $580/$310/$2.00 per inch. Back issues: $1.00. Pub's reviews. §Jewish affairs or interests.

SKYWRITING, Blue Mountain Press, Martin Grossman, 511 Campbell St, Kalamazoo, MI 49007, 616-349-3924. Poetry, fiction, interviews, reviews, criticism. "*SKYWRITING* attempts to remain as open as possible, so there are no real biases concerning style. We are interested in quality poetry, and fiction as it presents itself, and have in the past published work by Haines, Merwin, Charles Wright, Paul Zweig, Paul Nelson, Ira Sadoff, Stokes, Goldbarth, Matthews, Edson, Shelton, Scott and Woods. From our fifth issue on, we will 'feature' a poet, and present critical articles, interviews, more personal views, as well as the poets newest work." 2/yr; sub price: $5.00-3 issues; per copy: $2.00; sample: $2.00. 1971. 50pp; 9 x 6. of. circ. 400. Reporting time: 2 weeks to 2 months. Payment: copies. Mag copyrighted, copyright reverts to author upon pub. Ads: $60/$35. Discounts: 30% 5 copies minimum. Back issues: No. 1-$5.00; No. 2-$10.00; No. 3-$50.00; No. 4/5-$100.00; No. 6-$5.00. Pub'd 1 issue 1976; expects 2 issues 1977, 2 issues 1978. Pub's reviews: 1 in 1976. §all areas. CCLM.

THE SLACKWATER REVIEW, Confluence Press, Inc., M.K. Browning, Art Center, Lewis-Clark Campus, Lewiston, ID 83501, 208-746-2341. Poetry, fiction, articles, art, photos, interviews, criticism, reviews. "Prose 5-6 pages—poetry 1/2 to full page—focus on Northwest and Intermountain regional productions—do take unusually good materials from other areas. Wm. Stafford, Wm. P. Root, Jim Ikyren" 2/yr; 1-yr sub price: $4.00; per copy: $2.50. 100pp; 5½ x 11. of. circ. 500-1,000. Reporting time: 2-3 months. Payment: poetry 35 cents a line; prose 2 cents word when funds allow. Copyrighted, does not revert to author. Discounts: standard 40 percent retail; 50 percent wholesale. Pub's reviews. §Books & chapbooks of Northwest & Intermountain Region Writers. COSMEP.

Sleepy Hollow Restorations, Saverio Procario, Bruce D. MacPhail, Ray A. Freiman, Box 245, Tarrytown, NY 10591, 914-631-8200. Non-fiction. "Historical Material. American history and literature, pre-1900." avg. price, cloth: $15.00; paper: $4.00. 300pp; 6 x 9. of. avg. press run 2,000. Reporting time: 1 month. Payment: 5-10 percent. Copyrights for author. Discounts: 40 percent trade, jobber. Pub'd 4 titles 1976; expects 4 titles 1977, 5 titles 1978.

SLICK PRESS, Linda Williams, 5336 So. Drexel, Chicago, IL 60615, 324-4941 (312). Poetry, fiction. "Am trying to publish unknown writers mostly." 2-4/yr; price per copy: $2.00; sample: Free only to bookstores, distributors, etc. $2.00 otherwise. 1976. 30pp; 8 x 11. †lp. circ. 100 per issue. Payment: none at present. Copyrighted, reverts after 6 mos. time in the future. COSMEP.

SLIT WRIST, Slit Wrist, Terry Swanson, 333 East 30 St., New York, NY 10016, MU-9-8768. Poetry, fiction, articles, interviews, criticism, letters, parts-of-novels, long-poems. "Highly individual long works, private journals, 'primary process' but with special feeling for language; Hannah Weiner, Jim Brodey." 2/yr; 1-yr sub price: $10.00; per copy: $5.00 - double issue; sample: $2.50 - single issue, $5.00 - double issue. 1976. 100 pp single issue - 200 pp double issue; 8½ x 11. of. circ. 500-1,000. Reporting time: 4 weeks. Payment in copies. Copyrighted, reverts to author. Ads: $40.00/$20.00/none yet. Discounts: 30 percent & up resale discount accding to qty. Back issues: $5.00. Pub'd 2 issues 1976; expects 2 issues 1977, 2 issues 1978. CCLM, COSMEP.

THE SLOUGH, Altruistic Enterprises, Charles B. Taylor, Patricia Guidry, English Department, University of Utah, Salt Lake City, UT 84103. Poetry, fiction, art, photos, interviews, plays, concrete art. Infrequent.; sub price: $4.00 - 3 issues.; per copy: $1.00; sample: $1.00. 1974. 48pp; 8½ x 11. †of. circ. 700. Reporting time: 6 weeks. Payment: none. Ads: $30/$15. COSMEP.

Slow Loris Press (see also RAPPORT), Anthony Petrosky, Patricia Petrosky, 6359 Morrowfield Ave, Pittsburgh, PA 15217. Poetry. "SLOW LORIS broadside series III: letterpressed poems on individual 9 by 12 strathmore papers. Poems by John Logan, Pablo Neruda, Tony Petrosky, Martha Dickey, David Ignatow, Mac Hammond, Charles Baxter, and Jerome Mazzaro. Drawings by Rose Graubart and Nahum Tschacbasov. Printed in a limited edition of 175 unsigned, 25 signed folios. 10 unsigned left: $5.00 apiece; 8 signed left: $15.00 apiece. SLOW LORIS broadside series IV: poems printed on various size sheets the largest being 11 by 17. Chapbooks for 1976: Ed Ochester *The End Of The Ice Age;* Gary Eddy, *Waking Up Late* and books by David Ignatow and Richard Hugo." avg. price, paper: $3.00-$5.00. 1971. 32pp; 6 x 9. lp. avg. press run 500-1,000. Reporting time: 3 months. Payment: Copies. Copyrights for author. Discounts: Vary. Pub'd 1 title 1976; expects 4 titles 1977, 4 titles 1978.

THE SMALL FARM, The Small Farm, Jeff Daniel Marion, P.O. Box 563, Jefferson City, TN 37760. Poetry, reviews, long-poems. "Any poet is welcome who has good poems to offer, poems that take our earth consciousness in new directions, that leave us marked,changed by the experience of the poem. We believe in the importance of the creative act as a means of self-renewal as a vital connection with the organic flow of all life processes. Too, we see poetry as a striving to clarify the life we're living right now. We prefer in poetry a language that is alive, springy, a surface that is deceptively simple, underneath which are all the profundities, mysteries, we want a poetry that speaks to us now in a language that renews earth realities and possibilities, a poetry coming from, and committed to specific places. Contributors have included Wendell Berry, Robert Morgan, Frank Steele, Thomas Johnson, William Stafford, Robert Bly, Joe Bruchac, Greg Kuzma, Ted Kooser, Jim

289

W. Miller, David Curry, and others. Issue #3 is devoted entirely to Robert Morgan's work.'' 2/yr; 1-yr sub price: $3.00; per copy: $2.00; sample: $2.00 plus postage. 1975. 60pp; 5½ x 8½. of. circ. 300. Reporting time: 3-4 weeks. Payment: 2 copies. Pub's reviews. §poetry/poetics.

SMALL MOON, The Poetry Co-Operative Of Boston, Drunken Juggler Press, Ed Cates, Ann Morganson, Kent Wittenberg, c/o 12 Cooney Street, Somerville, MA 02143, 868-1354. Poetry, art, photos, interviews, criticism, reviews, concrete art. "SMALL MOON is especially interested in New England writers and writers based outside the U.S. as well as political poetry. SMALL MOON introduced Henrik Bjelke, PEN Writer from Denmark, to this country in SMALL MOON No. 1 and No. 2, which contained critical essays and excerpts from his novel. First translations of Yannis Ritsos' NAKED WINDOW, Polish writers Julian Tuwim and Jerzy Grupinski and the German poet, Robert Musil." 2/yr; 1-yr sub price: $4.00; per copy: $0.50; sample: $0.50. 1974. 16-24pp; tabloid size. circ. 3,500. Reporting time: 2 months. Payment in copies. Copyrighted, reverts to author. Ads: $50.00/$25.00/$5.00. Discounts: $0.50 copy retail; bulk rate for university classes (they pay postage) all others should mail inquiry to editor. Back issues: $0.35 issue no. 1 plus $0.30 postage and handling. Pub's reviews. §All areas of poetry: esp. 1st publications, translations, esp. mags. that carry a wide selection of material i.e. essays, reviews, poetry, listings, etc. CCLM.

THE SMALL POND MAGAZINE OF LITERATURE, Napoleon St. Cyr, 10 Overland Dr., Stratford, CT 06497. Poetry, fiction, articles, art, satire, concrete art, reviews. "Max: Fiction 2500 words, poetry approx 100 lines, other prose 2500 words. Recent contributors, some nobodies-some somebodies." 3/yr; 1-yr sub price: $3.25; per copy: $1.25; sample: $1.25. 1964. 36-40pp; 5½ x 8. of. circ. 300 plus. Reporting time: 1-15 days. Payment: 2 copies. Copyrighted. Ads: $30/$18. Discounts: Inquire. Back issues: Inquire. Pub'd 3 issues 1976; expects 3 issues 1977, 3 issues 1978. Pub's reviews: 11 in 1976. §only poetry (books). CCLM, COSMEP, NESPA.

THE SMALL PRESS REVIEW, Dustbooks, Len Fulton, Editor-Publisher; Ellen Ferber, Associate Editor; Nancy Cahill, Assistant Editor, P.O. Box EE, Paradise, CA 95969, 916-877-6110. Photos, reviews. "SPR seeks to study and promulgate the small press and little magazine (i.e. the *independent* publisher) worldwide. It was started in 1966 as part of an effort by its publisher to get a grip on small press/mag information since no one at the time (or for some five years thereafter) seemed interested in doing it. It was also designed to promulgate the small press in a variety of ways. In its first eight years of life, as a quarterly and then a bi-monthly, it lost $5,000-$6,000 *per year* until making the break to monthly—breaking even almost at once. The goal is weekly—not so far away as the corporate demon-gods of American periodicals may think. It links with other Dustbooks small-press info titles in a more and more fitting way, updating the annual INTERNATIONAL DIRECTORY and feeding into the (also annual) SMALL PRESS RECORD of BOOKS in Print. SPR has a three-level monthly destiny which can be disrupted only in some higher Cause—and we suspect that Cause does not exist: 1) it supplies 'hard' information both *for* (lists of jobbers, bookstores, etc) and *of* (titles, addresses, prices) the small presses and little magazines; 2) it publicizes small mag/press activity; 3) it reviews small press titles in 200 words or less. SPR is always on the lookout for competently written reviews (yes, we have a 'style sheet'—write for it), as long as they hold to a page in length and review a title published by a small press. Our regular contributor list is a mile long but here's some: Pat Urioste ('Feedback' Editor), Merritt & Robin Michelle Clifton ('Small Press Chronology' Editors), Ken Fernstrom ('Canadian Editor'), Richard Marsh ('Firstborn' Editor), Welch D. Everman, Brown Miller, Robert Peters, Hugh Fox, A.D. Winans, Cheryl James Naiden, John Pyros, Geoffrey Cook, Neil Baldwin, Douglas Blazek, Patricia O'Toole, Foster Robertson, Alta, Carol Berge, Sam Hamill. Write for a free copy & see how they do it. We list all books and mags received each month, and print full-info listings monthly on new small presses and mags. We provide 'Updater' forms for this last type of listing." 12/yr; 1-yr sub price: $8.50 Indiv. - $13.50 Inst.; per copy: $1.00; sample: free. 1966. 20pp; 8½ x 11. †of. circ. 3,000. Reporting time: 3 weeks. Payment: by arrangement. Not copyrighted. Ads: $75/$45. Discounts: $8/yr via agents. Pub'd 12 issues 1976; expects 12 issues 1977, 12 issues 1978. Pub's reviews. §anything published by a small press. ALP, CCLM, COSMEP, LPS.

Small Press Writer's Review (see PERADAM PUBLISHING HOUSE)

THE SMITH, The Generalist Assn., Inc., Harry Smith, Sidney Bernard, 5 Beekman St., New York, NY 10038. "THE SMITH is a function of the Generalist Association, Inc., as is the NEWSLETTER ON THE STATE OF THE CULTURE ($12/yr, 10-12 issues). Joint imprint projects include *The Scene*. The most general mag, no pet esthetic theories, no arbitrary tests set before experience of the work itself. The enemy of civilization: anti-conventional, questions the given values. Anything goes as long as it's good. 2 reg. book format mags in main series plus 'bonus publications', including two issues of tabloid newspaper." 1-yr sub price: $8.00; sample: $1.00. 1964. 192pp; 6 x 9. lp. circ. 2,500. Payment: $5,$10, & up. no ads. Discounts: 40%, agents 15%. CCLM, COSMEP.

SMOKE, Windows Project, Dave Ward, 46 Elsinore Heights, Halewood, Liverpool L26 9TE, United Kingdom. Poetry, fiction, art, long-poems, collages, concrete art, photos, cartoons. "Tom Pickard, Jim Burns, Dave Calder" 3/yr; sub price: 50p/4 issues incl. post.; per copy: 10p plus post; sample: 10p plus post. 1974. 24pp; A5. of. circ. 500. Reporting time: as quickly as possible. Payment: £2.00 per contributor. no ads. Pub'd 3 issues 1976; expects 3 issues 1977, 3 issues 1978.

SmokeRoot (see also CUTBANK), Lex Runciman, Rick Robbins, Dept of English/Univ of Mont, Missoula, MT 59812. Poetry. "Chapbooks: 28pp maximum. Recent contributors: John Haines, Mary Swander." avg. price, paper: $2.25. 1976. 28pp; 5½ x 8½. †of. avg. press run 300. Reporting time: 1-2 mos. Payment: by arrangement. Copyrights for author. Discounts: standard bookstore discount. Pub'd 2 titles 1976. CCLM.

Smyrna Press, Dan Georgakas, Leonard Rubenstein, Elias Bokhara, Judy Janda, Box 841, New York, NY 10009. Poetry, fiction, art, parts-of-novels, collages. "We try to publish one-three books a year which combine the latest technical breakthroughs with a concern for social change that is essentially Marxist but undogmatic. Our current projects include an annual anthology that will combine art and politics as well as publications dealing with themes of sexual liberation. We can use good line drawings or woodcuts. We are doing three art books in 1976 which is a new departure for our press. Sample copies of literary books—50 ¢ sample copies of art books—$1.50." avg. price, cloth: $12.00; paper: $4.00. 1964. 60-96pp; 5½ x 8½. of. avg. press run 1,000 copies. Reporting time: 2-3 weeks. Payment: copies. Discounts: 40%. Pub'd 2 titles 1976; expects 3 titles 1977, 3 titles 1978. COSMEP.

SNAKEROOTS, Tobin Simon, Liberal Arts & Sci, Pratt Inst., Brooklyn, NY 11205. Poetry, fiction, plays. "Plays must be short, under 10 pages. Michael Hogan, Guy R. Beining, Barry Wallenstein, Michael Mc Mahon, Karla Hammond, Ron Padgett, Richard Perry, Marilyn Coffey." 2/yr. 1973. 50pp; 8 x 5. lp. circ. 1,000. Reporting time: 2-4 weeks. Payment: 3 copies.

SNARF, Kitchen Sink Enterprises, Denis Kitchen, P.O. Box 7, Princeton, WI 54968. Art, cartoons, satire, letters. "Underground comic format-size ranges from 1/4 page strips to several pages long. Recent contributors: Robert Crumb, Justin Green, Will Eisner, Harvey Kurtzman." 2/yr; 1-yr sub price: $1.50; per copy: $.75; sample: $.75. 1972. 36pp; 6¾ x 9¾. of. Reporting time: 2 wks. Payment: 10% royalty, pro-rated. no ads. Discounts: 40%. §comix-oriented.

Snow Press, Jessie Kachmar, PO Box 427, Morton Grove, IL 60053, 312-299-7605. Poetry. "*At This Time*, this press is limited to the work (poetry) of Jessie Kachmar" avg. price, cloth: $6.50; paper: $3.95. 1976. 102pp; 5½ x 8½. avg. press run 1,000. Copyrights for author. Discounts: 40 percent usual. Since the book is barely off press, still in process of negotiation. Pub'd 1 title 1976.

SNOWY EGRET, Humphrey A. Olsen, Editor & Bus. Mgr.; Wm. T. Hamilton, Literary Editor; Gary Elder, West Coast Contributor; Robert A. Henschen, Music Editor; June Kemp, Artist; Dan Short, Artist, 205 S. Ninth St., Williamsburg, KY 40769. Poetry, fiction, articles, satire, criticism, reviews, music, letters, parts-of-novels, long-poems. "Emphasis on natural history and man in relation to natural history from literary, artistic, philosophical point of view. Prose generally not more than 3,000 words but will consider up to 10,000; poetry generally less than page although long poems will be considered. Expanded coverage includes politics, population, play, aggression, space, solitude, human nature, sense and sensibility, in relation to nature. Rev. copies of books desired:

those returned that cannot be used. Originality of material or originality of treatment and literary quality and readability important. Payment on publication plus checking copy. Recent contributors Gary Elder, Ron McNicoln, Merritt Clifton, Charles Fishman, Wm. D. Elliott, John Eastman, Conrad Hyers, Ed Zahniser." 2/yr; 1-yr sub price: $3.00; per copy: $2.00; sample: $1.00. 1922. 60pp; 8½ x 11. †mi. circ. 400. Reporting time: 2 months. Payment: Prose, $2.00 mag page, poetry, min $2.00 a poem, $4.00 mag page on pub. Copyrighted. Ads: None. Discounts: 40 on single $2.00, same on 1/yr sub at $4.00. Back issues: all back issues $2. Pub'd 2 issues 1976; expects 2 issues 1977, 2 issues 1978. Pub's reviews: 30 in 1976. §peoples in relation to natural surroundings, fresh nature poetry, fiction, essays, criticism, philosophy, biography. CCLM, COSMEP-SOUTH.

Soap Box Publishing (see also SPEAK OUT), Agnes Haviland, Box 737, Stamford, CT 06904, 203-357-9591. Poetry, art. "Current books—LIFELINE, Jill Marker 40pp - 1976/VIRTUE CAN TAKE SHAPE AS ANAPAEST, Hal Eskesen- 1976/LEATHER BUTTERFLY, Constance Kendall-forthcoming." avg. price, paper: $2.00. 1971. 40pp; 5 x 8. †Stencil Duplicator. avg. press run 200 copies. Reporting time: 2 wks to 3 months. Payment: co-operative-10 percent royalty—print run split 50 percent between publisher and author. Copyrights for author. Discounts: 40 percent trade. CCLM, NESPA.

SOCCER WORLD, World Publications, World Publications, P.O. Box 366, Mtn. View, CA 94040. Fiction, articles, art, photos, cartoons, interviews. "SOCCER WORLD contains information for players, coaches, referees, managers, parents, young players, and fans-information on technique, tactics, conditioning, officiating and much more. The editor maintains control over all printed and published material." 12/yr; 1-yr sub price: $8.00; per copy: $.75; sample: free. 1974. 28pp; 9 x 11. of. circ. 22,000. Discounts: bulk rates. Back issues: $1.00. §sports/recreation/leisure activities.

SOCIAL POLICY, Frank Reissman, 184 Fifth Avenue, New York, NY 10010, 212-989-5280. Articles, art, photos, interviews, criticism, reviews, letters. "Articles run 2,000-4,000 words, on contemporary, social thought (education, economics, community development). Recent special issues dealt with 'self-help', 'older persons', 'mental health', 'education assessment', 'consumer education'. Contributors include Herbert Gans, Nat Hentoff, Michael Harrington, Tom Cottle, Marcia Guttentag, Jean Miller." 5/yr; 1-yr sub price: $10.00; per copy: $2.00. 1970. 64pp; 8½ x 11. lp. circ. 10,000. Reporting time: 2-4 weeks. Payment: none. Copyrighted. Ads: $300/$180. Discounts: 10% agent. Back issues: $3. Pub'd 5 issues 1976; expects 5 issues 1977, 5 issues 1978. Pub's reviews: 13 in 1976. §Nonfiction, social policy materials, esp. in area of economics and human services. COSMEP.

Socialist Party of Canada (see FULCRUM)

Society For Education In Film And Television (see SCREEN)

Soft Press, Robert Sward, 1050 Saint David St., Victoria, British Columbia V8S4Y8, Canada, 604-598-2173. Poetry, photos, collages. "No unsolicited material." avg. price, paper: $4.95. 1970. 64pp; 6 x 9. †of/lp. avg. press run 1,000. Payment: copies. Copyrights for author. Discounts: 40% bookstores/50% distributors. Pub'd 2 titles 1976. COSMEP.

SOFT STONE, An International Journal of the Arts, Karl C. Wang, 102-40 62nd Avenue Apt 6C, Forest Hills, NY 11275. Poetry, fiction, art, photos. "Best, not to try sending to SOFT STONE for a year or two, unless during this time, I can find a replacement (editor) willing to do the chores of editing. I look for creative work of high quality. Length and style make no difference, shall accept anything pleasing and attractive. Especially open to international writers, not necessarily well known. Features a particular poet or artist in each issue with a sizeable collection of their work: 1st issue featured Murat Namet-Nejat, and a 2nd issue Tom Joens, an American poet." irreg.; price per copy: $1.00; sample: $1.25. 1973. 72pp; 5½ x 8½. of. circ. 500. Reporting time: indefinite. Payment: copies only. Back issues: #1 issue tentatively priced at $1.50. §books of poems, stories, translations, art criticisms.

SOFT TIMES, O Press, E. T. Caldwell, Carol Line, Jim Spencer, Basil Tozer, 1338 N. Astor,

Milwaukee, WI 53202. Poetry, fiction, articles, art, photos, cartoons, interviews, satire, criticism, reviews, music, letters, collages, concrete art. 6/yr; 1-yr sub price: $5.00; per copy: $0.50; sample: $0.89. 1975. 60pp; varies. †of. circ. 5,000. Reporting time: 2 weeks-2 months. Payment: copies-& cash if available. Copyrighted, reverts to author. Ads: $75.00/$40.00/$0.10. Discounts: negotiable. Back issues: $1.00. Pub's reviews. §from random insanity to lucid hallucinations. ILIE.

Sol Press, R. Bruce Allison, 107 Minneola St., Hinsdale, IL 60521. "Not accepting manuscripts." †of.

SOLANA, Jeanne Fogler, Barb Weigel, Mary Hartcivili, Terri Anderson, Lola L. Lucas, 11822 Kramper Lane, St. Louis, MO 63128, 314-843-5930. Poetry, fiction, articles, art, photos, reviews, plays. "SOLANA is intended as a vehicle for women to express themselves. Poetry, short fiction, artwork, photographs, concise essays on topics of interest to women, and reviews of women writers will be considered. We like and appreciate receiving feminist work, but we do not insist on a feminist orientation. What we do insist on is quality. We will not print anything that we feel is poorly done, even if we agree with its viewpoint." 2/yr; 1-yr sub price: $3.00; per copy: $1.50; sample: $1.00. 1976. 40-50pp; 7 x 8½. mi/of. circ. 300. Reporting time: 4-6 weeks. Payment: 2 copies. Copyrighted, reverts to author. no ads. Back issues: $1.00 each. Only a few copies of I,1 available, but many of I,2 still on hand. Pub'd 2 issues 1976; expects 2 issues 1977, 2 issues 1978. Pub's reviews: 2 in 1976. §topics of interest to women in lit.

SOLAR AGE, Bruce Anderson, Sandra Oddo, Martin McPhillips, 200 East Main Street, Port Jervis, NY 12771, 914-856-6663. Articles, photos, cartoons, interviews, reviews, letters. 12/yr; 1-yr sub price: $20.00; per copy: $1.95. 1976. 35pp; 8¼ x 11-1/8. of. Reporting time: 1 month. Copyrighted, does not revert to author. Ads: $650.00/$500.00/$0.55. Discounts: jobbers - 50 percent; retail - 25-30 percent. Back issues: $2.50. §Solar energy. COSMEP.

THE SOLE PROPRIETOR, Al Fogel, 2770 NW 32 Ave., Miami, FL 33142. Poetry, reviews. "Devoted exclusively to high caliber contemporary poetry. Continue to welcome outstanding contemporary poetry in all of its forms & manifestations, altho preferential treatment accorded those poems in the following genres: (1) Meta- (2) Prose- (3) Found (4) Surreal (5) Post-objectivist (6) Long/Developmental/Sequence. In addition, TSP has a special per-issue feature: 'Small Press Tour De Force' in which outstanding poems from recent (past 6 months) small press magazines are re-printed with cash prizes & copies of TSP awarded to author(s) & editor(s) from which poems have been selected. Small press mags with a circulation under 1,000 are invited to send recent publications for possible inclusion. First & subsequent issues of TSP have featured: Antin, Samperi, Heller, Ignatow, Halvard Johnson, Jane Augustine, Rachel Blau DuPlessis, L.L. Zeiger, David Walker, Kostelanetz, Cooley, Vinz, Saner, etc." 2/yr; 1-yr sub price: $4.00; per copy: $2.00; sample: $2.00. 1976. 32pp; 8 x 11. of. circ. 300. Reporting time: 1-2 wks. Payment: contrib copy + monetary remuneration. Back issues: No. 1, $20.00; No. 2, $10.50; No. 3, $2.00. Pub'd 2 issues 1976; expects 2 issues 1977, 2 issues 1978. COSMEP, CCLM.

SOLEIL BLANK: a forum of progressive literature, Carl D. Clark, 3007 University, Austin, TX 78705, 512-472-7415. Poetry, fiction, articles, criticism, letters, parts-of-novels, long-poems, collages, plays, concrete art. "*SOLEIL BLANK* will publish progressive literature (and literature combined with otheraarts). Progressive literature is defined as that which starts from some established form or type (be it conventional, experiment 1 or avante-garde) and progresses beyond the normal formal/content bounds of that form." 6/yr. 1977. 4pp; 8½ x 11. Reporting time: 1 day. Payment: none. Not copyrighted. Ads: none. Discounts: none. Pub'd 1 issue 1976.

Solo Press (see CAFE SOLO)

SOMA-HAOMA, Salt-works Press, Tom Bridwell, Edward Harper, Box 649, Dennis, MA 02638. Poetry, fiction, art, photos, music, long-poems. "Fine hand-set letterpress printing-limited runs of block prints & other graphics, silk-screening (often includes actual items). Real photos. Conceptually packaged-cans or boxes or whatever.." 2/yr; sub price: $24.00-2 issues; per copy: $12.00. 1973. 80-120pp; 8½ x 11. †lp. circ. 200. Reporting time: 6 weeks. Payment: copies. Copyrighted. Ads:

293

None. Discounts: None. Back issues: Available. Pub'd 1 issue 1976; expects 2 issues 1977, 2 issues 1978. §poetry/photo/modern fiction.

SOME, Release Press, Harry Greenberg, Alan Ziegler, Larry Zirlin, Lois Morris, Associate, 309 W. 104 St. Apt. 9D, New York, NY 10025. Poetry, fiction, articles, art, photos, reviews, long-poems. "We select material we ourselves would like to come across as readers. Recent contributors: Tate, Bly, Boggis, Stokes, Anderson, Benedikt, Gutstein, Loney, Knott, Piercy, Yau, Edson, Moritz, Kellman, Love, Phillipps, Inez, Orr, Seidman, Zavatsky, Lazar, Haymes, Safane, Lux, a symposium on poetry readings; *some* 7/8 is in a box, including broadsides, photos, a pencil, a play, death warrents, a catalogue, etc." 2/yr; 1-yr sub price: $5.00 individuals/$9.00 institutions; per copy: $2.50; sample: $2.50. 1972. 72pp; 5½ x 8½. †of. circ. 1,250. Reporting time: 2-6 weeks. Payment: copies. Copyrighted, reverts to author. no ads. Discounts: 40 percent discount for orders above 5. Back issues: Inquire. Pub'd 1 issue 1976; expects 2 issues 1977. Pub's reviews. §all. CCLM.

SOME FRIENDS, Some Friends Press, Terry J. Cooper, P.O. Box 3395, Tyler, TX 75701. Poetry, fiction, articles, art, photos, interviews. 1-2/yr; 1-yr sub price: $2.50; per copy: $1.75; sample: $1.25. 1972. 40pp; 8 x 11. of. circ. 500-1,500. Reporting time: 6 wks-4 mos. Payment: 3 issues. Ads: $75/$50. Back issues: $1.50/ea. Pub's reviews. §poetry/short stories. CCLM, COSMEP.

Some of Us Press, Lee Lally, Ed Zahniser, 4110 Emery Pl. N.W., Washington, DC 20016. Poetry. "Beth Joselow, Bob Hershon, Robert Slater. Not soliciting new mss." avg. price, paper: $1.00. 1972. 36pp; 8½ x 5. lp. Reporting time: 3 weeks. Payment: 3 copies. Discounts: 40%. COSMEP.

Some Other Newsletter (see UNPUBLISHED EDITIONS)

SONG: A Magazine of Verse and Essay, Richard Behm, 808 Illinois, Stevens Pt, WI 54481, 715-344-6836. Poetry, articles, criticism, reviews, letters, long-poems. "SONG began as a whim, but it is something other than that now. The editorial slant is still towards poetry written in rhyme and meter. However, I am very interested in more free verse which demonstrates a crafted awareness of sound, as well as variations and experiments with traditional forms, rhyme patterns, and meters. Essays, personal and critical, are sought. SONG is a year behind in its publishing schedule and I hope contributors and subscribers will accept my apologies for the long delay. Following is a breakdown of SONG'S future issues: Issue 2, Sonnets, July 1977; Issue 3/4, a large double issue containing much of SONG'S backlog of material, October 1977; Issue 5, a special issue devoted to the work of a new poet, January 1978; Issue 6 and Issue 7 will also be published in 78. These will deal with translations, and verse light and bawdy. I will be happy to read manuscripts of a more general nature, but with the understanding that any poems accepted will not appear for some time to come. Contributors to the first three issues include: Eberhart, Aloff, Wagner, Eckman, Turco, Langton, R.P. Dickey, Richard Grossman, Judy Neeld, David Lunde, Gordon Weaver, Norma Farber, H.A. Maxson, Judson Crews, Michael Johnson, et al." 1/yr and occasional ancillary publications; 1-yr sub price: $2.50; per copy: $2.50; sample: $2.50. 1975. Varies 50-100pp; 8½ x 5½. of. Reporting time: 4-12 weeks. Payment: 1 contributors copy. Copyrighted, reverts to author. Ads: $20/$15. Discounts: 20% on orders of 10 or more copies by educational institutions or workshops. Back issues: $2.50 each. Expects 2 issues 1977, 2 or 3 issues 1978. Pub's reviews. §poetry/criticism/essays on craft of poetry.

A SONGSMITH'S JOURNAL, PhoeniXongs, James Durst, Box 622, Northbrook, IL 60062, 312-498-3981. Poetry, fiction, articles, art, photos, cartoons, interviews, satire, music, letters. 4/yr; 1-yr sub price: $3.00; $5.00; $10.00; or $25.00; per copy: $0.75; sample: $0.75. 1976. 12pp; 8½ x 11. of. circ. 2,500. Copyrighted. Back issues: $1.00. COSMEP.

SOU'WESTER, Pantagraph (Bloomington, Ill) Lloyd Kropp, Linda Williamson, Mary Diesel, Terry Perkins, Southern Illinois University, Edwardsville, IL 62025. Poetry, fiction, satire, long-poems. "We have no particular editorial biases or taboos. We publish the best poetry and fiction we can find." 3/yr; 1-yr sub price: $4.00; per copy: $1.50; sample: $1.50. 1960. 92pp; 9 x 12. of. circ. 500. Reporting time: 4-6 wks. Payment: copies (also cash prizes). Discounts: 20% off for orders over 4 copies. Back issues: $1.50 per copy. COSMEP.

SOUNDINGS, Peter Garland, c/o Apt 216E, 4201 Cathedral Ave. N.W., Washington, DC 20016. Articles, art, photos, interviews, criticism, music. "To date, SOUNDINGS has published 9 issues and 3 books. It will cease this year with issue 10 ($4-late summer or early fall). SOUNDINGS book #3 was *Magic Animals*, consisted of a Yuman Indian song cycle transcribed by the early 20th century ethnomusicologist Frances Densmore, and Mimbres (extinct Pueblo culture) pottery designs rendered by Victoria Brown." irreg.; price per copy: $3.00-$4.00; sample: free. 1972. 160pp; 8½ x 11. of. circ. 400. Reporting time: 1 week. Payment: none. Discounts: for bulk orders 40%.

SOURCE, LAD (Literary Arts Div) of Queens Council on the Arts, Jack Donahue, Margaret Stetler, Richard Vetere, c/o 46-38 202 St., Bayside, NY 11361, 144-30 Roosevelt Ave., Flushing, NY 11354. Poetry, fiction, art, photos, criticism, reviews, long-poems. "In first issue: David Ignatow, Stephen Stepanchev, Elsa Colligan, Miriam Solan and winners of recent Queens college and H.S. writing contests & more. Special interest in Queens writers, although we publish writers outside the borough. We're looking for new as well as established writers to submit to SOURCE." 1-yr sub price: $1.50; per copy: $1.50; sample: inquire. 1976. 40pp; 5½ x 8½. of. circ. 800. Reporting time: 1-2 mos. Payment: 2 copies. §poetry/fiction/new mags similar to ours.

SOUTH CAROLINA REVIEW, Frank Day, Managing Editor; Richard Calhoun, Robert Hill, William Koon, Asst. Editor, English Dept, Clemson Univ., Clemson, SC 29631. Poetry, fiction, articles, interviews, satire, criticism, reviews. "Joyce Carol Oates, Mark Steadman, Stephen Dixon." 2/yr; 1-yr sub price: $2.00; per copy: $1.50. 1968. 84pp. circ. 600. Reporting time: 2 weeks. Payment: copies. Pub's reviews. §poetry/fiction/literary history/criticism. CCLM.

SOUTH DAKOTA REVIEW, Dakota Press, Box 111, University Exchange, Vermillion, SD 57069, 605-677-5229. Fiction, poetry, art. 4/yr; 1-yr sub price: $6.00; per copy: $1.50. 1963. 120pp; 6 x 9. lp/of. circ. 700. Reporting time: Varies-average, 2 weeks. Payment: Copies, 1-4. Copyrighted. Discounts: 40 percent to bookstores. Back issues: Most are available. Pub'd 4 issues 1976; expects 4 issues 1977, 4 issues 1978. Pub's reviews. CCLM, COSMEP.

South Head Press (see POETRY AUSTRALIA)

SOUTHERN EXPOSURE, Institute for Southern Studies, Bob Hall, Managing Editor, P.O. Box 230, Chapel Hill, NC 27514. Poetry, fiction, articles, art, photos, interviews, reviews. "All material must be related to the South. Since issues are generally focused on particular themes, a query letter can be helpful. We'll let you know what topics we're planning to cover. Anything goes. We have published two regular issues (120 pages) and one double issue (220) each year. In the future we plan to publish two general issues and two special theme issues per year." 4/yr; 1-yr sub price: $8.00 ($12.00-libraries); per copy: $2.50; sample: $2.50. 1973. 120pp; 8½ x 11. of. circ. 5,000. Reporting time: 8 weeks. Payment: $75.00-$200.00. Ads: $200.00/$100.00. Discounts: 40% 5 or more. Pub'd 4 issues 1976; expects 4 issues 1977, 4 issues 1978. Pub's reviews. §Southern related to the South. COSMEP.

SOUTHERN HUMANITIES REVIEW, Eugene Current-Garcia, Norman Brittin, 9090 Haley Center, Auburn Univ., Auburn, AL 36830, 205-826-4606. Poetry, fiction, articles, interviews, satire, criticism, reviews, parts-of-novels. "W.H. Auden, Joyce Carol Oates, Tom Sinclair, Bo Ball." 4/yr; 1-yr sub price: $6.00; per copy: $2.00; sample: $2.00. 1966. 100pp; 6 x 9. lp. circ. 500. Reporting time: 1 month. Payment: none. Copyrighted, reverts to author upon request. Ads: none. Discounts: none. Pub'd 5 issues 1976; expects 4 issues 1977, 4 issues 1978. Pub's reviews: 150 in 1976.

SOUTHERN LIBERTARIAN MESSENGER, John T. Harllee, P.O. Box 1245, Florence, SC 29503. Poetry, articles, cartoons, satire, reviews, letters, art, news items. 12/yr; 1-yr sub price: $3.00; per copy: $.25; sample: $.25 or free. 1972. 10pp; 8½ x 11. †mi/of. circ. 400. Reporting time: variable. Payment: no payment, except complimentary subscriptions. Not copyrighted. Ads: $15/$8/$.25 line. Back issues: $0.25 if available. Pub'd 13 issues 1976; expects 12 issues 1977, 12 issues 1978. Pub's reviews: 50 in 1976. §libertarian, politics, economics, science fiction. LPS.

SOUTHERN POETRY REVIEW, Guy Owen, Mary C. Williams, Dept. of English, North Carolina State Univ., Raleigh, NC 27607. "SPR is not a regional mag-though we have a special interest in young Southern talent. We lean toward short poems in 'the modern mode.' No light verse, no nature poems. Book reviews are assigned. (We do not consider poems during the summer months.)" 3/yr; 1-yr sub price: $4.00; per copy: $4.00; sample: $1.00. 1958. 60pp. Circ. 700-1M. Reporting time: 1 wk to 1 mo. Payment: $3/poem plus contrib. copy. no ads. Discounts: 30%. Back issues: $1. CCLM, COSMEP, COSMEPA.

‡**SOUTHERN QUARTERLY,** Box 78, Southern Stn., USM, Hattiesburg, MS 39401.

SOUTHERN REVIEW, Kevin Margarey, F.H. Mares, (Adelaide); A.P. Reimer, (Sydney), Dept. of English, Univ. of Adelaide, Adelaide, S. 5001, Australia. Poetry, fiction, articles, interviews, criticism, reviews, parts-of-novels. "Literary and inter-disciplinary essays; poems; short stories. M.L.A. Style Sheet. Articles for critical exchange section welcomed." 3/yr; 1-yr sub price: A$12.00/A$10.00 individuals; per copy: a$4.50 ($5.00 posted); sample: free. 1963. 92pp (276pp per year); 16cm x 24cm. lp. circ. 700. Reporting time: 3 months. Payment: poems A$8.00/stories A$30.00. Ads: A$100/A$50. Discounts: agents A$8.00/students A$7.50. Back issues: $2.00 per issue to 1975. Pub's reviews. §literary criticism/literature and it's relation to history, philosophy, anthropology, etc.

THE SOUTHERN REVIEW, L.S.U. Press, Donald E. Stanford, Louis P. Simpson, Drawer D, University Station, Baton Rouge, LA 70893. Poetry, fiction, articles, interviews, criticism, reviews, letters, parts-of-novels, long-poems. "We emphasize craftsmanship and intellectual contest. We favor articles on contemporary literature and on the history and culture of the South. Recent contributors—Malcolm Cowley, Frank Kermode, Hayden Carruth, Roy Fuller, David Wagoner, Matthew Josephson, Thomas Parkinson, Martin Turnell, Howard Baker." 4/yr; 1-yr sub price: $5.00; per copy: $1.50; sample: free. 1935. 275pp; 6¾ x 10. of. circ. 3,000. Reporting time: one month. Payment: poetry $20-$50 a page/prose $12-$20 a page. Ads: $100/$60. Discounts: 30%. Pub's reviews. §Contemporary Literature, Fiction, Poetry, Culture of the South. CCLM.

Southwest Research and Information Center (see THE WORKBOOK)

SOUTHWEST REVIEW, Southern Methodist University Press, Margaret L. Hartley, Southern Methodist Univ., Dallas, TX 75275, 214-692-2263. "Contemporary literature and discussion combining quality fiction and verse with studies in current affairs, historical research, literary criticism, accounts of achievements in the lively arts, essays of personal opinion, and book reviews." 4/yr; 1-yr sub price: $5.00; per copy: $1.50; sample: gratis. 1915. 98pp; 6 x 9. lp. circ. 1,000. Reporting time: 3 months. Copyright by SMU Press. Ads: $60.00 (one time), $50.00 (four times)/$32.50 (one time), $27.50 (four times). Discounts: 25 percent to agencies. Back issues: available on request.

SPAFASWAP, Spafaswap, Lois J. Long, Ph.D., 1070 Ahern, La Puente, CA 91746, 213-962-3910. Poetry, art, photos, cartoons, criticism, reviews. "We are now limiting to poetry. Reviews and other columns are in-house. We consider the magazine to be a show case of poetic form and we publish as wide a variety of poetry as we can find. We do like our poetry to be positive. No porno. Cooperative basis only." 6/yr; 1-yr sub price: $6.00; per copy: $1.00; sample: $1.00. 1969. 40pp; 5½ x 8½. of. circ. 300. Reporting time: promptly (same day). Payment: copy. Ads: $2.00. Discounts: this problem has never come up. Back issues: $1 when available. Pub'd 6 issues 1976; expects 6 issues 1977. Pub's reviews.

SPANNER, E. M. Press, Allen Fisher, 18 Hayes Court, London SW2 4EX, United Kingdom. Articles, poetry, art, reviews, interviews, criticism, music. "Usually 10 pages, typed." 1-yr sub price: £4.00; per copy: 50p; sample: 50p. 1974. 10pp; A4. lo/mi. circ. varies. Reporting time: 3 months. Discounts: 5 plus 40%. Back issues: Last 2 at 50p each. Pub'd 6 issues 1976; expects 15 issues 1977.

SPARROW POVERTY PAMPHLETS, Sparrow Press, Felix Stefanile, Selma Stefanile, 103

Waldron St, West Lafayette, IN 47906. Poetry. "Strict format: 20 to 32 typed pages, no more, no less. We will not 'edit' your MSS stick to format. We only have the honest bias of our personal taste which, admittedly, is fallible. Nevertheless, *Sparrow* Poems are now in just about all the major anthologies in the country, from Little, Brown to Untermeyer, so we must do something right. (This brings money to our poets.) We are growing tired of the confessional cliche' the long, leaky poem has become, and our up-coming issues opt for the short poem. We have always been an eclectic magazine. In the past we have published Corman's word-count poems, Vassar Miller's sonnets. No style prejudices, but the poet has to love language. Recent *Sparrow* poets—John Fandel, Roger Pfingston, Tom Montag. Poet-in-the schools whiz-kids, creative writing teacher's pets, ideologues: don't call us, we'll call you. We urge writer's to inspect a copy before sending, 75 percent of what we get is quite simply not the kind of writing we 'want.'" 2/yr; 1-yr sub price: $3.00 indiv/$3.50 libraries; per copy: $1.50; sample: $1.00. 1954. 32pp; 5½ x 8½. of. circ. 800. Reporting time: 3 to 6 weeks. Payment: 2 free copies of the pamphlet, plus modest advance against royalties, plus 20 percent of income after cost. Copyrighted. no ads. Discounts: 40% to our agents/20% to classes more than 7. Back issues: issues before No. 31 are collector's items, from $4.00-$25.00 each. Pub'd 2 issues 1976; expects 2 issues 1977, 3 issues 1978. CCLM.

Sparrow Press (see also Vagrom Chap Books), Felix Stefanile, Editor; Selma Stefanile, Editor, 103 Waldron St., West Lafayette, IN 47906. Poetry, criticism. "*VAGROM CHAP BOOKS* by invitation only. Some poets published: Corman, Mills, Echman." avg. price, paper: $3.00. 1954. 8-108pp; 5½ x 8½. of/lp. avg. press run 250-1,000. Payment: 2 free copies, modest advance against royalties; plus 20 percent of income after cost. Our books sell. Copyrights for author. Discounts: 40 percent to agents. Pub'd 1 title 1976; expects 1 title 1977, 2 titles 1978. CCLM.

SPC (see THE TOYSUN)

SPEAK OUT, Soap Box Publishing, Agnes D'Ottavio, Box 737, Stamford, CT 06904, 203-357-9591. Poetry, art, cartoons, reviews. "Poems must be under 30 lines. No love poems. William Joyce, Douglas Blazek, Carol Adler, Karla Hammond, El Gilbert." 4/yr; 1-yr sub price: $5.00; per copy: $1.25; sample: $1.00. 1971. 40pp; 5 x 8. †stencil duplicator. circ. 100. Reporting time: 2-12 weeks. Payment: single copy. Copyrighted, reverts to author Ads: $50.00/$26.00/$0.10. Discounts: 40 percent trade. Back issues: $2.00 if available. Pub's reviews. §anything except Lesbianism/Gay. CCLM, NESPA.

SPEAK 2, Speak 2 Press, David C. Childers, 211B South 2nd Street, Wilmington, NC 28401. Poetry. "Shorter poems—1—50 lines. No biases. Poems by John Tagliabue,Von Underwood, James Lark, Richard Williams, Amon Liner & Geoff Mangum & Fred Chappell have appeared. SPEAK 2 is a broadside sheet." 4 in 1976. 1 in 1977. Depends on financial state of the editor.; 1-yr sub price: sase; per copy: free; sample: sase. 1974. 4pp; 8½ x 5½. mi. circ. 300-500. Distributed by hand, & mail. Reporting time: 2 days-4 mo. Payment: copies.

SPEAKOUT, Christine Root, Cheryl Shenkle, P.O. Box 6165, Albany, NY 12206. Poetry, fiction, articles, art, interviews, reviews, letters. "Feminist monthly news journal published for and by women of upstate New York." 11/yr; 1-yr sub price: $3.50; per copy: $.35; sample: 1 free. 1971. 20pp; 8½ x 11. mi/of. circ. 650. Reporting time: 60 days. Payment: none. Ads: $30/$20/10 words free to subscribers. Discounts: 10% to a periodical jobber. Back issues: $.35 per (not all dates available). Pub's reviews. §women, child care, prisons. COSMEP.

Special Aviation Publications, Nick Pocock, Alvena Prause Pocock, Box 672, Hillsboro, TX 76645. "Publishers of books. First title: *Did W.D. Custead Fly First?* by Nick Pocock. Presentation and discussion of evidence that little known aeronautical pioneer W.D. Custead flew before Wright Brothers. Illustrated with photographs, maps and drawings. Aviation related only." avg. price, paper: $2.95. 1974. of. Reporting time: 1 month. Discounts: 40 percent dealers. Expects 1 title 1977, 1 title 1978. COSMEP, ASWA.

SPECTRE (see also Spectre Press), Jon M. Harvey, 18 Cefn Road, Mynachdy, Cardiff CF4 3HS, United Kingdom. Articles, poetry, fiction, art, cartoons, satire, reviews, interviews, criticism, letters, long-poems, plays. "Anything up to 20,000 words. Fantasy-orientated material. Recent Contributors: Andrew Darlington, Richard Tierney, Ramsey Campbell, Dr. Dirk W. Mosig and Alex Kernaghan." infrequent; avg. price, cloth: £2/4 issues; paper: 50p; other: 50p. 1975. 48pp; 5½ x 8¼. litho. avg. press run 500. Reporting time: 1-2 months. Payment: copies only. Discounts: 25% for dealer & minor contributor 50% for major dealer.

Spectre Press (see also CTHULHU, SPECTRE), Jon M. Harvey, Publisher, 18 Cefn Road, Mynachdy, Cardiff CF4 3HS, United Kingdom. Poetry, fiction, articles, art, cartoons, satire, long-poems, plays. "For example: *Lovecraftian Characters And Other Things,* an art portfolio by Jim Pitts; *The Compassion Of Time,* a general greetings card, illustrated and containing a short story. And three anthologies of prose fictions: *Dreams Of A Dark Hue, Dark Words-Gentle Sounds* and *By Day And Night.* Will publish any fantasy item of interest, of maximum length 20,000 words: collections of articles and/or fiction on aspects of fantasy; also one-author collections of prose, poetry and/or art work." avg. price, cloth: varies; paper: varies; other: varies. 1976. pp varies; varies. litho. avg. press run 750 copies. Reporting time: 1-2 months. Payment: copies only. Buys first U.K. rights only. Discounts: agent, 50 percent; bulk, 40 percent for 10-49 copies; 50 percent for 50 or more copies. Pub'd 4 titles 1976; expects 5 titles 1977.

Spectrum Productions, Dan Schlossky, Adrienne Schizzano, 979 Casiano Rd., Los Angeles, CA 90049. Poetry, fiction, plays. "We are interested in receiving inquiries (not mss.) in the field of translations of European drama before the twentieth century." COSMEP.

THE SPHINX, Gordon Turner, English Dept, Univ Of Regina, Regina, SN S4S0A2, Canada. Articles, criticism, reviews. "4000 ww; sociological & pyschological approaches to literature; David Bleich, Andrew Brink, Leslie Fiedler." 2/yr; 1-yr sub price: $3.00; per copy: $1.50; sample: $1.00. 1974. 65pp; 8½ x 11. of. circ. 450. Reporting time: 5-6 weeks. Payment: none. Pub's reviews. §fiction; criticism of above kinds.

THE SPICY MEATBALL, 75 Press, Sue Willis, Karen Hubert, 236 Clinton St, Brooklyn, NY 11201. Poetry, fiction, articles, art, photos, cartoons, interviews, satire, parts-of-novels, long-poems, collages, plays. "We are using almost strictly work from P.S. 75 in Manhattan but every once in a while we take outside contributors. Everything is written by children themselves. We have lately expanded into Comics (*Bang, Pest*), and novels—one very good one is *Teresa Inez Drew* by Tanya Pendleton available for $1.50." 1 or 2 per yr; 1-yr sub price: $3.00; per copy: $2.00; sample: $2.00. 1972. 10-128pp; varies. †mi/of. circ. 1,000. Reporting time: 2 months. Payment: copies. Pub'd 4 issues 1976; expects 2-4 issues 1977, 2-4 issues 1978. §children's only.

Spindrift Press, Richard N. Hayton, P.O. Box 3252, Catonsville, MD 21228. Fiction, satire. "In 1975 published THE KING and THE CAT by Thomas Starling, a novel of political satire. $6.95/cloth. Hope for 1 or 2 books a year written from a radical perspective. At present submissions not solicited." 1974. of. COSMEP.

Spirit Mound Press, Box 111, University Exch., Vermillion, SD 57069. 1974. lp. Pub'd 2 titles 1976.

THE SPIRIT THAT MOVES US, The Spirit That Moves Us, Inc. (Formerly Emmess Press), Morty Sklar, P.O. Box 1585, Iowa City, IA 52240, 319-338-5761. Poetry, art, photos, cartoons, long-poems, collages, concrete art. "My only prejudices are those of personal taste. Will publish anything that grabs me; prefer work that comes from feeling. I like translations from all languages. Recent contributors: Anselm Hollo, Michael Lally, Barbara Holland, Pablo Neruda, John Batki, Cinda Wormley Kornblum, David Hilton, Sheila Heldenbrand, Richard Kostelanetz, Tom Veitch, Hermann Hesse. We're IRS tax-exempt, which means donations are tax-deductible. We put poetry with artwork in the buses. Special Chilean issue, Spring 1978." 3/yr, 2/yr with more pages each beginning with Vol. 3 in Fall 1977.; 1-yr sub price: $3.00-yr plus $0.75 postage; per copy: $1.00 plus $.25 postage; sample: $1.00 plus $0.25 postage-ea. 1975. 48 pp, 64 pp beginning with Vol. 3 in Fall 1977.; 5½ x 8½. of. circ. 800. Reporting time: 1-2 weeks. Payment: copies, money when possible. Copyright By The Spirit That Moves Us, for the authors. Ads: $40/$25. Discounts: 40% for 5 or more, 25% for less than 5, (bookstores) classroom 25% for 10 or more. Back issues: Vol. 1, No. 1 is now $1.50; Vol. 1, No. 2 is still $1.00; Vol. 1, No. 3 & Vol. 2, No. 1 are now rare & longer available for sale, but will be offered to patrons ($25 contributions, which are tax-deductible). Pub'd 3 issues 1976; expects 3 issues 1977, 2 issues 1978. Pub's reviews: none in 1976. CCLM, COSMEP, PD.

The Spirit That Moves Us, Inc. (Formerly Emmess Press) (see also THE SPIRIT THAT MOVES US), Morty Sklar, Ed-Publ., P.O. Box 1585, Iowa City, IA 52240, 319-338-5569. Poetry. *"The Spirit That Moves Us, Inc.* also puts poetry with drawings in the buses and presents free poetry readings. Books to date: *Riverside* poems by Morty Sklar (1974: Letterpress); *The Poem You Asked For* poems by Marianne Wolfe (1977: Offset); *An Actualist Anthology* poems by Anselm Hollo, David Hilton, Cinda Kornblum, John Batki, Morty Sklar, Darrel Gray, Sheila Heldenbrand and 7 others who lived & interacted in Iowa City in the early 70's, but who come from New York City, Saint Louis, Hungary, Finland, San Francisco & elsewhere, and whose work expresses affirmation and feeling in many different ways (1977: Perfectbound or hardcover; 144 pages; photos & drawings). Forthcoming: Attila Jozsef: his poems (transl. from the *Magyar* by John Batki; winter 1977). Donations to *The Spirit That Moves Us* are IRS tax-deductible." avg. price, cloth: $6.50; paper: $2.00. 1974. 16-144pp; 5½ x 8½. †lp/of. avg. press run 1,000. Reporting time: Booked thru 1978 for books; mss welcome for the mag, tho: 5 minutes to a month. Payment: 10 percent of run. Copyrights revert to authors. Discounts: usual. Pub'd 1 title 1976; expects 3 titles 1977, 3 titles 1978. COSMEP, CCLM.

Spiritual Community Publications (see also SPIRITUAL COMMUNITY GUIDE), Parmatma Singh, Box 1080, San Rafael, CA 94902, 415-457-2990. Articles, art, photos, interviews, reviews. "We encourage corrections, additions and advice." 1970. 5½ x 8½. of. avg. press run 15,000. Copyrights for author. Discounts: 40% stores/50% distributors. Expects 1 title 1978. COSMEP.

SPIT IN THE OCEAN, Intrepid Trips Information Service, Ken Kesey, Ken Babbs, David Butkovich, Walt Curtis, Ed McClanahan, Timothy Leary, Lee Mars, 85829 Ridgeway Rd, Pleasant Hill, OR 97401. "SPIT IN THE OCEAN will consist of seven issues total over however many years it takes. Each issue will have a seperate 'guest' editor who picks his/her theme. First issue published in Jan. 1974, 2nd issue published in March, 1976." occasional; sub price: 3 issues for $5.00/7 issues for $10.00; per copy: $2.00; sample: $2.00. 1974. 128pp; 8½ x 5¼. of. circ. 2,000. Reporting time: no set time. Payment: proportional share of eventual profits-if any. Back issues: $2.00. COSMEP.

Split-Leaf Press (see also THE WESTERLY REVIEW). COSMEP, CCLM.

SPLIT LEVEL, Split Level Publishing House, Harry Peters, Box 791, Winnipeg, MB R3C1P7, Canada. Poetry, fiction, art, satire, collages, plays, concrete art. "If the poetry doesn't have the *impact* of a Mack Truck (idea-wise) or the punch of M. Ali (humor-wise) then we send it back. Recent Canadian contributors of note: Ivan Berg, Marilyn Julian and John Ditsky. Graphic Artist Superb—Bela Egyedi." 2/yr; 1-yr sub price: $2.00; per copy: $1.00; sample: $1.00. 1974. 32pp; 4 x 7. circ. 150. Reporting time: 2 mos. Payment: 10 copies. Back issues: all three for $2.50. COSMEP.

THE SPOON RIVER QUARTERLY, The Spoon River Poetry Press, David R. Pichaske, Bradley University, Peoria, IL 61606. Poetry, art. "Interested only in quality poetry that is readable. Avoids poetry that is directly or indirectly about poetry, style, or its own self." 4/yr; 1-yr sub price: $4.50; per copy: $1.50; sample: $1.50. 1976. 40pp; 5½ x 8½. of. circ. 300. Reporting time: 1 month. Payment: none. Copyrighted, assigned to author on request. Discounts: 20% bulk, classroom, agent. Pub'd 4 issues 1976; expects 4 issues 1977, 4 issues 1978.

SPORTSWOMAN MAGAZINE, CM Publications, Molly Tyson, 119 Paul Drive Box 4450, San Rafael, CA 94902. 10/yr; 1-yr sub price: $6.50; per copy: $.75; sample: $.75. 1972. 56pp; 10-7/8 x 8-3/8. circ. 12,000. Reporting time: 2 months. Payment: $1 per column inch/$10 per b & w photo. Ads: b & w $520/$275. Discounts: 3-5 subs $5.50 per/6-10 $5.00 per. Back issues: $.75. Pub's reviews. §sports w/ emphasis on women writers or subject.

Spring Church Book Company, Britt Horner, Ed Ochester, PO Box 127, Spring Church, PA 15686. "Contemporary poetry at a discount: all publishers, with growing emphasis on small press; hardback & paperback. Annotated catalog and update lists free on request. Also issue annotated lists of homesteading and gardening books, and children's titles. We have issued books in conjunction with Quixote Press—e.g., *Natives: An Anthology of Contempory American Poetry,* Erica Jong, Marge Piercy, Dave Etter, Victor Contoski, et al, $2.00—but are not reading manuscripts at present." 1973. 6pp; 8½ x 11. of. Discounts: 5/40%—bookstores prepay first orders.

‡**Spring Rain Press,** Box 15319 Wedgewood Stn., Seattle, WA 98115. CCLM.

Sproing Books, Eric Wickstrom, Lois Wickstrom, 1150 St Paul St, Denver, CO 80206. "Right now we have a backlog of stuff by ourselves and friends that is waiting for us to afford the printing costs. Our basic theme is living our own lives within the establishment by helping them to leave us alone." 1973. 8½ x 5½. of.

THE SQUATCHBERRY JOURNAL, The Squatchberry Journal, Edgar Lavoie, Box 205, Geraldton, Ontario P0T1M0, Canada, 807-854-1184. Poetry, fiction, articles, art, photos, cartoons, interviews, satire, reviews. "This is a regional magazine featuring the fact and fiction, photographs and drawings, arising from experience in Northern Ontario." 2/yr; 1-yr sub price: $3.50; per copy: $2.00; sample: $2.00 or free, depending on circumstances. 1975. 72pp; 6 x 9. of. circ. 400. Reporting time: almost immediately. Payment: a copy of the edition. Copyrighted, reverts to author. Ads: none permitted. Discounts: none. Back issues: $2.00 or free, depending on circumstances. Pub'd 2 issues 1976. Pub's reviews: 2 in 1976. §only material featuring experiences of Northern Ontario.

SQUEEZE BOX, Paper Tiger Press, Mardy Murphy, 334 N Vassar, Wichita, KS 67208. Poetry, art. "Short (one page) fiction and prose poems, imagist poems, contributors: Marge Piercy, Denise Levertov, Lisel Mueller, Colette Inez, Tom McKeon, James Mechem." 3/yr; 1-yr sub price: $3.50; per copy: $1.00; sample: $1.00. 1973. 45pp; 5½ x 8. of. circ. 500. Reporting time: 6 wks. Payment: 3 copies. Back issues: $1.00. §women's poetry. CCLM, COSMEP.

Staff Press (see FROM THE FIELD)

Stagecoach Pub. Co. Ltd. (see also CANADA WEST), T. W. Paterson. avg. price, cloth: $11.95; paper: $5.95. 1975. 200pp; 6 x 9. of. avg. press run 10,000. Reporting time: 6 weeks. Payment: standard terms. Copyrights for author. Discounts: regular discounts to various jobbers, schools, etc. Pub'd 6 titles 1976.

STAND, Jon Silkin, Lorna Tracy, A.G. Jones, Neil Astley, 19 Haldane Tce, Newcastle-on-Tyne NE23 AN, United Kingdom. Poetry, fiction, reviews, criticism. 4/yr; 1-yr sub price: $5.50; per copy: $1.50; sample: $1.50. 1952. 80pp; 6-1/10 x 8. lp. circ. 5,000. Reporting time: 1-2 mos. Payment: $10.00/poem; $10.00/1,000 words. Ads: $100.00 & pro rata. Pub'd 4 issues 1976; expects 4 issues 1977, 4 issues 1978. Pub's reviews: 8 in 1976. CCLM.

STAR-WEB PAPER, All This & Less Publishers, Thomas Michael Fisher, Regents 509 NMSU, Las Cruces, NM 88003. Poetry, fiction, articles, art, photos, cartoons, interviews, satire, criticism, reviews, music, letters, parts-of-novels, long-poems, collages, plays, concrete art, news items, non-fiction. "After a two and a half year wait in getting an issue out after number five, we finally did it. STAR-WEB PAPER number six is out on offset, 8½ x 11, containing sixty pages of collage, poetry, drawings, letters, essays, prose, photos and more, by robert kelly, ray cosseboom, ronald h. bayes, helen luster, kenneth stange, a.d. winans, john tagliabue, albert drake, f.a. nettelbeck, richard harper, richard snyder, j.m. bennett, thomas michael fisher, jim mcCurry, gerald lange, stephen leggett, steve richmond, guy r. beining, judson crews, paul payack, and others. with number seven, out problee before this directory (this is 5/18/77) STAR-WEB PAPER institutes a review section of books and magazines of the small press and otherwise. STAR-WEB PAPER has come a long way since its founding, but we have retained the original spirit of community energy; subscribed to by approximately fifteen major universities in the u.s. and canada, SWP is available on microfilm, and is listed in six directories and indexes of periodicals. bookstores have begun enquiring about the magazine, and in general, the project is going well. our major problem has been (ho-hum) dollars, and we may decide upon an annual appearance. in past issues, STAR-WEB PAPER has presented the work of ed dorn, george bowering, james bertolino, charles olson, robert creeley, jonathan williams, john cage, hugh fox, lyn lifshin, george montgomery, anselm hollo, len fulton, david meltzer, peter wild, and many others. this is one of the trademarks of SWP: it encourages submissions by unknown and little known writers, and if such work is considered 'publishable' in STAR-WEB PAPER, it is printed, regardless of who a writer is or isn't. the greatest joy is to 'discover' work of merit for the first time, and much of the best material in the magazine has come from unknowns. we want to engage in mutual flier-exchange programs - send us your fliers or announcements for our outgoing mail, and we'll send you some of ours. books and magazines also wanted for review. hasta luego!" 60 cycles per second/irregular.; sub price: $7.00 - 4 issues individual, $15.00 - 5 issues institutions.; per copy: $2.00 plus post; sample: $2.00 plus post. 1973. 60pp; 8½ x 11. †mi/of. circ. by osmosis. Reporting time: 2 weeks. Payment: copies. Copyrighted. Ads: By arrangement. Discounts: By arrangement. Back issues: No. 2 $2.50 plus post, No. 3 $2.50 plus post, No. 5 $2.50 plus post, No. 6 $2.00 plus post. Expects 3 issues 1977, 2 issues 1978. Pub's reviews. §arts, literature, photography, earth, native American. CCLM, COSMEP.

STAR WEST, S-B Gazette, Leon Spiro, Box 731, Sausalito, CA 94965. Poetry, cartoons, satire, concrete art. "Short, dynamic, multi-lingual poetry. Satire, Chicano, Black, etc, wide open. Ronald Crowe, Anna Moresi, Maria Auguello, Albert Chantraine, Mark Axelrod, Teresinka Pereira, Sonia Kury, Erin St. Mawr, Nazim Hickmet, Dora La Flamme, Felix Leon, Laureate, French Academy's David Gitin, Angela S. de Hoyos, Jean Coutsocheras, Paul Fericano, Sidney Tyler." 4/yr; 1-yr sub price: $6.60; per copy: $1.00; sample: $1.00. 1963. 8½ x 14. of. circ. 800-2,000. Reporting time: 2 weeks. Payment: 5 copies.

STARDANCER, Stardance Publications, Michael S. Prochak, Co-Editor; Michael R. Graham, Co-Editor; Cheryl Shores, Art Editor, P.O. Box 128, Athens, OH 45701. Poetry, fiction, articles, art, photos, interviews, satire, criticism, reviews, music, letters, parts-of-novels, long-poems, collages, plays. "Our goal is to provide a means whereby individuals may cast off out moded and restrictive standards of art, literature, philosophy, and the self in order to ferret out and express creatively their relationship with their environment, their age, their universe, their art, and themselves. We'll consider material of any length, but quality is a must. We look for new ideas, approaches, and contents dealing with matter of an experimental, neo-romantic, mythic, or visionary nature, or of an evolutionary strain, but maintain an eclectic editorial approach. See sample for examples. Recent contributors include Brian Swann, George Hitchcock, John Weigel, Greg Kuzma, Lawrence Ferlinghetti, David Schloss, Daniel Halpern, & we await Alaine Robbe-Grillet, Colin Wilson, and Terry Stokes. We are, however, more concerned with the vision than the name." 3/yr; 1-yr sub price: $4.00; per copy: $1.50; sample: $1.00. 1975. 52pp; 5½ x 8½. of. circ. 500. Reporting time: 6 weeks maximum. Payment: contributors copy of magazine & 30 percent discount to 3 copies. Copyrighted, reverts to author. Discounts: Only discount is for trade—30-40 percent, and bulk-10 copies min-30 percent. Pub'd 2 issues 1976; expects 3 issues 1977, 3 issues 1978. Pub's reviews. §New arts, literature, and anything of an evolutionary nature. COSMEP.

Starogubski Press, Bonnie Bluh, P.O. Box 46, GPO, Brooklyn, NY 11202. "Published: WOMAN TO WOMAN: EUROPEAN FEMINISTS. If I have the time or can afford workers I will publish other books. Starogubski has been a glorious, rewarding experience. Financially forget it. I wish I could say different." 1974. 317pp; 5½ x 8. lp.

Starvation Studios (see POOR FARM)

STARWIND, The Starwind Press, Elbert Lindsey Jr., Box 3346, Columbus, OH 43210. Poetry, fiction, articles, art, cartoons, interviews. "We are looking for sf dark and heroic fantasy. Our prime requisite is good storytelling that is logically constructed. Preferred length is 2,000 to 10,000 words. We also need articles on interpretative analysis of pro authors and interviews with sf writers and editors. Preferred length is 4,000 to 10,000 words. *Starwind* is published in the fall and spring." 2/yr; sub price: $6.00/2 yrs; per copy: $1.50 (plus 50 ¢ postage); sample: $1.50 (plus 50 cents postage).

1974. 60pp; 8½ x 11. of. circ. 2,500 printed. Reporting time: 6-8 weeks. Payment: 1/2 cent/word on publication for fiction, articles, and interviews. Ads: $45/$25/$.10 word. Discounts: 20% on consignment minimum 10. COSMEP.

STATIONS, Membrane Press, Karl Young, P.O. Box 11601 Shorewood, Milwaukee, WI 53211. Poetry, fiction, articles, art, photos, parts-of-novels, long-poems, collages, plays, concrete art. "Concentrate on 4-6 contributors per issue, with emphasis on works in progress, works in series, longpoems, attempts at change, sizeable selections. Due to the nature of the magazine, I can't publish a lot of contributors. I don't recommend sending unsolicited material unless you've thoroughly examined issues published so far and have a good idea of what I'm looking for. Richard Kostelanetz, Rochelle Owens, George Economou, Toby Olson, Kathleen Wiegner, Carol Berge, John Shannon, Victor Contoski, John Jacob, Hilary Ayer, Martin J. Rosenblum, Peter Anastas." irreg.; sub price: $6.00-4 issues, individuals; $10.00-4 issues, institutions; per copy: $2.00-individuals; $3.00-institutions. 100pp; 5 x 8. †of. circ. 500. Reporting time: forever & two days. Payment: copies only. Ads: advertising: negotiable. Discounts: 40% trade disc or consignment. Back issues: No. 3 & 4, $3.00, individuals; $4.00, institutions; No. 2, $1.50; individuals; $2.50, institutions; No. 1, $10.00. Pub'd 1 issue 1976. COSMEP.

Steel Rail Publishing, P O Box 6813 Station A, Toronto, Ontario, Canada. Poetry, fiction, articles, art, photos, cartoons, interviews, satire, plays. "Most of our publications will be book length material, any consideration of shorter works would only be possible in the context of a collection of essays, poems, etc. on a particular subject or theme. We are looking primarily for contemporary historical material about Canada or material that relates to Canada." avg. price, cloth: $10.95 - $12.95; paper: $4.95 - $6.95. 1976. 200pp; 5¼ x 8¼. of. avg. press run 3,000-5,000. Reporting time: 2-3 weeks. Payment: 10 percent of retail on cloth, 5 percent on paper. Copyrights for author. Discounts: Trade 40 percent graduated bulk discount schedule, Education 20 percent, Wholesale 40 percent. ACP, CBA, CBIC.

STEPPENWOLF, Philip Boatright, Jean Shannon, P.O. Box 55045, Omaha, NB 68155. Poetry, articles, criticism, reviews. "Especially interested in the longer poem, translations (must be accompanied by a copy of the work in its original language), articles and critical comment. Request no more unsolicited mss. until further notice." CCLM.

STILE, Dennis Ray, P.O. Box 336, Jonesboro, TN 37569. Poetry, art, reviews, letters, long-poems, concrete art. "The poetry published in STILE will continue to range from sonnets to surrealism. (Surreal sonnets, anyone?) This may sound like the mag. does not have an editorial direction, wrong from the start! The bias is 'who would want knobs/on a door that grabbed back?' This is just to say that a two lines from a poem of the IMAGINATION has more weight than a refrigerator full of plums. If one is not sure, read the poetry of H.R. Hays. A special Kenneth Patchen issue is planned for fall '76. Poems in his spirit. No odes, please." 2/yr; sample price: $1.00. 1974. 56pp; 5½ x 8. of/le. Reporting time: 1 day to two wks. Payment: 2 copies (more upon request). Pub's reviews. §poetry. COSMEP.

STINKTREE, Stinktree Press, Thomas Johnson, 130 Sears Street, Ithaca, NY 14750. Poetry, art, reviews, letters, long-poems. "I'll be soliciting for the next two issues and so will not be reading other than what i ask to see." irreg; 1-yr sub price: $3.75; per copy: $1.95; sample: $1.95. 1971. 48-60pp; 5½ x 8½. of. circ. 300. Reporting time: 3 months. Payment: copies. Discounts: 1/3 off. Back issues: #4 - $2.50. Expects 2 issues 1977, 2 issues 1978. Pub's reviews. §poetry. CCLM.

Stinktree Press (see also STINKTREE), Thomas Johnson, 130 Sears St., Ithaca, NY 14850. Poetry. "Will consider chapbook mss. in late 1977-early 1978. Have published books by Ken Smith, Kotaro Takamura, Hans Enzensberger, Jorge De Lima. Mss. should be 16-20 pp."

Stock Poetry, B. E. Stock, 630 E. 14 St. No. 3, New York, NY 10009, 212-673-0781. Poetry, fiction, long-poems. avg. price, paper: $1.00. 1976. 18 pp (so far: 1,6,7,21,100 pp done); 9 x 12. †lp. avg. press run 100. as yet I publish only myself. Copyrights for author. Discounts: as prices are rock bottom I would expect retailers to add margin instead. Pub'd 7 titles 1976; expects 2 titles 1977. COSMEP, ASW.

THE STONE, Rich Jorgensen, 3978 26th St, San Francisco, CA 94131, 415-648-5392. Poetry, fiction, art, photos, cartoons. "Mostly we publish poetry of the body's land, love. The Stone is elemental." 1/yr; 1-yr sub price: $2.00; per copy: $2.00; sample: $2.00 negotiable. 1967. 96pp; 5½ x 8½. of. circ. 1M. Reporting time: 1 week. Payment: 2 copies/contributor. Copyrighted. Discounts: 40% to the trade. Back issues: $2 if avail. Pub'd 1 issue 1976; expects 1 issue 1977, 1 issue 1978. CCLM, COSMEP.

STONE COUNTRY, Stone Country Press, Judith Neeld, Editor and Publisher; Pat McCormick, Art; Robert Blake Truscott, Reviews, 20 Lorraine Road, Madison, NJ 07940. Poetry, art, articles, interviews, criticism, reviews. "We publish mature poetry from poets of all ages, in styles from the traditional to the experimental and anywhere in between. However, even traditional poems should be handled with contemporary language and outlook. This is not a magazine for beginners. Recent contributors: Thomas Johnson, Jon Lang, Frances Minturn Howard, Maxine Kumin, A. M. Miller, Martin Robbins, Tom O'Grady, Freya Manfred, Janice Thaddeus. We present the Phillips Award each issue; $25.00 to the poem deemed best by a panel of poets and critics." 3/yr; 1-yr sub price: $3.75; per copy: $1.50; sample: $1.25. 1971. 40pp; 8½ x 5½. of. circ. about 500. Reporting time: one month. Payment: Copies plus prize for poetry (see above); modest cash payments for cover art and prose commentaries/reviews. Copyrighted, reverts to author. Ads: $12.00/$8.50. Discounts: usual. Back issues: $1, if available. Pub'd 3 issues 1976; expects 3 issues 1977, 3 issues 1978. Pub's reviews: 9 in 1976. §poetry. CCLM, COSMEP.

‡**Stone-Marrow Press,** Univ. Of Cincinnati, 248 McMicken Ave., Cincinnati, OH 45221.

STONE MOUNTAIN REVIEW, Stuart P. Radowitz, 857 N. Broadway, Massapequa, NY 11758. Poetry, interviews, criticism, reviews. "Stone Mountain is primarily a poetry magazine but is open to all literary poems. Interested in the critical aware reviews, clean, beautiful poems, experimental; we are growing and will try to be responsive to our readers. Contributors include: Dunn, Piercy, Blazek, Lietz, Palmer, Lifshin, Crow, Booth." irregular; 1-yr sub price: $2.50; per copy: $2.50; sample: $2.50. 1974. 48-64pp; 5½ x 8½. of. circ. 500. Reporting time: 1-3 mo. Payment: copies. Ads: $70/$50. Discounts. 40% trade. Pub's reviews §poetry. COSMEP.

Stone Press (see also HAPPINESS HOLDING TANK), Albert Drake, Barbara Drake, 1790 Grand River, Okemos, MI 48864. Poetry. "Small books and pamphlets. Recently published Peter Nye, Judith Root, Barbara Drake, and a 72 pp. book by Judith Goren. Also publish posters: Richard Kostelanetz, Harley Elliott, William Stafford, Earle Birney, Anselm Hollo, etc. Six posters for $1.25. Poetry Pack ($4) includes 2 issues of the magazine, book, pamphlet, 3 posters, postcards, etc." avg. price, paper: $1.00. 1968. †of. avg. press run 300-500. Reporting time: 1-3 weeks. Discounts: 25 percent.

The Stone Press (see J STONE PRESS WEEKLY)

STONE SOUP, A Magazine By Children, Children's Art Foundation, Inc., Gerry Mandel, William Rubel, Bx 83, Santa Cruz, CA 95063, 408-426-5557. Poetry, fiction, art, reviews, parts-of-novels, plays, photos, letters, long-poems. "All material written & drawn by children 3-13." 5/yr; 1-yr sub price: $7.00; per copy: $1.50; sample: $1.25. 1973. 48pp; 5¾ x 8½. of. circ. 5,000. Reporting time: 3 wks. Payment: copy. Copyrighted, does not revert to author. Ads: none. Discounts: Schedule available upon request. Back issues: Prices upon request. Pub'd 5 issues 1976; expects 5 issues 1977, 5 issues 1978. Pub's reviews: 12 in 1976. §childrens books. CCLM.

Stone Wall Press, Inc, Henry C. Wheelwright, 5 Byron St, Boston, MA 02108. "Non-fiction—outdoor material regional to northeastern USA or national with photos or illustrations. Optimally combining progmatic material with adventures, humor, and overriding sense of ecology" avg. price, paper: $4.95. 1972. 175pp; 6 x 9. of. avg. press run 4-5,000. Reporting time: a week. Copyrights for author. Pub'd 2 titles 1976; expects 4 titles 1977.

STONECLOUD, Pacific Perceptions, Inc., Dan Ilves, Rick Smith, 3718 Vinton No. 5, Los Angeles, CA 90034, 213-204-0590. Poetry, fiction, articles, art, photos, interviews, satire, parts-of-novels, long-poems, plays. "Bukowski, Beining, Locke, Lifshin, Peters, Tagliabue, Wakoski, Winans, Zawadiwsky...Pacific Perceptions, Inc. is a non-profit, tax exempt organization. All donations are tax deductible. Manuscripts accepted between September and May. Not accepting or reading manuscripts at all until further notice. Publication of magazine temporarily suspended." 1/yr; sub price: 3/$8.95; per copy: $2.95; sample: $2.00. 1972. 140pp; 8½ x 11. of. circ. 2,000. Reporting time: 6-8 weeks. Payment: in copies. Magazine copyrighted by Pacific Perceptions. All rights held by authors on their own works. Ads: $45/$25. Discounts: Institution rate: 3 issues for $10.00. Discounts available upon request. Complete sets while available. Issues 1 thru 6 for $10.50. Back issues: $2.50 per issue, all back issues available. Pub'd 1 issue 1976; expects 1 issue 1977. CCLM, COSMEP, LPSC.

STONEY LONESOME, Nosferatu, Richard Pflum, David Wade, Roger Pfingston, 2600 Dekist, Bloomington, IN 47401. Poetry, art, photos, long-poems, concrete art. "Named after a rocky gulch in Brown County. Highwaymen made the journey perilous. Editors reflect three divergent sensibilities & seek work alive to the possibilities of mother tongue, deep image, sharply honed & (except for concrete poems) vibrant in oral powers. We're down on *bathos,* weak diction self-consciously pretty poems, didacticism, moralizing, over-description & busy-ness. Recently published D. Locke, W. Barnstone, M.E. Solt, L. Lifshin, R. Pfingston, S. Gilbert, R. Grillo, J. Folks, O. Siporin, J. Roman, V. Shreve, M. Allen, M. Satterfield." more or less annual; 1-yr sub price: $2.75; per copy: $2.75; sample: $2.75. 1969. 114pp; 7 x 8¾. of. circ. 300 local. Reporting time: 2 weeks to 2 month. Payment: 1 copy. Copyrighted, reverts to author. Discounts: 30% off 5 copies. Pub'd 1 issue 1976; expects 1 issue 1977, 1 issue 1978. CCLM.

STONY HILLS: The New England Alternative Press Review, Rat & Mole, Diane Kruchkow, Box 715, Newburyport, MA 01950, 617-465-9451. Articles, art, photos, cartoons, interviews, criticism, reviews, letters. "Covers material: 1)published by a NEngland small press or mag. 2)written by a N.E. writer-published by a small press. 3)about N.E. published by a small press" 3/yr; 1-yr sub price: $1.50; per copy: $0.75; sample: $0.75. 1977. 12pp; 11 x 17. of. circ. 2,000. Reporting time: 1 week. Payment: copies. Copyrighted. Ads: $75.00/$50.00. Discounts: more than 5 copies-40 percent. §New England small press material. COSMEP, NESPA.

STORY QUARTERLY, Fran Katz, Pamela Painter Skeen, Dolores Weinberg, 720 Central Ave, Highland Park, IL 60035. Fiction, art, interviews, letters, parts-of-novels. "*STORY QUARTERLY* seeks to be an open forum of the short story; featuring: a generous number of stories in a wide range of styles and forms. Also: guest columns on the state of the story; interviews with story writers; parts-of-novels, found fiction; letters to the editor. Our bias is toward instantly recognizable talent as opposed to instantly recognizable names. Please do not study the publication with an eye toward imitation/slant but send us your own truest work and vision. We would like to see more non-imitative break-through experimentation consistent with at least its own sense of control. Recent contributors: Jerry Bumpus, Anne Brashler, Kelly Cherry, Daniel Curley, Stephen Dixon, Gail Godwin, Phillip Green, Richard Kostelanetz, Joyce Carol Oates, Henry H. Roth, James Park Sloan, Meredith Sue Willis." 4/yr; 1-yr sub price: $6.50; per copy: $1.75; sample: $1.00. 1974. 128pp; 6¾ x 9¾. of. circ. 3,000. Reporting time: 3 months. Payment: 6 copies. Copyrighted. Ads: $200/$100. Back issues: $1.50. Pub'd 3 issues 1976; expects 4 issues 1977, 4 issues 1978. CCLM, COSMEP.

THE STRAIT, Cathy J. Teevan, Editor in Chief, 1300 Elmwood Ave, Buffalo, NY 14222. Poetry, fiction, articles, art, photos, cartoons, interviews, satire, criticism, reviews, music, letters. "Middle-of-the-road publication offering voice for far left-right activists in community, and certain vocal minority groups: gay campus activities, campus Marxists and Stalinists, Women's Caucus, community Nazis, currently. Subject matter is not censored or abridged, except for grammatical or space editing, with prime criteria appropriateness for college/Buffalo audience. Graphics appreciated." 50/yr; 1-yr sub price: $4.00 by mail non-students; per copy: free on campus; sample: $.25. 1971. 24-28pp. of. circ. 10,000. Reporting time: 2 weeks. Payment: on request. Ads: $120/$75/$.15-word. Back issues: $1.00; very limited. Pub's reviews. §Subjects of interest to young adults; also education, art ,journalism/broadcasting, exceptional ed (lgst. majors). APS.

STRANGE FAECES, Strange Faeces Press, Opal L. Nations, Ellen Nations, P.O. Box 81, Barton, VT 05822. Poetry, fiction, art, photos, cartoons, satire, letters, parts-of-novels, collages, concrete art. "1) 4-5 page length 2) speculative 3) bias *for*- bad taste, brutal & unusual, bias *against* 99% small magazine so called poetry & interlectual claptrap 4) Mike Bulteau & Bruce Hutchinson. Submissions by request only." 3-4/yr, dependant on funding; 1-yr sub price: $9.00; per copy: $2.00; sample: $2.00. 1969. 50-60pp; Varies with each issue. of. circ. 500. Payment: none. Rights remain with authors & artists. Discounts: 40 percent bookstores only. Back issues: All sold. CCLM, COSMEP.

Strawberry Press, Maurice Kenny, 11 Broadway, Room 933, New York, NY 10004, 212-425-5979. Poetry, art. "*Strawberry Press* publishes the poetry of Native American Indian poets only as it is felt that the open forum for Native American poets is closing to not only the young poets of this country, but to established poets as well who seem, often, to be ignored in both the small press & established press except in the 'special issue' sense. Poets recently published include: Norman Russell, Joseph Bruchac, Wendy Rose, Lance Henson, Maurice Kenny, Rokwaho, Karoniaktatie, Carol Lee Sanchez, Duane Niatum, Peter Blue Cloud, Adrian C. Louis, and artists: Kahones, Sharol Graves and Helen Rundell." avg. price, paper: chapbooks...$1.50/signed $3.00; other: broadsides...$0.50/signed $1.50. 1976. pp varies; varies. of. avg. press run chapbooks 500 in a limited issue: broadsides 250 in a limited issue. Reporting time: 3 weeks. Payment: payment to poet and artist, and copies. Copyrights for author. Discounts: trade/jobber/classroom...40 percent. Pub'd 4 titles 1976; expects 12 titles 1977.

STREET CRIES, Robbie Woliver, Aaron Fischer, Pat Velaquez, 33 Edi Ave., Plainview, NY 11803. Poetry, art, photos, interviews, reviews, long-poems, concrete art. "STREET CRIES is devoted to those writers and artists usually by passed by more traditional magazines (e.g. the institutionalized, feminists, children, prisoners,etc.) as well as the professional established writer. STREET CRIES is a Bi-lingual (Spanish & English) literary and art magazine which prides itself on it's innovative projects/concepts and dedication to the writer/artist. Now attempting to run solely through mailing list, so try to send name & address rather than unsolicited material." 3-4/yr; price per copy: $2.00; sample: $2.00. 1972. 98pp; 5½ x 8½. of. circ. 5,000. Reporting time: up to 1 mo. Payment; copies. Ads: $75/$40. Back issues: men's consciousness issue-$3.00. CCLM, COSMEP.

STREET MAGAZINE, Street Press, Dan Murray, Graham Everett, Box 555, Port Jefferson, NY 11777. Poetry, fiction, articles, art, photos, cartoons, interviews, criticism, reviews, collages, concrete art, non-fiction. "Looking for poems, regional & human perspective, prose, graphics, photos, reviews, statements of writing. Returns up to 3 mos. Vol 1 No. 4: Interview with Jack Kerouac, plus poems and reviews. Vol 2 No. 1: Conversation with Robert Bly, plus poems and reviews. Vol 2 No. 2: Black Mountain Issue, poems, articles and perspectives. (available). Vol 2 No. 3: H. R. Hayes and Spanish America: translations of Spanish American poets; articles on and by H. R. Hayes. Vol 2 No. 4: Beat/Energy Issue: poems and articles on Energy. Early Greenwich Village memories and articles on Kerouac." 2/yr; sub price: $6.00/4 issues; per copy: $1.50. 1973. 60pp; 5½ x 8. †of. circ. 750. Reporting time: 8 weeks. Payment: 2 copies. Copyrighted, revert to authors. Discounts: 40%. Back issues: cost + postage. Pub'd 2 issues 1976; expects 3 issues 1977. Pub's reviews: 8 in 1976. §poetry. CCLM, COSMEP.

THE STRUGGLE, United Struggle Press, Harry Jackson, 175 Fifth Avenue, New York, NY 10010, 212-677-6868. Articles, art, photos, cartoons, interviews, reviews, letters. "THE STRUGGLE is a bimonthly journal reporting on the struggles and organizing of the poor in this country and worldwide. Contributions from progressive activists, scholars (pol. sci., sociology). Articles include current history and events, and broader analytic writings." 6/yr; 1-yr sub price: Indiv: $6.00, Inst. $12.00; per copy: $1.00; sample: $1.00. 1976. 32pp; 8½ x 11. of. circ. 3,000. Articles received on contribution basis-no payment. Not copyrighted. Pub's reviews. §History, social thought, socialist literature. COSMEP.

STUDIA CELTICA, University of Wales Press, J.E. Caerwyn Williams, University of Wales Press, 6 Gwennyth St., Cathays, Cardiff CF2 4YD, United Kingdom. "Devoted mainly to philosophical and linguistic studies of the Celtic languages with some contributions on Celtic archaeology and early Celtic history." 1/yr; sub price: £1.50. £3.00 per volume/£6.00 per double volume from volume XII-XIII due in 78. Pub'd 2 issues 1976; expects 2 issues 1977, 2 issues 1978.

STUDIES IN DESIGN EDUCATION AND CRAFT, Studies in Education Ltd., John Eggleston, Keele University, Keele, Staffordshire ST5 5BG, United Kingdom, 0782-621111. Articles, cartoons, photos, reviews, news items, interviews, criticism, letters, concrete art, non-fiction. "Prints articles on new developments and practice of design education in schools and colleges." 2/yr; 1-yr sub price: £8.00; per copy: £4.00; sample: £1.25. 1966. 80pp; 25cm x 18cm. of. circ. 3,000. Reporting time: max 1 mo. usually two wks. Payment: none. Copyrighted, held by magazine. Ads: £50.00/ £25.00. Discounts: 10 percent series disc/w ads. Back issues: £4.00. Pub'd 2 issues 1976; expects 2 issues 1977, 2 issues 1978. Pub's reviews: 30 in 1976. §Craft, art, design, education.

STUDIES IN LABOUR HISTORY, John L. Noyce, Publ., John L. Noyce, P.O. Box 450, Brighton BN18GR, United Kingdom. Articles, reviews. "Radical A 'Peoples' history-bias toward modern British-history." 1/yr; price per copy: $5.00. 1976. 60pp; A4. †of/dupli. circ. 300 plus. Reporting time: we try. Payment: free copy. Ads: details on application. Discounts: 20 percent to trade. Pub'd 1 issue 1976; expects 1 issue 1977, 1 issue 1978. Pub's reviews: 20 in 1976. §Social History.

STUDIES IN POETRY: A GRADUATE JOURNAL, Tommy P. Allen, Wendell Broom, Debra Munn, Daryl Jones, Eugene Korkowski, Dept of English, Texas Tech Univ, Lubbock, TX 79409. Poetry, articles, interviews, criticism. "STUDIES IN POETRY seeks original poetry and poetry explication by graduate students. Preference will be given to poems of under forty lines and explications of under three thousand words treating a poem or group of poems written in English. Essays should conform to *The MLA Style Sheet,* 2nd edition. Contributors whose manuscripts are accepted will be encouraged to register their own copyrights." 1-2/yr; sub price: $2.50-2 issues; per copy: $1.50; sample: $1.50. 1976. 40pp; 6 x 9. of. circ. 300. Reporting time: 1-3 months. Payment: copies only. Not copyrighted. Discounts: to contributors. Back issues: $1.00. Pub'd 1 issue 1976; expects 2 issues 1977, 2 issues 1978.

STUDIO INTERNATIONAL, Studio International (Journal) Ltd., Richard Cork, 14 West Central St., London, England WC1A 1JH, United Kingdom. Articles, art, criticism, letters, photos. 6/yr; 1-yr sub price: £11.00 UK, $34 abroad; per copy: £2.00 UK, $6 abroad. 1893. 100pp. Ads: £160.00/£87.00/£2.40 for min 20 words. Discounts: students sub £10 UK $30 abroad. Back issues: £3.00. Pub'd 6 issues 1976; expects 4 issues 1977.

STUFFED CROCODILE, Killaly Press, Clarke E. Leverett, 764 Dalkeith Ave., London, Ontario N5X1R8, Canada. Poetry. "No restrictions on source, style, length. English or French preferred." 4/yr; 1-yr sub price: $4.00; per copy: $1.00; sample: $1.00. 1972. 24pp; 7 x 8½. †mi. circ. 300. Reporting time: 2 mos. Payment: $5.00/item, s.o. cost. Discounts: 33-1/3. Back issues: $1.50. §Canadian only/literature/art/drama.

STUMP, Ciccone, Knapp, Naccarato, Novesky, Perchan, 6395 Colby St, Oakland, CA 94618. Poetry, fiction, long-poems. "The subscription is a patronage. Life Time subscribers accepted. Concentrate energy on solicited special issues. Polite interest in unsolicited material, but read us first. #1 sold out. #2, Jack Hirschman issue still available. #3 out June 1976. Will consider contemporary poetry in translation." irregular; 1-yr sub price: $10.00-$25.00; per copy: $2.00. 1973. 60pp; 5 x 7. †of. Reporting time: immediate. Payment: Am. currency & copies. Discounts: 10% surcharge to institutions.

SUMMER BULLETIN, Yorkshire Dialect Society, Ben T. Dyson, 47 Timothy Lane, Batley, West Yorkshire, United Kingdom. 1/yr. 1954. 40pp; 8 x 6. of. circ. 850.

Summer Thought, Peter Steiner, PO Box 1420, Banff, Alberta T0L0C0, Canada, 762-4055. Poetry, photos. avg. price, cloth: $10.50; paper: $5.95. 1969. 160pp; 6 x 9. lp. avg. press run 10,000. Reporting time: 2 weeks. Payment: 10 percent 12½ reprint. Copyrights for author. Discounts: 40 percent trade/20 percent classroom. CBA.

Summit University Press, Elizabeth Clare Prophet, PO Box 7018, Pasadena, CA 91109, 213-797-1131. "We publish only materials brought forth through 'Church Universal and Triumphant', an activity of the Great White Brotherhood dedicated to the spiritual upliftment of all mankind." avg. price, cloth: $10.50; paper: $3.50; other: $2.95. 1958. 200pp; 5¼ x 8¼. †of. avg. press run 10,000 books. We print only our own books. Payment: none. Copyrights for author. Discounts: 40 percent to bookstores and libraries, 50 percent to distributors.

‡**SUN, Sun Publishing Co.**, PO Box 4383, Albuquerque, NM 87106.

SUN, Bill Zavatsky, 456 Riverside Drive-5B, New York, NY 10027. Poetry, fiction, interviews, criticism, reviews, letters, parts-of-novels, long-poems, plays. "No unsolicited material. Recent contributors: John Ashbery, Harvey Shapiro, George Economou, Rochelle Owens, Hugh Seidman, Ron Padgett, Phillip Lopate, Maureen Owen, etc." 2/yr; sub price: $5.00/3 issues; per copy: varies; sample: $2.00. 1966 (as SUNDIAL). 150pp; 5½ x 8½. of. circ. 1,000. No unsolicited material. Payment: copies. Discounts: trade 5 copies, 40%. inquire with bookpeople, Sun's distributor, for their rates. Pub's reviews. §Books of poetry; books on or about poetry; translations of poetry; biographies of poets; anthologies of poetry, etc. CCLM, COSMEP.

THE SUN, NORTH CAROLINA'S MAGAZINE OF IDEAS, Sy Safransky, PO Box 732, 412 W. Rosemary St, Chapel Hill, NC 27514, 942-5282. Poetry, fiction, articles, art, photos, cartoons, interviews, satire, criticism, reviews, letters, parts-of-novels, long-poems, collages, news items, non-fiction. "Interested in articles on any subject, of any length, that enrich our common space." 11/yr; 1-yr sub price: $8.00 (intro), $9.00 (renewal); per copy: $1.00; sample: free. 1974. 56pp; 8¼ x 10¼. †of. circ. 1,000. Reporting time: 1 month. Payment varies, query first. Copyrighted, reverts to author. Ads: $150.00/$80.00/$1.00 (line). Discounts: varies. Back issues: Half-price. Pub'd 11 issues 1976; expects 10 issues 1977, 11 issues 1978. Pub's reviews. §all areas. COSMEP.

SUN & MOON: A Quarterly of Literature and Art, Sun & Moon/La-Bas, Douglas Messerli, Howard N. Fox, 4330 Hartwick Rd, #418, College Park, MD 20740, 301-864-6921. Poetry, fiction, articles, art, interviews, criticism, letters, parts-of-novels, plays, concrete art. "While we primarily print contemporary art and literature, occasionally we reprint older material which is relevant to the literature and art of today. Recent contributors include Keith Abbott, John Baldessari, Djuna Barnes, Tom Clark, Clark Coolidge, Agnes Denes, Stephen Dixon, Larry Eigner, Kenward Elmslie, Theodore Enslin, Charles Henri Ford, Barbara Guest, Peter Hutchinson, Michael Lally, Lucy Lippard, Ron Padgett, Joseph Shannon, Gilbert Sorrentino, Anne Truitt, Tom Veitch and Douglas Woolf." 3/yr; 1-yr sub price: $10.00 (Individuals) $15.00 (Institutions); per copy: $3.00. 1976. 80-150pp; 5½ x 8½. of. Reporting time: 1-3 weeks. Payment: none. Copyrights all material unless copyrighted by author previous to publication. Discounts: 40% for agents and bookstores. Back issues: $2.50. Pub'd 3 issues 1976; expects 3 issues 1977, 3 issues 1978. Pub's reviews: 4 in 1976. §Contemporary poetry and fiction, art related works. CCLM.

SUN CENTER NEWS, Sun Center, Skip Whitson, PO Box 4372, Albuquerque, NM 87106. 12/yr. 1976. 4pp; 10 x 13¼. of. circ. 5,000. Ads: $130/$72. Pub's reviews.

SUN-LOTUS HAIKU, Sun-Lotus Books, R. Clarence Matsui-Allard, Editor; Kinuko Matsui-Allard, Associate Editor, 125 West Merrimack St, Manchester, NH 03101. Poetry, articles, art, interviews, criticism, reviews, letters, concrete art. "#1 will contain some reprints of Robert Bly's translations of Basho and Issa; new translations of Shiki Masaoka by Hiroaki Sato; new material by Gary Hotham, Lloyd Gold and others. S-LH needs haiku, senryu and one line poems; translations; short-short prose under 500 words in any way relating to the above. Both traditional and experimental forms are welcome. Authors of prose should query first. S-LH will be primarily concerned with making these forms, especially haiku, more accepted forms in American poetry. Sun-Lotus Books will publish one to three booklets of poetry a year, but work will be solicited by us directly to authors of our choice. No unsolicited manuscripts here. S-L Books will publish *Sun-Lotus Poetry Journal* on an irregular basis. Manuscripts here by invitation." 4/yr & irreg.; 1-yr sub price: $2.50 (U.S.) $3.00 (FOREIGN); per copy: $.50; sample: $.50. 1975. 8-32pp; 5½ x 4¼. of. circ. 300. Reporting time: 1 to 21 days. One payment of $5.00, two of $1.00 and three copies. Ads: $24/$12. Back issues: $.50 each. Pub's reviews. §Poetry, especially haiku, senryu and one-line poems, also short poems-books dealing with these subjects in any way.

Sun Publishing Co. (see also SUN), Skip Whitson, P.O. Box 4383, Albuquerque, NM 87106, 505-255-6550. avg. price, cloth: $10.00; paper: $4.00. 1974. 150pp; 6 x 9. of. avg. press run 1,000. Reporting time: 2-3 months. Payment: 8 percent. Copyright to Sun Pub Co. Discounts: 20 percent to 50 percent. Pub'd 21 titles 1976; expects 52 titles 1977, 130 titles 1978.

SUN TRACKS: An American Indian Literary Magazine, Sun Tracks, Larry Evers, Ann Brudevold, SUPO Box 20788, Univ of Arizona, Tucson, AZ 85721, 884-1836. Poetry, fiction, articles, art, photos, interviews, parts-of-novels, long-poems. "We publish literary material by and about American Indians." 2/yr; 1-yr sub price: $4.00; per copy: $2.00; sample: $2.00. 1971. 44pp; 8½ x 11. of. circ. 400. Reporting time: 3 months. Payment: 5 copies. Copyrighted, reverts to author. Discounts: 20 percent on 10 copies or more. Back issues: $2.00 per issue. Pub'd 2 issues 1976. §American Indian literature. CCLM, BCC.

SUNBURY (a poetry magazine), Sunbury Press, Virginia Scott, Joan Murray, Box 274 Jerome Ave Station, Bronx, NY 10468. Poetry. "'Affirming women, working class, Third World. Fay Chiang, Elouise Loftin, Joan Murray, Marge Piercy, Ellen Bissert, Quincy Troupe, Lorraine Sutton, V. Scott, Richard Oyama, Sharon Barba.'" 3/yr; 1-yr sub price: $5.00; per copy: $1.75 plus post.; sample: $1.75 plus postage. 1973. 88pp; 5-3/8 x 8¼. of. circ. 1500. Reporting time: 1-6 mos. Payment: in copies. Ads: none. Discounts: 40% for ten copies or more. CCLM, COSMEP, NESPA.

Suncat Enterprises (see CROSSROADS QUARTERLY)

Sunken Forum Press (see also ANTHOLOGY: Montreal Poets), Keitha K. MacIntosh, Dewittville, Quebec J0S1C0, Canada, 514-264-2866. Poetry, fiction. "*Sunken Forum Press* published *Shattered Glass & Other Fragments,* poetry fiction by Keitha MacIntosh in 1976. (still available, retail $3.50). Other Montreal poets are being published this year. *Montreal Poems III* now available, $3.00 retail. Guest poet Al Purdy plus Louis Dudek, Artie Gold, Stephen Morrissey & sixteen other Montreal poets." avg. price, paper: $2.50. 1974. 50pp; 8 x 10. of. avg. press run 1,000. Cannot accept unsolicited material. No payment. Copyrights for author. Discounts: 20-30 percent. Pub'd 5 titles 1976; expects 10 titles 1977.

Sunrise Press, John Leibolo, PO Box 742, Chandler, AZ 85224, 967-4251. Poetry, fiction, long-poems, plays. "Length of material is limited to less than 150 printed pages. All subjects considered." avg. price, cloth: $8.95. 1976. 111pp; 8½ x 11. of. avg. press run 500-1,000 copies. Reporting time: 2 weeks. Payment: negotiable. Copyrights for author. Discounts: negotiable.

SUNSHINE, J. Mark Press, Mark Fischer, Box J, Babylon, NY 11702. Poetry. "1-3 poems, 3-16 lines, and return envelope. No nursery rhymes! Sincere poetry of nature, seasons, and animals for young adults. This publication is supervised by an eleven-year-old editor who was 'born into' the field, and raised with it!" 4/yr; price per copy: $4.50; sample: $3.50. 1975. 40pp; 8½ x 5½. †of. circ. 2,000. Reporting time: 2-4 weeks. Payment: prizes for best poems. Ads: none. Back issues: $3.50 paperback $7.95 hardcover. §poetry.

SUNSPARK, Sunspark Press, Don Carnahan, Box 6341, St. Pete Beach, FL 33736. "Supplement which updates guide to alternative periodicals. First issue published in May, 1977 with new listings and changes. Second supplement planned for Fall, 1977." 2/yr; 1-yr sub price: $2.00; per copy: $1.00; sample: $1.00. 1976. 8½ x 11 Newsletter. of. Not copyrighted. Discounts: bulk-5 copies plus-40 percent. Pub'd 1 issue 1976; expects 2 issues 1977. §Homesteading, environment, spirtual, community, social change, natural living, health & nutrition, arts & crafts, outdoors, children.

Sunspark Press (see also SUNSPARK), Don Carnahan, Box 6341, St. Pete Beach, FL 33736. "*G.A.P.* is a directory of magazines, journals and newsletters devoted to creative, natural lifestyles. Lists prices, sub. rates, addresses and descriptions for over 400 periodicals on environment, homesteading, spirituality, arts and crafts, outdoor recreation, survival health and nutrition, alternative energy, commonity and children, and social change." avg. price, paper: $2.50; other: $1.00 for supplement. 1976. 52pp; 8½ x 11. of. avg. press run 1,000. Does not copyright for author. Discounts: 2-5 copies 30 percent; 6-10 copies 36 percent; 11-24 copies 40 percent; 25 plus copies 43 percent. Pub'd 1 title 1976; expects 2 titles 1977.

THE SUNSTONE REVIEW, The Sunstone Press, Sandra Edelman, PO Box 2321, Santa Fe, NM 87501, 505-988-4418. Poetry, fiction, articles, photos, art, interviews, criticism, reviews. "Have an annual Indian issue" 4/yr; 1-yr sub price: $6.00; per copy: $2.00; sample: $2.00. 1971. 50pp; 6 x 9. of. circ. 500. Reporting time: 30 days. Payment: copies. Copyrighted. Ads: $100/$50. Discounts: 20%. Back issues: $2.00. Pub'd 4 issues 1976; expects 4 issues 1977, 4 issues 1978. Pub's reviews. §poetry, literature, Southwest history. COSMEP.

Sunyata Press (see also NOMEN), Jak English, Susan Clark. 1975. 50-100pp; 9 x 6. avg. press run 3-500. Reporting time: Irreg 2-6 weeks. Payment: 2 copies. Pub'd 1 title 1976; expects 4 titles 1977.

SURFSIDE POETRY REVIEW, William Linehan, George Betar, PO Box 289, Surfside, CA 90743. Poetry, fiction, articles, interviews, criticism, reviews, parts-of-novels, long-poems, plays. "'Our only standard is quality; decent, mature work that has something important to say and realizes it in an interesting manner. We shall undoubtedly print some work we should not and reject some work we should. For this human failure, we apologize beforehand." 3/yr; 1-yr sub price: $3.50; per copy: $1.00; sample: $.50. 1972. 52pp; 5½ x 8. of. circ. 500. Reporting time: 2-3 months. Payment: 2 copies. Ads: none. Discounts: best to query. Back issues: $1.00 per issue, when available. Pub's reviews. COSMEP.

The Swallow Press Inc. (Book Publisher), Durrett Wagner, Donna Ippolito, 811 W. Junior Terrace, Chicago, IL 60613, 312-871-2760. Poetry, fiction, articles, art, photos, interviews, criticism, long-poems, plays, news items, non-fiction. "We distribute the books of: Chicago Review Press, Bardian House, J. B. Pal, Artists & Alchemists" avg. price, cloth: $10.00; paper: $4.95. 250pp; 6 x 9. avg. press run 2,000-5,000. Reporting time: 3-6 months. Payment: Standard royalty 10 percent cl, 7½ percent pa. Copyright in author's name. Discounts: 1 copy 10 percent; 2-4, 30 percent; 5-49, 40 percent; 50-99, 41 percent; 100-199, 42 percent; 200-299, 43 percent; 300-399, 44 percent; 400-499, 45 percent; 500-up, 46 percent. Short discount 20 percent. SCOP 40 percent. Expects 20 titles 1977, 20 titles 1978. ABA.

Swamp Press (see also TIGHTROPE), Jo Mish, Frank Pondolfino, Ed Rayher, Bob Rayher, 300 Main St, Oneonta, NY 13820. Poetry, art, satire, criticism, reviews, letters, long-poems. "Fine papers used in all magazines & chapbooks." avg. price, paper: $1.50. 1975. 20-40pp; Varies. †lp. avg. press run 300. Reporting time: 1 month. Payment: Copies/chapbook rates worked out. Copyrights for author. Pub'd 3 titles 1976; expects 5 titles 1977, 5 titles 1978. COSMEP.

Sweet Pine Press, R. A. Swanson, Rt 1 Box 52, Harrah, WA 98933. Poetry. "Interested mainly in Native American poets (No blatant racism, please)" 1975. †lp. Reporting time: 30 days.

Sydon, Inc., Sy M. Kahn, Don Gray, 451 South Regent St., Stockton, CA 95204. "Has not published in recent years, tho probably will within next year. We are not currently seeking material." 1965. lp. Payment: 10% royalties. COSMEP.

Synergistic Press, Bud Johns, Judith Clancy, 3965 Sacramento St., San Francisco, CA 94118, 415-EV7-8180. Poetry, articles, art, letters. "Our interests are wide ranging, which is best shown are our three titles in print: *The Ombibulous Mr. Mencken,* a humorous biography of H. L. Mencken; *Last Look At The Old Met,* a personal portrait in drawings and text of the old Metropolitan Opera House, and *Bastard In The Ragged Suit,* the published work of a leading protetarian writer of the '20s and '30s, with selections from manuscript fragments and drawings during the last two decades of his life when he didn't submit his work for publication, plus a biographical introduction. To date all of our titles have been developed internally and that probably be true of a majority of our titles in the immediate future." avg. price, cloth: $12.50; paper: $2.95. 1968. varies, have published from 52-216pp. of. avg. press run 3,000-5,000. Reporting time: 1 month. To date payment has varied with title. Copyrights for author. Discounts: trade: single copies, 30 percent; 2-5, 35 percent, 6-11, 37 percent; 12-49, 40 percent, 50 or more, 44 percent; wholesaler/jobber discounts upon request. Pub'd 2 titles 1976; expects 1 title 1977.

Synergy Magazine (see Energy Blacksouth Press)

SYRACUSE Guide, Barbara Dufford, Greg Djanikian, Jon Lang, Poetry Editors, 500 S. Warren St., Syracuse, NY 13202, 315-472-4541. Poetry, fiction, articles, art, photos, cartoons, interviews, satire, criticism, reviews, letters. "Magazine emphasizes articles of general interest to Central New Yorkers (or by present or former Central N.Y.ERS), but will consider other things. Has not yet published fiction but would like to—short (3,000 word top). Magazine carries program listing of Central N.Y.'s concert music station, WONO-FM." 12/yr; 1-yr sub price: $9.00; per copy: $1.00; sample: free. 1975. 44pp; 8½ x 11. of. circ. 3,000. Reporting time: 1 month. Payment: $5.00-published poem; $15.00-basic published article fee, plus 3 copies. Copyrighted, reverts to author. Ads: $150.00/$90.00/$0.25. Discounts: quantities over 10, less than 100-60 cents/copy; over 100-50 cents/copy. Back issues: limited quantities-free. Pub'd 12 issues 1976; expects 12 issues 1977, 12 issues 1978. Pub's reviews. §Central New York; music.

SYZYGY-A Journal of Fiction and Sketches, Cincinnati Women's Press, Dorothy Weil, Ceil Waldrip, 3901 Ledgewood Dr., Cincinnati, OH 45229. Fiction. "Cincinnati Women's Press is Ohio's first small press incorporated by women. Founders Dorothy Weil and Ceil Waldrip hope to offer an outlet for fiction for new and published writers. Our journal emphasizes the woman's point of view, but we welcome manuscripts from men also. All writers are eligible to contribute. We plan to add a third issue as soon as possible and to include non-fiction and poetry as well. The journal is a product of a non-profit organization and we can offer no payment for material accepted. Send SASE." 2/yr; 1-yr sub price: $5.00; per copy: $2.00.

SZ/Press, Suzanne Zavrian, Daniel Kurland, P.O. Box 383, Cathedral Station, New York, NY 10025. "3-4 books per year, approx. $3.00 each. Poetry, prose, experimental arts."

T TABLOID STORY, Lucy Frost, 3 Winson Green Rd., Canterbury, Victoria 3126, Australia. Fiction. 6/yr; 1-yr sub price: $3.00; per copy: $.50. 1972. 4pp; tabloid. Payment: $80 per 1000. Ads: none. Back issues: 6 issues for $3.00.

Talakin Press, Leigh K. Johnson, Publisher, P O Box 143, Clarkdale, AZ 86324.

TALES, Barry Glassner, Jonathan Moreno, Box 24226, St Louis, MO 63130. Fiction. "Recent contribs: Ron Carter, V. J. Emmett, Barry Lopez,F. Waage, Howard Schwartz, Joyce Carol Oates. We receive too many straight stories following the traditional straight formulae and too many experimental stories following the traditional experimental formulae." 4/yr; 1-yr sub price: $3.00; per copy: $1.00; sample: $1.00. 1970. 16pp; tabloid. of. circ. 12,000. Reporting time: 2-4 months. Payment: copies. Ads: $390/$210. Discounts: 15% agency discount on ads, substantial discount for classroom use. Back issues: $2.00 each. Pub's reviews. §fiction only. CCLM.

TALISMAN, Blythe Ayne, 132 Cora, San Francisco, CA 94134. Poetry, fiction, art, photos. sub price: $2.50/6 issues; per copy: $.39. 1973. 32pp; 3½ x 4¼. of. circ. 300. CCLM, COSMEP.

Talonbooks, David Robinson, Karl Siegler, Dwight Gardiner, Poetry; Peter Hay, Drama, 201-1019 East Cordova, Vancouver, British Columbia V6A 1M8, Canada, 604-255-5915. Poetry, fiction, art, photos, long-poems, plays, criticism, letters. "*Talonbooks* is one of the leading Canadian literary publishers. The press publishes almost exclusively only poetry, drama and fiction-and is the major publisher of contemporary drama in Canada." avg. price, paper: $2.95-$4.75. 1967. 128pp; 5½ x 8½. †of. avg. press run poetry-1,000; drama-3,000; fiction-3,000-5,000 (first printings). Payment: 10% royalty of retail sale price. Discounts: 37 percent trade-40 percent for 100 plus copies, 25 percent educational, 20 percent libraries & individuals. All shipping prepaid. Pub'd 17 titles 1976; expects 18 titles 1977. ACP, BCPG, COSMEP.

Tamal Vista Publications, P. W. DeFremery, 222 Madrone Ave, Larkspur, CA 94939, 362-0888.

avg. price, cloth: $7.95. 1976. 96pp; 9 x 12. of. avg. press run 2. Reporting time: 1 month. Copyrights for author. Discounts: 0-4 equals 0; 5-10 20 percent; 10-49 40 percent; 50-100 43 percent; wholesellers 50 percent. COSMEP.

Tamarack Press (see WISCONSIN TRAILS)

Tamarisk (see also APOCALYPSE), Dennis Barone, 188 Forest Ave, Ramsey, NJ 07446, 201-327-7469. Poetry, fiction, art, photos, collages. "*Tamarisk* grew out of *APOCALYPSE*. Tamarisk, that old testament tree, to be before Apocalypse. Quieter, smaller, smarter; of any length—printing what comes, in someway, by way of ear, not mail. Recent publications include a chapbook by Ron Atkinson, '*And Quiet, And Slow, And The Rain Fell Like Petals, And The People Went Oh,*' with drawings by Cormac Tully. Having small, scalelike leaves and clusters of pink flowers—*Tamarisk*.'' avg. price, paper: $1.00. 1975. 40pp; 5½ x 8½. of. avg. press run 250. Reporting time: 2 yrs to not at all. Copyrights for author. Pub'd 1 title 1976; expects 2 titles 1977, 3 titles 1978. NESPA.

Tamarix (see THE SALT CEDAR)

TANGENTS, Don Slater, Joseph Hansen, 6715 Hollywood Blvd. #210, Hollywood, CA 90028. Poetry, fiction, articles, art, interviews, reviews, letters. "Seeds of the American sexual revolution, discussions of the studies of Alfred Kinsey. Reader at large, tangents reprint (discussion of books on homosexuality in 1960s). $.35 Selected bibliography of homosexuality." irregular; price per copy: $1.00. 1965. 6 x 9. lp. circ. 3,000. Payment: in copies & subs. no ads. Discounts: 50%. Back issues: $.50 apiece (not all available).

The Tantivy Press (see FOCUS ON FILM)

TAR RIVER POETS, East Carolina University Poetry Forum Press, Vernon Ward, Department of English, East Carolina University, Greenville, NC 27834. "Among recent featured contributors have been Gerda Nischan, Douglas McReynolds, Robert Waters Grey, and Julia Fields" 1-2/yr; price per copy: $1.25-$2.00. 1960. 48pp; 6 x 8¾. of. circ. 1,000. Payment varies. Pub's reviews §poetry.

Taramara, Unltd., Marcia M. Dreiss-Tarasovic, 5644 No. 7 Forbes, Pittsburgh, PA 15217, 412-422-8981. Poetry. "Currently doing *ONLY* poetry Broadsides-eventually plan on moving to chapbooks—style is art background with poetry overlay." avg. price, other: $3.00 broadsides. 1976. 1pp; 18 x 24. †silkscreen. avg. press run 500. Reporting time: as soon as poss. Payment: prices. Author retains copyright. COSMEP.

Task Force on Gay Liberation (see A GAY BIBLIOGRAPHY)

Tau Delta Phi Press, Box 4, SJSU, San Jose, CA 95192. "Tau Delta Phi biennially issues two publications, *The Tower List,* including student ratings of SJSU professors, circulation 15,000, and *The Tower Anthology Of The San Jose Movement In Fiction,* self-explanatory, circulation 500. In charge of *The Tower List's* 7th edition are Wayne Gribling, J. Michael Gonzales, and Pat Alvarez. *Tower Anthology* editor-in-chief for the 2nd edition is Merritt Clifton, assistant editor Nick Baptista. First edition contributors were Clifton, Thomas Livingston, Tom Suddick, Dennis Shelley, Ray Pitts, Stella Zamvil, Nils Peterson, Fred Handsfield, Dale C. Dalton, Richard Amyx, Marylou Lewandowski, Robert Burdette Sweet, and Ron Vinyard; copies still available at $1.25/each. Second edition contributors will include Clifton, Suddick, Vinyard, Joe Izzo, Jon Ilgen, George Terry Chapman, and others, with introduction by Baptista. $1.00; out in May '76."

Taurean Horn Press (see also MINI TAUR SERIES), 601 Leavenworth #45, San Francisco, CA 94109. "Publications in print: *Honeydew,* an anthology; *Blind Annie's Cellar* by Paul Vane. MINI-TAUR SERIES: *Black Birds & Other Birds* by Mary Francis Glaggett; *Message Bringer Woman* by Carol Lee Sanchez." avg. price, paper: $3.00. avg. press run 500. Pub'd 1 title 1976; expects 2 titles 1977.

TAWTE: Texas Artists Writers and Thinkers in Exile, Thorp Springs Press, Paul Foreman, Bob Burleson, 2311-C Woolsey, Berkeley, CA 94705. Poetry, fiction, articles, art, photos, cartoons, interviews, criticism, reviews, music, letters, parts-of-novels, long-poems, collages, plays. "Recent contributors: Bert Almon, Rodger Scott, Joanie Whitebird, Susan Buchanan, Charles Taylor, James Cody, Gerald Haslam." 1-2/yr; sub price: $6.00-4 copies; per copy: $1.50; sample: $1.50. 1974. 64pp; 8½ x 11. of. circ. 1,200. Reporting time: 3 months to 1 yr. Payment varies. Copyrighted. Ads: inquire. Discounts: 33-1/3% trade, 20% classroom. Back issues: $5.00 each. §Fiction, poetry, art, general concerning the state of Texas. COSMEP.

Teachers and Writers (see also TEACHERS AND WRITERS MAGAZINE), Miguel Ortiz, 186 West 4th Street, New York, NY 10014, 212-691-6590. Articles, interviews, reviews. avg. price, paper: $4.00. 1968. 160pp; 6 x 9. of. avg. press run 3,000. Reporting time: one month. Payment: advance on royalty. Copyrights for author. Discounts: none. Pub'd 2 titles 1976; expects 3 titles 1977, 2 titles 1978.

TEACHERS AND WRITERS MAGAZINE, Teachers and Writers Press, Miguel Ortiz, 186 West 4th Street, New York, NY 10014, 212-691-6590. Articles, interviews, letters. 3/yr; 1-yr sub price: $5.00; per copy: $2.00; sample: $2.00. 1967. 50pp; 8½ x 11. of. circ. 2,500. Reporting time: one month. Payment: $25.00-$50.00. Copyrighted, does not revert to author. Discounts: none. Back issues: $2.00 an issue. Pub'd 3 issues 1976; expects 3 issues 1977, 3 issues 1978.

Ted Smith/Graphics (see GRAFIKTRAKTS)

Tegwar Press (see also SALT), Robert Currie, Barbara Sapergia, Geoffrey Ursell, 1119 13th Ave. NW, Moose Jaw, Sask. S6H4N5, Canada. Poetry. "Short stories. No book publishing. Editorial address: 2226 McTavish, Regina, Sask., Canada, S4T3X2." 1969. †mi. Reporting time: 1-2 months.

TELEPHONE, Telephone Books, Maureen Owen, Box 672, Old Chelsea Sta., New York City, NY 10011. Poetry, fiction, cartoons, letters, collages. "Britt Wilkie, Michael Flory, Janine Pomy Vega, Bob Dumont, Charlie Vermont, Ruth Krauss, Tony Towle, Susan Howe, David Moe, Richard Snyder, Erik Satie, Red Grooms, Carol Pierman, Joe Johnson, Maria Gitin, Peggy Garrison, Bruce Andrews, Joe Brainard." 2/yr; sub price: $4.50-3 copies (All checks made out to: Maureen Owen); per copy: $1.50 (All checks made out to: Maureen Owen); sample: $1.00. 1969. 100pp; 8½ x 14. of. circ. 700. Reporting time: 1 month. Payment: none. Copyrighted. Ads: none. Discounts: none. Back issues: $4 per copy (most out of print). Expects 2 issues 1978. CCLM, COSMEP, NESPA, WDG, BC.

Telephone Books (see also TELEPHONE), Maureen Owen, Box 672, Old Chelsea Sta, New York, NY 10011. Poetry, fiction. "In 1976 we'll publish books by Fanny Howe, Janine Pomy Vega, Yuki Hartman, Rebecca Wright." avg. price, paper: $1.50 All cks made out to: Maureen Owen. 40pp; 5½ x 8½. of. avg. press run 750. Payment: In copies. Copyrights for author. Expects 4 titles 1977. CCLM, NESPA, COSMEP, WDG, BC.

TELEPOEM, Telepoetics (396-8978), Loren-Paul Caplin, 230 San Juan, Venice, CA 90291. Poetry. "Since we change the poems so often (we go through 5-12 poems a week) we are able to use a great many poems. All kinds are accepted but we tend to lean toward shortish (not exceeding 25 lines) narrative. All poems are read in same dry monotones. Looking to shock the complacency of the curious caller as well as satisfying the ear of the afficionado. Between 100-500 a week and just starting." 2-4 per wk; sample price: free. Reporting time: 1-3 wks.

Telepoetics (396-8978) (see TELEPOEM)

TELOS, Telos Press, Paul Piccone, Sociology Dept, Washington Univ, St Louis, MO 63130, 314-863-0100, EXT. 4383. Articles, criticism, reviews. 4/yr; 1-yr sub price: $10.00; per copy: $2.50; sample: $2.50. 1968. 264pp; 6 x 9. of. circ. 3,000. Reporting time: 6 mos. Payment: none. Ads: $200.00/$125.00. Discounts: 30% bulk orders; 10% agent. Pub'd 4 issues 1976; expects 4 issues 1977, 4 issues 1978. Pub's reviews: 25 in 1976. §left-wing philosophy, lit. criticism, politics.

Telos Press (see also TELOS), C/O Sociology Dept, Washington Univ, St Louis, MO 63130, 314-863-0100, EXT. 4383. Articles, criticism, reviews. avg. price, cloth: $7.00; paper: $3.00. 1970. 200pp; Varies. of. avg. press run 4,000. Reporting time: 6 months. Payment: None. Copyrights for author. Discounts: usual is 30%. Other can be arranged. Pub'd 2 titles 1976; expects 2 titles 1977, 2 titles 1978.

Ten Penny Players, Inc., B. Fisher Perry, 799 Greenwich Street, New York, NY 10014, 212-929-3169. Poetry, fiction, plays. "Age range 3-12 years. Varying lengths: 8 pp - 34 pp. At present doing a series of read aloud and playscripts, fully illustrated by B Fisher Perry. We stress an integration of language and picture so that the material can be used either as a book to read or a book to perform." avg. price, paper: $3.00. 1975. 34pp; 4½ x 6. †of/lp. avg. press run 200 copies. No unsolicited manuscripts please. Payment: Negotiable. Copyrights for author. Discounts: Standard 60/40. NYSSPA.

10 POINT 5, A Magazine of the Arts, Oz Publications, Inc., Peter Jensen, David Zeltzer, Karen Kramer, Peter Wallace, Amedee Smith, 1035401/2 Ferry St., Eugene, OR 97401. Poetry, fiction, art, photos, cartoons, interviews, satire, parts-of-novels, collages, plays, concrete art. "We like to have about 25 contributors/issue, so we go for shorter material in written works. We do full page graphics, as well as smaller accent graphics. Recent artists: Mary Byrne, Rogene Zaharie, Syd Baker.Recent writers: David Johnson, Karen McPherson, David Zeltzer, Peter Jensen, Thea, Jerry Yanuck." 3/yr; 1-yr sub price: $2.00; per copy: $.50; sample: $.75. 1975. 32pp; 8½ x 11. of. circ. 2,000. Reporting time: 2 months. Payment: 2 copies. Ads: $15 for 2 lines patron's listing. Discounts: none. Back issues: 50¢/each. §exchange with other arts magazines.

‡**Ten Speed Press,** PO Box 4310, Berkeley, CA 94704.

Tendon Press (see NORTH STONE REVIEW)

TENDRIL, Tendril, George Murphy, Chuck Ozug, Moira Linehan, Mark Cohen, Box 512, Green Harbor, MA 02041, 617-834-4137. Poetry, art. "Occaisional graphics. Biases, poetry that is 'concise, imagistic, and emotive'." 2/yr; 1-yr sub price: $3.50; per copy: $2.00; sample: $2.00. 1977. 30-40pp; 5½ x 8½. circ. 200. Reporting time: 2-6 weeks. Payment: copies. Not copyrighted. no ads. Discounts: negotiable. Back issues: $1.00. CCLM, COSMEP.

TENNYSON RESEARCH BULLETIN, Tennyson Society, Tennyson Society Publications Board, Tennyson Research Centre, Central Library, Free School Lane, Lincoln LN2 1EZ, United Kingdom. Articles, criticism, letters. "Subs ($5.00 personal; $12.00 institutional) includes all publications issued in the year. Includes all notes and queries relating to *TENNYSON* and select articles up to 5,000 words. A cumulative index covering 1967 to 71 (Vol. 1) and 1972-76 (Vol. 2) has now been issued and is available free." 1/yr; 1-yr sub price: with membership; per copy: Back numbers only 1967-73 $2.40; 1974-5 $3.60 each copy. 1967. 21.5 x 13.7cm. lp. circ. 500. Discounts: 25% trade.

Territorial Press (see DACOTAH TERRITORY)

Texas Christian University Press (see DESCANT)

TEXAS COUNTRY MAGAZINE, Ransehc Publishing, Inc., Lynne Chesnar, Publisher; Guida Jackson, Editor-in-Chief, P.O. Box 966, Alief, TX 77411. Articles, art, photos, cartoons, interviews, reviews, music, letters, news items, non-fiction. "*TEXAS COUNTRY MAGAZINE* is dedicated to the preservation of pure country soul, especially Texan. We'd rather have articles about people (with B/W glossies), but might not pass up a good piece of poetry or fiction. We're heavy on music, especially bluegrass and progressive country, but we also like western artists, craftsmen, cooks, cowboys, farmers, ranchers, folk dancers, honky-tonk proprietors, whoever. We edit prose." 6/yr; sub price: $5.00/6 issues; per copy: $1.00; sample: $1.00. 1976. 28-32pp; 8 x 11. of. circ.

15,000. Reporting time: 6 weeks. Payment: copies only plus free ad. Buys all rights but will reassign poetry & fiction on request. Ads: $456.00/$234.00/$0.10. Discounts: 45 percent-20 copies or more. Back issues: $1.00. Pub'd 6 issues 1976; expects 6 issues 1977, 6 issues 1978. Pub's reviews.

TEXAS OBSERVER, Jim Hightower, 600 W. 7th, Austin, TX 78701, 512-477-0746. Articles, art, photos, cartoons, criticism, reviews. "Primarily political and social topics; populist/progressive point of view." 25/yr; 1-yr sub price: $12.00; per copy: $.50; sample: free. 1954. 24pp; 8½ x 11. of. circ. 12,000. Reporting time: 4 weeks. Payment: $10 to $50. Copyrighted. Ads: $300.00/$150.00/$0.30. Discounts: 10 or more copies to same address: 20¢ per issue. Back issues: 50 ¢. Pub'd 25 issues 1976; expects 25 issues 1977, 25 issues 1978. Pub's reviews: 4 in 1976. §political or sociological.

TEXAS PORTFOLIO, B. Weberlein, Publisher, Dwight Fullingin, Editor; Gayle Faget, Art Editor; Mary Danaczko, Consulting Editor, 123 Eleventh Avenue, North, Texas City, TX 77590, 713-948-3703. Poetry, fiction, articles, art, photos, interviews, satire, reviews, letters, parts-of-novels. "Recent contributors: Maxine Kumin, Brian Swann, D. C. Berry, Naomi Shihab." 2/yr; 1-yr sub price: $4.00; per copy: $2.00; sample: $1.00. 1976. 32pp; 8½ x 11. of. circ. 500. Reporting time: 8 weeks. Payment: Contributor's copies. Ads: $60/$30. Discounts: 40% to all. Back issues: $2.00 each if available. Pub's reviews. §Poetry, fiction, graphics, art. COSMEP.

‡**TEXAS QUARTERLY,** Box 7517 University Stn., Austin, TX 78712.

THEATRE ACROSS AMERICA, Theatre Sources, Inc., Mike Firth, 104 N. St. Mary, Dallas, TX 75214. Articles, photos, interviews, reviews, letters, news items. "Looking for material of moderate length, instructional style, how-to in the theatre. *No* reviews of plays in performance (books or scripts ok). Reasonable do-it-yourself equipment ideas wanted." 5/yr; 1-yr sub price: $5.00; per copy: $1.00; sample: $1.00. 1975. 8-12pp; 8½ x 11. of. circ. 75. Reporting time: 1 month min. Payment: $0.01 a word. Ads: $20/$10. Back issues: $1. Pub'd 4 issues 1976; expects 5 issues 1977, 5 issues 1978. Pub's reviews: 4 in 1976. §Theatre/practical solutions to problems.

THEATRE DESIGN AND TECHNOLOGY, U.S. Institute for Theatre Technology, Inc., Thomas Watson, Editor; Donald Swinney, Managing Editor & Advertising Director; Tony Courtade, Herb Greggs, Richard D. Thompson, Fred M. Wolff, Associate Editors, 1 Hillside Road, Newark, DE 19711, 302-731-5468. Articles, photos, interviews, reviews, letters, news items. "*Scope* of the *Journal* includes the range of interests set forth in the Institute's statement of policy: 'The Institute's first concern is the physical aspects of the theatre, as its architecture, engineering, administration, and the basic conditions of presentation. All these phases stand obviously at the service of the final fruition in the theatre, the presentation itself, where the skills of actor and playwright and director are the most conspicuous, aided by all the intricate collaboration of the stage through services of the designer, costumer, lighting designer and the various technicians.' Articles will reflect the opinion of the stated author in every case: except for officially designated Institute notices, opinions stated do not necessarily constitute sentiment of the Institute or recommended practice. Opinionated statements which tend to stimulate serious thought and thus further the art of the theatre are always to be encouraged." 4/yr; 1-yr sub price: $12.00-libraries only; per copy: $3.50; sample: $3.50. 1965. 40pp; 8½ x 11. of. circ. 2,950. Reporting time: 6 weeks. Payment: none. Copyrighted, held by magazine after publication unless author wishes separate copyright. Ads: $250/$150. Discounts: 10% for annual contract. Back issues: $3.50. Pub'd 4 issues 1976; expects 4 issues 1977, 4 issues 1978. Pub's reviews: 26 in 1976. §books only, scenography, theatre production, engineering, architecture.

Theatre Sources, Inc. (see PROLOG, THEATER ACROSS AMERICA)

THEATRE SURVEY-THE American Journal of Theatre History, Attilio Favonni, Executive Editor, Univ. Pittsubrgh, 1117 Cathedral of Learning, Pittsburgh, PA 15260. Articles, criticism. "*TS* is a scholarly journal and requires full documentation. *TS* publishes in the field of theatre history, as distinguished from the history of the drama or dramatic interpretation and criticism. Articles should be submitted in triplicate and follow the format in the latest edition of U. Chicago Press's *Manual of Style*." 2/yr with occasional special issues; sub price: $5.00/yr domestic $5.50/yr foreign; per copy: $2.50; sample: free. 1961. 90pp; 6 x 9. of. circ. 981. Reporting time: 4 months. Payment: none. Discounts: none. Back issues: $2.50. §theatre history only.

The Thimble Press (see SIGNAL)

THIRD COAST ARCHIVES, House Of Words, Jeffrey Winke, C. Rossiter, 207 E. Buffalo St. No. 518, c/o House of Words, Milwaukee, WI 53202. Poetry, fiction, art, long-poems, concrete art, photos, cartoons. "We call ourselves 'free-form, contemporary, independent.' Our favorite material falls somewhere between the absurdities that grace the average street sheet and the dull stuff too often found in 'academic' publications. Slight bias favoring Wisc. writers." Quarterly (with a year-end double issue); 1-yr sub price: $5.00; per copy: $1.00; sample: $1.00. 1976. 20-35pp; 8½ x 5½. of. circ. 150. Reporting time: usually 2 to 8 weeks. Payment: copy. Copyrighted. Ads: $25.00 (back cover)/$15.00 (back cover)/no classified. Discounts: 40 percent plus postage on 5 copies or more. Back issues: all are $1.00 each. Pub's reviews. §contemporary, experimental, also haikus.

THIRD EYE, P.T. Lally, Carol Covill, 250 Mill St., Williamsville, NY 14221. Poetry, fiction, long-poems. "Prefer free verse (if only to avoid contrived phrases). Would like to see more poetry of social relevance. Will use prose (if brief)." 4/yr; 1-yr sub price: $5.50; per copy: $1.50; sample: $1.00. 1976. 48pp; 8½ x 6¾. of. circ. 325. Reporting time: 3 weeks. Payment: None, cash awards beginning 1977 - 7 cash prizes per issue. Copyrighted, reverts to author. no ads. Discounts: None. Back issues: $1. Pub'd 3 issues 1976; expects 4 issues 1977, 4 issues 1978. Pub's reviews: none in 1976.

THE THIRD PRESS REVIEW, The Third Press (Joseph Okpaku Publishing Co. Inc.), Joseph Okpaku, 444 Central Park West, New York, NY 10025. Articles, interviews, reviews. "Leopold Sedar Senghor, Wole Soyinka, Sol Gordon, Ph. D., Richard Kostelanetz." 6/yr; 1-yr sub price: $9.00; per copy: $2.00. 1975. 70pp; 8½ x 11. of. Reporting time: two months. Pub's reviews. §African Studies/Black writings.

THIRD RAIL, Third Rail Press, Doren Robbins, Uri Hertz, 9721 Monte Mar Dr., Los Angeles, CA 90035. Poetry, fiction, articles, art, photos, interviews, satire, criticism, reviews, parts-of-novels, long-poems, collages. "We print poetry, prose, and artwork of a contemplative, surreal, anarchist nature. Recent contributors: Henry Miller, Kenneth Rexroth, Robert Bly, Gary Robbins, Walter Lowenfels, George Hitchcock, and Shinkichi Takahashi." 1/yr; 1-yr sub price: $2.00; per copy: $2.00; sample: $2.00. 1975. 50-75pp; 5½ x 8½. †of. Reporting time: 2-6 wks. Payment: copies (2). Ads: $50/$25/$10. Discounts: up to 10 copies 20% over 40%. Back issues: $2.00. Pub's reviews.

3RD THING MAGAZINE OF POETRY AND GRAPHICS, Hudson River Press, Shaun Farragher, Marlene Tartaglione, P.O. Box 270, Edgewater, NJ 07020. Poetry, art, photos, reviews, long-poems, collages, concrete art. "For the next year we will not need new submissions of poetry. We are especially interested in receiving art work and photography for possible publication. We are especially interested in collage and conceptual photography. The Focus Arts Center closed this past year and this magazine no longer has any association with Focus 2 Community Center, Inc. Recent contributions include Joel Oppenheimer, Eve Merriam, Hugh Seidman, and Konstantinos Lardas. Two issues planned for 1976-77. We are also interested in receiving all small press publications for review and exchange." 2/yr; 1-yr sub price: $4.00; per copy: $2.00; sample: free with SASE. 1974. 64pp; 8½ x 11. of. circ. 500. Reporting time: month. Payment: none. Ads: exchange ads only. Discounts: free to alternate schools, prisoners, to anyone who cannot afford it. (please send SASE 9x12). Pub's reviews. §poetry/photography/art.

Third World Publications Ltd., 151 Stratford Road, Birmingham B111RD, United Kingdom, 021-773-6572. "UK agents for Tanzania Publishing House & distributors for the East African Publishing House, & Progressive South African Publishers, and several UK organisations campaigning on Third World issues." avg. price, cloth: £4.00; paper: 20p to £7.50. 1972. Discounts: Trade: 33-1/3 percent. Bulk: 10 percent (over £20.00 value) larger discounts negotiable on big orders.

13th MOON, 13th Moon, Inc., Ellen Marie Bissert, P.O. Box 3, Inwood Station, New York, NY 10034, 212-942-6761. Poetry, fiction, articles, art, photos, interviews, criticism, reviews, letters,

315

parts-of-novels, long-poems, collages, plays, concrete art. "13th MOON is a literary magazine publishing work by women whoever we choose to be. Eclectic. No biases in content. Interested only in good work by women. Published Rochelle Owens, Kathleen Spivack, Karen Swenson, Alix Kates Shulman as well as a long interview with concrete-conceptual poet Amelia Etlinger with nine photos of her work. Open." 2/yr; sub price: $4.50/for 3 issues; per copy: current double issue $3.00; sample: $3.00. 1973. 64-96pp; 6 x 9. of. circ. 2,500. Reporting time: 3 wks-2mos. Payment: copies. Discounts: the usual 40% discount on orders of 5 or more. Back issues: back issues sold only to libraries. Pub'd 1 issue 1976; expects 2 issues 1977, 2 issues 1978. Pub's reviews: 9 in 1976. §Small press books by women/literature by women/women's literary history by women. CCLM, NESPA.

Thistledown Press, Glen Sorestad, Sonia Sorestad, Neil Wagner, Susan Wagner, 668 East Place, Saskatoon, Saskatchewan S7J2Z5, Canada, 374-1730. Poetry, art. avg. price, cloth: $7.00; paper: $3.00. 1975. 50pp; 7 x 8½. of. avg. press run 600 copies. Reporting time: 1 month-6 weeks. Payment: 10 books plus 10 percent net profit. Copyrights for author. Discounts: bookstore/jobber: 1-9 copies 20 percent, 10 or more 40 percent. schools: 10-25 copies 20 percent, 26 or more 30 percent. Pub'd 5 titles 1976; expects 5 titles 1977.

THOMAS HARDY YEARBOOK, Toucan, J Stevens-Cox, Mt Durand, St Peter Port, Guernsey CI, United Kingdom. Articles, poetry, photos, news items, interviews, criticism, letters, non-fiction. "1,000-3,000 words" 1/yr; 1-yr sub price: £3.00; per copy: £3.00; sample: £3.00. 1970. 100pp; Qto. lp. circ. 3,000. Reporting time: 1 month. Payment: by arrangement. Ads: £10.00/£5.00. Back issues: £5.00. Pub'd 1 issue 1976; expects 1 issue 1977, 1 issue 1978. Pub's reviews: 25 in 1976.

THOREAU JOURNAL QUARTERLY, Thoreau Fellowship, Richard F. Fleck, Literary Editor; Mary P. Sherwood, Managing Editor, P.O. Box 551, Old Town, ME 04468, (literary) English Dept., Univ. of Wyoming, Laramie, WY 82070. Poetry, articles, photos, criticism, reviews, plays. "Critical articles, outdoor articles, poetry, plays relating to Henry David Thoreau. Articles should be no more than 15 typed pages and poetry no longer than 2 typed pages. Plays or dramatic sketches up to 15 typed pages." 4/yr; 1-yr sub price: $4.00; per copy: $1.00. 1968. 32pp; 9 x 6. of. circ. 500. Reporting time: 3-4 wks. Payment: copies only.

Thorp Springs Press (see also TAWTE, HYPERION), Paul Foreman, Foster Robertson, 2311-C Woolsey, Berkeley, CA 94705. Poetry, parts-of-novels, plays, news items. avg. price, cloth: $7.50 - $8.00; paper: $3.00; other: pamphlet $1.00. 1971. 90pp; 8½ x 5½. †of. avg. press run 1,000. Reporting time: Up to 1 year. Copyrights for author. Discounts: Bkst/40 percent returns in saleable condition if in 6 months; jobbers/10 percent 1-10 copies / 20 percent 11-50 copies. Expects 10-12 titles 1977.

THOUGHTS FOR ALL SEASONS: The Magazine of Epigrams, Valley Press, Michel Paul Richard, State University College At Geneseo, Geneseo, NY 14454. Art, satire. "Form: One sentence or one paragraph original thoughts. Art work: Pen and ink or etchings." 2/yr; 1-yr sub price: $4.00; per copy: $2.00; sample: $2.00. 1976. 44pp; 8½ x 11. of. Reporting time: 30 days. Payment: none. Ads: $50/$25. Discounts: none. §epigrams and aphorisms, as well as essays on the epigram as a literary form.

THREE CENT PULP, Pulp Press, Pulp Press Ed. Board, Box 48806 Stn. Bental, Vancouver, Canada, 604-687-4233. Poetry, fiction, articles, art, photos, cartoons, interviews, satire, criticism, reviews, letters, parts-of-novels, concrete art, non-fiction. "New poetry, fiction, drama, art, and occasional political and literary essays. Has published over 175 authors and artists from 4 continents. Entirely supported by subscribers." 24/yr; sub price: $10.00 (24 issues); per copy: $0.03; sample: free. 1972. 4pp; 5½ x 8½. †of. circ. 1,100. Reporting time: 1 month. Payment: copies. Copyrighted, reverts to author. Discounts: 100 percent to bookstores. Back issues: complete volumes only $25 ea (scarce). Pub'd 24 issues 1976; expects 24 issues 1977, 24 issues 1978. §literary/political. CPPA.

THREE RIVERS POETRY JOURNAL, Three Rivers Press, Gerald Costanzo, P.O. Box 21, Carnegie-Mellon University, Pittsburgh, PA 15213. Poetry, articles, reviews. "Recent contributors include Dave Smith, Charles Wright, Vern Rutsala, Jay Meer, Gerald Stern, Linda Pastan, Stanley

Plumly, Leonard Nathan, and Paula Rankin. We continue to publish work in each issue by new writers. We are able to read manuscripts only between September 1 and April 30. We do not wish to receive xerox copies of poems, nor are we able to accept submissions bearing postage due. Reviews are by invitation only, from previous contributors." 2/yr; sub price: $5.00/4 issues; per copy: $1.50; sample: $1.50. 1972. 60pp; 8½ x 5½. circ. 1,000. Reporting time: 2 weeks-2 mos. Payment: copies. Ads: exchange ads only. Discounts: 40% on ten or more copies. Back issues: available only through Xerox University Microfilms. Pub'd 2 issues 1976; expects 2 issues 1977, 2 issues 1978. Pub's reviews: 16 in 1976. §Poetry/poetics. CCLM.

Three Rivers Press (see also THREE RIVERS POETRY JOURNAL), Gerald Costanzo, Editor, P.O. Box 21, Carnegie-Mellon University, Pittsburgh, PA 15213. Poetry. "We are in the process of phasing out book production with Three Rivers Press in order to devote full time and energy to the Carnegie-Mellon University Press Poetry Series. In 1977 we've produced John Calvin Rezmerski's second collection, *An American Gallery*. We have one more book scheduled and will be reading no more manuscripts for that series. Three Rivers Press will continue to produce THREE RIVERS POETRY JOURNAL and its poetry on buses program." avg. price, paper: $2.95; other: $10.00 signed, cloth. 1973. †of/lp. avg. press run 1,000. Reporting time: 2-3 months. Pub'd 2 titles 1976; expects 2 titles 1977.

THREE SISTERS, Georgetown University, Jody Falco, David Ringold, Elizabeth Joyce, Jeffrey Steinman, Box 969, Hoya Station, Washington, DC 20057. Poetry, fiction, articles, art, photos, criticism, reviews, parts-of-novels, long-poems, plays. "Recent appearances have included Kunitz, Stafford, Flint, and Lifshin, but the bulk of what we publish is by new writers and artists." 3/yr; 1-yr sub price: $5.00; per copy: $2.00; sample: $2.00. 1971. 48pp; 8½ x 11. of. circ. 2,500. Reporting time: 4-6 weeks. Payment: copies. Discounts: none. Back issues: $2/issue. Pub's reviews. §fiction/poetry/mostly.

The Three Trees Press, Wenceslaus Horak, Box 70, Post. Station V, Toronto, Ontario M6R3A4, Canada, 924-0894. Poetry, fiction. "Biases, Original, well defined artistic values. Positive human approach." avg. price, cloth: $6.95; paper: $3.95. 1976. 64pp; 5¼ x 8. of. avg. press run 1,000. Reporting time: 1-2 months. Payment: 5 percent of the sale price, or 10 percent from net. Does not copyright for author. Discounts: 40 percent, 45 percent, 20 percent, 10 percent commission, 50 percent. Pub'd 8 titles 1976.

Thresh Publications, Christine Thresh, Robert Thresh, 441-443 Sebastopol Ave., Santa Rosa, CA 95401. "No set minimum-maximum length. Our titles vary from 24 page booklets to 160 page books (paperbacks only). We publish limited non-fiction subjects. Primary emphasis has been fiber arts, but we are now expanding to other 'how-to' and informational areas of interest to homesteaders. Recent books: WARPING ALL BY YOURSELF by Cay Garrett (160pp); LET'S TRY MUSHROOMS FOR COLOR by Miriam Rice (40pp); ANYONE CAN BUILD A SPINNING WHEEL by W.C. West (32pp)." of. Reporting time: 6 wks. Payment: royalty. COSMEP, COSMEP-WEST.

Thunder City Press, Steven Ford Brown, Editor; Sandra S. Thompson, Co-Editor, PO Box 11126, Birmingham, AL 35202, 205-870-7281. Poetry, fiction, art, photos. "Recent books by Pier Giorgio Di Cicco, Steven Ford Brown, Michael Swindle, Ellen Bonnie, Robert Lynn Penny. Books forthcoming by Charles Entrekin, D.C. Berry, Alan P. Perlis, James F. Mersmann. Poems that break out the windows of the head. Good images. Original use of language." avg. price, paper: $2.00. 1975. 36pp; 5½ x 8½. †of/lp. avg. press run 500 but almost everyone of our books goes into second & third printings. Reporting time: 1 month at the most. Payment: according to the individual. Copyrights for author. Discounts: negotiable. Pub'd 3 titles 1976; expects 6 titles 1977, 8 titles 1978. COSMEP, COSMEP-SOUTH.

Tide Publications (see THE LESBIAN TIDE)

Tideline Press, Leonard Seastone, P.O. Box 786, Tannersville, NY 12485. Poetry, art, parts-of-novels, long-poems. "Like to keep the text under 30 pages. Style preference varies: must be something that takes me someplace, grabs me by the throat and makes the blood to rise. Recently

Ronald Baatz, Mariquita Platov, Lyn Lifshin, Leonard Seastone, Peter Wild, Sheila Heldenbrand; Future: William Matthews, George Crane and possibly Robert Bly.'' 1972. pp varies; varies. †Washington hand-press. Reporting time: usually same day SASE. Payment: copies. Discounts: 1 copy-20% 2-4 copies 30% 5 or more 40%.

TIGHTROPE, Swamp Press, Jo Mish, Ed Rayher, Robert Rayher, Frank Pondolfino, 300 Main St., Oneonta, NY 13820. Poetry, art, articles, long-poems, photos, satire, criticism, reviews, letters. "We do appreciate writers who remember the sounds of words. The three rules of the imagists would be good to look at before submitting. Recent contributors-Mike Newell, Jo Mish, Pier Giorgio Di Cicco, Bela Egyedi.'' 2/yr; 1-yr sub price: $3.00; per copy: $1.50; sample: $1.00. 1975. 28pp; 4½ x 6. †lp. circ. 300. Reporting time: 1 month. Payment: copies. Copyrighted, reverts to author. Back issues: See samples. Pub's reviews §Poetry. COSMEP.

TIME/OUT, Creative Communications, Carol Ann Piggres, 928 Cleveland Ave, Racine, WI 53405, 414-633-3621. Poetry, fiction, articles, art. "We produce a non-sexist, multi-racial magazine for children. We have a humanistic outlook. We encourage children to be creative, to explore their potential, to believe in themselves. We like open-ended material.'' 4/yr; 1-yr sub price: $3.00; per copy: $0.75; sample: $0.75. 1975. 20pp; 6 x 8¾. of. circ. 1,000. Reporting time: up to 2 months as our editorial office is in The Netherlands. Payment: $2.00-$15.00 (higher in special cases). Copyrighted, reverts to author. Discounts: 20 percent commission to agent, 25 percent discount on classroom bulk orders of 15 or more. Pub's reviews. §juveniles, books for adults who work with children. COSMEP.

TIME BARRIER EXPRESS, Ralph M. Newman, PO Box 1109, White Plains, NY 10602, 914-793-2649. Articles, photos, cartoons, interviews, criticism, reviews, letters, news items, non-fiction. "*TIME BARRIER EXPRESS* magazine covers the history of rock & roll music, particularly from the 1950's and 60's. Special emphasis on the artists of that era and on the collection of their recordings. Special features include complete discographies and labelographies, vintage photos and reports of current events in this field.'' 8/yr; 1-yr sub price: $8.00; per copy: $1.25; sample: $1.50. 1974. 36pp; 8½ x 11. of. circ. 10,000. Reporting time: 2 months before publication. Payment: negotiable. Copyrighted, reverts if requested. Ads: $75.00/$40.00/$0.15. Discounts: Discounts available on orders of 10 or more to the same address. Back issues: available back issues are $1.50. Pub'd 8 issues 1976; expects 8 issues 1977, 8 issues 1978. Pub's reviews: 40 in 1976. §Magazines, books and recordings which encompass the subjects described above.

TIMEPAD, Carl D. Clark, 3007 University, Austin, TX 78705, 472-7415. Poetry, fiction, articles, art, photos, cartoons, interviews, satire, criticism, reviews, music, letters, parts-of-novels, long-poems, collages, plays, concrete art. "Devoted.'' irreg; price per copy: varies; sample: write us. 1977. 1pp; 11 x 17. of. circ. varies. Reporting time: 1 day. Payment: copy. Copyrighted. Ads: none. Discounts: write us. Pub's reviews.

Times Change Press, Moonlight, Tom Wodetzki, Box 187, Albion, CA 95410. Articles, criticism, non-fiction. "We seek book length ms. which will further fundamental social change and personal growth.'' avg. price, cloth: $9.00; paper: $3.00. 1970. 150pp; 5¼ x 7. of. avg. press run 3,000. Reporting time: 1 month. Payment: some money, not alot. Copyrights for author. Discounts: 40% to retail. Expects 4 titles 1977, 4 titles 1978. COSMEP.

Tino Publications (see ORGAN DIGEST)

TINTAN, Editorial Pocho Che, Alejandro Murguia, PO Box 1959, San Francisco, CA 94101, 415-431-5549. Poetry, fiction, articles, art, photos, cartoons, interviews, satire, criticism, reviews, music, long-poems. "Latin American and Chicano oriented. Recent contributors: Roberto Marquez Fernando Alegria, Victor H. Cruz'' 4/yr; 1-yr sub price: $6.00; per copy: $1.50; sample: $1.50. 1975. 32pp; 11 x 13. of. circ. 2,500. Reporting time: 3-6 months. Copyrighted, reverts to author. Ads: $300.00/$160.00. Discounts: 33 percent trade/33 percent bulk/33 percent agent/33 percent jobber. Back issues: $1.50. Expects 3-4 issues 1977, 4 issues 1978. Pub's reviews. §latin american & chicano art. lit crit. polit. music etc. COSMEP.

TITMOUSE, Titmouse Supernatural, Linda Hoffman, Avron Hoffman, 720 West 19th Ave., Vancouver, B.C., Canada. Poetry, fiction, cartoons, satire, collages. "Dedicated to the hidden treasures of contemporary life; the far-out & the easy-to-read, non sexist & non-racist element of a dwindling counter-culture. Recent contributors, *Nicanor* Parra, *Nicanor* Snyder, *Nicanor* Edson & *Nicanors* Jaffee, Becker, & Cohen." irreg.; sub price: 3 copies $3.00; per copy: $1.00; sample: $1.00. 1939. 53pp; 8½ x 5½. of. circ. 400. Reporting time: varies. Payment: copies. COSMEP.

To The Lighthouse Press (see PROVINCETOWN POETS)

Todd Tarbox Books, Todd Tarbox, Shirley Tarbox, 2523 Ashton Rd., Jackson, MI 49203. "Children & photography." avg. price, cloth: Varies.; paper: Varies.; other: Varies. 1975. pp varies.; Varies. of/lp. avg. press run Varies. Reporting time: 4 weeks on solicited manuscripts. Variety of payment arrangements. Copyright varies. Discounts: Write for details. Pub'd 2 titles 1976; expects 2 titles 1977, 5 titles 1978. Bookbuilders Of Boston.

Tombouctou Books, Michael Wolfe, Box 265, Bolinas, CA 94924, 415-868-0322. Poetry, fiction, criticism, long-poems. "We are publishing four books this year, all perfect bound, in runs of 500 to 1,000. The titles are: *Lewis MacAdams' News From Niman Farm,* 48 pp., $2.50. *Lawrence Kearney's Five,* 72 pp., $3.00 (Illustration by Terry Bell); Duncan McNaughton's, *Sumeriana,* 80 pp., $3.00 (Illust. by Arthur Okamura); Bobbie Hawkins' *Frenchy & Cuban Pete & Other Stories,* 80 pp., $3.50 (Cover by painter)." 1975. 5½ x 8½. †of. avg. press run 500-2,000. No unsolicited manuscripts. Write first. Payment varies. Copyrights for author. Discounts: Query Serendipity Books Distributor. Pub'd 2 titles 1976; expects 4 titles 1977, 4 titles 1978. COSMEP.

Tonatiuh International Inc. (see GRITO DEL SOL)

Toothpaste Press (see also DENTAL FLOSS MAGAZINE), Allan Kornblum, Cinda Kornblum, PO Box 546, 626 E. Main, West Branch, IA 52358, 319-643-2604. Poetry. "1977 titles: Morty Sklar, *The Night We Stood Up For Our Rights* ($4.00/$15.00), Anselm Hollo, *Heavy Jars* ($4.00/$15.00 - July, 1977), Joseph Ceravolo, *Transmigration Solo* (fall, 1977). Due to grant pressures, we're unable to consider new manuscripts until current backlog is taken care of." avg. price, cloth: $15.00; paper: $4.00; other: $2.00. 1970. 35pp; varies. †lp. avg. press run 600. Reporting time: 6-8 weeks. Payment: 10% of copies. Discounts: 1-4 copies, 25 percent; 5 & over, 40 percent (bookstores), libraries & individuals, standing orders 10 percent. Pub'd 5 titles 1976; expects 5 titles 1977, 4 titles 1978. COSMEP.

TOTAL LIFESTYLE- The Bicentennial Magazine of Natural Living, The First Ozark Press, Carey Carpenter, P.O. Box 1137, Harrison, AR 72601. Poetry, articles, cartoons, interviews, reviews, letters. "TOTAL LIFESTYLE is for people seeking the better life...for the homesteader who is already on the land, or those who are searching for ways to get there...with personal contact ads to help our readers find people places and things...articles on self-sufficiency, alternative energy, organic gardening, parents and children, being in tune with God and Nature. Recent articles on Natural Childbirth (twelve part series now running through 1976), Astrology, Herbal Healing, Communities and Families, Spiritual Awareness, Companion Planting for Pest Control, Alternate Energy Sources, How to Find Your Land, How to, Where, and Who With. Practical advice to help people achieve the better life, not pipe dreams. Recipes, poems, and short fillers; 500 to 1500 word articles on how-to, or how-not-to, as one reaches for the better life in the country and in the city. The practical, yet harmonious approach to natural living, is our editorial intent." 12/yr; 1-yr sub price: $12.00; per copy: $1.50; sample: $1.00. 1976. 36-48pp; 7 x 8½. †of. circ. 2,700. Reporting time: 30-60 days. Payment: low to moderate-varies; query first if payment rate is important. Ads: $200/$120/$.05 for indiv. $.20 for commercial. Discounts: write for current policy. Back issues: $2.50 to $1.50, depending on issue. Query w/SASE. Pub's reviews. §energy, ecology, country living, community & family, education (especially alternative education), science, cottage industries, spiritual awareness, those stated, any which fit the principal, yet harmonious approach to Natural Living, catalogs for the homesteader, do-it-yourself projects, alternatives, generally. COSMEP.

TOTTEL'S, Ron Silliman, 3028 California, San Francisco, CA 94115, 415-922-1923. Poetry.

"Our interests are specific: Writing in which language is the center of activity, as such. TOTTEL'S is not 'experimental' in its bias (the most common mistake which would-be contributors make). Almost all of our work is solicited." irreg. 1-3/yr; 1-yr sub price: inquire. 1970. 40pp; 8½ x 11. of. circ. 150-200. Reporting time: Discourage submissions, so we reject them in the return mail. Payment: copies. Not copyrighted. Ads: none. Discounts: none available. Back issues: inquire: most are o.p. §Poetry, art, politics, philosophy, natural sciences. CCLM.

Toucan (see also THOMAS HARDY YEARBOOK), James Stevens-Cox, Gregory Stevens-Cox, Birling Mt. Durand, St Peter Port, Guernsey, Great Britain, 45091. Non-fiction. avg. price, cloth: £6.00; paper: £1.00. 1931. 48pp; A4. †Various. avg. press run 1,000. Payment: By arrangement. Pub'd 42 titles 1976; expects 25 titles 1977, 25 titles 1978.

TOUCHSTONE, Houston Writers Workshop, Guida Jackson, Managing Editor, Drawer 42331, Houston, TX 77042. Poetry, fiction, articles, art, photos, cartoons, interviews, satire, criticism, reviews, music, letters, non-fiction. "Special Haiku section; other poetry length to 18 lines-prose limited to 1,500 words. Touchstone explores one social issue each quarter but espouses no particular causes, grinds no axes." 4/yr; 1-yr sub price: $6.00; per copy: $1.50; sample: $1.50. 1976. 32pp; 8½ x 11. of. circ. 1,000. Reporting time: 6 weeks. Payment: copies only-one cash award each quarter. Discounts: 45 percent-20 or more copies. Back issues: $1.50. Pub'd 3 issues 1976; expects 4 issues 1977, 4 issues 1978. Pub's reviews. §poetry/fiction/social reform.

Toulouse Press, Sylvia Hikins, 14 Harringay Ave, Liverpool, England L18 1JE, United Kingdom. Poetry, articles, cartoons, satire. "The press is affiliated to the Merseyside Arts Association. It publishes poetry books and booklets. Its aim is to publish high quality books at the lowest possible price." avg. price, paper: $2.00. 1972. 60pp; 6 x 8½. avg. press run 500. Payment: negotiable. Copyrights for author. Discounts: 1/3 retailers. Pub'd 2 titles 1976; expects 3 titles 1977, 1 title 1978. ALP.

TOWARD REVOLUTIONARY ART (TRA), TRA, Eli Shul, John Levin, Dan Cassidy, Fernando Barreiro, Ernie Brill, Ingrid Badenburg, P.O. Box 40909, San Francisco, CA 94140. Poetry, fiction, articles, art, photos, cartoons, interviews, satire, criticism, reviews, music, letters, parts-of-novels, long-poems, collages, plays. 4/yr; 1-yr sub price: $5.00; per copy: $1.25; sample: $1.25. 1973. 48pp; 8½ x 11. of. circ. 5,000. Reporting time: 2 months. Payment: occasional honorariums. Discounts: 5-10 30% 10-up 40%. Back issues: $2.00. Pub's reviews. §culture. CCLM, COSMEP.

THE TOWN FORUM JOURNAL & COMMUNITY REPORT, The Town Forum, Inc., Christopher Canfield, Cerro Gordo Ranch, Dorena Lake, Cottage Grove, OR 97424, 503-942-7720. Articles, art, photos, interviews, reviews, letters, news items, non-fiction. 4/yr; 1-yr sub price: $8.00; per copy: $2.00; sample: $2.00. 1972. 60pp; 8½ x 11. of. circ. 5,000. Reporting time: 30 days. Payment: negotiable. Copyrighted. Ads: $100.00/$50.00/$0.10. Back issues: series 1 (4 books)-$6.00; series 2 (4 books)-$8.00. Pub'd 2 issues 1976; expects 4 issues 1977, 4 issues 1978. Pub's reviews. §communities/ecology.

THE TOY SUN, SPC Press, Laura Djalezni, Box 306, 102 Charles St, Boston, MA 02114. Poetry, photos, cartoons, satire, criticism, reviews, music, letters, collages, concrete art. "Eccentric, experimental, topical prose, poems, visuals. All manifestos." 3/yr; 1-yr sub price: $5.00; per copy: $0.25; sample: $0.25. 1976. 12pp; 11½ x 16¼. of. circ. 2,000. Reporting time: 1 month. Payment: none. Not copyrighted. Ads: $20.00/$10.00/$0.20. Discounts: none. Pub's reviews. §Political, experimental.

TRA (see TOWARD REVOLUTIONARY ART)

TRACKS, A Journal of Artists' Writings, Herbert George, P.O. Box 557, Old Chelsea Station, New York, NY 10011. "TRACKS is intended to serve as a forum for artists of all persuasions, serving primarily as an open-space an area in which individual or fashionable ideologies are surrendered to the general interests of the art community. First, it provides a medium for writings normally ignored in the scheduling of catalogues and the general art media. Its format insures that these works are presented as *artists'* writings, immune from editorial alteration or comment. Also, the magazine can admit a wide variety of material, from the most theoretical of texts to journal entries and letters. Foreign texts have been, and will continue to be, translated so that they will be increasingly accessible to artists and writers who speak only English. Finally, although TRACKS aims to present issues current in the art community, it is anticipated that the simultaneous publication of contemporary and historic texts will prevent it from becoming an homage to purely temporal concerns." 3/yr; 1-yr sub price: $5.50; per copy: $2.00; sample: $2.00. 1974. 75pp; 9 x 5¾. of. circ. 1,400. Reporting time: 2-3 months. Payment: none. Discounts: even trade with other magazines, 40% discount on orders of 10 or more, all other regular price. Back Issues: Volume I #1 is out of print and costs $6.00 for those that are available. CCLM.

Trans-Anglo Books, Spencer Crump, Editorial Director, P.O. Box 38, Corona del Mar, CA 92625. 1962.

Trans-Oceanic Trouser Press, Inc. (see TROUSER PRESS)

TRANSFORMACTION, John Lyle, Harpford, Sidmouth, Devon EX10 0NH, United Kingdom. Articles, poetry, art, cartoons, photos, reviews, interviews, criticism, letters, plays, collages. "Material commissioned from adherents of international surrealist movement only." irreg.; price per copy: 75p; sample: 75p. 1967. 36pp; A5. †of. Payment: none. Ads: none. Pub'd 1 issue 1976; expects 2 issues 1977. Pub's reviews. §Surrealism, painting, writing, cinema, dada.

TRANSIENCE QUARTERLY, Guild of Alternative Artists, Von D'Van, 19731 Forrer, Detroit, MI 48235, 313-272-3128. Poetry, fiction, articles, art, photos, cartoons, reviews, music, letters, satire, collages, non-fiction. "Page long or 2 pages—original complementary illustrations and artwork, interested in imaginative literature, black & white photos, hand calligraphy copy ready, based on changing themes, madness as liberation, roadlife, minds, write for projected themes or suggest one—" 4/yr; 1-yr sub price: $6.00; per copy: $2.00; sample: $2.00. 1976. 40pp; 8½ x 11. of. circ. 2,000. Reporting time: 30 days. Payment: App. $20.00/page. Copyrighted, reverts to author. Ads: None. Discounts: Schools $1.30/copy; wholesale $1.20/copy (10); distributors $1.00/copy (10). Back issues: None. Expects 4 issues 1977, 4 issues 1978. Pub's reviews. §Original artwork, non-commercial, visionary, prophetic, resources for counter-culture. GAA.

THE TRANSIENT, The Transientpress (TRANSKEN), Ken Saville, Felix Farm, Country Music Editor, Box 4662, Albuquerque, NM 87106. "We've evolved into an occasional publication made up of various bits of assorted words and visuals. Much of the transient is hand assembled and each copy is different. Do not send submissions! The work we use is solicited from the transnational postal exchange art lunacy circuit, or from locals. To see what we're doing send a handmade postcard. Recent contributors: Carl Johansen, Chuck Stake, John M. Bennett, Felix Farm, Henn Haus, Sallye Forth." irreg.; 1-yr sub price: $3.00; per copy: varies; sample: $1.00 plus postage. 1973. 8pp; varies. of. circ. 200. Reporting time: 2 weeks. Payment: copies. Copyright reverts to author on publication. Ads: none. Discounts: none. Back issues: send for publication checklist. Pub'd 1 issue 1976; expects 2 issues 1977, 3 issues 1978. §experimental, avant-garde, dada, country music.

TRANSLATION, Robert Payne, William Jay Smith, Frank MacShane, Dallas Galvin, Managing Editor, 307A Mathematics, Columbia University, New York, NY 10027, 212-280-2305. Poetry. "Interested in literary translations-fiction or poetry-articles about translations. We often publish excerpts before book publication. Especially interested in less well known languages from Asia and Africa. Contributors to most recent issue include: Burton Watson, Robert Bly, Tomas Transtromer, Donald Keene, W.S. Merwin, Hori Tatsuo, Gunnar Ekelof, Robert Payne." 2/yr plus newsletters; 1-yr sub price: $6.00; per copy: $4.00; sample: $4.00. 1973. 120pp; 9 x 6. lp. circ. 2,500 plus. Reporting time: 3 months. Payment: small. Copyrighted. Ads: $100.00/$50.00. Discounts: none. Pub'd 1 issue 1976; expects 2 issues 1977, 2 issues 1978. CCLM.

The Trauma Works (see THE ILLUSTRATED ORB)

Traumwald Press, Helen Bugbee, Suite 10, 3550 Lake Shore Drive, Chicago, IL 60657. COSMEP.

Treacle Press, Bruce R. McPherson, 4615 Cedar Ave., Philadelphia, PA 19143. Poetry, fiction, art. "Books published: *Shamp Of The City-Solo* by Jaimy Gordon; *Realignment* by Clayton Eshleman; *Poem From Memory* by Keith Waldrop (book); *Love Is Weal, Love Is Woe* by Jaimy Gordon (broadside). The Treacle Story Series: *A Movie Starring the Late Cary Grant and an As-yet Unsigned Actress* by Tom Ahern, *Smithsong* by Michael Brondoli, *The Sex Token* by James Shreeve, *Wind Scales* by Keith Waldrop, *Volume One* (Nos: 1-4). No unsolicited mss." avg. price, cloth: $8.00; paper: $3.00. 1973. 50-150pp; varies. of/lp/silkscreen. avg. press run 1,000. Reporting time: 2 weeks-2 months. Payment: royalties and copies. Copyrights for author. Discounts: 40 percent to the trade for 5 or more assorted. Pub'd 5 titles 1976; expects 5 titles 1977, 5 titles 1978. COSMEP, NESPA, CRISP.

TREE, Tree Books, David Meltzer, P.O. Box 9005, Berkeley, CA 94709. Poetry, articles. "Each issue utilizes works which adhere to specific themes. #6: Messiah; #7: Golem; #8: Angel." 2/yr; 1-yr sub price: $8.00; per copy: $4.00. 1970. 180pp. of. circ. 1,100. Reporting time: 2 wks - 1 mo. Payment: copies only. CCLM.

Tree Frog Press, Allan Shute, 10717 106th Avenue, Edmonton, Alberta T5H3Y9, Canada, 403-425-1505. Fiction. "Children's literature. Mostly interested in Western Canadian authors." avg. price, cloth: $4.95; paper: $2.95. 1971. 64pp; Varies. †of. avg. press run 3,000. Reporting time: 6 weeks. Copyrights for author. Discounts: 40 percent (bulk negotiable). APA, ACP.

TREES, Arbor, Joan Dibble Shambaugh, Old Winter St, Lincoln, MA 01773. Poetry, fiction, art. "Use material in the nature of the title" 1/yr; price per copy: $1.50; sample: $1.50. 1975. 6 x 8. of. circ. 250. Payment: copies. Copyrighted. Pub'd 1 issue 1976.

Trent University (see JOURNAL OF CANADIAN STUDIES)

Tribal Press (see MEASURE)

Trike, David Christopher Arnold, Keith Shein, P.O. Box 732, Pismo Beach, CA 93449. Poetry, fiction, art, photos, long-poems, collages, concrete art. avg. price, paper: $4.00. 1976. pp varies; varies. of/lp. avg. press run 500. Does not copyright for author. Pub'd 2 titles 1976. CCLM, COSMEP, LPS.

Trinity Press (see QUOZ?)

TRIQUARTERLY, Elliott Anderson, Editor; Mary Kinzie, Exec. Editor, University Hall 101, North West Univ., Evanston, IL 60201, 312-492-3490. 3/yr; 1-yr sub price: $12.00. 1964. 256pp; 6 x 9. Payment varies. CCLM.

TRIVIUM, University Of Wales Press, Rhys S. Jones, Dept. Of French, St. David's University College, Lampeter, Dyfed SA48 7ED, United Kingdom. Articles, reviews, criticism. "Articles: av. length - 5,000 words. Book reviews: av. length - 500 words. Bias: towards the humanitess." 1/yr; 1-yr sub price: £2 individuals; £3 institutions. 1966. 160pp; 9 x 6. lp/of. circ. 300. Reporting time: 3-4 weeks. Payment: None. Copyright vested in editor of TRIVIUM. Back issues: Vols. 1-10 £2 individuals, £3 institutions. Pub'd 1 issue 1976; expects 1 issue 1977, 1 issue 1978. Pub's reviews: 21 in 1976.

TROUSER PRESS, Trans-Oceanic Trouser Press, Inc., Ira A. Robbins, Editor-in-Chief; Dave Schulps, Mag. Ed.; Jim Green, Assoc. Ed., 147 W. 42nd St, New York, NY 10036, 212-354-4376. Articles, photos, interviews, criticism, reviews, music, letters, non-fiction. "Biased against American rock music in favor of British rock music. Articles run 5,000-8,000 words. Reviews 300-600." 10/yr; 1-yr sub price: $10.00; per copy: $1.25; sample: $1.25. 1974. 48pp; 8½ x 11. of. circ. 10,000. Reporting time: 1 month. Payment: $25-50 for features. Copyrighted. Ads: $300.00/$175.00/$0.30. Discounts: sold for 70 percent of cover on orders over 10 copies. Back issues: No. 9-$3.00/No. 13-$5.00 remainder available (No. 14-20) are $1.00 ea. Pub'd 6 issues 1976; expects 7 issues 1977, 10 issues 1978. Pub's reviews: 50 in 1976. §rock music, pop culture.

Trouser Press (see ANAESTHESIA REVIEW)

TRUCHA, Trucha Publications, Inc., Josie Mora, Box 5223, Lubbock, TX 79417. Poetry, fiction, articles, art, photos, cartoons, interviews, satire, criticism, reviews, music, letters, collages, plays. "Bilingual, bicultural (Spanish-English) literature, art & expression for young & old. Chicano & Third World" 4/yr; 1-yr sub price: $5.00; per copy: $2.00; sample: $2.00. 1971. 30pp; 6 x 9. †of. circ. 5,000. Reporting time: 2 wks. Ads: $250/$150/none. Discounts: 30% on trade or bulk. Back issues: not available. Pub's reviews. §Chicano/Third World/bilingual/bicultural. CPA (Chicano Press Association).

TRUCK, Truck Press, David Wilk, 1141 James Ave, St Paul, MN 55105. Poetry, fiction, articles, art, photos, cartoons, criticism, letters, parts-of-novels, long-poems, collages, concrete art. "Request enquiry before submission, am mostly not interested in poetry-as-beautiful-words am truly tired of receiving unsolicited manuscripts from people who have never read the magazine. All biases are those of the editor only, this a one person show-the only standards I can think of have to do with what I like or not, but experience shows that I like poems that say something about the world and not just the poet moaning about life boring boring & terrible. See Charles Olson for details, also Duncan, Zukofsky, & Creeley. Recent contributors have included Paul Metcalf, Jonathan Williams, Richard Grossinger, Laura Chester, Jane Augustine, Jayne Anne Phillips, Bill Corbett, Lorine Niedecker, Daphne Marlatt, Bob Bertholf, George Quasha, Robert Kelly, Clayton Eshleman, and many others you haven't heard of yet. Natural history, the nature of nature, the poet engaged in active exploration of the universe, all that good stuff. Lately I am cranky about all sorts of publisher's complaints which I will gladly relieve myself of at the drop of a hat." 2-3/yr; sub price: $7.50/3 issues/$15.00 overseas/sub runs by no. not by calendar year.; per copy: $3.00; sample: $3.00. 1970. 220pp; 6 x 9. of. circ. 600-1,000. Reporting time: indefinite. Payment: copies only except when have grants. Copyrighted in name of editor but for contributors. Discounts: bulk (25 or more of any one thing)-50% otherwise standard trade discount agent/agency subscriptions 20% single copies 10%. Back issues: Back issues: 1-10 are rare, $5.00 each or $40.00 the set 11-17 at cover price also the complete set, current (thru No. 17) $60.00. No. 16 now op-$10.00. Pub'd 1 issue 1976; expects 2 issues 1977, 2 issues 1978. CCLM, COSMEP, NESPA.

Truck Press (see also TRUCK), David Wilk, Editor & Publisher, 1141 James Ave, St Paul, MN 55105. "Four books in '76: *Houses* by Jonis Agee, *Place I-XXXVII* by Allen Fisher, *Sweethearts* by Jayne Anne Phillips and William Bronk, *An Essay* by Cid Corman. So far in 1977, *Graphite* by Linda Parker, *Untinears And Antennae for Maurice Ravel* by Jonathan Williams, *Living By The Sword* by Felton Eaddy and *Tree Taking Root* by David Wilk. Later in the year, books by Michael McClure, Robert Ferguson, Lindy Hough, Becky Newth and others. All books are distributed thru Serendipity Books Distribution, 1790 Shattuck Ave., Berkeley, Ca 94709; please direct all orders and catalog requests to them. Unsolicited manuscripts will not be accepted as there is simply no time to read them all; please inquire first, brief description or outline is helpful. Same biases of taste as for the magazine. No moaners and groaners please. Latest (ad)venture is *Aquila Rose*, a chapbook series one may subscribe to; each issue features the work of one person. $1.50 each or $6.00 for six issues." 1975. †of/lp. avg. press run 600. Reporting time: indefinite. Payment: copies & cash negotiable. Discounts: Query distributor. Pub'd 4 titles 1976; expects 6 titles 1977 8 titles 1978.

TRULY FINE PRESS, A Review, Truly Fine Press, Jerry Madson, P.O. Box 891, Bemidji, MN 56601. Poetry, reviews, fiction. "Mode is avant-garde. Have published Jon Miller, John Judson, James Magorian to name a few. Plus review of Bukowski." irreg.; 1-yr sub price: $4.00; per copy: $1.00; sample: Free. 1976. †mi. Reporting time: 2-4 weeks. Payment: 3 copies. Not copyrighted. §small press works.

Truly Fine Press (see also TRULY FINE PRESS, A Review), Jerry Madson, P.O. Box 891, Bemidji, MN 56601. Poetry, fiction. "Truly Fine Press has in the past published a pamphlet series. And also published Minnesota's first tabloid novel." avg. price, cloth: Varies; paper: Varies; other: Varies. 1973. Varies. †mi/of/lp. avg. press run Varies. Reporting time: 2-4 weeks. Payment: 3 copies. Copyrights for author. Pub'd 5 titles 1976.

Trunk Press, Judson Jerome, Hancock, MD 21750, 717-294-3345. Poetry, fiction, satire, long-poems, plays, non-fiction. "Author pays printing costs, owns all copies. Only take books about which we have personal enthusiasm." avg. price, cloth: $6.00; paper: $2.00. 1976. 20-200pp; 5½ x 8½. of. avg. press run 500-1,000. Reporting time: 2 wks. Payment: author gets all, except 50 percent of sales through mail order distribution. Copyright by *Trunk Press*. Pub'd 6 titles 1976; expects 10 titles 1977. COSMEP.

TSA'ASZI', William L. Rada, Lonna Lawrence, Advisors, Box 356, Ramah, NM 87321. Poetry, fiction, articles, art, photos, cartoons, interviews, satire, criticism, reviews, music, letters, parts-of-novels, long-poems, plays. "This magazine is produced by Navajo high school students about Navajo culture. Materials must be relevant to Navajo culture and preferably student produced." 4/yr; 1-yr sub price: $7.00; per copy: $2.00; sample: $2.00. 1971. 65pp; 7 x 10. of. circ. 1,200. Discounts: 25% of single issues to dealers. §Navajo culture.

TUGBOAT, Frick and Friends, Arthur J.F. Frick, Gen. Ed.; Carole Collier, Music Ed.; Billy Dwyer, Art Ed.; John Linthicum, Poetry Ed.; Ted Melnechuk, Science Ed., Box 15234, San Diego, CA 92115. Poetry, fiction, articles, art, photos, cartoons, interviews, satire, criticism, reviews, music, letters, parts-of-novels, long-poems, collages, plays, concrete art. "TUGBOAT is an interdisciplinary publication based on the premise that fields of thought are not simply exclusive from each other and that their publication together may provide access to stimulating exchange. TUGBOAT wishes to provide the reader with a variety of ideas in art, literature, science, music, philosophy and human concerns. TUGBOAT'S objective is to be an effective international tool for keeping contact with developments in diverse fields, enabling the reader to experience both actual work and expository discussion about what is currently going on. Recent contributors: John Baldessari, Jacob Bronowski, Newton & Helen Harrison, Richard Kostelanetz, Pauline Oliveros, Roger Reynolds, Harry Partch." 4/yr; 1-yr sub price: $15.00; per copy: $3.00; sample: $3.00. 1975. 40-48pp; 8½ x 11. of. circ. 1,000. Reporting time: 2-8 weeks. Payment: none. Ads: $100/$50/none. Discounts: none. Back issues: same as present issues.

‡**Tundra Books Of Northern New York,** M. Engelhart, 18 Cornelia St., P.O. Box 1030, Plattsburg, NY 12901.

‡**Turkey Press,** Harry E. Reese, 34 Fort Ave., Cranston, RI 02905.

Turtle Island Foundation (see NEW WORLD JOURNAL)

TUUMBA, Tuumba Press, Lyn Hejinian, 2639 Russell Street, Berkeley, CA 94705. Poetry, fiction, articles, interviews, letters, parts-of-novels, long-poems, plays. "Each issue will be devoted to the work of one writer or the written work of one artist; this may include fiction, poetry, essays, interviews, statements, and manifestoes. As to style and bias, I hope they are inclusive rather than exclusive. Contributors in 1976 include: Barbara Baracks, Susan Howe, John Woodall, T.R. Uthco, Lyn Hejinian, Barry Eisenberg, and Kenneth Irby." 6/yr; 1-yr sub price: $6.00; per copy: $2.00; sample: $2.00. 1976. 20pp; 6 x 9. †lp. circ. 100-400. Reporting time: immediate. Payment: 25 copies. Copyrights for author. Ads: none. Discounts: usual to stores & distributors. Back issues: $2.00. Pub'd 10 issues 1976; expects 6 issues 1977, 6 issues 1978. COSMEP.

TUVOTI Books (see THE UNSPEAKABLE VISIONS OF THE INDIVIDUAL)

Tvrt Press-Viper's Tongue Books, Ted Castle, Leandro Katz, 25 East Fourth Street, New York, NY 10003. "We publish rare works of art and literature. No unsolicited material is considered." 1970. of. Discounts: trade discount 40% if more than $25 retail value is ordered.

TWELFTH KEY, Applegarth Follies, Penny Chalmers, Box 40, Stn. B, London, Ontario N6A4V3, Canada, 519-432-6137. Poetry. "Each issue is thematic: please write for a flyer. Only unpublished work, please." 3/yr; 1-yr sub price: $9.00; per copy: $3.50; sample: $3.50. 1976. 90pp; 5 x 8. †of. circ. 500. Reporting time: 14 days. Payment: one copy of the issue concerned. Copyrighted, reverts to author. Ads: none. Discounts: see Applegarth Follies. Expects 3 issues 1977, 3 issues 1978.

1250 Press (see also ANDROGYNE), Ken Weichel, 930 Shields, San Francisco, CA 94132, 586-2697. Poetry, fiction, articles, art, photos, criticism, collages, plays. avg. price, cloth: $1.00-$4.00. 1971. †of. avg. press run 500 copies. Reporting time: 3 weeks. Copyrights for author. COSMEP, COSMEP-WEST.

23 CLUB SERIES, Intrepid Press, Allen DeLoach, P.O. Box 1423, Buffalo, NY 14214. "Experimental prose." irreg. 1971. 8½ x 11. of. By request. Payment: copies only. no ads. Discounts: none. Back issues: Available. COSMEP.

TWIGS, Appalachian Studies Center, Pikeville College Press, Dr. Leonard Roberts, Dr. Harold Branam, Sandy Branam, Art, College Box 2, Pikeville, KY 41501, 432-3161. Poetry, fiction, articles, interviews, criticism, parts-of-novels. "Poetry-40 lines; stories-3,000 words; No biases. Guy Owen, David Axelrod, Emilie Glen, Irene Wanner, James Stuart." 2-3/yr; 1-yr sub price: $5.00; per copy: $2.50; sample: $1.50. 1965. 100-120pp; 5 x 8. of. circ. under 500. Reporting time: 6 weeks. Payment: copies, awards of $25.00. Copyrighted, reverts on request. Ads: none. Discounts: Contributors-50 percent—jobbers-20 percent—sub services-20 percent. Back issues: as issued, varies from $1.00 to $5.00. CCLM, COSMEP.

Twin Oaks Community (see LEAVES OF TWIN OAKS)

Two-Eighteen Press, Tom Johnson, P. O. Box 218 Village Station, New York City, NY 10014, 212-255-1723. "So far just a one-man show." avg. price, paper: $4.00. 1974. 100pp. of. avg. press run 1,000. Reporting time: 1 week. Does not copyright for author. Discounts: Dealers 40 percent, distributors 50 percent.

TWO HANDS NEWS, B. Madden, 1125 Webster, Chicago, IL 60614. "News of the poetry scene in Chicago. Reviews of readings & books, listing of all area readings." 9/yr; 1-yr sub price: Free or $4.00 first-class mail subscr. 1976. 4-8pp; 11 x 8. of. circ. 1,000. §poetry only.

TWO SCORE OR LESS FOR WORDS, The Yellow Chicken Press, Lawrence Skinner, Production Coordinator, P.O. Box 1146, Las Vegas, NV 89101. "Only one restriction: Must not exceed forty, 60 space, lines. Can be camera ready copy for 5 wide, 7½ deep, area. Photos with words considered." 4/yr; 1-yr sub price: $9.00; per copy: $3.00; sample: $3.00. 1976. 80pp; 5½ x 8½. of. circ. 500. Reporting time: 1 week. Payment: Contributor copy. no ads. COSMEP, Western World Haiku Scoiety.

Twowindows Press, Don Gray, 2644 Fulton St., Berkeley, CA 94704. Poetry, fiction, art, parts-of-novels, poetry. "We tend to do small but well made books. Ms should run 12-20 pp. in book form. Style and content open." 1967. 32pp. †lp. Reporting time: varies. Payment: 10% of edition.

Tyndall Creek Press, David Beecher, 17 Ashford St., Allston, MA 02134. Poetry. "'Publishers of good contemporary poets in quality paperbacks' now, with a list of three books, we are currently doing a book by Peter F. Neumeyer, HOMAGE TO JOHN CLARE. Submissions are welcome." 1971. 68pp; 5½ x 8. of. Reporting time: 1 month. Payment: free copies. Discounts: 40% off to wholesalers 50% in volume or frequency.

TYPEWRITER, Bird in the Bush, R. Thomas Caldwell, P.O. Box 409, Iowa City, IA 52240. Poetry. "Visual-spatial-graphic representation of language. Bob Cobbing, Hugh Fox, Michael Gibbs, Karl Kempton, Richard Kostelanetz, Peter Mayer, Maurizio Nannucci, Ruth Rehfeldt, Jiri Valoch." 1/yr; 1-yr sub price: $1.00; per copy: $1.00; sample: $1.00. 1971. 35pp. of/lp. circ. 300. Reporting time: 1 wk-1 year. Payment: in copies. Discounts: 10-15%. CCLM.

TZADDIKIM, Judaic Book Service, Steven L. Maimes, 3726 Virden Avenue, Oakland, CA 94619. Art, criticism, reviews, poetry, photos. "TZADDIKIM is a catalogue-bibliography of specialized Judaic books. TZADDIKIM REVIEW contains book reviews and book notes. We sell, distribute and publish Jewish Books. All books are available by mail order." 2/yr; 1-yr sub price: $2.00; per copy: varies; sample: $.25. 1972. 24pp; 8½ x 5½. of. circ. 4,000. Reporting time: 2

weeks. Payment: copies/books. Copyrighted. Ads: Inquire for rates. Discounts: Free to libraries, trade $0.50 each. Back issues: $0.25. Pub'd 2 issues 1976; expects 2 issues 1977, 2 issues 1978. Pub's reviews: 80 in 1976. §Jewish books/Jewish mysticism/poetry/new age/folklore. CCLM, COSMEP.

U.S. Institute for Theatre Technology, Inc. (see THEATRE DESIGN AND TECHNOLOGY)

USITT NEWSLETTER, Herb Greggs, 1501 Broadway, Room 1408, New York, NY 10036, 212-354-5360. Articles, art, cartoons, interviews, reviews, letters, news items. 1961. 20pp; 8½ x 11. of. circ. 3,000. Reporting time: 2 weeks. Not copyrighted. Expects 5 issues 1977, 5 issues 1978.

US1 WORKSHEETS, US1 Poets' Cooperative, Rotating panel, 21 Lake Drive, Roosevelt, NJ 08555, 609-448-5096. Poetry, fiction, articles, art, photos, cartoons, interviews, satire, music, parts-of-novels, long-poems. "Fiction should not be over 15 double-spaced pages. Poetry must be shorter than book length. A wide range of tastes represented in the rotating panel of editors. No restriction on subject or point of view. We read unsolicited mss., but accept very few." 2-3/yr; sub price: $4.00 (10 issues); per copy: $0.50; sample: $0.50. 1973. 12pp; 11 x 17½. of. circ. 1,000. Reporting time: 1 week to 4 months. Payment: 2 copies. Copyrighted, reverts to author. Discounts: inquire. Back issues: Inquire. No. 1 and No. 2 have become quite rare. Pub'd 3 issues 1976; expects 3 issues 1977, 3 issues 1978. Pub's reviews. §contemporary poetry and fiction. CCLM, COSMEP

UGLY DUCKLING, Urban Refugee Press, Keith Richmond, Susan Jane March, 23 Hazlemere Rd, Penn, High Wycombe, Bucks HP108AD, United Kingdom, Penn (049481) 3629. Poetry, fiction, articles, art, cartoons, criticism, reviews, letters, news items. "We see *UGLY DUCKLING* as a centre for discussion. We don't intend to exclude any topics, points of view, or types of poetry, or to limit the horizons of *UGLY DUCKLING* in any way. We publish the best work of the established small press poets alongside many new poets-we do everything to encourage new poets, for they represent the future." 3/yr; sub price: 75 pence for 3 issues; per copy: 26½ pence [20p for UD; 6½p for post]; sample: 26½ pence [20p for UD; 6½p for post]. 1975. 20 pp [plus 12 pp letters/discussion supplement]; 6 x 8½. of. circ. 180. Reporting time: 3 days. Payment: none. The magazine as a collection is copyright Keith Richmond/Urban Refugee Press. Individual contributors retain copyright over their individual contributions. Ads: $4.00/$2.00/not applicable. Discounts: one-third discount on five copies i.e., 90 pence for five [instead of £1.32½ p]. Back issues: 15 pence/30 cents per issue. Pub'd 3 issues 1976; expects 3 issues 1977. Pub's reviews: 62 in 1976. §any underground/alternative magazine [poetry/fiction/art/music/politics/comics].

THE U*N*A*B*A*S*H*E*D LIBRARIAN, THE "HOW I RUN MY LIBRARY GOOD" LETTER, Marvin H. Scilken, Editor; Mary P. Scilken, Assoc. Editor, G.P.O. Box 2631, New York, NY 10001. Articles, cartoons, satire, criticism, reviews. "U*L seeks long (and especially short) articles on innovative procedures; forms used in libraries. Articles should be complete to enable the reader to 'do it' with little or no research. Single paragraph 'articles' are ok with U*L." 4/yr; 1-yr sub price: $10.00; per copy: $2.50 foreign postage add 10% including Canada. 1971. 32pp; 8½ x 11. of. No payment. Back issues: (all are in print) are $2.50 each add 10 percent foreign including Canada postage. Expects 4 issues 1977, 4 issues 1978. Pub's reviews. §library subjects only.

UNAKA RANGE, Rt. 1-Box 58A, Bryson City, NC 28713. Poetry, fiction, long-poems. "emphasizes review by excerpt" 4-6/yr. 1976. 10-12pp; 9½ x 11. of. circ. 1,200. Payment: copies. Not copyrighted. Pub's reviews. §poetry, fiction, non-fiction prose.

Undena Publications, Giorgio Buccellati, P.O. Box 97, Malibu, CA 90265. 1974. 8½ x 11. of.

Under Dorset Skies (see DORSET POETS SOCIETY)

UNDER THE SIGN OF PISCES: Anais Nin and Her Circle, The Ohio State University Libraries Publications Committee, Richard R. Centing, 1858 Neil Avenue Mall, Columbus, OH 43210. Articles, photos, interviews, criticism, reviews. "Want biographical and bibliographic articles about Anais Nin and her circle (Henry Miller, *et al*). Studies on the art of diary keeping. Length of material limit: ten pages double-spaced. Style: informal or MLA- take your pick. Note: make checks for subscriptions payable to: The Ohio State University Libraries Publications Committee." 4/yr; 1-yr sub price: $5.00 a year, 1977.; per copy: $2.00. 1970. 16pp; 5½ x 8½. of. circ. 400. Reporting time: 2 weeks. Payment: one copy. Ads: $20/$10. Back issues: Back issues: all back issues in print at $3.50 a volume (1970-1976). Pub'd 4 issues 1976; expects 4 issues 1977, 4 issues 1978. Pub's reviews. §books about autobiography/modern women writers/anything on Henry Miller and Lawrence Durrell/Nin's circle or times.

UNDERCURRENTS, Undercurrents Ltd., 27 Clerkenwell Close, London EC10AT, England. Articles, cartoons, reviews, letters. 6/yr; 1-yr sub price: $7.50; per copy: $1.25; sample: back nos. free. 1972. 48pp; A4. of. circ. 10,000. Payment: nil. Copyrighted. Ads: $85.00/$41.00. Discounts: terms supplied on request. Pub'd 6 issues 1976; expects 6 issues 1977, 6 issues 1978. Pub's reviews. §science & politics.

UNDERTOW, Brown Miller, 50 Phelan Ave, San Francisco, CA 94112, 415-239-3141. Poetry, fiction, articles, art, photos, cartoons, interviews, satire, collages, plays. "Emphasis on poetry, the very highest quality being written. Prose should not exceed 2,500 words. Welcome all styles and content, unknown as well as previously published writers." 1/yr; sub price: Copies free to anyone who sends a self-addressed 9 x 12 envelope plus 26 cents postage. 1977. 60pp; 8½ x 11. of. circ. 1,500. Reporting time: 2 weeks to 2 months. Payment: 2 copies. Copyrighted, reverts to author. Ads: Query. Discounts: Query.

UNDINE, Renaissance Press, Michael McKenzie, Ilmars Pureng, 244 Fifth Ave., New York, NY 10001. Poetry, fiction, art. "Mag is printed entirely in calligraphy. Recent contributors include : Harvey Shapiro, Hollander, Malanga, Kostelanetz, Ignatow, and Halpern." 2/yr; sub price: $10.00/4 issues; per copy: $3.00; sample: $2.50. 1974. 125pp; 6 x 8. of. circ. 1,000. Reporting time: varies. Payment: copies.

UNEXPECTED, Otherworlds Media, Nadra Ballentine, Jene Ballentine, 1394 Frank St., Honolulu, HI 96816. Poetry, fiction, art, photos, parts-of-novels, long-poems, plays. "Heavy on the surreal, the bizarre, the tragi-comic. No length requirements or limits." 2/yr; 1-yr sub price: $8.00; per copy: $4.00. 1974. 100pp; 7 x 8½. of. circ. 1M. Reporting time: 2 mos. Ads: $100/$60. Discounts: 40%. Back issues: $.50 ea.

UNICORN: A Miscellaneous Journal, Karen Rockow, Editor; Stuart Silverman, Assoc. Editor, 345 Harvard St. 3B, Cambridge, MA 02138, 617-354-0124. Poetry, fiction, articles, cartoons, interviews, satire, criticism, reviews, letters, collages, concrete art. "We are looking for all types of material, particularly lively articles and reviews (serious and whimsical) on all topics. We are using very little poetry and fiction these days, and reading it very slowly. We're swamped. We favor well-written pieces on the more off-beat and fun aspects of popular culture, folklore and literature; use MLA style for any footnotes. Please-no intellectualese, studied incomprehensibility or pomposity, we pay $10.00 for front covers; $5.00 for back covers. Summer: Box 118, Salisbury, VT. 05769, 802-352-4236." irreg.; 1-yr sub price: $2.50/$3.50 libraries/$4.50 overseas; per copy: $1.00/$1.50 libraries. 1967. 28-32pp; 8½ x 11. of. circ. 700. Reporting time: 2-4 wks (summers & poetry/short stories longer). Payment: $5 honararium for essays plus copies & off prints. Ads: Query. Discounts: 35% on 10 or more. Back issues: All in print at single issue prices. Pub'd 1 issue 1976; expects 2 issues 1977, 2-3 issues 1978. Pub's reviews: 14 in 1976. §popular culture, folklore, gardening, progressive education, childrens lit. CCLM, COSMEP.

UNICORN, Mike Reis, Editor-in-Chief; Vicki Aversa, Associate Editor; D. R. Belz, Associate Editor; Bob Farmer, Associate Editor; Mike Schultz, Associate Editor, 4501 North Charles Street, Baltimore, MD 21210, 301-323-1010. Poetry, fiction, art, photos. "Fiction no longer than 10 double-spaced typed pages. Recent contributors: Phillip McCaffrey, Paul Lake, Bruce Guernsey,

James Reiss, Devy Bendit, Jesse Glass, Jr., Dyanne Fancey, Linda Pastan. No taboos, except submissions of poor quality." 4/yr; 1-yr sub price: $4.00; per copy: $1.00; sample: $1.00. 1975. 28pp; 5½ x 8½. mi/of. circ. 1,200. Reporting time: 8-10 weeks, longer in summer months. Payment in copies (three). Copyrighted, reverts to author. Discounts: none. Back issues: back issues available-what we have on hand, at $0.75 per copy. Pub'd 4 issues 1976; expects 4 issues 1977, 4 issues 1978. Pub's reviews. §Poetry and fiction. CCLM, COSMEP, Pen Prison Writers Project.

UNICORN JOURNAL, Unicorn Press, Teo Savory, P.O. Box 3307, Greensboro, NC 27402. "We have no plans for issuing another Journal before at *least* two years from now. But the Journal has existed, still sells. Only we do not accept any unsolicited MSS." temporarily suspended; price per copy: $3.00. 1968. 125pp; 5 x 9. lp. circ. 2,000. CCLM.

United Struggle Press (see THE STRUGGLE)

Unity Press, Inc., Stephen Levine, 113 New St., Santa Cruz, CA 95060, 408-427-2020. Nonfiction. "5 books a year. Meditation books, planet lore, how to, be here now." avg. price, cloth: $9.95; paper: $4.95. 1971. 196pp; 5½ x 8½. of. avg. press run 10,000 copies. Reporting time: 2 weeks. Payment: 15 percent monies received. Copyrights for author. Pub'd 2 titles 1976; expects 4 titles 1977, 6 titles 1978. COSMEP.

Unity Press (see COME-UNITY)

UNIVERSITY JOURNAL, David A. Downes, Dept. English, CSU, Chico, CA 95926. Poetry, fiction, articles, art, interviews, satire, criticism, reviews, letters, parts-of-novels, plays. "5-700 words. George Keithley, Clark Brown, W.H. Hutchinson, Lawrence Clark Powell, Robert Bellah." 3/yr. 1974. 28pp; 8½ x 11. †of. circ. 1,500. Reporting time: 6 weeks. Payment: 0. Pub's reviews.

University Of Alabama Press (see ALABAMA REVIEW)

University of California Press (see FILM QUARTERLY)

University of New Hampshire Student Press (see HARMONY)

University of Oregon Press (see NORTHWEST REVIEW)

University of the Trees Press, Christopher Hills, PO Box 644, Boulder Creek, CA 95006, 408-338-3855. avg. price, paper: $7.95. 1975. 300pp; varies. avg. press run 10,000. Payment: 10 percent. Copyrights for author. Discounts: 40 percent retail, 50 percent distr. Pub'd 5 titles 1976; expects 10 titles 1977, 10 titles 1978.

University Of Utah Press (see WESTERN HUMANITIES REVIEW)

UNIVERSITY OF WINDSOR REVIEW, University of Windsor Press, Eugene McNamara, c/o University of Windsor, Windsor, Ontario N9B3P4, Canada. Poetry, fiction, articles, art, criticism, reviews. "We try to offer a balance of essays, fiction, poetry, and reviews—but we seem to have developed into a platform for some really excellent fiction and poetry especially: W.D. Valgardson, Joyce Carol Oates, Tom Wayman etc." 2/yr; 1-yr sub price: $3.50; per copy: $1.75; sample: $1.75. 1966. 100pp; 5¾ x 9. lp. circ. 750. Reporting time: 6 weeks. Payment: $25.00 for story or essay, $10.00 for poem. Copyrighted, reverts to author. Discounts: 40 percent. Back issues: please write. Pub's reviews. §current fiction and poetry. COSMEP.

University of Wisconsin Press (see CONTEMPORARY LITERATURE)

University Press (see THE SHAW REVIEW)

‡**UNIVERSUM,** Artia Praque 1, Vesmeckach 20, Czechoslovakia.

UNMUZZLED OX, Michael Andre, Box 840, Canal St. Station, New York City, NY 10013. Poetry, fiction, articles, art, photos, interviews, criticism, reviews, music, letters, parts-of-novels. "I try to edit a magazine which would be my favorite magazine if I didn't even edit it. That leads me to publish favorite people, like Creeley, Corso, Berrigan, Lewitt, Rivers, Eleanor Antin, James Wright, Ray Johnson. It's fun, as well, to try to create a personality for the magazine which, through design and patter, would embody the collective spirit of our contributors; we haven't succeeded." 4/yr; 1-yr sub price: $8.00; per copy: $2.00; sample: $2.00. 1971. 140pp; 8½ x 5½. of. circ. 4,000. Reporting time: 2 weeks. Payment: none. Ads: $65/$35. Discounts: 40%. Back issues: 1-6:$12 each 7-13 cover price. §art & literature. CCLM, COSMEP.

Unpublished Editions (see also SOME OTHER NEWSLETTER), Alison Knowles, PO Box 26, West Glover, VT 05875. *"Unpublished Editions* is now a cooperative of avant-garde poets, artists and musicians, carrying on the tradition of Dick Higgin's former *Something Else Press,* and doing 11 titles a year (1977)." avg. price, cloth: $18.00; paper: $5.00; other: $50.00. 1972. 100pp; 6 x 9. of. avg. press run 1,000. No mss. accepted. Payment: 45 percent. Copyright in artists' names. Discounts: 40%. Pub'd 7 titles 1976; expects 11 titles 1977. COSMEP, NESPA.

THE UNSPEAKABLE VISIONS OF THE INDIVIDUAL, TUVOTI Books, Arthur Winfield Knight, Kit Knight, PO Box 439, California, PA 15419. Poetry, fiction, articles, art, photos, interviews, satire, criticism, reviews, letters, parts-of-novels, long-poems, collages, non-fiction. "Jack Kerouac, William Burroughs, Gary Snyder, Allen Ginsberg, Gregory Corso, Lawrence Ferlinghetti, Carolyn Cassady, Michael McClure, Carl Solomon, Herbert Huncke, Diane Di Prima, John Clellon Holmes, Philip Whalen, Neal Cassady, & Peter Orlovsky. Particularly interested in beat writing. Have used photographs by Elsa Dorfman, Fred W. McDarrah & Jill Krementz." 1/yr; 1-yr sub price: $8.00; per copy: varies; sample: $2.00. 1971. 176pp; 8½ x 11. of. circ. 2,000. Reporting time: 2 months. Payment: 2 contributor's copies. Ads: $500.00/$250.00. Discounts: query. Back issues: Back issues: Vol 1(No 1,2,3), $60; Vol. 2(No 1,2,3), $35; Vol. 3(No 1,2,3), $15; Vol. 4(The Beat Book), $10. Vol. 5 (The Beat Diary), $10.95. Prices subject to change on collector's editions. Expects 2 issues 1977, 2 issues 1978. Pub's reviews: none in 1976. §literary-esp. Beat literature. CCLM, COSMEP.

UP FROM UNDER (A Magazine By, For And About Women), Editorial Collective, 1377 Ninth Ave, San Francisco, CA 94122. Poetry, fiction, articles, art, photos, cartoons, interviews, satire, letters, parts-of-novels, collages. "Do not print or use any material by men. In the past we have used material by Alix Schulman and Tillie Olsen." 2/yr; sub price: $3.00/5 issues; per copy: $.60. 1969. 64pp; 8 x 11. of. circ. 5,000. Reporting time: 2-3 mos. Payment: none. Ads: none. Discounts: 5 issues for institutions $5.00, orders of 10 or more 1/3 discount or 40 cents. Back issues: same as cover. §feminist nature/labor/fiction perhaps how-to books for women/autobiographies. COSMEP.

JOHN UPDIKE NEWSLETTER, Herb Yellin, 19073 Los Alimos St., Northridge, CA 91326, 360-5804. Articles, criticism. "About John Updike—short" 4/yr; 1-yr sub price: $5.00. 1976. 4-6pp; 8½ x 11. of. Payment: none. Not copyrighted. Discounts: trade discounts. §Modern fiction & poetry.

Uphill Underground Press (see LIVE FREE QUARTERLY)

URBAN & SOCIAL CHANGE REVIEW, Karen Wolk Feinstein, Boston College, McGuinn Hall, Chestnut Hill, MA 02167. Articles, photos, criticism, reviews. "Articles usually 12-20 typewritten pages. Theme: Urban & Social Change. bias: Article should have implications for application to solve social problems or ameliorate urban crisis." 2/yr; 1-yr sub price: $5.00; per copy: $2.50; sample: free. 1967. 32pp; 8½ x 11. lp. circ. 1,500. Reporting time: 2 months. Payment: none. Ads: All done on complimentary, exchange basis. Back issues: $2.00. Pub's reviews. §urban studies, social problems, social change.

Urban Refugee Press (see UGLY DUCKLING)

URBANE GORILLA, Raven Publications, Ed Tork, 29 Parker Rd, Sheffield S10 1BN, United

Kingdom. Poetry, fiction, long-poems. 9 monthly; 1-yr sub price: £1.00 ($6.00); per copy: 50p or $4.00 inc. p&p; sample: 50p or $4.00 inc. p&p. 1970. 68pp; A4. litho. circ. 1,000. Reporting time: 2-3 months. Payment: none. Copyrighted. Ads: £20.00 equals $35.00/page pro rata. Discounts: Rate on enquiry. Back issues: 50p or $4.00 inc. p&p. Pub'd 1 issue 1976; expects 2 issues 1977, 2 issues 1978.

Urion Press, A.H. Rosenus, L.L. Wynne, John Pittman, Box 2244, Eugene, OR 97402. Fiction. "Reprints, low-fat fiction. The objective is to publish staples, books that will be read thirty years from today as well as now. If a book is right, we then wait another year before making a final decision on it. If you are in a rush, not here. We especially invite suggestions for reprints in the area of Western Americana. Recent titles include an original novel by David Middlebrook, and a reprint of The Indian History of the Modoc War. SASE with submissions please." 1 bk/yr. 1972. of. Reporting time: 2-3 mos. Discounts: bkstrs 40% on orders over 3/jobbers 50% on orders over 10/library disc 20%. COSMEP.

UROBOROS (was ALLEGANY POETRY), Allegany Mountain Press, Ford F. Ruggieri, Helen Ruggieri, 111 N. 10th St., Olean, NY 14760, 716-372-0935. Poetry, fiction, articles, art, photos, cartoons, interviews, satire, criticism, reviews, letters, letters, parts-of-novels, long-poems, collages, concrete art. "Length: fiction up to 6000 words; criticism/reviews up to 500 words; poetry-no restrictions; art work-no restrictions; photographs-8 x 10 glossies. Style: poetry, fiction, art-no restrictions; criticism, reviews on small press literature only. Biases: contemporary & ancient myth, folk tales, archetypal perceptions, experimental edges, visions, dreams, satire, sense of humor. Generally open to anything that moves, means and/or is." 2/yr; sub price: 3 issues for 5 dollars; per copy: $2.00; sample: $1.25. 1974. 80pp; 5½ x 8½. †of. circ. 400. Reporting time: 2 to 4 weeks. Payment: copies. Copyrighted. Ads: $50/$25. Discounts: 40% discount for 5 or more copies. Pub'd 2 issues 1976; expects 2 issues 1977, 2 issues 1978. Pub's reviews: 6 in 1976. §poetry, fiction, state of the arts. CCLM, COSMEP, NYSSPA.

‡**UT,** University Of Tampa, Tampa, FL 33602. CCLM.

UTOPIAN EYES: A JOURNAL OF PRACTICAL UTOPIAN FANTASY, Performing Arts Social Society, Inc. (a nonprofit collective of artists and writers), Even Eve, Brother Jud, Bluejay Way, Geo Logical, Utopian Eyes c/o Storefront Classroom, PO Box 1174, San Francisco, CA 94101. "All writing is done by members of the collective or utopian network. *UTOPIAN EYES* features articles on communal living procedures that work, input on how to overcome negative conditioning & a comic strip called ' Far *Out West,*' plus lots of art & thought-provoking ideas. In addition to publishing *UTOPIAN EYES* on a quarterly basis, the collective publishes *The Storefront Classroom,* a bimonthly ecology newspaper. *UTOPIAN EYES* and *Storefront Classroom* are $5.00 a year together; $3.75 a year for the magazine alone. $25.00 year for 4 listings (1 per issue) of 40 words each, in any category." 4/yr; 1-yr sub price: $3.75; per copy: $1.00; sample: $1.00. 1975. 48pp; 8½ x 11. of. circ. 10,000. Payment: none. Discounts: distributors can obtain Utopian Eyes for 50% off cover price with credit for returns. Back issues: Back issues: $0.75 per copy, for Utopian Society members; otherwise $1.00 per copy. Pub'd 4 issues 1976; expects 4 issues 1977, 4 issues 1978. Pub's reviews. §If mtl. pertains to utopias, community, & relevant subject matter.

UZZANO, Uzzano Press, Robert Schuler, Editor, c/oShimer College, Mount Carroll, IL 61053, 208 South State Rd., Upper Darby, PA 19082, 815-244-6575. Poetry, fiction, art, photos, satire, parts-of-novels, long-poems. "Receptive to all styles and forms of prose and poetry. We like poems with strong images and rhythms. Very interested in nature poetry. Want to see more good short stories. We'll read carefully whatever you've judged to be your best work. Have published: Brainard, Cooley, McGrath, Dubie, Gunderson, Kelly, Keithley, Witherup, Vinz, Adcock, Nelson." 3/yr; 1-yr sub price: $5.00; per copy: $1.50; sample: $1.50. 1975. 50pp; 8½ x 6. of. circ. 500. Reporting time: 2-4 weeks. Payment: 3 copies per contributor; cash when available. Copyrighted. Discounts: 40 percent. Back issues: $1.00 for Nos. 1 & 2; $2.00 for No. 3; $2.25 for No. 4. Pub'd 3 issues 1976; expects 3 issues 1977, 3 issues 1978. COSMEP, CCLM.

V

VAGABOND, Vagabond Press, John Bennett, PO Box 879, Ellensburg, WA 98926. Poetry, fiction, articles, art, photos, interviews, reviews, letters, parts-of-novels, plays. "Some recent contributors: Al Masarik, T. L. Kryss, Kent Taylor, Gerda Penfold, Marvin Malone, Lyn Lifshin, Linda King, Charles Potts, Jerry Bumpus, D. E. Steward, Steve Richmond, William Wantling, Nila Northsun, Marcus Grapes, Tom Robbins, Rich Mangelsdorff, etc." 4/yr; 1-yr sub price: $5.00; per copy: $1.50; sample: $1.25. 1966. 90pp; 7 x 8½. †of/other/silkscreen. circ. 900. Reporting time: fast. Payment: copies, bread when available. Ads: $100.00/$60.00/$0.10. Discounts: 40% trade disc.; orders for $30 or over-50%. Pub'd 2 issues 1976; expects 3 issues 1977, 4 issues 1978. Pub's reviews: 5 in 1976. §poetry, fiction.

Vagrom Chapbooks (see SPARROW PRESS)

VAJRA BODHI SEA, Buddhist Text Translation Society, 1731 15th St, San Francisco, CA 94103, 861-9672. Poetry, fiction, articles, art, photos, interviews, reviews, letters. "*VAJRA BODHI SEA* is the monthly journal of the Sino-American Buddhist Association, printing translations of Buddhist texts, biographies of Buddhist Masters, feature articles, World Buddhist News, poetry, language lessons, and a calendar of Buddhist Holidays and events." 12/yr; 1-yr sub price: $14.00; per copy: $2.00; sample: $0.00. 1970. 40pp; 5½ x 8½. of. circ. 500. Payment: $14.00 per year (same for all). Copyrighted, reverts to author. Discounts: bulk, non-profit organization. Back issues: Prices vary from $100.00 to $2.00 dependent on rarity of issues. Pub's reviews. §buddhism.

Valkyrie Press, Inc. (see also POETRY VENTURE), Marjorie Schuck, Publisher, President, Owner, 2135 1st Ave. S., St. Petersburg, FL 33712. Poetry, fiction, art, criticism, long-poems, non-fiction. "We are book publishers with our own full-scale modern book production and printing equipment including typesetting, layout, design, camera, offset presses, bindery. At present, we strive to reach effectively not the mass market, but the market representing people willing and anxious to buy specialized books of quality in production and worth in content. Our concern is for genuine excellence to maintain our imprint and to help the works of our authors sell even years from first publication. We operate on a flexible, generous Publisher-Author Contract: straight royalty, cooperative, and/or subsidy-with a widescale promotional and publicity program." avg. price, cloth: $6.00; paper: $3.95. 1972. 96pp; 5½ x 8½. †of. avg. press run 1,000. Reporting time: 2-6 mos. Payment: 3 contract bases - see comments in No. 11 above. Copyrights for author. Discounts: 40% and up. Pub'd 8 titles 1976; expects 15 titles 1977, 15 titles 1978.

Valley Press (see THOUGHTS FOR ALL SEASONS)

Van Dyk Publications, Adrian C. Van Dyk Jr., 303 Wikiup Dr., Santa Rosa, CA 95401, 707-544-6103. Poetry. "Three books of poetry have been published: *Love In The Valley*, and *Whisper Love In The Wind*, are available at $1.95 ea., *Love Is A Special Feeling*, the latest publication, is priced at $2.95. Order from above address with 50 cents for postage and handling. *Love In The Valley* is now into its second edition, special discount to libraries and on larger orders. Please contact the author for further information. The poetry has been endorsed by such prominent authors as Jessamyn West and Lawrence Ferlinghetti." avg. price, other: $1.95-$2.95. 1975. 40-112pp; 5½ x 8. lp. avg. press run 1,000. do not solicit mss. Author is copyrighted. Discounts: libraries may purchase at cost, bookstores at 40 percent discount (orders over 10). Pub'd 2 titles 1976.

VANDERBILT POETRY REVIEW, Vanderbilt University Press, Frank Judge, David Cheatham, c/o Rochester Routes, 50 Inglewood Drive, Rochester, NY 14619. "THE VANDERBILT POETRY REVIEW publishes poetry, poetry translations and interviews. We are interested in quality; though long poems will be read and considered, we prefer to print shorter (20-30 line) pieces. Past issues have included established poets like Auden, Bly, and Heyen as well as new and younger writers. We have also published special issues devoted to contemporary Canadian poetry and to contemporary Italian poetry. Due to funding problems, we have temporarily suspended publication while unearthing new sources. Back issues Nos. 1-4 may be purchased at the above address for $3.00 each." 2/yr; 1-yr sub price: $4.00; per copy: $2.00; sample: $3.00. 1972. 64pp; 5½ x 8½. of. circ. 1,000. Reporting time: 1 month. Payment: 2 copies. Copyrighted. Back issues: No. 1-4 $3.00 each. Expects 1 issue 1977.

VANGUARD, Wedge Publishing Foundation, Bonnie M. Greene, 229 College St, Toronto, Ontario M5T 1R4, Canada, 416-979-2442. Poetry, fiction, articles, interviews, satire, criticism, reviews, letters. "To 1800 words, more by arrangement. Style: Follow U. of Chicago *Manual Of Style*. Biases: This is a radical, christian idea magazine, offering, informed commentary on the important events and ideas shaping North American culture. Since we're working for social change, potential contributors should definitely query before submitting articles." 6/yr; 1-yr sub price: $8.00; per copy: $1.50; sample: $.50. 1971. 32pp; 8½ x 11. of. circ. 2,000. Reporting time: 3-4 weeks. Payment: up to $50 to authors making less than $6,000/yr; others paid in copies. Ads: $200/$100/none. Discounts: books-40 percent, mag. 40 (return) 50 percent no return, no disc. for inst. Back issues: $.50 copy. Pub'd 9 issues 1976; expects 6 issues 1977, 6 issues 1978. Pub's reviews: 153 in 1976. §political affairs, economics, education, psychology, arts, some theology.

Vanguard Books, Ashley Bullitt, Edythe Anderson, P.O. Box 3566, Chicago, IL 60654. "Publishers and distributors of literature reflecting current social struggles. Reprints, and original material, full length books and pamphlets. Looking for manuscripts of a socially progressive nature, histories, biographies, autobiographies analysis, or fiction." avg. price, paper: $3.95. 1975. 250pp; 5½ / 8½. of. avg. press run 5,000. Discounts: bkstrs 40%, textbook dis. with full return privileges 20%, libraries 20%. Pub'd 3 titles 1976; expects 3 titles 1977, 7 titles 1978. COSMEP.

The Vanity Press, Sonya Jones, Lydia Anne Moore, PO Box 15064, Atlanta, GA 30333. Poetry, fiction. "The Vanity Press intends to publish poetry and fiction by women. Vanity is a collective: Author pays 10% of production costs-retains editorial rights. No agents. Work must be submitted by author. Editors will work closely with authors. No standard rejection slips-each submission given thorough and serious consideration and returned with comments. Vanity is an alternative to 'New York The Goat'." 1976. of. Reporting time: 2 weeks. Payment: negotiable. Discounts: 40%.

VANTAGE POINT, Jeff Bradford, Karen Johnson, PO Box 62, Danville, KY 40422, 606-236-9933. Poetry, fiction, art, photos, letters, long-poems, plays, concrete art. "Poems and short stories should be of reasonable length (3-5 pages)." 3/yr; 1-yr sub price: $3.00; per copy: $1.00; sample: free. 1968. 35pp; 8 x 11. of/lp/xerox. Reporting time: 6-12 weeks. Payment: copies of mag. Not copyrighted. Ads: $25.00/$15.00/0. Discounts: available on request. §poetry/literature. COSMEP.

VECTOR, British Science Fiction Association Limited, Christopher Fowler, 72 Kenilworth Ave., Southcote Reading RG3 3DN, United Kingdom, 0734-594890. Articles, art, cartoons, photos, reviews, interviews, criticism, letters, poetry, fiction, satire, news items. "We are the official organ of the BSFA. We publish serious critical material on science fiction. No limit on length of articles. Recent contributors include J.G. Ballard (interviewed), Brian Aldiss, John Brunner, Ian Watson, John Clute, Mark Adlard, Ursula Le Guin, Edmund Cooper, James Blish." 6/yr; sub price: 6 issues - $7.00 (Air mail - $10.00) (Institutions - $11.00); per copy: 60p; sample: 60p. 1958. 32pp; A4. photo-litho. circ. 800. Reporting time: 3 weeks. No payment. Copyrighted, reverts to author. Ads: £30.00 or $50.00/other sizes pro rata. Discounts: 33-1/3 to dealer. Back issues: Most available. Write for price list. Pub'd 8 issues 1976; expects 6 issues 1977.

VECTOR MAGAZINE, Bart Rains, c/o Ball State News, Ball State Univ., Muncie, IN 47306. Poetry, fiction, photos. "Recent contributors include: Dennis E. Hensley, Mike Early, Sonia Hunter, Judith Shafer, Mike Fallon." 12/yr; 1-yr sub price: no charge. 1974. Payment: copies.

VEGETARIAN HEALTH REVIEW AND DIGEST, Vegetus Publications, Frank Ray Rifkin, Andrew Rifkin, Box 221, Haverford, PA 19041. Poetry, fiction, articles, art, photos, cartoons, interviews, satire, criticism, reviews. "Subjects relating to Nutrition, Vegetarianism, Animal Welfare" 4/yr; sub price: $6.00-2 yr, 8 issues; per copy: $.50; sample: $1.00. 1976. 32pp; tabloid. of. circ. 110,000. Reporting time: 60 days. Payment: negotiable. Ads: $500.00/$250.00/$45.00. Pub's reviews. COSMEPA.

VEGETARIAN WORLD, William Blanchard, Suite 216 8235 Santa Monica Blvd., Los Angeles, CA 90046, 213-654-7002. Poetry, articles, photos, cartoons, interviews, letters, satire, criticism, news items. "All submissions must be relevant to the vegetarian movement. Most are freely contributed." 4/yr; 1-yr sub price: $2.00; per copy: $0.50; sample: $0.75. 1974. 32pp; 11 x 17. of. circ. 30,000. Reporting time: 30 days. Payment: negotiate. Ads: $680.00/$360.00/personal only: $10.00/50 words. Discounts: Flexible-40 percent retail, 60 percent distributor is usual. Back issues: $0.75. Pub'd 4 issues 1976; expects 4 issues 1977, 4 issues 1978. Pub's reviews: 3 in 1976. §Vegetarianism, world food crisis, health, animals.

Vegetus Publications (see VEGETARIAN HEALTH REVIEW AND DIGEST)

Vehicule Press (see also DAVINCI MAGAZINE), Si Dardick, Artie Gold, Andre Farkas, George Bowering, Alden Nowlan, David McFadden, Ken Norris, Guy Lavoie, 1000 Clark St., Montreal, Quebec H2Z1J9, Canada. "VEHICULE PRESS publishes and distributes (by mail). Write for our current catalogue. We distribute art books/editions, poetry, catalogues (art) and small press publications. In Spring 1977 we published books by George Bowering, Claudia Lapp, John McAuley, Opal L. Nations, Andre Farkas. Forthcoming Fall 1977: an anthology of Montreal poets of the 70's and a book by Stephen Morrissey." avg. price, paper: $3.00; other: $3.00 less 10 percent. 1973. 60pp; 5¼ x 8. †of. avg. press run 500-1,000. Reporting time: 60 days. Payment: Copies plus royalties. Copyrights for author. Discounts: Trade 40 pc, distributors/50 pc, universities-20 pc. Pub'd 3 titles 1976; expects 7 titles 1977, 7 titles 1978. COSMEP, NESPA, CBIC, AMI, ARWS, NA.

VEINS, St. Mawr Jazz Poetry Project, John H. Kennedy, Box 615, Middlebury, VT 05753. Poetry, articles, art, interviews, music, long-poems. " *VEINS* is now a cassette mag. publishing jazz poetry, poetic drama, music; poetry, and interviews. All submissions should be on tape cassettes unless previous arrangements for us to do the recording have been made. Interested in multi-media experiments with music & poetry. Primarily interested in jazz poetry any length. International university circulation. Also interviews." irregular; 1-yr sub price: $2.50/tape; sample: $0.24 stamp (back printed issues). 1973 (print) 1977 (tape). 60 pp min.; 60 min. tape cassette. Magnetic tape cassette recorder. circ. irregular. Reporting time: 1 wk. Payment: copies. Copyrights: if you are concerned, secure your own; assign us one time rights. Discounts: 40% bulk, min. 20. Back issues: free for $0.24 stamp. §poetry & music (also poetics), CCLM, NESPA.

THE VELVET LIGHT TRAP: Review of Cinema, Arizona Jim Co-Op, John Davis, Old Hope Schoolhouse, Cottage Grove, WI 53527. Articles, interviews, criticism, reviews. "Our specialty is the serious critical evaluation of America's film past. We do not give priority to recent releases nor do we indulge in nostalgia. Each issue is devoted to one subject or theme (a studio, a genre, a decade, etc.,). Many of our contributors come from the academic community, but this is not by design. We encourage anyone who feels the urge to write to contribute. We do not favor any political or critical perspective over others in deciding what to print. The main things we look for are: that the person has something to say, that he makes his arguments in a logical and organized fashion, that the piece is somewhere between 10 and 20 double-spaced pages, that the basic facts are straight, and that the writing style is understandable (not graceful or beautiful)." 4/yr; 1-yr sub price: $4.00; per copy: $1.00; sample: $1.00. 1968. 64pp; 8½ x 11. of. circ. 2,400. Reporting time: 2 weeks. Ads: $64/$32. Discounts: 10% agency discount. Back issues: Double the cover price. Pub's reviews §film. COSMEP.

VELVET WINGS, Paradoxical Press, Sarah Kennedy, 1228 Oxford St., Berkeley, CA 94709, 415-843-4630. Poetry, fiction, art, long-poems. "Hope to do an issue devoted to women prisoners, another to children (0-18 years) writers and perhaps an issue to outstanding women writers...Recent contributors include Lyn Lifshin, Alta, John Oliver Simon, Julia Viuograd, Emilie Glen, Pancho Aguila etc." 2-3/yr; 1-yr sub price: $4.00; per copy: $1.50; sample: depends on who it's going to. 1976. 50-70pp; varies. †of. circ. 500-750. Reporting time: 2 weeks to 3 months. Payment: 3 copies of magazine. Copyrighted, reverts to author. Discounts: 40 percent to trade, bulk. Back issues: don't got none yet. Pub'd 1 issue 1976; expects 2 issues 1977, 2-3 issues 1978. COSMEP.

Ventura Press, Raymond Barrio, P.O. Box 2268, Sunnyvale, CA 94087. Fiction. "My own private self-publishing press." avg. price, paper: $2.75. †of. Pub'd 1 title 1976; expects 1 title 1977, 3 titles 1978.

VER POETS VOICES/BROADSHEETS/POETRY POST/VERMOUTH, Ver Poets, M. E. Badman, 61 & 63 Chiswell Green Lane, St. Albans, Herts AL23AG, United Kingdom. Poetry, articles, art, criticism, reviews. "Our members, whose work only we use, are some of them published poets-Mole, Gurney, Jaffin, Ivimy, etc. Others are beginners or have not had any breaks. All types of work acceptable if in our opinion it works in one way or another. Single poets series—selections by individual poets, price varies with no. pages, usually 20P-25P. Also foldcard poems, 10P if illustrated, 5P if not." irreg.; 1-yr sub price: £2.00 per annum; per copy: 60p post free. 1966. 30-40pp; varies. †dup. circ. 300. Reporting time: 2 wks to 2 mos. No payment. Copyright left with author. Ads: None. Discounts: If pushed, 33-1/3 percent, but we are not funded to cover discounts. Back issues: 40p post free. Pub'd 3 issues 1976; expects 4 issues 1977. Pub's reviews: 2 in 1976. SAAA, EAA.

Veritie Press, Inc., Elizabeth Boyer, PO Box 222, Novelty, OH 44072. Fiction. "Have published only two books in our first two years. *Marguerite De La Rogue, A Story Of Survival* and *Freydis And Gudrid* both by Elizabeth Boyer. Both are historical novels based on fact. We are not yet ready to accept submissions." 1975.

Verlag Guenther Emig, Postfach 2225, 7500 Karlsruhe 1; West Germany. 1973.

VERMONT CHILDREN'S MAGAZINE, Ed Osborn, PO Box 941, Burlington, VT 05401, 425-2359. Poetry, fiction, art, photos, music, letters. "Our magazine is a college of work done by Vermont elementary school children. We try to let their inclinations dictate the subject areas." 4/yr. 1975. 24pp; 8½ x 11. of. circ. 20,000. Reporting time: 2 months max. Payment: none-all contributors are children. Copyrighted, does not revert except by request. Discounts: VT. elementary schools receive the magazine at cost (or less) as we are trying to support it with grants. Back issues: our circulation precludes a stockpiling of past issues. §children's literature, education, publishing. CCLM.

Vermont Crossroads Press, Inc., Constance C. Montgomery, Co-Pres.; Raymond A. Montgomery, Co-Pres., Box 30, Waitsfield, VT 05673. Poetry, fiction, photos. "Publishing hard cover & soft cover books for the school-library market & the trade mkt. currently 60% children's books 40% adult-price range from $1.95-$6.95." avg. price, cloth: $4.95; paper: $4.95. 1974. of. avg. press run 5,000. Pub'd 3 titles 1976; expects 6 titles 1977, 6 titles 1978.

Vesta Publications, PO Box 1641, Cornwall, Ont. K6H 5V6, Canada, 613-932-2135. Poetry, fiction, criticism, plays. 1974. 100pp. †of. Reporting time: 2 months. Payment: 10 paper; 10 hard. Discounts: 40-50 percent. Pub'd 9 titles 1976; expects 16 titles 1977, 20 titles 1978.

VIA, Antonio Cussen, Laura Rirkin, Marki Smith, 103 Sproul Hall, University of California, Berkeley, CA 94720, 642-2103. Poetry, fiction, articles, interviews, criticism, reviews, parts-of-novels, long-poems. "Length should not exceed 15 pages. *Via* wishes to further the interaction among the writers of the Americas. Publishes works in English, Spanish and Portuguese. First issue had works by Leonard Michaels, Nathaniel Tam, Jose Miguel Oviedo and Haroldo de Campos." 2/yr; 1-yr sub price: $4.00; per copy: $2.00; sample: $2.00. 1976. 90pp; 5½ x 8½. of. circ. 750. Reporting time: 4 weeks. Payment: 2 copies. Copyrighted, reverts to author. Back issues: $2.00. Pub's reviews. §American & Latin American lit. & criticism. COSMEP.

VICTIMOLOGY AN INTERNATIONAL JOURNAL, Visage Press Inc., Emilio C Viano, P O Box 39045, Washington, DC 20016, 202-686-5302. Articles, photos, interviews, reviews, letters, news items. 4/yr; 1-yr sub price: $17.00 indiv. $25.00 instit.; per copy: $5.00; sample: $5.00. 1975. 200pp; 6½ x 10. circ. 2,500. Reporting time: 6-8 weeks. Payment: payment per story for nonacademics negotiable. Query first. Magazine is copyrighted, retains all rights. Ads: $150.00/$85.00. Discounts: 10 percent jobbers and subscription agencies for domestic circulation only. Back issues: $7.00. Pub'd 4 issues 1976; expects 4 issues 1977, 4 issues 1978. Pub's reviews: 25 in 1976. §Victimization in general, rape, consumerism, compensation to victims, genocide, etc. Environmental issues, prevention of victimization thru different measures. COSMEP, COSMEP-SOUTH.

VIEW FROM THE SILVER BRIDGE, Bill Standeven, 201 Alder St, Campbell River, B. C. V9W 2N5, Canada. Poetry, fiction, articles, art, photos, reviews. "Material must include telling language, words that speak out to the reader, must include a sense of magic—as if something meaningful were unfolding before the reader's very eyes. I prefer a loose and open style, involving a sense of vulnerability. The bias of this magazine is towards quality, a sense of life at the moment it is written that *has* to be written down. Some recent contributors: Roderick Haig-Brown, Allan Fry, Robert Sward, Mike Doyle." 3/yr; 1-yr sub price: $3.00; per copy: $1.00; sample: $.50. 1973. 32pp; 5½ x 8½. †mi. circ. 250. Reporting time: 1 week. Payment: by merit, or copies. Back issues: $.75 each. Pub's reviews. §fiction, poetry, drama.

VIEWPOINT AQUARIUS, Jean Coulsting, Rex Dutta, c/oFish Tanks Ltd, 49 Blandford St., London W1 3AF, United Kingdom. Articles, poetry, photos, reviews, news items, interviews, criticism, letters, concrete art. "Very serious, informative, going deeper than 'nuts and bolts' of the Orthodox, penetrating to the hidden laws within: for flying saucers, occult, yoga, meditation, theosophy." 11/yr; 1-yr sub price: $7.00; per copy: $0.50; sample: free. 1971. 30pp; foolscap. Reporting time: 10. Back issues: $0.50.

VILE, Banana Productions, Anna Banana, Bill Gaglione, 1183 Church St, San Francisco, CA 94114. Fiction, articles, art, photos, cartoons, satire, reviews, letters, parts-of-novels, collages. "Average length, 500-1,000 words, occasionally use longer (good) work. Poetry, none-the-less new issue contains 21 poems, used mainly as space fillers-not a feature. Style-Dada-Iconoclastic. Current issue incl. works from: John M. Bennett, Robin Crozier, Ken Friedman, Geoff Hendricks, Ray Johnson, Genesis P. Orridge, Richard Morris, Opal Nations, Robert Rehfeldt, etc. Pub's reviews of art shows, events & performances. Not of books unless they are art-related." 2/yr; 1-yr sub price: $7.00; per copy: $3.00; sample: $3.00. 1974. 100pp; 8½ x 11. of. circ. 1,000. Reporting time: 2-3 months. Payment: copies only. Copyrighted. Ads: $200.00/$100.00/$10.00 col. inch. Discounts: none. Back issues: First two not available, 3rd available at $5.00/copy, 4th will be back issue before directory comes out and will be available for $3.00/copy. Expects 2 issues 1978. CCLM.

Violet Press, Fran Winant, PO Box 398, New York, NY 10009. Poetry, art, photos. "We are a lesbian feminist press. 1-2 books per year." 1971. 64pp; 5½ x 8½. of Reporting time: 1-2 months. Payment: contributors' copies. Discounts: 40% U.S.A. discount on orders of 3 or more copies of any title. COSMEP, NESPA.

Visage Press, Inc. (see also VICTIMOLOGY), Emilio C. Viano, Editor-in-Chief, 3409 Wisconsin Avenue NW, Washington, DC 20016, 202-686-5302. Fiction, photos, plays, non-fiction. "Publishes fiction and non-fiction. Willing to publish controversial material." avg. price, cloth: $12.00; paper: $6.00. 1976. 198-640pp; varies. of. avg. press run 2,000. Reporting time: 8 weeks. Payment: depends, negotiable—query first with outline. Retains all rights. is copyrighted. Discounts: 10 percent. Pub'd 1 title 1976; expects 3 titles 1977, 10 titles 1978. COSMEP, COSMEP-SOUTH, AAP.

The Visart Press, 1847 N. Beverly Glen Blvd, Los Angeles, CA 90024. "Manuscripts *not* accepted or asked for, except by invitation only for 1976 &1977." avg. price, paper: $3.50. 1975. avg. press run 500. Discounts: none.

THE VOICE, Joan G. Gibson, PO Box 26615, San Jose, CA 95159. "No advertising accepted. Articles contributed. Occult, Spiritual." 4/yr; 1-yr sub price: $2.25; per copy: $.60; sample: $.30. 36pp; 5½ x 8½. †of. circ. 500. Back issues: $.50. §Metaphysics.

VORT, Vort Works Ink/Vort World Hdqs, Barry Alpert, 1708 Tilton Dr, Silver Spring, MD 20902. Interviews, criticism. "All unappropriate material submitted by individuals who have obviously not considered the magazine's established format will be *burned on receipt.* This editor knows who he wants to publish and will contact those individuals directly. Please look at back issues before bothering even to inquire, with SASE." 1-yr sub price: $7.50; per copy: $3.50; sample: $5.00 libraries. 1972. 160pp; 8½ x 11. mi/of. Reporting time: irregular. Payment: copies. Copyrighted, reverts to author. Discounts: 40 percent trade, 20 percent classroom. Back issues: $7.50 plus postage for 3. Pub'd 1 issue 1976; expects 2-3 issues 1977. §artists' writing, practical criticism, poetry, interviews. CCLM.

THE VOYEUR, Open Window Society Inc., Jody Azzouni, 301 Hicks, Brooklyn, NY 11201. Poetry, fiction, articles, art, photos, cartoons, interviews, satire, criticism, reviews, music, letters, parts-of-novels, long-poems, collages, plays, concrete art, news items, non-fiction. "No restrictions on length except for full length novels and plays. Long pieces are subject to serialization. Recent contributors are: Joseph Semenovich, Barbara Holland, J. Azzouni, James Jurado, Joe Reccardi, Patricia Eakins, Michael Blanchard." 12/yr; 1-yr sub price: $4.00; per copy: free (by mail, $.50 a copy plus $.35 handling). 1974. 16pp; 7 x 8½. of. circ. 30,000. Reporting time: 2 months. Payment: Cash & copies (both vary). Copyrighted. Ads: $250.00/$150.00. Discounts: none. Back issues: No. 1 $5.00, Vol. 1 No. 2-13 $1.00 each. Volume 1 entire $15.00. Volume 2 1-12 each $0.75. Entire $7.50. Pub'd 12 issues 1976; expects 12 issues 1977, 12 issues 1978. Pub's reviews. CCLM.

W **A WAKE NEWSLITTER, Studies Of James Joyce's Finnegans Wake,** Clive Hart, Fritz Senn, Department of Literature, University of Essex, Wivenhoe Park, Colchester, Essex CO4 3SQ, United Kingdom. Articles, criticism. "Articles on Joyces's Finnegans Wake, with occasional notes and articles on other books by Joyce. No other material normally included. Short articles preferred. The bias is exegetical rather than critical." 6/yr; 1-yr sub price: £6.00; per copy: £1.00; sample: free. 1962. 24pp; A5. lo. circ. 700. Reporting time: 24 hrs. Payment: nil. no ads. Discounts: none. Back issues: £6.00 p.a. £1.00 single copies.

Walden Press (see also HURON REVIEW), 423 South Franklin Ave, Flint, MI 48503. Poetry, fiction. "Autobiographical material where author has found direction, need and energy to be creative and love others; also encourage seniors to retell the 1920's and 1930's" avg. price, paper: $3.95. 1965. 140-185pp. lp. avg. press run 1,000. Reporting time: 1 week. Payment: 20 percent. Copyrights for author. Discounts: 50 percent. Pub'd 1 title 1976; expects 3 titles 1978. Lib of Congress.

Waldrop Publications, P.O. Box 396, Mt Baldy, CA 91759. " book: *Boy, Girl, and Garden,* by Stanley Waldrop."

Walloon Street Press (see WALUNA)

WALLPAPER, Richard Eichen, Recaz Klita, Acadamon, Room 205, Hebrew University, Givat Ram, Jerusalem, Israel. "Essays & fiction under 2,000 words. Barry Chamish, Michael Tannenbaum." irreg.; price per copy: Il2.50, No U.S. price listed. 1975. Broadside format; Roughly 2 feet by three feet. lp.

Walnut Press, Bruce Thompson, 4252 N. Brown Ave, Scottsdale, AZ 85251, 602-946-4440. Non-fiction. "Length of material at discretion of author, no biases. Bruce S. Thompson, recent contrib." avg. price, cloth: $8.95; paper: $5.95. 1976. 250pp; 6 x 9. avg. press run 3,000. Reporting time: 2 wks. Payment: 30% of net, end of month. Copyrights for author. Discounts: trade—40 percent, agent/jobber—46 percent, bulk—50 percent. Pub'd 1 title 1976; expects 3 titles 1977, 6 titles 1978. COSMEP, WBPA.

WALUNA, THE SOHO REVIEW, Walloon Street Press, Doris Lane, 72 Wooster St, New York, NY 10012. Poetry, fiction, photos, cartoons, criticism, reviews, parts-of-novels, long-poems, plays. "Cover photo & end story subject always 'soho'." 2/1976 3/1977; 1-yr sub price: $9.00; per copy: $3.50. 1976. 100-150pp; 7½ x 8. of. circ. 1,000. Reporting time: 90 days. Payment: none. Copyrighted, reverts to author. Ads: $200.00/$100.00. Pub'd 1 issue 1976; expects 3 issues 1977, 4 issues 1978. Pub's reviews. §Fiction & poetry & photography & art. COSMEP.

WASHINGTON INTERNATIONAL ARTS LETTER, Daniel Millsaps, Box 9005, Washington, DC 20003, Box 9005, Washington, DC 20003. "We publish financial information for the arts and artists. Federal actions and grants; private foundation and business corporation arts program information. And we have the following titles in books: GRANTS AND AID TO INDIVIDUALS IN THE ARTS (now in 2nd ed. 3rd to come out Jan 77 $12.95) and PRIVATE FOUNDATIONS AND BUSINESS CORPS ACTIVE IN ARTS/HUMANITIES/EDUCATION Vol 2. ($45)."′ 10/yr; 1-yr sub price: $16: individuals/$32: institutions; sample: $2.00. 1962. 8pp per issue; 8½ x 11 inches. of. circ. 15,030. Back issues: Write for schedule. Pub'd 10 issues 1976; expects 10 issues 1977, 10 issues 1978. Pub's reviews: 300 in 1976. §all arts.

WASHINGTON REVIEW, A Quarterly Review of the Arts, Friends of the Washington Review of the Arts, Inc., Jean Lewton, Managing Editor; Patricia Griffith, Clarissa Wittenberg, Elizabeth Brunazzi, 404 10th Street SE, Washington, DC 20003, 202-546-4319. Poetry, fiction, articles, art, photos, cartoons, interviews, satire, criticism, reviews, letters, parts-of-novels, long-poems, collages, plays. "Articles: 2,000 words at most. Review: 500-1,000 words. Interested in in-depth articles on all arts, with particular emphasis on DC. Recent contributors: Patricia Griffith, Ted Greenwald, Doris Grumbach, E. Ethelbert Miller, William Christenberry." 4/yr; 1-yr sub price: $4.00; per copy: $0.75; sample: $1.00. 1975. 32 pp tabloid; 11¼ x 16. of. circ. 3,000. Reporting time: 2 months. Payment: In issues. Copyrighted, reverts to author. Ads: $100.00/$60.00/$0.10. Discounts: 15 percent bulk discount, 15 percent classroom, 10 percent agencies, 40 percent to bookstores for resale. Back issues: $1.50. Pub's reviews. §Arts, history, philosophy, social commentary. COSMEP.

Washington Writers Publishing House, Grace Cavalieri, Deidra Baldwin, Robert Sargent, Roberta Pilk, 1010 Vermont Ave, NW, Room 920, Washington, DC 20005. Poetry. avg. price, paper: $2.00. 1975. 32pp; 6 x 9. of. avg. press run 500. Payment: none. Copyright held by authors. Discounts: bulk orders-10 or more titles. Pub'd 5 titles 1976.

WASHOUT REVIEW, Washout Publishing Co., Nan C. Johnson, Sarah Provost, PO Box 2752, Schenectady, NY 12309. Poetry, art, photos. "Poems preferably under 40 lines; variety of styles. Recent contributors: Elaine Dallman, Mark Nepo, Janet Seery, Peggy Seely, Toni O. Zimmerman, Susan Baumann, Mary I. Cuffe, Lee Meitzen Grue, Joel Dailey, Madeleine Hennessy, Kathryn Poppino, Susan Shafarzek, Joan Colby, Dennis Holzman, Alice Fulton, Sydney Lea, Lyn Lifshin, Christine Zawadiwski." 4/yr; 1-yr sub price: $5.00; per copy: $1.95; sample: $1.50. 1975. 64pp; 5½ x 8½. of. circ. 500. Reporting time: 2-5 weeks. Payment: in copies (2). Ads: none. Discounts: 40%-10 or more copies, 33-1/3%-1 to 9 copies. Back issues: $1.50. Pub'd 4 issues 1976; expects 4 issues 1977, 4 issues 1978. COSMEP, CCLM.

WATERS, More Waters, Rocky Karlage, Thomas Early, Joe Darwish, PO Box 19341, Cincinnati, OH 45219, 513-861-5528. Poetry, fiction, art, photos, reviews, parts-of-novels, criticism. "No set biases, except poetry must be intelligent and 'hard-worked'. If we have a bias, it is quality. Wish to encourage short fiction, criticism. Recent contributors: Peter Wild, Lynn Shoemaker, William Stafford, Greg Kuzma, Lyn Lifshin, Robert Peters, Robert Hudzik, Albert Stainton, James Bertolino, F. Keith Wahle, Dallas Wiebe, Marina Rivera. 'More Waters' supplement No. 1 featured Lyn Lifshin." 3/yr; 1-yr sub price: $3.00; per copy: $1.00; sample: $0.80. 1974. 30-50pp; 5½ x 8½. †of. circ. 400. Reporting time: 2 weeks-1 month. Payment: 2 copies. Copyright: common law/yes. Discounts: 20 percent discount to libraries on sample copy; potential subscribers. Back issues: no discount. Pub'd 2 issues 1976; expects 3 issues 1977, 3 issues 1978. Pub's reviews. §Contemporary poetry and criticism, fiction. CCLM, Ohio Arts Council.

Watershed Intermedia (see also BLACK BOX), Alan D. Austin, P.O. Box 4174, Washington, DC 20015, 202-547-2727. Poetry, interviews, music, plays. "*WATERSHED* issues single cassettes of authors reading/performing their poetry. There are three series: the '*Signature*' series, featuring the work of major, established poets not otherwise available on records or tapes; the '*Premiere*' series featuring the work of newer poets who prefer audio to print; and the '*Archive*' series—recordings from the past generation which should have been available, but weren't." avg. price, other: $7.95 (cassette). 1976. (45-60 min playing time); Single audiocassettes. †Audiocassette duplication. avg. press run No limit. Reporting time: Varies. Payment: Royalty. Copyrights remain with authors; audio copyright (Form 'N') held in trust for duration of contract. Discounts: Trade: 40 percent min. 5. Pub'd 1 title 1976; expects 15 titles 1977, 25 titles 1978. COSMEP.

WAVES, Bernice Lever, Robert Casto, Rm. 128, Founders College, York University, Downsview, Ontario M3T1P3, Canada. Poetry, fiction, articles, art, photos, interviews, satire, criticism, reviews, letters, parts-of-novels. "Fiction-1,000 to 10,000 wds. Reviews-500 to 2,500 wds. Our bias is towards reviews of Canadian writing but we print original poetry and fiction in English or French from any country. Recent contributors: Layton, Birney, Purdy, Bissett, Livesay, and interviews with Laurence and Atwood." 3/yr; 1-yr sub price: $5.00; per copy: $2.00; sample: $1.00. 1972. 80pp; 5 x 8. of. circ. 1,000. Reporting time: 2-4 wks. Payment: sample copies. Ads: exchange. Back issues: $2.00 each. Pub'd 3 issues 1976; expects 2 issues 1977, 3 issues 1978. Pub's reviews: 10 in 1976. §contemporary fiction & poetry. CPPA.

Wayside Press (see also **WAYSIDE QUARTERLY**), Joan Atwater, Mary Radcliffe, P.O. Box 475, Cottonwood, AZ 86326. "Our 'motto' is 'books for living', and we are interested in reflective, serious, intelligent material, and are always interested in new poets who show promise." avg. price, cloth: varies; paper: $3.00-$7.00; other: $2.00-$5.00. 1972. pp varies; varies. †mi. avg. press run 250. Reporting time: within a month. Payment: to be discussed. Does not copyright for author. Discounts: 30 percent trade. Pub'd 12 titles 1976.

WAYSIDE QUARTERLY, Wayside Press, Joan Atwater, Mary Radcliffe, P.O. Box 475, Cottonwood, AZ 86326. Poetry, articles, art, interviews, reviews, letters. "We print material that reflects a serious view of life, everyday matters of living, appreciation of natural world. We have a nutritional section and can use material on remedies, recipes, and sane living." 4/yr; 1-yr sub price: $2.00; per copy: $0.50; sample: on request free. 1972. 72pp; 5½ x 8½. †mi. circ. 500. Reporting time: 1 month or sooner. Payment: copies only so far. Not copyrighted. Pub'd 4 issues 1976. Pub's reviews.

Waystar Books (see **A DRIFTGLIDE IN TIME**)

B. Weberlein, Publisher (see **TEXAS PORTFOLIO**)

WEBSTER REVIEW, Nancy Schapiro, Harry J. Cargas, Webster College, Webster Groves, MO 63119. "WEBSTER REVIEW publishes contempoary American and international literature. We are interested in fiction of any length, poetry, interviews, essays, and English translations of contemporary writing from all countries. Recent contributors have included: Donald Finkel, Istvan Csurka, Elie Wiesel, Nhat Hanh, Roland Flint, Allen Shepherd, Yehuda Amichai and Howard Schwartz." 4/yr; 1-yr sub price: $5.00; per copy: $1.25; sample: free. 1974. 64pp; 7 x 5. circ. 400. Reporting time: 1 month. Payment: 2 free copies. Discounts: 25%. CCLM, COSMEP.

Wedge Publishing Foundation (see also **VANGUARD**), Bonnie M. Greene, 229 College St., Toronto, Ont. M5T1R4, Canada, 416-979-2442. Non-fiction. "The books we publish approach areas such as education, economics, politics, philosophy, art, from a distinct, or christian perspective." avg. price, paper: $3.95. 1970. 200pp; 5½ x 8½. of. avg. press run 3,000. Discounts: 40 percent. Pub'd 1 title 1976; expects 4 titles 1977.

Weekly Guardian Associates (see **GUARDIAN**)

WEID: The Sensibility Revue, Olivant Press, D.V. Smith, Chief Ed.; Charles Guenther, Poetry; J.H. Fredrick, Fiction, PO Box 1409, Homestead, FL 33030, 2935 Russell Blvd., St. Louis, MO 63104. Poetry, fiction, articles, art, photos, cartoons, interviews, satire, criticism, reviews, letters, parts-of-novels, long-poems, collages, plays, concrete art. "Mss. to Charles Guenther, 2935 Russell Bl, St. Louis, MO 63104." 3/yr; 1-yr sub price: $5.00; per copy: $1.75; sample: $1.75 individual/Free institution. 1952. 100pp; 5 x 7. †of. circ. Confidential. Reporting time: 1 month. Payment: confidential. Copyrighted, reverts to author. Ads: Book rate-no ads permitted. Discounts: Agency 30%. Pub'd 13 issues 1976; expects 3 issues 1977, 3 issues 1978. Pub's reviews: 15 in 1976. §poetry & essays. CCLM, COSMEP.

WELLSIANA, The World Of H.G. Wells, High Orchard Press, Eric Ford, Exec; Royston King, Technical, High Orchard, 125 Markyate Rd, Dagenham, Essex RM8 2LB, United Kingdom.

"Literary and sociological bias for worldwide dissemination of life, works, times, influences, contemporaries on and about, upon and from British Author H.G. Wells (1866-1976)." 2-3/yr; 1-yr sub price: £2; per copy: 50p; sample: £1. 1970. A5. lo/dup. circ. 600. Discounts: agents 20%. Back issues: in bulk 20% list.

WEST COAST POETRY REVIEW, West Coast Poetry Review Press, William L. Fox, Bruce McAllister, Wm. Ransom, 1127 Codel Way, Reno, NV 89503, 702-786-1625. Poetry, interviews, criticism, letters, long-poems, collages, concrete art. "See magazine. Looking for experimental/visual works to balance our backlog of conventional material. People we would like to see work from: Antins (both), Robert Lax, Merwin and Strand, dsh. Recent contributors: Emmett Williams and Dick Higgins, Ian Hamilton Finlay, Dennis Saleh, Hugh Fox with John Brockman, Carolyn Stoloff. We are not interested in automatic writing, surrealism, or naive concrete—tho all of those we like to see used to good ends." 2/yr; 1-yr sub price: $7.00; per copy: $2.00; sample: $2.00. 1970. 84pp; 6 x 9. of. circ. 500-2,000. Reporting time: 1 week. Payment: 2 copies. Copyright permission (for reprints, etc.) must be obtained from publisher-all we ask is published notice of permission and a copy of book in which work appears. Ads: exchange. Discounts: 40% trade. Back issues: Inquire. Pub'd 2 issues 1976; expects 2 issues 1977, 2 issues 1978. Pub's reviews: 4 in 1976. §poetry, fiction, experimental. CCLM.

West Coast Poetry Review Press (see also WEST COAST POETRY REVIEW), William L. Fox, Bruce McAllister, William Ransom, 1127 Codel Way, Reno, NV 89503, 702-786-1625. Poetry, fiction, art. *"The Road To Tamazunchale,* a novel by Ron Arias; *Going Places,* William Stafford; *Ground Zero,* Thomas Johnson; *Soft Where, Inc.;* Aaron Marcus (experimental typography and conceptual art); *Me Too,* Raymond Federman; *Selected Ponds,* Ian Hamilton Finlay (photos). Titles due from Mary Ellen Solt, George Hitchcock, Don Gordon, D. S. Long, Richard Kostelanetz and others. Query first." avg. price, paper: $3.00. 1973. 80pp; 6 x 9. of. avg. press run 1,000. Reporting time: 1 week. Payment: copies. Copyrights for author. Discounts: 40 percent trade. Pub'd 2 titles 1976; expects 4 titles 1977, 4 titles 1978.

THE WEST CONSCIOUS REVIEW, Scarecrow Books, Paul F. Fericano, 1050 Magnolia #2, Millbrae, CA 94030. Poetry, criticism, reviews, letters. "Immensely overstocked. *The West Conscious Review* will be going 'unconscious' in 1978. We will still be around, but any issues put out in that year will be from solicited contributors. Any changes, updates, miraculous recoveries, and drunken stupors will be reported in issues of *Small Press Review*. (John Wayne and Victor Mature are upset about this too.)" irregular/usually 2-year; price per copy: $1.00; sample: free to anyone who sends postage or a photo of the 3 stooges. 1975. 36pp; 5½ x 8½. of. circ. 300. Reporting time: 1-2 weeks. Payment: copies. Copyrighted. Back issues: some still available. COSMEP.

WEST END MAGAZINE, Gail Darrow Kaliss, Box 354, Jerome Ave. Station, Bronx, NY 10468. Poetry, fiction, articles, art, photos. "We try to publish work of high literary quality which also serves to promote postive social and personal change. Recent contributors include Margaret Randall, Ntozake Shange, Bill Herron." 4/yr; 1-yr sub price: $5.00; per copy: $1.00; sample: $1.00. 1971. 48pp; 7 x 8½. †of. circ. 1,500. Reporting time: 10 days to 3-4 months. Payment: In copies. Copyrights return to authors. Pub'd 2 issues 1976; expects 4 issues 1977, 4 issues 1978. CCLM, COSMEP, NESPA.

WESTART, Westart Publications, Jean L. Gouzens, PO Box 1396, Auburn, CA 95603. Articles, art, photos, interviews, criticism, reviews, letters, collages, concrete art. 24/yr; 1-yr sub price: $6.00; per copy: $.30; sample: free. 1962. 20pp; 10 x 15. of. circ. 7,200. Ads: $90.00/$50.00/$.05 word. Discounts: on request. Back issues: Available thru xerox University Microfilms. Pub's reviews. §Arts, art techniques, crafts, craft techniques.

Westburg Associates, Publishers (see also NORTH AMERICAN MENTOR MAGAZINE), John E. Westburg, Gen'l. Ed.; Mildred Westburg, Gen'l. Ed; Martial R. Westburg, Art Ed., 1745 Madison Street, Fennimore, WI 53809, 608-822-6237. Poetry, fiction, articles, art, criticism, reviews. "Open for discussion on use of any kind of material." avg. price, cloth: Between $5.00 and $10.00.; paper: Between $5.00 and $10.00.; other: Between $5.00 and $10.00. 1964. Between 50 and 200.pp; 8½ x 11 or 8½ x 5½. avg. press run Varies, but short runs only, less than 3,000. Reporting time: 6 months or more. Payment varies, but negotiable, but generally no payment made. Copyrights for author. Discounts: None. Pub'd 1 title 1976; expects 2 titles 1977, 3 titles 1978. COSMEP, CCLM.

THE WESTERLY REVIEW, Split-Leaf Press, May Eliot, R. Wujcik, Dana F. Neugent, Patricia Hval, 229 Post Rd, Westerly, RI 02891. Poetry, fiction, art, reviews, parts-of-novels. "Poetry, Short Fiction, and Letters. Manuscripts accompanied by S.A.S.E. are welcome." 3/yr; 1-yr sub price: $6.00; per copy: $2.00. 1976. 50pp; 6 x 8. †of/lp. circ. 250. Reporting time: 2 mos. Payment: copy. Rights revert to authors upon publication. no advertising. Discounts: 30% to anyone on orders of 5 copies or more. Back issues: Vol. 1 No. 1 $3.00, others $1.50. Pub'd 3 issues 1976; expects 3 issues 1977, 3 issues 1978. Pub's reviews. COSMEP, CCLM.

WESTERN AMERICAN LITERATURE, Thomas J. Lyon, UMC 32, Utah State Univ., Logan, UT 84322. Articles, reviews. 4/yr; 1-yr sub price: $7.00; per copy: $1.75. 1966. 80pp; 6 x 9. circ. 700. Reporting time: 2 mos. Payment: 3 copies. Ads: $75/$40.

THE WESTERN CRITIC, The Western Critic, Dwight Jensen, Box 591, Boise, ID 83701. Articles, art, photos, cartoons, interviews, satire, criticism, reviews, letters. "Will consider poetry, which we have printed, and fiction, which we never have." irregular; sub price: 12 issues, $5.00; per copy: $.60; sample: $.60. 1969. 48pp; 8 x 11. of. circ. 1,650. Reporting time: 2-3 weeks. Payment: $5 to $100 per article, usually $15-$25. Ads: $40/$25. Pub's reviews. §The west, the arts, ecology, food, or politics.

WESTERN HUMANITIES REVIEW, Jack Garlington, Editor, University of Utah, Salt Lake City, UT 84112, 801-581-7438. Poetry, fiction, articles, art, interviews, satire, criticism, reviews, parts-of-novels, long-poems, plays, concrete art, non-fiction. "We prefer 2-3,000 words; We like humor, articles with real meaning. Recent contributors: Philip Stevick, William Joyce, Brewster Ghiselin, William Stafford, Jack Matthews, Virgil Aldrich, E R Apffel, Earle Birney." 4/yr; 1-yr sub price: $10.00 (Institutions) $6.00 (Individuals); per copy: $2.00; sample: $2.00. 1947. 96pp; 6¾ x 10. lp. circ. 1,100. Reporting time: 1 month if rejected; longer if accepted. Payment: Up to $100.00 for stories and articles; up to $35.00 for poems; up to $25.00 for reviews. Copyrighted, reverts to author on request. Ads: $75.00/$40.00. Discounts: 25 percent to agents. Back issues: Depends on year. Pub'd 4 issues 1976; expects 4 issues 1977, 4 issues 1978. Pub's reviews: 22 in 1976. §All but novels (we don't review them) Poetry, scholarly works in any area of the humanities, fiction. CCLM, COSMEP.

WESTERN POETRY QUARTERLY, Western Poetry Press, Joseph Rosenzweig, Mildred Rosenzweig, 3253 Q San Amadeo, Laguna Hills, CA 92653. Poetry, reviews. "To 24 lines of poetry—will accept longer poems of *exceptional* quality. Publish *all* types of poetry—only criteria are high technical quality vividness of imagery & uniqeness of approach." 4/yr; 1-yr sub price: $4.00; per copy: $1.25; sample: $1.00. 1973. 31-35pp; 5½ x 8½. of. circ. 200. Reporting time: 7 to 14 days. Payment: 1 copy of issue in which poem appears & 3 cash awards per issue. Copyrighted, reverts to author. Discounts: trade, classroom $1.00 per copy. Back issues: same as when first issued. Pub's reviews. §poetry collections-or books about poetry. CCLM, COSMEP.

Western Washington State College (see JEOPARDY)

WESTERN WORLD REVIEW, Robert E. Sagehorn, PO Box 2714, Culver City, CA 90230. "Articles, reviews, criticism, essays. 'Good' non-fiction on politics, economics, media, philosophy or most anything." 4/yr; 1-yr sub price: $3.00; sample: $.50/sample. 1965. 40pp; 8½ x 7. of. circ. under 500. Reporting time: 2 wks. Payment: copies only. COSMEP.

Westwind Press, A.S. Parrish, Director, Route 1, Box 64, Farmington, WV 26571, 304-287-7160. Fiction, art. 1974. Very small staff, cannot consider unsolicited mss. Copyrights for author. Discounts: Libraries 25 percent. New schedule of prices not yet established. All orders in USA and Canada postpaid. Expects 1 title 1977, 1 title 1978.

WEYFARERS, Guildford Poets Press, John Emuss, David Colbeck, Margaret George, Eric Harrison, Peter Owtram, 10 Ashcroft, Shalford, Surrey, United Kingdom. Poetry. 3/yr; 1-yr sub price: £1; per copy: 35p. 1972. 32pp; 8 x 6. lo. circ. 250. Reporting time: 2 mo. No payment. Copyrighted. Discounts: 25% trade. Pub'd 3 issues 1976; expects 3 issues 1977, 3 issues 1978.

WHAT'S A NICE HILLBILLY LIKE YOU . . . ?, Appalachian Press, Gail Amburgey, David Chaffins, Pauletta Hansel, 107 Earwood St, Beckley, WV 25801. Poetry, fiction, articles, photos. "John Beecher, Don West, Peter Laska, Bob Snyder, Roger Hicks. We print poems, fiction, and other writings by Appalachians. This implies no particular stylistic bias." 4/yr; 1-yr sub price: $3.50; per copy: $1.00; sample: $1.00. 1974. 32pp; 6 x 8. of. circ. 500. Reporting time: 2 mos. Payment: free copy. §Books on Appalachia or by Appalachians. COSMEP.

WHAT'S NEW ABOUT LONDON, JACK?, London Northwest, David H. Schlottmann, 929 South Bay Rd., Olympia, WA 98506. Articles, interviews, criticism, reviews. "Jack London (author) news/fan magazine, a co-operative venture between subscriber & publisher. Subscribers (and others) send in any news they may find, along with all details available. Items vary from trivia to major. Of related interest, THE CHANEY CHRONICAL is a companion magazine devoted to London's father, and THE WOLF is an annual issued each January 12." irreg.; sub price: $5.00/10 issues; per copy: $.60; sample: postage/sample. 1971. 10-12pp; 8½ x 11. mi. circ. 80. Reporting time: a.s.a.p.

What's Your Line Graphics (see BERKELEY JOURNAL OF SOCIOLOGY)

WHITE ARMS MAGAZINE, Rene White, B. Schwartz, Box 302, Howe, IN 46746. Articles, art, photos, interviews, letters. "The Drag Queen Digest. Drag queens our specialty-what they think, where they go, who they know; parties, fashion, recipes, gossip, etc etc etc. You may be the drag queen were looking for. That certain smile that elusive style. White Arms has-will feature such drag queens as B. Schwartz, Jacqueline Joan Johnston (Tacky Jacky), Amanda Reckinwith (A. Ahol), Anna Bannana, Opal Nations etc. Also coming up, Audrey Hepburn look-alike contest. B Schwartz is the sure winner, but you might make runner-up. Represent *your* state in this much-anticipated spectacle. White Arms Magazine is the only little magazine to receive an 'f' rating in *all* categories of Samisdat Review's Little Magazine Symposium. Also that magazine referred to WAM as the National Enquirer of Little Magazines. Can we be anything but flattered. Plus White Arms Magazette, keeping you up on all the behind-the-scenes gossip. With Jimmy's death, things are a little sad, but Rene White has decided to continue the magazine. Grief purifies. A nose for news, a heart for art. Art for Art's ache. All the little axioms that make life bearable. Love, Rene." irreg.; 1-yr sub price: $5.00; per copy: varies; sample: $.20 postage. 1974. 12-60pp; varies. †of. circ. 1,000. Reporting time: soon. Payment: copies. Ads: $10/$5. Back issues: some free with postage. §Drag Queens.

White Bear Books (see THE RED BOOK)

White Bones Press (see BONES)

White Crescent Press (see BEDFORDSHIRE MAGAZINE)

The White Ewe Press (see also THE MILL), Kevin Urick, Box 996, Adelphi, MD 20783, 301-439-1470. Fiction. "Due to financial limitations cannot consider unsolicited book length material. First book publication coming out in 1977. Seems like time. A collection of short stories by Kevin Urick. See listing for magazine." avg. price, paper: $3.00. 1976. 88pp; 6 x 9. of. avg. press run 500 copies. Payment: see 11. Copyrights for author. Discounts: Trade: 40 percent on 3 or more copies. None on less. Will bargain on other. Will exchange. Pub'd 1 title 1976; expects 3 titles 1977, 3 titles 1978. COSMEP, Washington Writers Center.

White Mountain Publishing Company, Guy Lockwood, 13801 N. Cave Creek Rd, Phoenix, AZ 85022, 971-2720. Non-fiction. "Books, booklets. Our first book at printer-publication date: May 1, 1977 future work on books & booklets, in progress." avg. price, cloth: $12.95; paper: $7.95. 1976.

330pp; 5½ x 8½. of. avg. press run 5,000. Reporting time: can't predict. Payment: 10 percent gross or 50-50 profit w/investment. Copyrights for author. Discounts: 45 percent to book & catalog. Expects 2 titles 1977. COSMEP.

WHITE MULE, Thomas Abrams, 2710 E. 98th Ave., Tampa, FL 33612. Poetry, reviews. "Southern surrealism-Van Brock, Willie Reader, Pattie Perry Minchen, Robert Smith, John Hatcher, James Blaine, John Calderazzo, M. Patamia, Chuck Henry, Steven Colburn." 4/yr; price per copy: $1.00; sample: $1.00. 1975. 40pp; varies. of. circ. 300. Payment: copies and a smile. Back issues: priceless. Pub's reviews. §poetry.

WHITE PINE, White Pine Press, Dennis Maloney, 109 Duerstein St., Buffalo, NY 14210, 716-825-8671. Poetry, long-poems. "WHITE PINE is now appearing as one poet per issue usually in chapbook form-an occasional anthology is anticipated. A small series of short poems or a long poem. Recent contributors include: Barry Gifford, Lyn Lifshin, Juan Ramon Jimenez, Han-Shan, Lu Yu, Anselm Hollo, Edith Shiffert. Biases: sense of place and shamanistic poetics and translations." 4/yr; 1-yr sub price: $5.00; per copy: $1.50; sample: $1.25. 1974. 20pp; 5½ x 8½. of. circ. 500. Reporting time: 2 weeks-1 month. Payment: copies. Copyrighted. Discounts: 40% trade discount. Back issues: #1,2 & 3-$1.00 each. Pub'd 8 issues 1976; expects 4 issues 1977, 4 issues 1978. CCLM, COSMEP, NESPA, COSMEP-SOUTH, COSMEP-EAST.

White Urp Press (see ABBEY)

WHOLE EARTH, 11 George St, Brighton, Sussex BN21RH, United Kingdom. Poetry, articles, art, photos, cartoons, interviews, reviews, letters. "Major articles 1,500 words-short news articles. Large emphasis on graphics." 4-5/yr; 1-yr sub price: $4.00; per copy: $1.00; sample: $0.50. 1974. 24pp. of. circ. 1,500. Payment: none. Not copyrighted. Ads: $30.00/$15.00/$0.02. Discounts: 37½ percent cash within 7 days of delivery, otherwise 20 percent. Back issues: no. 1 25 cents, no. 3/4/5 50 cents, no. 6 75 cents. Pub's reviews. §agriculture, community, crafts, ecology, foods, energy. APS.

WIA NEWSLETTER, Women in the Arts Foundation, Inc., Mary Vaughan, 435 Broome St, New York, NY 10013, 212-966-5894. Articles, interviews, letters. "Length-200 to 1,000 words-must be on women's art movement or topics relevant to women artists." 10/yr; 1-yr sub price: $5.00 ($6.00 institution); sample: free. 1971 (for organization) 1973 (for newsletter). 6pp; 8½ x 11. of. circ. 1,000. No payment. Not copyrighted. Ads: $35.00/$17.50. Discounts: trade-free, subscription in exchange for free subscription; 20 percent discount to jobber or agent. Back issues: free for single copy; 50 cents/pc. otherwise. Pub'd 10 issues 1976. Pub's reviews: 5 in 1976. §women's visual art & writing.

Wild & Woolley, Michael Wilding, Pat Woolley, P.O. Box 41, Glebe NSW 2037, Australia. Fiction. "We are small press book publisher, concentrating on Australian writers, doing an average of six titles per year. We publish prose, comix, politics. Our authors include Vicki Viidikas, Robert Adamson, Ron Cobb, Michael Wilding, Antigone Kefala, Rudi Krausmann and Kris Hemensley. We are interested in co-publishing with US and UK small presses. Co-published authors include Jon Silkin, Henry James Korn and Didier Coste. Wild & Woolley represent City Lights Books in Australia and New Zealand. The Wild share is Michael Wilding, the Woolley part is Pat Woolley." 1974. of. Reporting time: 3 months. Payment: royalties. COSMEP, COSMEPA, AIPA.

WILD FENNEL, Pauline Palmer, Editor, 2510 48th Street, Bellingham, WA 98225. Poetry, fiction, articles, art, cartoons, interviews, satire, criticism, reviews, letters. "Especially interested in humor, personal essays, light and/or satirical social comment. Some short fiction of the fantasy and sf genre. A very limited amount of poetry, but especially like short poems that show the poet as human with a sense of humor." 2/yr; 1-yr sub price: $2.00; per copy: $1.00; sample: $1.00. 1970. 24-32pp; 8 x 10. of. circ. 200-500. Reporting time: 3-4 wks. Payment: copies only. Pub'd 2 issues 1976; expects 2 issues 1977, 2-3 issues 1978.

Wild Horses & The Potted Plant, Pamela Portugal, Helen Stephens, Sidney Damon, Jody Shane-Main, Nancy Portugal, 2145 Everding, Eureka, CA 95501, 707-442-7127. Poetry, fiction, articles, art, cartoons, music. "Also: The Potted Plant in The Artifactory, 226 Hamilton Ave., Palo Alto, CA 94301. Phone: 415-327-9815 Tues & Thurs. Published 2 books: *THE POTTED PLANT ORGANIC CARE HANDBOOK,* and *A PLACE FOR HUMAN BEINGS.*" avg. price, paper: $5.75. 1972. 328pp; 7½ x 10. †of. avg. press run 4,000. Reporting time: infinite. Copyrights for author. Discounts: 40-55. Pub'd 1 title 1976; expects 1 title 1977, 1 title 1978. ARTIFACTORY.

Wilderness Press, Thomas Winnett, 2440 Bancroft Way, Berkeley, CA 94704, 415-843-8080. Non-fiction. "Ms. to 50,000 words-guidebook to a camping-hiking area based on complete coverage by author of every place described. Heavy conservation bias." avg. price, cloth: $16.95; paper: $4.95. 1967. 212pp; Varies. of. avg. press run 5,000. Reporting time: 1 month. Payment: royalty. Copyrights for author. Discounts: 40% to retail stores. Pub'd 5 titles 1976; expects 10 titles 1977, 5 titles 1978.

WILLAMETTE VALLEY OBSERVER, Kenneth J. Doctor, 1065 High St., Eugene, OR 97401, 503-687-0376. Articles, interviews, satire, letters, non-fiction. 51/yr; 1-yr sub price: $8.00; per copy: $.25; sample: $.25. 1975. 24pp; 10¼ x 15. of. circ. 5,000. Reporting time: 1 mo. Payment varies. Copyrighted, reverts to author. Ads: $285.00/$142.50/$0.10. Back issues: 50¢. Pub'd 24 issues 1976; expects 45 issues 1977, 51 issues 1978. Pub's reviews. §environment, art, music, children, sports.

Molly M. Willett, Molly M. Willett, P.O. Box 689, Mill Valley, CA 94941, 415-388-3692. Photos, interviews. "One book: *A Woman Psychologist's Own Process Of Self Development.*" avg. price, paper: $5.95. 1976. †litho. Discounts: 30 percent trade.

William Blackwood & Sons Ltd. (see also BLACKWOOD'S MAGAZINE), David Fletcher, 32 Thistle Street, Edinburgh EH2 1HA, United Kingdom, 031-225-3411. "Mat'l used: monographs on Scottish subjects. New series of commissioned booklets." avg. price, paper: 85p. 1804. 64pp; 210 mm x 147 mm. †lp/of. avg. press run 5,000. Payment: By negotiation. Copyright is property of authors. Discounts: 33-1/3 percent. Expects 6 titles 1977, 12 titles 1978. PA.

William L. Bauhan, Publisher, William L. Bauhan, Dublin, NH 03444. "Specialize in New England regional books, authors/non-fiction. Recent titles: OF EARTH, poems by Douglas Worth, A CELEBRATION, poems by Henry Chapin, MORE THAN LAND: Stories of New England Country Life by Herman Chase, ON THE TRAIL OF STODDARD GLASS, by Anne Field, MAXFIELD PARRISH PRINTS by Marian S. Sweeney, AFTER THE BEGINNING poems by Sarah Singer." of/lp. Reporting time: month or so. Payment: 10% of list price; less on poetry & small editions. Discounts: 40% off on 5 or more copies. flat 20% off on textbooks, ltd. editions. NESPA.

WILLMORE CITY, Willmore City Press, Alex N. Scandalios, Jim Gautney, Byron Whalen, Joan Smith, P O Box 1601, Carlsbad, CA 92008. Poetry, fiction, articles, art, photos, cartoons, interviews, letters, parts-of-novels, long-poems, plays. "Includes a directory of graduate writing programs. Published as a double-issue, one of which features a specific school-Long Beach State, Univ. of Iowa, Univ. of Mass., Amherst-thus far. Recent contributors: Gerald Locklin, John Bennett, Edward Field, Donald Junkins, James Tate, Jay Neurenberg, and a whole bunch more." 4/yr; 1-yr sub price: $4.50; per copy: $2.75; sample: $2.75. 1974. 140 pp, Perfect bound.; 5½ x 8½. †of. circ. 1,000. Reporting time: 6 weeks. Payment: Copies and writing awards for poetry and fiction. ($20.00 ea.). Copyrighted, reverts to author. Ads: $100.00/$50.00. Discounts: 40 percent. Back issues: 40 percent off. Pub's reviews. §Fiction and poetry.

Willmore City Press (see also WILLMORE CITY), Alex N. Scandalios, Jim Gautney, P O Box 1601, Carlsbad, CA 92008. Poetry, fiction. "We are not looking for book submissions. Within the next year we are hoping to publish books by the following authors: Edward Field, Linda Brown, Janet Pnelan, Leanne Bitterolf, Alex N. Scandalios." avg. price, paper: $2.50. 1976. 40-60 pp, Perfect bound; 5½ x 8½. †of/lp. avg. press run 500. Reporting time: 4-6 weeks. Payment: 15 percent of net profit. Copyrights for author. Discounts: 40 percent trade discount.

WIN MAGAZINE, Dwight Ernest, Mary Mayo, Mark Morris, Susan Pines, Murray Rosenblith, Box 547, Rifton, NY 12471. Poetry, articles, art, photos, cartoons, interviews, satire, reviews, letters. "WIN is a weekly publication of the Peace Movement. We publish articles of interest to radical pacifist people and organizers of direct action campaigns, political analysis for and from the radical left. Recent contributors include Dave McReynolds, Harvey Wasserman, Miriam Wolf Wasserman, Grace Paley, Art Waskow, the Berrigans, Murray Bookchin, Claudia Dreifus, Marty Jezer, Craig Karpel, Staughton Lynd, and many others. Word length: 650-2000 words or more. No guidelines available, but anyone may request a sample copy for an idea of our style and bias. WIN is available on Microfilm from Xerox University Microfilms." 52/yr; sub price: $11.00/yr individuals $15.00/yr libraries free/prisoners; per copy: $.30; sample: free upon request. 1966. 24-32pp; 8½ x 11. of. circ. 7,000. Reporting time: 2-6 weeks. Payment: none. Ads: $150/$85/$2/10 words. Discounts: 40% to bookstores, 15% agency discount on ads, sub agents should write for info. Back Issues: 50¢ most, $1 or $1.50 on others; bulk 10 or more 50% additional discount. Pub's reviews. §political, social change, non-violence, sociology, anarchism, social and economic thought, non-violent direct action experiences. COSMEP, APS, LNS News Service.

Winbooks, Fred Rosen, Box 547, Rifton, NY 12471. "Publisher of THINKING LIKE A WOMAN by Leah Fritz, with an afterword by Barbara Deming. WINBOOKS is actively seeking writers to publish."

WIND MAGAZINE, The Wind Press, Quentin R. Howard, RFD Rt. 1 Box 810, Pikeville, KY 41501, 606-437-6963. Poetry, fiction, articles, interviews, criticism, reviews, parts-of-novels, plays. "No set length on anything. No biases. Josephine Jacobsen, Larry Rubin, Dave Etter, Eve Triem, John Unterecker, John Tagliabue, Lewis Turco, George Scarbrough, Norma Farber, R. P. Dickey, John F. Bennett, Bruce D. Brown, Lillie D. Chaffin, Jesse Stuart, James Still." 4/yr; 1-yr sub price: $4.50-yr, $5.50-yr instit, $6.50-yr foreign; per copy: $1.25; sample: $1.25. 1971. 96pp; 5½ x 8½. of. circ. 500. Reporting time: 1-2 wks. Payment: copies only. Copyrighted, reverts to author. Ads: $50/$25/$.10 class./wd. Discounts: none. Back issues: $1.50/ea. Pub'd 4 issues 1976; expects 4 issues 1977, 4 issues 1978. Pub's reviews. CCLM, COSMEP, SSSL, AWP.

Windfall, Joel Rosen, Molly Hegarty, 160 Hancock, Cambridge, MA 02139. Poetry, fiction, cartoons, satire, parts-of-novels. "Anthologies of short fiction." avg. price, paper: $2.00; other: $2.50. 1976. 75pp; 6 x 9. †lp/of. avg. press run 500. Reporting time: 1 month. Payment in copies (usually 20 percent of the edition). Copyrights for author. Discounts: 40 percent. Pub'd 6 titles 1976; expects 2 titles 1977, 2 titles 1978. Pub's reviews. CRISP.

Windflower Press, Ted Kooser, P.O. Box 82213, Lincoln, NB 68501. Poetry. "Windflower Press publishes books of poetry. We are not currently reading unsolicited manuscripts." avg. price, cloth: $6.95; paper: $2.95. 1967. 64pp; 5½ x 8. of. avg. press run 500. Reporting time: 2 weeks. Payment: by contract. Copyright by contract. Discounts: 40 percent to bookstores for orders of 5 copies or more; 20 percent otherwise. Pub'd 1 title 1976; expects 1 title 1977. COSMEP.

THE WINDLESS ORCHARD, Indiana Univ Eng Dept, Ft. Wayne, IN 46805. Poetry, criticism. 4/yr; 1-yr sub price: $7.00; per copy: $2.00; sample: $2.00. 1970. circ. 400. Reporting time: 1-9 weeks. Pub'd 3 issues 1976; expects 4 issues 1977, 4 issues 1978. Pub's reviews.

The Windmill Press, Charles Krouse, 1369 Linwood Drive, Holland, MI 49423, 616-335-2688. Poetry. "Owner & founder has published one, and is currently working on a 2nd; is in the mkt. for other work but costs of production usually require some money from the publisher. Writers seem to promote their work more if their own cash is at stake. We started the venture as a way of getting out of the closet and letting others know we are HERE and are writing and publishing. A hedge against oblivion. Published THOUGHTS & POEMS, Lorraine Gezon, currently working with other local poets and encouraging some 'mute, inglorious Miltons' to correct that often fatal condition. We find non-literate, art noveau, low-skill stuff palling. Word-mongers should possess a lot of plain old skill." avg. price, paper: $2.00. 1975. 60pp; varied. †of/lp. avg. press run 500. Reporting time: flexible. Payment: none yet—negotiable. Does not copyright for author. Discounts: subject to negotiation.

WINDOW, Window Press, Dan Johnson, Paul Deblinger, Trisha Tatam, Nan Barbour, 7005 Westmoreland Ave., Takoma Park, MD 20012. Poetry, fiction, art, photos, interviews, reviews, letters. "No particular bias. Would prefer to print several poems by a given poet. Recent poems by Henry Taylor, Linda Pastan, William Claire, and John Engels." 3/yr; sub price: $6.00 - 4 issues; per copy: $1.75; sample: $1.00. 1976. 72pp; 5½ x 8½. of. circ. 750. Reporting time: 6 weeks. Payment: 2 copies. Ads: $60.00/$40.00. Discounts: 40 percent. Back issues: $1.75. Pub'd 3 issues 1976; expects 3 issues 1977, 3 issues 1978. Pub's reviews. §poetry/criticism/fiction. WWC.

WINDOWS IN THE STONE, Free Books Inc., Ronnie Lane, 7437 Eastern S.E., Grand Rapids, MI 49508. Poetry, fiction, art, photos, cartoons, satire, long-poems. "Eric Greinke, Ben Tibbs, Dave Cope, Bruce Rizzon, Pam Greinke, Sue Cope, Paul Payack. 'My taste runs from macabre to sf, rhymes to prose if in a surrealistic (without being abstract) hybrid. With art it depends on the individual thing.'" 2/yr; 1-yr sub price: free; per copy: free; sample: free. 1974. 80-100pp; varies. †of. circ. 5,000. Reporting time: slow, deliberate. Payment: copies. Back issues: no back copies available.

Windows Project (see also SMOKE), Dave Ward, 46 Elsinore Heights, Halewood, Liverpool L269TE, United Kingdom. Poetry, fiction, art, photos, cartoons, long-poems, collages, concrete art. avg. price, paper: 30P booklet/10P SMOKE. 1974. 24pp; A4 (booklet)/A5 (SMOKE). of. avg. press run 500. Reporting time: As quickly as possible. Payment: yes/negotiable. Discounts: 33 percent. Expects 1 title 1977, 1 title 1978.

The Wine Press, James Ramholz, 4504 N. Mc Vicker, Chicago, IL 60630. Poetry, parts-of-novels, long-poems. 3-6/yr; price per copy: varies. 1972. 12pp; 8½ x 5½. †of/lp. circ. 500. Reporting time: immediately/week. Payment: copies only (10%). Discounts: 40% to bookstores.

WINE RINGS, Joyce Odam, Ann Menebroker, 2432-48th Ave., c/o Odam, Sacramento, CA 95822, Rt. 1, Box 821, c/o Menebroker, Wilton, CA 95693. "Poetry, not over a page long." 4/yr; 1-yr sub price: $2.00; per copy: $.50; sample: $.50. 1975. 4-8pp; 8½ x 11. †mi. circ. 200. Reporting time: 2 wks to 2 mos. Payment: copy.

WINGED OX, Eugene Warren, 107 South Rolla, Rolla, MO 65401. "First and so far only issue: *Icons* by John Morgan. No unsolicited." irreg.; price per copy: varies; sample: $.30. 1975. 12pp. of. circ. 500. Payment: copies. Discounts: 40%.

Winston-Paramount Books (see BEST POETS OF THE 20th CENTURY, NOTABLE AMERICAN POETS)

WIP, Windfall, Paul Acker, Joel Rosen, Marlene Youmans, c/oEnglish Department, Box 1852, Brown Univ., Providence, RI 02912. Poetry, fiction, art. "Biases: We have a positive horror of meaningless assertions. The trite, the stilted or tautological better look to their nouns. Recent contributors: Denise Levertov, Terry Stokes, Michael Harper, Robert Peters, Alan Dugan, Robert Hayden, William Bronk." 3/yr; 1-yr sub price: $3.00; per copy: $.95; sample: $.95. 1975. 36pp; 8½ x 7. †of. circ. 400. Reporting time: 1 month. Payment: copies. Back issues: $1.50 per. §poetry/prose. CRISP.

The Wire Press (see also JOURNAL OF THE HELLENIC DIASPORA, COFFEE HOUSE), Dino Siotis, 329 San Jose Ave, San Francisco, CA 94110. Poetry. *"Chroniche Of Exile-poems* by Greece's greatest poet, Yannis Ritsos." avg. price, paper: $2.95. 1974. 96pp; 8½ x 5. †of. avg. press run 3,000. Copyrights for author. Discounts: 40 percent bookstores. Expects 2 titles 1977, 3 titles 1978. CCLM.

Wisconsin Dance Council (see DANCE DIMENSIONS)

WISCONSIN REVIEW, Wisconsin Review, Charles Dahlen, Judith Wittig, Karen Waugh, Box 145 Dempsey Hall, University of Wisconsin-Oshkosh, Oshkosh, WI 54901, 414-424-2267. Poetry, fiction, art, photos, cartoons, interviews, reviews, parts-of-novels, long-poems, plays. "Doug

Flaherty, Tom McKeown, Lyn Lifshin, R.D. Swets and Anick O'Meara. Please do not submit more than five pages of poetry at one time. Do not submit poetry and fiction with only one S.A.S.E. Do not submit during May, June, & July." 4/yr; 1-yr sub price: $3.00; per copy: $0.75; sample: $0.75. 1966. 75pp; 8½ x 11. of. circ. 1,000. Reporting time: 0-3 months. Payment: copies. Copyrighted, reverts to author. Back issues: $1.00/issue. Pub'd 4 issues 1976; expects 4 issues 1977, 4 issues 1978. Pub's reviews. §poetry and shortstories.

WISCONSIN TRAILS, Tamarack Press, Jill Dean, Maggie Dewey, Mary Bradish, 517 N. Segoe Rd., P.O. Box 5650, Madison, WI 53705. Poetry, articles, photos. "Tamarack Press at present is interested in books about nature and the environment, heritage, and folklore, and guides to city and countryside as well as outdoor sports. Submissions should contain outline and sample chapters." 4/yr; 1-yr sub price: $10.00; per copy: $2.50. 1960. 44pp; 9 x 12. of. circ. 23,500. Reporting time: 2-3 weeks-magazine; 1 month-books. Discounts: sub agency discount, all other universal disc. sched. Back issues: reg. issues $2.00/rare issues $4.00. Pub's reviews. §outdoor sports/activities/anything dealing w/Wisconsin.

WITCHCRAFT DIGEST MAGAZINE (THE WICA NEWSLETTER), Hero Press, Leo Louis Martello, Suite 1B, 153 West 80th St., New York, NY 10024. "Prospective contributors should familiarize themselves with our theology-philosophy as outlined in Dr. Martello's book *WITCHCRAFT: The Old Religion;* or Patricia Crowther's *Witch Blood: Autobiography of a Witch High Priestess* or her *The Witches Speak.* We're Pre-Christian Pagans, naturalists, and the Old Religion has NOTHING to do with Christian-defined Satanism, devil-worship etc. Anyone sending in a self-addressed stamped envelope will receive our FREE lists of Old Religion books and publications." 1/yr; 1-yr sub price: $1.25. 1970. 24pp; 8½ x 11. of. circ. 3,500. Reporting time: immediately. Payment: 1 cent per word. Ads: $100/$50/$.20. Discounts: 40%. Pub's reviews. §witchcraft, occult, psychology, religion.

Witwatersrand University Press (see ENGLISH STUDIES IN AFRICA)

Wolf House Books (see THE LONDON COLLECTOR)

THE WOMAN ACTIVIST, Flora Crater, 2310 Barbour Road, Falls Church, VA 22043. Articles. "The woman activist could be classified as a newsletter. I call it a political action bulletin for women's rights." 12/yr; 1-yr sub price: $10.00; per copy: $1.00; sample: $.25. 1971. 8pp; 8½ x 11. of. circ. 300. Reporting time: 3 weeks. Payment: none. Ads: $.20 wd. Pub'd 12 issues 1976; expects 12 issues 1977, 12 issues 1978. Pub's reviews: 5 in 1976. §women/politics/feminism.

Woman Press, Marie J. Kuda, Box 59330, Chicago, IL 60645. Poetry, fiction, art, photos, criticism, parts-of-novels, long-poems, plays. "Annotated bibliography monograph, anthology, poetry. A lesbian press." 1974. †of/lp. Discounts: 40%. COSMEP.

WOMAN SPIRIT, Collective, Box 263, Wolf Creek, OR 97497. Poetry, fiction, articles, art, photos, cartoons, interviews, criticism, reviews, music, letters, long-poems, collages, plays. "Our audience is women. Only women contribute. We use 'she' and 'her' as generic terms. Unpublished women are encouraged to submit personal experiences, about their inner growth, and original art work (in black and white only). Originality, authenticity and positive attitudes towards women, their lives, changes and potential. 500 to 5000 words, graphics up to 8 x 10. Seasonal material (related to equinoxes and solstices) is used as appropriate and themes are developed which relate to cycles of monthly (moon) changes, yearly (sun) changes and life time development (aging). We are feminist, in the Women's Movement, see our magazine as going to the roots (radical) of women's experiences to rebuild a humane culture. We do not publish personal love poetry, love stories etc." 4/yr; 1-yr sub price: $6.00; per copy: $2.00. 1974. 64pp; 8½ x 11. of. circ. 5M. Reporting time: 3-6 mos. Payment: 2 copies. CCLM.

Woman's Soul Publishing Inc. (see PAID MY DUES)

WOMANCHILD, Womanchild Press, Julie Scheinman, 84 Birch St., Worcester, MA 01603, 617-756-4426. Poetry, long-poems. "Wants poems of clarity in any style or form. Now accepting book-length mss for chapbook series. Recent contributors include Lifshin, Malanga, Gayle Harvey, Roberta Gould, S.R. Lavin." 1/yr; price per copy: $2.00. 1976. 40pp; 6 x 9. †lp. circ. 300. Reporting time: 2-4 weeks. Payment: 3 copies. Discounts: 10 or more 50% off, cash basis. Back issues: $5.00. Pub'd 1 issue 1976; expects 1 issue 1977, 1 issue 1978.

WOMANSMITH, Womansmith, The Womansmith Collective, 243 N. Idaho Ave., Massapequa, NY 11758. Poetry, fiction, articles, art, photos, cartoons, interviews, satire, criticism, reviews, music, parts-of-novels, long-poems, collages, plays, concrete art. "We want to publish women's work, unknown women to provide ratification of our shared experiences & visions." sub price: 4 issues: $5.00; per copy: $1.50 plus $.35 (p.t.h.); sample: $1.85. 1975. 48pp; 8½ x 7. of. Reporting time: 2-6 months. No payment. Ads: $20.00 to women-owned business. Discounts: bulk prices-5 issues or more $1.00 per issue. §women's books-feminist studies.

WOMEN: A Journal of Liberation, Collective, 3028 Greenmount Ave, Baltimore, MD 21218. Poetry, fiction, articles, art, photos, cartoons, interviews, satire, criticism, reviews, letters, parts-of-novels, long-poems. "We are a socialist-feminist journal. Issues are by theme—eg 'aging', 'The cost of living.' Only publish material by women. Material should be informal (nonacademic) in style." 2-3/yr; sub price: 1 vol./4 issues: $5.00 individual; per copy: $1.25; sample: $1.25. 1969. 64pp; 8½ x 11. circ. 12,000. Reporting time: 5 months. Payment: none. Back issues: damaged copies $.50. Pub's reviews. §women's & political. COSMEP.

WOMEN & FILM, Siew-Hwa Beh, Saunie Salyer, PO Box 4501, Berkeley, CA 94704. Poetry, fiction, articles, art, photos, cartoons, interviews, criticism, reviews, letters, long-poems, collages. "Length of material & style determined by subject/writer. Flexible. Requirements-interested in experimental material." 3/yr; sub price: $3.00/yr, $5.50/yr institutional; per copy: $1.50. 1972. 80-100pp; 8½ x 11. circ. 6M. Reporting time: 1-3 mos. Ads: $200/$150/no class/wd. Discounts: 1/3 bulk, 1/4 agent. Back issues: #'s 3-4, $2.25; issues 1 & 2 are o.o.p. COSMEP.

The Women And Literature Collective, Box 441, Cambridge, MA 02138, 617-266-2082. Art, photos, criticism, reviews, parts-of-novels. "Book: *Women and Literature,* an annotated bibliography of women writers" avg. price, paper: $3.50; other: $3.50 plus 25 cents postage. 1973. 212pp; 5½ x 7½. of. avg. press run 5,000. Payment: flat rate. Copyrights for author. Discounts: teacher, 20 percent off for 5-15 copies; 30 percent off for more than 15 copies. 40 percent bookstore discount for more than 5 copies. Pub'd 1 title 1976. COSMEP.

Women Artists Newsletter (Press), Cynthia Navaretta, Box 3304, Grand Central, New York City, NY 10017, 212-682-4716. Articles, art, photos, interviews, criticism, reviews, letters, collages, concrete art. 10/yr; avg. price, cloth: $5.00; paper: $0.50; other: $0.50. 1975. 8pp; 8½ x 11. of. avg. press run 5,000. Reporting time: 2—3 weeks. Payment: Not at present; anticipated in near future. Copyrights for author. Discounts: jobber & agent 20%; bookstores, galleries 50%; classroom 40%. Back issues: $0.50. Pub's reviews. §art, (visual arts, film, dance) women. CCLM, COSMEP.

WOMEN ARTISTS NEWSLETTER, Women Artists Newsletter (Press), Cynthia Navaretta, Judy Seigel, 3304 Grand Central Sta, New York City, NY 10017, 212-682-4716. Articles, art, photos, cartoons, interviews, criticism, reviews, letters, collages, concrete art. "Lucy Lippard, Miriam Schapiro, Jonathan Price, Susan Mango" 10/yr; 1-yr sub price: $5.00; per copy: $0.50; sample: $0.50. 1975. 8pp; 8½ x 11. of. Reporting time: 3 weeks. Payment: signed articles 5 column inches in print or larger $10.00 less than 5-$5. Copyrighted. Ads: $80.00/$5.00. Discounts: group rate of 5 or more $3.50/issue—jobber $4.00/subscription. Back issues: 50 cents per copy. Pub's reviews. §art, feminist. CCLM, COSMEP.

WOMEN IN STRUGGLE, J. C. Taylor, Box 324-DB, Winneconne, WI 54986. 6/yr; sub price: 10 issues $3.00; per copy: free on request with SASE. 1970. 8pp; 8½ x 11. of. circ. controlled. Copyrighted. Pub'd 2 issues 1976; expects 6 issues 1977, 6 issues 1978. COSMEP.

Women In The Arts Foundation, Inc. (see WIA NEWSLETTER)

Women Library Workers (see also WOMEN LIBRARY WORKERS NEWSLETTER), Helen Josephine, Ed. of Newsletter Only, 555 29th St, San Francisco, CA 94131, 415-527-5836. "Editor(s) Carole Leita, Mary McKenney, Sue Critchfield, share a directory of feminist library workers (first edition published as *Sisters Have Resources Everywhere,* a directory of feminist librarians) is a directory of feminist library workers. Names, addresses and brief self-descriptions of almost 200 women in the U.S. and Canada who are interested in sharing information, skills, and friendship with other feminists. Entries are geographically arranged; subject and name indexes are included." avg. price, paper: $2.00 prepaid; other: $2.50 if invoiced. 1975. 50pp; 5½ x 8½. of. avg. press run 1,000. Reporting time: varies. Payment: none. Does not copyright for author. Expects 1 title 1978.

WOMEN LIBRARY WORKERS NEWSLETTER, Women Library Workers, Helen Josephine, 555 29th St, San Francisco, CA 94131, 415-527-5836. Articles, art, photos, interviews, criticism, reviews. "WLW Newsletter contains news and information of interest to members of this feminist library workers organization." 6/yr; 1-yr sub price: $5.00; per copy: $1.00; sample: free. 1975. 16pp; 5½ x 8½. of. circ. 550. Reporting time: 1 month. Payment: none available at present. Not copyrighted. Ads: no paid advertising. Discounts: 10 percent to vendors. Back issues: $1.00 each, as available. Pub'd 6 issues 1976; expects 6 issues 1977, 6 issues 1978. Pub's reviews. §feminism, libraries & information services.

WOMEN STUDIES ABSTRACTS, J and J Printing, Sara Stauffer Whaley, PO Box 1, Rush, NY 14543. "Contains abstracts of articles from selected periodicals on all aspects of women's lives. Any periodical wanting to be considered for possible inclusion should write and send a sample copy." 4/yr; 1-yr sub price: $20.00 institutional $25.00; per copy: $5.00 ($6.00 to library); sample: $3.00, to libraries free. 1972. 96pp; 5-7/8 x 9. of. circ. 1,500. Reporting time: 1 month. Payment: $100-$200 for bibliographic essay. Copyrighted, reverts to author. Ads: $100.00/$60.00. Discounts: To bookstores-40% off institutional rate. Pub'd 4 issues 1976; expects 4 issues 1977, 4 issues 1978. Pub's reviews. §Women. COSMEP.

Women Writing Press, Andrea Chesman, Alison Colbert, Polly Joan, Rd 3, Newfield, NY 14867. Poetry, articles, art, photos, interviews, criticism, reviews, letters. "Not currently soliciting." avg. price, paper: $3.00. 1974. pp varies; Varies. of. avg. press run 1,000. Reporting time: 2-4 mos. Payment: free copies to contributors. Copyrights for author. Discounts: 40 percent price for 5 or more copies bookstores. Back issues: $.50. Pub'd 1 title 1976; expects 3 titles 1977.

Women's Heritage Association Trust (see AUNTIE BELLUM)

Women's History Research Center, Inc. (see also FEMALE ARTISTS PAST & PRESENT also, FILMS BY AND/OR ABOUT WOMEN), Vicki Lynn Hill, '74 Ed; Louisa Moe, '75 Ed. 72pp; 7 x 8½. of. avg. press run 1,000. Discounts: 30-40 percent discount to book dealers buying at least 5 copies.

Women's Institute for Freedom of the Press, Donna Allen, Editor, 3306 Ross Place, N.W., Washington, DC 20008, 202-966-7783. Non-fiction. "Studies of communication system, particularly as it affects women, is our major interest, although we will consider related material, especially documentary or source material, about women in media." 1972. 6 x 9. of. Reporting time: 2 months. Discounts: bulk-40 percent on 5 or more. Expects 2 titles 1977, 2 titles 1978.

Women's Studies, Wendy Martin, Dept. of English, Queens College, CUNY, Flushing, NY 11367. Articles, reviews. 3/yr; 1-yr sub price: $14.50. 1971. 100pp. circ. 2,000. Pub's reviews.

WOMEN'S STUDIES NEWSLETTER, The Feminist Press, Florence Howe, Box 334, Old Westbury, NY 11568, 516-997-7660. Articles, reviews. "News, issues, events in women's studies; articles are from 1,200 to 2,000 words usually." 4/yr; 1-yr sub price: $7.00 individuals/$12.00 institutions/foreign, $10.00 individual/$15.00 institution; per copy: $2.00; sample: $2.00. 1972. 16pp; 8½ x 11. circ. 1,500 to 2,000. Payment: we do not pay contributors. Copyrighted, does not revert to author. Ads: $125.00/$75.00/$0.25. Discounts: none. Back issues: $2.00 each. Pub'd 4 issues 1976; expects 3 issues 1977, 4 issues 1978. Pub's reviews. §Women's studies.

WOOD IBIS, Place Of Herons, James Cody, 2404 Riverside Farms Rd., Austin, TX 78741. Poetry, fiction, articles, art, criticism, reviews, music, letters, parts-of-novels, long-poems. "Nature, shamanism, ethnopoetry, tribal, regionalism, Texas, The South, native Americans, mythology, literature (prose), poetry. Villanueva, Lawless, Gifford, Calvello, Fowler, Arcos, Sanchez, Blue Cloud, Cardenas, Garcia, Camarillo." Irregular, at least once a year.; 1-yr sub price: $5.00; per copy: $1.25; sample: $1.25. 1974. 60-100pp; 8½ x 5½. of. circ. 1,000. Reporting time: Varies. Payment: Copies, hope to pay in future. Ads: $50.00/$25.00. Back issues: No. 1/$5.00 ea. No. 2 $1.25 ea. Expects 2 issues 1977, 1-2 issues 1978. Pub's reviews. §Nature, shamanism, ethnopoetry, tribal, regionalism, Texas, the South, Native Americans, mythology, general poetry.

Woodbine Press, Bruce McPherson, 4615 Cedar Ave, Philadelphia, PA 19143, 65 Allen Ave, E. Prov., RI 02915. Poetry, long-poems. "*Woodbine Press* publishes books of poetry, concentrating on longpoems and works in verse. Books published: *Sea Agon* by Alexandra Griukhes, *The Rose Of The West* by Jaimy Gordon, *The Name Encanyoned River* by Clayton Eshleman, *Hymns To The Night* by Novalis (trans. by Dick Higgins). Please note: separate address for all non-editorial correspondence & orders. Paul Woodbine, Publisher/65 Allen Avenue/Riverside, R.I. 02915." avg. price, cloth: $8.00; paper: $4.00. 1975. 40pp; varies. †lp. avg. press run 500. Reporting time: 2 weeks to 2 months. Payment: copies and royalties. Copyrights for author. Discounts: 40 percent to the trade for 5 or more assorted. Pub'd 2 titles 1976; expects 3 titles 1977, 4 titles 1978. COSMEP.

Wooden Needle Press (see THE MODULARIST REVIEW)

Woods Hole Press, PO Box 44, Woods Hole, MA 02543. †of. COSMEP.

Woolman Press (see PORT TOWNSEND JOURNAL)

Woolmer/Brotherson Ltd., Robert Brotherson, Andes, NY 13731, 914-676-3218. Poetry. avg. price, cloth: $5.95. 1971. varies with contents. †of/lp. avg. press run quite varied. Reporting time: 6 weeks. Payment: 10 percent paid twice a year. Copyrights for author. Discounts: We are members of STOP and give 40 percent discount on single copies ordered on STOP form. Pub'd 1 title 1976; expects 3 titles 1977, 3 titles 1978.

Word-Camera (see also AFTER-IMAGE), Joe Magri, Ray Sibol, PO Box 10144, Towson, MD 21204. Poetry, fiction, satire, parts-of-novels, plays. "WORD-CAMERA seeks experimental material (strictly). Poetry/Prose/Plays/Stories/Novels...(all these terms are used loosely). We're more interested in the solidity of words as they imply ideas, than the solidity of ideas using words as their implications. Brevity is important (but not absolutely necessary). We look for manuscripts from writers who feel that the most important issue is getting into print (and not the print itself). Therefore, we're not ashamed to say our format is MIMEO. Those writer's who have reservations about MIMEO should avoid us (tritely) like the plague. We will publish as many good manuscripts as money allows. Manuscripts cannot be returned unless accompanied by sufficient return postage." avg. price, cloth: varies. 1976. varies 30-60pp; 8½ x 11. †mi. avg. press run varies. Reporting time: promptly. Payment: pays copies only. Copyright by arrangement.

Word And Action (Dorset), Co-Operative, 186 Newstead Road, Weymouth, Dorset DT40DY, United Kingdom, 03057-74205. Poetry. "In association with theatre and writing service. Publishers of Chesil (magazine of Chesil poets); W & A(D), anthology of work by poets born in or living in Dorset, first issue 1975, thereafter annual. Poets in Dorset-series of individual poets. W & A (D) Book Club." avg. price, paper: 80p-50p. 1972. Anthology-60 pp, Individual poets-18pp; A5. of. avg. press run 600 (Anthologies); 200 (Individual booklets). Payment: Copies/no payments at present. Copyrights for author. Expects 6 titles 1977, 7 titles 1978.

WORD GARDEN, Joyce Farag, Shawky Farag, PO Box 2245, Springfield, IL 62705, 217-523-9865. Poetry, fiction, articles, art, cartoons, interviews, satire, criticism, reviews, music, letters, long-poems, plays, news items, non-fiction. "We are featuring translations of Arabic Poetry. We will consider carefully all material submitted and publish the best we receive. Prefer short articles and poems—any subject. Recent contributors—Stella Craft Tremble, Alexandre Amprimoz, Lynn Pezze, Lavanch Reyon Hall, Joanne Benger, Tim Van Schmidt." 2-6/yr; price per copy: $2.00; sample: $2.00. 1977. 75pp; 5½ x 8½. of. circ. 1,000. Reporting time: 1 week-2 months. Payment: None, please send postage for return. We will give cash awards for superior material. Copyrighted, reverts to author. Ads: $50.00/$25.00/$0.10. Back issues: $1.50. Expects 3 issues 1977, 4 issues 1978. §all areas.

THE WORD-SMITH, Stephen J. Pike, 3827 Walnut St., Philadelphia, PA 19104. Poetry, fiction, articles, cartoons, interviews, criticism, reviews, parts-of-novels, long-poems. "Contributors: Steve Berg, Doug Blazek, W. S. DiPiero, George Economou, Larry Eigner, Michael Heller, Ted Enslin, Alexandra Grilikhes, John Montague, Richard Murphy, David Ignatow, Thomas Kinsella, Richmond Lattimore, Lyn Lifshin, M. L. Rosenthal, Rhoda Schwartz, Theodore Weiss and many others. We try to be unbiased, but since that's impossible, we settle for not encouraging the cute or the precious; we try to find the best work of honest craftsman artists." 2/yr; 1-yr sub price: $3.00; per copy: $1.50; sample: $1.00 (while available). 1974. 35pp; 8½ x 11½. of. circ. 500. Reporting time: Has been slow. We hope to reply within 2 weeks. Payment: Copies. Whenever possible we have helped contributors get payment through outside sources or, in one case, through book publication. Ads: $50/$30. Discounts: 40% off to bookstores, 45% if they pay cash for copies, same for classroom or anyone buying over 5 copies. Pub's reviews. §poetry, criticism, experimental prose.

Word Wheel Books, Inc., Richard H. Raymond, Acting President, 540 Santa Cruz Ave, Menlo Park, CA 94025. "We have published several books, no magazines. *Eggs And Peanut Butter, Seven Laws Of Money, The Pure Gamble,* & *Finger Pickin Dominoes.* . . concerning alternative education economics & lifestyles."

The Word Works, Inc., Deirdra Baldwin, Jim Beall, Yolanda Gerritsen, 5033 V St., NW, Washington, DC 20007, 202-338-7435. avg. price, paper: $3.00. 1974. 50pp; 5½ x 8½. of. avg. press run 500. Reporting time: 3 mos. Payment: 10 percent of run. Copyright reverts to author upon pub. Discounts: 40 percent. Pub'd 2 titles 1976; expects 3 titles 1977, 5 titles 1978.

The WorDoctor Publications, Rolf Gompertz, PO Box 9761, North Hollywood, CA 91606, 213-980-3576. "Self-publisher only, at this time. *'My Jewish Brother Jesus'* (Biblical novel)." avg. price, cloth: $6.95; paper: $3.95. 1974. 208pp; 5½ x 8½. of. avg. press run 1,000 copies. Copyrights for author. Discounts: 40 percent to book stores; 50 percent to distributors; 10 percent to libraries. Expects 1 title 1977. COSMEP.

THE WORKBOOK, Southwest Research and Information Center, Katerine Montague, Peter Montague, PO Box 4524, Albuquerque, NM 87106, 505-265-0461. Articles, criticism, reviews. "Style-articles showing people who are concerned with specific problems & how they can become involved. Action oriented. Bias-politics are leftist oriented. Contributors-Michael Jacobson, Egan O'Connor. Richard Morgan, James Sullivan, Sandra Simons, Dan Butler, Steve Goldin." 10/yr; sub price: $7.00/yr students, $10.00/yr individuals, $20.00/yr institutions; per copy: $1.00; sample: free. 1974. 48pp; 8½ x 10½. of. circ. 1,000. Payment: none. Copyrighted by Southwest Research & Information Center. Ads: none. Discounts: Trade-40% agent 40%. Back issues: $1.00. Pub'd 10 issues 1976; expects 10 issues 1977, 10 issues 1978. Pub's reviews. §Action oriented, dealing with environmental, consumer & social problems. COSMEP.

Workers' Press (see PROLETARIAT)

THE WORKING CRAFTSMAN, Marilyn Heise, Editor, Publisher, Box 42, Northbrook, IL 60062, 312-498-2250. "Articles of interest to professional or part-time craftsmen, teachers, students, shops/galleries, suppliers. How to succeed in the business of crafts; selling, exhibiting hints, events to enter, trends, book reviews, news, new products. Contributors primarily professional craftsmen." 4 plus 1 special issue/yr; 1-yr sub price: $9.00; per copy: $2.25; sample: $2.25. 1971. 40pp; 8½ x 11. of. circ. 10,000. Reporting time: 2 wks. Payment: $5 to $35. Back issues: $.50.

The Workingman's Press, Barry Gifford, Gary Wilkie, C/O Serendipity Books, 1790 Shattuck Avenue, Berkeley, CA 94709, 415-848-4777. Poetry, fiction. "We are interested primarily in contemporary poetry. Recent authors include Ginsberg, Big Eagle, Corr, Gifford, Jammes." avg. price, paper: $2.50. 1975. 25-30pp; 5½ x 8½. of. avg. press run 500-1,000 copies. Reporting time: 1 week to 3 months. Payment varies. Copyrights for author. Discounts: Distributed exclusively by Serendipity Books Distribution. 40 percent discount to bookstores. Pub'd 2 titles 1976; expects 3 titles 1977, 3 titles 1978.

Workshop Press Ltd. (see also **NEW POETRY**), Norman Hidden, 2 Culham Court, Granville Rd, London N44JB, United Kingdom, 01-348-4054. "No unsolicited material required" 1967. lp. Reporting time: up to 1 mo. Payment: 10 percent royalty. Copyrights for author. Discounts: 33-1/3 percent on bulk orders. Pub'd 1 title 1976.

WORLD OF POETRY, World Of Poetry Press, John T. Campbell, Eddie-Lou Cole, Julie Joy, 1841 Garden HWY, Sacramento, CA 95833. Articles, art, photos, cartoons, interviews, satire, criticism, reviews, letters. "Slant to the beginner usually, using 'How To' format. Keep manuscript down to 2 or 3 pages typed. Recent contributors: Irma g. Rhodes, Leonard Nimoy, Marvin Miller. We need articles on current poets making news, with photos, etc." 12/yr; 1-yr sub price: $10.00; per copy: $1.00; sample: free. 1975. 4pp; 8½ x 11. of. circ. 25,000. Reporting time: 2 weeks. Payment: $.05-$.10 per word. Ads: $600.00/$350.00/$.01 per word. Discounts: bulk, classroom, institution, agent: 50%. Back issues: $1.00 each. Pub's reviews. §poetry.

World Publications (see **AQUATIC WORLD, BIKE WORLD, DOWN RIVER, GYMNASTICS WORLD, NORDIC WORLD, RUNNER'S WORLD, SELF-DEFENSE WORLD, SOCCER WORLD**)

World University Service (see **THE NEW QUARTERLY**)

THE WORMWOOD REVIEW, The Wormwood Review Press, Marvin Malone, Ernest Stranger, Art Ed., PO Box 8840, Stockton, CA 95204, 209-466-8231. Poetry, reviews, long-poems, collages, concrete art. "Poetry and prose-poems to 300+ lines reflecting the temper and depth of present human scene. All types and schools from traditional-economic through concrete, dada and extreme avant-garde. Special fondness for prose poems/fables. Each issue has yellow-page section devoted to one poet or topic (e.g. Bukowski, Wantling, Jon Webb, Micheline, Crews, Locklin, Koertge, Dick Higgins, Ian Hamilton Finlay, Steve Richmond, John Currier, Wm. Burroughs, etc)." 4/yr; sub price: $3.50/yr, $5.50/yr institutions; per copy: $1.50; sample: $1.50. 1959. 40-44pp; 5½ x 8½. of. circ. 700. Reporting time: 2-8 wks. Payment: 3-5 copies or cash equivalent. Copyrighted, rights reassigned on request to author. Discounts: $1.50 retail copy costs agent $0.90. Back issues: Nos. 16-23, 25-64 ($1.50 per) Nos. 1-15 & 24 (priced upon request, when available). Pub'd 4 issues 1976; expects 4 issues 1977, 4 issues 1978. Pub's reviews: many in 1976. §Poetry/experimental prose. CCLM, COSMEP.

The Worn-Out Press (see **MCLEAN COUNTY POETRY REVIEW**)

WRIT, Roger Greenwald, Two Sussex Ave, Toronto M5S 1J5, Canada. Poetry, fiction, reviews, parts-of-novels, long-poems. "Sewn binding. We have an open policy; we're looking for good writing regardless of format; we'll print work that's intellectual and difficult if we think it's good and work that's colloquial, breezy, 'experimental' or whatever if we think it's good. We've printed large amounts of fiction and hope to continue doing so (number four was a special fiction issue); we've almost made a specialty of short (page or less) prose forms. We'll consider translations of poetry or fiction too. We do not court people with names, since they have ample opportunity to appear elsewhere. We print only work that has not yet appeared in print." 1-2/yr; sub price: Institutions $7.00 for 2 issues personal: $5.00 for 2 issues NB: not per calendar year; per copy: $2.50; sample: $2.00 or free on inspection. 1970. 100pp; 6 x 9. of. circ. 800. Reporting time: Generally 1 month; longer May-August. Payment: Copies only. Copyright by the authors. Ads: None. Discounts: bookstores 40% of sale price, subscription agencies none, classroom & other bulk purchases-by arrangement. Back issues: $2.50 each for Nos. 2, 3, 5, 7; $5.00 each for Nos. 1, 4, 6, 8. Pub'd 1 issue 1976; expects 1 issue 1977, 1 issue 1978. Pub's reviews: none in 1976. §Poetry, fiction.

WRITE ON, Northland Library, Laura Shelley, Librarian, 120 Three Degree Rd, Pittsburgh, PA 15237, 412-366-3350. Poetry, fiction, articles, art, cartoons, interviews, satire, criticism, reviews, long-poems, concrete art, non-fiction. "We now distribute in community only. We are not selling copies or giving out free ones by mail except to contributors." 3/yr; sample price: $1.00. 1974. 50pp; 5 x 8½. †mi. circ. 300-500. Reporting time: 8 weeks. Payment: 3 free copies. Copyrighted, reverts to author upon publication. Pub'd 2 issues 1976; expects 2 issues 1977, 2 issues 1978. Pub's reviews: 1 in 1976.

Writer Unlimited Agency (see WRITERS INK)

Writers & Scholars (see INDEX ON CENSORSHIP)

Writers' Cooperative, Wayne Robbins, PO Box 457, Montreal, Quebec H4A 3P8, Canada. Poetry, fiction, parts-of-novels, long-poems, plays. "One joins the writers' cooperative for $18. Each member receives 6 books for the membership fee and has the right to submit manuscripts for publication with us. Ten full-length works by previously unpublished writers produced to date. We always react in writing to each MS submitted." 1972. 6¼ x 9. of. Reporting time: 5-6 weeks. Payment: none. Discounts: none.

WRITERS IN RESIDENCE, Armchair Press, Mark Berman, P.O. Box 393, Tiffin, OH 44883, 419-447-4167. Poetry, fiction, art, photos, interviews, reviews, long-poems. 2/yr; 1-yr sub price: $3.00; per copy: $1.50; sample: $1.00. 1973. 64pp; 8½ x 8½. of. circ. 300. Reporting time 2 months. Payment: copies. Copyrighted. Ads: $50.00/$25.00/$0.05 per word. Back issues: $1.00. Expects 1 issue 1977, 2 issues 1978. Pub's reviews. §poetry/fiction. CCLM, COSMEP.

WRITERS INK, Writer Unlimited Agency, Inc., David B. Axelrod, John C. Hand, RR 3, Box 147-A, Rocky Point L.I., NY 11778, 516-744-6160. Articles, art, photos, cartoons, interviews, satire, criticism, reviews, collages. "Maximum article or story length 500 w. Though longer material might be serialized. Filler, humor for writers used. Limited to L.I. authors or items/ads of interest to L.I. literary scene." 10/yr; 1-yr sub price: $6.00; per copy: $0.60; sample: free. 1975. 4-12pp; 5 x 7. of. circ. 1,000. Reporting time: immediately (maximum 2 weeks). Payment: 50 cents col. inch or $2.00 per poem or photo *if* available. Copyrighted, reverts to author. Ads: $15.00/$8.00/$0.25. Discounts: None-but free to worthy folks or groups—sold, $6.00 yearly rate direct by 1st class mail from WU. Expects 6 issues 1977, 10 issues 1978. Pub's reviews. §all aids to writers, general interest and of course, L.I. works, mags., books. COSMEP, NESPA, LIPS, Lit. Assoc., East Endarts Council, Long Island Publ. Service.

WRITERS' RESOURCES, Bruce Shatswell, Ann Morganson, 48 Kinnaird St Apt 3, Cambridge, MA 02139, 617-492-3248. Articles, interviews, criticism, reviews, letters. "Average review length: half-page to 2 pages (500-1,200 words). We have a regional focus, accepting material from outside as well (region: northeast). News and reviews: calendar, writers' classifieds. Contributors: John Crawford, Jane Barnes, Paul Kahn etc." 6/yr; 1-yr sub price: $5.00; per copy: $0.75; sample: $0.50. 1976. 24-28pp; 5½ x 8½. of. circ. 750. Reporting time: 1 month. Payment: 5 copies. Copyright transfer easily arranged. Ads: $18.00/$10.00/free. Discounts: Free to mental hospital & prison writing programs. 40 percent bookstore discount. (consignment). Back issues: Same as regular issues, unless supply is exhausted (No. 5 unavailable). Pub'd 5 issues 1976; expects 6 issues 1977, 6 issues 1978. Pub's reviews: 28 plus in 1976. §Poetry, fiction, drama, children's books, criticism. COSMEP, NESPA.

Writing Center Press (see ARS POETICA)

Wwhimsy Press, Ronald Vincent Voigt, 1822 Northview Dr., Arnold, MO 63010. Poetry. "This is a private press which prints/publishes/distributes only (and *only)* the output of Ronald Voigt." 1953. of. Payment: none.

‡**Wyrd Press,** Janey Tannenbaum, 131 West St., Warwick, NY 10990.

WYRD, The Magazine of Illustrated Fantasy, Chaosium, Greg Stafford, PO Box 6302, Albany, CA 94706. Poetry, fiction, articles, art, photos, cartoons, interviews, satire, reviews, letters, parts-of-novels, long-poems, collages, non-fiction. "Traditional & modern fantasy fiction, art features/portfolios, (assigned) supportive art, (some) comics, poetry (prefer short humor, oral poetry, or epics); reviews on fantasy subjects. Looking for emotive fiction with an integral sense of fantasy & imagination." 2-4/yr; sub price: $6.00-3 issues; per copy: $2.50; sample: $2.50. 1973. 92-96pp; 7 x 8½. †mi/of. circ. 500. Reporting time: 1-2 mo. Payment:40¢1/4 cent/word fict., poetry, some reviews; or by arrangement. $2.50/page for art, $5.00 for cover; or by arrangement. Copyrighted, reverts to author upon publication. Ads: not at present, trade only. Discounts: 6 copies w/get 40 percent off, no returns. Back issues: only No. 6 (current issue) available. Pub'd 1 issue 1976; expects 3 issues 1977, 3 issues 1978. Pub's reviews: 1 in 1976. §art or any fantasy subjects, epic poetry.

X   X, A JOURNAL Of The ARTS, X Press, George Myers Jr., P.O. Box 2648, Harrisburg, PA 17105. Poetry, fiction, articles, art, interviews, criticism, reviews, letters, concrete art. "Kostelanetz, Grossinger, Skellings,Galen Green, John M. Bennett, Henry Miller, Opal and Ellen Nations, Montag, R. C. Morse, Woodward, Arthur Craven, Duane Ackerson, Elaine Dallman, Zirlin. Interested in those who are interested in the small presses. X will sometimes purchase (discount) a number of already published chapbooks and distribute to subscribers. Patrons who contribute $12.00 or more will be listed in 4 issues." 6/yr; sub price: $8.00 for 4 consecutive issues; per copy: $2.50. 1976. 50pp; 5½ x 8½. of. circ. 400. Reporting time: 2-3 weeks. Payment: copy. Copyrighted, reverts to author. Ads: $30.00/$20.00. Discounts: none. Back issues: same. Pub'd 1 issue 1976; expects 2 issues 1977, 3 issues 1978. Pub's reviews: 35 in 1976. §art, post-modernist literature letters, interviews, arts & poetry. COSMEP, CCLM.

X Press Press, David Gershator, Phillis Gershator, 524 Henry St., Brooklyn, NY 11231, 212-625-4245. Poetry, plays. "Interested in quality, energy, talent. Chapbooks by Enid Dame, Irving Stettner, Fritz Hamilton, Jack Alchemy, & David Gershator. To be published: Althea Romeo, Ivan Arguelles, Charles Haseloff, Don Lev, & Funice Wolfgram. So far, cooperative publication by invitation, but plans may change." avg. price, paper: $1.50. 1976. 40pp; 5½ x 8½. of. avg. press run 500. Reporting time: 1 month. Payment: yes. Copyrights for author. Discounts: jobber-50 percent; trade-40 percent. Pub'd 1 title 1976; expects 5 titles 1977, 6 titles 1978. COSMEP, NESPA.

XANADU, Pleasure Dome Press, Charles Fishman, George William Fisher, Beverly Lawn, Coco Gordon, 1704 Auburn Road, Wantagh, NY 11793, 516-826-4964. Poetry, art, photos, long-poems, reviews, news items. "We are still replying to all submissions, with a personal note. Poems to 60 lines are most welcome, though longer work will be considered. We like to see at least 5 poems by an individual at one time. Poems with strong visual impact, concrete language: poems rooted in the human. This is not a place for amateur or closet poets. Contributors include: Blazek, Bruchac, Inez, Kramer, McElroy, McMahon, Miller, Swann, and many others, known & unknown. S.A.S.E. must be included." 2/yr; 1-yr sub price: $2.50; per copy: $1.50; sample: $1.50. 1975. 64pp; 5½ x 8½. of. circ. 1,000. Reporting time: 2-6 wks. (normally take longer on material that comes close). We buy copyright for author, reassign-upon request for reprints in collections of poems, anthologies. Discounts: 10 percent on orders of $20.00 or more, in any combination of titles (PLEASURE DOME PRESS also included.). Back issues: $1.50 each. Pub'd 2 issues 1976; expects 2 issues 1977, 2 issues 1978. CCLM.

XANTHIPPE, Mog Duff, c/o Women's Center, SJSU, 177 S. 10th, San Jose, CA 95192. Poetry, fiction, articles, art, cartoons, satire. "Feminist material only-15 pages typed would be our top limit. (By feminist we mean by women, *about* women, and true to women's experience.)" 1/yr; price per copy: $.75; sample: $.75. 1971. 40pp. of. circ. 300. Reporting time: varies!. Payment: 3 copies. Ads: none. Discounts: 1/3 off to bookstores etc. Back issues: $.50. §feminist writing-women's biographies.

XENHARMONIC BULLETIN, Electronic Music Enterprises, Ivor Darreg, 349 1/2 W. California Ave., Glendale, CA 91203, 213-243-3477. Articles, reviews, music, letters. "*Xenharmonic* means a kind of music which does not sound like the ordinary 12-tone temperament as on the piano or organ keyboard. Encouragement for builders of new instruments and composers in new scale-systems. Will be open to contributors after 1977, letters welcome." 3-4/yr; price per copy: $1.00. 1974. 10pp; 8½ x 11. of. circ. 200. Back issues: Available on request. Pub'd 2 issues 1976; expects 2 issues 1977, 3 or 4 issues 1978. Pub's reviews: 2 in 1976.

XENHARMONIKON, John H. Chalmers Jr., 10819 Shannon Hills Drive, Houston, TX 77099, 713-498-0055. Articles, art, photos, reviews, music. "Xenharmonikon, was coined in imitation of the title of Ptolemy's Treatise on Greek Music, 'The Harmonike' (the word is derived from *xenos* (uncommon) and *harmonike* (musical science) and should be constaved as a genitive plural.) I am interested in articles on various aspects of experimental music-new instruments, keyboards, scores etc. The journal is balanced between advocates of equal temperaments (17,19,22,24,31,41,etc tones per octave) and just intonation in the expanded sense of Partch and Fokker. Recent contributors include Lou Harrison, Erv Wilson, Ivor Darreg and George Secor. Specifications and descriptions of the Secor generalized keyboard Scalatron and the Hackleman-Wilson 19-tone clavichord were published in 1975, scores by Darreg, Lou Harrison and his students have also appeared. I am very interested too in the application of electronic and computor technology to Xenharmonics." 1-2/yr; 1-yr sub price: $6.00; per copy: $3.00; sample: $3.00. 1974. 60pp; 8½ x 11. of. circ. 100. Reporting time: by arrangement. Payment: copies only. Copyrighted, reverts to author. no ads at present. Discounts: none. Back issues: $3.00 ea for No. 4 & 5 others from Xerox Univ. micro film. Pub'd 1 issue 1976; expects 1-2 issues 1977, 1-2 issues 1978. Pub's reviews: 0 in 1976. §Experimental music, electronic music.

XTRAS, From Here Press, William J. Higginson, Box 2702, Paterson, NJ 07509. Poetry, fiction, parts-of-novels, long-poems, plays. "Whole issues devoted to single author or group. In 1975: #1, translations by WJH (thistle/brilliant/morning); #2, haiku, senryu, haibun by Alan Pizzarelli (Zenryu); #3, poems of vision & recollection by Penny Bihler (House by the Sea); #4, haiku & sequences by Elizabeth Searle Lamb (in this blaze of sun); #5, poems from a workshop by Paterson teenagers & senior citizens (I can tell you more....) Publication is cooperative; author supplies cost of materials, photography, etc. ($100-300), we supply editorial knowhow, mechanicals, typesetting, printing, binding and distribute. This is not vanity publishing; if we wouldn't publish it with our own £ we won't do it with yours. Authors receive substantial number of copies, refund of initial expenses through sales, and eventually split 50/50 if we're lucky. Do not send whole ms with initial query; 8-10 pages of material, and letter indicating extent of project, # copies author personally desires, etc. will result in rejection or an offer, to be confirmed on receipt of whole ms.SASE., of course." sub price: $6/4 issues; institutions, $10/4 issues; sample: none. 1975. 25-40pp; 5½ x 8½. †of. circ. 500-1,000. Reporting time: immed. COSMEP.

Y Y GWYDDONYDD, University Of Wales Press, Glyn O. Phillips, 6 Gwennyth St., Cathays, Cadiff, Wales, United Kingdom, 0222-31919. Articles. 4/yr; sub price: 25p/yr per port; per copy: 50p; sample: 25p. 1962. 50pp; A4. Ads: £50.00/£25.00. Discounts: booksellers 25%. Pub'd 4 issues 1976; expects 4 issues 1977, 4 issues 1978. Pub's reviews. §Science.

THE YALE REVIEW, J. E. Palmer, Editor; Mary Price, Managing Editor, 1902A Yale Station, New Haven, CT 06520. Poetry, fiction, articles, criticism, reviews, non-fiction. 4/yr; sub price: $12.00/yr institutions $10.00/yr individuals; per copy: $3.00; sample: $3.00. 1911. 160 pp plus 12 to 24 pp front matter; 6-3/8 x 9-1/8. of/lp. circ. 6,000. Reporting time: 1-3 months. Payment: on publication. Copyright Yale University, no reversion to author except by request for transfer. Ads: $250/$115. Discounts: distributor, 50%, agent 20% bookstores 10%. Back issues: on request. Pub'd 4 issues 1976; expects 4 issues 1977, 4 issues 1978. Pub's reviews: 34 in 1976. §literature, history, fiction, poetry, economics, biography, arts & architecture, politics, foreign affairs. CCLM.

‡**YALE/THEATRE, Yale University Press,** 222 York St., New Haven, CT 06520. CCLM.

YANAGI, Louis Patler, Bill Barrett, Box 466, Bolinas, CA 94924, 415-868-0292. Poetry, parts-of-novels, long-poems. "General policy is to publish a large selection of a relatively few poets, with each issue edited for readability, cover-to-cover. Contributors: Tom Clark, Bill Berkson, Ed Janders, Joan Wieners." 1/yr. 1974. 80pp; 8½ x 11. †mi/of. circ. 400. Reporting time: 6 weeks. Payment: 2 copies. Copyrighted, reverts to author. Discounts: YANAGI is distributed free to poets, donations are asked from bookstores and institutions. Back issues: Contact Serendipidy Books, Berkeley, Ca. §Poetry and poetics. CCLM, COSMEP.

YARDBIRD READER, Yardbird Publishing Co., Inc., Ishmael Reed, Box 2370, Sta A, Berkeley, CA 94702. Music, letters, collages, concrete art. 2/yr; price per copy: $4.95; sample: $3.50. 1972. 200-336pp; 5½ x 8½. lp. circ. 3,000. Payment: copies; an occasional $25.00-$50.00 honorarium. Copyrighted. Ads: $150.00/$100.00/0. Discounts: 40% regular bookstore; 27% college textbooks; 30% orders 5 or less. Back issues: prior to 3 most recent issues—$3.00. Pub'd 1 issue 1976; expects 2 issues 1977. §fiction/poetry/plays. CCLM, COSMEP.

Yardbird Wing Editions (see also YARDBIRD READER), Al Young, Box 2370, Station A, Berkeley, CA 94702. "Book length variable." avg. price, paper: $5.00. 1975. 250pp; 5½ x 8½. lp. avg. press run 2,000. Payment: 10% on 1st 5,000; 15% above 5,000. Copyrights for author. Discounts: 40% general trade; 27% classroom. Pub'd 3 titles 1976; expects 2 titles 1977. COSMEP.

Yarrow Press (see CHOOMIA)

Years Press (see CENTERING)

YELLOW BRICK ROAD, Emerald City Press, Robert Matte Jr., Paul H. Cook, 107 W. 7th St, Tempe, AZ 85281, 602-966-7505. Poetry, fiction, art, photos. "In poetry we consider anything of quality but shudder at, sleeve poems (heartthrob), traditional religious, and stuff pitting the poet against the universe. Content can range from surreal-absurd-humorous to heavy duty. Fiction must be under six pages double spaced. Poetry biases apply to style. We seek interesting graphics (B&W) as well as photographs, especially ones with roads. Every other issue on special theme, i.e. the legends, laundromats. We welcome submissions from old pros and newcomers. We're just folks. Contributors have included: Ron Koertge, Emilie Glen, Harley Elliott, Charles Bukowski, Lyn Lifshin, Gerry Locklin, John Bennett, Doug Blazek, Gerda Penfold, G. P. Skratz, GOD, A. D. Winans, Charles Webb, Opal Nations, Michael Hogan, Geraldine King. Also publish poetry books. No unsolicited manuscripts. Catalog sent upon request." 3/yr; sub price: $3.00/yr individuals, $4.50/yr institutions; per copy: $1.00; sample: $1.00. 1974. 40pp; 5½ x 8½. of. circ. 400. Reporting time: 2 wks-2 months. Payment: contrib copies and poss small monetary payment. Copyrighted, reverts to author. Ads: $50/$30/none. Discounts: 40% discount on five or more copies. Back issues: YBR No. 1 $25.00; Nos. 2,3,4 $10.00; others $1.00. Pub'd 3 issues 1976; expects 3 issues 1977, 3 issues 1978. Pub's reviews: 15 in 1976. §poetry, short fiction, graphics. CCLM, COSMEP.

YELLOW BUTTERFLY BROADSIDES, Laurence Fallis, Guadalupe Fallis, Box 3 BD, University Stn., Las Cruces, NM 88003. "Currently concentrating on broadsides. Essential to query first before submission." irreg.; 1-yr sub price: $2.00; per copy: $.50; sample: SASE. 1972. 8½ x 11. of. circ. 100. Reporting time: immediate. Payment: 20 copies. Ads: no ads. Pub'd 4 issues 1976; expects 10 issues 1977, 10 issues 1978.

The Yellow Chicken Press (see TWO SCORE OR LESS FOR WORDS)

The Yellow Press (see MILK QUARTERLY)

York Press, Dr. Saad Elkhadem, P.O. Box 1172, Fredericton, New Brunswick E3B5C8, Canada, 455-6501. Criticism. "Manuscripts—preferably between 80 and 120 typewritten pages—should be prepared in conformity with the second edition of the *MLA Style Sheet;* spelling and hyphenation according to *Webster*. Areas of special interest include comparative literature, literary criticism, and creative writing of an experimental nature." avg. price, paper: $5.00. 1975. 100pp; 5 x 8. of. avg. press run 1,000. Reporting time: 4 weeks. Payment: differs from case to case. Copyright depends on other arrangements. Discounts: 1-5 copies, 20 percent; 5 or more, 40 percent. Pub'd 3 titles 1976.

Yorkshire Dialect Society (see SUMMER BULLETIN TRANSACTIONS OF THE YORKSHIRE DIALECT SOCIETY)

Young Publications, Lincoln B. Young, 531 N. Gay St. (PO Box 3455), Knoxville, TN 37917. Poetry. "Any length, any style, any subject except pornography or racist material." avg. price, cloth: $14.95; paper: $9.95. 1957. 300pp; 8½ x 7. †of. avg. press run 2,000. Reporting time: up to 6 months. No payment. Copyrights for author. Discounts: We offer discounts to booksellers and to contributors only. Pub'd 1 title 1976; expects 2 titles 1977, 2 titles 1978. COSMEP.

Z

Z, Z Press, Inc., Kenward Elmslie, Poets Corner, Calais, VT 05648. Poetry, fiction, long-poems, plays. "The editor strongly discourages the submission of unsolicited material, as the magazine is a one-man operation, and a real time pressure is at work. Recent contributors: Ashbery, Lally, Dlugos, Schuyler, Gooch, Coolidge, Wieners, Brownstein, Winkfield, Abbott, Nolan, Towle, O'Hara, Koch, Elmslie, Winch, Hawkins." 2/yr; price per copy: $2.50; sample: $2.50. 1973. 120pp; 6 x 9. circ. 1,200. Reporting time: variable. Payment: none (except for 2 issues funded by CCLM). Ads: none. Discounts: 40% to bookstores. Back issues: $2.50. Pub'd 1 issue 1976; expects 1 issue 1977, 1 issue 1978. CCLM, COSMEP.

Z REVUE, Z Revue Collective, 41 Norman St., Leicester, United Kingdom, 0533-549652. Poetry, fiction, articles, art, photos, cartoons, interviews, satire, criticism, reviews, letters, long-poems, collages, plays, non-fiction. "Run by a revolutionary organisation (well maybe) of anarchists." Annual; 1-yr sub price: $0.50; per copy: $0.50; sample: $0.50. 1975. 32pp; A5. of. circ. 1,000. Payment: None. None. Ads: None. Discounts: 33-1/3 percent. Back issues: $0.50. Pub'd 2 issues 1976; expects 1 issue 1977, 1 issue 1978. Pub's reviews: 8 in 1976. §Mainly anarchist. AABC.

ZAHIR, Diane Kruchkow, Box 715, Newburyport, MA 01950, 617-465-9451. Poetry, fiction, articles, art, cartoons, interviews, criticism, reviews, letters. "No. 8 features New England poets. No. 9-new issue features Spanish Journals of Hugh Fox, Dick Higgins on Immanentism, Sklar on Actualism plus plenty of great poetry." 2/yr; 1-yr sub price: $3.00; per copy: $1.50 plus $0.30 postage; sample: $1.50 plus $0.30 postage. 1970. 64pp; 5½ x 8½. of. circ. 600. Reporting time: 6 weeks. Payment: 1 or 2 copies. Copyrighted. Ads: $40.00/$25.00. Discounts: worked individually. Back issues: $2.00. Pub'd 1 issue 1976; expects 2 issues 1977, 2 issues 1978. Pub's reviews: CCLM, COSMEP, NESPA.

Zartscorp, Inc. Books, Lynn Zelevansky, Paul Zelevansky, 267 West 89th Street, New York, NY 10024, 724-5071. Poetry, fiction, art, photos, concrete art. avg. price, cloth: $12.00; paper: $5.95. 1975. 80pp; 8½ x 11. of. avg. press run 500-1,000. Author has copyright of work. We have copyright of book. Discounts: 10 percent libraries/other: 1-4 books 20 percent/5-10 books 40 percent. Pub'd 1 title 1976; expects 1 title 1977. COSMEP.

ZEPHYRUS IMAGE, Zephyrus Image, Holbrook Teter, Michael Myers, 4460 Pine Flat Rd, Healdsburg, CA 95448, 707-433-3543. 1-yr sub price: $2.00; per copy: $2.00; sample: $2.00. 1970. 20pp; varies. †lp. circ. 200. Reporting time: 6 months. Payment: none. Not copyrighted. Pub'd 2 issues 1976; expects 3 issues 1977.

ZEUGMA, Zeugma Press, Merrill Kaitz, 25 Jeanette Ave., Belmont, MA 02178. Poetry, criticism, long-poems. "ZEUGMA looks for: traditional forms as well as new, literacy if not extensive vocabulary, major poems as well as miniature, perceptive observation of any subject, people and culture as well as nature, self and emotions, and sometimes, the bizarre, whimsical or surprising.

Criticism from the writers point of view, but not impressionist. Recent contributors Mark Helprin, Rachel Hadas, Susan Weiner, Carol Dine, Dona Stein, Tom Hart, Margaret Condon, L.A. Raphals, E.B. Olson, Hugh Rogers, Martin Robbins, Louis Phillips, David McCann, Nina Nyhart, Harold Bond." 4/yr; 1-yr sub price: $5.00; per copy: $1.50; sample: free with SASE. 1975. 36pp; 6 x 9. lp. circ. 250. Reporting time: 6-12 weeks. Payment: 3 copies. Ads: $100. Discounts: none. Back issues: 1st 2 issues $2.00 each. §poetry/poetry criticism/literary criticism/fiction. CCLM, COSMEP, NESPA.

Ziesing Bros.' Publishing Company, 768 Main St., Willimantic, CT 06226, 203-423-5836/8162. Poetry, fiction, articles, criticism, long-poems. "Taylor, Alexander: *Zadar*. Butterick, George F.: *Reading Genesis By the Light of a Comet*. Above are books of poems. We're also interested in remainders. We are currently remaindering James Scully's *Avenue of the Americas*." avg. price, paper: $2.95. 1976. 50pp; 5¾ x 8¾. of. avg. press run 1,000 copies. Reporting time: 2-3 months. Payment: contract. Does not copyright for author. Discounts: to the trade: 40%/to jobber: 50-55%. Expects 2 titles 1977.

ZIGGURAT Annual International Anthology of the Fine Arts, Ziggurat Publications, Joshua, 2546 South Kinnickinnic, Milwaukee, WI 53207. Poetry, fiction, articles, art, photos, cartoons, interviews, satire, criticism, reviews, music, letters. 1/yr; price per copy: $1.00; sample: no sample. 1966. 100pp; 8½ x 11. of. circ. 1,000. Reporting time: 2-3 months. Payment: 2 copies. Ads: $50(1X)/$30(1X)/$100(1X) inside cover. Pub's reviews. §poetry.

‡**ZONA, Ramaclo Brothers,** Marbella #66, San Juan, PR 00907.

ZONE ONE, Zonepress, Jay Heller, Peter Cherches, Steve Lackow, Dennis Deforge, Jonathan Seckofsky, Michael Friedman, PO Box 194, Bay Station, Brooklyn, NYC, NY 11235, 212-625-2770. Poetry, fiction, articles, art, photos, music, long-poems. "Zone seeks high quality art of any form—restaurant review to epic poem, dramatic monlogue to love song; pastoral elegy to cookie recipe." 2 or more/yr; price per copy: $2.00; sample: $1.25. 1976. 96pp; 8½ x 11. of. circ. 700. Reporting time: immediately if possible-never more than 6-8 weeks. Payment: 3 copies plus reduced rates for extra copies (ie 5 for $7.50). Copyrighted, reverts to author. Pub's reviews. §Any creative arts journals. COSMEP.

Zonepress (see also ZONE ONE), Jay Heller, Peter Cherches, Steve Lackow, Dennis DeForge, Johnathan Seckofsky, Michael Friedman, PO Box 194, Bay Station, Brooklyn NYC, NY 11235, 212-625-2770. Poetry, fiction, articles, art, photos, cartoons, interviews, satire, criticism, reviews, music, parts-of-novels, long-poems, collages, plays. "Zonepress will be glad to accept any creative endeavor as a submission and/or possible artistic endeavor for the group's involvement." avg. price, paper: $2.00. 1976. 96p,; 8½ x 11. of. avg. press run 700. Reporting time: As soon as possible-never more than 6-8 weeks. Payment: in copies (3) & reduced rate for contributors. Copyrights for author. Expects 2 titles 1977, 3 titles 1978. COSMEP.

ZVEZDA, Mark Osaki, Steven Mikulan, Meats Elliott, c/o Student Activities, 103 Sproul Hall, University of California, Berkeley, CA 94702, 415-843-4216. Poetry, fiction, art, photos, reviews, parts-of-novels, long-poems, collages, concrete art. "Not reading unsolicited material at this time. Inquiries are welcome however. Please send to: P. O. Box 9024, Berkeley, CA 94709." 2/yr; 1-yr sub price: $2.00; per copy: $1.00; sample: $0.50. 1976. 30-40pp; 8½ x 11. of. circ. 500 plus. Reporting time: 1-3 months. Payment: 2 copies. Copyrighted, reverts to author. Discounts: trade. Back issues: $0.50 if available. Pub's reviews §Poetry, fiction/visual arts, graphics.

Keep your Directory up-to-date with a subscription to

small press review

a monthly magazine

. **listings** OF NEW PRESSES
NEW MAGS
ADDRESS CHANGES

. **reviews** OF SMALL PRESS BOOKS
LITTLE MAGAZINES

. **news** FROM THE SMALL PRESS WORLD

$8/year individuals
$14/2 years
$18/3 years

$13.50/year institutions
$21/2 years
$27.50/3 years

FROM **DUSTBOOKS**

Subject Index

AFRICAN LITERATURE, AFRICA, AFRICAN STUDIES

AFRICA NEWS
AFRICA TODAY
THE AFRICAN BOOK PUBLISHING RECORD
AFRICAN LITERATURE TODAY
BA SHIRU
THE BLACK SCHOLAR: Journal of Black Studies and Research
CAFETERIA
Challenge Press
CIE
Conch Magazine Ltd. (Publishers)
CONCH MAGAZINE
CONCH REVIEW OF BOOKS
CONFRONTATION/CHANGE REVIEW
ENGLISH STUDIES IN AFRICA-A Journal of the Humanities
FREEDOMWAYS
HOO-DOO BlackSeries
Lawrence Hill & Company, Publishers, Inc.
LSM Information Center
LSM NEWS
THE THIRD PRESS REVIEW
Third World Publications Ltd.
Tombouctou Books
TRANSLATION
WOOD IBIS

AGRICULTURE

Circle Press
CONFRONTATION/CHANGE REVIEW
COUNTRYSIDE
THE ELEMENTS
RAIN: JOURNAL OF APPROPRIATE TECHNOLOGY
RFD
VEGETARIAN WORLD
White Mountain Publishing Company

ALCOHOL, ALCOHOLISM

DRINKWATCHERS' NEWSLETTER
Gullistan Press

ANARCHIST

Aberdeen Peoples Press
Abyss/Augtwofive
AGAINST THE WALL
CONQUEST
THE DANDELION
FREEDOM
GATEAVISA
INDIVIDUAL LIBERTY
Kropotkin's Lighthouse Publications
THE MATCH
NEW ART EXAMINER
ONE DOLLAR
OUR GENERATION
PAUNCH
PEACE NEWS "For Non-Violent Revolution"
QUOZ?
651
THIRD RAIL
TIMEPAD
Z REVUE

ANTHROPOLOGY, ARCHAEOLOGY

ALCHERINGA:ETHNOPOETICS
ART AND ARCHAEOLOGY NEWSLETTER
Cat's Pajamas Press
Chandler & Sharp Publishers, Inc.
LA CONFLUENCIA
CONFRONTATION/CHANGE REVIEW
COQUI QUARTERLY
THE DALHOUSIE REVIEW
Free Life Editions
IO
JOURNAL OF CALIFORNIA ANTHROPOLOGY
Malki Museum Press
THE NEW SCHOLAR: Studies, Essays, Reviews
Packard Publications
EL PALACIO
POEMCARDS
Regent Graphic Services
Ross-Erikson Publishers, Inc.
SEVEN STARS FICTION QUARTERLY
Undena Publications
Westburg Associates, Publishers

ANTIQUES

ANTIQUE PHONOGRAPH MONTHLY
THE ANTIQUER
APM Press
A. COLLECTOR'S ITEM
Padre Productions
Sleepy Hollow Restorations

ARCHITECTURE

Capra Press
THE CHARIOTEER
Cheshire Books
Erewon Press
GLASS
GRASS ROOTS
Levenson Press
MODERN LITURGY
THE MODULARIST REVIEW
Oregon Historical Society
Peregrine Smith, Inc.
RAIN: JOURNAL OF APPROPRIATE TECHNOLOGY
Regent Graphic Services
STUDIO INTERNATIONAL
THEATRE DESIGN AND TECHNOLOGY
THE TOWN FORUM JOURNAL & COMMUNITY REPORT

ARTS

ACA REPORTS
ACCEPTANCE
ACID SWITCH
Acid Switch Press
Acrobat Books
Air Press
All This & Less Publishers
ALLEGRA
Allegra Press
ALPHA
AMERICAN ARTS PAMPHLET SERIES
American-Canadian Publishers, Inc.

American Revolutionary Political Pamphlets
ANN ARBOR REVIEW
Archangel Books
THE ARDENT SABOTEUR: a journal of amnemonics
ARETE
Arion Press
ART & LITERARY DIGEST
Art Official Inc.
ARTE QUINCENAL
Arterial Books
Artists & Alchemists Publications
AVALANCHE
AXIOM (Atlantic Canada's Magazine)
AZU-THE INFINITE MAN
BASTARD ANGEL
THE BEAD JOURNAL
Beau Geste Press/Libro Accion Libre
Bellevue Press
BETELGEUSE CHAPBOOK SERIES/NEWEDI FICTION SERIES
Beyond Baroque Foundation Publications, includes Beyond Baroque/newforms, NEW Magazine. Arts & Letters (formerly NeWLetterS), and NewBooks.
BIG DEAL
Biohydrant Publications
BLACK GRAPHICS INTERNATIONAL
BLACK MARIA
BLACK MOSS
BLUE UNICORN
BOOK ARTS
BOTTOMFISH MAGAZINE
"BRILLIANT CORNERS": A Magazine of The Arts
BUCKLE
CAIM
CALIFORNIA STATE POETRY QUARTERLY
CALYX
CANTO LIBRE-A Bilingual Quarterly of Latin American Peoples Art
THE CAPILANO REVIEW
CELEBES
THE CENTENNIAL REVIEW
Center For Cuban Studies
THE CHARIOTEER
CHOMO-URI
CHOUTEAU REVIEW
CINEMA/QUEBEC
Circle Press
CIRCULAR LETTER
Clatworthy Colorvues
THE CLOVER PATCH
COASTLINE MAGAZINE
THE COFFEEHOUSE
COMBINATIONS, A JOURNAL OF PHOTOGRAPHY
CONTEMPORARY ART/SOUTHEAST
THE COPPER COUNTRY ANTHEM
CRAWL OUT YOUR WINDOW
Crawl Out Your Window Press
CREACION
CRISS-CROSS ART COMMUNICATIONS
CROSSCURRENTS
DADAZINE
DANCE DIMENSIONS
DANCE HERALD
DANCE IN CANADA
DAY BY DAY
Daylight Press
THE DEKALB LITERARY ARTS JOURNAL
DESCANT
Ecart Publications
EH?
ELAN VITAL: Journal of Creative Adventures
THE EMISSARY

THE FAMOUS SCIENCE FICTION CHAPBOOK (series)
THE FAULT
FEMALE ARTISTS PAST & PRESENT
THE FEMINIST ART JOURNAL
FILE MAG
FIREWEED
FIRST ENCOUNTER
FOLK MASS AND MODERN LITURGY
FOLLIES
Free Books Inc
FROM THE FIELD: A Magazine of Art and Verse
Full Court Press
GEGENSCHEIN QUARTERLY, NeoNeo Do-Do
THE GENEVA POND BUBBLES
GLASS
Gleniffer Press
THE GOODFELLOW REVIEW OF CRAFTS
The Green Hut Press
Hearsay Press
HECTOR AND HECTOR
HEIRS
HERESIES: A FEMINIST PUBLICATION ON ART AND POLITICS
The Heron Press
HINDSIGHT
The Hosanna Press
THE HUDSON REVIEW
IMPULSE
INTERMEDIA
International Center for Environmental Research-ICER Press
IRON
IS (pronounced 'eyes')
J and J House
LE JARDIN DU MONDE: The Journal of International Casafundanda
JOURNAL OF CALIFORNIA ANTHROPOLOGY
Kelsey St. Press
KONGLOMERATI
Konglomerati Press
Kontexts Publications
KRZYK (OUTCRY)
LAOMEDON REVIEW
Leathern Wing Scribble Press
LEFT CURVE
LIGHT
LODGISTIKS
LOST AND FOUND TIMES
LUDD'S MILL
Luna Bisonte Prods
MAGIC SAM
MAKARA
Malki Museum Press
THE SUPPLEMENT TO THE BULLETIN OF THE MARYLAND WRITERS COUNCIL
Mattole Press
Middle Earth Books Inc.
MIDNIGHT
THE MISSISSIPPI MUD
MODERN LITURGY
THE MODULARIST REVIEW
THE MOOSEHEAD REVIEW
MUSEUM OF TEMPORARY ART (MOTA) MAGAZINE
NEW ART EXAMINER
NEW BOSTON REVIEW
NEW LETTERS
NEW MAGAZINE: Arts & Letters
NEW QUARTERLY CAVE
NEW YORK ARTS JOURNAL
Newedi Press
NEWORLD
NEXUS
Noumenon Press

O Press/Heavy Evidence
O. O. L. P. (Out of London Press)
ONE SHOT DEAL
ONTARIO REVIEW
Peradam Publishing House
Peregrine Smith, Inc.
PERFORMING ARTS JOURNAL
PERMAFROST
PHOEBE
Pikeville College Press
THE POETRY MAILING LIST
Poltroon Press
POSTCARD ART/POSTCARD FICTION
PRAXIS: A Journal of Radical Perspectives on the Arts
PRIMER
PROVINCETOWN POETS
QUARTET
QUEEN STREET MAGAZINE
QUOZ?
Red Studio Press
Resource Publications
Rough Life Press
ROUNDTABLE
S Press Books
Saint Heironymous Press, Inc.
SALOME: A LITERARY DANCE MAGAZINE
SAN JOSE STUDIES
SANDWICHES
SCHMUCK ANTHOLOGICAL
Scrimshaw Press
SECOND COMING
Second Coming Press
Seripress
THE SHORE REVIEW
Smyrna Press
SOFT STONE, An International Journal of the Arts
SOFT TIMES
THE SQUATCHBERRY JOURNAL
STAR-WEB PAPER
STONECLOUD
STREET CRIES
STUDIO INTERNATIONAL
SUN & MOON: A Quarterly of Literature and Art
SYRACUSE Guide
Teachers and Writers
TEACHERS AND WRITERS MAGAZINE
10 POINT 5, A Magazine of the Arts
TOWARD REVOLUTIONARY ART (TRA)
TRACKS, A Journal of Artists' Writings
TRANSIENCE QUARTERLY
THE TRANSIENT
Treacle Press
TUUMBA
Tvrt Press-Viper's Tongue Books
Two-Eighteen Press
UNIVERSITY JOURNAL
UNMUZZLED OX
Unpublished Editions
Vehicule Press
Ventura Press
VILE
WASHINGTON REVIEW, A Quarterly Review of the Arts
WASHOUT REVIEW
WAVES
Wedge Publishing Foundation
West Coast Poetry Review Press
WESTART
Westburg Associates, Publishers
WHITE ARMS MAGAZINE
WIA NEWSLETTER
William L. Bauhan, Publisher
WOMANSMITH

Women Artists Newsletter (Press)
WOMEN ARTISTS NEWSLETTER
X, A JOURNAL Of The ARTS
Zartscorp, Inc. Books
ZIGGURAT Annual International Anthology of the Fine Arts
ZONE ONE
ZVEZDA

ASIA, INDOCHINA, CHINA

THE ASIA MAIL
BULLETIN OF CONCERNED ASIAN SCHOLARS
INDOCHINA CHRONICLE
INDOCHINA RESOURCE CENTER
JOURNAL OF SOUTH ASIAN LITERATURE
Lawrence Hill & Company, Publishers, Inc.
THE NEW QUARTERLY
TRANSLATION
WOOD IBIS

ASIAN-AMERICAN

THE ASIA MAIL
BRIDGE MAGAZINE
ISTHMUS
WOOD IBIS

AVIATION

Parachuting Publications
PARACHUTIST
Special Aviation Publications

BERRYMAN, JOHN

JOHN BERRYMAN STUDIES

BIBLIOGRAPHY

THE AFRICAN BOOK PUBLISHING RECORD
AMERICAN LITERATURE
AUSTRALASIAN SMALL PRESS REVIEW
Critiques Livres
ELAN POETIQUE LITTERAIRE ET PACIFISTE
A GAY BIBLIOGRAPHY
Gleniffer Press
IRISH BOOKLORE
Ithaca Press
Library Research Associates
LUNA
Maro Verlag
John L Noyce, Publisher (formerly Smoothie Pub)
Sable Publishing Corporation
TANGENTS
TZADDIKIM
The Women And Literature Collective

BILINGUAL

Children's Book Press/Emprenta de Libros Enfantiles

BIOGRAPHY

Canongate Publishing Ltd.
Challenge Press
Clean Energy Press
Creative Arts Book Company
THE EMISSARY
Gleniffer Press
HYACINTHS AND BISCUITS
Ithaca Press
Lawrence Hill & Company, Publishers, Inc.

Maryland Historical Press
Parable Press (formerly June McLaughlin Press)
The Rather Press
Sagarin Press
Simon & Pierre Publishing Co. Ltd.
SOUTH DAKOTA REVIEW
Synergistic Press
Westburg Associates, Publishers

BLACK

AFRO-AMERICANS in NEW YORK LIFE & HISTORY
AMERICAN ARTS PAMPHLET SERIES
BLACK/AMERICAN LITERATURE FORUM
BLACK FORUM
THE BLACK POSITION
THE BLACK SCHOLAR: Journal of Black Studies and Research
BOPP
Challenge Press
CODA: Canada's Jazz Magazine
THE CRISIS
DANCE HERALD
FREEDOMWAYS
Garrett Park Press
Harlo Press
HOO-DOO BlackSeries
Impact Publishers, Inc.
ISTHMUS
Lawrence Hill & Company, Publishers, Inc.
LIVING BLUES
Maryland Historical Press
OBSIDIAN: BLACK LITERATURE IN REVIEW
Pathfinder Press, Inc
Place of Herons
WEID: The Sensibility Revue
WOOD IBIS

BLAKE, WILLIAM

BLAKE, AN ILLUSTRATED QUARTERLY

BOOK COLLECTING, BOOKSELLING

ALA/SRRT NEWSLETTER
The Basilisk Press
BOOK ARTS
BOOK BUYER'S GUIDE/MARKETPLACE
BOOK REPORT
Cold Mountain Press
DENTAL FLOSS MAGAZINE
FINE PRINT; A Review for the Arts of the Book
Franklin Book Company
Gleniffer Press
PEOPLE'S BOOKSELLER
SCIENCE FICTION BAZAAR
JOHN UPDIKE NEWSLETTER

BOOK REVIEWING

ABRAXAS
AEOLIAN-HARP
ALA/SRRT NEWSLETTER
THE ANTIGONISH REVIEW
ASPEN ANTHOLOGY
AUSTRALASIAN SMALL PRESS REVIEW
BASTARD ANGEL
BIBLIOTHEQUE D'HUMANISME ET RENAISSANCE
THE BLACK CAT
BOOK BUYER'S GUIDE/MARKETPLACE
BOOK EXCHANGE
BOOK REPORT
BOOKS & BOOKMEN
BOOKS IN CANADA: A National Review Of Books
BOOKSELLER
BOOKSWEST
BRICK: A Journal Of Reviews
BRITISH BOOK NEWS
BUTT: A Quarterly
C.S.P. WORLD NEWS
CAFETERIA
CANADIAN AUTHOR & BOOKMAN
THE CATHARTIC
THE CHOWDER REVIEW
COASTLINE MAGAZINE
COMPASS
CONCH REVIEW OF BOOKS
CONRADIANA
CP Graham Press
CROSSCOUNTRY
DACOTAH TERRITORY
THE DALHOUSIE REVIEW
DAY BY DAY
DELAP'S F & SF REVIEW
THE DICKENSIAN
THE EMISSARY
ENGLISH STUDIES IN AFRICA-A Journal of the Humanities
FICTION WEST
FILM HERITAGE
FILM INDEX
FORESIGHT MAGAZINE
Franklin Book Company
FROZEN WAFFLES
Gullistan Press
THE ILLUSTRATED ORB
INDIAN TRUTH
IN VICTUS
ISTHMUS
KENTUCKY FOLKLORE RECORD
LAUGHING BEAR
THE LITERARY MONTHLY (formerly Pacific Sun Literary Quarterly)
LITERARY SKETCHES
NATIONAL BOOK REVIEW
THE NEW YORK CULTURE REVIEW
NORTHEAST RISING SUN
NORTHERN NEW ENGLAND REVIEW
NOSTOC
OHIOANA QUARTERLY
THE ORCHARD
Orchard Press
PAINTED BRIDE QUARTERLY
PLEXUS. Bay Area Women's Newspaper
POETRY FLASH
POETRY QUARTERLY (previously CURLEW)
PORCH
THE PRE-RAPHAELITE REVIEW
QUILL & QUIRE
RAIN: JOURNAL OF APPROPRIATE TECHNOLOGY
ROAD/HOUSE
SAN FRANCISCO REVIEW OF BOOKS
SELECT PRESS REVIEW
SEX NEWS
THE SHORE REVIEW
THE SMALL PRESS REVIEW
STONY HILLS: The New England Alternative Press Review
STUDIO INTERNATIONAL
THE THIRD PRESS REVIEW
TRIVIUM
TZADDIKIM
WESTERN WORLD REVIEW
WRITERS INK

BRONTES

BRONTE SOCIETY TRANSACTIONS

BUSINESS & ECONOMICS

Bell Springs Publishing Company
Bethesda Books
Challenge Press
THE EMISSARY
Grossmont Press, Inc.
Hiddigeigei Books
Olympus Publishing Company
PACIFIC RESEARCH
Phillip M. Perry
Programmed Studies Inc
RAIN: JOURNAL OF APPROPRIATE TECHNOLOGY
Red Bean Revue
Simon & Pierre Publishing Co. Ltd.
Wedge Publishing Foundation
Word Wheel Books, Inc.

CALIFORNIA

Carousel Press
1250 Press

CANADA

ART & LITERARY DIGEST
BOREAL
BRITISH COLUMBIA HISTORICAL NEWS
CANADA WEST
CANADIAN CHILDREN'S LITERATURE
CANADIAN DIMENSION
CANADIAN FRONTIER
CANADIAN LITERATURE
CANADIAN PUBLIC POLICY- Analyse de Politiques
CANADIAN THEATRE REVIEW
ESSAYS ON CANADIAN WRITING
Highway Book Shop
House of Anansi Press Limited/Publishing Co.
Hurtig Publishers
JOURNAL OF CANADIAN FICTION
JOURNAL of CANADIAN STUDIES
LAST POST
Prairie Publishing Company
Press Porcepic Limited
RAINCOAST CHRONICLES
Stagecoach Pub. Co. Ltd.

CELTIC

CARN (a link between the Celtic nations)
STUDIA CELTICA

CHAUCER, GEOFFREY

CHAUCER REVIEW

CHICANO/A

CARACOL
CARTA ABIERTA
DE COLORES
LA CONFLUENCIA
EL FUEGO DE AZTLAN
GRITO DEL SOL: A Chicano Quarterly
Lawrence Hill & Company, Publishers, Inc.
MANGO
THE NEW SCHOLAR: Studies, Essays, Reviews
Place of Herons

Pleasant Hill Press
LA RAZON MESTIZA/LA MUJER es la TIERRA
REVISTA CHICANO-RIQUENA
SEERS RIO GRANDE WEEKLY
TINTAN
TRUCHA
Ventura Press
WOOD IBIS

CHILDREN, YOUTH

Academy Press Limited
Aldebaran Review
All About Us
Artistic Endeavors, Inc.
ASPO NEWSLETTER
The B & R Samizdat Express
The Bookstore Press
CANADIAN CHILDREN'S LITERATURE
CANADIAN CHILDREN'S MAGAZINE
Carousel Press
Catex Press
Cedar House Enterprises
Cobblesmith
CREATIVE GUITAR INTERNATIONAL
The Crossing Press
E & R Marlin, Publishers
THE EMISSARY
FPS: A MAGAZINE OF YOUNG PEOPLE'S LIBERATION
Gleniffer Press
Harvest Press
Impact Publishers, Inc.
In Between Books
JABBERWOCKY
Joyful World Press
Kelsey St. Press
Knollwood Publishing Company
Lenape Publishing Ltd.
Magic Circle Press
The Mediaworks
Milky Way-Kosmos
Multinational Media
New Plays for Children
NEW SCHOOLS EXCHANGE NEWSLETTER
New Seed Press
NOUS JOURNAL
Parable Press (formerly June McLaughlin Press)
PAZ PRINT/PERIPHERY
Pegana Press
Peradam Publishing House
Phillip The Grasshopper
THE PLANET QUARTERLY
Prologue Publications
St. Luke's Press
The Saturday Centre
Scotty Macgreger Publications
SIGNAL, Approaches To Children's Books
Simon & Pierre Publishing Co. Ltd.
THE SPICY MEATBALL
Sproing Books
STONE SOUP, A Magazine By Children
SUNSHINE
Ten Penny Players, Inc.
The Three Trees Press
TIME/OUT
Todd Tarbox Books
Tree Frog Press
VERMONT CHILDREN'S MAGAZINE
Vermont Crossroads Press, Inc.

CITIES

AFRO-AMERICANS in NEW YORK LIFE & HISTORY

Artistic Endeavors, Inc.
Challenge Press
COASTLINE MAGAZINE
International Publishers Co., Inc.
RAIN: JOURNAL OF APPROPRIATE TECHNOLOGY
SELF-RELIANCE
SHELTERFORCE
URBAN & SOCIAL CHANGE REVIEW
ZONE ONE

CLASSICAL STUDIES

ARION, A Journal of Humanities and the Classics
ART AND ARCHAEOLOGY NEWSLETTER
THE DALHOUSIE REVIEW
The Elizabeth Press
Westburg Associates, Publishers

CLAUDEL, PAUL

CLAUDEL STUDIES

COMICS

ARCADE-THE COMICS REVUE
BUGLE-AMERICAN
COSMIC CIRCUS
THE ILLUSTRATED ORB
Real Free Press Foundation
SNARF
THE SPICY MEATBALL
Wild & Woolley

COMMUNICATION, MEDIA, JOURNALISM

Around Publishing
CANADIAN AUTHOR & BOOKMAN
CIE
FOLIO
INDEX ON CENSORSHIP
THE LITTLE AROUND JOURNAL
MEDIA REPORT TO WOMEN
Mercer House Press
NEW PERIODICALS INDEX
PASSAGES
PRAXIS: A Journal of Radical Perspectives on the Arts
RAIN: JOURNAL OF APPROPRIATE TECHNOLOGY
ST. LOUIS JOURNALISM REVIEW
Unpublished Editions
Women's Institute for Freedom of the Press

COMMUNISM, MARXISM, LENINISM

THE CALL/EL CLARIN
ISTHMUS
Lawrence Hill & Company, Publishers, Inc.
Liberator Press
METANOIA, An Independent Journal of Radical Lutheranism
PRAXIS: A Journal of Radical Perspectives on the Arts
PROLETARIAT
QUIXOTE, QUIXOTL
THE RAG

COMMUNITY

Aberdeen Peoples Press
Circle Press
CITY MINER
CLAIMANTS NEWSPAPER (Claimants Unite)
COMMUNITIES
COMMUNITY ACTION
COMMUNITY SERVICE NEWSLETTER- in serial with: COMMUNITY COMMENTS

Creative Book Company
THE EMISSARY
FOLLIES
MOLE EXPRESS
PEACE NEWS "For Non-Violent Revolution"
ProActive Press
RAIN: JOURNAL OF APPROPRIATE TECHNOLOGY
ROCHDALE'S ALTERNATIVE PAPER
SCHMUCK ANTHOLOGICAL
SELF-RELIANCE
SHINAKI
SYRACUSE Guide
Trunk Press
UTOPIAN EYES: A JOURNAL OF PRACTICAL UTOPIAN FANTASY
WOOD IBIS

COMPUTERS

COMPUTER MUSIC JOURNAL
CREATIVE COMPUTING
Creative Computing Press
DR. DOBB'S JOURNAL OF COMPUTER CALISTHENICS & ORTHODONTIA
Dymax
Minicomputer Press
People's Computer Co.
PEOPLE'S COMPUTERS
PMS/King Publishing
RAIN: JOURNAL OF APPROPRIATE TECHNOLOGY
Resource Publications

CONRAD, JOSEPH

CONRADIANA

CONSERVATION

BUSH LEAGUE
Clean Energy Press
CRY CALIFORNIA
THE ELEMENTS
THE EMISSARY
GREENPEACE
HIGH COUNTRY NEWS
HIGH COUNTRY NEWS
HUMANIST IN CANADA
Lawrence Hill & Company, Publishers, Inc.
THE MOTHER EARTH NEWS
R.O. Beatty & Associates
RAIN: JOURNAL OF APPROPRIATE TECHNOLOGY
REBUTTAL! The Bicentennial Newsletter of Truth
ROUND NOTES
Vermont Crossroads Press, Inc.
Wilderness Press

CONSUMER

THE NEW HARBINGER: A JOURNAL OF THE COOPERATIVE MOVEMENT

CRAFTS, HOBBIES

ACA REPORTS
THE ANTIQUER
ART & LITERARY DIGEST
BAMCA
THE BEAD JOURNAL
Carma Press
A. COLLECTOR'S ITEM
COSMOPOLITAN CONTACT
FINE PRINT; A Review for the Arts of the Book
Full Court Press

Gleniffer Press
THE GOODFELLOW REVIEW OF CRAFTS
GRASS ROOTS
Gullistan Press
Hunter Publishing, Co.
Lodestar Publishing
Minicomputer Press
THE MOTHER EARTH NEWS
Old Time Bottle Publishing Company
Peregrine Smith, Inc.
Pleasant Hill Press
PMS/King Publishing
R & D Services
Richboro Press
Seagull Books, NOPCO, Ltd.
STUDIES IN DESIGN EDUCATION AND CRAFT
Tamal Vista Publications
TRIVIUM
WESTART
THE WORKING CRAFTSMAN

CRITICISM

ABRAXAS
ABYSS
ALGOL: The Magazine About Science Fiction
Algol Press
American-Canadian Publishers, Inc.
AMERICAN LITERATURE
THE ANTIGONISH REVIEW
ARIZONA QUARTERLY
THE ARK RIVER REVIEW
ATLANTIC PROVINCES BOOK REVIEW
ATTENTION PLEASE
THE BARD
BEAU FLEUVE SERIES
BIBLIOTHEQUE D'HUMANISME ET RENAISSANCE
BIRD EFFORT
Black Cat Books
The Blue Oak Press
THE BODY POLITIC- Gay Liberation Journal
BOUNDARY 2
BUTT: A Quarterly
CAFETERIA
CAMELS COMING NEWSLETTER
CANADIAN AUTHOR & BOOKMAN
CANADIAN CHILDREN'S LITERATURE
CANADIAN FICTION MAGAZINE
CANADIAN LITERATURE
Chandler & Sharp Publishers, Inc.
THE CHARIOTEER
THE CHOWDER REVIEW
CINEASTE MAGAZINE
CLAUDEL STUDIES
COASTLINE MAGAZINE
CONCERNING POETRY
CONRADIANA
CONTACT/11: A Bimonthly Poetry Review Magazine
CONTEMPORARY ART/SOUTHEAST
THE CONTEMPORARY LITERARY SCENE
CONTEMPORARY LITERATURE
COUNTERSPY
CREATIVE MOMENT
THE CRITICAL REVIEW
CRITIQUE: Studies in Modern Fiction
CROSSCURRENTS
Cumbria Poetry Centre
THE D.H. LAWRENCE REVIEW
DAMASCUS ROAD
THE DICKINSON REVIEW
THE DURHAM UNIVERSITY JOURNAL
ECHO

EMILY DICKINSON BULLETIN
ENTROPY NEGATIVE
ESSAYS ON CANADIAN WRITING
GENRE
THE GRACKLE: Improvised Music In Transition
GREAT CIRCUMPOLAR BEAR CULT
Green Knight Press
GUARD THE NORTH
THE GYPSY SCHOLAR: A Graduate Forum for Literary Criticism
HAPPINESS HOLDING TANK
Harvest Publishers
HARVEST QUARTERLY
Hearthstone Press
HIGGINSON JOURNAL OF POETRY
THE HOLLINS CRITIC
HUMANIST IN CANADA
HYPERION A Poetry Journal
ICONOCLAST
ICONOMATRIX
THE INTERNATIONAL FICTION REVIEW
INVISIBLE CITY
ISLANDS, A New Zealand Quarterly of Arts & Letters
LE JARDIN DU MONDE: The Journal of International Casafundada
JOHN BERRYMAN STUDIES
JOURNAL of CANADIAN STUDIES
JOURNAL OF MODERN LITERATURE
JOURNAL OF NARRATIVE TECHNIQUE
JUMP CUT, A Review of Contemporary Cinema
Kylix Press
LITERARY SKETCHES
LONG POND REVIEW
THE MARKHAM REVIEW
MEANJIN QUARTERLY
MINUTES & PROCEEDINGS
MODERN LANGUAGE QUARTERLY
MODERNIST STUDIES: Literature & Culture 1920-1940
MOONS AND LION TAILES
Mosaic Press/Valley Editions
MOUNTAIN SUMMER
THE NEW YORK CULTURE REVIEW
NEWEST REVIEW
NORTHEAST/JUNIPER BOOKS
ONE
OUT THERE MAGAZINE
PARTISAN REVIEW
PAUNCH
Pentagram Press
PEQUOD
PHOEBE
PLOUGHSHARES
POET & CRITIC
Poetry Eastwest
POETRY FLASH
THE POETRY MISCELLANY
POETRY WALES
POINT OF CONTACT/PUNTO DE CONTACTO
PRAXIS: A Journal of Radical Perspectives on the Arts
THE PRE-RAPHAELITE REVIEW
Press Porcepic Limited
QUEEN STREET MAGAZINE
Raindust Press
Rat & Mole Press
RIVERSIDE QUARTERLY
RUNE
S Press Books
S.H.Y.
ST. CROIX REVIEW
SALMAGUNDI
Samisdat Associates
SCHOLIA SATYRICA

SHAKESPEARE NEWSLETTER
SHOCKS
THE SHORE REVIEW
SKYWRITING
Sleepy Hollow Restorations
SONG: A Magazine of Verse and Essay
SOUTHERN HUMANITIES REVIEW
Sparrow Press
THE SPHINX
STEPPENWOLF
STONE COUNTRY
STONY HILLS: The New England Alternative Press Review
THE STRAIT
STUDIES IN POETRY: A GRADUATE JOURNAL
TELOS
VECTOR
THE VELVET LIGHT TRAP: Review of Cinema
Ventura Press
VORT
Westburg Associates, Publishers
THE WESTERN CRITIC
WRITERS' RESOURCES
THE YALE REVIEW

CUBA

AREITO
CENTER NEWSLETTER

DADA, SURREALISM

AIEEE
Alphaville Books
American-Canadian Publishers, Inc.
ANDROGYNE
ATARAXIA
AUSTIN PULPWOOD
BANANA RAG
BASTARD ANGEL
BIRD EFFORT
Blue Horse
BOMBAST POETRY REVIEW
BUTT: A Quarterly
Caligula Books
THE CITY MOON
DADAZINE
EH?
Hh
IMAGES AND INFORMATION (Sort of an Art Magazine)
ISTHMUS
LIGHT TIMES
MUSEUM OF TEMPORARY ART (MOTA) MAGAZINE
OXYMORON: Journal Of Convulsive Beauty
PANJANDRUM POETRY JOURNAL
THE POETIC HARDWARE PRESS
QUOZ?
Rumba Train Press
651
SKYWRITING
Thunder City Press
TRANSFORMACTION
VILE

DANCE

AMERICAN DANCE GUILD NEWSLETTER
DANCE DIMENSIONS
DANCE HERALD
DANCE IN CANADA
DANCE SCOPE
EDDY
ENGLISH DANCE AND SONG

FOLK MASS AND MODERN LITURGY
MODERN LITURGY
QUEEN STREET MAGAZINE
Resource Publications
SALOME: A LITERARY DANCE MAGAZINE

DICKENS, CHARLES

THE DICKENSIAN

DICKINSON, EMILY

EMILY DICKINSON BULLETIN
HIGGINSON JOURNAL OF POETRY

DRAMA

Bern Porter Books
BOPP
CANADIAN AUTHOR & BOOKMAN
CANADIAN THEATRE REVIEW
Casa Editorial
THE CHARIOTEER
CHIMERA-A Complete Theater Piece
CTR Publications
Dolphin-Moon
DRAMATIKA
Dramatika Produce
EDWARDIAN DRAMA & LITERATURE
EVENT
FOLK MASS AND MODERN LITURGY
GALLIMAUFRY
The Heron Press
Illuminations Press
LIBRE PRESS
Litmus, Inc.
Living Poets Press
Love Street Books
MODERN LITURGY
New Plays for Children
NEW VOICES
PHOEBE
Playwrights Co-op
Prairie Books
PROLOG
Resource Publications
SHAKESPEARE NEWSLETTER
Simon & Pierre Publishing Co. Ltd.
THE SLOUGH
Spectrum Productions
Talonbooks
Ten Penny Players, Inc.
THEATRE ACROSS AMERICA
THEATRE DESIGN AND TECHNOLOGY
THEATRE SURVEY-THE American Journal of Theatre History
Westburg Associates, Publishers
X Press Books
ZONE ONE

EARTH, NATURAL HISTORY, ANIMALS

AKWESASNE NOTES
Alex Aiken
BLACKBERRY
The Boxwood Press
BRITISH NATURALISTS' ASSOCIATION (PUBLISHERS)
Capra Press
Chronicle Books
COEVOLUTION QUARTERLY
COQUI QUARTERLY
COUNTRY-SIDE

THE COUNTRYMAN
Creative Ventures
DOGS IN CANADA
THE ELEMENTS
THE EMISSARY
Falconiforme Press Ltd.
Gen Guides Book Co.
George Sroda, Publisher
THE GREEN REVOLUTION
International Marine Publishing Co.
KUKSU: Journal of Backcountry Writing
MANITOBA NATURE (formerly ZOOLOG)
MEXICO WEST
Miller Pond Books
Miocene Press
NATIONAL FISHERMAN
Peradam Publishing House
QUEEN STREET MAGAZINE
THE SALT CEDAR
SERIATIM: A Journal of Ecotopia
SNOWY EGRET
Stone Wall Press, Inc
TRUCK
Walnut Press
Wilderness Press
WOOD IBIS

ECOLOGY, FOODS

ALTERNATIVES- Perspectives on Society and Environment
Autumn Press, Inc.
Bookworm Publishing Company
BRITISH NATURALISTS' ASSOCIATION (PUBLISHERS)
Bull Publishing Co.
BUSH LEAGUE
Butterfly Press
COEVOLUTION QUARTERLY
COUNTRY-SIDE
THE COUNTRYMAN
COUNTRYSIDE
The Crossing Press
Dawn Horse Press
DAY BY DAY
THE ECOLOGIST
ELAN POETIQUE LITTERAIRE ET PACIFISTE
GARLIC TIMES
Grasshopper Press
GREENPEACE
HUMANIST IN CANADA
John Muir Publications
Kitchen Harvest
THE MACROBIOTIC
Midpress Books
THE MOTHER EARTH NEWS
NATURAL LIFE
Naturegraph Publishers, Inc.
New Vegetarian Press
THE NORTH AMERICAN REVIEW
NORTH COUNTRY STAR
NOT MAN APART
Omango d' Press
PEACE NEWS "For Non-Violent Revolution"
Peace Press
PEOPLE & ENERGY
Place of Herons
POSTCARD ART/POSTCARD FICTION
RAIN: JOURNAL OF APPROPRIATE TECHNOLOGY
SCHMUCK ANTHOLOGICAL
SECOND GROWTH
SEERS RIO GRANDE WEEKLY
SELF-RELIANCE
SERIATIM: A Journal of Ecotopia
Sproing Books

TOTAL LIFESTYLE- The Bicentennial Magazine of Natural Living
THE TOWN FORUM JOURNAL & COMMUNITY REPORT
1250 Press
VEGETARIAN HEALTH REVIEW AND DIGEST
VEGETARIAN WORLD
Walnut Press
White Mountain Publishing Company
WHOLE EARTH
Wild Horses & The Potted Plant

EDUCATION

All About Us
Ash Lad Press
ASSERT NEWSLETTER
BRIARPATCH REVIEW: A Journal of Right Livelihood and Simple Living
CANADIAN CHILDREN'S MAGAZINE
CEDAR ROCK
Challenge Press
DE COLORES
LA CONFLUENCIA
Creative Book Company
CREATIVE COMPUTING
Creative Computing Press
EDCENTRIC MAGAZINE
Edgepress
Elm Tree Press
THE EMISSARY
ETC: A Review of General Semantics
ETC Publications
The Feminist Press
FPS: A MAGAZINE OF YOUNG PEOPLE'S LIBERATION
FUTURES INFORMATION INTERCHANGE
THE GREAT BLAFIGRIA IS/THE GREAT COMPASSION
The Harian Press
House of Anansi Press Limited/Publishing Co
HUMANIST IN CANADA
Impact Publishers, Inc.
IN TOUCH
INTERFACE JOURNAL: Alternatives in Higher Education
JOURNAL OF WORLD EDUCATION
K-State Press
MASTHEAD: A Journal For Teaching History With Old Newspapers
Mattole Press
Mercer House Press
MODERN LITURGY
NATIONAL ON-CAMPUS REPORT
NEW SCHOOLS EXCHANGE NEWSLETTER
NOUS JOURNAL
Olympus Publishing Company
PEOPLE'S COMPUTERS
Pruett Publishing Company
Scotty Macgreger Publications
SCREEN
SESAME
SEX NEWS
SIGNAL, Approaches To Children's Books
STONE SOUP, A Magazine By Children
STUDIES IN DESIGN EDUCATION AND CRAFT
Teachers and Writers
TEACHERS AND WRITERS MAGAZINE
UNIVERSITY JOURNAL
Wedge Publishing Foundation
Westbury Associates, Publishers
WOMEN'S STUDIES NEWSLETTER
Word Wheel Books, Inc.

ENERGY

ALTERNATIVE SOURCES of ENERGY MAGAZINE

Cheshire Books
COEVOLUTION QUARTERLY
THE EMISSARY
HIGH COUNTRY NEWS
HIGH COUNTRY NEWS
HUMANIST IN CANADA
Lawrence Hill & Company, Publishers, Inc.
NATURAL LIFE
NRG
PEOPLE & ENERGY
RAIN: JOURNAL OF APPROPRIATE TECHNOLOGY
SELF-RELIANCE
SOLAR AGE
STREET MAGAZINE
Walnut Press
WOOD IBIS

ENGLISH

BOSTON UNIVERSITY JOURNAL
BOUNDARY 2
BROWNING SOCIETY NOTES
CANADIAN AUTHOR & BOOKMAN
THE CENTENNIAL REVIEW
Chandler & Sharp Publishers, Inc.
COLLEGE ENGLISH
THE DALHOUSIE REVIEW
DRIFTWOOD-EAST
ESSAYS ON CANADIAN WRITING
GAZEBO
THE GYPSY SCHOLAR: A Graduate Forum for Literary Criticism
HYPERION A Poetry Journal
John Parke Custis Press
JOURNAL OF NARRATIVE TECHNIQUE
LAUGHING BEAR
THE MAINSTREETER
THE MODERN LANGUAGE JOURNAL
MODERNIST STUDIES: Literature & Culture 1920-1940
PAUNCH
Peregrine Smith, Inc.
QUEEN STREET MAGAZINE
Richboro Press
SCHOLIA SATYRICA
THE SHAW REVIEW
Sleepy Hollow Restorations
THE SLOUGH
THE SPHINX
TABLOID STORY
THOREAU JOURNAL QUARTERLY
Thorp Springs Press
Tyndall Creek Press
VIA
Westburg Associates, Publishers
THE YALE REVIEW

FICTION

ABBEY
Acrobat Books
AFTER-IMAGE
THE AGNI REVIEW
AIS EIRI
THE ALCHEMIST
ALDEBARAN
ALEPH
Allegany Mountain Press
ANAESTHESIA REVIEW
Angst World Library
Anthelion Press, Inc.
THE ANTIGONISH REVIEW
THE ANTIOCH REVIEW
APALACHEE QUARTERLY
Arbor
ARCADE-THE COMICS REVUE
THE ARK RIVER REVIEW
Around Publishing
AS IS
ASCENT
ASPEN ANTHOLOGY
AZU Press
The B & R Samizdat Express
The Babbington Press
BACHY
BACK ROADS
Back Roads Press
BARATARIA REVIEW
BARBEQUE PLANET
BARTHOLOMEW'S COBBLE
Basement Workshop, Inc.
BASTARD ANGEL
Bear Hug Books
THE BELLINGHAM REVIEW
BERKELEY POETS COOPERATIVE
BETELGEUSE CHAPBOOK SERIES/NEWEDI FICTION SERIES
BEZOAR
The Bieler Press
BIG MOON
BIG SCREAM
BIRD EFFORT
Black Sparrow Press
THE BLACK WARRIOR REVIEW
BLACKWOOD'S MAGAZINE
BLANK TAPE
Blue Horse
BLUE MOON NEWS
Blue Moon Press, Inc.
Blue Mountain Press
Blue Wind Press (Dynamite Books; Overdrive Books)
BOX 749
BOXSPRING
BRAVADO
Cambric Press
CANADIAN AUTHOR & BOOKMAN
CANADIAN FICTION MAGAZINE
THE CAPILANO REVIEW
Capra Press
The Carolina Wren Press
Carpenter Press
Casa Editorial
Cat Anna Press
Catalyst
CATALYST 1987
CENTER
Challenge Press
THE CHARIOTEER
CHARITON REVIEW
Chthon Press
CIMARRON REVIEW
CITY 4
City Lights Books
The City Moon
City Slicker Press
Cloud Marauder Press
COASTLINE MAGAZINE
CODA: Poets & Writers Newsletter
COE REVIEW
THE COLORADO QUARTERLY
CONNECTICUT FIRESIDE
CONTRABAND MAGAZINE
Copper Beech Press
Cornerstone Press
Coteau Books

Court Street Chap-Book Series
Creative Arts Book Company
CROW'S NEST
CTHULHU
Curbstone Press
The Curlew Press
CURTAINS
DARK HORSE
DARK TOWER
Daughters Publishing Co., Inc.
Dawn Valley Press
DECEMBER MAGAZINE
DELIRIUM
DESCANT
Deuce of Clubs Press
DIANA'S BIMONTHLY
Dodo Press
DOGSOLDIER
Dolphin-Moon
Dovetail Press
Duck Down Press
Dustbooks
Eads Street Press
THE EAR IN A WHEATFIELD
EARTH'S DAUGHTERS
The Ecco Press
EEL
EPOCH
Equus Publishers
ESPONTANEO
EUREKA REVIEW
EVENT
Excello & Bollard
EXIT
THE FALCON
FAS Publishing/Fleetwood Art Studio, Inc.
FICTION
FICTION INTERNATIONAL
FICTION WEST
The Figures
FIRELANDS ARTS REVIEW
First Person
FLOATING ISLAND
FOR THE TIME BEING
Forum Literati
FOUR QUARTERS
Free Books Inc
THE FRONT
Funch Press
GALLIMAUFRY
GLASSWORKS
GOETHE'S NOTES
Goldermood Rainbow Press
GRAFIKTRAKTS
GRANITE
GRAYDAY MAGAZINE
GREEN'S MAGAZINE
GRUB STREET
Halty Ferguson Publishing Co.
HAND BOOK
HANGING LOOSE
HARBINGER
The Harian Press
HARVEST
Helix House
HELLCOAL ANNUAL
Hibiscus Press
Hiddigeigei Books
House of Anansi Press Limited/Publishing Co.
HURON REVIEW
ICARUS
IMAGE MAGAZINE
IN A NUTSHELL
INCUS
INLET
Interface Unlimited
THE INTERNATIONAL FICTION REVIEW
International Publishers Co., Inc.
Iris Press
Isat Pragbhara Press
ISLANDS, A New Zealand Quarterly of Arts & Letters
ISTHMUS
Ithaca House
Ithaca Press
JEOPARDY
JOURNAL OF CANADIAN FICTION
JUICE
KANSAS QUARTERLY
KARAKI
KARAMU
Kent Publications, Kent School
KOSMOS
THE LAKE SUPERIOR REVIEW
LAKES & PRAIRIES; A Journal of Writings
Lamplighters Roadway Press
LAUGHING BEAR
THE LAUREL REVIEW
Lawrence Hill & Company, Publishers, Inc.
Libra Press
LITTLE CAESAR
LONG POND REVIEW
LOOK QUICK
LOWLANDS REVIEW
LUCKY HEART BOOKS
LUNCH
Lynx House Press
MEANJIN QUARTERLY
MEASURE
MERLIN PAPERS
METAMORPHOSIS
Micah Publications
THE MIDATLANTIC REVIEW
MIKROKOSMOS
MILK QUARTERLY
THE MILL
MINOTAUR
THE MISSISSIPPI MUD
MISSISSIPPI REVIEW
MISSISSIPPI VALLEY REVIEW
THE MODULARIST REVIEW
MODUS OPERANDI
MOJO NAVIGATOR(E)
MONUMENT IN CANTOS AND ESSAYS
MOONDANCE
Mosaic Press/Valley Editions
MULCH
Nada
Nairn Publishing House
NAUSEA
NEBULA
THE NEW INFINITY REVIEW
THE NEW KENT QUARTERLY
NEW LETTERS
THE NEW RENAISSANCE, A Magazine of Ideas & Opinions, Emphasizing Literature & The Arts
NEW RIVER REVIEW
NEW STORIES
NEW VOICES
NewBooks
Newedi Press
Newsnovel Publishers
NEXUS
NIMROD
"NITTY GRITTY"
THE NORTH AMERICAN REVIEW
THE NORTH CAROLINA REVIEW

NORTHERN JOURNEY
NORTHERN NEW ENGLAND REVIEW
NORTHWEST REVIEW
Old Adobe Press
ONCE
ONE
ONE: The Writer's Magazine of Fiction and Poetry
Oolichan Books
Out of the Ashes Press
OYEZ REVIEW
PACIFIC POETRY AND FICTION REVIEW
PANACHE
Parable Press (formerly June McLaughlin Press)
Paradoxical Press
PARAGRAPH: A QUARTERLY OF GAY FICTION
Parallax Press
THE PAWN REVIEW
Peaceweed Press
Pegana Press
Penmaen Press
The Penumbra Press
PEQUOD
Peradam Publishing House
Perivale Press
PERMAFROST
Philmer Enterprises
PHOEBE
PIGIRON
Pikeville College Press
Pilot Press Books
THE PLANET QUARTERLY
PLOUGHSHARES
POCKET PAL
The Pocket Pal Press
Poet Gallery Press
POETRY-WINDSOR-POESIE
Pogo Press
The Pomegranate Press
PORT TOWNSEND JOURNAL
PRAIRIE SCHOONER
Press Porcepic Limited
Pressed Curtains
PROTEUS
Puckerbrush Press
PUERTO DEL SOL
Puerto Del Sol Press
PULP
PYRAMID
QUARRY WEST
QUARTERLY REVIEW OF LITERATURE
QUARTERLY WEST
QUARTET
QUIXOTE, QUIXOTL
THE RAG
Raven Publications
RE:PRINT (AN OCCASIONAL MAGAZINE)
Rebis Press
RED CEDAR REVIEW
Red Dust
RED FOX REVIEW
Regent Graphic Services
Release Press
RIPPLES
RIVER BOTTOM MAGAZINE (Baseball, Floating and Nickle Times)
ROCKBOTTOM
ROCKY MOUNTAIN REVIEW
Ross-Erikson Publishers, Inc.
ROUNDTABLE
Sagarin Press
SAGEBLOOM
St. Luke's Press

SAMISDAT
Samisdat Associates
The Saturday Centre
SATURDAY CLUB BOOK OF POETRY (sub-title: SCOP)
Seagull Publications
SEEMS
SENECA REVIEW
SEQUOIA
SEVEN STARS FICTION QUARTERLY
SEVEN STARS POETRY
Seventh Dream Press
SHELLY'S
SHENANDOAH
THE SHORE REVIEW
Sicilian Antigruppo
Simon & Pierre Publishing Co. Ltd.
Singing Wind Publications
SKYWRITING
SLICK PRESS
SLIT WRIST
THE SLOUGH
THE SMALL POND MAGAZINE OF LITERATURE
Smyrna Press
SNAKEROOTS
SOLANA
SOME
SOU'WESTER
SOURCE
SOUTH CAROLINA REVIEW
SOUTHERN REVIEW
Spindrift Press
SPIT IN THE OCEAN
THE SQUATCHBERRY JOURNAL
STARWIND
Stock Poetry
STORY QUARTERLY
STRANGE FAECES
STUMP
SUN
Sunken Forum Press
Sunrise Press
SURFSIDE POETRY REVIEW
The Swallow Press Inc. (Book Publisher)
SYZYGY-A Journal of Fiction and Sketches
TABLOID STORY
TALES
TELEPHONE
THIRD EYE
13th MOON
TITMOUSE
TOUCHSTONE
TRANSLATION
Treacle Press
TREES
Truly Fine Press
1250 Press
Twowindows Press
US1 WORKSHEETS
UNDERTOW
UNDINE
UNEXPECTED
UNICORN
Unpublished Editions
JOHN UPDIKE NEWSLETTER
Urion Press
UROBOROS (was ALLEGANY POETRY)
UZZANO
VAGABOND
The Vanity Press
VELVET WINGS
Ventura Press
Veritie Press, Inc.

Verlag Guenther Emig
Vermont Crossroads Press, Inc.
Vesta Publications
VIEW FROM THE SILVER BRIDGE
VILE
THE VOYEUR
WALLPAPER
WALUNA, THE SOHO REVIEW
WATERS
West Coast Poetry Review Press
Westburg Associates, Publishers
THE WESTERLY REVIEW
Westwind Press
WHAT'S A NICE HILLBILLY LIKE YOU . . . ?
The White Ewe Press
Wild & Woolley
WILLMORE CITY
Willmore City Press
Windfall
WINDOW
WINDOWS IN THE STONE
WIP
WISCONSIN REVIEW
Word-Camera
The Workingman's Press
WRIT
WRITE ON
Writers' Cooperative
WRITERS IN RESIDENCE
XANTHIPPE
YELLOW BRICK ROAD
Z
ZONE ONE

FILM, VIDEO

AVALANCHE
CANADIAN AUTHOR & BOOKMAN
CINEASTE MAGAZINE
CLASSIC FILM COLLECTOR
CRISS-CROSS ART COMMUNICATIONS
DADAZINE
DECEMBER MAGAZINE
Ecart Publications
FILM
FILM CULTURE
Film Culture Non-Profit, Inc.
FILM HERITAGE
FILM INDEX
FILM LIBRARY QUARTERLY
FILM QUARTERLY
FOCUS ON FILM
JUMP CUT, A Review of Contemporary Cinema
Kontexts Publications
Levenson Press
THE MODULARIST REVIEW
Phillip M. Perry
PRAXIS: A Journal of Radical Perspectives on the Arts
RAIN: JOURNAL OF APPROPRIATE TECHNOLOGY
SCREEN
THE TOY SUN
THE VELVET LIGHT TRAP: Review of Cinema
WOMEN & FILM
Women's History Research Center, Inc.

FOLKLORE

ARTE QUINCENAL
BITTERSWEET
THE CHARIOTEER
LA CONFLUENCIA
THE DRAMA REVIEW
HOO-DOO BlackSeries

KENTUCKY FOLKLORE RECORD
KENTUCKY FOLKLORE SERIES
LORE AND LANGUAGE
The Middle Atlantic Press
Perivale Press
Pleasant Hill Press
Raintree
Sleepy Hollow Restorations
STREET MAGAZINE
TSA'ASZI'
UNICORN: A Miscellaneous Journal
WISCONSIN TRAILS
WOOD IBIS

FRANCE, FRENCH

POESIE - U.S.A.

GAELIC

Club Leabhar Highland Book Club
GAIRM

GAMES

AQUATIC WORLD
BIKE WORLD
DOWN RIVER
J'ADOUBE!
Kanthaka Press
Kontexts Publications
NORDIC WORLD
NORTHWEST CHESS
RUNNERS WORLD
SELF DEFENSE
SOCCER WORLD

GARDENING

Bing America Publications
Bookworm Publishing Company
Brombacher Books
THE EMISSARY
GRASS ROOTS
Harvest Press
THE MOTHER EARTH NEWS
RAIN: JOURNAL OF APPROPRIATE TECHNOLOGY
Spring Church Book Company
TOTAL LIFESTYLE- The Bicentennial Magazine of Natural Living
Wild Horses & The Potted Plant

GAY

THE ADVOCATE
BASTARD ANGEL
BIG MAMA RAG
THE BODY POLITIC- Gay Liberation Journal
Catalyst
Diana Press, Inc
DIGNITY
FAG RAG
A GAY BIBLIOGRAPHY
GAY COMMUNITY NEWS
GAY LEFT
GAY LITERATURE
GAY NEWS
GAY SUNSHINE: A Journal of Gay Liberation
GAY TIDE
GAYELLOW PAGES
Good Gay Poets Press
GPU NEWS
INTEGRITY: Gay Episcopal Forum

371

THE LAMPETER MUSE
THE LESBIAN TIDE
OFF OUR BACKS
OUT
Out & Out Books
PARAGRAPH: A QUARTERLY OF GAY FICTION
PEACE NEWS "For Non-Violent Revolution"
Pink Triangle Press
RFD
SAPPHO
SCHMUCK ANTHOLOGICAL
SPORTSWOMAN MAGAZINE
TANGENTS
Unpublished Editions
Violet Press
WEID: The Sensibility Revue
WHITE ARMS MAGAZINE
Woman Press

GERMAN

NEW GERMAN STUDIES

GRAPHICS

A SHOUT IN THE STREET: a journal of literary and visual art
THE ALTERNATIVE PRESS
APPLEGARTH'S FOLLY
ATHAENA
BACK ROADS
Back Roads Press
Basement Workshop, Inc.
BASTARD ANGEL
THE BEAUREGARD BUGLE BOY HERALD-TRIBUNE
BERGEN POETS
BETELGEUSE CHAPBOOK SERIES/NEWEDI FICTION SERIES
BIRTHSTONE
Blue Horse
Carolyn Bean Associates, Publishing
Cherry Valley Editions
CLOWN WAR
COSMIC CIRCUS
Creative Ventures
The Curlew Press
DADAZINE
DRAGONFLY: A Quarterly Of Haiku
EN PASSANT POETRY QUARTERLY
FINE PRINT: A Review for the Arts of the Book
GLASSWORKS
GRAFIKTRAKTS
GRUB STREET
Holmgangers Press
The Hosanna Press
Ilkon Press
THE ILLUSTRATED ORB
JAM TO-DAY
KONGLOMERATI
Kontexts Publications
LAUGHING BEAR
LOVE LIGHTS
The New Poets Series
Newedi Press
NICOTINE SOUP
No Dead Lines
PADAN ARAM
PHANTASM
PIGIRON
Pleasure Dome Press (Long Island Poetry Collective Inc.)
The Pray Curser Press
Queens College Press
RADAR
RAIN: JOURNAL OF APPROPRIATE TECHNOLOGY

THE RECORD SUN
RIVER STYX
ROUNDTABLE
Saint Heironymous Press, Inc.
THE SHORE REVIEW
SPLIT LEVEL
THE STONE
STRANGE FAECES
Swamp Press
TEXAS PORTFOLIO
3RD THING MAGAZINE OF POETRY AND GRAPHICS
13th MOON
Thistledown Press
TIGHTROPE
TIMEPAD
THE TRANSIENT
TREES
Trike
TWELFTH KEY
VILE
XANADU

GREEK

THE COFFEEHOUSE

HAIKU

BONSAI: A Quarterly of Haiku
DRAGONFLY: A Quarterly Of Haiku
HIGH/COO: A Quarterly of Short Poetry
High/Coo Press
MIDWEST CHAPARRAL
Swamp Press
TIGHTROPE
WESTERN POETRY QUARTERLY

HEALTH

Aslan Enterprises
Badger Creek Press
Bull Publishing Co.
Butterfly Press
THE CRITICAL LIST
Elm Tree Press
THE EMISSARY
FORESIGHT MAGAZINE
GARLIC TIMES
Golden West Books
THE GROVE
Gullistan Press
HEALTH/PAC BULLETIN
Henry Philips Publishing Company
Images Press
Impact Publishers, Inc.
MEDICAL HISTORY
THE MOTHER EARTH NEWS
Omango d' Press
RAIN: JOURNAL OF APPROPRIATE TECHNOLOGY

HISTORY

AFRO-AMERICANS in NEW YORK LIFE & HISTORY
ALBERTA HISTORY
AMEX-CANADA MAGAZINE
THE ANTIQUER
BIBLIOTHEQUE D'HUMANISME ET RENAISSANCE
Biscuit City Press
BRITISH COLUMBIA HISTORICAL NEWS
BULLETIN OF CONCERNED ASIAN SCHOLARS
CANADA WEST
CANADIAN FRONTIER
CANADIAN SLAVONIC PAPERS

CANADIAN STEAM MAGAZINE
CANNIBAL
Challenge Press
COASTLINE MAGAZINE
Communication Creativity
LA CONFLUENCIA
Creative Books
THE DALHOUSIE REVIEW
Golden West Books
GRAND RIVER REVIEW/CAPITOL CITY MOON
Great Basin Press
Harvest Publishers
HARVEST QUARTERLY
THE JOURNAL of PSYCHOHISTORY
Les Femmes Publishing
Library Research Associates
Maryland Historical Press
MASTHEAD: A Journal For Teaching History With Old Newspapers
Miocene Press
MODERN LANGUAGE QUARTERLY
Monad Press
Nevada Publications
New Review Books
NEW REVIEW OF EAST-EUROPEAN HISTORY
NEW WORLD JOURNAL
THE NORTH WIND
Northwoods Press, Inc.
OCCULT AMERICANA
Oregon Historical Society
EL PALACIO
Peoples Press
Peregrine Smith, Inc.
Prairie Publishing Company
Pruett Publishing Company
RADICAL AMERICA
RAINCOAST CHRONICLES
The Rather Press
SALTHOUSE
Second Porcupine
Sleepy Hollow Restorations
Stagecoach Pub. Co. Ltd.
Steel Rail Publishing
STUDIES IN LABOUR HISTORY
Summer Thought
TANGENTS
Vanguard Books
Veritie Press, Inc.
Wedge Publishing Foundation
Westburg Associates, Publishers
William L. Bauhan, Publisher

HOLOGRAPHY

Pentangle Press
THEATRE DESIGN AND TECHNOLOGY

HOW-TO

A Harmless Flirtation With Wealth
The Adobe Press
Ana-Doug Publishing
Badger Creek Press
Bell Springs Publishing Company
Bing America Publications
BITTERSWEET
The Bookstore Press
Bookworm Publishing Company
BRIARPATCH REVIEW: A Journal of Right Livelihood and Simple Living
Brownstone Publishers, Inc.
Butterfly Press

Capra Press
Carma Press
Carousel Press
Cobblesmith
Communication Creativity
The Communication Press
COUNTRY WOMEN
Dustbooks
E & R Marlin, Publishers
Food For Thought Publications
G P Enterprises—JOB HUNTER'S FORUM
Gullistan Press
HAPPINESS HOLDING TANK
Hunter Publishing, Co.
Jalmar Press, Inc.
John Muir Publications
Lincoln Publishing Company
LIVING IN THE OZARKS NEWSLETTER
Lonely Planet Publications
Midpress Books
Moon Publications
THE MOTHER EARTH NEWS
Old Time Bottle Publishing Company
Opportunities Unlimited Publications
Programmed Studies Inc
Pushcart Press
R & D Services
Racz Publishing Co.
RAIN: JOURNAL OF APPROPRIATE TECHNOLOGY
RICH'S SUCCESS NEWS
Running Press
Seagull Books, NOPCO, Ltd.
Second Back Row Press
Tamal Vista Publications
THEATRE ACROSS AMERICA
Thresh Publications
Unity Press, Inc.
Vermont Crossroads Press, Inc.
THE WOMAN ACTIVIST
THE WORKBOOK

HUMANISM

Carolyn Bean Associates, Publishing
Gleniffer Press
Gullistan Press
THE HUMANIST
HUMANIST IN CANADA
HYPERION A Poetry Journal
ISTHMUS
THE PHOENIX
POETS ON:
REBUTTAL! The Bicentennial Newsletter of Truth
S.A. Growth Press
STREET MAGAZINE
TIME/OUT
Vermont Crossroads Press, Inc.

HUMOR

A Harmless Flirtation With Wealth
Amen-Ra Publishing Co
AQUILA MAGAZINE
B & H BOOKS
The Communication Press
THE EMISSARY
FRONT STREET TROLLEY
Landmark Publishing
MAL DE MER
Miller Pond Books
Perivale Press
PHILOLOGOS

373

REPARTEE
Resource Publications
RESOURCES
SNARF
SPLIT LEVEL
STRANGE FAECES
THOUGHTS FOR ALL SEASONS: The Magazine of Epigrams
Ventura Press
THE WEST CONSCIOUS REVIEW
WILD FENNEL
The WorDoctor Publications
ZONE ONE

IDAHO

IDAHO HERITAGE

ILLINOIS

POETRY &

INDEXES & ABSTRACTS

C.I.S.S.
THE DALHOUSIE REVIEW
RAIN: JOURNAL OF APPROPRIATE TECHNOLOGY
WOMEN STUDIES ABSTRACTS

IRELAND

IRISH BOOKLORE

JEFFERS, ROBINSON

Quintessence Publications

JOYCE, JAMES

JAMES JOYCE QUARTERLY
A WAKE NEWSLITTER, Studies Of James Joyce's Finnegans Wake

KANSAS

COTTONWOOD REVIEW

KENTUCKY

KENTUCKY FOLKLORE RECORD

LABOR

ABOUT UNIONS
GREEN MOUNTAIN QUARTERLY
INDUSTRIAL WORKER
INTERNATIONAL SOCIALIST REVIEW
The Jacek Publishing Company
Labor Arts Books
THE MILITANT
Prairie Publishing Company
PROLETARIAT
STUDIES IN LABOUR HISTORY

LANGUAGE

BA SHIRU
CANADIAN AUTHOR & BOOKMAN
Daylight Press
THE EMISSARY
ETC: A Review of General Semantics
HYPERION A Poetry Journal
IF LIFE, THEN ONE AMONG AT LEAST FOUR
JOURNAL OF CALIFORNIA ANTHROPOLOGY

Kontexts Publications
LAUGHING BEAR
Litmus, Inc.
LORE AND LANGUAGE
Malki Museum Press
MICHIGAN GERMANIC STUDIES
THE MODERN LANGUAGE JOURNAL
NRG
Tom Ockerse Editions
OSIRIS
STAR WEST
Thorp Springs Press
TOTTEL'S
TRUCHA
TYPEWRITER

LATIN AMERICA

AZU Press
CANTO LIBRE-A Bilingual Quarterly of Latin American Peoples Art
Center For Cuban Studies
Place of Herons
TINTAN
VIA
WOOD IBIS

LAW

Brownstone Publishers, Inc.

LAWRENCE, D. H.

THE D.H. LAWRENCE REVIEW

LESBIANISM

ALBATROSS
Back Row Press
CONDITIONS
GAY COMMUNITY NEWS
GPU NEWS
LESBIAN CONNECTION
LESBIAN VOICES
MAJORITY REPORT
The Naiad Press, Inc.
Out & Out Books
PEACE NEWS "For Non-Violent Revolution"
SINISTER WISDOM
13th MOON
WEID: The Sensibility Revue
Woman Press

LIBERTARIAN

AGAINST THE WALL
THE DANDELION
Free Life Editions
ILLINOIS LIBERTARIAN
INDIVIDUAL LIBERTY
LIMIT! (The National Newsletter Of The Libertarian Republican Alliance)
PEACE NEWS "For Non-Violent Revolution"
PHILOLOGOS
SOUTHERN LIBERTARIAN MESSENGER
STREET MAGAZINE

LIBRARIES

ALA/SRRT NEWSLETTER
THE BIBLIOTHECK
BOOKLEGGER MAGAZINE

CIE
COLLECTORS' NETWORK NEWS
EMERGENCY LIBRARIAN
EXPRESSION
FILM LIBRARY QUARTERLY
Gleniffer Press
HENNEPIN COUNTY LIBRARY CATALOGING BULLETIN
LIBRARIANS FOR SOCIAL CHANGE
LIBRARY REVIEW
John L Noyce, Publisher (formerly Smoothie Pub)
QUILL & QUIRE
RAIN: JOURNAL OF APPROPRIATE TECHNOLOGY
LA RAZON MESTIZA/LA MUJER es la TIERRA
ROCKINGCHAIR
Scarecrow Press
SIPAPU
THE U*N*A*B*A*S*H*E*D LIBRARIAN, THE "HOW I RUN MY LIBRARY GOOD" LETTER
Women Library Workers
WOMEN LIBRARY WORKERS NEWSLETTER

LITERARY REVIEW

A
ABYSS
AGENDA
AISLING
AKROS
All This & Less Publishers
AMERICAN ARTS PAMPHLET SERIES
ANN ARBOR REVIEW
ANTAEUS
THE ANTIGONISH REVIEW
APHRA
ARION, A Journal of Humanities and the Classics
ARIZONA QUARTERLY
ASPECT
ASPEN ANTHOLOGY
ATLANTIC PROVINCES BOOK REVIEW
AURA Literary Arts Review
BACONIANA
BALL STATE UNIVERSITY FORUM
BARTLEBY'S REVIEW
BASTARD ANGEL
BEDFORDSHIRE MAGAZINE
Beyond Baroque Foundation Publications, includes Beyond Baroque/newforms, NEW Magazine. Arts & Letters (formerly NeWLetterS), and NewBooks.
BIG SKY
BIRD EFFORT
BLACK/AMERICAN LITERATURE FORUM
BLACK MOSS
THE BLACK POSITION
BLACKBERRY
BLACKWOOD'S MAGAZINE
BOOKS IN CANADA: A National Review Of Books
BOOKSWEST
BOSS
BOSTON UNIVERSITY JOURNAL
BRITISH JOURNAL OF AESTHETICS
BUTT: A Quarterly
CAFE SOLO
CAFETERIA
THE CALIFORNIA QUARTERLY
Cambric Press
CANADIAN AUTHOR & BOOKMAN
CANADIAN FICTION MAGAZINE
THE CANADIAN FORUM
CANADIAN LITERATURE
CANNIBAL
CENTER
Challenge Press
THE CHARIOTEER

CHARITON REVIEW
CHELSEA
CHICAGO REVIEW
CHOUTEAU REVIEW
THE CHOWDER REVIEW
COLORADO-NORTH REVIEW
CONFRONTATION
THE CONTEMPORARY LITERARY SCENE
CONTEMPORARY LITERATURE IN TRANSLATION
COTTONWOOD REVIEW
CRITIQUE: Studies in Modern Fiction
CUTBANK
THE D.H. LAWRENCE REVIEW
THE DALHOUSIE REVIEW
THE DENVER QUARTERLY
DESCANT
DREMPLES
EAR MAGAZINE
EAST RIVER REVIEW
EDGE
ELAN POETIQUE LITTERAIRE ET PACIFISTE
THE FAULT
FICTION INTERNATIONAL
THE FIDDLEHEAD
FIREWEED
GALAXIA 71
GAY LITERATURE
GEGENSCHEIN
THE GEORGIA REVIEW
GLOBAL TAPESTRY JOURNAL
THE GREAT BLAFIGRIA IS/THE GREAT COMPASSION
Great Raven Press
GREAT WORKS
THE GREEN FUSE
GRONK
GRUB STREET
THE HAMPDEN-SYDNEY POETRY REVIEW
HAPPINESS HOLDING TANK
THE HARVARD ADVOCATE
Harvest Publishers
HARVEST QUARTERLY
HECTOR AND HECTOR
HEIRS
Hellcoal Press
THE HOLLINS CRITIC
House of Anansi Press Limited/Publishing Co.
THE HUDSON REVIEW
HYACINTHS AND BISCUITS
HYPERION A Poetry Journal
ICONOMATRIX
INDEX ON CENSORSHIP
INDIAN Literature
INTERSTATE
INVICTUS
ISLANDS, A New Zealand Quarterly of Arts & Letters
ISTHMUS
JAMES JOYCE QUARTERLY
JAWBONE
JEFFERSONIAN REVIEW
JOURNAL OF CANADIAN FICTION
JOURNAL OF MODERN LITERATURE
JOURNAL OF SOUTH ASIAN LITERATURE
JULES VERNE VOYAGER
KANSAS QUARTERLY
KAYAK
Kontexts Publications
LAOMEDON REVIEW
LAUGHING BEAR
LETTERS
LINQ
LONG ISLAND REVIEW
LOOSE LIPS SINK SHIPS
MADRONA

MAINE EDITION
THE MALAHAT REVIEW
THE MARKHAM REVIEW
THE MASSACHUSETTS REVIEW
THE MICKLE STREET REVIEW
THE MIDWEST QUARTERLY
MONTANA GOTHIC
MONTEMORA
MOUNTAIN REVIEW
MOVING OUT: Feminist Literary & Arts Journal
NANTUCKET REVIEW
NEW BOSTON REVIEW
NEW EDINBURGH REVIEW
NEW HOPE
NEW LITERATURE & IDEOLOGY
NEW MAGAZINE: Arts & Letters
THE NEW MOON
NEW ORLEANS REVIEW
THE NEW REVIEW (formerly THE REVIEW)
NEW YORK ARTS JOURNAL
NEWEST REVIEW
NEWORLD
NORTH AMERICAN MENTOR MAGAZINE
NORTH COAST POETRY
NORTH COUNTRY
NORTHWOODS JOURNAL
THE NOTEBOOK & OTHER REVIEWS
Notebook Press
OBSIDIAN: BLACK LITERATURE IN REVIEW
OCCURRENCE
OFF OUR BACKS
THE OHIO REVIEW
OHIOANA QUARTERLY
OLD FRIENDS
OSIRIS
OTHER PRESS POETRY REVIEW
OUTRIGGER
OVERLAND
PANJANDRUM POETRY JOURNAL
PARNASSUS: POETRY IN REVIEW
PARTISAN REVIEW
PEACE & PIECES REVIEW
PEMBROKE MAGAZINE
PERMAFROST
THE PHOENIX
PILGRIMS OF THE ARTS
PLATFORM
PLOUGHSHARES
POET & CRITIC
POETRY NATION REVIEW
POETRY VENTURE
PORTLAND REVIEW
PRAIRIE SCHOONER
PRIMER
PROSPICE
PUDDINGSTONE
QUEEN'S QUARTERLY: A Canadian Review
RA: A Journal of Popular Culture and the Arts
RED WEATHER
THE REMINGTON REVIEW
REVISTA CHICANO-RIQUENA
The Rose Bower Press
RUFUS
RUSSIAN LITERATURE TRIQUARTERLY
SAINT ANDREWS REVIEW
SAM HOUSTON LITERARY REVIEW
SAMISDAT
SAMPHIRE
SAN FRANCISCO REVIEW OF BOOKS
SAN JOSE STUDIES
SAN MARCOS REVIEW
SF COMMENTARY

SHAVIAN—JOURNAL OF BERNARD SHAW
SHAW NEWSLETTER
THE SHAW REVIEW
SHENANDOAH
THE SHORE REVIEW
613 MAGAZINE
THE SLACKWATER REVIEW
THE SMITH
SOLANA
THE SOLE PROPRIETOR
SOUTHERN HUMANITIES REVIEW
SOUTHERN REVIEW
THE SOUTHERN REVIEW
STAND
STAR-WEB PAPER
STARDANCER
STATIONS
STILE
STONE MOUNTAIN REVIEW
STONECLOUD
THE SUNSTONE REVIEW
Swamp Press
TANGENTS
Tau Delta Phi Press
TAWTE: Texas Artists Writers and Thinkers in Exile
10 POINT 5, A Magazine of the Arts
13th MOON
THOREAU JOURNAL QUARTERLY
THREE RIVERS POETRY JOURNAL
THREE SISTERS
TIGHTROPE
TRUCK
TUUMBA
UGLY DUCKLING
UNDER THE SIGN OF PISCES: Anais Nin and Her Circle
UNIVERSITY OF WINDSOR REVIEW
UNMUZZLED OX
VANDERBILT POETRY REVIEW
VECTOR MAGAZINE
Vehicule Press
VORT
WAVES
WEBSTER REVIEW
WEID: The Sensibility Revue
WEST COAST POETRY REVIEW
Westburg Associates, Publishers
WESTERN AMERICAN LITERATURE
WESTERN HUMANITIES REVIEW
Women's Studies
THE WORD-SMITH
THE WORMWOOD REVIEW
THE YALE REVIEW
ZIGGURAT Annual International Anthology of the Fine Arts
ZONE ONE

LITERATURE (GENERAL)

A SHOUT IN THE STREET: a journal of literary and visual art
ACID SWITCH
Air Press
ALLEGRA
Allegra Press
ALPHA
American Revolutionary Political Pamphlets
ANN ARBOR REVIEW
Anthelion Press, Inc.
APPLEGARTH'S FOLLY
The Aquila Publishing Co. Ltd.
Archangel Books
AUSTIN PULPWOOD
AZU-THE INFINITE MAN
AZU Press

BETELGEUSE CHAPBOOK SERIES/NEWEDI FICTION SERIES
BIG DEAL
BIRD EFFORT
BLACK FORUM
BOTTOMFISH MAGAZINE
BROWNING SOCIETY NOTES
Calliopea Press
CALYX
CANADIAN AUTHOR & BOOKMAN
CARACOL
CAROLINA QUARTERLY
Cassandra Publications
CELEBES
THE CHARIOTEER
CHOOMIA - COLLECTIONS OF CONTEMPORARY POETRY
Cider Press
CIRCULAR LETTER
CITY MINER
THE CLOVER PATCH
CRAWL OUT YOUR WINDOW
Crawl Out Your Window Press
CREACION
THE DEKALB LITERARY ARTS JOURNAL
EARTH'S DAUGHTERS
FICTION WEST
FIGMENT
THE FOOLKILLER
Foundations for the Redefinition of Sanity
EL FUEGO DE AZTLAN
Gleniffer Press
Great Basin Press
Great Works Editions
GREENHOUSE REVIEW
THE HAMPDEN-SYDNEY POETRY REVIEW
The Harian Press
THE HARVARD ADVOCATE
Holmgangers Press
HYPERION A Poetry Journal
ILLUMINATIONS
IO
"JOINT" CONFERENCE
KONTAKTE
Lame Johnny Press, Associates
LAUGHING BEAR
Lawton Press
LETTERS
THE LITERARY MONTHLY (formerly Pacific Sun Literary Quarterly)
Mainespring Press
MANGO
The Menard Press
MICHIGAN GERMANIC STUDIES
MODUS OPERANDI
Mudborn Press
THE MYSTERIOUS BARRICADES
NEW COLLAGE MAGAZINE
THE NEW LAUREL REVIEW
NEW QUARTERLY CAVE
THE NEW RENAISSANCE, A Magazine of Ideas & Opinions, Emphasizing Literature & The Arts
The New South Company
NEW STORIES
Newedi Press
NEWSLETTER
NICOTINE SOUP
THE NORTH AMERICAN REVIEW
North Atlantic Books
NORTHWOODS JOURNAL
Northwoods Press, Inc.
THE NOTEBOOK & OTHER REVIEWS
Notebook Press
NOUS: a journal of arts and ideas
ONTARIO REVIEW
Petronium Press
Phenomenon Press
Place of Herons
POETRY &
Porphyrion Press
PRAXIS: A Journal of Radical Perspectives on the Arts
PULP
Pulp Press
Queens College Press
QUIXOTE, QUIXOTL
Raintree
Raven Publications
ROOF
ROOM OF ONE'S OWN
The Rose Bower Press
S.H.Y.
St. Luke's Press
SALMAGUNDI
THE SALT CEDAR
A SELECTED FEW/THE PEOPLE'S GALLERY
Sibyl-Child Press
SIBYL-CHILD: A Women's Arts & Culture Journal
SINISTER WISDOM
SOLEIL BLANK: a forum of progressive literature
SOUTH DAKOTA REVIEW
Steel Rail Publishing
STREET MAGAZINE
SUN & MOON: A Quarterly of Literature and Art
The Swallow Press Inc. (Book Publisher)
Synergistic Press
13th MOON
Thorp Springs Press
THREE CENT PULP
UNAKA RANGE
THE UNSPEAKABLE VISIONS OF THE INDIVIDUAL
Westburg Associates, Publishers
WESTERN HUMANITIES REVIEW
WOOD IBIS
X, A JOURNAL Of The ARTS
YARDBIRD READER
Yardbird Wing Editions
York Press
ZONE ONE

LONDON, JACK

THE CHANEY CHRONICAL
THE LONDON COLLECTOR
WHAT'S NEW ABOUT LONDON, JACK?

LOVECRAFT, H. P.

CTHULHU

LYTTON, BULWER

THE BULWER LYTTON CHRONICLE

MAGAZINES

AURA Literary Arts Review
BUTT: A Quarterly
CALIFORNIA PELICAN MAGAZINE
CENTERING: A Magazine of Poetry
CONFRONTATION
THE DENVER QUARTERLY
EXPRESSIVE ARTS REVIEW
GNOSTICA
GRAVIDA

HAPPINESS HOLDING TANK
Harvest Publishers
HARVEST QUARTERLY
Heidelberg Graphics
HYPERION A Poetry Journal
INTERMEDIA
LA-BAS: A Newsletter of Experimental Poetry & Poetics
Loverseed Press
THE SUPPLEMENT TO THE BULLETIN OF THE MARYLAND WRITERS COUNCIL
MOVING OUT: Feminist Literary & Arts Journal
NATIONAL BOOK REVIEW
NEW PERIODICALS INDEX
NEW POETRY
OREGON TIMES MAGAZINE
POETRY QUARTERLY (previously CURLEW)
POETRY TORONTO NEWSLETTER
PROVINCETOWN POETS
THE SHORE REVIEW
THE SMALL PRESS REVIEW
SPORTSWOMAN MAGAZINE
STONE SOUP, A Magazine By Children
THE STRAIT
SUNSPARK
Sunspark Press
13th MOON
VERMONT CHILDREN'S MAGAZINE
WHITE MULE
WILLAMETTE VALLEY OBSERVER
WOMEN STUDIES ABSTRACTS
ZIGGURAT Annual International Anthology of the Fine Arts

MATHEMATICS

Dymax
Ilkon Press
MATHEMATICAL SPECTRUM

MEDIEVAL

Resource Publications

MEN

GATEAVISA
JOURNAL OF CALIFORNIA ANTHROPOLOGY
Malki Museum Press
MEN'S
Programmed Studies Inc
RECON
Red Alder Books
RFD

MIDDLE EAST

ARARAT
MERIP REPORTS

MILITARY, VETERANS

Alex Aiken
East River Anthology
FIGHT BACK
The Salamander Imprint

MUSIC

AMERICAN FIDDLERS NEWS
ANTIQUE PHONOGRAPH MONTHLY
APM Press
The Avondale Press
CODA: Canada's Jazz Magazine
COMPUTER MUSIC JOURNAL
CONTEMPORARY KEYBOARD MAGAZINE
CREATIVE GUITAR INTERNATIONAL
DANCE HERALD
EAR MAGAZINE
ENGLISH DANCE AND SONG
FOLK MASS AND MODERN LITURGY
Foundations for the Redefinition of Sanity
Glouchester Press
GOLD TURKEY
THE GRACKLE: Improvised Music In Transition
INDIAN HOUSE
JOURNAL OF CALIFORNIA ANTHROPOLOGY
LIVING BLUES
Malki Museum Press
The Mediaworks
Merlin Press
MODERN LITURGY
MUSIC AND LETTERS
THE MYSTERIOUS BARRICADES
New Woman Press
ORGAN DIGEST
OUT THERE MAGAZINE
PAID MY DUES: Journal of Women and Music
PhoeniXongs
RELIX
Resource Publications
Roberton Publications
ROCK-N-ROLL NEWS
Roxbury Poetry Enterprises
Shinn Music Aids
THE SHORE REVIEW
SING OUT! The Folk Song Magazine
A SONGSMITH'S JOURNAL
SOUNDINGS
TEXAS COUNTRY MAGAZINE
TIME BARRIER EXPRESS
TROUSER PRESS
Two-Eighteen Press
VEINS
XENHARMONIC BULLETIN
XENHARMONIKON

NATIVE AMERICAN

AKWESASNE NOTES
ALBERTA HISTORY
Clearwater Publishing Company, Inc.
LA CONFLUENCIA
Heidelberg Graphics
Heyday Books
Hurtig Publishers
INDIAN HOUSE
INDIAN TRUTH
THE INDIAN VOICE
JOURNAL OF CALIFORNIA ANTHROPOLOGY
Lawrence Hill & Company, Publishers, Inc.
Malki Museum Press
MANY SMOKES
The Middle Atlantic Press
Naturegraph Publishers, Inc.
THE NEW SCHOLAR: Studies, Essays, Reviews
Packard Publications
Peregrine Smith, Inc.
Place of Herons
The Proof Press
SCREE
Strawberry Press
SUN TRACKS: An American Indian Literary Magazine
Sweet Pine Press
TSA'ASZI'
WOOD IBIS

NEW ENGLAND

GARGOYLE

NEW ZEALAND

ISLANDS, A New Zealand Quarterly of Arts & Letters

NEWSLETTER

ALA/SRRT NEWSLETTER
AMERICAN DANCE GUILD NEWSLETTER
ASPO NEWSLETTER
THE BULLETIN BOARD
CAMELS COMING NEWSLETTER
CENTER NEWSLETTER
THE CITY MOON
CODA: Poets & Writers Newsletter
COMMON SENSE
COMMUNITY SERVICE NEWSLETTER- in serial with: COMMUNITY COMMENTS
CONRADIANA
COSMEP NEWSLETTER
DAY BY DAY
EAR MAGAZINE
ELBOW DRUMS
FEMINIST BULLETIN
FIT
Gleniffer Press
LAST POST
LAUGHING BEAR
LESBIAN CONNECTION
LIBERTE
LIFELINE
LIMIT! (The National Newsletter Of The Libertarian Republican Alliance)
LIVING IN THE OZARKS NEWSLETTER
LOCUS: The Newspaper of the Science Fiction Field
MINUTES & PROCEEDINGS
NEWSLETTER
THE ORIGINAL ART REPORT (TOAR)
PEOPLE'S BOOKSELLER
POETIPS
POETRY NEWSLETTER
POETS' LEAGUE of GREATER CLEVELAND NEWSLETTER
SEX NEWS
SHINAKI
SIPAPU
SOUTHERN LIBERTARIAN MESSENGER
WASHINGTON INTERNATIONAL ARTS LETTER
WOMEN IN STRUGGLE
WORLD OF POETRY
WRITERS' RESOURCES

NIN, ANAIS

UNDER THE SIGN OF PISCES: Anais Nin and Her Circle

OCCULT

AQUARIAN AGENT-ASTROLOGY 77 (78)
Artists & Alchemists Publications
ASI
ASI Publishers, Inc.
ASTROLOGY '77—The New Aquarian Agent
B & H BOOKS
Blue Crow Press
BOTH SIDES NOW
Butterfly Press
Cat Anna Press
CONQUEST
COSMIC CIRCUS
CRCS Publications
CROSSROADS QUARTERLY
DECARABIA
GNOSTICA
Gullistan Press
JACKSONVILLE POETRY QUARTERLY: Proclamations of the Arcane Order
Les Femmes Publishing
Multinational Media
Rialto Books
Summit University Press
SUN CENTER NEWS
TALISMAN
VIEWPOINT AQUARIUS
THE VOICE
WITCHCRAFT DIGEST MAGAZINE (THE WICA NEWSLETTER)
WOOD IBIS

OUTDOORS, SPORTS, BOATING

ALL ABOUT BOATING
AQUATIC WORLD
BIKE WORLD
BUSH LEAGUE
Circle Press
DOWN RIVER
FIGHTING WOMAN NEWS
FISH & GAME SPORTSMAN
Florida Sun-Gator Publishing Co.
GROUND SKIMMER
THE GROVE
GYMNASTICS WORLD
Heyday Books
MEXICO WEST
NORDIC WORLD
PARACHUTIST
RUNNERS WORLD
SELF DEFENSE
SIGNPOST
Signpost Publications
SOCCER WORLD
SPORTSWOMAN MAGAZINE
Stone Wall Press, Inc
Wilderness Press
WISCONSIN TRAILS

PHILATELY

Philatelic Directory Publishing Co

PHILOSOPHY

Agape
Artists & Alchemists Publications
Asylum Publishing
BOTH SIDES NOW
BRITISH JOURNAL OF AESTHETICS
BUTT: A Quarterly
Butterfly Press
C.S.P. WORLD NEWS
Challenge Press
COLLABORATION
DAEDALUS, Journal of the American Academy of Arts and Sciences
Desserco Publishing
DIVINE TOAD SWEAT
Edgepress
THE EMISSARY
EUROPEAN JUDAISM
GESAR- The Magazine of Buddhism in the West
THE HUMANIST
HUMANIST IN CANADA

HUNDELOCH
IF LIFE, THEN ONE AMONG AT LEAST FOUR
ILLYRIAN REVUE
THE INDEPENDENT JOURNAL OF PHILOSOPHY
The Independent Philosophy Press
THE INTERNATIONAL NEW AGE NEWSLETTER
Les Femmes Publishing
LIVE FREE QUARTERLY
LODGISTIKS
THE MACROBIOTIC
Newsnovel Publishers
NOUS: a journal of arts and ideas
O. O. L. P. (Out of London Press)
Open Window Books
OPINION
Rialto Books
Seed Center
SUN CENTER NEWS
TELOS
Telos Press
University of the Trees Press
Wayside Press
WAYSIDE QUARTERLY
Wedge Publishing Foundation
WESTERN WORLD REVIEW
WOOD IBIS
Ziesing Bros.' Publishing Company

PHOTOGRAPHY

Alchemist/Light Publishing
Arterial Books
BOMBAY DUCK
THE CAPE ROCK
Clatworthy Colorvues
COMBINATIONS, A JOURNAL OF PHOTOGRAPHY
CQ, CONTEMPORARY QUARTERLY: POETRY AND ART
Creative Books
Druid Books
EVENT
ExPress
THE GOLIARDS
Great Star Press
Images Press
IMPRESSIONS
International Center for Environmental Research-ICER Press
JOURNAL OF CALIFORNIA ANTHROPOLOGY
Malki Museum Press
MCLEAN COUNTY POETRY REVIEW
Not-For-Sale-Press
Open Window Books
OVO MAGAZINE
Padma Press
PAUNCH
PHOEBE
PIGIRON
R.O. Beatty & Associates
Salt-Works Press
Scrimshaw Press
SHAMAN
THE SLOUGH
SOMA-HAOMA
Todd Tarbox Books
WALUNA, THE SOHO REVIEW
THE WINDLESS ORCHARD
Zartscorp, Inc. Books
ZONE ONE

POETRY

A
A
A Press Ltd.

AB INTRA
ABBEY
ABERDEEN UNIVERSITY REVIEW
Abyss/Augtwofive
Ad Hoc Press
The Adobe Press
AEOLIAN-HARP
AFTER-IMAGE
AGENDA
THE AGNI REVIEW
Ahsahta
AISLING
AKROS
THE ALCHEMIST
Alchemist/Light Publishing
ALCHERINGA:ETHNOPOETICS
Aldebaran Review
ALDEBARAN
ALEPH
Alice James Books
ALIVE & KICKING!
ALL-TIME FAVORITE POETRY
Allegany Mountain Press
Alleluia Press
THE ALLEY CAT READINGS
ALLIN
Allonge Press
The Ally Press
Alphabox Press
THE ALTERNATIVE PRESS
Amen-Ra Publishing Co
AMERICAN POETRY REVIEW
ANAESTHESIA REVIEW
ANDROGYNE
Angel Hair Books
ANN ARBOR REVIEW
THE ANTIOCH REVIEW
APALACHEE QUARTERLY
Apple-wood Press
AQUILA MAGAZINE
The Aquila Publishing Co. Ltd.
Arbor
Arc Publications
THE ARCHER
ARETE
Ariel Press
Arion Press
ARION'S DOLPHIN
THE ARK RIVER REVIEW
Armchair Press
AS IS
ASPECT
ASPEN ANTHOLOGY
Astro Black Books
Asylum Publishing
Asylum's Press
ATARAXIA
ATHAENA
Atlantis Editions
ATTENTION PLEASE
AUDIT/POETRY
B & H BOOKS
BACHY
BACK DOOR
BACK ROADS
Back Roads Press
BALL OCCASIONAL
BARATARIA REVIEW
BARBEQUE PLANET
BARDIC ECHOES
BARTHOLOMEW'S COBBLE
BARTLEBY'S REVIEW
Basement Workshop, Inc.

380

The Basilisk Press
BASTARD ANGEL
Bear Hug Books
BEAU FLEUVE SERIES
Bellevue Press
THE BELLINGHAM REVIEW
BELOIT POETRY JOURNAL
BERGEN POETS
BERKELEY POETRY REVIEW
BERKELEY POETS COOPERATIVE
Born Porter Books
BEST FRIENDS
BEST IN POETRY
BEST POETS OF THE 20th CENTURY
BETELGEUSE CHAPBOOK SERIES/NEWEDI FICTION SERIES
BEZOAR
The Bieler Press
BIG MOON
BIG SCREAM
BIG SKY
Biohydrant Publications
BIRD EFFORT
BIRTHSTONE
BITS
Bits Press
THE BITTER OLEANDER
BITTERROOT
BLACK BOOK
BLACK BOX MAGAZINE
THE BLACK CAT
Black Cat Books
Black Sparrow Press
THE BLACK WARRIOR REVIEW
BLACKBERRY
BLACKBERRY
THE BLACKBIRD CIRCLE
BLACKSMITH ANTHOLOGY
The Blacksmith Press
BLACKWOOD'S MAGAZINE
BLANK TAPE
BLEB
Blewointmentpress
BLOODROOT
Blue Crow Press
BLUE MOON NEWS
Blue Moon Press, Inc.
Blue Mountain Press
The Blue Oak Press
BLUE PIG
BLUE UNICORN
Blue Wind Press (Dynamite Books; Overdrive Books)
Boa Editions
BOMBAST POETRY REVIEW
BONES
BONSAI, A Quarterly of Haiku
BOSS
BOX 749
BOXSPRING
"BRILLIANT CORNERS": A Magazine of The Arts
Bristol Arts Centre
BROADSIDE
BUCKLE
Buffalo Books
BUFFALO GNATS
THE BULLETIN BOARD
BUTT: A Quarterly
CAFE SOLO
CAFETERIA
CAIM
CALIFORNIA PELICAN MAGAZINE
THE CALIFORNIA QUARTERLY

CALIFORNIA STATE POETRY QUARTERLY
CALIFORNIA STATE POETRY QUARTERLY
Caligula Books
Calliopea Press
Cambric Press
CANADIAN AUTHOR & BOOKMAN
THE CANADIAN FORUM
Canongate Publishing Ltd.
THE CAPE ROCK
THE CAPILANO REVIEW
Capra Press
CAROLINA QUARTERLY
The Carolina Wren Press
CAROUSEL QUARTERLY OF POETRY
Carpenter Press
Casa Editorial
Cascade Farm Enterprises
Cassandra Publications
Catalyst
CATALYST 1987
THE CATHARTIC
Cat's Pajamas Press
Caveman Publications Ltd.
Cedar Creek Press
CEDAR ROCK
CELEBRATION
THE CENTENNIAL REVIEW
Center For Contemporary Poetry
CENTERGRAM
Centergram Press
CENTERING: A Magazine of Poetry
THE CHARIOTEER
CHARITON REVIEW
CHELSEA
CHERNOZEM
Cherry Tree Press
Cherry Valley Editions
CHIAROSCURO
CHOOMIA - COLLECTIONS OF CONTEMPORARY POETRY
THE CHOWDER REVIEW
Chthon Press
Cider Press
CIMARRON REVIEW
CIRCLE
Circle Press
CIRCUS MAXIMUS
CITY 4
City Lights Books
City Slicker Press
Cleveland State Univ. Poetry Center
Cloud Marauder Press
CLOWN WAR
Cobra Press
CODA: Poets & Writers Newsletter
COE REVIEW
Cold Mountain Press
COLLEGE ENGLISH
The Commentators Press
CONCERNING POETRY
CONNECTICUT FIRESIDE
CONTACT/11: A Bimonthly Poetry Review Magazine
CONTEMPORARY POETS
CONTEMPORARY POETS, JOURNAL OF
CONTRABAND MAGAZINE
Copper Beech Press
Copper Canyon Press/Copperhead
Cornerstone Press
Coteau Books
COTTONWOOD REVIEW
Court Street Chap-Book Series
CP Graham Press

381

CQ, CONTEMPORARY QUARTERLY: POETRY AND ART
CREATIVE MOMENT
Creative Ventures
Croissant & Company
Cross Country Press, Ltd.
CROSSCOUNTRY
The Crossing Press
CROW'S NEST
Cumbria Poetry Centre
Curbstone Press
The Curlew Press
CURTAINS
CUTBANK
CYCLO * FLAME
DACOTAH TERRITORY
DADAZINE
DAIMON
THE DALHOUSIE REVIEW
DAMASCUS ROAD
DARK HORSE
DARK TOWER
Dawn Valley Press
DECARABIA
Deciduous
DELIRIUM
DENTAL FLOSS MAGAZINE
DESCANT
DESCANT
Desert First Works, Inc.
Deuce of Clubs Press
DIAL-A-POEM POETS LP'S
DIANA'S BIMONTHLY
THE DICKINSON REVIEW
A DIFFERENT DRUMMER — THE POET'S JOURNAL
Dodo Press
DOGSOLDIER
Dollar of Soul Press
Dolphin Editions
Dolphin-Moon
Dovetail Press
DRAGONFLY: A Quarterly Of Haiku
Dragon's Teeth Press
DREMPLES
A DRIFTGLIDE IN TIME
DRIFTWOOD-EAST
Druid Books
Duck Down Press
Dustbooks
Eads Street Press
THE EAR IN A WHEATFIELD
EARTH'S DAUGHTERS
EAST RIVER REVIEW
The Ecco Press
ECHO
ECO CONTEMPORANEO
The Edge Press
EEL
ELAN POETIQUE LITTERAIRE ET PACIFISTE
The Elizabeth Press
Elpenor Books
THE EMISSARY
EN PASSANT POETRY QUARTERLY
ENDYMION
Equal Time Press
Equus Publishers
Erebus Press
Erewon Press
ETC: A Review of General Semantics
EUREKA REVIEW
EVENT
Excello & Bollard
EXIT

EXPLORATION
EXPRESSIVE ARTS REVIEW
THE FALCON
Fallen Angel Press
Fantome Press
FAS Publishing/Fleetwood Art Studio, Inc.
THE FIDDLEHEAD
FIELD
The Figures
FIRELANDS ARTS REVIEW
Fireweed Press
FIRST ENCOUNTER
FIT
Five Trees Press
FLOATING ISLAND
FOR THE TIME BEING
Forum Literati
The Four Humours Press
FOUR QUARTERS
THE FOUR ZOAS JOURNAL OF POETRY & LETTERS
Free Books Inc
FREE LANCE, A Magazine of Poetry & Prose
FROM HERE
FROM THE FIELD: A Magazine of Art and Verse
THE FRONT
FRONT STREET TROLLEY
Frontier Press
FROZEN WAFFLES
Funch Press
THE FURTHER RANGE
GALLERY SERIES/POETS
Galloping Dog Press
GARGOYLE
GAZEBO
GEGENSCHEIN QUARTERLY, NeoNeo Do-Do
THE GENEVA POND BUBBLES
THE GEORGIA REVIEW
Ghost Dance: THE INTERNATIONAL QUARTERLY OF EXPERIMENTAL POETRY
Ghost Dance Press
Glass Bell Press
GLASSWORKS
Gleniffer Press
GOETHE'S NOTES
Goethe's Notes Press
Golden Atom Publications
Golden Mountain Press
Goldermood Rainbow Press
THE GOLIARDS
Good Gay Poets Press
GRAFIKTRAKTS
GRAHAM HOUSE REVIEW
GRANITE
Granny Soot Publications
GRAVIDA
GRAYDAY MAGAZINE
Gray Flannel Press
The Graywolf Press
GREAT CIRCUMPOLAR BEAR CULT
Great Raven Press
Great Society Press
GREAT WORKS
Great Works Editions
THE GREATER GOLDEN HILL POETRY EXPRESS
THE GREEN FUSE
THE GREEN HORSE FOR POETRY
Green Horse Press
Green Horse Publications
The Green Hut Press
Green Knight Press
GREEN RIVER REVIEW
Green River Press

GREEN'S MAGAZINE
THE GREENFIELD REVIEW
GREENHOUSE REVIEW
Greenhouse Review Press
Grist Press
GRIST
GRONK
Grossmont Press, Inc.
GRUB STREET
Guildford Poets Press
Gullistan Press
HAIKU MAGAZINE
Halty Ferguson Publishing Co.
HAND BOOK
HANGING LOOSE
HAPPINESS HOLDING TANK
HARBINGER
HARD PRESSED
HARVEST
HAWK PRESS Hawk Press
Headland Publications
Hearsay Press
Hearthstone Press
Helikon Press
Helix House
HELLCOAL ANNUAL
Hellric Publications
The Heron Press
The Heyeck Press
Hh
Hibiscus Press
Hierophant Press
HIGGINSON JOURNAL OF POETRY
HIGH/COO: A Quarterly of Short Poetry
High/Coo Press
Hippopotamus Press
HIRAM POETRY REVIEW
Hit & Run Press
Hoddypoll Press
HOLLOW SPRING REVIEW OF POETRY
The Hosanna Press
HOT WATER REVIEW
House of Anansi Press Limited/Publishing Co.
House of Keys: The Atlanta Poetry Collective, Inc.
House Of Words
HUERFANO
The Huffman Press
HUNDELOCH
HURON REVIEW
HYACINTHS AND BISCUITS
HYPERION A Poetry Journal
ICARUS
ICARUS
ILLUMINATIONS
Illuminations Press
ILLYRIAN REVUE
IMAGE MAGAZINE
IMAGES
IMPACT, AN INTERNATIONAL QUARTERLY OF CONTEMPORARY POETRY
IMPEGNO '70
IN A NUTSHELL
In Between Books
INCUS
INDIAN Literature
INLET
INQUEST
Interim Books
Interim Press
International Books
INTERNATIONAL POETRY REVIEW
INTREPID

INVISIBLE CITY
Iris Press
IRON
Iron Mountain Press
IS (pronounced 'eyes')
Isat Pragbhara Press
ISLANDS, A New Zealand Quarterly of Arts & Letters
ISTHMUS
Ithaca House
J and J House
J STONE PRESS WEEKLY
The Jackpine Press
JAM TO-DAY
JAWBONE
JEOPARDY
JOURNAL OF NEW JERSEY POETS
JUICE
Jungle Garden Press
KALDRON
The Kanchenjunga Press (San Francisco & Vancouver)
KANSAS QUARTERLY
KARAKI
KARAMU
KAYAK
KEEPSAKE POEMS
Kelsey St. Press
KONGLOMERATI
Konglomerati Press
KONTAKTE
Kontexts Publications
KOSMOS
KRAX
Kropotkin's Lighthouse Publications
KUKSU: Journal of Backcountry Writing
KULCHUR Foundation
Kylix Press
LA-BAS: A Newsletter of Experimental Poetry & Poetics
La-bas
THE LAKE SUPERIOR REVIEW
LAKES & PRAIRIES; A Journal of Writings
THE LAMPETER MUSE
Lamplighters Roadway Press
LANELLE'S LETTER BOX
LAUGHING BEAR
THE LAUREL REVIEW
Lawton Press
Leathern Wing Scribble Press
Leaves of Grass Press, Inc.
LEMMING
Lenape Publishing Ltd.
L'Epervier Press
LETTERS
Libra Press
LIGHT
LINES REVUE
LINQ
Litmus, Inc.
LITTACK SUPPLEMENT
LITTLE CAESAR
THE LITTLE MAGAZINE
THE LITTLE REVIEW
Little Wing Publishing
Living Poets Press
LOCAL TENDERNESS
Lodestar Press
LONG ISLAND REVIEW
LONG POND REVIEW
LOOK QUICK
LOON
LOST AND FOUND TIMES
LOVE LIGHTS
Love Street Books
Loverseed Press

383

LOWLANDS REVIEW
LUCILLE
LUCKY HEART BOOKS
LUDD'S MILL
Luna Bisonte Prods
LUNCH
Lynx House Press
MADRONA
MAGIC SAM
MAINE EDITION
Mainespring Press
THE MAINSTREETER
Malpelo
The Mandeville Press
MANROOT
THE MARGARINE MAYPOLE ORANGOUTANG EXPRESS
MARILYN: A Magazine of New Poetry
Maro Verlag
MATI
MCLEAN COUNTY POETRY REVIEW
Meanings Press
MEANJIN QUARTERLY
MEASURE
Membrane Press
The Menard Press
MERLIN PAPERS
Merlin Press
METAMORPHOSIS
THE MICKLE STREET REVIEW
MICROMEGAS
THE MIDATLANTIC REVIEW
Middle Earth Books Inc.
MIDNIGHT
MIDWEST CHAPARRAL
MIKROKOSMOS
MILK QUARTERLY
Milky Way-Kosmos
THE MILL
MINI-TAUR SERIES
MINOTAUR
MISSISSIPPI REVIEW
MISSISSIPPI VALLEY REVIEW
MR. COGITO
THE MODULARIST REVIEW
Mojave Books
MOJO NAVIGATOR(E)
Mole Press
MOMENTUM
Momentum Press
MONTANA GOTHIC
MONTEMORA
NEWSLETTER - MONTREAL POETS' INFORMATION EXCHANGE
MONUMENT IN CANTOS AND ESSAYS
MOONDANCE
MOONS AND LION TAILES
THE MOOSEHEAD REVIEW
Mosaic Press/Valley Editions
MOUNTAIN SUMMER
MOUTH OF THE DRAGON
Mu Publications
MULCH
MUNDUS ARTIUM: A Journal of International Literature & Art
Nada
Nairn Publishing House
NAUSEA
NEBULA
NEW COLLAGE MAGAZINE
NEW EARTH TRIBE NEWSPACK
THE NEW INFINITY REVIEW
NEW JERSEY POETRY MONTHLY
THE NEW KENT QUARTERLY

THE NEW LAUREL REVIEW
NEW LETTERS
New London Pride
THE NEW MOON
NEW ORLEANS REVIEW
NEW POETRY
NEW POETRY
The New Poets Series
NEW RIVER REVIEW
New Rivers Press, Inc.
NEW VOICES
NEW WORLD JOURNAL
NewBooks
Newedi Press
NEXUS
THE NIAGARA MAGAZINE
NIMROD
"NITTY GRITTY"
No Dead Lines
Nobodaddy Press
NOE VALLEY POETS WORKSHOP
NOMEN
NORTH AMERICAN MENTOR MAGAZINE
THE NORTH AMERICAN REVIEW
North Atlantic Books
THE NORTH CAROLINA REVIEW
NORTH COAST POETRY
NORTHEAST/JUNIPER BOOKS
NORTHERN JOURNEY
NORTHERN LIGHT
NORTHERN NEW ENGLAND REVIEW
NORTHWEST REVIEW
NOSTOC
NOTABLE AMERICAN POETS
Noumenon Press
O Press
O Press/Heavy Evidence
O. O. L. P. (Out of London Press)
OCCULT AMERICANA
OCCURRENCE
Tom Ockerse Editions
THE OHIO REVIEW
OINK!
Old Time Bottle Publishing Company
Olivant Press
OMENS POETRY MAGAZINE
Omphalos Press (J-Jay Publications Ltd.)
ONE
ONE: The Writer's Magazine of Fiction and Poetry
Oolichan Books
OPEN PLACES
Openings Press
ORBIS
THE ORCHARD
Orchard Press
ORIGINS
OUT OF SIGHT
Out of the Ashes Press
OUT THERE MAGAZINE
Outland Press
OUTPOSTS
OUTRIGGER
Ox Head Press
Oxus Press
OYEZ REVIEW
PACIFIC POETRY AND FICTION REVIEW
PADAN ARAM
PAINTBRUSH: A Journal of Poetry, Translations & Letters
PAINTED BRIDE QUARTERLY
PALERMO ANTIGRUPPO
PANACHE
Pancake Press

PANJANDRUM POETRY JOURNAL
Paradoxical Press
Parallax Press
PARNASSUS: POETRY IN REVIEW
THE PAWN REVIEW
PAZ PRINT/PERIPHERY
PEACE & PIECES REVIEW
Peace & Pieces Foundation
Peaceweed Press
PEMBROKE MAGAZINE
Penmaen Press
Pennyworth Press
Pentagram Press
The Penumbra Press
PEQUOD
Peradam Publishing House
Perivale Press
PERMAFROST
Permanent Press
Petronium Press
PHANTASM
Phenomenon Press
PHOEBE
PhoeniXongs
PIANETA FRESCO
PICK
PIGIRON
Pilot Press Books
Pirate Press
Place of Herons
THE PLANET QUARTERLY
PLANTAGENET PRODUCTION, Recording Library of the Spoken Word
Platform Poets
Pleasure Dome Press (Long Island Poetry Collective Inc.)
PLOUGHSHARES
POCKET PAL
POCKET POETRY
POEM
THE POEM COMPANY
POEMCARDS
POESIE - U.S.A.
POET
POET & CRITIC
Poet Gallery Press
Poet Papers
Poet Press India
THE POETIC HARDWARE PRESS
POETIPS
POETRY
POETRY AUSTRALIA
POETRY CUMBRIA
Poetry Eastwest
POETRY FLASH
POETRY IN MOTION
POETRY INFORMATION
THE POETRY MAILING LIST
THE POETRY MISCELLANY
POETRY NEWSLETTER
POETRY NIPPON
POETRY NOW
POETRY/PEOPLE
POETRY QUARTERLY (previously CURLEW)
POETRY REVIEW
POETRY SURVEY
POETRY TEXAS
POETRY TORONTO NEWSLETTER
POETRY VENTURE
POETRY VIEW
POETRY WALES
POETRY-WINDSOR-POESIE
POETS' LEAGUE of GREATER CLEVELAND NEWSLETTER

POETS ON:
POETS YEARBOOK
Pogo Press
POINTS OF AWARENESS
Poltroon Press
The Pomegranate Press
PORCH
Porphyrion Press
PRAIRIE SCHOONER
PRAXIS: A Journal of Radical Perspectives on the Arts
Prescott Street Press
Press Porcepic Limited
Pressed Curtains
PRIMAVERA
PRIMIPARA
Prism Books
PROMONTORY
PROSPICE
PROTEUS
Puckerbrush Press
PUDDINGSTONE
PUERTO DEL SOL
Puerto Del Sol Press
PULP
PYRAMID
Quark Press
QUARRY WEST
QUARTERLY REVIEW OF LITERATURE
QUARTERLY WEST
QUARTET
The Quarto Press
Quintessence Publications
QUINTESSENCE
QUIXOTE, QUIXOTL
RADAR
THE RAG
Ragnarok Press
Rainbow Press
Rainbow Resin
Raincrow Press
Raindust Press
Raintree

RAPPORT
RASPBERRY PRESS (magazine)
Rat & Mole Press
Raven Publications
RE:PRINT (AN OCCASIONAL MAGAZINE)
Rebis Press
Red Alder Books
Red Bean Revue
RED CEDAR REVIEW
Red Dust
RED FOX REVIEW
Red Hill Press, Los Angeles & Fairfax
Red Ochre Press
Red Studio Press
RED WEATHER
Red Weather Press
Release Press
RHINO
RIPPLES
RIVER BOTTOM MAGAZINE (Baseball, Floating and Nickle Times)
RIVER STYX
RIVERSEDGE
Riversedge Press
ROAD/HOUSE
ROAD APPLE REVIEW
ROCKBOTTOM
ROCKY MOUNTAIN REVIEW
ROOF
The Rosetta Press

385

Rough Life Press
ROUNDTABLE
Roxbury Poetry Enterprises
RUFUS
Rumba Train Press
RUNE
S Press Books
Sagarin Press
SAGEBLOOM
SAILING THE ROAD CLEAR
SAINT ANDREWS REVIEW
St. Luke's Press
The Salamander Imprint
SALT
Salt-Works Press
SALTHOUSE
Samisdat Associates
SAN JOSE STUDIES
SAN MARCOS REVIEW
Sand Dollar
SANDWICHES
The Saturday Centre
SATURDAY CLUB BOOK OF POETRY (sub-title: SCOP)
The Sceptre Press
SCREE
SCREEN DOOR REVIEW
Sea Pen Press
SECOND COMING
Second Coming Press
SECOND GROWTH
Second Porcupine
SEEMS
SEER OX: American Senryu Magazine
A SELECTED FEW/THE PEOPLE'S GALLERY
SENECA REVIEW
SEQUOIA
Seripress
Sesame Press
SEVEN STARS POETRY
Seven Woods Press
Seventh Dream Press
SHAMAN
SHAMELESS HUSSY REVIEW
SHELL
SHELLY'S
SHENANDOAH
SHOCKS
THE SHORE REVIEW
Sicilian Antigruppo
Singing Wind Publications
SKYWRITING
SLICK PRESS
SLIT WRIST
THE SLOUGH
Slow Loris Press
THE SMALL FARM
SMALL MOON
THE SMALL POND MAGAZINE OF LITERATURE
SMOKE
SmokeRoot
Smyrna Press
SNAKEROOTS
Snow Press
SNOWY EGRET
Soap Box Publishing
Soft Press
SOFT TIMES
SOLANA
THE SOLE PROPRIETOR
SOMA-HAOMA
SOME
SOME FRIENDS

Some of Us Press
SONG: A Magazine of Verse and Essay
A SONGSMITH'S JOURNAL
SOU'WESTER
SOURCE
SOUTH CAROLINA REVIEW
SOUTHERN POETRY REVIEW
SOUTHERN REVIEW
THE SOUTHERN REVIEW
SPAFASWAP
SPARROW POVERTY PAMPHLETS
Sparrow Press
SPEAK 2
Spectrum Productions
THE SPIRIT THAT MOVES US
The Spirit That Moves Us, Inc. (Formerly Emmess Press)
SPIT IN THE OCEAN
THE SPOON RIVER QUARTERLY
Spring Church Book Company
SQUEEZE BOX
STAR WEST
STATIONS
STEPPENWOLF
STILE
STINKTREE
Stinktree Press
Stock Poetry
THE STONE
STONE COUNTRY
STONE MOUNTAIN REVIEW
Stone Press
STONEY LONESOME
STRANGE FAECES
Strawberry Press
STREET CRIES
STREET MAGAZINE
STUDIES IN POETRY: A GRADUATE JOURNAL
STUFFED CROCODILE
STUMP
SUN
SUN-LOTUS HAIKU
SUN TRACKS: An American Indian Literary Magazine
SUNBURY (a poetry magazine)
Sunken Forum Press
Sunrise Press
SUNSHINE
THE SUNSTONE REVIEW
Sunyata Press
SURFSIDE POETRY REVIEW
The Swallow Press Inc. (Book Publisher)
Swamp Press
Sweet Pine Press
Sydon, Inc.
TALISMAN
Talonbooks
TAR RIVER POETS
Taurean Horn Press
TELEPHONE
Telephone Books
TELEPOEM
TEXAS PORTFOLIO
THIRD COAST ARCHIVES
THIRD EYE
THIRD RAIL
3RD THING MAGAZINE OF POETRY AND GRAPHICS
13th MOON
Thistledown Press
Thorp Springs Press
THREE RIVERS POETRY JOURNAL
Three Rivers Press
THREE SISTERS
The Three Trees Press

386

Thunder City Press
Tideline Press
TIGHTROPE
TITMOUSE
Tombouctou Books
Toothpaste Press
TOTTEL'S
TOUCHSTONE
Toulouse Press
THE TOY SUN
TRANSIENCE QUARTERLY
TRANSLATION
Traumwald Press
Treacle Press
TREE
TREES
Trike
TRUCHA
Truck Press
TRULY FINE PRESS, A Review
Truly Fine Press
Trunk Press
TWELFTH KEY
TWO HANDS NEWS
TWO SCORE OR LESS FOR WORDS
Twowindows Press
Tyndall Creek Press
TYPEWRITER
US1 WORKSHEETS
UGLY DUCKLING
UNAKA RANGE
UNDERTOW
UNDINE
UNEXPECTED
UNICORN
UNICORN JOURNAL
Unpublished Editions
UROBOROS (was ALLEGANY POETRY)
UZZANO
VAGABOND
Valkyrie Press, Inc.
Van Dyk Publications
VANDERBILT POETRY REVIEW
The Vanity Press
VECTOR MAGAZINE
VEINS
VELVET WINGS
VER   POETS
Verlag Guenther Emig
Vermont Crossroads Press, Inc.
Vesta Publications
VIEW FROM THE SILVER BRIDGE
VILE
THE VOYEUR
WALUNA, THE SOHO REVIEW
WASHOUT REVIEW
WATERS
Wayside Press
WAYSIDE QUARTERLY
WEID: The Sensibility Revue
WEST COAST POETRY REVIEW
West Coast Poetry Review Press
THE WEST CONSCIOUS REVIEW
WEST END MAGAZINE
Westburg Associates, Publishers
THE WESTERLY REVIEW
WESTERN POETRY QUARTERLY
WEYFARERS
WHAT'S A NICE HILLBILLY LIKE YOU . . . ?
WHITE MULE
WHITE PINE
WILLMORE CITY

Willmore City Press
WIND MAGAZINE
Windfall
Windflower Press
THE WINDLESS ORCHARD
The Windmill Press
WINDOW
WINDOWS IN THE STONE
Windows Project
The Wine Press
WINE RINGS
WINGED OX
WIP
The Wire Press
WISCONSIN REVIEW
WOMANCHILD
Women Writing Press
WOOD IBIS
Woodbine Press
Woolmer/Brotherson Ltd.
Word-Camera
Word And Action (Dorset)
WORD GARDEN
THE WORD-SMITH
The Word Works, Inc.
The Workingman's Press
WORLD OF POETRY
THE WORMWOOD REVIEW
WRIT
WRITE ON
Writers' Cooperative
WRITERS IN RESIDENCE
Wwhimsy Press
X Press Press
XANADU
XANTHIPPE
XTRAS
YANAGI
YELLOW BRICK ROAD
YELLOW BUTTERFLY BROADSIDES
Young Publications
Z
ZAHIR
ZEUGMA
Ziesing Bros.' Publishing Company
ZIGGURAT Annual International Anthology of the Fine Arts
ZONE ONE
Zonepress
ZVEZDA

POLITICAL SCIENCE

AFRICA TODAY
AMEX-CANADA MAGAZINE
AREITO
BERKELEY BARB
CANADIAN DIMENSION
CANADIAN PUBLIC POLICY- Analyse de Politiques
CANADIAN SLAVONIC PAPERS
Challenge Press
Chandler & Sharp Publishers, Inc.
Critiques Livres
CURRENT (a reprint magazine)
DPG Publishing Co./Dumont Press Graphics
THE ELEMENTS
Glide Publications
THE GREAT BLAFIGRIA IS/THE GREAT COMPASSION
Harvest Publishers
HARVEST QUARTERLY
THE INDEPENDENT JOURNAL OF PHILOSOPHY
The Independent Philosophy Press
INDIVIDUAL LIBERTY

INTERCONTINENTAL PRESS
International Publishers Co., Inc.
INTERNATIONAL SOCIALIST REVIEW
Lawrence Hill & Company, Publishers, Inc.
LEAVES OF TWIN OAKS
LIBERTE
LSM NEWS
MARKET FOR LIBERTY
MERIP REPORTS
Merlin Press
Mojave Books
Monad Press
NEW LITERATURE & IDEOLOGY
NEW POLITICS
New Review Books
NEW REVIEW OF EAST-EUROPEAN HISTORY
North Country Press
NORTHERN NEIGHBORS
OUR GENERATION
Peace Press
PROLETARIAT
QUEST: A Feminist Quarterly
RADICAL AMERICA
REBUTTAL! The Bicentennial Newsletter of Truth
RECON
REPARTEE
ST. CROIX REVIEW
SCHISM: A Journal of Divergent American Opinion
SING OUT! The Folk Song Magazine
Spindrift Press
THE STRUGGLE
TOWARD REVOLUTIONARY ART (TRA)
Vanguard Books
Wedge Publishing Foundation
Westburg Associates, Publishers
WIN MAGAZINE
THE WOMAN ACTIVIST

POLITICS

BOTH SIDES NOW
C.I.S.S.
THE CANADIAN FORUM
Challenge Press
THE CHELSEA JOURNAL
DAY BY DAY
FAG RAG
FOCUS/ MIDWEST
GATEAVISA
GUARDIAN
The Jacek Publishing Company
LIBERAL NEWS
Liberator Press
LIMIT! (The National Newsletter Of The Libertarian Republican Alliance)
MAKARA
THE MILITANT
SOUTHERN EXPOSURE
TEXAS OBSERVER
UNDERCURRENTS
WEST END MAGAZINE

PRINTING, PUBLISHING

BETELGEUSE CHAPBOOK SERIES/NEWEDI FICTION SERIES
Biscuit City Press
FINE PRINT; A Review for the Arts of the Book
The Four Humours Press
Gleniffer Press
The Graywolf Press
HAPPINESS HOLDING TANK

Newedi Press
PASSAGES
Pentagram Press
The Pray Curser Press
QUILL & QUIRE
Raincrow Press

PRISON

Aldebaran Review
CONSTRUCTIVE ACTION FOR GOOD HEALTH
CRIME AND SOCIAL JUSTICE, ISSUES IN CRIMINOLOGY.
Harlo Press
"JOINT" CONFERENCE
OFF OUR BACKS
SPEAK OUT
Taramara, Unltd.

PSYCHOLOGY

Adventure Trails Research and Development Laboratories
ALTERNATIVE TO ALIENATION
ANIMA
Ash Lad Press
ASSERT NEWSLETTER
Back Roads Press
Butterfly Press
Chandler & Sharp Publishers, Inc.
CHANGE
CITY MINER
CLARITY
CONSTRUCTIVE ACTION FOR GOOD HEALTH
CRCS Publications
Down There Press
DREAMS AND INNER SPACES
E & E Enterprises
THE EMISSARY
Food For Thought Publications
Gullistan Press
THE HUMANIST
HUMANIST IN CANADA
HUMPTY DUMPTY
Images Press
Impact Publishers, Inc.
Jalmar Press, Inc.
THE JOURNAL of PSYCHOHISTORY
K-State Press
Les Femmes Publishing
Litmus, Inc.
RT: A Journal of Radical Therapy (formerly ROUGH TIMES)
S.A. Growth Press
SELF AND SOCIETY
Starogubski Press
UTOPIAN EYES: A JOURNAL OF PRACTICAL UTOPIAN FANTASY
Waldrop Publications
Wild Horses & The Potted Plant
Molly M. Willett

PUBLIC AFFAIRS

THE ADVOCATE
THE ANTIOCH REVIEW
AXIOM (Atlantic Canada's Magazine)
BRAVADO
CANADIAN DIMENSION
CANADIAN PUBLIC POLICY- Analyse de Politiques
Chandler & Sharp Publishers, Inc.
COSMOPOLITAN CONTACT
COUNTERSPY
THE CRISIS

CURRENT (a reprint magazine)
DAY BY DAY
EDCENTRIC MAGAZINE
Glide Publications
GUARDIAN
House of Anansi Press Limited/Publishing Co.
HUMANIST IN CANADA
THE INDIAN VOICE
INDIVIDUAL LIBERTY
INDOCHINA CHRONICLE
THE INSURGENT SOCIOLOGIST
LAST POST
LIBERATION MAGAZINE
MAIL ORDER USA
NOT MAN APART
ONE DOLLAR
OREGON TIMES MAGAZINE
ProActive Press
QUEEN'S QUARTERLY: A Canadian Review
RAIN: JOURNAL OF APPROPRIATE TECHNOLOGY
RECON
RIKKA
SEERS RIO GRANDE WEEKLY
SOCIAL POLICY
TAWTE: Texas Artists Writers and Thinkers in Exile
TEXAS OBSERVER
Thorp Springs Press
URBAN & SOCIAL CHANGE REVIEW
VANGUARD
THE WESTERN CRITIC

QUOTATIONS

THE MONTHLY JOURNAL OF GREAT QUOTATIONS

REFERENCE

AMERICAN FIDDLERS NEWS
The Avondale Press
FLEA MARKET QUARTERLY ALMANAC
Garrett Park Press
GAYELLOW PAGES
GRANTS AND AWARDS AVAILABLE TO AMERICAN WRITERS
HENNEPIN COUNTY LIBRARY CATALOGING BULLETIN
Kanthaka Press
PEOPLE'S YELLOW PAGES of the SAN FRANCISCO BAY AREA
POETRY INFORMATION
POETRY SURVEY
Poets & Writers of New Jersey
POETS YEARBOOK
Racz Publishing Co.
Reference Service Press
REFERENCE SERVICES REVIEW
RESOURCES
Running Press
Scarecrow Press
SUNSPARK
Sunspark Press
WASHINGTON INTERNATIONAL ARTS LETTER
Woolmer/Brotherson Ltd.
THE WORKBOOK
York Press

RELIGION

Agape
Alleluia Press
Ananda Publications
Anti-Ocean Press
Back Row Press
BOTH SIDES NOW
BRITH
Buddhist Text Translation Society
CLARITY
CS JOURNAL
DAY BY DAY
DHARMA SARA
DIGNITY
DIVINE TOAD SWEAT
THE DRAMA REVIEW
EUROPEAN JUDAISM
FOLK MASS AND MODERN LITURGY
GESAR- The Magazine of Buddhism in the West
Glide Publications
HARMONY
HOLY BEGGARS' GAZETTE
HUMANIST IN CANADA
THE INQUIRER
Inquiry Press
INTEGRITY: Gay Episcopal Forum
JOURNAL OF CALIFORNIA ANTHROPOLOGY
Kurios Press
Malki Museum Press
MANY SMOKES
METANOIA, An Independent Journal of Radical Lutheranism
MODERN LITURGY
MOVEMENT
NEW THOUGHT
NOMEN
OCCULT AMERICANA
OPINION
Parable Press (formerly June McLaughlin Press)
PROMONTORY
Resource Publications
REYNARD QUAKER FELLOWSHIP OF THE ARTS
Ross-Erikson Publishers, Inc.
SEER OX: American Senryu Magazine
SHIRHADASH/NEW SONG
613 MAGAZINE
Soft Press
Summit University Press
Sunyata Press
TREE
TZADDIKIM
VAJRA BODHI SEA
VANGUARD
WEID: The Sensibility Revue
WITCHCRAFT DIGEST MAGAZINE (THE WICA NEWS-LETTER)
The WorDoctor Publications

REPRINTS

BOTH SIDES NOW
CURRENT (a reprint magazine)
Peradam Publishing House
Peregrine Smith, Inc.
POCKET POETRY
Press Pacifica
RE:PRINT (AN OCCASIONAL MAGAZINE)
THE RECORD SUN
The Runeskald Press
Urion Press

ROMANIAN STUDIES

MIORITA

SAN FRANCISCO

PEOPLE'S YELLOW PAGES of the SAN FRANCISCO BAY AREA

SCIENCE

Adventure Trails Research and Development Laboratories
ALTERNATIVE SOURCES of ENERGY MAGAZINE
Aslan Enterprises
The Boxwood Press
Boyd & Fraser Publishing Company
THE CENTENNIAL REVIEW
CREATIVE COMPUTING
Creative Computing Press
DAEDALUS, Journal of the American Academy of Arts and Sciences
Florida Sun-Gator Publishing Co.
IMPACT, AN INTERNATIONAL QUARTERLY OF CONTEMPORARY POETRY
Inquiry Press
Levenson Press
MEDICAL HISTORY
Prairie Books
RAIN: JOURNAL OF APPROPRIATE TECHNOLOGY
The Runeskald Press
SCIENCE FOR THE PEOPLE
UNDERCURRENTS
University of the Trees Press

SCIENCE FICTION

ALGOL: The Magazine About Science Fiction
Algol Press
Angst World Library
Around Publishing
Back Roads Press
BLACK LITE
British Science Fiction Assoc. Ltd.
CROSSROADS QUARTERLY
DARK FANTASY
de la Ree Publications
DELAP'S F & SF REVIEW
Deuce of Clubs Press
A DRIFTGLIDE IN TIME
ELAN VITAL: Journal of Creative Adventures
ENTROPY NEGATIVE
EXPLORATION
THE FAMOUS SCIENCE FICTION CHAPBOOK (series)
Fantome Press
FICTION WEST
GEGENSCHEIN
Golden Atom Publications
GUARD THE NORTH
IT COMES IN THE MAIL
Kent Publications, Kent School
LETTERS
LIMIT! (The National Newsletter Of The Libertarian Republican Alliance)
LOCUS: The Newspaper of the Science Fiction Field
LUNA
MAYBE, Worlds of Fandom
MODUS OPERANDI
Pegana Press
POETRY/PEOPLE
RIVERSIDE QUARTERLY
SCHMUCK ANTHOLOGICAL
SCIENCE FICTION BAZAAR
SF COMMENTARY
Shadow Press
SPECTRE
Spectre Press
STARWIND
STRANGE FAECES
VECTOR
WILD FENNEL
WYRD, The Magazine of Illustrated Fantasy

SCOTLAND

Scottish Arts Council

SHAKESPEARE

THE BARD

SHAW, G. B.

THE SHAW REVIEW

SOCIALIST

THE BODY POLITIC- Gay Liberation Journal
CLAIMANTS NEWSPAPER (Claimants Unite)
COMMUNITIES
CRIME AND SOCIAL JUSTICE, ISSUES IN CRIMINOLOGY.
FIREWEED
GAY LEFT
ISTHMUS
LSM NEWS
METANOIA, An Independent Journal of Radical Lutheranism
MOVEMENT
MOVING ON
THE MYSTERIOUS BARRICADES
Pathfinder Press, Inc
Pink Triangle Press
PRAXIS: A Journal of Radical Perspectives on the Arts
STREET MAGAZINE
THE STRUGGLE
WOMEN: A Journal of Liberation

SOCIETY

ALTERNATIVE TO ALIENATION
ALTERNATIVES- Perspectives on Society and Environment
Being Incorporated
BERKELEY BARB
BERKELEY JOURNAL OF SOCIOLOGY
Boyd & Fraser Publishing Company
BUGLE-AMERICAN
Chandler & Sharp Publishers, Inc.
THE CHELSEA JOURNAL
COASTLINE MAGAZINE
LA CONFLUENCIA
COSMOPOLITAN CONTACT
CRIME AND SOCIAL JUSTICE, ISSUES IN CRIMINOLOGY.
CROSSCURRENTS
E & E Enterprises
ETC Publications
FOCUS/ MIDWEST
FOLIO
Free Life Editions
FULCRUM
GAY COMMUNITY NEWS
GAY TIDE
Glide Publications
GREEN MOUNTAIN QUARTERLY
THE GREEN REVOLUTION
THE HUMANIST
HUMPTY DUMPTY
ICONOCLAST
THE INSURGENT SOCIOLOGIST
JOURNAL OF CALIFORNIA ANTHROPOLOGY
LEAVES OF TWIN OAKS
LEFT CURVE
LIBERATION MAGAZINE
Loverseed Press
METANOIA, An Independent Journal of Radical Lutheranism
THE MIDWEST QUARTERLY

NEW POLITICS
The New South Company
North Country Press
NORTHERN NEIGHBORS
NORTHWEST PASSAGE
ONE SHOT DEAL
PEACE NEWS "For Non-Violent Revolution"
PEDESTRIAN RESEARCH
RIKKA
SCHISM: A Journal of Divergent American Opinion
SCIENCE FOR THE PEOPLE
SELF AND SOCIETY
THE SMITH
SOCIAL POLICY
SPEAK OUT
THOUGHTS FOR ALL SEASONS: The Magazine of Epigrams
Times Change Press
URBAN & SOCIAL CHANGE REVIEW
VICTIMOLOGY AN INTERNATIONAL JOURNAL
Visage Press, Inc.
WIN MAGAZINE
Winbooks
WORD GARDEN

SOUTH

AUNTIE BELLUM
SOUTHERN EXPOSURE

SOUTHWEST

Lodestar Publishing

SPIRITUAL

Ananda Publications
Artists & Alchemists Publications
Being Incorporated
BOTH SIDES NOW
Butterfly Press
COLLABORATION
CS JOURNAL
Dawn Horse Press
DHARMA SARA
DREAMS AND INNER SPACES
EXPLORATION
FORESIGHT MAGAZINE
THE GREAT BLAFIGRIA IS/THE GREAT COMPASSION
HARMONY
HOLY BEGGARS' GAZETTE
Images Press
THE INTERNATIONAL NEW AGE NEWSLETTER
J. Buchs Publications
JOURNAL OF CALIFORNIA ANTHROPOLOGY
Kanthaka Press
The Kober Press
LIGHT TIMES
Little Wing Publishing
Malki Museum Press
MODERN LITURGY
NEW THOUGHT
Resource Publications
Seed Center
THE SEEKER NEWSLETTER
Spiritual Community Publications
TREE
TZADDIKIM
Unity Press, Inc.
University of the Trees Press
THE VOICE
Wild Horses & The Potted Plant
WINGED OX

TAPES & RECORDS

BLACK BOX MAGAZINE
The Commentators Press
DIAL-A-POEM POETS LP'S
GOLD TURKEY
INDIAN HOUSE
Lava Mt
PLANTAGENET PRODUCTION, Recording Library of the Spoken Word
Resource Publications
ROCK-N-ROLL NEWS
ROCKINGCHAIR
Saline Productions
TIME BARRIER EXPRESS
XENHARMONIC BULLETIN

TENNYSON, ALFRED

TENNYSON RESEARCH BULLETIN

TEXAS

TAWTE: Texas Artists Writers and Thinkers in Exile
TEXAS COUNTRY MAGAZINE

THEATRE

BRITISH THEATRE INSTITUTE NEWSLETTER & REPORT
CANADIAN THEATRE REVIEW
CHIMERA-A Complete Theater Piece
CLAUDEL STUDIES
DADAZINE
DRAMATIKA
Dramatika Produce
LIBRE PRESS
MIME JOURNAL
Multinational Media
PERFORMING ARTS JOURNAL
Playwrights Co-op
PRAXIS: A Journal of Radical Perspectives on the Arts
PROLOG
Resource Publications
THEATRE ACROSS AMERICA
THEATRE DESIGN AND TECHNOLOGY
THEATRE SURVEY-THE American Journal of Theatre History
The Visart Press

THIRD WORLD, MINORITIES

AFRICA NEWS
Challenge Press
Conch Press Ltd. (Publishers)
CONCH MAGAZINE
THE GREENFIELD REVIEW
HERA, INC.
ISTHMUS
Lawrence Hill & Company, Publishers, Inc.
LSM Information Center
MINORITY RIGHTS GROUPS REPORTS
PEACE NEWS "For Non-Violent Revolution"
RAIN: JOURNAL OF APPROPRIATE TECHNOLOGY
The Salamander Imprint
SUNBURY (a poetry magazine)
Third World Publications Ltd.
WOOD IBIS

THOMAS, DYLAN

ORIEL

391

THOREAU, H. D.

THOREAU JOURNAL QUARTERLY

TRANSLATION

Anti-Ocean Press
Apple-wood Press
BASTARD ANGEL
BIRD EFFORT
THE BITTER OLEANDER
BLEB
Boa Editions
CENTER NEWSLETTER
THE CHARIOTEER
CHARITON REVIEW
Cherry Valley Editions
CHIAROSCURO
THE COFFEEHOUSE
CONTEMPORARY LITERATURE IN TRANSLATION
CURTAINS
THE EAR IN A WHEATFIELD
ENDYMION
Engendra Press Ltd.
EXIT
FROM HERE
Green Horse Press
HAIKU MAGAZINE
HYPERION A Poetry Journal
Interim Press
International Books
INTERNATIONAL POETRY REVIEW
INVISIBLE CITY
LIGHT
THE LITTLE REVIEW
The Menard Press
MICROMEGAS
Mudborn Press
MUNDUS ARTIUM: A Journal of International Literature & Art
OINK!
PAINTBRUSH: A Journal of Poetry, Translations & Letters
PEQUOD
Perivale Press
Pirate Press
POETRY WALES
Prescott Street Press
Pressed Curtains
RAPPORT
Raven Publications
Red Hill Press, Los Angeles & Fairfax
RUSSIAN LITERATURE TRIQUARTERLY
The Salamander Imprint
SHIRHADASH/NEW SONG
THE SHORE REVIEW
Slow Loris Press
SMALL MOON
THE SPIRIT THAT MOVES US
The Spirit That Moves Us, Inc. (Formerly Emmess Press)
STAR WEST
STEPPENWOLF
STINKTREE
Stinktree Press
STRANGE FAECES
SUN-LOTUS HAIKU
TRANSLATION
UNICORN JOURNAL
VANDERBILT POETRY REVIEW
WEBSTER REVIEW
WEID: The Sensibility Revue
Westburg Associates, Publishers
WHITE PINE
WOOD IBIS

YARDBIRD READER
ZONE ONE

TRANSPORTATION, TRAVEL

CANADIAN STEAM MAGAZINE
Chronicle Books
CRIME AND SOCIAL JUSTICE, ISSUES IN CRIMINOLOGY
ExPress
Golden West Books
Grasshopper Press
Kurios Press
Landmark Publishing
Lonely Planet Publications
MEXICO WEST
Miocene Press
Moon Publications
NOMAD
Padre Productions
PEDESTRIAN RESEARCH
Prologue Publications
RAIN: JOURNAL OF APPROPRIATE TECHNOLOGY
Sol Press
SOUTH DAKOTA REVIEW
Spiritual Community Publications
Summer Thought

TWAIN, MARK

MARK TWAIN JOURNAL

U.S.S.R.

CANADIAN SLAVONIC PAPERS
Merlin Press

VISUAL ARTS

THE ORIGINAL ART REPORT (TOAR)
The Visart Press

VOELCKER, HUNCE

Panland Books

WALES

ORIEL
Y GWYDDONYDD

WASHINGTON, D. C.

WASHINGTON REVIEW, A Quarterly Review of the Arts

WELLS, H. G.

WELLSIANA, The World Of H.G. Wells

WISCONSIN

WISCONSIN TRAILS

WOLFE, THOMAS

Croissant & Company

WOMEN

Academy Press Limited
ALBATROSS
Alice James Books

Allonge Press
ANIMA
APHRA
Ariel Press
Artists & Alchemists Publications
AUNTIE BELLUM
BEST FRIENDS
BIG MAMA RAG
BLACK MARIA
BLACKSMITH ANTHOLOGY
The Blacksmith Press
BLOODROOT
BONES
BOOKLEGGER MAGAZINE
THE BRIGHT MEDUSA
BROADSHEET
CAFE SOLO
Canadian Women's Educational Press
CHOMO-URI
CONDITIONS
COUNTRY WOMEN
Daughters Publishing Co., Inc.
Diana Press, Inc
Down There Press
EARTH'S DAUGHTERS
EMERGENCY LIBRARIAN
FEMALE ARTISTS PAST & PRESENT
THE FEMINIST ART JOURNAL
FEMINIST BULLETIN
The Feminist Press
FIGHTING WOMAN NEWS
Five Trees Press
Glass Bell Press
Glide Publications
THE GREATER GOLDEN HILL POETRY EXPRESS
Grist Press
GRIST
Henry Philips Publishing Company
HERA, INC.
HERESIES: A FEMINIST PUBLICATION ON ART AND POLITICS
The Heyeck Press
House of Anansi Press Limited/Publishing Co.
HUMANIST IN CANADA
Impact Publishers, Inc.
Incunabula Collection Press
JOURNAL OF CALIFORNIA ANTHROPOLOGY
Joyful World Press
Kelsey St. Press
Know, Inc.
Lawrence Hill & Company, Publishers, Inc.
Les Femmes Publishing
LESBIAN CONNECTION
THE LESBIAN TIDE
LESBIAN VOICES
Magic Circle Press
MAJORITY REPORT
Malki Museum Press
MATI
MAYBE, Worlds of Fandom
MEDIA REPORT TO WOMEN
MEN'S
Merlin Press
Moon Books
MOVING OUT: Feminist Literary & Arts Journal
The Naiad Press, Inc.
NEW DIRECTIONS FOR WOMEN
New Woman Press
Northwest Matrix
OFF OUR BACKS
OUR GENERATION
Out & Out Books
OUT OF SIGHT

PAID MY DUES: Journal of Women and Music
Pathfinder Press, Inc
PEACE NEWS "For Non-Violent Revolution"
Peoples Press
Philmer Enterprises
PLEXUS, Bay Area Women's Newspaper
POSTCARD ART/POSTCARD FICTION
Press Gang Publishers
Press Pacifica
PRIMAVERA
PRIMIPARA
Programmed Studies Inc
QUEST: A Feminist Quarterly
Ragnarok Press
RAIN: JOURNAL OF APPROPRIATE TECHNOLOGY
Reference Service Press
ROOM
ROOM OF ONE'S OWN
ROOTS OF CREATION
SAPPHO
SCHMUCK ANTHOLOGICAL
Seagull Publications
SHAMELESS HUSSY REVIEW
Sibyl-Child Press
SIBYL-CHILD: A Women's Arts & Culture Journal
SISTER COURAGE
SOLANA
SPEAKOUT
SPORTSWOMAN MAGAZINE
SQUEEZE BOX
Starogubski Press
SUNBURY (a poetry magazine)
Taramara, Unltd.
13th MOON
Times Change Press
UNDER THE SIGN OF PISCES: Anais Nin and Her Circle
UP FROM UNDER (A Magazine By, For And About Women)
The Vanity Press
VICTIMOLOGY AN INTERNATIONAL JOURNAL
Violet Press
WEID The Sensibility Revue

WIA NEWSLETTER
Winbooks
THE WOMAN ACTIVIST
Woman Press
WOMAN SPIRIT
WOMANCHILD
WOMANSMITH
WOMEN: A Journal of Liberation
WOMEN & FILM
The Women And Literature Collective
Women Artists Newsletter (Press)
WOMEN ARTISTS NEWSLETTER
WOMEN IN STRUGGLE
Women Library Workers
WOMEN LIBRARY WORKERS NEWSLETTER
WOMEN STUDIES ABSTRACTS
Women Writing Press
Women's History Research Center, Inc.
Women's Institute for Freedom of the Press
Women's Studies
WOMEN'S STUDIES NEWSLETTER
XANTHIPPE

WORKER

THE CALL/EL CLARIN
INDUSTRIAL WORKER
Labor Arts Books
QUIXOTE, QUIXOTL
SISTER COURAGE
SUNBURY (a poetry magazine)

U. S. Regional Index

ALABAMA

RA: A Journal of Popular Culture and the Arts, Ra Press, PO Box 1043, Auburn, AL 36830
SOUTHERN HUMANITIES REVIEW, 9090 Haley Center, Auburn Univ., Auburn, AL 36830, 205-826-4606
AURA Literary Arts Review, The University of Alabama In Birmingham, Box 348 NBSB, University Station, Birmingham, AL 35294, 205-934-3618
Ragnarok Press, 1719 13th Ave So, Birmingham, AL 35205, 205-933-6366
REPARTEE, P.O. Box 3232-A, Birmingham, AL 35205
Thunder City Press, PO Box 11126, Birmingham, AL 35202, 205-870-7281
POEM, Huntsville Literary Association, PO Box 1247, West Station, Huntsville, AL 35807
EPOS, Department of English, Troy State University, Troy, AL 36081
THE BLACK WARRIOR REVIEW, P.O. Box 2936, University, AL 35486, 205-348-7839

ALASKA

MINOTAUR, Minotaur Press, 2923B Rose, Anchorage, AK 99504
PERMAFROST, Box 80625, Fairbanks, AK 99708

ARIZONA

Border-Mountain Press, P.O. Box 1296, Benson, AZ 85602
Sunrise Press, PO Box 742, Chandler, AZ 85224, 967-4251
Talakin Press, P O Box 143, Clarkdale, AZ 86324
Wayside Press, P.O. Box 475, Cottonwood, AZ 86326
WAYSIDE QUARTERLY, Wayside Press, P.O. Box 475, Cottonwood, AZ 86326
IN VICTUS, J & A Publications, c/o Iacono, 4521 West Greenway Rd., Glendale, AZ 85306
Padma Press, PO Box 56, Oatman, AZ 86433
BONSAI, A Quarterly of Haiku, Bonsai Press/Jama Press, P. O. Box 7211, Phoenix, AZ 85011
Golden West Publishers, 4113 N. Longview, Phoenix, AZ 85014
Hunter Publishing, Co., P.O. Box 9533, Phoenix, AZ 85068, 602-944-1022
ORGAN DIGEST, Tino Publications, 4001 East Fanfol, Phoenix, AZ 85028, 602-996-9335
White Mountain Publishing Company, 13801 N. Cave Creek Rd, Phoenix, AZ 85022, 971-2720
NEW THOUGHT, International New Thought Alliance, 4533 Scottsdale Rd. 208, Scottsdale, AZ 85251, 602-945-0744
ONE: The Writer's Magazine of Fiction and Poetry, One Books, PO Box W, Scottsdale, AZ 85252
Walnut Press, 4252 N. Brown Ave, Scottsdale, AZ 85251, 602-946-4440
YELLOW BRICK ROAD, Emerald City Press, 107 W. 7th St, Tempe, AZ 85281, 602-966-7505
ARIZONA QUARTERLY, Univ. Of Arizona, Tucson, AZ 85721, 602-884-1029
BLUE MOON NEWS, Blue Moon Press, Inc., c/o English Dept., University of Arizona, Tucson, AZ 85721, 602-884-1387
Blue Moon Press, Inc., c/o English Dept., University of Arizona, Tucson, AZ 85721, 602-884-1387
Desert First Works, Inc., 3870 N. Vine Ave., Tucson, AZ 85719, 602-793-2859
HUERFANO, Daran, Inc., Box 49155, Tucson, AZ 85717
SUN TRACKS: An American Indian Literary Magazine, Sun Tracks, SUPO Box 20788, Univ of Arizona, Tucson, AZ 85721, 884-1836
THE MATCH, P.O. Box 3488, Tuscon, AZ 85722

ARKANSAS

THE D.H. LAWRENCE REVIEW, Box 2474, University of Arkansas, Fayetteville, AR 72701
THE INTERNATIONAL NEW AGE NEWSLETTER, The High Foundation, P.O. Box 1137, Harrison, AR 72601
TOTAL LIFESTYLE- The Bicentennial Magazine of Natural Living, The First Ozark Press, P.O. Box 1137, Harrison, AR 72601
LIVING IN THE OZARKS NEWSLETTER, Living In The Ozarks, Pettigrew, AR 72752
NEW SCHOOLS EXCHANGE NEWSLETTER, Pettigrew, AR 72752

CALIFORNIA

ASPO NEWSLETTER, PO Box 6112, Albany, CA 94706, 415-527-5849
Carousel Press, P.O. Box 6061, Albany, CA 94706, 415-527-5849
METANOIA, An Independent Journal of Radical Lutheranism, 1018 9th Street No. 47, University Village, Albany, CA 94710
Sand Dollar, 1205 Solano Avenue, Albany, CA 94706
WYRD, The Magazine of Illustrated Fantasy, Chaosium, PO Box 6302, Albany, CA 94706
COUNTRY WOMEN, Country Women Press, P.O. Box 208, Albion, CA 95410
Times Change Press, Box 187, Albion, CA 95410
Quintessence Publications, 356 Bunker Hill Mine Road, Amador City, CA 95601, 209-267-5470
WESTART, Westart Publications, PO Box 1396, Auburn, CA 95603

JOURNAL OF CALIFORNIA ANTHROPOLOGY, Malki Museum Press, Business Offices Malki Museum, Inc., 11-795 Fields Road Morongo Indian, Banning, CA 92220, 714-787-3885 or 787-3346
Malki Museum Press, 11-795 Fields Road, Morongo Indian Reservation, Banning, CA 92220, 714-849-7289
Red Alder Books, Box 545, Ben Lomond, CA 95005
Aldebaran Review, 2209 California, Berkeley, CA 94703
Archangel Books, 2922 Otis C, Berkeley, CA 94703, 415-843-0169
Ariel Press, Box 9183, Berkeley, CA 94709
BALL OCCASIONAL, Crosscut Saw Unltd., 1806 Bonita, Berkeley, CA 94709
Banyan Tree Books, 2300 Le Conte Avenue, Berkeley, CA 94709, 415-548-0737
BERKELEY BARB, P.O. Box 1247, Berkeley, CA 94701
BERKELEY JOURNAL OF SOCIOLOGY, What's Your Line Graphics, 410 Barrows Hall, University of California, Berkeley, CA 94720
BERKELEY POETS COOPERATIVE, Berkeley Poets Workshop and Press, P.O. Box 459, Berkeley, CA 94701, 415-652-6806
Blue Wind Press (Dynamite Books; Overdrive Books), 820 Miramar, Berkeley, CA 94707, 415-526-1905
THE BRIGHT MEDUSA, The Bright Medusa Press, Box 9321, Berkeley, CA 94709
CALIFORNIA PELICAN MAGAZINE, Eshelman Hall, University of California, Berkeley, CA 94720
CARTA ABIERTA, 3408 Dwinelle Hall-UC-, Berkeley, CA 94720, 415-642-0240
Catex Press, 1150 Spruce St, Berkeley, CA 94707
CENTER, 2617 Benvenue, Berkeley, CA 94704, 415-845-2860
CITY MINER, City Miner, P.O. Box 176, Berkeley, CA 94701, 415-524-1162
Creative Arts Book Company, 833 Bancroft Way, Berkeley, CA 94710, 415-848-4777
CRIME AND SOCIAL JUSTICE, ISSUES IN CRIMINOLOGY., P.O. Box 4373, Berkeley, CA 94704
Erewon Press, PO Box 4253, Berkeley, CA 94704
FEMALE ARTISTS PAST & PRESENT, Women's History Research Center, Inc., 2325 Oak St, Berkeley, CA 94708, 415-548-1770
The Figures, 2016 Cedar, Berkeley, CA 94709, 415-843-3120
FILM QUARTERLY, Univ. of California Press, University of California Press, Berkeley, CA 94720
FOLIO, 2207 Shattuck Ave., Berkeley, CA 94704
EL FUEGO DE AZTLAN, 3408 Dwinelle Hall, Univ of Calif, Berkeley, CA 94720
Full Court Press, Box 4520, Berkeley, CA 94704, 415-845-7645
GARLIC TIMES, Lovers Of The Stinking Rose/Midpress Books, 1043 Cragmont Av., Berkeley, CA 94708, 527-1958
THE GOODFELLOW REVIEW OF CRAFTS, Full Court Press, PO Box 4520, Berkeley, CA 94704, 415-845-7645
Great Star Press, 1117 High Court, Berkeley, CA 94708
GRITO DEL SOL: A Chicano Quarterly, Tonatiuh International Inc., 2150 Shattuck Ave, Berkeley, CA 94704
Heyday Books, Box 9145, Berkeley, CA 94709
Hipparchia Press, Netzahaulcoyotl Historical Society, 2845 Buena Vista Way, Berkeley, CA 94708
HYPERION A Poetry Journal, Thorp Springs Press, 2311-C Woolsey, Berkeley, CA 94705
ILLUMINATIONS, Illuminations Press, 1900 9th Street 8, Berkeley, CA 94710, 415-849-2102
Illuminations Press, 1900 9th Street 8, Berkeley, CA 94710, 415-849-2102
Images Press, P.O. Box 9444, Berkeley, CA 94709, 415-843-8834
INDOCHINA CHRONICLE, Indochina Resource Center, P.O. Box 4000-D, Berkeley, CA 94704, 415-548-2546
INDOCHINA RESOURCE CENTER, Indochina Chronicle, P.O. Box 4000 D, Berkeley, CA 94704, 415-548-2546
JUMP CUT, A Review of Contemporary Cinema, P.O. Box 865, Berkeley, CA 94701
Kelsey St. Press, 2824 Kelsey St., Berkeley, CA 94705, 841-2044
The Kober Press, P.O. Box 4155, Berkeley, CA 94704, 415-845-1790
Midpress Books, 1043 Cragmont Ave., Berkeley, CA 94708, 527-1958
Moon Books, PO Box 9223, Berkeley, CA 94709, 444-0465
Neon Sun, P.O. Box 2191, Station A, Berkeley, CA 94702
NEW WORLD JOURNAL, Turtle Island Foundation, 2845 Buena Vista Way, Berkeley, CA 94708
OYEZ, PO Box 5134, Berkeley, CA 94705
Paradoxical Press, 1228 Oxford St, Berkeley, CA 94709, 415-843-4630
PLEXUS, Bay Area Women's Newspaper, 2600 Dwight Way 209, Berkeley, CA 94704
Poltroon Press, 2315 Carleton Street, Berkeley, CA 94704
ProActive Press, P.O. Box 296, Berkeley, CA 94701, 415-549-0839
The Proof Press, PO Box 1256, Berkeley, CA 94720
THE RECORD SUN, 982 University Avenue, Berkeley, CA 94710
Reed, Cannon, & Johnson, 2140 Shattuck #311, Berkeley, CA 94704
RIVERSIDE QUARTERLY, Boggs Box 1111, Berkeley, CA 94701
Saint Heironymous Press, Inc., PO Box 9431, Berkeley, CA 94709, 415-549-1405
TAWTE: Texas Artists Writers and Thinkers in Exile, Thorp Springs Press, 2311-C Woolsey, Berkeley, CA 94705
Thorp Springs Press, 2311-C Woolsey, Berkeley, CA 94705
TREE, Tree Books, P.O. Box 9005, Berkeley, CA 94709
TUUMBA, Tuumba Press, 2639 Russell Street, Berkeley, CA 94705
Twowindows Press, 2644 Fulton St., Berkeley, CA 94704
VELVET WINGS, Paradoxical Press, 1228 Oxford St., Berkeley, CA 94709, 415-843-4630
VIA, 103 Sproul Hall, University of California, Berkeley, CA 94720, 642-2103
Wilderness Press, 2440 Bancroft Way, Berkeley, CA 94704, 415-843-8080
WOMEN & FILM, PO Box 4501, Berkeley, CA 94704
The Workingman's Press, C/O Serendipity Books, 1790 Shattuck Avenue, Berkeley, CA 94709, 415-848-4777
YARDBIRD READER, Yardbird Publishing Co., Inc., Box 2370, Sta A, Berkeley, CA 94702
Yardbird Wing Editions, Box 2370, Station A, Berkeley, CA 94702
ZVEZDA, c/o Student Activities, 103 Sproul Hall, University of California, Berkeley, CA 94702, 415-843-4216
Pentangle Press, 132 Lasky Dr., Beverly Hills, CA 90212

BIG SKY, Box 389, Bolinas, CA 94924
Leaves of Grass Press, Inc., P.O. Box 129, Bolinas, CA 94924
Tombouctou Books, Box 265, Bolinas, CA 94924, 415-868-0322
YANAGI, Box 466, Bolinas, CA 94924, 415-868-0492
BIG MOON, 167 Riverside Dr, Boulder Creek, CA 95006
Circle Press, PO Box N, Boulder Creek, CA 95006, 408-338-2141
ROUND NOTES, Circle Press, PO Box N, Boulder Creek, CA 95006, 408-338-2141
University of the Trees Press, PO Box 644, Boulder Creek, CA 95006, 408-338-3855
HYACINTHS AND BISCUITS, Hummingbird Press, box 392, Brea, CA 92621
ATTENTION PLEASE, Hearthstone Press, 708 Inglewood Drive, Broderick, CA 95605
THE GREEN FUSE, Hearthstone Press, 708 Inglewood Dr, Broderick, CA 95605
Hearthstone Press, 708 Inglewood Drive, Broderick, CA 95605, 916-372-0250
Down There Press, PO Box 2086, Burlingame, CA 94010, 415-342-9867
POET, Poet Press India, 208 W. Latimer Ave., Campbell, CA 95008, 408-379-8555
Poet Press India, 208 W. Latimer Ave., Campbell, CA 95008, 408-379-8555
WILLMORE CITY, Willmore City Press, P O Box 1601, Carlsbad, CA 92008
Willmore City Press, P O Box 1601, Carlsbad, CA 92008
Creative Books, P.O. Box 5162, Carmel, CA 93921
The California/Pendleton Press, P.O. Box 731, Carmel Valley, CA 93924, 408-659-2886
Heidelberg Graphics, P.O. Box 3404, Chico, CA 95927, 916-342-6582
PHANTASM, Heidelberg Graphics, PO Box 3404, Chico, CA 95927, 916-342-6582
UNIVERSITY JOURNAL, Dept. English, CSU, Chico, CA 95926
MARILYN: A Magazine of New Poetry, 150 West Ninth Street, Claremont, CA 91711
Trans-Anglo Books, P.O. Box 38, Corona del Mar, CA 92625
Chandler & Sharp Publishers, Inc., 5643 Paradise Drive Suite 10, Corte Madera, CA 94925, 415-924-7822
BACK ROADS, Back Roads Press, Box 543, Cotati, CA 94928, 707-937-0618
Back Roads Press, Box 543, Cotati, CA 94928, 707-937-0618
COASTLINE MAGAZINE, New Horizens Communications Group Press, P.O. Box 914, Culver City, CA 90230
DELAP'S F & SF REVIEW, 11863 West Jefferson Blvd., Culver City, CA 90230, 213-432-1192
Desserco Publishing, P.O. Box 2433, Culver City, CA 90230, (213) 320-9101
Peace Press, 3828 Willat Ave., Culver City, CA 90230, 213-838-7387
WESTERN WORLD REVIEW, PO Box 2714, Culver City, CA 90230
BOTTOMFISH MAGAZINE, Bottomfish, 21250 Stevens Crk., Cupertino, CA 95014, 408-996-4550
THE CALIFORNIA QUARTERLY, 100 Sproul Hall, Univ of Calif, Davis, CA 95616
CRCS Publications, 111 G Street, Suite 29, Davis, CA 95616, 916-756-5074
LEMMING, 1125 H St. Apt. 22, Davis, CA 94616
American Revolutionary Political Pamphlets, 704 Nob Avenue, Del Mar, CA 92014, 755-1258
CRAWL OUT YOUR WINDOW, Crawl Out Your Window Press, 704 Nob Ave, Del Mar, CA 92014, 714-755-1258
Crawl Out Your Window Press, 704 Nob Ave, Del Mar, CA 92014, 714-755-1258
POSTCARD ART/POSTCARD FICTION, Martha Rosler, RFD 168 Z, Del Mar, CA 92014
Holmgangers Press, 11 El Centro, Diablo, CA 94528
The Adobe Press, 264 Cottonpatch, El Cajon, CA 92020
Bing America Publications, 1555 Murray Avenue, El Cajon, CA 92020
Cedar House Enterprises, PO Box 70, El Granada, CA 94018, 415-726-4096
Dharma Publishing, 5856 Doyle St., Emeryville, CA 94608
GESAR- The Magazine of Buddhism in the West, Dharma Publishing, 5856 Doyle St., Emeryville, CA 94608
POETRY NOW, 3118 K Street, Eureka, CA 95501
Wild Horses & The Potted Plant, 2145 Everding, Eureka, CA 95501, 707-442-7127
INVISIBLE CITY, Red Hill Press, 6 San Gabriel Drive, Fairfax, CA 94930
Jungle Garden Press, 47 Oak Rd, Fairfax, CA 94930
Red Hill Press, Los Angeles & Fairfax, 6 San Gabriel Dr, Fairfax, CA 94930
COSMOPOLITAN CONTACT, Pantheon Press, P. O. Box 1566, Fontana, CA 92335
PEQUOD, Fiction, P.O. Box 491, Forest Knolls, CA 94933
Lamplighters Roadway Press, Freestone Box #1, 500 Bohemian Hwy., Freestone, CA 95472
A DRIFTGLIDE IN TIME, Waystar Books, 3138 W. Dakota, 229, Fresno, CA 93711
GAY LITERATURE, English Dept./CSUF, Fresno, CA 93740
Hit & Run Press, P. O. Box 1041, Ft. Bragg, CA 95437, 707-964-0843
LANELLE'S LETTER BOX, 142 West Brookdale Place, Fullerton, CA 92632
Badger Creek Press, PO Box 728, Galt, CA 95632, 916-687-7295
Dragon's Teeth Press, Adams Acres, El Dorado Nat. Forest, Georgetown, CA 95634
XENHARMONIC BULLETIN, Electronic Music Enterprises, 349 1/2 W. California Ave., Glendale, CA 91203, 213-243-3477
PRAXIS: A Journal of Radical Perspectives on the Arts, Praxis, P.O. Box 207, Goleta, CA 93017
KALDRON, Rainbow Resin Press, 441 North 6th St., Grover City, CA 93433, 805-481-2360
Rainbow Resin, 441 North 6th Street, Grover City, CA 93433, 805-481-2360
Naturegraph Publishers, Inc., P. O. Box 1075, Happy Camp, CA 96039, 916-496-5353
ZEPHYRUS IMAGE, Zephyrus Image, 4460 Pine Flat Rd, Healdsburg, CA 95448, 707-433-3543
THE ALLEY CAT READINGS, Bombshelter Press, 1092 Loma Drive, Hermosa Beach, CA 90254
ELAN VITAL: Journal of Creative Adventures, Elan Vital Publications, P O Box 209, Hermosa Beach, CA 90254, 372-0190
TANGENTS, 6715 Hollywood Blvd. #210, Hollywood, CA 90028
MEXICO WEST, Baja Trail Publications, Inc., P.O. Box 6088, Huntington Beach, CA 92646, 714-836-9203
Rough Life Press, 734 Venice Way, Inglewood, CA 90302
Little Wing Publishing, 865-E Emb. del Mar, Isla Vista, CA 93017

Bear Hug Books, 1636 Ocean View, Kensington, CA 94707, 524-2107
BLUE UNICORN, 22 Avon Road, Kensington, CA 94707, 415-526-8439
CALIFORNIA STATE POETRY QUARTERLY, 22 Avon Road, Kensington, CA 94707, 526-8439
GROUND SKIMMER, Box 66306, 11312½ Venice Blvd, L. A., CA 90066
Copley Books, 7776 Ivanhoe Avenue, P O Box 957, La Jolla, CA 92038, 714-454-1842
SPAFASWAP, Spafaswap, 1070 Ahern, La Puente, CA 91746, 213-962-3910
International Center for Environmental Research-ICER Press, 141 Emerald Bay, Laguna Beach, CA 92651
WESTERN POETRY QUARTERLY, Western Poetry Press, 3253 Q San Amadeo, Laguna Hills, CA 92653
Tamal Vista Publications, 222 Madrone Ave, Larkspur, CA 94939, 362-0888
ACADEMY AWARDS OSCAR ANNUAL, ESE California, 509 N. Harbor Blvd., Lattabra, CA 90631
Bell Springs Publishing Company, Box 322, Laytonville, CA 95454, 707-984-7117
NAUSEA, Russ Haas Press (Nausea Publications), P.O. Box 4261, Long Beach, CA 90804
Acrobat Books, 409 N. Las Palmas, Los Angeles, CA 90004, 213-933-7796
THE ALLEY CAT READINGS, Bombshelter Press, 725 Sweetzer, Los Angeles, CA 90069
BACHY, Papa Bach Paperbacks, 11317 Santa Monica Blvd., Los Angeles, CA 90025
THE BEAD JOURNAL, P.O. Box 24c47, Los Angeles, CA 90024, 213-838-7539
BOOKSWEST, BooksWest, Inc., 3757 Wilshire Blvd, Los Angeles, CA 90010, 213-383-8362
CQ, CONTEMPORARY QUARTERLY: POETRY AND ART, L/A House, Box 41110, Los Angeles, CA 90041, 213-254-4455
DREAMS AND INNER SPACES, Edendale PO 26556, Los Angeles, CA 90026
John Parke Custis Press, 875 Fifth Avenue, Los Angeles, CA 90005
THE LESBIAN TIDE, Tide Publications, 8855 Cattaragus Ave., Los Angeles, CA 90034
Levenson Press, P.O.B. 19606, Los Angeles, CA 90019
Lodestar Publishing, 3075 West Seventh Street, Los Angeles, CA 90005, 213-387-9781
MOMENTUM, Momentum Press, 10508 W. Pico Blvd., Los Angeles, CA 90064
Momentum Press, 10508 W. Pico Blvd., Los Angeles, CA 90064
NEWORLD, 1308 S. New Hampshire Ave., Los Angeles, CA 90029
Phillip The Grasshopper, Box 54119, Los Angeles, CA 90054, (213) 662-0188
Reference Service Press, 9023 Alcott Street, Los Angeles, CA 90035, 213-271-1955
ROUNDTABLE, 170 So. Hobart, Los Angeles, CA 90004
SEER OX: American Senryu Magazine, Seer Ox, PO Box 42923, Los Angeles, CA 90050
Spectrum Productions, 979 Casiano Rd., Los Angeles, CA 90049
STONECLOUD, Pacific Perceptions, Inc., 3718 Vinton No. 5, Los Angeles, CA 90034, 213-204-0590
THIRD RAIL, Third Rail Press, 9721 Monte Mar Dr., Los Angeles, CA 90035
VEGETARIAN WORLD, Suite 216 8235 Santa Monica Blvd., Los Angeles, CA 90046, 213-654-7002
The Visart Press, 1847 N. Beverly Glen Blvd, Los Angeles, CA 90024
Opportunities Unlimited Publications, P.O. Box AA, Magalia, CA 95954
Undena Publications, P.O. Box 97, Malibu, CA 90265
Cheshire Books, P.O. Box 7616, Menlo Park, CA 94025, 415-854-0393
COMPUTER MUSIC JOURNAL, People's Computer Co., 1263 El Camino, P. O. Box E, Menlo Park, CA 94025, 415-323-3111
DR. DOBB'S JOURNAL OF COMPUTER CALISTHENICS & ORTHODONTIA, People's Computer Co., 1263 El Camino, P. O. Box E, Menlo Park, CA 94025, 415-323-3111
Dymax, PO Box 310, Menlo Park, CA 94025, 415-323-6117
People's Computer Co., 1010 Doyle St, Menlo Park, CA 94025, 415-323-3111
PEOPLE'S COMPUTERS, People's Computer Co., 1263 El Camino, P. O. Box E, Menlo Park, CA 94025, 415-323-3111
Prologue Publications, P.O. Box 640, Menlo Park, CA 94025, 322-5034
Word Wheel Books, Inc., 540 Santa Cruz Ave, Menlo Park, CA 94025
Druid Heights Books, 685 Camino Del Canyon, Muir Woods, Mill Valley, CA 94941
Molly M. Willett, P.O. Box 689, Mill Valley, CA 94941, 415-388-3692
Celestial Arts, 231 Adrian Rd., Millbrae, CA 94030
CROW'S NEST, Scarecrow Books, 1050 Magnolia 2, Millbrae, CA 94030
Les Femmes Publishing, 231 Adrian Road, Millbrae, CA 94030, 415-692-4500
Scarecrow Books, 1050 Magnolia No. 2, Millbrae, CA 94030
THE WEST CONSCIOUS REVIEW, Scarecrow Books, 1050 Magnolia #2, Millbrae, CA 94030
BIG MOON, PO Box 2024, Modesto, CA 95354
BOMBAST POETRY REVIEW, PO Box 3752, Modesto, CA 95352
LITTLE CAESAR, 231 W. Olive, Monrovia, CA 91016, 213-358-1556
Panland Books, Box 83, Monte Rio, CA 95462
PACIFIC RESEARCH, Pacific Studies Center, 867 W. Dam, Mountain View, CA 94041, 415-969-1545
Waldrop Publications, P.O. Box 396, Mt Baldy, CA 91759
AQUATIC WORLD, World Publications, Po Box 366, c/o World Publications, Mtn. View, CA 94040
BIKE WORLD, World Publications, P.O. Box 366, Mtn. View, CA 94040
DOWN RIVER, World Publication's, World Publications, P.O. Box 366, Mtn. View, CA 94040
GYMNASTICS WORLD, World Publications, c/o World Publications, P.O. Box 366, Mtn. View, CA 94040
NORDIC WORLD, World Publications, PO Box 366, Mtn. View, CA 94040
RUNNERS WORLD, World Publications, World Publications, P.O. Box 366, Mtn. View, CA 94040
SELF DEFENSE, World Publications, P.O. Box 366, Mtn. View, CA 94040
SOCCER WORLD, World Publications, P.O. Box 366, Mtn. View, CA 94040
FICTION WEST, Fiction West, 3012 Vichy Ave., Napa, CA 94558
Ananda Publications, 900 Alleghany Star Rt., Nevada City, CA 95959, 916-265-5877
KUKSU: Journal of Backcountry Writing, Kuksu Press, Box 980 Alleghany Star Rt., Nevada City, CA 95959
The Blue Oak Press, 2555 Newcastle Road, Newcastle, CA 95658, 916-663-3474
Malpelo, 1916 Court Avenue, Newport Beach, CA 92663
THE ARCHER, Camas Press, P.O. Box 9488, No. Hollywood, CA 91609

The WorDoctor Publications, PO Box 9761, North Hollywood, CA 91606, 213-980-3576
Kent Publications, Kent School, 18301 Halsted St, Northridge, CA 91324, 213-349-5088
JOHN UPDIKE NEWSLETTER, 19073 Los Alimos St., Northridge, CA 91326, 360-5804
Cloud Marauder Press, 5153 Shafter Ave., Oakland, CA 94618, 415-654-7116
COSMIC CIRCUS, Cosmic Brain Trust, 521 33rd St., Oakland, CA 94609, 415-658-0233
HOLY BEGGARS' GAZETTE, Judaic Book Service, 3726 Virden Ave., Oakland, CA 94619
J STONE PRESS WEEKLY, The Stone Press, 5399½ Bryant, Oakland, CA 94618
JUICE, Juice Press, 5402 Ygnacio, Oakland, CA 94601, 415-532-5621
LOOSE LIPS SINK SHIPS, California Syllabus (Cal-Syl Press), P.O. Box 2764, Oakland, CA 94602
LSM Information Center, P.O. Box 2077, Oakland, CA 94604, 635-4863
LSM NEWS, LSM Press, LSM Information Center, P.O. Box 2077, Oakland, CA 94604
NORTH COUNTRY STAR, North Country Star, PO Box 24081, Oakland, CA 94623, 415-655-1335
The Rather Press, 3200 Guido Street, Oakland, CA 94602
Rebis Press, 5806 Lawton Ave., Oakland, CA 94618, 415-655-5695
Scrimshaw Press, 6040 Claremont Ave, Oakland, CA 94618, 415-658-2323
STUMP, 6395 Colby St, Oakland, CA 94618
TZADDIKIM, Judaic Book Service, 3726 Virden Avenue, Oakland, CA 94619
THE RED BOOK, White Bear Books, Box 402, Occidental, CA 95465
Bookworm Publishing Company, P.O. Box 3037, Ontario, CA 91761, 714-984-9419
THE MACROBIOTIC, First Feather Press, 1544 Oak St, Oroville, CA 95965
Racz Publishing Co., PO Box 287, Oxnard, CA 93032, 805-483-8843
The Boxwood Press, 183 Ocean View Blvd, Pacific Grove, CA 93950
THE DELPHYS FORUM, P.O. Box 677, Pacific Palisades, CA 90272, 213-454-8659
ETC Publications, P.O. Drawer 1627-A, Palm Springs, CA 92262, 714-325-5352
Bull Publishing Co., P O Box 208, Palo Alto, CA 94302, 415-322-2855
Fels and Firn Press, 1036 Colorado Ave., Palo Alto, CA 94303, 415-321-0696
Seed Center, PO Box 591, Palo Alto, CA 94302, 493-6121
Dustbooks, Box 1056, Paradise, CA 95969, 916-877-6110
THE SMALL PRESS REVIEW, Dustbooks, P.O. Box EE, Paradise, CA 95969, 916-877-6110
FOLLIES, P O Box 5231, Pasadena, CA 91107, 213-358-6255
RUFUS, Gyst Publications, PO Box 16, Pasadena, CA 91102
Summit University Press, PO Box 7018, Pasadena, CA 91109, 213-797-1131
Old Adobe Press, P.O. Box 115, Penngrove, CA 94951, [Haslam]707-763-7362
Trike, P.O. Box 732, Pismo Beach, CA 93449
BUSH LEAGUE, Bush League, 7777 W. 91st #E-1144, Playa del Rey, CA 90291
Edgepress, Box 64, Point Reyes, CA 94956, 415-663-1511
FLOATING ISLAND, Floating Island Publications, P.O. Box 516, Point Reyes Station, CA 94956
No Dead Lines, 241 Bonita, Portola Valley, CA 94025
The Kanchenjunga Press (San Francisco & Vancouver), 22 Rio Vista Lane, Red Bluff, CA 96080
Mojave Books, 7040 Darby Ave., Reseda, CA 91335, 213-342-3403
Brombacher Books, 691 South 31st Street, Richmond, CA 94804, 415-232-5380
Newsnovel Publishers, 3969 University Ave, Riverside, CA 92501
THE LITERARY MONTHLY (formerly Pacific Sun Literary Quarterly), PO Box 1445, Ross, CA 94957, 415-383-4500
Creative Book Company, PO Box 21-4998, Sacramento, CA 95821, 916-489-4390
Deuce of Clubs Press, P.O. Box 4682, Sacramento, CA 95825
HARD PRESSED, Ellen's Old Alchemical Press, 2850 3rd Ave, Sacramento, CA 95818
Hibiscus Press, P.O. Box 22248, Sacramento, CA 95822
IN A NUTSHELL, Hibiscus Press, P.O. Box 22248, Sacramento, CA 95822
Jalmar Press, Inc., 391 Munroe Street, P. O. Box 255038, Sacramento, CA 95825, 916-481-1134
MAL DE MER, Press of Arden Park, 861 Los Molinos Way, Sacramento, CA 95825
ROCK-N-ROLL NEWS, Communications Company, The, 2815 J St, Sacramento, CA 95816, 916-446-1455
WINE RINGS, 2432-48th Ave., c/o Odam, Sacramento, CA 95822
WORLD OF POETRY, World Of Poetry Press, 1841 Garden HWY, Sacramento, CA 95833
A Harmless Flirtation With Wealth, P.O. Box 9779, San Diego, CA 92109, 714-270-3908
Ana-Doug Publishing, 2830 Chicago St, San Diego, CA 92117, 714-275-2211
CAFETERIA, Cafeteria Press, P.O. Box 16191, San Diego, CA 92116
Communication Creativity, P O Box 17210, San Diego, CA 92117, 714-276-7171
FEMINIST BULLETIN, Center for Women's Studies & Services, 908 F St., San Diego, CA 92101
The Feminist Poetry & Graphics Center, 2561 B Street, San Diego, CA 92102, 714-239-3664
THE GREATER GOLDEN HILL POETRY EXPRESS, The Feminist Poetry & Graphics Center, 2829 Broadway, San Diego, CA 92102, 714-239-3664
Grossmont Press, Inc., 7071 Convoy Court, San Diego, CA 92111
THE NEW SCHOLAR: Studies, Essays, Reviews, The New Scholar, Center for Iberian and Latin American Studies, University of California, San Diego, CA 92093
PACIFIC POETRY AND FICTION REVIEW, English Office, San Diego State University, San Diego, CA 92182, 714-466-0675
POEMCARDS, Realities, P.O. Box 33512, San Diego, CA 92103, 714-280-8359
SCIENCE FICTION BAZAAR, P.O. Box 11272, San Diego, CA 92111
THE SEEKER NEWSLETTER, The Love Project, PO Box 7601, San Diego, CA 92107
SEVEN STARS POETRY, Realities, P.O. Box 33512, San Diego, CA 92103, 714-280-8359
TUGBOAT, Frick and Friends, Box 15234, San Diego, CA 92115
Alchemist/Light Publishing, 231 Dorland St, P.O. Box 5530, San Francisco, CA 94101, 415-863-3421
ANDROGYNE, 1250 Press, 930 Shields, San Francisco, CA 94132, 586-2697

Anthelion Press, Inc., 101 Townsend St., San Francisco, CA 94107, 415-957-1277
ARCADE-THE COMICS REVUE, The Print Mint, Inc., Po Box 40474, San Francisco, CA 94140
ARETE, 830 Hyde St. #6, San Francisco, CA 94109
Arion Press, 566 Commercial St, San Francisco, CA 94111, 415-981-8974
Banana Productions, 1183 Church St., San Francisco, CA 94114, 415-648-5174
BANANA RAG, Banana Productions, 1183 Church St., San Francisco, CA 94114
BARTLEBY'S REVIEW, 3152 Lyon St., San Francisco, CA 94123
BASTARD ANGEL, PO Box 3449, San Francisco, CA 94119
BIRTHSTONE, PO Box 27394, San Francisco, CA 94127
BOMBAY DUCK, 3035 Fillmore, San Francisco, CA 94123
BOOKLEGGER MAGAZINE, Booklegger Press, 555 29th St., San Francisco, CA 94131
Boyd & Fraser Publishing Company, 3627 Sacramento St., San Francisco, CA 94118, 415-346-0686
BRIARPATCH REVIEW: A Journal of Right Livelihood and Simple Living, Portola Institute, 330 Ellis Street, San Francisco, CA 94102
Buddhist Text Translation Society, 1731 15th Street, San Francisco, CA 94103, 415-861-9672
Buffalo Books, 15 Gladstone Dr., San Francisco, CA 94112, 415-586-2247
BULLETIN OF CONCERNED ASIAN SCHOLARS, 604 Mission #1001, San Francisco, CA 94105
CAMELS COMING NEWSLETTER, PO Box 703, San Francisco, CA 94101
Carolyn Bean Associates, Publishing, 48 Second Street, San Francisco, CA 94105, 415-398-6011
Casa Editorial, 3128 24th Street, San Francisco, CA 94110
Cassandra Publications, 160 Caselli Avenue, San Francisco, CA 94114, 626-6047
Children's Book Press/Emprenta de Libros Enfantiles, 1461 9th Ave., San Francisco, CA 94122, 415-664-8500
Chronicle Books, 870 Market Street Suite 915, San Francisco, CA 94102, 415-777-7240
City Lights Books, 261 Columbus Ave., San Francisco, CA 94133
THE COFFEEHOUSE, The Wire Press, 392 San Jose Ave, San Francisco, CA 94110
COMMON SENSE, 2811 Mission St., San Francisco, CA 94110
The Communication Press, P O Box 22541, San Francisco, CA 94122, 415-566-3921
COSMEP NEWSLETTER, PO Box 703, San Francisco, CA 94101
CRY CALIFORNIA, California Tomorrow (nonprofit, educational foundation), 681 Market Street, Room 1059, San Francisco, CA 94105
DADAZINE, Dadaland Press, 1183 Church St., San Francisco, CA 94114
Dawn Horse Press, P.O. Box 99637, San Francisco, CA 94109, 621-1158
ExPress, Box 31123, San Francisco, CA 94131, 824-8938
FINE PRINT; A Review for the Arts of the Book, 2107 Van Ness Ave. 303, San Francisco, CA 94120
Five Trees Press, 660 York St, San Francisco, CA 94117
Frontier Press, 1419-12th Ave., San Francisco, CA 94122, 415-665-6071
GAY SUNSHINE: A Journal of Gay Liberation, Gay Sunshine Press, P.O. Box 40397, San Francisco, CA 94140
Gay Sunshine Press, Inc., P.O. Box 40397, San Francisco, CA 94140
Glide Publications, 330 Ellis St, San Francisco, CA 94117
Golden Mountain Press, PO Box 2387, San Francisco, CA 94126
HEIRS, Heirs Press, 657 Mission St., San Francisco, CA 94105
Hiddigeigei Books, P.O. Box 5031, San Francisco, CA 94103
Hoddypoll Press, 226 Rose St., San Francisco, CA 94102
INTERMEDIA, Intermedia, 243 Grand View Ave, San Francisco, CA 94114
ISTHMUS, Isthmus Poetry Foundation, PO Box 6877, San Francisco, CA 94101, 415-668-5605
Joyful World Press, 468 Belvedere Street, San Francisco, CA 94117, 415-566-2787
KOSMOS, Milky Way-Kosmos, 130 Eureka, San Francisco, CA 94114, 415-863-4861
LEFT CURVE, Left Curve Publications, 1230 Grant St. Box 302, San Francisco, CA 94133
LOCUS: The Newspaper of the Science Fiction Field, Locus Publications, Box 3938, San Francisco, CA 94119, 415-339-9196
LOVE LIGHTS, Boustrophedon Deserted X (Mag), #354 1230 Grant Ave, San Francisco, CA 94133
Mattole Press, PO Box 22324, San Francisco, CA 94122
Milky Way-Kosmos, 130 Eureka, San Francisco, CA 94114, 415-863-4861
MINI-TAUR SERIES, Taurean Horn Press, 601 Leavenworth 45, San Francisco, CA 94109
NICOTINE SOUP, Sea of Storms, P.O. Box 22613, San Francisco, CA 94122, 567-9091
NOE VALLEY POETS WORKSHOP, Cassandra Publications, 160 Caselli Ave, San Francisco, CA 94114
Not-For-Sale-Press, 243 Grand View Ave, San Francisco, CA 94114, 415-647-4290
NOT MAN APART, Friends of the Earth, 529 Commercial St, San Francisco, CA 94111
OUT THERE MAGAZINE, Pedestrian Press, 552 25th Ave, San Francisco, CA 94121
Pancake Press, 54 Aqua Vista Way, San Francisco, CA 94131, 415-648-3573
PANJANDRUM POETRY JOURNAL, Panjandrum Press, Inc., 99 Sanchez St, San Francisco, CA 94114
PARAGRAPH: A QUARTERLY OF GAY FICTION, The Antares Foundation, Box 14051, San Francisco, CA 94114
PEACE & PIECES REVIEW, Peace And Pieces Foundation, PO Box 99394, San Francisco, CA 94109
Peace & Pieces Foundation, Box 99394, San Francisco, CA 94109
Peoples Press, 2680 21st St, San Francisco, CA 94110
PEOPLE'S YELLOW PAGES of the SAN FRANCISCO BAY AREA, P.O. Box 31291, San Francisco, CA 94131
POETRY FLASH, 144 Hugo, San Francisco, CA 94122, 415-731-9084
QUOZ?, Trinity Press, Box 1320, San Francisco, CA 94101
LA RAZON MESTIZA/LA MUJER es la TIERRA, Concilio Mujeres, P.O. Box 27524, San Francisco, CA 94127
ROOM, P.O. Box 40610, San Francisco, CA 94110
S.H.Y., Eberhard Ebner, Jeffrey Miller, 556 Larkin St., San Francisco, CA 94102
SAN FRANCISCO REVIEW OF BOOKS, 2140 Vallejo St., San Francisco, CA 94123
SECOND COMING, Second Coming Press, P.O. Box 31249, San Francisco, CA 94131
Second Coming Press, PO Box 31249, San Francisco, CA 94131

SHOCKS, Momo's Press, Box 14061, San Francisco, CA 94114
THE STONE, 3978 26th St, San Francisco, CA 94131, 415-648-5392
Synergistic Press, 3965 Sacramento St., San Francisco, CA 94118, 415-EV7-8180
TALISMAN, 132 Cora, San Francisco, CA 94134
Taurean Horn Press, 601 Leavenworth #45, San Francisco, CA 94109
TINTAN, Editorial Pocho Che, PO Box 1959, San Francisco, CA 94101, 415-431-5549
TOTTEL'S, 3028 California, San Francisco, CA 94115, 415-922-1923
TOWARD REVOLUTIONARY ART (TRA), TRA, P.O. Box 40909, San Francisco, CA 94140
1250 Press, 930 Shields, San Francisco, CA 94132, 586-2697
UNDERTOW, 50 Phelan Ave, San Francisco, CA 94112, 415-239-3141
UP FROM UNDER (A Magazine By, For And About Women), 1377 Ninth Ave, San Francisco, CA 94122
UTOPIAN EYES: A JOURNAL OF PRACTICAL UTOPIAN FANTASY, Performing Arts Social Society, Inc. (a nonprofit collective of artists and writers), Utopian Eyes c/o Storefront Classroom, PO Box 1174, San Francisco, CA 94101
VAJRA BODHI SEA, Buddhist Text Translation Society, 1731 15th St, San Francisco, CA 94103, 861-9672
VILE, Banana Productions, 1183 Church St, San Francisco, CA 94114
The Wire Press, 329 San Jose Ave, San Francisco, CA 94110
Women Library Workers, 555 29th St, San Francisco, CA 94131, 415-527-5836
WOMEN LIBRARY WORKERS NEWSLETTER, Women Library Workers, 555 29th St, San Francisco, CA 94131, 415-527-5836
CALIFORNIA STATE POETRY QUARTERLY, 3218 Impala Dr. 9, San Jose, CA 95117, 408-379-0303
Cobra Press, 15381 Chelsea Dr, San Jose, CA 95124
FOLK MASS AND MODERN LITURGY, Resource Publications, 7291 Coronado Dr. #3, San Jose, CA 95129
LESBIAN VOICES, Ms. Atlas Press, 120 E. San Carlos Street, San Jose, CA 95112, 408-289-1088
MANGO, 329 So. Willard A, San Jose, CA 95126, 297-2077 (408)
MERLIN PAPERS, Merlin Press, PO Box 5602, San Jose, CA 95150
Merlin Press, P. O. Box 5602, San Jose, CA 95150
Ms. Atlas Press, 120 E. San Carlos, San Jose, CA 95112, 408-289-1088
Resource Publications, 7291 Coronado Dr, San Jose, CA 95070
SAN JOSE STUDIES, San Jose State University, San Jose State Univ., San Jose, CA 95192, 408-277-3460
Tau Delta Phi Press, Box 4, SJSU, San Jose, CA 95192
THE VOICE, PO Box 26615, San Jose, CA 95159
XANTHIPPE, c/o Women's Center, SJSU, 177 S. 10th, San Jose, CA 95192
SHAMELESS HUSSY REVIEW, Shameless Hussy, P.O. Box 424, San Lorenzo, CA 94580
ASSERT NEWSLETTER, Impact Publishers, Inc., PO Box 1094, San Luis Obispo, CA 93406, 805-543-5911
CAFE SOLO, Solo Press, 1209 Drake Circle, San Luis Obispo, CA 93401
A. COLLECTOR'S ITEM, Padre Productions, PO Box 1275, San Luis Obispo, CA 93406, 805-543-5404
Erin Hills Publishers, 1390 Fairway Dr, San Luis Obispo, CA 93401
Impact Publishers, Inc., PO Box 1094, San Luis Obispo, CA 93406, 805-543-5911
Padre Productions, PO Box 1275, San Luis Obispo, CA 93406, 805-543-5404
Golden West Books, PO Box 8136, San Marino, CA 91108, 213-283-3446
THE ADVOCATE, 1730 S. Amphlett, Suite 225, San Mateo, CA 94402, 415-573-7100
B & H BOOKS, Fur Line Press, 330 Paloma Ave, San Rafael, CA 94901, 415-456-0941
Spiritual Community Publications, Box 1080, San Rafael, CA 94902, 415-457-2990
SPORTSWOMAN MAGAZINE, CM Publications, 119 Paul Drive Box 4450, San Rafael, CA 94902
Being Incorporated, Box 641, Santa Barbara, CA 93102
Black Sparrow Press, PO Box 3993, Santa Barbara, CA 93105
Capra Press, 631 State St., Santa Barbara, CA 93101, 805-966-4590
Great Granny Press, 829 West Anapamu, Santa Barbara, CA 93101, 805-966-9532
Harvest Publishers, 907 Santa Barbara Street, Santa Barbara, CA 93101
HARVEST QUARTERLY, Harvest Publishers, 907 Santa Barbara Street, Santa Barbara, CA 93101
Mudborn Press, 209 W. De la Guerra, Santa Barbara, CA 93101, 805-962-9996
Parachuting Publications, P.O. Box 4232-Q, Santa Barbara, CA 93103, 805-968-7277
ROCKBOTTOM, Mudborn Press, 209 W. De La Guerra, Santa Barbara, CA 93101, 805-962-9996
Ross-Erikson Publishers, Inc., 1825 Grand Ave, Santa Barbara, CA 93101, 966-2691
Clatworthy Colorvues, 111½ Riverview St, Santa Cruz, CA 95062, 408-426-6401
Green Horse Press, PO Box 1691, Santa Cruz, CA 95061
GREENHOUSE REVIEW, Greenhouse Review Press, 126 Escalona Dr., Santa Cruz, CA 95060, 408-426-4355
Greenhouse Review Press, 126 Escalona Dr., Santa Cruz, CA 95060, 408-426-4355
Harvest Press, P.O. Box 1265, Santa Cruz, CA 95061, 415-335-5015
KAYAK, Kayak Press, 325 Ocean View, Santa Cruz, CA 95062
QUARRY WEST, College V, College v, University of Calif, Santa Cruz, CA 95064
RADAR, Santa Cruz Poetry Center, 108 Locust St, Santa Cruz, CA 95060
RICH'S SUCCESS NEWS, P.O. Box 587, Santa Cruz, CA 95061, 408-427-3959
STONE SOUP, A Magazine By Children, Children's Art Foundation, Inc., Bx 83, Santa Cruz, CA 95063, 408-426-5557
Unity Press, Inc., 113 New St., Santa Cruz, CA 95060, 408-427-2020
Lincoln Publishing Company, Box 5249, Santa Monica, CA 90405
Project Press, 710 Wilshire #106, Santa Monica, CA 90401
LOON, P.O. Box 11633, Santa Rosa, CA 95406
Thresh Publications, 441-443 Sebastopol Ave., Santa Rosa, CA 95401
Van Dyk Publications, 303 Wikiup Dr., Santa Rosa, CA 95401, 707-544-6103
CONTEMPORARY KEYBOARD MAGAZINE, Keyboard Players International, Box 907 (12333 Saratoga-Sunnyvale Rd.), Saratoga, CA 95070
MODERN LITURGY, Resource Publications, Box 444, Saratoga, CA 95070

PMS/King Publishing, 12625 Lido Way, Saratoga, CA 95070
Artists & Alchemists Publications, 215 Bridgeway, Sausalito, CA 94965, 914-332-0326
THE BLACK SCHOLAR: Journal of Black Studies and Research, P.O. Box 908, Sausalito, CA 94965, 415-332-3130
COEVOLUTION QUARTERLY, Box 428, Sausalito, CA 94965, 415-332-1716
In Between Books, Star Route, Box 271, Sausalito, CA 94965, 388-8048
STAR WEST, S-B Gazette, Box 731, Sausalito, CA 94965
Multinational Media, 228 Burlwood Dr., Scotts Valley, CA 95066, 408-438-0253
THE ORCHARD, Orchard Press, 2855 Old Gravenstein Hwy South, Sebastopol, CA 95472
Orchard Press, 2855 Old Gravenstein Hwy. South, Sebastopol, CA 95472
Pleasant Hill Press, 2600 Pleasant Hill Rd, Sebastopol, CA 95472
Hierophant Press, 15141 Sutton St., Sherman Oaks, CA 91403
Harlo Press, PO Box B-65577, E-207, Soledad, CA 93960
MANROOT, ManRoot Books, Box 982, South San Francisco, CA 94080
Helix House, 1520 Helix St, Spring Valley, CA 92077, 714-461-1185
New Seed Press, P.O. Box 3016, Stanford, CA 94305
SEQUOIA, Storke Publications Bldg., Stanford, CA 94305
Sydon, Inc., 451 South Regent St., Stockton, CA 95204
THE WORMWOOD REVIEW, The Wormwood Review Press, PO Box 8840, Stockton, CA 95204, 209-466-8231
BAMCA, 1505 Lochinvar Ave., Sunnyvale, CA 94087, 408-248-7220
The Commentators Press, P.O. Box 61297, Sunnyvale, CA 94088
IMPACT, AN INTERNATIONAL QUARTERLY OF CONTEMPORARY POETRY, The Commentators' Press, P.O. Box 61297, Sunnyvale, CA 94088
LITERARY CONTESTS & AWARDS NEWSLETTER, The Commentators' Press, P.O. Box 61297, Sunnyvale, CA 94088
Ventura Press, P.O. Box 2268, Sunnyvale, CA 94087
SURFSIDE POETRY REVIEW, PO Box 289, Surfside, CA 90743
Poet Papers, P.O. Box 528, Topanga, CA 90290
THE FAULT, The Fault Press, 33513 6th St., Union City, CA 94587
BERKELEY POETRY REVIEW, c/o Office of Student Activities, 103 Sproul Hall, Univ of Calif, Berkeley, CA 94720
The Green Hut Press, Book Orders: P.O. Box 55144, Valencia Hills, CA 91355, 805-259-5290
The Green Hut Press, 24051 Rotunda Rd, Valencia Hills, CA 91355
MIDNIGHT, Moon publications, PO Box 7574, Van Nuys, CA 91409
Perivale Press, 13830 Erwin Street, Van Nuys, CA 91401, 213-785-4671
ACCEPTANCE, Conceptual Non-Press, 230 San Juan, Venice, CA 90291
Beyond Baroque Foundation Publications, includes Beyond Baroque/newforms, NEW Magazine. Arts & Letters (formerly NeWLetterS), and NewBooks., 1639 W. Washington Blvd., Venice, CA 90291, 213-392-5763
BEYOND BAROQUE LIBRARY of SMALL PRESS PUBLICATIONS, Beyond Baroque Foundation, 1639 W. Washington Blvd., Venice, CA 90291, 213-392-5763
LIGHT TIMES, St. John's Bread Church, 3028 Stanford, Venice, CA 90291, 823-6233
TELEPOEM, Telepoetics (396-8978), 230 San Juan, Venice, CA 90291
Creative Ventures, 1000 East Kaweah, Visalia, CA 93277
Gen Guides Book Co., 5409 Lenvale, Whittier, CA 90601, 213-692-5492
EUREKA REVIEW, Orion Press, P.O. Box 366, Willows, CA 95988
WINE RINGS, Rt. 1, Box 821, c/o Menebroker, Wilton, CA 95693
Konocti Books, Route 1, Box 216, Winters, CA 95694
SIPAPU, Konocti Books, Route 1, Box 216, Winters, CA 95694, 916-662-3364; 916-752-1032
The Heyeck Press, 25 Patrol Ct., Woodside, CA 94062

COLORADO

ASPEN ANTHOLOGY, The Aspen Leaves Literary Foundation, Box 3185, Aspen, CO 81611, 303-925-8750
Adventure Trails Research and Development Laboratories, Laughing Coyote Mt., Black Hawk, CO 80422
The Mediaworks, P.O. Box 4494, Boulder, CO 80303, 303-494-1439
Aslan Enterprises, P.O. Box 1858, Boulder, CO 80306, 303-449-1515
THE COLORADO QUARTERLY, University of Colorado, Hellems 134, University of Colorado, Boulder, CO 80309
CRISS-CROSS ART COMMUNICATIONS, Criss-Cross, PO Box 2022, Boulder, CO 80302, 442-5832 (303)
Lodestar Press, P.O. Box 4657, Boulder, CO 80306
LOOK QUICK, Quick Books, P.O. Box 4434, Boulder, CO 80306
THE MODERN LANGUAGE JOURNAL, McKenna 30A, University of Colorado, Boulder, CO 80309, 303-492-7036
NEW PERIODICALS INDEX, The Mediaworks Ltd., P.O. Box 4494, Boulder, CO 80306, 303-494-1439
Pegana Press, P.O. Box 2148, Boulder, CO 80302
Pruett Publishing Company, 3235 Prairie Avenue, Boulder, CO 80301, 303-449-4919
AFRICA TODAY, Africa Today Associates, Cherrington Hall, Univ of Denver, Denver, CO 80210
The Ally Press, 1764 Gilpin St, Denver, CO 80218
BIG MAMA RAG, 1724 Gaylord, Denver, CO 80206
DELIRIUM, Libra Press, 1827 Elm St., Denver, CO 80220
THE DENVER QUARTERLY, University of Denver, Denver, CO 80210
Libra Press, 1827 Elm St., Denver, CO 80220, 309-399-1644
Mustang Press, P.O. Box 9007, Denver, CO 80209
New Vegetarian Press, 1764 Gilpin St, Denver, CO 80218
Sproing Books, 1150 St Paul St, Denver, CO 80206
ROCKY MOUNTAIN REVIEW, Atlatl Press, PO Box 1848, Durango, CO 81301, 303-247-2857
L'Epervier Press, 1219 East Laurel, Fort Collins, CO 80521
THE SALT CEDAR, Tamarix House, Route 3, Box 652, Fort Collins, CO 80521, 303-568-7472

Raincrow Press, 501 Vivian, Ft Collins, CO 80521
COLORADO-NORTH REVIEW, University Center, Greeley, CO 80639, 303-353-4647
THE EMISSARY, Eden Valley Press, Inc., P.O. Box 328, Loveland, CO 80537, 303-667-0599

CONNECTICUT

The Harian Press, 47 Hyde Blvd, Ballston SPA, CT 12020, 518-885-7397
POETS ON:, Box 255, Chaplin, CT 06235, 203-455-9671
CONNECTICUT FIRESIDE, Fireside Press, P.O. Box 5293, Hamden, CT 06518
COLLEGE ENGLISH, National Council of Teachers of English, Wesleyan University, Middletown, CT 06457, 203-347-9411, EX 491
Parallax Press, 1160 South Main St., Middletown, CT 06457
The Jacek Publishing Company, 38 Morris Lane, Milford, CT 06460, 203-874-4544
THE YALE REVIEW, 1902A Yale Station, New Haven, CT 06520
RED FOX REVIEW, Mohegan Community College, Norwich, CT 06360
SAILING THE ROAD CLEAR, Box 238, Old Mystic, CT 06372
New Plays for Children, Box 273, Rowayton, CT 06853
HARVEST, Art Press, New Britain, Conn., 238 Meriden Ave, Southington, CT 06489
Soap Box Publishing, Box 737, Stamford, CT 06904, 203-357-9591
SPEAK OUT, Soap Box Publishing, Box 737, Stamford, CT 06904, 203-357-9591
THE SMALL POND MAGAZINE OF LITERATURE, 10 Overland Dr., Stratford, CT 06497
BARTHOLOMEW'S COBBLE, 19 Howland Rd., West Hartford, CT 06107, 203-521-6053
Magic Circle Press, 10 Hyde Ridge Rd, Weston, CT 06880
Lawrence Hill & Company, Publishers, Inc., 24 Burr Farms Road, Westport, CT 06880, 203-226-9392
Omango d' Press, PO Box 255, Wethersfield, CT 06109, 203-242-4294
Curbstone Press, 321 Jackson Street, Willimantic, CT 06226, 456-2432
Ziesing Bros.' Publishing Company, 768 Main St., Willimantic, CT 06226, 203-423-5836/8162

DELAWARE

THEATRE DESIGN AND TECHNOLOGY, U.S. Institute for Theatre Technology, Inc., 1 Hillside Road, Newark, DE 19711, 302-731-5468
EN PASSANT POETRY QUARTERLY, 1906 Brant Rd, Wilmington, DE 19810
Lenape Publishing Ltd., 608 Whitby Dr., Wilmington, DE 19803, 302-652-1248

DISTRICT OF COLUMBIA

THE AMERICAN SCHOLAR, 1811 Q St., NW, Washington, DC 20009, 202-C05-3808
BLACK BOX MAGAZINE, Watershed Intermedia, PO Box 4174, Washington, DC 20015
COUNTERSPY, Fifth Estate Publishing Company, 647 Ben Franklin Station, Washington, DC 20044, 202-466-3424
EEL, Eel Press, 3314 Mt. Pleasant NW No. 2, Washington, DC 20010
THE ELEMENTS, The Elements, 1901 Q St N.W., Washington, DC 20009
HOO-DOO BlackSeries, Energy BlackSouth Press, Box 4174, Washington, DC 20015
"JOINT" CONFERENCE, King Publications, P.O. Box 19332, Washington, DC 20036
MAIL ORDER USA, PO Box 19083, Washington, DC 20036
MEDIA REPORT TO WOMEN, 3306 Ross Pl. N.W., Washington, DC 20008, 202-363-0812
MERIP REPORTS, P.O. Box 3122, Columbia Heights Station, Washington, DC 20010
MUSEUM OF TEMPORARY ART (MOTA) MAGAZINE, Mota Press, 1206 G Street NW, Washington, DC 20005, 202-296-6689
OFF OUR BACKS, Off Our Backs, 1724 20th st. N.W., Washington, DC 20009, 202-234-8072
PARACHUTIST, Corporate Press, 806 15th St. NW. Suite 444, Washington, DC 20005
PEOPLE & ENERGY, 1757 S Street NW, Washington, DC 20009, 202-332-4252
QUEST: A Feminist Quarterly, Quest: A Feminist Quarterly, Inc., PO Box 8843, Washington, DC 20003
SELF-RELIANCE, Institute for Local Self-Reliance, 1717 18th St. NW, Washington, DC 20009
Some of Us Press, 4110 Emery Pl. N.W., Washington, DC 20016
SOUNDINGS, c/oApt 216E, 4201 Cathedral Ave. N.W., Washington, DC 20016
THREE SISTERS, Georgetown University, Box 969, Hoya Station, Washington, DC 20057
VICTIMOLOGY AN INTERNATIONAL JOURNAL, Visage Press Inc., P O Box 39045, Washington, DC 20016, 202-686-5302
Visage Press, Inc., 3409 Wisconsin Avenue NW, Washington, DC 20016, 202-686-5302
WASHINGTON INTERNATIONAL ARTS LETTER, Box 9005, Washington, DC 20003
WASHINGTON INTERNATIONAL ARTS LETTER, Box 9005, Washington, DC 20003
WASHINGTON REVIEW, A Quarterly Review of the Arts, Friends of the Washington Review of the Arts, Inc., 404 10th Street SE, Washington, DC 20003, 202-546-4319
Washington Writers Publishing House, 1010 Vermont Ave, NW, Room 920, Washington, DC 20005
Watershed Intermedia, P.O. Box 4174, Washington, DC 20015, 202-547-2727
Women's Institute for Freedom of the Press, 3306 Ross Place, N.W., Washington, DC 20008, 202-966-7783
The Word Works, Inc., 5033 V St., NW, Washington, DC 20007, 202-338-7435

FLORIDA

RIVERSIDE QUARTERLY, Sapiro Box 14451, University Station, Gainesville, FL 32604
KONGLOMERATI, Konglomerati Press, 5719 29th Avenue South, Gulfport, FL 33707, 813-343-3633
Konglomerati Press, 5719 29th Avenue South, Gulfport, FL 33707, 813-343-3633

Olivant Press, P.O. Box 1409, Homestead, FL 33030
WEID: The Sensibility Revue, Olivant Press, PO Box 1409, Homestead, FL 33030
BOTH SIDES NOW, Free People Press, 1232 Laura St., P. O. Box 13079, Jacksonville, FL 32206
JACKSONVILLE POETRY QUARTERLY: Proclamations of the Arcane Order, Arcane Order, 5340 Weller Ave., Jacksonville, FL 32211, 904-724-4185
POCKET POETRY, Pocket Poetry Press, PO Box 70, Key West, FL 33040
THE SOLE PROPRIETOR, 2770 NW 32 Ave., Miami, FL 33142
Florida Sun-Gator Publishing Co., P.O. Box 365, Oviedo, FL 32765, 671-6543, 671-3633
NEW COLLAGE MAGAZINE, New Collage Press, 5700 North Trail, Sarasota, FL 33580, 919-355-7671, Ex 203
SUNSPARK, Sunspark Press, Box 6341, St. Pete Beach, FL 33736
Sunspark Press, Box 6341, St. Pete Beach, FL 33736
POETRY VENTURE, Valkyrie Press, Inc., 2135 1st Ave. South, St. Petersburg, FL 33712
Valkyrie Press, Inc., 2135 1st Ave. S., St. Petersburg, FL 33712
APALACHEE QUARTERLY, D.D.B. Press, Po Box 20106, Tallahassee, FL 32304
PEOPLE'S BOOKSELLER, P.O. Box 20049, Tallahassee, FL 32304
PHILOLOGOS, PO Box 2586, Tallahassee, FL 32304
SCHOLIA SATYRICA, English Department, University of South Florida, Tampa, FL 33620, 974-2421
WHITE MULE, 2710 E. 98th Ave., Tampa, FL 33612

GEORGIA

THE GEORGIA REVIEW, Univ. of Georgia, Athens, GA 30602, 404-542-3481
CONTEMPORARY ART/SOUTHEAST, Contemporary Art/Southeast, Inc., PO Box 7873, Station C, Atlanta, GA 30357
CRITIQUE: Studies in Modern Fiction, Dept. of English, Georgia Tech, Atlanta, GA 30332
DAIMON, House of Keys, P O Box 7952, Atlanta, GA 30357, 404-876-0529
House of Keys: The Atlanta Poetry Collective, Inc., P O Box 7952, Atlanta, GA 30357, 404-876-0529
The Vanity Press, PO Box 15240, Atlanta, GA 30333
Blue Horse, P.O. Box 6061, Augusta, GA 30906
THE DEKALB LITERARY ARTS JOURNAL, 555 N. Indian Creek Dr, Clarkston, GA 30021
GRAYDAY MAGAZINE, Point Blanc Press, 2830 Napier Ave., Macon, GA 31204
ATARAXIA, The Madisonian, Madison, Ga. 30650, 204 Highland Ave., Madison, GA 30650, 404-342-0820

HAWAII

Clean Energy Press, 3593-a Alani Dr, Honolulu, HI 96822, 808-988-4155
Petronium Press, 1255 Nuuanu Ave, #1813, Honolulu, HI 96817
UNEXPECTED, Otherworlds Media, 1394 Frank St., Honolulu, HI 96816
Press Pacifica, PO Box 47, Kailua, HI 96734, 808-261-6594

IDAHO

Ahsahta, Boise State University, Department of English, Boise, ID 83725, 208-385-1246
IDAHO HERITAGE, Idaho Heritage, Inc., P O Box 9365, Boise, ID 83707, 208-345-0060
R.O. Beatty & Associates, P.O. Box 763/611 North Fifth, Boise, ID 83701, 208-343-4949
THE WESTERN CRITIC, The Western Critic, Box 591, Boise, ID 83701
THE SLACKWATER REVIEW, Confluence Press, Inc., Art Center, Lewis-Clark Campus, Lewiston, ID 83501, 208-746-2341

ILLINOIS

RHINO, 1420 North Av., Bannockburn, IL 60015, 312-945-0382
ROAD/HOUSE, Road/House, 900 West 9th St., Belvidere, IL 61008, 543-9581
KARAMU, English Dept, Eastern Illinois Univ., Charleston, IL 61920, 217-581-5013
Academy Press Limited, 360 N. Michigan, Chicago, IL 60601, 312-782-9826
Ad Hoc Press, 1372 W. Estes No. 2N, Chicago, IL 60626, 312-761-3702
BLACK MARIA, 815 W. Wrightwood, Chicago, IL 60614
THE BLACK POSITION, Broadside Press, 7428 S. Evans Ave., Chicago, IL 60619
"BRILLIANT CORNERS": A Magazine of The Arts, Ad Hoc Press, 1372 W. Estes #2N, Chicago, IL 60626, 312-761-3702
THE CALL/EL CLARIN, Call Publications, Box 5597, Chicago, IL 60680
Chicago New Art Association, 230 E. Ohio, RM. 207, Chicago, IL 60611, 312-642-6236
CHICAGO REVIEW, University of Chicago, Faculty Exchange Box C, Chicago, IL 60637
DECEMBER MAGAZINE, December Press, 4 E. Huron, Chicago, IL 60611
Elpenor Books, P O Box 3152, Chicago, IL 60654, 312-929-0906
GALLERY SERIES/POETS, Harper Square Press, 401 W. Ontario St., c/o Artcrest Products, Chicago, IL 60610
ILLINOIS LIBERTARIAN, Libertarian Party of Illinois, (editor) 5301 S. Kimbark Ave., Chicago, IL 60615
ILLINOIS LIBERTARIAN, Libertarian Party of Illinois, (press address) Box 1776, Chicago, IL 60690
INDUSTRIAL WORKER, 752 W. Webster, Chicago, IL 60614, 312-549-5045
LAKES & PRAIRIES; A Journal of Writings, Pioneer Press, P.O. Box A 3454, Chicago, IL 60690
Liberator Press, P.O. Box 7128, Chicago, IL 60680
LIVING BLUES, 2615 N. Wilton, Chicago, IL 60611
LONG ISLAND REVIEW, Box 900, Chicago, IL 60690
MATI, Ommation Press, 5548 N. Sawyer, Chicago, IL 60625
MILK QUARTERLY, The Yellow Press, 2394 Blue Island Ave, Chicago, IL 60608
MOVING ON, New American Movement, 4327 N Milwaukee, Chicago, IL 60647, 312-252-7151

NEW ART EXAMINER, Chicago New Art Association, 230 E. Ohio, Chicago, IL 60611, 312-642-6236
OINK!, Oink! Press, 7021 N. Sheridan Rd, Chicago, IL 60626
THE ORIGINAL ART REPORT (TOAR), P.O. Box 1641, Chicago, IL 60690
OUT THERE MAGAZINE, Out There Press, 6944 W George St, Chicago, IL 60634, 312-745-8988
OYEZ REVIEW, 430 S Michigan, Chicago, IL 60605, 312-341-2017
POETRY, 1228 N. Dearborn Parkway, Chicago, IL 60610
POETRY &, P O Box A3298, Chicago, IL 60690
PRIMAVERA, Matrix, Ida Noyes Hall, Univ. of Chicago, Chicago, IL 60637
PROLETARIAT, Workers' Press, PO Box 3774, Merchandise Mart, Chicago, IL 60654
RIVERSIDE QUARTERLY, Smith 1346 W. Howard, Chicago, IL 60626
SALOME: A LITERARY DANCE MAGAZINE, 5548 N. Sawyer, Chicago, IL 60625
SHAKESPEARE NEWSLETTER, Univ. of Illinois, Chicago Circle, Chicago, IL 60680, 312-996-3289
SLICK PRESS, 5336 So. Drexel, Chicago, IL 60615, 324-4941 (312)
The Swallow Press Inc. (Book Publisher), 811 W. Junior Terrace, Chicago, IL 60613, 312-871-2760
Traumwald Press, Suite 10, 3550 Lake Shore Drive, Chicago, IL 60657
TWO HANDS NEWS, 1125 Webster, Chicago, IL 60614
Vanguard Books, P.O. Box 3566, Chicago, IL 60654
The Wine Press, 4504 N. Mc Vicker, Chicago, IL 60630
Woman Press, Box 59330, Chicago, IL 60645
Eads Street Press, 402 Stanton Lane, Crete, IL 60417
SHADES OF LIGHT, Shades of Light Press, Crete-Monee High School, Crete, IL 60417
SEEMS, Dept. of English, Northern Illinois Univ., DeKalb, IL 60115
SOU'WESTER, Pantagraph (Bloomington, Ill), Southern Illinois University, Edwardsville, IL 62025
PASSAGES, Passages Press, Box 14, Evanston, IL 60204, 312-492-1288
TRIQUARTERLY, University Hall 101, North West Univ., Evanston, IL 60201, 312-492-3490
LIVE FREE QUARTERLY, Uphill Underground Press, Live Free Inc., PO Box 743, Harvey, IL 60426
STORY QUARTERLY, 720 Central Ave, Highland Park, IL 60035
Sol Press, 107 Minneola St., Hinsdale, IL 60521
MISSISSIPPI VALLEY REVIEW, Dept. of English, Western Ill. University, Macomb, IL 61455
Snow Press, PO Box 427, Morton Grove, IL 60053, 312-299-7605
UZZANO, Uzzano Press, c/oShimer College, Mount Carroll, IL 61053
EXPLORATION, Exploration Press, Dept. of English, Illinois State University, Normal, IL 61761
MCLEAN COUNTY POETRY REVIEW, The Worn-Out Press, 101 East Sycamore, Normal, IL 61761
PhoeniXongs, P.O. Box 622 (orders), 1652 Longvalley Drive (correspondence), Northbrook, IL 60062, 312-498-3981
A SONGSMITH'S JOURNAL, PhoeniXongs, Box 622, Northbrook, IL 60062, 312-498-3981
THE WORKING CRAFTSMAN, Box 42, Northbrook, IL 60062, 312-498-2250
Cat's Pajamas Press, 527 Lyman, Oak Park, IL 60304
MOJO NAVIGATOR(E), Cat's Pajamas Press, 527 Lyman, Oak Park, IL 60304
THE SPOON RIVER QUARTERLY, The Spoon River Poetry Press, Bradley University, Peoria, IL 61606
LUCKY HEART BOOKS, Salt Lick Press, Box 1064, Quincy, IL 62301
OPINION, Opinion Publications, PO Box 1885, Rockford, IL 61110
WORD GARDEN, PO Box 2245, Springfield, IL 62703, 217-523-9865
Kitchen Harvest, 3N 681 Bittersweet Drive, St. Charles, IL 60174, 312-584-4084
ASCENT, English Dept,, U of Illinois, Urbana, IL 61801
Peradam Publishing House, P.O. Box 85, Urbana, IL 61801, 815-367-7070

INDIANA

FROZEN WAFFLES, Pitjon Press/Backback Media, 321 N. Indiana, Bloomington, IN 47401, 813-336-9117
THE MINNESOTA REVIEW, Box 211, Bloomington, IN 47401
Raintree, 4043 Morningside Dr, Bloomington, IN 47401, 812-332-6561
STONEY LONESOME, Nosferatu, 2600 Dekist, Bloomington, IN 47401
THE WINDLESS ORCHARD, Indiana Univ Eng Dept, Ft. Wayne, IN 46805
REVISTA CHICANO-RIQUENA, Indiana University Northwest, 3400 Broadway, Gary, IN 46408, 219-980-6692
WHITE ARMS MAGAZINE, Box 302, Howe, IN 46746
JOURNAL OF THE HELLENIC DIASPORA, The Wire Press, P.O. Box 22334, Indianapolis, IN 46222
PRIMER, Primer Press, 502 E. 38 St, #14F, Indianapolis, IN 46205
Around Publishing, 541 Mentone, Mentone, IN 46539
THE LITTLE AROUND JOURNAL, Around Publishing, PO Box 541, Mentone, IN 46539
BALL STATE UNIVERSITY FORUM, Ball State Univ., Muncie, IN 47303
VECTOR MAGAZINE, c/o Ball State News, Ball State Univ., Muncie, IN 47306
BLACK/AMERICAN LITERATURE FORUM, Indiana State University, Indiana State University, Parsons Hall 237, Terre Haute, IN 47809, 812-232-6311, Ext. 2664
HIGH/COO: A Quarterly of Short Poetry, High/Coo Press, 26-11 Hilltop Dr., W. Lafayette, IN 47906, 463-6969
High/Coo Press, 26-11 Hilltop Dr., W. Lafayette, IN 47906, 463-6969
SPARROW POVERTY PAMPHLETS, Sparrow Press, 103 Waldron St, West Lafayette, IN 47906
Sparrow Press, 103 Waldron St., West Lafayette, IN 47906

IOWA

HECTOR AND HECTOR, 1112 ISU Station, Ames, IA 50010
POET & CRITIC, Iowa State University Press, English Dept., ISU, 203 Ross Hall, Ames, IA 50010
THE NORTH AMERICAN REVIEW, Univ. Of Northern Iowa, Cedar Falls, IA 50613, 319-266-8487/273-2681

COE REVIEW, 1220 First Ave NE, Cedar Rapids, IA 52402, 319-398-1563
R & D Services, PO Box 644, Des Moines, IA 50303, 515-262-5397
International Books, International Writing Program, Univ of Iowa, Iowa City, IA 52240, 319-353-5920
IOWA REVIEW, U of Iowa Printing Service, 321 EPB, Univ. Of Iowa, Iowa City, IA 52242
THE SPIRIT THAT MOVES US, The Spirit That Moves Us, Inc. (Formerly Emmess Press), P.O. Box 1585, Iowa City, IA 52240, 319-338-5569
The Spirit That Moves Us, Inc. (Formerly Emmess Press), P.O. Box 1585, Iowa City, IA 52240, 319-338-5569
TYPEWRITER, Bird in the Bush, P.O. Box 409, Iowa City, IA 52240
The Penumbra Press, Box 12, Lisbon, IA 52253
Toothpaste Press, PO Box 546, 626 E. Main, West Branch, IA 52358, 319-643-2604
DENTAL FLOSS MAGAZINE, Toothpaste Press, P.O. Box 546, 626 E. Main, Westbranch, IA 52358, 319-643-2604

KANSAS

MIDWEST CHAPARRAL, 5508 Osage, Kansas City, KS 66106
COTTONWOOD REVIEW, Cottonwood Review, Box J, Kansas Union, Univ. of Kansas, Lawrence, KS 66045
K-State Press, College of Education, K.S.U., Manhattan, KS 66506, 913-532-5533
KANSAS QUARTERLY, Denison Hall, Kansas St. Univ., Manhattan, KS 66506, 913-532-6716
THE MIDWEST QUARTERLY, Pittsburg State University, Pittsburg State University, Pittsburg, KS 66762
FROM THE FIELD: A Magazine of Art and Verse, Staff Press, Box 295, Sterling, KS 67579
THE FAMOUS SCIENCE FICTION CHAPBOOK (series), Apocalypse Press, P.O. Box 1821, Topeka, KS 66601
THE ARK RIVER REVIEW, c/o A.G. Sobin Box 14 WSU, Wichita, KS 67208, 316-832-1075
GAZEBO, Wichita State Univ Post Office, Wichita State University, Wichita, KS 67208, 316-689-3130
MIKROKOSMOS, Mikropress, Box 14 Dept of English, Wichita State University, Wichita, KS 67208
OUT OF SIGHT, Caprice Out Of Sight, Box 32, Wichita, KS 67201
SQUEEZE BOX, Paper Tiger Press, 334 N Vassar, Wichita, KS 67208

KENTUCKY

KENTUCKY FOLKLORE RECORD, Kentucky Folklore Society, Box u-169, Western Ky. University, Bowling Green, KY 42101, 502-745-3043
KENTUCKY FOLKLORE SERIES, Kentucky Folklore Society, Box U-169, Western Ky. Univ., Bowling Green, KY 42101, 502-745-3043
VANTAGE POINT, PO Box 62, Danville, KY 40422, 606-236-9933
THE BLACKBIRD CIRCLE, The Blackbird Press, Inc., Box 99112, Jeffersontown, KY 40299
Love Street Books, P.O. Box 58163, Louisville, KY 40258
Pikeville College Press, Pikeville, KY 41501, 432-3161
TWIGS, Appalachian Studies Center, Pikeville College Press, College Box 2, Pikeville, KY 41501, 432-3161
WIND MAGAZINE, The Wind Press, RFD Rt. 1 Box 810, Pikeville, KY 41501, 606-437-6936
MOUNTAIN REVIEW, Box 660, Whitesburg, KY 41856
SNOWY EGRET, 205 S. Ninth St., Williamsburg, KY 40769

LOUISANA

THE SOUTHERN REVIEW, L.S.U. Press, Drawer D, University Station, Baton Rouge, LA 70893
THE NEW LAUREL REVIEW, Lawhead Press, PO Box 1083, Chalmette, LA 70044, 504-271-4209
Agape, P.O. Box 192, Franklin, LA 70538
Isat Pragbhara Press, Rt. 1, Box 143-C, Houma, LA 70360, 504-872-9701
LIBERTE, Box 2932, LaFayette, LA 70502
BARATARIA REVIEW, The New South Press, 1918½ Dauphine, New Orleans, LA 70116
LOWLANDS REVIEW, 8204 Maple No. 1, New Orleans, LA 70118
NEW ORLEANS REVIEW, Loyola University, New Orleans, LA 70118, 504-865-2294
QUINTESSENCE, Quintessence Press, 166 Albany Ave., Shreveport, LA 71105

MAINE

Cobblesmith, Route One, Ashville, ME 04607, 207-963-7071
Bern Porter Books, 22 Salmond Road, Belfast, ME 04915, 207-338-3763
BLACKBERRY, Box 186, Brunswick, ME 04011
International Marine Publishing Co., 21 Elm Street, Camden, ME 04843, 207-236-4326
Meanings Press, 36 Megunticook St., Camden, ME 04843
NATIONAL FISHERMAN, International Marine Pub Co, 21 Elm St., Camden, ME 04843, 207-236-4344
NORTH COAST POETRY, North Coast Press, PO Box 56, East Machias, ME 04630
Friends of Malatesta, Inc., P.O. Box 937, Ellsworth, ME 04605
The Bookstore Press, Box 191, RFD 1, Freeport, ME 04032, 207-963-7071
SHAMAN, Shaman, Inc., 47 Fletcher St. Kennebunk, ME 04043
Mercer House Press, P.O. Box 681, Kennebunkport, ME 04046
Great Raven Press, P.O. Box 1112, Lewiston, ME 04240, 784-0523
THOREAU JOURNAL QUARTERLY, Thoreau Fellowship, P.O. Box 551, Old Town, ME 04468
Puckerbrush Press, 76 Main St., Orono, ME 04473, 207-866-4868
CONTRABAND MAGAZINE, Contraband Press, P.O. Box 4073, Sta. A, Portland, ME 04101
Contraband Press, P.O. Box 4073, Sta A, Portland, ME 04101
METAMORPHOSIS, Metamorphosis Books, Rumford, ME 04276

LETTERS, Mainespring Press, Box 82, Stonington, ME 04681
Mainespring Press, Box 82, Stonington, ME 04681, 207-367-2484
MAINE EDITION, 22 Bridge St, Topsham, ME 04086

MARYLAND

THE MILL, The White Ewe Press, Box 996, Adelphi, MD 20783
The White Ewe Press, Box 996, Adelphi, MD 20783, 301-439-1470
G P Enterprises—JOB HUNTER'S FORUM, 132 Pinecrest Drive, Annapolis, MD 21403, 301-261-2320
The Runeskald Press, P.O. Box 612, Annapolis, MD 21404
CAIM, Dolphin-Moon, 1829 Colonial Road, Baltimore, MD 21207
CELEBRATION, 2707 Lawina Road, Baltimore, MD 21216
Diana Press, Inc, 12 West 25th St., Baltimore, MD 21218
Dolphin-Moon, 1829 Colonial Rd, Baltimore, MD 21207
J and J House, P.O. Box 15019, Baltimore, MD 21209
THE SUPPLEMENT TO THE BULLETIN OF THE MARYLAND WRITERS COUNCIL, Maryland Writers Council, 16 West Franklin St, Baltimore, MD 21201
The New Poets Series, 541 Piccadilly Rd., Baltimore, MD 21204, 301-828-8783
Seventh Dream Press, 10-B Fallridge Court, Baltimore, MD 21207, 301-298-2371
UNICORN, 4501 North Charles Street, Baltimore, MD 21210, 301-323-1010
WOMEN: A Journal of Liberation, 3028 Greenmount Ave, Baltimore, MD 21218
AS IS, As Is, 6302 Owen Pl., Bethesda, MD 20034, 301-229-0142
Bethesda Books, PO Box 34567, Bethesda, MD 20034, 301-320-4675
EMILY DICKINSON BULLETIN, Higginson Press, 4508 38th St., Brentwood, MD 20722
HIGGINSON JOURNAL OF POETRY, Higginson Press, 4508 38th St., Brentwood, MD 20722
M.O. Publishing Company, P.O. Box 136, Brookeville, MD 20729
MODUS OPERANDI, M.O. Publishing Company, P.O. Box 136, Brookeville, MD 20729, 301-774-2900
Spindrift Press, P.O. Box 3252, Catonsville, MD 21228
LA-BAS: A Newsletter of Experimental Poetry & Poetics, La-bas, Box 509 Hollywood Sta., College Park, MD 20740, 301-864-6921
La-bas, Box 509 Hollywood Sta., College Park, MD 20740, 301-864-6921
SUN & MOON: A Quarterly of Literature and Art, Sun & Moon/La-Bas, 4330 Hartwick Rd, #418, College Park, MD 20740, 301-864-6921
ABBEY, White Urp Press, 5011-2 Green Mountain Circle, Columbia, MD 21044
THE GREEN REVOLUTION, The School of Living, c/o School of Living, Freeland, MD 21053
Garrett Park Press, Garrett Park, MD 20766
Trunk Press, Hancock, MD 21750, 717-294-3345
Sibyl-Child Press, 6906 West Park Dr., Hyattsville, MD 20783, 301-422-7493/9140
SIBYL-CHILD: A Women's Arts & Culture Journal, Sibyl-Child Press, 6906 West Park Dr., Hyattsville, MD 20783, 301-422-7493/9140
Maryland Historical Press, 9205 Tuckerman St, Lanham, MD 20801, 301-577-2436
ICARUS, Icarus Press, P.O. Box 8, Riderwood, MD 21139
CS JOURNAL, R.S.H. Publications Worldwide, Suite 302, 818 Roeder Road, Silver Spring, MD 20910, 301-588-7896
VORT, Vort Works Ink/Vort World Hdqs, 1708 Tilton Dr, Silver Spring, MD 20902
ALEPH, 7319 Willow Ave, Takoma Park, MD 20012
Red Ochre Press, 8215 Flower Ave, Takoma Park, MD 20012
WINDOW, Window Press, 7005 Westmoreland Ave., Takoma Park, MD 20012
AFTER-IMAGE, Word-Camera Press, PO Box 10144, Towson, MD 21204
ICARUS, Icarus Press, 1015 Kenilworth Drive, Towson, MD 21204
Word-Camera, PO Box 10144, Towson, MD 21204
GOETHE'S NOTES, Goethe's Notes Press, 254 N. Gorsuch Rd, Westminister, MD 21157, 848-3690
Goethe's Notes Press, 254 N Gorsuch Rd., Westminister, MD 21157, 848-3690

MASSACHUSETTS

SISTER COURAGE, Box 296, Allston, MA 02134, 617-661-2689
Tyndall Creek Press, 17 Ashford St., Allston, MA 02134
BOXSPRING, Hampshire College, Amherst, MA 01002
CHOMO-URI, 506 Goodell Hall, University of Mass, Amherst, MA 01003, 413-545-0883
Food For Thought Publications, PO Box 331, Amherst, MA 01002, 413-584-7984
FUTURES INFORMATION INTERCHANGE, 166 Hills South, University of Massachusetts, Amherst, MA 01003, 413-545-0981
Green Knight Press, P.O. Box 512, Amherst, MA 01002
Lynx House Press, PO Box 800, Amherst, MA 01002, 413-367-2865
THE MASSACHUSETTS REVIEW, Memorial Hall, Univ. of Mass, Amherst, MA 01003, 413-545-2689
MICROMEGAS, 84 High Point Dr., Amherst, MA 01002, 413-256-8637
Parable Press (formerly June McLaughlin Press), 136 Gray Street, Amherst, MA 01002, 413-253-5634
THE PRE-RAPHAELITE REVIEW, Rat & Mole Press, P.O. Box 111, Amherst, MA 01002
Rat & Mole Press, P.O. Box 111, Amherst, MA 01002
BUTT: A Quarterly, Butt Press, 156 Pleasant St., Arlington, MA 02174
THE NEW RENAISSANCE, A Magazine of Ideas & Opinions, Emphasizing Literature & The Arts, 9 Heath Road, Arlington, MA 02174
ZEUGMA, Zeugma Press, 25 Jeanette Ave., Belmont, MA 02178
HOLLOW SPRING REVIEW OF POETRY, Hollow Spring Press, PO Box 76, Berkshire, MA 01224, 413-499-2709
ALCHERINGA:ETHNOPOETICS, Alcheringa, 745 Commonwealth Ave., Boston, MA 02215, 617-353-4026

ARION, A Journal of Humanities and the Classics, Boston University, 270 Bay State Rd, Boston, MA 02134
Artistic Endeavors, Inc., PO Box 8916, Boston, MA 02114, 617-227-1967
Ave Victor Hugo Publishing, 339 Newberry St., Boston, MA 02115
BOSTON UNIVERSITY JOURNAL, 775 Commonwealth Ave., Boston, MA 02215
DIGNITY, 755 Boylston St. Room 413, Boston, MA 02116
FAG RAG, Fag Rag Varieties, Inc., Box 331, Kenmore Station, Boston, MA 02115, 617-426-4469
FICTION MAGAZINE, Ave Victor Hugo Publ., 339 Newbury St., Boston, MA 02115, 617-266-7746
GALILEO, Ave Victor Hugo Publ., 339 Newberry St, Boston, MA 02115
GAY COMMUNITY NEWS, GCN Inc., 22 Bromfield St., Boston, MA 02108, 617-426-4469
Good Gay Poets Press, Box 277, Astor Station, Boston, MA 02123
The Heron Press, 36 Bromfield St., Boston, MA 02108
Stone Wall Press, Inc, 5 Byron St, Boston, MA 02108
THE TOY SUN, SPC Press, Box 306, 102 Charles St, Boston, MA 02114
Autumn Press, Inc., 7 Littell Road, Brookline, MA 02146, 617-738-5680
Kanthaka Press, P.O. Box 696, Brookline Village, MA 02147, 617-734-8146
THE AGNI REVIEW, The Agni Press, P.O. Box 349, Cambridge, MA 02138
Alice James Books, 138 Mount Auburn St., Cambridge, MA 02138
Apple-wood Press, Box 2870, Cambridge, MA 02139, 617-868-5408
ARION'S DOLPHIN, Dolphin Editions, Box 313, Cambridge, MA 02138
BLACKSMITH ANTHOLOGY, The Blacksmith Press, 5 Walnut Ave, Cambridge, MA 02140, 868-5753
The Blacksmith Press, 5 Walnut Ave., Cambridge, MA 02140
DAEDALUS, Journal of the American Academy of Arts and Sciences, American Academy of Arts and Sciences, 7 Linden Street, Cambridge, MA 02138
DARK HORSE, c/o Barnes, 47a Dana St., Cambridge, MA 02138
Dolphin Editions, Box 313, Cambridge, MA 02138
Grist Press, 195 Lakeview Ave., Cambridge, MA 02138
GRIST, Grist Press, 195 Lakeview Ave., Cambridge, MA 02138
Halty Ferguson Publishing Co., 376 Harvard Street, Cambridge, MA 02138, 617-868-6190
THE HARVARD ADVOCATE, 21 South St., Cambridge, MA 02138, 617-495-7820
INTEGRITY: Gay Episcopal Forum, Integrity, Inc., 99 Brattle St., Cambridge, MA 02138
LIBERATION MAGAZINE, 186 Hampshire St., Cambridge, MA 02139, 617-354-0492
PADAN ARAM, 52 Dunster Street, Harvard U, Cambridge, MA 02138, 495-2807
PHONE-A-POEM, Box 193, Cambridge, MA 02141, 617-492-1144
The Pilot School Co-operative, C/O Heather A. Ryan, 2 Bancroft Street, Cambridge, MA 02139, 617-864-9341
Pitcairn Press Inc., 388 Franklin St, Cambridge, MA 02139
THE PLANET QUARTERLY, The Pilot School Co-operative, c/o Heather A. Ryan, 2 Bancroft Street, Cambridge, MA 02139, 617-864-9341
PLOUGHSHARES, Box 529, Cambridge, MA 02139
Quark Press, Box 193, Cambridge, MA 02141
RESOURCES, Box 134, Harvard Square, Cambridge, MA 02138
UNICORN: A Miscellaneous Journal, 345 Harvard St. 3B, Cambridge, MA 02138, 617-354-0124
Windfall, 160 Hancock, Cambridge, MA 02139
The Women And Literature Collective, Box 441, Cambridge, MA 02138, 617-266-2082
WRITERS' RESOURCES, 48 Kinnaird St Apt 3, Cambridge, MA 02139, 617-492-3248
URBAN & SOCIAL CHANGE REVIEW, Boston College, McGuinn Hall, Chestnut Hill, MA 02167
Chthon Press, 39 Hawthorne Village, Concord, MA 01742
OSIRIS, Box 297, Deerfield, MA 01342
Salt-Works Press, Box 649, Dennis, MA 02638, 617-385-3948
SOMA-HAOMA, Salt-works Press, Box 649, Dennis, MA 02638
CHOOMIA - COLLECTIONS OF CONTEMPORARY POETRY, Yarrow Press, P.O. Box 107, Framingham, MA 01701
BEZOAR, P.O. Box 535, Gloucester, MA 01930
TENDRIL, Tendril, Box 512, Green Harbor, MA 02041, 617-834-4137
Morning Star Press, Poplar Hill Road, RFD, Haydenville, MA 01039, 413-665-4754
THE PHOENIX, Morning Star Press, Morning Star Farm, RFD, Haydenville, MA 01039, 413-665-4754
AB INTRA, Hellric Publications, 39 Eliot St., Jamaica Plain, MA 02130
ESPONTANEO, Hellric Publications, 39 Eliot St., Jamaica Plain, MA 02130
GARGOYLE, Gargoyle, 160 Boylston St. no. 3, Jamaica Plain, MA 02130
Hellric Publications, 39 Eliot St, Jamaica Plain, MA 02130
PYRAMID, Hellric Publications, 39 Eliot St., Jamaica Plain, MA 02130
SCIENCE FOR THE PEOPLE, Science for the People, 9 Walden St., Jamaica Plain, MA 02130
Angel Hair Books, Box 718, Lenox, MA 01240
Arbor, Old Winter Street, Lincoln, MA 01773
EKISTICS, Athens Center of Ekistics, Page Farm Road, Lincoln, MA 01773, 617-259-9144
Penmaen Press, Old Sudbury Road, Lincoln, MA 01773, 617-259-0842
TREES, Arbor, Old Winter St, Lincoln, MA 01773
Ithaca Press, P.O. Box 853, Lowell, MA 01853
MASTHEAD: A Journal For Teaching History With Old Newspapers, Living History Classrooms Pub. Co., P O Box 1009, Marblehead, MA 01945, 617-581-0198
Micah Publications, 255 Humphrey St, Marblehead, MA 01945
The Pomegranate Press, PO Box 181, N. Cambridge, MA 02140
RADICAL AMERICA, Box B, N. Cambridge, MA 02140
NANTUCKET REVIEW, P.O. Box 1444, Nantucket, MA 02554
Roxbury Poetry Enterprises, 301 Marked Tree Road, Needham, MA 02192

STONY HILLS: The New England Alternative Press Review, Rat & Mole, Box 715, Newburyport, MA 01950, 617-465-9451
ZAHIR, Box 715, Newburyport, MA 01950, 617-465-9451
FIGMENT, 34 Andrew St, Newton, MA 02161, 617-628-4571
BLUE PIG, Sand Project Press/US, 23 Cedar Street, Northampton, MA 01060
MULCH, Mulch Press, P.O. Box 598, Northampton, MA 01060
PROVINCETOWN POETS, To the Lighthouse Press, 216 Bradford St., Provincetown, MA 02657
ABYSS, Abyss Publications, P.O. Box C, Somerville, MA 02143
Abyss/Augtwofive, PO Box C, Somerville, MA 02143, 617-666-1804
ASPECT, 66 Rogers Ave., Somerville, MA 02144
Drunken-Juggler Press, 12 Cooney St, Somerville, MA 02143
NEW BOSTON REVIEW, Boston Critic, Inc., 77 Sacramento St., Somerville, MA 02143
SMALL MOON, The Poetry Co-Operative Of Boston, Drunken Juggler Press, c/o 12 Cooney Street, Somerville, MA 02143, 868-1354
Phillip M. Perry, P O Box 2319, Springfield, MA 01101, 413-737-1685
The Babbington Press, P.O. Box 98, Stow, MA 01775, (617) 568-8024
Programmed Studies Inc, P.O. Box 113, Stow, MA 01775, 617-897-2130
PANACHE, Panache Books, PO Box 77, Sunderland, MA 01375, 413-367-2762
RT: A Journal of Radical Therapy (formerly ROUGH TIMES), Box 89, W. Somerville, MA 02144
NOSTOC, 101 Nehoiden Rd, Waban, MA 02168
SHELL, 362 Waban Ave, Waban, MA 02168, 617-244-3258
THE FOUR ZOAS JOURNAL OF POETRY & LETTERS, The Four Zoas Press, RFD, Ware, MA 01082
The B & R Samizdat Express, PO Box 161, West Roxbury, MA 02132, 617-469-2269
THE POETRY MISCELLANY, P.O. Box 175, Williamstown, MA 01267, 413-458-3214
Woods Hole Press, Pxx 44, Woods Hole, MA 02543
WOMANCHILD, Womanchild Press, 84 Birch St., Worcester, MA 01603, 617-756-4426

MICHIGAN

ANAESTHESIA REVIEW, Trouser Press, 732 S. Forest St no. 5, Ann Arbor, MI 48104
ANN ARBOR REVIEW, Ann Arbor Review Press, Washtenaw Community College, Fred Wolven, editor, Ann Arbor, MI 48106, 313-971-6300 ex 407
CHIAROSCURO, Chiaroscuro Press, 2624 Roseland Dr., Ann Arbor, MI 48103, 313-761-5530
FPS: A MAGAZINE OF YOUNG PEOPLE'S LIBERATION, Youth Liberation Press, Inc., 2007 Washtenaw, Ann Arbor, MI 48104
Kylix Press, 1485 Maywood, Ann Arbor, MI 48103, (313) 761-5399
MICHIGAN GERMANIC STUDIES, Michigan Germanic Studies, Inc., Department of German, University of Michigan, Ann Arbor, MI 48109, (313) 764-5357
THE NEW HARBINGER: A JOURNAL OF THE COOPERATIVE MOVEMENT, North American Student Cooperative Organization (NASCO), Box 1301, Ann Arbor, MI 48106, 313-663-0889
REFERENCE SERVICES REVIEW, Pierian Press, P.O. Box 1808, Ann Arbor, MI 48106, 313-434-5530
RIPPLES, Shining Waters Press, P.O. Box 52, Ann Arbor, MI 48107
RUSSIAN LITERATURE TRIQUARTERLY, Ardis, 2901 Heatherway, Ann Arbor, MI 48104, 313-971-2367
SALTHOUSE, 1562 Jones Dr., Ann Arbor, MI 48105
THE NOOOK & OTHER REVIEWS, Notebook Press, P O Box 180, Birmingham, MI 48012
Notebook Press, P O Box 180, Birmingham, MI 48012
AEOLIAN-HARP, 1395 James St., Burton, MI 48529
THE LONDON COLLECTOR, Wolf House BOOKS, P.O. Box 209, Cedar Springs, MI 49319
BLACK GRAPHICS INTERNATIONAL, Black Graphics International, P.O. Box 732, Detroit, MI 48206
Clover Press, Box 313, Detroit, MI 48231
Glass Bell Press, 5053 Commonwealth, Detroit, MI 48208, 414-898-7972
GREEN'S MAGAZINE, Clover Press, Box 313, Detroit, MI 48231
MOVING OUT: Feminist Literary & Arts Journal, 4866 Third & Warren, Wayne State University, Detroit, MI 48202
SEVEN STARS FICTION QUARTERLY, Realities, 3635 Nottingham, Detroit, MI 48224
TRANSIENCE QUARTERLY, Guild of Alternative Artists, 19731 Forrer, Detroit, MI 48235, 313-272-3128
Cat Anna Press, P.O. Box 301, Dexter, MI 48130
ALLEGRA, Allegra Press, 526 Forest, E. Lansing, MI 48823, 517-351-5977
Allegra Press, 526 Forest, E. Lansing, MI 48823, 517-351-5977
THE CENTENNIAL REVIEW, 110 Morrill Hall, Mich. State Univ., E. Lansing, MI 48824, 517-355-1905
CENTERING: A Magazine of Poetry, Years Press, ATL EBH, Michigan State University, E. Lansing, MI 48824
Ghost Dance: THE INTERNATIONAL QUARTERLY OF EXPERIMENTAL POETRY, Ghost Dance Press, 526 Forest, E. Lansing, MI 48823, 351-5977
Ghost Dance Press, 526 Forest, E. Lansing, MI 48823
Inquiry Press, P.O. Box 1766, E. Lansing, MI 48823
JOURNAL OF SOUTH ASIAN LITERATURE, Asian Studies Center, Mich State Univ, Asian Studies Ctr., E. Lansing, MI 48823
LESBIAN CONNECTION, P.O. Box 811, E. Lansing, MI 48823
LOCAL TENDERNESS, Old Marble Press, P.O. Box 1701, E. Lansing, MI 48823
RED CEDAR REVIEW, 325 Morrill Hall, Dept. of English, Mich. State Univ., E. Lansing, MI 48824, 517-355-9656
THE GYPSY SCHOLAR: A Graduate Forum for Literary Criticism, Dept. of English, Michigan State U., East Lansing, MI 48824
HURON REVIEW, Walden Press, 423 South Franklin Ave., Flint, MI 48503
Walden Press, 423 South Franklin Ave, Flint, MI 48503
BARDIC ECHOES, Bardic Echoes Brochures, 1036 Emerald Ave., N.E., Grand Rapids, MI 49503, 616-454-9120
BIG SCREAM, Nada, 696 48th St SE, Grand Rapids, MI 49508, 616-531-1442
Cider Press, 1821 Burton St. S.E., Grand Rapids, MI 49506, 616-243-6840

FOR THE TIME BEING, P.O. Box 7144, Grand Rapids, MI 49507
Free Books Inc, 7437 Eastern SE, Grand Rapids, MI 49508
Nada, 696 48th St SE, Grand Rapids, MI 49508, 616-531-1442
Pilot Press Books, PO Box 2662, Grand Rapids, MI 49501
THE RAG, Roaring Aardvark Press, 850 Reynard St SE, Grand Rapids, MI 49507
WINDOWS IN THE STONE, Free Books Inc., 7437 Eastern S.E., Grand Rapids, MI 49508
THE ALTERNATIVE PRESS, 3090 Copeland Rd, Grindstone City, MI 48467
THE COPPER COUNTRY ANTHEM, The Book Concern, Box 330, Hancock, MI 49930, 906-482-1250
Anti-Ocean Press, 148 Pasadena, Highland Park, MI 48203, 313-869-6663
Fallen Angel Press, 1913 West McNichols C-6, Highland Park, MI 48203, 313-864-0982
SHIRHADASH/NEW SONG, Anti-Ocean Press, 148 Pasadena, Highland Park, MI 48203, 313-869-6663
The Windmill Press, 1369 Linwood Drive, Holland, MI 49423, 616-335-2688
THE LAKE SUPERIOR REVIEW, Box 724, Ironwood, MI 49938
Todd Tarbox Books, 2523 Ashton Rd., Jackson, MI 49203
Blue Mountain Press, 511 Campbell St., Kalamazoo, MI 49007, 349-3924
THE NEW MOON, Humble Hills Press, 2147 Oakland Dr, Kalamazoo, MI 49008
SKYWRITING, Blue Mountupress,11CampbsSt, KalamazoMI 49007, 616-349-3924
GRAND RIVER REVIEW/CAPITOL CITY MOON, Grand River Review, PO Box 15052, Lansing, MI 48901
HAPPINESS HOLDING TANK, Stone Press, 1790 Grand River, Okemos, MI 48864
Stone Press, 1790 Grand River, Okemos, MI 48864
SCREEN DOOR REVIEW, Arbitrary Closet Press, Box 54, Onondaga, MI 49264
THE ILLUSTRATED ORB, The Trauma Works, P.O. Box 111, Royal Oak, MI 48068
INTERNATIONAL POETRY REVIEW, Green River Press, SVSC Box 56, Univ. Center, MI 48710
GREEN RIVER REVIEW, Green River Press, SVSC Box 56, University Center, MI 48710
Green River Press, SVSC Box 56, University Center, MI 48710
JOURNAL OF NARRATIVE TECHNIQUE, English Dept, Eastern Michigan University, Ypsilanti, MI 48197

MINNESOTA

RASPBERRY PRESS (magazine), Raspberry Press, Rte. 6 Box 459, Bemidji, MN 56601, 218-751-8497
TRULY FINE PRESS, A Review, Truly Fine Press, P.O. Box 891, Bemidji, MN 56601
Truly Fine Press, P.O. Box 891, Bemidji, MN 56601
HENNEPIN COUNTY LIBRARY CATALOGING BULLETIN, 7001 York Ave. S., Secretary, Technical Services Division,Hennepin Co. Library, Edina, MN 55435, 612-830-4980
MEN'S, M.E.N. International, P.O. Box 189, Forest Lake, MN 55025
Red Studio Press, Route 1 Box 155, Loretto, MN 55357
Ox Head Press, 414 N 6th St, Marshall, MN 56258
ALTERNATIVE SOURCES of ENERGY MAGAZINE, Alternative Sources of Energy, Inc., Rt. 2, Box 90A, Milaca, MN 56353
LITTLE FREE PRESS, 715 E. 14th St., Minneapolis, MN 55404
MOONS AND LION TAILES, Permanent Press, Box 8434, Lake Street Station, Minneapolis, MN 55408, 612-377-4384
DACOTAH TERRITORY, Territorial Press, P.O. Box 775, Moorhead, MN 56560
Carma Press, Box 12633, St Paul, MN 55112, 612-633-6845
THE DANDELION, 1985 Selby Ave, St Paul, MN 55104, 612-646-8917
TRUCK, Truck Press, 1141 James Ave, St Paul, MN 55105
Truck Press, 1141 James Ave, St Paul, MN 55105
Back Row Press, PO Box 12845, St. Paul, MN 55112, 612-633-1685
CONQUEST, 318 Summit Ave., St. Paul, MN 55102
GNOSTICA, Llewellyn Publications, Box 3383, St. Paul, MN 55165
ST. CROIX REVIEW, Box 244, Stillwater, MN 55082
Knollwood Publishing Company, Box 735, Willmar, MN 56201, 612-235-4950

MISSISSIPPI

MISSISSIPPI REVIEW, Mississippi Review, Box 37, Southern Station, Hattisburg, MS 39401

MISSOURI

Wwhimsy Press, 1822 Northview Dr., Arnold, MO 63010
REBUTTAL! The Bicentennial Newsletter of Truth, The First Ozark Press, P.O. Box 1126, Branson, MO 65716
THE CAPE ROCK, Southeast Missouri State Univ., English Dept, Southeast Missouri State, Cape Girardeau, MO 63701, 314-334-8211 ext. 278
The Hosanna Press, 405 South Ann St, Columbia, MO 65201, 314-442-6755
MONUMENT IN CANTOS AND ESSAYS, Monument Press, 508 Mexico Gravel Road, Columbia, MO 65201
OPEN PLACES, Box 2085, Stephens College, Columbia, MO 65201, 314-442-2211
Singing Wind Publications, P.O. Box 1426, Columbia, MO 65201, 314-442-6543
Raindust Press, PO Box 1823, Independence, MO 64055
CHOUTEAU REVIEW, 10016, Kansas City, MO 64111, 816-444-0060
THE FOOLKILLER, The Foolkiller, 2 W 39th, Kansas City, MO 64111, 816-531-9226
NEW LETTERS, University of Missouri, 5346 Charlotte, Kansas City, MO 64110, 816-276-1168
SEX NEWS, 7140 Oak, Kansas City, MO 64114
CHARITON REVIEW, Language & Literature, Northeast Missouri St. Univ., Kirksville, MO 63501, 816-665-5121
MARK TWAIN JOURNAL, Mark Twain Journal, Kirkwood, MO 63122

BITTERSWEET, Lebanon High School, 777 Brice St., Lebanon, MO 65536, 417-532-9829
GRAFIKTRAKTS, Ted Smith/Graphics, 300 W. 3rd, Rolla, MO 65401
WINGED OX, 107 South Rolla, Rolla, MO 65401
TALES, Box 24226, St Louis, MO 63130
TELOS, Telos Press, Sociology Dept, Washington Univ, St Louis, MO 63130, 314-863-0100, EXT. 4383
Telos Press, C/O Sociology Dept, Washington Univ, St Louis, MO 63130, 314-863-0100, EXT. 4383
ICARUS, Missouri Western State College, St. Joseph, MO 64507
Cornerstone Press, P.O. Box 28048, St. Louis, MO 63119, 314-225-3892
FOCUS/ MIDWEST, Focus/ Midwest Publishing Co., Inc., St. Louis Journalism Review, 928a N. McKnight, St. Louis, MO 63132, 314-991-1698
IMAGE MAGAZINE, Cornerstone Press, P.O. Box 28048, St. Louis, MO 63119, 314-225-3892
RIVER STYX, Big River Association, 7420 Cornell Ave., St. Louis, MO 63130, 314-725-0602
ST. LOUIS JOURNALISM REVIEW, FOCUS/ Midwest Publishing Co., Inc., 928A N. McKnight, St. Louis, MO 63132, 314-991-1698
SOLANA, 11822 Kramper Lane, St. Louis, MO 63128, 314-843-5930
WEID: The Sensibility Revue, Olivant Press, 2935 Russell Blvd., St. Louis, MO 63104
WEBSTER REVIEW, Webster College, Webster Groves, MO 63119

MONTANA

Circle Press, 419 So. Grand, Bozeman, MT 59715
Calliopea Press, 701 Longstaff, Missoula, MT 59801, 406-549-6945
CUTBANK, SmokeRoot, English Dept., U. of Montana, Missoula, MT 59801
MONTANA GOTHIC, Black Stone Press, P.O. Box 756, Missoula, MT 59801
SmokeRoot, Dept of English/Univ of Mont, Missoula, MT 59812

NEBRASKA

AMERICAN FIDDLERS NEWS, American Old Time Fiddlers Assoc., 6141 Morrill Avenue, Lincoln, NB 68507, 402-466-5519
PRAIRIE SCHOONER, 201 Andrews Hall, Univ. of Nebr., Lincoln, NB 68588
Windflower Press, P.O. Box 82213, Lincoln, NB 68501
CHERNOZEM, Big Deal Press, Gen. Delivery, No. Platte, NB 69101
STEPPENWOLF, P.O. Box 55045, Omaha, NB 68155

NEVADA

Duck Down Press, Box 761, Fallon, NV 89406
SCREE, Duck Down Press, Box 761, Fallon, NV 89406
Nevada Publications, Box 15444, Las Vegas, NV 89114
TWO SCORE OR LESS FOR WORDS, The Yellow Chicken Press, P.O. Box 1146, Las Vegas, NV 89101
Great Basin Press, Box 11162, Reno, NV 89510, 702-329-0709
The Naiad Press, Inc., P.O. Box 5025, Washington Stn., Reno, NV 89513, 816-633-4136
WEST COAST POETRY REVIEW, West Coast Poetry Review Press, 1127 Codel Way, Reno, NV 89503, 702-786-1625
West Coast Poetry Review Press, 1127 Codel Way, Reno, NV 89503, 702-786-1625

NEW HAMPSHIRE

William L. Bauhan, Publisher, Dublin, NH 03444
HARMONY, University of New Hampshire Student Press, M.U.B. Rm. 153, University of N.H., Durham, NH 03824
SELECT PRESS REVIEW, Select Press Book Service, Inc., 14 South Street, Manchester, NH 03055, 613-673-8255
SUN-LOTUS HAIKU, Sun-Lotus Books, 125 West Merrimack St, Manchester, NH 03101
NORTHERN NEW ENGLAND REVIEW, PO Box 825, Franklin Pierce College, Rindge, NH 03461
Blue Crow Press, 48 Salmon Falls Rd. (Box A), Rochester, NH 03867
DECARABIA, Blue Crow Press, 48 Salmon Falls Rd (Box-A), Rochester, NH 03867

NEW JERSEY

Alleluia Press, 672 Franklin Tpke Box 103, Allendale, NJ 07401, 201-327-3513
THE MICKLE STREET REVIEW, 330 Mickle St., Camden, NJ 08103
BOOK BUYER'S GUIDE/MARKETPLACE, Franklin Book Company, PO Box 208, East Millstone, NJ 08873, 201-873-2156
Franklin Book Company, PO Box 208, East Millstone, NJ 08873, 201-873-2156
ALBATROSS, P.O. Box 2046, Central Station, East Orange, NJ 07019, 201-OR-4-4111
SHELTERFORCE, 31 Chestnut Street, East Orange, NJ 07018
3RD THING MAGAZINE OF POETRY AND GRAPHICS, Hudson River Press, P.O. Box 270, Edgewater, NJ 07020
THE REMINGTON REVIEW, 505 Westfield Ave., Elizabeth, NJ 07208
GRAHAM HOUSE REVIEW, Graham House Press, Box 489, Englewood, NJ 07631, 201-871-4498
BERGEN POETS, 218 Gramercy Place, Glen Rock, NJ 07452, 201-652-7016
BUFFALO GNATS, Buffalo Gnats Press, PO Box 163, Glen Rock, NJ 07452, 201-652-7016
E & E Enterprises, P.O. Box 405, Howell, NJ 07731
Circle Publications, PO Box 34, Lyndhurst, NJ 07071, 201-438-1326
JOURNAL OF NEW JERSEY POETS, Fairleigh Dickinson Univ., English Dept., Madison, NJ 07940, 01-377-4700
The Literary Review, Fairleigh Dickinson University, 285 Madison Avenue, Madison, NJ 07940

STONE COUNTRY, Stone Country Press, 20 Lorraine Road, Madison, NJ 07940
Scarecrow Press, P O Box 656, Metuchen, NJ 08840, 201-548-8600
THE FURTHER RANGE, 27 Oval Road, Milburn, NJ 07041
CREATIVE COMPUTING, Creative Computing Press, P.O. Box 789-M, Morristown, NJ 07960, 201-540-0445
Creative Computing Press, 51 Dumont Place, Morristown, NJ 07960, 201-540-0445
CAROUSEL QUARTERLY OF POETRY, Carousel Publishers, Box 111, Mt Laurel, NJ 08054, 609-871-0612
PARTISAN REVIEW, 1 Richardson St., Rutgers University, New Brunswick, NJ 08903
SECOND GROWTH, 121 Somerset St, New Brunswick, NJ 08903
Incunabula Collection Press, 277 Hillside Ave, Nutley, NJ 07110
ROOTS OF CREATION, Incunabula Collection Press, 277 Hillside Av., Nutley, NJ 07110
LUNA, Luna Publications, 655 Orchard St., Oradell, NJ 07649
IF LIFE, THEN ONE AMONG AT LEAST FOUR, P.O. Box 282, Palisades Park, NJ 07650
FROM HERE, From Here Press, Box 2702, Paterson, NJ 07509
HAIKU MAGAZINE, From Here Press, Box 2702, Paterson, NJ 07509
XTRAS, From Here Press, Box 2702, Paterson, NJ 07509
Great Society Press, 451 Heckman St. Apt. 308, Phillipsburg, NJ 08865, 201-859-6134
LETTERS, Mainespring Press, Box 175, Princeton, NJ 08540, 207-367-2484
QUARTERLY REVIEW OF LITERATURE, Quarterly Review of Literature, 26 Haslet Ave, Princeton, NJ 08540, 921-6976
Tamarisk, 188 Forest Ave, Ramsey, NJ 07446, 201-327-7469
US1 WORKSHEETS, US1 Poets' Cooperative, 21 Lake Drive, Roosevelt, NJ 08555, 609-448-5096
LUNCH, 220 Montross Ave, Rutherford, NJ 07070
ILLYRIAN REVUE, Kneechee Press, P.O. Box 450, Saddle Brook, NJ 07662
NEW JERSEY POETRY MONTHLY, New Jersey Poetry Press, P.O. Box 824, Saddle Brook, NJ 07662, 201-445-9436
de la Ree Publications, 7 Cedarwood Lane, Saddle River, NJ 07458
Poets & Writers of New Jersey, 2514 Tack Circle, Scotch Plains, NJ 07076
A DIFFERENT DRUMMER—THE POET'S JOURNAL, Addrummer Press Ltd., 18 Union St Rt, Toms Rvr., NJ 08753, 201-341-0835
AGAINST THE WALL, PO Box 444, Westfield, NJ 07091
NEW DIRECTIONS FOR WOMEN, New Directions For Women, Inc., 223 Old Hook Road, Westwood, NJ 07675, 201-666-4677

NEW MEXICO

BEST FRIENDS, Best Friends, 329 Montclaire NE, Albuquerque, NM 87108, 268-9105
THE BLACK CAT, Black Cat Books, PO Box 4926, Albuquerque, NM 87106
Black Cat Books, PO Box 4926, Albuquerque, NM 87106
BLACKBERRY, P.O. Box 4757, Albuquerque, NM 87106
BLAKE, AN ILLUSTRATED QUARTERLY, Dept. of English, Univ. of New Mexico, Albuquerque, NM 87131, 505-277-3103
DE COLORES, Pajarito Publications, 2633 Granite NW, Albuquerque, NM 87104
LA CONFLUENCIA, P.O. Box 409, Albuquerque, NM 87103
THE MARGARINE MAYPOLE ORANGOUTANG EXPRESS, Anonymous Owl Press, 3213 Wellesley, NE 2, Albuquerque, NM 87107
Packard Publications, 11521 Snow Heights N.E., Albuquerque, NM 87112, 505-293-5493
Red Earth Press, P.O. Box 26641, Albuquerque, NM 87125
SAN MARCOS REVIEW, San Marcos Press, P.O. Box 4368, Albuquerque, NM 87106
SEERS RIO GRANDE WEEKLY, New Mexico News Collective, P.O. Box 4940, Albuquerque, NM 87106, 505-247-1518
SUN CENTER NEWS, Sun Center, PO Box 4372, Albuquerque, NM 87106
Sun Publishing Co., P.O. Box 4383, Albuquerque, NM 87106, 505-255-6550
THE TRANSIENT, The Transientpress (TRANSKEN), Box 4662, Albuquerque, NM 87106
THE WORKBOOK, Southwest Research and Information Center, PO Box 4524, Albuquerque, NM 87106, 505-265-0461
A, A Press Ltd., Box 311, Laguna, NM 87026, 505-455-7692
A Press Ltd., Box 311, Laguna, NM 87026
All This & Less Publishers, Regents 509 NMSU, Las Cruces, NM 88003
PUERTO DEL SOL, Puerto Del Sol Press, Box 3E, Las Cruces, NM 88003, 505-646-3932
Puerto Del Sol Press, Box 3E, Las Cruces, NM 88003
STAR-WEB PAPER, All This & Less Publishers, Regents 509 NMSU, Las Cruces, NM 88003
YELLOW BUTTERFLY BROADSIDES, Box 3 BD, University Stn., Las Cruces, NM 88003
Duende Press, Box 571, Placitas, NM 87043
American-Canadian Publishers, Inc., Drawer 2078, Portales, NM 88130, 505-356-4082
TSA'ASZI', Box 356, Ramah, NM 87321
THE GREAT BLAFIGRIA IS/THE GREAT COMPASSION, Blafigria Press, PO Box 1054, Santa Fe, NM 87501
John Muir Publications, P.O. Box 613, Santa Fe, NM 87501, 505-982-1387
EL PALACIO, Museum of New Mexico Press, P.O. Box 2087, Santa Fe, NM 87503
Second Porcupine, PO Box 548, Santa Fe, NM 87501, 505-988-2995
THE SUNSTONE REVIEW, The Sunstone Press, PO Box 2321, Santa Fe, NM 87501, 505-988-4418
INDIAN HOUSE, Indian House, Box 472, Taos, NM 87571

NEW YORK

A SELECTED FEW/THE PEOPLE'S GALLERY, 206 Elm St, Albany, NY 12210
SPEAKOUT, P.O. Box 6165, Albany, NY 12206
Woolmer/Brotherson Ltd., Andes, NY 13731, 914-676-3218
THE LAMPETER MUSE, Lampeter Editions, Bard College, Annandale-On-Hudson, NY 12504

BEST POETS OF THE 20th CENTURY, Winston-Paramount Books, Drawer J, Babylon, NY 11702
NOTABLE AMERICAN POETS, Winston-Paramount Books, Box j, Babylon, NY 11702
SUNSHINE, J. Mark Press, Box J, Babylon, NY 11702
THE MIDATLANTIC REVIEW, P O Box 398, Baldwin Place, NY 10505
ONCE, The Country Press, P O Box 398, Baldwin Place, NY 10505
SOURCE, LAD (Literary Arts Div) of Queens Council on the Arts, c/o46-38 202 St., Bayside, NY 11361
GRAVIDA, Gravida, Ltd., Box 118, Bayville, NY 11709
GRUB STREET, Grub Street, P.O. Box 91, Bellmore, NY 11710, 212-733-3922
Bellevue Press, 60 Schubert St., Binghamton, NY 13905, 607-729-0819
BOUNDARY 2, State University of New York, Binghamton, NY 13901
Iris Press, 27 Chestnut St., Binghamton, NY 13905, 607-722-6679
Ishtar Press, Inc., Comparative Literature, State Univ of New York, Binghamton, NY 13901, 607-798-2319
PAINTBRUSH: A Journal of Poetry, Translations & Letters, Ishtar Press, Inc., Comparative Literature, State Univ of New York, Binghamton, NY 13901
CONTEMPORARY POETS, JOURNAL OF, Box 444, Brentwood, NY 11717
EXPRESSIVE ARTS REVIEW, Box 444, Brentwood, NY 11717
Boa Editions, 92 Park Avenue, Brockport, NY 14420, 716-637-3844
BLACK FORUM, Black Forum Magazine, PO Box 1090, Bronx, NY 10451
SUNBURY (a poetry magazine), Sunbury Press, Box 274 Jerome Ave Station, Bronx, NY 10468
WEST END MAGAZINE, Box 354, Jerome Ave. Station, Bronx, NY 10468
Erebus Press, 4 Merestone Terrace, Bronxville, NY 10708, 914-793-4663
THE GRACKLE: Improvised Music In Transition, The Grackle, Box 244 Vanderveer Station, Brookly, NY 11210
ALA/SRRT NEWSLETTER, ALA Social Responsibilities Round Table, 60 Remsen St, #10E, Brooklyn, NY 11201
ANTIQUE PHONOGRAPH MONTHLY, APM Press, 650 Ocean Ave., Brooklyn, NY 11226, 212-941-6835
APM Press, 650 Ocean Avenue, Brooklyn, NY 11226, 212-941-6835
Assembling Press, ASSEMBLING, Box 1967, Brooklyn, NY 11202
BITTERROOT, Blythbourne Station, P.O. Box 51, Brooklyn, NY 11219
BLANK TAPE, Permanent Press, Box 371, Brooklyn, NY 11230
THE BULLETIN BOARD, 190 East 21st St. 6D, Brooklyn, NY 11226
CLOWN WAR, Clown War Press, P.O. Box 1093, Brooklyn, NY 11202
CONDITIONS, Conditions, PO Box 56, Van Brunt Sta., Brooklyn, NY 11215, 212-857-5351/768-2453
CONFRONTATION, English Dept., Long Island University, Brooklyn, NY 11201
EAST RIVER REVIEW, Daniel Stokes, Publisher, 1807-60th St, Brooklyn, NY 11204
THE FEMINIST ART JOURNAL, The Feminist Art Journal, Inc., 41 Montgomery Place, Brooklyn, NY 11215
HANGING LOOSE, Hanging Loose Press, 231 Wyckoff St, Brooklyn, NY 11217
INCUS, 457 Avenue Y, Brooklyn, NY 11223, 214-375-5801
LIMIT! (The National Newsletter Of The Libertarian Republican Alliance), 1811 East 34th St, Brooklyn, NY 11234
Living Poets Press, 838 Carroll St., Brooklyn, NY 11215
MULCH, Mulch Press, 326A Fourth St., Brooklyn, NY 11215
THE NEW YORK CULTURE REVIEW, The New York Culture Review Press, 1807 60th St, Brooklyn, NY 11204
Out & Out Books, 476 Second St, Brooklyn, NY 11215, 212-499-9227
RELIX, PO Box 94, Brooklyn, NY 11229, 212-998-1100
Seagull Publications, 1736 East 53 Street, Brooklyn, NY 11234, 212-338-6622
SHANTIH, Box 125, Bay Ridge St., Brooklyn, NY 11220
613 MAGAZINE, Kol Hai, Inc., P.O. Box 168, Brooklyn, NY 11223
SNAKEROOTS, Liberal Arts & Sci, Pratt Inst., Brooklyn, NY 11205
THE SPICY MEATBALL, 75 Press, 236 Clinton St, Brooklyn, NY 11201
Starogubski Press, P.O. Box 46, GPO, Brooklyn, NY 11202
THE VOYEUR, Open Window Society Inc., 301 Hicks, Brooklyn, NY 11201
X Press Press, 524 Henry St., Brooklyn, NY 11231, 212-625-4245
Zonepress, PO Box 194, Bay Station, Brooklyn NYC, NY 11235, 212-625-2770
ZONE ONE, Zonepress, PO Box 194, Bay Station, Brooklyn, NYC, NY 11235, 212-625-2770
AFRO-AMERICANS in NEW YORK LIFE & HISTORY, The Afro-American Historical Association Of The Niagara Frontier, Inc., P.O. Box 1663, Buffalo, NY 14216
AUDIT/POETRY, Audit, 18 Allenhurst Rd, Buffalo, NY 14214
BEAU FLEUVE SERIES, Intrepid Press, P.O. Box 1423, Buffalo, NY 14214
BUCKLE, State Univ/1300 Elmwood Av, English Dept., Buffalo, NY 14222, 716-886-7033
THE CATHARTIC, 76 Hinman, Buffalo, NY 14216
Conch Magazine Ltd. (Publishers), 102 Normal Avenue, (Symphony Circle), Buffalo, NY 14213, 716-885-3686
CONCH MAGAZINE, Conch Magazine, Ltd., 102 Normal Avenue, Buffalo, NY 14213, 716-885-3686
CONCH REVIEW OF BOOKS, Conch Magazine, Ltd., 102 Normal Ave., Buffalo, NY 14213, 716-885-3686
EARTH'S DAUGHTERS, 944 Kensington Ave, Buffalo, NY 14215
THE HUMANIST, 923 Kensington Ave., Buffalo, NY 14215, 716-837-0306
INTREPID, Intrepid Press, P.O. Box 1423, Buffalo, NY 14214
Labor Arts Books, 1064 Amherst St., Buffalo, NY 14216, 716-873-4131
THE NIAGARA MAGAZINE, 369 Pennsylvania Street, Buffalo, NY 14201
PAUNCH, 123 Woodward Ave, Buffalo, NY 14214, 716-836-7532
THE STRAIT, 1300 Elmwood Ave, Buffalo, NY 14222
23 CLUB SERIES, Intrepid Press, P.O. Box 1423, Buffalo, NY 14214
WHITE PINE, White Pine Press, 109 Duerstein St., Buffalo, NY 14210, 716-825-8671
Ash Lad Press, P.O. Box 396, Canton, NY 13617, 315-386-8820
FICTION INTERNATIONAL, Dept. of English, St. Lawrence Univ., Canton, NY 13617

Sagarin Press, 26 High St, Chatham, NY 12037, 518-392-3094
Cherry Valley Editions, Box 303, Cherry Valley, NY 13320, 607-264-3204
NORTHEAST RISING SUN, Box 303, Cherry Valley, NY 13320, 607-264-3204
Nobodaddy Press, 20 College Hill Rd., Clinton, NY 13323, 315-853-6946
POETRY IN MOTION, Nobodaddy Press, 20 College Hill Rd., Clinton, NY 13323, 315-853-6946
Philatelic Directory Publishing Co, Box 150, Clinton Corners, NY 12514
THE PHILATELIC JOURNALIST, The Philatelic Directory, Box 150, Clinton Corners, NY 12514, 914-266-3150
NEW VOICES, P. O. Box 308, Clintondale, NY 12515
Grasshopper Press, P.O. Box 331, DeWitt, NY 13214
BIRD EFFORT, Bird Effort Press, 25 Mudford Avenue, Easthampton, NY 11937, 516-324-4156
A SHOUT IN THE STREET: a journal of literary and visual art, Queens College Press, English Dept. Queens College, Flushing, NY 11367, 212-520-7238
PULP, 46-48 Robinson St., Flushing, NY 11355
Queens College Press, Writers & Artists Series, English Dept, Queens College, Flushing, NY 11367, 212-520-7238
SOURCE, LAD (Literary Arts Div) of Queens Council on the Arts, 144-30 Roosevelt Ave., Flushing, NY 11354
Women's Studies, Dept. of English, Queens College, CUNY, Flushing, NY 11367
THE MODULARIST REVIEW, Wooden Needle Press, 65-45 Yellowstone Blvd., Forest Hills, NY 11375, 212-896-4103
SOFT STONE, An International Journal of the Arts, 102-40 62nd Avenue Apt 6C, Forest Hills, NY 11375
The Basilisk Press, P.O. Box 71, Fredonia, NY 14063
OBSIDIAN: BLACK LITERATURE IN REVIEW, 10 Georges Place, Fredonia, NY 14063, 716-672-2082
THOUGHTS FOR ALL SEASONS: The Magazine of Epigrams, Valley Press, State University College At Geneseo, Geneseo, NY 14454
Rialto Books, Box 343, Geneva, NY 14456
SENECA REVIEW, Hobart & William Smith Colleges, Geneva, NY 14456
COMBINATIONS, A JOURNAL OF PHOTOGRAPHY, Combinations Press, Middle Grove Road, Greenfield Center, NY 12833, 518-584-4612
THE GREENFIELD REVIEW, The Greenfield Review Press, P.O. Box 80, Greenfield Center, NY 12833, 518-584-1728
DRINKWATCHERS' NEWSLETTER, Gullistan Press, PO Box 179, Haverstraw, NY 10927, 914-429-4844
Gullistan Press, P.O. Box 179, Haverstraw, NY 10927, 914-429-4844
JOURNAL OF WORLD EDUCATION, 3 Harbor Hill Dr, Huntington, NY 11743, 516-427-0723
BONES, White Bones Press, Box 333, Islip, NY 11751
Court Street Chap-Book Series, 114 West Court Street, Ithaca, NY 14850, 607-273-0509
EPOCH, 251 Goldwin Smith Hall, Cornell Univ., Ithaca, NY 14850
Ithaca House, 108 N. Plain St, Ithaca, NY 14850, 607-272-1233
STINKTREE, Stinktree Press, 130 Sears Street, Ithaca, NY 14850
Stinktree Press, 130 Sears St., Ithaca, NY 14850
ALIVE & KICKING!, 35-50 85th St., Jackson Heights, NY 11372, 212-HA6-8788
BRAVADO, Bravado Feature Service/BFS Press, 37-40 75th St., Jackson Heights, NY 11372
J&C Transcripts, Box 15, Kanona, NY 14856
STONE MOUNTAIN REVIEW, 857 N. Broadway, Massapequa, NY 11758
WOMANSMITH, Womansmith, 243 N. Idaho Ave., Massapequa, NY 11758
POESIE - U.S.A., P O Box 811, Melville, NY 11746, 516-549-3438
Porphyrion Press, 4053 Middle Grove Road, Middle Grove, NY 12850, 518-587-9809
Library Research Associates, Dunderberg Road, Monroe, NY 10950, 914-783-1144
COLLABORATION, Matagiri, Matagiri, Mt. Tremper, NY 12457
ALL-TIME FAVORITE POETRY, J. Mark Press, Box 2057, N. Babylon, NY 11703
BEST IN POETRY, J. Mark Press, Box 2057, N. Babylon, NY 11703
NATIONAL BOOK REVIEW, J. Mark Press, Box 2057, N. Babylon, NY 11703
POETIPS, J. Mark Press, Box 2057, N. Babylon, NY 11703
THE JOURNAL of PSYCHOHISTORY, Psychohistory Press, 2315 Broadway, NY, NY 10024
The Elizabeth Press, 103 Van Etten Blvd, New Rochelle, NY 10804
Lawton Press, 230 Pelham Road 5P, New Rochelle, NY 10805, 914-576-1435
ACA REPORTS, 570 Seventh Ave., 1546 Broadway #820, New York, NY 10018, 212-354-6655
AIS EIRI, 553 W. 51st St., New York, NY 10019, 212-757-3318
ALGOL: The Magazine About Science Fiction, Algol Press, P.O. Box 4175, New York, NY 10017, 212-643-9011
Algol Press, P.O. Box 4175, New York, NY 10017, 212-643-9011
Allonge Press, 215 Thompson St No. 13, New York, NY 10011, 212-868-3330
Amen-Ra Publishing Co, P.O. Box 481, New York, NY 10462, 212-824-3122
AMERICAN DANCE GUILD NEWSLETTER, American Dance Guild, Inc. (see also DANCE SCOPE), 1619 Broadway, Rm. 603, New York, NY 10019
ANTAEUS, The Ecco Press, 1 West 30th St., New York, NY 10001, 212-736-2599
APHRA, Box 893 Ansonia Station, New York, NY 10023
AQUARIAN AGENT-ASTROLOGY 77 (78), ASI, 127 Madison Ave, New York, NY 10016, 212-679-5676
AREITO, PO Box 1124, New York, NY 10009
ART AND ARCHAEOLOGY NEWSLETTER, Otto F. Reiss, Publisher, 243 East 39th Street, New York, NY 10016
ASI, 127 Madison Ave., New York, NY 10016, 212-679-5676
ASI Publishers, Inc., 127 Madison Ave, New York, NY 10016, 212-679-5676
ASTROLOGY '77 — The New Aquarian Agent, ASI Publishers, Inc., 127 Madison Ave, New York, NY 10016, 212-679-5676
Asylum's Press, 464 Amsterdam Ave, New York, NY 10024, 212-799-4475
AVALANCHE, Center for New Art Activities Inc, 93 Grand Street, New York, NY 10013
AZU-THE INFINITE MAN, Azu Press, Equus Publishers, 146 West 29th St, New York, NY 10001, 212-947-0528
AZU Press, 146 West 29th St, New York, NY 10001, 212-947-0528
Basement Workshop, Inc., 199 Lafayette St., New York, NY 10012

BIG DEAL, Big Deal Press, P.O. Box 830, Peter Stuyvesant Sta., New York, NY 10009
BLEB, Bleb Press, Box 322 Times Square Station, New York, NY 10036, 612-339-5162
BOOK ARTS, The Center for Book Arts, 15 Bleeker St, New York, NY 10012
BOPP, Ayanna Press, 542 W. 112 No. 5-f, New York, NY 10025, 749-7544
BOSS, Boss Books, Box 370, Madison Square Station, New York, NY 10010
BOX 749, Seven Square Press of The Printable Arts Society, Inc., Box 749, Old Chelsea Station, New York, NY 10011
BRIDGE MAGAZINE, 199 Lafayette St. 7th fl., New York, NY 10012
Brownstone Publishers, Inc., 360 Lexington Avenue, New York, NY 10017
CANTO LIBRE-A Bilingual Quarterly of Latin American Peoples Art, Center for Cuban Studies, 220 East 23rd St, New York, NY 10010
Center For Cuban Studies, 220 East 23rd St, New York, NY 10010
CENTER NEWSLETTER, Center for Cuban Studies, 220 East 23rd St., New York, NY 10010
THE CHARIOTEER, Parnassos, Greek Cultural Society Of New York, PO Box 2928, Grand Central Station, New York, NY 10017
CHELSEA, Box 5880, Grand Central Station, New York, NY 10017
CINEASTE MAGAZINE, 333 Sixth Ave, New York, NY 10014
CITY 4, Faculty Press, 152 Finley Hall, CCNY 138 St & Convent Ave, New York, NY 10031
THE CITY MOON, The City Moon, PO Box 842, Canal St. Station, New York, NY 10013, 212-674-0288
The City Moon, PO Box 842, Canal St. Station, New York, NY 10013, 212-674-0288
Clearwater Publishing Company, Inc., 75 Rockefeller Plaza, New York, NY 10019
CODA: Poets & Writers Newsletter, Poets & Writers, Inc., 201 West 54th St., New York, NY 10019
CONTACT/11: A Bimonthly Poetry Review Magazine, Contact/11 Publications, 11 Broadway, New York, NY 10004, 212-425-5979
CONTEMPORARY POETS, 100 Sullivan St., New York, NY 10012
COPY CORNUCOPIA, The Direct Marketing Writers Guild, 516 Fifth Avenue, New York, NY 10016
COUNCIL ON INTERRACIAL BOOKS FOR CHILDREN BULLETIN, 1841 Broadway, New York, NY 10023, 212-757-5339
THE CRISIS, Crisis Publishing Company, Inc., 1790 Broadway, New York, NY 10019
CROSSROADS QUARTERLY, Suncat Enterprises, 1471 Second Avenue Apt. 19, New York, NY 10021
DANCE HERALD, Dance Herald Press, 243 West 63st, New York, NY 10023
DANCE SCOPE, American Dance Guild, Inc., 1619 Broadway, Rm. 603, New York, NY 10019
Daughters Publishing Co., Inc., 22 Charles St., New York, NY 10014, 212-243-8252
DIAL-A-POEM POETS LP'S, Giorno Poetry Systems Records, 222 Bowery, New York, NY 10012, 212-925-6372
Dovetail Press, 427 West 113th Street, New York, NY 10025
THE DRAMA REVIEW, 51 West 4th St. Room 300, New York, NY 10012, 212-598-2597
DRAMATIKA, Dramatika Produce, 390 Riverside Dr., New York, NY 10025
Dramatika Produce, 390 Riverside Dr., New York, NY 10025
EAR MAGAZINE, Ear, 32 East Second St., apt 22, New York, NY 10003
EDDY, Eddy Dance Foundation, Inc., 124 Chambers St, New York, NY 10007, 212-962-1327
ENDYMION, 562 W. End Ave Apt 6A, New York, NY 10024
Equal Time Press, 463 West St. Apt D 1016, New York, NY 10014
Equus Publishers, 146 West 29th St., New York, NY 10001
EUROPEAN JUDAISM, UAHC, European Judaism, 838 5th Ave, New York, NY 10021
FICTION, Fiction, Inc., Box 112 Stuyvesant Station, New York, NY 10009
FIGHTING WOMAN NEWS, 9 East 48th St, New York, NY 10017, 212-868-3330
FILM CULTURE, Film Culture Non-Profit Inc., G. P. O. Box 1499, New York, NY 10001
Film Culture Non-Profit, Inc., G. P. O. Box 1499, New York, NY 10001
FILM LIBRARY QUARTERLY, Box 348, Radio City Station, New York, NY 10019
Free Life Editions, 41 Union Square West, New York, NY 10003, 212-989-3750
FREEDOMWAYS, Freedomways Associates, Inc., 799 Broadway, Suite 542, New York, NY 10003
The Future Press, P.O. Box 73, Canal St., New York, NY 10013
GEGENSCHEIN QUARTERLY, NeoNeo Do-Do, 291-293 7th Ave, 10th Floor, New York, NY 10001
GRANTS AND AWARDS AVAILABLE TO AMERICAN WRITERS, P.E.N. American Center, 156 Fifth Ave, New York, NY 10010
GUARDIAN, Weekly Guardian Associates, 33 W 17th St, New York, NY 10011, 212-691-0404
HEALTH/PAC BULLETIN, 17 Murray Street, New York, NY 10007
HERESIES: A FEMINIST PUBLICATION ON ART AND POLITICS, Heresies Collective, PO Box 766 Canal St. Station, New York, NY 10013
Ilkon Press, 210 Riverside Drive No. 6G, New York, NY 10025, 212-663-2579
INTERCONTINENTAL PRESS, P.O. Box 116, Varick Street Station, New York, NY 10014
Interim Books, Box 35, Village Station, New York, NY 10014
International Publishers Co., Inc., 381 Park Ave. South, New York, NY 10016
INTERNATIONAL SOCIALIST REVIEW, 14 Charles Lane, New York, NY 10014
Kulchur Foundation, 888 Park Ave., New York, NY 10021, 988-5193
THE LITTLE MAGAZINE, Box 207 Cathedral Station, New York, NY 10025
MAJORITY REPORT, 74 Grove St, New York, NY 10014, 212-691-4950
THE MILITANT, 14 Charles Lane, New York, NY 10014, 212-929-3486
MINUTES & PROCEEDINGS, Haiku Society of America, Inc., 333 East 47th St., New York, NY 10017
Monad Press, 410 West Street, New York, NY 10014
MONTEMORA, The Montemora Foundation, Box 336, Cooper Station, New York, NY 10003, 212-255-2733
MOUTH OF THE DRAGON, Box 107, New York, NY 10003
THE MYSTERIOUS BARRICADES, Rainbow Press, 1332 Riverside Drive, New York, NY 10033, 212-928-8108
THE NEW EARTH REVIEW, New Earth Books, 58 St. Marks Pl, New York, NY 10003
NEW POLITICS, 507 Fifth Ave, New York, NY 10017
THE NEW QUARTERLY, World University Service, World University Service, 20 West 40th St, New York, NY 10018
New Rivers Press, Inc., PO Box 578, Cathedral Sta., New York, NY 10025

NEW YORK ARTS JOURNAL, 560 Riverside Drive, New York, NY 10024
O Press, 138 Sullivan St, New York, NY 10012
O. O. L. P. (Out of London Press), 12 West 17th St, New York, NY 10011
PARNASSUS: POETRY IN REVIEW, 205 West 89th Street, New York, NY 10024, (212) 787-3569
Pathfinder Press, Inc, 410 West Street, New York, NY 10014
PEDESTRIAN RESEARCH, 170 Broadway, Rm 201, New York, NY 10038
PEQUOD, Poetry, 282 W. 4th St., New York, NY 10014
PERFORMING ARTS JOURNAL, P.O. Box 858, Peterstuyvesant Station, New York, NY 10009, 212-260-7586
Permanent Press, 1040 Park Avenue, New York, NY 10028
Poet Gallery Press, 224 West 29th St, New York, NY 10001
THE POETIC HARDWARE PRESS, 1815 Riverside Drive 4k, New York, NY 10034, 212-942-4692
THE POETRY MAILING LIST, The Poetry Mailing List, 77 Franklin St., New York, NY 10013, 212-442-8432
Poets & Writers, Inc., 201 West 54th Street, New York, NY 10019, 212-757-1766
Rainbow Press, 1332 Riverside Drive, New York, NY 10033, 212-928-8108
RE:PRINT (AN OCCASIONAL MAGAZINE), Seven Square Press of the Printable Arts Society, Inc., c/o BOX 749, Box 749 Old Chelsea Station, New York, NY 10011
Red Dust, 218 E. 81st St, New York, NY 10028
Release Press, 309 W. 104 St. Apt. 9D, New York, NY 10025
ROOF, 300 Bowery, c/o Sherry, New York, NY 10012, 212-677-7911
Seven Woods Press, P.O. Box 32, Village Station, New York, NY 10014
SING OUT! The Folk Song Magazine, 270 Lafayette Street, New York, NY 10001
SLIT WRIST, Slit Wrist, 333 East 30 St., New York, NY 10016, MU-9-8768
THE SMITH, The Generalist Assn., Inc., 5 Beekman St., New York, NY 10038
Smyrna Press, Box 841, New York, NY 10009
SOCIAL POLICY, 184 Fifth Avenue, New York, NY 10010, 212-989-5280
SOME, Release Press, 309 W. 104 St. Apt. 9D, New York, NY 10025
Stock Poetry, 630 E. 14 St. No. 3, New York, NY 10009, 212-673-0781
Strawberry Press, 11 Broadway, Room 933, New York, NY 10004, 212-425-5979
THE STRUGGLE, United Struggle Press, 175 Fifth Avenue, New York, NY 10010, 212-677-6868
SUN, 456 Riverside Drive-5B, New York, NY 10027
SZ/Press, P.O. Box 383, Cathedral Station, New York, NY 10025
Teachers and Writers, 186 West 4th Street, New York, NY 10014, 212-691-6590
TEACHERS AND WRITERS MAGAZINE, Teachers and Writers Press, 186 West 4th Street, New York, NY 10014, 212-691-6590
Telephone Books, Box 672, Old Chelsea Sta, New York, NY 10011
Ten Penny Players, Inc., 799 Greenwich Street, New York, NY 10014, 212-929-3169
THE THIRD PRESS REVIEW, The Third Press (Joseph Okpaku Publishing Co. Inc.), 444 Central Park West, New York, NY 10025
13th MOON, 13th Moon, Inc., P.O. Box 3, Inwood Station, New York, NY 10034, 212-942-6761
TRACKS, A Journal of Artists' Writings, P.O. Box 557, Old Chelsea Station, New York, NY 10011
TRANSLATION, 307A Mathematics, Columbia University, New York,,NY 10027, 212-280-2305
TROUSER PRESS, Trans-Oceanic Trouser Press, Inc., 147 W. 42nd St, New York, NY 10036, 212-354-4376
Tvrt Press-Viper's Tongue Books, 25 East Fourth Street, New York, NY 10003
USITT NEWSLETTER, 1501 Broadway, Room 1408, New York, NY 10036, 212-354-5360
THE U*N*A*B*A*S*H*E*D LIBRARIAN, THE "HOW I RUN MY LIBRARY GOOD" LETTER, G.P.O. Box 2631, New York, NY 10001
UNDINE, Renaissance Press, 244 Fifth Ave., New York, NY 10001
Violet Press, PO Box 398, New York, NY 10009
WALUNA, THE SOHO WEEKLY, Walloon Street Press, 72 Wooster St, New York, NY 10012
WIA NEWSLETTER, Women in the Arts Foundation, Inc., 435 Broome St, New York, NY 10013, 212-966-5894
WITCHCRAFT DIGEST MAGAZINE (THE WICA NEWSLETTER), Hero Press, Suite 1B, 153 West 80th St., New York, NY 10024
Zartscorp, Inc. Books, 267 West 89th Street, New York, NY 10024, 724-5071
ARARAT, 628 Second Ave, New York City, NY 10016
Foundations for the Redefinition of Sanity, 463 West St. Apt 318C, New York City, NY 10014, 212-929-3833
GAYELLOW PAGES, Renaissance House, box 292 Village Station, New York City, NY 10014
Hearsay Press, 115 West Broadway, New York City, NY 10013, (212) 349-4234
Helikon Press, 120 West 71st Street, New York City, NY 10023
THE HUDSON REVIEW, The Hudson Review, Inc., 65 East 55th St., New York City, NY 10022, 212-755-9040
Lava Mt, 235 W 76th St, New York City, NY 10023, 874-3631
LIGHT, P.O. Box 1105 Stuyvesant, New York City, NY 10009
New Earth Books, 58 St. Marks Pl., New York City, NY 10003, 212-673-1682
POINT OF CONTACT/PUNTO DE CONTACTO, 110 Bleecker St. 16B, New York City, NY 10012, 212-260-6346
PULP, 720 Greenwich St. Apt 4H, New York City, NY 10014
TELEPHONE, Telephone Books, Box 218 Village Station, New York City, NY 10014, 212-255-1723
Two-Eighteen Press, P. O. Box 218 Village Station, New York City, NY 10014, 212-255-1723
UNMUZZLED OX, Box 840, Canal St. Station, New York City, NY 10013
Women Artists Newsletter (Press), Box 3304, Grand Central, New York City, NY 10017, 212-682-4716
WOMEN ARTISTS NEWSLETTER, Women Artists Newsletter (Press), 3304 Grand Central Sta, New York City, NY 10017, 212-682-4716
CENTERGRAM, Centergram Press, 401 N Plank Rd, Newburgh, NY 12550
Centergram Press, 401 N Plank Rd, Newburgh, NY 12550
Women Writing Press, Rd 3, Newfield, NY 14867
The Feminist Press, Box 334, Old Westbury, NY 11568
WOMEN'S STUDIES NEWSLETTER, The Feminist Press, Box 334, Old Westbury, NY 11568, 516-997-7660

Allegany Mountain Press, 111 N. 10th St., Olean, NY 14760, 716-372-0935
UROBOROS (was ALLEGANY POETRY), Allegany Mountain Press, 111 N. 10th St., Olean, NY 14760, 716-372-0935
Swamp Press, 300 Main St, Oneonta, NY 13820
TIGHTROPE, Swamp Press, 300 Main St., Oneonta, NY 13820
First Person, Washington Springs Rd, Palisades, NY 10964
STREET CRIES, 33 Edi Ave., Plainview, NY 11803
STREET MAGAZINE, Street Press, Box 555, Port Jefferson, NY 11777
SOLAR AGE, 200 East Main Street, Port Jervis, NY 12771, 914-856-6633
WIN MAGAZINE, Box 547, Rifton, NY 12471
Winbooks, Box 547, Rifton, NY 12471
EXIT, Rochester Routes/Creative Arts Projects, 50 Inglewood Drive, Rochester, NY 14619, 271-8552
Golden Atom Publications, P.O. Box 1101, Rochester, NY 14603
VANDERBILT POETRY REVIEW, Vanderbilt University Press, c/o Rochester Routes, 50 Inglewood Drive, Rochester, NY 14619
WRITERS INK, Writer Unlimited Agency, Inc., RR 3, Box 147-A, Rocky Point L.I., NY 11778, 516-744-6160
AKWESASNE NOTES, Mohawk Nation, Rooseveltown, NY 13683
WOMEN STUDIES ABSTRACTS, J and J Printing, PO Box 1, Rush, NY 14543
SALMAGUNDI, Salmagundi, Skidmore College, Saratoga Springs, NY 12866, 518-584-5000 (ext 302)
WASHOUT REVIEW, Washout Publishing Co., PO Box 2752, Schenectady, NY 12309
LONG POND REVIEW, English Dept, Suffolk Community College, Selden Long Island, NY 11784
Scotty Macgreger Publications, 10 Pineacre Dr., Smithtown, NY 11787
GRANITE, Granite Publications, Box 1367, Southampton, NY 11968
GLASSWORKS, Glassworks Press, PO Box 163, Rosebank sta, Staten Island, NY 10305
THE MARKHAM REVIEW, Horrmann Library, Wagner College, Staten Island, NY 10301
THE ANTIQUER, 318 Highland Ave, Syracuse, NY 13203
THE BITTER OLEANDER, The Bitter Oleander Press, 310 Bradford Parkway, Syracuse, NY 13224
CONSTRUCTIVE ACTION FOR GOOD HEALTH, The American Conference of Therapeutic Selfhelp/Selfhealth/Social Clubs (ACT), B 1104 Ross Towers, 710 Lodi St., Syracuse, NY 13203, 315-471-4644
ONE SHOT DEAL, Pulpart Forms Unltd., 1530 East Genesee St., Syracuse, NY 13210
SYRACUSE Guide, 500 S. Warren St., Syracuse, NY 13202, 315-472-4541
Tideline Press, P.O. Box 786, Tannersville, NY 12485
Sleepy Hollow Restorations, Box 245, Tarrytown, NY 10591, 914-631-8200
The Crossing Press, R.D. 3, Trumansburg, NY 14886, 607-387-6217
INTERFACE JOURNAL: Alternatives in Higher Education, Interface, P.O. Box 970, Utica, NY 13503
NEWSLETTER, Long Island Poetry Collective, Inc, 2441 Riverside Drive, Wantagh, NY 11793, 516-826-8724
Pleasure Dome Press (Long Island Poetry Collective Inc.), 2441 Riverside Drive, Wantagh, NY 11793, 516-826-8724
XANADU, Pleasure Dome Press, 1704 Auburn Road, Wantagh, NY 11793, 516-826-4964
TIME BARRIER EXPRESS, PO Box 1109, White Plains, NY 10602, 914-793-2649
THIRD EYE, 250 Mill St., Williamsville, NY 14221
Cross Country Press, Ltd., PO Box 21081, Woodhaven, NY 11421, 212-896-7648
CROSSCOUNTRY, Cross Country Press, Ltd., PO Box 21081, Woodhaven, NY 11421, 212-896-7648
ATHAENA, 2 Sadore Lane, Yonkers, NY 10710
Pushcart Press, P.O. Box 845, Yonkers, NY 10701

NORTH CAROLINA

UNAKA RANGE, Rt. 1-Box 58A, Bryson City, NC 28713
The Carolina Wren Press, P O Box 209, Carrboro, NC 27510, 919-967-8666
CAROLINA QUARTERLY, PO Box 1117, Chapel Hill, NC 27514, 919-933-0244
CHANGE, 1825 North Lake Shore Dr, Chapel Hill, NC 27514, 919-942-2994
HYPERION A Poetry Journal, Thorp Springs Press, Subs: 2-D Chase Park, Chapel Hill, NC 27514
SOUTHERN EXPOSURE, Institute for Southern Studies, P.O. Box 230, Chapel Hill, NC 27514
THE SUN, NORTH CAROLINA'S MAGAZINE OF IDEAS, PO Box 732, 412 W. Rosemary St, Chapel Hill, NC 27514, 942-5282
The New South Company, P.O. Box 3891, Dilworth Station, Charlotte, NC 28203, 704-334-3440
Red Clay Books, 6366 Sharon Hills Rd, Charlotte, NC 28210, 704-366-9624
SINISTER WISDOM, 3116 Country Club Dr, Charlotte, NC 28205, 704-377-0333
AFRICA NEWS, Africa News Service, Inc., P.O. Box 3851, Durham, NC 27702, 919-286-3910
AMERICAN LITERATURE, Duke University Press, 6667 College Station, Durham, NC 27708
UNICORN JOURNAL, Unicorn Press, P.O. Box 3307, Greensboro, NC 27402
TAR RIVER POETS, East Carolina University Poetry Forum Press, Department of English, East Carolina University, Greenville, NC 27834
THE MOTHER EARTH NEWS, PO Box 70, Hendersonville, NC 28739
Mole Press, C/O English Program, St. Andrews College, Laurinburg, NC 28352
SAINT ANDREWS REVIEW, St. Andrews College, Laurinburg, NC 28352, 919-276-3652
PEMBROKE MAGAZINE, P.O. Box 756, Pembroke, NC 28372
THE NORTH CAROLINA REVIEW, The N. C. Review Press, 3329 Granville Dr., Raleigh, NC 27609
SOUTHERN POETRY REVIEW, Dept. of English, North Carolina State Univ., Raleigh, NC 27607
SPEAK 2, Speak 2 Press, 211B South 2nd Street, Wilmington, NC 28401
The Jackpine Press, 3381 Timberlake Lane, Winston-Salem, NC 21706

NORTH DAKOTA

THE DICKINSON REVIEW, Div. of English, Dickinson State College, Dickinson, ND 58601
BLOODROOT, 316 Harvard St, Grand Forks, ND 58201, 701-777-4300

NORTH COUNTRY, Dept English, U. of N.D., Grand Forks, ND 58201

OHIO

BACK DOOR, P.O. Box 481, Athens, OH 45701
Croissant & Company, Route 1, Box 51, Athens, OH 45701, 614-593-8339
THE OHIO REVIEW, Ellis Hall, Ohio University, Athens, OH 45701, 614-594-5889
The Rosetta Press, P O Box 771, Athens, OH 45701, 614-592-4822
STARDANCER, Stardance Publications, P.O. Box 128, Athens, OH 45701
BETELGEUSE CHAPBOOK SERIES/NEWEDI FICTION SERIES, Newedi Press, Dept. of English, Bowling Green University, Bowling Green, OH 43403
BLACK BOOK, ,Dept. of English, Bowling Green State Univ., Bowling Green, OH 43403
THE GREEN HORSE FOR POETRY, The Green Horse Press, c/oCreative Writing Program, Bowling Green Univ., Bowling Green, OH 43403
MEASURE, The Tribal Press, P.O. Box 161, Bowling Green, OH 43402
Newedi Press, Dept. of English, Bowling Green University, Bowling Green, OH 43403
BOOK REPORT, Book Report, P.O. Box 266, Campbell, OH 44405
J'ADOUBE!, Cincinnati Chess Federation, P O Box 30072, Cincinnati, OH 45230, 513-232-3204
SYZYGY-A Journal of Fiction and Sketches, Cincinnati Women's Press, 3901 Ledgewood Dr., Cincinnati, OH 45229
WATERS, More Waters, PO Box 19341, Cincinnati, OH 45219, 513-861-5528
BITS, Bits Press, c/o Dept of English, Case Western Reserve University, Cleveland, OH 44106, 216-368-2359
Cleveland State Univ. Poetry Center, Dept English, Cleveland State Univ, Cleveland, OH 44115, 216-687-3986
DARK TOWER, University Center Rm. 7, Cleveland State University, Cleveland, OH 44115
Deciduous, 4208½ Whitman Avenue, Cleveland, OH 44113, 216-631-1454
FREE LANCE, A Magazine of Poetry & Prose, 6005 Grand Ave., Cleveland, OH 44104
POETS' LEAGUE of GREATER CLEVELAND NEWSLETTER, League Books, PO Box 6055, Cleveland, OH 44101
FIREWEED, Fireweed Press, Box 9888, Columbus, OH 43206, 614-262-3395
Fireweed Press, Box 9888, Columbus, OH 43206, 614-262-3395
LOST AND FOUND TIMES, Luna Bisonte Prods, Casa Del Sensitive, 137 Leland Ave, Columbus, OH 43214
LOST AND FOUND TIMES, Luna Bisonte Prods, Casa Del Sensitive, 118 E. Longview, Columbus, OH 43202
Luna Bisonte Prods, 137 Leland Ave, Columbus, OH 43214
OHIOANA QUARTERLY, 1105 Ohio Dept Bldg., 65 S. Front St, Columbus, OH 43215, 614-466-3831
STARWIND, The Starwind Press, Box 3346, Columbus, OH 43210
UNDER THE SIGN OF PISCES: Anais Nin and Her Circle, The Ohio State University Libraries Publications Committee, 1858 Neil Avenue Mall, Columbus, OH 43210
Challenge Press, C/O Economic Research Center, Inc., 32 College St., Dayton, OH 45407, 513-275-8637
CONFRONTATION/CHANGE REVIEW, Challenge Press, 32 College St., Dayton, OH 45407, 513-275-8637
FILM HERITAGE, University of Dayton, Box 652, University of Dayton, Dayton, OH 45469
IMAGES, English Dept, Wright State Univ., Dayton, OH 45435
NEXUS, Wright State University, Dayton, OH 45431, 513-873-2782
HAND BOOK, C/O Mernit, 72 Spring St., Delaware, OH 43015
HAND BOOK, 72 Spring St, Delaware, OH 43015
HIRAM POETRY REVIEW, Box 162, Hiram, OH 44234, 216-569-3211
Cambric Press, 912 Strowbridge Dr., Huron, OH 44839, 419-433-4221
FIRELANDS ARTS REVIEW, Cambric Press, Firelands Campus, Huron, OH 44839, 419-433-4221
THE NEW KENT QUARTERLY, Quarterly Press, 239 Student Center, Kent State University, Kent, OH 44240, 216-672-7951
SHELLY'S, Engine Press, 501 Franklin St, Kent, OH 44240
SCHISM: A Journal of Divergent American Opinion, Schism Publishing Company, 3 West Highland Court, Mount Vernon, OH 43050, 614-392-8586
Veritie Press, Inc., PO Box 222, Novelty, OH 44072
FIELD, Rice Hall, Oberlin College, Oberlin, OH 44074
POCKET PAL, The Pocket Pal Press, 131 E. College Street, Oberlin, OH 44074, 216-774-5548
The Pocket Pal Press, 131 E. College Street, Oberlin, OH 44074, 216-774-5548
OCCULT AMERICANA, Box 667, Painesville, OH 44077
Carpenter Press, Route 4, Pomeroy, OH 45769, 614-992-7520
THE NEW INFINITY REVIEW, P.O. Box 554, South Point, OH 45680, 614-377-4182
Armchair Press, P.O. Box 393, Tiffin, OH 44883, 419-447-4167
BROADSIDE, Armchair Press, P.O. Box 393, Tiffin, OH 44883, 419-447-4167
WRITERS IN RESIDENCE, Armchair Press, P.O. Box 393, Tiffin, OH 44883, 419-447-4167
Interface Unlimited, P.O. Box 8583, Toledo, OH 43623
Fantome Press, 720 North Park Avenue, Warren, OH 44483
THE ANTIOCH REVIEW, The Antioch Review, Inc., PO Box 148, Yellow Springs, OH 45387, 513-767-7386
COMMUNITY SERVICE NEWSLETTER- in serial with: COMMUNITY COMMENTS, Community Service, Inc., Box 243, Yellow Springs, OH 45387
PIGIRON, Pigiron Press, P.O. Box 237, Youngstown, OH 44501, 216-744-2258

OKLAHOMA

Open Window Books, P.O. Box 949, Chickasha, OK 73018, 405-224-3217
GENRE, University of Oklahoma, Dept. of English 760 Van Vleet Oval, Norman, OK 73069
Cedar Creek Press, P.O. Box 1051, Stillwater, OK 74074
CIMARRON REVIEW, Okla. State University Press, Oklahoma State University, Stillwater, OK 74074

JAMES JOYCE QUARTERLY, University of Tulsa, 600 S. College, Tulsa, OK 74104
NIMROD, University of Tulsa, Nimrod University of Tulsa, 600 S. College, Tulsa, OK 74104

OREGON

MARKET FOR LIBERTY, 1903 E. 38th, Albany, OR 97321
NRG, 30½ Dewey No. 4, Ashland, OR 97520
FLEA MARKET QUARTERLY ALMANAC, Maverick Publications, Box 243, Bend, OR 97701
CALYX, Calyx, A Northwest Feminist Review, Route 2, Box 118, Corvallis, OR 97330, 503-753-8891
THE TOWN FORUM JOURNAL & COMMUNITY REPORT, The Town Forum, Inc., Cerro Gordo Ranch, Dorena Lake, Cottage Grove, OR 97424, 503-942-7720
Cascade Farm Enterprises, Route 1, Box 259, Estacada, OR 97023, 503-630-4690
EDCENTRIC MAGAZINE, Center for Educational Reform, Inc., PO Box 1802, Eugene, OR 97401
THE INSURGENT SOCIOLOGIST, c/o Department of Sociology, Univ. of Oregon, Eugene, OR 97403
Northwest Matrix, 1628 E. 19th, Eugene, OR 97403, 503-687-8660
NORTHWEST REVIEW, University of Oregon Press, 369 P.L.C., University of Oregon, Eugene, OR 97405, 503-686-3957
10 POINT 5, A Magazine of the Arts, Oz Publications, Inc., 1035401/2 Ferry St., Eugene, OR 97401
Urion Press, Box 2244, Eugene, OR 97402
WILLAMETTE VALLEY OBSERVER, 1065 High St., Eugene, OR 97401, 503-687-0376
MR. COGITO, Box 627, Pacific Univ., Forest Grove, OR 97116
SERIATIM: A Journal of Ecotopia, Communities, PO Box 117, McMinnville, OR 97128
Shinn Music Aids, PO Box 192, Medford, OR 97501, 664-2317
SPIT IN THE OCEAN, Intrepid Trips Information Service, 85829 Ridgeway Rd, Pleasant Hill, OR 97401
CIRCLE, Circle Forum, P.O. Box 176, Portland, OR 97207
DRAGONFLY:A Quarterly Of Haiku, J & C Transcripts, 4102 N.E. 130th Pl., Portland, OR 97230
GLASS, The Evergreen Publishing Corporation, 7830 S.W. 40th Avenue, Portland, OR 97219, 503-245-4444
THE MISSISSIPPI MUD, Mud Press, 3125 S.E. Van Water, Portland, OR 97202
MR. COGITO, John Gogol, 8744 SE Rural, Portland, OR 97226
ONE DOLLAR, One Dollar Publishing, 919 SW Taylor #706, Portland, OR 97205
Oregon Historical Society, 1230 S.W. Park Avenue, Portland, OR 97205, 503-222-1741
OREGON TIMES MAGAZINE, New Oregon Publishers, Inc., 1000 SW 3rd, Portland, OR 97204
Out of the Ashes Press, P.O. Box 42384, Portland, OR 97242
PORTLAND REVIEW, P.O. Box 751, Portland, OR 97207
Prescott Street Press, 407 Postal Building, Portland, OR 97204
RAIN: JOURNAL OF APPROPRIATE TECHNOLOGY, The Rain Umbrella, 2270 NW Irving Street, Portland, OR 97210, 503-227-5110
Old Time Bottle Publishing Company, 611 Lancaster Dr. N.E., Salem, OR 97301
Rumba Train Press, 4497 Barrett Street S., Salem, OR 97302, 399-1640
New Woman Press, Box 56, Wolf Creek, OR 97497
RFD, 4525 Lower Wolf Creek Rd, Wolf Creek, OR 97497
WOMAN SPIRIT, Box 263, Wolf Creek, OR 97497

PENNSYLVANIA

Kurios Press, 743 Woodleave Rd./Box 946, Bryn Mawr, PA 19010, 215-527-4635
THE UNSPEAKABLE VISIONS OF THE INDIVIDUAL, TUVOTI Books, PO Box 439, California, PA 15419
ANIMA, Conococheague Associates, Inc., 1053 Wilson Avenue, Chambersburg, PA 17201
JOHN BERRYMAN STUDIES, Rook Press, Inc., 805 West First Avenue, Derry, PA 15627
Rook Press, Inc., 805 West First Avenue, Derry, PA 15627
X, A JOURNAL Of The ARTS, X Press, P.O. Box 2648, Harrisburg, PA 17105
VEGETARIAN HEALTH REVIEW AND DIGEST, Vegetus Publications, Box 221, Haverford, PA 19041
COMPASS, RD 1 Box 584, Honey Brook, PA 19344
CLASSIC FILM COLLECTOR, 734 Philadelphia St, Indiana, PA 15701
Outland Press, Lewisville, PA 19351
THE FALCON, Belknap Hall, Mansfield State College, Mansfield, PA 16933
THE CLOVER PATCH, The Clover Patch, Inc., 75 Church St., Montrose, PA 18801, 717-278-3950
Dawn Valley Press, Box 58, New Wilmington, PA 16142
East River Anthology, 114 N 6th St., Perkasie, PA 18944
AQUILA MAGAZINE, Roq Press, Box 174-B, Petersburg, PA 02725, 814-667-2336
Middle Earth Books Inc., 1134 Pine St, Phila, PA 19107
AMERICAN POETRY REVIEW, 1616 Walnut St., Room 405, Philadelphia, PA 19103, 215-732-6770
Atlantis Editions, P.O. Box 2776, Philadelphia, PA 19120
CHIMERA: A Complete Theater Piece, HS Press, 340 East Mechanic St., Philadelphia, PA 19144
CIE, Museoroom, 8 Longford St, Philadelphia, PA 19136, 612-222-2096/227-2240
FOUR QUARTERS, LaSalle College, Philadelphia, PA 19141
A GAY BIBLIOGRAPHY, Task Force on Gay Liberation, P.O. Box 2383, Philadelphia, PA 19103
HERA, INC., 328 South 17th St, Philadelphia, PA 19103, 215-732-2420
HOT WATER REVIEW, Hotwater, 42 W. Washington Lane, Philadelphia, PA 19144
INDIAN TRUTH, Indian Rights Association, 1505 Race St., Philadelphia, PA 19102, 215-563-8349
JOURNAL OF MODERN LITERATURE, Temple Univ., Philadelphia, PA 19122
OCCURRENCE, 928 Pine, Apt 12-B, Philadelphia, PA 19107
PAINTED BRIDE QUARTERLY, Painted Bride Press, 527 South St, Philadelphia, PA 19147
PASS-AGE: A Futures Journal, 3617 Powelton Ave, Philadelphia, PA 19104, 215-387-6294

POETRY NEWSLETTER, Dept. of English, Temple University, Philadelphia, PA 19122
RECON, Recon Publications, P.O. Box 14602, Philadelphia, PA 19134
ROCKINGCHAIR, Cupola Productions, P.O. Box 27, Philadelphia, PA 19105
Running Press, 38 South 19th Street, Philadelphia, PA 19103, 215-567-5080
Treacle Press, 4615 Cedar Ave., Philadelphia, PA 19143
Woodbine Press, 4615 Cedar Ave, Philadelphia, PA 19143
THE WORD-SMITH, 3827 Walnut St., Philadelphia, PA 19104
Know, Inc., P.O. Box 86031, Pittsburgh, PA 15221
RAPPORT, The Slow Loris Press, 6359 Morrowfield Avenue, Pittsburgh, PA 15217
Slow Loris Press, 6359 Morrowfield Ave, Pittsburgh, PA 15217
Taramara, Unltd., 5644 No. 7 Forbes, Pittsburgh, PA 15217, 412-422-8981
THEATRE SURVEY-THE American Journal of Theatre History, Univ. Pittsubrgh, 1117 Cathedral of Learning, Pittsburgh, PA 15260
THREE RIVERS POETRY JOURNAL, Three Rivers Press, P.O. Box 21, Carnegie-Mellon University, Pittsburgh, PA 15213
Three Rivers Press, P.O. Box 21, Carnegie-Mellon University, Pittsburgh, PA 15213
WRITE ON, Northland Library, 120 Three Degree Rd, Pittsburgh, PA 15237, 412-366-3350
Minicomputer Press, Box 1, Richboro, PA 18954, 215-355-6084
Richboro Press, Box 1, Richboro, PA 18954, 215-355-6084
LIBRE PRESS, Scranton Theatre Libre, 512-514 Brooks Bldg, Scranton, PA 18510, 717-342-3608
Spring Church Book Company, PO Box 127, Spring Church, PA 15686
PIVOT, Mayer Press, 221 S. Barnard, State College, PA 16801, 814-238-8887
Regent Graphic Services, P.O. Box 8372, Swissvale, PA 15218, 412-371-7128
CHAUCER REVIEW, The Pennsylvania State University Press, 215 Wagner Bldg., University Park, PA 16802
THE SHAW REVIEW, University Press (Penn State University), S-234 Burrowes Building, University Park, PA 16802
UZZANO, Uzzano Press, 208 South State Rd., Upper Darby, PA 19082, 815-244-6575
The Middle Atlantic Press, Box 263, Wallingford, PA 19086, 215-565-2445
INDIVIDUAL LIBERTY, P.O. Box 1147, Warminster, PA 18974, 215-675-6830
DAMASCUS ROAD, Damascus Road Press, 6271 Hill Drive, Wescosville, PA 18106
FIT, The Fit Press, 4 Riverside Drive, Wilkes-Barre, PA 18702, 717-822-3024
Philmer Enterprises, 617 Wayfield Rd, Wynnewood, PA 19096, 215-896-6630
CIRCUS MAXIMUS, Garretson Graphics, P O Box 3251, York, PA 17402

PUERTO RICO

COQUI QUARTERLY, Cibola Studio, P O Box E, Carolina, PR 00630, 809-726-8382
CREACION, Asociacion Poncena Pro Arte Y Cultura (APPAC), Box 111, Estacion 6-UCPR, Ponce, PR 00731

RHODE ISLAND

ALDEBARAN, Roger Williams College, Bristol, RI 02809
BLACK LITE, Box 8214, Cranston, RI 02920, 401-944-8867
Woodbine Press, 65 Allen Ave, E. Prov., RI 02915
Biscuit City Press, 146 Biscuit City Road, Kingston, RI 02881, 401-783-8851
DRIFTWOOD-EAST, 95 Carter Avenue, P.O. Box 2262, Pawtucket, RI 02861, 401-723-5184
Copper Beech Press, Box 1852 Brown Univ., Providence, RI 02912, 401-863-2393
DIANA'S BIMONTHLY, 71 Elmgrove Ave., Providence, RI 02906
Gray Flannel Press, P.O. Box 9181, Providence, RI 02940
HARBINGER, P.O. Box 235, Annex Sta, Providence, RI 02901
HELLCOAL ANNUAL, Hellcoal Press, Box 4 SAO, Brown University, Providence, RI 02912
Hellcoal Press, Box SAO, Brown Univ., Providence, RI 02912
Tom Ockerse Editions, 37 Woodbury Street, Providence, RI 02906, 401-331-0783
WIP, Windfall, c/oEnglish Department, Box 1852, Brown Univ., Providence, RI 02912
ANYART JOURNAL, Anyart Contemporary Arts Center, 259 Water Street, Warren, RI 02885, 245-9005
THE WESTERLY REVIEW, Split-Leaf Press, 229 Post Rd, Westerly, RI 02891

SOUTH CAROLINA

SOUTH CAROLINA REVIEW, English Dept, Clemson Univ., Clemson, SC 29631
AUNTIE BELLUM, Womens Heritage Association Trust, 615 Woodrow St, Columbia, SC 29205, 803-799-4012
SOUTHERN LIBERTARIAN MESSENGER, P.O. Box 1245, Florence, SC 29503
CREATIVE MOMENT, Poetry Eastwest, Box 391, Sumter, SC 29150
Poetry Eastwest, Box 391, Sumter, SC 29150

SOUTH DAKOTA

Lame Johnny Press, Associates, Box 66, Hermosa, SD 57744, 605-255-4228
Astro Black Books, P O Box 46, Sioux Falls, SD 57101, 605-338-0277
Dakota Press, Swes, University of South Dakota, Vermillion, SD 57069, 605-677-5281
SOUTH DAKOTA REVIEW, Dakota Press, Box 111, University Exchange, Vermillion, SD 57069, 605-677-5229
Spirit Mound Press, Box 111, University Exch., Vermillion, SD 57069

TENNESSEE

MAYBE, Worlds of Fandom, IMK, c/o 835 Chatt. Bk. Bg., Chattanooga, TN 37402, 615-267-2000
THE SMALL FARM, The Small Farm, P.O. Box 563, Jefferson City, TN 37760
STILE, P.O. Box 336, Jonesboro, TN 37659
PAZ PRINT/PERIPHERY, House of Paz, P.O. Box 8267, Univ. of Tenn. Station, Knoxville, TN 37916
PUDDINGSTONE, Puddingstone Press, Box 8800, University Station, Knoxville, TN 37916
Young Publications, 531 N. Gay St. (PO Box 3455), Knoxville, TN 37917
MOONDANCE, Moonbeam Publications, 1321 Swallow Lane, Memphis, TN 38116
St. Luke's Press, 1474 Harbert, Memphis, TN 38104, 901-276-8028
BARBEQUE PLANET, Project House Foundation, Inc., 2513-B Ashwood, Nashville, TN 37212
FRONT STREET TROLLEY, 2125 Acklen Ave., Nashville, TN 37212, 615-297-8025
MOUNTAIN SUMMER, Ex Libris at the University Press, 'Glen Antrim', Sewanee, TN 37375
Book Publishing Co., 156 Drakes Lane, Summertown, TN 38483, 615-964-3571

TEXAS

Ransehc Publishing, Inc., Box 966, Alief, TX 77411, 713-467-5664
TEXAS COUNTRY MAGAZINE, Ransehc Publishing, Inc., P.O. Box 966, Alief, TX 77411
CREATIVE GUITAR INTERNATIONAL, Mockingbird Press, Box 7, Alpine, TX 79830
Biography Press, 1240 W. Highland Ave., Rt. 1 Box 745, Aransas Pass., TX 78336, 512-758-3870
Sable Publishing Corporation, P.O. Box 788, Arlington, TX 76010, 817-265-5001
ACID SWITCH, Acid Switch Press, 3007 University Avenue, Austin, TX 78705, 512-472-7415
Acid Switch Press, 3077 University, Austin, TX 78705, 512-472-7415
THE ARDENT SABOTEUR: a journal of amnemonics, 3007 University, Austin, TX 78705, 512-472-7415
AUSTIN PULPWOOD, Red Bean Revue, 501 Park Blvd, Austin, TX 78751, 512-247-3706
THE BEAUREGARD BUGLE BOY HERALD-TRIBUNE, 3007 University, Austin, TX 78705, 512-472-7415
CANNIBAL, 3007 University, Austin, TX 78705, 512-472-7415
CIRCULAR LETTER, 3007 University, Austin, TX 78705, 512-472-7415
Cold Mountain Press, 4705 Sinclair Ave, Austin, TX 78756
EH?, 3007 University, Austin, TX 78705, 512-472-7415
GOLD TURKEY, 3007 University, Austin, TX 78705, 512-472-7415
HUNDELOCH, 3007 University, Austin, TX 78705, 512-472-7415
INTERSTATE, Noumenon Press, P.O. Box 7068, U.T. Sta., Austin, TX 78712
Latitudes Press, 3514 Lafayette Ave, Austin, TX 78722
LUCILLE, Lucille Press, No. 5 Kern Ramble, Austin, TX 78722
Noumenon Press, PO Box 7068, University Station, Austin, TX 78712
NOUS: a journal of arts and ideas, 3007 University, Austin, TX 78705, 512-472-7415
Place of Herons, 2404 Riverside Farms Rd., Austin, TX 78741
Prairie Books, 501 Park Blvd, Austin, TX 78751, 512-454-6133
THE RAG, 2330 Guadalupe, Austin, TX 78705
Red Bean Revue, 501 Park Blvd, Austin, TX 78751, 247-3706
Salient Books, 3007 University, Austin, TX 78705, 512-472-7415
Saline Productions, 3007 University, Austin, TX 78705, 512-472-7415
651, 3007 University, Austin, TX 78705, 472-7415
SOLEIL BLANK: a forum of progressive literature, 3007 University, Austin, TX 78705, 512-472-7415
TEXAS OBSERVER, 600 W. 7th, Austin, TX 78701, 512-477-0746
TIMEPAD, 3007 University, Austin, TX 78705, 472-7415
WOOD IBIS, Place Of Herons, 2404 Riverside Farms Rd., Austin, TX 78741
QUARTET, 1119 Neal Pickett Dr., College Station, TX 77840
ICONOCLAST, P.O. Box 7013, Dallas, TX 75209
THE PAWN REVIEW, 2806 Reagan Apt. 204, Dallas, TX 75219
PROLOG, Theater Sources, Inc., 104 N. St. Mary, Dallas, TX 75214
SOUTHWEST REVIEW, Southern Methodist University Press, Southern Methodist Univ., Dallas, TX 75275, 214-692-2263
THEATRE ACROSS AMERICA, Theatre Sources, Inc., 104 N. St. Mary, Dallas, TX 75214
Funch Press, 1101 Tori Lane, Edinburg, TX 78539
RIVERSEDGE, Riversedge Press, PO Box 1547, Edinburg, TX 78539
Riversedge Press, PO Box 1547, Edinburg, TX 78539
DESCANT, Texas Christian University Press, English Department, TCU, Fort Worth, TX 76129
Special Aviation Publications, Box 672, Hillsboro, TX 76645
Butterfly Press, PO Box 19571, Houston, TX 77024, 713-464-7570
Forum Literati, P.O. Box 79464, Houston, TX 77079, 467-2398
HOO-DOO BlackSeries, Energy BlackSouth Press, 2805 Southmore, Houston, TX 77004
Houston Writers Workshop, Drawer 42331, Houston, TX 77042
IN ORBIT: A Journal of Earth Literature, Energy BlackSouth Press, 2805 Southmore, Houston, TX 77004
J. Buchs Publications, 5301 Richmond, 24B, Houston, TX 77056
SAGEBLOOM, Forum Literati, P.O. Box 79464, Houston, TX 77079, 467-2398
TOUCHSTONE, Houston Writers Workshop, Drawer 42331, Houston, TX 77042
XENHARMONIKON, 10819 Shannon Hills Drive, Houston, TX 77099, 713-498-0055
SAM HOUSTON LITERARY REVIEW, Sam Houston State University Press, English Department, Sam Houston State University, Huntsville, TX 77340
CLAUDEL STUDIES, University of Dallas Station, Irving, TX 75061

AISLING, PO Box 998, LaMarque, TX 77568
CONRADIANA, Texas Tech Press, Dept. of English, Box 4530, Texas Tech University, Lubbock, TX 79409
STUDIES IN POETRY: A GRADUATE JOURNAL, Dept of English, Texas Tech Univ., Lubbock, TX 79409
TRUCHA, Trucha Publications, Inc., Box 5223, Lubbock, TX 79417
CEDAR ROCK, Cedar Rock, Inc., 1121 Madeline, New Braunfels, TX 78130, 512-625-6002
MUNDUS ARTIUM: A Journal of International Literature & Art, Mundus Artium Press, Box 688, Richardson, TX 75080
CYCLO * FLAME, Cyclotron Press, 212 W. First St., San Angelo, TX 76901
CARACOL, Caracol, PO Box 7577, San Antonio, TX 78207, 512-228-9838
POETRY TEXAS, Poetry Texas Press, Division of Humanities, College of the Mainland, Texas City, TX 77590
TEXAS PORTFOLIO, B. Weberlein, Publisher, 123 Eleventh Avenue, North, Texas City, TX 77590, 713-948-3703
SOME FRIENDS, Some Friends Press, P.O. Box 3395, Tyler, TX 75701

UTAH

Peregrine Smith, Inc., PO Box 667, Layton, UT 84041
WESTERN AMERICAN LITERATURE, UMC 32, Utah State Univ., Logan, UT 84322
Altruistic Enterprises, 184 Q Street 2, English Department, Univ. of Utah, Salt Lake City, UT 84103
Litmus, Inc., 574 3rd Ave, Salt Lake City, UT 84103
Olympus Publishing Company, 1670 East 13th South, Salt Lake City, UT 84105
QUARTERLY WEST, Quarterly West, 312 Olpin Union, U. of Utah, Salt Lake City, UT 84112, 801-581-3938
THE SLOUGH, Altruistic Enterprises, English Department, University of Utah, Salt Lake City, UT 84103
WESTERN HUMANITIES REVIEW, University of Utah, Salt Lake City, UT 84112, 801-581-7438

VERMONT

STRANGE FAECES, Strange Faeces Press, P.O. Box 81, Barton, VT 05822
DIVINE TOAD SWEAT, The Neo-American Church, Inc., 423 Northgate, North Ave, Burlington, VT 05401
Landmark Publishing, Box 3287, Burlington, VT 05401, 802-863-5333
VERMONT CHILDREN'S MAGAZINE, PO Box 941, Burlington, VT 05401, 425-2359
Z, Z Press, Inc., Poets Corner, Calais, VT 05648
The Crow's Mark Press, Johnson, VT 05656
THE MONTHLY JOURNAL OF GREAT QUOTATIONS, Adams Publishing, Box 512, Manchester, VT 05255, 803-362-9890
VEINS, St. Mawr Jazz Poetry Project, Box 615, Middlebury, VT 05753
JAM TO-DAY, P.O. Box 249, Northfield, VT 05663
CURRENT (a reprint magazine), Plainfield, VT 05667
IO, North Atlantic Books, RFD 2 Box 135, Plainfield, VT 05667, 802-454-7845
North Atlantic Books, RFD 2, Box 135, Plainfield, VT 05667, 802-454-7845
SAMISDAT, Samisdat Associates, Box 231, Richford, VT 05476
Samisdat Associates, Box 231, Richford, VT 05476
Biohydrant Publications, R.F.D. 3, St. Albans, VT 05478
Miller Pond Books, RFD, Thetford Center, VT 05075
Vermont Crossroads Press, Inc., Box 30, Waitsfield, VT 05673
Unpublished Editions, PO Box 26, West Glover, VT 05875

VIRGINIA

THE ASIA MAIL, Potomac Asia Communications, P O Box 1044, Alexandria, VA 22313
The Huffman Press, 110 S. Columbus St., Alexandria, VA 22314, 703-836-7160
GALLIMAUFRY, Gallimaufry, 3208 N. 19th Rd., Arlington, VA 22201
PROTEUS, Proteus Press, 1004 N. Jefferson St., Arlington, VA 22205
AIEEE, Alphaville Books, PO Box 3424, Charlottesville, VA 22903
Alphaville Books, Box 3424, Charlottesville, VA 22903
JEFFERSONIAN REVIEW, PO Box 3864, Charlottesville, VA 22903
OXYMORON: Journal Of Convulsive Beauty, Alphaville Books/Sleep & Dream Lab., P.O. Box 3424, Charlottesville, VA 22903, 804-977-5685
OLD FRIENDS, Glebe Press, c/o Culpeper News, 146 N. Main St, Culpeper, VA 22701
Mu Publications, Box 612, Dahlgren, VA 22448
The Pray Curser Press, c/oErwin R. Bergdoll, Elm Bank, Dutton, VA 23050, 804-693-2823
Iron Mountain Press, Box 28, Emory, VA 24327, 703-944-5363
PHOEBE, G.M.U. 4400 University Dr., Fairfax, VA 22030
April Dawn Publishing Company, Po Box 4433, Falls Church, VA 22044
THE WOMAN ACTIVIST, 2310 Barbour Road, Falls Church, VA 22043
The Rose Bower Press, Rt 3, Box 252, Farmville, VA 23901, 804-223-8209
THE HAMPDEN-SYDNEY POETRY REVIEW, P.O. Box 126, Hampden-Sydney, VA 23943, 804-223-4381
THE HOLLINS CRITIC, P.O. Box 9538, Hollins College, VA 24020
CP Graham Press, Box 5, Keswick, VA 22947
SHENANDOAH, Journalism Laboratory Press, Washington and Lee University, P.O. Box 722, Lexington, VA 24450
COMMUNITIES, Community Publications Cooperative, Box 426, Louisa, VA 23093, 703-894-5126
LEAVES OF TWIN OAKS, Twin Oaks Community, Rt. 4 Box 17, Louisa, VA 23093, 703-894-5126
Northwoods Press, Inc., RR 1, Meadows of Dan, VA 24120, 703-952-2588
NORTHWOODS JOURNAL, Northwoods Press, Inc., RR 1, Meadows of Dan, VA 24120, 703-952-2388
IT COMES IN THE MAIL, Purple Mouth Press, 713 Paul Street, Newport News, VA 23605

INLET, Virginia Wesleyan College, Norfolk, VA 23502
NEW RIVER REVIEW, Highlands Press, Radford College Stat., Radford, VA 24142
THE CONTEMPORARY LITERARY SCENE, Salem Press, Inc., Dept. of English, Va. Commonwealth Univ., Richmond, VA 23284
LITERARY SKETCHES, Box 711, Williamsburg, VA 23185, 804-229-2901

WASHINGTON

Creative Ventures, Route 8, Box 8835, Bainbridge Island, WA 98110, 209-734-3503
THE BELLINGHAM REVIEW, Signpost Press, 2600 Hampton Place, Bellingham, WA 98225
CONCERNING POETRY, English Department, Western Wash. State College, Bellingham, WA 98225
THE GOLIARDS, Goliards Press, 3515 18th St, Bellingham, WA 98225
JEOPARDY, Western Washington State University, Humanities 362 W.W.S.C., Bellingham, WA 98225
NORTHWEST PASSAGE, Box 105, South Bell Station, Bellingham, WA 98225
WILD FENNEL, 2510 48th Street, Bellingham, WA 98225
Peaceweed Press, Tolstoy Farm, Rt. 3 Box 70, Davenport, WA 99122
VAGABOND, Vagabond Press, PO Box 879, Ellensburg, WA 98926
Sweet Pine Press, Rt 1 Box 52, Harrah, WA 98933
SIGNPOST, Signpost Publications, 16812 36th Ave W, Lynnwood, WA 98036, 206-743-3947
Signpost Publications, 16812 36th Ave W, Lynnwood, WA 98036, 206-743-3947
THE CHANEY CHRONICAL, London Northwest, 929 South Bay Rd, Olympia, WA 98506
NORTHWEST CHESS, P O Box 2951, Olympia, WA 98507, 206-753-3841
WHAT'S NEW ABOUT LONDON, JACK?, London Northwest, 929 South Bay Rd., Olympia, WA 98506
Goldermood Rainbow Press, 331 W. Bonneville, Pasco, WA 99301, 509-547-5525
"NITTY GRITTY", Goldermood Rainbow Press, 331 W. Bonneville, Pasco, WA 99301, 509-547-5525
Copper Canyon Press/Copperhead, P.O. Box 271, Port Townsend, WA 98368
The Graywolf Press, P.O. Box 142, 2210 S. Peabody, Port Townsend, WA 98368, 206-385-1160
PORT TOWNSEND JOURNAL, Woolman Press, 933 Tyler St, Port Townsend, WA 98368
Angst World Library, 2307 22nd Ave. E, Seattle, WA 98112
Henry Philips Publishing Company, 19316-3rd Avenue N.W., Seattle, WA 98177, 206-542-8483
HINDSIGHT, And/Or (alternative gallery space, not a press), 1525 10th Ave., Seattle, WA 98122, 324-5880
LE JARDIN DU MONDE: The Journal of International Casafundada, Casafundada, P.O. Box 5385, Seattle, WA 98105
JAWBONE, Jawbone Press, 17023 5th Avenue NE, Seattle, WA 98155
MADRONA, Gemini, 4730 Latona N.E., Seattle, WA 98105
MODERN LANGUAGE QUARTERLY, 4045 Brooklyn Ave. N.E., Seattle, WA 98195
North Country Press, P.O. Box 12223, Seattle, WA 98112
PORCH, Porch Publications, 1019 E. Pike, Seattle, WA 98122, 206-325-5614
Sea Pen Press, 2216 NE 46th, Seattle, WA 98105, LA2-8113
DOGSOLDIER, Dogsoldier Press, E. 2933 Queen, Spokane, WA 99207
MANY SMOKES, Bear Tribe, P.O. Box 9167, Spokane, WA 99209
DHARMA SARA, Dharma Sara Publications, P.O. Box 247, Sumas, WA 98295
LAUGHING BEAR, Laughing Bear Press, Box 14, Woodinville, WA 98072, 206-524-2314

WEST VIRGINIA

WHAT'S A NICE HILLBILLY LIKE YOU . . . ?, Appalachian Press, 107 Earwood St, Beckley, WV 25801
THE LAUREL REVIEW, West Virginia Wesleyan College, Buckhannon, WV 26201, 303-473-8006
Glouchester Press, PO Box 1044, Fairmont, WV 26554, 304-366-1441
Westwind Press, Route 1, Box 64, Farmington, WV 26571, 304-287-7160
THE LITTLE REVIEW, Little Review Press, Marshall University, English Department, Huntington, WV 25701

WISCONSIN

George Sroda, Publisher, Amherst Jct., WI 54407
GREAT CIRCUMPOLAR BEAR CULT, Bear Cult Press, Box 468, Ashland, WI 54806
BELOIT POETRY JOURNAL, Beloit Poetry Journal, P.O. Box 2, Beloit, WI 53511
THE VELVET LIGHT TRAP: Review of Cinema, Arizona Jim Co-Op, Old Hope Schoolhouse, Cottage Grove, WI 53527
RED WEATHER, Red Weather Press, PO Box 1104, Eau Claire, WI 54701, 715-834-9870
Red Weather Press, PO Box 1104, Eau Claire, WI 54701, 715-834-9870
Druid Books, Ephraim, WI 54211
MARGINS, P.O. Box A, Fair Water, WI 53931
NORTH AMERICAN MENTOR MAGAZINE, Westburg Associates, Publishers, Post Office Drawer 69, Fennimore, WI 53809
Westburg Associates, Publishers, 1745 Madison Street, Fennimore, WI 53809, 608-822-6237
RIVER BOTTOM MAGAZINE (Baseball, Floating and Nickle Times), River Bottom Press, Box 252, Iola, WI 54945
City Slicker Press, 2325 52 St, Kenosha, WI 53140, 414-657-7883
Center For Contemporary Poetry, Murphy Library, Univ of Wisconsin, La Crosse, WI 54601, 608-784-6050, Ext 237
Elm Tree Press, P O Box 1364-185, La Crosse, WI 54665
NORTHEAST/JUNIPER BOOKS, Juniper Press, 1310 Shorewood Dr., LaCrosse, WI 54601
ABRAXAS, 2322 Rugby Row, Madison, WI 53705
BA SHIRU, University of Wisconsin, 1456 Van Hise, Madison, WI 53706
THE CHOWDER REVIEW, 2858 Kingston Dr, Madison, WI 53713
COLLECTORS' NETWORK NEWS, Acq Sec/State Histrcl Soc, 816 State Street, Madison, WI 53706, 608-262-9584

CONTEMPORARY LITERATURE, University of Wisconsin Press, 7141 Helen C. White Hall, University of Wisconsin, Madison, WI 53706
FAS Publishing/Fleetwood Art Studio, Inc., 6613 Seybold Rd, Madison, WI 53719
INQUEST, Quest Publishing, 853 Williamson St., Madison, WI 53703
NATIONAL ON-CAMPUS REPORT, Magna Publishing Co., 621 N. Sherman Ave, Madison, WI 53704
QUIXOTE, QUIXOTL, Quickoats, 151 E Gilman, Madison, WI 53703
WISCONSIN TRAILS, Tamarack Press, 517 N. Segoe Rd., P.O. Box 5650, Madison, WI 53705
POETRY VIEW, Post-Crescent, 1125 Valley Rd., Menasha, WI 54952
NEW EARTH TRIBE NEWSPACK, R.V.K. Publishing Co., P.O. Box 264, Menomonee Falls, WI 53051
POETRY/PEOPLE, R. V. K. Publishing Co., PO Box 264 du, Menomonee Falls, WI 53051
BUGLE-AMERICAN, P.O. Box 12318, Milwaukee, WI 53212
DANCE DIMENSIONS, Wisconsin Dance Council, 3236 N. Bartlett Ave., Milwaukee, WI 53211
GPU NEWS, Liberation Publications, Inc., PO Box 92203, Milwaukee, WI 53202, 414-276-0612
House Of Words, 207 E. Buffalo St. No. 518, Milwaukee, WI 53202
Membrane Press, P.O. Box 11601-Shorewood, Milwaukee, WI 53211
O Press/Heavy Evidence, 1338 N. Astor, Milwaukee, WI 53202
PAID MY DUES: Journal of Women and Music, Woman's Soul Publishing, Inc., P.O. Box 11646, Milwaukee, WI 53211, 414-263-7792
Pentagram Press, P.O. Box 11609, Milwaukee, WI 53211
THE SHORE REVIEW, Shore Press, 2931 So. 57 St., Milwaukee, WI 53219
SOFT TIMES, O Press, 1338 N. Astor, Milwaukee, WI 53202
STATIONS, Membrane Press, P.O. Box 11601 Shorewood, Milwaukee, WI 53211
THIRD COAST ARCHU, House Of Words, 207 E. Buffalo St. No. 518, c/o House of Words, Milwaukee, WI 53202
ZIGGURAT Annual International Anthology of the Fine Arts, Ziggurat Publications, 2546 South Kinnickinnic, Milwaukee, WI 53207
PRIMIPARA, Impress Inc, PO Box 171, Oconto, WI 54153
GREEN MOUNTAIN QUARTERLY, Green Mountain Editions, 460 N. Main Street, Oshkosh, WI 54901
ROAD APPLE REVIEW, 3263 Shorewood Dr., Oshkosh, WI 54901
WISCONSIN REVIEW, Wisconsin Review, Box 145 Dempsey Hall, University of Wisconsin-Oshkosh, Oshkosh, WI 54901, 414-424-2267
SNARF, Kitchen Sink Enterprises, P.O. Box 7, Princeton, WI 54968
TIME/OUT, Creative Communications, 928 Cleveland Ave, Racine, WI 53405, 414-633-3621
MIME JOURNAL, Route 3, Spring Green, WI 53588, 608-588-2514
THE MAINSTREETER, The Scopcraeft Press, Dept of English, Univ of Wisc, Stevens Pt, WI 54481
SONG: A Magazine of Verse and Essay, 808 Illinois, Stevens Pt, WI 54481, 715-344-6836
The Bieler Press, 124 North Page Street, Stoughton, WI 53589
COUNTRYSIDE, Countryside Publications Ltd., Route One, Waterloo, WI 53594
WOMEN IN STRUGGLE, Box 324-DB, Winneconne, WI 54986

WYOMING

HIGH COUNTRY NEWS, Box K, 331 Main St., Lander, WY 82520, 332-4877 (307)
HIGH COUNTRY NEWS, Box K, Lander, WY 82520, 307-332-4877
ETC: A Review of General Semantics, International Society for General Semantics (ISGS), Univ of Wyoming, Laramie, WY 82070
THOREAU JOURNAL QUARTERLY, Thoreau Fellowship, (literary) English Dept., Univ. of Wyoming, Laramie, WY 82070

The Englewood Readings
By Terence Clarke

Selected Essays
By Rich Mangelsdorff

Anti-Matter
By C.M. Stanbury II

Night Conversations With None Other
By Shreela Ray

— Dustbooks —
P.O. BOX 1056
PARADISE, CA 95969

Distributors

The following is a list of some 140 book distributors, book jobbers and magazine agents. Most of them have an active account with Dustbooks, though some of them are new small press/magazine distributors funded (initially) by a Ford Foundation grant via the Coordinating Council of Literary Magazines (80 8th Ave. NYC 10011). This past spring we sent a survey to all 140 in this list; those with more complete information in their listings are those who answered the survey. Generally, an **Agent** (A) sells magazine subscriptions to libraries and other institutions (in the case of Dustbooks it handles the **Small Press Review**); a **jobber** (J) sells single copies of books to these same institutions; and a **distributor** (D) is a wholesaler who sells in quantity to bookstores, though will often mailorder single titles as the listings indicate. We suggest enclosing a SASE when writing for information to any of these listings; and always query before sending copies of books or magazines for possible distribution.

Abrahams Magazine Service Inc., 56 E. 13th St., NYC 10003 (A)

Academic Library Service, 141 NE 38th Terrace, Oklahoma City, OK 73105 (J)

ACP Distributors, 105 Pine Rd., Sewickley, PA 15143 (D)

Albert J. Phiebig, Books, P.O. Box 352, White Plains, NY 10602 (J)

Alesco, 404 Sette Drive, Paramus, NJ 07652 (J)

Alesco, Box 1488, Madison, WI 53701 (J)

Alexander Horn, P.O. Box 2163, Allemagne, Germany (J)

Aloe Book Agency, P.O. Box 4349, Johannesburg, South Aftica 2000 (J)

Ambassador Book Service Inc., 1415 Newbridge Rd., N. Bellmore, NY 11710 (J)

American Jewish Congress, 15 East 84th St., NYC 10028 (J)

Atlantis Distributors, 1725 Carondelet, New Orleans, LA 70130 (D)

Bacon Pamphlet Service, East Chatham, NY 12060 (J)

Baker & Taylor Co. (J): Gladiola Ave., Momence, IL 60954; 380 Edison Way, Reno, NV 89502; Commerce, GA 30529; Box 931, Clarksville, TX 75426; 50 Kirby Ave., Somerville, NJ 08876.

Ballen Booksellers, 667 Austin Blvd., Commack, LI, NY 11725 (J)

R.E. Banta, Bookseller, Crawfordsville, IN 47933 (J)

BCN Agencies PTY LTD, 161 Sturt St., Melbourne, Victoria, 3205 Australia

Before Columbus Foundation, P.O. Box 2370, Sta. A, Berkeley, CA 94702 (D). Covers primarily west and southwest; multi-cultural and multi-lingual literature; carries 16 titles, 100% small press; will ship mailorder and send catalogue.

The Benjamin & Matthew Book Co., Route One, Ashville, ME 05607 (D). Covers New England and other areas in the Northeast; carries cookbooks, alternative energy, children's books, how-to books; about 200 titles, 10% small press but growing; will ship mailorder and send catalogue.

Berkeley Educational Paperbacks, 2480 Bancroft Way, Berkeley, CA 94704 (J)

Beverly Books Inc., 36 East Prince St., Linden, NJ 07036 (J)

Black Box, P.O. Box 4174, Washington, DC 20015 (D). Covers USA; carries all 20 Century poetry available on audiotape; represents 21 producers/publishers; 240 titles, 30% small press; will ship mailorder and send descriptive listing catalogue free. Complete annotated catalogue is $2.00.

Blackwell, B.H. Ltd., Broad St., Oxford, UK OXI 3BV (J)

Blackwell North America, 10300 S.W. Allen Blvd., Beaverton, OR 97005 (J); also: 1001 Fries Mill Rd., Blackwood, NJ 08012.

Blackwell's AOB Dept., 33 St. Aldates, Oxford, U.K. OX1 3BQ (J)

Book & Periodical Acq. Ltd., 33 Coronet Rd., Toronto, Ont., Canada M8Z 2L9 (J)

The Book Bus, Joe Flaherty, c/o Visual Studies Workshop, 4 Elton St., Rochester, NY 14607 (D). Covers New England, New York, Ohio, Pennsylvania; carries literature and visual arts; 325 titles, 100% small press; does some mailorder and will send catalogue.

Bookazine Co. Inc., 303 West 10th St., NYC 10014 (J)

Bookimpen Booksellers, Molenstraat 20, Den Haag, Netherlands (J)

Bookpeople, 2940 7th St., Berkeley, CA 94710 (D)

Booksmith Distributing, 30 Superior Drive, Natick, MA 01760 (J)

Bro-Dart Books, 500 Arch St., Williamsport, PA 17701 (J)

Charles W. Clark Co. Inc., 564 Smith St., Farmingdale, NY 11735 (J)

Charles Sessler Inc., 1308 Walnut St., Philadelphia, PA 19107 (J)

Chaucer & Co., 2402 California 409, San Francisco, CA 94115 (J)

Clark Subscription Agency, 17-19 Washington Ave., Tenaply, NJ 07670 (A)

Claude Gill Subscriptions, Aldermaston Court, Aldermaston, Reading, UK RG7 4PF (A)

Cold Mountain Poetry, Ryan Petty, 4705 Sinclair Ave., Austin, TX 78756 (D)

COSMEP-East, 527 South St., Philadelphia, PA 19147 (D)

COSMEP-South Distribution Co-op, Box 209, Carrboro, NC 27510 (D). Covers the south mostly; carries poetry, fiction, non-fiction; 260 titles, 100% small press; will ship mailorder and send catalogue.

COSMEP Van Project, P.O. Box 209 Carrboro, NC 27510 (D). Promotes small presses/ magazines; covers southeast and middle-Atlantic states; carries 1,000 titles, 100% small press; will ship mailorder and send catalogue.

COSMEP-West, P.O. Box 31249, San Francisco, CA 94131 (D). Covers 11 western states, all general subject areas; carries 66 presses, 99% small press; will ship mailorder and send catalogue.

Coutts Library Service Inc., 736-738 Cayuga St., Lewiston, NY 14092 (J)

Customer Book Service, Box 281-Montgomery Cn, Rocky Hill, NJ 08553 (J)

Davis Agency, P.O. Box 2382, London, Ont., Canada N6A 5A7 (A)

Dawson Subscription Agency, 6 Thornecliffe Park, Toronto, Ont., Canada (A)

Dayton Hudson Booksellers, 9340 James Ave. So., Minneapolis, MN 55431 (D)

Dekker En Nordmanns, O.Z. Voorburgwal 239, Amsterdam-c, Netherlands (J)

DeWolfe & Fiske Inc., 10 Pequot Park, Canton, MA 02021 (J)

Diliart, Vallarta No. 1696, Guadalajara, Jal., Mexico (J)

Dimonstein Book Co. Inc., 38 Portman Rd., New Rochelle, NY 10801 (J)

the distributors, 702 S. Michigan, South Bend, IN 46618 (D). Covers midwest; carries paperbound books, 7,000 titles, 35% small press; ships only orders rec'd from bookstores and will send catalogue.

Drown News Agency, 15172 Golden West Circle, Westminster, CA 92683 (D)

Eastern Book Co., 131 Middle St., Portland, ME 04112 (J)

EBS Inc Book Service, 290 Broadway, Lynbrook, NY 11563 (J)

EBSCO Industries, 1st Ave. at 13th St., Birmingham, AL 33203 (A)

EBSCO Industries, 2727 Bryant St., #100, Denver, CO 80211 (A)

Edco-Vis Associates, Box 158, Middleton, WI 53562 (J)

Educational Services Division (see Shar-Frey Inc.)

El Camino Real, P.O. Box 25426-A, Denver, CO 80225 (J)

Ellsworth Magazine Service, 332 S. Michigan Ave., Chicago, IL 60604 (A)

Emery-Pratt Co., 1966 W. Main St., Owosso, MI 48567 (J)

Energy Blacksouth, 2805 Southmore, Houston, TX 77004 (D). Covers area from Houston to Washington, DC; carries 50% poetry, 40% other literary, 80% third world; 300 titles, 99% small press; will ship mailorder and send catalogue.

Exclusive Books Pty Ltd., P.O. Box 17554, Hillbrow, So. Africa 2038 (J)

Eyre's Mag & Book Service Ltd., 123-6420 Silver Ave., Burnaby, BC, Canada V5H 2Y5 (J)

F.W. Faxon Co., 15 Southwest Parkway, Westwood, MA 02090 (A)

Gnomon Distribution, P.O. Box 106, Frankfort, KY 40601 (D). Distributes nationally (U.S.) for Gnomon Press and the Jargon Society; carries literature and photography; 25 titles, 100% small press; will ship by mail and send catalogue.

Grahame Library & Subscription Center, 35-51 Mitchell St., N. Sydney, Australia 2060 (A)

Grayson Book Service Inc., 138 S. Van Brunt St., Englewood, NJ 07631 (J)

Hawaiian Magazine Distributors, 222 Koula St., Honolulu, HI 96813 (D)

Herbert Lang & Cie Ag., Munzgraben 2 CH-3011, Switzerland (J)

Huntting, 300 Burnett Rd., Chicopee, MA 01020 (J)

Instructor Subscription Agency, Instructor Park, Dansville, NY 14437 (A)

International Service Co., 333 Fourth Ave., Indialantic, FL 32903 (A)

International University Booksellers, 101 5th Ave., NYC 10003 (J)

Jende-Hagan Co., P.O. Box 177, Frederick, CO 80530 (J)

Jostens Library Services, 1301 Cliff Rd., Burnsville, MN 55337 (J)

Key Book Service Inc., 425 Asylum St., Bridgeport; CT 06610 (J)

Kleins of Westport, 4450 Main St., Westport, CT 06880 (J)

Kunst Und Wissen Erich, 7000 Stuttgart 1, W. Germany (J)

Kurt Staheli & Co., Buchhandlung, Bahnhofstrasse 70, Zurich, Switzerland CH-8021 (J)

Leigh M. Railsback, 1276 North Lake Ave., Pasadena, CA 91104 (J)

Literary Publishers of Southern California (LPSC), 1639 W. Washington Blvd., Venice, CA 90291 (D). Covers regional Southern California; carries literary, children's, educational, non-fiction, art books, women's books, records, etc.; 100 titles, 95% small press; will ship mailorder and send catalogue.

Louis Goldberg, 2018 Haines St., Philadelphia, PA 19138 (J)

Magazine Co-op, Box 840 Canal Street Sta., NYC 10013 (A). Sells subscriptions nationally (U.S.); all literary magazines; carries 41 titles, 100% small magazine; no mailorder, no catalogue.

Marshall Field & Co., 111 N. State St., Chicago, IL 60690 (J)

Martinus Nijhoff B.V., P.O. Box 269, H.R. 4309 Den Haa, Netherlands (J)

Maryknoll Publications, Maryknoll, NY 10545 (J)

Matagiri, Mt. Tremper, NY 12457 (D). Covers U.S. and Canada; carries philosophy and yoga of Sri Aurobindo, related works, education, health, poetry; 350 titles, 20% small press; will ship mailorder and send catalogue.

McGregor Magazine Agency, Mt. Morris, IL 61054 (A)

Meier & Frank Co., 1438 NW Irving, Portland, OR 97209 (J)

Mexican Book Service, Loft Bookshop in Village, St. Peters, PA 19470 (J)

Midwest Library Service, 11400 Dorsett Rd., Maryland Hts., MO 63043 (J)

Monash Books, 301 Dennis Dr., Daly City, CA 94051 (J)

Moore-Cottrell Subscription Agency, North Cohocton, NY 14868 (A)

Moseley Mail Order, 38 Newbury St., Boston, MA 02116 (J)

N.M. Preyer, CPO Box 833 Christchurch, NZ

National Educational Aids Inc., Box 5753, 516 A Beltline Blvd., Columbia, SC 29250 (J,D) Covers all areas, carries 8,000 titles; will ship mailorder and send catalogue.

NESPD (New England Small Press Distribution), 45 Hillcrest Place, Amherst, MA 01002 (D) Covers New England; carries 47 small presses/mags; 100% small press; will ship mailorder and send catalogue.

New England Mobile Bookfair, 82-84 Needham St., Newton Highlands, MA 02161 (D)

Olympic Agency, 909 South 28th St., Tacoma, WA 98409 (A)

Ourobouros, 5830 Ayala Ave., Oakland, CA 94609 (D)

P & H Bliss, P.O. Box 1079, Middletown, CT 06457 (J)

P.N.R. Subscription Service, 7241 Garden Grove Blvd., Suite M, Garden Grove, CA 92641 (A)

Quality Books Inc., 400 Anthony Trail, Northbrook, IL 60062 (J,D). Distributes internationally; carries 200,000 books in Spanish as well as several thousand remainders; 10% small press; will ship by mail and send catalogue.

Read-More Publ., 140 Cedar St., NYC 10006 (A)

Regent Book Co., 107 Prospect Pl., Hillsdale, NJ 07642 (J)

Reginald F. Fennell Subscription Service, Jackson, MI 49201 (A)

Reprint Distribution Service, P.O. Box 245, Kent, CT 06757 (D)

Rigley Book Co., P.O. Box 26012, San Francisco, CA 94126 (D)

Scholtens & Zoon B.V. 21 5063, Grote Mrkt 43 44, Groningen, Netherlands (J)

Scoham Bookshelf, 5 Atherton St., Roxbury, MA 02119 (D)

Second Back Row Press, P.O. Box 197, North Sydney N.S.W. Australia 2060 (D). Covers Australia and New Zealand; carries general books; specializes in alternative technology, feminism, education, children's books; 500+ titles, 75% small press; will ship mailorder and send catalogue.

Select Press Book Service, 14 South Street, Milford, NH 03055 (D)

Serendipity Book Distribution, 1790 Shattuck Ave., Berkeley, CA 94709 (D). Covers U.S.; carries poetry, fiction, essays, criticism; 1,000 titles, 95% small press; will ship mailorder and send catalogue.

Shar-Frey Inc., Educational Services Div., 580 Bloomfield Ave., Bloomfield, NJ 07003 (J). Covers New Jersey, New York, Penna; carries all paperback books for schools and libraries; 15,000 titles, 2% small press; no mail order, no catalogue.

Silers Inc., 130 Carondelet St., New Orleans, LA 70130 (J)

Small Press Book Center, 3841-B 24th St., San Francisco, CA 94114 (D). Distributes catalogue to California, Oregon, Washington, Hawaii; 3,000 titles, 100% small press; no mailorder but will send catalogue.

Small Press Book Club, P.O. Box 100, Paradise, CA 95969 (D). International distribution; carry all subjects but emphasis is on the creative; carry 10-20 titles per "Selectionlist" issued bi-monthly; 100% small press; will ship mailorder and will send catalogue ("Selectionlist").

Small World Books, 1407 Ocean Front Walk, Venice, CA 90291 (J)

Social Innovation, 1506 19th St. NW, Washington, DC 20036 (A)

Southern Library Bindery Co., 2952 Sidco Dr., Nashville, TN 37204 (J)

Southwest Literary Express, 901 Pinon, Las Cruces, NM 88001 (D). Covers New Mexico and the southwest; carries literary magazines, small press books -- multi-lingual, multi-ethnic; 80 titles, 100% small press; does some mailorder, will send catalogue.

Spread Eagle Distribution, 19731 Forrer, Detroit, MI 48235 (D). The "communications central for the arts, crafts, entertainment and alternative publishing in Detroit."

Spring Church Book Co., P.O. Box 127, Spring Church, PA 15686 (D)

Squire Magazine Agency, 6009 Pinewood Rd., Oakland, CA 94611 (A)

Standard Book Suppliers, Adelaide, So. Australia 5000 (J)

Stechert MacMillan, 7250 Westfield Ave., Pennsauken, NJ 08110 (J)

Stechert MacMillan, 54 Rue Boissanade, Paris, France 75014 (J)

Sundance Paperback Dist., Newtown Rd., Littleton, MA 01460 (D)

Taylor Carlisle, 115 E. 23rd St., NYC 10010 (J)

Truck Distribution Service, 1141 James Ave., St. Paul, MN 55105 (D). Covers Minn., Wisc., Iowa and anywhere else worldwide; carries primarily literature, also women, ecology/alternatives; 600-750 titles and growing; 97% small press; will ship mailorder and send catalogue.

429

The Turner Subscription Agency, 235 Park Ave. So., NYC 10003 (A). Covers world in all subjects; 70,000 titles; will ship mailorder and will send catalogue.

United Methodist Publishing House, 5th & Grace Sts., Richmond, VA 23261 (J)

Universal Periodical Service, 826 S. NW Hwy, Barrington, IL 60010 (A)

University Press Book Service, 302 5th Ave., NYC 10011 (J)

Vancouver Magazine Service Ltd., 3455 Gardner Ct., Burnaby 2, BC, Canada (A)

Walter J. Johnson Inc., 355 Chestnut, Norwood, NJ 07648 (J)

Weeger-Pride Book Co., Waterford Rd., No. Bridgton, ME 04057 (J)

Women in Distribution, P.O. Box 8858, Washington, DC 20003 (D)

The Women's Distribution Group, c/o Maureen Owen, Box 672 Old Chelsea Sta., NYC 10011 (D). Covers U.S.; carries books and magazines published & distributed by women; 21 titles, 100% small press; will ship mailorder and send catalogue.

William Reeves Publishers & Booksellers, 1A Norbury Crescent, London, UK (J)

ORGANIZATION ACRONYMS

AAA/American Anthropological Association
AABC/Affiliated to Anarchist Black Cross
AASLH/American Association for State and Local History
AAP/Association of American Publishers
ABA/American Booksellers Association
ACP/Association of Canadian Publishers
AIGA/American Institute of Graphic Art
AIP/Artists in Print
AIPA/Australia Independent Publishers Association
ALMS/Association of Little Magazines (UK)
ALP/Association of Little Presses (UK)
APA/Alberta Publishers Association
APS/Alternative Press Service
ASCAP/American Society of Composers, Artists and Producers
ASW/American Society of Writers
ASWA/Aviation-Space Writers Association
B of B/Bookbuilders of Boston
BPS/British Printing Society
CBA/Canadian Books Association
CBIC/Canadian Books Info Centre
CBPA/Conneticut Book Publishers Association
CCLM/Coordinating Council of Literary Magazines
CELJ/Council of Editors of Learned Journals
CHA/Canadian Historical Association
CNS/Canadian News Service
COSMEP/Committee of Small Magazine Editors and Publishers
COSMEPA/Committee of Small Magazine Editors and Publishers Australasia
CPPA/Canadian Periodical Publishers Association
CRISP/Committee of Rhode Island Small Presses
EAA/Eastern Arts Association
EPAA/Educational Press Association of America
FLG/Feminist Literary Guild
GAA/Guild of Alternative Artists

IFA/International Fiction Association
IPA/Independent Publishers of Australia
IPA/Irish Publishers Association
LPS/Libertarian Press Service
LPSC/Literary Publishers of Southern California
MPA/Magazine Publishers Association
MPW/Maine Publishers and Writers
NESPA/New England Small Press Association
NCPA/Northern California Publicists Association
NYSSPA/New York State Small Press Association
OAC/Ohio Arts Council
PA/Publishers Association
SAAA/St. Albans Arts Association
PANP/People Against Nuclear Power
PBC/Philadelphia Book Clinic
PHS/Printing Historical Society
SCCIPHC/Superior California Club of International Printing House Craftsmen
SGPA/Scottish General Publishers Association
STWP/Society of Technical Writers and Publishers
UAPS (E)/United Alternative Press Service (Europe)
WBPA/Western Book Publishers Association
WDG/Women's Distribution Group
WIFP/Women's Institute for Freedom of the Press
WIP/Women in Print
WPA/Western Publishers Association
WWC/Washington Writers Center
WWHS/Western World Haiku Society

NEW BOOKS CATALOGUE 1977-1978
includes outstanding critical comments on each book plus a book summary and price

ILLUSTRATED
DRAMA
ANTHOLOGIES
and
CHILDREN'S
PLAYS
FICTION
DANCE
AND
ART
BOOKS

Please write for a catalogue to —

Simon & Pierre
P.O. Box 280 Adelaide St. Postal Stn., Toronto M5C 2J4

300 to 300,000 good reasons to try BookCrafters/LithoCrafters.

Good reasons like flexibility. We won't look down our nose if you want 300 copies. On the other hand, we won't be embarrassed about 300,000. LithoCrafters has the facilities and the people to produce your book the way you want it done. And BookCrafters has the technology to save you a bundle—on your medium-to-long run.

Good reasons like time, money, and quality. Your Litho-Crafters/BookCrafters rep will work with you to achieve a fine balance between your printed product, schedule, and budget. He'll advise you on choices like the sheet-fed quality of Litho-Crafters' offset work or the incredibly fast turnaround of the complete in-line flexographic system at BookCrafters.

Good reasons like you. We know who's the boss, and we're on-line to help you keep on top of things from the moment you first contact us to the time you approve the finished product.

Call us now and get to know us before you plan the next book. We think you'll like us.

BookCrafters (703) 371-3800
Post Office Box 892, Fredricksburg, Virginia 22401

(313) 475-9145   **LithoCrafters**
Post Office Box 1266, Ann Arbor, Michigan 48106

New York, New York (212) 759-2002   Los Altos, California (415) 941-5870

Booklist	Quarterly The Plains Distribution Service publishes a thirty-two page booklist introducing fifteen titles, carefully selected by our reading committee, and mailed to over three thousand individuals and libraries throughout the country. The Plains Booklist is free upon request, with only one catch; due to the high cost of printing, we must pull your name off the list if we don't hear from you after two mailings. Some of the authors of books selected and distributed through the Booklist include: William Kloefkorn, Thomas McGrath; Greg Kuzma, John Judson, Mark Vinz, Jenne Andrews, Meridel LeSueur, Fredrick Manfred, Gerald Vizenor, Cary Waterman, James Moore, Carl Rakosi, David Ray, Kathleen Wiegner, Daniel Lusk, Roland Flint, Franklin Brainard, Robert Bly, David Etter, James L. White and Tom Montag. A backlist of all previous Booklist titles, still in stock, is available.
Criteria	Any small press or writer from the states of Wyoming, Montana, South Dakota, North Dakota, Minnesota, Nebraska, Kansas, Wisconsin, Illinois, Iowa, Indiana, Michigan or Ohio may submit a review copy of their book(s) for possible promotion and distribution via our quarterly Booklists.
Magazine List	The Chowder Review, Dacotah Territory, Dental Floss, Margins, North American Review, Northeast, North Stone Review, South Dakota Review and The Spirit That Moves Us are all members of our Magazine Committee. Further information on these magazines, our sample subscription program and creative writing packets is available by requesting a free copy of our annual Magazine Brochure.
Criteria	Any magazine published in Minnesota, Iowa, North Dakota, South Dakota or Wisconsin may submit one copy of the last three issues for possible membership in our Magazine Committee when it expands or replaces current membership.
Magazine Directory	A Directory of Midwestern Little Magazines will be given away free with purchases from our Booklists, when specifically requested and as long as they are in print, or otherwise sold for 75¢.

The Plains Distribution Service, Inc.
A service for Midwestern small presses and little magazines

P.O. Box 3112
Room 406
Block 6, 620 Main
Fargo, North Dakota 58102
Ph. (701) 235-5636

"The homebrew revival has spawned its first new literature, a book that taps brewhouse knowledge and experience."...*New Hampshire Times*

"Beer culture...the pie of life seen through the bottom of a beer glass."...*High Times*

"An effervescent mixture of beermaking how-to and the philosophy behind it. Like its subject, Mountain Brew is spicy, clear and light. Also like its subject, Mountain Brew gets the job done when circumstances say its time to get down to business."... **Harrowsmith Magazine**

"More like a beer party than like a brewing session...Mountain Brew packs a variety of recipes for every palate, a pot pourri of beer anecdotes. The information is all there."... **The Advocate**, Amherst, Mass.

"Zen and the art of beer brewing. Mountain Brew will go just fine with your suds and pretzels."...*Granite State Independence*

MOUNTAIN BREW

Available from Miller Pond Books, RFD Thetford Center, Vermont 05075.
Distributed by RPM. /2.25

WITHOUT YOU, WE WOULD BE "JUST ANOTHER" MAGAZINE.

Phantasm

BI-MONTHLY MAGAZINE

Current literary events, poetry, award-winning graphic art, features, guest columns, interviews, fiction, illustrated articles, special issues and editorials.

If it's

POETRY

and it's available

ON TAPE

*we either have it, or
we'll get it for you!*

write for our catalog:
**BLACK BOX / Box 4174
Wash., DC 20015**

Clip this ad for $1 discount on any tape.

S 7

Publishers of short-run
and unique books,
perfect or edition bound;
or journals, booklets,
pamphlets, reprints,
promotional material,
et cetera;
who need
photocomposition
and layout,
fine offset printing,
and binding;
who are looking
for one supplier to
take total responsibility
to get your publication
right, on time, and at
the right price;

you are looking for...

Publications Trade Press

1390 W. Fulton Street
Chicago, Illinois 60607

COMPLETE BOOK MANUFACTURING SERVICE

Universal manufactures books by the thousands —textbooks ... novels ... religious material ... books of every size ...

UNIVERSAL'S PLASTIC MAGAZINE BINDERS

... with Patented "TWIN LOCK" can never be pilfered. Telephone or write with your magazine requirements.

UNIVERSAL BOOKBINDERY, INC.
P.O. Box 159, San Antonio, Texas 78291 ● (512) 225-6551

Poets & Writers WIN
Contests   Awards
Fellowships   Grants

● NEW ●
Literary Contests & Awards
NEWSLETTER

COMPLETE LISTINGS OF CURRENT CONTEST
Information for ●Poets ●Writers ●Literary Agents

Subscription (6 issues) $12.00   **THE COMMENTATORS' PRESS**
Send $2.00 for   P.O. Box 61297
Sample Copy To   Sunnyvale, CA 94088

The Phœnix—a radical humanitarian literary magazine—is internationally in allegiance with all human mutants in the spreading mutiny against the inherent ancient crime of war; in allegiance with all libertarians who oppose social injustice and the denial of individual conscience; in sympathy with all revolutionists who struggle against the suppression of human rights in any and all ways apart from terrorist violence which is ever indistinguishable from the hateful violence of tyranny.

The Phœnix encourages individuals to refuse to pay taxes; to refuse to submit to military service; and to no longer remain in passive collaboration with the detention camps, prisons, convict slave labor, secret police, torturers, murderers, and executioners in the rival anti-human States of contemporary society.

The Phœnix publishes voices of affirmation, intercession, protest and reconciliations: stories, diaries, serialized novels, poems, woodcuts and line drawings. Letterpress printing. 224 to 360 pages per issue. Subscription to the four Nos. of each volume is $10 in America; $12 abroad. Special lowered subscription rates are available for students, reader groups, and writers. Free subscriptions on request to workers' libraries, radical groups & organizations, and to prison libraries wherever permitted. If you can afford to subscribe please do so now. Subscriptions are a life-line to us.

THE PHOENIX
Morning Star Farm West Whately
via RFD Haydenville Massachusetts 01039

MAINSPRING PRESS

Prints LETTERS Magazine
(Since 1968)

For readers of general literary interests. High quality authors (Carlos Baker, David Ray, George Garrett..). Free sample copy and submissions if SASE.

Prints WINDFALL POEMS
Sponsors MAINE WRITERS WORKSHOP

June to Dec. annually for writers in residence and one-week seminars July & Aug. in poetry, fiction (incl. novel, scifiction), juveniles, nonfiction, basics, drama.

Sponsors annual WINDFALL PRIZE POETRY CONTEST 1st Prize $1,000.

Quality book mms publication subsidies. Bx.82D Stonington Me. 04681   Ph. 207-367-2484

Small Press Information

1 INTERNATIONAL DIRECTORY OF LITTLE MAGAZINES AND SMALL PRESSES

$8.95/paperback; $11.95/cloth
27/4 year subscription/paperback
$36/4 year subscription/cloth
ISBN 0-913218-04-9/pa
ISBN 0-913218-05-7/cl

2 DIRECTORY OF SMALL MAGAZINE/PRESS EDITORS AND PUBLISHERS

8th Edition - 1977-78

$6.95/copy paperback
$21/4 year subscription
ISBN 0-913218-06-5

3 SMALL PRESS RECORD OF BOOKS

$8.95/paperback
$27/4 year subscription

ISBN 0-913218-03-0

4  small press review

ONGOING *MONTHLY*

$8/year individuals
$14/2 years
$18/3 years

$13.50/year institution:
$21/2 years
$27.50/3 years

Dustbooks

P.O. Box 1056,
Paradise, CA 95969

Write for complete list of titles.

See order blank on last page

Dustbooks Order Form

Item	Price	Quantity
Directory:Little Mags/Presses paper	$8.95	
cloth	$11.95	
Directory:Small Mag/Press Editors	$6.95	
Small Press Record of Books in Print	$8.95	
Small Press Review 1yr.	$8.00/indiv. $13.50/inst.	
2yr.	$14.00/indiv. $21.00/inst.	
3yr.	$18.00/indiv. $27.50/inst.	
The Publish-it Yourself Handbook	$5.00/paper $10.00/cloth	
How To Publish Your Own Book	$4.95/paper $6.95/cloth	
The Writer Publisher	$4.95/paper $7.95/cloth	
American Odyssey	$4.50/paper $7.95/cloth	
Moving To Antarctica	$3.95/paper $7.95/cloth	
Captive Voices	$3.95/paper $7.95/cloth	
The Far Side of The Storm	$4.00/paper $9.00/cloth	
Honey Dwarf	$2.50/paper $6.95/cloth	
The Gragoman	$2.95/paper $7.95/cloth	
Anti-Matter	$2.95/paper $7.95/cloth	
Milk of Wolves	$6.95/paper	
Dark Other Adam Dreaming	$2.95/paper $8.95/cloth	
Selected Essays of Rich Mangelsdorff	$2.95/paper	
Conjuring A Counter-Culture	$2.50/paper $5.95/cloth	
The Poetry of Pop	$2.50/paper	
Peeple	$2.00/paper	
The Englewood Readings	$2.50/paper $6.95/cloth	
Night Conversations with None Other	$2.95/paper $6.95/cloth	
Mr. & Mrs. Mephistopheles & Son	$2.50/paper	
Arnulfsaga	$1.50/paper	
Togethering in Happyland	$2.50/paper	
The Source	$1.50/paper	
Love Ode	$1.50/paper	
Once	$1.50/paper	
Mind Dances	$1.00/paper	
Guide to Women's Publishing	$3.95/paper $8.95/cloth	
Co-op Publishing Handbook	$3.95/paper $8.95/cloth	
In The Absence of Humans:Wilderness Poems	$2.95/paper $7.95/cloth	

_____ PLEASE SEND LATEST SMALL PRESS BOOK CLUB SELECTION LIST!

Total _____

California Residents add 6% Sales Tax _____

Add $.75 Postage and Handling _____

Total Enclosed _____

NAME _____

ADDRESS _____

BOOKSELLERS: 25% discount/2-10 copies; 40% 11-25; 50%/26+

Dustbooks   P.O. Box 1056,   Paradise, CA 95969